SPECIAL INDIAN EDITION

NINTH EDITION

Project Management

A Socio-Technical Approach

About the Authors

Erik W. Larson is professor emeritus of project management at the College of Business, Oregon State University. He teaches executive, graduate, and undergraduate courses on project management and leadership. His research and consulting activities focus on project management. He has published numerous articles on matrix management, product development, and project partnering. He has been honored with teaching awards from both the Oregon State University MBA program and the University of Oregon Executive MBA program. He has been a member of the Project Management Institute since 1984. In 1995 he worked as a Fulbright scholar with faculty at the Krakow Academy of Economics on modernizing Polish business education. He was a visiting professor at Chulalongkorn University in Bangkok, Thailand, and at Baden-Wuerttemberg Cooperative State University in Bad Mergentheim, Germany. He received a B.A. in psychology from Claremont McKenna College and a Ph.D. in management from State University of New York at Buffalo. He is a certified Project Management Professional (PMP) and Scrum master.

Clifford F. Gray is professor emeritus of management at the College of Business, Oregon State University. He has personally taught more than 100 executive development seminars and workshops. Cliff has been a member of the Project Management Institute since 1976 and was one of the founders of the Portland, Oregon, chapter. He was a visiting professor at Kasetsart University in Bangkok, Thailand, in 2005. He was the president of Project Management International, Inc. (a training and consulting firm specializing in project management) 1977–2005. He received his B.A. in economics and management from Millikin University, MBA from Indiana University, and doctorate in operations management from the College of Business, University of Oregon. He is a certified Scrum master.

Pinyarat Sirisomboonsuk is an assistant professor of management at the College of Business, The University of Texas Permian Basin. She teaches courses in project management, operations management, business logistics, risk management in supply chains, and business statistics for both undergraduate and graduate levels in either face-to-face or online formats. Her primary research interests are in the areas of project management, operations management, and supply chain management, which incorporate concepts from strategic management and organizational theory. She has been a member of the Project Management Institute since 2007. She completed her bachelor's degree in economics with first class honors from Chulalongkorn University in Thailand and received her MBA from Oregon State University. She holds a Ph.D. in Operations Management (minor in Industrial Engineering) from Texas Tech University. In 2014, she earned her Project Management Professional (PMP) credential.

Rohit Joshi is currently working as Dean-Academics and is Professor in Operations Management and Quantitative Techniques at IIM Shillong. He was a member of the Board of Governors at IIM Shillong 2023–25. He is a Fulbright fellow and has done his Postdoctoral Research work at UCLA. He obtained his Ph.D from the Department of Management Studies, IIT Delhi. He has received his master's in technology from Malviya National Institute of Technology, Jaipur, in industrial engineering and his bachelor's degree in mechanical engineering. Prof. Joshi has more than 20 years of work experience in the industry and academia. His areas of interest in consulting and teaching assignments include Supply Chain Management, Operations Management, Six Sigma and Lean Thinking, Business Statistics, Project Management, Value Engineering, Design Thinking, and Creative Problem Solving. Prof. Joshi has written and published several research papers in top rated international journals.

SPECIAL INDIAN EDITION

NINTH EDITION

Project Management

A Socio-Technical Approach

Erik W. Larson
Oregon State University

Clifford F. Gray
Oregon State University

Pinyarat Sirisomboonsuk
The University of Texas Permian Basin

Rohit Joshi
IIM Shillong

McGraw Hill

McGraw Hill Education (India) Private Limited

Published by McGraw Hill Education (India) Private Limited
Registered Office: Anjana Complex No: 5/90 A, Butt Road, St. Thomas Mount, Chennai – 600016

Special Indian Edition (SIE) 2025

First reprint 2025

This edition can be exported from India only by the publisher

Sales Territories: India, Pakistan, Nepal, Bangladesh, Sri Lanka and Bhutan

Print Edition:
ISBN (13): 978-93-6444-368-5
ISBN (10): 93-6444-368-3

E-Book Edition:
ISBN (13): 978-93-6444-641-9
ISBN (10): 93-6444-641-0

02 03 04 05 06 RAJ 29 28 27 26 25

Typeset at APS Compugraphics, 4G, PKT 2, Mayur Vihar Phase-III, Delhi 96 and Printed and Bound in India at Rajkamal Electric Press, Plot No. 2, Phase – IV, Kundli, Sonepat, Haryana

Cover Image Source: Shutterstock
Cover Designer: Gyanendra Swamy

Visit us at: www.mheducation.co.in
Write to us at: support.india@mheducation.com
CIN: U80302TN2010PTC111532
Toll Free Number: 1800 103 5875

"Man's mind, once stretched by a new idea, never regains its original dimensions."

Oliver Wendell Holmes, Jr.

To my family, who have always encircled me with love and encouragement—my parents (Samuel and Charlotte), my wife (Mary), my sons and their wives (Kevin and Dawn, Robert and Sally), and their children (Ryan, Carly, Connor, and Lauren).

C.F.G.

"The reasonable man adapts himself to the world; the unreasonable one persists in trying to adapt the world to himself. Therefore all progress depends on the unreasonable man."

Bernard Shaw, Man and Superman

To Ann, whose love and support have brought out the best in me. To our girls Mary, Rachel, and Tor-Tor for the joy and pride they give me. And to our grandkids, Mr. B, Livvy, Jasper Jones!, Ya Ya, Juni, and Calliwumpas, whose future depends upon effective project management. Finally, to my muse, Neil—walk on!

E.W.L.

"You can do anything you set your mind to."

Benjamin Franklin

To my parents (Penphim and Ophas) for their unconditional love, their support, their faith in me, and allowing me to choose the direction of my life. To my Thai and U.S. teachers, instructors, professors, and mentors, I am forever indebted. Thanks to all of you for instilling within me not only knowledge but also motivation to achieve and always do my best. The examples all of you set are with me as a guide forever.

P.S.

"Dream is not that which you see while sleeping it is something that does not let you sleep."

A P J Abdul Kalam

To Sonu, Navya, Neelaksh and my parents for their unwavering love, support and inspiration, which have been my guiding light in this journey.

R.J.

Preface

Our motivation in writing this text continues to be to provide a realistic, socio-technical view of project management. In the past, textbooks on project management focused almost exclusively on the tools and processes used to manage projects and not the human dimension. This baffled us, since people, not tools, complete projects! While we firmly believe that mastering tools and processes is essential to successful project management, we also believe that the effectiveness of these tools and methods is shaped and determined by the prevailing culture of the organization and interpersonal dynamics of the people involved. Thus, we try to provide a holistic view that focuses on both the technical and social dimensions and how they interact to determine the fate of projects.

Audience

This text is written for a wide audience. It covers concepts and skills that are used by managers to propose, plan, budget, manage and lead project teams to successful completions of their projects. The text should prove useful to students and prospective project managers in helping them understand why organizations have developed a formal project management process to gain a competitive advantage. Readers will find the concepts and techniques discussed in enough detail to be immediately useful in new-project situations. Practicing project managers will find the text to be a valuable guide and reference when dealing with typical problems that arise in the course of a project. Managers will also find the text useful in understanding the role of projects in the missions of their organizations. Analysts will find the text useful in helping to explain the data needed for project implementation as well as the operations of inherited or purchased software.

Members of the Project Management Institute will find the text is well structured to meet the needs of those wishing to prepare for PMP (Project Management Professional) or CAPM (Certified Associate in Project Management) certification exams. The text has in-depth coverage of the most critical topics found in PMI's *Project Management Body of Knowledge* (PMBOK) and its supplement guidebook, *Process Groups: A Practice Guide*. People at all levels in the organization assigned to work on projects will find the text useful not only in providing them with a rationale for the use of project management processes but also because of the insights they will gain into how to enhance their contributions to project success.

Our emphasis is not only on how the management process works but also, and more importantly, on *why* it works. The concepts, principles, and techniques are universally applicable. That is, the text does not specialize by industry type or project scope. Instead, the text is written for the individual who will be required to manage a variety of projects in a variety of organizational settings. In the case of some small projects, a few of the steps of the techniques can be omitted, but the conceptual framework applies to all organizations in which projects are important to survival. The approach can be used in pure project organizations such as construction, research organizations, and engineering consultancy firms. At the same time, this approach will benefit organizations that carry out many small projects while the daily effort of delivering products or services continues.

Content

In this and other editions, we continue to try to resist the forces that engender scope creep and focus only on essential tools and concepts that are being used in the real world. We have been guided by feedback from reviewers, practitioners, teachers, and students. Some changes are minor and incremental, designed to clarify and reduce confusion. Other changes are significant. They represent new developments in the field or better ways of teaching project management principles. Below are major changes to the ninth edition.

- The title of the text has been changed to ***Project Management: A Socio-Technical Approach.*** This more accurately captures the emphasis not only on the techniques associated with project management but also on what ultimately determines success—people and how they use these techniques to complete projects. All material has been reviewed and revised based on the latest edition of *Project Management Body of Knowledge* (PMBOK), Seventh Edition, 2020. Note that the newest edition represents a *major shift* in PMBOK toward focusing not only on terms and processes but also behavioral issues associated with managing projects. This has been the focus of this text from the beginning.
- The impact of COVID-19 pandemic on project execution is discussed throughout the text.
- Some of the Snapshots from Practice have been expanded to more fully cover the examples.
- New student exercises and cases have been added to chapters.
- The Snapshot from Practice boxes feature a number of new examples of project management in action.
- The Instructor's Manual contains a listing of current YouTube videos that correspond to key concepts and Snapshots from Practice.

Overall the text addresses the major questions and challenges the authors have encountered over their 80 combined years of teaching project management and consulting with practicing project managers in domestic and foreign environments. These questions include the following: How should projects be prioritized? What factors contribute to project failure or success? How do project managers orchestrate the complex network of relationships involving vendors, subcontractors, project team members, senior management, functional managers, and customers that affect project success? What project management system can be set up to gain some measure of control? How are projects managed when the customers are not sure what they want? How do project managers work with people from foreign cultures?

Project managers must deal with all these concerns to be effective. All of these issues and problems represent linkages to a socio-technical project management perspective. This text focuses not only project management methodology but also on the behavioral skills and cultural awareness necessary to be successful. The chapter content of the text has been placed within an overall framework that integrates these topics in a holistic manner. Cases and snapshots are included from the experiences of practicing managers. The future for project managers is exciting. Careers will be built on successfully managing projects.

Online Resources

Numerous learning resources are available online that include Practice Ops student manual, practice videos and MS Project tutorials for students. These can be accessed at *www.mheducation.co.in*. For instructors, in addition to these, instructor manual, PowerPoint Slides and Practice Ops instructor manual are also given. These can be accessed at *https://connect. mheducation.com*. Please refer to the book's cover for more information on how to access the online resources.

Acknowledgments

We would like to thank Scott Bailey for his work on the Connect assessments and Test Bank, and Ronny Richards for his quality assurance reviews.

Next, it is important to note that the text includes contributions from numerous students, colleagues, friends, and managers gleaned from professional conversations. We want them to know we sincerely appreciate their counsel and suggestions. Almost every exercise, case, and example in the text is drawn from a real-world project. Special thanks to managers who graciously shared their current project as ideas for exercises, subjects for cases, and examples for the text. John A. Drexler, Jim Moran, John Sloan, Pat Taylor, and John Wold, whose work is printed, are gratefully acknowledged. Special gratitude is due Robert Breitbarth of

Interact Management, who shared invaluable insights on prioritizing projects. University students and managers deserve special accolades for identifying problems with earlier drafts of the text and exercises.

We are indebted to the reviewers of past editions who shared our commitment to elevating the instruction of project management. We thank you for your many thoughtful suggestions and for making our book better. Of course, we accept responsibility for the final version of the text.

Paul S. Allen, Rice University
Victor Allen, Lawrence Technological University
Kwasi Amoako–Gyampah, University of North Carolina–Greensboro
Gregory Anderson, Weber State University
Mark Angolia, East Carolina University
Joseph Aranyosi, University of Phoenix
Brian M. Ashford, North Carolina State University
Dana Bachman, Colorado Christian University
Robin Bagent, College of Southern Idaho
Scott Bailey, Troy University
Nabil Bedewi, Georgetown University
Anandhi Bharadwaj, Emory University
James Blair, Washington University–St. Louis
Mary Jean Blink, Mount St. Joseph University
S. Narayan Bodapati, Southern Illinois University at Edwardsville
Warren J. Boe, University of Iowa
Thomas Calderon, University of Akron
Alan Cannon, University of Texas–Arlington
Susan Cholette, San Francisco State
Denis F. Cioffi, George Washington University
Rebecca Clemons, Indiana University East
Robert Cope, Southeastern Louisiana University
Kenneth DaRin, Clarkson University
Ron Darnell, Amberton University
Jason Deane, Virginia Tech University
Burton Dean, San Jose State University
Joseph D. DeVoss, DeVry University
David Duby, Liberty University
Michael Ensby, Clarkson University
Charles Franz, University of Missouri, Columbia
Larry Frazier, City University of Seattle
Raouf Ghattas, DeVry University
Edward J. Glantz, Pennsylvania State University
Michael Godfrey, University of Wisconsin–Oshkosh
Jay Goldberg, Marquette University
Robert Groff, Westwood College
Raffael Guidone, New York City College of Technology
Brian Gurney, Montana State University–Billings
Owen P. Hall, Pepperdine University
Chaodong Han, Towson University
Bruce C. Hartman, University of Arizona
Jacob Heller, Tarleton State University
Mark Huber, University of Georgia
Richard Irving, York University
Marshall Issen, Clarkson University
Robert T. Jones, DePaul University
Susan Kendall, Arapahoe Community College
George Kenyon, Lamar University
Robert Key, University of Phoenix
Elias Konwufine, Keiser University
Dennis Krumwiede, Idaho State University
Rafael Landaeta, Old Dominion University
Eldon Larsen, Marshall University
Eric T. Larson, Rutgers University
Philip Lee, Lone Star College–University Park
Charles Lesko, East Carolina University
Richard L. Luebbe, Miami University of Ohio
Linh Luong, City University of Seattle
Steve Machon, DeVry University-Tinley Park
Andrew Manikas, University of Louisville
William Matthews, William Patterson University
Lacey McNeely, Oregon State University
Carol Miller, Community College of Denver
William Moylan, Lawrence Technological College of Business
Ravi Narayanaswamy, University of South Carolina–Aiken
Muhammad Obeidat, Southern Polytechnic State University

Michael Pace, Texas A&M University
Edward Pascal, University of Ottawa
James H. Patterson, Indiana University
Steve Peng, California State University–East Bay
Nicholas C. Petruzzi, University of Illinois–Urbana/Champaign
Abirami Radhakrishnan, Morgan State University
Emad Rahim, Bellevue University
Tom Robbins, East Carolina University
Rory Rodney, Post University
Tim Rodgers, University of Colorado
Art Rogers, City University
Linda Rose, Westwood College
Pauline Schilpzand, Oregon State University
Teresa Shaft, University of Oklahoma
Russell T. Shaver, Kennesaw State University
William R. Sherrard, San Diego State University
Erin Sims, DeVry University–Pomona
Donald Smith, Texas A&M University
Kenneth Solheim, DeVry University–Federal Way
Christy Strbiak, U.S. Air Force Academy
Dr. Susan Sweeney, Wilmington University
Peter Sutanto, Prairie View A&M University
Jon Tomlinson, University of Northwestern Ohio
Oya Tukel, Cleveland State University
David A. Vaughan, City University
Mahmoud Watad, William Paterson University
Fen Wang, Central Washington University
Cynthia Wessel, Lindenwood University
Larry R. White, Eastern Illinois University
Ronald W. Witzel, Keller Graduate School of Management
G. Peter Zhang, Georgia State University

In addition, we would like to thank our colleagues in the College of Business at Oregon State University for their support and help in completing this project. In particular, we recognize Lacey McNeely, Prem Mathew, and Jeewon Chou for their helpful advice and suggestions. We also wish to thank the many students who helped us at different stages of this project, most notably Neil Young, Saajan Patel, Katherine Knox, Dat Nguyen, and David Dempsey. Mary Gray deserves special credit for editing and working under tight deadlines on earlier editions.

Finally, we want to extend our thanks to all the people at McGraw-Hill Education for their efforts and support. First, we would like to thank Stephanie DeRosa, and David Ploskonka, for providing editorial direction, guidance, and management of the book's development for the eighth edition. And we would also like to thank Sandy Wille, Sandy Ludovissy, Egzon Shaqiri, Beth Cray, and Angela Norris for managing the final production, design, supplement, and media phases.

For the Indian adaptation, I, Rohit Joshi, extend my gratitude to my colleagues at the IIM Shillong, for their support in bringing this project to completion. In particular, I am deeply grateful to Prof. D P Goyal for his valuable advice and insights. I also appreciate the contributions of numerous students who assisted at various stages, with special thanks to our PGPEx students of the 2024 batch for their immense support. Additionally, I acknowledge the dedicated efforts of Navneet Kumar, Aishwarya Ganapathy, and Pratiti Ghosh from McGraw Hill (India) for their meticulous editing and commitment to meeting tight deadlines.

Erik W. Larson
Clifford F. Gray
Pinyarat Sirisomboonsuk
Rohit Joshi

Publisher's Note

McGraw-Hill Education (India) invites suggestions and comments from you, all of which can be sent to *support.india@mheducation.com* (kindly mention the title and author name in the subject line).

Piracy-related issues may also be reported.

Note to Student

You will find the content of this text highly practical, relevant, and current. The concepts discussed are relatively simple and intuitive. As you study each chapter we suggest you try to grasp not only how things work but also why things work. You are encouraged to use the text as a handbook as you move through the three levels of competency:

I know.

I can do.

I can adapt to new situations.

The field of project management is growing in importance and at an exponential rate. It is nearly impossible to imagine a future management career that does not include management of projects. Resumes of managers will soon be primarily a description of their participation in and contributions to projects.

Good luck on your journey through the text and on your future projects.

Chapter-by-Chapter Revisions for the Ninth Edition

Chapter 1: Modern Project Management

- New Snapshot: PMI's 50 Most Influential Projects: 1969–2019.
- New Appendix: A Guide to the Project Management Body of Knowledge (PMBOK Guide) Seventh Edition and Its Ancillaries.
- New Snapshot: Infosys Adopting Agile.
- New Case: Delhi Metro: Driving Excellence in Urban Infrastructure.

Chapter 2: Organization Strategy and Project Selection

- Revised Snapshot: IBM's Watson Project.
- New Snapshot: Is This the End of Airbnb?
- New segment on behavioral biases that affect project selection.
- Snapshot: Project Code Names revised.
- New Snapshot: Organizational Strategy for Indian Railways.
- New Case: Reliance Jio's 6G Market Entry Strategy.

Chapter 3: Organization: Structure and Culture

- New Snapshot: 2021 PMO of the Year Moffitt Cancer Center.
- New Snapshot: Infosys' Flat Organizational Structure.
- New Research Highlight: Multinational Project and Organizational Culture – Case of India and Russia.

Chapter 4: Defining the Project

- Requirements is now discussed under defining a project.
- New Snapshot: The Bradley Fighting Vehicle.
- New section on Software Solutions and Emerging Trends in Project Management.

Chapter 5: Estimating Project Times and Costs

- New segment on four aspects of estimating.
- New Case: Tata Steel's Kalinganagar Plant.
- New Case: Electrification of Mumbai-Ahmedabad Bullet Train.

Chapter 6: Developing a Project Schedule

- Snapshot: Concurrent Engineering (Fast Tracking) updated.
- A new project network exercise.
- New Case: Freight Corridor Project.
- Appendix 6.1: Step-by-Step MS Project Demonstration of Book Questions.

Chapter 7: Managing Risk

- An example of how pandemic created an opportunity for project is included in the text.
- Minor revisions made to tables to provide better clarity.
- New Case: Smart Cities Mission – Risk Assessment and Mitigation Strategies.

Chapter 8: Scheduling Resources and Costs

- New case: Midnight Sun II Project.
- New Snapshot: Indian Telecom Company – PMO for Scheduling Resources and Costs.
- Appendix 8.2: MS Project Demonstration of Resource Allocation, Leveling and Costing.

Chapter 9: Reducing Project Duration

- Snapshot 9.1: Smartphone Wars updated.
- New Snapshot: Operation Warp Speed.
- New Case: Chandrayaan Mission.

Chapter 10: Being an Effective Project Manager

- Reliance on virtual communication methods is discussed.
- New Snapshot: Fighting Zoom Fatigue.
- New Snapshot: Organizational Strategy for Dedicated Freight Corridors (DFC).

Chapter 11: Managing Project Teams

- Managing Virtual Teams section has been updated and expanded.
- Managing hybrid teams where people work part time at home is discussed.
- New Case: L&T-IBM Collaboration: Pioneering India's Semiconductor Revolution.

Chapter 12: Outsourcing: Managing Interorganizational Relations

- New case: Umdanso Project.

Chapter 13: Progress and Performance Measurement and Evaluation

- Snapshot: Guidelines for Setting Milestones has been revised.
- New Snapshot: Oregon State University's Regional Coastal Research Vessels (RCRV) Project.

Chapter 14: Project Closure

- Discussion of project retrospectives has been updated and revised.
- New Research Highlight: Why Is It Difficult to Pull the Plug on Projects?
- New Case: Project Closure of L&T-IBM Semiconductor.

Chapter 15: Agile Project Management

- Introduction revised.
- Discussion of hybrid project management is expanded.
- New Snapshot: Adopting Agile Project Management at Infosys and TCS.

Chapter 16: International Projects

- New Snapshot: Avoiding Communication Catastrophes When Emailing Across Cultures.
- New Case: Bharti Airtel's Expansion into Africa.
- New Case: Tata Motors' Acquisition of Jaguar Land Rover: A Strategic Perspective.

Appendix Two: Computer Project Exercises

- Updated two computer exercises.

List of Indian Snapshots and Cases

Snapshots

- Infosys Adopting Agile 13
- Organizational Strategy for Indian Railways 56
- Infosys' Flat Organizational Structure 100
- Indian Telecom Company – PMO for Scheduling Resources and Costs 330
- Organizational Strategy for Dedicated Freight Corridors (DFC) in Indian Railways 418
- Adopting Agile Project Management at Infosys and TCS 649

Cases

- Delhi Metro: Driving Excellence in Urban Infrastructure 27
- Reliance Jio's 6G Market Entry Strategy 80
- Tata Steel's Kalinganagar Plant 189
- Electrification of Mumbai-Ahmedabad Bullet Train 91
- Freight Corridor Project 240
- Smart Cities Mission—Risk Assessment and Mitigation Strategies 287
- Chandrayaan Mission 404
- Navigating Communication Challenges in Global Remote Teams 449
- Poor Communication Leads to Loss of Customer 450
- L&T-IBM Collaboration: Pioneering India's Semiconductor Revolution 495
- Project Closure of L&T-IBM Semiconductor 628
- Agile Project Management in AEC Industry 661
- Agile Project Management by Zebra Ltd. 662
- Agile in Education Industry 663
- Bharti Airtel's Expansion into Africa 700
- Tata Motors' Acquisition of Jaguar Land Rover: A Strategic Perspective 703

Brief Contents

Preface vii

1. Modern Project Management 1
2. Organization Strategy and Project Selection 38
3. Organization: Structure and Culture 87
4. Defining the Project 125
5. Estimating Project Times and Costs 158
6. Developing a Project Schedule 197
7. Managing Risk 251
8. Scheduling Resources and Costs 301
9. Reducing Project Duration 368
10. Being an Effective Project Manager 410
11. Managing Project Teams 451
12. Outsourcing: Managing Interorganizational Relations 503
13. Progress and Performance Measurement and Evaluation 543
14. Project Closure 601
15. Agile Project Management 632
16. International Projects 665

APPENDIX

One Solutions to Selected Exercises 707

Two Computer Project Exercises 720

GLOSSARY 736

ACRONYMS 743

PROJECT MANAGEMENT EQUATIONS 744

SOCIO-TECHNICAL APPROACH TO PROJECT MANAGEMENT 745

INDEX 746

Contents

Preface vii

Chapter 1
Modern Project Management 1

1.1 What Is a Project? 5
What a Project Is Not 6
Program versus Project 8
The Project Life Cycle 8
The Project Manager 9
Being Part of a Project Team 11
1.2 Agile Project Management 12
1.3 Current Drivers of Project Management 13
Compression of the Product Life Cycle 15
Knowledge Explosion 16
Triple Bottom Line (Planet, People, Profit) 16
Increased Customer Focus 16
Small Projects Represent Big Problems 16
1.4 Project Management Today: A Socio-Technical Approach 17
Summary 19

Chapter 2
Organization Strategy and Project Selection 38

2.1 Why Project Managers Need to Understand Strategy 40
2.2 The Strategic Management Process: An Overview 40
Four Activities of the Strategic Management Process 43
2.3 The Need for a Project Priority System 45
Problem 1: Behavioral Biases 45
Problem 2: The Implementation Gap 47
Problem 3: Organization Politics 47
Problem 4: Resource Conflicts and Multitasking 48
2.4 Project Classification 49
2.5 Phase Gate Model 50
2.6 Selection Criteria 52
Financial Criteria 52
Nonfinancial Criteria 54
Two Multi-Criteria Selection Models 54
2.7 Applying a Selection Model 58
Project Classification 58
Sources and Solicitation of Project Proposals 59
Ranking Proposals and Selection of Projects 60
2.8 Managing the Portfolio System 64
Senior Management Input 64
Governance Team Responsibilities 64
Balancing the Portfolio for Risks and Types of Projects 64
Summary 66

Chapter 3
Organization: Structure and Culture 87

3.1 Project Management Structures 89
Organizing Projects within the Functional Organization 89
Organizing Projects as Dedicated Teams 91
Organizing Projects within a Matrix Arrangement 96
Different Matrix Forms 98
3.2 Project Management Office (PMO) 100
3.3 What Is the Right Project Management Structure? 103
Organization Considerations 103
Project Considerations 103
3.4 Organizational Culture 104
What Is Organizational Culture? 105
Identifying Cultural Characteristics 107
3.5 Implications of Organizational Culture for Organizing Projects 109
Summary 113

Chapter 4
Defining the Project 125

4.1 Step 1: Defining the Project Scope 127
Employing a Project Scope Checklist 127
4.2 Step 2: Establishing Project Priorities 132

4.3 Step 3: Creating the Work Breakdown Structure 134
Major Groupings in a WBS 134
How a WBS Helps the Project Manager 135
A Simple WBS Development 136
4.4 Step 4: Integrating the WBS with the Organization 139
4.5 Step 5: Coding the WBS for the Information System 141
4.6 Process Breakdown Structure 142
4.7 Responsibility Matrices 143
4.8 Project Communication Plan 146
4.9 Software Solutions and Emerging Trends in Project Management 148
Summary 150

Chapter 5
Estimating Project Times and Costs 158

5.1 Factors Influencing the Quality of Estimates 160
Planning Horizon 160
Project Complexity 161
People 161
Project Structure and Organization 161
Padding Estimates 161
Organizational Culture 161
Other Factors 162
5.2 Estimating Guidelines for Times, Costs, and Resources 162
5.3 Top-Down versus Bottom-Up Estimating 164
5.4 Methods for Estimating Project Times and Costs 166
Top-Down Approaches for Estimating Project Times and Costs 166
Bottom-Up Approaches for Estimating Project Times and Costs 170
A Hybrid: Phase Estimating 171
5.5 Level of Detail 173
5.6 Types of Costs 175
Direct Costs 175
Direct Project Overhead Costs 175
General and Administrative (G&A) Overhead Costs 175
5.7 Refining Estimates 176
5.8 Creating a Database for Estimating 178
5.9 Mega Projects: A Special Case 179
Summary 182

Chapter 6
Developing a Project Schedule 197

6.1 Developing the Project Network 198
6.2 From Work Package to Network 199
6.3 Constructing a Project Network 201
Terminology 201
Basic Rules to Follow in Developing Project Networks 201
6.4 Activity-on-Node (AON) Fundamentals 202
6.5 Network Computation Process 205
Forward Pass—Earliest Times 206
Backward Pass—Latest Times 208
Determining Slack (or Float) 209
6.6 Using the Forward and Backward Pass Information 212
6.7 Level of Detail for Activities 213
6.8 Practical Considerations 213
Network Logic Errors 213
Activity Numbering 213
Use of Computers to Develop Networks 214
Calendar Dates 214
Multiple Starts and Multiple Projects 214
6.9 Extended Network Techniques to Come Closer to Reality 217
Laddering 217
Use of Lags to Reduce Schedule Detail and Project Duration 217
An Example Using Lag Relationships—the Forward and Backward Pass 221
Hammock Activities 222
Summary 223

Chapter 7
Managing Risk 251

7.1 Risk Management Process 253
7.2 Step 1: Risk Identification 254
7.3 Step 2: Risk Assessment 258
Probability Analysis 261
7.4 Step 3: Risk Response Development 262
Mitigating Risk 262
Avoiding Risk 263
Transferring Risk 263
Escalating Risk 265
Retaining Risk 265
7.5 Contingency Planning 265
Technical Risks 267
Schedule Risks 268
Cost Risks 268
Funding Risks 268
7.6 Opportunity Management 269
7.7 Contingency Funding and Time Buffers 270
Contingency Reserves 271
Management Reserves 271

Time Buffers 272
7.8 Step 4: Risk Response Control 272
7.9 Change Control Management 273
Summary 276

Chapter 8
Scheduling Resources and Costs 301

8.1 Overview of the Resource Scheduling Problem 303
8.2 Types of Resource Constraints 304
8.3 Classification of a Scheduling Problem 306
8.4 Resource Allocation Methods 306
Assumptions 306
Time-Constrained Projects: Smoothing Resource Demand 306
Resource-Constrained Projects 308
8.5 Computer Demonstration of Resource-Constrained Scheduling 313
The Impacts of Resource-Constrained Scheduling 317
8.6 Splitting Activities 320
8.7 Benefits of Scheduling Resources 321
8.8 Assigning Project Work 322
8.9 Multiproject Resource Schedules 323
8.10 Using the Resource Schedule to Develop a Project Cost Baseline 324
Why a Time-Phased Budget Baseline Is Needed 324
Creating a Time-Phased Budget 325
Summary 331

Chapter 9
Reducing Project Duration 368

9.1 Rationale for Reducing Project Duration 370
9.2 Options for Accelerating Project Completion 371
Options When Resources Are Not Constrained 371
Options When Resources Are Constrained 374
9.3 Project Cost-Duration Graph 376
Explanation of Project Costs 376
9.4 Constructing a Project Cost-Duration Graph 379
Determining the Activities to Shorten 379
A Simplified Example 380
9.5 Practical Considerations 383
Using the Project Cost-Duration Graph 383
Crash Times 384
Linearity Assumption 384
Choice of Activities to Crash Revisited 384
Time Reduction Decisions and Sensitivity 386
9.6 What If Cost, Not Time, Is the Issue? 386
Reduce Project Scope 387
Have Owner Take on More Responsibility 387
Outsource Project Activities or Even the Entire Project 387
Brainstorm Cost Savings Options 387
Summary 388

Chapter 10
Being an Effective Project Manager 410

10.1 Managing versus Leading a Project 412
10.2 Engaging Project Stakeholders 413
10.3 Influence as Exchange 417
Task-Related Currencies 419
Position-Related Currencies 420
Inspiration-Related Currencies 421
Relationship-Related Currencies 421
Personal-Related Currencies 421
10.4 Social Network Building 422
Mapping Stakeholder Dependencies 422
Management by Wandering Around (MBWA) 424
Managing Upward Relations 427
Leading by Example 428
10.5 Ethics and Project Management 431
10.6 Building Trust: The Key to Exercising Influence 433
10.7 Qualities of an Effective Project Manager 434
Summary 437

Chapter 11
Managing Project Teams 451

11.1 The Five-Stage Team Development Model 454
11.2 Situational Factors Affecting Team Development 456
11.3 Building High-Performance Project Teams 458
Recruiting Project Members 458
Conducting Project Meetings 459
Establishing Team Norms 461
Establishing a Team Identity 464
Creating a Shared Vision 465
Managing Project Reward Systems 467
Orchestrating the Decision-Making Process 469
Managing Conflict within the Project 471
Rejuvenating the Project Team 474
11.4 Managing Virtual Project Teams 476
Mixed Project Teams 480

Hybrid Project Teams 480

11.5 Project Team Pitfalls 481

Groupthink 481

Bureaucratic Bypass Syndrome 481

Team Spirit Becomes Team Infatuation 482

Going Local 482

Summary 483

Chapter 12

Outsourcing: Managing Interorganizational Relations 503

12.1 Outsourcing Project Work 505

12.2 Request for Proposal (RFP) 509

Selection of Contractor from Bid Proposals 510

12.3 Best Practices in Outsourcing Project Work 511

Well-Defined Requirements and Procedures 511

Extensive Training and Team-Building Activities 513

Well-Established Conflict Management Processes in Place 514

Frequent Review and Status Updates 516

Co-location When Needed 517

Fair and Incentive-Laden Contracts 518

Long-Term Outsourcing Relationships 518

12.4 The Art of Negotiating 519

1. Separate the People from the Problem 520

2. Focus on Interests, Not Positions 521

3. Invent Options for Mutual Gain 522

4. When Possible, Use Objective Criteria 523

Dealing with Unreasonable People 523

12.5 A Note on Managing Customer Relations 524

Summary 527

Chapter 13

Progress and Performance Measurement and Evaluation 543

13.1 Structure of a Project Monitoring Information System 544

What Data Are Collected? 544

Collecting Data and Analysis 545

Reports and Reporting 545

13.2 The Project Control Process 546

Step 1: Setting a Baseline Plan 546

Step 2: Measuring Progress and Performance 546

Step 3: Comparing Plan against Actual 546

Step 4: Taking Action 546

13.3 Monitoring Time Performance 547

Tracking Gantt Chart 547

Control Chart 547

Milestone Schedules 549

13.4 Earned Value Management (EVM) 549

The Need for Earned Value Management 549

Percent Complete Rule 553

What Costs Are Included in Baselines? 553

Methods of Variance Analysis 554

13.5 Developing a Status Report: A Hypothetical Example 556

Assumptions 556

Baseline Development 556

Development of the Status Report 557

13.6 Indexes to Monitor Progress 561

Performance Indexes 562

Project Percent Complete Indexes 563

Software for Project Cost/Schedule Systems 563

Additional Earned Value Rules 564

13.7 Forecasting Final Project Cost 565

13.8 Other Control Issues 567

Technical Performance Measurement 567

Scope Creep 569

Baseline Changes 570

The Costs and Problems of Data Acquisition 574

Summary 575

Chapter 14

Project Closure 601

14.1 Types of Project Closure 603

14.2 Wrap-up Closure Activities 606

14.3 Project Audits 609

The Project Audit Process 610

Project Retrospectives 612

14.4 Project Audits: The Big Picture 614

Level 1: Ad Hoc Project Management 615

Level 2: Formal Application of Project Management 616

Level 3: Institutionalization of Project Management 616

Level 4: Management of Project Management System 616

Level 5: Optimization of Project Management System 617

14.5 Post-implementation Evaluation 618

Team Evaluation 618

Individual, Team Member, and Project Manager Performance Reviews 619

Summary 622

Chapter 15
Agile Project Management 632

15.1 Traditional versus Agile Methods 634
15.2 Agile PM 636
15.3 Agile PM in Action: Scrum 639
Roles and Responsibilities 640
Scrum Meetings 641
Product and Sprint Backlogs 643
Sprint and Release Burndown Charts 644
15.4 Extreme Programming and Kanban 646
Extreme Programming (XP) 646
Kanban 647
15.5 Applying Agile PM to Large Projects 648
15.6 Limitations and Concerns 650
15.7 Hybrid Project Management 651
Summary 652

Chapter 16
International Projects 665

16.1 Environmental Factors 667
Legal/Political Factors 667
Security 668
Geography 669
Economic Factors 669
Infrastructure 671
Culture 672
16.2 Project Site Selection 674
16.3 Cross-Cultural Considerations: A Closer Look 675
Adjustments 676
Working in Mexico 679
Working in France 681
Working in Saudi Arabia 682
Working in China 683
Working in the United States 684
Summary Comments about Working in Different Cultures 686
Culture Shock 687
16.4 Selection and Training for International Projects 690
Summary 692

Appendix One: Solutions to Selected Exercises 707

Appendix Two: Computer Project Exercises 720

Glossary 736

Acronyms 743

Project Management Equations 744

A Socio-Technical Approach to Project Management 745

Index 746

CHAPTER ONE

1 Modern Project Management

LEARNING OBJECTIVES

After reading this chapter you should be able to:

1-1 Understand why project management (PM) is crucial in today's world.

1-2 Distinguish a project from routine operations.

1-3 Identify the different stages of a project life cycle.

1-4 Describe how Agile PM is different from traditional PM.

1-5 Understand that managing projects involves balancing the technical and sociocultural dimensions of the project.

OUTLINE

1.1 What Is a Project?

1.2 Agile Project Management

1.3 Current Drivers of Project Management

1.4 Project Management Today: A Socio-Technical Approach

Summary

Text Overview

Appendix 1.1: 2021 PMI: A Guide to the Project Management Body of Knowledge (PMBOK Guide) Seventh Edition and Its Ancillaries

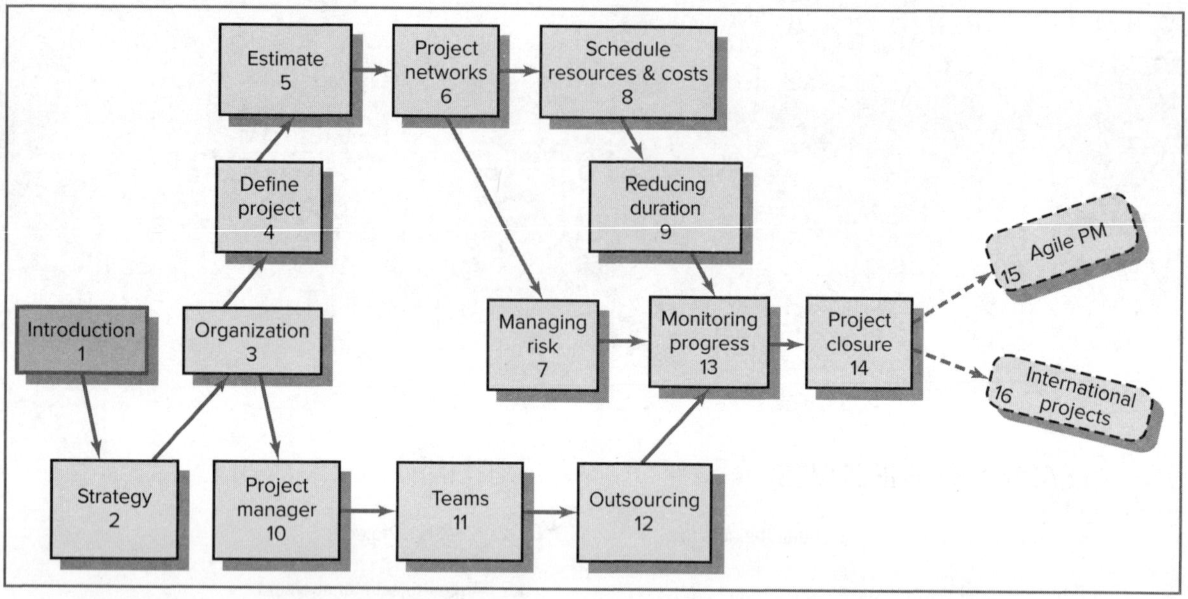

All of humankind's greatest accomplishments—from building the great pyramids to discovering a cure for polio to putting a footprint on the moon—began as a project.

LO 1-1

Understand why project management (PM) is crucial in today's world.

Ever since the first edition, we have opened our text with the line: "This is a good time to be reading a book about project management." This is more true today than ever before. Business leaders and experts have recognized that project management is critical to sustainable economic growth. New jobs and competitive advantage are achieved by constant innovation, developing new products and services, and improving both productivity and quality of work. This is the world of project management. Project management provides people with a powerful set of tools that improves their ability to plan, implement, and manage activities to accomplish specific objectives. But project management is more than just a set of tools; it is a contact sport that requires building collaborative relationships among a diverse cast of stakeholders. Exciting opportunities await people skilled in project management.

The project approach has long been the style of doing business in the construction industry, U.S. Department of Defense contracts, and Hollywood, as well as big consulting firms. Now, project management has spread to all avenues of work. Today, project teams carry out everything from port expansions to hospital restructuring to upgrading information systems. They are creating next-generation fuel-efficient vehicles, developing sustainable sources of energy, and exploring the farthest reaches of outer space. The impact of project management is most profound in high-tech industries, where the new folk heroes are young professionals whose Herculean efforts lead to the constant flow of new hardware and software products.

Project management is not limited to the private sector. Project management is also a vehicle for doing good deeds and solving social problems. Endeavors such as providing emergency aid to areas hit by natural disasters, devising a strategy for reducing crime and drug abuse within a city, or organizing a community effort to renovate a public playground would and do benefit from the application of modern project management techniques.

Perhaps the best indicator of demand for project management can be seen in the rapid expansion of the Project Management Institute (PMI), a professional organization for project managers. PMI membership has grown from 93,000 in 2002 to more than 686,000 in 2021. See Snapshot from Practice 1.1: The Project Management Institute for information regarding professional certification in project management.

It's nearly impossible to pick up a newspaper or business periodical and not find something about projects. This is no surprise! Approximately $2.5 trillion (about 25 percent of the U.S. gross national product) is spent on projects each year in the United States alone. Other countries are increasingly spending more on projects. Millions of people around the world consider project management the major task in their profession.

Many people who excel at managing projects never have the title of project manager. They include accountants, lawyers, administrators, scientists, contractors, coaches, public health officials, teachers, and community advocates whose success depends upon being able to lead and manage project work. For some, the very nature of their work is project driven. Projects may be cases for lawyers, audits for accountants, events for artists, and renovations for contractors. For others, projects may be a small but

SNAPSHOT FROM PRACTICE 1.1 The Project Management Institute*

The Project Management Institute (PMI) was founded in 1969 as an international society for project managers. Today, PMI has members from more than 200 countries/territories and more than 686,000 members. PMI professionals come from virtually every major industry, including aerospace, automotive, business management, construction, engineering, financial services, information technology, pharmaceuticals, healthcare, and telecommunications.

PMI provides certification as a **Project Management Professional (PMP)**—someone who has documented sufficient project experience, agreed to follow the PMI code of professional conduct, and demonstrated mastery of the field of project management by passing a comprehensive examination based on the Project Management Body of Knowledge (PMBOK), which is in its 6th edition. The number of people earning PMP status has grown dramatically in recent years. In 1996, there were fewer than 3,000 certified Project Management Professionals. By 2023, more than 1.3 million people have passed the PMP exam.

Just as the CPA exam is a standard for accountants, passing the PMP exam may become the standard for project managers. Some companies are requiring that all their project managers be PMP certified. Moreover, many job postings are restricted to PMPs. Job seekers, in general, are finding that being PMP certified is an advantage in the marketplace.

PMI added a certification as a **Certified Associate in Project Management (CAPM).** CAPM is designed for project team members and entry-level project managers, as well as qualified undergraduate and graduate students who want a credential to recognize their mastery of the project management body of knowledge. CAPM does not require the extensive project management experience associated with the PMP. In fact, students often qualify for taking the CAPM exam by taking a course on project management. For more details on PMP and CAPM, google PMI to find the current website for the Project Management Institute.

This text provides a solid foundation for passing either exam. However, we personally found it necessary to study a good PMP/CAPM exam "prep book" to pass the exam. This is recommended, given the format and nature of the exam. Project management is not a multiple choice profession.

*C. McGaughy, K. Whitby, L. Schofield, and H. McLarnon, "March 2023 PMI Fact File Stats," www.projectmanagement.com. Accessed 5/5/23; Project Management Institute, *2021 Annual Report: Year of Impact,* www.pmi.org. Accessed 5/4/23.

critical part of their work. For example, a high school teacher who teaches four classes a day is responsible for coaching a group of students to compete in a national debate competition. A store manager who oversees daily operations is charged with developing an employee retention program. A sales account executive is given the additional assignment of team lead to launch daily deals into a new city. A public health official who manages a clinic is also responsible for organizing a Homeless Youth Connect event. For these and others, project management is not a title but a critical job requirement. It is hard to think of a profession or a career path that would not benefit from being good at managing projects.

Not only is project management critical to most careers, but also the skill set is transferable across most businesses and professions. Project management fundamentals are universal. The same project management methodology that is used to develop a new product can be adapted to create new services, organize events, refurbish aging operations, and so forth. In a world where it is estimated that each person is likely to experience three to four career changes, managing projects is a talent worthy of development.

The significance of project management can also be seen in the classroom. Twenty years ago, major universities offered one or two classes in project management, primarily for engineers. Today, most universities offer multiple sections of project management classes, with the core group of engineers being supplemented by business students majoring in marketing, management information systems (MIS), and finance,

SNAPSHOT FROM PRACTICE 1.2 A Dozen Examples of Projects Given to Recent College Graduates

1. **Business information:** Join a project team charged with installing a new data security system.
2. **Physical education:** Design and develop a new fitness program for senior citizens that combines principles of yoga and aerobics.
3. **Marketing:** Execute a sales program for a new home air purifier.
4. **Industrial engineering:** Manage a team to create a value chain report for every aspect of a key product from design to customer delivery.
5. **Chemistry:** Develop a quality control program for an organization's drug production facilities.
6. **Management:** Implement a new store layout design.
7. **Pre-med neurology student:** Join a project team linking mind mapping to an imbedded prosthetic that will offer people with blindness an option to improve their vision.
8. **Sports communication:** Join the athletics staff at Montana State University to promote women's basketball.
9. **Systems engineer:** Become a project team member of a project to develop data mining of medical papers and studies related to drug efficacy.
10. **Accounting:** Work on an audit of a major client.
11. **Public health:** Research and design a medical marijuana educational program.
12. **English:** Create a web-based user manual for a new electronics product.

John Fedele/Blend Images

as well as students from other disciplines such as oceanography, health sciences, computer sciences, and liberal arts. These students are finding that their exposure to project management is providing them with distinct advantages when it comes time to look for jobs. More and more employers are looking for graduates with project management skills. See Snapshot from Practice 1.2: A Dozen Examples of Projects Given to Recent College Graduates for examples of projects given to recent college graduates. The logical starting point for developing these skills is understanding the uniqueness of a project and of project managers.

1.1 What Is a Project?

LO 1-2

Distinguish a project from routine operations.

What do the following headlines have in common?

Millions Watch World Cup Finals
Citywide WiFi System Set to Go Live
Hospitals Respond to New Healthcare Reforms
Apple's New iPhone Hits the Market
City Receives Stimulus Funds to Expand Light Rail System

All of these events are projects.

Holly Hildreth/McGraw Hill

The Project Management Institute provides the following definition of a project:

A **project** is a temporary endeavor undertaken to create a unique product, service, or result.

Like most organizational efforts, the major goal of a project is to satisfy a customer's need. Beyond this fundamental similarity, the characteristics of a project help differentiate it from other endeavors of the organization. The major characteristics of a project are as follows:

1. An established objective.
2. A defined lifespan with a beginning and an end.
3. Usually, the involvement of several departments and professionals.
4. Typically, doing something that has never been done before.
5. Specific time, cost, and performance requirements.

First, projects have a defined objective—whether it is constructing a 12-story apartment complex by January 1 or releasing version 2.0 of a specific software package as quickly as possible. This singular purpose is often lacking in daily organizational life in which workers perform repetitive operations each day.

Second, because there is a specified objective, projects have a defined endpoint, which is contrary to the ongoing duties and responsibilities of traditional jobs. Instead of staying in one job, individuals often move from project to project, working with different groups of people. For example, after helping to install a security system, an IT engineer may be assigned to develop a database for a different client.

Third, unlike much organizational work that is segmented according to functional specialty, projects typically require the combined efforts of a variety of specialists. Instead of working in separate offices under separate managers, project participants, whether they be engineers, financial analysts, marketing professionals, or quality control specialists, work together under the guidance of a project manager to complete a project.

The fourth characteristic of a project is that it is nonroutine and has some unique elements. This is not an either/or issue but a matter of degree. Obviously, accomplishing something that has never been done before, such as building an electric automobile or landing two mechanical rovers on Mars, requires solving previously unsolved problems and using breakthrough technology. On the other hand, even basic construction projects that involve established sets of routines and procedures require some degree of customization that makes them unique. See Snapshot from Practice 1.3: London Calling: Seattle Seahawks versus Oakland Raiders for an unusual change in routine.

Finally, specific time, cost, and performance requirements bind projects. Projects are evaluated according to accomplishment, cost, and time spent. These triple constraints impose a higher degree of accountability than typically found in most jobs. These three also highlight one of the primary functions of project management, which is balancing the trade-offs among time, cost, and performance while ultimately satisfying the customer.

What a Project Is Not

Projects should not be confused with everyday work. A project is not routine, repetitive work! Ordinary daily work typically requires doing the same or similar work over and over, while a project is done only once; a new product or service exists when the project is completed. Examine the list in Table 1.1 that compares routine, repetitive work and projects. Recognizing the difference is important because too often resources can be used up on daily operations, which may not contribute to longer-range organization strategies that require innovative new products.

SNAPSHOT FROM PRACTICE 1.3 London Calling: Seattle Seahawks versus Oakland Raiders*

On October 7, 2018, the National Football League (NFL) Seattle Seahawks walked off the field having played their best game of the season, only to fall short to the undefeated Los Angeles Rams, 33-31. Next on the schedule was an away game with the Oakland Raiders. Instead of heading about 670 miles south to Oakland, California, however, the Seahawks flew nearly 5,000 miles to London, England, eight time zones away, to spread the gospel of the NFL.

Sending an NFL team overseas during the season is no easy task. Advanced planning is critical. Players need passports. Accommodations have to be found and transportation arranged. The equipment staff sends supplies months in advance. All total, the Seahawks ended up shipping 21,000 pounds of gear and products, including 1,150 rolls of athletic tape, 2 tons of medical supplies, 350 power adapters, and 500 pairs of shoes!

Two of the biggest challenges the "Hawks" faced were jet lag and distractions. Many of the players and staff had never been overseas. London would be a strange, exciting experience. With this in mind, head coach Pete Carroll decided to fly early to London on Wednesday, October 10. This would allow players to better adjust their sleep patterns while providing some free time to explore London.

WEDNESDAY, OCTOBER 10

The Seahawks boarded a chartered jet that included 45 sleeping pods in first class for the veteran players. Coach Carroll and his staff sat in the first row of business class. Rookies and members of the practice squad sat behind them. Regardless of class, everyone got the same menu: beef filet, Cajun chicken, or herb-roasted salmon.

Typically, on flights to the east, Sam Ramsden, the team's director of health and player performance, tells players to stay awake so they will be tired and sleep well when they arrive. For the London trip, though, Ramsden reversed the program: he told players to sleep as much as possible on the flight so that when they arrived in London on Thursday afternoon, they would have enough energy to stay up until 9 or 10 p.m. and then get a full night's rest. "We try to protect their circadian rhythms as much as possible," Ramsden said. Circadian rhythm (also known as body clock) is a natural, internal system that's designed to regulate feelings of sleepiness and wakefulness over a 24-hour period.

Ramsden's staff gave each player special sleep kits that included blackout eye masks. Some players took melatonin or Ambien, while others used headphones that played the sounds of wind and rushing water to induce sleep.

THURSDAY, OCTOBER 11

The Seahawks landed on Thursday about 1:30 p.m. (5:30 a.m. Seattle time). Buses took them to a golf course resort north of London.

At night, the players let off some steam at a Topgolf facility. Here organized into groups of four, they tried to hit golf balls into giant holes to score points. Jeers rang out every time they were wildly off target.

FRIDAY, OCTOBER 12

After several hours of meetings and a practice, players were free to explore London. They scattered to the various corners of London. On returning to the resort before the 11:00 p.m. curfew, a few of the players complained about the warm English beer.

The Oakland Raiders arrived in London at 1:00 p.m., 53 hours before game time.

SATURDAY, OCTOBER 13

Coach Carroll likes to take his players to the stadium the day before a road game so they can visualize conditions ahead of time. At 1:30 p.m., the Seahawks drove to Wembley, where they saw their fully Seahawk-equipped locker room and the field, the most famous soccer pitch in England. The field appeared slick, so the equipment manager had longer screw-in cleats available for the players. The Hawks returned to their resort for their normal pregame evening routine.

GAMEDAY, OCTOBER 14

During the course of the game, the TV announcers commented several times that the Raiders seemed sluggish, while the Seahawks were sharp and focused. The Seahawks dominated the game, winning 27–3.

David Lee/Shutterstock

*G. Bell, "Seahawks Arrive in London. Why Twins Shaquill and Shaquem Griffin Did Not Travel Here Equally," thenewstribune.com, October 11, 2018. K. Belson, "Four Thousand Miles for the W," nytimes.com, October 20, 2018; Accessed 10/22/18.

TABLE 1.1 Comparison of Routine Work with Projects

Routine, Repetitive Work	Projects
Taking class notes	Writing a term paper
Daily entering sales receipts into the accounting ledger	Setting up a sales kiosk for a professional accounting meeting
Responding to a supply-chain request	Developing a supply-chain information system
Practicing scales on the piano	Writing a new piano piece
Routine manufacture of an Apple iPod	Designing an iPod that is approximately 2 × 4 inches, interfaces with PC, and stores 10,000 songs
Attaching tags on a manufactured product	Wire-tag projects for GE and Walmart

Program versus Project

In practice, the terms *project* and *program* cause confusion. They are often used synonymously. *A* **program** *is a group of related projects designed to accomplish a common goal over an extended period of time.* Each project within a program has a project manager. The major differences lie in scale and time span.

Program management is the process of *managing* a group of ongoing, interdependent, related *projects* in a coordinated way to achieve strategic objectives. For example, a pharmaceutical organization could have a program for curing cancer. The cancer program includes and coordinates *all* cancer projects that continue over an extended time horizon (Gray, 2011). Coordinating all cancer projects under the oversight of a cancer team provides benefits not available from managing them individually. This cancer team also oversees the selection and prioritizing of cancer projects that are included in their special "Cancer" portfolio. Although each project retains its own goals and scope, the project manager and team are also motivated by the higher program goal. Program goals are closely related to broad strategic organization goals.

The Project Life Cycle

LO 1-3

Identify the different stages of a project life cycle.

Another way of illustrating the unique nature of project work is in terms of the **project life cycle.** The life cycle recognizes that projects have a limited lifespan and that there are predictable changes in the level of effort and focus over the life of the project. There are a number of different life-cycle models in project management literature. Many are unique to a specific industry or type of project. For example, a new-software development project may consist of five phases: definition, design, code, integration/test, and maintenance. A generic cycle is depicted in Figure 1.1.

The project life cycle typically passes sequentially through four stages: defining, planning, executing, and closing. The starting point begins the moment the project is given the go-ahead. Project effort starts slowly, builds to a peak, and then declines to delivery of the project to the customer.

1. **Defining stage.** Specifications of the project are defined; project objectives are established; teams are formed; major responsibilities are assigned.
2. **Planning stage.** The level of effort increases, and plans are developed to determine what the project will entail, when it will be scheduled, whom it will benefit, what quality level should be maintained, and what the budget will be.
3. **Executing stage.** A major portion of the project work takes place—both physical and mental. The physical product is produced (e.g., a bridge, a report, a software program). Time, cost, and specification measures are used for control. Is the project

FIGURE 1.1
Project Life Cycle

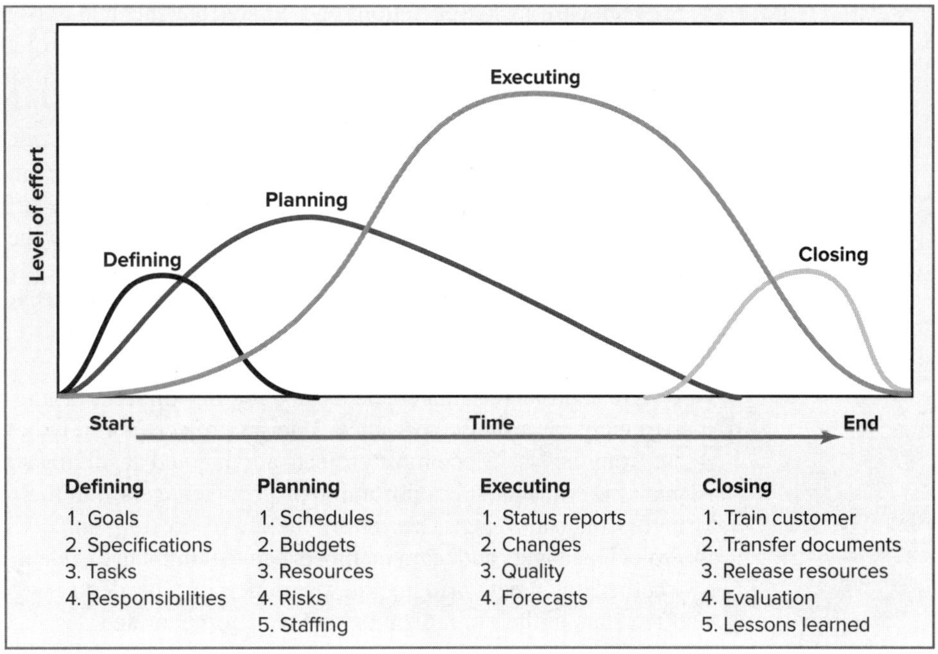

on schedule, on budget, and meeting specifications? What are the forecasts of each of these measures? What revisions/changes are necessary?

4. **Closing stage.** Closing includes three activities: delivering the project product to the customer, redeploying project resources, and conducting a post-project review. Delivery of the project might include customer training and transferring documents. Redeployment usually involves releasing project equipment/materials to other projects and finding new assignments for team members. Post-project reviews include not only assessing performance but also capturing lessons learned.

In practice, the project life cycle is used by some project groups to depict the timing of major tasks over the life of the project. For example, the design team might plan a major commitment of resources in the defining stage, while the quality team would expect their major effort to increase in the latter stages of the project life cycle. Because most organizations have a portfolio of projects going on concurrently, each at a different stage of each project's life cycle, careful planning and management at the organization and project levels are imperative.

The Project Manager

At first glance, project managers perform the same functions as other managers. That is, they plan, schedule, motivate, and control. However, what makes them unique is that they manage temporary, nonrepetitive activities to complete a fixed-life project. Unlike functional managers, who take over existing operations, project managers create a project team and organization where none existed before. They must decide what and how things should be done instead of simply managing set processes. They must meet the challenges of each phase of the project life cycle and even oversee the dissolution of their operation when the project is completed.

Project managers must work with a diverse troupe of characters to complete projects. They are typically the direct link to the customer and must manage the tension between customer expectations and what is feasible and reasonable. Project managers provide direction, coordination, and integration to the project team, which is often made up of part-time participants loyal to their functional departments. They often must work with a cadre of outsiders—vendors, suppliers, and subcontractors—who do not necessarily share their project allegiance.

Project managers are ultimately responsible for performance (frequently with too little authority). They must ensure that appropriate trade-offs are made among the time, cost, and performance requirements of the project. At the same time, unlike their functional counterparts, project managers often possess only rudimentary technical knowledge to make such decisions. Instead, they must orchestrate the completion of the project by inducing the right people, at the right time, to address the right issues and make the right decisions.

While project management is not for the timid, working on projects can be an extremely rewarding experience. Life on projects is rarely boring; each day is different from the last. Since most projects are directed at solving some tangible problem or pursuing some useful opportunity, project managers find their work personally meaningful and satisfying. They enjoy the act of creating something new and innovative. Project managers and team members can feel immense pride in their accomplishments, whether it is a new bridge, a new product, or a needed service. Project managers are often stars in their organization and well compensated.

Good project managers are always in demand. Every industry is looking for effective people who can get the right things done on time. See Snapshot from Practice 1.4: Ron Parker for an example of someone who leveraged his ability to manage projects to build a successful career in the glass products industry. Clearly, project management is a challenging and exciting profession. This text is intended to provide the necessary knowledge, perspective, and tools to enable students to accept the challenge.

SNAPSHOT FROM PRACTICE 1.4 Ron Parker

1986	BS Business Administration—Oregon State University
1986–1990	Food Products Manufacturing
1990–1994	Wood Products Manufacturing
1994–Current	Glass Products Manufacturing

Upon completion of my business degree at Oregon State University, I was recruited by a Fortune 100 food products company for a first-line production supervisor position. In that role, an opportunity came up for me to manage a project that involved rolling out a new statistical package-weight-control program throughout the factory. Successfully completing that project was instrumental in accelerating my career within the company, advancing from supervisor to product manager in less than three years.

After four years in food products, I accepted an offer to join a wood products manufacturing company. Initially, my role in this company was human resource manager. My HR responsibilities included managing several projects to improve safety and employee retention. Successful completion of these projects led to a promotion to plant manager. In the plant manager role, I was tasked with building and managing a new wood door manufacturing factory. After successfully taking that factory to full production, I was promoted again, to corporate manager of continuous improvement. This "culture change" project involved implementing total quality management throughout 13 different manufacturing factories as well as all the indirect and support functions within the corporation. Shortly after we successfully ingrained this new culture in the company, the owner passed away, leading me to look for other employment.

I was able to leverage my previous experience and success to convince the owner of a struggling glass fabrication company to hire me. In this new role as general manager, I was tasked with turning the company around. This was my largest project yet. Turning a company around involves a myriad of smaller improvement projects spanning from facilities and equipment improvements to product line additions and deletions to sales and marketing strategy and everything in between. In four years we successfully turned the company around to the extent that the owner was able to sell the company and comfortably retire.

Successfully turning that glass company around got the attention of a much larger competitor of ours, resulting in an offer of employment. This new offer involved the start-up of a $30M high-tech glass manufacturing facility in another state. We were able to take that facility from a dirt field to the highest-volume manufacturing facility of its kind in the world in just three years. After building and operating this factory at a world-class benchmark level for eight years, I came across a new and exciting opportunity to help expand a strong glass fabrication company in Canada. I spent four years successfully transitioning this Canadian company from a medium-sized glass fabrication facility to one of the largest and most successful of its kind in North America.

After tiring of the "Great White North," I found an opportunity to tackle the largest and most impactful project of my career. I'm currently VP of operations in a venture-funded, high-tech, start-up company. In this role, I'm overseeing the construction and start up of the first full-scale, high-volume electrochromic glass fabrication factory in the world. This new project involves building a company from the ground up and taking an exciting new technology from the lab to full-scale commercialization. Success in this role, although still far from being certain, will eventually revolutionize the glass industry through the introduction of a product that dramatically improves the energy efficiency and occupant comfort of buildings around the world.

Looking back on my career, it is apparent that my degree of success has largely been the result of taking on and successfully completing successively larger and increasingly impactful projects.

There's a saying that's always resonated with me: "If your only tool is a hammer, all your problems look like nails." Good tools are hard to come by and heavy to carry around. I like my tool bag filled with generalist tools: things like communication skills, leadership, common sense, judgment, reasoning, logic, and a strong sense of urgency. I often wonder how much more I could have accomplished, had I actually studied project management and had more of that toolset in my bag. With a bag full of strong generalist tools, you can tackle any problem in any business. Project management is clearly one of those skills where the better you are at it, the higher your chances of success in any business environment. Having the tools is only part of the equation, though. To be successful, you must also be willing to run at problems/opportunities when everyone else is running away from them.

Ron Parker

Being Part of a Project Team

Most people's first exposure to project management occurs while working as part of a team assigned to complete a specific project. Sometimes this work is full time, but in most cases, people work part-time on one or more projects. They must learn how to juggle their day-to-day commitments with additional project responsibilities. They may join a team with a long history of working together, in which case roles and norms are firmly established. Alternatively, their team may consist of strangers from different departments and organizations. As such, they endure the growing pains of a group evolving into a team. They need to be a positive force in helping the team coalesce into an effective project team.

Not only are there people issues, but project members are also expected to use project management tools and concepts. They develop or are given a project charter or scope statement that defines the objectives and parameters of the project. They work with others to create a project schedule and budget that will guide project execution. They need to understand project priorities so they can make independent decisions. They must know how to monitor and report project progress. Although much of this book is written from the perspective of a project manager, the tools, concepts, and methods are critical to everyone working on a project. Project members need to know how to avoid the dangers of scope creep, manage the critical path, engage in timely risk management, negotiate, and utilize virtual tools to communicate.

1.2 Agile Project Management

LO 1-4

Describe how Agile PM is different from traditional PM.

Traditional project management focuses on thorough planning up front. Planning requires predictability. For plans to be effective, managers have to have a good understanding of what is to be accomplished and how to do it. For example, when it comes to building a bridge, engineers can draw upon proven technology and design principles to plan and build the bridge. Not all projects enjoy such predictability. Figure 1.2 speaks to this issue.

Project uncertainty varies according to the extent the project scope is known and stable and the technology to be used is known and proven. Many projects, like the bridge project, product extensions, events, marketing campaigns, and so forth have well-established scopes and use proven technology, which provide predictability for effective planning. However, when the project scope and/or technology is not fully known, things become much less predictable and plan-driven methods suffer. Such was the case for software development projects where it was estimated that in 1995 American firms and agencies spent $81 billion for canceled software projects (The Standish Group, 1995). Fast forward to 2021, the cost of poor software quality in the United States was estimated to be over $2 trillion because of unsuccessful projects, software failure, and inferior quality legacy systems (Krasner, 2022).

Enter **Agile project management (Agile PM).** Agile methodologies emerged out of frustration with using traditional project management processes to develop software. Software projects are notorious for having unstable scopes in which end-user

FIGURE 1.2
Project Uncertainty

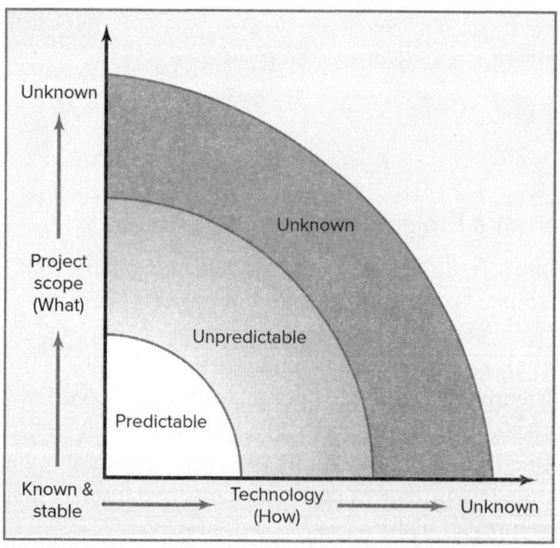

requirements are discovered not defined up front. Agile PM is now being used across industries to manage projects with high levels of uncertainty. Examples of people encountering high-uncertainty work include software systems engineers, product designers, explorers, doctors, lawyers, and many problem-solving engineers.[1]

Fundamentally, Agile PM employs an incremental, iterative process sometimes referred to as a "rolling wave" approach to complete projects (see Figure 1.3). Instead of trying to plan for everything up front, the scope of the project evolves. That is, the final project design/outcome is not known in great detail and is continuously developed through a series of incremental iterations (*waves*). Iterations typically last from one to four weeks. The goal of each iteration is to make tangible progress such as defining a key requirement, solving a technical problem, or creating desired features to demonstrate to the customer. At the end of each iteration, progress is reviewed, adjustments are made, and a different iterative cycle begins. Each new iteration subsumes the work of the previous iterations until the project is completed and the customer is satisfied.

Agile PM focuses on active collaboration between the project team and customer representatives, breaking projects into small functional pieces, and adapting to changing requirements.

It is not simply a question of either/or. Agile methods are often used up front in the defining phase to establish specifications and requirements, and then traditional methods are used to plan, execute, and close the project. Agile methods are also used to address certain technical issues on a project while most of the project work is being managed in the traditional way. Hybrid project management has emerged as the name given to this blending of traditional and agile methodologies.

The internal dynamics on Agile projects is quite different from the traditional PM approach. Agile works best in small teams of four to eight members. Instead of directing and integrating the work of others, the project manager serves as a facilitator and coach. The team manages itself, deciding who should do what and how it should be done.

Agile PM will be discussed in depth in Chapter 15 and where appropriate throughout the text.

FIGURE 1.3 **Rolling Wave Development**

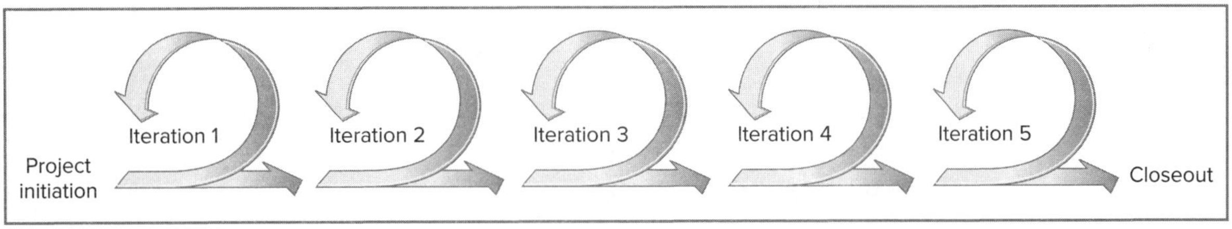

1.3 Current Drivers of Project Management

Project management is no longer a special-need management. It is rapidly becoming a standard way of doing business. See Snapshot from Practice 1.5: Project Management in Action: 2019. An increasing percentage of the typical firm's effort is being devoted to projects. The future promises an increase in the importance and role of projects in contributing to the strategic direction of organizations. Several reasons for this are discussed briefly in this section.

[1] It should be noted that PMBOK Guide also includes Incremental and Iterative as two additional approaches, which are beyond the scope of this text. Search pmi.org for further details.

SNAPSHOT FROM PRACTICE 1.5 Infosys Adopting Agile

Infosys embarked on a large-scale Agile transformation to overcome inefficiencies in project delivery, better align with evolving client needs, and foster a culture of innovation. This strategic shift aimed to modernize software delivery processes and scale Agile practices across diverse teams, ultimately driving operational agility and enhancing customer satisfaction. The primary objectives of this transformation were to reduce project delivery timelines by 20% within a year, increase responsiveness to client requirements, and transition delivery teams to Agile frameworks such as Scrum and Kanban. Infosys also integrated DevOps practices like Continuous Integration/Continuous Deployment (CI/CD) to streamline development cycles, improve quality, and accelerate time-to-market.

However, the transition came with significant technical challenges, including integrating Agile with legacy systems, especially in BFSI (Banking, Financial Services, and Insurance) projects. Operational hurdles like workforce resistance and the need for change management and upskilling added further complexity. Infosys addressed these through training programmes, leadership support, and fostering a mindset shift within delivery teams. The transformation brought measurable outcomes, including improved team collaboration, faster client feedback loops, and enhanced productivity. It highlighted the importance of continuous upskilling, change management, and client education, offering a valuable blueprint for Indian IT firms navigating similar transformations. Infosys's success showcases how structured project management can integrate Agile principles to achieve flexibility, efficiency, and innovation at scale.

AGILE TRANSFORMATION SUCCESS AT INFOSYS

Infosys's Agile adoption has delivered tangible results through pilot project success stories, innovative frameworks, and sustainable practices, highlighting the real-world impact of Agile methodologies.

- **Pilot project success stories:** In a BFSI project, Infosys transitioned from the Waterfall model to Agile, achieving a 25% reduction in delivery timelines and improving defect detection rates by 15% during the development phase. Similarly, in collaboration with a retail client, Infosys deployed Agile for product development, enhancing time-to-market by 18% while significantly improving end-user satisfaction scores. These successes demonstrate the efficiency gains and customer-centric outcomes enabled by Agile adoption.
- **Agile scaling frameworks:** To scale Agile practices across large portfolios, Infosys employed the Scaled Agile Framework (SAFe), ensuring alignment among diverse teams and improving client communication. The use of Programme Increments (PIs) fostered structured planning, milestone tracking, and seamless cross-team coordination.
- **Innovation in tools and techniques:** Infosys introduced self-developed dashboards to measure Agile maturity and team efficiency, enabling data-driven decision-making. By integrating DevOps and automating 70% of the deployment pipeline, Infosys ensured faster and smoother Agile adoption while maintaining quality.

CRITICAL CHALLENGES AND SOLUTIONS

- **Resistance to change:** Infosys overcame resistance through leadership workshops, peer mentoring, and incentivized Agile certifications, fostering a culture of Agile acceptance.
- **Legacy system compatibility:** Infosys collaborated with technology partners to develop middleware solutions (e.g., API development), ensuring seamless integration with legacy platforms. This resulted in a 12% reduction in delivery timelines.

Metric	Pre-Agile	Post-Agile	Improvement
Delivery Time	6 months	4.5 months	25% reduction
Defect Detection Rate	78%	90%	15% improvement
Client Satisfaction Scores	7.5/10	09/10	20% increase
Deployment Automation	30%	70%	40% improvement

AGILE PRACTICE SUSTAINABILITY

Infosys aligned its Agile journey with Green IT initiatives, reducing its operational carbon footprint by 40% through cloud transitions. By minimising dependencies on physical resources, such as printed documentation, Infosys saved thousands of reams of paper annually, showcasing its commitment to sustainability alongside operational excellence.

Infosys's innovative approach to scaling Agile, addressing challenges, and aligning with sustainability goals highlights its success as a leader in Agile transformation.

REFERENCES

Gupta, S., & Kapoor, P. (2020). "Adopting Scaled Agile Framework (SAFe) for Large Enterprises: A Case Study of Infosys." *Journal of Agile Development Practices*.

Ramaswamy, V., & Sundararajan, M. (2018). "Agile Transformation at Infosys: Challenges and Outcomes." *International Journal of IT Project Management*.

Gupta, S., & Kapoor, P. (2020). "Adopting Scaled Agile Framework (SAFe) for Large Enterprises: A Case Study of Infosys." *Journal of Agile Development Practices*.

Infosys White Paper (2019): "Driving Large-Scale Agile Transformation for Business Excellence." *Infosys Knowledge Institute*.

Compression of the Product Life Cycle

One of the most significant driving forces behind the demand for project management is the shortening of the product life cycle. For example, today in high-tech industries the product life cycle is averaging 6 months to 3 years. Only 30 years ago, life cycles of 10 to 15 years were not uncommon. *Time-to-market* for new products with short life cycles has become increasingly important. A common rule of thumb in the world of high-tech product development is that a 6-month project delay can result in a 33 percent loss in product revenue share. Speed, therefore, becomes a competitive advantage; more and more organizations are relying on cross-functional project teams to get new products and services to the market as quickly as possible.

SNAPSHOT FROM PRACTICE 1.6 Project Management in Action: 2019*

Businesses and nonprofits thrive and survive based on their ability to manage projects that produce products and services that meet market needs. Here is a small sample of projects that are important to their companies' futures.

INTUITIVE SURGICAL INC.: MONARCH PROJECT

The Monarch platform is an AI-driven robot featuring two arms with a long, blue tube attached that allows a doctor to steer a camera and other surgical implements deep inside the body. Intuitive hopes to one day use robots to not only diagnose but also treat lung cancer.

WALT DISNEY/MARVEL STUDIOS: CAPTAIN MARVEL

Captain Marvel is a superhero film based on Marvel Comics character Carol Danvers/Captain Marvel. The film stars Academy Award–winner Brie Larson in the title role. It is Marvel's first female-led superhero movie and is seen by many as a response to D.C.'s popular *Wonder Woman* film.

PROJECT C.U.R.E.: CARGO

Cargo projects deliver semi-trailer-sized cargo containers carrying medication donations to underresourced hospitals, clinics, and community health centers in developing countries. Each 40-foot container delivers an average $4 million worth of medical supplies and equipment.

SIKORSKY-BOEING: DEFIANT PROJECT

Boeing and Sikorsky have teamed up to develop a prototype for the next-generation military helicopter. The SB-1 Defiant is being built to travel faster, longer, and more quietly than other models. At stake is a billion-dollar-plus contract with the U.S. Department of Defense.

AUDI: E-TRON SUV

E-tron is Audi's first entry into the all-electric vehicle market. It is a fully equipped, luxury SUV with a 220-mile range. With a starting price of $74,800, it is meant to compete against Tesla's electric SUV and Jaguar's I-Pace, as well as establish Audi as a significant player in the growing all-electric market.

DOMINICAN REPUBLIC: TROPICAL FOREST RESTORATION

In many parts of the tropics, deforestation results in areas dominated by colonizing ferns. The Dominican restoration project involves manually removing ferns and planting native trees and shrubs.

*M. Chafkin, "This Robot Can Detect Lung Cancer," *BusinessWeek,* April 2, 2018; D. Coggan, "Production Underway on Marvel Studios' 'Captain Marvel,'" Marvel.com, March 3, 2018; "C.U.R.E. Cargo," projectcure.org. Accessed 2/15/19; K. Rockwood, "The Next Wave," *PM Network,* June 2018, pp. 6–7; Society for Ecological Restoration, "Dominican Republic: Restoring Tropical Forest at Sites Dominated by Anthropogenic Fern Thickets," ser-rrc.org. Accessed 2/25/19; "The Audi e-tron SUV Is an Electric Shot at Tesla," techcrunch.com, September 9, 2018. Accessed 2/22/19.

Knowledge Explosion

The growth in new knowledge has increased the complexity of projects because projects encompass the latest advances. For example, building a road 30 years ago was a somewhat simple process. Today, each area has increased in complexity, including materials, specifications, codes, aesthetics, equipment, and required specialists. Similarly, in today's digital, electronic age it is becoming hard to find a new product that does not contain at least one microchip. The same is likely to be true for artificial intelligence (AI). Product complexity has increased the need to integrate divergent technologies. Project management has emerged as the key discipline for achieving this task.

Triple Bottom Line (Planet, People, Profit)

The threat of global warming has brought sustainable business practices to the forefront. Businesses can no longer simply focus on maximizing profit to the detriment of the environment and society. Efforts to reduce carbon imprints and utilize renewable resources are realized through effective project management. The impact of this movement toward sustainability can be seen in changes in the objectives and techniques used to complete projects. For example, achieving a high LEED certification award is often an objective on construction projects.[2]

Increased Customer Focus

Increased competition has placed a premium on customer satisfaction. Customers no longer simply settle for generic products and services. They want customized products and services that cater to their specific needs. This mandate requires a much closer working relationship between the provider and the receiver. Account executives and sales representatives are assuming more of a project manager's role as they work with their organization to satisfy the unique needs and requests of clients.

Increased customer attention has also prompted the development of customized products and services. For example, 25 years ago buying a set of golf clubs was a relatively simple process: you picked out a set based on price and feel. Today, there are golf clubs for tall players and short players, clubs for players who tend to slice the ball and clubs for those who hook the ball, high-tech clubs with the latest metallurgic discovery guaranteed to add distance, and so forth. Project management is critical both to developing customized products and services and to sustaining lucrative relationships with customers.

Small Projects Represent Big Problems

The velocity of change required to remain competitive or simply keep up has created an organizational climate in which hundreds of projects are implemented concurrently. This climate has created a multiproject environment and a plethora of new problems. Sharing and prioritizing resources across a portfolio of projects is a major challenge for senior management. Many firms have no idea of the problems involved with the inefficient management of small projects. Small projects typically carry the same or more risk as large projects. Small projects are perceived as having little impact on the bottom line because they do not demand large amounts of scarce resources and/or money. Because so many small projects are going on concurrently and because the perception of the inefficiency impact is small, measuring inefficiency is usually nonexistent. Unfortunately, many small projects soon add up to large sums of money.

[2] LEED certification was developed by Leadership in Energy and Environmental Design (LEED) and is one of the most popular green building certification programs used worldwide.

Many customers and millions of dollars are lost each year on small projects in product and service organizations. Small projects can represent hidden costs not measured in the accounting system.

Organizations with many small projects going on concurrently face the most difficult project management problems. A key question becomes one of how to create an organizational environment that supports multiproject management. A process is needed to prioritize and develop a portfolio of small projects that supports the mission of the organization.

In summary, there are a variety of environmental forces interacting in today's business world that contribute to the increased demand for good project management across all industries and sectors.

1.4 Project Management Today: A Socio-Technical Approach

LO 1-5

Understand that managing projects involves balancing the technical and sociocultural dimensions of the project.

Project management has shaped the world we live (see Snapshot from Practice 1.6: PMI's 50 Most Influential Projects 1969–2019). Managing projects is a multidimensional process (see Figure 1.4). The first dimension is the technical side of the management process, which consists of the formal, disciplined, purely logical parts of the process. This technical dimension consists of project management methodology: planning, scheduling, and controlling projects. Clear project scope statements are written to link the project and customer and to facilitate planning and control. Creation of the deliverables and work breakdown structures facilitates planning and monitoring the progress of the project. The work breakdown structure serves as a database that links all levels in the organization, major deliverables, and all work—right down to the tasks in a work package. Effects of project changes are documented and traceable. Thus, any change in one part of the project is traceable to the source by the integrated linkages of the system. This integrated information approach can provide all project managers and the customer with decision information appropriate to their level and needs. A successful project manager will be well trained in the technical side of managing projects.

FIGURE 1.4
A Socio-Technical Approach to Project Management

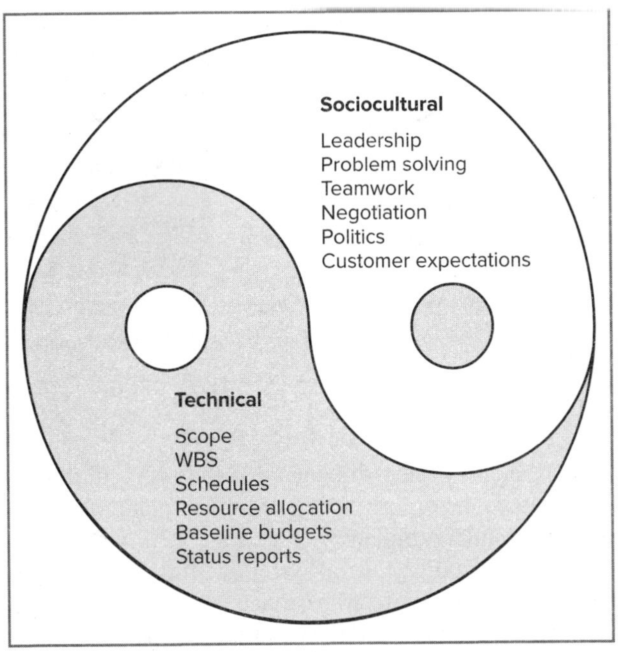

SNAPSHOT FROM PRACTICE 1.7 PMI's 50 Most Influential Projects 1969–2019*

To commemorate its 50th year, the Project Management Institute (PMI) undertook a yearlong research initiative: to identify the 50 most influential projects of the last 50 years. They reached out to more than 400 experts—from leading academics to influential authors, their Global Executive Council as well as to their global chapter communities. Thousands of projects were examined, with the overriding criteria: Did they reshape our expectations, defy convention, and transform an industry or our culture in ways that continue to reverberate? The final selections provide an inspirational reflection on what project work has enabled and the central role project management has played in creating the world we live in. The top five projects were:

1. **World Wide Web**—*for single-handedly revolutionizing how we live, work, think, and play.*
2. **Apollo 11**—*for proving risk management and out-of-this-world ambitions can make the impossible possible.*
3. **Intel 4004**—*for creating the microprocessor that democratized the power of computing.*
4. **Euro**—*for flawlessly executing the largest monetary changeover in the industry.*
5. **Human Genome Project**—*for rising above usual silos and unlocking the building block of humanity and enabling unparallel innovation in medicine and life sciences.*

Other projects cited included:

- **Singles Day**—*for creating the largest e-commerce day in the world and fundamentally shifting how we shopped.*
- **Prius Automobile**—*for forcing the auto industry toward a more sustainable future.*
- **1985 Live Aid Concert**—*for re-imaging the magnitude and model of philanthropy with a major dose of celebrity.*
- **Rwanda National Unity and Reconciliation Commission**—*for forging a path to recovery/redemption amid severe trauma.*
- **Walt Disney World**—*for setting the bar on immersive entertainment and then raising it again and again.*
- **Magnetic Resonance Imaging (MRI)**—*for taking much of the mystery out of medicine.*
- **iPod**—*for being able to contain one thousand songs in your pocket and being the gateway product to the i-universe.*
- **Global Polio Eradication Program**—*for creating the world's largest health initiative and bringing a deadly disease to the brink of extinction.*
- **Wikipedia**—*for tapping the world's collective knowledge with a radically collaborative online encyclopedia.*

It should be noted that most of these "projects" consisted of a series of projects often conducted by different people and organizations. Many would be considered programs.

Johnson Space Center/NASA

*PMI, "The World's 50 Most Influential Projects 1969–2019," *PMNetwork*, April 2019, pp. 9–60.

The second and opposing dimension is the sociocultural side of project management. In contrast to the orderly world of project planning, this dimension involves the much messier, often contradictory and paradoxical world of implementation. It centers on creating a temporary social system within a larger organizational environment that combines the talents of professionals working to complete the project. Project managers must try to shape a project culture that stimulates teamwork and high levels of personal motivation as well as a capacity to quickly identify and resolve problems that threaten project work. Things rarely go as planned and project managers must be able to steer the project back on track or alter directions when necessary.

The sociocultural dimension also involves managing the interface between the project and the external environment. Project managers have to assuage and shape the expectations of customers, sustain the political support of top management, and negotiate with their functional counterparts, monitor subcontractors, and so on. Overall, the manager must build a cooperative social network among an often divergent set of stakeholders with different standards, commitments, and perspectives.

Some suggest that the technical dimension represents the "science" of project management, while the sociocultural dimension represents the "art" of managing a project. Frankly, we believe there is less art behind managing projects as the term would suggest. Best practices and research exist to suggest there is more science behind managing the sociocultural dimension than previously existed. This text has a reflection of this progress.

To be successful, a manager must be a master of both. Unfortunately, some project managers become preoccupied with the planning and technical dimension of project management. Often their first real exposure to project management is through project management software, and they become infatuated with network charts, Gantt diagrams, and performance variances; they attempt to manage a project from a distance. Conversely, there are other managers who manage projects by the "seat of their pants," relying heavily on charisma and organizational politics to complete a project. Good project managers work with others to balance their attention to both the technical and sociocultural aspects of project management.

Summary

Project management is a critical skill set in today's world. A project is defined as a nonroutine, one-time effort limited by time, resources, and performance specifications designed to meet customer needs. One of the distinguishing characteristics of project management is that it has both a beginning and an end and typically consists of four phases: defining, planning, executing, and closing. Successful implementation requires both technical and social skills. Project managers have to plan and budget projects as well as orchestrate the contributions of others.

Text Overview

This text is written to provide the reader with a comprehensive, socio-technical understanding of project management. The text focuses on not only project methodology but also on how people apply these methods to successfully complete projects. Following this introductory chapter, Chapter 2 focuses on how organizations go about evaluating and selecting projects. Special attention is devoted to the importance of aligning project selection to the mission and strategy of the firm. The organizational environment in which projects are implemented is the focus of Chapter 3. The discussion of matrix management and other organizational forms is augmented by a discussion of the significant role the culture of an organization plays in the implementation of projects.

The next six chapters focus on developing a plan for the project; after all, project success begins with a good plan. Chapter 4 deals with defining the scope of the project and developing a work breakdown structure (WBS). The challenge of formulating cost and time estimates is the subject of Chapter 5. Chapter 6 focuses on utilizing the information from the WBS to create a project plan in the form of a timed and sequenced network of activities.

Risks are a potential threat to every project, and Chapter 7 examines how organizations and managers identify and manage risks associated with project work. Resource allocation is added to the plan in Chapter 8, with special attention devoted to how resource limitations impact the project schedule. After a resource schedule is established, a project time-phased budget is developed. Finally, Chapter 9 examines strategies for reducing ("crashing") project time either prior to the initiation of the project or in response to problems or new demands placed on the project. Throughout all these technical discussions, the sociocultural aspects are highlighted.

Chapters 10 through 12 focus on project implementation and the sociocultural side of project management. Chapter 10 focuses on the role of the project manager as a leader and stresses the importance of managing project stakeholders within the organization. Chapter 11 focuses on the core project team; it combines the latest information on team dynamics with leadership skills/techniques for developing a high-performance project team. Chapter 12 continues the theme of managing project stakeholders by discussing how to outsource project work and negotiate with contractors, customers, and suppliers.

Chapter 13 focuses on the kinds of information managers use to monitor project progress, with special attention devoted to the key concept of earned value. The project life cycle is completed with Chapter 14, which covers closing out a project and the important assessment of performance and lessons learned. Agile project management, a much more flexible approach to managing projects with high degree of uncertainty, is the subject of Chapter 15. Finally, so many projects today are global; Chapter 16 focuses on working on projects across cultures.

Throughout this text, you will be exposed to the major aspects of the project management process. However, a true understanding of project management comes not from knowing what a scope statement is, or the critical path, or partnering with contractors, but from comprehending how the different elements of the project management system interact to determine the fate of a project. If by the end of this text, you come to appreciate and begin to master both the technical and sociocultural dimensions of project management, you should have a distinct competitive advantage over others aspiring to work in the field of project management.

Key Terms

Agile project management (Agile PM), *12*
Certified Associate in Project Management (CAPM), *3*
Program, *8*
Project, *5*
Project life cycle, *8*
Project Management Professional (PMP), *3*

Review Questions

1. Define a project. What are five characteristics that help differentiate projects from other functions carried out in the daily operations of the organization?
2. What are some of the key environmental forces that have changed the way projects are managed? What has been the effect of these forces on the management of projects?
3. Describe the four phases of the traditional project life cycle. Which phase do you think would be the most difficult one to complete?
4. What kinds of projects is Agile PM best suited for and why?
5. The technical and sociocultural dimensions of project management are two sides of the same coin. Explain.

SNAPSHOT FROM PRACTICE

Discussion Questions

1.1 *The Project Management Institute*

1. If you were a student interested in pursuing a career in project management, how important do you think being a CAPM would be?
2. How valuable do you think being certified PMP is?

1.3 *London Calling: Seattle Seahawks versus Oakland Raiders*

1. Why was it important to give players and staff a chance to explore London one evening?
2. What are one or two lessons you learned from this Snapshot?

1.4 *Ron Parker*

1. Do you agree with Ron Parker's statement "To be successful, you must also be willing to run at problems/opportunities when everyone else is running away from them"?

1.7 *PMI's 50 Most Influential Projects 1969–2019*

1. Do you agrcc with thc top fivc choices? What choices would you have recommended?

Exercises

1. Review the front page of your local newspaper and try to identify all the projects contained in the articles. How many were you able to find?
2. Individually, identify what you consider to be humanity's greatest achievements in the last five decades. Now share your list with three to five other students in the class and come up with an expanded list. Review these great achievements in terms of the definition of a project. What does your review suggest about the importance of project management?
3. Individually, identify projects assigned in previous terms. Were both sociocultural and technical elements factors in the success or difficulties in the projects?
4. Check out the Project Management Institute's home page at www.pmi.org.
   a. Review general information about PMI as well as membership information.
   b. See if there is a local PMI chapter. If not, where is the closest one?
   c. Use the search function at the PMI home page to find information on Project Management Body of Knowledge (PMBOK). What are the major knowledge areas of PMBOK?
   d. Explore other links that PMI provides. What do these links tell you about the nature and future of project management?

References

Benko, C., and F. W. McFarlan, *Connecting the Dots* (Boston: HBS Press, 2003).

Cohen, D. J., and R. J. Graham, *The Project Manager's MBA* (San Francisco: Jossey-Bass, 2001).

Darnell, R., "The Emerging Role of the Project Manager," *PM Network,* 1997.

Derby, C., and O. Zwikael, "The Secret of (Defining) Success," *PM Network,* August 2012, pp. 20–22.

Gray, C., "Program Management, a Primer," *PM World Today,* August 2011, pp. 1–7.

Jonas, D., "Empowering Project Portfolio Managers: How Management Involvement Impacts Project Management Performance," *International Journal of Project Management,* vol. 28, no. 8 (2010), pp. 818–31.

Krasner, H., *The Cost of Poor Software Quality in the U.S.: A 2022 Report,* www.it-cisq.org. Accessed 5/5/23.

Mortensen, M., and H. K. Gardner, "The Overcommitted Organization," *Harvard Business Review,* September/October 2017, pp. 58–65.

PMI/Agile Alliance, *Agile Practice Guide* (Chicago: Independent Publishers Group, 2017).

Project Management Institute, *A Guide to the Project Management Body of Knowledge (PMBOK)* (Newton Square, PA: PMI Publishing, 2017).

Project Management Institute, *Leadership in Project Management Annual* (Newton Square, PA: PMI Publishing, 2006).

Schwaber, K., *Agile Project Management with Scrum* (Redmond, WA: Microsoft Press, 2004).

The Standish Group, *CHAOS Summary 1995* (Dennis, MA: Standish, 1995).

The Standish Group, *CHAOS Summary 2009* (Dennis, MA: Standish, 2009).

Stewart, T. A., "The Corporate Jungle Spawns a New Species: The Project Manager," *Fortune,* September 1996, pp. 14–15.

Case 1.1

A Day in the Life—2024

Troi, the project manager of a large information systems project, arrives at her office early to get caught up with work before her co-workers and project team arrive. However, as she enters the office she meets Akeem, one of her fellow project managers, who also wants to get an early start on the day. Akeem has just completed a project overseas. They spend 10 minutes socializing and catching up on personal news.

Troi walks to her desk and opens her laptop. She was at her client's site the day before until 7:30 p.m. and has not checked her e-mail or voice mail since 4:30 p.m. the previous day. She has 2 voicemails, 16 e-mails, and 10 posts on her team Slack channel.[1] She spends 15 minutes reviewing her schedule and "to-do" lists for the day before responding to messages that require immediate attention.

Troi spends the next 25 minutes going over project reports and preparing for the weekly standup meeting. Her manager who just arrived at the office, interrupts her. They spend 20 minutes discussing the project. He shares a rumor about a potential acquisition he's heard about. She tells him she hasn't heard anything but will keep him posted if she does.

The 9:00 a.m. project status meeting starts 15 minutes late because two of the team members have to finish a job for a client. Several people go to the cafeteria to get coffee and doughnuts while others discuss last night's baseball game. The team members arrive, and the remaining 45 minutes of the progress review meeting surface project issues that have to be addressed and assigned for action.

After the meeting, Troi goes down the hallway to meet with Achara, another IS project manager. They spend 30 minutes reviewing project assignments, since the two

[1] Slack is a communications program designed to manage the flow of information on a project. See slack.com.

of them share personnel. Achara's project is behind schedule and in need of help. Troi offers to free up some of the team's time to help her get back on track.

Troi returns to her office and makes several phone calls and returns several e-mails before walking downstairs to visit with members of her project team. Her intent is to follow up on an issue that surfaced in the status report meeting. However, her simple, "Hi, you all, how are things going?" elicits a stream of disgruntled responses. After listening patiently for over 20 minutes, she realizes that among other things several of the client's managers are beginning to request features that were not in the original project scope statement. She tells her people that she will get on this right away.

Returning to her office, she tries to call her counterpart, John, at the client firm but is told that he is not expected back from lunch for another hour. At this time, Eddie drops by and says, "How about lunch?" Eddie works in the finance office and they spend the next half hour in the company cafeteria gossiping about internal politics. She is surprised to hear that Jonah Johnson, the director of systems projects, may join another firm. Jonah has always been a powerful ally.

She returns to her office, answers a few more e-mails, catches up on Slack, and finally gets through to John. They spend 30 minutes going over the problem. The conversation ends with John promising to do some investigating and get back to her as soon as possible.

Troi goes outside to the company's atrium, where she sits next to a creek, meditating for 30 minutes.

Troi then takes the elevator to the third floor and talks to the purchasing agent assigned to her project. They spend the next 30 minutes exploring ways of getting the necessary equipment to the project site earlier than planned. She finally authorizes express delivery.

When she returns to her desk, her watch reminds her that she is scheduled to participate in a Zoom meeting at 2:30 p.m. It takes 10 minutes for everyone to get online due to problems with the technology. During this time, Troi catches up on some e-mail. She spends the next hour exchanging information about the technical requirements associated with a new version of a software package they are using on systems projects like hers.

Troi decides to stretch her legs and goes on a walk down the hallway, where she engages in brief conversations with various co-workers. She goes out of her way to thank Chandra for his thoughtful analysis at the status report meeting. She returns to find that John has left a message for her to call him back ASAP. She contacts John, who informs her that according to his people, her firm's marketing rep had made certain promises about specific features her system would provide. He doesn't know how this communication breakdown occurred, but his people are pretty upset over the situation. Troi thanks John for the information and immediately takes the stairs to where the marketing group resides.

She asks to see Mary, a senior marketing manager. She catches up on Slack updates on her phone while she waits for 10 minutes before being invited into her office. After a heated discussion, she leaves 40 minutes later with Mary agreeing to talk to her people about what was promised and what was not promised.

She goes downstairs to her people to give them an update on what is happening. They spend 30 minutes reviewing the impact the client's requests could have on the project schedule. She also shares with them the schedule changes she and Achara had agreed to. After she says good night to her team, she heads upstairs to her manager's office and spends 20 minutes updating him on key events of the day. She returns to her office and spends 30 minutes reviewing e-mails, her team Slack channel, and project documents. She logs on to the MS Project schedule of her project and spends the next

30 minutes working with "what-if" scenarios. She reviews tomorrow's schedule and writes some personal reminders before starting off on her 30-minute commute home.

1. How effectively do you think Troi spent her day?
2. What does the case tell you about what it is like to be a project manager?

Case 1.2

The Hokies Lunch Group[1]

PART A

Fatma settled down for lunch at the Yank Sing Chinese restaurant. She was early and took the time to catch up on her e-mail. Soon she would be joined by Jasper and Viktoria, two fellows 2014 grads from Virginia Tech in Blacksburg, Virginia.

Jasper worked as a software engineer for a start-up company that wanted to expand the boundaries of sharing economy. Viktoria was an electrical engineer who worked for a German healthcare company in San Francisco. They had met each other at a Silicon Valley alumni reception hosted by Virginia Tech. Each of them felt a bit like a fish out of water on the West Coast, so they decided to have lunch together each month. The lunch evolved into a professional support group. A major part of each of their jobs was managing projects, and they found it useful to share issues and seek advice from each other.

Fatma worked for a very successful Internet company whose founders believed that everyone in the firm should devote three days a year to community service projects. The company was partnering with several companies in the construction industry to renovate abandoned buildings for low-income families. The next project was the renovation of an empty warehouse into eight two-bedroom apartments. Fatma was part of the core team in charge of scheduling and managing work assignments.

Viktoria and Jasper entered the restaurant together. Viktoria was the first to move to the Bay Area. She was currently working on the next-generation neural stimulator ("PAX 2"). Neural stimulators are electronic devices that doctors implant in patients with wires connected to sources of pain in the patient's spine. In the past, patients would have to have an operation to replace the stimulator battery every 10 years. PAX 2 was being designed to take advantage of new battery technologies and use a rechargeable battery. In concept, this battery system would eliminate the need for replacement surgeries and allow the implanted battery to be recharged externally. Viktoria's team had just completed the second prototype and was entering a critical testing phase. It had been tricky trying to predict the lifespan of the new rechargeable battery without testing it in real-time. She was anxious to begin seeing the test results.

Jasper was working for a start-up company after doing contract work for his first nine months in San Francisco. He was sworn to secrecy about the project and all Fatma and Viktoria knew was that the project had something to do with sharing economy. He was working with a small development team that included colleagues from Bangalore, India, and Malmo, Sweden.

After ordering and chit-chatting a bit, Fatma started the discussion. "I will be glad when this week is over," she said. "We've been struggling defining the scope of the

[1] Hokies is the name associated with Virginia Tech athletic teams.

project. At first glance our project seems relatively simple, build eight two-bedroom apartments in an old warehouse. But there are a lot of unanswered questions. What kind of community space do we want to have? How efficient should the energy system be? What kind of furniture? Everybody wants to do a good job, but when does low-income housing morph into middle-income housing?"

Viktoria offered, "Scope defining is one of the things my company does very well. Before a project is authorized, a detailed scope statement is developed that clearly defines the project objectives, priorities, budget, requirements, limits, and exclusions. All of the key stakeholders sign off on it. It is really important to identify priorities up-front. I know on the PAX 2 project that scope is the number one priority. I know that no matter how long it takes it is imperative that my work is done right."

Fatma responded, "That's exactly what my project manager is preparing for Friday's meeting. I guess that one of the things you have to do as a project manager is end discussions. He is going to make the tough calls and finalize the project scope so we can begin planning."

Jasper interjected, "You all are so lucky; for the most part your scope remains the same. In my work the scope is constantly changing. You show the founders a feature they wanted, and they say, well, if you can do that, can you do this? You know it's going to happen, but you really can't plan for it."

Jasper went on, "We do know what our number one priority is: *time*. There are a lot of players trying to move in to the 'space' we are working on. We have to demonstrate we are ahead of the pack if we are going to continue to get VC funding.[2]"

Jasper said that despite the pressure, his project had been a lot of fun. He especially liked working with his Swedish and Indian counterparts, Askel and Sree. They worked like a global tag team on their part of the project. Jasper would code and then pass his work on to Sree, who would work on it and pass it on to Askel, who would eventually hand it off to Jasper. Given the time zones, they were able to have at least one person working on the code around the clock.

Jasper said it was hard at first working with someone he hadn't met personally other than on a video screen. Trust was an issue. Everyone was trying to prove themselves. Eventually, a friendly competition arose across the team. The programmers exchanged funny cartoons and YouTube videos. He showed Fatma and Viktoria a YouTube video about scope creep that got a chuckle from everyone.

They made plans to meet next at the new Peruvian restaurant on SE 8th Street.

PART B

The Peruvian cilantro/lime ceviche was a big hit at the next lunch. Viktoria began their discussion by reporting, "I have good and bad news. The bad news is that our first prototype failed its tests miserably. The good news is that I have a smart project manager. She knew this could happen, so she mitigated the risk by having us working on two alternative battery technologies. The alternative technology is passing all of the tests. Instead of falling behind months, we are only days behind schedule."

This precipitated a discussion of risk management. Fatma reported that there had been a two-day session on risk management for the renovation project. They spent the first day brainstorming what could go wrong, and the second day coming up with strategies for dealing with risks. A big help was the risk report that was generated after the last project. The report detailed all of the problems that had occurred on the last renovation project as well as recommendations. Fatma said, "I couldn't believe how much time and attention was devoted to safety, but as my project manager said, 'all it takes is one bad accident to shut down a project for weeks, even months.'"

[2] New venture capital funding.

Jasper reported that on his project they spent very little time on risk management. His project was driven by a build-test mentality. "Everybody assumes that daily testing eliminates problems, but when it's time to integrate different features, that's when the real bugs will emerge," Jasper said.

Jasper went on to say that things were not going well at work. They had missed their second straight milestone, and everyone was feeling the pressure to show results. "I even slept by my cubicle three nights ago," Jasper confessed. Fatma asked, "How many hours are you working?" "I don't know, at least 70, maybe 80 hours," Jasper answered. He went on to say, "This is a high-stakes project, with a BIG upside if successful. I am doing some of my best programming and we'll just have to see what happens."

Jasper showed them a cartoon that was being circulated across his team. The caption read "When did you want it done? Yesterday."

Fatma turned to her friends and said, "I need some advice. As you know, I'm responsible for scheduling work assignments. Well, some of my colleagues have been pretty aggressive in lobbying for choice assignments. Everyone wants to work alongside Bruno or Reese. Suddenly I am everyone's friend, and certain people are going way out of their way to do favors for me. I am sure they think it will influence my decisions. It's getting awkward and I am not sure what to do."

"Quid pro quo," answered Jasper, "that's how the business world works. You scratch my back and I'll scratch yours. Within reason, I don't have a problem with someone taking advantage of their position to garner favors and build relationships."

Viktoria said, "I disagree. You don't want to be seen as someone whose influence can be bought. You need to think what's best for the company. You need to ask yourself what Bruno and Reese would want you to do. And if you don't know, ask them."

After much discussion, Fatma left the restaurant leaning toward Viktoria's advice, but she wasn't sure what the guidelines should be.

PART C

It took two months for the Hokies lunch group to get together again. Jasper had canceled the last meeting because of work, so Viktoria and Fatma saw a movie together instead.

Jasper was the last person to arrive at the Russian bakery and it was clear from the look on his face that things were not going well. He sat down, avoiding eye contact, before blurting, "I'm out of work." "What do you mean?" Fatma and Viktoria cried. Jasper explained after months and months of work they had been unable to demonstrate a functional product.

Jasper went on to say, "Despite our best efforts we couldn't deliver. The founders couldn't get an ounce of second-round venture funding, so they decided to cut their losses and kill the project. I just spent the best six months of my programming life for nothing."

Fatma and Viktoria tried to comfort their friend. Fatma asked Jasper how the others were taking the news. Jasper said the Swedish programmer, Askel, took the news very hard. He went on to say, "I think he was burning a lot of bridges at home with the long work hours and now he has nothing to show for it. He started blaming us for mistakes we never made." Sree, his Indian counterpart, was a different story. "Sree seemed to shrug her shoulders." Jasper added, "She said, 'I know I am a good programmer. There are lots of opportunities here in Bangalore.'"

Fatma broke the silence that followed by saying to Jasper, "Send me your resume. My company is always looking for top-notch programmers and it is a really great company. Can you believe it, the two founders, Bruno and Reese, are working side by side with everyone on renovating the warehouse? In fact, people were amazed at how good Bruno was with sheet rock. A big part of my job now is scheduling their time so they can work with as many different people as possible. They really want to use the project to get to know their employees. This hasn't been easy. I have had to juggle their calendars, their abilities, and work opportunities."

Viktoria interjected, "You're using Microsoft Project to do this?" "Not really," responded Fatma. "At first I tried scheduling their work in Microsoft Project, but it was too cumbersome and time-consuming. Now I just use the Project master schedule and each of their calendars to schedule their work. This seems to work best."

Viktoria added, "Yeah, Microsoft Project is a great program, but you can get lost trying to get it to do everything. Sometimes all you need is an Excel sheet and common sense."

Viktoria felt awkward, given what had happened to Jasper. She was just wrapping up the successful PAX 2 project. She was also getting ready for a well-deserved holiday in Vietnam paid for by her project bonus. "I hate closing out a project," Viktoria said. "It's so boring. Document, document, document! I keep kicking myself for not tracking things when they happened. I am spending most of my time scouring my computer for files. I can't wait to take off to Vietnam."

Viktoria went on to say, "The only thing I liked doing was the project retrospective."

Jasper asked, "What's a project retrospective?" Viktoria answered, "It's when the project team gets together and reviews what went well and what didn't and identifies lessons learned that we can apply to future projects. For example, one of the things we learned was that we needed to bring the manufacturing people on board a lot sooner in the design process. We focused on designing the very best product possible, regardless of cost. We found out later that there were ways for reducing production costs without compromising quality."

Fatma added, "We do that, too, at the end of our projects, but we call it an audit."

Fatma asked Viktoria, "Do you know what your next assignment will be?" "No," she replied, "I will probably go back to my department and do some testing. I'm not worried. I did good work. I am sure someone will want me for their project."

Jasper chimed in, "I sure hope someone wants me for their next project." Fatma and Viktoria immediately went into action, trying to lift their friend's spirits.

A little while later, they walked out of the restaurant and gave each other hugs. Fatma reminded Jasper to send her his latest resume.

1. For each part (A, B, C), what phase of the project life cycle is each project in? Explain.
2. What are two important things you learned about working on projects from the case? Why are they important?

Case 1.3

Delhi Metro: Driving Excellence in Urban Infrastructure

The Delhi Metro is not merely a transportation project; it stands as a hallmark of innovative project management and a transformative milestone in India's urban mobility landscape. Conceived to address Delhi's escalating traffic congestion, deteriorating air quality, and overstretched public transport system, the project was envisioned as a solution that would redefine the standards of infrastructure development in the country.

Initiated in the late 1990s, the Delhi Metro Rail Corporation (DMRC) spearheaded this ambitious venture with a clear vision: to create a world-class, sustainable, and efficient mass transit system. The project was unprecedented in scale and complexity, requiring meticulous planning, stakeholder collaboration, and advanced technological integration. It brought together government bodies, international consultants, and financial institutions, establishing a model of multi-agency coordination and public-private partnerships.

From its inception, the project adopted global best practices in project management, including rigorous cost control, time-bound delivery, risk management, and quality assurance. The adoption of cutting-edge technologies, such as modern tunnelling methods and automated systems, combined with meticulous execution, ensured the project adhered to international standards while catering to the unique challenges of Delhi's urban landscape.

What makes the Delhi Metro truly exemplary in the context of project management is its ability to deliver results efficiently despite the constraints of dense population, financial limitations, and environmental concerns. The project was completed in phases, demonstrating an agile and phased approach to implementation, allowing for continuous learning and adaptation. Its success story highlights the role of leadership, stakeholder alignment, and robust project governance in achieving large-scale infrastructure goals.

Today, the Delhi Metro serves as a model of project excellence, offering key insights into the effective management of scope, time, cost, and quality in infrastructure development. It is a testament to how disciplined project management can turn ambitious visions into reality, setting benchmarks for urban mobility projects worldwide.

KEY STAKEHOLDERS

- **Government bodies:** Key enablers included the Delhi Government, Urban Development Ministry, and various municipal authorities, which provided critical policy support and regulatory oversight.
- **DMRC leadership and management:** Led by visionaries like Dr. E. Sreedharan, the "Metro Man of India," the DMRC's team demonstrated exceptional leadership, planning, and execution to steer the project to success.
- **Financial institutions:** International organisations, notably the Japan International Cooperation Agency (JICA), played a pivotal role by providing funding, technical expertise, and long-term financial support.
- **Citizens and commuters:** The people of Delhi NCR, including public interest groups and daily commuters, remained the ultimate beneficiaries and key stakeholders whose needs and feedback shaped the project's objectives.

The Delhi Metro Project Life Cycle was meticulously planned and executed in well-defined phases, each aligning with specific objectives and activities to ensure the project's seamless delivery. The phases were broken down into manageable sub-phases, allowing for structured progress and efficient resource allocation. For each phase, the Delhi Metro Rail Corporation (DMRC) undertook a series of critical activities, ranging from feasibility studies, detailed project planning, and stakeholder engagement to execution, quality assurance, and risk management. By systematically managing the project through clearly delineated phases and activities, DMRC demonstrated an exemplary approach to the project life cycle, ensuring timely completion while maintaining international standards of safety, quality, and efficiency.

Phase	Objective	Sub Phases	Specific Activities Performed by DMRC
Initiation Phase	To define the project's groundwork, involve key stakeholders, and create feasibility.	**Feasibility Studies**	Technical, environmental and financial studies defined if the project is viable. Analysis concerned traffic patterns, required land and funds sources.
		Stakeholder Identification	The authorities consulted local governments, environmental agencies and bodies entrusted with urban planning to align objectives.
		Scope Definition	The Delhi Metro defined a multi-phased development programme and identified well-defined milestones for civil works, construction of stations and procuring rolling stock.
Planning Phase	To design a detailed roadmap covering every aspect of the project.	**Work Breakdown Structure**	The works were segregated into tunnelling, elevated tracks, and station construction. In the case of this work decomposition and concentration, it was helpful.
		Scheduling and Budgeting	Gantt Charts and the Critical Path Method (CPM) applied for scheduling.
		EVM	Earned Value Management (EVM) was used for cost control.
		Risk Management	DMRC estimated potential risks as including delays in land acquisition and regulatory approvals. Contingency plans were designed and prepared for these challenges.
Execution Phase	To construct, install, and operationalize the metro system.	**Resource Management**	The execution of the Delhi Metro project involved a very complex process, requiring effective utilisation of resources, and their coordination with the various stakeholders.
		Construction and Procurement	The project incorporated vendor selection based on competitive bidding. Contractors and suppliers were selected considering quality standards and compliance with legal terms.
		Specialized equipment	TBMs were used for difficult activities such as underground tunnelling.
		Usage of Resource	Labor, equipment, and materials were committed according to deadlines.
		Funds Allocation	Intelligent use of the fund involved international loan, government support, and internal budgeting.
		Communications	Providing the stakeholders with regular updates on work progress through dashboards and meetings. Public sensitization was encouraged so that the public would be aware of the construction works to minimize disturbance.
Monitoring and Control Phase	To track progress, ensure quality, and address challenges during construction.	**Monitoring and Control**	Tools like Primavera and MS Project gave real-time monitoring of the project schedule. Adaptive strategies brought timelines and budgets back on track within hours.
Closing Phase	To finalize the project, conduct reviews, and hand over operations.	**Testing Handover**	These tests ensured that the operation was efficient and that passengers were secure. These included rigorous tests on signalling, track alignment, and the performance of rolling stock.
		Stakeholder Sign-Offs	Safety certificates from the regulatory body. Final approval from funding agencies and the government.
		Training	Staff for DMRC was trained on metro operations, maintenance, and emergency procedures.
		Post-Implementation Reviews	Findings in comparison to the actual outcome elaborated on the successes achieved and areas where there was a need for improvement.

OPERATIONAL CHALLENGES

The Delhi Metro project, despite its remarkable success, encountered significant operational challenges during its execution. These challenges were effectively managed through innovative strategies, rigorous planning, and proactive decision-making by the Delhi Metro Rail Corporation (DMRC).

- **Delays and cost overruns:** One of the most pressing challenges was the delay caused by land acquisition and regulatory clearances, which often stretched over weeks or months. Delays of this nature risked cost escalations and timeline disruptions. To mitigate this, DMRC adopted a parallel processing approach, starting construction in areas where clearances had already been secured while awaiting approvals for others. This dynamic strategy helped ensure steady progress and minimized the overall impact on project schedules.
- **Workforce management:** Managing a heterogeneous workforce comprising contractors, engineers, laborers, and specialists was a daunting task. Effective communication, clear role definitions, and regular performance reviews were critical in aligning diverse teams towards the project's goals. DMRC implemented well-structured management systems to ensure seamless coordination and accountability, fostering collaboration despite the complexities of a large-scale infrastructure project.
- **Environmental and social concerns:**
    - **Community impacts:** The construction process inevitably caused disturbances to nearby communities, including noise pollution and traffic disruptions. DMRC proactively addressed these issues by implementing noise reduction measures and devising comprehensive traffic management plans to minimize inconvenience. Additionally, community relocation was planned meticulously to ensure fair compensation and resettlement.
    - **Sustainable practices:** DMRC prioritized environmental sustainability by incorporating innovative practices into the project's framework. Measures such as rainwater harvesting, the use of energy-efficient trains, and the installation of solar panels showcased DMRC's commitment to eco-friendly development. These initiatives not only reduced the project's environmental footprint but also set a precedent for sustainable infrastructure projects in the future.

By addressing these operational challenges through strategic planning, stakeholder collaboration, and innovative solutions, DMRC was able to overcome obstacles and deliver the Delhi Metro project successfully. Its ability to manage delays, workforce dynamics, and environmental concerns reflects a robust project management approach and highlights the importance of agility and adaptability in large-scale infrastructure development.

CRITICAL OUTCOMES

The Delhi Metro has emerged as a lifeline for millions of commuters, fundamentally transforming urban mobility in the National Capital Region (NCR). By significantly reducing travel time and transportation expenses, it has provided a fast, reliable, and cost-effective alternative to traditional modes of public and private transport. One of the most notable outcomes of the Delhi Metro is its role as a benchmark for efficiency in large-scale infrastructure projects. The project was completed with a strong emphasis on timely delivery and cost control, showcasing disciplined project management practices and setting new standards for execution and accountability.

Furthermore, the Delhi Metro project exemplifies transparency in infrastructure development. From its planning stages to execution, the Delhi Metro Rail Corporation (DMRC) prioritized open communication, stakeholder engagement, and clear reporting mechanisms, ensuring trust and confidence among government bodies, financial institutions, and the public. On the sustainability front, the Delhi Metro stands out as a model for environmentally conscious development. With initiatives such as energy-efficient trains, solar power installations, and rainwater harvesting systems, DMRC integrated green practices into its operations. This commitment to sustainability not only reduced its environmental footprint but also demonstrated how large-scale projects can align with long-term ecological goals.

The Delhi Metro's success has redefined urban transportation by enhancing commuter convenience, improving air quality, and decongesting road traffic. Its outcomes extend beyond mobility to inspire confidence in India's ability to undertake and deliver complex infrastructure projects. The Delhi Metro has set a precedent for future urban transit systems, both domestically and globally, emphasising efficiency, transparency, and sustainability as key pillars of modern infrastructure development.

Key Features of Delhi Metro Technology Adoption

Technology	Description	Impact
Automatic Train Control (ATC)	System for managing train movement, speed, and schedule adherence	Improved punctuality by 95%
Supervisory Control and Data Acquisition (SCADA)	Remote monitoring and control of operational infrastructure	Reduced downtime by 30%
Regenerative Braking	Energy recovery system for trains	30% reduction in energy consumption
Rooftop Solar Panels	Solar energy solutions installed across stations	Reduced carbon footprint by 112,500 tons

IMPACT AND LESSONS LEARNED

The Delhi Metro project has revolutionized urban mobility in Delhi NCR, providing a cleaner, faster, and more reliable mode of transportation. By significantly improving connectivity and reducing road congestion, it has enhanced the quality of life for millions of commuters while addressing critical environmental concerns like vehicular emissions. Its success has had a far-reaching impact, inspiring the development of similar metro projects across cities in India, transforming public transportation systems on a national scale.

LESSONS LEARNED AS A PROJECT MANAGER

- **Visionary leadership:** The role of leaders like Dr. E. Sreedharan was instrumental in overcoming challenges while keeping the team focused on the project's core objectives. His unwavering commitment and decisive leadership ensured smooth progress despite complexities, serving as a powerful lesson in project governance and accountability.

- **Early stakeholder involvement:** Engaging key stakeholders—government bodies, financial institutions, contractors, and the public—early in the project lifecycle proved critical to its success. The DMRC maintained open channels of communication, ensuring alignment of objectives, proactive issue resolution, and effective delivery of outcomes.
- **Agile principles in project execution:** While the Delhi Metro primarily involved civil and infrastructure development, the adoption of Agile principles for software components and operational adjustments demonstrated the value of flexibility and adaptability. The ability to accommodate changes and respond swiftly to challenges became a cornerstone of the project's management approach.
- **Adoption of technology:** The Delhi Metro employs the latest technologies, including ATC, ATO, and SCADA, with a view to achieving greater efficiency and safety in operations. The SCADA system brings remote train, track, and station monitoring along with their control, thus greatly minimising operational down time.
- **Sustainability practices:** The DMRC became the world's first metro system to gain certification from the United Nations in carbon credits. Solar panels installed on rooftops at the metro stations generated millions of savings in energy costs and went a long way in reducing the carbon footprint. Energy-efficient trains with regenerative braking systems helped reduce electricity consumption by 30%.
- **Public engagement initiatives:** Public campaigns for proper metro usage and awareness about safety norms represented DMRC's social responsibility efforts, that helped increase ridership satisfaction. For instance, the "Be the Change" campaign was directed at passengers on cleanliness and citizen's responsibilities.
- **Critical issues and solutions for land acquisition:** A multi-layered process involved a close coordination with the local authorities, community consultation, and compensation packages for the affected locals. The grievance redressal mechanism was a support to have minimal displacement.
- **Workforce integration:** DMRC employed diverse workforces from contractors and international consultants, promoting intercultural collaboration. Weekly reviews ensured alignment on quality and deadlines.
- **Broader implications:** The Delhi Metro stands as a textbook example of robust project management frameworks in action. It highlights the importance of careful planning, risk management, stakeholder coordination, and a strong focus on sustainability. The project's success underscores that large-scale infrastructure development can achieve its objectives when managed with discipline, vision, and innovation.

The success of the Delhi Metro has inspired and led to the replication of its model in several cities across India. These cities have adopted similar project management frameworks, technological advancements, and sustainability practices to develop their metro systems. The following are notable examples where the Delhi Metro model has been successfully replicated:

- **Bengaluru Metro (Namma Metro):** Karnataka's capital implemented a metro system to address its traffic congestion and enhance urban mobility.

- **Chennai Metro:** Designed to provide an efficient and eco-friendly mass transit system in Tamil Nadu's capital city.
- **Hyderabad Metro:** A public-private partnership (PPP) project in Telangana that follows the Delhi Metro's operational and technological benchmarks.
- **Kolkata Metro (Expansion Projects):** While Kolkata Metro was India's first metro system, its subsequent expansions adopted modern practices inspired by the Delhi Metro model.
- **Mumbai Metro:** The financial capital of India has developed and is expanding its metro system to ease the burden on road and rail infrastructure.
- **Jaipur Metro:** Rajasthan's capital introduced its metro system following the Delhi Metro's model, including sustainability practices and phased implementation.
- **Lucknow Metro:** A modern metro system in Uttar Pradesh's capital city that mirrors the efficiency and punctuality standards set by Delhi Metro.
- **Kochi Metro:** Kerala's first metro project incorporated sustainability features such as solar-powered stations, inspired by Delhi Metro's eco-friendly initiatives.
- **Nagpur Metro:** Maharashtra's city adopted best practices from the Delhi Metro to improve urban transportation infrastructure.
- **Ahmedabad Metro:** Gujarat's metro system was developed with project management frameworks similar to those employed in Delhi.
- **Pune Metro:** A newer metro project aimed at alleviating the growing congestion in the city, modelled after Delhi's successful implementation.
- **Kanpur Metro:** Uttar Pradesh's industrial hub has adopted modern metro practices similar to Delhi Metro for efficiency and sustainability.

These metro systems demonstrate how the Delhi Metro's success has become a blueprint for urban mobility across India, setting standards for project execution, stakeholder coordination, sustainability, and operational excellence.

REFERENCES

Sreedharan, E., & Mittal, A. K. (2015). Restoring the Urban Infrastructure: Case Study of Delhi Metro. *Journal of Urban Infrastructure Development*, 8(2), 23–35.

Mann, A. (2019). India's Infrastructure Development: Lessons Learned from the Delhi Metro. *International Journal of Infrastructure and Transportation*, 14(1), 45–57.

Centre for Public Impact. (2017). The Construction of the Delhi Metro. Retrieved from https://centreforpublicimpact.org/public-impact-fundamentals/the-construction-of-the-delhi-metro/.

Appendix 1.1

2021 PMI: A Guide to the Project Management Body of Knowledge (PMBOK Guide) Seventh Edition and Its Ancillaries

In 2021, PMI took two major steps in the right direction by publishing a significant revision of *PMBOK Guide* and introducing the *Standard for Project Management (SPM).* The new, seventh edition of *PMBOK Guide* adopts a systems perspective instead of the previous process orientation. Processes are still important to managing projects, but the *PMBOK Guide,* seventh edition, utilizes a more socio-technical approach to focus on the delivery of ***value.*** Value may come in the form of a new product or service, improving efficiency and operations, sustaining benefits, or having a positive social or environmental impact.

The *SPM* sets forth for the first time, 12 principles that provide foundational guidelines for managing projects. The principles are broadly based so there is no one best way to apply them, but rather they need to be "tailored" to the situation. These principles are consistent with the philosophy and approach the authors have championed since our first edition. Figure A1.1 displays how PMI summarizes the 12 principles and their relationship to project performance domains.

Also in 2023, PMI released a new book, entitled *Process Groups: A Practice Guide.* This book contains a discussion of all the processes that made up the earlier, sixth edition of *PMBOK Guide.* Now PMI has both a process-based guide and a principle-based standard. There is a significant need for both. The process-based guide provides "how to" knowledge or procedural knowledge necessary to manage projects. The message of the seventh edition of *PMBOK Guide* is this must be done while applying the 12 principles and 10 performance domains that are extolled by the seventh edition of *PMBOK Guide.*[1]

It is worth noting that the newest version of *PMBOK Guide* is not intended for students or first-time aspiring project managers who know nothing about project management. The material provides less procedural knowledge in the sense of a "cookbook" that tells you what to do step-by-step. Most project management textbooks start with a definition of project management and then discussion of scope followed by a determination of tasks from the work breakdown structure (WBS), followed by a sequencing of those tasks, estimates of the task durations, assignment of resources, scheduling, and costs, etc. In most books, there is a lot of procedural substance; not so for the seventh edition of *PMBOK Guide.* It appears this newest edition is intended for a seasoned project management professional who must be insightful enough to know where the principle-based declarative knowledge can be applied.

The seventh edition of *PMBOK Guide* does not provide many examples of how and where the principles and performance domains can be applied. Fortunately, this is one of the strengths of this text.

This text was never intended as a primer for taking the PMP or CAPM exam. Our goal was to share our passion for managing projects and provide readers with essential

[1] In essence, the *Process Groups: A Practice Guide* now contains most of the information covered in *PMBOK Guide*, 6th edition.

FIGURE A1.1 Relationship between 12 project management principles and project performance domains

Principles of Project Management			
Be a diligent, respectful and caring steward	Create a collaborative team environment	Effectively engage with stakeholders	Focus on value
Recognize, evaluate, and respond to system interactions	Demonstrate leadership behaviors	Tailor based on context	Build quality into processes and deliverables
Navigate complexity	Optimize risk responses	Embrace adaptability and resiliency	Enable change to achieve the envisioned future state

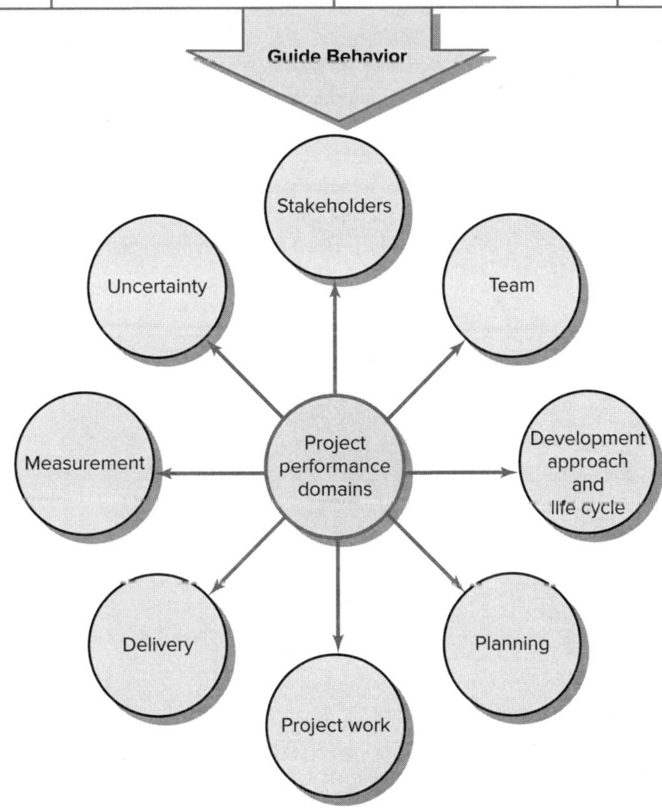

Source: Project Management Institute, *A Guide to Project Management Body of Knowledge PMBOK Guide,* seventh edition (Pennsylvania: Project Management Institute, 2021), p. PGS1:5.

insights and tools to be successful. The text is based on research on project management, hundreds of interviews and discussions with project professionals, and our own experience managing projects. We are confident that we are providing the student with a solid foundation for passing either exam. See Exhibit A1.1 for a cross-reference of *PMBOK Guide* concepts to text topics.

EXHIBIT A1.1 Cross-Reference of *Project Management Body of Knowledge* (PMBOK, 7th ed.) Concepts to Text Topics

Chapter 1	**Modern Project Management**
2.3.1	Development, Cadence, and Life Cycle Relationship
2.3.2	Delivery Cadence
2.3.3	Development Approaches
2.3.5	Life Cycle and Phase Definitions
4.2.7.4	Process Groups
Chapter 2	**Organizational Strategy and Project Selection**
2.3.4.1	Product, Service, or Result
Chapter 3	**Organization: Structure and Culture**
2.2.1	Project Team Management and Leadership
2.2.2	Project Team Culture
2.3.4.3	Organization
2.4.3	Project Team Composition and Structure
Chapter 4	**Defining the Project**
2.3.4.1	Product, Service, or Result
2.4.2.1	Delivery
2.4.4	Communication
2.5.2	Balancing Competing Constraints
2.5.4	Project Communication and Engagement
2.6.2	Deliverables
Chapter 5	**Estimating Project Times and Costs**
2.4.2.2	Estimating
4.4.2	Estimating
Chapter 6	**Developing a Project Schedule**
2.4.2.3	Schedules
Chapter 7	**Managing Risk**
2.4.7	Changes
2.5.7	Monitoring New Work and Changes
2.8.1	General Uncertainty
2.8.4	Volatility
2.8.5	Risk
Chapter 8	**Scheduling Resources and Cost**
2.4.2.4	Budget
2.4.5	Physical Resources
2.5.5	Managing Physical Resources
Chapter 9	**Reducing Project Duration**
2.4.2.3	Schedules
Chapter 10	**Being an Effective Project Manager**
2.1.1	Stakeholder Engagement
2.2.4	Leadership Skills
Chapter 11	**Managing Project Teams**
2.2.3	High-Performing Project Teams
2.2.5	Tailoring Leadership Styles
2.5.3	Maintaining Project Team Focus
4.2.6.1	Tuckman Ladder
4.2.7.1	Conflict Model
Chapter 12	**Outsourcing: Managing Interorganizational Relations**
2.4.6	Procurement
2.5.6	Working with Procurements
4.2.7.2	Negotiation
Chapter 13	**Progress and Performance Measurement and Evaluation**

2.4.8	Metrics
2.5.1	Project Processes
2.5.7	Monitoring New Work and Changes
2.7.1	Establishing Effective Measures
2.7.2	What to Measure
2.7.3	Presenting Information
2.7.4	Measurement Pitfalls
2.7.5	Troubleshooting Performance
Chapter 14	**Project Closure**
2.5.8	Learning throughout the Project
2.6.4	Suboptimal Outcomes
Chapter 15	**Agile Project Management**
2.3.4.2	Project
2.5.7	Monitoring New Work and Changes
2.7.3	Presenting Information
Chapter 16	**International Projects**
–	–

Design elements: Snapshot from Practice, Highlight box, Case icon: Sky Deswigns/Shutterstock

CHAPTER TWO

2 Organization Strategy and Project Selection

LEARNING OBJECTIVES

After reading this chapter you should be able to:

2-1 Explain why it is important for project managers to understand their organization's strategy.

2-2 Identify the significant role projects contribute to the strategic direction of the organization.

2-3 Understand the need for a project priority system.

2-4 Distinguish among three kinds of projects.

2-5 Describe how the phase gate model applies to project management.

2-6 Apply financial and nonfinancial criteria to assess the value of projects.

2-7 Understand how multi-criteria models can be used to select projects.

2-8 Apply an objective priority system to project selection.

2-9 Understand the need to manage the project portfolio.

OUTLINE

2.1 Why Project Managers Need to Understand Strategy

2.2 The Strategic Management Process: An Overview

2.3 The Need for a Project Priority System

2.4 Project Classification

2.5 Phase Gate Model

2.6 Selection Criteria

2.7 Applying a Selection Model

2.8 Managing the Portfolio System

Summary

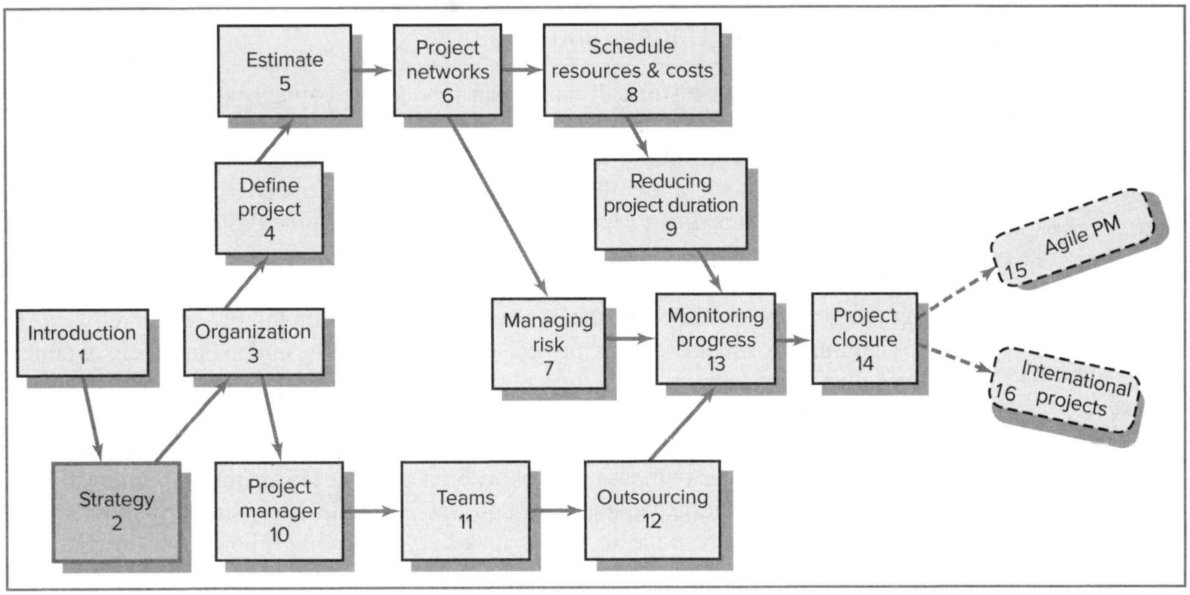

A vision without a strategy remains an illusion.

—Lee Bolman, Professor of Leadership, University of Missouri–Kansas City.

Strategy is fundamentally deciding how the organization will compete. Organizations use projects to convert strategy into new products, services, and processes needed for success. For example, Intel's major strategy is one of differentiation. Intel relies on projects to create specialty chips for products other than computers, such as autos, security, cell phones, and air controls. Another strategy is to reduce project cycle times. Procter and Gamble, NEC, General Electric, and AT&T have reduced their cycle times by 20–50 percent. Toyota and other auto manufacturers are now able to design and develop new cars in two to three years instead of five to seven years. Projects and project management play the key role in supporting strategic goals. It is vital for project managers to think and act strategically.

Aligning projects with the strategic goals of the organization is crucial for business success. Today's economic climate is unprecedented by rapid changes in technology, global competition, financial uncertainty, and disease outbreaks. These conditions make strategy/project alignment even more essential for success.

The larger and more diverse an organization, the more difficult it is to create and maintain a strong link between strategy and projects. How can an organization ensure this link? The answer requires integration of projects with the strategic plan. Integration assumes the existence of a strategic plan and a process for prioritizing projects by their contribution to the plan. A key factor to ensure the success of integrating the plan with projects is an open and transparent selection process for all participants to review.

This chapter presents an overview of the importance of strategic planning and the process for developing a strategic plan. Typical problems encountered when strategy and projects are not linked are noted. A generic methodology that ensures integration by creating strong linkages of project selection and priority to the strategic plan is then discussed. The intended outcomes are clear organization focus, best use of scarce organization resources (people, equipment, capital), and improved communication across projects and departments.

2.1 Why Project Managers Need to Understand Strategy

LO 2-1

Explain why it is important for project managers to understand their organization's strategy.

Project management historically has been preoccupied solely with the planning and execution of projects. Strategy was considered to be under the purview of senior management. This is old-school thinking. New-school thinking recognizes that project management is at the apex of strategy and operations. Shenhar speaks to this issue when he states, "It is time to expand the traditional role of the project manager from an operational to a more strategic perspective. In the modern evolving organization, project managers will be focused on business aspects, and their role will expand from getting the job done to achieving the business results and winning in the marketplace."[1]

There are two main reasons project managers need to understand their organization's mission and strategy. The first reason is so they can make appropriate decisions and adjustments. For example, how a project manager would respond to a suggestion to modify the design of a product to enhance performance will vary depending upon whether his/her company strives to be a product leader through innovation or to achieve operational excellence through low-cost solutions. Similarly, how a project manager would respond to delays may vary depending upon strategic concerns. A project manager will authorize overtime if his/her firm places a premium on getting to the market first. Another project manager will accept the delay if speed is not essential.

The second reason project managers need to understand the strategic implications of their project is so they can be effective project advocates. Project managers have to be able to demonstrate to senior management how their project contributes to their firm's mission in order to garner their continued support. Project managers need to be able to explain to stakeholders why certain project objectives and priorities are critical in order to secure buy-in on contentious trade-off decisions. Finally, project managers need to be able to redirect teams' efforts when they drift off course. Being able to explain why a suggestion or course of action is not appropriate in terms of strategic objectives will go a long way in building support within the team (Brown, Hyer, & Ettenson, 2013).

For these reasons, project managers will find it valuable to have a solid understanding of strategic management and project selection processes, which are discussed next.

2.2 The Strategic Management Process: An Overview

LO 2-2

Identify the significant role projects contribute to the strategic direction of the organization.

Strategic management is the process of assessing "what we are" and deciding and implementing "what we intend to be and how we are going to get there." Strategy describes how an organization intends to compete with the resources available in the existing and perceived future environment. Two major dimensions of strategic management are responding to changes in the external environment and allocating the firm's scarce resources to improve its competitive position. Constant scanning of the external environment for changes is a major requirement for survival in a dynamic competitive environment. The second dimension is the internal responses to new action programs aimed at enhancing the competitive position of the firm. The nature of the responses depends on the type of business, environment volatility, competition, and organizational culture.

Strategic management provides the theme and focus of the future direction of the organization. It supports consistency of action at every level of the organization. It encourages integration because effort and resources are committed to common goals and strategies. Strategic management is a continuous, iterative process aimed at developing an integrated and coordinated long-term plan of action. Objectives

[1] Shenhar, A., and D. Dvie, *Reinventing Project Management* (Boston: Harvard Business School Press, 2007), p. 5.

are set, and then translated into actions by implementing projects. See Snapshot from Practice 2.1: IBM's Watson Project for an example of how IBM tried to use a TV game show to signal a shift in strategic focus.

SNAPSHOT FROM PRACTICE 2.1 IBM's Watson Project*

On February 2010, millions of people were glued to their television sets to watch IBM's Watson outclass two former champion contestants on the *Jeopardy* quiz show. Watson performed at human expert levels in terms of precision, confidence, and speed during the show.

Watson's triumph announced to the world IBM's shift in strategic focus toward artificial intelligence (AI) driven business services. IBM's management thought the technology behind Watson could do for the company what mainframe computer once did—be an engine for growth and profits for decades.

WATSON PROJECT DESCRIPTION

AI has advanced significantly in recent years. Watson goes beyond IBM's chess-playing supercomputer of the late 1990s. Chess is finite, logical, and reduced easily to mathematics. Watson's work is ill-defined and involves dealing with abstraction and the circumstantial nature of language. Since Watson's system can understand natural language, it can extend the way people interact with computers.

The IBM Watson project took three intense years of research and development by a core team of about 20. Eight university teams working on specific challenge areas augmented these researchers.

Watson depends on over 200 million pages of structured and unstructured data and a program capable of running trillions of operations per second. With this information backup, it attacks a *Jeopardy* question by parsing the question into small pieces. With the question parsed, the program then searches for relevant data. Using hundreds of decision rules, the program generates possible answers. These answers are assigned a confidence score to decide if Watson should risk offering an answer and how much to bet.

WHAT HAPPENED NEXT?

IBM invested millions of dollars in the next few years into promoting Watson as a benevolent digital assistant that would help hospitals and farms as well as offices and factories. The potential uses, IBM suggested, were boundless, from spotting new market opportunities to tackling cancer and climate change. An IBM report called it "the future of knowing."

Sean Gallup/Getty Images

A decade since the *Jeopardy* victory, Watson has yet to revolutionize industries nor significantly lift IBM's fortunes. Touted efforts in healthcare have fallen far short of expectations. Dreams of creating digital physician assistant which would analyze medical data and assist in diagnosis and treatment never got out of the development phase. Potential cancer treatment applications never materialized. On the AI front, IBM still trails rivals—Amazon, Microsoft, and Google—in cloud computing and AI.

The company's missteps with Watson began with its focus on big and difficult initiatives (i.e., cancer treatment) intended to generate both acclaim and sizable revenue for IBM. Experts noted that while Watson was a remarkable achievement, it was custom-built for a quiz show. Applying the technology to real-world settings has been problematic.

Now IBM describes Watson as a learning journey for the company. There have been wrong turns and setbacks, IBM says, but that comes with trying to commercialize pioneering technology.

Beside all was not a loss. Watson is being used to build models and develop applications to help business make predictions, automate processes, and interact with users and customers. In 2021, IBM reported more than 40,000 Watson customers across 20 industries worldwide, more than double the number four years ago. While Watson is no longer the next big thing, it has evolved into a solid business for IBM.

* D. Ferrucci, E. Brown, J. Chu-Carroll, J. Fan, D. Gondek, A. Kaylanp, A. Lally, J. Murdock, E. Nyborg, J. Prager, N. Schaefer, and C. Wetty, "Building Watson," *AI Magazine*, Fall 2010, pp. 59–79; S. Lohr, "What ever happened to IBM's Watson?" *New York Times*, July 16, 2021. Accessed 8/4/22.

Strategy can decide the survival of an organization. Most organizations are successful in *formulating* strategies for the course(s) they should pursue. However, the problem in many organizations is *implementing* strategies—that is, making them happen. Integration of strategy formulation and implementation often does not exist.

The components of strategic management are closely linked, and all are directed toward the future success of the organization. Strategic management requires strong links among mission, goals, objectives, strategy, and implementation. The mission gives the general purpose of the organization. Goals give global targets within the mission. Objectives give specific targets to goals. Objectives give rise to the formulation of strategies to reach objectives. Finally, strategies require actions and tasks to be implemented. In most cases, the actions to be taken represent projects. Figure 2.1 shows a schematic of the strategic management process and major activities required.

FIGURE 2.1 **Strategic Management Process**

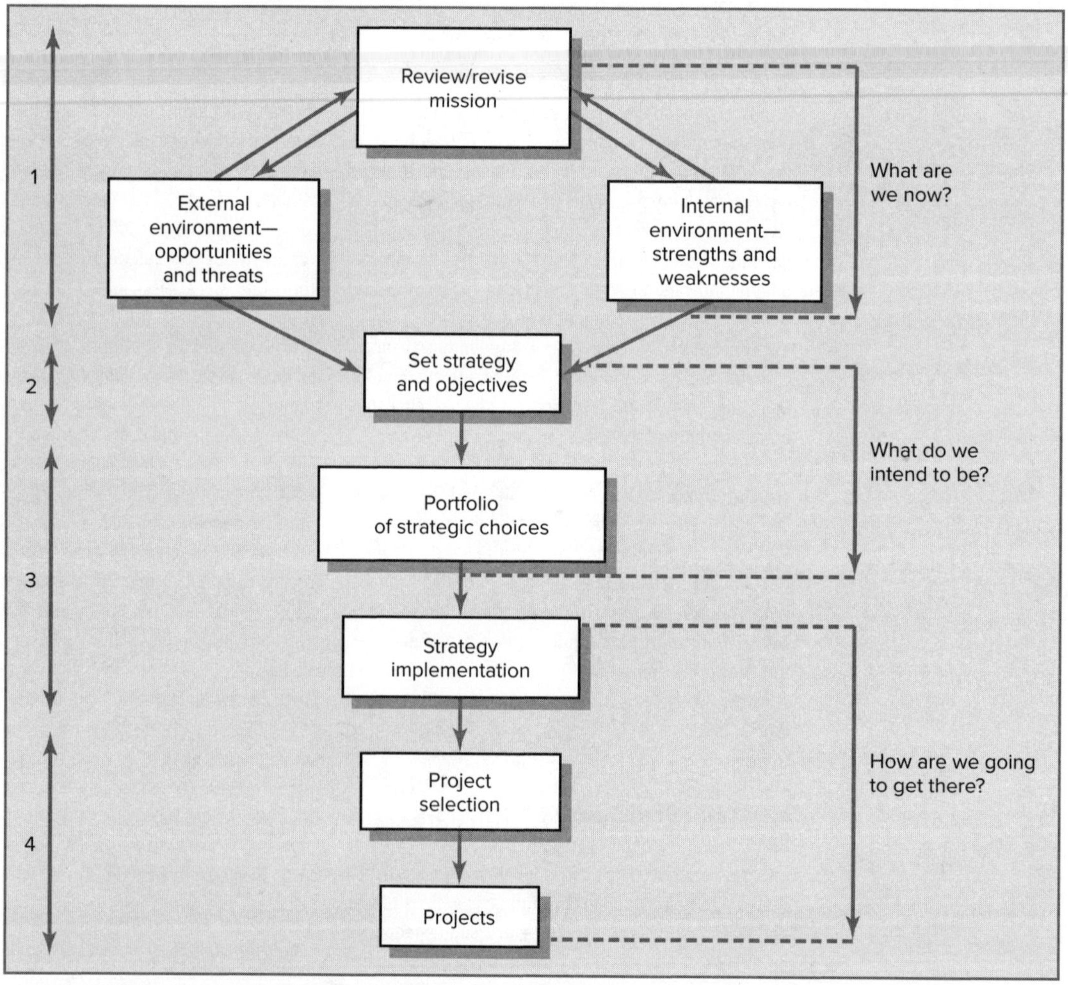

Four Activities of the Strategic Management Process

The typical sequence of activities of the strategic management process is outlined here; a description of each activity then follows.

1. Review and define the organizational mission.
2. Analyze and formulate strategies.
3. Set objectives to achieve strategies.
4. Implement strategies through projects.

Review and Define the Organizational Mission

The mission identifies "what we want to become," or the raison d'être. Mission statements identify the scope of the organization in terms of its product or service. A written mission statement provides focus for decision making when shared by organizational managers and employees. Everyone in the organization should be keenly aware of the organization's mission. For example, at one large consulting firm, partners who fail to recite the mission statement on demand are required to buy lunch. The mission statement communicates and identifies the purpose of the organization to all stakeholders. Mission statements can be used for evaluating organization performance.

Traditional components found in mission statements are major products and services, target customers and markets, and geographical domain. In addition, statements frequently include organizational philosophy, key technologies, public image, and contribution to society. Including such factors in mission statements relates directly to business success.

Mission statements change infrequently. However, when the nature of the business changes or shifts, revised mission, and strategy statements may be required.

More specific mission statements tend to give better results because of a tighter focus. Mission statements decrease the chance of false directions by stakeholders. For example, compare the phrasing of the following mission statements:

Provide hospital design services.
Provide data mining and analysis services.
Provide information technology services.
Provide high-value products to our customers.

Clearly, the first two statements leave less chance for misinterpretation than the others. A rule-of-thumb test for a mission statement is that, if the statement can be anybody's mission statement, it will not provide the guidance and focus intended. The mission sets the parameters for developing objectives.

Analyze and Formulate Strategies

Formulating strategy answers the question of *what* needs to be done to reach objectives. Strategy formulation includes determining and evaluating alternatives that support the organization's objectives and selecting the best alternative. The first step is a realistic evaluation of the past and current position of the enterprise. This step typically includes an analysis of "who are the customers" and "what are their needs as they (the *customers*) see them."

The next step is an assessment of the internal and external environments. What are the internal strengths and weaknesses of the enterprise? Examples of internal strengths or weaknesses are core competencies, such as technology, product quality, management talent, low debt, and dealer networks. Managers can alter internal strengths and weaknesses. Opportunities and threats usually represent external forces for change such as technology, industry structure, and competition. Competitive benchmarking tools are sometimes used to assess current and future directions. Opportunities and threats are the flip sides of each other. That is, a threat can be perceived as an opportunity, or vice versa. Examples of perceived external threats are a slowing of the economy, a maturing life cycle, exchange rates, and government regulation. Typical opportunities are increasing demand, emerging markets, and demographics. Managers or individual firms have limited opportunities to influence such external environmental factors; however, notable exceptions have been new technologies such as Apple using the iPod to create a market to sell music. The keys are to attempt to forecast fundamental industry changes and stay in a proactive mode rather than a reactive one. This assessment of the external and internal environments is known as the SWOT (strengths, weaknesses, opportunities, and threats) analysis.

From this analysis, critical issues and strategic alternatives are identified. Critical analysis of the strategies includes asking questions: Does the strategy take advantage of our core competencies? Does the strategy exploit our competitive advantage? Does the strategy maximize meeting customers' needs? Does the strategy fit within our acceptable risk range? These strategic alternatives are winnowed down to a critical few that support the basic mission.

Strategy formulation ends with cascading objectives or projects assigned to lower divisions, departments, or individuals. Formulating strategy might range around 20 percent of management's effort, while determining *how* strategy will be implemented might consume 80 percent.

Set Objectives to Achieve Strategies

Objectives translate the organization strategy into specific, concrete, measurable terms. Organizational objectives set targets for all levels of the organization. Objectives pinpoint the direction managers believe the organization should move toward. Objectives answer in detail *where* a firm is headed and *when* it is going to get there. Typically objectives for the organization cover markets, products, innovation, productivity, quality, finance, profitability, employees, and consumers. In every case, objectives should be as operational as possible. That is, objectives should include a time frame, be measurable, be an identifiable state, and be realistic. Doran (1981) created the memory device shown in Exhibit 2.1, which is useful when writing objectives.

Each level below the organizational objectives should support the higher-level objectives in more detail; this is frequently called cascading of objectives. For example, if a firm making leather luggage sets an objective of achieving a 40 percent increase in sales through a research and development strategy, this charge is passed to the Marketing, Production, and R&D Departments. The R&D Department accepts the firm's strategy as their objective, and their strategy becomes the design and development of a new "pull-type luggage with hidden, retractable wheels." At this point, the objective becomes a project to be implemented—to develop the retractable-wheel luggage for market within six months within a budget of $500,000. In summary, organizational objectives drive projects.

EXHIBIT 2.1
Characteristics of Objectives

S	**Specific**	Be specific in targeting an objective
M	**Measurable**	Establish a measurable indicator(s) of progress
A	**Assignable**	Make the objective assignable to one person for completion
R	**Realistic**	State what can realistically be done with available resources
T	**Time related**	State when the objective can be achieved, that is, duration

Implement Strategies through Projects

Implementation answers the question of *how* strategies will be realized, given available resources. The conceptual framework for strategy implementation lacks the structure and discipline found in strategy formulation. Implementation requires action and task completion; the latter frequently means mission-critical projects. Therefore, implementation must include attention to several key areas.

First, task completion requires resources. Resources typically represent funds, people, management talents, technological skills, and equipment. Frequently, implementation of projects is treated as an "addendum" rather than an integral part of the strategic management process. However, multiple objectives place conflicting demands on organizational resources. Second, implementation requires a formal and informal organization that complements and supports strategy and projects. Authority, responsibility, and performance all depend on organization structure and culture. Third, planning and control systems must be in place to be certain project activities necessary to ensure strategies are effectively performed. Fourth, motivating project contributors will be a major factor for achieving project success. Finally, areas receiving more attention in recent years are **portfolio management** and prioritizing projects. Although the strategy implementation process is not as clear as strategy formulation, all managers realize that without implementation, success is impossible. Although the four major steps of the strategic management process have not been altered significantly over the years, the view of the time horizon in the strategy formulation process has been altered radically in the last two decades. Global competition, rapid innovation, and now the COVID-19 pandemic require being highly adaptive to short-run changes while being consistent in the longer run. See Snapshot: Is This the End of Airbnb? for an example of the role projects played in how a company persevered during the COVID-19 pandemic.

2.3 The Need for a Project Priority System

LO 2-3

Understand the need for a project priority system.

Implementation of projects without a strong **priority system** linked to strategy creates problems. Four of the most obvious problems are discussed in this section. A priority-driven **project portfolio** system can go a long way to reduce, or even eliminate, the impact of these problems.

Problem 1: Behavioral Biases

Project selection decisions are made by people, and as human beings, they are susceptible to biases. Two important human predispositions that relate to project selection are Optimism bias and Uniqueness bias.

Optimism bias is the tendency to be overly positive about the outcomes of planned activities (Kahneman, 2011). Project proponents often advocate based on an ideal future rather than rational assessment of gains, losses, and risks. Left on their own they tend to underestimate time/costs and overestimate benefits of projects. Note, this is *not* deliberate, it is a human predisposition, especially true for young professionals who consider themselves experts.

Uniqueness bias was originally identified by psychologists as the tendency for individuals to see themselves as more singular than they actually are, for example, healthier or cleverer than others (c.f., Alicke & Govorun, 2005; Suis & Wan, 1987). Danish researcher Bent Flyvbjerg applied this bias to project selection when he tried to explain why organizations ignore past histories and continue to fund megaprojects (i.e., bridges, airports, etc.) that go way over budget (Flyvbjerg, 2014). When confronted with negative data from other similar projects, proponents argue, "but this project is different, we

SNAPSHOT FROM PRACTICE Is This the End of Airbnb?*

When COVID-19 spread across the globe in 2020, the travel company Airbnb was in the process of registering to go public. Within weeks, Airbnb lost 80 percent of its business. "Is this the end of Airbnb?" a *Wired UK* headline asked.

Like most businesses, Airbnb's immediate response was to cut costs. Top management laid off 25 percent of the workforce! There was also a steep reduction in discretionary and capital expenditures, a slashing of executive salaries, and a suspension of all facilities build-outs. In other words, hundreds of projects were canceled. Top management at Airbnb redirected the remaining workforce efforts on sustaining their "core" business and finding innovative responses to the COVID-19 pandemic.

Focus on the Core Business: Co-founder Brian Chesky noted, "When the pandemic hit, we knew we couldn't pursue everything that we used to. We chose to focus on what is most unique about Airbnb—our core business of hosting. We got back to our roots and back to what is truly special about Airbnb—the everyday people who host their homes and offer experiences. We scaled back investments that did not directly support the core of our host community."

This move proved critical. As the pandemic deepened, people were looking more at local stays and this played to the advantage of Airbnb. They offered host deep cleaning guidance and re-tooled their websites to promote beachfront getaways and cabins tucked away in the woods. They found that people liked having a home all to themselves where they could be in their own bubble and have a kitchen to prepare their own food.

People also took advantage of the work attendance embargo to book extended stays in attractive locales (i.e., Hawaii, Mexico) and do their work remotely. Airbnb supported hosts efforts at creating virtual workspaces for lodgers. This turned out to be another big factor in the turnaround.

Creatively-led Projects: Severe constraints and limitations can often lead to even more inspiration. This was certainly the case with the Airbnb project teams. For example, when the In Person Experiences segment was suspended, this led to the creation of "Online Experiences." For example, instead of meeting a guide in St. Petersburg and going on an actual walking tour, you have a zoom meeting with a Russian guide who talks you through videos and pictures of the sites you would have seen. Airbnb projects teams worked with guides to set up and test their Experiences. Online Experiences turned out to be an extremely popular offering.

Airbnb has a long tradition providing disaster relief to local communities. In 2017, Airbnb launched "Open Homes"—a program that enabled host community to offer their homes for free to people impacted by disasters or fleeing conflicts. Within months, Open Homes was housing thousands of displaced people from such disasters as Hurricane Irma, Hurricane Maria, and the earthquake in Mexico City. These were locally driven projects that did not have to operate in the messy environment of a potentially deadly virus.

Airbnb redirected their energies to launching "Frontline Stays"—a global initiative to connect healthcare workers and first responders with free and subsidized stays during the COVID-19 pandemic. The initiative began with two pilot projects in Italy and France. Within days of working with local governments and medical officials, Airbnb announced that doctors, nurses, caregivers, and other medical support staff responding to the outbreak could have free or discounted access to accommodation through Airbnb.

The response was immediate and within weeks project teams expanded the program across the globe. Hosts worldwide offered more than 225,000 places to stay and helped accommodate tens of thousands of healthcare professionals, relief workers, and first responders.

In a large part due to their response to the COVID-19 pandemic crisis, Airbnb was able to launch a very successful initial public offering (IPO) on December 10, 2020. By the end of that day, the market value of Airbnb was $100 billion, which greatly exceeded market analysts' predictions.

*B. Chesky, What Makes Airbnb, Airbnb. *Airbnb News,* February 22, 2021, https://news.airbnb.com/what-makes-airbnbairbnb/#:~:text=We%20got%20back%20to%20ou,core%20of%20our%20host%20community. Accessed 12/12/22.

J. Temperton, Is This the End Of Airbnb? *Wired UK,* April 22, 2020, https://www.wired.co.uk/article/airbnb-coronavirus-losses Accessed 12/12/22.

are different, despite what others have done, we can do this." Flyvbjerg points out that by its very nature project management is susceptible to this bias since by most definition projects are "unique" (Flyvbjerg, 2021). Note again, there is no intended deception, rather project advocates truly believe their project is different.

Unchecked, the optimism and uniqueness biases can contribute to costly project decisions. This is why veteran managers, who are aware of these tendencies, need to be involved in selecting and prioritizing projects.

Problem 2: The Implementation Gap

In many organizations, top management formulate strategy and leave strategy implementation to functional managers. Within these broad constraints, more detailed strategies and objectives are developed by the functional managers. The fact that these objectives and strategies are made *independently* at different levels by functional groups within the organization hierarchy causes manifold problems.

Following are some symptoms of organizations struggling with strategy disconnect and unclear priorities.

- Conflicts frequently occur among functional managers and cause lack of trust.
- Frequent meetings are called to establish or renegotiate priorities.
- People frequently shift from one project to another, depending on current priority. Employees are confused about which projects are important.
- People are working on multiple projects and feel inefficient.
- Resources are not adequate.

Because clear linkages do not exist between strategy and action, the organizational environment becomes dysfunctional, confused, and ripe for ineffective implementation of organization strategy and, thus, of projects. The **implementation gap** is the lack of understanding and consensus of organization strategy among top and middle level managers.

A scenario the authors have seen repeated several times follows. Top management pick their top 20 projects for the next planning period, without priorities. Each functional department—Marketing, Finance, Operations, Engineering, Information Technology, and Human Resources—selects projects from the list. Unfortunately, independent department priorities across projects are not homogenous. A project that rates first in the IT Department can rate 10th in the Finance Department. Implementation of the projects represents conflicts of interest, with animosities developing over organizational resources. In a study of Deloitte Consulting, MacIntyre reports, "Only 23 percent of nearly 150 global executives considered their project portfolios aligned with the core business."[2]

Problem 3: Organization Politics

Politics exist in every organization and can have a significant influence on which projects receive funding and high priority. This is especially true when the criteria and process for selecting projects are ill-defined and not aligned with the mission of the firm. Project selection may be based not so much on facts and sound reasoning as on the persuasiveness and power of people advocating projects.

The term **sacred cow** is often used to denote a project that a powerful, high-ranking official is advocating. Case in point, a marketing consultant confided that he was once

[2] MacIntyre, J., "Stroke of Strategy," *PM Network,* November 2006, pp. 32–35.

hired by the marketing director of a large manufacturing firm to conduct an independent, external market analysis for a new product the firm was interested in developing. His extensive research indicated that there was insufficient demand to warrant the financing of this new product. The marketing director chose to bury the report and made the consultant promise never to make the information public. The director explained that this new product was the "pet idea" of the new CEO, who saw it as his legacy to the firm. The director went on to describe the CEO's irrational obsession with the project and how he referred to it as his "new baby." Like a parent fiercely protecting his child, the marketing director believed that he would lose his job if such critical information ever became known.

Project sponsors play a significant role in the selection and successful implementation of product innovation projects. Project sponsors are typically high-ranking managers who endorse and lend political support for the completion of a specific project. They are instrumental in winning approval of the project and in protecting the project during the critical development stage. The importance of project sponsors should not be taken lightly. For example, a PMI global survey of over 1,000 project practitioners and leaders over a variety of industries found those organizations having active sponsors on at least 80 percent of their projects/programs have a success rate of 75 percent, 11 percentage points above the survey average of 64 percent. Many promising projects have failed to succeed due to lack of strong sponsorship.[3]

The classic example of corporate politics can be seen in the ill-fated ALTO computer project at Xerox during the mid-1970s.[4] The project was a tremendous technological success; it developed the first workable mouse, the first laser printer, the first user-friendly software, and the first local area network. All of these developments were five years ahead of their nearest competitor. Over the next five years, this opportunity to dominate the nascent personal computer market was squandered because of internal in-fighting at Xerox and the absence of a strong project sponsor. (Apple's MacIntosh computer was inspired by many of these developments.)

Politics can play a role not only in project selection but also in the aspirations behind projects. Individuals can enhance their power within an organization by managing extraordinary and critical projects. Power and status naturally accrue to successful innovators and risk takers rather than to steady producers. Many ambitious managers pursue high-profile projects as a means for moving quickly up the corporate ladder. Unfortunately, some devious people will deliberately distort and misrepresent information in order to get their projects approved (Flyvbjerg et al., 2009; Kain, 1990; Wachs, 1989).

Many would argue that politics and project management should not mix. A more proactive response is that projects and politics invariably mix and that effective project managers recognize that any significant project has political ramifications. Likewise, top management need to develop a system for identifying and selecting projects that reduces the impact of internal politics and fosters the selection of the best projects for the firm.

Problem 4: Resource Conflicts and Multitasking

Most projects operate in a multiproject environment. This environment creates the problems of project interdependency and the need to share resources. For example, what would be the impact on the labor resource pool of a construction company if it

[3] PMI, "PMI's Pulse of the Profession," Project Management Institute, March 2012, p. 7.

[4] Smith, D. K., and R. C. Alexander, *Fumbling the Future: How Xerox Invented, Then Ignored the First Personal Computer* (New York: Macmillan, 1988).

EXHIBIT 2.2
Benefits of Project Portfolio Management

- Builds discipline into project selection process.
- Links project selection to strategic metrics.
- Prioritizes project proposals across a common set of criteria, rather than on politics or emotion.
- Allocates resources to projects that align with strategic direction.
- Balances risk across all projects.
- Justifies killing projects that do not support organization strategy.
- Improves communication and supports agreement on project goals.

should win a contract it would like to bid on? Will existing labor be adequate to deal with the new project—given the completion date? Will current projects be delayed? Will subcontracting help? Which projects will have priority? Competition among project managers can be contentious. All project managers seek to have the best people for their projects. The problems of sharing resources and scheduling resources across projects grow exponentially as the number of projects rises. In multiproject environments, the stakes are higher and the benefits or penalties for good or bad resource scheduling become even more significant than in most single projects (Mortensen & Gardner, 2017).

Resource sharing also leads to multitasking. Multitasking involves starting and stopping work on one task to go and work on another project, then returning to the work on the original task. People working on several tasks concurrently are far less efficient, especially where conceptual or physical shutdown and start-up are significant. Multitasking adds to delays and costs.

A multiproject organizational environment faces major problems without a priority system that is clearly linked to the strategic plan. Exhibit 2.2 lists a few key benefits of Project Portfolio Management; the list could easily be extended.

2.4 Project Classification

LO 2-4

Distinguish among three kinds of projects.

Many organizations find they have three basic kinds of projects in their portfolio: *compliance* (emergency—must do), *operational,* and *strategic* projects (see Figure 2.2). Compliance projects are typically those needed to meet regulatory conditions required to operate in a region; hence, they are called "must do" projects. Emergency projects, such as building an auto parts factory destroyed by a tsunami, recovering a crashed network, or developing new COVID-19 vaccines are examples of must do projects. Compliance and emergency projects usually have penalties if they are not implemented.

Operational projects are those that are needed to support current operations. These projects are designed to improve the efficiency of delivery systems, reduce product costs, and improve performance. Some of these projects, given their limited scope and cost, require only immediate manager approval, while bigger, more expensive projects need extensive review. Choosing to install a new piece of equipment is an example of the latter, while modifying a production process is an example of the former. Total quality management (TQM) projects are examples of operational projects.

Strategic projects are those that directly support the organization's long-run mission. They frequently are directed toward increasing revenue or market share. Examples of strategic projects are new products, new technologies, research, and development.[5]

[5] For a good, complete discussion on classification schemes found in practice, see: Crawford, L., B. Hobbs, and J. R. Turner, "Aligning Capability with Strategy: Categorizing of Projects to Do the Right Projects and Do Them Right," *Project Management Journal,* vol. 37, no. 2 (June 2006), pp. 38–50.

FIGURE 2.2
Project Classification

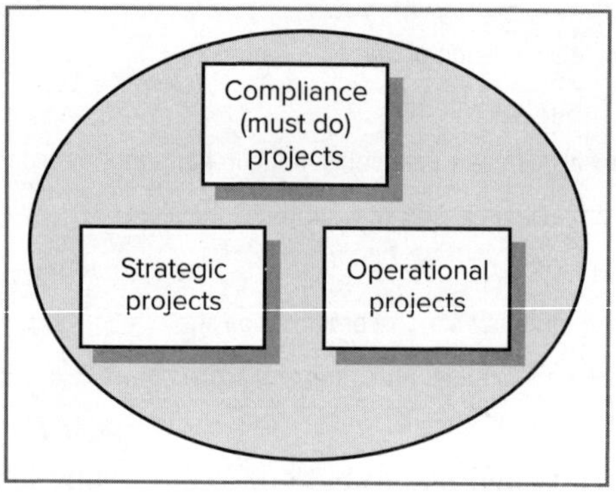

Frequently these three classifications are further decomposed by product type, organization divisions, and functions that will require different criteria for project selection. For example, the same criteria for the Finance or Legal Division would not apply to the Information Technology Department. This often requires different project selection criteria within the basic three classifications of strategic, operational, and compliance projects.

2.5 Phase Gate Model

LO 2-5

Describe how the phase gate model applies to project management.

Before we delve into the intricacies of project selection, we need to put this process in perspective. The selection process is the first part of the management system that spans the lifetime of the project. This system has been described as a series of gates that a project must pass through in order to be completed.[6] The purpose is to ensure that the organization is investing time and resources on worthwhile projects that contribute to its mission and strategy. Each gate is associated with a project phase and represents a decision point. A gate can lead to three possible outcomes: go (proceed), kill (cancel), or recycle (revise and resubmit). Figure 2.3 captures the **phase gate model.**

The first gate is invisible. It occurs inside the head of a person who has an idea for a project and must decide whether it is worth investing the time and effort to submit a formal proposal. This decision may be a gut reaction or involve informal research. Such research might include bouncing the idea off of colleagues or doing online research. It helps if the organization has a transparent project selection process where objectives and requirements for approval are well known. If not, many good ideas never see the light of day.

If the person believes his/her idea is worthwhile, then a project proposal is submitted conforming to the selection guidelines of the firm. Project proposals, as you will see, include such items as project objectives, business case, estimated costs, return on investment, risks, and resource requirements. Beyond the basic question of whether the proposal makes sense, management assesses how the project outcomes will contribute to the mission and strategy of the firm. For example, what strategic objectives does the project address? A second key question is "How well does the project fit with other projects?" Will it interfere with other, more important projects? Here the final question is whether this project is worthy of more planning.

[6] The original *stage-gate* model was pioneered by R. G. Cooper in *Product Leadership: Creating and Launching Superior New Products* (Cambridge, MA: Perseus, 2000).

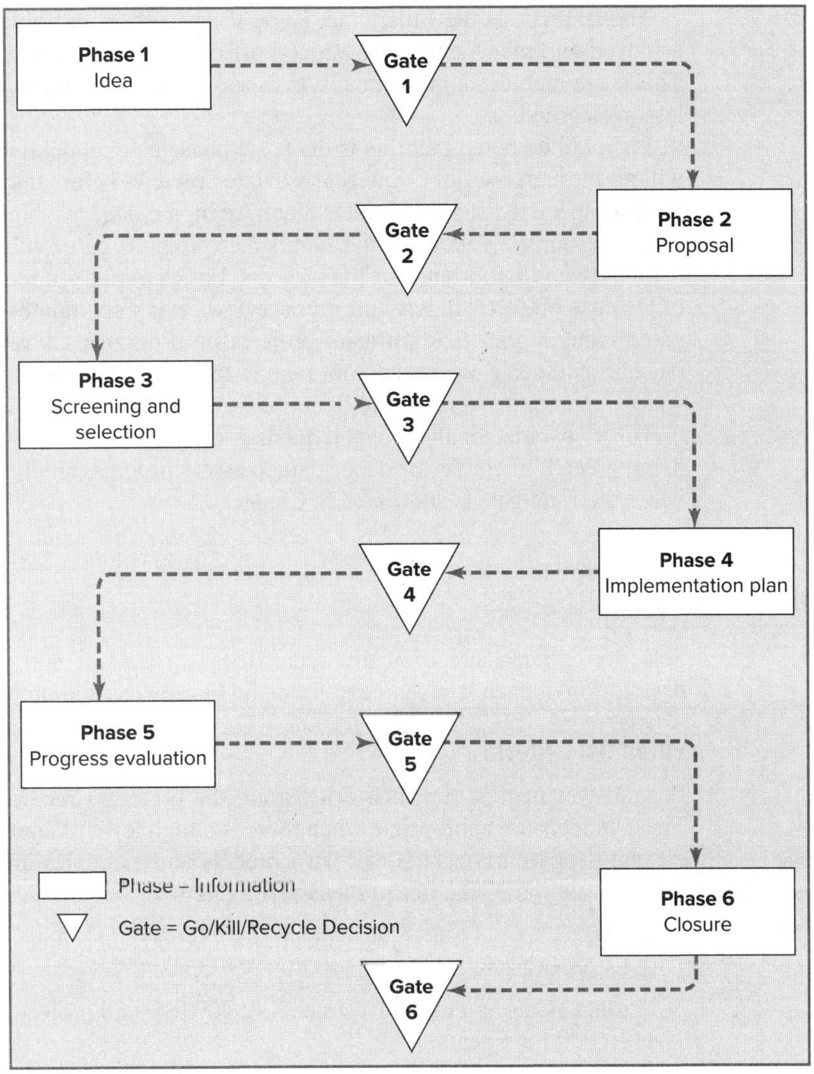

FIGURE 2.3
Phase Gate Process Diagram

If the preliminary proposal is approved, then a project manager and staff are assigned to develop a more comprehensive implementation plan. The preliminary proposal is revised and expanded. The plan now includes detailed information regarding schedule, costs, resource requirements, risk management, and so forth. Not only is the proposal assessed again in terms of strategic importance, but the implementation plan is scrutinized. Does the plan make sense? Do the numbers add up? Is it worth the risk? How much confidence is there in the plan? If affirmative, the green light is given to launch the project.

Once the project is under way there will likely be one or more progress reviews. The main purpose of progress review is to assess performance and determine what, if any, adjustments should be made. In some cases, the decision is made to cancel, or "kill," a project due to poor performance or lack of relevancy.

The last gate is the finish line. Here, the necessary customer acceptance has been achieved and management has signed off on the fulfillment of project requirements. This stage includes a project audit to assess project success as well as identifying key lessons learned.

It should be noted that this is the basic phase gate model. For many firms, projects will go through a series of internal escalated reviews before they obtain final approval. This is especially true for projects that have high risks, have high costs, and/or demand scarce resources. Likewise, the number of progress gates will vary depending upon the length and importance of the projects. For example, a three-year U.S. Department of Defense project will have progress reviews every six months. Finally, the described gate model applies to significant projects in terms of cost, resources, and/or importance. Small-scale projects do not require this level of inspection. Most often they are simply approved and reviewed by immediate superiors.

The remainder of this chapter focuses on gates 2 and 3, which lead to a project being green lighted. Performance data to assess progress are the subject of Chapter 13, while the final gate is addressed in Chapter 14.

2.6 Selection Criteria

Selection criteria are typically identified as *financial* and *nonfinancial*. A short description of each is given next, followed by a discussion of their use in practice.

Financial Criteria

LO 2-6

Apply financial and nonfinancial criteria to assess the value of projects.

For most managers, financial criteria are the preferred method to evaluate projects. These models are appropriate when there is a high level of confidence associated with estimates of future cash flows. Two models and examples are demonstrated in this section—**payback** and **net present value (NPV).**

Project A has an initial investment of $700,000 and projected cash inflows of $225,000 for 5 years.

Project B has an initial investment of $400,000 and projected cash inflows of $110,000 for 5 years.

1. The payback model measures the time it will take to recover the project investment. Shorter paybacks are more desirable. Payback is the simplest and most widely used model. Payback emphasizes cash flows, a key factor in business. Some managers use the payback model to eliminate unusually risky projects (those with lengthy payback periods). The major limitations of payback are that it ignores the time value of money, assumes cash inflows for the investment period (and not beyond), and does not consider profitability. The payback formula is:

$$\text{Payback period (yrs)} = \text{Estimated project cost/Annual savings}$$

Exhibit 2.3A compares the payback for project A and project B. The payback for project A is 3.1 years and for project B is 3.6 years. Using the payback method, both projects are acceptable, since both return the initial investment in less than five years and have returns on the investment of 32.1 percent and 27.5 percent. Payback provides especially useful information for firms concerned with liquidity and having sufficient resources to manage their financial obligations.

EXHIBIT 2.3A
Example Comparing Two Projects Using Payback Method
Microsoft Excel

	A	B	C	D	E	F	G	H	I	J
1					Exhibit 2.3A					
2										
3			Example Comparing Two Projects Using the Payback Method							
4										
5				Project A		Project B				Formulas
6										
7										
8		Investment		$700,000		$400,000				Project A: Payback = (D8/D9)
9		Annual savings		$225,000		$110,000				Project B: Payback = (F8/F9)
10										
11		Payback period*		3.1 years		3.6 years				
12										
13		Rate of return **		32.1%		27.5%				Project A: Rate of return = (D9/D8)
14										Project B: Rate of return = (F9/F8)
15	Project A: Accept. Less than 5 years and exceeds 15% desired rate.									
16										
17	Project B: Accept. Less than 5 years and exceeds 15% desired rate.									
18										
19	* Note: Payback does not use the time value of money.									
20	** Note: Rate of return is reciprocal of Payback.									
21										
22										

2. The net present value (NPV) model uses management's minimum desired rate of return (discount rate, for example, 15 percent) to compute the present value of all net cash inflows. If the result is positive (the project meets the minimum desired rate of return), it is eligible for further consideration. If the result is negative, the project is rejected. Thus, higher positive NPVs are desirable. Excel uses this formula:

$$\text{Project NPV} = I_0 + \sum_{t=1}^{n} \frac{F_t}{(1+k)^t}$$

where

I_0 = Initial investment (since it is an outflow, the number will be negative)
F_t = Net cash inflow for period t
k = Required rate of return
n = number of years

Exhibit 2.3B presents the NPV model using Microsoft Excel software. The NPV model accepts project A, which has a *positive* NPV of $54,235. Project B is rejected, since the NPV is *negative* $31,263. Compare the NPV results with the payback results. The NPV model is more realistic because it considers the time value of money, cash flows, and profitability.

EXHIBIT 2.3B
Example Comparing Two Projects Using Net Present Value Method
Microsoft Excel

J3

	A	B	C	D	E	F	G	H	I	J
1										
2				Exhibit 2.3B						
3										
4				Example Comparing Two Projects Using NPV						
5	Project A		Year 0	Year 1	Year 2	Year 3	Year 4	Year 5	Total	Formulas
6	Required	15%								
7	Outflows		-$700,000						-$700,000	
8	Inflows			$225,000	$225,000	$225,000	$225,000	$225,000	$1,125,000	
9	Net inflows			$225,000	$225,000	$225,000	$225,000	$225,000	$425,000	Project A: =C7+NPV(B6,D9:H9)
10	NPV	$54,235								
11										
12										
13	Project B									
14	Required	15%								
15	Outflows		-$400,000						-$400,000	
16	Inflows			$110,000	$110,000	$110,000	$110,000	$110,000	$550,000	
17	Net inflows			$110,000	$110,000	$110,000	$110,000	$110,000	$150,000	Project B: =C15+NPV(B14,D17:H17)
18	NPV	-$31,263								
19										
20										
21										
22	NPV comparison: Accept Project A—NPV is positive.									
23	Reject Project B—NPV is negative.									

In the NPV model, the discount rate (return on investment [ROI] hurdle rate) can differ for different projects. For example, the expected ROI on strategic projects is frequently set higher than operational projects. Similarly, ROIs can differ for riskier versus safer projects. The criteria for setting the ROI hurdle rate should be clear and applied consistently.

Unfortunately, pure financial models fail to include many projects where financial return is impossible to measure and/or other factors are vital to the accept or reject decision. One research study by Foti (2003) showed that companies using predominantly financial models to prioritize projects yielded unbalanced portfolios and projects that were not strategically oriented.

Nonfinancial Criteria

Financial return, while important, does not always reflect strategic importance. The past saw firms become overextended by diversifying too much. Now the prevailing thinking is that long-term survival is dependent upon developing and maintaining core competencies. Companies have to be disciplined in saying no to potentially profitable projects that are outside the realm of their core mission. This requires other criteria to be considered beyond direct financial return. For example, a firm may support projects that do not have high-profit margins for other strategic reasons, including

To capture larger market share.

To make it difficult for competitors to enter the market.

To develop an enabler product, which by its introduction will increase sales in more profitable products.

To develop core technology that will be used in next-generation products.

To reduce dependency on unreliable suppliers.

To prevent government intervention and regulation.

Less tangible criteria may also apply. Organizations may support projects to restore corporate image or enhance brand recognition. Many organizations are committed to corporate citizenship and support community development projects.

Two Multi-Criteria Selection Models

Since no single criterion can reflect strategic significance, portfolio management requires multi-criteria screening models. Two models, the checklist and multi-weighted scoring models, are described next.

Checklist Models

LO 2-7

Understand how multi-criteria models can be used to select projects.

The most frequently used method in selecting projects has been the checklist. This approach basically uses a list of questions to review potential projects and to determine their acceptance or rejection. Several of the typical questions found in practice are listed in Exhibit 2.4.

A justification of checklist models is that they allow great flexibility in selecting among many different types of projects and are easily used across different divisions and locations. Although many projects are selected using some variation of the checklist approach, this approach has serious shortcomings. Its major shortcomings are that it fails to answer the relative importance or value of a potential project to the organization and fails to allow for comparison with other potential projects. Each potential project will have a different set of positive and negative answers. How do you compare? Ranking and prioritizing projects by their importance is difficult, if

EXHIBIT 2.4
Sample Selection Questions Used in Practice

Topic	Question
Strategy/alignment	What specific organization strategy does this project align with?
Driver	What business problem does the project solve?
Sponsorship	Who is the project sponsor?
Risk	What is the impact of not doing this project?
Risk	How risky is the project?
Benefits, value, ROI	What is the value of the project to this organization?
Benefits, value, ROI	When will the project show results?
Objectives	What are the project objectives?
Organization culture	Is our organizational culture right for this type of project?
Resources	Will internal resources be available for this project?
Schedule	How long will this project take?
Finance/portfolio	What is the estimated cost of the project?
Portfolio	How does this project interact with current projects?

not impossible. This approach also leaves the door open to the potential opportunity for power plays, politics, and other forms of manipulation. To overcome these serious shortcomings, experts recommend the use of a multi-weighted scoring model to select projects, which is examined next.

Multi-Weighted Scoring Models

A weighted scoring model typically uses several weighted selection criteria to evaluate project proposals. Weighted scoring models generally include qualitative and/or quantitative criteria. Each selection criterion is assigned a weight. Scores are assigned to each criterion for the project, based on its importance to the project being evaluated. The weights and scores are multiplied to get a total weighted score for the project. Using these multiple screening criteria, projects can then be compared using the weighted score. Projects with higher-weighted scores are considered better.

Selection criteria need to mirror the critical success factors of an organization. For example, 3M set a target that 25 percent of the company's sales would come from products fewer than four years old versus the old target of 20 percent. Their priority system for project selection strongly reflects this new target. On the other hand, failure to pick the right factors will render the screening process useless in short order. See Snapshot from Practice 2.2: Crisis IT.

Figure 2.4 represents a project scoring matrix using some of the factors found in practice. The screening criteria selected are shown across the top of the matrix (e.g., stay within core competencies . . . ROI of 18 percent plus). Management weights each criterion (a value of 0 to a high of, say, 3) by its relative importance to the organization's objectives and strategic plan. Project proposals are then submitted to a project **priority team** or project office.

Each project proposal is then evaluated by its relative contribution/value added to the selected criteria. Values of 0 to a high of 10 are assigned to each criterion for each project. This value represents the project's fit to the specific criterion. For example, project 1 appears to fit well with the strategy of the organization, since it is given a value of 8. Conversely, project 1 does nothing to support reducing defects (its value is 0). Finally, this model applies the management weights to each criterion by importance using a value of 1 to 3. For example, ROI and strategic fit have a weight of 3, while urgency and core competencies have weights of 2. Applying the weight to each criterion, the priority team derives the weighted total points for each project.

SNAPSHOT FROM PRACTICE 2.2 Crisis IT*

In May 2007, Frontier Airlines Holdings hired Gerry Coady as chief information officer (CIO). Nearly a year later the airline filed for bankruptcy under Chapter 11. In an interview, Coady describes how he managed IT projects during the bankruptcy and recession crisis of 2008–2009.

Fundamentally, Coady faced a situation of too many projects and too few resources. Coady used a strategy of focusing on reducing the number of projects in the portfolio. He put together a steering committee of senior management that reviewed several hundred projects. The end result was a reduction to less than 30 projects remaining in the portfolio.

HOW CAN YOU GET TO A BACKLOG OF OVER 100 PROJECTS?

"There are never enough resources to get everything done." Backlogs build over time. Sacred cow projects get included in the selection system. Projects proposed from people who have left the airline still reside in the project portfolio. Non-value-added projects somehow make their way into the project portfolio. Soon the queue gets longer. With everyone in IT working on too many projects concurrently, project completion and productivity are slow.

WHICH PROJECTS REMAIN?

To cut the number of projects, the steering committee used a weighting scheme that reflected the airline's priorities, which were fly safe, generate revenue, reduce costs, and customer service. The weighting scheme easily weeded out the fluff. Coady noted that

Matej Kastelic/kasto/123RF

"by the time you get to the 20s the margin of differentiation gets narrower and narrower." Of the remaining projects, project sponsors had to have solid justification why their project was important. Reduction of the number of projects placed emphasis on high-value projects.

WHAT ADVICE DOES COADY HAVE FOR CRISIS MANAGEMENT?

In times of crisis, it is easier to take bold steps to make changes. But you need to have a clear vision of what you should be focusing on with the resources available. Coady suggests, "It comes back to really having a good idea of what the initial business case for a project is and what resources it is consuming, both people and otherwise."

* B. Worthen, "Crisis IT," *Wall Street Journal,* April 20, 2009, p. 6.

SNAPSHOT FROM PRACTICE 2.3 Organizational Strategy for Indian Railways

The Indian Railways' Dedicated Freight Corridor (DFC) project is a prime example of aligning organizational strategy with project management principles to achieve long-term success. The strategic goal of the DFC project is to enhance India's logistics infrastructure by creating dedicated, high-speed freight rail corridors. This alignment of organizational objectives and project goals is aimed at reducing transportation costs, improving efficiency, and accelerating movement of goods across the nation. The project is centred on fostering economic growth, increasing industrial productivity, and providing a sustainable, reliable mode of transport for goods.

WHAT ARE THE KEY STRATEGIC PRINCIPLES DRIVING THE DFC PROJECT?

- **Efficiency in freight transport:** The DFC is designed to create a world-class infrastructure that bypasses the bottlenecks caused by passenger traffic, enabling faster and more reliable freight movement. This approach directly impacts the project's efficiency goals by reducing congestion and improving capacity on the existing rail network.

- **Capacity enhancement and economic growth:** By developing dedicated freight corridors, the project addresses the increasing demand for freight transport and directly contributes to economic growth. This strategic objective is critical for India's industrial sectors, which rely on improved logistics for the timely delivery of goods.
- **Sustainability and eco-friendly solutions:** A key element of the project strategy is the use of electrification to reduce dependency on fossil fuels and lower carbon emissions. This reflects the organization's commitment to sustainability, integrating environmental considerations into the project's execution to minimize its ecological footprint.
- **Technological integration and innovation:** The project incorporates advanced technologies such as automation, AI, and real-time data analytics for traffic management and predictive maintenance. The adoption of these technologies ensures the project stays future-ready, increasing operational efficiency and enhancing the capacity of the freight network.

The scope of the DFC project involves several phases of project planning and execution, with meticulous alignment between organizational strategy and project management practices:

WHAT ARE THE PHASES AND STRATEGIC ALIGNMENTS INVOLVED IN THE DFC PROJECT'S SCOPE?

- **Feasibility analysis and planning:** This phase involves identifying optimal routes, conducting environmental impact assessments, and preparing a detailed project report (DPR) to ensure strategic alignment with national logistics and infrastructure goals.
- **Stakeholder engagement and approvals:** The project requires securing necessary government approvals for land acquisition, environmental clearance, and financing, which are essential for aligning the project with regulatory requirements and policies.
- **Infrastructure development:** The project focuses on constructing dedicated rail lines, freight terminals, and inter-modal logistics hubs, ensuring smooth integration with existing transportation networks. This ensures the project contributes to the broader logistics ecosystem, fostering greater coordination across the supply chain.
- **Procurement and technology integration:** The DFC project emphasizes procuring high-quality rolling stock (locomotives and freight cars) and installing signalling, electrification, and automation systems to enhance operational efficiency.
- **Testing, commissioning, and operational launch:** After thorough testing, the project transitions to launching freight services, marking the realization of strategic goals. Integration with the existing rail network ensures seamless movement of goods across the country.
- **Ongoing monitoring and maintenance:** As part of the long-term sustainability plan, the project includes provisions for continuous monitoring, maintenance, and upgrades to accommodate growing freight demand and ensure ongoing operational success.

From a project management standpoint, the DFC project integrates key risk management practices, addressing land acquisition delays, budgetary concerns, and engineering risks. Strategic management of these risks is essential for maintaining the project's timeline and budget, ensuring successful delivery. Additionally, the DFC project's performance can be assessed through key metrics such as freight turnaround time, capacity utilization, environmental impact, and customer satisfaction. These metrics provide valuable feedback on the project's success, ensuring that it aligns with both organizational and project-specific strategic goals.

In conclusion, the Indian Railways' DFC project demonstrates how effective project management can drive an organization's strategic vision, improve operational efficiencies, and contribute to broader economic goals. By integrating project management practices, such as thorough planning, risk mitigation, and technology integration, the DFC project stands as a model for successful execution of large-scale infrastructure initiatives that are aligned with the overall organizational strategy.

REFERENCES

Dedicated Freight Corridor Corporation of India Limited (DFCCIL) - http://www.dfccil.com/

Dedicated Freight Corridors (DFC) in India: A New Vision for Logistics, Source: Indian Railways, https://indianrailways.gov.in/

Indian Railways Dedicated Freight Corridor (DFC) Project: An Overview - Source: Economic Times

FIGURE 2.4 Project Screening Matrix

Criteria / Weight	Stay within core competencies	Strategic fit	Urgency	25% of sales from new products	Reduce defects to less than 1%	Improve customer loyalty	ROI of 18% plus	Weighted total
	2.0	3.0	2.0	2.5	1.0	1.0	3.0	
Project 1	1	8	2	6	0	6	5	66
Project 2	3	3	2	0	0	5	1	27
Project 3	9	5	2	0	2	2	5	56
Project 4	3	0	10	0	0	6	0	32
Project 5	1	10	5	10	0	8	9	102
Project 6	6	5	0	2	0	2	7	55
⋮								
Project *n*	5	5	7	0	10	10	8	83

For example, project 5 has the highest value of 102 [(2 × 1) + (3 × 10) + (2 × 5) + (2.5 × 10) + (1 × 0) + (1 × 8) + (3 × 9) = 102] and project 2 has a low value of 27. If the resources available create a cutoff threshold of 50 points, the priority team would eliminate projects 2 and 4. Project 5 would receive first priority, project *n* second, and so on. In rare cases where resources are severely limited and project proposals are similar in weighted rank, it is prudent to pick the project placing less demand on resources. Weighted multi-criteria models similar to this one are rapidly becoming the dominant choice for prioritizing projects.

At this point in the discussion it is wise to stop and put things into perspective. While selection models like the one in this section may yield numeric solutions to project selection decisions, models should not make the final *decisions*—the people using the models should. No model, no matter how sophisticated, can capture the total reality it is meant to represent. Models are tools for guiding the evaluation process so that the decision makers will consider relevant issues and reach a meeting of the minds as to which projects should be supported. This is a much more subjective process than calculations suggest.

2.7 Applying a Selection Model

LO 2-8

Apply an objective priority system to project selection.

Project Classification

It is not necessary to have exactly the same criteria for the different types of projects discussed in the previous section (strategic and operations). However, experience shows most organizations use similar criteria across all types of projects, with perhaps one or two criteria specific to the type of project—for example, strategic breakthrough versus operational.

Regardless of criteria differences among different types of projects, the most important criterion for selection is the project's fit to the organization strategy. Therefore, this criterion should be consistent across all types of projects and carry a high priority relative to other criteria. This uniformity across all priority models used can keep departments from suboptimizing the use of organizational resources. Project proposals should be classified by type so the appropriate criteria can be used to evaluate them.

Selecting a Model

In the past, financial criteria were used almost to the exclusion of other criteria. However, in the last two decades we have witnessed a dramatic shift to include multiple criteria in project selection. Concisely put, profitability alone is simply not an adequate measure of contribution; however, it is still an important criterion, especially for projects that enhance revenue and market share such as breakthrough R&D projects.

Today, senior management are interested in identifying the potential mix of projects that will yield the best use of human and capital resources to maximize return on investment in the long run. Factors such as researching new technology, public image, ethical position, protection of the environment, core competencies, and strategic fit might be important criteria for selecting projects. Weighted scoring criteria seem the best alternative to meet this need.

Weighted scoring models result in bringing projects into closer alignment with strategic goals. If the scoring model is published and available to everyone in the organization, some discipline and credibility are attached to the selection of projects. The number of wasteful projects using resources is reduced. Politics and sacred cow projects are exposed. Project goals are more easily identified and communicated using the selection criteria as corroboration. Finally, using a weighted scoring approach helps project managers understand how their project was selected, how their project contributes to organization goals, and how it compares with other projects. Project selection is one of the most important decisions guiding the future success of an organization.

Criteria for project selection are where the power of a portfolio starts to manifest itself. New projects are aligned with the strategic goals of the organization. With a clear method in place for selecting projects, project proposals can be solicited.

Sources and Solicitation of Project Proposals

As you would guess, projects should come from anyone who believes his/her project will add value to the organization. However, many organizations restrict proposals from specific levels or groups within the organization. This could be an opportunity lost. Good ideas are not limited to certain types or classes of organization stakeholders.

Figure 2.5A provides an example of a proposal form for an automatic vehicular tracking (Automatic Vehicle Location) public transportation project. Figure 2.5B presents a preliminary risk analysis for a 500-acre wind farm. Many organizations use risk analysis templates to gain a quick insight into a project's inherent risks. Risk factors depend on the organization and type of projects. This information is useful in balancing the project portfolio and identifying major risks when executing the project. Project risk analysis is the subject of Chapter 7.

In some cases, organizations will solicit ideas for projects when the knowledge requirements for the project are not available in the organization. Typically the organization will issue a Request for Proposal (RFP) to contractors/vendors with adequate experience to implement the project. In one example, a hospital published an RFP that asked for a bid to design and build a new operating room that used the latest technology. Several architecture firms submitted bids to the

FIGURE 2.5A
A Proposal Form for an Automatic Vehicular Tracking (AVL) Public Transportation Project

Project Proposal Form

Date: Jan 22, 2xxx   Proposal # 11   Sponsor J. Moran

Project classification?
Strategic ______ Operational X Compliance ______

What business problem does the project solve?
Increase customer satisfaction through kiosk, website, and mobile applications for bus, streetcar, and fast rail Enhance driver and traveler safety   Hyperlink to: AVL.tri-met.org

How does this project align with our organization strategy?
Increase customer ridership through better passenger travel planning & scheduling decisions
Faster response to accidents

What are the major deliverables of the project?
GPS vehicle tracking system, Internet access, schedule screen

What is the impact of not doing this project?
Not meeting ridership goals

What are the three major risks for this project?
Cost overruns   Integration of fast rail, bus, and streetcar systems
Hacking system

How will we measure success?
Increased ridership
Customer satisfaction
Meeting budget and schedule

Yes [X] No [ ] Will this project require internal resources?
Yes [X] No [ ] Available?

What is the estimated cost of the project? $10 million

How long will this project take? 22 Weeks

Oversight action: Accept [X] Return [ ]

Signature XXXXXX   Date: Feb. 7, 2xxx

hospital. The bids for the project were evaluated internally against other potential projects. When the project was accepted as a go, other criteria were used to select the best-qualified bidder.

Ranking Proposals and Selection of Projects

Culling through so many proposals to identify those that add the most value requires a structured process. Figure 2.6 shows a flow chart of a screening process beginning with the submission of a formal project proposal.[7] A senior priority team evaluates

[7] See Figure 12.3 for a template for evaluating contractors.

FIGURE 2.5B
Risk Analysis for a 500-Acre Wind Farm

Brief Risk Assessment

Purpose: To draw attention to apparent project risks that will need management attention.

What are the four major risks of this project?
1. *Government incentives curtailed*
2. *Land use injunction*
3. *Energy price decrease*
4. *New import tax*

Rank risks above by "probability" and "impact" on the chart below by High, Medium, or Low.

Risk Intensity Rating

Risk	Probability	Impact
1. *Government incentives curtailed*	*High*	*High*
2. *Land use injunction*	*Medium*	*High*
3. *Energy price decrease*	*Medium*	*Medium*
4. *New import tax*	*Low*	*High*

Check other project risk factors:

Complexity	Low [ ]	Average [X]	High [ ]
Resource skills	Good [X]	Okay [ ]	Lacking [ ]
Technology	Low [ ]	Average [X]	High [ ]

Reviewed by *Rachel* **Date** *April 1, 2xxx*

each proposal in terms of feasibility, potential contribution to strategic objectives, and fit within a portfolio of current projects. Given selection criteria and current portfolio, the priority team rejects or accepts the project.

If the project is approved, a project manager and staff are assigned to develop a detailed implementation plan. Once completed, the proposal with implementation plan is reviewed a second time. Veteran project managers are assigned to the priority team. They draw on their experience to identify potential flaws in the plan. Strategic value is again assessed, but within the context of a more detailed plan. Variances between what was estimated in the initial proposal and final estimates based on more complete research/planning are examined. If significant negative differences are found (e.g., the initial total cost estimate was $10 million but the final estimate was $12 million, or the end product will no longer include a key feature), the proposal will likely be deferred to more senior management to decide whether the project should still be approved. Otherwise, the project is approved and priority assigned. Management issues a project charter authorizing the project manager to form a project team and secure resources to begin project work.

FIGURE 2.6
Project Screening Process

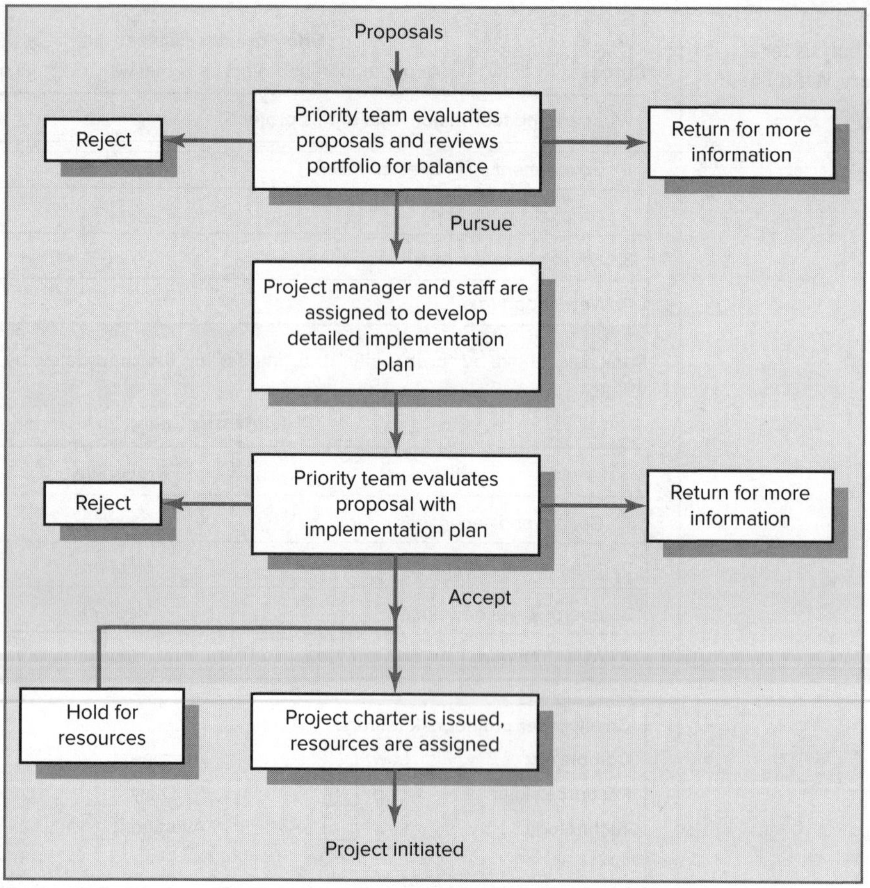

Figure 2.7 is a partial example of an evaluation form used by a large company to prioritize and select new projects. The form distinguishes between must and want objectives. If a project does not meet designated "must" objectives, it is not considered and is removed from consideration. Organization (or division) objectives have been ranked and weighted by their relative importance—for example, "Improve external customer service" carries a relative weight of 83 when compared to other want objectives. The want objectives are directly linked to objectives found in the strategic plan.

Impact definitions represent a further refinement to the screening system. They are developed to gauge the predicted impact a specific project would have on meeting a particular objective. A numeric scheme is created and anchored by defining criteria. To illustrate how this works, let's examine the $5 million in new sales objective. A "0" is assigned if the project will have no impact on sales or less than $100,000, a "1" is given if predicted sales are more than $100,000 but less than $500,000, a "2" if greater than $500,000. These impact assessments are combined with the relative importance of each objective to determine the predicted overall contribution of a project to strategic objectives. For example, project 26 creates an opportunity to fix field problems, has no effect on sales, and will have major impact

FIGURE 2.7
Priority Screening Analysis

		Project number			
Must objectives	**Must meet if impacts**	**...26**	**27**	**28**	**29**
All activities meet current legal, safety, and environmental standards	Yes-Meets objective No-Does not meet obj N/A-No impact	**N/A**			
All new products will have a complete market analysis	Yes-Meets objective No-Does not meet obj N/A-No impact	**Yes**			

Want objectives	**Relative Importance 1-100**	**Single project impact definitions**	**Weighted score**	**Weighted score**	**Weighted score**	**Weighted score**
Provides immediate response to field problems	**99**	0 = Does not address 1 = Opportunity to fix 2 = Urgent problem	**99**			
Create $5 million in new sales by 20xx	**88**	0 < $100,000 1 = $100,000–500,000 2 > $500,000	**0**			
Improve external customer service	**83**	0 = Minor impact 1 = Significant impact 2 = Major impact	**166**			
Total weighted score						
Priority						

on customer service. On these three objectives, project 26 would receive a score of 265 [99 + 0 + (2 × 83)]. Individual weighted scores are totaled for each project and are used to prioritize projects.

Responsibility for Prioritizing

Senior management should be responsible for prioritizing projects. It requires more than a blessing. Management will need to rank and weigh, in concrete terms, the objectives and strategies they believe are most critical to the organization. This public declaration of commitment can be risky if the ranked objectives later prove to be poor choices, but setting the course for the organization is top management's job. The good news is, if management is truly trying to direct the organization to a strong future position, a good project priority system supports their efforts and develops a culture in which everyone is contributing to the goals of the organization.

2.8 Managing the Portfolio System

LO 2-9

Understand the need to manage the project portfolio.

Managing the portfolio takes the selection system one step higher in that the merits of a particular project are assessed within the context of existing projects. At the same time it involves monitoring and adjusting selection criteria to reflect the strategic focus of the organization. This requires constant effort. The priority system can be managed by a small group of key employees in a small organization. Or in larger organizations, the priority system can be managed by the project office or a governance team of senior managers.

Senior Management Input

Management of a portfolio system requires two major inputs from senior management. First, senior management must provide guidance in establishing selection criteria that strongly align with the current organization strategies. Second, senior management must annually decide how they wish to balance the available organizational resources (people and capital) among the different types of projects. A preliminary decision of balance must be made by top management (e.g., 20 percent compliance, 50 percent strategic, and 30 percent operational) before project selection takes place, although the balance may be changed when the projects submitted are reviewed. Given these inputs the priority team or project office can carry out its many responsibilities, which include supporting project sponsors and representing the interests of the total organization.

Governance Team Responsibilities

The governance team, or project office, is responsible for publishing the priority of every project and ensuring the process is open and free of power politics. For example, most organizations using a governance team or project office use an electronic bulletin board to disperse the current portfolio of projects, the current status of each project, and current issues. This open communication discourages power plays. Over time the governance team evaluates the progress of the projects in the portfolio. If this whole process is managed well, it can have a profound impact on the success of an organization. See Snapshot from Practice 2.3: Project Code Names for the rationale behind titles given to projects.

Constant scanning of the external environment to determine if organizational focus and/or selection criteria need to be changed is imperative. Periodic priority review and changes need to keep current with the changing environment and keep a unified vision of organization focus. If projects are classified by must do, operation, and strategic, each project in its class should be evaluated by the same criteria. Enforcing the project priority system is critical. Keeping the whole system open and aboveboard is important to maintaining the integrity of the system and keeping new, young executives from going around the system.

Balancing the Portfolio for Risks and Types of Projects

A major responsibility of the priority team is to balance projects by type, risk, and resource demand. This requires a total organization perspective. Hence, a proposed project that ranks high on most criteria may not be selected because the organization portfolio already includes too many projects with the same characteristics—for example, project risk level, use of key resources, high cost, non-revenue-producing, and long durations. Balancing the portfolio of projects is as important as selecting projects. Organizations need to evaluate each new project in terms of what it adds to the project mix. Short-term needs must be balanced with long-term potential. Resource usage needs to be optimized across all projects, not just the most important project.

SNAPSHOT FROM PRACTICE 2.4 Project Code Names*

What do Yangtze, Operation Iceberg, and Get Blue have in common? They are all code names given to projects. Project code names are used for several reasons:

- To uniquely identify the project within the organization.

  Apple Corporation used to name major releases of MAC OS X after big cats such as Jaguar, Tiger, Panther, and Leopard but now names them after major California landmarks (e.g., Yosemite, Big Sur).

- To assist in maintaining secrecy of the project against rival concerns.

  The Chamber of Secrets sequel to the *Harry Potter* film series was code-named "Incident of 57th Street" to disguise the production from its increasingly rabid fan base, who would seek out filming locations and disrupt production.

- As a public relations tool to garner support for project objectives.

  Operation Just Cause was the name given by the U.S. government to the 1989 invasion of Panama, which ousted corrupt leader Manual Noriega.

- To inspire and elevate performance.

Jill Braaten/McGraw Hill

Revolution was used by Nintendo for its groundbreaking Wii video game console.

Often on small projects, names convey a playful sense of humor. For example, a set of interrelated software projects were all named after Smurf characters (Papa Smurf, Handy Smurf, Dreamy Smurf, and so on). Likewise, Ultraman, Sailor Moon, and Kamen Riders were names chosen by another set of project teams.

* G. C. Sieminski, "The Art of Naming Operations," *Parameters,* Autumn 1995, pp. 81–98; "Operation Know-It-All: The Indispensable Guide to Choosing Good Project Names," articulatemarketing.com. Accessed 12/20/15.

Two types of risk are associated with projects. First are risks associated with the total portfolio of projects, which should reflect the organization's risk profile. Second are specific project risks that can inhibit the execution of a project. In this chapter, we look only to balancing the organizational risks inherent in the project portfolio, such as market risk, ability to execute, time-to-market, and technology advances. Project-specific risks will be covered in detail in Chapter 7.

David and Jim Matheson studied R&D organizations and developed a classification scheme that could be used for assessing a project portfolio (see Figure 2.8).[8] They separated projects in terms of degree of difficulty and commercial value and came up with four basic types of projects:

Bread-and-butter projects are relatively easy to accomplish and produce modest commercial value. They typically involve evolutionary improvements to current products and services. Examples include software upgrades and manufacturing cost-reduction efforts.

Pearls are low-risk development projects with high commercial payoffs. They represent revolutionary commercial advances using proven technology. Examples include next-generation integrated circuit chips and subsurface imaging to locate oil and gas.

[8] Matheson, D., and J. Matheson, *The Smart Organization* (Boston: Harvard Business School Press, 1998), pp. 203–09.

FIGURE 2.8
Project Portfolio Matrix

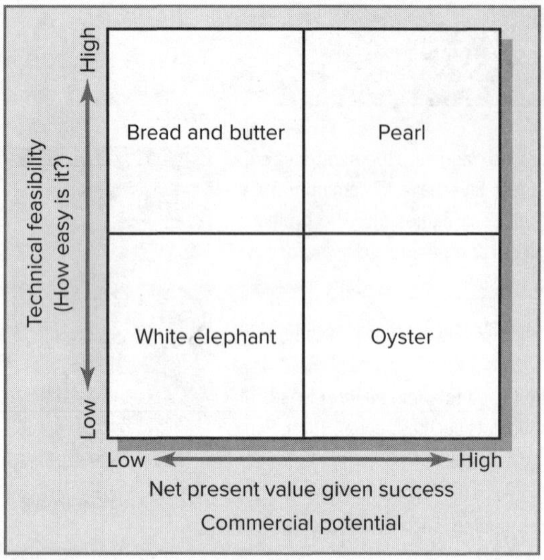

Oysters are high-risk, high-value projects. These projects involve technological breakthroughs with tremendous commercial potential. Examples include embryonic DNA treatments and new kinds of metal alloys.

White elephants are projects that at one time showed promise but are no longer viable. Examples include products for a saturated market and a potent energy source with toxic side effects.

The Mathesons report that organizations often have too many white elephants and too few pearls and oysters. To maintain strategic advantage, they recommend that organizations capitalize on pearls, eliminate or reposition white elephants, and balance resources devoted to bread-and-butter and oyster projects to achieve alignment with overall strategy. Although their research centers on R&D organizations, their observations appear to hold true for all types of project organizations.

Summary

Multiple competing projects, limited skilled resources, dispersed virtual teams, time-to-market pressures, and limited capital serve as forces for the emergence of project portfolio management that provides the infrastructure for managing multiple projects and linking business strategy with project selection. The most important element of this system is the creation of a ranking system that utilizes multiple, weighted criteria that reflect the mission and strategy of the firm. It is critical to communicate priority criteria to all organizational stakeholders so that the criteria can be the source of inspiration for new project ideas.

Every significant project selected should be ranked and the results published. Senior management must take an active role in setting priorities and supporting the priority system. Going around the priority system will destroy its effectiveness. Project review boards need to include seasoned managers who are capable of asking tough questions and distinguishing facts from fiction. Resources (people, equipment, and capital) for major projects must be clearly allocated and not conflict with daily operations or become an overload task.

The governance team needs to scrutinize significant projects in terms of not only their strategic value but also their fit with the portfolio of projects currently being implemented. Highly ranked projects may be deferred or even turned down if they upset the current balance among risks, resources, and strategic initiatives. Project selection must be based not only on the merits of the specific project but also on what it contributes to the current project portfolio mix. This requires a holistic approach to aligning projects with organization strategy and resources.

Key Terms

Implementation gap, *47*
Net present value (NPV), *52*
Optimism bias, *45*
Organization politics, *47*
Payback, *52*
Phase gate model, *50*
Portfolio management, *45*
Priority system, *45*
Priority team, *55*
Project portfolio, *45*
Project sponsor, *48*
Sacred cow, *47*
Strategic management, *40*
Uniqueness bias, *45*

Review Questions

1. Describe the major components of the strategic management process.
2. Explain the role projects play in the strategic management process.
3. How are projects linked to the strategic plan?
4. The portfolio of projects is typically represented by compliance, strategic, and operations projects. What impact can this classification have on project selection?
5. Why does the priority system described in this chapter require that it be open and published? Does the process encourage bottom-up initiation of projects? Does it discourage some projects? Why?
6. Why should an organization not rely only on ROI to select projects?
7. Discuss the pros and cons of the checklist versus the weighted factor method of selecting projects.

SNAPSHOT FROM PRACTICE

Discussion Questions

2.1 *IBM's Watson Project*

1. Why would IBM want to move from computer hardware to service products?
2. Was Project Watson a success or failure?

2.2 *Crisis IT*

1. What benefits did Frontier Airlines obtain by using a weighted scoring scheme to assess the value of projects?

2.4 *Project Code Names*

1. Can you think of a project code name not mentioned in the Snapshot? What function did it serve?

Is This the End of Airbnb?

1. What was the impact of COVID-19 pandemic on projects at Airbnb?
2. What are unique challenges facing "Frontline Stays" compared to "Open Homes"?

Exercises

1. You manage a hotel resort located on the South Beach on the Island of Kauai in Hawaii. You are shifting the focus of your resort from a traditional fun-in-the-sun destination to eco-tourism. (Eco-tourism focuses on environmental awareness and education.) How would you classify the following projects in terms of compliance, strategic, and operational?
   a. Convert the pool heating system from electrical to solar power.
   b. Build a four-mile nature hiking trail.
   c. Renovate the horse barn.
   d. Launch a new promotional campaign with Hawaii Airlines.
   e. Convert 12 adjacent acres into a wildlife preserve.
   f. Update all the bathrooms in condos that are 10 years old or older.
   g. Change hotel brochures to reflect eco-tourism image.
   h. Test and revise disaster response plan based on new requirements.

   How easy was it to classify these projects? What made some projects more difficult than others? What do you think you now know that would be useful for managing projects at the hotel?
2. Two new software projects are proposed to a young, start-up company.* The Alpha project will cost $150,000 to develop and is expected to have an annual net cash flow of $40,000. The Beta project will cost $200,000 to develop and is expected to have an annual net cash flow of $50,000. The company is very concerned about their cash flow. Using the payback period, which project is better from a cash flow standpoint? Why?
3. A five-year project has a projected net cash flow of $15,000, $25,000, $30,000, $20,000, and $15,000 in the next five years. It will cost $50,000 to implement the project. If the required rate of return is 20 percent, conduct a discounted cash flow calculation to determine the NPV.
4. You work for the 3T company, which expects to earn at least 18 percent on its investments. You have to choose between two similar projects. The following chart shows the cash information for each project. Which of the two projects would you fund if the decision were based only on financial information? Why?

Omega Year	Inflow	Outflow	Netflow	Alpha Year	Inflow	Outflow	Netflow
Y0	0	$225,000	−225,000	Y0	0	$300,000	−300,000
Y1	0	190,000	−190,000	Y1	$ 50,000	100,000	−50,000
Y2	$ 150,000	0	150,000	Y2	150,000	0	150,000
Y3	220,000	30,000	190,000	Y3	250,000	50,000	200,000
Y4	215,000	0	215,000	Y4	250,000	0	250,000
Y5	205,000	30,000	175,000	Y5	200,000	50,000	150,000
Y6	197,000	0	197,000	Y6	180,000	0	180,000
Y7	100,000	30,000	70,000	Y7	120,000	30,000	90,000
Total	1,087,000	505,000	582,000	Total	1,200,000	530,000	670,000

5. You are the head of the project selection team at SIMSOX.* Your team is considering three different projects. Based on past history, SIMSOX expects at least a rate of return of 20 percent.

* The solution to these exercises can be found in Appendix One.

Given the following information for each project, which one should be SIMSOX's first priority? Should SIMSOX fund any of the other projects? If so, what should be the order of priority based on return on investment?

Project: **Dust Devils**

Year	Investment	Revenue Stream
0	$500,000	0
1		50,000
2		250,000
3		350,000

Project: **Osprey**

Year	Investment	Revenue Stream
0	$250,000	0
1		75,000
2		75,000
3		75,000
4		50,000

Project: **Voyagers**

Year	Investment	Revenue Stream
0	$75,000	0
1		15,000
2		25,000
3		50,000
4		50,000
5		150,000

6. You are the head of the project selection team at Broken Arrow Records. Your team is considering three different recording projects. Based on past history, Broken Arrow expects at least a rate of return of 20 percent.

   Given the following information for each project, which one should be Broken Arrow's first priority? Should Broken Arrow fund any of the other projects? If so, what should be the order of priority based on return on investment?

Recording Project: **Time Fades Away**

Year	Investment	Revenue Stream
0	$600,000	0
1		600,000
2		75,000
3		20,000
4		15,000
5		10,000

Recording Project: **On the Beach**

Year	Investment	Revenue Stream
0	$400,000	0
1		400,000
2		100,000
3		25,000
4		20,000
5		10,000

Recording Project: **Tonight's the Night**

Year	Investment	Revenue Stream
0	$200,000	0
1		200,000
2		125,000
3		75,000
4		25,000
5		10,000

7. The Custom Bike Company has set up a weighted scoring matrix for evaluation of potential projects. Following are five projects under consideration.
   a. Using the scoring matrix in the following chart, which project would you rate highest? Lowest?
   b. If the weight for "Strong Sponsor" is changed from 2.0 to 5.0, will the project selection change? What are the three highest-weighted project scores with this new weight?
   c. Why is it important that the weights mirror critical strategic factors?

Project Screening Matrix

Criteria / Weight	Strong sponsor	Supports business strategy	Urgency	10% of sales from new products	Competition	Fill market gap	Weighted total
	2.0	5.0	4.0	3.0	1.0	3.0	
Project 1	9	5	2	0	2	5	
Project 2	3	7	2	0	5	1	
Project 3	6	8	2	3	6	8	
Project 4	1	0	5	10	6	9	
Project 5	3	10	10	1	8	0	

References

Adler, P. S., A. Mandelbaum, V. Nguyen, and E. Schwerer, "Getting the Most Out of Your Product Development Process," *Harvard Business Review,* vol. 74, no. 2 (2003), pp. 134–52.

Alicke, M. D., and O. Govorun, "The Better-than-Average Effect," in M.D. Alicke, D. A. Dunning, and J. I. Krueger (eds.), *The Self in Social Judgment (Studies in Self and Identity),* pp. 85–106 (Psychology Press, 2005).

Benko, C., and F. W. McFarlan, *Connecting the Dots: Aligning Projects with Objectives in Unpredictable Times* (Boston: Harvard Business School Press, 2003).

Boyer, C., "Make Profit Your Priority," *PM Network,* October 2003, pp. 37–42.

Brown, K., N. Hyer, and R. Ettenson, "The Question Every Project Team Should Answer," *Sloan Management Review,* vol. 55, no. 1 (2013), pp. 49–57.

Cohen, D., and R. Graham, *The Project Manager's MBA* (San Francisco: Jossey-Bass, 2001), pp. 58–59.

Descamps, J. P., "Mastering the Dance of Change: Innovation as a Way of Life," *Prism,* Second Quarter, 1999, pp. 61–67.

Doran, G. T., "There's a Smart Way to Write Management Goals and Objectives," *Management Review,* November 1981, pp. 35–36.

Floyd, S. W., and B. Woolridge, "Managing Strategic Consensus: The Foundation of Effectiveness Implementation," *Academy of Management Executives,* vol. 6, no. 4 (1992), pp. 27–39.

Flyvbjerb, B., "What You Should Know About Megaprojects and Why: An Overview," *Project Management Journal,* vol. 45, no. 2 (April/May 2014), pp. 6–19.

Flyvbjerg, B., "Top Ten Behavioral Biases in Project Management: An Overview," *Project Management Journal,* vol. 52, no. 6 (December 2021), pp. 531–46.

Flyvbjerg, B., M, Garbuio, and D. Lovallo, "Delusion and Deception in Large Infrastructure Projects: Two Models for Explaining and Preventing Executive Disaster," *California Management Review,* vol. 51, no. 2 (February 2009), pp. 170–93.

Foti, R., "Louder Than Words," *PM Network,* December 2002, pp. 22–29.

Foti, R., "Make Your Case, Not All Projects Are Equal," *PM Network,* July 2003, pp. 35–43.

Friedman, T. L., *Hot, Flat, and Crowded* (New York: Farrar, Straus, and Giroux, 2008).

Helm, J., and K. Remington, "Effective Project Sponsorship: An Evaluation of the Executive Sponsor in Complex Infrastructure Projects by Senior Project Managers," *Project Management Journal,* vol. 36, no. 1 (September 2005), pp. 51–61.

Hutchens, G., "Doing the Numbers," *PM Network,* March 2002, p. 20.

"IBM Wants to Put Watson in Your Pocket," *Bloomberg Businessweek,* September 17–23, 2012, pp. 41–42.

Johnson, R. E., "Scrap Capital Project Evaluations," *Chief Financial Officer,* May 1998, p. 14.

Kain, J. F., "Deception in Dallas: Strategic Misrepresentation in Rail Transit Promotion and Evaluation," *Journal of the American Planning Association,* vol. 56, no. 2 (1990), pp. 184–96.

Kahneman, D., *Thinking, Fast and Slow* (New York: Farrar, Straus and Giroux, 2011).

Kaplan, R. S., and D. P. Norton, "The Balanced Scorecard—Measures That Drive Performance," *Harvard Business Review,* January/February 1992, pp. 73–79.

Kenny, J., "Effective Project Management for Strategic Innovation and Change in an Organizational Context," *Project Management Journal,* vol. 34, no. 1 (2003), pp. 45–53.

Kharbanda, O. P., and J. K. Pinto, *What Made Gertie Gallop: Learning from Project Failures* (New York: Van Nostrand Reinhold, 1996), pp. 106–11, 263–83.

Korte, R. F., and T. J. Chermack, "Changing Organizational Culture with Scenario Planning," *Futures,* vol. 39, no. 6 (August 2007), pp. 645–56.

Leifer, R., C. M. McDermott, G. C. O'Connor, L. S. Peters, M. Price, and R. W. Veryzer, *Radical Innovation: How Mature Companies Can Outsmart Upstarts* (Boston: Harvard Business School Press, 2000).

Magretta, J., *Understanding Michael Porter: The Essential Guide to Competition and Strategy* (Boston: Harvard Business Press, 2011).

Milosevic, D. Z., and S. Srivannaboon, "A Theoretical Framework for Aligning Project Management with Business Strategy," *Project Management Journal,* vol. 37, no. 3 (August 2006), pp. 98–110.

Morris, P. W., and A. Jamieson, "Moving from Corporate Strategy to Project Strategy," *Project Management Journal,* vol. 36, no. 4 (December 2005), pp. 5–18.

Mortensen, M., and H. K. Gardner, "The Overcommitted Organization," *Harvard Business Review,* September/October 2017, pp. 58–65.

Motta, S., and R. H. Quintella, "Assessment of Non-Financial Criteria in the Selection of Investment Projects for Seed Capital Funding: The Contribution of Scientometrics and Patentometrics," *Journal of Technology Management Innovation,* vol. 7, no. 3 (2012), pp. 172–97.

Raskin, P., T. Banuri, G. Gallopin, P. Gutman, and A. Hammond, *Great Transitions: The Promise and Lure of the Times Ahead,* www.gtinitiative.org/documents/Great_Transitions.pdf. Accessed 6/3/08.

Schwartz, P., and D. Randall, "An Abrupt Climate Change Scenario and its Implications for United States National Security," Global Business Network, Inc., October 2003.

Shenhar, A., "Strategic Project Leadership: Focusing Your Project on Business Success," *Proceedings of the Project Management Institute Annual Seminars & Symposium,* San Antonio, Texas, October 3–10, 2002, CD.

Suis, J., and C. K. Wan, "In Search of the False-Uniqueness Phenomenon: Fear and Estimates of Social Consensus," *Journal of Personality and Social Psychology,* vol. 52, no. 1 (1987), pp. 211–7.

Swanson, S., "All Things Considered," *PM Network,* February 2011, pp. 36–40.

Wachs, M., "When Planners Lie With Numbers," *Journal of the American Planning Association,* vol. 55, no. 4 (1989), pp. 476–9.

Case 2.1

Hector Gaming Company

Hector Gaming Company (HGC) is an educational gaming company specializing in young children's educational games. HGC has just completed their fourth year of operation. This year was a banner year for HGC. The company received a large influx of capital for growth by issuing stock privately through an investment banking firm. It appears the return on investment for this past year will be just over 25 percent with zero debt! The growth rate for the last two years has been approximately 80 percent each year. Parents and grandparents of young children have been buying HGC's products almost as fast as they are developed. Every member of the 56-person firm is enthusiastic and looking forward to helping the firm grow to be the largest and best educational gaming company in the world. The founder of the firm, Sally Peters, has been written up in *Young Entrepreneurs* as "the young entrepreneur to watch." She has been able to develop an organizational culture in which all stakeholders are committed to innovation, continuous improvement, and organization learning.

Last year, 10 top managers of HGC worked with McKinley Consulting to develop the organization's strategic plan. This year the same 10 managers had a retreat in Aruba to formulate next year's strategic plan using the same process suggested by McKinley Consulting. Most executives seem to have a consensus of where the firm should go in the intermediate and long term. But there is little consensus on how this should be accomplished. Peters, now president of HGC, feels she may be losing control. The frequency of conflicts seems to be increasing. Some individuals are always requested for any new project created. When resource conflicts occur among projects, each project manager believes his or her project is most important. More projects are not meeting deadlines and are coming in over budget. Yesterday's management meeting revealed some top HGC talent have been working on an international business game for college students. This project does not fit the organization vision or market niche. At times it seems everyone is marching to his or her own drummer. Somehow more focus is needed to ensure everyone agrees on *how* strategy should be implemented, given the resources available to the organization.

Yesterday's meeting alarmed Peters. These emerging problems are coming at a bad time. Next week HGC is ramping up the size of the organization, number of new products per year, and marketing efforts. Fifteen new people will join HGC next month. Peters is concerned that policies be in place that will ensure the new people are used most productively. An additional potential problem looms on the horizon. Other gaming companies have noticed the success HGC is having in their niche market; one company tried to hire a key product development employee away from HGC. Peters wants HGC to be ready to meet any potential competition head on and to discourage any new entries into their market. Peters knows HGC is project driven; however, she is not as confident that she has a good handle on how such an organization should be managed—especially with such a fast growth rate and potential competition closer to becoming a reality. The magnitude of emerging problems demands quick attention and resolution.

Peters has hired you as a consultant. She has suggested the following format for your consulting contract. You are free to use another format if it will improve the effectiveness of the consulting engagement.

What is our major problem?
Identify some symptoms of the problem.
What is the major cause of the problem?

Provide a detailed action plan that attacks the problem. Be specific and provide examples that relate to HGC.

Case 2.2

Film Prioritization

The purpose of this case is to give you experience in using a project priority system that ranks proposed projects by their contribution to the organization's objectives and strategic plan.

COMPANY PROFILE

The company is the film division for a large entertainment conglomerate. The main office is located in Anaheim, California. In addition to the feature film division, the conglomerate includes theme parks, home videos, a television channel, interactive games, and theatrical productions. The company has been enjoying steady growth over the past 10 years. Last year total revenues increased by 12 percent to $32.2 billion. The company is engaged in negotiations to expand its theme park empire to mainland China and Poland. The film division generated $376 million in revenues, which was an increase of 7 percent over the past year. Profit margin was down 3 percent to 16 percent because of the poor response to three of the five major film releases for the year.

COMPANY MISSION

The mission for the firm is as follows:

> Our overriding objective is to create shareholder value by continuing to be the world's premier entertainment company from a creative, strategic, and financial standpoint.

The film division supports this mission by producing four to six high-quality, family entertainment films for mass distribution each year. In recent years, the CEO of the company has advocated that the firm take a leadership position in championing environmental concerns.

COMPANY "MUST" OBJECTIVES

Every project must meet the must objectives as determined by executive management. It is important that selected film projects not violate such objectives of high strategic priority. There are three must objectives:

1. All projects meet current legal, safety, and environmental standards.
2. All film projects should receive a PG or lower advisory rating.
3. All projects should not have an adverse effect on current or planned operations within the larger company.

COMPANY "WANT" OBJECTIVES

Want objectives are assigned weights for their relative importance. Top management is responsible for formulating, ranking, and weighting objectives to ensure that projects support the company's strategy and mission. The following is a list of the company's want objectives:

1. Be nominated for and win an Academy Award for Best Animated Feature or Best Picture of the Year.
2. Generate additional merchandise revenue (action figures, dolls, interactive games, music CD/DVDs).
3. Raise public consciousness about environmental issues and concerns.
4. Generate profit in excess of 18 percent.
5. Advance the state of the art in film animation and preserve the firm's reputation.
6. Provide the basis for the development of a new ride at a company-owned theme park.

ASSIGNMENT

You are a member of the priority team in charge of evaluating and selecting film proposals. Use the provided evaluation form to formally evaluate and rank each proposal. Be prepared to report your rankings and justify your decisions.

Assume that all of the projects have passed the estimated hurdle rate of 14 percent ROI. In addition to the brief film synopsis, the proposals include the following financial projections of theater and DVD sales: 80 percent chance of ROI, 50 percent chance of ROI, and 20 percent chance of ROI.

For example, for proposal #1 (Dalai Lama) there is an 80 percent chance that it will earn at least 8 percent return on investment (ROI), a 50/50 chance the ROI will be 18 percent, and a 20 percent chance that the ROI will be 24 percent.

FILM PROPOSALS

PROJECT PROPOSAL 1: MY LIFE WITH DALAI LAMA

This project is an animated, biographical account of the Dalai Lama's childhood in Tibet based on the popular children's book *Tales from Nepal.* The Lama's life is told through the eyes of "Guoda," a field snake, and other local animals who befriend the Dalai Lama and help him understand the principles of Buddhism.

Probability	80%	50%	20%
ROI	8%	18%	24%

PROJECT PROPOSAL 2: HEIDI

The project is a remake of the classic children's story with music written by award-winning composers Syskle and Obert. The big-budget film will feature top-name stars and breathtaking scenery of the Swiss Alps.

Probability	80%	50%	20%
ROI	2%	20%	30%

PROJECT PROPOSAL 3: THE YEAR OF THE ECHO

This project is a low-budget documentary that celebrates the career of one of the most influential bands in rock-and-roll history. The film will be directed by new-wave director Elliot Cznerzy and will combine concert footage and behind-the-scenes interviews spanning the 25-year history of the rock band the Echos. In addition to great music, the film will focus on the death of one of the founding members from a heroin overdose and reveal the underworld of sex, lies, and drugs in the music industry.

Probability	80%	50%	20%
ROI	12%	14%	18%

PROJECT PROPOSAL 4: ESCAPE FROM RIO JAPUNI

This project is an animated feature set in the Amazon rainforest. The story centers around Pablo, a young jaguar that attempts to convince warring jungle animals that they must unite and escape the devastation of local clear cutting.

Probability	80%	50%	20%
ROI	15%	20%	24%

PROJECT PROPOSAL 5: NADIA!

This project is the story of Nadia Comaneci, the famous Romanian gymnast who won three gold medals at the 1976 Summer Olympic Games. The low-budget film will document her life as a small child in Romania and how she was chosen by Romanian authorities to join their elite, state-run athletic program. The film will highlight how Nadia maintained her independent spirit and love for gymnastics despite a harsh, regimented training program.

Probability	80%	50%	20%
ROI	8%	15%	20%

PROJECT PROPOSAL 6: KEIKO—ONE WHALE OF A STORY

The story of Keiko, a famous killer whale, will be told by an imaginary offspring, Seiko, who in the distant future is telling her children about their famous grandfather. The big-budget film will integrate actual footage of the whale within a realistic animated environment using state-of-the-art computer imagery. The story will reveal how Keiko responded to his treatment by humans.

Probability	80%	50%	20%
ROI	6%	18%	25%

PROJECT PROPOSAL 7: GRAND ISLAND

This project is the true story of a group of junior-high biology students who discover that a fertilizer plant is dumping toxic wastes into a nearby river. The moderate-budget film depicts how students organize a grassroots campaign to fight local bureaucracy and ultimately force the fertilizer plant to restore the local ecosystem.

Probability	80%	50%	20%
ROI	9%	15%	20%

Project Priority Evaluation Form

Must objectives		Must meet if impacts	1	2	3	4	5	6	7
Meets all legal, safety and environmental standards		Y = yes N = no N/A = not applicable							
PG or G rating		Y = yes N = no N/A = not applicable							
No adverse effect on other operations		Y = yes N = no N/A = not applicable							
Want objectives	**Relative Importance 1–100**	**Single project impact definitions**	**Weighted Score**	**Weighted Score**	**Weighted Score**	**Weighted Score**	**Weighted Score**	**Weighted Score**	**Weighted Score**
Win Best Picture of the Year	**70**	0 = No potential 1 = Low potential 2 = High potential							
Win Best Animated Feature Film	**60**	0 = No potential 1 = Low potential 2 = High potential							
Generate additional merchandise revenue	**10**	0 = No potential 1 = Low potential 2 = High potential							
Raise environmental concerns	**55**	0 = No potential 1 = Low potential 2 = High potential							
Generate profit greater than 18%	**70**	0 < 18% 1 = 18–22% 2 > 22%							
Advance state of film animation	**40**	0 = No impact 1 = Some impact 2 = Great impact							
Provide basis for new theme ride	**10**	0 = No potential 1 = Low potential 2 = High potential							
		Total weighted score							
		Priority							

Case 2.3

Fund Raising Project Selection

The purpose of this "case exercise" is to provide you with experience in using a project selection process that ranks proposed projects by their contribution to an organization's mission and strategy.

FUND RAISING PROJECT

Assume you are a member of a class on project management. Each student will join a team of five to seven students who will be responsible for creating, planning, and executing a fund raising project for a designated charity. The fund raising project has two goals: (1) raise money for a worthy cause and (2) provide an opportunity for all team members to practice project management skills and techniques.

In addition to completing the project, a number of deliverables are required to complete this assignment. These deliverables include

a. Project proposal
b. Implementation plan
c. Risk management plan
d. Status report
e. Project reflections presentation
f. Project retrospective/audit

Approved projects will receive $400 seed money to be reimbursed upon completion of the project.

"MUST" OBJECTIVES

Every project must meet the "must" objectives as determined by the instructor. There are four must objectives:

1. All projects must be safe, be legal, and comply with university policies.
2. All projects must be capable of earning at least $1,000.
3. All projects must be able to be completed within nine weeks.
4. All projects must provide an opportunity for every member of the project team to experience and learn about project management.

Among the factors to consider for the last objective are the extent to which there is meaningful work for every member of the team, the degree of coordination required, the extent to which the team will have to work with external stakeholders, and the complexity of the project.

"WANT" OBJECTIVES

In addition to the must objectives, there are "want" objectives that the instructor would like to achieve.

1. Earn more than $1,000 for a charity.
2. Increase public awareness of the charity.
3. Provide a resume-worthy experience for students.
4. Be featured on local TV news.
5. Be fun to do.

ASSIGNMENT

You are a member of the class priority team in charge of evaluating and approving fund raising projects. Use the provided proposal evaluation form to formally evaluate and rank each proposal. Be prepared to report your rankings and justify your decision. You should assume that these projects would be held at your university or college.

FUND RAISING PROPOSALS

PROJECT PROPOSAL 1: HOOPS FOR HOPE

The project is a three-on-three basketball tournament to raise money for the Down Syndrome Association. The tournament will consist of three brackets: co-ed, male, and female teams. There will be a $100 entry fee per team and additional funds will be derived from the sale of commemorative T-shirts ($15). Winning teams will receive gift baskets consisting of donations from local businesses and restaurants. The event will be held at the university recreational center.

PROJECT PROPOSAL 2: SINGING FOR SMILES

The project will hold a karaoke competition with celebrity judges at a popular campus night spot. Funds will be raised by $10 admission at the door and a $2 raffle for prizes donated by local businesses. Funds will be donated to Smile Train, an international organization that performs cleft lip surgery at a cost of $250 per child. The event will feature pictures of children born with cleft lips, and with every $50 earned a piece of a picture puzzle will be added until the original picture is covered with a smiling face.

PROJECT PROPOSAL 3: HALO FOR HEROES

The project will be a Halo video game competition to be held over the weekend utilizing the college's big-screen electronic classrooms. Teams of four players will play each other in a single elimination tournament, with the grand prize being a Sony Play Station 5 donated by a local video game store. Entry fee is $40 per team, and individual players will be able to play in a loser's bracket for $10. All proceeds will go to the National Military Family Association.

PROJECT PROPOSAL 4: RAFFLE FOR LIFE

Organize a raffle contest. Raffle tickets will be sold for $10 a piece, with the winning ticket worth $500. Each of the six team members will be responsible for selling 50 raffle tickets. All profits will go to the American Cancer Society.

PROJECT PROPOSAL 5: HOLD'EM FOR HUNGER

Organize a Texas Hold'em poker tournament at a campus dining facility. It will cost $40 to enter the tournament with a $20 buy-back-in. Prizes include $300, $150, and $50 gift certificates to a large department store. Fifty percent of the gift certificates will be paid for by entry fees, while the remaining 50 percent is expected to be donated by the store. All players will be eligible to win two donated tickets to men's and women's basketball games. Funds raised will go to the local county food shelter.

PROJECT PROPOSAL 6: BUILD YOUR OWN BOX

The purpose of this project is to raise awareness of the plight of the homeless. Students will donate $25 to participate in building and living in a cardboard city on the university quad for one night. Building materials will be provided by local recycling centers and hardware stores. Hot soup will be provided by the team at midnight to all participants. Proceeds go to the local homeless shelter.

Project Priority Evaluation Form

Must objectives		**Must meet if impacts**	**1**	**2**	**3**	**4**	**5**	**6**
Be safe, legal, & comply with University Policies		Y = yes N = no						
Earn at least $1,000		Y = yes N = no						
Can be completed within 9 weeks		Y = yes N = no						
Opportunity to learn Project Management		Y = yes N = no						
Want objectives	**Relative Importance 1–100**	**Single project impact definitions**						
Earning potential	**90**	0: <$1,000 1: $1,000–1,500 2: $1,501–2,000 3: >$2,000						
Fun	**30**	0: None 1: Some fun 2: A lot of fun						
Increase awareness of charity	**30**	0: No potential 1: Low potential 2: High potential						
Resume worthy	**40**	0: No potential 1: Low potential 2: High potential						
Be featured on local TV news	**40**	0: No potential 1: Low potential 2: High potential						
		Total weighted score						
		Priority						

Design elements: Snapshot from Practice, Highlight box, Case icon: Sky Designs/Shutterstock

Case 2.4

Reliance Jio's 6G Market Entry Strategy

INTRODUCTION

Reliance Jio's foray into 6G technology marks a bold step towards establishing India as a global leader in next-generation telecommunications. With the exponential rise in digital connectivity demands, Jio aims to deliver unprecedented internet speed, ultra-low latency, and high-bandwidth connectivity through 6G infrastructure. The initiative reflects the company's commitment to fostering technological innovation, addressing the growing demands of India's urban and rural population, and aligning with global trends in connectivity and digital transformation.

OBJECTIVES

The primary objectives of Reliance Jio's 6G market entry are:

1. **Nationwide 6G network deployment:** Establish a robust infrastructure to roll out 6G networks across both urban and rural areas, ensuring seamless connectivity and bridging the digital divide.
2. **Global market leadership:** Position Reliance Jio as a leader in India's 6G ecosystem, leveraging its established competitive edge to expand influence on the global stage.
3. **Customer base expansion:** Attract early adopters and enhance user experience through innovative, next-generation services, increasing market share and customer satisfaction.
4. **Strategic partnerships:** Collaborate with global technology providers, telecom equipment suppliers, and regulators to accelerate the rollout of 6G infrastructure and ensure seamless adoption of new standards.
5. **New revenue streams:** Drive monetization by launching 6G-powered services such as Internet of Things (IoT), augmented reality (AR), virtual reality (VR), smart cities, connected vehicles, and other advanced applications.

SCOPE

The scope of Reliance Jio's 6G initiative focuses on comprehensive project lifecycle management:

1. **Market analysis and feasibility study:**
   a. Assess demand for 6G services in the Indian market.
   b. Evaluate competition, industry trends, and global advancements.
   c. Analyze technology readiness, spectrum availability, and regulatory landscapes.
2. **Regulatory approvals and licensing:**
   a. Obtain necessary approvals from Indian telecom regulatory bodies such as TRAI and DoT.
   b. Navigate spectrum allocation, licensing agreements, and compliance.
3. **Network infrastructure set-up:**
   a. Deploy 6G towers, fibre optic networks, and data centres to support the infrastructure.
   b. Integrate core network elements like servers, routers, and switches for optimal connectivity.
4. **Spectrum acquisition:**
   a. Participate in spectrum auctions for 6G frequencies.
   b. Negotiate spectrum-sharing agreements to ensure nationwide coverage.

5. Testing and deployment:

a. Conduct pilot testing in select urban and rural locations to optimize network performance.

b. Execute phased deployment, prioritizing major cities before expanding to Tier-2 and Tier-3 cities.

6. Customer acquisition and marketing:

a. Develop robust marketing campaigns to educate customers on the benefits of 6G technology.

b. Target individuals, enterprises, and government bodies to drive adoption.

7. Post-launch support and optimization:

a. Provide dedicated customer support to address initial challenges and ensure smooth user experience.

b. Monitor network performance, troubleshoot issues, and continuously optimize system performance.

Reliance Jio's entry into 6G is a strategically planned initiative underpinned by rigorous project management practices. From regulatory approvals and infrastructure deployment to market analysis and customer engagement, Jio aims to transform India's digital landscape while positioning itself as a global leader in the 6G revolution. Through innovation, collaboration, and meticulous execution, the project sets the stage for a future, where connectivity drives progress and prosperity.

KEY DELIVERABLES OR HIGH-LEVEL TASKS

Reliance Jio's market entry into 6G is a multi-faceted project involving critical deliverables to ensure a smooth rollout, technological readiness, and widespread adoption. These high-level tasks are aligned with global standards and project management frameworks:

1. Research and Development (R&D)

a. Development of 6G standards and protocols: Collaborate with international standardization bodies to define 6G specifications, ensuring technological leadership.

b. 6G hardware and infrastructure design: Innovate and test 6G-enabled hardware components, including antennas, base stations, and data transmission protocols to ensure efficiency and scalability.

c. Pilot testing and performance optimization: Conduct trials to validate the network's reliability, speed, and ultra-low latency under real-world conditions.

2. Network Infrastructure Deployment

a. 6G tower and base station installation: Nationwide rollout of 6G towers and base stations to provide seamless connectivity across urban and rural areas.

b. Fibre-optic backbone implementation: Establish a robust fibre-optic infrastructure to deliver high-speed, high-bandwidth data transfer critical for 6G operations.

3. Spectrum Licensing

a. **Acquisition of spectrum rights:** Actively participate in government-conducted 6G spectrum auctions to secure bandwidth required for nationwide coverage.
b. **Strategic spectrum utilization:** Plan spectrum allocation efficiently to optimize network performance and reduce latency.

4. Consumer Products

a. **Launch of 6G-compatible devices:** Partner with manufacturers to introduce 6G-ready smartphones, routers, wearables, and IoT devices.
b. **Introduction of Innovative Service Plans:** Develop customer-centric service plans to cater to individual users, enterprises, and niche segments such as smart cities and AR/VR platforms.

5. Digital Ecosystem Enhancement

a. **Integration of emerging technologies:** Seamlessly incorporate Artificial Intelligence (AI), Internet of Things (IoT), and edge computing capabilities to enhance service offerings.
b. **Expansion of Jio platforms:** Leverage 6G speeds to upgrade and scale platforms like JioTV, JioCinema, and JioSaavn, offering ultra-fast streaming and superior user experiences.

6. Marketing and Customer Engagement

a. **Brand positioning:** Establish Jio 6G as a pioneering solution for next-generation connectivity through targeted branding and communication campaigns.
b. **Customer acquisition strategies:** Implement pre-launch awareness programmes and post-launch engagement initiatives to attract early adopters and retain a growing customer base.
c. **Education and outreach:** Develop initiatives to educate businesses, enterprises, and individuals on the transformative benefits of 6G.

7. Partnerships and Alliances

a. **Collaborations with key stakeholders:** Forge strategic partnerships with global device manufacturers, software developers, cloud service providers, and telecom equipment suppliers to ensure smooth technology integration.
b. **Global alliances for innovation:** Align with international technology leaders to drive advancements in 6G infrastructure and applications.

The outlined deliverables reflect Reliance Jio's systematic approach to managing a complex, large-scale project like 6G market entry. From research and infrastructure development to stakeholder collaboration and customer engagement, each phase emphasizes core project management learning goals: meticulous planning, efficient resource allocation, risk mitigation, and continuous monitoring. By aligning technological advancements with strategic execution, Jio's 6G rollout offers valuable insights into managing innovation-driven projects, balancing time, cost, and scope while ensuring stakeholder satisfaction. This case provides a robust framework for understanding project lifecycle management, cross-functional coordination, and the adoption of cutting-edge solutions to achieve transformative outcomes.

Reliance Jio's 6G project follows a structured, multi-year plan, beginning with feasibility studies and spectrum licensing in the first two years. This is followed by pilot testing in metro cities, scaling nationwide deployment, and eventually expanding globally. The strategic focus is on infrastructure development, market penetration, and innovation in services, ensuring Jio becomes a leader in next-gen connectivity solutions.

Year	Milestone	Key Activities
Year 1	Feasibility Study and Planning	Complete market research and demand analysis. Finalize partnerships and alliances.
Year 2	Spectrum Licensing and R&D	Acquire 6G spectrum rights. Develop pilot projects for testing 6G infrastructure.
Year 3	Pilot Testing and Rollout	Conduct pilot testing in metro cities. Launch commercial services in selected areas.
Year 4	Nationwide Expansion	Scale infrastructure deployment across Tier 1, 2, and 3 cities. Roll out consumer products and services nationwide.
Year 5	Global Expansion and Enhancement	Begin international market entry. Introduce advanced features and additional services.

KEY PRINCIPLES OF RELIANCE JIO'S MARKET ENTRY STRATEGY

Reliance Jio's market entry strategy is a prime example of disruptive innovation, underpinned by careful organizational planning and project management principles. The approach focuses on five key principles that guided their strategy and helped overcome significant challenges.

1. **Disruptive Pricing:**

   Principle: Offering aggressively low tariffs, including free voice calls and affordable data services.

   Objective: To rapidly build a massive user base and facilitate widespread adoption across varied demographics, thus driving early market penetration.

2. **Ecosystem Play:**

   Principle: Providing a comprehensive digital ecosystem, encompassing JioFiber, JioTV, JioCinema, and JioSaavn.

   Objective: To create a compelling value proposition that not only attracts customers but also enhances their retention by providing a range of interconnected services.

3. **Technology Leadership:**

   Principle: Focusing on a future-ready 6G network, leapfrogging past legacy technologies such as 2G, 3G, 4G, and 5G.

   Objective: To position Jio as a technological leader, delivering high-speed, low-latency data services to stay ahead of market demands.

4. **Scalability and Accessibility:**

   Principle: Expanding infrastructure nationwide with strategic partnerships for both urban and rural penetration.

   Objective: To ensure widespread accessibility and enable seamless connectivity across India, regardless of geographic location.

5. **Digital Inclusion:**

   Principle: Offering low-cost smartphones bundled with Jio services, making technology accessible to first-time internet users, particularly in rural areas.

   Objective: To democratize internet access and bridge the digital divide in India.

CHALLENGES FACED BY RELIANCE JIO

1. **Regulatory and competitive resistance:** Competitors such as Airtel and Vodafone challenged Jio's policies on interconnection usage charges and its free calling services.
2. **Infrastructure investments:** Jio faced significant upfront capital requirements to build fibre optics networks, towers, and data centres.
3. **Customer acquisition costs:** The free service model initially resulted in high cash burn, making customer acquisition a financial strain.
4. **Network congestion:** The rapid growth in user base led to temporary network issues, impacting service quality.
5. **Skepticism from stakeholders:** Concerns about the sustainability of Jio's aggressive pricing model and its long-term profitability were prevalent among investors and industry analysts.

SOLUTIONS ADOPTED BY RELIANCE JIO

1. **Regulatory Engagement:** Jio actively collaborated with regulators to ensure compliance and leveraged favorable rulings to sustain its business model.
2. **Vertical Integration:** By integrating its operations vertically, from infrastructure development to content delivery, Jio reduced costs and increased control over its value chain.
3. **Innovative Financing:** Jio attracted strategic investments from global giants like Google and Facebook, ensuring financial stability and scalability.
4. **Scalable Infrastructure:** Jio invested in robust backend systems to scale its infrastructure and accommodate the surge in data traffic.
5. **Focus on Customer Experience:** Continuous network improvements and diversified service offerings allowed Jio to retain its growing customer base despite competitive pressures.
6. **Strategic Alliances:** Jio formed key partnerships with technology providers and service companies to foster innovation and expedite market penetration.

STRATEGIC OUTCOMES

1. **Market leadership:** Jio became India's largest telecom operator, dominating market share within a few years.
2. **Digital transformation enabler:** The company facilitated a mass shift towards digital services, significantly increasing internet adoption, especially in rural India.
3. **Industry disruption:** Jio's pricing model forced competitors to revise their own, disrupting the industry's pricing norms and business models.
4. **Business expansion:** Jio expanded beyond telecom, venturing into sectors like e-commerce, entertainment, and financial services, diversifying its portfolio.

This strategic combination of innovative principles, effective challenge management, and project execution made Reliance Jio a market leader and a textbook example of successful market entry and disruptive innovation.

REFERENCES

Mukherjee, S. (2019). "Jio's 6G Vision: A Step Toward Digital Transformation." Telecom Policy Review, 23(1), 14-20.

Rai, A. (2019). "The Jio Effect: Disrupting the Telecom Industry." *Journal of Business Strategy*, 40(2), 45–53.

Bhasin, H. (2020). "Reliance Jio's Market Entry Strategy." *Journal of Strategic Marketing*, 28(4), 301–312.

Kapoor, A. & Sharma, R. (2021). "Reliance Jio's Disruptive Innovation in Telecom: A Case Study." *Asian Journal of Management*, 12(2), 143–152.

Jha, A. & Yadav, P. (2021). "Reliance Jio: A Disruptive Force in India's Telecom Sector." *Journal of Strategic Management*, 16(1), 52–61.

Sharma, R. & Gupta, N. (2020). "Strategic Marketing and Leadership: A Case Study on Reliance Jio." *Journal of Marketing and Technology*, 7(4), 98–104

Soni, S. (2019). "The Impact of Jio's Market Strategy on Indian Telecom." *Indian Business Review*, 14(1), 34–40.

CHAPTER THREE

3 Organization: Structure and Culture

LEARNING OBJECTIVES

After reading this chapter you should be able to:

3-1 Identify different project management structures and understand their strengths and weaknesses.

3-2 Distinguish three different types of matrix structures and understand their strengths and weaknesses.

3-3 Describe how project management offices (PMOs) can support and improve project execution.

3-4 Understand organizational and project considerations that should be considered in choosing an appropriate project management structure.

3-5 Appreciate the significant role that organizational culture plays in managing projects.

3-6 Interpret the culture of an organization.

3-7 Understand the interaction between project management structure and the culture of an organization.

OUTLINE

3.1 Project Management Structures

3.2 Project Management Office (PMO)

3.3 What Is the Right Project Management Structure?

3.4 Organizational Culture

3.5 Implications of Organizational Culture for Organizing Projects

Summary

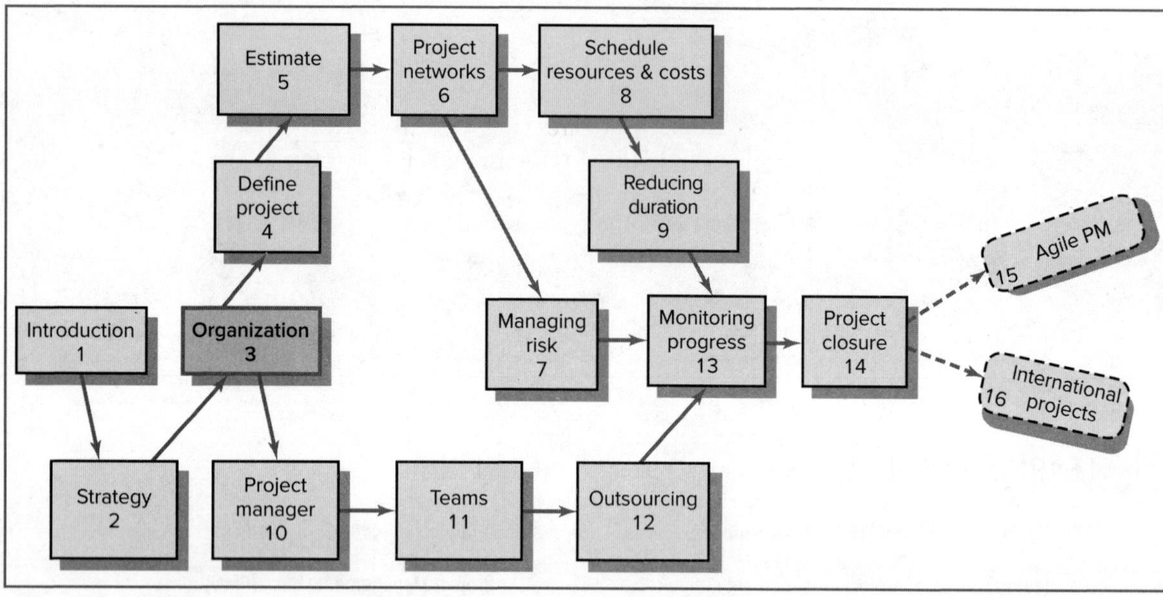

Culture eats strategy for breakfast.

Peter F. Drucker, *renown management thinker.*

Once management approves a project, then the question becomes, how will the project be implemented? This chapter examines three different project management structures used by firms to implement projects: functional organization, dedicated project teams, and matrix structure. Although not exhaustive, these structures and their variant forms represent the major approaches for organizing projects. The advantages and disadvantages of each of these structures are discussed as well as some of the critical factors that might lead a firm to choose one form over others.

Whether a firm chooses to complete projects within the traditional functional organization or through some form of matrix arrangement is only part of the story. Anyone who has worked for more than one organization realizes that there are often considerable differences in how projects are managed within certain firms even with similar structures. Working in a matrix system at AT&T is different from working in a matrix environment at Hewlett Packard. Many researchers attribute these differences to the organizational culture at AT&T and Hewlett Packard. A simple explanation of *organizational culture* is that it reflects the "personality" of an organization. Just as each individual has a unique personality, so each organization has a unique culture. Toward the end of this chapter, we examine in more detail what organizational culture is and the impact that the culture of the parent organization has on organizing and managing projects.

Both the project management structure and the culture of the organization constitute major elements of the enterprise environment in which projects are implemented.[1] It is important for project managers and participants to know the "lay of the land" so that they can avoid obstacles and take advantage of pathways to complete their projects.

[1] In addition to culture and structure, environmental factors also include geographical distribution, resource availability, IT capabilities, and the like.

3.1 Project Management Structures

LO 3-1

Identify different project management structures and understand their strengths and weaknesses.

A project management system provides a framework for launching and implementing project activities within a parent organization. A good system appropriately balances the needs of both the parent organization and the project by defining the interface between the project and parent organization in terms of authority, allocation of resources, and eventual integration of project outcomes into mainstream operations. With this in mind, we will start the discussion of project management structures.

Organizing Projects within the Functional Organization

One approach to organizing projects is to simply manage them within the existing functional hierarchy of the organization. Once management decides to implement a project, the different segments of the project are delegated to the respective functional units with each unit responsible for completing its segment of the project (see Figure 3.1). Coordination is maintained through normal management channels. For example, a tool manufacturing firm decides to differentiate its product line by offering a series of tools specially designed for left-handed individuals. Top management decides to implement the project, and different segments of the project are distributed to appropriate areas. The Industrial Design Department is responsible for modifying specifications to conform to the needs of left-handed users. The Production Department is responsible for devising the means for producing new tools according to these new design specifications. The Marketing Department is responsible for gauging demand and price as well as identifying distribution outlets. The overall project will be managed within the normal hierarchy, with the project being part of the working agenda of top management.

The functional organization is also commonly used when, given the nature of the project, one functional area plays a dominant role in completing the project or has a dominant interest in the success of the project. Under these circumstances, a high-ranking manager in that area is given the responsibility of coordinating the project. For example, the transfer of equipment and personnel to a new office would be managed by a top-ranking manager in the firm's Facilities Department. Likewise, a project involving the upgrading of the management information system would be managed by the Information Systems Department. In both cases, most of the project work would be done within the specified department, and coordination with other departments would occur through normal channels.

There are advantages and disadvantages for using the existing functional organization to administer and complete projects (Larson, 2004). The major advantages are the following:

1. **No change.** Projects are completed within the basic functional structure of the parent organization. There is no radical alteration in the design and operation of the parent organization.
2. **Flexibility.** There is maximum flexibility in the use of staff. Appropriate specialists in different functional units can temporarily be assigned to work on the project and then return to their normal work. With a broad base of technical personnel available within each functional department, people can be switched among different projects with relative ease.

FIGURE 3.1 **Functional Organizations**

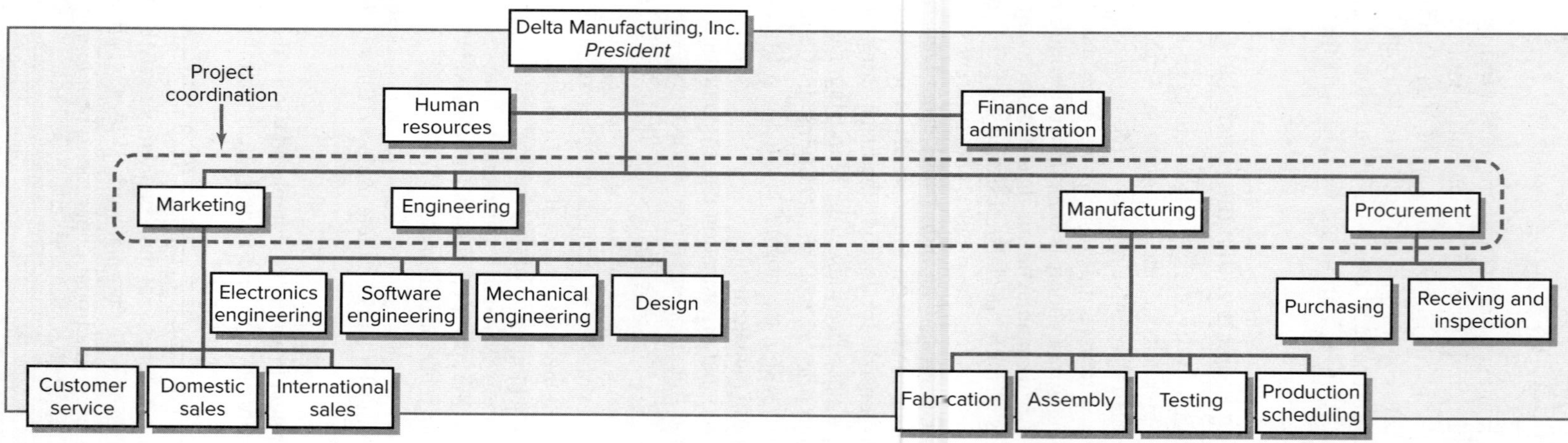

3. **In-depth expertise.** If the scope of the project is narrow and the proper functional unit is assigned primary responsibility, then in-depth expertise can be brought to bear on the most crucial aspects of the project.
4. **Easy post-project transition.** Normal career paths within a functional division are maintained. While specialists can make significant contributions to projects, their functional field is their professional home and the focus of their professional growth and advancement.

Just as there are advantages for organizing projects within the existing functional organization, there are also disadvantages. These disadvantages are particularly pronounced when the scope of the project is broad and one functional department does not take the dominant technological and managerial lead on the project:

1. **Lack of focus.** Each functional unit has its own core routine work to do; sometimes project responsibilities get pushed aside to meet primary obligations. This difficulty is compounded when the project has different priorities for different units. For example, the Marketing Department may consider the project urgent but the operations people consider it only of secondary importance. Imagine the tension if the marketing people have to wait for the operations people to complete their segment of the project before they proceed.
2. **Poor integration.** There may be poor integration across functional units. Functional specialists tend to be concerned only with their segment of the project and not with what is best for the total project.
3. **Slow.** It generally takes longer to complete projects through this functional arrangement. This is in part attributable to slow response time—project information and decisions have to be circulated through normal management channels. Furthermore, the lack of horizontal, direct communication among functional groups contributes to rework as specialists realize the implications of others' actions after the fact.
4. **Lack of ownership.** The motivation of people assigned to the project can be weak. The project may be seen as an additional burden that is not directly linked to their professional development or advancement. Furthermore, because they are working on only a segment of the project, professionals do not identify with the project.

Organizing Projects as Dedicated Teams

At the other end of the structural spectrum is the creation of a **dedicated project team.** These teams operate as units separate from the rest of the parent organization. Usually, a full-time project manager is designated to pull together a core group of specialists who work full time on the project. The project manager recruits necessary personnel from both within and outside the parent company. The subsequent team is physically separated from the parent organization and given marching orders to complete the project (see Figure 3.2).

The interface between the parent organization and the project teams will vary. In some cases, the parent organization maintains a tight rein through financial controls. In other cases, firms grant the project manager maximum freedom to get the project done as s/he sees fit. Lockheed Martin has used this approach to develop next-generation jet airplanes. See Snapshot from Practice 3.1: Skunk Works at Lockheed Martin.

In the case of firms where projects are the dominant form of business, such as a construction firm or a consulting firm, the entire organization is designed to support

FIGURE 3.2 **Dedicated Project Team**

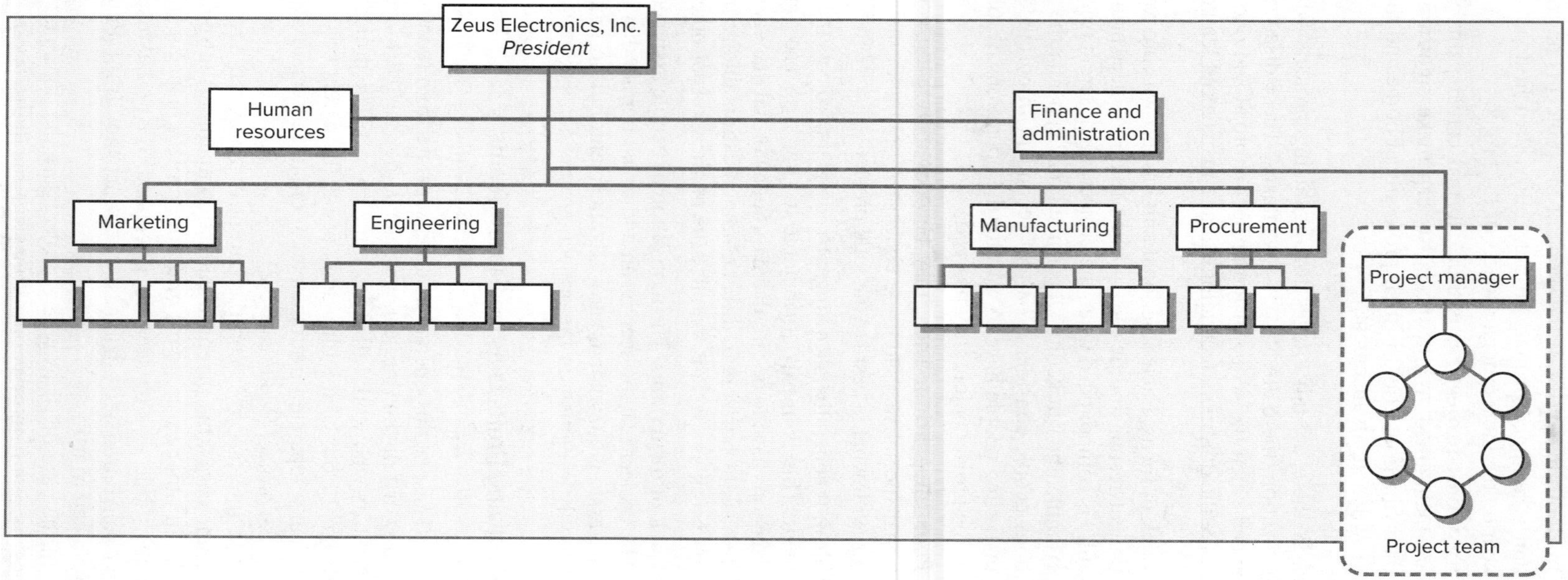

SNAPSHOT FROM PRACTICE 3.1 Skunk Works at Lockheed Martin*

Monty Rakusen/Getty Images

In project management folklore, *skunk works* is code for a small, dedicated team assigned to a breakthrough project. The first skunk works were created more than half a century ago by Clarence L. "Kelly" Johnson at Lockheed Aerospace Corporation. Kelly's project had two objectives: (1) to create a jet fighter, the Shooting Star, and (2) to do it as fast as possible. Kelly and a small band of engineering mavericks operated as a dedicated team unencumbered by red tape and the bureaucratic delays of the normal R&D process. The name was coined by team member Irvin Culver after the moonshine brewery deep in the forest in the popular cartoon strip Lil'Abner. The homemade whisky was euphemistically called kickapoo joy juice.

The project was a spectacular success. In just 43 days, Johnson's team of 23 engineers and teams of support personnel put together the first American fighter to fly at more than 500 miles per hour. Lockheed, like others, found that the management systems necessary to run a large manufacturing operation are not conducive to innovation. Instead, they choose to use agile dedicated teams that act as a well-funded start-up.

Lockheed has continued to use skunk works to develop a string of high-speed jets, including the F117 Nighthawk Stealth Fighter, as well as jet drone prototypes. Lockheed Martin has an official Skunk Works Division. Its charter is

> The Skunk Works is a concentration of a few good people solving problems far in advance—and at a fraction of the cost—by applying the simplest, most straightforward methods possible to develop and produce new products.

*"*Lockheed Martin Skunk Works*," www.lockheedmartin.com/us/aeronautics/skunkworks.html, accessed 1/22/15; J. Miller, *Lockheed Martin's Skunk Works* (New York: Specialty Publications, 1996).

project teams. Instead of one or two special projects, the organization consists of sets of quasi-independent teams working on specific projects. The main responsibility of traditional functional departments is to assist and support these project teams. For example, the Marketing Department is directed at generating new business that will lead to more projects, while the Human Resource Department is responsible for managing a variety of personnel issues as well as recruiting and training new employees. This type of organization is referred to in the literature as a **projectized organization** and is graphically portrayed in Figure 3.3. It is important to note that not all projects are dedicated project teams; personnel can work part time on several projects.

As in the case of functional organization, the dedicated project team approach has strengths and weaknesses (Larson, 2004). The following are recognized as strengths:

1. **Simple.** Other than taking away resources in the form of specialists assigned to the project, the functional organization remains intact with the project team operating independently.

FIGURE 3.3 Projectized Organization Structure

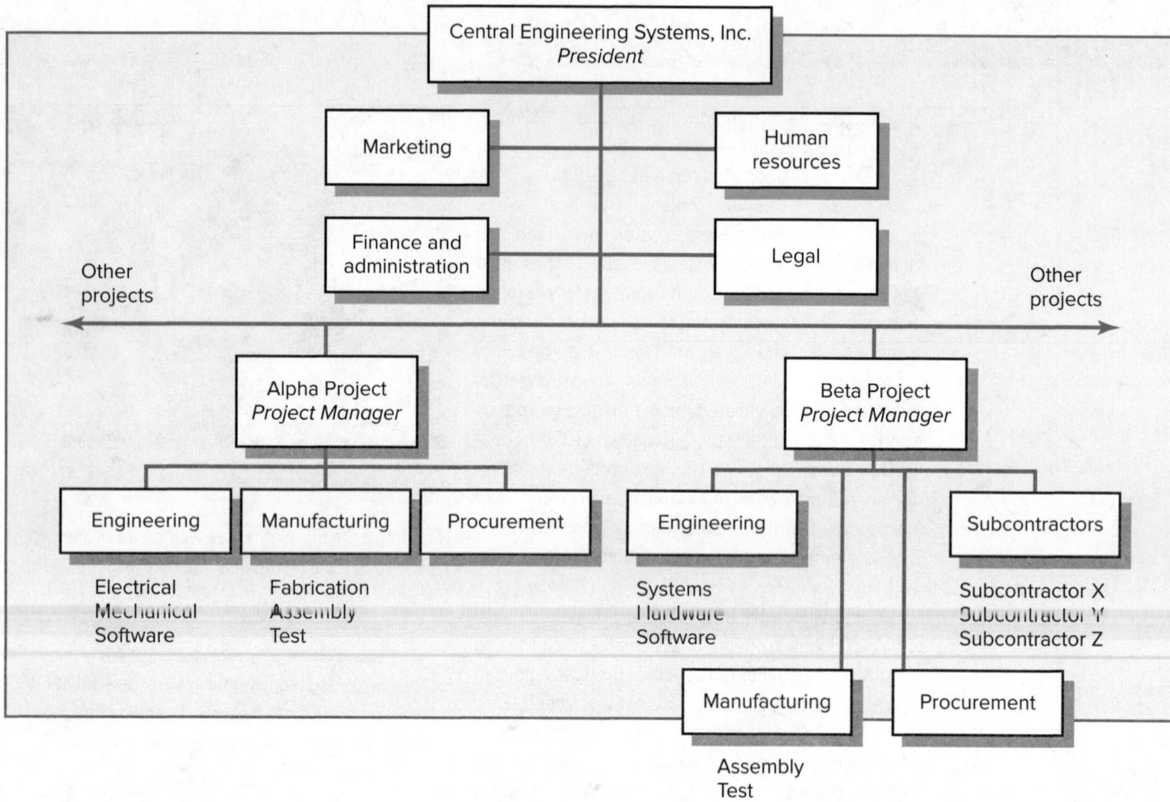

2. **Fast.** Projects tend to get done more quickly when participants devote their full attention to the project and are not distracted by other obligations and duties. Furthermore, response time tends to be quicker under this arrangement because most decisions are made within the team and are not deferred up the hierarchy.
3. **Cohesive.** A high level of motivation and cohesiveness often emerges within the project team. Participants share a common goal and personal responsibility toward the project and the team.
4. **Cross-functional integration.** Specialists from different areas work closely together and, with proper guidance, become committed to optimizing the project, not their respective areas of expertise.

In many cases, the project team approach is the optimum approach for completing a project when you view it solely from the standpoint of what is best for completing the project. Its weaknesses become more evident when the needs of the parent organization are taken into account:

1. **Expensive.** Not only have you created a new management position (project manager), but resources are also assigned on a full-time basis. This can result in duplication of efforts across projects and a loss of economies of scale.
2. **Internal strife.** Sometimes dedicated project teams become an entity in their own right and conflict emerges between the team and the remainder of the organization

(see Snapshot from Practice 3.2: The Birth of the Mac). This divisiveness can undermine not only the integration of the eventual outcomes of the project into mainstream operations but also the assimilation of project team members back into their functional units once the project is completed.

SNAPSHOT FROM PRACTICE 3.2 The Birth of the Mac*

One of the advantages of creating dedicated project teams is that project participants from different functional areas can develop into a highly cohesive work team that is strongly committed to completing the project. While such teams often produce Herculean efforts in pursuit of project completion, there is a negative dimension to this commitment that is often referred to in the literature as **projectitis.**

A we–they attitude can emerge between project team members and the rest of the organization. The project team succumbs to *hubris* and develops a holier-than-thou attitude that antagonizes the parent organization. People not assigned to the project become jealous of the attention and prestige being showered on the project team, especially when they believe that it is their hard work that is financing the endeavor. The tendency to assign project teams exotic titles such as "Silver Bullets" and "Tiger Teams," as well as to give them special perks, tends to intensify the gap between the project team and the rest of the organization.

Such appears to have been the case with Apple's highly successful Macintosh development team. Steve Jobs, who at the time was both the chairperson of Apple and the project manager for the Mac team, pampered his team with perks, including at-the-desk massages, coolers stocked with freshly squeezed orange juice, a Bosendorfer grand piano, and first-class plane tickets. No other employees at Apple got to travel first class. Jobs considered his team to be the elite of Apple and had a tendency to refer to everyone else as "Bozos" who "didn't get it." Engineers from the Apple II division, which was the bread and butter of Apple's sales, became incensed with the special treatment their colleagues were getting.

One evening at Ely McFly's, a local watering hole, the tensions between Apple II engineers seated at one table and those of a Mac team at another boiled over. Aaron Goldberg, a long-time industry consultant, watched from his barstool as the squabbling escalated. "The Mac guys were screaming, 'We're the future!' The Apple II guys were screaming, 'We're the money!' Then there was a geek brawl. Pocket protectors and pens were flying. I was waiting for a notebook to drop, so they would stop and pick up the papers."

Jill Braaten/McGraw Hill

Although comical from a distance, the discord between the Apple II and Mac groups severely hampered Apple's performance during the 1980s. John Sculley, who replaced Steve Jobs as chairperson of Apple, observed that Apple had evolved into two "warring companies" and referred to the street between the Apple II and Macintosh buildings as "the DMZ" (demilitarized zone).

*J. Carlton, *Apple: The Inside Story of Intrigue, Egomania, and Business Blunders* (New York: Random House, 1997), pp. 13–14; J. Sculley, *Odyssey: Pepsi to Apple. . . a Journey of Adventure, Ideas, and the Future* (New York: Harper & Row, 1987), pp. 270–79.

3. **Limited technological expertise.** Creating self-contained teams inhibits maximum technological expertise being brought to bear on problems. Technical expertise is limited somewhat to the talents and experience of the specialists assigned to the project. While nothing prevents specialists from consulting with others in the functional division, the we–they syndrome and the fact that such help is not formally sanctioned by the organization discourage this from happening.
4. **Difficult post-project transition.** Assigning full-time personnel to a project creates the dilemma of what to do with them after the project is completed. If other project work is not available, then the transition back to their original functional departments may be difficult because of their prolonged absence and the need to catch up with recent developments in their functional area.

Organizing Projects within a Matrix Arrangement

Matrix management is a hybrid organizational form in which a horizontal project management structure is "overlaid" on the normal functional hierarchy. In a matrix system, there are usually two chains of command, one along functional lines and the other along project lines. Instead of delegating segments of a project to different units or creating an autonomous team, project participants report simultaneously to both functional and project managers.

Companies apply this matrix arrangement in a variety of ways. Some organizations set up temporary matrix systems to deal with specific projects, whereas "matrix" may be a permanent fixture in other organizations. Let us first look at its general application and then proceed to a more detailed discussion of finer points. Consider Figure 3.4. There are three projects currently under way: A, B, and C. All three project managers (PM A–C) report to a director of project management, who supervises all projects. Each project has an administrative assistant, although the one for project C is only part time.

Project A involves the design and expansion of an existing production line to accommodate new metal alloys. To accomplish this objective, project A has assigned to it 3.5 people from Manufacturing and 6 people from Engineering. These individuals are assigned to the project on a part-time or full-time basis, depending on the project's needs during various phases of the project. Project B involves the development of a new product that requires the heavy representation of Engineering, Manufacturing, and Marketing. Project C involves forecasting changing needs of an existing customer base. While these three projects, as well as others, are being completed, the functional divisions continue performing their basic, core activities.

The matrix structure is designed to utilize resources optimally by having individuals work on multiple projects as well as being capable of performing normal functional duties. At the same time, the matrix approach attempts to achieve greater integration by creating and legitimizing the authority of a project manager. In theory, the matrix approach provides a dual focus between functional/technical expertise and project requirements that is missing in either the project team or functional approach to project management. This focus can most easily be seen in the relative input of functional managers and project managers over key project decisions (see Table 3.1).

FIGURE 3.4 **Matrix Organization Structure**

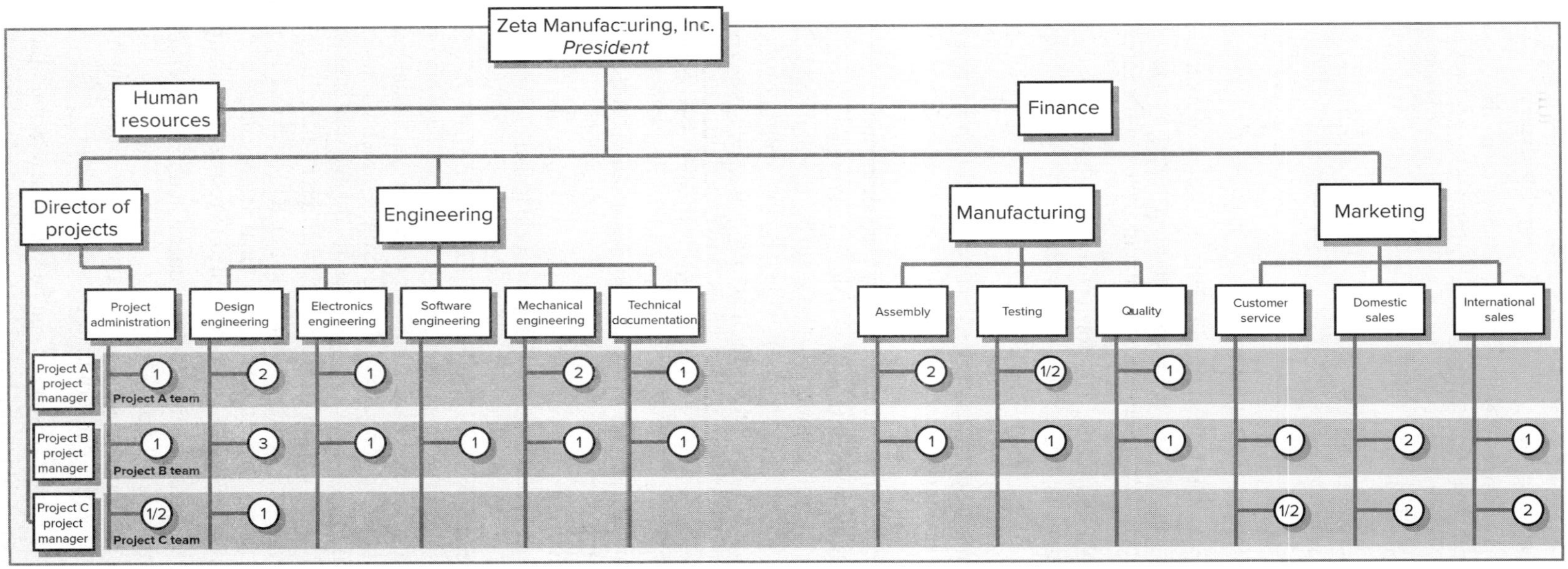

TABLE 3.1
Division of Project Manager and Functional Manager Responsibilities in a Matrix Structure

Project Manager	Negotiated Issues	Functional Manager
What has to be done?	Who will do the task?	How will it be done?
When should the task be done?	Where will the task be done?	
How much money is available to do the task?	Why will the task be done?	How will the project involvement impact normal functional activities?
How well has the total project been done?	Is the task satisfactorily completed?	How well has the functional input been integrated?

Different Matrix Forms

LO 3-2

Distinguish three different types of matrix structures and understand their strengths and weaknesses.

In practice there are really different kinds of matrix systems, depending on the relative authority of the project and functional managers (Bowen et al., 1994; Larson & Gobeli, 1987). Here is a thumbnail sketch of the three kinds of matrices:

- **Weak matrix.** This form is very similar to a functional approach with the exception that there is a formally designated project manager responsible for coordinating project activities. Functional managers are responsible for managing their segment of the project. The project manager basically acts as a staff assistant who draws the schedules and checklists, collects information on the status of work, and facilitates project completion. The project manager has indirect authority to expedite and monitor the project. Functional managers call most of the shots and decide who does what and when the work is completed.
- **Balanced matrix.** This is the classic matrix, in which the project manager is responsible for defining what needs to be accomplished, while the functional managers are concerned with how it will be accomplished. More specifically, the project manager establishes the overall plan for completing the project, integrates the contribution of the different disciplines, sets schedules, and monitors progress. The functional managers are responsible for assigning personnel and executing their segment of the project according to the standards and schedules set by the project manager. The merger of "what and how" requires both parties to work closely together and jointly approve technical and operational decisions.
- **Strong matrix.** This form attempts to create the "feel" of a project team within a matrix environment. The project manager controls most aspects of the project, including scope trade-offs and assignment of functional personnel. The project manager controls when and what specialists do and has final say on major project decisions. The functional manager has title over his or her people and is consulted on a need basis. In some situations, a functional manager's department may serve as a "subcontractor" for the project, in which case it has more control over specialized work. For example, the development of a new series of laptop computers may require a team of experts from different disciplines working on the basic design and performance requirements within a project matrix arrangement. Once the specifications have been determined, final design and production of certain components (e.g., power source) may be assigned to respective functional groups to complete.

Matrix management, both in general and in its specific forms, has unique strengths and weaknesses (Larson & Gobeli, 1987). The advantages and disadvantages of matrix organizations in general are noted in the following list, which only briefly highlights the specifics concerning different forms.

1. **Efficient.** Resources can be shared across multiple projects as well as within functional divisions. Individuals can divide their energy among multiple projects on an as-needed basis. This reduces the duplication required in a projectized structure.

2. **Strong project focus.** A stronger project focus is provided by having a formally designated project manager who is responsible for coordinating and integrating contributions of different units. This helps sustain a holistic approach to problem solving that is often missing in the functional organization.
3. **Easier post-project transition.** Because the project organization is overlaid on the functional divisions, specialists maintain ties with their functional group, so they have a homeport to return to once the project is completed.
4. **Flexible.** Matrix arrangements provide for flexible utilization of resources and expertise within the firm. In some cases, functional units provide individuals who are managed by the project manager. In other cases, the contributions are monitored by the functional manager.

The strengths of the matrix structure are considerable. Unfortunately, so are the potential weaknesses. This is due in large part to the fact that a matrix structure is more complicated and the creation of multiple bosses represents a radical departure from the traditional hierarchical authority system.

Furthermore, one does not install a matrix structure overnight. Experts argue that it takes three to five years for a matrix system to fully mature, so many of the following problems represent growing pains.

1. **Dysfunctional conflict.** The matrix approach is predicated on tension between functional managers and project managers who bring critical expertise and perspectives to the project. Such tension is viewed as a necessary mechanism for achieving an appropriate balance between complex technical issues and unique project requirements. While the intent is noble, the effect is sometimes analogous to opening Pandora's box. Legitimate conflict can spill over to a more personal level, resulting from conflicting agendas and accountabilities. Worthy discussions can degenerate into heated arguments that engender animosity among the managers involved.
2. **Infighting.** Any situation in which equipment, resources, and people are being shared across projects and functional activities lends itself to conflict and competition for scarce resources. Infighting can occur among project managers, who are primarily interested in what is best for their project.
3. **Stressful.** Matrix management violates the management principle of unity of command. Project participants have at least two bosses—their functional head and one or more project managers. Working in a matrix environment can be extremely stressful. Imagine working in an environment in which you are being told to do three conflicting things by three different managers.
4. **Slow.** In theory, the presence of a project manager to coordinate the project should accelerate its completion. In practice, however, decision making can get bogged down, as agreements have to be forged across multiple functional groups. This is especially true for the balanced matrix.

When the three variant forms of the matrix approach are considered, we can see that advantages and disadvantages are not necessarily true for all three forms of matrix. The strong matrix is likely to enhance project integration, diminish internal power struggles, and ultimately improve control of project activities and costs. On the downside, technical quality may suffer because functional areas have less control over their contributions. Finally, projectitis may emerge as the members develop a strong team identity.

The weak matrix is likely to improve technical quality as well as provide a better system for managing conflict across projects because the functional manager assigns personnel to different projects. The problem is that functional control is often maintained at the expense

SNAPSHOT FROM PRACTICE 3.3 Infosys' Flat Organizational Structure

Infosys, a global IT services leader, is undergoing significant restructuring to flatten its organizational hierarchy. The effort is to break down a five-tiered structure into two. The senior management has reviewed each layer closely to understand the overlaps in these layers. The idea is to fix greater responsibility and accountability on senior executives who are not billable resources but are people managers. This initiative is aimed at enhancing decision-making, empowering frontline leaders, and improving operational efficiency, particularly in the context of modern project management.

KEY HIGHLIGHTS OF THE RESTRUCTURING

- **Reduction in hierarchical layers:** Infosys plans to transition from a five-tiered structure to a two-tier model. This change will trim roles at job levels (JL) 7 and above, such as delivery managers, industry principals, AVPs, VPs, and SVPs. Currently, Infosys has over 30,000 employees in senior roles or what they call JL 6, 7, and 8. Around 13,000 employees are in JL7 levels and above.
- **Increased accountability:** Senior executives, particularly those in non-billable roles, will be given greater responsibility, focusing on aligning their contributions with business outcomes.
- **Enhanced agility:** By reducing managerial layers, the company aims to minimize reporting redundancies, enabling faster escalations, quicker decision-making, and better responsiveness to client needs.

IMPACT ON PROJECT MANAGEMENT

Infosys's flat and decentralized structure aligns with its goal of enhancing project delivery efficiency. This approach empowers leaders by granting them autonomy to make swift decisions and resolve conflicts effectively. It enables decision-makers to take ownership of their modules, facilitating cost-saving measures through prompt decisions on cost optimization, resource allocation, smoothing, and leveling. Additionally, the simplified reporting structure strengthens communication channels, fosters robust networking, and enhances collaboration among stakeholders.

The adoption of a flat organizational model reflects its readiness to address the rapidly evolving demands of modern project management. By implementing a leaner and more agile structure, the company becomes more responsive to customer needs. The restructuring of sales, delivery, BPO, and support services emphasizes better scope and time management, improved employee ownership, and overall cost optimization.

REFERENCES

https://www.peoplematters.in/news/employee-relations/infosys-to-restructure-to-flatten-organization-25870

IT major Infosys is undertaking a major restructuring. (2024). Times of India.

Balaji, S., & Murugaiyan, M. S. (2012). "Agile Methodology in Project Management." *International Journal of Information Technology and Business Management*

of poor project integration. The balanced matrix can achieve better balance between technical and project requirements, but it is a very delicate system to manage and is more likely to succumb to many of the problems associated with the matrix approach.

3.2 Project Management Office (PMO)

LO 3-3

Describe how project management offices (PMOs) can support and improve project execution.

A **project management office (PMO)**[2] is a centralized unit within an organization or a department that oversees and supports the execution of projects. PMOs emerged in response to the poor track record many companies experienced in finishing projects on time, within budget, and according to plan. Organizations began to devote staff to support and improve project implementation. Often PMOs played a critical role in helping matrix systems mature into more effective project delivery platforms. A 2022 study showed that 79 percent of U.S. organizations reported having a PMO (Cabanis-Brewin, 2022).

[2] Project management offices are also referred to as project offices, program offices, project support offices, and the like.

PMOs come in many different forms. In a small organization with few projects, the PMO may consist of just one professional assigned to support project efforts. In large, multinational firms, PMOs may involve hundreds, even thousands, of professionals operating at different levels and in different parts of the organization. Since 2003 the Project Management Institute (PMI) has recognized a PMO of the Year. Snapshot from Practice 3.3: 2018 PMO of the Year details the 2018 recipient. Subsequent Snapshot from Practice 2021 PMO of the Year features the 2021 recipient (Moffitt Cancer Center).

One interesting way of characterizing different kinds of PMOs has been set forth by Casey & Peck (2001), who describe certain PMOs in terms of being (1) a weather station, (2) a control tower, or (3) a resource pool. We have added a fourth kind, a command and control center that reflects recent developments. Each of these models performs a very different function within an organization.

- **Weather station.** The primary function of the weather station PMO is to track and monitor project performance. It is typically created to satisfy top management's need to stay on top of the portfolio of projects under way in the firm. Staff provides an independent forecast of project performance. The questions answered for specific projects include

  How are our projects progressing? Which ones are on track? Which ones are not?
  How are we doing in terms of cost? Which projects are over or under budget?
  What are the major problems confronting projects? Are contingency plans in place?
  What can the organization do to help the project?

SNAPSHOT FROM PRACTICE 3.4 2018 PMO of the Year: Telstra—Capital Planning & Delivery PMO, Melbourne, Australia*

From mobile networks to home Internet to pay TV, Telstra, Australia's largest telecom company, invests heavily in projects. In 2012, Telstra commissioned an assessment of how well the company managed large, strategic projects. The results were not good: roughly 30 percent of its investment programs and projects were not meeting its goals.

In response, Telstra launched the Capital Planning & Delivery Project Management Office (PMO) as a dedicated capability within the finance and strategy function of the firm. The PMO's overarching goal was to instill discipline around strategic capital planning and improve the overall effectiveness of the company's capital investment management. The PMO now includes 24 full-time staff overseeing a portfolio of 1,265 projects worldwide with an annual value of more than AU$3.77 billion.

The PMO team has implemented an enterprise-wide portfolio management system to track and improve ROI on all invested capital. At the outset of each major project, the PMO works with responsible managers to develop key performance indicators (KPIs) that outline how the project will contribute to Telstra's strategic mission. These KPIs are used on a monthly basis to monitor project performance and raise flags when slippage begins to occur. The PMO has the authority to shut down underperforming projects. The PMO also provides sponsors and managers with the necessary training to support successful project management. These efforts have paid off. In 2017, more than 75 percent of projects scored above benchmarks for schedule, budget, and quality. The PMO also helped Telstra save over AU$220 million over three years, thanks to a rigorous go/no-go stage-gate process.

"We've been able to ensure that the best projects with the best returns have been prioritized and executed with the right people," Rob Loader, one of the PMO staff members says. "That allows us to be first to market on specific initiatives in a very competitive environment."

*Project Management Institute press release, November 15, 2018.

- **Control tower.** The primary function of the control tower PMO is to improve project execution. It considers project management as a profession to be protected and advanced. Staff at the PMO identify best practices and standards for project management excellence. They work as consultants and trainers to support project managers and their teams.
- **Resource pool.** The goal of the resource pool PMO is to provide the organization with a cadre of trained project managers and professionals. It operates like an academy for continually upgrading the skills of a firm's project professionals. In addition to training, this kind of PMO also elevates the stature of project management within the organization.
- **Command and control center.** Unlike the support function performed by the other kinds of PMO, this type has direct authority over projects. It acts as a key decision maker across the life of a project, making sure the project is aligned with business objectives and conforms to accepted practices. Such PMOs make recommendations, approve significant changes, and even terminate projects.

Today most PMOs take on more than one of these roles. For example, a PMO may track projects, provide training, and institutionalize lessons learned. In recent years, PMOs have played a key role in helping organizations adapt Agile methods to their projects (Patel, 2018).

PMOs will continue to evolve and adapt. It is important to remember that the primary role of a PMO is to facilitate/enable projects, not do projects. Top management should not allow a PMO to usurp the technical aspects (scheduling, planning, budgeting, etc.) of completing a project. Those are the project manager's responsibilities.

SNAPSHOT FROM PRACTICE — 2021 PMO of the Year: Moffitt Cancer Center*

The Project Management Office (PMO) of the year award is intended to recognize individuals working in a PMO that has demonstrated superior project management abilities by adding value to its organization through its support of successful strategic initiatives. The 2021 recipient was Moffitt Cancer Center's Enterprise Project Management Team. Located in Tampa, Florida, the Moffitt Cancer Center is one of only 52 National Cancer Institutes designated comprehensive cancer centers. With more than 7,500 members, Moffitt has an economic impact in the state of $2.4 Billion.

Moffitt's Enterprise Project Management Team was instrumental in the First Connect initiative. This approach ensures patients can speak directly to a cancer expert from their care team within one business day of contacting Moffitt for an appointment. Furthermore, the team introduced standardized project management methodologies to serve the strategic initiatives across the organization and has served as coach and mentor on projects.

"Congratulations to the Moffitt Enterprise Project Management Team," said Yvette Tremonti, Moffitt executive. "This team was formed in early 2019 as part of Moffitt's new Process & Project Management Office to ensure we deliver on our strategic plan and equip others along the way. I am impressed by how this team has matured itself and helped the organization do the same. The team's collaborative approach with other shared services colleagues and operational areas is exemplary. I am proud of this team for achieving this prestigious award and the service to our patients it represents."

A summary of Moffitt's accomplishments can be found at: https://www.youtube.com/watch?v=gSW8dFshTw0.

*News Release, Moffitt Cancer Center, "Moffitt Cancer Center Recognized as Winner of Project Management Institute 2021 PMI Professional Awards," https://moffitt.org/newsroom/press-release-archive/moffitt-cancer-center-recognized-as-winner-of-project-management-institute-2021-pmi-professional-awards/, October 11, 2021. Accessed 6/5/22.

3.3 What is the Right Project Management Structure?

LO 3-4

Understand organizational and project considerations that should be considered in choosing an appropriate project management structure.

There is empirical evidence that project success is directly linked to the amount of autonomy and authority project managers have over their projects (Gray et al., 1990; Larson & Gobeli, 1987, 1988; Lechler & Dvir, 2010). However, most of this research is based on what is best for managing specific projects. It is important to remember what was stated in the beginning of the chapter—the best system balances the needs of the project with those of the parent organization. So what project structure should an organization use? This is a complicated question with no precise answers. A number of issues need to be considered at both the organization and project levels.

Organization Considerations

At the organization level, the first question that needs to be asked is, how important is project management to the success of the firm? That is, what percentage of core work involves projects? If over 75 percent of work involves projects, then an organization should consider a fully projectized organization. If an organization has both standard products and projects, then a matrix arrangement would appear to be appropriate. If an organization has very few projects, then a less formal arrangement is probably all that is required. Dedicated teams could be created on an as-needed basis and the organization could outsource project work.

A second key question involves resource availability. Remember, matrix evolved out of the necessity to share resources across multiple projects and functional domains while creating legitimate project leadership. For organizations that cannot afford to tie up critical personnel on individual projects, a matrix system would appear to be appropriate. An alternative would be to create a dedicated team but outsource project work when resources are not available internally.

Within the context of the first two questions, an organization needs to assess current practices and what changes are needed to more effectively manage projects. A strong project matrix is not installed overnight. The shift toward a greater emphasis on projects has a host of political implications that need to be worked through, requiring time and strong leadership. For example, we have observed many companies that make the transition from a functional organization to a matrix organization begin with a weak functional matrix. This is due in part to resistance by functional and department managers toward transferring authority to project managers. With time, these matrix structures eventually evolve into a project matrix.

Project Considerations

At the project level, the question is how much autonomy the project needs in order to be successfully completed. Hobbs and Ménard (1993) identify seven factors that should influence the choice of project management structure:

- Size of project.
- Strategic importance.
- Novelty and need for innovation.
- Need for integration (number of departments involved).
- Environmental complexity (number of external interfaces).
- Budget and time constraints.
- Stability of resource requirements.

The higher the levels of these seven factors, the more autonomy and authority the project manager and project team need to be successful.[3] This translates into using either a dedicated project team or a project matrix structure. For example, these structures should be used for large projects that are strategically critical and are new to the company, thus requiring much innovation. These structures are also appropriate for complex, multidisciplinary projects that require input from many departments, as well as for projects that require constant contact with customers to assess their expectations. Dedicated project teams should also be used for urgent projects in which the nature of the work requires people working steadily from beginning to end.

Many firms that are heavily involved in project management have created a flexible management system that organizes projects according to project requirements. For example, Chaparral Steel, a mini-mill that produces steel bars and beams from scrap metal, classifies projects into three categories: advanced development, platform, and incremental. Advanced development projects are high-risk endeavors involving the creation of a breakthrough product or process. Platform projects are medium-risk projects involving system upgrades that yield new products and processes. Incremental projects are low-risk, short-term projects that involve minor adjustments in existing products and processes. At any point in time, Chaparral might have 40–50 projects under way, of which only 1 or 2 are advanced, 3–5 are platform projects, and the remainder are small, incremental projects. The incremental projects are almost all done within a weak matrix with the project manager coordinating the work of functional subgroups. A strong matrix is used to complete the platform projects, while dedicated project teams are typically created to complete the advanced development projects. More and more companies are using this "mix and match" approach to managing projects.

3.4 Organizational Culture

LO 3-5

Appreciate the significant role that organizational culture plays in managing projects.

The decision for combining a discussion of project management structures and organizational cultures in this chapter can be traced to a conversation we, the authors, had with two project managers who worked for a medium-sized information technology firm.

The managers were developing a new operating platform that would be critical to the future success of their company. When they tried to describe how this project was organized, one manager began to sketch out on a napkin a complicated structure involving 52 different teams, each with a project leader and a technical leader! In response to our further probing to understand how this system worked, the manager stopped short and proclaimed, "The key to making this structure work is the culture in our company. This approach would never work at Company Y, where I worked before. But because of our culture here we are able to pull it off."

This comment, our observations of other firms, and research suggest there is a strong connection among project management structure, organizational culture, and project success.[4] We have observed organizations successfully manage projects within the traditional functional organization because the culture encouraged cross-functional

[3] For a more sophisticated discussion of contingency factors related to managing specific projects see: Shenhar, A. J., and D. Dvir, *Reinventing Project Management: The Diamond Approach to Successful Growth and Innovation* (Boston: Harvard Press, 2007).

[4] See, for example, Gu, V. C., J. J. Hoffman, Q. Cao, and M. J. Schniederjans, "The Effects of Organizational Culture and Environmental Pressures on IT Project Performance: A Moderation Perspective," *International Journal of Project Management,* vol. 32, no. 7 (2014), pp. 1170–81; Kerzner, H., *In Search of Excellence in Project Management* (New York: Von Nostrand Reinhold, 1997); Yazici, H., "The Role of Project Management Maturity and Organizational Culture in Perceived Performance," *Project Management Journal,* vol. 40, no. 3 (2009), pp. 14–33.

integration. Conversely, we have seen matrix structures break down because the culture of the organization did not support the division of authority between project managers and functional managers. We have also observed companies relying on independent project teams because the dominant culture would not support the innovation and speed necessary for success.

What Is Organizational Culture?

LO 3-6

Interpret the culture of an organization.

Organizational culture refers to a system of shared norms, beliefs, values, and assumptions that binds people together, thereby creating shared meanings (Deal & Kennedy, 1982). This system is manifested by customs and habits that exemplify the values and beliefs of the organization. For example, egalitarianism may be expressed in the informal dress worn at a high-tech firm. Conversely, mandated uniforms at a department store reinforce respect for the hierarchy.

Culture reflects the personality of the organization and, like an individual's personality, can enable us to predict attitudes and behaviors of organizational members. Culture is also one of the defining aspects of an organization that sets it apart from other organizations, even in the same industry.

Research suggests that there are 10 primary characteristics that, in aggregate, capture the essence of an organization's culture:[5]

1. **Member identity**—the degree to which employees identify with the organization as a whole rather than with their type of job or field of professional expertise.
2. **Team emphasis**—the degree to which work activities are organized around groups rather than individuals.
3. **Management focus**—the degree to which management decisions take into account the effect of outcomes on people within the organization.
4. **Unit integration**—the degree to which units within the organization are encouraged to operate in a coordinated or interdependent manner.
5. **Control**—the degree to which rules, policies, and direct supervision are used to oversee and control employee behavior.
6. **Risk tolerance**—the degree to which employees are encouraged to be aggressive, innovative, and risk seeking.
7. **Reward criteria**—the degree to which rewards such as promotion and salary increases are allocated according to employee performance rather than seniority, favoritism, or other nonperformance factors.
8. **Conflict tolerance**—the degree to which employees are encouraged to air conflicts and criticisms openly.
9. **Means versus ends orientation**—the degree to which management focuses on outcomes rather than on techniques and processes used to achieve those results.
10. **Open-system focus**—the degree to which the organization monitors and responds to changes in the external environment.

As shown in Figure 3.5, each of these dimensions exists on a continuum. Assessing an organization according to these 10 dimensions provides a composite picture of the organization's culture. This picture becomes the basis for feelings of shared

[5] Harrison, M. T., and J. M. Beyer, *The Culture of Organizations* (Englewood Cliffs, NJ: Prentice Hall, 1993); O'Reilly, C. A., J. Chatman, and D. F. Caldwell, "People and Organizational Culture: A Profile Comparison Approach to Assessing Person-Organization Fit," *Academy of Management Journal*, vol. 34, no. 3 (September 1991), pp. 487–516; Schein, E., *Organizational Culture and Leadership: A Dynamic* View (San Francisco, CA: Jossey-Bass, 2010).

FIGURE 3.5
Key Dimensions Defining an Organization's Culture

Dimension	Left pole	Right pole
1. Member identity	Job	Organization
2. Team emphasis	Individual	Group
3. Management focus	Task	People
4. Unit integration	Independent	Interdependent
5. Control	Loose	Tight
6. Risk tolerance	Low	High
7. Reward criteria	Performance	Other
8. Conflict tolerance	Low	High
9. Means-ends orientation	Means	Ends
10. Open-system focus	Internal	External

understanding that the members have about the organization, how things are done, and the way members are supposed to behave.

Culture performs several important functions in organizations. An organization's culture *provides a sense of identity* for its members. The more clearly an organization's shared perceptions and values are stated, the more strongly people can identify with their organization and feel a vital part of it. Identity generates commitment to the organization and reasons for members to devote energy and loyalty to the organization.

A second important function is that culture *helps legitimize the management system* of the organization. Culture helps clarify authority relationships. It provides reasons why people are in a position of authority and why their authority should be respected.

Most importantly, organizational culture *clarifies and reinforces standards of behavior.* Culture helps define what is permissible and inappropriate behavior. These standards span a wide range of behavior from dress code and working hours to challenging the judgment of superiors and collaborating with other departments. Ultimately culture *helps create social order* within an organization. Imagine what it would be like if members didn't share similar beliefs, values, and assumptions—chaos! The customs, norms, and ideals conveyed by the culture of an organization provide the stability and predictability in behavior that are essential for an effective organization. See Snapshot from Practice 3.4: Google-y for an example of this.

Although our discussion of organizational culture may appear to suggest one culture dominates the entire organization, in reality, this is rarely the case. *Strong* and *thick* are adjectives used to denote a culture in which the organization's core values and customs are widely shared within the entire organization. Conversely, a *thin* or *weak* culture is one that is not widely shared or practiced within a firm.

Even within a strong organizational culture, there are likely to be subcultures, often aligned within specific departments or specialty areas. As noted earlier in our discussion of project management structures, it is not uncommon for norms, values, and customs to develop within a specific field or profession such as marketing, finance, or operations. People working in the Marketing Department may have a different set of norms and values than those working in Finance.

Countercultures sometimes emerge within organizations that embody a different set of values, beliefs, and customs—often in direct contradiction with the culture

SNAPSHOT FROM PRACTICE 3.5 Google-y*

On entering the 24-hour Googleplex located in Mountain View, California, you feel that you are walking through a new-age college campus rather than the corporate office of a billion-dollar business. The interconnected low-rise buildings with colorful, glass-encased offices feature upscale trappings—free gourmet meals three times a day, free use of an outdoor wave pool, indoor gym and large child care facility and private shuttle bus service to and from San Francisco and other residential areas—that are the envy of workers across the Bay Area. These perks and others reflect Google's culture of keeping people happy and thinking in unconventional ways.

Jade/Blend Images

The importance of corporate culture is no more evident than in the fact that the head of Human Resources, Stacy Savides Sullivan, also has the title of chief culture officer. Her task is to try to preserve the innovative culture of a start-up as Google quickly evolves into a mammoth international corporation. Sullivan characterizes Google culture as "team-oriented, very collaborative and encouraging people to think nontraditionally, different from where they ever worked before—work with integrity and for the good of the company and for the good of the world, which is tied to our overall mission of making information accessible to the world." Google goes to great lengths to screen new employees to make sure not only that they have outstanding technical capabilities but also that they are going to fit Google's culture. Sullivan goes on to define a Google-y employee as somebody who is "flexible, adaptable, and not focusing on titles and hierarchy, and just gets stuff done."

Google's culture is rich with customs and traditions not found in most corporations. For example, project teams typically have daily "stand-up" meetings seven minutes after the hour. Why seven minutes after the hour? Because Google co-founder Sergey Brin once estimated that it took seven minutes to walk across the Google campus. Everybody stands to make sure no one gets too comfortable and no time is wasted during the rapid-fire update. As one manager noted, "The whole concept of the stand-up is to talk through what everyone's doing, so if someone is working on what you're working on, you can discover and collaborate not duplicate."

Another custom is "dogfooding." This is when a project team releases the functional prototype of a future product to Google employees for them to test drive. There is a strong norm within Google to test new products and provide feedback to the developers. The project team receives feedback from thousands of Google-ys. The internal focus group can log bugs or simply comment on design or functionality. Fellow Google-ys do not hold back on their feedback and are quick to point out things they don't like. This often leads to significant product improvements.

*S. K. Goo, "Building a 'Googley' Workforce," *Washington Post*, October 21, 2006; E. Mills, "Meet Google's Culture Czar," *CNET News.com*, April 27, 2007; H. Walters, "How Google Got Its New Look," *BusinessWeek*, May 10, 2010.

espoused by top management. How pervasive these subcultures and countercultures are affects the strength of the culture of the organization and the extent to which culture influences members' actions and responses.

Identifying Cultural Characteristics

Deciphering an organization's culture is a highly interpretative, subjective process that requires assessment of both current and past history. The student of culture cannot simply rely on what people report about their culture. The physical environment in which people work, as well as how people act and respond to different events that

FIGURE 3.6 Organizational Culture Diagnosis Worksheet

Power Corp.

I. Physical Characteristics:
Architecture, office layout, décor, attire

Corporate HQ is a 20-story modern building—president on top floor. Offices are bigger in the top floors than lower floors. Formal business attire (white shirts, ties, power suits, . . .). Power appears to increase the higher up you are.

II. Public Documents:
Annual reports, internal newsletters, vision statements

At the heart of the Power Corp. way is our vision . . . to be the global energy company most admired for its people, partnership, and performance.

Integrity. We are honest with others and ourselves. We meet the highest ethical standards in all business dealings. We do what we say we will do.

III. Behavior:
Pace, language, meetings, issues discussed, decision-making style, communication patterns, rituals

Hierarchical decision making, pace brisk but orderly, meetings start on time and end on time, subordinates choose their words very carefully when talking to superiors, people rarely work past 6:00 p.m., president takes top-performing unit on a boat cruise each year. . . .

IV. Folklore:
Stories, anecdotes, heroines, heroes, villains

Young project manager was fired after going over his boss's head to ask for additional funds.

Stephanie C. was considered a hero for taking complete responsibility for a technical error.

Jack S. was labeled a traitor for joining chief competitor after working for Power Corp. for 15 years.

occur, must be examined. Figure 3.6 contains a worksheet for diagnosing the culture of an organization. Although by no means exhaustive, the checklist often yields clues about the norms, customs, and values of an organization.

1. **Study the physical characteristics of an organization.** What does the external architecture look like? What image does it convey? Is it unique? Are the buildings and offices the same quality for all employees? Or are modern buildings and fancier offices reserved for senior executives or managers from a specific department? What are the customs concerning dress? What symbols does the organization use to signal authority and status within the organization? These physical characteristics can shed light on who has real power within the organization, the extent to which the organization is internally differentiated, and how formal the organization is in its business dealings.
2. **Read about the organization.** Examine annual reports, mission statements, press releases, and internal newsletters. What do they describe? What principles are espoused in these documents? Do the reports emphasize the people who work for the organization and what they do or the financial performance of the firm? Each emphasis reflects a different culture. The first demonstrates concern for the people who make up the company. The second may suggest a concern for results and the bottom line.
3. **Observe how people interact within the organization.** What is their pace—is it slow and methodical or urgent and spontaneous? What rituals exist within the organization? What values do they express? Meetings can often yield insightful information. Who are the people at the meetings? Who does the talking? To whom do they talk? How candid is the conversation? Do people speak for the organization

or for the individual department? What is the focus of the meetings? How much time is spent on various issues? Issues that are discussed repeatedly and at length are clues about the values of the organization's culture.

4. **Interpret stories and folklore surrounding the organization.** Look for similarities among stories told by different people. The subjects highlighted in recurring stories often reflect what is important to an organization's culture. For example, many of the stories that are repeated at Versatec, a Xerox subsidiary that makes graphic plotters for computers, involve their flamboyant co-founder, Renn Zaphiropoulos. According to company folklore, one of the very first things Renn did when the company was formed was to assemble the top management team at his home. They then devoted the weekend to handmaking a beautiful teak conference table, around which all future decisions would be made. This table came to symbolize the importance of teamwork and maintaining high standards of performance, two essential qualities of the culture at Versatec.

   One should also try to identify who the heroes and villains are in company folklore. What do they suggest about the culture's ideals? Returning to the Versatec story, when the company was eventually purchased by Xerox, many employees expressed concern that Versatec's informal, play hard/work hard culture would be overwhelmed by the bureaucracy at Xerox. Renn rallied the employees to superior levels of performance by arguing that if they exceeded Xerox's expectations they would be left alone. Autonomy has remained a fixture of Versatec's culture long after Renn's retirement.

   It is also important to pay close attention to the basis for promotions and rewards. What do people see as the keys to getting ahead within the organization? What contributes to downfalls? These last two questions can yield important insights into the qualities and behaviors the organization honors as well as the cultural taboos and behavioral land mines that can derail a career. For example, one project manager confided that a former colleague was sent to project management purgatory soon after publicly questioning the validity of a marketing report. From that point on, the project manager was extra careful to privately consult the Marketing Department whenever she had questions about their data.

With practice, an observer can assess how strong the dominant culture of an organization is and the significance of subcultures and countercultures. Furthermore, learners can discern and identify where the culture of an organization stands on the 10 cultural dimensions presented earlier and, in essence, begin to build a cultural profile for a firm. Based on this profile, conclusions can be drawn about specific customs and norms that need to be adhered to, as well as those behaviors and actions that violate the norms of a firm.

3.5 Implications of Organizational Culture for Organizing Projects

LO 3-7

Understand the interaction between project management structure and the culture of an organization.

Project managers have to be able to operate in several, potentially diverse, organizational cultures. First, on internal projects, they have to interact with the culture of their parent organization as well as the subcultures of various departments (e.g., Marketing, Accounting). On external projects, they also have to interact with the project's client or customer organizations. Finally, they often have to interact in varying degrees with a host of other organizations connected to the project. These organizations include suppliers and vendors, subcontractors, consulting firms, government and regulatory agencies, and in many cases community groups. Many of these organizations are likely to

FIGURE 3.7
Cultural Dimensions of an Organization Supportive of Project Management

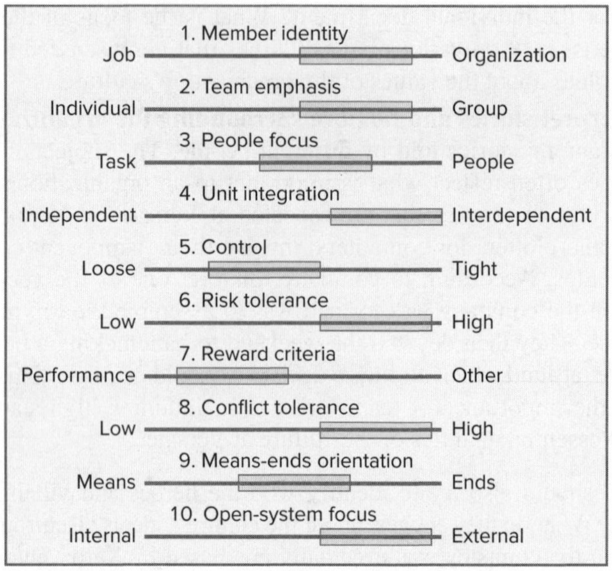

have very different cultures. Project managers have to be able to read and speak the culture they are working in to develop strategies, plans, and responses that are likely to be understood and accepted. Still, the emphasis of this chapter is on the relationship between organizational culture and project management structure, and it is necessary to defer further discussion of these implications until Chapters 10–12, which focus on leadership, team building, and outsourcing.

Earlier we stated that we believe there are strong relationships among project management structure, organizational culture, and successful project management. To explore these relationships further, let us return to the dimensions that can be used to characterize the culture of an organization. When examining these dimensions we could hypothesize that certain aspects of the culture of an organization would support successful project management, while other aspects would deter or interfere with effective management. Figure 3.7 attempts to identify which cultural characteristics create an environment conducive to completing most complex projects involving people from different disciplines.

Note that in many cases the ideal culture is not at either extreme. For example, a fertile project culture would likely be one in which management balances its focus on the needs of both the task and the people. An optimal culture would balance concern with output (ends) and processes to achieve those outcomes (means). In other cases, the ideal culture would be on one end of a dimension. For example, because most projects require collaboration across disciplines, it would be desirable that the culture of the organization emphasize working in teams and identifying with the organization, not just the professional domain. Likewise, it is important that the culture support a certain degree of risk taking and a tolerance for constructive conflict.

One organization that appears to fit this ideal profile is 3M. 3M has received acclaim for creating an entrepreneurial culture within a large corporate framework. The essence of its culture is captured in phrases that have been chanted often by 3Mers throughout its history: "Encourage experimental doodling." "Hire good people and leave them alone." "If you put fences around people, you get sheep. Give people the room they need." Freedom and autonomy to experiment are reflected in the "15 percent rule," which encourages technical people to spend up to 15 percent of their time on projects of their own choosing and initiative. This fertile culture has contributed to 3M's branching out into more than 60,000 products and 35 separate business units (Collins & Porras, 1994).

The metaphor we choose to describe the relationship between organizational culture and project management is that of a riverboat trip. Culture is the river and the project is the boat. Organizing and completing projects within an organization in which the culture is conducive to project management is like paddling downstream: much less effort is required. In many cases, the current can be so strong that steering is all that is required. Such is the case for projects that operate in a project-friendly environment where teamwork and cross-functional cooperation are the norms, where there is a deep commitment to excellence, and where healthy conflict is voiced and dealt with quickly and effectively.

Conversely, trying to complete a project in a toxic culture is like paddling upstream: much more time, effort, and attention are needed to reach the destination. This would be the situation in cultures that discourage teamwork and cooperation, that have a low tolerance for conflict, and where getting ahead is based less on performance and more on cultivating favorable relationships with superiors. In such cases, the project manager and his or her people have to overcome not only the natural obstacles of the project but also the prevailing negative forces inherent in the culture of the organization.

The implications of this metaphor are important. Greater project authority and time are necessary to complete projects that encounter a strong, negative cultural current. Conversely, less formal authority and fewer dedicated resources are needed to complete projects in which the cultural currents generate behavior and cooperation essential to project success.

The key issue is the degree of interdependency between the parent organization and the project team. In cases where the prevalent organizational culture supports the behaviors essential to project completion, a weaker, more flexible project management structure can be effective. For example, one of the major reasons Chaparral Steel is able to use a functional matrix to successfully complete incremental projects is that its culture contains strong norms for cooperation (Bowen et al., 1994). See Research Highlight 3.1: The Secret of Success for another example of how culture supports successful project management.

When the dominant organizational culture inhibits collaboration and innovation, it is advisable to insulate the project team from the dominant culture. Here it becomes necessary to create a self-sufficient project team. If a dedicated project team is impossible because of resource constraints, then at least a project matrix should be used where the project manager has dominant control over the project. In both cases, the managerial strategy is to create a distinct team subculture in which a new set of norms, customs, and values evolves that will be conducive to project completion.

Under extreme circumstances, this project culture could even represent a counterculture in that many of the norms and values are the antithesis of the dominant, parent culture. Such was the case when IBM decided to develop their personal computer quickly in 1980 (Smith & Reinertsen, 1995). They knew that the project could get bogged down by the overabundance of computer knowledge and bureaucracy in the company. IBM also realized that they would have to work closely with suppliers and make use of many non-IBM parts if they were to get to the market quickly. This was not the IBM way at the time, so IBM established the Personal Computer (PC) project team in a warehouse in Boca Raton, Florida, far from corporate headquarters and other corporate development facilities that existed within the organization.

Research Highlight 3.1

The Secret of Success*

In *The Secret of Success: The Double Helix of Formal and Informal Structures in an R&D Laboratory,* Polly Rizova revealed the results of a year-long investigation into the inner workings of a Fortune 500 R&D laboratory. Through interviews with key participants and analysis of social networking data, Rizova assessed the efficacy of six high-tech development projects.

Four critical success factors emerged from her research. One element that is crucial to success is a heavy reliance on open and unrestricted patterns of communication, coupled with a low degree of formal reporting. In other words, team members freely interacted with each other regardless of title, experience, or discipline.

A second key is having individuals on the project who are highly respected across the laboratory for their exceptional technical skills and experience. Similarly, it is also vital to have individuals involved in the project who are highly respected for their organizational expertise and experience. Having both "technical stars" and "organizational stars" on the project team is essential to success.

The final factor is a strong and sustained support for the project from the company's corporate management. What's more, her analysis revealed the interactive nature of the four conditions, namely, that no one condition was likely to produce successful outcomes on its own, but only when put together in a way in which they reinforce each other. Here the culture of the laboratory was seen as the key catalyst.

Rizova describes a matrix system in which people work on multiple projects simultaneously but with a different wrinkle. Individuals occupy different positions and play different roles depending upon the project. For example, it is common for a senior engineer to be the manager of one project and a researcher on another that is led by his or her subordinate. In essence, one must "boss" his or her own boss. At first glance, this formal structure should create destructive tensions. However, Rizova argues that the organizational culture of the lab is the glue that keeps things running smoothly.

She describes a culture in which the social norms of cooperation, respect, and civility are upheld and reproduced. It is a culture characterized by trust and a strong drive toward superior individual and organizational learning and achievement. The culture is captured in the comments of researchers:

> That is one of the nicest things around here. Your opinions are listened to. Superiors consider our advice. You will find that most of the projects here are a team effort.
>
> What I like most is the positive thinking and the "whatever it takes" attitude. Personality conflicts can be devastating. Here everyone helps you and supports you. There is no "I" in the word team.
>
> Very friendly environment. . . . I met new people and learned a lot from them. They do not mind sharing their expertise.

*P. S. Rizova, *The Secret of Success: The Double Helix of Formal and Informal Structures in an R&D Laboratory* (Stanford, CA: Stanford University Press, 2007).

Research Highlight 3.2

Multinational Project and Organizational Culture – Case of India and Russia

Multicultural project teams drive innovation and creativity but pose management challenges, especially in binational projects involving two equally represented cultures. A study by Titov (2020)* analyzed 175 projects in Russia and 200 in India, highlighting significant differences in organizational cultures and project management systems. Using GLOBE project data (2004), cultural similarities were assessed across 18 measures, revealing a high cultural distance between India and Russia.

The PMPQ model by Zwikael and Globerson (2018) compared 33 elements of project management systems through surveys of 378 managers. Findings offer tools and measures to enhance the effectiveness of binational project teams.

The study reveals significant differences between the organizational cultures of India and Russia, with a similarity index of 25.25, calculated using a clustering algorithm. The analysis shows a high cultural distance between the two nations, exceeding the distance between Russia and South Korea, Poland, or Argentina, and between India and Malaysia, Egypt, or Japan. India's project management system, evaluated through the PMPQ model, scored higher than Russia's on 28 out of 33 processes, indicating greater maturity. Without intervention, Indo-Russian projects may face systemic challenges due to these differences. Recommendations include intercultural communication training, assessing and improving the maturity of Russian project management systems, and aligning methodologies between the two countries.

*Sergei Titov, Alexandr Birukov, Elena Vichodtseva (2020), Organizational Culture and Project Management in India and Russia in the Context of Binational Projects, TEM Journal, Volume 9, Issue 2, Pages 601–605

Summary

This chapter examined two major characteristics of the parent organization that affect the implementation and completion of projects. The first is the formal structure of the organization and how it chooses to organize and manage projects. Although the individual project manager may have very little say as to how the firm chooses to manage projects, s/he must be able to recognize the options available as well as the inherent strengths and weaknesses of different approaches.

Three basic project management structures were described and assessed as to their weaknesses and strengths. Only under unique circumstances can a case be made for managing a project within the normal functional hierarchy. When thinking only in terms of what is best for the project, the creation of an independent project team is clearly favored. However, the most effective project management system appropriately balances the needs of the project with those of the parent organization. Matrix structures emerged out of the parent organization's need to share personnel and resources across multiple projects and operations while creating legitimate project focus. The matrix approach is a hybrid organizational form that combines elements of both the functional and the project team forms in an attempt to realize the advantages of both.

The second major characteristic of the parent organization that was discussed in this chapter is the concept of organizational culture. Organizational culture is the pattern of beliefs and expectations shared by an organization's members. Culture includes the behavioral norms, customs, shared values, and "rules of the game" for getting along and getting ahead within the organization. It is important for project managers to be "culture sensitive" so that they can develop appropriate strategies and responses and avoid violating key norms that would jeopardize their effectiveness within the organization. We opened this chapter with a quote from renowned management thinker, Peter Drucker: "Culture eats strategy for breakfast." One might say that the theme of this chapter is "Culture eats project structures for lunch." In both cases, we are alluding to the dominant role that the culture of an organization plays in pursuing objectives and managing projects. Regardless of how effective your strategy or project structure is supposed to be, the culture of your company ultimately determines success.

The interaction between project management structure and organizational culture is a complicated one. We have suggested that in certain organizations, culture encourages the implementation of projects. In this environment, the project management structure used plays a less decisive role in the success of the project. Conversely, for other organizations in which the culture stresses internal competition and differentiation, just the opposite may be true. The prevailing norms, customs, and attitudes inhibit effective project management, and the project management structure plays a more decisive role in the successful implementation of projects. At a minimum, under adverse cultural conditions, the project manager needs to have significant authority over the project team; under more extreme conditions, firms should physically relocate dedicated project teams to complete critical projects. In both cases, the managerial strategy should be to insulate project work from the dominant culture so that a more positive subculture can emerge among project participants.

The project management structure of the organization and the culture of the organization are major elements of the environment in which a project is initiated. Subsequent chapters will examine how project managers and professionals work within this environment to successfully complete projects.

Key Terms

Balanced matrix, *98*
Dedicated project team, *91*
Matrix, *96*
Organizational culture, *105*
Projectitis, *95*
Projectized organization, *93*
Project management office (PMO), *100*
Strong matrix, *98*
Weak matrix, *98*

Review Questions

1. What are the relative advantages and disadvantages of the functional, matrix, and dedicated team approaches to managing projects?
2. What distinguishes a weak matrix from a strong matrix?
3. Under what conditions would it be advisable to use a strong matrix instead of a dedicated project team?
4. How can project management offices (PMOs) support effective project management?
5. Why is it important to assess the culture of an organization before deciding what project management structure should be used to complete a project?
6. Other than culture, what other organizational factors should be used to determine which project management structure should be used?
7. What do you believe is more important for successfully completing a project—the formal project management structure or the culture of the parent organization?

SNAPSHOT FROM PRACTICE

Discussion Questions

3.1 *Skunk Works at Lockheed Martin*

1. Do you agree that true innovation can only come from a small group of dedicated professionals?

3.2 *The Birth of the Mac*

1. Is projectitis the price you pay for truly innovative projects?
2. What similarities and differences do you see between Lockheed's Skunk Works and Apple's Mac team?

3.4 *2018 PMO of the Year: Telstra—Capital Planning & Delivery PMO, Melbourne, Australia*

1. Which of the four kinds of PMOs described in the chapter does Telstra's PMO appear to be?

3.5 *Google-y*

1. How important do you think the perks Google employees receive are for maintaining the culture of Google?
2. How does the custom of "dogfooding" contribute to the culture at Google?

2021 PMO of the Year: Moffitt Cancer Center

1. Which of the four kinds of PMOs described in the chapter does the PMO at Moffitt Cancer Center appear to be?

Exercises

1. Going to college is analogous to working in a matrix environment in that most students take more than one class and must distribute their time across multiple classes. What problems does this situation create for you? How does it affect your performance? How could the system be better managed to make your life less difficult and more productive?
2. You work for LL Company, which manufactures high-end optical scopes for hunting rifles. LL Company has been the market leader for the past 20 years and has decided to diversify by applying its technology to develop a top-quality binocular. What kind of project management structure would you recommend they use for this project? What information would you like to have to make this recommendation and why?
3. You work for Barbata Electronics. Your R&D people believe they have come up with an affordable technology that will double the capacity of existing MP3 players and use an audio format that is superior to MP3. The project is code named KYSO (Knock Your Socks Off). What kind of project management structure would you recommend they use for the KYSO project? What information would you like to have to make this recommendation and why?
4. This chapter discussed the role of values and beliefs in forming an organization's culture. The topic of organizational culture is big business on the Internet. Many companies use their Web pages to describe their mission, vision, and corporate values and beliefs. There also are many consulting firms that advertise how they help organizations change their culture. The purpose of this exercise is for you to obtain information pertaining to the organizational culture for two different companies. You can go about this task by very simply searching the key words *organizational culture* or *corporate vision and values.* This search will identify numerous companies for you to use to answer the following

questions. You may want to select companies that you would like to work for in the future.

a. What are the espoused values and beliefs of the companies?

b. Use the worksheet in Figure 3.6 to assess the Web page. What does the Web page reveal about the culture of this organization? Would this culture be conducive to effective project management?

5. Use the cultural dimensions listed in Figure 3.5 to assess the culture of your school. Instead of employees, consider students, and instead of management, use faculty. For example, *member identity* refers to the degree to which students identify with the school as a whole rather than their major or option. Either as individuals or in small groups, rate the culture of your school on the 10 dimensions.

 a. Which dimensions were easy to evaluate and which were not?

 b. How strong is the culture of your school?

 c. What functions does the culture serve for your school?

 d. Do you think the culture of your school is best suited to maximizing your learning? Why or why not?

 e. What kind of projects would be easy to implement in your school and what kind of projects would be difficult, given the structure and culture of your school? Explain your answer.

6. You work as an analyst in the Marketing Department of Springfield International (SI). SI uses a weak matrix to develop new services. Management has created an extremely competitive organizational culture that places an emphasis upon achieving results above everything else. One of the project managers you have been assigned to help has been pressuring you to make his project your number one priority. He also wants you to expand the scope of your work on his project beyond what your marketing manager believes is necessary or appropriate. The project manager is widely perceived as a rising star within SI. Up to now you have been resisting the project manager's pressure and complying with your marketing manager's directives. However, your most recent interchange with the project manager ended by his saying, "I'm not happy with the level of help I am getting from you and I will remember this when I become VP of Marketing." How would you respond and why?

References

Block, T. R., and J. D. Frame, *The Project Office—a Key to Managing Projects Effectively* (Menlo Park, CA: Crisp Publications, 1998).

Block, T. R., and J. D. Frame, "Today's Project Office: Gauging Attitudes," *PM Network,* August 2001, pp. 13–16.

Bowen, H. K., K. B. Clark, C. A. Holloway, and S. C. Wheelwright, *The Perpetual Enterprise Machine* (New York: Oxford University Press, 1994).

Brown, S., and K. R. Eisenhardt, "Product Development: Past Research, Present Findings, and Future Directions," *Academy of Management Review,* vol. 20, no. 2 (1995), pp. 343–78.

Cabanis-Brewin, J., "The PMP at 20: New Research Findings Released," May 17, 2022, pmsolutions.com. Accessed 6/14/22.

Cameron, K. S., and R. E. Quinn, *Diagnosing and Changing Organizational Culture: Based on the Competing Values Framework* (Upper Saddle River, NJ: Prentice Hall, 2011).

Casey, W., and W. Peck, "Choosing the Right PMO Setup," *PM Network,* August 2001, pp. 40–47.

Collins, J. C., and J. I. Porras, *Built to Last: The Successful Habits of Visionary Companies* (New York: HarperCollins, 1994), pp. 150–58.

de Laat, P. B., "Matrix Management of Projects and Power Struggles: A Case Study of an R&D Laboratory," *Human Relations,* vol. 47, no. 9 (September 1994), pp. 1089–119.

Deal, T. E., and A. A. Kennedy, *Corporate Cultures: The Rites and Rituals of Corporate Life* (Reading, MA: Addison-Wesley, 1982).

Filipczak, B., "Beyond the Gates of Microsoft," *Training,* September 1992, pp. 37–44.

Graham, R. J., and R. L. Englund, *Creating an Environment for Successful Projects: The Quest to Manage Project Management* (San Francisco: Jossey-Bass, 1997).

Gray, C., S. Dworatschek, D. H. Gobeli, H. Knoepfel, and E. W. Larson, "International Comparison of Project Organization Structures: Use and Effectiveness," *International Journal of Project Management,* vol. 8, no. 1 (February 1990), pp. 26–32.

Hobbs, B., and P. Ménard, "Organizational Choices for Project Management," in Paul Dinsmore (ed.), *The AMA Handbook of Project Management* (New York: AMACOM, 1993).

Hobday, M., "The Project-Based Organization: An Ideal Form for Managing Complex Products and Systems?" *Research Policy,* vol. 29, no. 17 (2000), pp. 871–93.

Jassawalla, A. R., and H. C. Sashittal, "Cultures That Support Product-Innovation Processes," *Academy of Management Executive,* vol. 15, no. 3 (2002), pp. 42–54.

Johnson, C. L., M. Smith, and L. K. Geary, *More Than My Share in All* (Washington, D.C.: Smithsonian Institute Publications, 1990).

Kerzner, H., "Strategic Planning for the Project Office," *Project Management Journal,* vol. 34, no. 2 (2003), pp. 13–25.

Larson, E. W., "Project Management Structures," in P. Morris and J. Pinto (eds.), *The Wiley Handbook for Managing Projects* (New York: Wiley, 2004), pp. 48–66.

Larson, E. W., and D. H. Gobeli, "Matrix Management: Contradictions and Insights," *California Management Review,* vol. 29, no. 4 (Summer 1987), pp. 137–49.

Larson, E. W., and D. H. Gobeli, "Organizing for Product Development Projects," *Journal of Product Innovation Management,* vol. 5, no. 3 (September 1988), pp. 180–90.

Larsson, U. (ed.), *Cultures of Creativity: The Centennial Exhibition of the Nobel Prize* (Canton, MA: Science History Publications, 2001).

Laslo, Z., and A. I. Goldberg, "Matrix Structures and Performance: The Search for Optimal Adjustments to Organizational Objectives?" *IEEE Transactions in Engineering Management,* vol. 48, no. 12 (2001), pp. 144–56.

Lawrence, P. R., and J. W. Lorsch, *Organization and Environment* (Homewood, IL: Irwin, 1969).

Lechler, T., and D. Dvir, "An Alternative Taxonomy of Project Management Structures: Linking Project Management Structures and Project Success," *IEEE Transactions on Engineering Management,* vol. 57 (2010), pp. 198–210.

Majchrzak, A., and Q. Wang, "Breaking the Functional Mind-Set in Process Organizations," *Harvard Business Review,* September–October 1996, pp. 93–99.

Olson, E. M., O. C. Walker, Jr., and R. W. Ruekert, "Organizing for Effective New Product Development: The Moderating Role of Product Innovativeness," *Journal of Marketing,* vol. 59, no. 1 (January 1995), pp. 48–62.

Patel, B., "The Many Benefits of an Agile PMO: What You Should Know," www.forbes.com/. . ./the-many-benefits-of-an-agile-pmo-what-you-should-know, June 13, 2018. Accessed 8/28/18.

Pettegrew, A. M., "On Studying Organizational Culture," *Administrative Science Quarterly,* vol. 24, no. 4 (1979), pp. 570–81.

Powell, M., and J. Young, "The Project Management Support Office" in P. Morris and J. Pinto (eds.), *The Wiley Handbook for Managing Projects* (New York: Wiley, 2004), pp. 937–69.

Rebello, K., "Inside Microsoft," *Business Weekly,* July 15, 1996, pp. 56–67.

Shenhar, A. J., "From Theory to Practice: Toward a Typology of Project Management Styles," *IEEE Transactions in Engineering Management,* vol. 41, no. 1 (1998), pp. 33–48.

Shenhar, A. J., D. Dvir, T. Lechler, and M. Poli, "One Size Does Not Fit All—True for Projects, True for Frameworks," *Frontiers of Project Management Research and Application,* Proceedings of PMI Research Conference, Seattle, 2002, pp. 99–106.

Smith, P. G., and D. G. Reinertsen, *Developing Products in Half the Time* (New York: Van Nostrand Reinhold, 1995).

Stuckenbruck, L. C., *Implementation of Project Management* (Upper Darby, PA: Project Management Institute, 1981).

Youker, R., "Organizational Alternatives for Project Management," *Project Management Quarterly,* vol. 8, no. 1 (March 1977), pp. 24–33.

Case 3.1

Moss and McAdams Accounting Firm

Bruce Palmer had worked for Moss and McAdams (M&M) for six years and was just promoted to account manager. His first assignment was to lead an audit of Johnsonville Trucks. He was quite pleased with the five accountants who had been assigned to his team, especially Zeke Olds. Olds was an army vet who had returned to school to get a double major in accounting and computer sciences. He was on top of the latest developments in financial information systems and had a reputation for coming up with innovative solutions to problems.

M&M was a well-established regional accounting firm with 160 employees located across six offices in Minnesota and Wisconsin. The main office, where Palmer worked, was in Green Bay, Wisconsin. In fact, one of the founding members, Seth Moss, played briefly for the hometown NFL Packers during the late 1950s. M&M's primary services were corporate audits and tax preparation. Over the last two years, the partners decided to move more aggressively into the consulting business. M&M projected that consulting would represent 40 percent of their growth over the next five years.

M&M operated within a matrix structure. As new clients were recruited, a manager was assigned to the account. A manager could be assigned to several accounts, depending on the size and scope of the work. This was especially true in the case of tax preparation projects, where it was not uncommon for a manager to be assigned to 8–12 clients. Likewise, senior and staff accountants were assigned to multiple account teams. Ruby Sands was the office manager responsible for assigning personnel to different accounts at the Green Bay office. She did her best to assign staff to multiple projects under the same manager. This wasn't always possible, and sometimes accountants had to work on projects led by different managers.

M&M, like most accounting firms, had a tiered promotion system. New CPAs entered as junior or staff accountants. Within two years, their performance was reviewed and they were either asked to leave or promoted to senior accountant. Sometime during their fifth or sixth year, a decision was made to promote them to account manager. Finally, after 10–12 years with the firm, the manager was considered for promotion to partner. This was a very competitive position. During the last five years, only 20 percent of account managers at M&M had been promoted to partner. However, once a partner, they were virtually guaranteed the position for life and enjoyed significant increases in salary, benefits, and prestige. M&M had a reputation for being a results-driven organization; partner promotions were based on meeting deadlines, retaining clients, and generating revenue. The promotion team based its decision on the relative performance of the account manager in comparison to his or her cohorts.

One week into the Johnsonville audit, Palmer received a call from Sands to visit her office. There he was introduced to Ken Crosby, who had recently joined M&M after working nine years for a Big 5 accounting firm. Crosby was recruited to manage special consulting projects. Sands reported that Crosby had just secured a major consulting project with Springfield Metals. This was a major coup for the firm: M&M had competed against two Big 5 accounting firms for the project. Sands went on to explain that she was working with Crosby to put together his team. Crosby insisted that Zeke Olds be assigned to his team. Sands told him that this would be impossible because Olds was already assigned to work on the Johnsonville audit. Crosby persisted, arguing that Olds's expertise was essential to the Springfield project. Sands decided to work out a compromise and have Olds split time across both projects.

At this time Crosby turned to Palmer and said, "I believe in keeping things simple. Why don't we agree that Olds works for me in the mornings and you in the afternoons? I'm sure we can work out any problems that come up. After all, we both work for the same firm."

SIX WEEKS LATER

Palmer could scream whenever he remembered Crosby's words "After all, we both work for the same firm." The first sign of trouble came during the first week of the new arrangement when Crosby called, begging to have Olds work all of Thursday on his project. They were conducting an extensive client visit, and Olds was critical to the assessment. After Palmer reluctantly agreed, Crosby said he owed him one. The next week, when Palmer called Crosby to request that he return the favor, Crosby flatly refused and said any other time but not this week. Palmer tried again a week later and got the same response.

At first, Olds showed up promptly at 1:00 p.m. at Palmer's office to work on the audit. Soon it became a habit to show up 30–60 minutes late. There was always a good reason. He was in a meeting in Springfield and couldn't just leave, or an urgent task took longer than planned. One time it was because Crosby took his entire team out to lunch at the new Thai restaurant—Olds was over an hour late because of slow service. In the beginning Olds usually made up the time by working after hours, but Palmer could tell from conversations he overheard that this was creating tension at home.

What probably bothered Palmer the most were the e-mails and telephone calls Olds received from Crosby and his team members during the afternoons when he was supposed to be working for Palmer. A couple of times Palmer could have sworn that Olds was working on Crosby's project in his (Palmer's) office.

Palmer met with Crosby to talk about the problem and voice his complaints. Crosby acted surprised and even a little hurt. He promised things would change, but the pattern continued.

Palmer was becoming paranoid about Crosby. He knew that Crosby played golf with Olds on the weekends and could just imagine him badmouthing the Johnsonville project and pointing out how boring auditing work was. The sad fact was that there probably was some truth to what he was saying. The Johnsonville project was getting bogged down, and the team was slipping behind schedule. One of the contributing factors was Olds's performance. His work was not up to its usual standards. Palmer approached Olds about this, and Olds became defensive. Olds later apologized and confided that he found it difficult switching his thinking from consulting to auditing and then back to consulting. He promised to do better, and there was a slight improvement in his performance.

The last straw came when Olds asked to leave work early on Friday so that he could take his wife and kids to a Milwaukee Brewers baseball game. It turned out Springfield Metals had given Crosby their corporate tickets, and he decided to treat his team with box seats right behind the Brewers dugout. Palmer hated to do it, but he had to refuse the request. He felt guilty when he overheard Olds explaining to his son on the telephone why they couldn't go to the game.

Palmer finally decided to request an urgent meeting with Sands to resolve the problem. He got up enough nerve and put in the call only to be told that Sands wouldn't be back in the office until next week. As he put the receiver down, he thought maybe things would get better.

TWO WEEKS LATER

Sands showed up unexpectedly at Palmer's office and said they needed to talk about Olds. Palmer was delighted, thinking that now he could tell her what had been going on. But before he had a chance to speak, Sands told him that Olds had come to see her yesterday. She told him that Olds confessed he was having a hard time working on both Crosby's and Palmer's projects. He was having difficulty concentrating on the auditing work in the afternoon because he was thinking about some of the consulting issues that had emerged during the morning. He was putting in extra hours to try to meet both of the projects' deadlines, and this was creating problems at home. The bottom line was that he was stressed out and couldn't deal with the situation. He asked that he be assigned full time to Crosby's project. Sands went on to say that Olds didn't blame Palmer; in fact, he had a lot of nice things to say about him. He just enjoyed the consulting work more and found it more challenging. Sands concluded by saying, "I told him I understood, and I would talk to you about the situation and see what could be done. Frankly, I think we should pull him from your project and have him work full time on Crosby's project. What do you think?"

1. If you were Palmer at the end of the case, how would you respond?
2. What, if anything, could Palmer have done to avoid losing Olds?
3. What advantages and disadvantages of a matrix-type organization are apparent from this case?
4. What could the management at M&M do to manage situations like this more effectively?

Case 3.2

Horizon Consulting

Patti Smith looked up at the bright blue Carolina sky before she entered the offices of Horizon Consulting. It was Friday, which meant she needed to prepare for the weekly status report meeting. Horizon Consulting is a custom software development company that offers fully integrated mobile application services for iPhone™, Android™, Windows Mobile®, and BlackBerry® platforms. Horizon was founded by Lola Thrasher, a former marketing executive, who quickly saw the potential for digital marketing via smartphones. Horizon enjoyed initial success in sports marketing but quickly expanded to other industries. A key to their success was the decline in cost for developing smartphone applications, which expanded the client base. The decline in cost was primarily due to the learning curve and ability to build customized solutions on established platforms.

Patti Smith was a late bloomer who went back to college after working in the restaurant business for nine years. She and her former husband had tried unsuccessfully to operate a vegetarian restaurant in Golden, Colorado. After her divorce, she returned to University of Colorado, where she majored in management information systems (MIS) with a minor in marketing. While she enjoyed her marketing classes much more than her MIS classes, she felt the IT know-how she acquired would give her an advantage in the job market. This turned out to be true, as Horizon hired her to be an account manager soon after graduation.

Patti Smith was hired to replace Stephen Stills, who had started the restaurant side of the business at Horizon. Stephen was "let go," according to one account manager, for being a *prima donna* and hoarding resources. Patti's clients ranged from high-end restaurants to hole-in the-wall "mom and pop shops." She helped develop smartphone apps that let users make reservations, browse menus, receive alerts on daily specials, provide customer feedback, order take-out, and in some cases order delivery. As an account manager, she worked with clients to assess their needs, develop a plan, and create customized smartphone apps.

Horizon appeared to be a good fit for Patti. She had enough technical training to be able to work with software engineers and help guide them to produce client-ready products. At the same time, she could relate to the restaurateurs and enjoyed working with them on web design and digital marketing.

Horizon was organized into three departments: Sales, Software Development, and Graphics, with account managers acting as project managers. Account managers generally came from Sales and divided their time between projects and sales pitches to potential new clients. Horizon employed a core group of software engineers and designers, supplemented by contracted programmers when needed.

The first step in developing a smartphone application involved the account manager meeting with the client to define the requirements and vision for the application. The account manager then worked with a Graphic User Interface (GUI) designer to come up with a preliminary story board of how the application would function and look. Once the initial concept and requirements were approved, the account manager was assigned two pairs of software engineers. The first pair (app engineers) worked on the smartphone side of the application, while the second pair worked on the client side. Horizon preferred to have software engineers work in tandem so that they could check each other's work. The two app engineers typically worked full time on the application until it was completed, while the other engineers worked on multiple projects as needed. Likewise, GUI designers worked on the project at certain key stages in the product development cycle when their expertise was needed.

The head of Graphics managed the GUI designers' schedule, while the head of Software managed the software engineer assignments. At the end of each project, account managers submitted performance reviews of their team. The director of sales was responsible for the account managers' performance reviews based on customer satisfaction, generation of sales, and project performance.

Horizon believed in iterative development, and every two to three weeks account managers were expected to demonstrate the latest version of applications to clients. This led to useful feedback and in many cases redefinition of the scope of the project. Often clients wanted to add more functionality to their application once they realized what the software could do. Depending upon the complexity of the application and changes introduced once the project was under way, it typically took Horizon two to four months to deliver a finished product to a client.

Patti was currently working on three projects. One was for Shanghai Wok, a busy Chinese mom and pop restaurant in downtown Charlotte, North Carolina. The owners of Shanghai Wok wanted Horizon to create a smartphone app that would allow customers to order and pay in advance for meals they would simply pick up at a walk-up window. The second project was for Taste of India, which operated in Kannapolis, North Carolina. They wanted Horizon to create a phone app that would allow staff at the nearby bio-tech firms to order food that would be delivered on-site during lunch and dinner hours. The last project was for Nearly Normal, a vegetarian restaurant that wanted to send out e-mail alerts to subscribers that would describe in detail their daily fresh specials.

Lola Thrasher was an admirer of Google and encouraged a playful but focused environment at work. Employees were allowed to decorate their work spaces, bring pets to work, and play Ping-Pong or pool when they needed a break. Horizon paid its employees well, but the big payoff was the annual Christmas bonus. This bonus was based on overall company profits, which were distributed proportionately based on pay grade and performance reviews. It was not uncommon for employees to receive a 10–15 percent boost in pay at the end of the year.

STATUS REPORT MEETING

As was her habit, Patti entered the status report meeting room early. David Briggs was in the midst of describing the game-winning catch John Lorsch had made in last night's softball game. Horizon sponsored a co-ed city league softball team, which most of the account managers played on. Patti had been coaxed to play to ensure that the requisite number of "females" were on the field. She balked at the idea at first; softball wasn't really her sport, but she was glad she did. Not only was it fun but it gave her a chance to get to know the other managers.

Thrasher entered the room and everyone settled down to business. She started off as she always did, by asking if anybody had important news to bring to everyone's attention. Jackson Browne slowly raised his hand and said, "I am afraid I do. I just received notification from Apple iOS that they have rejected our TAT app." TAT was a phone app, which Jackson was the project lead on, that allowed subscribers to reserve and see in real time what swimming lanes were available at a prestigious athletic club. This announcement was followed by a collective groan. Before an Apple app could go operational it had to be submitted to and approved by Apple. Usually, this was not a problem, but lately Apple had been rejecting apps for a variety of reasons. Jackson went on to circulate the list of changes that had to be made before Apple would approve the app. The group studied the list and in some cases ridiculed the new requirements.

Ultimately Thrasher asked Jackson how long it would take to make the necessary changes and resubmit the app for approval. Jackson felt it would probably take two to three weeks at most. Thrasher asked who the engineers working on this project were. Patti's heart fell. One of the app engineers who had developed the TAT app was working on her Shanghai Wok project. She knew what was going to happen next. Thrasher announced, "OK, everyone, it only makes sense that these engineers are the best ones to finish what they had started, so they are all going to have to be reassigned back to the TAT project. Those affected are going to have to get together after this meeting and figure out how to replace them." The meeting then proceeded as planned, with all the account managers reporting the status of their projects and sharing relevant issues with the group.

POST-MEETING

As everyone filed out, Patti looked around to see who else was in her same boat. There were three other account managers as well as Jackson Browne. Resource assignments were a recurring issue at Horizon, given the nature of their work. Horizon had developed a policy where decisions were made based on project priority. Each project was assigned a Green, Blue, or Orange designation based on the company priority. Priority status was based on the extent to which the project contributed to the mission of the firm. The Shanghai Wok project, given its limited size and scope, was an Orange project, which was the lowest ranking. The list of available software engineers was displayed on the big screen. Patti was familiar with only a few of the names.

Leigh Taylor, who had the only Green project, immediately selected Jason Wheeler from the list. She had used him before and was confident in his work. Tom Watson and Samantha Stewart both had Blue Projects and needed to replace a mobile app engineer. They both immediately jumped on the name of Prem Mathew, claiming he was the best person for their project. After some friendly jousting, Tom said, "OK, Sam, you can have him; I remember when you helped me out on the Argos project; besides, my project is just beginning. I'll take Shin Chen." Everyone looked at Patti; she started by saying, "You know, I am familiar with only a few of these names; I guess I'll go with Mike Thu." Jackson interjected, "Hey, everyone, I am really sorry this happened, and I am sure Mike is a good programmer, but I recommend you work with Axel Gerthoff. I have used him before, and he is a very quick study and a joy to work with." This was a relief to Patti and she quickly took his advice. They left to submit a report to Thrasher detailing the decisions they each had made and the impact on their projects.

1. How successful was the post-meeting?
2. What factors contributed to the success or failure of this meeting?
3. What kind of project management structure does Horizon use? Is it the right structure? Explain.

Design elements: Snapshot from Practice, Highlight box, Case icon: Sky Designs/Shutterstock

CHAPTER FOUR

4 Defining the Project

LEARNING OBJECTIVES

After reading this chapter you should be able to:

4-1 Identify key elements of a project scope statement and understand why a complete scope statement is critical to project success.

4-2 Describe the causes of scope creep and ways to manage it.

4-3 Understand why it is important to establish project priorities in terms of cost, time, and performance.

4-4 Demonstrate the importance of a work breakdown structure (WBS) to the management of projects and how it serves as a database for planning and control.

4-5 Demonstrate how the organization breakdown structure (OBS) establishes accountability to organization units.

4-6 Describe a process breakdown structure (PBS) and when to use it.

4-7 Create responsibility matrices for small projects.

4-8 Create a communication plan for a project.

OUTLINE

4.1 Step 1: Defining the Project Scope

4.2 Step 2: Establishing Project Priorities

4.3 Step 3: Creating the Work Breakdown Structure

4.4 Step 4: Integrating the WBS with the Organization

4.5 Step 5: Coding the WBS for the Information System

4.6 Process Breakdown Structure

4.7 Responsibility Matrices

4.8 Project Communication Plan

4.9 Software Solutions and Emerging Trends in Project Management

Summary

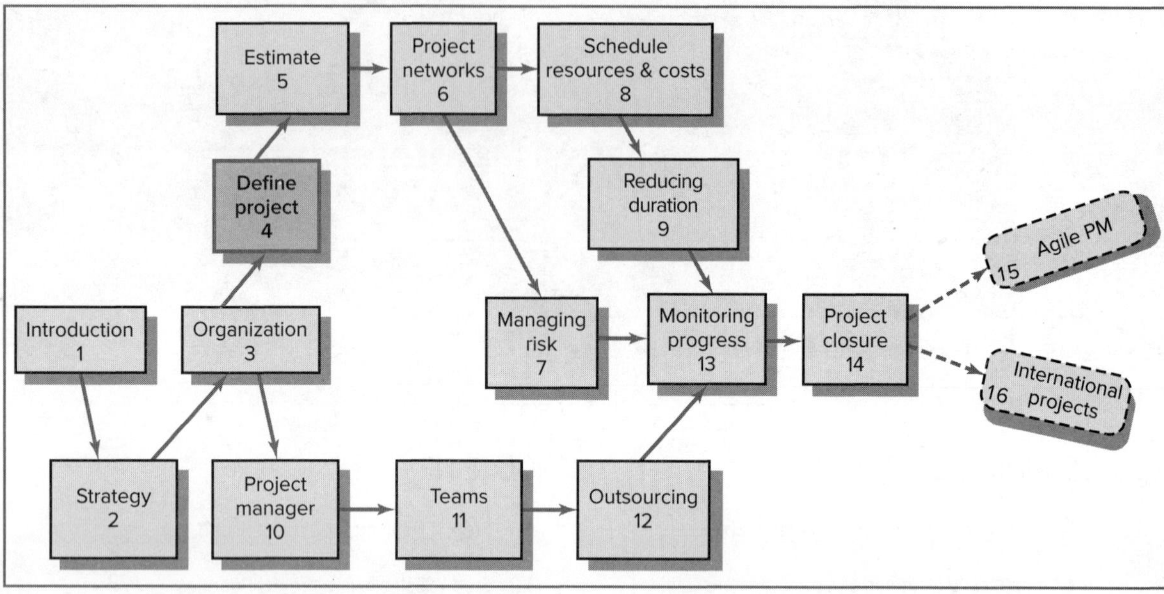

Select a dream
Use your dream to set a goal
Create a plan
Consider resources
Enhance skills and abilities
Spend time wisely
Start! Get organized and go
. . . it is one of those acro-whatevers, said Pooh.

—Roger E. Allen and Stephen D. Allen, Winnie-the-Pooh on Success (New York: Penguin, 1997), p. 10.

Project managers in charge of a single small project can plan and schedule the project tasks without much formal planning and information. However, when the project manager must manage several small projects or a large, complex project, a threshold is quickly reached in which the project manager can no longer cope with the detail.

This chapter describes a disciplined, structured method for selectively collecting information to use through all phases of the project life cycle, to meet the needs of all stakeholders (e.g., customer, management), and to measure performance against the strategic plan of the organization. The suggested method is a selective outline of the project called the *work breakdown structure.* The early stages of developing the outline ensure that all tasks are identified and that project participants have an understanding of what is to be done. Once the outline and its detail are defined, an integrated information system can be developed to schedule work and allocate budgets. This baseline information is later used for control.

In addition, the chapter presents a variant of the work breakdown structure called the *process breakdown structure* as well as *responsibility matrices* that are used for smaller, less complex projects. With the work of the project defined through the *work breakdown structure,* the chapter concludes with the process of creating a communication plan used to help coordinate project activities and follow progress.

The five generic steps described provide a structured approach for collecting the project information necessary for developing a work breakdown structure. These steps and the development of project networks found in the next chapters all take place concurrently, and several iterations are typically required to develop dates and budgets that can be used to manage the project. The old saying "We can control only what we have planned" is true; therefore, defining the project is the first step.

4.1 Step 1: Defining the Project Scope

LO 4-1

Identify key elements of a project scope statement and understand why a complete scope statement is critical to project success.

The project charter authorizes the project manager to begin to define the scope of the project. Defining the project scope sets the stage for developing a detailed project plan. Project scope is a definition of the end result or mission of your project—a product or service for your client/customer. The primary purpose is to define as clearly as possible the deliverable(s) for the end user and to focus project plans.

Research clearly shows that a poorly defined scope or mission is the most frequently mentioned barrier to project success. In a study involving more than 1,400 project managers in the United States and Canada, Gobeli and Larson (1990) found that approximately 50 percent of the planning problems relate to unclear definition of scope and goals. This and other studies suggest a strong correlation between project success and clear scope definition (Ashley et al., 1987; Pinto & Slevin, 1988; Standish Group, 2009). The scope document directs focus on the project purpose throughout the life of the project for the customer and project participants.

The scope should be developed under the direction of the project manager, customer, and other significant stakeholders. The project manager is responsible for seeing that there is agreement with the owner on project objectives, deliverables at each stage of the project, technical requirements, and so forth. For example, a deliverable in the early stage might be specifications; for the second stage, three prototypes for production; for the third, a sufficient quantity to introduce to market; and finally, marketing promotion and training.

Your project scope definition is a document that will be published and used by the project owner and project participants for planning and measuring project success. *Scope* describes what you expect to deliver to your customer when the project is complete. Your project scope should define the results to be achieved in specific, tangible, and measurable terms.

Employing a Project Scope Checklist

Clearly project scope is the keystone interlocking all elements of a project plan. To ensure that scope definition is complete, you may wish to use the following checklist:

Project Scope Checklist
1. Project objective
2. Product scope description
3. Justification
4. Deliverables
5. Milestones
6. Technical requirements
7. Limits and exclusions
8. Acceptance criteria

1. **Project objective.** The first step of project scope definition is to define the overall objective to meet your customer's need(s). For example, as a result of extensive market research a computer software company decides to develop a program that automatically translates verbal sentences in English to Russian. The project should be completed within three years at a cost not to exceed $1.5 million. Another example is to design and construct a portable hazardous-waste thermal treatment system in 13 months at a cost not to exceed $13 million. The project objective answers the questions of what, when, how much, and at times where.
2. **Product scope description.** This step is a detailed description of the characteristics of the product, service, or outcome of the project. The description is progressively elaborated throughout the project. The product scope answers the question "What end result is wanted?" For example, if the product is a cell phone, its product scope will be its screen size, battery, processor, camera type, memory, and so on. These descriptions are often based on product/end-user requirements. Requirements should be prioritized, for example, (1) lightweight, (2) AI (artificial intelligence) capability, (3) connection with other products, (4) attractive, etc. Requirements tend to start off general and become more detailed as more information about the requirements become known.
3. **Justification.** It is important that project team members and stakeholders know why management authorized the project. What is the problem or opportunity the project is addressing? This is sometimes referred to as the *business case* for the project, since it usually includes cost/benefit analysis and strategic significance. For example, on a new-release project, the justification may be an expected ROI of 30 percent and an enhanced reputation in the marketplace.
4. **Deliverables.** The next step is to define major deliverables—the expected, measurable outputs over the life of the project. For example, deliverables in the early design phase of a project might be a list of specifications. In the second phase, deliverables might be software coding and a technical manual. The next phase might be the prototype. The final phase might be final tests and approved software. Note: Deliverables and requirements are often used interchangeably.
5. **Milestones.** A **milestone** is a significant event in a project that occurs at a point in time. The milestone schedule shows only major segments of work; it represents first, rough-cut estimates of time, cost, and resources for the project. The milestone schedule is built using the deliverables as a platform to identify major segments of work and an end date—for example, testing complete and finished by July 1 of the same year. Milestones should be natural, important control points in the project. Achievement of a milestone should be easy for all project participants to recognize.
6. **Technical requirements.** More frequently than not, a product or service will have technical requirements to ensure proper performance. Technical requirements typically clarify the deliverables or define the performance specifications. For example, a technical requirement for a personal computer might be the ability to accept 120-volt alternating current or 240-volt direct current without any adapters or user switches. Another well-known example is the ability of 911 emergency systems to identify the caller's phone number and the location of the phone. Examples from information systems projects include the speed and capacity of database systems and connectivity with alternative systems. For understanding the importance of key requirements, see Snapshot from Practice 4.1: Big Bertha ERC II versus the USGA's COR Requirement.

SNAPSHOT FROM PRACTICE 4.1 Big Bertha ERC II versus the USGA's COR Requirement*

In 1991 Callaway Golf Equipment introduced their Big Bertha driver and revolutionized the golf equipment business. Big Bertha—named after the World War I German long-distance cannon—was much larger than conventional woods and lacked a hosel (the socket in the head of the club into which the shaft is inserted) so that the weight could be better distributed throughout the head. This innovative design gave the clubhead a larger sweet spot, which allowed a player to strike the golf ball off-center and not suffer much loss in distance or accuracy.

In 2000 Callaway introduced the Big Bertha ERC II forged titanium driver. "Designing the ERC II was a dream experience," said Richard C. Helmstetter, senior executive vice president of research and development and chief of new products. "We had no restrictions, so we were able to think outside the box to accomplish our goal of making the energy transfer from club to ball as efficient as possible. This allows golfers to generate more ball speed without swinging harder, which leads to greater distance. We used a combination of advanced new computer design technology and hands-on research with golfers from around the world. As a result, we created some design elements that go beyond any previous driver designs. Feedback from the players who have tested this driver indicates that our efforts dramatically improved the performance all golfers can expect to get from these drivers."*

However, there was a big problem. The new version of Bertha did not conform to the coefficient of restitution (COR) requirement established by the United States Golf Association (USGA). As a result, it was barred from use by golfers in North America who intended to play by the USGA's Rules of Golf.

The USGA felt that the integrity of the game was being threatened by technological advances. Players were hitting balls so much farther and straighter that golf courses around the world were being redesigned to make them longer and more difficult. This was expensive.

Val Thoermer/123RF

So in 1998, the USGA established performance thresholds for all new golf equipment. In order to prevent manufacturers from developing more powerful clubs, the USGA limited the COR of new golf equipment to 0.83. The COR was calculated by firing a golf ball at a driver out of a cannonlike machine at 109 miles per hour. The speed that the ball returned to the cannon could not exceed 83 percent of its initial speed (90.47 mph). The USGA called the ratio of incoming to outgoing velocity the coefficient of restitution (COR). Studies indicated that a 0.01 increase in COR resulted in two extra yards of carry. The Big Bertha ERC II's COR was 0.86.

After numerous efforts to get USGA to change its technical requirements, Callaway's engineers went back to the drawing board and in 2002 introduced Great Big Bertha II, which conformed to USGA's 0.83 COR restriction. They also continued to produce the ERC II.

* L. Dorman, and K. Mallory, "Callaway Golf Introduces ERC II Forged Titanium Driver—Its Hottest And Most Forgiving Driver Ever," www.https://www.topgolfcallawaybrands.com, October 24, 2000. Accessed 01/03/01.

7. **Limits and exclusions.** The limits of scope should be defined. Failure to do so can lead to false expectations and to expending resources and time on the wrong problem. The following are examples of limits: work on-site is allowed only between the hours of 8:30 a.m. and 5:00 p.m.; system maintenance and repair will be done only up to one month after final inspection; and the client will be billed for additional training beyond that prescribed in the contract. Exclusions further define the

boundary of the project by stating what is not included. Examples include: data will be collected by the client, not the contractor; a house will be built, but no landscaping or security devices added; software will be installed, but no training given.

8. **Acceptance criteria.** Acceptance criteria are a set of conditions that must be met before the deliverables are accepted. The following are examples: all tasks and milestones are complete, new service processes begin with a less than 1 percent defect rate, third-party certification is required, and customer on-site inspection is required.

Scope statements are twofold. There is a short, one- to two-page summary of key elements of the scope, followed by extended documentation of each element (e.g., a detailed milestone schedule or risk analysis report). See Snapshot from Practice 4.2: Scope Statement for an example of a summary page.

The project scope checklist in Step 1 is generic. Different industries and companies will develop unique checklists and templates to fit their needs and specific kinds of projects. A few companies engaged in contracted work refer to scope statements as "statements of work (SOWs)." Some organizations use the term *project charter.* However, the term project charter in the world of project management is a document that authorizes the project manager to form a team and initiate the project. This document is issued by upper management and provides the project manager with written authority to use organizational resources for project activities. Often the charter will include a brief scope description as well as such items as risk limits, business case, spending limits, and even team composition.

LO 4-2

Describe the causes of scope creep and ways to manage it.

Many projects suffer from **scope creep,** which is the tendency for the project scope to expand over time—usually by changing requirements, specifications, and priorities. Scope creep can have a positive or negative effect on the project, but in most cases scope creep means added costs and possible project delays. Changes in requirements, specifications, and priorities frequently result in cost overruns and delays. Examples are abundant—the Denver Airport baggage handling system, Boston's new freeway system ("The Big Dig"), the Sochi Winter Olympics, and the list goes on. On software development projects, scope creep is manifested in bloated products in which added functionality undermines ease of use. For a classic example of scope creep, see Snapshot from Practice the Bradley Fighting Vehicle.

Six of the most common causes of scope creep are

- **Poor requirement analysis.** Customers often don't really know what they want. "I'll know it when I see it" syndrome contributes to wasted effort and ambiguity.
- **Not involving users early enough.** Too often project teams think they know what the end user needs, only to find out later they were mistaken. The consequence is requirements are being adding as project progresses.
- **Underestimating project complexity.** Complexity and associated uncertainty naturally lead to changes in scope, since there are so many unknowns yet to be discovered.
- **Too many decision-makers.** Often in order to reduce conflict, unnecessary compromises are made.
- **Lack of change control.** A robust change control process is needed to ensure that only appropriate changes occur in the scope of the project.
- **Gold plating. Gold plating** refers to adding extra value to the project that is beyond the scope of the project. This is common in software projects where developers add features that they like.

SNAPSHOT FROM PRACTICE 4.2 Scope Statement

PROJECT OBJECTIVE

To construct a high-quality, custom house within five months at cost not to exceed $800,000 on lot 42A in Greendale, Oregon.

Ufulum/Shutterstock

PRODUCT SCOPE DESCRIPTION

A 2,200-square-foot, 2½-bath, 3-bedroom, finished home.

DELIVERABLES

- A finished garage, insulated, and sheetrocked.
- Kitchen appliances to include range, oven, microwave, and dishwasher.
- A high-efficiency gas furnace with programmable thermostat.
- Aluminum roofing.

MILESTONES

1. Permits approved—March 5.
2. Foundation poured—March 14.
3. Roof erected—April 7.
4. Drywall in. Framing, sheathing, plumbing, electrical, and mechanical inspections passed—June 12.
5. Final inspection—June 21.

TECHNICAL REQUIREMENTS

1. Home must meet local building codes.
2. All windows and doors must pass NFRC class 40 energy ratings.
3. Exterior wall insulation must meet an "R" factor of 21.
4. Ceiling insulation must meet an "R" factor of 38.
5. Floor insulation must meet an "R" factor of 25.
6. Garage will accommodate two large-size cars and one 20-foot Winnebago.
7. Structure must pass seismic stability codes.

LIMITS AND EXCLUSIONS

1. House will be built to the specifications and design of the original blueprints provided by the customer.
2. Owner is responsible for landscaping.
3. Refrigerator is not included among kitchen appliances.
4. Air conditioning is not included but prewiring is included.
5. Contractor reserves the right to contract out services.
6. Contractor is responsible for subcontracted work.
7. Site work is limited to Monday through Friday, 8:00 a.m. to 6:00 p.m.

CUSTOMER REVIEW

Linda and Dave Smith.

In many cases, these causes reflect a misfit—traditional project management methods being applied to high-uncertainty projects (remember Figure 1.2!). Instead of trying to establish plans up front, Agile project management should be applied to discover what needs to be done. On Agile projects, the scope is assumed to evolve rather than be prescribed. Scope creep is managed and reflects progress.

If the project scope needs to change, it is critical to have a sound change control process in place that records the change and keeps a log of all project changes. Change control is one of the topics of Chapter 7. Project managers in the field constantly suggest that dealing with changing requirements is one of their most challenging problems.

SNAPSHOT FROM PRACTICE The Bradley Fighting Vehicle*

In the annals of project management history, one of the most famous examples of scope creep is the development of the Bradley Fighting Vehicle (BFV) by the U.S. Army. The Bradley has been described by military officers and historians, as a weapon that means "all things to all people" and "a proverbial camel. . .that does nothing well."

In 1967, the Soviet Union introduced the BMP (Boyevaya Mashina Pyekhoty), an amphibious, tracked vehicle with tank and armored personnel carrier capabilities. Despite BMP's serious design flaw, a small hull size that could carry only "short" Soviet soldiers, the U.S. military was eager to build a vehicle that was part tank and part personnel carrier. The original requirements were for vehicle with a two-man turret, cannon, coaxial machine gun, and nine troop carry capacity.

The list of requirements grew as more agencies made recommendations and further additions to the design. The Office of Secretary of Defense advocated the inclusion of firing ports, a cannon, and antitank munitions, while armored officers wanted to increase firepower by adding long-range TOW-missiles. TOW stands for Tube-launched, Optically tracked, Wire-guided. Although there were concerns over the vehicles increase weight and cost, BMP development continued without design or cost trade-offs.

Meanwhile, the U.S. Army was also developing an armored reconnaissance scout vehicle. In 1976, the BMP project was merged with the scout project. At this point, it was decided to create a completely new vehicle platform. The rationale was that costs savings could be achieved since the two vehicles had common requirements.

In 1977, the Government Accounting Office (GAO) of Congress investigated the fighting vehicle's current swimming capability and reported that it was too heavy and that it took too long to inflate for water travel. The U.S. Army was still determined to push for retaining the amphibious requirements and including TOW missiles. Over the next four years, several design iterations followed before production began in 1981.

The exorbitant development cost overruns of the BFV caught the attention of the press and the public in 1980. Pentagon reformists seized on the BFV as an opportunity to display flaws in Department of Defense (DoD) weapons acquisitions, development, and testing procedures.

DoD critics were skeptical of the U.S. Army's failure to adequately simulate combat to test the overall effectiveness of the vehicle. The U.S. Army conducted limited field tests and liked to rely on tests of individual components and computer simulations to assess combat worthiness. When BFV was finally tested under maximum fire, it proved unsafe for personnel inside. The vehicle had to go back to the drawing board. Eventually, significant improvements were made in suspension, armor, and munitions storage to enhance survivability and combat effectiveness.

In the end, the final version of the BFV was quite different from the originally planned armored personnel carrier. It was 13 tons heavier than originally specified and carried less people. Furthermore, it took 16 years from the time the first requirements were set in 1964 to the time a vehicle was finally approved for production. Even after that more changes had to be made after combat simulation tests.

*L. Ayes, "The Bradley Fighting Vehicle," www.prezi.com. Accessed 12/24/2022; J. G. Burton, *The Pentagon Wars: Reformers Challenge the Old Guard* (Annapolis: Naval University Press, 1993).

4.2 Step 2: Establishing Project Priorities

LO 4-3

Understand why it is important to establish project priorities in terms of cost, time, and performance.

Quality and the ultimate success of a project are traditionally defined as meeting and/or exceeding the expectations of the customer and/or upper management in terms of the cost (budget), time (schedule), and performance (scope) of the project (see Figure 4.1). The interrelationship among these criteria varies. For example, sometimes it is necessary to compromise the performance and scope of the project to get the project done quickly or less expensively. Often the longer a project takes, the more expensive it becomes. However, a positive correlation between cost and schedule may not always be true. Other times project costs can be reduced by using cheaper, less efficient labor or equipment that extends the duration of the project. Likewise, as will be seen in

FIGURE 4.1
Project Management Trade-offs

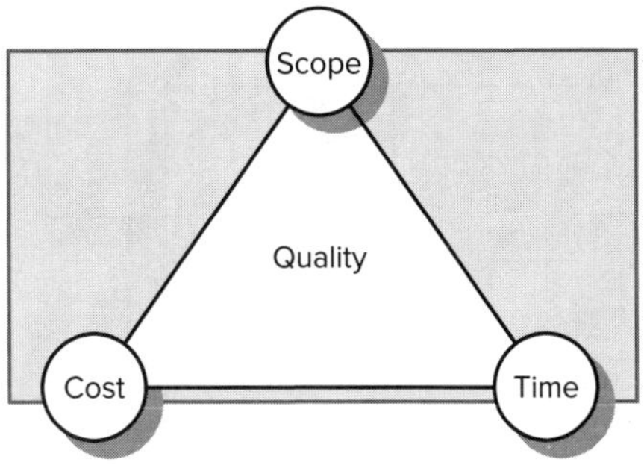

Chapter 9, project managers are often forced to expedite, or "crash," certain key activities by adding additional labor, thereby raising the original cost of the project.

One of the primary jobs of a project manager is to manage the trade-offs among time, cost, and performance. To do so, project managers must define and understand the nature of the priorities of the project. They need to have a candid discussion with the project customer and upper management to establish the relative importance of each criterion. For example, what happens when the customer keeps adding requirements? Or if midway through the project a trade-off must be made between cost and expediting, which criterion has priority?

One technique that is useful for this purpose is completing a **priority matrix** for the project to identify which criterion is constrained, which should be enhanced, and which can be accepted:

Constrain. The original parameter is fixed. The project must meet the completion date, specifications and scope of the project, or budget.

Enhance. Given the scope of the project, which criterion should be optimized? In the case of time and cost, this usually means taking advantage of opportunities to either reduce costs or shorten the schedule. Conversely, with regard to performance, enhancing means adding value to the project.

Accept. For which criterion is it tolerable not to meet the original parameters? When trade-offs have to be made, is it permissible to allow the schedule to slip, to reduce the scope and performance of the project, or to go over budget?

Figure 4.2 displays the priority matrix for the development of a new wireless router. Because *time*-to-market is important to sales, the project manager is instructed to take advantage of every opportunity to reduce completion time. In doing so, going over *budget* is acceptable, though not desirable. At the same time, the original *performance* specifications for the router as well as reliability standards cannot be compromised.

Priorities vary from project to project. For example, for many software projects time-to-market is critical, and companies like Microsoft may defer original scope requirements to later versions in order to get to the market first. Alternatively, for special event projects (conferences, parades, tournaments) time is constrained once the date has been announced, and if the budget is tight the project manager will compromise the scope of the project in order to complete the project on time.

Some would argue that all three criteria are always constrained and that good project managers should seek to optimize each criterion. If everything goes well on a project and no major problems or setbacks are encountered, their argument may be valid. However, this situation is rare, and project managers are often forced to make tough decisions that benefit one criterion while compromising the other two.

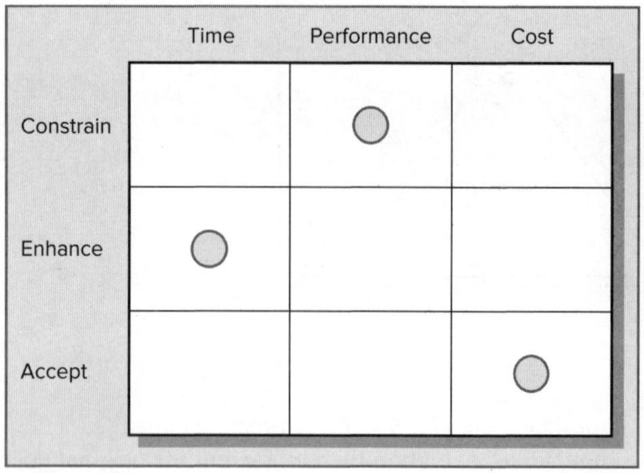

FIGURE 4.2
Project Priority Matrix

The purpose of this exercise is to define and agree on what the priorities and constraints of the project are so that when "push comes to shove," the right decisions can be made.

There are likely to be natural limits to the extent managers can constrain, enhance, or accept any one criterion. It may be acceptable for the project to slip one month behind schedule but no further or to exceed the planned budget by as much as $20,000. Likewise, it may be desirable to finish a project a month early, but after that cost conservation should be the primary goal. Some project managers document these limits as part of creating the priority matrix.

In summary, developing a priority matrix for a project *before the project begins* is a useful exercise. It provides a forum for clearly establishing priorities with customers and top management so as to create shared expectations and avoid misunderstandings. The priority information is essential to the planning process, where adjustments can be made in the scope, schedule, and budget allocation. Finally, the matrix is useful midway in the project for approaching a problem that must be solved.

One caveat must be mentioned; during the course of a project, priorities may change. The customer may suddenly need the project completed one month sooner, or new directives from top management may emphasize cost-saving initiatives. The project manager needs to be vigilant in order to anticipate and confirm changes in priorities and make appropriate adjustments.

4.3 Step 3: Creating the Work Breakdown Structure

LO 4-4

Demonstrate the importance of a work breakdown structure (WBS) to the management of projects and how it serves as a database for planning and control.

Major Groupings in a WBS

Once the scope and deliverables have been identified, the work of the project can be successively subdivided into smaller and smaller work elements. The outcome of this hierarchical process is called the **work breakdown structure (WBS).** Use of a WBS helps to assure project managers that all products and work elements are identified, to integrate the project with the current organization, and to establish a basis for control. Basically, the WBS is an outline of the project with different levels of detail.

Figure 4.3 shows the major groupings commonly used in the field to develop a hierarchical WBS. The WBS begins with the project as the final deliverable. Major project work deliverables/systems are identified first; then the subdeliverables necessary to accomplish the larger deliverables are defined. The process is repeated until the subdeliverable detail is small enough to be manageable and one person can be responsible. This subdeliverable is further divided into work packages. Because the lowest subdeliverable usually includes several work packages, the work packages are grouped by type of work—for example, design and testing. These groupings within a subdeliverable are called cost accounts. This grouping facilitates a system for monitoring project progress by work, cost, and responsibility.

How a WBS Helps the Project Manager

The WBS defines all the elements of the project in a hierarchical framework and establishes their relationships to the project end item(s). Think of the project as a large work package that is successively broken down into smaller work packages; the total project is the summation of all the smaller work packages. This hierarchical structure facilitates the evaluation of cost, time, and technical performance at all levels in the

FIGURE 4.3
Hierarchical Breakdown of the WBS

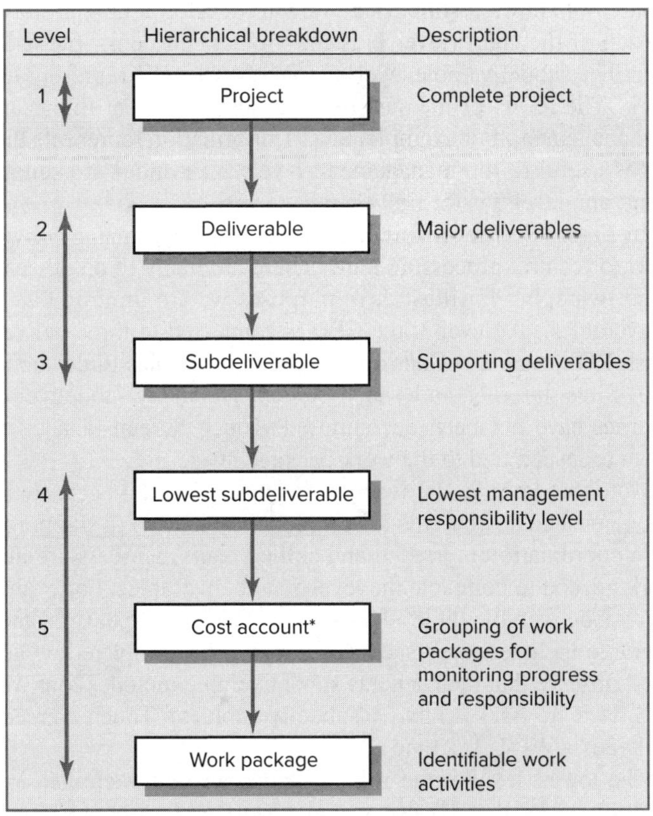

*This breakdown groups work packages by type of work within a deliverable and allows assignment of responsibility to an organization unit. This extra step facilitates a system for monitoring project progress (discussed in Chapter 13).

organization over the life of the project. The WBS also provides management with information appropriate to each level. For example, top management deals primarily with major deliverables, while first-line supervisors deal with smaller subdeliverables and work packages.

Each item in the WBS needs a time and cost estimate. With this information, it is possible to plan, schedule, and budget the project. The WBS also serves as a framework for tracking cost and work performance.

As the WBS is developed, organization units and individuals are assigned responsibility for executing work packages. This integrates the work and the organization. In practice, this process is sometimes called the organization breakdown structure (OBS), which will be further discussed later in the chapter.

Use of the WBS provides the opportunity to "roll up" (sum) the budget and actual costs of the smaller work packages into larger work elements so that performance can be measured by organization units and work accomplishment.

The WBS can also be used to define communication channels and assist in understanding and coordinating many parts of the project. The structure shows the work and responsible organization units and suggests where written communication should be directed. Problems can be quickly addressed and coordinated because the structure integrates work and responsibility.

A Simple WBS Development

Figure 4.4 shows a simplified WBS to develop a new prototype tablet computer. At the top of the chart (level 1) is the project end item—the E-Slim Tablet x-13 Prototype. The subdeliverable levels (2–5) below level 1 represent further decomposition of work. The levels of the structure can also represent information for different levels of management. For example, level 1 information represents the total project objective and is useful to top management; levels 2, 3, and 4 are suitable for middle management; and level 5 is for first-line managers.

In Figure 4.4, level 2 indicates there are two major deliverables—Hardware and CPU, or central processing unit. (There are likely to be other major deliverables such as software, but for illustrative purposes we are limiting our focus to just two major deliverables.) At level 3, the CPU is connected to three deliverables—Power Supply, Flash ROM, and I/O Controller. I/O Controller has three subdeliverables at level 4—USB Slots, Internet, and Touch Screen. The many subdeliverables for USB Slots and Internet have not been decomposed. Touch Screen (shaded) has been decomposed down to level 5 and to the work package level.

Note that level 2, Hardware, skips levels 3 and 4 because the final subdeliverables can be pushed down to the lowest manageable level 5; skipping levels 3 and 4 suggests little coordination is needed and skilled team members are already familiar with the work needed to complete the level 5 subdeliverables. For example, Hardware requires four subdeliverables at level 5—Frame, Cameras, Speakers, and Antenna. Each subdeliverable includes work packages that will be completed by an assigned organization unit. Observe that the Cameras subdeliverable includes four work packages—WP-C1, 2, 3, and 4. Back Light, a subdeliverable of Touch Screen, includes three work packages—WP-L 1, 2, and 3.

The lowest level of the WBS is called a **work package.** Work packages are short-duration tasks that have a definite start and stop point, consume resources, and

FIGURE 4.4 Work Breakdown Structure

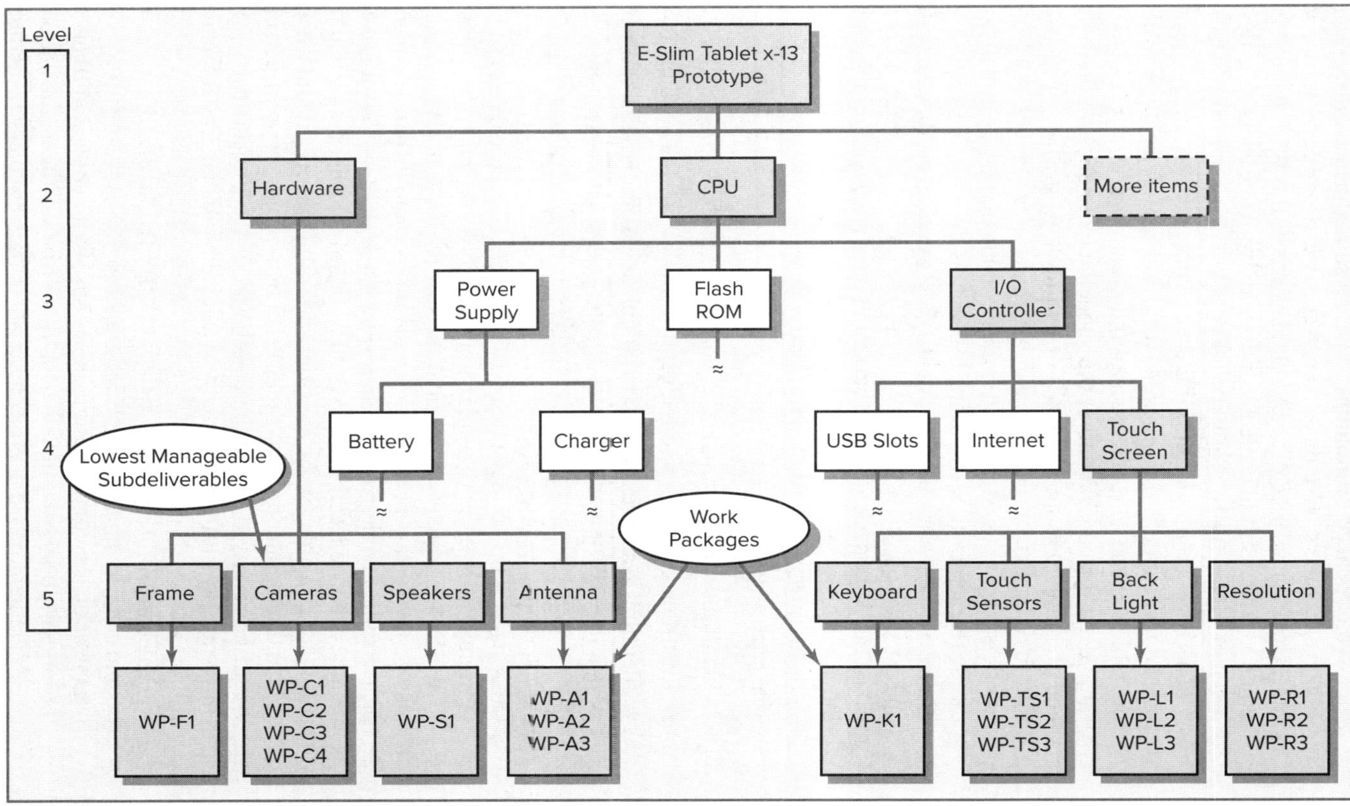

represent cost. Each work package is a control point. A work package manager is responsible for seeing that the package is completed on time, within budget, and according to technical specifications. Practice suggests a work package should not exceed 10 workdays or one reporting period. If a work package has a duration exceeding 10 days, check or monitoring points should be established within the duration—say, every three to five days—so progress and problems can be identified before too much time has passed. Each work package of the WBS should be as independent of other packages of the project as possible. No work package is described in more than one subdeliverable of the WBS.

There is an important difference from start to finish between the last work breakdown subdeliverable and a work package. Typically a work breakdown subdeliverable includes the outcomes of more than one work package from perhaps two or three departments. Therefore, the subdeliverable does not have a duration of its own and does not consume resources or cost money directly. (In a sense, of course, a duration for a particular work breakdown element can be derived from identifying which work package must start first [earliest] and which package will be the latest to finish; the difference from start to finish becomes the duration for the subdeliverable.) The higher elements are used to identify deliverables at different phases in the project and to develop status reports during the execution stage of the project life cycle. Thus, the work package is the basic unit used for planning, scheduling, and controlling the project.

In summary, each work package in the WBS

1. Defines work (what).
2. Identifies time to complete a work package (how long).
3. Identifies a time-phased budget to complete a work package (cost).
4. Identifies resources needed to complete a work package (how much).
5. Identifies a single person responsible for units of work (who).
6. Identifies monitoring points for measuring progress (how well).

Creating a WBS from scratch can be a daunting task. Project managers should take advantage of relevant examples from previous projects to begin the process.

WBSs are products of group efforts. If the project is small, the entire project team may be involved in breaking down the project into its components. For large, complex projects, the people responsible for the major deliverables are likely to meet to establish the first two levels of deliverables. In turn, further detail would be delegated to the people responsible for the specific work. Collectively this information would be gathered and integrated into a formal WBS by a project support person. The final version would be reviewed by the inner echelon of the project team. Relevant stakeholders (most notably customers) would be consulted to confirm agreement and revise when appropriate.

Project teams developing their first WBS frequently forget that the structure should be end-item, output oriented. First attempts often result in a WBS that follows the organization structure—design, marketing, production, and finance. If a WBS follows the organization structure, the focus will be on the organization function and processes, rather than the project output or deliverables. In addition, a WBS with a process focus will become an accounting tool that records costs by function rather than a tool for "output" management. Every effort should be made to develop a WBS that is output oriented in order to concentrate on concrete deliverables. See Snapshot from Practice 4.3: Creating a WBS.

SNAPSHOT FROM PRACTICE 4.3 Creating a WBS

Figure 4.4 represents the classic WBS in which the project is broken down to the lowest manageable deliverable and subsequent work packages. Many situations do not require this level of detail. This begs the question of how far you should break down the work. There is no set answer to this question. However, here are some tips given by project managers:

Break down the work until you can do an estimate that is accurate enough for your purposes. If you are doing a ballpark estimate to see if the project is worthy of serious consideration, you probably do not need to break it down beyond major deliverables. On the other hand, if you are pricing a project to submit a competitive bid, then you are likely to go down to the work package level.

The WBS should conform to how you are going to schedule work. For example, if assignments are made in terms of days, then tasks should be limited as best as possible to one day or more to complete. Conversely, if hours are the smallest unit for scheduling, then work can be broken down to one-hour increments.

Final activities should have clearly defined start/end events. Avoid open-ended tasks like "research" or "market analysis." Take it down to the next level in which deliverables/outcomes are more clearly defined. Instead of ending with market analysis, include items such as "identify market share," "list user requirements," or "write a problem statement."

If accountability and control are important, then break the work down so that one individual is clearly responsible for the work. For example, instead of stopping at product design, take it to the next level and identify specific components of the design (e.g., electrical schematics or power source) that different individuals will be responsible for creating.

The bottom line is that the WBS should provide the level of detail needed to manage the specific project successfully.

4.4 Step 4: Integrating the WBS with the Organization

LO 4-5

Demonstrate how the organization breakdown structure (OBS) establishes accountability to organization units.

The WBS is used to link the organization units responsible for performing the work. In practice, the outcome of this process is the **organization breakdown structure (OBS).** The OBS depicts how the firm has organized to discharge work responsibility. The purposes of the OBS are to provide a framework to summarize organization unit work performance, identify the organization units responsible for work packages, and tie the organization unit to cost control accounts. Recall that, cost accounts group similar work packages (usually under the purview of a department). The OBS defines the organization subdeliverables in a hierarchical pattern in successively smaller and smaller units. Frequently the traditional organization structure can be used. Even if the project is completely performed by a team, it is necessary to break down the team structure for assigning responsibility for budgets, time, and technical performance.

As in the WBS, the OBS assigns the lowest organization unit the responsibility for work packages within a cost account. Herein lies one major strength of using the WBS and OBS; they can be *integrated* as shown in Figure 4.5. The intersection of work packages and the organization unit creates a project control point **(cost account)** that integrates work and responsibility. For example, at level 5, Touch Sensors has three work packages that have been assigned to the Design, Quality Control Test, and Production Departments. The intersection of the WBS and OBS represents the set of work packages necessary to complete the subdeliverable located immediately above and the organization unit on the left responsible for accomplishing the packages at the intersection. Note that the Design Department is responsible for five different work packages across the Hardware and Touch Screen deliverables.

FIGURE 4.5 Integration of WBS and OBS

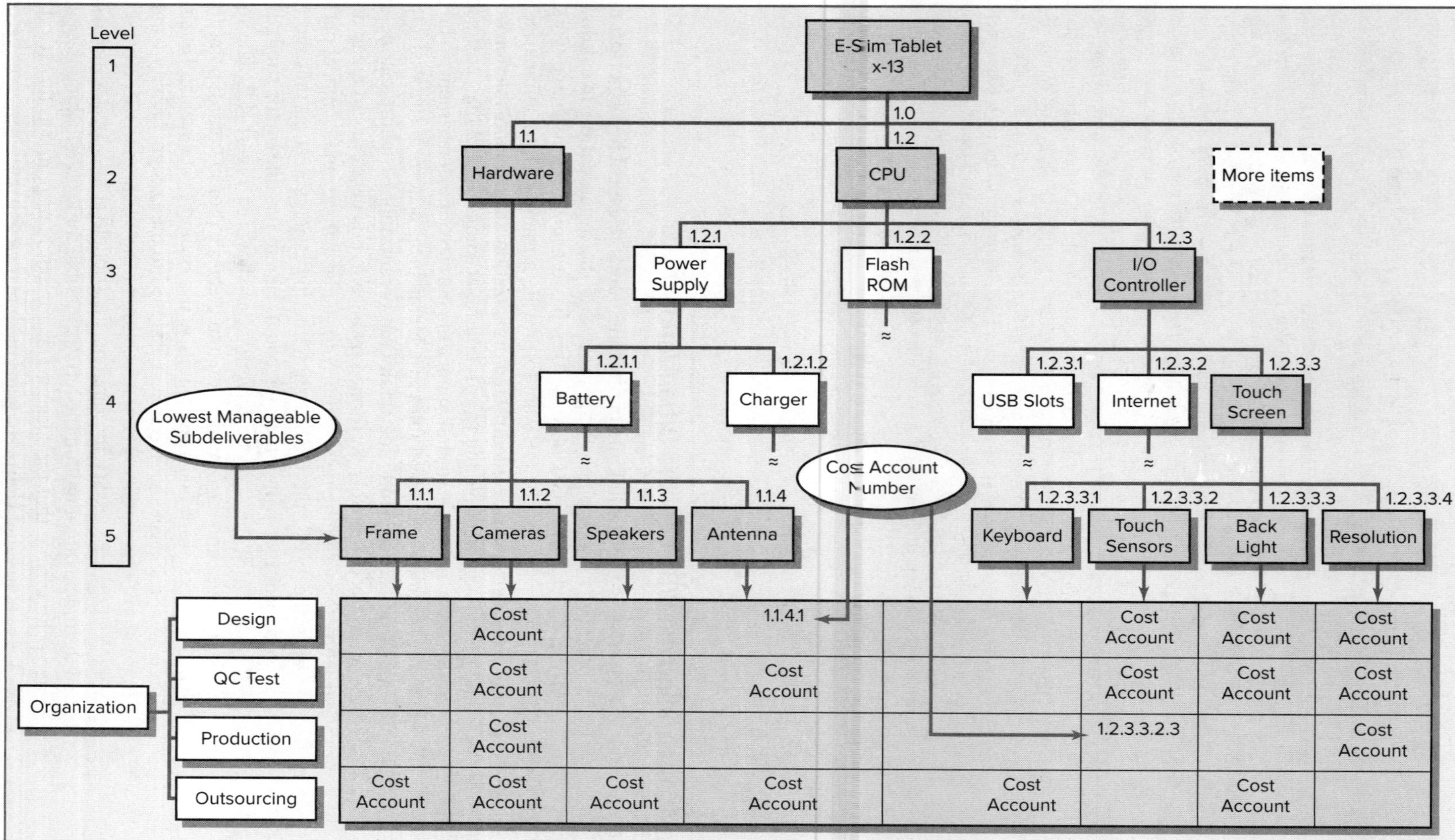

Later we will use the intersection as a cost account for management control of projects. For example, the Cameras element requires the completion of work packages whose primary responsibility will include the Design, QC Test, Production, and Outsourcing Departments. Control can be checked from two directions—outcomes and responsibility. In the execution phase of the project, progress can be tracked vertically on deliverables (client's interest) and tracked horizontally by organization responsibility (owner's interest).

4.5 Step 5: Coding the WBS for the Information System

Gaining the maximum usefulness of a breakdown structure depends on a coding system. The codes are used to define levels and elements in the WBS, organization elements, work packages, and budget and cost information. The codes allow reports to be consolidated at any level in the structure. The most commonly used scheme in practice is numeric indention. A portion of the E-Slim Tablet x-13 Prototype project is presented in Exhibit 4.1.

EXHIBIT 4.1
Coding the WBS

	ⓘ	Task Mode	WBS	Task Name
1			**1**	**E-Slim Tablet x-13 Prototype**
2			**1.1**	**Hardware**
3			1.1.1	Frame
4			1.1.2	Cameras
5			1.1.3	Speakers
6			1.1.4	Antenna
7			**1.2**	**CPU**
8			**1.2.1**	**Power Supply**
9			1.2.1.1	Battery (more items)
10			1.2.1.2	Charger (more items)
11			1.2.2	Flash ROM
12			**1.2.3**	**I/O Controller**
13			1.2.3.1	USB Slots (more items)
14			1.2.3.2	Internet (more items)
15			**1.2.3.3**	**Touch Screen**
16			**1.2.3.3.1**	**Keyboard**
17			1.2.3.3.1.1	Work package K1
18			**1.2.3.3.2**	**Touch Sensors**
19			1.2.3.3.2.1	Work package TS1
20			1.2.3.3.2.2	Work package TS2
21			1.2.3.3.2.3	Work package TS3
22			1.2.3.3.3	Back Light (more items)
23			1.2.3.3.4	Resolution (more items)

Microsoft Project

Note that the project identification is 1.0. Each successive indention represents a lower element or work package. Ultimately the numeric scheme reaches down to the work package level, and all tasks and elements in the structure have an identification code. The "cost account" is the focal point because all budgets, work assignments, time, cost, and technical performance come together at this point.

This coding system can be extended to cover large projects. Additional schemes can be added for special reports. For example, adding a "23" after the code could indicate a site location, an elevation, or a special account such as labor. Some letters can be used as special identifiers such as "M" for materials or "E" for engineers. You are not limited to only 10 subdivisions (0–9); you can extend each subdivision to large numbers—for example, 0.1–0.99 or 0.1–0.9999. If the project is small, you can use whole numbers. The following example is from a large, complex project:

3R–237A–P2–33.6

where 3R identifies the facility, 237A represents elevation and the area, P2 represents pipe 2 inches wide, and 33.6 represents the work package number. In practice, most organizations are creative in combining letters and numbers to minimize the length of WBS codes.

On larger projects, the WBS is further supported with a **WBS dictionary** that provides detailed information about each element in the WBS. The dictionary typically includes the work package level (code), name, and functional description. In some cases, the description is supported with specifications. The availability of detailed descriptions has an added benefit of dampening scope creep.

4.6 Process Breakdown Structure

LO 4-6

Describe a process breakdown structure (PBS) and when to use it.

The WBS is best suited for design and build projects that have tangible outcomes such as an offshore mining facility or a new car prototype. The project can be decomposed, or broken down, into major deliverables, subdeliverables, further subdeliverables, and ultimately work packages. It is more difficult to apply WBS to less tangible, *process-oriented* projects in which the final outcome is a product of a series of steps or phases. Here, the big difference is that the project evolves over time with each phase affecting the next phase. Information systems projects typically fall in this category—for example, creating an extranet website or an internal software database system. Process projects are driven by performance requirements, not by plans/blueprints. Some practitioners choose to utilize a **process breakdown structure (PBS)** instead of the classic WBS.

Figure 4.6 provides an example of a PBS for a software development project. Instead of being organized around deliverables, the project is organized around phases. Each of the five major phases can be broken down into more specific activities until a sufficient level of detail is achieved to communicate what needs to be done to complete that phase. People can be assigned to specific activities, and a complementary OBS can be created, just as is done for the WBS. Deliverables are not ignored but are defined as outputs required to move to the next phase. The software industry often refers to a PBS as the "waterfall method," since progress flows downward through each phase.[1]

[1] The limitations of the waterfall method for software development have led to the emergence of Agile project management methods that are the subject of Chapter 15.

FIGURE 4.6 **PBS for Software Development Project**

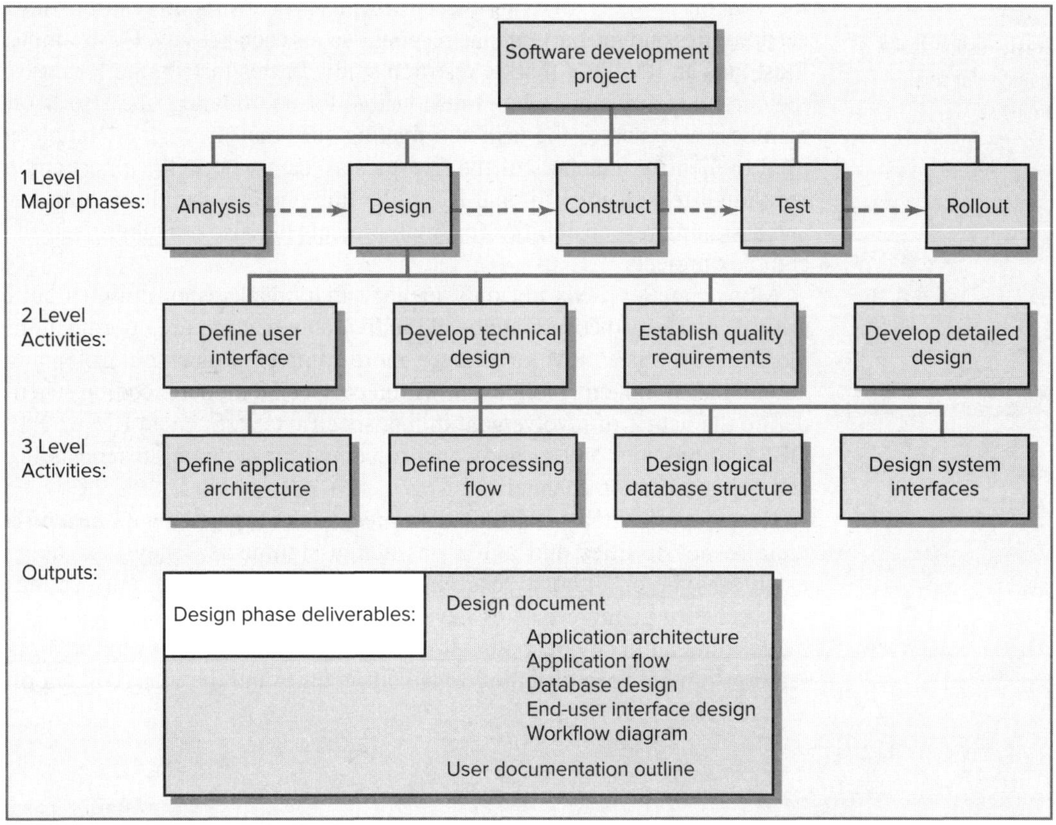

Checklists that contain the phase exit requirements are developed to manage project progress. These checklists provide the means to support phase walk-throughs and reviews. Checklists vary depending upon the project and activities involved but typically include the following details:

- Deliverables needed to exit a phase and begin a new one.
- Quality checkpoints to ensure that deliverables are complete and accurate.
- Sign-offs by all responsible stakeholders to indicate that the phase has been successfully completed and that the project should move on to the next phase.

As long as exit requirements are firmly established and deliverables for each phase are well defined, the PBS provides a suitable alternative to the standard WBS for projects that involve extensive development work.

4.7 Responsibility Matrices

In many cases, the size and scope of the project do not warrant an elaborate WBS or OBS. One tool that is widely used by project managers and task force leaders of small projects is the **responsibility matrix** (RM). The RM (sometimes called a linear

LO 4-7

Create responsibility matrices for small projects.

responsibility chart) summarizes the tasks to be accomplished and who is responsible for what on a project. In its simplest form, an RM consists of a chart listing all the project activities and the participants responsible for each activity. For example, Figure 4.7 illustrates an RM for a market research study. In this matrix, the R is used to identify the committee member who is responsible for coordinating the efforts of other team members assigned to the task and making sure that the task is completed. The S is used to identify members of the five-person team who will support and/or assist the individual responsible. Simple RMs like this one are useful not only for organizing and assigning responsibilities for small projects but also for subprojects of large, more complex projects.

More complex RMs not only identify individual responsibilities but also clarify critical interfaces between units and individuals that require coordination. For example, Figure 4.8 is an RM for a larger, more complex project to develop a new piece of automated equipment. Notice that within each cell a numeric coding scheme is used to define the nature of involvement in that specific task. Such an RM extends the WBS/OBS and provides a clear and concise method for depicting responsibility, authority, and communication channels.

Responsibility matrices provide a means for all participants in a project to view their responsibilities and agree on their assignments. They also help clarify the extent or type of authority exercised by each participant in performing an activity in which two or more parties have overlapping involvement. By using an RM and by defining authority, responsibility, and communications within its framework, the relationship between different organization units and the work content of the project is made clear.

FIGURE 4.7 **Responsibility Matrix for a Market Research Project**

	Project Team				
Task	Richard	Duy	Dave	Linda	Izabella
Identify target customers	R	S		S	
Develop draft questionnaire	R	S	S		
Pilot-test questionnaire		R		S	
Finalize questionnaire	R	S	S	S	
Print questionnaire					R
Prepare mailing labels					R
Mail questionnaires					R
Receive and monitor returned questionnaires				R	S
Input response data			R		
Analyze results		R	S	S	
Prepare draft of report	S	R	S	S	
Prepare final report	R		S		

R = Responsible
S = Supports/assists

FIGURE 4.8 **Responsibility Matrix for the Conveyor Belt Project**

	Organization							
Deliverables	Design	Development	Documentation	Assembly	Testing	Purchasing	Quality Assur.	Manufacturing
Architectural designs	1	2			2		3	3
Hardware specifications	2	1				2	3	
Kernel specifications	1	3						3
Utilities specifications	2	1			3			
Hardware design	1			3		3		3
Disk drivers	3	1	2					
Memory management	1	3			3			
Operating system documentation	2	2	1					3
Prototypes	5		4	1	3	3	3	4
Integrated acceptance test	5	2	2		1		5	5

1 Responsible
2 Support
3 Consult
4 Notification
5 Approval

4.8 Project Communication Plan

LO 4-8

Create a communication plan for a project.

Once the project deliverables and work are clearly identified, creating an internal communication plan is vital. Stories abound of poor communication as a major contributor to project failure. Having a robust communication plan can go a long way toward mitigating project problems and can ensure that customers, team members, and other stakeholders have the information to do their jobs.

The communication plan is usually created by the project manager and/or the project team in the early stage of project planning.

Communication is a key component in coordinating and tracking project schedules, issues, and action items. The plan maps out the flow of information to different stakeholders and becomes an integral part of the overall project plan. The purpose of a project communication plan is to express what, who, how, and when information will be transmitted to project stakeholders so schedules, issues, and action items can be tracked.

Project communication plans address the following core questions:

- What information needs to be collected and when?
- Who will receive the information?
- What methods will be used to gather and store information?
- What are the limits, if any, on who has access to certain kinds of information?
- When will the information be communicated?
- How will it be communicated?

Developing a communication plan that answers these questions usually entails the following basic steps:

1. **Stakeholder analysis.** Identify the target groups. Typical groups could be the customer, sponsor, project team, project office, or anyone else who needs project information to make decisions and/or contribute to project progress. A common tool found in practice to initially identify and analyze major project stakeholders' communication needs is presented in Figure 4.9.[2] What is communicated and how are influenced by stakeholder interest and power. Some of these stakeholders may have the power to

FIGURE 4.9
Stakeholder Communications

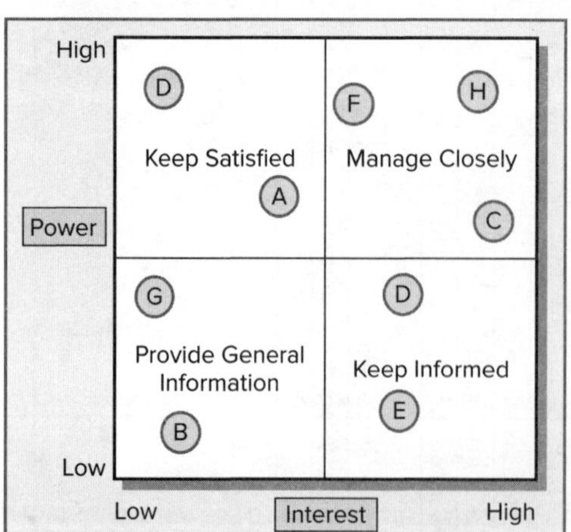

[2] For a more elaborate scheme for assessing stakeholders, see: Bourne, L. *Stakeholder Relationship Management* (Farnham, UK: Gower, 2009).

either block or enhance your project. By identifying stakeholders and prioritizing them on the "Power/Interest" map, you can plan the type and frequency of communications needed. (More on stakeholders will be discussed in Chapter 10.)

For example, on a typical project, you want to manage closely the professionals doing the work, while you want to satisfy senior management and the project sponsor with periodic updates. Unions and operation managers interested in capacity should be kept informed, while you would only need to provide general information to the legal, public relations, and other departments.

2. **Information needs.** What information is pertinent to stakeholders who contribute to the project's progress? The simplest answer to this question can be obtained by asking the various individuals what information they need and when they need it. For example, top management needs to know how the project is progressing, whether it is encountering critical problems, and the extent to which project goals are being realized. This information is required so that they can make strategic decisions and manage the portfolio of projects. Project team members need to see schedules, task lists, specifications, and the like so they know what needs to be done next. External groups need to know any changes in the schedule and performance requirements of the components they are providing. Frequent information needs found in communication plans are

Project status reports	Deliverable issues
Changes in scope	Team status meetings
Gating decisions	Accepted request changes
Action items	Milestone reports

3. **Sources of information.** When the information needs are identified, the next step is to determine the sources of information. That is, where does the information reside? How will it be collected? For example, information relating to the milestone report, team meetings, and project status meetings would be found in the minutes and reports of various groups.
4. **Dissemination modes.** In today's world, traditional status report meetings are being supplemented by e-mail, teleconferencing, SharePoint, and a variety of database sharing programs to circulate information. In particular, many companies are using the cloud database to create a "virtual project office" to store project information. Project management software feeds information directly to the cloud platform so that different people have immediate access to relevant project information. In some cases, appropriate information is routed automatically to key stakeholders. Backup paper hardcopy to specific stakeholders is still critical for many project changes and action items.
5. **Responsibility and timing.** Determine who will send out the information. For example, a common practice is to have the note taker of meetings forward the minutes or specific information to the appropriate stakeholders. In some cases, the responsibility lies with the project manager or project office. Timing and frequency of distribution appropriate to the information need to be established.

The advantage of establishing a communication plan is that instead of responding to information requests, you are controlling the flow of information. This reduces confusion and unnecessary interruptions, and it can provide project managers greater autonomy. Why? By reporting on a regular basis how things are going and what is happening, you allow senior management to feel more comfortable about letting the team complete the project without interference. See Figure 4.10 for a sample Shale Oil research project communication plan.

FIGURE 4.10 **Shale Oil Research Project Communication Plan**

What Information	*Target Audience*	*When?*	*Method of Communication*	*Provider*
Milestone report	Senior management and project manager	Bimonthly	E-mail and hardcopy	Project office
Project status reports & agendas	Staff and customer	Weekly	E-mail and hardcopy	Project manager
Team status reports	Project manager and project office	Weekly	E-mail	Team recorder
Issues report	Staff and customer	Weekly	E-mail	Team recorder
Escalation reports	Staff and customer	When needed	Meeting and hardcopy	Project manager
Outsourcing performance	Staff and customer	Bimonthly	Meeting	Project manager
Accepted change requests	Project office, senior mgmt., customer, staff, and project mgr.	Anytime	E-mail and hardcopy	Design department
Oversight gate decisions	Senior management and project manager	As required	E-mail meeting report	Oversight group or project office

The importance of establishing a plan up front for communicating important project information cannot be overstated. Many of the problems that plague a project can be traced back to insufficient time devoted to establishing a well-grounded internal communication plan.

4.9 Software Solutions and Emerging Trends in Project Management

Project management tools are designed to help project managers and stakeholders effectively manage tasks, ensure timely reporting, and streamline project workflows. Often called 'PM tools', they typically include software solutions available for purchase or free online. These tools provide a structured approach to planning, execution, monitoring, and project closure, ensuring efficiency and effectiveness. In today's VUCA world, PM tools are invaluable for handling projects ranging from simple to highly complex. They enhance resource management, tracking, and overall project visibility, ensuring better communication among stakeholders. Features like Gantt charts, WBS, and Agile boards enable system-level project planning. Given below is a list of popular PM tools used across industries such as IT, manufacturing, and infrastructure.

a. **Microsoft Project:** A product of the widely trusted brand Microsoft, it is used by millions worldwide. Designed to integrate various project management functionalities from its sister tools, it offers a robust solution for managing individual projects. However, Microsoft Project is less favored for handling multiple concurrent projects. It has features like, timeline visualization using Gantt charts, resource allocation and workload balancing, risk assessment and budget tracking.

b. **Asana:** It is a widely used project management software designed for businesses of all sizes. This versatile platform combines file storage, project roadmaps, dashboards, and more within an intuitive and visually appealing interface. Ideal for task tracking, team collaboration, and deadline management, Asana's customizable workflows and user-friendly design make it especially popular among startups and medium-sized enterprises. Key features include task assignment and tracking, custom workflows and project templates, and seamless integration with tools like Slack, Zoom, and Google Drive.

c. **Wrike:** It is a versatile work management platform used by over 20,000 companies and 2.4 million users in 140+ countries. It offers features like resource planning, time-tracking, budgeting, automation, and AI tools to streamline workflows, predict risks, and generate reports. While there is a learning curve for advanced features, many users find it worthwhile for scaling and growth. Key features include Kanban boards for task management, customizable Gantt charts for tracking progress, and real-time analytics for performance insights. With 400+ app integrations, including Google Drive, Slack, and Adobe CC, Wrike ensures seamless collaboration across teams and tools.

d. **Monday:** Monday.com is a popular project management software offering a range of templates and tools to boost team productivity. While its user-friendly interface and features like automations, customizable dashboards, and templates make it a top choice, its spreadsheet-like layout can become cluttered, risking key information being overlooked. Additionally, it lacks native proofing features and advanced analytics for complex organizations. Key features include custom dashboards for real-time project monitoring, powerful automation for task reminders, and a library of 100 templates to streamline project initiation. Although it has fewer integrations than competitors, it syncs with popular apps like Google, Slack, and Salesforce.

e. **Adobe Workfront:** It is a project management solution primarily favored by marketing teams, offering a wide array of features suitable for enterprise-sized organizations. With Gantt charts, reporting, advanced dashboards, and strong proofing and asset management capabilities, it justifies its premium pricing. However, some users find the latest UX lacks ease of use and collaboration, leading to limited adoption. Additionally, the DAM function can be buggy, causing delays in publication. Key features include the Scenario Planner for outcome prediction, strategic goal-setting for team alignment, and detailed dashboards for monitoring workflows. While it integrates seamlessly with Creative Cloud, third-party integrations are limited.

f. **Basecamp:** It is an easy-to-use platform ideal for small teams that need essential project management tools like scheduling, collaboration, and monitoring features. Its simple interface and pricing based on requirements, rather than the number of users, make it appealing to smaller or growing teams. The short learning curve is another advantage. However, Basecamp may lack the advanced features needed for larger, cross-functional teams, such as customizable Gantt charts or Kanban boards. Key features include to-do lists, message boards, and project scheduling. While integration options are more limited than some alternatives, Basecamp still supports third-party app integrations for additional functionalities.

g. **Jira:** Originally developed as a software solution, Jira is now part of the Atlassian Group and offers a comprehensive platform that includes Jira Software, Jira Core, and Jira Work Management, catering to teams of all sizes. While its customizable interface and ease of data import/export are beneficial, Jira is limited to Agile methodology and lacks built-in features for resource planning, proofing, and project reporting. Key features include customizable dashboards, unique search functionality, and tailored work request forms for efficient task management. Jira integrates seamlessly with other Atlassian products, enhancing team collaboration.

h. **Zoho Projects:** Zoho Projects, developed by the Indian software giant Zoho Corporation, part of the Zoho suite, provides a project management solution that integrates seamlessly with other Zoho tools like CRM and sales platforms, making it particularly beneficial for current users, especially in the real estate sector. It excels in task management and automation, promoting efficient collaboration and project oversight. However, it lacks a multi-select option for custom fields, which can complicate data entry, and sometimes displays code alongside the data. Key features include Blueprint for task mapping, issue management for bug tracking, and Gantt charts for visual project management. While it offers fewer integrations, it supports essential software like Google and Microsoft.

i. **Smartsheet:** Based on the traditional spreadsheet model, it is a visually rich project management platform that uses cloud-based spreadsheets and automated workflows for efficient task and project management. While it offers advanced tools and capabilities ideal for larger organizations, it may have a steep learning curve for users unfamiliar with spreadsheets, and its add-ons can be costly. Key features include automated workflows for streamlined delivery, content management tools like progress dashboards and resource management, and detailed dashboards for visualizing project and team data. Smartsheet integrates with over 100 apps, with additional options via Zapier and Automate.io.

j. **Primavera P6:** Oracle Primavera P6 is a robust project, program, and portfolio management tool designed for planning, managing, and executing projects. Used across various industries, including construction, manufacturing, energy, and IT, it has been supporting both large and small projects worldwide for over 30 years. Known for its high performance, Primavera P6 is particularly favored for large-scale projects in construction, engineering, and oil & gas. Key features include advanced resource and risk management, multi-project management capabilities, and integration with Building Information Modeling (BIM), making it ideal for complex, high-stakes projects across diverse sectors.

The dynamic landscape of project management is continuously evolving with advancements in technology and the growing need for collaborative, efficient, and scalable tools. Selecting the right project management tool depends on the size of the team, the complexity of projects, and organizational goals. By leveraging these tools effectively, teams can enhance productivity, streamline processes, and achieve project success in an increasingly competitive environment. Whether for small teams or large enterprises, the diverse options available ensure that there is a tailored solution for every project management need.

Summary

The project scope definition, priorities, and work breakdown structure are the keys to nearly every aspect of managing the project. The scope definition provides focus and emphasis on the end item(s) of the project. Establishing project priorities allows managers to make appropriate trade-off decisions. The WBS structure helps ensure that all tasks of the project are identified and provides two views of the project—one on deliverables and one on organization responsibility. The WBS avoids having the project driven by organization function or by a finance system. The structure forces attention to realistic requirements of personnel, hardware, and budgets. Use of the structure provides a powerful framework for project control that identifies deviations from the plan, identifies responsibility, and spots areas for improved performance. No well-developed project plan or control system is possible without a disciplined, structured approach. The WBS, OBS, and cost account codes provide this discipline. The WBS serves as the database for developing the project network, which establishes the timing of work, people, equipment, and costs.

The PBS is often used for process-based projects with ill-defined deliverables. In small projects, responsibility matrices may be used to clarify individual responsibility.

Clearly defining your project is the first and most important step in planning. The absence of a clearly defined project plan consistently shows up as the major reason for project failures. Whether you use a WBS, PBS, or responsibility matrix will depend primarily on the size and nature of your project. Whatever method you use, definition of your project should be adequate to allow for good control as the project is being implemented. Follow-up with a clear communication plan for coordinating and tracking project progress will help you keep important stakeholders informed and avoid some potential problems.

Key Terms

Acceptance criteria, *130*
Cost account, *139*
Gold plating, *130*
Milestone, *128*
Organization breakdown structure (OBS), *139*
Priority matrix, *133*
Process breakdown structure (PBS), *142*
Product scope description, *128*
Responsibility matrix, *143*
Scope creep, *130*
Scope statement, *130*
WBS dictionary, *142*
Work breakdown structure (WBS), *134*
Work package, *136*

Review Questions

1. What are the eight elements of a typical scope statement?
2. What questions does a project objective answer? What would be an example of a good project objective?
3. What does it mean if the priorities of a project include Time-constrain, Scope-accept, and Cost-enhance?
4. What kinds of information are included in a work package?
5. When would it be appropriate to create a responsibility matrix rather than a full-blown WBS?
6. How does a communication plan benefit the management of projects?

SNAPSHOT FROM PRACTICE

Discussion Questions

4.1 *Big Bertha ERC II versus the USGA's COR Requirement*

1. How did Helmstetter's vision conflict with USGA rules?
2. How could this mistake have been avoided?

4.2 *Scope Statement*

1. How does this scope statement discourage scope creep?
2. Where do you think the most likely sources of scope creep will occur on this construction project? Is this scope "creep" bad?

4.3 *Creating a WBS*

1. Why is it important that final activities not be open-ended?

The Bradley Fighting Vehicle

1. What were the major causes of scope creep on the BFV Project?
2. How could the DoD reduce the extensive scope creep that occurred on the BFV project?

Exercises

1. You are in charge of organizing a dinner-dance concert for a local charity. You have reserved a hall that will seat 30 couples and have hired a jazz combo.
   a. Develop a scope statement for this project that contains examples of all the elements. Assume that the event will occur in four weeks. Provide your best estimate of the dates for milestones.
   b. What would the priorities likely be for this project?
2. In small groups, identify real-life examples of a project that would fit each of the following priority scenarios:
   a. Time-constrain, Scope-enhance, Cost-accept
   b. Time-accept, Scope-constrain, Cost-accept
   c. Time-constrain, Scope-accept, Cost-enhance
3. Develop a WBS for a project in which you are going to build a bicycle. Try to identify all of the major components and provide three levels of detail.
4. You are the parent of a family of four (kids ages 13 and 15) planning a weekend camping trip. Develop a responsibility matrix for the work that needs to be done prior to starting your trip.
5. Develop a WBS for a local stage play. Be sure to identify the deliverables and organization units (people) responsible. How would you code your system? Give an example of the work packages in one of your cost accounts. Develop a corresponding OBS that identifies who is responsible for what.
6. Use an example of a project you are familiar with or are interested in. Identify the deliverables and organization units (people) responsible. How would you code your system? Give an example of the work packages in one of your cost accounts.
7. Develop a communication plan for an airport security project. The project entails installing the hardware and software system that (1) scans a passenger's eyes, (2) fingerprints the passenger, and (3) transmits the information to a central location for evaluation.
8. Go to an Internet search engine (e.g., Google) and type in "project communication plan." Check three or four results that have ".gov" as their source. How are they similar or dissimilar? What would be your conclusion concerning the importance of an internal communication plan?
9. Your roommate is about to submit a scope statement for a spring concert sponsored by the entertainment council at Western Evergreen State University (WESU). WESU is a residential university with over 22,000 students. This will be the first time in six years that WESU has sponsored a spring concert. The entertainment council has budgeted $60,000 for the project. The event is to occur on

June 5. Since your roommate knows you are taking a class on project management he has asked you to review his scope statement and make suggestions for improvement. He considers the concert a resume-building experience and wants to be as professional as possible. Following is a draft of his scope statement. What suggestions would you make and why?

WESU Spring Music Concert

Project Objective

To organize and deliver a 6-hour music concert

Product Scope Description

An all-age, outdoor rock concert

Justification

Provide entertainment to WESU community and enhance WESU's reputation as a destination university

Deliverables

- Concert security
- Contact local newspapers and radio stations
- Separate beer garden
- Six hours of musical entertainment
- Design a commemorative concert T-shirt
- Local sponsors
- Food venues
- Event insurance
- Safe environment

Milestones

1. Secure all permissions and approvals
2. Sign big-name artist
3. Contact secondary artists
4. Secure vendor contracts
5. Advertising campaign
6. Plan set-up
7. Concert
8. Clean-up

Technical Requirements

1. Professional sound stage and system
2. At least five performing acts
3. Restroom facilities
4. Parking
5. Compliance with WESU and city requirements/ordinances

Limits and Exclusions

- Seating capacity for 8,000 students
- Performers are responsible for travel arrangements to and from WESU
- Performers must provide their own liability insurance
- Performers and security personnel will be provided lunch and dinner on the day of the concert
- Vendors contribute 25 percent of sales to concert fund
- Concert must be over at 12:15 a.m.

Customer Review: WESU

References

Ashley, D. B., C. S. Lurie, and E. J. Jaselskis, "Determinants of Construction Project Success," *Project Management Journal,* vol. 18, no. 2 (June 1987), pp. 69–79.

Chilmeran, A. H., "Keeping Costs on Track," *PM Network,* 2004, pp. 45–51.

Gary, L., "Will Project Scope Cost You—or Create Value?" *Harvard Management Update,* January 2005.

Gobeli, D. H., and E. W. Larson, "Project Management Problems," *Engineering Management Journal,* vol. 2 (1990), pp. 31–36.

Ingebretsen, M., "Taming the Beast," *PM Network,* July 2003, pp. 30–35.

Katz, D. M., "Case Study: Beware 'Scope Creep' on ERP Projects," CFO.com, March 27, 2001.

Kerzner, H., *Project Management: A Systems Approach to Planning,* 8th ed. (New York: Van Nostrand Reinhold, 2003).

Luby, R. E., D. Peel, and W. Swahl, "Component-Based Work Breakdown Structure," *Project Management Journal,* vol. 26, no. 2 (December 1995), pp. 38–44.

Murch, R., *Project Management: Best Practices for IT Professionals* (Upper Darby, NJ: Prentice Hall, 2001).

Pinto, J. K., and D. P. Slevin, "Critical Success Factors across the Project Life Cycle," *Project Management Journal,* vol. 19, no. 3 (June 1988), pp. 67–75.

Pitagorsky, G., "Realistic Project Planning Promotes Success," *Engineer's Digest,* vol. 29, no. 1 (2001).

PMI Standards Committee, *Guide to the Project Management Body of Knowledge* (Newton Square, PA: Project Management Institute, 2017).

Posner, B. Z., "What It Takes to Be a Good Project Manager," *Project Management Journal,* vol. 18, no. 1 (March 1987), pp. 52–4.

Raz, T., and S. Globerson, "Effective Sizing and Content Definition of Work Packages," *Project Management Journal,* vol. 29, no. 4 (1998), pp. 17–23.

The Standish Group, *CHAOS Summary 2009,* pp. 1–4.

Tate, K., and K. Hendrix, "Chartering IT Projects," *Proceedings, 30th Annual, Project Management Institute* (Philadelphia: Project Management Institute, 1999), CD.

Microsoft (2023). "Microsoft Project Features and Benefits".

Zoho Corporation (2023). "Zoho Projects Overview."

Atlassian (2023). "Jira Software for Agile Teams."

Primavera (2023). "Primavera P6 Features."

Tech Mahindra (2023). "AI in Project Management."

Larsen & Toubro (2023). "Project Management Practices in Infrastructure."

Case 4.1

Celebration of Colors 5K

Jamal was having an ale with his girlfriend, Sierra, when the subject of the Omega Theta Pi 5K-run project came up. Jamal has been chosen to chair the 5K-charity run for his fraternity. At the time, Jamal thought it would look good on his resume and wouldn't be too difficult to pull off. This would be the first running event Omega Theta Pi had organized. In the past, Delta Tau Chi always organized the spring running event. However, Delta Tau Chi had been dissolved after a highly publicized hazing scandal.

Jamal and his brothers at Omega Theta Pi thought that organizing a 5K-run would be a lot more fun and profitable than the normal spring cleaning service they offered the local community. Early on in the discussions, everyone agreed that partnering with a sorority would be an advantage. Not only would they help manage the event, but they would have useful contacts to recruit sponsors and participants. Jamal pitched the fundraising idea to the sisters at Delta Nu, and they agreed to co-manage the event. Olivia Pomerleau volunteered and was named co-chair by Delta Nu.

Jamal told Sierra about the task force's first meeting, which was held last night and included five members from each living group. Olivia and Jamal tried, but failed, to meet beforehand due to scheduling conflicts. The meeting began with the attendees introducing themselves and telling what experience they had had with running events. Only one person had not run at past events, but no one had been involved in managing an event other than volunteering as intersection flaggers.

Olivia then said she thought the first thing they should decide on was the theme of the 5K-race. Jamal hadn't thought much about this, but everyone agreed that the race had to have a theme. People began to suggest themes and ideas based on other runs they knew about. The group seemed stumped when Olivia said, "Do you know that the last Friday in March is a full moon? In India, *Holi,* the celebration of colors, occurs on the last full moon day in March. Maybe you've seen pictures of this, but this is where people go wild tossing dye and color water balloons at each other. I looked it up and the Holi festival signifies a victory of good over evil, the arrival of spring and the end of winter. It is a day to meet others, play, laugh, and forgive and forget. I think it would be neat if we organized our 5K-run as a Holi festival. At different points in the race we would have people toss dye on runners. The run would end with a giant water balloon fight. We could even see if Evergreen [the local Indian restaurant] would cater the event!"

Jamal and the other boys looked at each other, while the girls immediately supported the idea. The deal maker occurred when Olivia showed a YouTube video of a similar event last year at a university in Canada that had over 700 participants and raised over $14,000.

Once the theme was decided the discussion turned into a free-for-all of ideas and suggestions. One member said she may know an artist who could create really neat T-shirts for the event. Others wondered where to get the dye and if it is safe. Another talked about the importance of a website and creating a digital account for registration. Others began to argue whether the run should be done on campus or through the streets of their small college town. One by one students excused themselves due to other commitments. With only a few members remaining Jamal and Olivia adjourned the meeting.

While Jamal took a sip of his IPA (India Pale Ale) beer, Sierra pulled a book out of her knapsack. "Sounds like what you need to do is create what my project management professor calls a WBS for your project." She pointed to a page in her project management textbook showing a diagram of a WBS.

1. Make a list of the major deliverables for the 5k-run color project and use them to develop a draft of the work breakdown structure for the project that contains, when appropriate, at least three levels of detail.
2. How would developing a WBS alleviate some of the problems that occurred during the first meeting and help Jamal organize and plan the project?

Case 4.2

The Home Improvement Project

Lukas Nelson and his partner, Anne, and their three daughters had been living in their house for over five years when they decided it was time to make some modest improvements. One area they both agreed needed an upgrade was the bathtub. Their current house had one standard shower/bathtub combination. Lukas was 6 feet four and could barely squeeze into it. In fact, he had taken only one bath since they moved in. He and Anne both missed soaking in the older, deep bathtubs they enjoyed when they lived back East.

Fortunately, the previous owners, who had built the house, had plumbed the corner of a large exercise room in the basement for a hot tub. They contacted a trusted remodeling contractor, who assured them it would be relatively easy to install a new bathtub and it shouldn't cost more than $2,500. They decided to go ahead with the project.

First, the Nelsons went to the local plumbing retailer to pick out a tub. They soon realized that for a few hundred dollars more they could buy a big tub with water jets (a Jacuzzi). With old age on the horizon a Jacuzzi seemed like a luxury that was worth the extra money.

Originally the plan was to install the tub using the simple plastic frame the bath came with and install a splash guard around the tub. Once Anne saw the tub, frame, and splashguard in the room she balked. She did not like how it looked with the cedar paneling in the exercise room. After significant debate, Anne won out, and the Nelsons agreed to pay extra to have a cedar frame built for the tub and use attractive tile instead of the plastic splashguard. Lukas rationalized that the changes would pay for themselves when they tried to sell the house.

The next hiccup occurred when it came time to address the flooring issue. The exercise room was carpeted, which wasn't ideal when getting out of a bathtub. The original idea was to install relatively cheap laminated flooring in the drying and undressing area adjacent to the tub. However, the Nelsons couldn't agree on the pattern to use. One of Anne's friends said it would be a shame to put such cheap flooring in such a nice room. Her friend felt they should consider using tile. The contractor agreed and said he knew a tile installer who needed work and would give them a good deal.

Lukas reluctantly agreed that the laminated options just didn't fit the style or quality of the exercise room. Unlike the laminated floor debate, both Anne and Lukas immediately liked a tile pattern that matched the tile used around the tub. Anxious not to delay the project, they agreed to pay for the tile flooring.

Once the tub was installed and the framing was almost completed, Anne realized that something had to be done about the lighting. One of her favorite things to do was to read while soaking in the tub. The existing lights didn't provide sufficient illumination for doing so. Lukas knew this was "nonnegotiable" and they hired an electrician to install additional lighting over the bathtub.

While the lighting was being installed and the tile was being laid, another issue came up. The original plan was to tile only the exercise room and use remnant rugs to cover the area away from the tub where the Nelsons did their exercises. The Nelsons were very happy with how the tile looked and fit with the overall room. However, it clashed with the laminated flooring in the adjacent bathroom. Lukas agreed with Anne that it really made the adjacent bathroom look cheap and ugly. He also felt the bathroom was so small it wouldn't cost much more.

After a week, the work was completed. Both Lukas and Anne were quite pleased with how everything turned out. It cost much more than they had planned, but they planned to live in the house until the girls graduated from college, so they felt it was a good long-term investment.

Anne had the first turn using the bathtub, followed by their three girls. Everyone enjoyed the Jacuzzi. It was 10:00 p.m. when Lukas began running water for his first bath. At first the water was steaming hot, but by the time he was about to get in, it was lukewarm at best. Lukas groaned, "After paying all of that money I still can't enjoy a bath."

The Nelsons rationed bathing for a couple weeks, until they decided to find out what, if anything, could be done about the hot water problem. They asked a reputable heating contractor to assess the situation. The contractor reported that the hot water tank was insufficient to service a family of five. This had not been discovered before because baths were rarely taken in the past. The contractor said it would cost $2,800 to replace the existing water heater with a larger one that would meet their needs. The heating contractor also said if they wanted to do it right they should replace the existing furnace with a more energy-efficient one. A new furnace would not only heat the house but also indirectly heat the water tank. Such a furnace would cost $11,500, but with the improved efficiency and savings in the gas bill, the furnace would pay for itself in 10 years. Besides, the Nelsons would likely receive tax credits for the more fuel-efficient furnace.

Three weeks later, after the new furnace was installed, Lukas settled into the new bathtub. He looked around the room at all the changes that had been made and muttered to himself, "And to think that all I wanted was to soak in a nice, hot bath."

1. What factors and forces contributed to scope creep in this case?
2. Is this an example of good or bad scope creep? Explain.
3. How could scope creep have been better managed by the Nelsons?

CHAPTER FIVE

5 Estimating Project Times and Costs

LEARNING OBJECTIVES

After reading this chapter you should be able to:

5-1 Understand estimating project times and costs is the foundation for project planning and control.

5-2 Identify different aspects of estimating.

5-3 Describe guidelines for estimating time, costs, and resources.

5-4 Describe the methods, uses, and advantages and disadvantages of top-down and bottom-up estimating methods.

5-5 Distinguish different kinds of costs associated with a project.

5-6 Suggest a scheme for developing an estimating database for future projects.

5-7 Understand the challenge of estimating mega projects and describe steps that lead to better informed decisions.

5-8 Define a "white elephant" in project management and provide examples.

A5-1 Use learning curves to improve task estimates.

OUTLINE

5.1 Factors Influencing the Quality of Estimates

5.2 Estimating Guidelines for Times, Costs, and Resources

5.3 Top-Down versus Bottom-Up Estimating

5.4 Methods for Estimating Project Times and Costs

5.5 Level of Detail

5.6 Types of Costs

5.7 Refining Estimates

5.8 Creating a Database for Estimating

5.9 Mega Projects: A Special Case

Summary

Appendix 5.1: Learning Curves for Estimating

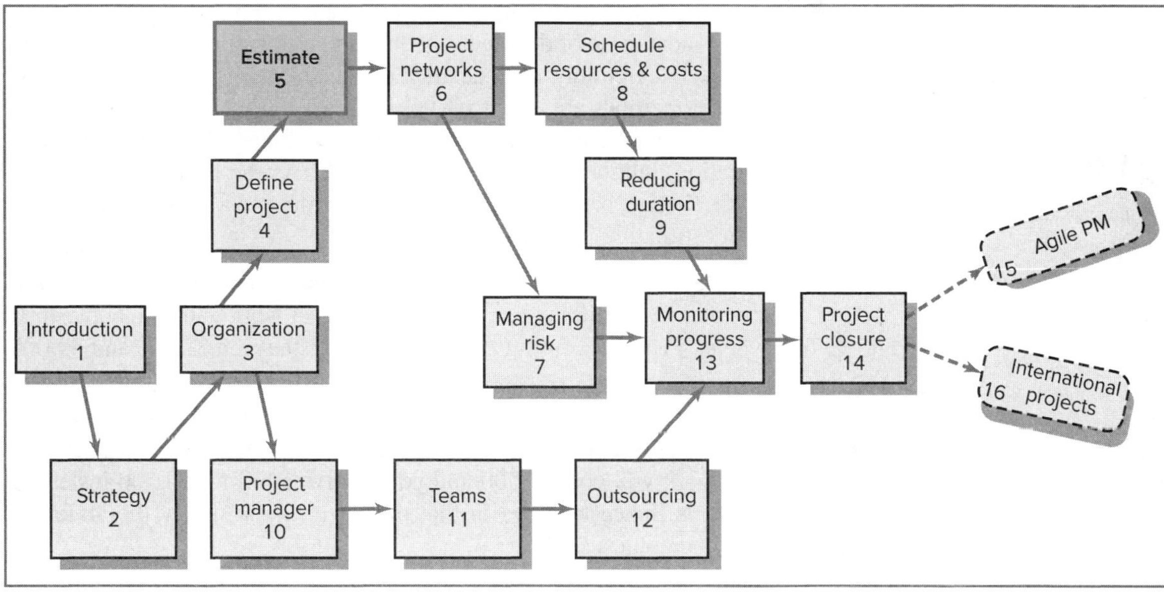

Plans are of little importance, but planning is essential.

— Winston Churchill, former British prime minister

LO 5-1

Understand estimating project times and costs is the foundation for project planning and control.

Estimating is the process of forecasting or approximating the time and cost of completing project deliverables. Estimating processes are frequently classified as top-down and bottom up. Top-down estimates are usually done by senior management. Management will often derive estimates from analogy, group consensus, or mathematical relationships. Bottom-up estimates are typically performed by the people who are doing the work. Their estimates are based on estimates of elements found in the work breakdown structure. Exhibit 5.1 summarizes some of the key reasons for estimating.

All project stakeholders prefer accurate cost and time estimates, but they also understand the inherent uncertainty in all projects. Inaccurate estimates lead to false expectations and consumer dissatisfaction. Accuracy is improved with greater effort, but is it worth the time and cost? Estimating costs money! Project estimating becomes a trade-off, balancing the benefits of better accuracy against the costs for securing increased accuracy.

Cost, time, and budget estimates are the lifeline for control; they serve as the standard for comparison of actual and plan throughout the life of the project. Project status reports depend on reliable estimates as the major input for measuring variances and

EXHIBIT 5.1
Why Estimating Time and Cost Is Important

- Estimates are needed to support good decisions.
- Estimates are needed to schedule work.
- Estimates are needed to determine how long the project should take and its cost.
- Estimates are needed to determine whether the project is worth doing.
- Estimates are needed to develop cash flow needs.
- Estimates are needed to determine how well the project is progressing.

taking corrective action. Ideally, the project manager, and in most cases the customer, would prefer to have a database of detailed schedule and cost estimates for every work package in the project. Regrettably, such detailed data gathering is not always possible or practical, and other methods are used to develop project estimates.

LO 5-2

Identify different aspects of estimating.

Estimates are a quantitative assessment of the likely outcome or amount of a variable like cost, duration, number of people required, etc. As the project evolves estimates are likely to change based on current information and circumstances. Four different aspects of estimating include (PMI, 2021):

1. **Range.** Range refers to the number of potential outcomes that could be expected to occur. For example, your building contractor reports that work will take between 10 and 15 days versus 11 and 13 days. Or the cost will be between \$2,000 and \$3,000.
2. **Accuracy.** Accuracy refers to the correctness of an estimate. For example, if your building contractor completes the work in 9 days then despite being done early the estimate was not accurate. Conversely, an accurate estimate would be one when you are told the work will cost \$2,500 and you receive a bill for \$2,500 instead of \$2,450. Accuracy is linked to range in that the lower the accuracy the larger the number potential outcomes.
3. **Precision.** Precision refers to the degree of exactness associated with the estimate. For example, your contractor reports the work will be done in 15 days instead of "by the end of the month." Or the work should cost \$850 instead of less than a thousand. Precision is different from accuracy in that you can have a very detailed estimate that is far off the mark.
4. **Confidence.** Confidence refers to the degree of trust one has in the estimate. While we would be remiss not to acknowledge that confidence is often based on a "gut feel," it is usually linked to probability. Your contractor is 90 percent sure that the work will be done by Friday, or there is less than a fifty-fifty (50/50) chance we can get the work done for under \$2,000.

As a project progresses, there should be an improvement in the quality of estimates. During the defining stage, estimates will be less precise, accurate, and have a broad range with limited confidence. During the execution stage, one can factor past performance, workforce dynamics, and a better understanding of the challenges into estimates. This information should yield more precise, accurate estimates with greater confidence.

5.1 Factors Influencing the Quality of Estimates

A typical statement in the field is the desire to "have a 95 percent probability of meeting time and cost estimates." *Past experience* is a good starting point for developing time and cost estimates. But past experience estimates must almost always be refined by other considerations to reach the 95 percent probability level. Factors related to the uniqueness of the project will have a strong influence on the accuracy of estimates. Project, people, and external factors all need to be considered to improve the quality of estimates for project times and costs.

Planning Horizon

The quality of the estimate depends on the *planning horizon;* estimates of current events are close to 100 percent accurate but are reduced for more distant events. For example, cost estimates for a party you are organizing this weekend should be much more accurate than the estimates for a party that will take place in six months. Now imagine how difficult it would be to estimate the total cost of a four-year transportation project. The accuracy of time and cost estimates should improve as you move from the conceptual phase to the point where individual work packages are defined.

Project Complexity

Time to implement new *technology* has a habit of expanding in an increasing, nonlinear fashion. Sometimes poorly written scope specifications for new technology result in errors in estimating times and costs.

People

The *people* factor can influence the quality of time and cost estimates. For example, accuracy of estimates depends on the skills of the people making the estimates. How familiar are they with the task they are estimating?

Project Structure and Organization

Which *project structure* is chosen to manage the project will influence time and cost estimates. One of the major advantages of a dedicated project team is the speed gained from concentrated focus and localized project decisions. This speed comes at an additional cost of tying up personnel full time. Conversely, projects operating in a matrix environment may reduce costs by more efficiently sharing personnel across projects but may take longer to complete, since attention is divided and coordination demands are higher.

Padding Estimates

In some cases, people are inclined to *pad estimates.* For example, if you are asked how long it takes you to drive to the airport, you might give an average time of 30 minutes, assuming a 50/50 chance of getting there in 30 minutes. If you are asked the fastest you could possibly get there, you might reduce the driving time to 20 minutes. Finally, if you are asked how long the drive would take if you absolutely had to be there to meet with the president, it is likely you would increase the estimate to, say, 50 minutes to ensure not being late.

In work situations where we are asked for time and cost estimates, most of us are inclined to add a little padding to reduce the risk of being late. If everyone at all levels of the project adds a little padding to reduce risk, the project duration and cost are seriously overstated. This phenomenon causes some managers or owners to call for a 10–15 percent cut in time and/or cost for the project. Of course, the next time the game is played, the person estimating cost and/or time will pad the estimate to 20 percent or more. Clearly, such games defeat chances for realistic estimates, which is what is needed to be competitive.

Organizational Culture

Organizational culture can significantly influence project estimates. In some organizations, padding estimates are tolerated and even privately encouraged. Other organizations place a premium on accuracy and strongly discourage estimating gamesmanship. Organizations vary in the importance they attach to estimates. The prevailing belief in some organizations is that detailed estimating takes too much time and is not worth the effort or that it's impossible to predict the future. Other organizations subscribe to the belief that accurate estimates are the bedrock of effective project management.

Organizational culture shapes every dimension of project management; estimating is not immune to this influence.

Other Factors

Finally, *nonproject factors* can impact time and cost estimates. For example, equipment downtime can alter time estimates. National holidays, vacations, and legal limits can influence project estimates. Project priority can influence resource assignment and impact time and cost.

Project estimating is a complex process. The quality of time and cost estimates can be improved when these variables are considered in making the estimates. Estimates of time and cost together allow the manager to develop a time-phased budget, which is imperative for project control. Before discussing macro and micro estimating methods for times and costs, a review of estimating guidelines will remind us of some of the important "rules of the game" that can improve estimating.

5.2 Estimating Guidelines for Times, Costs, and Resources

LO 5-3

Describe guidelines for estimating time, costs, and resources.

Managers recognize time, cost, and resource estimates must be accurate if project planning, scheduling, and controlling are to be effective. However, there is substantial evidence suggesting poor estimates are a major contributor to projects that have failed. Therefore, every effort should be made to see that initial estimates are as accurate as possible, since the choice of no estimates leaves a great deal to luck and is not palatable to serious project managers. Even though a project has never been done before, a manager can follow seven guidelines to develop useful work package estimates.

1. **Responsibility.** At the work package level, estimates should be made by the person(s) most familiar with the task. Draw on their expertise! Except for supertechnical tasks, those responsible for getting the job done on schedule and within budget are usually first-line supervisors or technicians who are experienced and familiar with the type of work involved. These people will not have some preconceived, imposed duration for a deliverable in mind. They will give an estimate based on experience and best judgment. A secondary benefit of using those responsible is the hope they will "buy in" to seeing that the estimate materializes when they implement the work package. If those involved are not consulted, it will be difficult to hold them responsible for failure to achieve the estimated time. Finally, drawing on the expertise of team members who will be responsible helps to build communication channels early.
2. **The use of several people to estimate.** It is well known that a cost or time estimate usually has a better chance of being reasonable and realistic when several people with relevant experience and/or knowledge of the task are used (sometimes called "crowdsourcing"). True, people bring different biases based on their experience. But discussion of the individual differences in their estimate leads to consensus and tends to eliminate extreme estimate errors.
3. **Normal conditions.** When task time, cost, and resource estimates are determined, they are based on certain assumptions. *Estimates should be based on normal conditions, efficient methods, and a normal level of resources.* Normal conditions are sometimes difficult to discern, but it is necessary to have a consensus in the organization as to what normal conditions mean in this project. If the normal workday is eight hours, the time estimate should be based on an eight-hour day. Similarly, if the normal workday is two shifts, the time estimate should be based on a two-shift workday. Any time estimate should reflect efficient methods for the resources normally available.

The time estimate should represent the normal level of resources—people or equipment. For example, if three programmers are available for coding or two road graders are available for road construction, time and cost estimates should be based on these normal levels of resources unless it is anticipated the project will change what is currently viewed as "normal." In addition, possible conflicts in demand for resources on parallel or concurrent activities should not be considered at this stage. The need for adding resources will be examined when resource scheduling is discussed in a later chapter.

4. **Time units.** Specific time units to use should be selected early in the development phase of the project network. *All task time estimates need consistent time units.* Estimates of time must consider whether normal time is represented by calendar days, workdays, workweeks, person days, single shift, hours, minutes, etc. In practice, the use of workdays is the dominant choice for expressing task duration. However, in projects such as a heart transplant operation, minutes probably would be more appropriate as a time unit. One such project that used minutes as the time unit was the movement of patients from an old hospital to an elegant new one across town. Since there were several life-endangering moves, minutes were used to ensure patient safety so that proper emergency life-support systems would be available if needed. The point is, network analysis requires a standard unit of time. When computer programs allow more than one option, some notation should be made of any variance from the standard unit of time. If the standard unit of time is a five-day workweek and the estimated activity duration is in calendar days, it must be converted to the normal workweek.
5. **Independence.** Estimators should treat each task as independent of other tasks that might be integrated by the WBS. Use of first-line managers usually results in considering tasks independently; this is good. Top managers are prone to aggregate many tasks into one time estimate and then deductively make the individual task time estimates add to the total. If tasks are in a chain and performed by the same group or department, it is best not to ask for all the time estimates in the sequence at once to avoid the tendency for a planner or a supervisor to look at the whole path and try to adjust individual task times in the sequence to meet an arbitrary imposed schedule or some rough "guesstimate" of the total time for the whole path or segment of the project. This tendency does not reflect the uncertainties of individual activities and generally results in optimistic task time estimates. In summary, each task time estimate should be considered independently of other activities.
6. **Contingencies.** *Work package estimates should not include allowances for contingencies.* The estimate should assume normal or average conditions, even though every work package will not materialize as planned. For this reason, top management needs to create an extra fund for contingencies that can be used to cover unforeseen events.
7. **Risk assessment added to the estimate to avoid surprises to stakeholders.** It is obvious some tasks carry more time and cost risks than others. For example, a new technology usually carries more time and cost risks than a proven process. Simply identifying the degree of risk lets stakeholders consider alternative methods and alter process decisions. A simple breakdown by optimistic, most likely, and pessimistic for task time could provide valuable information regarding time and cost. See Chapter 7 for further discussion of project risk.

Where applicable, these guidelines will greatly help to avoid many of the pitfalls found so often in practice.

5.3 Top-Down versus Bottom-Up Estimating

LO 5-4

Describe the methods, uses, and advantages and disadvantages of top-down and bottom-up estimating methods.

Since estimating efforts cost money, the time and detail devoted to estimating are important decisions. Yet when estimating is considered, you as a project manager may hear statements such as these:

> *Rough order of magnitude is good enough. Spending time on detailed estimating wastes money.*
> *Time is everything; our survival depends on getting there first! Time and cost accuracy is not an issue.*
> *The project is internal. We don't need to worry about cost.*
> *The project is so small. We don't need to bother with estimates. Just do it.*

However, there are sound reasons for using top-down or bottom-up estimates. Table 5.1 depicts conditions that suggest when one approach is preferred over another.

Top-down estimates usually are derived from someone who uses experience and/or information to determine the project duration and total cost. However, these estimates are sometimes made by top managers who have very little knowledge of the component activities used to complete the project. For example, a mayor of a major city making a speech noted that a new law building would be constructed at a cost of $23 million and would be ready for occupancy in two and one-half years. Although the mayor probably asked for an estimate from someone, the estimate could have come from a luncheon meeting with a local contractor who wrote an estimate (guesstimate) on a napkin. This is an extreme example, but in a relative sense this scenario is frequently played out in practice. See Snapshot from Practice 5.1: Portland Aerial Tram for another example of this. The question actually is, do these estimates represent low-cost, efficient methods? Seldom. The fact that the estimate came from the top can influence people responsible to "do what it takes to make the estimate."

If possible and practical, you want to push the estimating process down to the work package level for **bottom-up estimates** that establish low-cost, efficient methods. This process can take place after the project has been defined in detail. Good sense suggests project estimates should come from the people most knowledgeable about the estimate needed. The use of several people with relevant experience with the task can improve the time and cost estimate. The bottom-up approach at the work package level can serve as a check on cost elements in the WBS by rolling up the work packages and associated cost accounts to major deliverables. Similarly, resource requirements can be checked. Later, the time, resource, and cost estimates from the work packages can be consolidated into time-phased networks, resource schedules, and budgets that are used for control.

TABLE 5.1 Conditions for Preferring Top-Down or Bottom-Up Time and Cost Estimates

Condition	Top-Down Estimates	Bottom-Up Estimates
Strategic decision making	X	
Cost and time important		X
High uncertainty	X	
Internal, small project	X	
Fixed-price contract		X
Customer wants details		X
Unstable scope	X	

SNAPSHOT FROM PRACTICE 5.1 Portland Aerial Tram*

The Portland Tram is an aerial tramway in Portland, Oregon. The tram carries passengers between the city's south waterfront and the main Oregon Health & Science University (OHSU) campus, which is located high on a bluff overlooking the waterfront. The tram ride takes four minutes and rises over 500 feet. The tram was jointly funded by OHSU, the city of Portland, and south waterfront property owners.

OHSU was the driving force behind the project. OHSU argued that the tram was needed so it could expand its operations to the south waterfront, where there were plans to build several major facilities. The tram would also reduce traffic congestions and make it easier for OHSU employees to commute to work. OHSU is a major player in the Oregon economy, with an estimated annual economic impact of over $4 billion and over 35,000 jobs.

The OHSU tram would be one of only two city trams in the United States, and advocates championed the idea that the tram would become an icon for the city like Seattle's Space Needle.

OHSU political clout helped gain approval by the Portland city council for the project in 2003. The initial cost estimate was $15 million, with the city directly responsible for $2 million. A public review in 2004 revealed a new cost estimate of $18.5 million. A second review in 2005 led to a cost readjustment of $40 million with a construction delay of six months.

In 2006 a change in city leadership led to an independent audit being conducted on the tram project. The audit revealed that OSHU managers knew as early as 2003 that the cost of the tram would be in excess of $15.5 million but withheld the information from city officials.

Public reaction was immediate and harsh. City Commissioner Randy Leonard accused the OHSU leadership of an "outrageous shell game . . . all at the expense of taxpayers." The city of Portland threatened to pull out of the project. OHSU protested vigorously, threatening a lawsuit, should the tram be canceled. Negotiations ensued.

Rigucci/Shutterstock

A revised funding plan and budget were agreed upon in April 2006, by a 3–2 vote of the city council. This plan required concessions from all parties involved and called for a final budget of $57 million, with direct contributions from the city of $8.5 million, or nearly 15 percent of the overall budget. This final budget was met, and the tram was opened to the public on January 27, 2007.

Budget concerns were not the only problem facing the tram project. Many residents in the neighborhood beneath the tram were concerned that the tram would be an invasion of privacy and lead to lower property values. The residents were promised that the overhead power lines would be buried, but as a cost saving measure the plans were scrapped. One irate homeowner living below the track placed a sign on his backyard fence stating "F%&! The Tram." The sign was not visible from the street, only from the air. Lawsuits ensued.

The city ultimately negotiated with each resident living under the tramway and offered fair market value for their homes.

*R. Gragg and A. Scott, "From Controversy to Icon: Portland's Aerial Tram Turns 10," *Oregon Broadcasting Network,* February 12, 2017, www.opb.org/radio/. Accessed 2/14/19; S. Moore, "Audit: Tram Costs Shoot Skyward—Again," *Portland Mercury,* www.portlandmercury.com, February 2, 2006. Accessed 2/20/19; E. Njus, "Portland Aerial Tram Marks Its 10th Anniversary," *Oregonian,* www.oregonlive.com. Accessed 2/2/19.

The bottom-up approach also provides the customer with an opportunity to compare the low-cost, efficient method approach with any imposed restrictions. For example, if the project completion duration is imposed at two years and your bottom-up analysis tells you the project will take two and one-half years, the client can now consider the trade-off of the low-cost method versus compressing the project to two years—or in rare cases canceling the project. Similar trade-offs can be compared for different levels of resources or increases in technical performance. The assumption is any movement away from the low-cost, efficient method will increase costs—for example, overtime. The preferred approach in defining the project is to make rough top-down estimates, develop the WBS/OBS, make bottom-up estimates, develop schedules and budgets, and reconcile differences between top-down and bottom-up estimates. These steps should be done *before* final negotiation with either an internal or external customer.

In conclusion, the ideal approach is for the project manager to allow enough time for both the top-down and bottom-up estimates to be worked out so that a complete plan based on reliable estimates can be offered to the customer. In this way false expectations are minimized for all stakeholders and negotiation is reduced.

5.4 Methods for Estimating Project Times and Costs

Top-Down Approaches for Estimating Project Times and Costs

At the strategic level, top-down estimating methods are used to evaluate the project proposal. Sometimes much of the information needed to derive accurate time and cost estimates is not available in the initial phase of the project—for example, design is not finalized. In these situations top-down estimates are used until the tasks in the WBS are clearly defined.

Consensus Method

This method simply uses the pooled experience of senior and/or middle managers to estimate the total project duration and cost. It typically involves a meeting where experts discuss, argue, and ultimately reach a decision as to their best guesstimate. Firms seeking greater rigor will use the Delphi Method to make these macro estimates. See Snapshot from Practice 5.2: The Delphi Method.

It is important to recognize that these first top-down estimates are only a rough cut and typically occur in the "conceptual" stage of the project. The top-down estimates are helpful in initial development of a complete plan. However, such estimates are sometimes significantly off the mark because little detailed information is gathered. At this level, individual work items are not identified. Or, in a few cases, the top-down estimates are not realistic because top management "wants the project." Nevertheless, the initial top-down estimates are helpful in determining whether the project warrants more formal planning, which would include more detailed estimates. Be careful that macro estimates made by senior managers are not dictated to lower-level managers who might feel compelled to accept the estimates even if they believe resources are inadequate.

Ratio Method

Top-down methods (sometimes called parametric) usually use ratios, or surrogates, to estimate project times or costs. Top-down **ratio methods** are often used in the concept, or "need," phase of a project to get an initial duration and cost estimate for the project. For example, contractors frequently use number of square feet to estimate the cost and time to build a house; that is, a house of 2,700 square feet might cost \$200 per square foot (2,700 feet × \$200 per square foot equals \$540,000). Likewise, knowing the square feet and dollars per square foot, experience suggests it should take approximately 150 days to complete. Two other common examples of top-down cost estimates are the cost for a new plant estimated by capacity size and a software product estimated by features and complexity.

SNAPSHOT FROM PRACTICE 5.2 The Delphi Method

Originally developed by the RAND Corporation in 1969 for technological forecasting, the **Delphi Method** is a group decision process about the likelihood that certain events will occur. The Delphi Method makes use of a panel of experts familiar with the kind of project in question. The notion is that well-informed individuals, calling on their insights and experience, are better equipped to estimate project costs/times than theoretical approaches or statistical methods. Their responses to estimate questionnaires are anonymous, and they are provided with a summary of opinions.

Experts are then encouraged to reconsider, and if appropriate, to change their previous estimate in light of the replies of other experts. After two or three rounds it is believed that the group will converge toward the "best" response through this consensus process. The midpoint of responses is statistically categorized by the median score. In each succeeding round of questionnaires, the range of responses by the panelists will presumably decrease and the median will move toward what is deemed to be the "correct" estimate.

A movie exec would use the Delphi Method to decide whether to invest in the remaking of a classic film, like *Gunga Din.*[1] He is concerned because both the screenwriter and director insist on shooting the film on location in Rajasthan, India. He recruits five experts who have worked on film projects overseas, two recently in India. He provides each of them with a detailed summary proposal that describes the requirements as well as the 75-day shooting schedule. He asks them to respond to an estimating questionnaire concerning the costs of certain deliverables (e.g., accommodations, sets) as well as total operational costs, ignoring the lead actors' contracts. He is surprised by the disparity between those who have worked in India and the others. After several rounds, where opinions and ideas are exchanged, he has a fairly good idea of what the total costs are likely to be as well as the risks involved. When he combines this information with market research, he concludes that the project is not worth the investment.

One distinct advantage of the Delphi Method is that the experts never need to be brought together physically. The process also does not require complete agreement by all panelists, since the majority opinion is represented by the median. Since the responses are anonymous, the pitfalls of ego, domineering personalities, and the bandwagon or halo effect in responses are all avoided.

[1] *Gunga Din* is a 1939 adventure film that tells the tale of three British officers in Rajasthan, India, who, thanks to a water boy (Gunga Din), survive a rebel revolt.

Apportion Method

This method is an extension to the ratio method. **Apportionment** is used when projects closely follow past projects in features and costs. Given good historical data, estimates can be made quickly with little effort and reasonable accuracy. This method is very common in projects that are relatively standard but have some small variation or customization.

Anyone who has borrowed money from a bank to build a house has been exposed to this process. Given an estimated total cost for the house, banks and the FHA (Federal Housing Authority) authorize pay to the contractor by completion of specific segments of the house. For example, foundation might represent 3 percent of the total loan, framing 25 percent, plumbing and heating 15 percent, etc. Payments are made as these items are completed. An analogous process is used by some companies that apportion costs to deliverables in the WBS—given average cost percentages from past projects. Figure 5.1 presents an example similar to one found in practice. Assuming the total project cost is estimated, using a top-down estimate, to be \$500,000, the costs are apportioned as a percentage of the total cost. For example, the costs apportioned to the "Document" deliverable are 5 percent of the total, or \$25,000. The subdeliverables "Doc-1 and Doc-2" are allocated 2 and 3 percent of the total—\$10,000 and \$15,000, respectively.

FIGURE 5.1
Apportion Method of Allocating Project Costs Using the Work Breakdown Structure

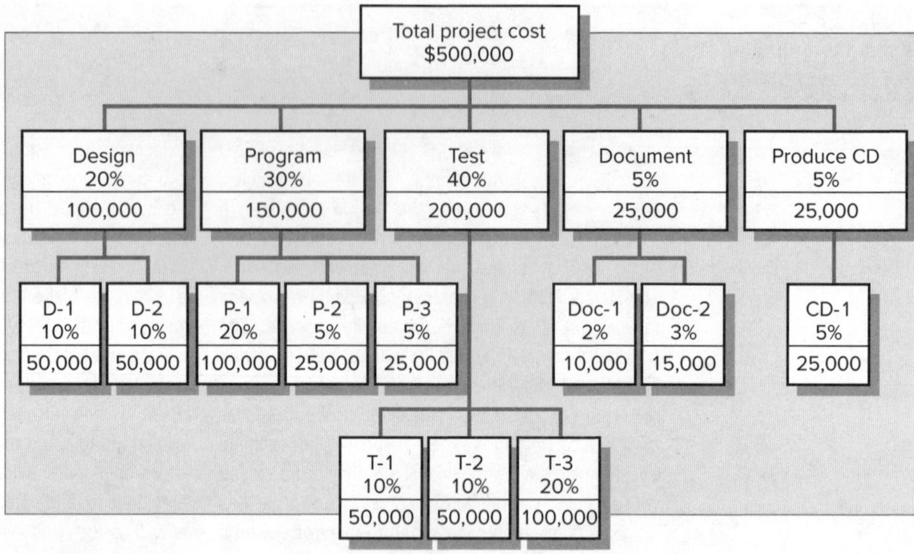

Function Point Methods for Software and System Projects

In the software industry, software development projects are frequently estimated using weighted macro variables called **function points** or major parameters such as number of inputs, number of outputs, number of inquiries, number of data files, and number of interfaces. These weighted variables are adjusted for a complexity factor and added. The total adjusted count provides the basis for estimating the labor effort and cost for a project (usually using a regression formula derived from data of past projects). This latter method assumes adequate historical data by type of software project for the industry—for example, MIS systems. In the U.S. software industry, one person-month represents on average five function points. A person working one month can generate on average (across all types of software projects) about five function points. Of course, each organization needs to develop its own average for its specific type of work. Such historical data provide a basis for estimating the project duration. Variations of this top-down approach are used by companies such as IBM, Bank of America, Sears Roebuck, HP, AT&T, Ford Motors, GE, DuPont, and many others. See Tables 5.2 and 5.3 for a simplified example of function point count methodology.

From historical data, the organization developed the weighting scheme for complexity found in Table 5.2. Function points are derived from multiplying the number of kinds of elements by weighted complexity.

TABLE 5.2
Simplified Basic Function Point Count Process for a Prospective Project or Deliverable

	Complexity Weighting			
Element	**Low**	**Average**	**High**	**Total**
Number of *inputs*	____ × 2 +	____ × 3 +	____ × 4	= ____
Number of *outputs*	____ × 3 +	____ × 6 +	____ × 9	= ____
Number of *inquiries*	____ × 2 +	____ × 4 +	____ × 6	= ____
Number of *files*	____ × 4 +	____ × 8 +	____ × 12	= ____
Number of *interfaces*	____ × 5 +	____ × 10 +	____ × 15	= ____

TABLE 5.3
Example: Function Point Count Method

Software Project 13: Patient Admitting and Billing			
15	Inputs	Rated complexity as low	(2)
5	Outputs	Rated complexity as average	(6)
10	Inquiries	Rated complexity as average	(4)
30	Files	Rated complexity as high	(12)
20	Interfaces	Rated complexity as average	(10)

Application of Complexity Factor

Element	Count	Low	Average	High	Total
Inputs	15	× 2			= 30
Outputs	5		× 6		= 30
Inquiries	10		× 4		= 40
Files	30			× 12	= 360
Interfaces	20		× 10		= 200
				Total	660

Table 5.3 shows the data collected for a specific task or deliverable: Patient Admitting and Billing—the number of inputs, outputs, inquiries, files, and interfaces along with the expected complexity rating. Finally, the application of the element count is applied and the function point count total is 660. Given this count and the fact that 1 person-month has historically been equal to 5 function points, the job will require 132 person-months (660/5 = 132). Assuming you have 10 programmers who can work on this task, the duration would be approximately 13 months. The cost is easily derived by multiplying the labor rate per month times 132 person-months. For example, if the monthly programmer rate is $8,000, then the estimated cost would be $1,056,000 (132 × 8,000). Although function point metrics are useful, their accuracy depends on adequate historical data, the currency of the data, and the relevancy of the project/deliverable to past averages.

Learning Curves

Some projects require that the same task, group of tasks, or product be repeated several times. Managers know intuitively that the time to perform a task improves with repetition. This phenomenon is especially true of tasks that are labor intensive. In these circumstances, the pattern of improvement phenomenon can be used to predict the reduction in time to perform the task. From empirical evidence across *all* industries, the pattern of this improvement has been quantified in the **learning curve** (also known as improvement curve, experience curve, and industrial progress curve), which is described by the following relationship:

Each time the output quantity doubles, the unit labor hours are reduced at a constant rate.

In practice the improvement ratio may vary from 60 percent, representing very large improvement, to 100 percent, representing no improvement at all. Generally, as the difficulty of the work decreases the expected improvement also decreases and the improvement ratio that is used becomes greater. One significant factor to consider is the proportion of labor in the task in relation to machine-paced work. Obviously, a lower percentage of improvement can occur only in operations with high labor content. Appendix 5.1 at the end of the chapter provides a detailed example of how the improvement phenomenon can be used to estimate time and cost for repetitive tasks.

The main disadvantage of top-down approaches to estimating is simply that the time and cost for a specific task are not considered. Grouping many tasks into a common basket encourages errors of omission and the use of imposed times and costs.

Micro, bottom-up estimating methods are usually more accurate than macro methods.

Bottom-Up Approaches for Estimating Project Times and Costs

Template Method

If the project is similar to past projects, then **template methods** can be used as a starting point for the new project. Templates are created based on the costs of previous, similar projects. Differences in the new project can be noted and past times and costs adjusted to reflect these differences. For example, a ship repair drydock firm has a set of standard repair projects (i.e., templates for overhaul, electrical, mechanical) that are used as starting points for estimating the cost and duration of any new project. Differences from the appropriate standardized project are noted (for times, costs, and resources) and changes are made. This approach enables the firm to develop a potential schedule, estimate costs, and develop a budget in a very short time span. Development of such templates in a database can quickly reduce estimate errors.

Parametric Procedures Applied to Specific Tasks

Just as parametric techniques such as cost per square foot can be the source of top-down estimates, the same technique can be applied to specific tasks. For example, as part of an MS Office conversion project, 36 different computer workstations needed to be converted. Based on past conversion projects, the project manager determined that on average one person could convert three workstations per day. Therefore, the task of converting the 36 workstations would take three technicians four days [(36/3)/3]. Similarly, to estimate the wallpapering allowance on a house remodel, contractors figured a cost of $7 per square yard of wallpaper and $4 per square yard to install it, for a total cost of $11. By measuring the length and height of all the walls, they were able to calculate the total area in square yards and multiply it by $11.

Range Estimating

When do you use range estimating? **Range estimating** works best when work packages have significant uncertainty associated with the time or cost to complete. If the work package is routine and carries little uncertainty, using the people most familiar with the work package is usually the best approach. They are likely to know best how to estimate work packages durations and costs. However, when work packages have significant uncertainty associated with the time or cost to complete, it is a prudent policy to require three time estimates—low, average, and high (borrowed from PERT methodology that uses probability distributions). The low to high give a range within which the average estimate will fall. Determining the low and high estimates for the activity is influenced by factors such as complexity, technology, newness, and familiarity.

How do you get the estimates? Since range estimating works best for work packages that have significant uncertainty, having a group determine the low, average, and high cost or duration gives best results. Group estimating tends to refine extremes by bringing more evaluative judgments to the estimate and potential risks. The judgment of others in a group helps to moderate extreme perceived risks associated with a time or cost estimate. Involving others in making activity estimates gains buy-in and credibility to the estimate.

FIGURE 5.2
Range Estimating Template

	A	B	C	D	E	F	G	H
1	Project number: 18				Project Manager: Dawn O'Connor			
2	Project description:	New Organic Wine Launch			Date: 2/17/2xxx			
3			Organic Wine Launch Project					
4			Range Estimates					
5								
6	WBS	Description	Low	Average	High	Range	Risk	
7	ID		Estimate	Estimate	Estimate		Level	
8			Days	Days	Days	Days		
9								
10	102	Approval	1	1	3	2	low	
11	103	Design packaging	4	7	12	8	medium	
12	104	ID potential customers	14	21	35	21	high	
13	105	Design bottle logo	5	7	10	5	low	
14	106	Contract kiosk space	8	10	15	7	medium	
15	107	Construct kiosk	4	4	8	4	medium	
16	108	Design fair brochure	6	7	12	6	high	
17	109	Trade journal advertising	10	12	15	5	medium	
18	110	Production test	10	14	20	10	high	
19	111	Produce to inventory	5	5	10	5	high	
20	112	Business card scanner hookup	1	2	3	2	low	
21	113	Video hook up	2	2	4	2	medium	
22	114	Event rehearsal	2	2	5	3	high	

Microsoft Corporation

Figure 5.2 presents an abridged estimating template using three time estimates for work packages developed by a cross-functional group or groups of project stakeholders. The group estimates show the low, average, and high for each work package. The Risk Level column is the group's independent assessment of the degree of confidence that the actual time will be very close to the estimate. In a sense, this number represents the group's evaluation of many factors (e.g., complexity, technology) that might impact the average time estimate. In our example, the group feels work packages 104, 108, 110, 111, and 114 have a high chance that the average time may vary from expected. Likewise, the group's confidence feels the risk of work packages 102, 105, and 112 not materializing as expected is low.

How do you use the estimate? Group range estimating gives the project manager and owner an opportunity to assess the confidence associated with project times (and/or costs). For example, a contractor responsible for building a high-rise apartment building can tell the owner that the project will cost between $3.5 and $4.1 million and take between six and nine months to complete. The approach helps to reduce surprises as the project progresses. The range estimating method also provides a basis for assessing risk, managing resources, and determining the project contingency fund. (See Chapter 7 for a discussion of contingency funds.) Range estimating is popular in software and new product projects where up-front requirements are fuzzy and not well known. Group range estimating is often used with phase estimating, which is discussed next.

A Hybrid: Phase Estimating

This approach begins with a top-down estimate for the project and then refines estimates for phases of the project as it is implemented. Some projects by their nature cannot be rigorously defined because of the uncertainty of design or the final product. These projects are often found in aerospace projects, IT projects, new technology projects, and construction projects where design is incomplete. In these projects, phase or life-cycle estimating is frequently used.

Phase estimating is used when an unusual amount of uncertainty surrounds a project and it is impractical to estimate times and costs for the entire project. Phase

FIGURE 5.3
Phase Estimating over Project Life Cycle

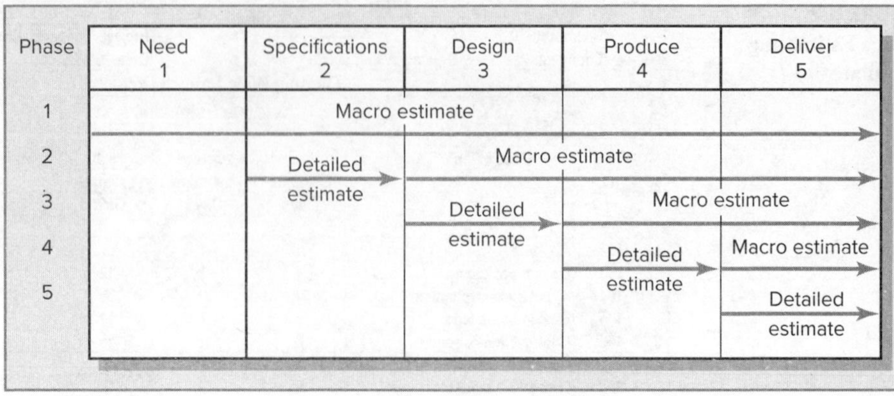

estimating uses a two-estimate system over the life of the project. A detailed estimate is developed for the immediate phase and a macro estimate is made for the remaining phases of the project. Figure 5.3 depicts the phases of a project and the progression of estimates over its life.

For example, when the project need is determined, a macro estimate of the project cost and duration is made so analysis and decisions can be made. Simultaneously a detailed estimate is made for deriving project specifications and a macro estimate for the remainder of the project. As the project progresses and specifications are solidified, a detailed estimate for design is made and a macro estimate for the remainder of the project is computed. Clearly, as the project progresses through its life cycle and more information is available, the reliability of the estimates should be improving. See Snapshot from Practice 5.3: Estimate Accuracy.

Phase estimating is preferred by those working on projects where the final product is not known and the uncertainty is very large—for example, the development of reusable rockets or domestic robots. The commitment to cost and schedule is only necessary over the next phase of the project, and commitment to unrealistic future schedules and costs based on poor information is avoided. This progressive macro/micro method provides a stronger basis for using schedule and cost estimates to manage progress during the next phase.

Unfortunately, your customer—internal or external—will want an accurate estimate of schedule and cost the moment the decision is made to implement the project. Additionally, the customer who is paying for the project often perceives phase estimating as a blank check because costs and schedules are not firm over most of the project life cycle. Even though the reasons for phase estimating are sound and legitimate, most customers have to be sold on its legitimacy. A major advantage for the customer is the opportunity to change features, re-evaluate the project, or even cancel it in each new phase. In conclusion, phase estimating is very useful in projects that possess huge uncertainties concerning the final nature (shape, size, features) of the project.

See Figure 5.4 for a summary of the differences between top-down and bottom-up estimates.

Obtaining accurate estimates is a challenge. Committed organizations accept the challenge of coming up with meaningful estimates and invest heavily in developing their capacity to do so. Accurate estimates reduce uncertainty and support a discipline for effectively managing projects.

SNAPSHOT FROM PRACTICE 5.3 Estimate Accuracy

The smaller the element of a work package, the more accurate the overall estimate is likely to be. The extent of this improvement varies by type of project. The following table is developed to reflect this observation. For example, information technology projects that determine their time and cost estimates in the conceptual stage can expect their "actuals" to err up to 200 percent over cost and duration and, perhaps, as much as 30 percent under estimates. Conversely, estimates for buildings, roads, and so on, made after the work packages are clearly defined, have a smaller error in actual costs and times of 15 percent over estimate and 5 percent less than estimate. Although these estimates vary by project, they can serve as ballpark numbers for project stakeholders selecting how project time and cost estimates will be derived.

Time and Cost Estimate Accuracy by Type of Project

	Bricks and Mortar	Information Technology
Conceptual stage	+60% to −30%	+200% to −30%
Deliverables defined	+30% to −15%	+100% to −15%
Work packages defined	+15% to − 5%	+ 50% to − 5%

FIGURE 5.4
Top-Down and Bottom-Up Estimates

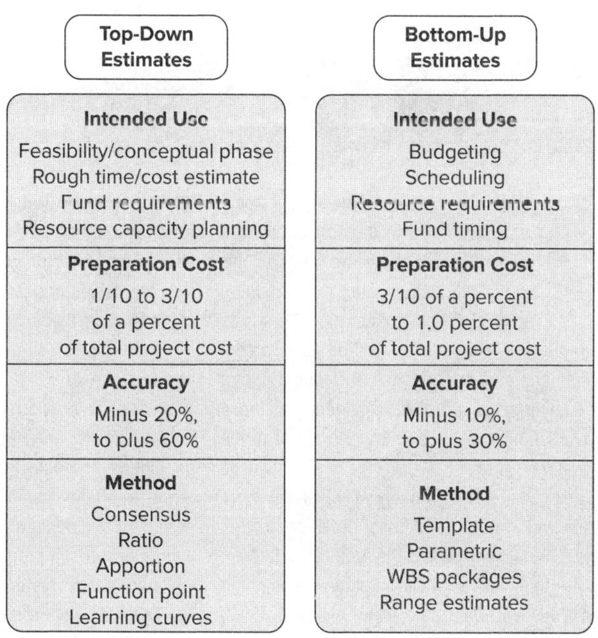

5.5 Level of Detail

Level of detail is different for different levels of management. At any level, the detail should be no more than is necessary and sufficient. Top management interests usually center on the total project and major milestone events that mark major accomplishments—for example, "build oil platform in the north sea" or "complete prototype." Middle management might center on one segment of the project or one milestone. First-line managers' interests may be limited to one task or work package. One of the beauties of WBS is the ability to aggregate network information so each level of management can have the kind of information necessary to make decisions.

Getting the level of detail in the WBS to match management needs for effective implementation is crucial, but the delicate balance is difficult to find. See Snapshot from Practice 5.4: Level of Detail. The level of detail in the WBS varies with the complexity of the project; the need for control; the project size, cost, and duration; and other factors. If the structure reflects excessive detail, there is a tendency to break the work effort into department assignments. This tendency can become a barrier to success, since the emphasis will be on departmental outcomes rather than on deliverable outcomes. Excessive detail also means more unproductive paperwork. Note that if the level of the WBS is increased by one, the number of cost accounts may increase geometrically. On the other hand, if the level of detail is not adequate, an organization unit may find the structure falls short of meeting its needs. Fortunately, the WBS has built-in flexibility. Participating organization units may expand their portion of the structure to meet their special needs. For example, the Engineering Department may wish to further break their work on a deliverable into smaller packages by electrical, civil, and mechanical. Similarly, the Marketing Department may wish to break their new product promotion into TV, radio, periodicals, and newspapers.

SNAPSHOT FROM PRACTICE 5.4 Level of Detail—Rule of Thumb

Practicing project managers advocate keeping the level of detail to a minimum. But there are limits to this suggestion. One of the most frequent errors of new project managers is to forget that the task time estimate will be used to control schedule and cost performance. A frequent rule of thumb used by practicing project managers says that a task duration should not exceed 5 workdays or at the most 10 workdays, if workdays are the time units used for the project. Such a rule probably will result in a more detailed network, but the additional detail pays off in controlling schedule and cost as the project progresses.

Suppose the task is "build prototype computer-controlled conveyor belt," the time estimate is 40 workdays, and the budget $300,000. It may be better to divide the task into seven or eight smaller tasks for control purposes. If one of the smaller tasks gets behind because of problems or a poor time estimate, it will be possible to take corrective action quickly and avoid delaying successive tasks and the project. If the single task of 40 workdays is used, it is possible that no corrective action would be taken until day 40, since many people have a tendency to "wait and see" or avoid admitting they are behind or passing on bad news; the result may mean far more than 5 days behind schedule.

The 5- to 10-day rule of thumb applies to cost and performance goals. If using the rule of thumb suggested in the previous paragraph results in too many network tasks, an alternative is available, but it has conditions. The activity time can be extended beyond the 5- to 10-day rule only *if* control monitoring checkpoints for segments of the task can be established so clear measures of progress can be identified by a specific percent complete.

This information is invaluable to the control process of measuring schedule and cost performance—for example, payments for contract work are paid on "percent complete" basis. Defining a task with clear definable start and end points and intermediate points enhances the chances of early detection of problems, corrective action, and on-time project completion.

5.6 Types of Costs

LO 5-5

Distinguish different kinds of costs associated with a project.

Assuming work packages are defined, detailed cost estimates can be made. Here are typical kinds of costs found in a project:

1. Direct costs
   a. Labor
   b. Materials
   c. Equipment
   d. Other
2. Direct project overhead costs
3. General and administrative (G&A) overhead costs

The total project cost estimate is broken down in this fashion to sharpen the control process and improve decision making.

Direct Costs

These costs are clearly chargeable to a specific work package. **Direct costs** can be influenced by the project manager, project team, and individuals implementing the work package. These costs represent real cash outflows and must be paid as the project progresses; therefore, direct costs are usually separated from overhead costs. Lower-level project rollups frequently include only direct costs.

Direct Project Overhead Costs

Direct overhead rates more closely pinpoint which resources of the organization are being used in the project. Direct project **overhead costs** can be tied to project deliverables or work packages. Examples include the salary of the project manager and temporary rental space for the project team. Although overhead is not an immediate out-of-pocket expense, it is *real* and must be covered in the long run if the firm is to remain viable. These rates are usually a ratio of the dollar value of the resources used—for example, direct labor, materials, equipment. For example, a direct labor burden rate of 20 percent would add a direct overhead charge of 20 percent to the direct labor cost estimate. A direct charge rate of 50 percent for materials would carry an additional 50 percent charge to the material cost estimate. Selective direct overhead charges provide a more accurate project (job or work package) cost than does using a blanket overhead rate for the whole project.

General and Administrative (G&A) Overhead Costs

These represent organization costs that are not directly linked to a specific project. They are carried for the duration of the project. Examples include organization costs across all products and projects such as advertising, accounting, and senior management above the project level. Allocation of G&A costs varies from organization to organization. However, G&A costs are usually allocated as a percent of total direct cost or a percent of the total of a specific direct cost such as labor, materials, or equipment.

Given the totals of direct and overhead costs for individual work packages, it is possible to cumulate the costs for any deliverable or for the entire project. A percentage can be added for profit if you are a contractor. A breakdown of costs for a proposed contract bid is presented in Figure 5.5.

FIGURE 5.5
Contract Bid Summary Costs

Direct costs	$ 80,000
Direct overhead	$ 20,000
Total direct costs	$100,000
G&A overhead (20%)	$ 20,000
Total costs	$120,000
Profit (20%)	$ 24,000
Total bid	$144,000

FIGURE 5.6
Three Views of Cost

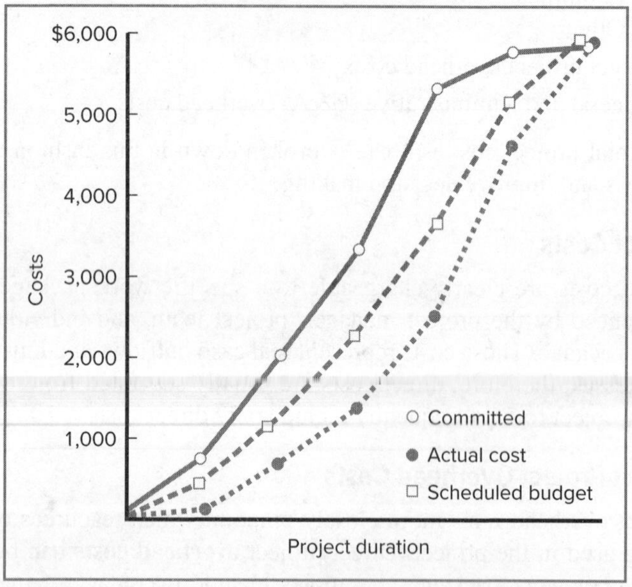

Perceptions of costs and budgets vary depending on their users. The project manager must be very aware of these differences when setting up the project budget and when communicating these differences to others. Figure 5.6 depicts these different perceptions. The project manager can commit costs months before the resource is used. This information is useful to the financial officer of the organization in forecasting future cash outflows. The project manager is interested in when the budgeted cost is expected to occur and when the budgeted cost actually is charged (earned); the respective timings of these two cost figures are used to measure project schedule and cost variances.

5.7 Refining Estimates

As described in Chapter 4, detailed work package estimates are aggregated and "rolled up" by deliverable to estimate the total direct cost of the project. Similarly, estimated durations are entered into the project network to establish the project schedule and determine the overall duration of the project. Experience tells us that for many projects the total estimates do not materialize and the actual costs and schedule of some projects significantly exceed original work package–based estimates. In order to compensate for the problem of actual cost and schedule exceeding estimates, some project managers adjust total costs by some multiplier (e.g., total estimated costs × 1.20).

The practice of adjusting original estimates by 20 percent or even 100 percent begs the question of why, after investing so much time and energy on detailed estimates, the numbers could be so far off. There are a number of reasons for this, most of which can be traced to the estimating process and the inherent uncertainty of predicting the future. Following are some of those reasons.

- **Interaction costs are hidden in estimates.** According to the guidelines, each task estimate is supposed to be done independently. However, tasks are rarely completed in a vacuum. Work on one task is dependent upon prior tasks, and the hand-offs between tasks require time and attention. For example, people working on prototype development need to interact with design engineers after the design is completed, whether to simply ask clarifying questions or to make adjustments in the original design. Similarly, the time necessary to coordinate activities is typically not reflected in independent estimates. Coordination is reflected in meetings and briefings as well as time necessary to resolve disconnects between tasks. Time, and therefore cost, devoted to managing interactions rises exponentially as the number of people and different disciplines involved increases on a project.
- **Normal conditions do not apply.** Estimates are supposed to be based on normal conditions. While this is a good starting point, it rarely holds true in real life, especially when it comes to the availability of resources. Resource shortages, whether in the form of people, equipment, or materials, can extend original estimates. For example, under normal conditions, four bulldozers are typically used to clear a certain site size in five days, but the availability of only three bulldozers would extend the task duration to eight days. Similarly, the decision to outsource certain tasks can increase costs as well as extend task durations, since time is added to acclimating outsiders to the particulars of the project and the culture of the organization.
- **Things go wrong on projects.** Design flaws are revealed after the fact, extreme weather conditions occur, accidents happen, and so forth. Although you shouldn't plan for these risks to happen when estimating a particular task, the likelihood and impact of such events need to be considered.
- **Project scope and plans change.** As one gets further and further into the project, a manager obtains a better understanding of what needs to be done to accomplish the project. This may lead to major changes in project plans and costs. Likewise, if the project is a commercial project, changes often have to be made midstream to respond to new demands by the customer and/or competition. Unstable project scopes are a major source of cost overruns. While every effort should be made up front to nail down the project scope, it is becoming increasingly difficult to do so in our rapidly changing world.
- **People are overly optimistic.** There is solid research indicating that people tend to overestimate how quickly they can get things done (Buehler, Griffin, & Ross, 1994; Lovallo & Kahneman, 2003).
- **People engage in strategic misrepresentation.** There is growing evidence that some project promoters underestimate the costs of projects and overestimate project benefits in order to win approval. This appears to be particularly true for large-scale public works projects, which have a notorious habit of coming in way over budget (remember Snapshot from Practice 5.1: Portland Aerial Tram).

The reality is that for many projects not all of the information needed to make accurate estimates is available, and it is impossible to predict the future. The challenge is further compounded by human nature and the political dynamics associated with gaining project approval. The dilemma is that without solid estimates the credibility of the project plan is eroded. Deadlines become meaningless, budgets become rubbery, and accountability becomes problematic.

Such challenges will influence the final time and cost estimates. Even with the best estimating efforts, it may be necessary to revise estimates based on relevant information *prior to* establishing a baseline schedule and budget.

Effective organizations adjust estimates of specific tasks once the risks, resources, and particulars of the situation have been more clearly defined. They recognize that the rolled-up estimates generated from a detailed estimate based on the WBS are just the starting point. As they delve further into the project-planning process, they make appropriate revisions in both the time and cost of specific activities. They factor the final assignment of resources into the project budget and schedule. For example, when they realize that only three instead of four bulldozers are available to clear a site, they adjust both the time and cost of that activity. They adjust estimates to account for specific actions to mitigate potential risks on the project. For example, to reduce the chances of design code errors, they add the cost of independent testers to the schedule and budget. Finally, organizations adjust estimates to take into account abnormal conditions. For example, if soil samples reveal excessive ground water, then they adjust foundation costs and times.

There will always be some mistakes, omissions, and adjustments that will require additional changes in estimates. Fortunately, every project should have a change management system in place to accommodate these situations and any impact on the project baseline. Change management and contingency funds will be discussed in Chapter 7.

5.8 Creating a Database for Estimating

LO 5-6

Suggest a scheme for developing an estimating database for future projects.

The best way to improve estimates is to collect and archive data on past project estimates and actuals. Saving historical data—estimates and actuals—provides a knowledge base for improving project time and cost estimating. Creating an estimating database is a "best practice" among leading project management organizations.

Some organizations, such as Boeing and IBM, have large estimating departments of professional estimators that have developed large **time and cost databases.** Others collect these data through the project office. This database approach allows the project estimator to select a specific work package item from the database for inclusion. The estimator then makes any necessary adjustments concerning the materials, labor, and equipment. Of course, any items not found in the database can be added to the project—and ultimately to the database if desired. Again, the quality of the database estimates depends upon the experience of the estimators, but over time the data quality should improve. Such structured databases serve as feedback for estimators and as benchmarks for cost and time for each project. In addition, comparison of estimate and actual for different projects can suggest the degree of risk inherent in estimates. See Figure 5.7 for the structure of a database similar to those found in practice.

FIGURE 5.7
Estimating Database Templates

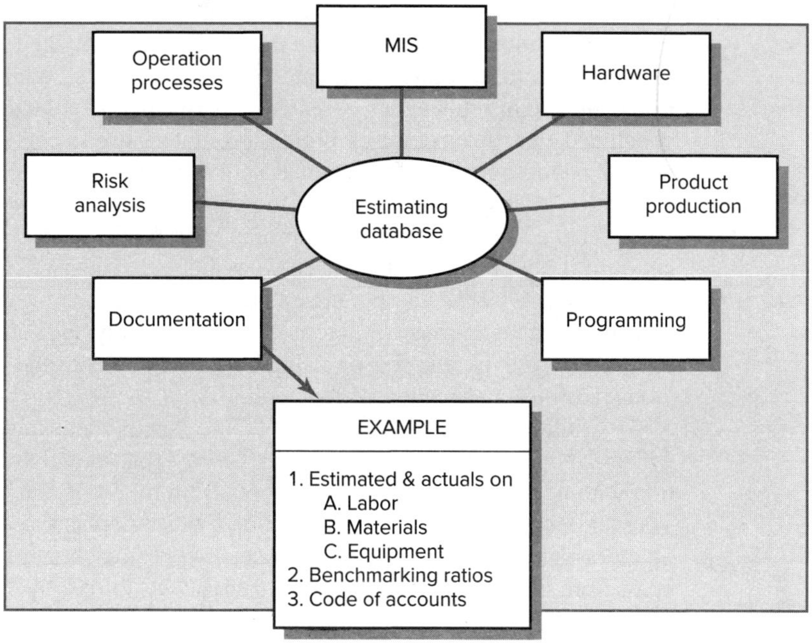

5.9 Mega Projects: A Special Case

LO 5-7

Understand the challenge of estimating mega projects and describe steps that lead to better informed decisions.

Mega projects are large-scale, complex ventures that typically cost $1 billion or more, take many years to complete, and involve multiple private and public stakeholders. They are often transformational, and impact millions of people (Flyvbjerg, 2014). Examples include high-speed rail lines, airports, healthcare reform, the Olympics, development of new aircraft, and so forth. What do these projects have in common beyond scope and complexity? They all tend to go way over budget and fall behind schedule. For example, the new Denver airport that opened in 1995 had cost overruns of 200 percent and was completed two years later than planned. The "Chunnel," the 31-mile-plus tunnel that connects France with England, was 80 percent over budget. These are but two examples of many public works and other large-scale projects in which costs came in way over than planned. In a study of government infrastructure projects, Flyvbjerg found costs for bridges and tunnels, roads, and rails to be underestimated 34 percent, 20 percent, and 45 percent, respectively, from baseline estimates (Flyvbjerg, Bruzelius, & Rothengatter, 2003)!

Mega projects often involve a double whammy. Not only did they cost much more than expected, but they underdelivered on benefits they were to provide. The Denver airport realized only 55 percent of forecasted traffic during its first year of operation. The Chunnel traffic revenues have been one-half of what was predicted with internal rate of return of −14.5 percent! Again Flyvbjerg's study revealed a consistent pattern of underusage on most infrastructure projects (Flyvbjerg et al., 2003), including only a 5 percent forecasted usage for the Kolkata (Calcutta) metro in India!

So why does there appear to be a consistent pattern of overestimating benefits and underestimating costs? Many argue the sheer complexity and long time horizon make it impossible to accurately estimate costs and benefits. While this is certainly true, Flyvbjerg and his colleagues' research suggests that other factors come into play. They concluded that in most cases project promoters use deception to promote projects not for public good but for personal gain, political or economic. Deception may be deliberate, or may be the product of overzealousness, optimism, and ignorance (Flyvbjerg et al., 2003). In some cases, promoters rationalize that nothing great would ever get built if people knew in advance what the real costs and challenges involved were (Hirschman, 1967).

On some mega projects, there is a triple whammy. Not only are they over budget and under value, but the cost of maintaining them exceeds the benefits received. These kinds of projects are called **white elephants.**

LO 5-8

Define a "white elephant" in project management and provide examples.

A "white elephant" suggests a valuable, but burdensome, possession, which its owner cannot easily dispose of and whose cost (particularly upkeep) is out of proportion with its usefulness. The term derives from the story that the Kings of Siam (now Thailand) would often make a present of a white elephant to courtiers who had fallen out of favor with the king. At first glance, it was a great honor to receive such a revered beast from the king. However, the true intent was to ruin the recipient by forcing him to absorb the costs of taking care of the animal.

Examples of white elephants abound. While traveling across southern China one of the authors was struck by the palatial stature of the Trade Expo buildings each city had. It was as if each city had tried to outdo its neighbor in terms of grandeur. When asked how often they were used, city officials would say once or twice a year. The 2015 FIFA scandal brought attention to the hidden costs of hosting the World Cup. South Africa built six new world-class stadiums for the 2010 competition. None of the post–World Cup revenue generated from these stadiums exceeds their maintenance cost (Molloy & Chetty, 2015).

White elephants are not limited to buildings and stadiums. Air France had to mothball the Concorde, the world's fastest commercial airline, because maintenance costs and noise restrictions did not justify a three-flights-a-week schedule. It is not uncommon in our personal lives to acquire white elephants, such as underutilized vacation homes or yachts.

Flyvbjerg and others argue that cost overrun is not the price of doing big things and that we are capable of making better informed decisions on mega projects. The first step is to assume there is optimism bias and even deception on the part of promoters. Proposals should require a thorough review by impartial observers who do not have vested interest in the project. Some if not all financial risk should be absorbed by promoters and those who benefit financially from the project. Sustainable business practices should be used and maintenance costs be integrated into the forecasted cost/benefit analyses of projects. See Snapshot from Practice 5.5: Avoiding the Curse of the White Elephant to see how British organizers tried to avoid the curse of the white elephant in the 2012 Olympic games.

SNAPSHOT FROM PRACTICE 5.5 Avoiding the Curse of the White Elephant*

Once, hosting the Olympics was considered the crown prize and a tremendous source of national pride. Seven cities competed to host the 1992 Winter Olympics. For the 2022 Winter Olympics only Beijing and Almaty (Kazakhstan) submitted bids. Oslo (Norway), the favorite, withdrew application due to a lack of public support. Likewise, Boston withdrew application for the 2024 Summer Olympics in the face of public outcry.

Why the outcry? Because of the legacy of exorbitant cost overruns and draining maintenance costs. The Olympics has a long history of expensive white elephants. For example, the Beijing National Stadium, nicknamed the *Bird's Nest,* built at a cost of $480 million for the 2008 Olympic games, requires over $10 million each year to maintain and has no regular tenant.

Some have attributed the Greek economic meltdown to exorbitant debt accrued from hosting the 2004 summer games (Flyvbjerg, 2014). "It felt good at the time because we were the center of the world, and we got to show off our country," says gymnast Christos Libanovnos of the Hellenic Gymnastics Federation. "But what did it cost? So much money—billions of euros. And now we are bankrupt, and everything just gets worse and worse every day. It's hard not to see a connection. It's hard not to think that maybe it wasn't worth it."[1]

Perhaps the most infamous example of an Olympic white elephant is the 1976 Montreal Olympic Stadium. Originally nicknamed the *Big O,* due to its unique doughnut design, the stadium soon became known across Canada as the *Big Owe.* Estimated to cost $134 million, it took Canadian taxpayers 30 years to pay off the final $1.1 billion debt. To make matters worse, the stadium was not completely finished by the time the Olympics opened. The stadium has not had a main tenant since 2004, when the successful Montreal Expos moved to Washington, D.C.

The London 2012 Olympics organizers were committed to reducing the Olympic financial hangover. In particular, they were well aware of hidden post-Olympic maintenance costs of buildings that were no longer in demand. One advantage they had over less developed countries is that the infrastructure and many of the arenas were already in place and the Olympics provided a necessary upgrade. They built temporary arenas for less popular sports. For example, after the games the water polo arena was deconstructed and materials recycled. The 12,000-seat basketball arena was designed to be portable so it could be used in future Olympics. Scalability was another key consideration. For example, during the Olympics over 17,000 people watched swimming events in the newly constructed aquatic center. The aquatic center was downsized to a 2,500-person capacity after the Olympics and is now open to the public.

Sophie Vigneault/123RF

In recognition of its achievements, London 2012 Olympics won Gold in the Environmental and Sustainability category of the 6th International Sports Events awards. "We set out with a huge promise to the world, to deliver the most sustainable Olympic Games of modern times," says David Stubbs, London 2012's Head of Sustainability. "Seven years, nine million visitors, and 2,484 medals later, that's exactly what we achieved."

[1] J. Sanborn, "Was It Worth It? Debit-Ridden Greeks Question the Cost of the 2004 Olympics," *Time,* July 9, 2012, p. 33.

*"London 2012's Sustainability Legacy Lives On," Olympic.org. July 31, 2013. Accessed 10/10/15.

In particular, Flyvbjerg advocates an external view based on the outcome of similar projects completed in the past. It is called **reference class forecasting (RCF)** and involves three major steps:

1. Select a reference class of projects similar to your potential project, for example, cargo ships or bridges.
2. Collect and arrange outcome data as a distribution. Create a distribution of cost overruns as a percentage of the original project estimate (low to high).
3. Use the distribution data to arrive at a realistic forecast. Compare the original cost estimate for the project with the reference class projects. Take, for example, a three-mile-long rail tunnel project. Tunnel advocates estimate that it will cost $100 million. Analyses of similar tunnel projects in the region indicate that on average they are 34 percent over budget. If the proponents cannot come up with a reasonable explanation for why this project will be different, decision makers should assume that the tunnel will cost at least $134 million.

The benefits of RCF are compelling:

- Outside empirical data mitigates human bias.
- Political, strategic, and promoter forces have difficulty ignoring outside RCF information.
- RCF serves as a reality check for funding large projects.
- RCF helps executives avoid unsound optimism.
- RCF leads to improved accountability.
- RCF provides a basis for project contingency funds.

The use of RCF is increasing as governments and organizations require this method to be used to temper project promoters' estimates and reduce cost/benefit inaccuracies.

Summary

Quality time and cost estimates are the bedrock of project control. Past experience is the best starting point for these estimates. The quality of estimates is influenced by other factors such as people, technology, and downtimes. Companies that excel record past experiences and create an estimation database that provides quick and accurate information on the cost of specific work packages.

Using top-down estimates is good for initial and strategic decision making or in situations where the costs associated with developing better estimates have little benefit. However, in most cases, the bottom-up approach to estimating is preferred and more reliable because it assesses each work package, rather than the whole project, section, or deliverable of a project. Estimating time and costs for each work package facilitates development of the project schedule and a time-phased budget, which are needed to control the project as it is implemented. Using the estimating guidelines will help eliminate many common mistakes made by those unacquainted with estimating times and costs for project control.

The level of time and cost detail should follow the old phrase "no more than is necessary and sufficient." Managers must remember to differentiate among committed outlays, actual costs, and scheduled costs. It is well known that up-front efforts in clearly defining project objectives, scope, and specifications vastly improve time and cost estimate accuracy.

Culture plays a significant role in estimating. If the focus is on what went wrong instead of who is to blame, then people should be more forthright in sharing their experiences and insights. However, if you work in a punitive organizational culture that is only concerned with results, you are likely to be much more guarded in what you share and may even pad estimates out of self-protection.

Finally, large-scale mega projects like subway systems or football stadiums often suffer from underestimated costs and overestimated benefits. They also can evolve into white elephants whose cost of maintenance exceeds benefits. Steps must be taken to remove bias and compare mega project estimates with similar projects that have been done in the past.

Key Terms

Accuracy of estimate, *160*
Apportionment, *167*
Bottom-up estimates, *164*
Confidence in estimate, *160*
Delphi Method, *167*
Direct costs, *175*
Estimate, *159*
Function points, *168*
Learning curve, *169*
Overhead costs, *175*
Phase estimating, *171*
Precision of estimate, *160*
Range estimating, *170*
Ratio method, *166*
Reference class forecasting (RCF), *182*
Template method, *170*
Time and cost databases, *178*
Top-down estimates, *164*
White elephant, *180*

Review Questions

1. Why are accurate estimates critical to effective project management?
2. How does the culture of an organization influence the quality of estimates?
3. What are the differences between bottom-up and top-down estimating approaches? Under what conditions would you prefer one over the other?
4. What are the major types of costs? Which costs are controllable by the project manager?
5. Why is it difficult to estimate mega project (e.g., airport, stadium) costs and benefits?
6. Define a white elephant in project management. Provide a real-life example.
7. Briefly explain four different aspects of estimating.

SNAPSHOT FROM PRACTICE

Discussion Questions

5.1 *Portland Aerial Tram*

1. Can you think of a local public project that had significant cost overruns like the Portland Tram project?
2. Do you agree with the statement that "nothing great would ever be built if people knew in advance what the real costs and challenges were"?

5.2 *The Delphi Method*

1. What kinds of estimates are best suited for this method?

5.3 *Estimate Accuracy*

1. Why is the range so much higher for IT projects than construction projects?

5.5 *Avoiding the Curse of the White Elephant*

1. Can you identify personal examples of white elephants?
2. What else do you think Olympic organizers could do to make the event more sustainable?

Exercises

1. Calculate the direct cost of labor for a project team member using the following data:
   Hourly rate: $50/hr
   Hours needed: 120
   Overhead rate: 40%

2. Calculate the direct and total direct costs of labor for a project team member using the following data:

   Hourly rate: $50/hr

   Hours needed: 100

   Overhead rate: 30%

3. The Munsters have been saving money in order to buy a house. They figure that, given current interest rates, they could afford a $500,000 home. Before looking at houses on the market they decide to explore the possibility of building a new home. The Munsters figure they could buy a suitable lot for $90,000–$95,000. At a minimum, they want to build a 2,200-square-foot house. The cost for a house of the quality they desire is $200 per square foot. Given this information, should the Munsters pursue the option of building a new house?

4. Mrs. Publinsky and her husband, Xander, are planning their dream house. The lot for the house sits high on a hill with a beautiful view of the White Mountains. The plans show the size of the house to be 2,900 square feet. The average price for a lot and house similar to this one has been $250 per square foot. Fortunately, Xander is a retired plumber and feels he can save money by installing the plumbing himself. Mrs. Publinsky feels she can take care of the interior decorating. They both feel they can complete the exterior painting with the help of their two sons.

   The following average cost information is available from a local bank that makes loans to local contractors and dispenses progress payments to contractors when specific tasks are verified as complete.

25%	Excavation and framing complete
8%	Roof and fireplace complete
3%	Wiring roughed in
6%	Plumbing roughed in
5%	Siding on
17%	Windows, insulation, walks, plaster, and garage complete
9%	Furnace installed
4%	Plumbing fixtures installed
5%	Exterior painting complete
4%	Light fixtures installed, finish hardware installed
6%	Carpet and trim installed
4%	Interior decorating
4%	Floors laid and finished

   a. What is the estimated cost for the Publinskys' house if they use contractors to complete all of the house?

   b. Estimate what the cost of the house would be if the Publinskys used their talents to do some of the work themselves.

5. Exercise Figure 5.1 is a project WBS with cost apportioned by percentages. If the total project cost is estimated to be $800,000, what are the estimated costs for the following deliverables?

   a. Design

   b. Programming

   c. In-house testing

What weaknesses are inherent in this estimating approach?

EXERCISE FIGURE 5.1
WBS Figure

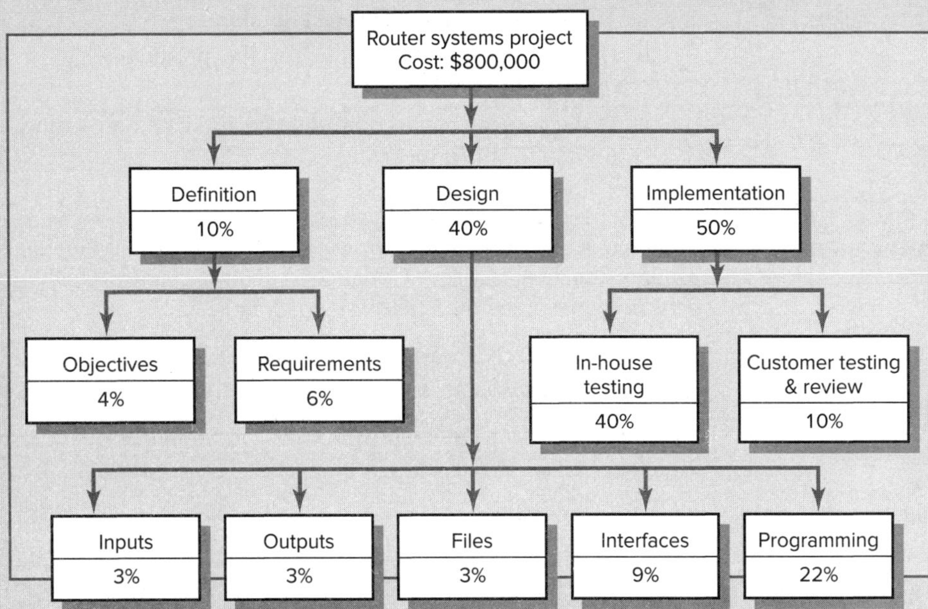

6. Assume you are the project manager for the Tidal 2 software project. You have been asked to calculate the expected cost for the project. Your company's database indicates that developers can handle eight function points each person-month and that the cost per developer at your firm is $7,000 per month. You and your team of five developers have come up with the following requirements:

Elements	Count	Complexity
Inputs	10	Low
Outputs	4	Low
Inquiries	4	High
Files	28	Medium
Interfaces	18	High

Using the "complexity weighting" scheme shown in Table 5.2 and the information provided, calculate the total number of function points, the estimated cost, and the estimated duration of the Tidal 2 project.

7. Omega 2 Project. Using the "complexity weighting" scheme shown in Table 5.2 and the following function point complexity weight table, estimate the total function point count. Assume historical data suggest five function points equal one person a month and six people have been assigned to work on the project.

Complexity Weight Table		
Number of inputs	15	Rated complexity low
Number of outputs	20	Rated complexity average
Number of inquiries	10	Rated complexity average
Number of files	30	Rated complexity average
Number of interfaces	50	Rated complexity high

a. What is the estimated project duration?
b. If 20 people are available for the project, what is the estimated project duration?
c. If the project must be completed in six months, how many people will be needed for the project?

References

Buehler, R., D. Griffin, and M. Ross, "Exploring the 'Planning Fallacy': Why People Underestimate Their Task Completion Times," *Journal of Personality and Social Psychology,* vol. 67, no. 3 (1994), pp. 366–81.

Dalkey, N. C., D. L. Rourke, R. Lewis, and D. Snyder, *Studies in the Quality of Life: Delphi and Decision Making* (Lexington, MA: Lexington Books, 1972).

Flyvbjerg, B., "Curbing Optimism Bias and Strategic Misrepresentation in Planning: Reference Class Forecasting in Practice," *European Planning Studies,* vol. 16, no. 1 (January 2008), pp. 3–21.

Flyvbjerg, B., "From Nobel Prize to Project Management: Getting Risks Right," *Project Management Journal,* vol. 37, no. 3 (August 2006), pp. 5–15.

Flyvbjerg, B., "Top Ten Behavioral Biases in Project Management: An Overview," *Project Management Journal,* vol. 52, no. 6 (2021), pp. 531–46.

Flyvbjerg, B., "What You Should Know about Megaprojects and Why: An Overview," *Project Management Journal,* vol. 45, no. 2 (April/May 2014), pp. 6–19.

Flyvbjerg, B., N. Bruzelius, and W. Rothengatter, *Mega Projects and Risk: An Anatomy of Ambition* (UK: Cambridge University Press, 2003).

Gray, N. S., "Secrets to Creating the Elusive 'Accurate Estimate,'" *PM Network,* August 2001, p. 56.

Hirschman. A. O., "The Principle of the Hiding Hand," *The Public Interest,* Winter 1967, pp. 10–23.

Jeffery, R., G. C. Low, and M. Barnes, "A Comparison of Function Point Counting Techniques," *IEEE Transactions on Software Engineering,* vol. 19, no. 5 (1993), pp. 529–32.

Jones, C., *Applied Software Measurement* (New York: McGraw-Hill, 1991).

Jones, C., *Estimating Software Costs* (New York: McGraw-Hill, 1998).

Kharbanda, O. P., and J. K. Pinto, *What Made Gertie Gallop: Learning from Project Failures* (New York: Von Nostrand Reinhold, 1996).

Lovallo, D., and D. Kahneman, "Delusions of Success: How Optimism Undermines Executives' Decisions," *Harvard Business Review,* July 2003, pp. 56–63.

Magne, E., K. Emhjellenm, and P. Osmundsen, "Cost Estimation Overruns in the North Sea," *Project Management Journal,* vol. 34, no. 1 (2003), pp. 23–29.

McLeod, G., and D. Smith, *Managing Information Technology Projects* (Cambridge, MA: Course Technology, 1996).

Molloy, E., and T. Chetty, "The Rocky Road to Legacy: Lessons from the 2010 FIFA World Cup South Africa Stadium Program," *Project Management Journal,* vol. 46, no. 3 (June/July 2015), pp. 88–107.

Project Management Institute, *A Guide to the Project Management Body of Knowledge, 7th ed.,* (Newton Square, PA: PMI Publishing, 2021).

Shenhar, A., and V. Holzmann, "The Three Secrets of Megaprojects Success: Clear Strategic, Vision, Total Alignment, and Adapting to Complexity," *Project Management Journal,* vol. 48, no. 6 (2017), pp. 29–46.

Soderlund, J., S. Sankaran, and C. Biesenthal, "The Past and Present of Megaprojets," *Project Management Journal,* vol. 48, no. 6 (2017), pp. 5–16.

Symons, C. R., "Function Point Analysis: Difficulties and Improvements," *IEEE Transactions on Software Engineering,* vol. 14, no. 1 (1988), pp. 2–11.

Walters, D. J., P. Fernbach, C. Fox, and S. Sloman, "Known Unknowns: A Critical Determinant of Confidence and Calibration," *Management Science,* vol. 63, no. 12 (2017), pp. 3999–4446.

Case 5.1

Sharp Printing, AG

Three years ago the Sharp Printing (SP) strategic management group set a goal of having a color laser printer available for the consumer and small business market for less than $200. A few months later the senior management met off-site to discuss the new product. The results of this meeting were a set of general technical specifications along with major deliverables, a product launch date, and a cost estimate based on prior experience.

Shortly afterward a meeting was arranged for middle management explaining the project goals, major responsibilities, project start date, and importance of meeting the product launch date within the cost estimate. Members of all departments involved attended the meeting. Excitement was high. Although everyone saw the risks as high, the promised rewards for the company and the personnel were emblazoned in their minds. A few participants questioned the legitimacy of the project duration and cost estimates. A couple of R&D people were worried about the technology required to produce the high-quality product for less than $200. But given the excitement of the moment, everyone agreed the project was worth doing and doable. The color laser printer project was to have the highest project priority in the company.

Lauren was selected to be the project manager. She had 15 years of experience in printer design and manufacture, which included successful management of several projects related to printers for commercial markets. Since she was one of those uncomfortable with the project cost and time estimates, she felt getting good bottom-up time and cost estimates for the deliverables was her first concern. She quickly had a meeting with the significant stakeholders to create a WBS identifying the work packages and organization unit responsible for implementing the work packages. Lauren stressed that she wanted time and cost estimates from those who would do the work or were the most knowledgeable, if possible. Getting estimates from more than one source was encouraged. Estimates were due in two weeks.

The compiled estimates were placed in the WBS/OBS. The corresponding cost estimate seemed to be in error. The cost estimate was $1,250,000 over the top-down senior management estimate; this represented about a 20 percent overrun! Furthermore, the bottom-up time estimate based on the project network was four months longer than the top management time estimate. Another meeting was scheduled with the significant stakeholders to check the estimates and to brainstorm for alternative solutions. At this meeting, everyone agreed the bottom-up cost and time estimates appeared to be accurate. Following are some of the suggestions from the brainstorming session.

- Change scope.
- Outsource technology design.
- Use the priority matrix (found in Chapter 4) to get top management to clarify their priorities.
- Partner with another organization or build a research consortium to share costs and to share the newly developed technology and production methods.
- Cancel the project.
- Commission a break-even study for the laser printer.

Very little in the way of concrete savings was identified, although there was consensus that time could be compressed to the market launch date, but at additional costs.

Lauren met with the marketing (Connor), production (Kim), and design (Gage) managers, who yielded some ideas for cutting costs, but nothing significant enough to have a large impact. Gage remarked, "I wouldn't want to be the one to deliver the message to top management that their cost estimate is $1,250,000 off! Good luck, Lauren."

1. At this point, what would you do if you were the project manager?
2. Was top management acting correctly in developing an estimate?
3. What estimating techniques should be used for a mission-critical project such as this?

Case 5.2

Post-Graduation Adventure

Josh and Mike met as roommates during freshman year at Macalester College in St. Paul, Minnesota. Despite a rocky start they became best friends. They are planning a two-week adventure together to celebrate their graduation in June. Josh has never been to Europe and wants to visit France or Spain. Mike spent a semester abroad in Aarhus, Denmark, and traveled extensively in northern Europe. Even though Mike has never been to France or Spain, he wants to go to someplace more exotic, like South Africa or Vietnam. For the past week, they have been arguing over where they should go. Josh argues that it will cost too much to fly to South Africa or Vietnam, while Mike counters that it will be much cheaper to travel in Vietnam or South Africa once they are there. They agree that they can spend no more than $4,000 each on the trip and could be gone for only two weeks.

One evening when they were arguing with each other over beers with friends, Sara said, "Why don't you use what you learned in your project management class to decide what to do?" Josh and Mike looked at each other and agreed that made perfect sense.

1. Assume you are either Mike or Josh; how would you go about making a decision using project management methodology?
2. Looking first at only cost, what decision would you make?
3. After cost, what other factors should be considered before making a decision?

Case 5.3

Tata Steel's Kalinganagar Plant

OVERVIEW OF TATA STEEL'S KALINGANAGAR PLANT

Kalinganagar Plant, Odisha, India, is one of Tata Steel's largest and most advanced facilities. The demand for steel from India's growing infrastructure and construction sector has been increasing, so the plant at Kalinganagar has been expanded several times to make Tata Steel a major player in the global market.

GROWTH TRIGGER/REASONS FOR PROJECT INITIATION

The Kalinganagar expansion sought to fill India's enormous steel growth requirement. Very large infrastructure development in the form of highways, railways, and rapid urbanization called for increased steel production capacities. Tata Steel planned to increase production to meet these demands, which would be all the better for cementing its leadership in India's steel marketplace. Besides achieving economies of scale and increasing production capacity, the project aimed to optimize technological capabilities, minimize operations costs and improve working efficiency. The Tata Steel Kalinganagar plant has been a leading spearhead towards achieving set targets that reflect the direction lines of India's National Steel Policy 2017. Under this policy, the government envisions increasing domestic steel production to achieve a state of self-sufficiency.

KEY STAKEHOLDERS

Government Bodies

The central and state governments, regulatory bodies, and other local municipal corporations have been engaged by the project for key clearances, land acquisition, and environmental clearances. Private firms like Tata Steel, the leading investor, teamed up with several contractors, subcontractors, and importers of equipment together from India and abroad. Public affected local people received compensation and resettlement packages.

SCOPE AND OBJECTIVES

The project involved a series of expansions and upgrades to strengthen production capabilities, improve integration with advanced technology, and respond to rising demand. It was also designed to meet environmental standards and facilitate sustainable growth.

KEY DELIVERABLES

A fresh set of steel production lines and blast furnaces, introduced in phases. Current improvement in production from 3 MTPA to 8 MTPA with further capacity expansion to 16 MTPA. For example, it must be an eco-friendly technology and practice, say, a facility for recycling wastes or for water treatment.

PROJECT MANAGEMENT FRAMEWORK

PROJECT INITIATION

For this multiple-stage project, Tata Steel conducted stringent feasibility studies that covered technical, economic, and environmental studies. The various feasibility studies were critical steps in determining viability, cost estimation, and risk assessment. Several stakeholders collaborated to receive the needed clearances. Environmental clearances, especially for installing blast furnaces and significant raw material procurement, were required for the project. Approvals were obtained from the government under India's environmental policies, the main emphasis of which was minimum ecological damage.

RISK ASSESSMENT AND COST-BENEFIT ANALYSIS

Risk management consideration is characterized by the project management structure adopted by Tata Steel. Such a cost-benefit analysis ensured that the ROI for the project was in line with the heavy upfront capital expenditure of ₹25,000 for Phase I and ₹27,000 crore for Phase II.

PROJECT PLANNING

Tata Steel prepared a detailed WBS to break up the huge project into smaller, manageable tasks. This breaking was critical and necessary to allocate resources, manage timelines, and set project milestones. The WBS allowed the team to focus on all the elements involved in plant development, from site preparation and procurement to equipment installation to commissioning.

RESOURCE ALLOCATION

The third critical area of project planning was resource allocation. Due to the size of this project, Tata Steel had to ensure the availability of skilled labor, raw materials, and advanced machinery. This involved coordination at the international supplier level for specific equipment and a large workforce over several shifts with tight deadlines. Labor unions were approached well in advance to avoid any disputes.

BUDGET AND TIMELINE ESTIMATES

This preliminary budget and timeline estimate is based on industry standard practice and experience in designing and constructing steel plants. Gantt charts and the Critical Path Method (CPM) tools were also used to track the team's work towards efficient resource utilization.

RISK MANAGEMENT FRAMEWORK

A delay in clearances at the regulatory level, erratic fluctuations in global steel prices, and sudden disruption of supply chains have posed challenges. Tata Steel has prepared contingency plans that include maintaining buffer stock for critical materials and collaborating with local suppliers to streamline the logistics. The project team has also devised strategies to fast-track environmental clearances, thus reducing the time taken to obtain such clearances.

Case 5.4

Electrification of Mumbai-Ahmedabad Bullet Train

Indian Railways, one of the world's largest rail networks, is undergoing major modernization to enhance capacity and efficiency. The key initiatives include high-speed corridors, station modernization, and Dedicated Freight Corridors to accommodate growing passenger and freight demands. Infrastructure development, including bullet trains and rail electrification, aims to reduce dependency on fossil fuels while meeting India's rising transportation needs. The primary stakeholders involved in these projects include the government, private sector, and the general public. The Ministry of Railways and the Indian Government oversee planning and execution, while private contractors, suppliers, and technology partners such as Alstom and Siemens contribute expertise and resources. Additionally, citizens, businesses, and communities impacted by railway upgrades play a crucial role in shaping the implementation of the project.

SCOPE AND OBJECTIVES

The modernization efforts encompass constructing new rail lines, electrifying existing networks, implementing advanced signalling systems, and redeveloping stations. The overarching goal is to enhance operational efficiency, reduce travel time, and meet the increasing demand for passenger and freight transport.

ESSENTIAL DELIVERABLES

Major deliverables include the development of high-speed rail corridors, such as the Mumbai-Ahmedabad Bullet Train, electrification of key railway lines and stations, and the introduction of international-standard passenger amenities and station designs.

PROJECT MANAGEMENT FRAMEWORK

PROJECT INITIATION

Before execution, Indian Railways conducts comprehensive feasibility studies addressing technical, economic, and environmental factors. These studies guide cost estimation, risk assessment, and regulatory compliance. Collaboration with government authorities and private consultants ensures necessary approvals, including environmental clearances for land acquisition and material procurement.

RISK ASSESSMENT AND COST-BENEFIT ANALYSIS

Risk management is integral to project planning. High-risk assessments focus on potential challenges such as land acquisition disputes, environmental concerns, and budget overruns. The National Rail Plan provides a strategic foundation to evaluate project feasibility and promote sustainable rail transport solutions.

PROJECT PLANNING

To manage large-scale projects effectively, a Work Breakdown Structure (WBS) is used. For example, the Mumbai-Ahmedabad Bullet Train project is divided into distinct phases, including land acquisition, track laying, and station development. This approach facilitates systematic resource allocation and budget control. Proper resource allocation is critical, ensuring the availability of skilled labor, timely procurement of essential materials such as rails and electrification components, and access to heavy machinery for tasks like tunnel construction. Budget estimates and project timelines are derived from industry standards and past experiences. Scheduling tools like Gantt charts and the Critical Path Method (CPM) are employed to monitor progress and optimize resource utilization.

KEY RISKS AND MITIGATION STRATEGIES

Potential risks include regulatory delays, political challenges, land acquisition disputes, and budget overruns due to global material cost inflation. Mitigation strategies include incorporating buffer times, fostering multiple supplier relationships to prevent material shortages, and maintaining dedicated teams to engage with communities and facilitate land acquisition.

PROJECT TIMELINE AND KEY MILESTONES

A structured timeline with key milestones ensures effective project monitoring and timely completion. Through these modernization efforts, Indian Railways aims to revolutionize rail transport, enhance operational efficiency, and contribute to India's long-term infrastructure growth.

Project Timeline with Milestones

Phase	Milestone	Expected Duration
Feasibility Studies and Approvals	Feasibility study completion and government approval	6 months
Land Acquisition	90% of land acquired	12 months
Design and Planning	Final design approval	6 months
Procurement	Contracting and procurement of materials	6 months
Construction	Completion of electrification works (section-wise)	18 months
Testing and Commissioning	Final testing of trains and systems	6 months
Project Handover	Full operationalization	2 months

Cost Breakdown Table: Indicative cost breakdown for the electrification project

Cost Item	Estimated Cost (INR Crore)	Percentage of Total Cost
Feasibility and Planning	50	5%
Land Acquisition	200	20%
Design and Engineering	150	13%
Procurement of Materials	300	30%
Construction and Electrification	400	40%
Signalling and Communication Systems	100	10%
Testing and Commissioning	50	5%
Contingency	50	3%
Total Project Cost	**1300**	**100%**

Appendix 5.1

LEARNING OBJECTIVES

After reading this appendix you should be able to:

A5-1 Use learning curves to improve task estimates.

LO A5-1

Use learning curves to improve task estimates.

Learning Curves for Estimating

A forecast estimate of the time required to perform a work package or task is a basic necessity for scheduling the project. In some cases, the manager simply uses judgment and past experience to estimate work package time or uses historical records of similar tasks.

Most managers and workers intuitively know that improvement in the amount of time required to perform a task or group of tasks occurs with repetition. Workers can perform tasks better/quicker the second time and each succeeding time they perform them (without any technological change). It is this pattern of improvement that is important to the project manager and project scheduler.

This improvement from repetition generally results in a reduction of labor hours for the accomplishment of tasks and results in lower project costs. From empirical evidence across *all* industries, the pattern of this improvement has been quantified in the *learning curve* (also known as improvement curve, experience curve, and industrial progress curve), which is described by the following relationship:

Each time the output quantity doubles, the unit labor hours are reduced at a constant rate.

For example, assume that a manufacturer has a new contract for 16 prototype units and a total of 800 labor hours were required for the first unit. Past experience has indicated that on similar types of units the improvement rate has been 80 percent. This relationship of improvement in labor hours is shown below:

Unit		Labor Hours
1		800
2	$800 \times 0.80 =$	640
4	$640 \times 0.80 =$	512
8	$512 \times 0.80 =$	410
16	$410 \times 0.80 =$	328

By using Table A5.1 unit values, similar labor hours per unit can be determined. Looking across the 16 unit level and down the 80 percent column, we find a ratio of 0.4096. By multiplying this ratio times, the labor hours for the first unit, we obtain the per unit value:

$$0.4096 \times 800 = 327.68 \text{ or } 328 \text{ hours}$$

That is, the 16th unit should require close to 328 labor hours, assuming an 80 percent improvement ratio.

Obviously, a project manager may need more than a single unit value for estimating the time for some work packages. The cumulative values in Table A5.2 provide factors for computing the cumulative total labor hours of all units. In the previous example, for the first 16 units, the total labor hours required would be

$$800 \times 8.920 = 7{,}136 \text{ hours}$$

TABLE A5.1
Learning Curves Unit Values

Units	60%	65%	70%	75%	80%	85%	90%	95%
1	1.0000	1.0000	1.0000	1.0000	1.0000	1.0000	1.0000	1.0000
2	0.6000	0.6500	0.7000	0.7500	0.8000	0.8500	0.9000	0.9500
3	0.4450	0.5052	0.5682	0.6338	0.7021	0.7729	0.8462	0.9219
4	0.3600	0.4225	0.4900	0.5625	0.6400	0.7225	0.8100	0.9025
5	0.3054	0.3678	0.4368	0.5127	0.5956	0.6857	0.7830	0.8877
6	0.2670	0.3284	0.3977	0.4754	0.5617	0.6570	0.7616	0.8758
7	0.2383	0.2984	0.3674	0.4459	0.5345	0.6337	0.7439	0.8659
8	0.2160	0.2746	0.3430	0.4219	0.5120	0.6141	0.7290	0.8574
9	0.1980	0.2552	0.3228	0.4017	0.4930	0.5974	0.7161	0.8499
10	0.1832	0.2391	0.3058	0.3846	0.4765	0.5828	0.7047	0.8433
12	0.1602	0.2135	0.2784	0.3565	0.4493	0.5584	0.6854	0.8320
14	0.1430	0.1940	0.2572	0.3344	0.4276	0.5386	0.6696	0.8226
16	0.1296	0.1785	0.2401	0.3164	0.4096	0.5220	0.6561	0.8145
18	0.1188	0.1659	0.2260	0.3013	0.3944	0.5078	0.6445	0.8074
20	0.1099	0.1554	0.2141	0.2884	0.3812	0.4954	0.6342	0.8012
22	0.1025	0.1465	0.2038	0.2772	0.3697	0.4844	0.6251	0.7955
24	0.0961	0.1387	0.1949	0.2674	0.3595	0.4747	0.6169	0.7904
25	0.0933	0.1353	0.1908	0.2629	0.3548	0.4701	0.6131	0.7880
30	0.0815	0.1208	0.1737	0.2437	0.3346	0.4505	0.5963	0.7775
35	0.0728	0.1097	0.1605	0.2286	0.3184	0.4345	0.5825	0.7687
40	0.0660	0.1010	0.1498	0.2163	0.3050	0.4211	0.5708	0.7611
45	0.0605	0.0939	0.1410	0.2060	0.2936	0.4096	0.5607	0.7545
50	0.0560	0.0879	0.1336	0.1972	0.2838	0.3996	0.5518	0.7486
60	0.0489	0.0785	0.1216	0.1828	0.2676	0.3829	0.5367	0.7386
70	0.0437	0.0713	0.1123	0.1715	0.2547	0.3693	0.5243	0.7302
80	0.0396	0.0657	0.1049	0.1622	0.2440	0.3579	0.5137	0.7231
90	0.0363	0.0610	0.0987	0.1545	0.2349	0.3482	0.5046	0.7168
100	0.0336	0.0572	0.0935	0.1479	0.2271	0.3397	0.4966	0.7112
120	0.0294	0.0510	0.0851	0.1371	0.2141	0.3255	0.4830	0.7017
140	0.0262	0.0464	0.0786	0.1287	0.2038	0.3139	0.4718	0.6937
160	0.0237	0.0427	0.0734	0.1217	0.1952	0.3042	0.4623	0.6869
180	0.0218	0.0397	0.0691	0.1159	0.1879	0.2959	0.4541	0.6809
200	0.0201	0.0371	0.0655	0.1109	0.1816	0.2887	0.4469	0.6757
250	0.0171	0.0323	0.0584	0.1011	0.1691	0.2740	0.4320	0.6646
300	0.0149	0.0289	0.0531	0.0937	0.1594	0.2625	0.4202	0.5557
350	0.0133	0.0262	0.0491	0.0879	0.1517	0.2532	0.4105	0.6482
400	0.0121	0.0241	0.0458	0.0832	0.1453	0.2454	0.4022	0.6419
450	0.0111	0.0224	0.0431	0.0792	0.1399	0.2387	0.3951	0.6363
500	0.0103	0.0210	0.0408	0.0758	0.1352	0.2329	0.3888	0.6314
600	0.0090	0.0188	0.0372	0.0703	0.1275	0.2232	0.3782	0.6229
700	0.0080	0.0171	0.0344	0.0659	0.1214	0.2152	0.3694	0.6158
800	0.0073	0.0157	0.0321	0.0624	0.1163	0.2086	0.3620	0.6098
900	0.0067	0.0146	0.0302	0.0594	0.1119	0.2029	0.3556	0.6045
1,000	0.0062	0.0137	0.0286	0.0569	0.1082	0.1980	0.3499	0.5998
1,200	0.0054	0.0122	0.0260	0.0527	0.1020	0.1897	0.3404	0.5918
1,400	0.0048	0.0111	0.0240	0.0495	0.0971	0.1830	0.3325	0.5850
1,600	0.0044	0.0102	0.0225	0.0468	0.0930	0.1773	0.3258	0.5793
1,800	0.0040	0.0095	0.0211	0.0446	0.0895	0.1725	0.3200	0.5743
2,000	0.0037	0.0089	0.0200	0.0427	0.0866	0.1683	0.3149	0.5698
2,500	0.0031	0.0077	0.0178	0.0389	0.0606	0.1597	0.3044	0.5605
3,000	0.0027	0.0069	0.0162	0.0360	0.0760	0.1530	0.2961	0.5530

TABLE A5.2
Learning Curves Cumulative Values

Units	60%	65%	70%	75%	80%	85%	90%	95%
1	1.000	1.000	1.000	1.000	1.000	1.000	1.000	1.000
2	1.600	1.650	1.700	1.750	1.800	1.850	1.900	1.950
3	2.045	2.155	2.268	2.384	2.502	2.623	2.746	2.872
4	2.405	2.578	2.758	2.946	3.142	3.345	3.556	3.774
5	2.710	2.946	3.195	3.459	3.738	4.031	4.339	4.662
6	2.977	3.274	3.593	3.934	4.299	4.688	5.101	5.538
7	3.216	3.572	3.960	4.380	4.834	5.322	5.845	6.404
8	3.432	3.847	4.303	4.802	5.346	5.936	6.574	7.261
9	3.630	4.102	4.626	5.204	5.839	6.533	7.290	8.111
10	3.813	4.341	4.931	5.589	6.315	7.116	7.994	8.955
12	4.144	4.780	5.501	6.315	7.227	8.244	9.374	10.62
14	4.438	5.177	6.026	6.994	8.092	9.331	10.72	12.27
16	4.704	5.541	6.514	7.635	8.920	10.38	12.04	13.91
18	4.946	5.879	6.972	8.245	9.716	11.41	13.33	15.52
20	5.171	6.195	7.407	8.828	10.48	12.40	14.64	17.13
22	5.379	6.492	7.819	9.388	11.23	13.38	15.86	18.72
24	5.574	6.773	8.213	9.928	11.95	14.33	17.10	20.31
25	5.668	6.909	8.404	10.19	12.31	14.80	17.71	21.10
30	6.097	7.540	9.305	11.45	14.02	17.09	20.73	25.00
35	6.478	8.109	10.13	12.72	15.64	19.29	23.67	28.86
40	6.821	8.631	10.90	13.72	17.19	21.43	26.54	32.68
45	7.134	9.114	11.62	14.77	18.68	23.50	29.37	36.47
50	7.422	9.565	12.31	15.78	20.12	25.51	32.14	40.22
60	7.941	10.39	13.57	17.67	22.87	29.41	37.57	47.65
70	8.401	11.13	14.74	19.43	25.47	33.17	42.87	54.99
80	8.814	11.82	15.82	21.09	27.96	36.80	48.05	62.25
90	9.191	12.45	16.83	22.67	30.35	40.32	53.14	69.45
100	9.539	13.03	17.79	24.18	32.65	43.75	58.14	76.59
120	10.16	14.16	19.57	27.02	37.05	50.39	67.93	90.71
140	10.72	15.08	21.20	29.67	41.22	56.78	77.46	104.7
160	11.21	15.97	22.72	32.17	45.20	62.95	86.80	118.5
180	11.67	16.79	24.14	34.54	49.03	68.95	95.96	132.1
200	12.09	17.55	25.48	36.80	52.72	74.79	105.0	145.7
250	13.01	19.28	28.56	42.08	61.47	88.83	126.9	179.2
300	13.81	20.81	31.34	46.94	69.66	102.2	148.2	212.2
350	14.51	22.18	33.89	51.48	77.43	115.1	169.0	244.8
400	15.14	23.44	36.26	55.75	84.85	127.6	189.3	277.0
450	15.72	24.60	38.48	59.80	91.97	139.7	209.2	309.0
500	16.26	25.68	40.58	63.68	98.85	151.5	228.8	340.6
600	17.21	27.67	44.47	70.97	112.0	174.2	267.1	403.3
700	18.06	29.45	48.04	77.77	124.4	196.1	304.5	465.3
800	18.82	31.09	51.36	84.18	136.3	217.3	341.0	526.5
900	19.51	32.60	54.46	90.26	147.7	237.9	376.9	587.2
1,000	20.15	34.01	57.40	96.07	158.7	257.9	412.2	647.4
1,200	21.30	36.59	62.85	107.0	179.7	296.6	481.2	766.6
1,400	22.32	38.92	67.85	117.2	199.6	333.9	548.4	884.2
1,600	23.23	41.04	72.49	126.8	218.6	369.9	614.2	1001.
1,800	24.06	43.00	76.85	135.9	236.8	404.9	678.8	1116.
2,000	24.83	44.84	80.96	144.7	254.4	438.9	742.3	1230.
2,500	26.53	48.97	90.39	165.0	296.1	520.8	897.0	1513.
3,000	27.99	52.62	98.90	183.7	335.2	598.9	1047.	1791.

By dividing the total cumulative hours (7,136) by the units, the average unit labor hours can be obtained:

7,136 labor hours/16 units = 446 average labor hours per unit

Note how the labor hours for the 16th unit (328) differs from the average for all 16 units (446). The project manager, knowing the average labor costs and processing costs, could estimate the total prototype costs. (The mathematical derivation of factors found in Tables A5.1 and A5.2 can be found in Jelen, F. C., and J. H. Black, *Cost and Optimization Engineering,* 2nd ed. New York: McGraw-Hill, 1983).

FOLLOW-ON CONTRACT EXAMPLE

Assume the project manager gets a follow-on order of 74 units; how should s/he estimate labor hours and cost? Going to the cumulative Table A5.2, we find at the 80 percent ratio and 90 total units intersection—a 30.35 ratio.

800 × 30.35 =	24,280 labor hours for 90 units
Less previous 16 units =	7,136
Total follow-on order =	17,144 labor hours
17,144/74 equals 232 average labor hours per unit	

Labor hours for the 90th unit can be obtained from Table A5.1: 0.2349 × 800 = 187.9 labor hours. (For ratios between given values, simply estimate.)

Exercise A5.1

Norwegian Satellite Development Company (NSDC)
Cost Estimates
for
World Satellite Telephone Exchange Project

NSDC has a contract to produce eight satellites to support a worldwide telephone system (for Alaska Telecom, Inc.) that allows individuals to use a single, portable telephone in any location on earth to call in and out. NSDC will develop and produce the eight units. NSDC has estimated that the R&D costs will be NOK (Norwegian Krone) 12,000,000. Material costs are expected to be NOK 6,000,000. They have estimated that the design and production of the first satellite will require 100,000 labor hours, and an 80 percent improvement curve is expected. Skilled labor cost is NOK 300 per hour. Desired profit for all projects is 25 percent of total costs.

A. How many labor hours should the eighth satellite require?
B. How many labor hours for the whole project of eight satellites?
C. What price would you ask for the project? Why?
D. Midway through the project your design and production people realize that a 75 percent improvement curve is more appropriate. What impact does this have on the project?
E. Near the end of the project, Deutsch Telefon AG requests a cost estimate for four satellites identical to those you have already produced. What price will you quote them? Justify your price.

CHAPTER SIX

6 Developing a Project Schedule

LEARNING OBJECTIVES

After reading this chapter, you should be able to

6-1 Understand the linkage between WBS and the project network.

6-2 Diagram a project network using AON methods.

6-3 Calculate early, late, and slack activity times.

6-4 Identify and understand the importance of managing the critical path.

6-5 Distinguish free slack from total slack.

6-6 Demonstrate understanding and application of lags in compressing projects or constraining the start or finish of an activity.

OUTLINE

6.1 Developing the Project Network

6.2 From Work Package to Network

6.3 Constructing a Project Network

6.4 Activity-on-Node (AON) Fundamentals

6.5 Network Computation Process

6.6 Using the Forward and Backward Pass Information

6.7 Level of Detail for Activities

6.8 Practical Considerations

6.9 Extended Network Techniques to Come Closer to Reality

Summary

Appendix 6.1: Step-by-Step MS Project Demonstration of Book Questions

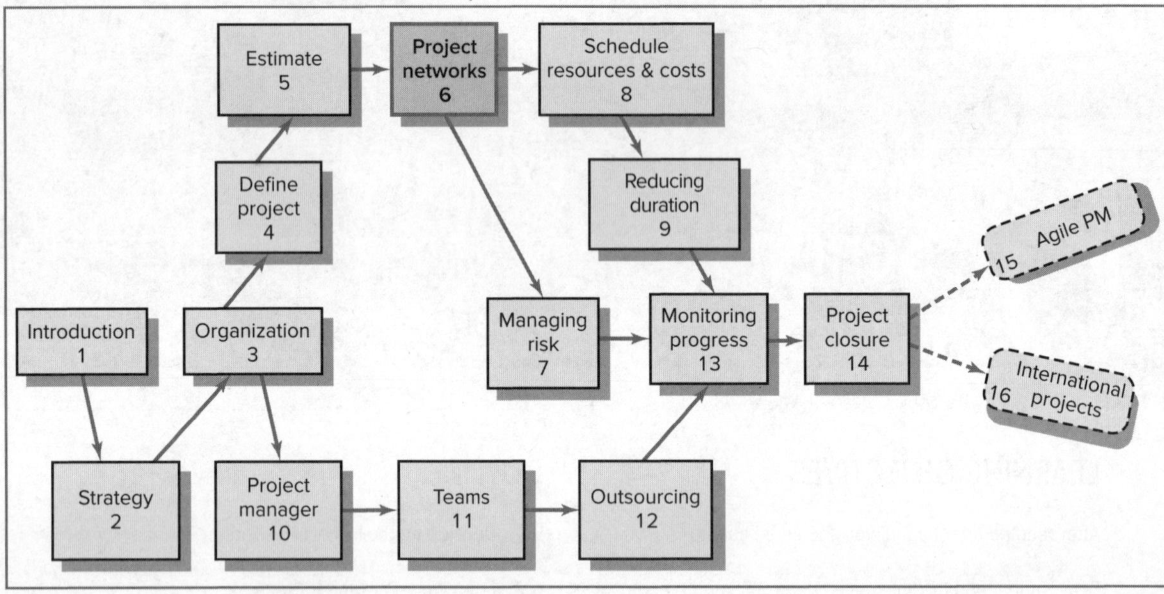

I keep six honest serving men (they taught me all I knew); their names are What and Why and When and How and Where and Who.

—Rudyard Kipling, noted journalist and author, 1865–1936.

6.1 Developing the Project Network

The project network is the tool used for planning, scheduling, and monitoring project progress. The network is developed from the information collected for the WBS and is a graphic flow chart of the project job plan. The network depicts the project activities that must be completed, the logical sequences, the interdependencies of the activities to be completed, and in most cases the times for the activities to start and finish along with the longest path(s) through the network—the *critical path.* The network is the framework for the project information system that will be used by the project managers to make decisions concerning project time, cost, and performance.

Developing the project networks takes time for someone or some group to develop; therefore, they cost money! Are networks really worth the struggle? The answer is definitely yes, except in cases where the project is considered trivial or very short in duration.[1] The network is easily understood by others because the network presents a graphic display of the flow and sequence of work through the project. Once the network is developed, it is very easy to modify when unexpected events occur as the project progresses. For example, if materials for an activity are delayed, the impact can be quickly assessed and the whole project revised in only a few minutes with the computer. These revisions can be communicated to all project participants quickly (e.g., via e-mail or project website).

[1] On these projects the simpler Responsibility Matrix will do (see Chapter 4).

The project network provides other invaluable information and insights. It provides the basis for scheduling labor and equipment. It enhances communication that melds all managers and groups together in meeting the time, cost, and performance objectives of the project. It provides an estimate of project duration rather than picking a random project completion date or someone's preferred date. The network gives the times when activities can start and finish and when they can be delayed. It provides the basis for budgeting the cash flow of the project. It identifies which activities are "critical" and, therefore, should not be delayed if the project is to be completed as planned. It highlights which activities to consider if the project needs to be compressed to meet a deadline.

There are other reasons project networks are worth their weight in gold. Basically, project networks minimize surprises by getting the plan out early and allowing corrective feedback. A commonly heard statement from practitioners is that the project network represents three-quarters of the planning process. Perhaps this is an exaggeration, but it signals the perceived importance of the network to project managers in the field.

6.2 From Work Package to Network

LO 6-1

Understand the linkage between WBS and the project network.

Project networks are developed from the WBS. The project network is a visual flow diagram of the sequence, interrelationships, and dependencies of all the activities that must be accomplished to complete the project. *An **activity** is an element in the project that consumes time—for example, work or waiting.* Work packages from the WBS are used to build the activities found in the project network. An activity can include one or more work packages. The activities are placed in a sequence that provides for orderly completion of the project. Networks are built using nodes (boxes) and arrows (lines).

Integrating the work packages and the network represents a point where the management process often fails in practice. The primary explanations for this failure are that (1) different groups (people) are used to define work packages and activities and (2) the WBS is poorly constructed and not deliverable/output oriented. Integration of the WBS and project network is crucial to effective project management. The project manager must be careful to guarantee continuity by having some of the same people who defined the WBS and work packages develop the network activities.

Networks provide the project schedule by identifying dependencies, sequencing, and timing of activities, which the WBS is not designed to do. The primary inputs for developing a project network plan are work packages. Remember, a work package is defined independently of other work packages, has definite start and finish points, requires specific resources, includes technical specifications, and has cost estimates for the package. However, dependency, sequencing, and timing of each of these factors are not included in the work package. A network activity can include one or more work packages.

Figure 6.1 shows a segment of the WBS example and how the information is used to develop a project network. The lowest-level deliverable in Figure 6.1 is "circuit board." The cost accounts (design, production, test, software) denote project work, organization unit responsible, and time-phased budgets for the work packages. Each cost account represents one or more work packages. For example, the design cost account has two work packages (D-1-1 and D-1-2)—specifications and documentation. The software and production accounts also have two work packages. Developing a network requires sequencing tasks from all work packages that have measurable work.

FIGURE 6.1
WBS/Work Packages to Network

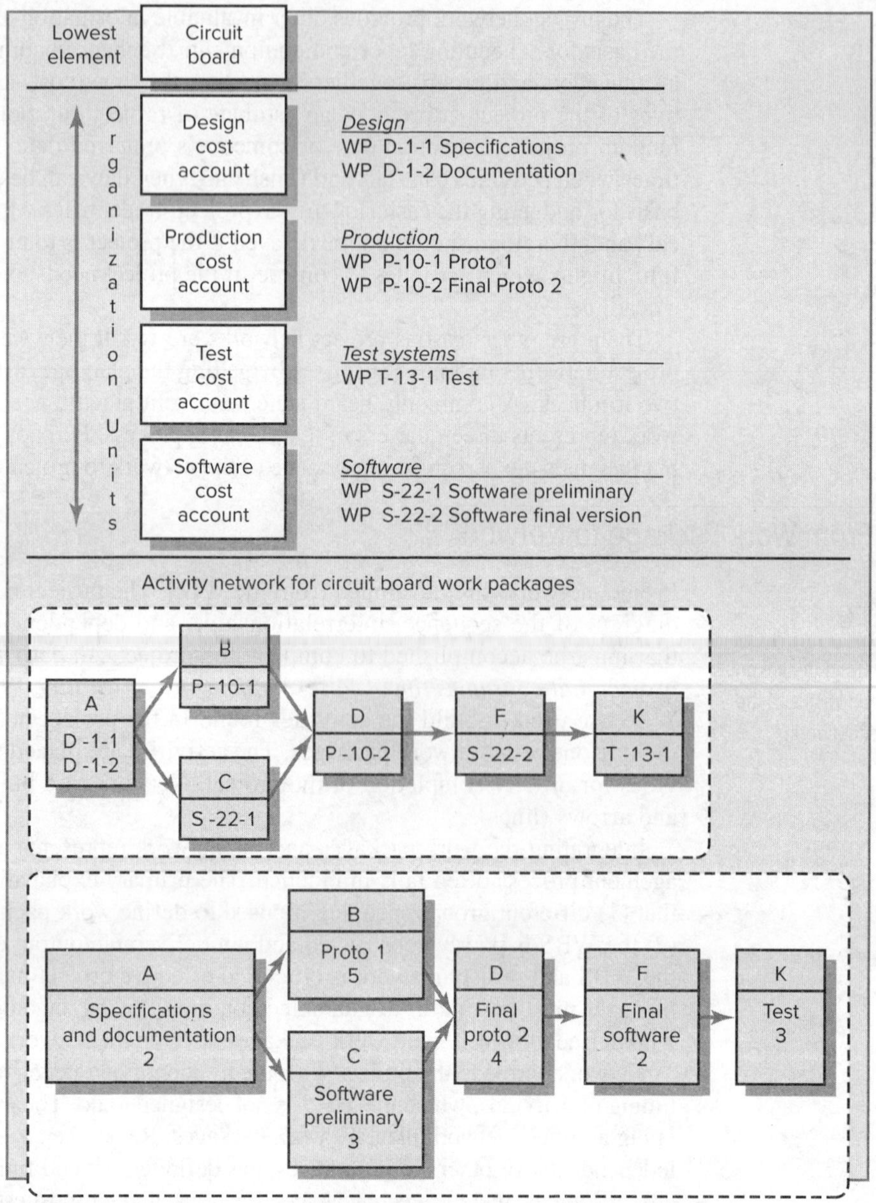

Figure 6.1 traces how work packages are used to develop a project network. You can trace the use of work packages by the coding scheme. For example, activity A uses work packages D-1-1 and D-1-2 (specifications and documentation), while activity C uses work package S-22-1. This methodology of selecting work packages to describe activities is used to develop the project network, which sequences and times project activities. Care must be taken to include all work packages. *The manager derives activity time estimates from the task times in the work package.* For example, activity B (proto 1) requires five weeks to complete; activity K (test) requires three weeks to complete. After computing the activity **early times** and **late times,** the manager can schedule resources and time-phase budgets (with dates).

6.3 Constructing a Project Network

LO 6-2

Diagram a project network using AON methods.

Terminology

Every field has its jargon that allows colleagues to communicate comfortably with each other about the techniques they use. Project managers are no exception. Here are some terms used in building project networks:

Activity. For project managers, an *activity* is an element of the project that requires time. It may or may not require resources. Typically an activity consumes time—either while people work or while people wait. Examples of the latter are time waiting for contracts to be signed, materials to arrive, drug approval by the government, and budget clearance. Activities usually represent one or more tasks from a work package. Descriptions of activities should use a verb/noun format—for example, develop product specifications.

Parallel activities. These are activities that can take place at the same time, if the manager wishes. However, the manager may choose to have parallel activities *not* occur simultaneously.

Burst activity. This activity has more than one activity immediately following it (more than one dependency arrow flowing from it).

Merge activity. This is an activity that has more than one activity immediately preceding it (more than one dependency arrow flowing to it).

Path. This is a sequence of connected, dependent activities.

Critical path. When this term is used, it means the path(s) with the longest duration through the network; if an activity on the path is delayed, the project is delayed the same amount of time.

Basic Rules to Follow in Developing Project Networks

The following eight rules apply in general when developing a project network:

1. Networks flow typically from left to right.
2. An activity cannot begin until all preceding connected activities have been completed.
3. Arrows on networks indicate precedence and flow. Arrows can cross over each other.
4. Each activity should have a unique identification number.
5. An activity identification number must be larger than that of any activities that precede it.
6. Looping is not allowed (in other words, recycling through a set of activities cannot take place).
7. Conditional statements are not allowed (i.e., this type of statement should not appear: if successful, do something; if not, do nothing).
8. Experience suggests that when there are multiple starts, a common start node can be used to indicate a clear project beginning on the network. Similarly, a single project end node can be used to indicate a clear ending.

Read Snapshot from Practice 6.1: The Yellow Sticky Approach to see how these rules are used to create project networks.

SNAPSHOT FROM PRACTICE 6.1 The Yellow Sticky Approach (for Constructing a Project Network)

In practice, small project networks (25–100 activities) are frequently developed using yellow Post-it® stickers.

The following are the requirements for such a project:

1. Project team members and a facilitator.
2. One yellow sticker (3 × 4 inches or larger) for each activity with the description of the activity printed on the sticker.
3. Erasable whiteboard with marker pen (a long, 4-foot-wide piece of butcher paper can be used in place of the whiteboard).

All of the yellow stickers are placed in easy view of all team members. The team begins by identifying those activity stickers that have no predecessors. Each of these activity stickers is then attached to the whiteboard. A start node is drawn, and a dependency arrow is connected to each activity.

Given the initial network start activities, each activity is examined for immediate successor activities. These activities are attached to the whiteboard and dependency arrows drawn. This process is continued until all of the yellow stickers are attached to the whiteboard with dependency arrows. (Note: The process can be reversed, beginning with those activities that have no successor activities and connecting them to a project end node. The predecessor activities are selected for each activity and attached to the whiteboard with dependency arrows marked.)

When the process is complete, the dependencies are recorded in the project software, which develops a project network along with the critical path(s) and early, late, and slack times. This methodology sensitizes team members early to the interdependencies among activities of the project. But more importantly, the methodology empowers team members by giving them input into the important decisions they must implement later.

FangXiaNuo/Getty Images

6.4 Activity-on-Node (AON) Fundamentals

Historically, two methods have been used to develop project networks: **activity-on-node (AON)** and **activity-on-arrow (AOA).** Over time the availability of advanced computer graphics improved the clarity and visual appeal of the AON method. Today the activity-on-node method has come to dominate nearly all project network plans. For this reason, we have limited our discussion to AON methods. Figure 6.2 shows a few typical uses of building blocks for the AON network construction. An activity is represented by a *node* (box). The node can take many forms, but in recent years the node represented as a rectangle (box) has dominated. The dependencies among activities are depicted by *arrows* between the rectangles (boxes) on the AON network. The arrows indicate how the activities are related and the sequence in which things must be accomplished. The length and slope of the arrow are arbitrary and set for the convenience of drawing the network. The letters in the boxes serve here to identify the activities while you learn the fundamentals of network construction and analysis. In practice, activities have identification numbers and descriptions.

FIGURE 6.2
Activity-on-Node Network Fundamentals

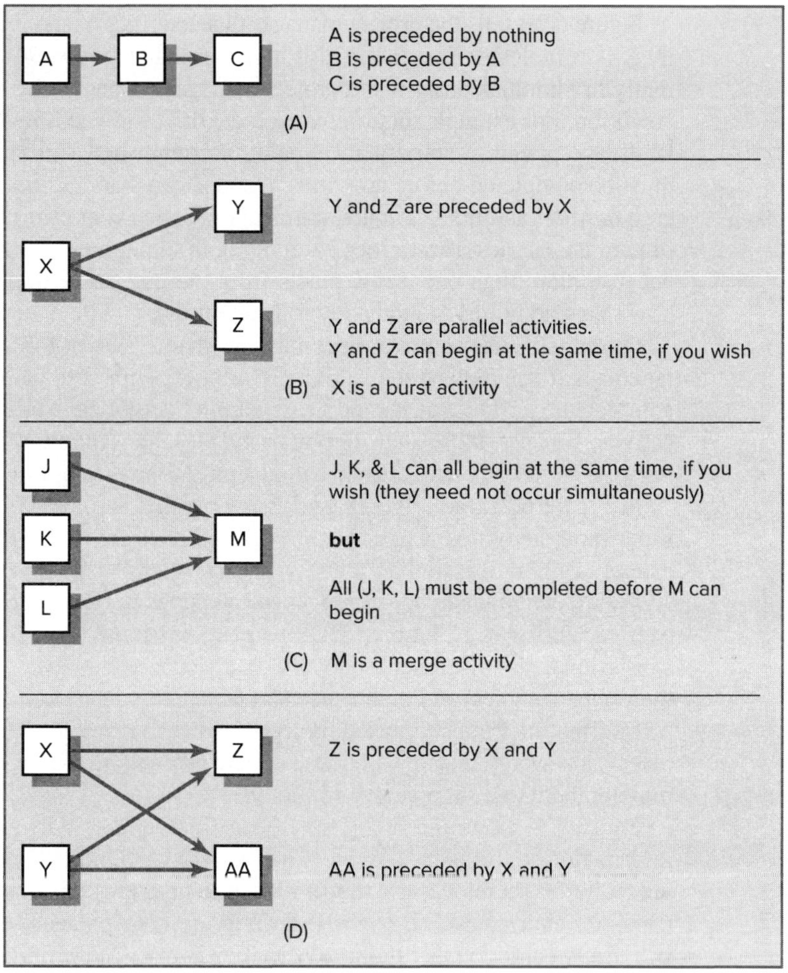

There are three basic relationships that must be established for activities included in a project network. The relationships can be found by answering the following three questions for each activity.

1. Which activities must be completed immediately *before* this activity? These activities are called *predecessor* activities.
2. Which activities must immediately *follow* this activity? These activities are called *successor* activities.
3. Which activities can occur *while* this activity is taking place? This is known as a *concurrent* or *parallel* relationship.

Sometimes a manager can use only questions 1 and 3 to establish relationships. This information allows the network analyst to construct a graphic flow chart of the sequence and logical interdependencies of project activities.

Figure 6.2A is analogous to a list of things to do where you complete the task at the top of the list first and then move to the second task, etc. This figure tells the project manager that activity A must be completed before activity B can begin and that activity B must be completed before activity C can begin.

Figure 6.2B tells the project manager that activities Y and Z cannot begin until activity X is completed. This figure also indicates that activities Y and Z can occur concurrently or simultaneously if the project manager wishes; however, it is not a necessary condition. For example, pouring a concrete driveway (activity Y) can take place while landscape planting (activity Z) is being accomplished, but land clearing (activity X) must be completed before activities Y and Z can start. Activities Y and Z are considered *parallel* activities. Parallel paths allow concurrent effort, which may shorten the time to do a series of activities. Activity X is sometimes referred to as a *burst* activity because more than one arrow bursts from the node. The number of arrows indicates how many activities immediately follow activity X.

Figure 6.2C shows the project manager that activities J, K, and L can occur simultaneously if desired and that activity M cannot begin until activities J, K, and L are all completed. Activities J, K, and L are parallel activities. Activity M is called a *merge* activity because more than one activity must be completed before activity M can begin. Activity M could also be called a milestone—a significant accomplishment.

In Figure 6.2D, activities X and Y are parallel activities that can take place at the same time; activities Z and AA are also parallel activities. But activities Z and AA cannot begin until activities X and Y are both completed. Given these fundamentals of AON, we can practice developing a simple network. Remember, the arrows can cross over each other (e.g., Figure 6.2D), be bent, or be any length or slope. Neatness is not a criterion for a valid, useful network—only accurate inclusion of all project activities, their dependencies, and their time estimates.

Information for a simplified project network is given in Table 6.1. This project represents a new automated warehouse system for picking frozen food package orders and moving them to a staging area for delivery to stores.

Figure 6.3 shows the first steps in constructing the AON project network from the information in Table 6.1. We see that activity A (Define Requirements) has nothing preceding it; therefore, it is the first node to be drawn. Next, we note that activities B (Assign Team) and C (Design Hardware) are both preceded by activity A. We draw two arrows and connect them to activities B and C. This segment shows the project manager that activity A must be completed before activities B and C can begin. After A is completed, B and C can take place concurrently, if desired. Figure 6.4 shows the completed network with all of the activities' sequences and dependencies.

The information in Figure 6.4 is tremendously valuable to those managing the project. However, estimating the duration for each activity will further increase the value of the network. A realistic project plan and schedule require reliable time estimates for project activities. The addition of time to the network allows us to estimate how long

TABLE 6.1
Network Information

AUTOMATED WAREHOUSE Order Picking System		
Activity	**Description**	**Preceding Activity**
A	Define Requirements	None
B	Assign Team	A
C	Design Hardware	A
D	Code Software	B
E	Build and Test Hardware	C
F	Develop Patent Request	C
G	Test Software	D
H	Integrate Systems	E, F, G

FIGURE 6.3
Automated Warehouse—Partial Network

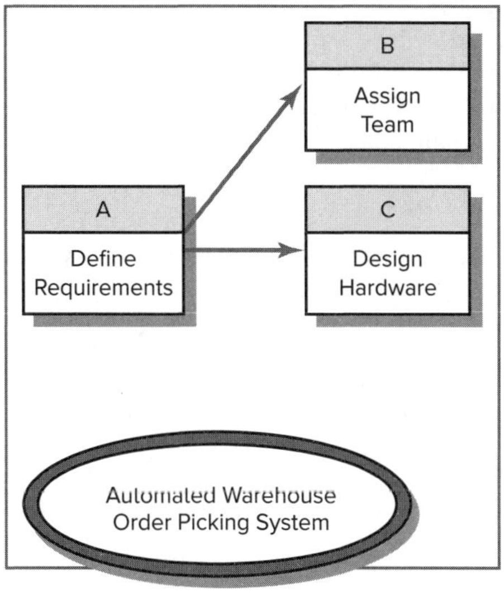

FIGURE 6.4 Automated Warehouse—Completed Network

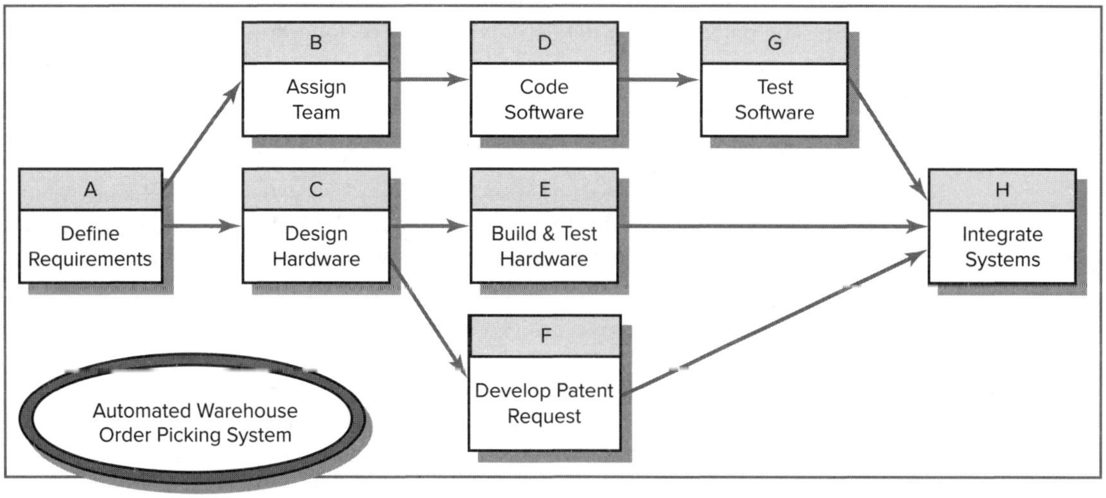

the project will take. When activities can or must start, when resources must be available, which activities can be delayed, and when the project is estimated to be complete are all determined from the times assigned. Deriving an activity time estimate necessitates early assessment of resource needs in terms of material, equipment, and people. In essence, the project network with activity time estimates links the planning, scheduling, and controlling of projects.

6.5 Network Computation Process

LO 6-3

Calculate early, late, and slack activity times.

Drawing the project network places the activities in the right sequence for computing the start and finish times of activities. Activity time estimates are taken from the task times in the work package and added to the network (review Figure 6.1). Performing a few simple computations allows the project manager to complete a process known as the forward and backward pass. Completion of the *forward and backward pass* will answer the following questions.

Forward Pass—Earliest Times

1. How soon can the activity start (early start—ES)?
2. How soon can the activity finish (early finish—EF)?
3. How soon can the project be finished (expected time—TE)?

Backward Pass—Latest Times

1. How late can the activity start (late start—LS)?
2. How late can the activity finish (late finish—LF)?
3. Which activities represent the critical path (CP)? This is the longest path in the network, which, when delayed, will delay the project.
4. How long can the activity be delayed (slack or float—SL)?

The terms in parentheses represent the acronyms used in most texts and computer programs and by project managers. The forward and backward pass process is presented next.

Forward Pass—Earliest Times

The forward pass starts with the first project activity(ies) and traces each path (chain of sequential activities) through the network to the last project activity(ies). As you trace along the path, you *add* the activity times. The longest path denotes the project completion time for the plan and is called the critical path (CP). Table 6.2 lists the activity times in workdays for the Automated Warehouse project example we used for drawing a network.

Figure 6.5 shows the network with the activity time estimate found in the node (see "DUR" for duration in the legend). For example, activity A (Define Requirements) has an activity duration of 10 workdays, and activity E (Build & Test Hardware) has a duration of 50 days. The forward pass begins with the project start time, which is usually time zero. (Note: Calendar times can be computed for the project later in the planning phase.)

In our Automated Warehouse example, the early start time for the first activity (activity A) is zero. This time is found in the upper left corner of the activity A node in Figure 6.6. The early finish for activity A is 10 days (EF = ES + DUR, or 0 + 10 = 10). Next, we see that activity A is the predecessor for activities B (Assign Team) and C (Design Hardware). Therefore, the earliest activities B and C can begin is the instant in time when activity A is completed; this time is 10 days. You can now see in Figure 6.6

TABLE 6.2
Network Information

AUTOMATED WAREHOUSE
Order Picking System

Activity	Description	Preceding Activity	Activity Time
A	Define Requirements	None	10 workdays
B	Assign Team	A	5
C	Design Hardware	A	25
D	Code Software	B	20
E	Build & Test Hardware	C	50
F	Develop Patent Request	C	15
G	Test Software	D	35
H	Integrate Systems	E, F, G	15

FIGURE 6.5 Activity-on-Node Network

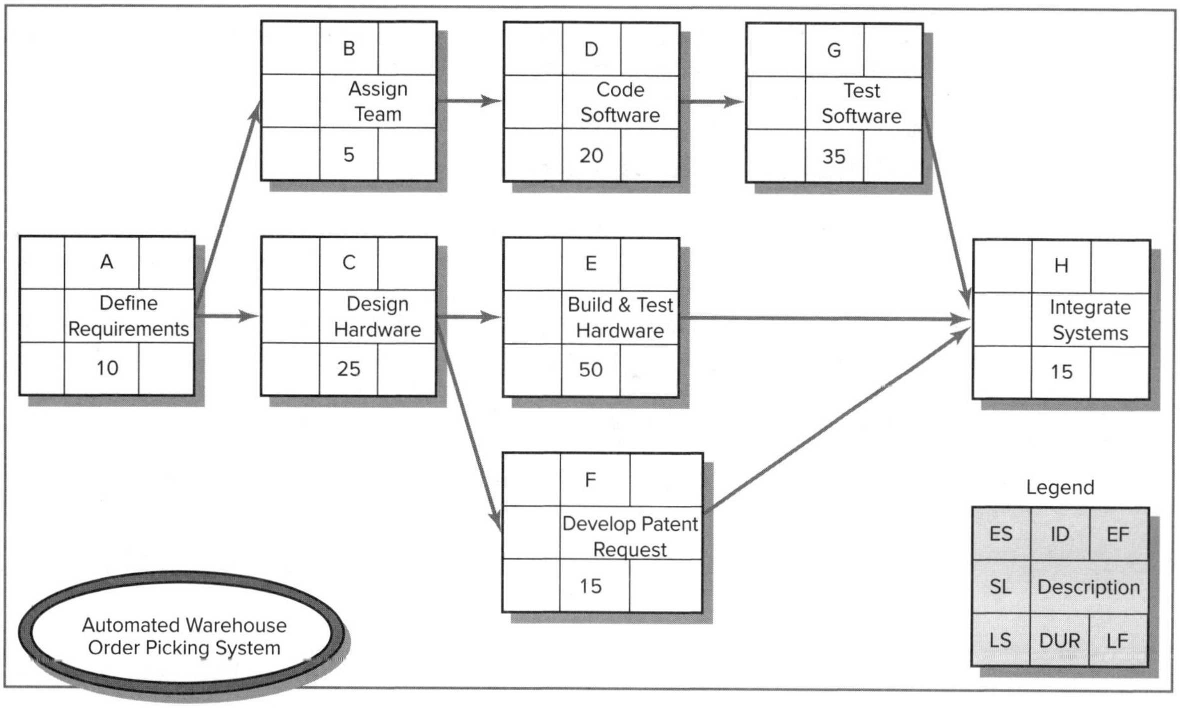

FIGURE 6.6 Activity-on-Node Network Forward Pass

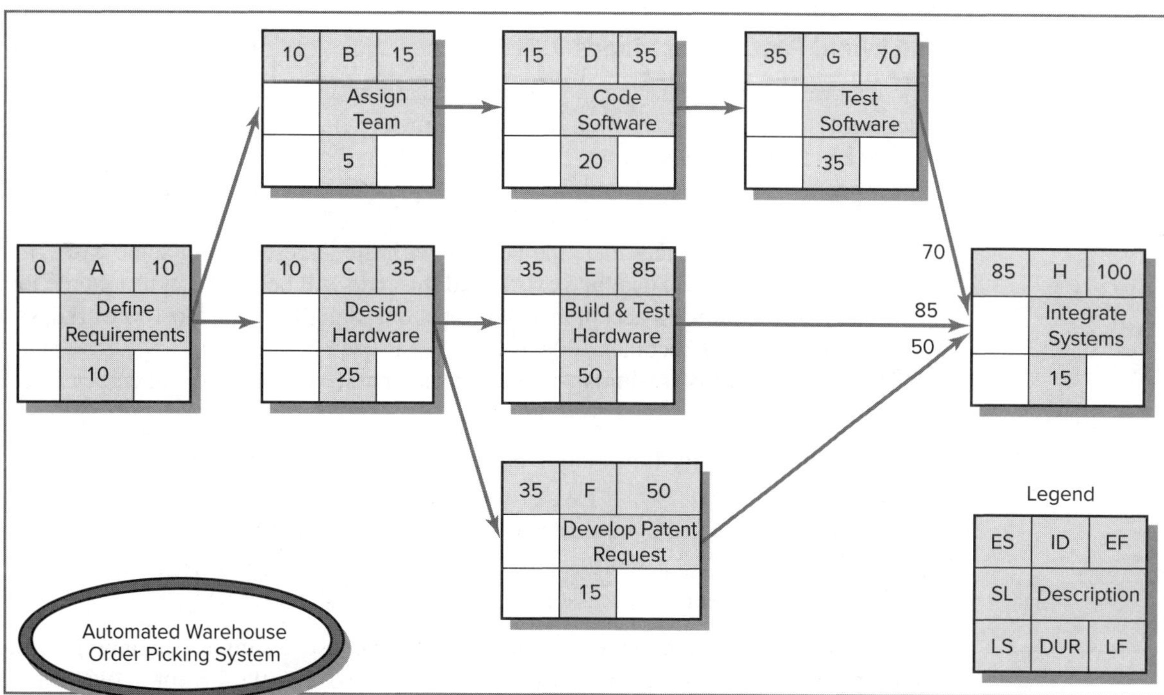

that activities B and C have an early start (ES) of 10 days. Using the formula EF = ES + DUR, the early finish (EF) times for activities B and C are 15 and 35 days. Following the same process of moving along each network path, the early start and finish times for selected activities are shown here:

Activity D: ES = 15	EF = 15 + 20 = 35	Activity F: ES = 35	EF = 35 + 15 = 50
Activity E: ES = 35	EF = 35 + 50 = 85	Activity G: ES = 35	EF = 35 + 35 = 70

Activity H (Integrate Systems) is a merge activity because it is preceded by more than one activity. The early start (ES) of a merge activity depends on the early finish (EF) of all activities that merge to it. In this project, activity H is preceded by activities E, F, and G. Which activity controls the ES of activity H? The answer is activity E. In Figure 6.6, the EF times are 85, 50, and 70. Since 85 days is the largest EF time, activity E controls the ES for activity H, which is 85. If activity E is delayed, activity H will be delayed. The early finish for activity H or the project is 100 days (EF = ES + DUR, or 85 + 15 = 100).

The forward pass requires that you remember just three things when computing early activity times:

1. You *add* activity times along each path in the network (ES + DUR = EF).
2. You carry the early finish (EF) to the next activity where it becomes its early start (ES), *or*
3. If the next succeeding activity is a *merge* activity, you select the *largest* early finish number (EF) of *all* its immediate predecessor activities.

The three questions derived from the forward pass have been answered; that is, early start (ES), early finish (EF), and the project expected duration (TE) times have been computed. The backward pass is the next process to learn.

Backward Pass—Latest Times

The backward pass starts with the last project activity(ies) on the network. You trace backward on each path, *subtracting* activity times to find the late start (LS) and late finish (LF) times for each activity. Before the backward pass can be computed, the late finish for the last project activity(ies) must be selected. In early planning stages, this time is usually set equal to the early finish (EF) of the last project activity (or in the case of multiple finish activities, the activity with the largest EF). In some cases, an imposed project duration deadline exists, and this date will be used. Let us assume for planning purposes we can accept the EF project duration (TE) equal to 100 workdays. The LF for activity H becomes 100 days (EF = LF) (see Figure 6.7).

The backward pass is similar to the forward pass; you need to remember three things:

1. You *subtract* activity times along each path starting with the project end activity (LF – DUR = LS).
2. You carry the LS to the preceding activity to establish its LF, *or*
3. If the next preceding activity is a *burst* activity; in this case you select the *smallest* LS of all its immediate successor activities to establish its LF.

Let us apply these rules to our Automated Warehouse example. Beginning with activity H (Integrate Systems) and an LF of 100 workdays, the LS for activity H is 85 days (LF – DUR = LS, or 100 – 15 = 85). The LS for activity H becomes the LF

FIGURE 6.7 Activity-on-Node Network Backward Pass

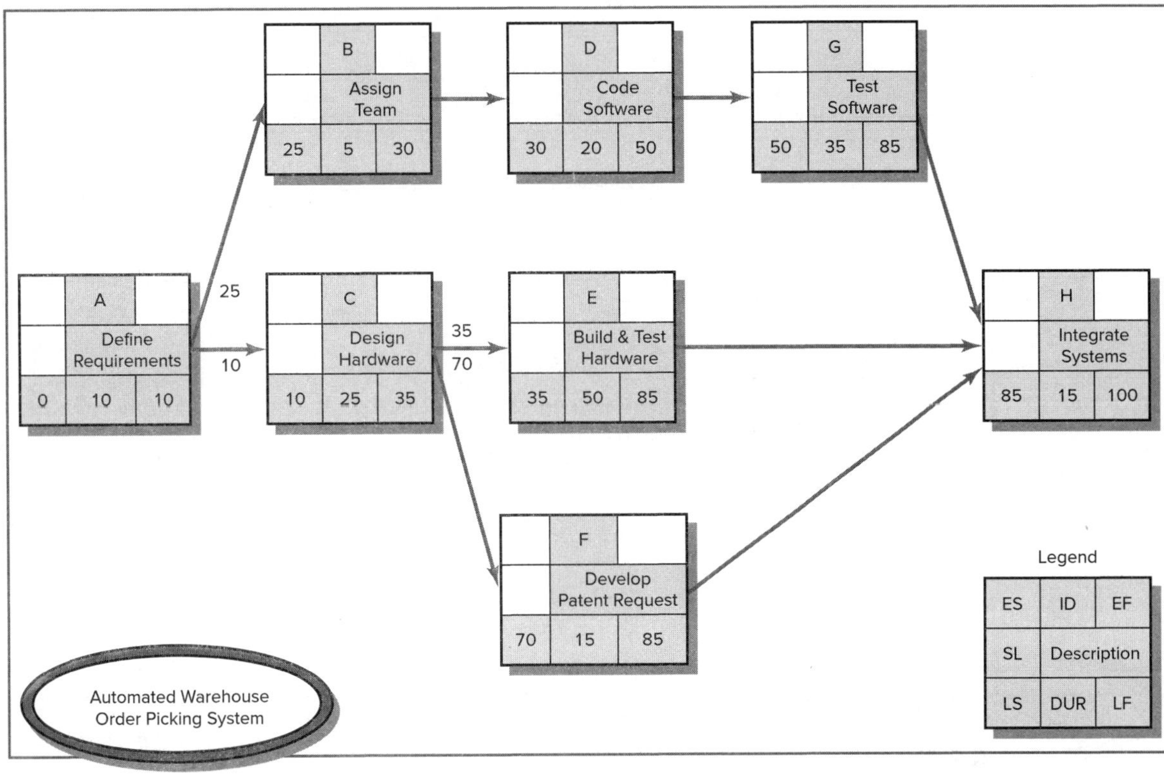

for activities E, F, and G. Moving backward on the network, the late starts for E, F, and G are shown here (LS = LF – DUR):

Activity E: LS = 85 – 50 = 35	Activity G: 85 – 35 = 50
Activity F: LS = 85 – 15 = 70	

At this point, we see that activity C is a *burst* activity that ties to (precedes) activities E and F. The late finish for activity C is controlled by the LS of activities E and F. The *smallest* LS of activities E and F (LS's = 35 and 70) is activity E. This establishes the LF for activity C. The LS for activity C becomes 10. Moving backward to the first project activity, we note it is also a *burst* activity that links to activities B and C. The LF of activity A is controlled by activity C, which has the smallest LS of 10 days. Given an LF of 10 days, the LS for activity is time period zero (LS = 10 – 10 = 0). The backward pass is complete, and the latest activity times are known. Figure 6.8 shows the completed network with all the early, late, and slack times included. Slack can be important to managing your project.

LO 6-4

Identify and understand the importance of managing the critical path.

Determining Slack (or Float)

Total Slack

When the forward pass and backward pass have been computed, it is possible to determine which activities can be delayed by computing "slack," or "float." **Total slack** *tells us the amount of time an activity can be delayed and not delay the project.* Stated

FIGURE 6.8 **Forward and Backward Pass Completed with Slack Times**

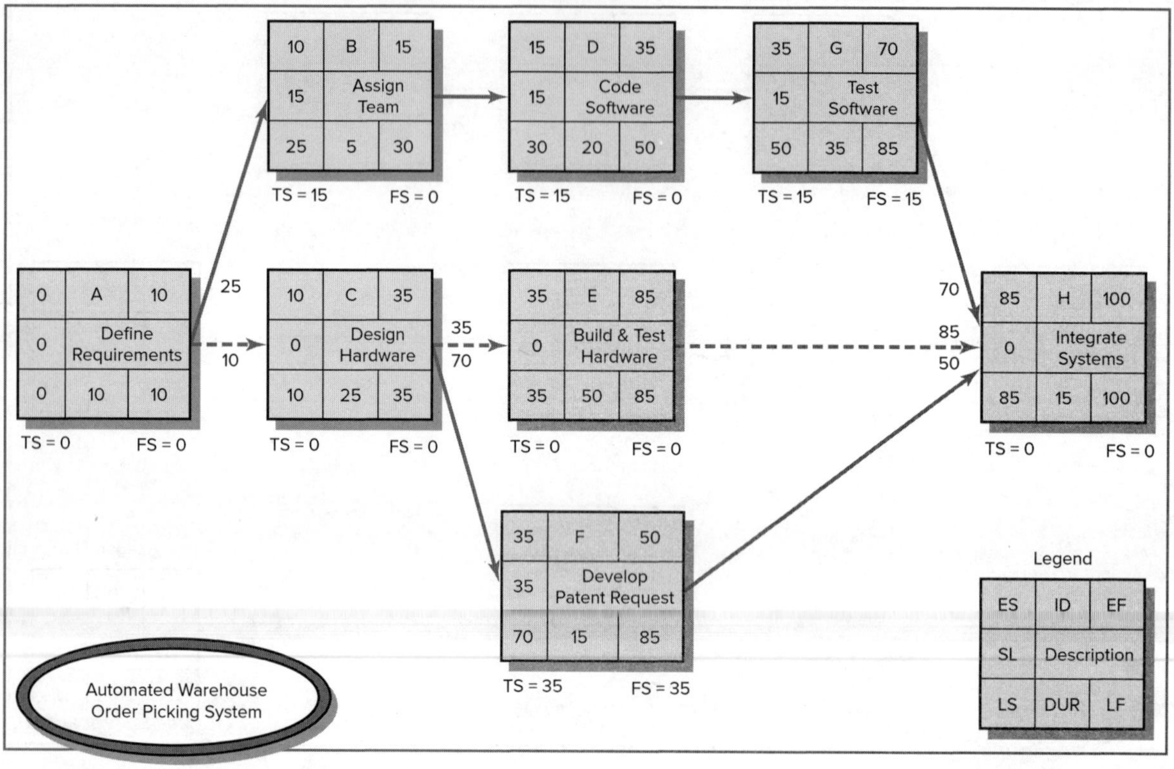

differently, *total slack is the amount of time an activity can exceed its early finish date without affecting the project end date or an imposed completion date.*

Total slack, or float, for an activity is simply the difference between the LS and ES (LS – ES = SL) or between the LF and EF (LF – EF = SL). For example, in Figure 6.8, the total slack for activity D is 15 workdays, for activity F is 35 days, and for activity E is zero. If total slack of one activity in a path is used, the ES for all activities that follow in the chain will be delayed and their slack reduced. Use of total slack *must be coordinated* with all participants in the activities that follow in the chain.

After slack for each activity is computed, the critical path(s) is (are) easily identified. When the LF = EF for the end project activity, the critical path can be identified as those activities that also have LF = EF or a slack of zero (LF – EF = 0 or LS – ES = 0). *The critical path is the network path(s) that has (have) the least slack in common.* This awkward arrangement of words is necessary because a problem arises when the project finish activity has an LF that differs from the EF found in the forward pass—for example, an imposed duration date. If this is the case, the slack on the critical path will *not* be zero; it will be the difference between the project EF and the imposed LF of the last project activity. For example, if the EF for the project is 100 days, but the imposed LF or target date is set at 95 days, all activities on the critical path have a slack of minus 5 days. Of course, this would result in a late start 5 days for the first project activity—a good trick if the project is to start now. Negative slack occurs in practice when the critical path is delayed.

In Figure 6.8, the critical path is marked with dashed arrows—activities A, C, E, and H. Delay of any of these activities will delay the total project by the same

SNAPSHOT FROM PRACTICE 6.2 The Critical Path

The critical path method (CPM) has long been considered the "Holy Grail" of project management. Here are comments made by veteran project managers when asked about the significance of the critical path in managing projects:

- I try to make it a point whenever possible to put my best people on critical activities or on those activities that stand the greatest chance of becoming critical.
- I pay extra attention when doing risk assessment to identifying those risks that can impact the critical path, either directly or indirectly, by making a noncritical activity so late that it becomes critical. When I've got money to spend to reduce risks, it usually gets spent on critical tasks.
- I don't have time to monitor all the activities on a big project, but I make it a point to keep in touch with the people who are working on critical activities. When I have the time, they are the ones I visit to find out firsthand how things are going. It's amazing how much more I can find out from talking to the rank and file who are doing the work and by reading the facial expressions of people—much more than I can gain from a number-driven status report.
- When I get calls from other managers asking to "borrow" people or equipment, I'm much more generous when it involves resources from working on noncritical activities. For example, if another project manager needs an electrical engineer who is assigned to a task with five days of slack, I'm willing to share that engineer with another project manager for two to three days.
- The most obvious reason the critical path is important is because these are the activities that impact completion time. If I suddenly get a call from above saying they need my project done two weeks earlier than planned, the critical path is where I schedule the overtime and add extra resources to get the project done more quickly. In the same way, if the project schedule begins to slip, it's the critical activities I focus on to get back on schedule.

number of days. Since actual projects may have many critical activities with numerous preceding dependencies, coordination among those responsible for critical activities is crucial. Critical activities typically represent about 10 percent of the activities of the project. Therefore, project managers pay close attention to the critical path activities to be sure they are not delayed. See Snapshot from Practice 6.2: The Critical Path.

We use the term **sensitivity** to reflect the likelihood the original critical path(s) will change once the project is initiated. Sensitivity is a function of the number of critical or near-critical paths. A network schedule that has only one critical path and noncritical activities that enjoy significant slack would be labeled insensitive. Conversely, a sensitive network would be one with more than one critical path and/or noncritical activities with very little slack. Under these circumstances, the original critical path is much more likely to change once work gets under way on the project. How sensitive is the Automated Warehouse schedule? Not very, since there is only one critical path and the two other noncritical paths have 15 and 35 days of slack, which suggests considerable flexibility. Project managers assess the sensitivity of their network schedules to determine how much attention they should devote to managing the critical path.

LO 6-5

Distinguish free slack from total slack.

Free Slack (Float)

Free slack (FS) is unique. *It is the amount of time an activity can be delayed without delaying any immediately following (successor) activity.*[2] Free slack can never be negative.

[2] An alternative way of defining FS is the amount of time an activity can exceed its early finish date without affecting the early start date of any successor(s).

Only activities that occur at the end of a chain of activities, where you have a merge activity, can have free slack. See Figure 6.8, the Automated Warehouse project.

In Figure 6.8, activity G has free slack of 15 days, while activities B and D do not. In this case, activity G is the last activity in the upper path, and it merges to activity H. Hence, to delay activity G up to 15 days *does not delay any following activities and requires no coordination with managers of other activities.* Conversely, if either activity B or activity D is delayed, the managers of following activities need to be notified that the slack has been used so they can adjust their start schedules. For example, if activity B is delayed 5 days, the manager of activity B should notify those in charge of the following activities (D and G) that their slack has been reduced to 10 time units and their early start will be delayed 5 days. In this example, activity D cannot then start until day 20, which reduces activity D slack to 10 days (LS − ES = SL or 30 − 20 = 10). Free slack for activity G is also reduced to 10 days.

Free slack occurs at the last activity in a chain of activities. In some situations, the "chain" has only one link. Activity F in Figure 6.8 is an example. It has free slack of 35 days. Note that it needs no coordination with other activities—unless a delay exceeds the free slack of 35 days. (Note: The moment you exceed all free slack available, you delay the project and must coordinate with others who are impacted.)

The distinction between free and total slack at first glance seems trivial, but in reality it is very important. When you are responsible for a late activity that has zero free slack, you impact the schedules of subsequent activities. You should notify the managers of the remaining activities in the chain that you will be late. Again, note that total slack is shared across the whole path. Alternatively, if you are responsible for an activity that has free slack when you start, you do not need to notify anyone as long as your work does not absorb all of the slack!

6.6 Using the Forward and Backward Pass Information

Returning to the Automated Warehouse project network in Figure 6.8, what does a slack of 35 days for activity F (Develop Patient Request) mean for the project manager? In this specific case, it means activity F can be delayed 35 days. In a larger sense, the project manager soon learns that free slack is important because it allows flexibility in scheduling scarce project resources—personnel and equipment—that are used on more than one parallel activity or another project.

Knowing the four activity times of ES, LS, EF, and LF is invaluable for the planning, scheduling, and controlling phases of the project. The ES and LF tell the project manager the time interval in which the activity should be completed. For example, activity G (Test Software) must be completed within the time interval 35 and 85 days; the activity can start as early as day 35 or finish as late as day 85. Conversely, activity C (Design Hardware) must start on day 10, or the project will be delayed.

When the critical path is known, it is possible to tightly manage the resources of the activities on the critical path so no mistakes are made that will result in delays. In addition, if for some reason the project must be expedited to meet an earlier date, it is possible to select those activities, or a combination of activities, that will cost the least to shorten the project. Similarly, if the critical path is delayed and the time must be made up by shortening some activity or activities on the critical path to make up any negative slack, it is possible to identify the activities on the critical path that cost the least to shorten. If there are other paths with very little slack, it may be necessary to shorten activities on those paths also.

6.7 Level of Detail for Activities

Time-phasing work and budgets of the project mandate careful definition of the activities that make up the project network. Typically, an activity represents one or more tasks from a work package. How many tasks you include in each activity sets the level of detail. In some cases, it is possible to end up with too much information to manage, and this can result in increased overhead costs. Managers of small projects have been able to minimize the level of detail by eliminating some of the preliminary steps to drawing networks. Larger firms also recognize the cost of information overload and are working to cut down the level of detail in networks.

6.8 Practical Considerations

Network Logic Errors

Project network techniques have certain logic rules that must be followed. One rule is that conditional statements such as "if test successful build proto, if failure redesign" are not permitted. The network is not a decision tree; it is a project plan that we assume will materialize. If conditional statements were allowed, the forward and backward pass would make little sense. Although in reality a plan seldom materializes as we expect in every detail, it is a reasonable initial assumption. You will see that once a network plan is developed, it is an easy step to make revisions to accommodate changes.

Another rule that defeats the project network and computation process is *looping.* Looping is an attempt by the planner to return to an earlier activity. Recall that the activity identification numbers should always be higher for the activities following an activity in question; this rule helps to avoid the illogical precedence relationships among the activities. An activity should only occur once; if it is to occur again, the activity should have a new name and identification number and should be placed in the right sequence on the network. Figure 6.9 shows an illogical loop. If this loop were allowed to exist, this path would perpetually repeat itself. Many computer programs catch this type of logic error.

Activity Numbering

Each activity needs a unique identification code—a letter or a number. In practice, very elegant schemes exist. Most schemes number activities in ascending order—that is, each succeeding activity has a larger number so that the flow of the project activities is toward project completion. It is customary to leave gaps between numbers (1, 5, 10, 15, . . .). Gaps are desirable so you can add missing or new activities later. Because it is nearly impossible to draw a project network perfectly, numbering networks is frequently not done until after the network is complete.

In practice, you will find computer programs that accept numeric, alphabetic, or a combination of activity designations. Combination designations are often used to identify

FIGURE 6.9
Illogical Loop

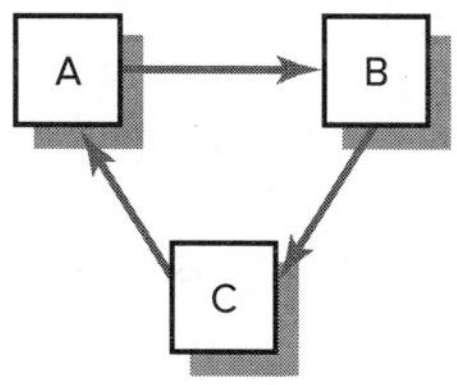

cost, work skill, department, and location. As a general rule, activity numbering systems should be ascending and as simple as possible. The intent is to make it as easy as you can for project participants to follow work through the network and locate specific activities.

Use of Computers to Develop Networks

All of the tools and techniques discussed in this chapter can be used with the computer software currently available. Two examples are shown in Figure 6.10 and Figure 6.11. Figure 6.10 presents a generic AON computer output for the Automated Warehouse Order Picking System project. Observe that these computer outputs use numbers to identify activities. The critical path is identified by the nodes (activities) 2, 4, 6, and 9. The activity description is shown on the top line of the activity node. The activity start time (ES) and identification are on the second line. The finish time (EF) and duration are on the third line of the node. The project starts on January 1 and is planned to finish May 20. Note this sample computer network has included non-workdays of holidays and weekends.

Figure 6.11 presents an early-start **Gantt chart.**[3] Bar charts are popular because they present an easy-to-understand, clear picture on a time-scaled horizon. They are used during planning, resource scheduling, and status reporting. The format is a two-dimensional representation of the project schedule, with activities down the rows and time across the horizontal axis. In this computer output, the shaded bars represent the activity durations. The extended lines from the bars represent slack. For example, "Test Software" (ID # 8) has a duration of 35 days (shaded area of the bar) and 15 days of slack (represented by the extended line). The bar also indicates that Test Software has an early start of February 19 and would finish April 8 but can finish as late as April 29 because it has 15 days of slack. When calendar dates are used on the time axis, Gantt charts provide a clear overview of the project schedule and can often be found posted on the walls of project offices. Unfortunately, when projects have many dependency relationships, the dependency lines soon become overwhelming and defeat the simplicity of the Gantt chart.

Project management software can be a tremendous help in the hands of those who understand and are familiar with the tools and techniques discussed in this text. However, there is nothing more dangerous than someone using the software with little or no knowledge of how the software derives its output. Mistakes in input are very common, and someone skilled in the concepts, tools, and information system is needed to recognize that errors exist so that false actions are avoided.

Calendar Dates

Ultimately you will want to assign calendar dates to your project activities. If a computer program is not used, dates are assigned manually. Lay out a calendar of workdays (exclude non-workdays) and number them. Then relate the calendar workdays to the workdays on your project network. Most computer programs will assign calendar dates automatically after you identify start dates, time units, non-workdays, and other information.

Multiple Starts and Multiple Projects

Some computer programs require a common start and finish event in the form of a node—usually a circle or rectangle—for a project network. Even if this is not a requirement, it is a good idea because it avoids "dangler" paths. Dangler paths give the impression that the project does not have a clear beginning or ending. If a project has more than one activity that can begin when the project is to start, each path is a dangler

[3] Gantt charts were introduced over 100 years ago by Henry Gantt.

FIGURE 6.10 Automated Warehouse Order Picking System Network

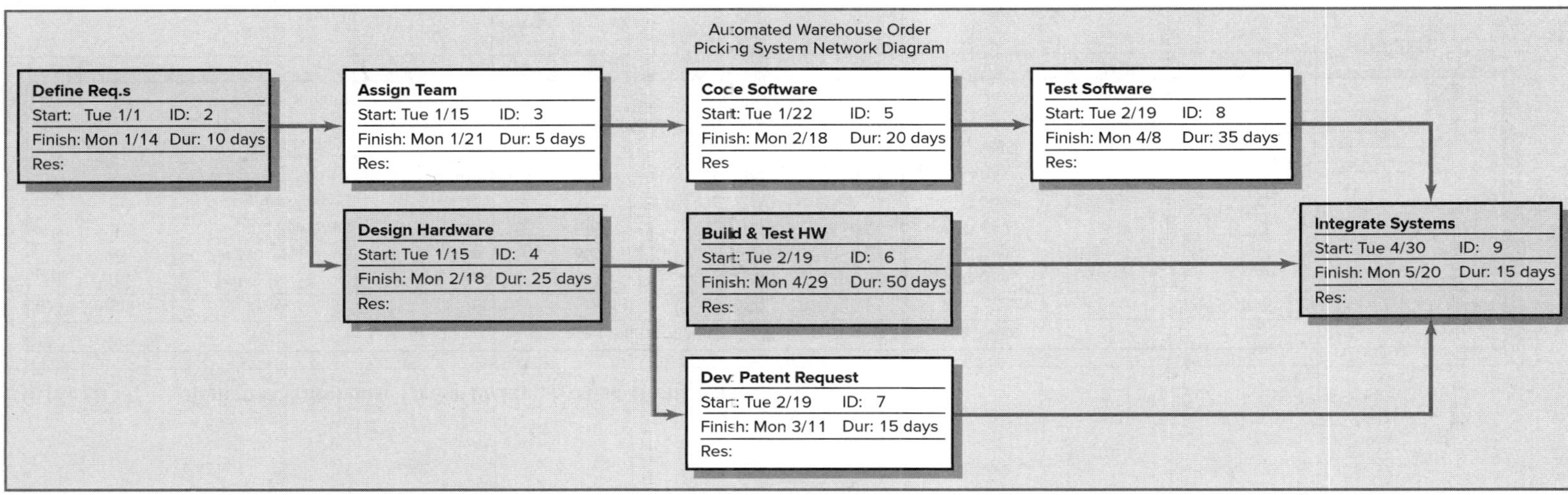

FIGURE 6.11 Automated Warehouse Order Picking System Gantt Chart

Automated Warehouse Order Picking System Schedule Table

ID	Duration	Task Name	Start	Finish	Late Start	Late Finish	Free Slack	Total Slack
2	10	Define Req.s	Tue 1/1	Mon 1/14	Tue 1/1	Tue 1/15	0 days	0 days
3	5	Assign Team	Tue 1/15	Mon 1/21	Tue 2/5	Mon 2/11	0 days	15 days
4	25	Design Hardware	Tue 1/15	Mon 2/18	Tue 1/15	Mon 2/18	0 days	0 days
5	20	Code Software	Tue 1/22	Mon 2/18	Tue 2/12	Mon 3/11	0 days	15 days
6	50	Build and Test HW	Tue 2/19	Mon 4/29	Tue 2/19	Mon 4/29	0 days	0 days
7	15	Dev. Patent Request	Tue 2/19	Mon 3/11	Tue 4/9	Mon 4/29	35 days	35 days
8	35	Test Software	Tue 2/19	Mon 4/8	Tue 3/12	Mon 4/29	15 days	15 days
9	15	Integrate Systems	Tue 4/30	Mon 5/20	Tue 4/30	Mon 5/20	0 days	0 days

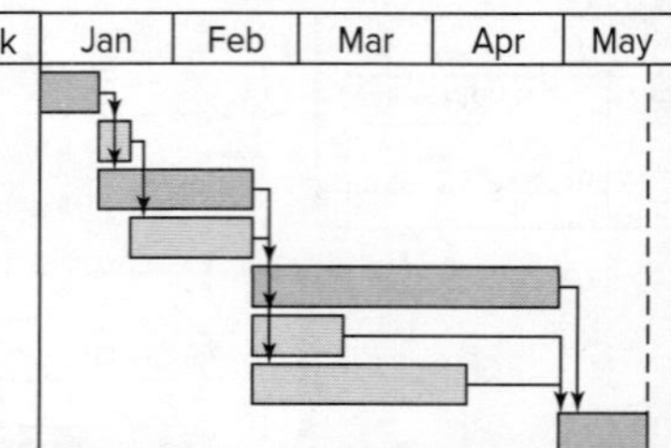

path. The same is true if a project network ends with more than one activity; these unconnected paths are also called danglers. Danglers can be avoided by tying dangler activities to a common project start or finish node.

When several projects are tied together in an organization, using a common start and end node helps to identify the total planning period of all projects. Use of pseudo or dummy wait activities from the common start node allows different start dates for each project.

6.9 Extended Network Techniques to Come Closer to Reality

LO 6-6

Demonstrate understanding and application of lags in compressing projects or constraining the start or finish of an activity.

The method for showing relationships among activities in the previous sections is called the finish-to-start relationship because it assumes all immediately preceding connected activities must be completed before the next activity can begin. In an effort to come closer to the realities of projects, some useful extensions have been added. The use of *laddering* was the first obvious extension practitioners found very useful.

Laddering

The assumption that all immediately preceding activities must be 100 percent complete is too restrictive for some situations found in practice. This restriction occurs most frequently when one activity overlaps the start of another and has a long duration. Under the standard finish-to-start relationship, when an activity has a long duration and will delay the start of an activity immediately following it, the activity can be broken into segments and the network drawn using a *laddering* approach so the following activity can begin sooner and not delay the work. This segmenting of the larger activity gives the appearance of steps on a ladder on the network, thus the name. The classic example used in many texts and articles is laying pipe, because it is easy to visualize. The trench must be dug, pipe laid, and the trench refilled. If the pipeline is one mile long, it is not necessary to dig one mile of trench before the laying of pipe can begin or to lay one mile of pipe before refill can begin. Figure 6.12 shows how these overlapping activities might appear in an AON network using the standard finish-to-start approach.

Use of Lags to Reduce Schedule Detail and Project Duration

The use of *lags* has been developed to offer greater flexibility in network construction. *A lag is the minimum amount of time a dependent activity must be delayed to begin or end.* The use of lags in project networks occurs primarily for two reasons:

1. When activities of long duration delay the start or finish of successor activities, the network designer normally breaks the activity into smaller activities to avoid the long delay of the successor activity. Use of lags can avoid such delays and reduce network detail.
2. Lags can be used to constrain the start and finish of an activity.

FIGURE 6.12
Example of Laddering Using Finish-to-Start Relationship

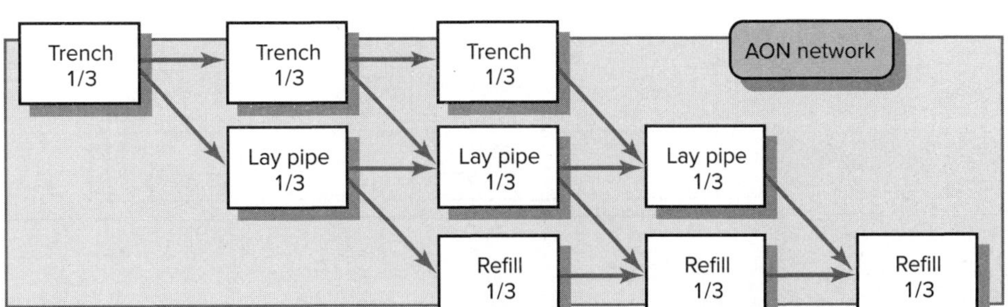

FIGURE 6.13
Finish-to-Start Relationship

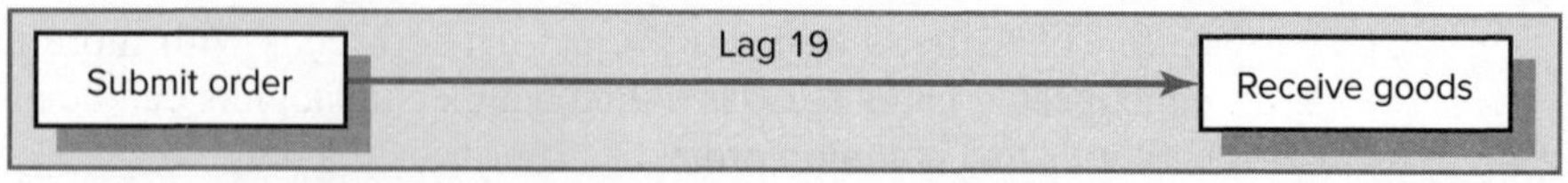

The most commonly used relationship extensions are start-to-start, finish-to-finish, and combinations of these two. These relationship patterns are discussed in this section.

Finish-to-Start Relationship

The finish-to-start relationship represents the typical, generic network style (used in the early part of the chapter). However, there are situations in which the next activity in a sequence must be delayed even when the preceding activity is complete. For example, removing concrete forms cannot begin until the poured cement has cured for two time units. Figure 6.13 shows this **lag relationship** for AON networks. Finish-to-start lags are frequently used when ordering materials. For example, it may take 1 day to place orders but take 19 days to receive the goods. The use of finish-to-start allows the activity duration to be only 1 day and the lag 19 days. This approach ensures the activity cost is tied to placing the order only, rather than charging the activity for 20 days of work. This same finish-to-start lag relationship is useful to depict transportation, legal, and mail lags.

The use of finish-to-start lags should be carefully checked to ensure their validity. Conservative project managers and those responsible for completion of activities have been known to use lags as a means of building in a "slush" factor to reduce the risk of being late. A simple rule to follow is that the use of finish-to-start lags must be justified and approved by someone responsible for a large section of the project. The legitimacy of lags is not usually difficult to discern. The legitimate use of the additional relationship shown can greatly enhance the network by more closely representing the realities of the project.

Start-to-Start Relationship

An alternative to segmenting the activities, as we did earlier, is to use a start-to-start relationship. Typical start-to-start relationships are shown in Figure 6.14. Figure 6.14A

FIGURE 6.14
Start-to-Start Relationship

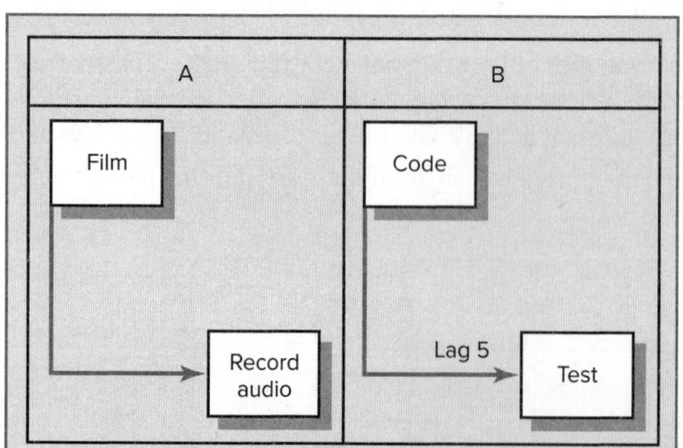

FIGURE 6.15
Use of Lags to Reduce Project Duration

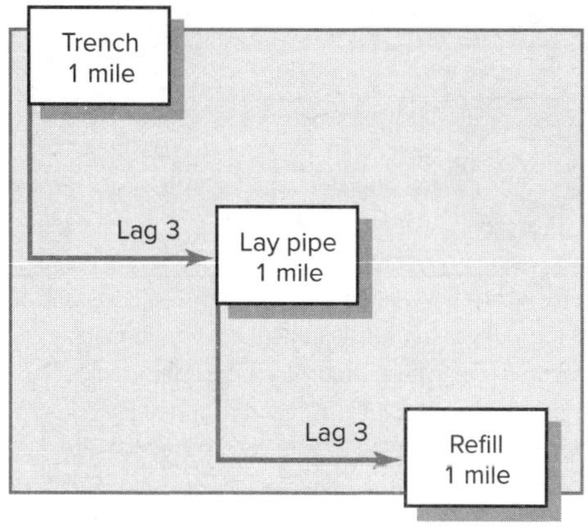

shows the start-to-start relationship with zero lag in which on a movie set you would want filming and recording audio to start simultaneously. Figure 6.14B shows the same relationship with a lag of five time units. It is important to note that the relationship may be used with or without a lag. If time is assigned, it is usually shown on the dependency arrow of an AON network.

In Figure 6.14B, testing cannot begin until five time units after coding begins. This type of relationship typically depicts a situation in which you can perform a portion of one activity and begin a following activity before completing the first. This relationship can be used on the pipe-laying project. Figure 6.15 shows the project using an AON network. The start-to-start relationship reduces network detail and project delays by using lag relationships.

It is possible to find compression opportunities by changing finish-to-start relationships to start-to-start relationships. A review of finish-to-start critical activities may point out opportunities that can be revised to be parallel by using start-to-start relationships. For example, in place of a finish-to-start activity "design house, then build foundation," a start-to-start relationship could be used in which the foundation can be started, say, five days (lag) after design has started—assuming the design of the foundation is the first part of the total design activity. This start-to-start relationship with a small lag allows a sequential activity to be worked on in parallel and to compress the duration of the critical path. This same concept is frequently found in projects in which concurrent engineering is used to speed completion of a project. **Concurrent engineering,** which is highlighted in Snapshot from Practice 6.3: Concurrent Engineering, basically breaks activities into smaller segments so that work can be done in parallel and the project expedited (Turtle, 1994). Start-to-start relationships can depict the concurrent engineering conditions and reduce network detail. Of course, the same result can be accomplished by applying the "laddering" technique and breaking an activity into small packages that can be implemented in parallel. However, laddering significantly increases the network and tracking detail when used repeatedly.

Next we discuss two other lags which are much rarer in practice.

SNAPSHOT FROM PRACTICE 6.3 Concurrent Engineering (Fast Tracking)*

In the old days, when a new product development project was initiated by a firm, it would start its sequential journey in the Research and Development Department. Concepts and ideas would be worked out and the results passed to the Engineering Department, which sometimes reworked the whole product. This result would be passed to Manufacturing, where it might be reworked once more in order to ensure the product could be manufactured using existing machinery and operations. Quality improvements were initiated after the fact once defects and improvement opportunities were discovered during production. This sequential approach to product development required a great deal of time, and it was not uncommon for the final product to be totally unrecognizable when compared to original specifications.

Given the emphasis on speed to the market, companies have abandoned the sequential approach to product development and have adopted a more holistic approach, called concurrent engineering. In a nutshell, *concurrent engineering* entails the active involvement of all the relevant specialty areas throughout the design and development process. The traditional, chainlike sequence of finish-to-start relationships is replaced by a series of start-to-start lag relationships as soon as meaningful work can be initiated for the next phase. Figure 6.16 summarizes the dramatic gains in time to market achieved by this approach.

Within the world of project management, this approach is also called *fast tracking*. General Motors used this approach to design the very first American hybrid car, the Chevy Volt. From the very beginning, specialists from Marketing, Engineering, Design, Manufacturing, Quality Assurance, and other relevant departments were involved in every stage of the project. Not only did the project meet all of its objectives, but it was completed ahead of schedule.

Operation Warp Speed, the U.S. government effort to bring effective COVID-19 vaccines to the public, relied heavily on fast tracking. Instead of waiting for vaccines to be approved, manufacturing and distribution systems were being created while drugs were in development. The hope was, once a vaccine was approved, all systems would be go for release to the public.

*"Chevrolet Volt Hits Road, Ahead of Schedule," *The New York Times*, June 25, 2009. Accessed 6/2/11.

FIGURE 6.16 New Product Development Process

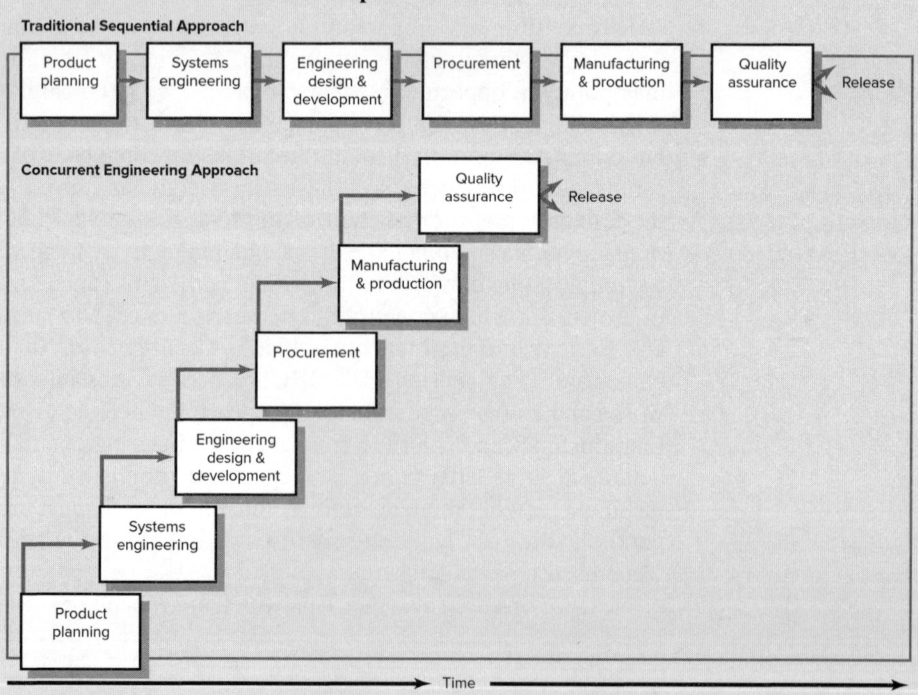

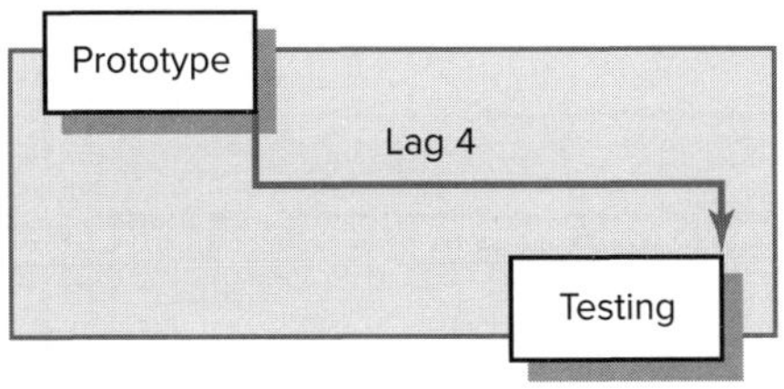

FIGURE 6.17
Finish-to-Finish Relationship

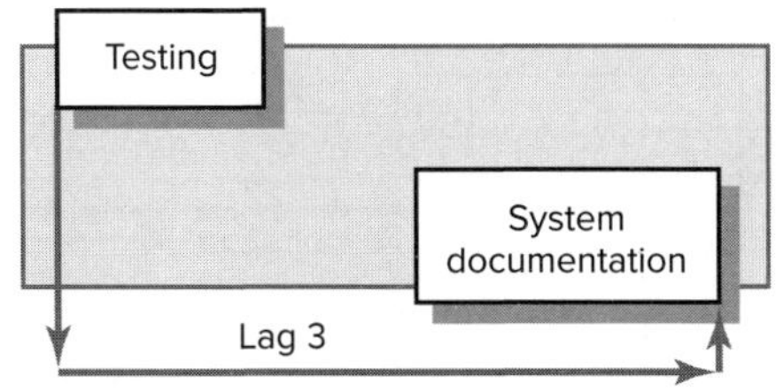

FIGURE 6.18
Start-to-Finish Relationship

Finish-to-Finish Relationship

This relationship is shown in Figure 6.17. The finish of one activity depends on the finish of another activity. For example, testing cannot be completed any earlier than four days after the prototype is complete. Note that this is not a finish-to-start relationship because the testing of subcomponents can begin before the prototype is completed, but four days of "system" testing is required after the prototype is finished.

Start-to-Finish Relationship

This relationship represents situations in which the finish of an activity depends on the start of another activity. For example, system documentation cannot end until three days after testing has started (see Figure 6.18). All the relevant information to complete the system documentation is produced after the first three days of testing.

Combinations of Lag Relationships

More than one lag relationship can be attached to an activity. These relationships are usually start-to-start and finish-to-finish combinations tied to two activities. For example, debug cannot begin until two time units after coding has started. Coding must be finished four days before debug can be finished (see Figure 6.19).

An Example Using Lag Relationships—the Forward and Backward Pass

The forward and backward pass procedures are the same as explained earlier in the chapter for finish-to-start relationships (without lags). The modifying technique lies in the need to check each new relationship to see if it alters the start or finish time of another activity.

An example of the outcome of the forward and backward pass is shown in Figure 6.20. Order hardware depends upon the design of the system (start-to-start). Three days into the design of the system (activity A), it is possible to order the required hardware (activity B). It takes four days after the order is placed (activity B) for the hardware to arrive so it can begin to be installed (activity C). After two days of installing the software system (activity D), the testing of the system can begin (activity E). System testing (activity E) can be completed one day after the software is installed (activity D). Preparing system documentation (activity F) can begin once the design is completed (activity A), but it cannot be completed until two days after testing the system (activity E) is completed. This final relationship is an example of a finish-to-finish lag.

Note how an activity can have a critical finish and/or start. Activities E and F have critical finishes (zero slack), but their activity starts have 3 and 11 days of slack. It is

FIGURE 6.19
Combination Relationships

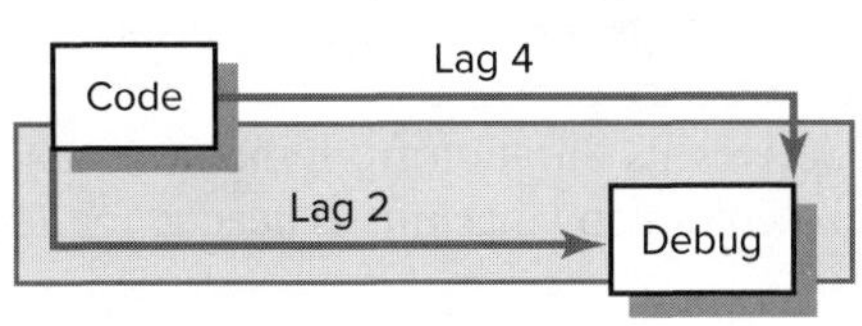

FIGURE 6.20 Network Using Lags

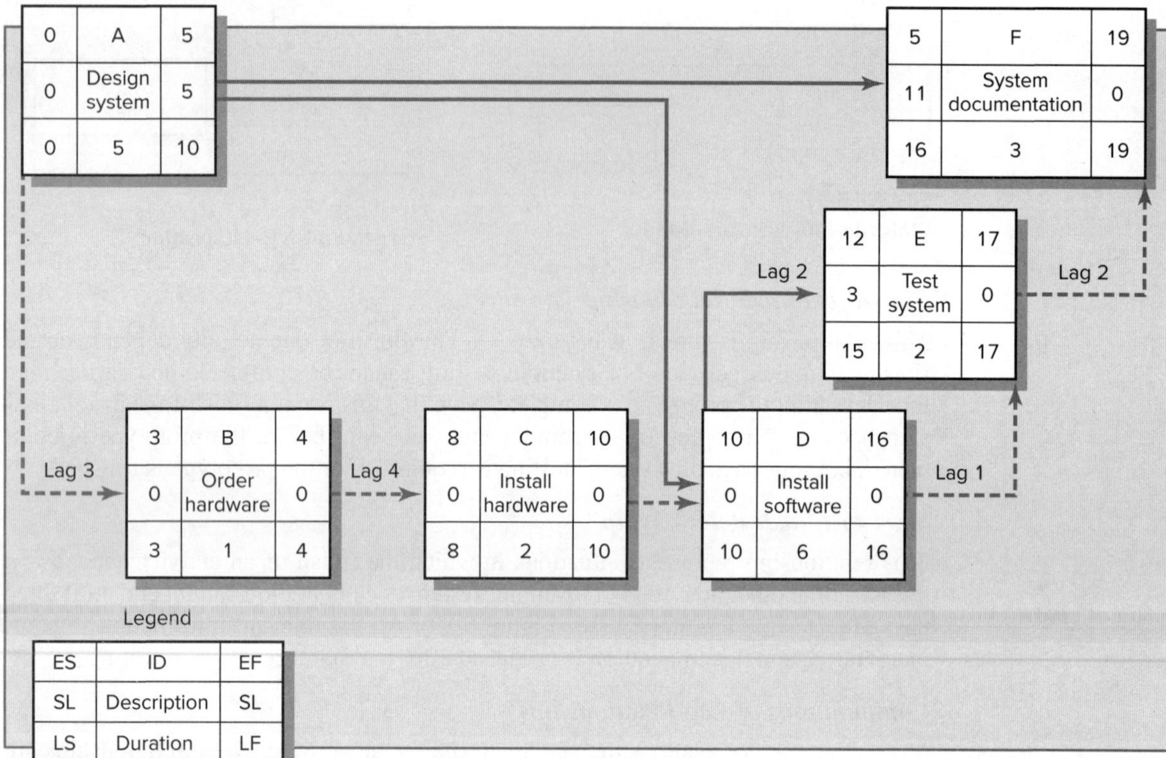

only the finishes of activities E and F that are critical. Conversely, activity A has zero slack to start but has five days of slack to finish. So, for example, the project team realizes that they have some flexibility in scheduling a portion of the testing work (activity E) up until the installation of software (activity D), at which time they know to be ready to complete the testing within one day after the installation.

The critical path follows activity start and finish constraints that occur due to the use of the additional relationships available and the imposed lags. You can identify the critical path in Figure 6.20 by following the dashed line on the network.

If a lag relationship exists, each activity must be checked to see if the start or finish is constrained. For example, in the forward pass, the EF of activity E (test system) (17) is controlled by the finish of activity D (install software) and the lag of one time unit (16 + lag 1 = 17). Finally, in the backward pass, the LS of activity A (design system) is controlled by activity B (order hardware) and the lag relationship to activity A (3 – 3 = 0).

Hammock Activities

Another of the extended techniques uses a **hammock activity.** This type of activity derives its name because it spans over a segment of a project. The hammock activity duration is determined *after* the network plan is drawn. Hammock activities are frequently used to identify the use of fixed resources or costs over a segment of the project. Typical examples of hammock activities are inspection services, consultants, and construction management services.

A hammock activity derives its duration from the time span between other activities. For example, a special color copy machine is needed for a segment of a tradeshow

FIGURE 6.21 Hammock Activity Example

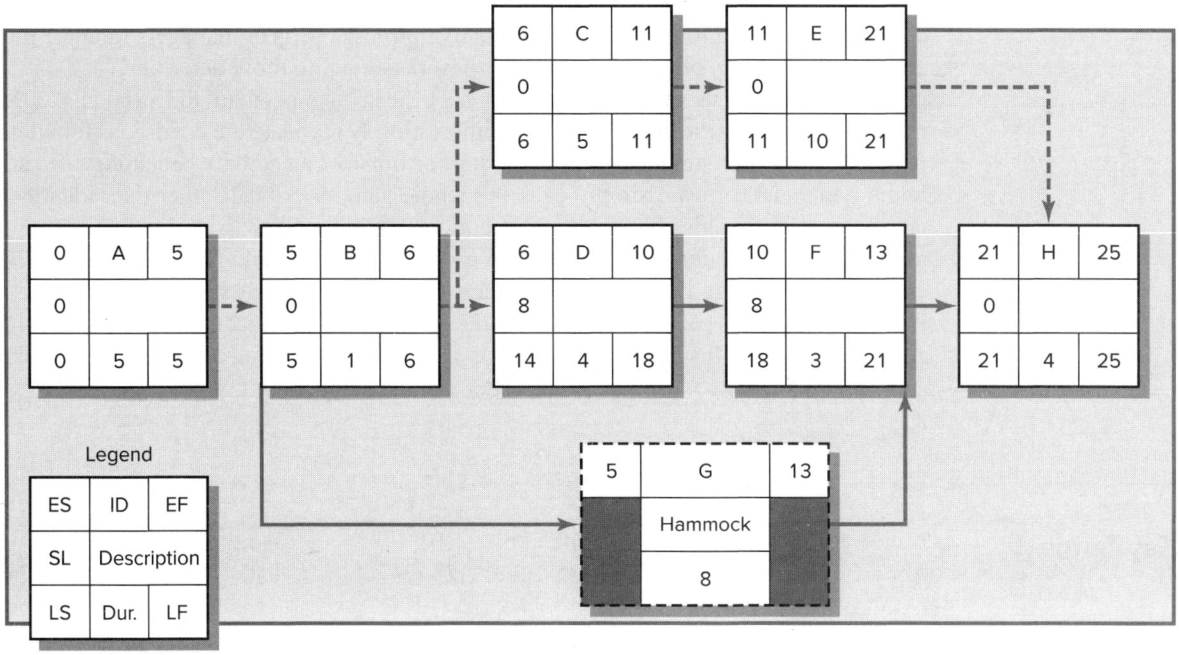

publication project. A hammock activity can be used to indicate the need for this resource and to apply costs over this segment of the project. This hammock is linked from the start of the first activity in the segment that uses the color copy machine to the end of the last activity that uses it. The hammock duration is simply the difference between the EF for the last activity and the ES of the first activity. The duration is computed after the forward pass and hence has no influence on other activity times. Figure 6.21 provides an example of a hammock activity used in a network. The duration for the hammock activity is derived from the early start of activity B and the early finish of activity F—that is, the difference between 13 and 5, or 8 time units. The hammock duration will change if any ES or EF in the chain-sequence changes. Hammock activities are very useful in assigning and controlling indirect project costs.[4]

Another major use of hammock activities is to aggregate sections of a project. This is similar to developing a subnetwork, but the precedence is still preserved. This approach is sometimes used to present a "macro network" for upper management levels. Using a hammock activity to group activities can facilitate getting the right level of detail for specific sections of a project.**Design elements:** Snapshot from Practice, Highlight box, Case icon: Sky Designs/Shutterstock

Summary

Many project managers feel the project network is their most valuable exercise and planning document. Project networks sequence and time-phase the project work, resources, and budgets. Work package tasks are used to develop activities for networks.

Every project manager should feel comfortable working in an AON environment. The AON method uses nodes (boxes) for activities and arrows for dependencies. The forward and backward pass establishes early and late times for activities as well as slack.

[4] In order to designate G as a hammock activity in MS Project 2021, you would copy and paste for activity G the start date of activity B and the finish date for activity F.

The critical path is the longest activity path(s) through the network. Any delay in an activity on the critical path will delay the project completion, assuming everything else goes according to plan. On time-sensitive projects, project managers monitor the critical path closely, often assigning their best personnel to those activities.

Several extensions and modifications have been appended to the original AON method. Lags allow the project planner to more closely replicate the conditions found in practice. The use of lags can result in the start or finish of an activity becoming critical. Some computer software simply calls the whole activity critical rather than identifying the start or finish as being critical. Caution should be taken to ensure that lags are not used as a buffer for possible errors in estimating time. Finally, hammock activities are useful in tracking the costs of resources used for a particular segment of a project. Hammock activities can also be used to reduce the size of a project network by grouping activities for simplification and clarity. All of the discussed refinements to the original AON methodology contribute toward better planning and control of projects.

Key Terms

Activity, 201
Activity-on-arrow (AOA), 202
Activity-on-node (AON), 202
Burst activity, 201
Concurrent engineering, 219
Critical path, 201
Early time, 200
Free slack (FS), 211
Gantt chart, 214
Hammock activity, 222
Lag relationship, 218
Late time, 200
Merge activity, 201
Parallel activities, 201
Path, 201
Sensitivity, 211
Total slack, 209

Review Questions

1. How does the WBS differ from the project network?
2. How are WBS and project networks linked?
3. Why bother creating a WBS? Why not go straight to a project network and forget the WBS?
4. Why is slack important to the project manager?
5. What is the difference between free slack and total slack?
6. Why are lags used in developing project networks?
7. What is a hammock activity and when is it used?

SNAPSHOT FROM PRACTICE

Discussion Questions

6.2 *The Critical Path*

1. Why is it important to identify the critical path before starting a project?
2. On what kind of projects would the critical path be irrelevant?

6.3 *Concurrent Engineering (Fast Tracking)*

1. What are the disadvantages of concurrent engineering (fast tracking)?
2. What kinds of projects should avoid using concurrent engineering?

Exercises

Creating a Project Network

1. Here is a partial work breakdown structure for a wedding. Use the method described in Snapshot from Practice 6.1: The Yellow Sticky Approach to create a network for this project.

Note: Do not include summary tasks in the network (i.e., 1.3, Ceremony, is a summary task; 1.2, Marriage license, is not a summary task). Do not consider who would be doing the task in building the network. For example, do not arrange "hiring a band" to occur after "florist" because the same person is responsible for doing both tasks. Focus only on technical dependencies between tasks.

Hint: Start with the last activity (wedding reception), and work your way back to the start of the project. Build the logical sequence of tasks by asking the following question: in order to have or do this, what must be accomplished immediately before this? Once completed, check forward in time by asking this question: is this task the only thing that is needed immediately before the start of the next task?

Work Breakdown Structure

1. Wedding project
   - 1.1 Decide on date
   - 1.2 Marriage license
   - 1.3 Ceremony
     - *1.3.1 Rent church*
     - *1.3.2 Florist*
     - *1.3.3 Create/print programs*
     - *1.3.4 Hire photographer*
     - *1.3.5 Wedding ceremony*
   - 1.4 Guests
     - *1.4.1 Develop guest list*
     - *1.4.2 Order invitations*
     - *1.4.3 Address and mail invitations*
     - *1.4.4 Track RSVPs*
   - 1.5 Reception
     - *1.5.1 Reserve reception hall*
     - *1.5.2 Food and beverage*
       - *1.5.2.1 Choose caterer*
       - *1.5.2.2 Decide on menu*
       - *1.5.2.3 Make final order*
     - *1.5.3 Hire DJ*
     - *1.5.4 Decorate reception hall*
     - *1.5.5 Wedding reception*

Drawing AON Networks

2. Draw a project network from the following information. What activity(ies) is a burst activity? What activity(ies) is a merge activity?

ID	Description	Predecessor
A	Survey site	None
B	Excavate site	A
C	Install power lines	B
D	Install drainage	B
E	Pour foundation	C, D

3. Draw a project network from the following information.* What activity(ies) is a burst activity? What activity(ies) is a merge activity?

ID	Description	Predecessor
A	Identify topic	None
B	Research topic	A
C	Draft paper	B
D	Edit paper	C
E	Create graphics	C
F	References	C
G	Proof paper	D, E, F
H	Submit paper	G

4. Draw a project network from the following information. What activity(ies) is a burst activity? What activity(ies) is a merge activity?

ID	Description	Predecessor
A	Contract signed	None
B	Survey designed	A
C	Target market identified	A
D	Data collection	B, C
E	Develop presentation	B
F	Analyze results	D
G	Demographics	C
H	Presentation	E, F, G

5. Draw a project network from the following information. What activity(ies) is a burst activity? What activity(ies) is a merge activity?

ID	Description	Predecessor
A	Order review	None
B	Order standard parts	A
C	Produce standard parts	A
D	Design custom parts	A
E	Software development	A
F	Manufacture custom parts	C, D
G	Assemble	B, F
H	Test	E, G

AON Network Times

6. From the following information, develop an AON project network. Complete the forward and backward pass, compute activity slack, and identify the critical path. How many days will the project take?

ID	Description	Predecessor	Time
A	Survey site	None	2
B	Excavate site	A	4
C	Install power lines	B	3
D	Install drainage	B	5
E	Pour foundation	C, D	3

*The solution to this exercise can be found in Appendix One.

7. The project information for the custom order project of the Air Control Company is presented here. Draw a project network for this project. Compute the early and late activity times and slack times. Identify the critical path.

ID	Description	Predecessor	Time
A	Order review	None	2
B	Order standard parts	A	3
C	Produce standard parts	A	10
D	Design custom parts	A	13
E	Software development	A	18
F	Manufacture custom hardware	C, D	15
G	Assemble	B, F	10
H	Test	E, G	5

8. You have signed a contract to build a garage for the Simpsons. You will receive a $500 bonus for completing the project within 17 working days. The contract also contains a penalty clause in which you will lose $100 for each day the project takes longer than 17 working days.

   Draw a project network, given the following information. Complete the forward and backward pass, compute activity slack, and identify the critical path. Do you expect to receive a bonus or a penalty on this project?

ID	Description	Predecessor	Time (days)
A	Prepare site	None	2
B	Pour foundation	A	3
C	Erect frame	B	4
D	Roof	C	4
E	Windows	C	1
F	Doors	C	1
G	Electrical	C	3
H	Rough-in-frame	D, E, F, G	2
I	Door opener	F, G	1
J	Paint	H, I	2
K	Cleanup	J	1

9. You are creating a customer database for the Hillsboro Hops minor league baseball team. Draw a project network, given the information in the table that follows. Complete the forward and backward pass, compute activity slack, and identify the critical path.

   How long will this project take? How sensitive is the network schedule? Calculate the free slack and total slack for all noncritical activities.

ID	Description	Predecessor	Time (days)
A	Systems design	None	2
B	Subsystem A design	A	1
C	Subsystem B design	A	1
D	Subsystem C design	A	1
E	Program A	B	2
F	Program B	C	2
G	Program C	D	2
H	Subsystem A test	E	1
I	Subsystem B test	F	1
J	Subsystem C test	G	1
K	Integration	H, I, J	3
L	Integration test	K	1

10. K. Nelson, project manager of Print Software, Inc., wants you to prepare a project network; compute the early, late, and slack activity times; determine the planned project duration; and identify the critical path. His assistant has collected the following information for the color printer drivers software project:

ID	Description	Predecessor	Time (days)
A	External specifications	None	8
B	Review design features	A	2
C	Document new features	A	3
D	Write software	A	60
E	Program and test	B	40
F	Edit and publish notes	C	2
G	Review manual	D	2
H	Alpha site	E, F	20
I	Print manual	G	10
J	Beta site	H, I	10
K	Manufacture	J	12
L	Release and ship	K	3

11. A large Southeast city is requesting federal funding for a park-and-ride project.* One of the requirements in the request application is a network plan for the design phase of the project. Sophie Kim, the chief engineer, wants you to develop a project network plan to meet this requirement. She has gathered the activity time estimates and their dependencies shown here. Show your project network with the activity early, late, and slack times. Mark the critical path.

ID	Description	Predecessor	Time
A	Survey	None	5
B	Soils report	A	20
C	Traffic design	A	30
D	Lot layout	A	5
E	Approve design	B, C, D	80
F	Illumination	E	15
G	Drainage	E	30
H	Landscape	E	25
I	Signage	E	15
J	Bid proposal	F, G, H, I	10

12. You are creating a customer database for the Lehigh Valley IronPigs minor league baseball team. Draw a project network, given the following information. Complete the forward and backward pass, compute activity slack, and identify the critical path.

How long will this project take? How sensitive is the network schedule? Calculate the free slack and total slack for all noncritical activities.

ID	Description	Predecessor	Time (days)
A	Systems design	None	2
B	Subsystem A design	A	1
C	Subsystem B design	A	2
D	Subsystem C design	A	1
E	Program A	B	2
F	Program B	C	10
G	Program C	D	3
H	Subsystem A test	E	1
I	Subsystem B test	F	1
J	Subsystem C test	G	1
K	Integration	H, I, J	3
L	Integration test	K	1

* The solution to this exercise can be found in Appendix One.

13. You are responsible for choosing a critical software product from competing vendors. There are many qualified vendors to select from. You will need to solicit formal proposals from each of these qualified vendors, evaluate them using a prototype, elicit final bids, and make the ultimate decision as to which vendor and accompanying software to use. A list of major tasks required to decide among the various competing software products is provided below. Also given are the predecessor tasks together with the number of days required to accomplish each task.

    Draw your project network, compute the activity early, late, and slack times, and determine the critical path. How long will the project take? How sensitive is the network schedule?

ID	Description	Predecessor	Time (days)
A	Interview management	None	2
B	Interview operations	None	4
C	Interview technical staff	None	2
D	Prepare requirements document	A, B, C	2
E	Prepare request for proposal and transmit	D	2
F	Await receipt of proposals	E	14
G	Write acceptance criteria	E	2
H	Prototype solution	E	10
I	Test prototype	H	5
J	Develop project plan	H	3
K	Evaluate proposals	F, G, I, J	2
L	Request and receive final bid	K	1
M	Make vendor decision	L	1

14. You are completing a group term paper.* Given the project network that follows, complete the forward and backward pass, compute activity slack, and identify the critical path. Use this information to create a Gantt chart for the project. Be sure to show slack for noncritical activities.

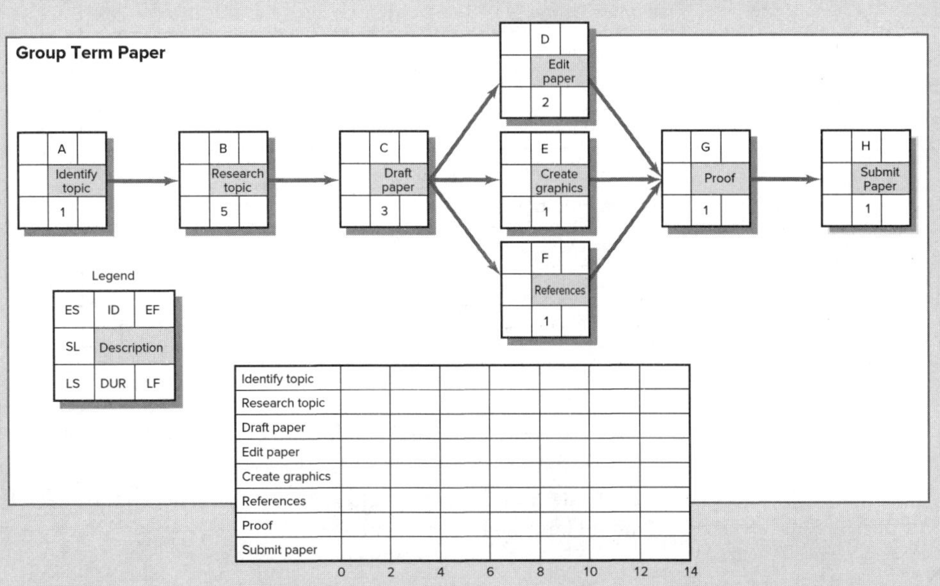

* The solution to this exercise can be found in Appendix One.

15. You are managing a product upgrade project for Bangkokagogo. Given the project network that follows, complete the forward and backward pass, compute activity slack, and identify the critical path. Use this information to create a Gantt chart for the project. Be sure to show slack for noncritical activities.

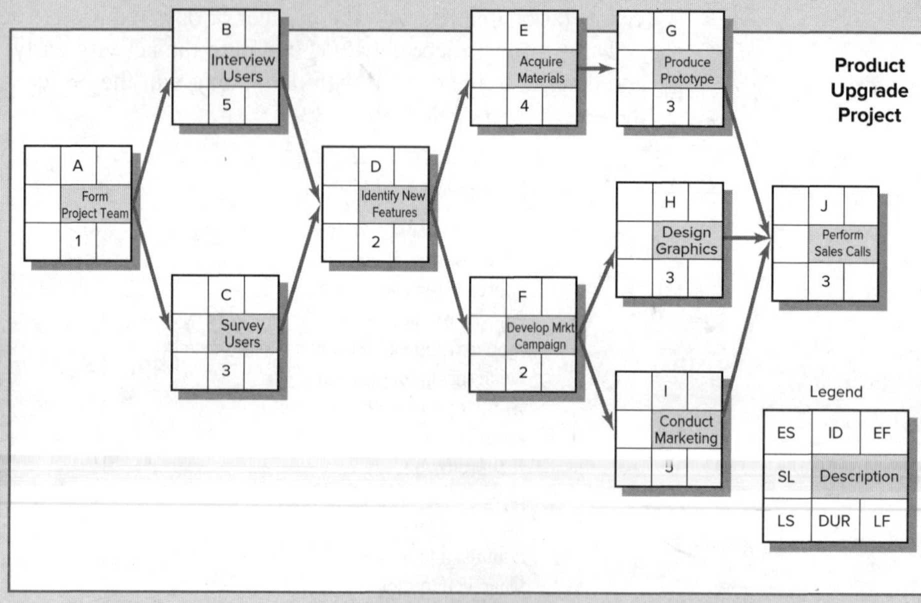

Product Upgrade Project Gantt Chart

	1	2	3	4	5	6	7	8	9	10	11	12	13	14	15	16	17	18
Form Project Team																		
Interview Users																		
Survey Users																		
ID New Features																		
Acquire Materials																		
Dev Mrkt Campaign																		
Produce Prototypes																		
Design Graphics																		
Conduct Marketing																		
Perform Sales Calls																		

16. You are creating a database for the Oklahoma City Thunder NBA basketball team. Given the project network that follows, complete the forward and backward pass, compute activity slack, and identify the critical path. Use this information to create a Gantt chart for the project.

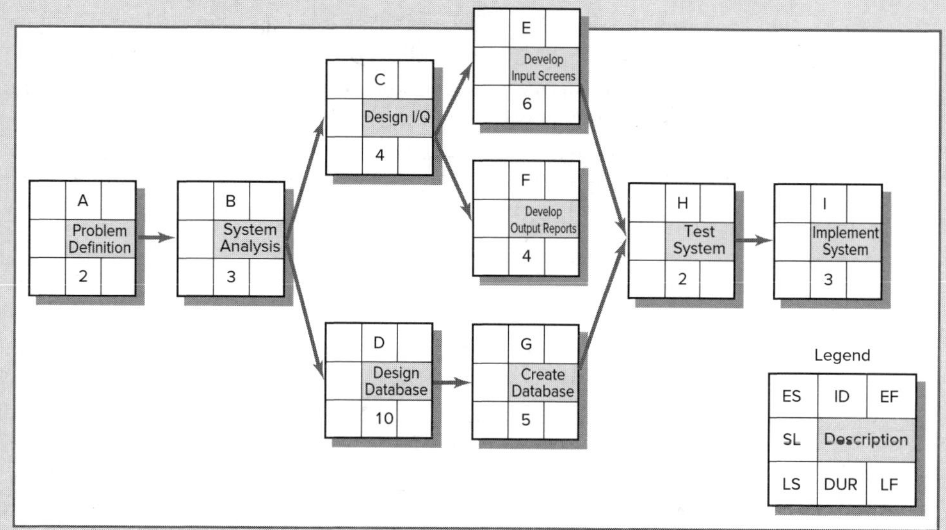

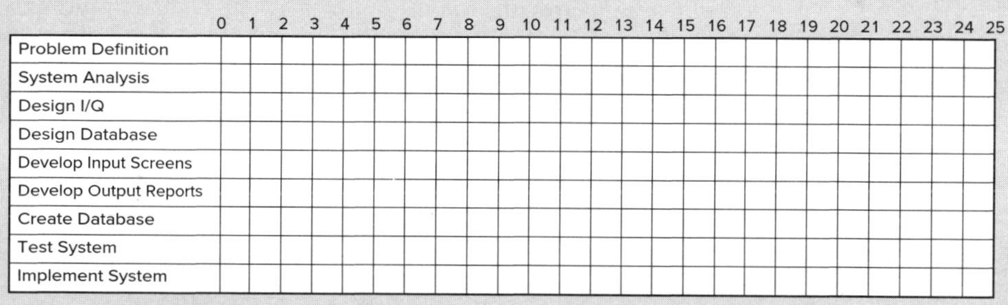

Computer Exercises

17. The Planning Department of an electronics firm has set up the activities for development and production of a new MP4 player. Given the following information, develop a project network using Microsoft Project. Assume a five-day workweek and the project starts on January 6, 2025.

Activity ID	Description	Activity Predecessor	Activity Time (weeks)
1	Staff	None	2
2	Develop market program	1	3
3	Select channels of distribution	1	8
4	Patent	1	12
5	Pilot production	1	4
6	Test market	5	4
7	Ad promotion	2	4
8	Set up for production	4, 6	16

The project team has requested that you create a network for the project and determine if the project can be completed in 45 weeks.

18. Using Microsoft Project, set up the network and determine the critical path for phase 1 of the Whistler Ski Resort project. The project workweek will be five days (M–F).

Whistler Ski Resort Project

Given the fact that the number of skiing visitors to Whistler, B.C., Canada, has been increasing at an exciting rate, thanks to the 2010 Winter Olympics, the Whistler Ski Association has been considering construction of another ski lodge and ski complex. The results of an economic feasibility study just completed by members of the staff show that a winter resort complex near the base of Whistler Mountain could be a very profitable venture. The area is accessible by car, bus, train, and air. The board of directors has voted to build the 10-million-dollar complex recommended in the study. Unfortunately, due to the short summer season, the complex will have to be built in stages. The first stage (year 1) will contain a day lodge, chair lift, rope tow, generator house (for electricity), and parking lot designed to accommodate 400 cars and 30 buses. The second and third stages will include a hotel, an ice rink, a pool, shops, two additional chair lifts, and other attractions. The board has decided that stage one should begin no later than April 1 and be completed by October 1, in time for the next skiing season. You have been assigned the task of project manager, and it is your job to coordinate the ordering of materials and construction activities to ensure the project's completion by the required date.

After looking into the possible sources of materials, you are confronted with the following time estimates. Materials for the chair lift and rope tow will take 30 days and 12 days, respectively, to arrive once the order is submitted. Lumber for the day lodge, generator hut, and foundations will take 9 days to arrive. The electrical and plumbing materials for the day lodge will take 12 days to arrive. The generator will take 12 days to arrive. Before actual construction can begin on the various facilities, a road to the site must be built; this will take 6 days. As soon as the road is in, clearing can begin concurrently on the sites of the day lodge, generator house, chair lift, and rope tow. It is estimated that the clearing task at each site will take 6 days, 3 days, 36 days, and 6 days, respectively. The clearing of the main ski slopes can begin after the area for the chair lift has been cleared; this will take 84 days.

The foundation for the day lodge will take 12 days to complete. Construction of the main framework will take an additional 18 days. After the framework is completed, electrical wiring and plumbing can be installed concurrently. These should take 24 and 30 days, respectively. Finally, the finishing construction on the day lodge can begin; this will take 36 days.

Installation of the chair lift towers (67 days) can begin once the site is cleared, lumber delivered, and foundation completed (6 days). Also, when the chair lift site has been cleared, construction of a permanent road to the upper towers can be started; this will take 24 days. While the towers are being installed, the electric motor to drive the chair lift can be installed; the motor can be installed in 24 days. Once the towers are completed and the motor installed, it will take 3 days to install the cable and an additional 12 days to install the chairs.

Installation of the towers for the rope tow can begin once the site is cleared and the foundation is built and poured; it takes 4 days to build the foundation, pour the concrete, and let it cure and 20 days to install the towers for the rope tow. While the towers are being erected, installation of the electric motor to drive the rope tow can begin; this activity will take 24 days. After the towers and motor are installed, the rope tow can be strung in 1 day. The parking lot can be cleared once the rope tow is finished; this task will take 18 days.

The foundation for the generator house can begin at the same time as the foundation for the lodge; this will take 6 days. The main framework for the generator house can begin once the foundation is completed; framing will take 12 days. After the house is framed, the diesel generator can be installed in 18 days. Finishing construction on the generator house can now begin and will take 12 more days.

Assignment

1. Identify the critical path on your network.
2. Can the project be completed by October 1?

Optical Disk Preinstallation Project

19. The optical disk project team has started gathering the information necessary to develop the project network—predecessor activities and activity times in weeks. The results of their meeting are found in the following table.

Activity	Description	Duration	Predecessor
1	Define scope	6	None
2	Define customer problems	3	1
3	Define data records and relationships	5	1
4	Mass storage requirements	5	2, 3
5	Consultant needs analysis	10	2, 3
6	Prepare installation network	3	4, 5
7	Estimate costs and budget	2	4, 5
8	Design section "point" system	1	4, 5
9	Write request proposal	5	4, 5
10	Compile vendor list	3	4, 5
11	Prepare mgmt. control system	5	6, 7
12	Prepare comparison report	5	9, 10
13	Compare system "philosophies"	3	8, 12
14	Compare total installation	2	8, 12
15	Compare cost of support	3	8, 12
16	Compare customer satisfaction level	10	8, 12
17	Assign philosophies points	1	13
18	Assign installation cost	1	14
19	Assign support cost	1	15
20	Assign customer satisfaction points	1	16
21	Select best system	1	11, 17, 18, 19, 20
22	Order system	1	21

The project team has requested that you create a network for the project and determine if the project can be completed in 45 weeks.

Lag Exercises

20. From the following information, compute the early, late, and slack times for each activity. Identify the critical path.

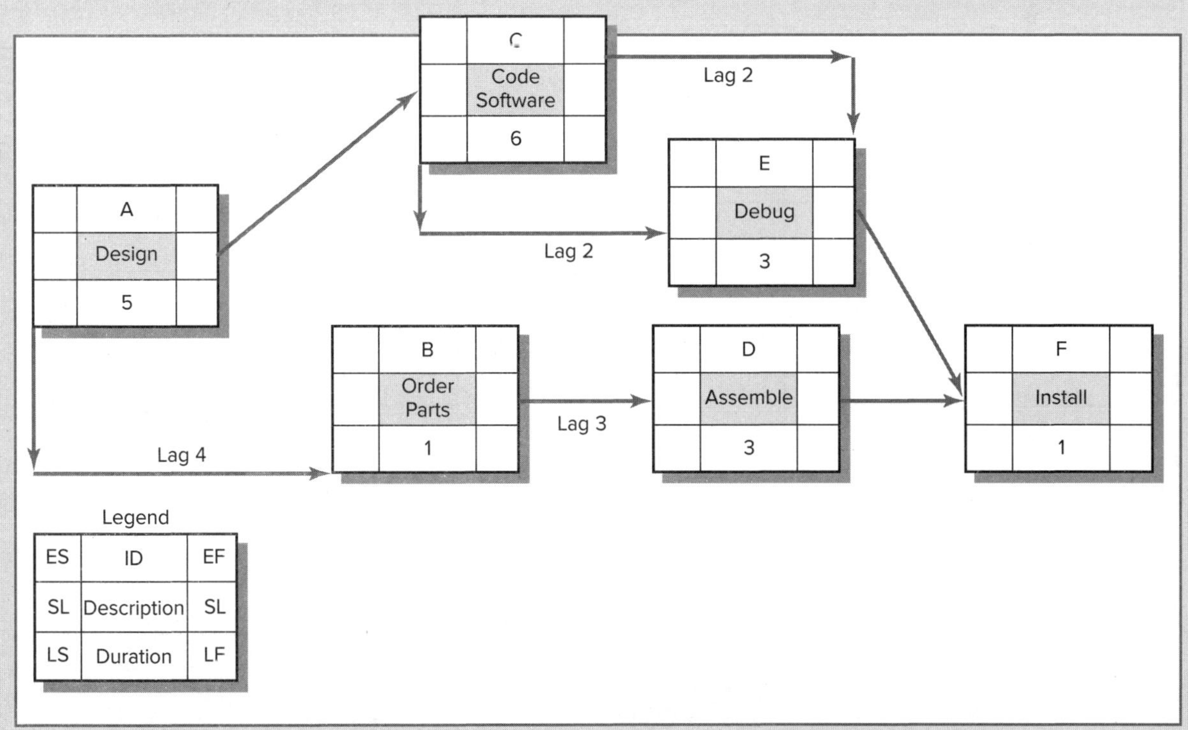

21. Given the following information, compute the early, late, and slack times for the project network. Which activities on the critical path have only the start or finish of the activity on the critical path?

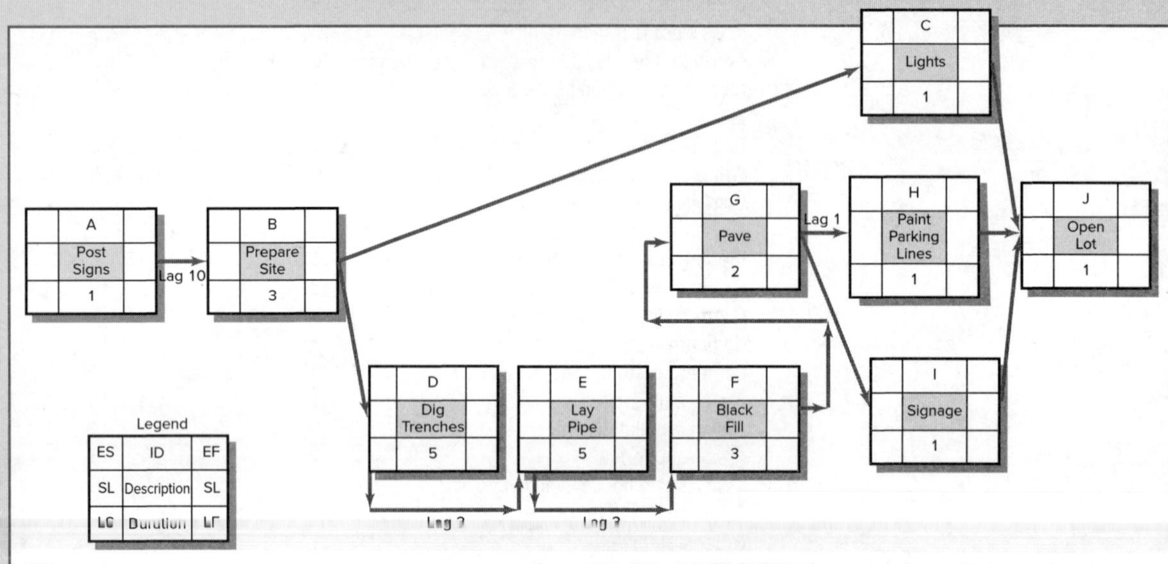

22. Given the information in the following lag exercises, compute the early, late, and slack times for the project network.* Which activities on the critical path have only the start or finish of the activity on the critical path?

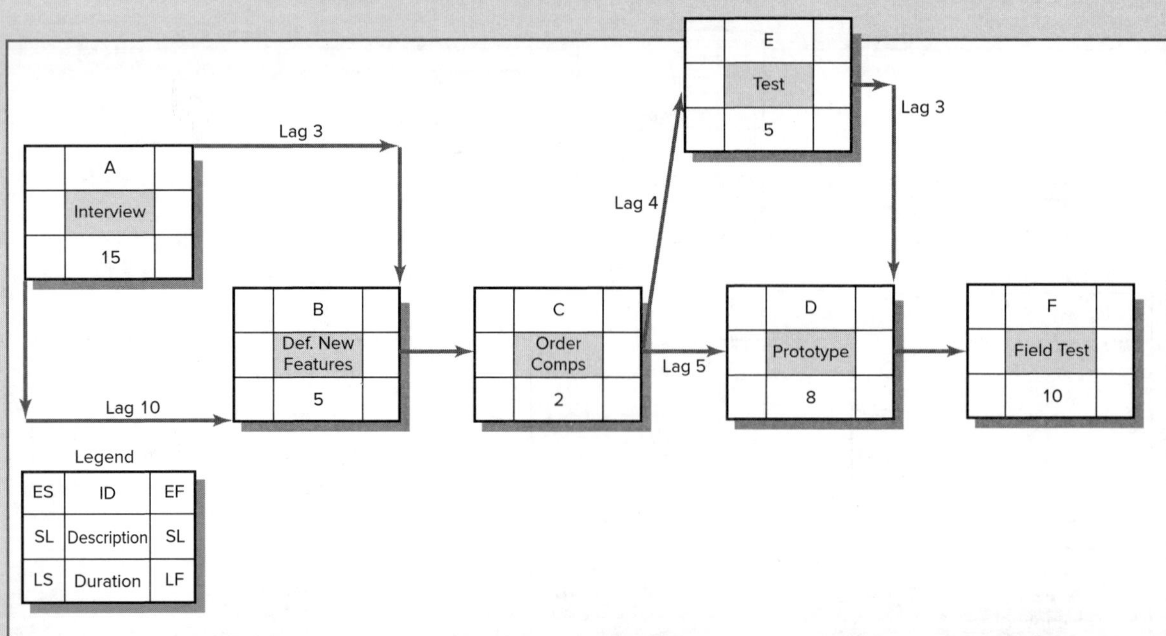

* The solution to this exercise can be found in Appendix One.

23. Given the following network, compute the early, late, and slack time for each activity. Clearly identify the critical path.

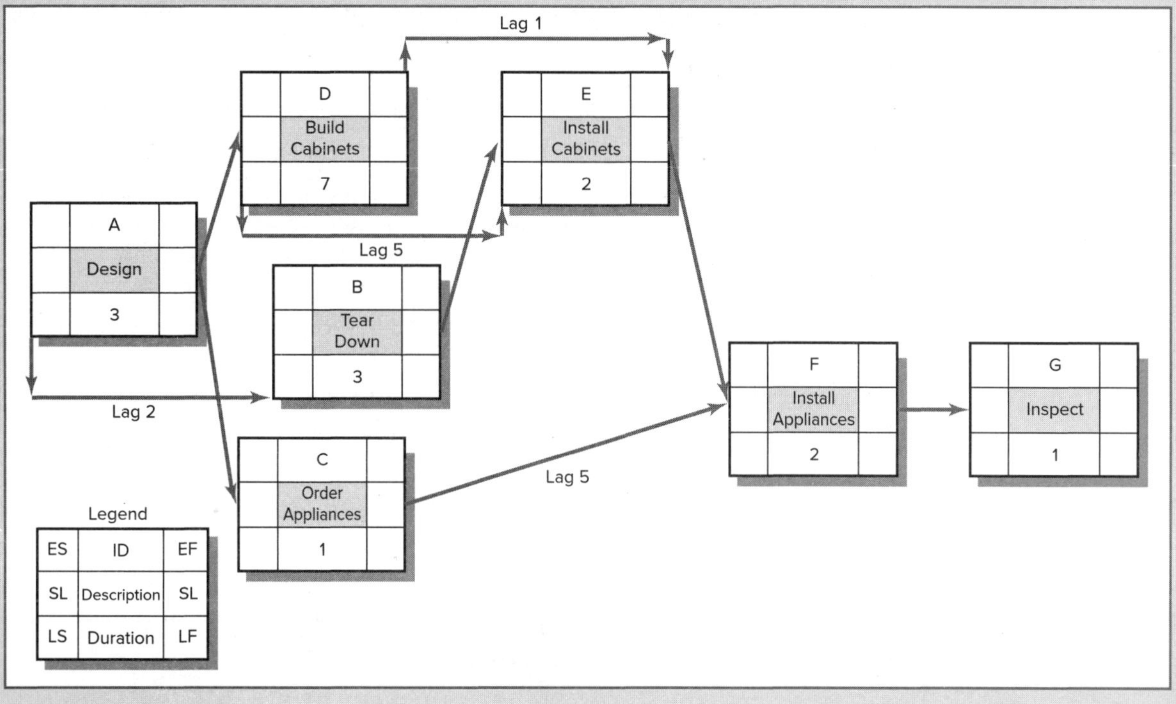

CyClon Project

24. The CyClon project team has started gathering the information necessary to develop a project network—predecessor activities and activity time in days. The results of their meeting are found in the following table.

Activity	Description	Duration	Predecessor
1	***CyClon Project***		
2	Design	10	
3	Procure prototype parts	10	2
4	Fabricate parts	8	2
5	Assemble prototype	4	3, 4
6	Laboratory test	7	5
7	Field test	10	6
8	Adjust design	6	7
9	Order stock components	10	8
10	Order custom components	15	8
11	Assemble test production unit	10	9, 10
12	Test unit	5	11
13	Document results	3	12

Part A. Create a network based on the information in the table. How long will the project take? What is the critical path?

Part B. Upon further review, the team recognize that they missed three finish-to-start lags. Procure prototype parts will involve only 2 days of work but it will take 8 days for the parts to be delivered. Likewise, Order stock components will take 2 days of work and 8 days for delivery and Order custom components will take 2 days of work and 13 days for delivery.

Reconfigure the CyClon schedule by entering the three finish-to-start lags. What impact did these lags have on the original schedule? On the amount of work required to complete the project?

Part C. Management is still not happy with the schedule and wants the project completed as soon as possible. Unfortunately, they are not willing to approve additional resources. One team member pointed out that the network contained only finish-to-start relationships and that it might be possible to reduce project duration by creating start-to-start lags. After much deliberation, the team concluded that the following relationships could be converted into start-to-start lags:

- Procure prototype parts could start 6 days after the start of Design.
- Fabricate parts could start 9 days after the start of Design.
- Laboratory test could begin 1 day after the start of Assemble prototype.
- Field test could start 5 days after the start of Laboratory test.
- Adjust design could begin 7 days after the start of Field test.
- Order stock and Order custom components could begin 5 days after Adjust design.
- Test unit could begin 9 days after the start of Assemble test production unit.
- Document results could start 3 days after the start of Test unit.

Reconfigure the CyClon schedule by entering all nine start-to-start lags. What impact did these lags have on the original schedule (Part A)? How long will the project take? Is there a change in the critical path? Is there a change in the sensitivity of the network? Why would management like this solution?

References

Gantt, H. L., *Work, Wages and Profit,* published by *The Engineering Magazine,* New York, 1910; republished as *Work, Wages and Profits* (Easton, PA: Hive, 1974).

Gray, C. F., *Essentials of Project Management* (Princeton, NJ: PBI, 1981).

Kelly, J. E., "Critical Path Planning and Scheduling: Mathematical Basis," *Operations Research,* vol. 9, no. 3 (May/June 1961), pp. 296–321.

Levy, F. K., G. L. Thompson, and J. D. West, "The ABCs of the Critical Path Method," *Harvard Business Review,* vol. 41, no. 5 (1963), pp. 98–108.

Rosenblatt, A., and G. Watson, "Concurrent Engineering," *IEEE Spectrum,* July 1991, pp. 22–37.

Turtle, Q. C., *Implementing Concurrent Project Management* (Englewood Cliffs, NJ: Prentice Hall, 1994).

Case 6.1

Advantage Energy Technology Data Center Migration*—Part A

Brian Smith, network administrator at Advanced Energy Technology (AET), has been given the responsibility of implementing the migration of a large data center to a new office location. Careful planning is needed because AET operates in the highly competitive petroleum industry. AET is one of five national software companies that provide an accounting and business management package for oil jobbers and gasoline distributors. A few years ago AET jumped into the "application service provider" world. Their large data center provides clients with remote access to AET's complete suite of application software systems. Traditionally, one of AET's primary competitive advantages has been the company's trademark IT reliability. Due to the complexity of this project, Brian will have to use a parallel method of implementation. Although this will increase project costs, a parallel approach is essential if reliability is not to be compromised.

Currently, AET's data center is located on the second floor of a renovated old bank building in downtown Corvallis, Oregon. The company is moving to a new, one-level building in the recently developed industrial complex at the Corvallis International Airport. On February 1, Brian is formally assigned the task by the vice president of operations, Sasha Whitmore, with the following guidelines:

- From start to finish, it is anticipated the entire project will take three to four months to complete.
- It is essential that AET's 235 clients suffer no downtime.

Whitmore advises Brian to come back to the Executive Committee on February 15 with a presentation on the scope of the project that includes costs, "first-cut" timeline, and proposed project team members.

Brian had some preliminary discussions with some of AET's managers and directors from each of the functional departments and then arranged for a full-day scope meeting on February 4 with a few of the managers and technical representatives from Operations, Systems, Facilities, and Applications. The scope team determined the following:

- Three to four months is a feasible project timeline, and first-cut cost estimate is $80,000–$90,000 (this includes the infrastructure upgrade of the new site).
- Critical to the "no-downtime" requirement is the need to completely rely on AET's remote disaster recovery "hot" site for full functionality.
- Brian will serve as project manager of a team consisting of one team member each from Facilities, Operations/Systems, Operations/Telecommunications, Systems and Applications, and Customer Service.

Brian's Executive Committee report was positively received and, after a few modifications and recommendations, he was formally charged with responsibility for the project. Brian recruited his team and scheduled their first team meeting (March 1) as the initial task of his project-planning process.

Once the initial meeting is conducted Brian can hire the contractors to renovate the new data center. During this time Brian will figure out how to design the network. Brian

* Prepared by James Moran, a project management instructor at the College of Business, Oregon State University.

estimates that screening and hiring a contractor will take about one week and that the network design will take about two weeks. The new center requires a new ventilation system. The manufacturer's requirements include an ambient temperature of 67 degrees to keep all of the data servers running at optimal speeds. The ventilation system has a lead time of three weeks. Brian will also need to order new racks to hold the servers, switches, and other network devices. The racks have a two-week delivery time.

The data center supervisor requested that Brian replace all of the old power supplies and data cables. Brian will need to order these as well. Because Brian has a great relationship with the vendor, they guarantee that it will take only one week lead time for the power supplies and the data cables. Once the new ventilation system and racks arrive, Brian can begin installing them. It will take one week to install the ventilation system and three weeks to install the racks. The renovation of the new data center can begin as soon as the contractors have been hired. The contractors tell Brian that construction will take 20 days. Once the construction begins and after Brian installs the ventilation system and racks, the city inspector must approve the construction of the raised floor.

The city inspector will take two days to approve the infrastructure. After the city inspection and after the new power supplies and cables have arrived, Brian can install the power supplies and run the cables. Brian estimates that it will take five days to install the power supplies and one week to run all of the data cables. Before Brian can assign an actual date for taking the network offline and switching to the hot remote site, he must get approval from each of the functional units ("switchover approval"). Meetings with each of the functional units will require one week. During this time he can initiate a power check to ensure that each of the racks has sufficient voltage. This will require only one day.

Upon completion of the power check, he can take one week to install his test servers. The test servers will test all of the primary network functions and act as a safeguard before the network is taken offline. The batteries must be charged, ventilation installed, and test servers up and running before management can be assured that the new infrastructure is safe, which will take two days. Then they will sign off the primary systems check, taking one day of intense meetings. They will also set an official date for the network move.

Brian is happy that everything has gone well thus far and is convinced that the move will go just as smoothly. Now that an official date is set, the network will be shut down for a day. Brian must move all of the network components to the new data center. Brian will do the move over the weekend—two days—when user traffic is at a low point.

ASSIGNMENT

1. Generate a priority matrix for AET's system move.
2. Develop a WBS for Brian's project. Include duration (days) and predecessors.
3. Using a project-planning tool, generate a network diagram for this project.

   Note: Base your plan on the following guidelines: eight-hour days, five-day weeks except for when Brian moves the network components over a weekend, no holiday breaks, and March 3, 2025, is the project start date. Ordering ventilation system, new racks, and power supplies/cables takes only one actual day of work. The remaining days are the time necessary for the vendors to fill and ship the order to Brian. So use finish-to-start lags here. Assume that five days after the start of the renovation of the data center that the raised floor will be ready for inspection (a start-to-start lag).

Case 6.2

Ventura Baseball Stadium—Part A

The G&E Company is preparing a bid to build the new 47,000-seat Shoreline baseball stadium. The construction must start on June 10, 2019, and be completed in time for the start of the 2022 season. A penalty clause of $500,000 per day of delay beyond April 3rd is written into the contract.

Percival Young, the president of the company, expressed optimism at obtaining the contract and revealed that the company could net as much as $5 million on the project. He also said that if they were successful, the prospects of future projects would be bright, since there is a projected renaissance in building classic ballparks with modern luxury boxes.

ASSIGNMENT

Given the information provided in Table 6.3, construct a network schedule for the stadium project and answer the following questions:

1. Can the project be completed by the April 3rd deadline? How long will it take?
2. What is the critical path for the project?
3. Based on the schedule, would you recommend that G&E pursue this contact? Why? Include a one-page Gantt chart for the stadium schedule.

TABLE 6.3 **Ventura Baseball Stadium Case**

ID	Activity	Duration	Predecessor(s)
1	***Baseball Stadium***		
2	Clear stadium site	60 days	—
3	Demolish building	30 days	2
4	Set up construction site	30 days	2
5	Drive support piling	120 days	2
6	Pour lower concrete bowl	120 days	5
7	Pour main concourse	120 days	4, 6
8	Install playing field	90 days	4, 6
9	Construct upper steel bowl	120 days	4, 6
10	Install seats	140 days	7, 9
11	Build luxury boxes	90 days	7, 9
12	Install jumbotron	30 days	7, 9
13	Stadium infrastructure	120 days	7, 9
14	Construct steel canopy	75 days	10
15	Light installation	30 days	14
16	Build roof supports	90 days	6
17	Construct roof	180 days	16
18	Install roof tracks	90 days	16
19	Install roof	90 days	17, 18
20	Inspection	20 days	8, 11, 13, 15, 19

Case Appendix

Technical Details for the Ventura Baseball Stadium

The baseball stadium is an outdoor structure with a retractable roof. The project begins with clearing the site, an activity that lasts 60 days. Once the site is clear, work can start simultaneously on the structure itself and demolition of an adjacent building site. This demolition is necessary to create a construction stage for storing materials and equipment. It will take 30 days to demolish the buildings and another 30 days to set up the construction site.

The work on the stadium begins by driving 160 support pilings, which will take 120 days. Next comes the pouring of the lower concrete bowl (120 days). Once this is done and the construction site has been set up, then the pouring of the main concourse (120 days), installation of the playing field (90 days), and construction of the upper steel bowl can occur.

Once the concourse and upper bowl are completed, work can start simultaneously on building the luxury boxes (90 days), installing the seats (140 days), installing the Jumbotron (30 days), and installing the stadium infrastructure (120 days), which includes bathrooms, lockers, restaurants, etc. Once the seats are installed, then the steel canopy can be constructed (75 days), followed by installation of the lights (30 days). The retractable roof represents the most significant technical challenge to the project. Building the roof track supports (90 days) can begin after the lower concrete bowl is constructed. At this time the dimensions of the roof can be finalized and the construction of the roof at a separate site can begin (180 days). After the roof supports are completed, then the roof tracks can be installed (90 days). Once the tracks and roof are completed, then the roof can be installed and made operational (90 days). Once all activities are completed, it will take 20 days to inspect the stadium.

For purposes of this case assume the following:

1. The following holidays are observed: January 1, Martin Luther King Day (third Monday in January), Memorial Day (last Monday in May), July 4th, Labor Day (first Monday in September), Thanksgiving Day (fourth Thursday in November), December 25 and 26.
2. If a holiday falls on a Saturday, Friday will be given as an extra day off, and if it falls on a Sunday, Monday will be given as a day off.
3. The construction crew works Monday through Friday.

Case 6.3

Freight Corridor Project

India's Freight Corridor Project is one of the flagship projects undertaken by the Ministry of Railways, for improving inefficiency within freight transport systems in the country. Dedicated corridors, unutilized for any other kind of movement, will provide faster and more reliable goods transport. The two major corridors currently under construction are the Eastern Corridor connecting Punjab and West Bengal and the Western Corridor connecting Delhi and Mumbai, targeting to improve industrial connectivity.

OBJECTIVES AND SCOPE

The Freight Corridor Project would reverse freight traffic on to dedicated lines to decongest passenger rail networks, thereby improving the speed and frequency of passenger trains. A major push of this project aims at developing an affordable logistics system wherein logistics cost as a percentage of GDP is brought down from 13–14% to less than 10% in line with the international benchmark. The project further emphasizes sustainability in the environmental sphere by providing energy-efficient in rail transport, which is more environmentally friendly than road transport, thereby decreasing drastically the greenhouse gas emissions. The work reflects in its pursuits the connecting of major ports with the industrial zones with the objective of strengthening the industrial backbone of India, inducting economic growth, and making the country more competitive in the world market.

KEY DELIVERABLES AND MILESTONES

Ambitious milestones have been set to implement the Freight Corridor Project in the least possible time and in an absolutely efficient manner. Land acquisition for both the Eastern and the Western corridors should be fully completed by 2025 as this lays the foundation stone for all subsequent construction works. In parallel, the project concentrates on signaling and electrification systems that are state-of-the-art and bolster operational efficiency and safety of freight trains. Multi-modal logistics parks along the corridors are also envisaged. Logistics hubs are designed to accommodate an integrated mode of inter-modal transportation so that the rail, road and sea transport are utilized appropriately, adding value to the freight ecosystem.

KEY STAKEHOLDERS

- **Government:** Ministry of Railways, State governments responsible for land acquisition
- **Private Sector:** Contractors involved in infrastructure development, Logistics companies managing freight operations
- **Local Communities:** Landowners and residents impacted by construction activities

PROJECT MANAGEMENT FRAMEWORK

Initiation

Feasibility Studies: Detailed surveys conducted to assess freight demand, cost-effectiveness, and alignment with industrial zones. For example, studies highlighted the potential to increase the average speed of goods trains from 25 km/h to over 70 km/h.

Approvals: Required clearances included environmental impact assessments and funding agreements with agencies like the World Bank and Japan International Cooperation Agency (JICA).

Planning: Work Breakdown Structure (WBS)*

Phases	Duration (in Days)	Number of Resources
1. Land Acquisition	365	15
Identify required land parcels	120	5
Negotiate with landowners	180	7
Compensation and resettlement	65	3
2. Construction of Infrastructure	1,095	50
Tracks	730	25
Bridges	365	15
Tunnels	365	10
3. Installation of Systems	730	30
Electrification	365	15
Signaling	365	15
4. Testing and Commissioning	730	20
Trial runs of trains	365	10
Safety certification	120	5
Operational handover	245	5

1. **Timeline Management:** A Gantt chart ensures tracking the timeline of tasks like land acquisition, construction milestones, and system installation over several years.

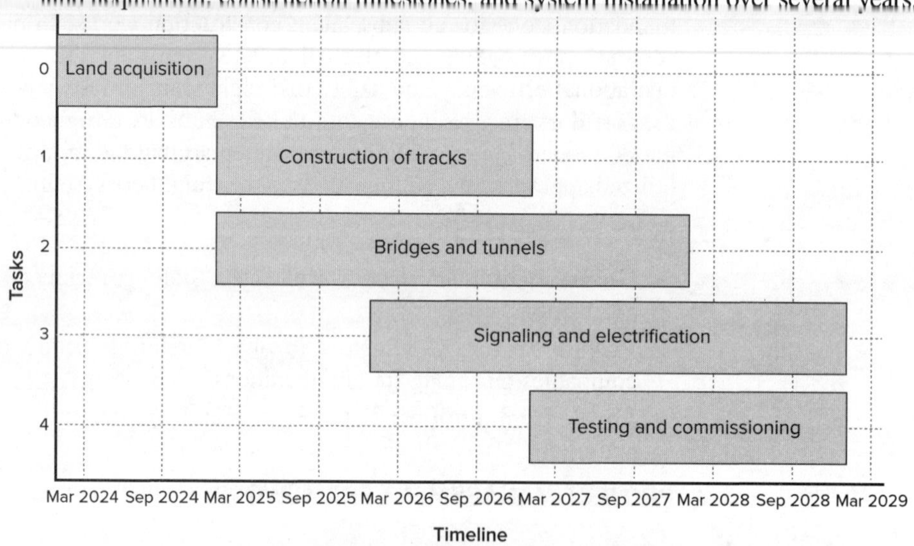

Freight Corridor Project Gantt Chart

Budgeting: A budget of ₹81,000 crore was allocated, ensuring proper monitoring to prevent cost overruns.

Risk Management: A dedicated grievance redressal cell was established to handle landowner disputes. Flexibility in schedules was implemented to account for delays.

PROJECT EXECUTION AND RESOURCE MANAGEMENT

RESOURCE ALLOCATION AND MANAGEMENT

- Advanced track-laying technologies, including pre-cast slab tracks, were introduced to accelerate construction.

* The figures are indicative (for duration and number of resources)

- Workforce mobilization across multiple states, with emphasis on skill training for local workers.

PROCUREMENT CHALLENGES

- Delays in material delivery due to supply chain disruptions.
- Resolution through framework agreements with multiple suppliers to ensure continuity.
- Communication and Stakeholder Management:

INTER-MINISTRY COORDINATION

- Regular meetings between the Ministry of Railways and state governments to resolve land-related disputes.
- Awareness campaigns conducted in affected areas to highlight long-term benefits of the project.

MONITORING AND CONTROL

- Use of drones for aerial surveys to monitor construction progress in real time.
- Deployment of software like Primavera for schedule management and EVM for performance evaluation.

PROJECT CHALLENGES

Technical Challenges: The Freight Corridor Project introduced advanced technologies, such as pre-cast slab tracks and electrification systems, which demanded significant innovation and expertise. For example, ensuring seamless integration of these systems requires extensive workforce training and meticulous planning. Similar challenges were faced during the Delhi Metro project, where tunnel boring machines were adopted for the first time in India to navigate dense urban areas. Furthermore, adapting to varied terrains and climatic conditions along the Eastern and Western corridors added complexity. Drone technology was leveraged for aerial surveys, enabling real-time monitoring and minimizing errors in construction alignment.

Operational Challenges: Operationally, the project faced substantial delays, primarily in land acquisition, where over 85% of the required land was held up due to disputes regarding compensation. For instance, in certain regions of Punjab and Uttar Pradesh, resistance from farmers delayed progress by months. Such delays always translated to cost overruns, taking the estimated budget higher to ₹81,000 crore. Similarly, supply chain disruptions during the COVID-19 pandemic caused material delivery postponements that emphasize the requirement for robust contingency planning.

Environmental and Social Issues: Some of the key environmental concerns were deforestation and disruption to local ecosystems. For example, along the Western Corridor in the Aravalli region, construction required extensive environmental impact assessments to minimize ecological damage. Compensatory afforestation and eco-sensitive construction techniques were undertaken to minimize harm. Socially, there was displacement of more than 20,000 individuals along the corridors, and a rehabilitation and resettlement program needed to be well-enforced. Public consultations and grievance redressal mechanisms had become an important tool for addressing the concerns of affected communities.

Sustainability Measures: This was the thrust of the project—to set the course toward reducing greenhouse gas emissions by promoting rail rather than road freight transport.

Multi-modal logistics parks with integrated renewable energies, such as solar and wind power, were designed to enhance energy efficiency. This not only neutralized environmental impact but also served as a model for sustainable infrastructure development within the Freight Corridor Project.

PROJECT CLOSURE AND EVALUATION

Completion: The Freight Corridor Project will meet its target for operationalization by 2025. This is when dedicated freight corridors will decongest the passenger networks, enhance industrial connectivity, and reduce logistics costs to less than 10% of the GDP. For instance, freight train speeds are anticipated to increase to over 70 km/h from 25 km/h today, which means a tremendous reduction in time taken. Logistics hubs on these corridors will strengthen the overall freight ecosystem, bringing together road, rail, and sea transport.

Handover and Operationalization: The handover to logistics operators will be phased, with such operationalization. Systems like centralized traffic management and integrated logistics hubs will ensure streamlined transitions to regular operating conditions. Tools which enable real-time monitoring include IoT-based systems in logistics hubs which enhance operational efficiency.

KEY TAKEAWAYS

- Key achievements of the project include innovative technologies leveraged, and robust stakeholder engagement. Improvements to be made to this project include better pre-construction planning and anticipating challenges related to land acquisition. For instance, early-stage consultations with the community of similar projects—the Mumbai Metro Rail Project—have facilitated effective acquisition of land with less delay.
- The Freight Corridor Project is one such iconic venture transforming India's freight transportation landscape with the efficiency and cost reduction profile it has adopted. The emphasis here is put into sustainability along with technological integration as a benchmark for future infrastructure. For example, decongesting passenger rail networks through the introduction of dedicated freight lines does improve the overall rail transport system.

REFERENCES

- Ministry of Housing and Urban Affairs. (n.d.). Smart Cities Mission: Transforming urban living. Government of India. Retrieved from https://smartcities.gov.in
- World Bank. (n.d.). India's Dedicated Freight Corridor Project. Retrieved from https://www.worldbank.org
- Japan International Cooperation Agency (JICA). (n.d.). Collaborative efforts in India's infrastructure development. Retrieved from https://www.jica.go.jp
- Ministry of Railways, Government of India. (n.d.). Official updates on freight corridor projects and timelines. Retrieved from https://indianrailways.gov.in
- Dedicated Freight Corridor Corporation of India Ltd. (DFCCIL). Updates on freight corridor projects. Retrieved from https://dfccil.com.

Appendix 6.1

LEARNING OBJECTIVES

After reading this appendix you should be able to:

LO A6-1 Observe Hands-on demonstration of Example 1: Table 6.2 in MS Project

LO A6-1

Observe Hands-on demonstration of Example 1: Table 6.2 in MS Project

Step-by-Step MS Project Demonstration of Book Questions

Example 1: Table 6.2 This section demonstrates step by step process of the Project depicted in Table 6.2 through MS Project.

Step 1: Once the MS Project is installed. Open the application, start with a *Blank Project* option of the list. This will show the Project screen as below.

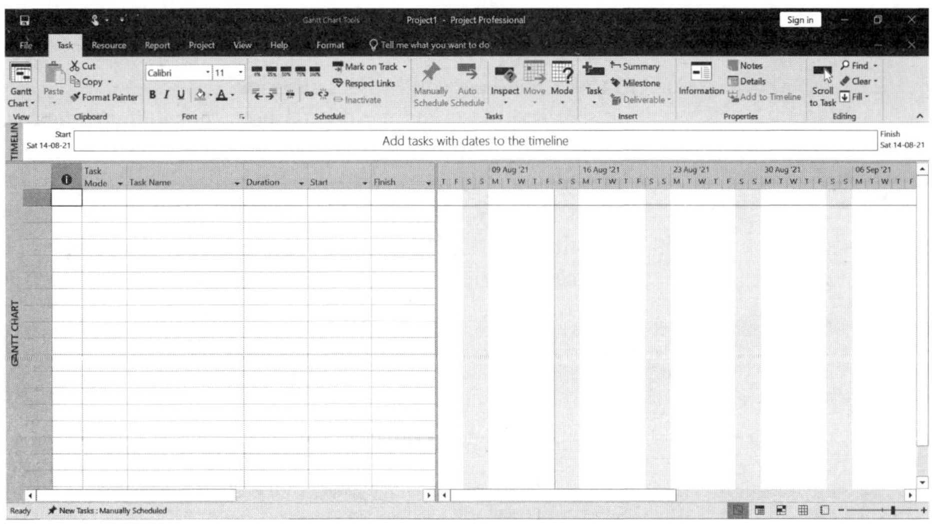

The Project screen shows two parts. The left side depicts the Task or Activity details that are to be planned and the right side presents the visualization of project schedule.

Step 2: Setup the basic project information. Go to Project Tab>Project Information. Here we can indicate the project start date and add some more information, like calendar type, priority of project across the project portfolio etc.

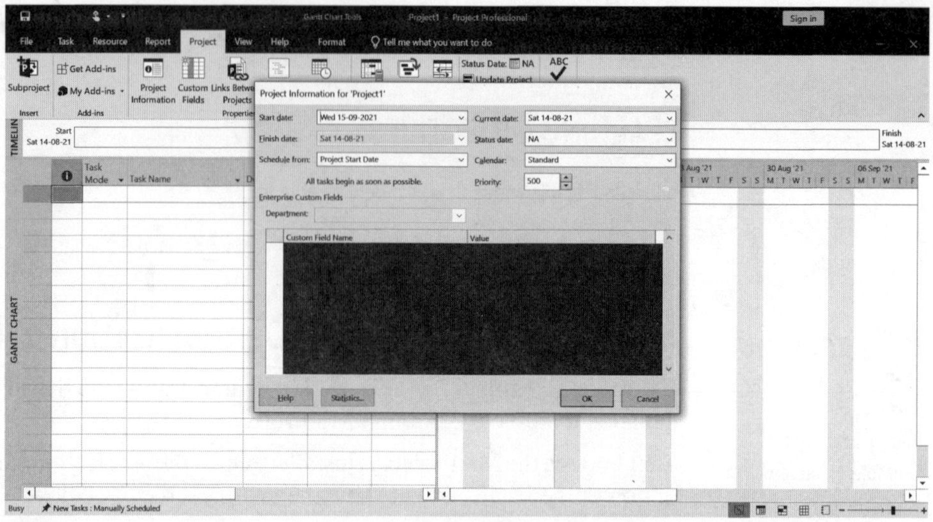

Step 3: Quickly scan through the default setting, and we may like to change a few.

a. Go to File and choose Project Options.
b. You can see the complete details here, not many things we would like to change here, but we should know that as a policy for various projects running at same time we can change default setting for better consistency across the project.
c. Display Tab: You can change currency to your home country currency.
d. Schedule Tab: It is very important as it may help us in scheduling the calendar.
e. Advance Tab: Here we can keep the standard rate of Man, Machine,and Material to depict how much do they cost per unit time or quantity.

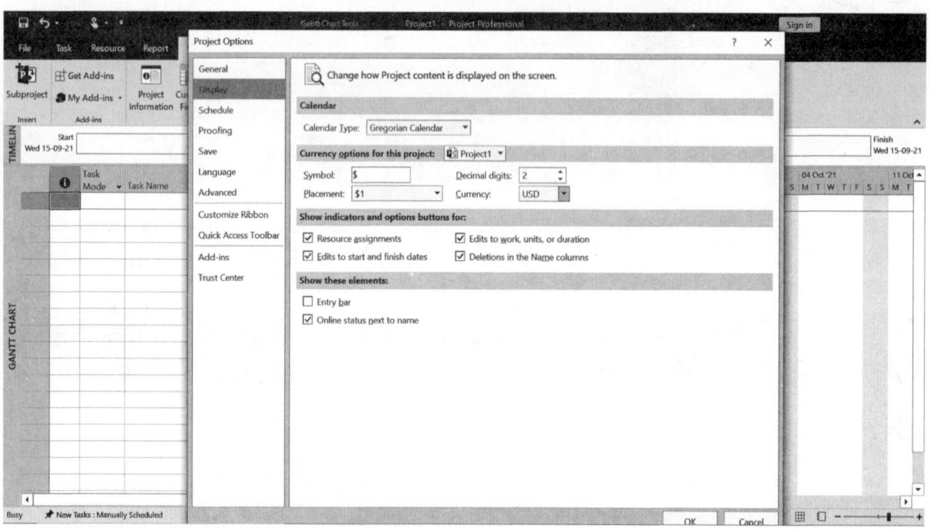

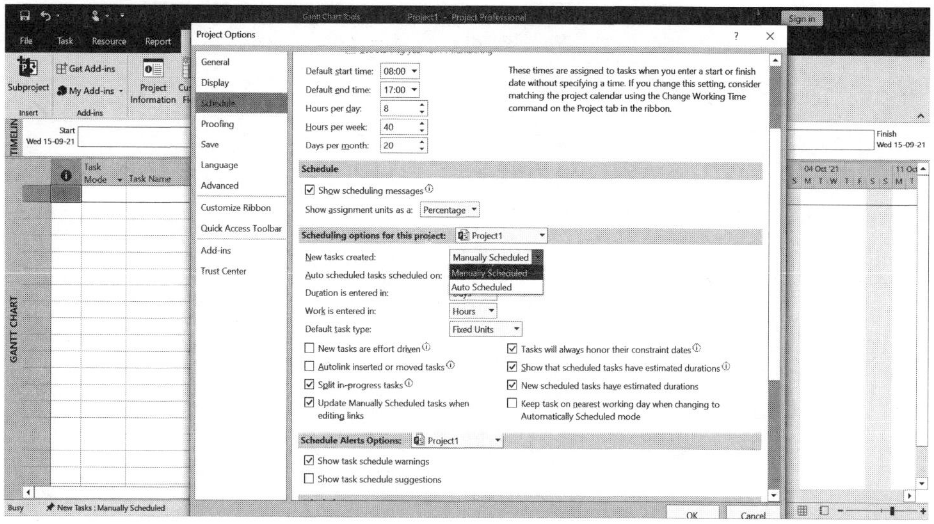

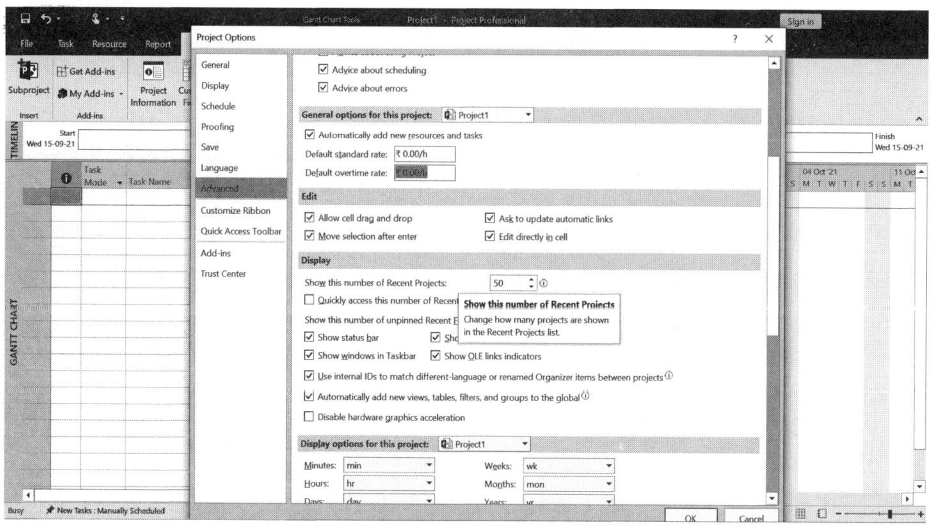

These values can always change within a project too.

Step 4: We need to enter the tasks now. For demonstration purpose, let us take network information given in Table 6.2 (refer to page 206)

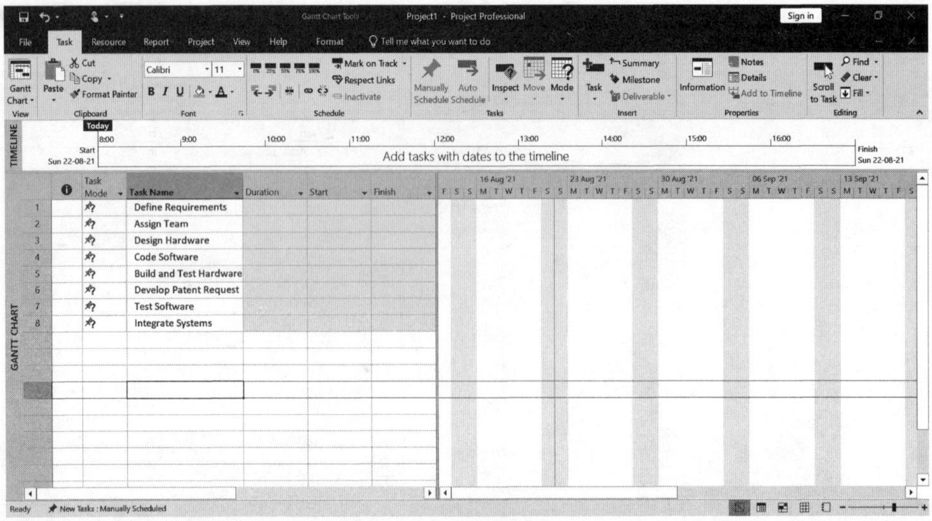

By default, we kept the task mode as Manually Scheduled. It is better to change it to Auto Scheduled for one task and drag the same to define for others tasks, similar to Excel dragging of cells.

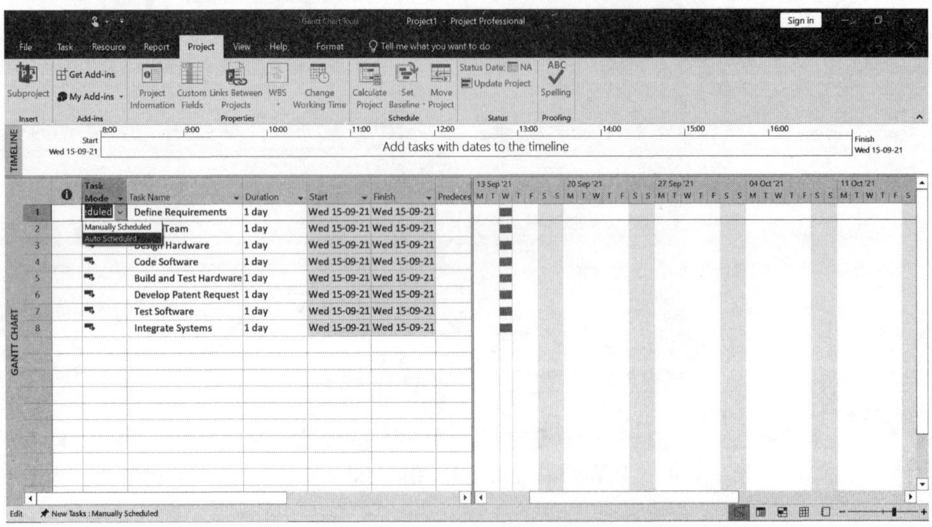

Now all the tasks are given 1 day as default task duration time and the start date is 15 Sep 2021 as we entered in Step 1. In the right pane one day duration is depicted in the Gantt chart.

Step 5: Enter Task duration and Task relationship with other tasks (Predecessors).

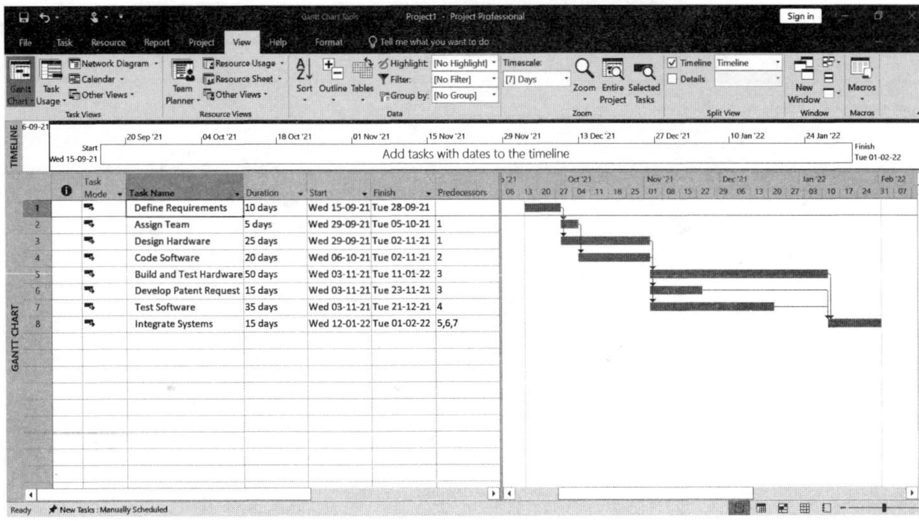

Step 6: Identification of Critical Tasks and slacks: Go to Format Tab, and check the Critical Tasks and Slack boxes.

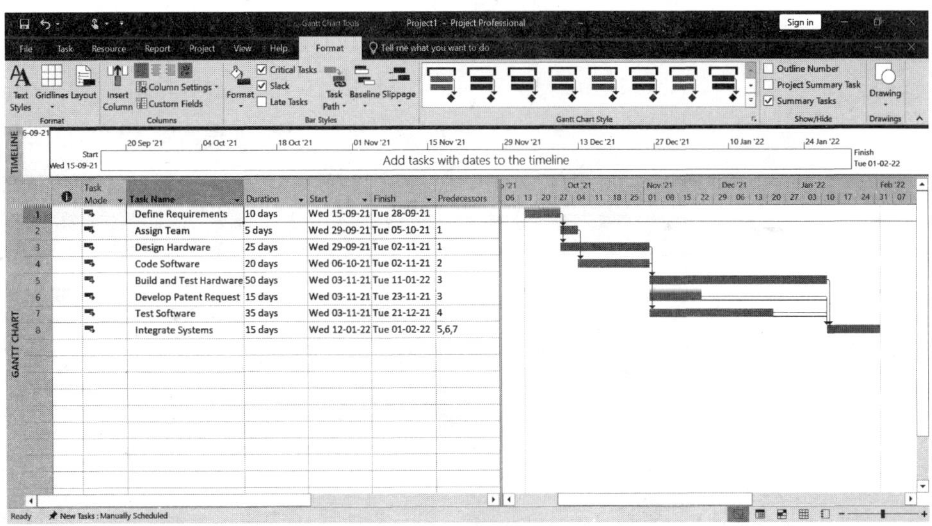

Step 7: To find the total project time. Add a row on the top of the given tasks. Select all the below tasks and get these right indented. The right indent groups the activities under one heading, which is Automated warehouse in our case.

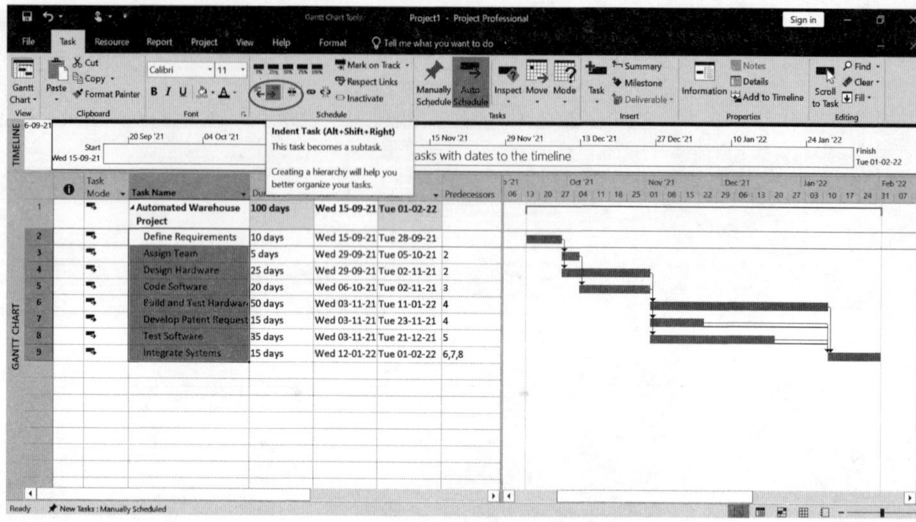

We can match the software result with the manual result as depicted in Figure 6.8, where the dashed activities show the Critical path. Here activity A,C,E, and H are represented by 1,3,5,8. Delay in any of these activities would have direct implication on the overall project duration which is 100 days.

Problem 18 Optical Disk Preinstallation Project: Solving through MS Project

Next is the MS Project Task Entry for the Optical Disk Preinstallation project. We have assumed that the project is scheduled to start on Sep 15, 2021 and there will be 5 days (Monday – Friday).

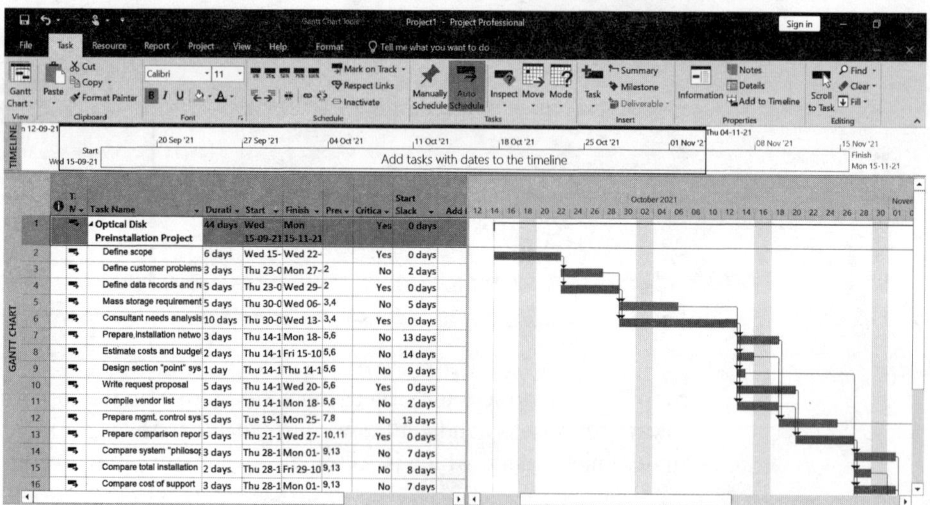

The estimated completion time is 44 weeks, so yes, the project can be completed in 45 weeks if everything goes as planned.

Note: We can also find the critical activity or Slack in the Task pane, by adding a column named *Critical* from the dropdown list.

Design elements: Snapshot from Practice, Highlight box, Case icon: Sky Designs/Shutterstock

CHAPTER SEVEN

7 Managing Risk

LEARNING OBJECTIVES

After reading this chapter you should be able to:

7-1 Describe the risk management process.

7-2 Understand how to identify project risks.

7-3 Assess the significance of different project risks.

7-4 Describe the five responses to managing risks.

7-5 Understand the role contingency plans play in the risk management process.

7-6 Understand opportunity management and describe the five approaches to responding to opportunities in a project.

7-7 Understand how contingency funds and time buffers are used to manage risks on a project.

7-8 Recognize the need for risk management being an ongoing activity.

7-9 Describe the change control process.

A7-1 Calculate basic PERT simulation projections.

OUTLINE

7.1 Risk Management Process

7.2 Step 1: Risk Identification

7.3 Step 2: Risk Assessment

7.4 Step 3: Risk Response Development

7.5 Contingency Planning

7.6 Opportunity Management

7.7 Contingency Funding and Time Buffers

7.8 Step 4: Risk Response Control

7.9 Change Control Management

Summary

Appendix 7.1: PERT and PERT Simulation

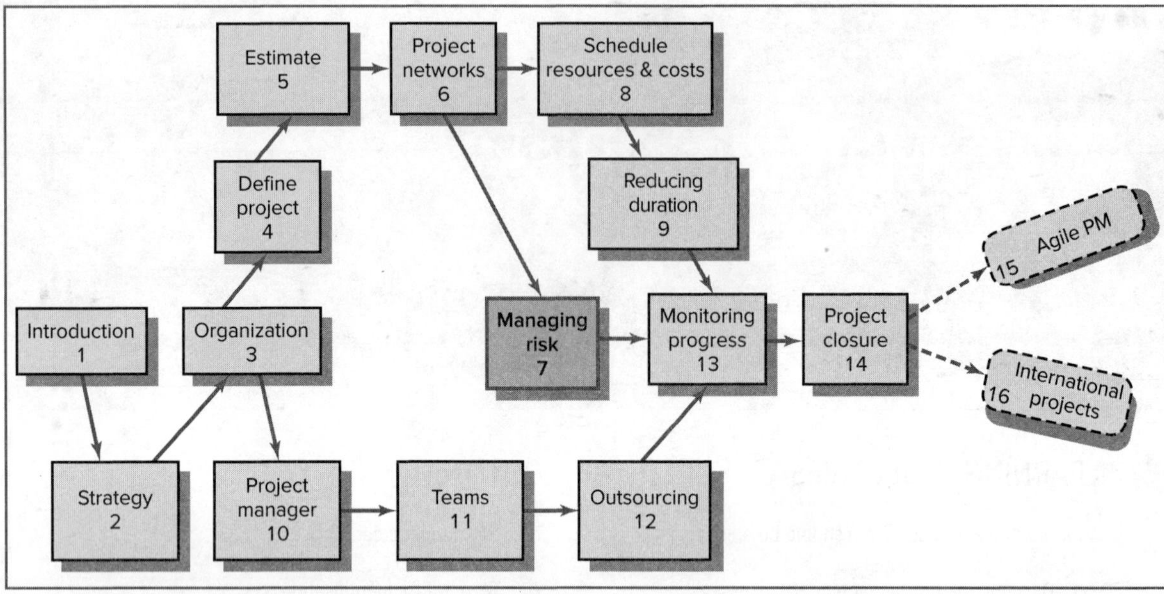

"The biggest risk is not taking any risk."

—Mark Zuckerberg, founder and CEO of FACEBOOK.

Every project manager understands risks are inherent in projects, deliveries are delayed, accidents happen, people get sick, etc. No amount of planning can overcome **risk,** or the inability to control chance events. In the context of projects, risk is an uncertain event or condition that if it occurs, has a positive or negative effect on project objectives. A risk has a cause and, if it occurs, a consequence. For example, a cause may be a flu virus or change in scope requirements. The event is that team members get stricken with the flu or the product has to be redesigned. If either of these uncertain events occurs, it will impact the cost, schedule, and quality of the project.

Some potential risk events can be identified before the project starts—such as equipment malfunction or change in technical requirements. Risks can be anticipated consequences, like schedule slippages or cost overruns. Other risks are beyond most people's imagination, like the COVID-19 pandemic or the 2008 financial meltdown.

While risks can have positive consequences such as unexpected price reductions in materials, the primary focus of this chapter is on what can go wrong and the risk management process.

Risk management attempts to recognize and manage potential and unforeseen trouble spots that may occur when the project is implemented. Risk management identifies as many risk events as possible (what can go wrong), minimizes their impact (what can be done about the event before the project begins), manages responses to events that do materialize (contingency plans), and provides contingency funds to cover risk events that actually materialize.

For a humorous, but ultimately embarrassing, example of poor risk management see Snapshot from Practice 7.1: Giant Popsicle Gone Wrong.

SNAPSHOT FROM PRACTICE 7.1 Giant Popsicle Gone Wrong*

An attempt to erect the world's largest popsicle in New York City ended with a scene straight out of a disaster film, but much stickier.

The 25-foot-tall, 17½-ton treat of frozen juice melted faster than expected, flooding Union Square in downtown Manhattan with kiwi-strawberry–flavored fluid.

Bicyclists wiped out in the stream of goo. Pedestrians slipped. Traffic was, well, frozen. Firefighters closed off several streets and used hoses to wash away the thick, sweet slime.

The Snapple Company, a leading maker of soft beverages, had been trying to promote a new line of frozen treats by setting a record for the world's largest popsicle but called off the stunt before the frozen giant was pulled fully upright by a construction crane.

Authorities said they were worried the 2½-story popsicle would collapse.

Brian Smith/Zuma Press, Inc.

Organizers were not sure why it melted so quickly. "We planned for it. We just didn't expect for it to happen so fast," said Snapple spokesperson Lauren Radcliffe. Lauren said the company would offer to pay the city for the clean-up costs.

*Associated Press, June 23, 2005.

7.1 Risk Management Process

LO 7-1

Describe the risk management process.

Figure 7.1 presents a graphic model of the risk management challenge. The chances of a risk event occurring (e.g., an error in time estimates, cost estimates, or design technology) are greatest during the early stages of a project. This is when uncertainty is highest and many questions remain unanswered. As the project progresses toward completion, risk declines as the answers to critical issues (Will the technology work? Is the timeline feasible?) are resolved. The cost impact of a risk event, however, increases over the life of the project. For example, the risk event of a design flaw occurring after a prototype has been made has a greater cost or time impact than if the flaw were discovered during the planning phase of the project.

The cost of mismanaged risk control early on in the project is exemplified by the ill-fated 1999 NASA Mars Climate Orbiter. Investigations revealed that Lockheed Martin had botched the design of critical navigation software. While flight computers on the ground did calculations based on pounds of thrust per second, the spacecraft's computer software used metric units called newtons. A check to see if the values were compatible was never done. "Our check and balances processes did not catch an error like this that should have been caught," said Ed Weiler, NASA's associate administrator for space science. "That is the bottom line" (*Orlando Sentinel,* 1999). If the error had been discovered early, the correction would have been relatively simple and inexpensive. Instead, the error was never discovered, and after the nine-month journey to the red planet, the $125-million probe approached Mars at too low an altitude and burned up in the planet's atmosphere.

FIGURE 7.1
Risk Event Graph

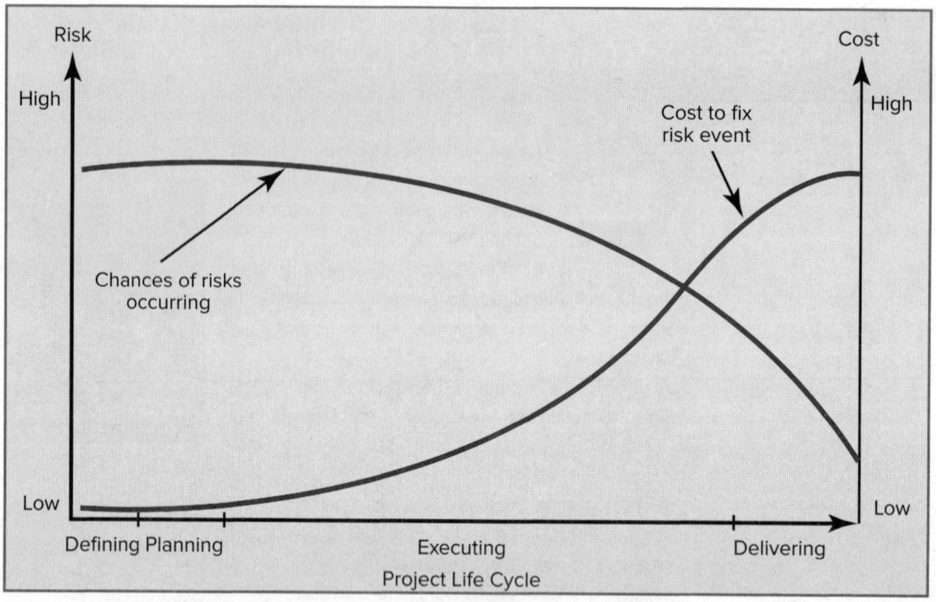

Following the 1999 debacle, NASA instituted a more robust risk management system, which has produced a string of successful missions to Mars, including the dramatic landing of the *Curiosity* rover in August 2012.[1]

Risk management is a proactive, rather than reactive, approach. It is a preventive process designed to ensure that surprises are reduced and that negative consequences associated with undesirable events are minimized. It also prepares the project manager to take action when a time, cost, and/or technical advantage is possible. Successful management of project risk gives the project manager better control over the future and can significantly improve the chances of reaching project objectives on time and within budget and of meeting required technical (functional) performance.

The sources of project risks are unlimited. There are external sources, such as inflation, market acceptance, exchange rates, and government regulations. In practice, these risk events are often referred to as "threats" to differentiate them from those that are not within the project manager's or team's responsibility area. (Later we will see that budgets for such risk events are placed in a "management reserve" contingency budget.) Since such external risks are usually considered before the decision to go ahead with the project, they will be excluded from the discussion of project risks. However, external risks are extremely important and must be addressed.

The major components of the risk management process are depicted in Figure 7.2. Each step will be examined in more detail in the remainder of the chapter.

7.2 Step 1: Risk Identification

LO 7-2

Understand how to identify project risks.

The risk management process begins by trying to generate a list of all the possible risks that could affect the project. Typically the project manager pulls together, during the planning phase, a risk management team consisting of core team members and other relevant stakeholders. Research has demonstrated that groups make more

[1] Landau, E., "Mars Landing Went 'Flawlessly,' Scientists Say," CNN.com. Accessed 8/14/12.

FIGURE 7.2
The Risk Management Process

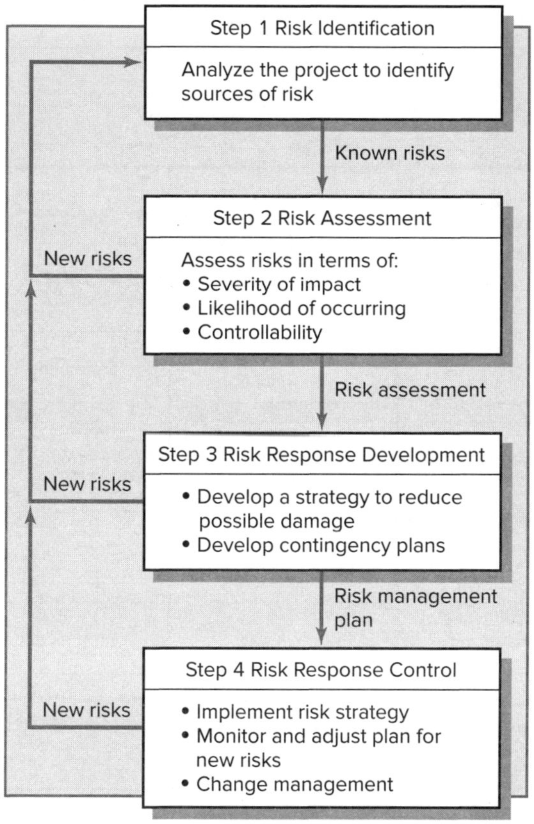

accurate judgments about risks than individuals do (Snizek & Henry, 1989). The team uses brainstorming and other problem-identifying techniques to identify potential problems. Participants are encouraged to keep an open mind and generate as many probable risks as possible. More than one project has been bushwhacked by an event that members thought was preposterous in the beginning. Later during the assessment phase, participants will have a chance to analyze and filter out unreasonable risks.

One common mistake that is made early in the risk identification process is to focus on objectives and not on the events that could produce consequences. For example, team members may identify failing to meet the schedule as a major risk. What they need to focus on are the events that could cause this to happen (e.g., poor estimates, adverse weather, shipping delays). Only by focusing on actual events can potential solutions be found.

Organizations use **risk breakdown structures (RBSs)** in conjunction with work breakdown structures (WBSs) to help management teams identify and eventually analyze risks. Figure 7.3 provides a generic example of an RBS. The focus at the beginning should be on risks that can affect the whole project, as opposed to a specific section of the project or network. For example, the discussion of funding may lead the team to identify the possibility of the project budget being cut after the project has started as a significant risk event. Likewise, when discussing the market, the team may identify responding to new product releases by competitors as a risk event.

FIGURE 7.3 The Risk Breakdown Structure (RBS)

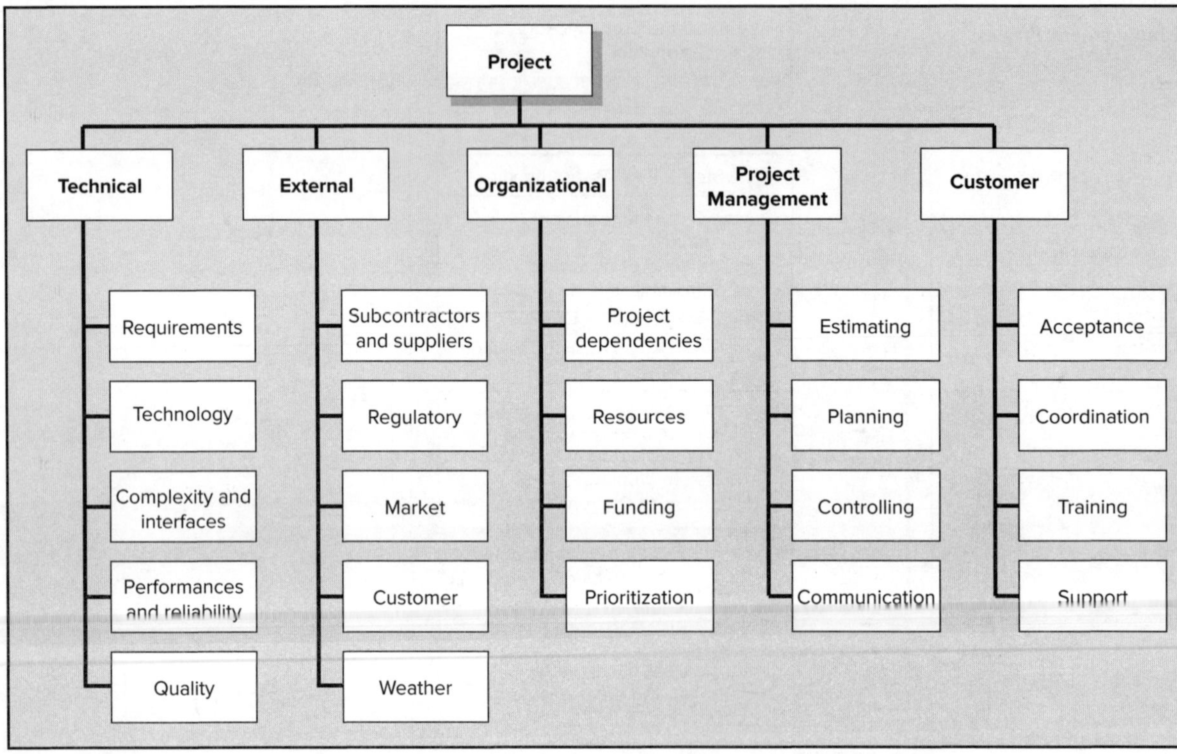

After the macro risks have been identified, specific areas can be checked. An effective tool for identifying specific risks is the risk breakdown structure. The use of the RBS reduces the chance a risk event will be missed. On large projects, multiple risk teams are organized around specific deliverables and submit their risk management reports to the project manager. See Snapshot from Practice 7.2: Terminal 5—London Heathrow Airport for an example of a project that would have benefited from a more robust RBS.

A risk profile is another useful tool. A **risk profile** is a list of questions that address traditional areas of uncertainty on a project. These questions have been developed and refined from previous, similar projects. Figure 7.4 provides a partial example of a risk profile.

Good risk profiles, like RBSs, are tailored to the type of project in question. For example, building an information system is different from building a new car. They are organization specific. Risk profiles recognize the unique strengths and weaknesses of the firm. Finally, risk profiles address both technical and management risks. For example, the profile shown in Figure 7.4 asks questions about design, such as "Does the design depend upon unrealistic assumptions?" The questions may lead the team to identify that the technology will not work under extreme conditions as a risk. Similarly, questions about work environment ("Do people cooperate across functional boundaries?") may lead to the identification of potential communication breakdowns between Marketing and R&D as a risk.

Risk profiles are generated and maintained usually by personnel from the project office. They are updated and refined during the post-project audit (see Chapter 14). These profiles, when kept up to date, can be a powerful resource in the risk management process. The collective experience of the firm's past projects resides in their questions.

SNAPSHOT FROM PRACTICE 7.2 Terminal 5—London Heathrow Airport*

The queen announced to a select audience at the ribbon-cutting ceremony for Terminal 5 at London Heathrow Airport, "It gives me great pleasure to open Terminal 5—the 21st-century gateway to Britain and, to us, the wider world."

At the cost of over $5 billion British Airways (BA) was banking on Terminal 5 eliminating what had commonly been called the "Heathrow hassle." Over the past decade, Heathrow had earned a reputation for baggage delays, long queues, and lost luggage, so much so that premium passengers were avoiding landing there and paying extra to land in ultra-modern hubs, like Amsterdam and Frankfurt.

Terminal 5 was designed by a world-famous architect and featured sweeping views of London; wide, open spaces; and rows of luxury shops, including Tiffany's and a Gordon Ramsey restaurant. It was designed to handle 30 million customers a year with state-of-the-art departure lounges. It included a sophisticated baggage setup designed to handle 12,000 bags per hour and eliminate the Heathrow hassle.

March 28, the opening day of the terminal, started ominously. The first warning came at 4:00 a.m., when many of the staff and passengers began showing up late because they could not find parking. The road signs outside the terminal were not clear, and people said they were given the wrong information once inside. Once the staff arrived at work, many were unable to log in to the computer system due to inadequate training. As a result, the processing of passengers began to bog down, and the luggage began to stack up. Technical glitches with the baggage system emerged. An underground conveyor system became clogged up. By noon, BA had had to cancel 20 flights. By 5:00 p.m., BA had suspended the checking in of all luggage. This meant passengers at the airport had the choice of flying with just hand baggage, getting an alternative flight, or claiming a refund. Of all the planes that left that day, one in three had no luggage!

That was only day 1; flights were canceled all week and BA brought in hundreds of volunteers to tackle the baggage mountain. In the end, over 28,000 suitcases were shipped to Milan, where they were sorted out away from the turmoil in London.

The opening of Terminal 5 was an embarrassment, with hundreds of canceled flights and thousands of lost bags. It cost BA over $32 million and two senior executives their jobs. BA later admitted that customers were deserting in wake of the Terminal 5 fiasco, with passenger numbers down 7 percent.

What are the lessons to be learned? There are many. The first is that on complex projects there is a tendency to focus on the technical challenges and shortchange the human side of the project. Remember, projects are socio-technical systems! A more robust RBS may have revealed the need for more training and a walk-through before the terminal became operational.

One also must question the wisdom of going fully operational on day 1. Going from operating zero flights one day to 380 is a formidable task. A more prudent approach may have been to limit the flights the first week to work out the kinks and ensure success.

*"Terminal 5 Fiasco: The New 'Heathrow Hassle,'" *The Independent*, March 28, 2008; "What Did Go Wrong at Terminal 5?" news.bbc.co.uk, March 30, 2008. Accessed 9/25/18.

Historical records can complement or be used when formal risk profiles are not available. Project teams can investigate what happened on similar projects in the past to identify potential risks. For example, a project manager can check the on-time performance of selected vendors to gauge the threat of shipping delays. IT project managers can access "best practices" papers detailing other companies' experiences converting software systems. Inquiries should not be limited to recorded data. Savvy project managers tap the wisdom of others by seeking the advice of veteran project managers.

The risk identification process should not be limited to just the core team. Input from customers, sponsors, subcontractors, vendors, and other stakeholders should be solicited. Relevant stakeholders can be formally interviewed or included on the risk management team. Not only do these players have a valuable perspective, but by

FIGURE 7.4
Partial Risk Profile for Product Development Project

Technical Requirements

Are the requirements stable?

Design

Does the design depend on unrealistic or optimistic assumptions?

Testing

Will testing equipment be available when needed?

Development

Is the development process supported by a compatible set of procedures, methods, and tools?

Schedule

Is the schedule dependent upon the completion of other projects?

Budget

How reliable are the cost estimates?

Quality

Are quality considerations built into the design?

Management

Do people know who has authority for what?

Work Environment

Do people work cooperatively across functional boundaries?

Staffing

Is staff inexperienced or understaffed?

Customer

Does the customer understand what it will take to complete the project?

Contractors

Are there any ambiguities in contractor task definitions?

involving them in the risk management process they also become more committed to project success.[2]

One of the keys to success in risk identification is attitude. While a "can do" attitude is essential during implementation, project managers have to encourage critical thinking when it comes to risk identification. The goal is to find potential problems before they happen.

The RBS and risk profiles are useful tools for making sure no stones are left unturned. At the same time, when done well the number of risks identified can be overwhelming and a bit discouraging. Initial optimism can be replaced with griping and cries of "What have we gotten ourselves into?" It is important that project managers set the right tone and complete the risk management process so members regain confidence in themselves and the project.

7.3 Step 2: Risk Assessment

LO 7-3

Assess the significance of different project risks.

Step 1 produces a list of potential risks. Not all of these risks deserve attention, however. Some are trivial and can be ignored, while others pose serious threats to the welfare of the project. Managers have to develop methods for sifting through the list of risks, eliminating inconsequential or redundant ones, and stratifying worthy ones in terms of importance and need for attention.

Scenario analysis is the easiest and most commonly used technique for analyzing risks. Team members assess the significance of each risk event in terms of

- Probability of the event.
- Impact of the event.

Simply stated, risks need to be evaluated in terms of the likelihood the event is going to occur and the impact or consequences of its occurrence. A project manager being

[2] The Delphi Method (see Snapshot from Practice 5.2) is a popular technique for involving stakeholders.

struck by lightning at a work site would have a major negative impact on the project, but the likelihood of such an event is so low that the risk is not worthy of consideration. Conversely, people do change jobs, so an event like the loss of key project personnel would have not only an adverse impact but also a high likelihood of occurring in some organizations. If so, then it would be wise for that organization to be proactive and mitigate this risk by developing incentive schemes for retaining specialists and/or engaging in cross-training to reduce the impact of turnover.

The quality and credibility of the risk analysis process require that different levels of risk probabilities and impacts be defined. These definitions vary and should be tailored to the specific nature and needs of the project. For example, a relatively simple scale ranging from "very unlikely" to "almost certainly" may suffice for one project, whereas another project may use more precise numeric probabilities (e.g., 0.1, 0.3, 0.5, . . .).

Impact scales can be a bit more problematic, since adverse risks affect project objectives differently. For example, a component failure may cause only a slight delay in project schedule but a major increase in project cost. If controlling cost is a high priority, then the impact would be severe. If, on the other hand, time is more critical than cost, then the impact would be minor.

Because impact ultimately needs to be assessed in terms of project priorities, different kinds of impact scales are used. Some scales may simply use rank-order descriptors, such as "low," "moderate," "high," and "very high," whereas others use numeric weights (e.g., 1–10). Some may focus on the project in general, whereas others focus on specific project objectives. The risk management team needs to establish up front what distinguishes a 1 from a 3 or "moderate" impact from "severe" impact. Figure 7.5 provides an example of how impact scales could be defined, given the project objectives of cost, time, scope, and quality.

FIGURE 7.5 **Defined Conditions for Impact Scales of a Risk on Major Project Objectives (examples for negative impacts only)**

	Relative or Numeric Scale				
Project Objective	1 Very Low	2 Low	3 Moderate	4 High	5 Very High
Cost	Insignificant cost increase	< 10% cost increase	10–20% cost increase	20–40% cost increase	> 40% cost increase
Time	Insignificant time increase	< 5% time increase	5–10% time increase	10–20% time increase	> 20% time increase
Scope	Scope decrease barely noticeable	Minor areas of scope affected	Major areas of scope affected	Scope reduction unacceptable to sponsor	Project end item is effectively useless
Quality	Quality degradation barely noticeable	Only very demanding applications are affected	Quality reduction requires sponsor approval	Quality reduction unacceptable to sponsor	Project end item is effectively useless

Documentation of scenario analyses can be seen in various risk assessment forms used by companies. Figure 7.6 is a partial example of a risk assessment form used on an information systems project involving an operating systems (OS) upgrade.

Notice that in addition to evaluating the severity and probability of risk events, the team also assesses when the event might occur and its detection difficulty. Detection difficulty is a measure of how easy it would be to detect that the event was going to occur in time to take mitigating action, that is, how much warning there would be. So in the OS upgrade example, the detection scale would range from 5 = no warning to 1 = lots of time to react.

Often, organizations find it useful to categorize the severity of different risks into some form of risk assessment matrix. The matrix is typically structured around the impact and likelihood of the risk event. For example, the risk matrix presented in Figure 7.7 consists of a 5 × 5 array of elements with each element representing a different set of impact and likelihood values.

FIGURE 7.6
Risk Assessment Form

Risk Event	Likelihood	Impact	Detection Difficulty	When
Interface problems	4	4	4	Conversion
System freezing	2	5	5	Start-up
User backlash	4	3	3	Postinstallation
Hardware malfunctioning	1	5	5	Installation

FIGURE 7.7
Risk Severity Matrix

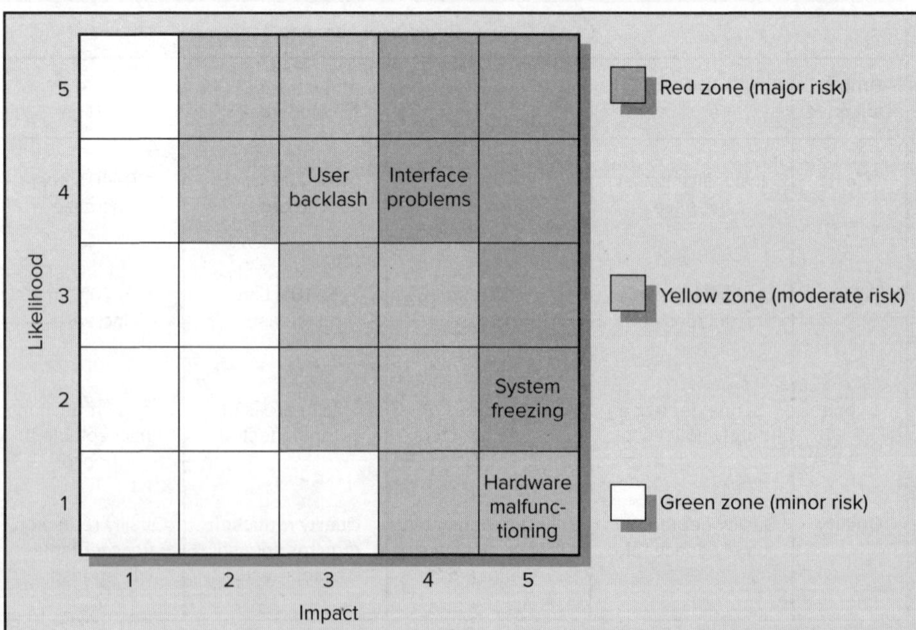

The matrix is divided into red, yellow, and green zones representing major, moderate, and minor risks, respectively. The red zone is centered on the top right corner of the matrix (high impact/high likelihood), while the green zone is centered on the bottom left corner (low impact/low likelihood). The moderate-risk yellow zone extends down the middle of the matrix. Since the impact is generally considered more important than likelihood (a 10 percent chance of losing $1,000,000 is usually considered a more severe risk than a 90 percent chance of losing $1,000), the red zone (major risk) extends farther down the high-impact column.

Using the OS upgrade project again as an example, interface problems and system freezing would be placed in the red zone (major risk), while user backlash and hardware malfunctioning would be placed in the yellow zone (moderate risk).

The **risk severity matrix** provides a basis for prioritizing which risks to address. Red zone risks receive first priority followed by yellow zone risks. Green zone risks are typically considered inconsequential and ignored unless their status changes.

Failure Mode and Effects Analysis (FMEA) extends the risk severity matrix by including ease of detection in the equation:

$$\text{Impact} \times \text{Probability} \times \text{Detection} = \text{Risk Value}$$

Each of the three dimensions is rated according to a 5-point scale. For example, detection is defined as the ability of the project team to discern that the risk event is imminent. A score of 1 would be given if even a chimpanzee could spot the risk coming. The highest detection score of 5 would be given to events that could only be discovered after it was too late (e.g., system freezing). Similar anchored scales would be applied for the severity of impact and the probability of the event occurring. The weighting of the risks is then based on their overall score. For example, a risk with an impact in the "1" zone with a very low probability and an easy detection score might score a 1 ($1 \times 1 \times 1 = 1$). Conversely, a high-impact risk that is highly probable and impossible to detect would score 125 ($5 \times 5 \times 5 = 125$). This broad range of numeric scores allows for easy stratification of risk according to overall significance.

No assessment scheme is absolutely foolproof. For example, the weakness of the FMEA approach is that a risk event rated Impact = 1, Probability = 5, and Detection = 5 would receive the same weighted score as an event rated Impact = 5, Probability = 5, and Detection = 1! This underscores the importance of *not* treating risk assessment as simply an exercise in mathematics. Risk assessment tools should be used to guide discussions, not to make decisions. There is no substitute for an engaged discussion of key risk events.

Probability Analysis

There are many statistical techniques available to the project manager that can assist in assessing project risk. Decision trees have been used to assess alternative courses of action using expected values. Statistical variations of net present value (NPV) have been used to assess cash flow risks in projects. Correlations between past projects' cash flow and S-curves (cumulative project cost curve—baseline—over the life of the project) have been used to assess cash flow risks.

PERT (program evaluation and review technique) and PERT simulation can be used to review activity and project risk. PERT and related techniques take a more macro perspective by looking at overall cost and schedule risks. Here the focus is not on individual events but on the likelihood the project will be completed on time and within budget. These methods are useful in assessing the overall risk of the project and the need for such things as contingency funds, resources, and time. The use of

PERT simulation is increasing because it uses the same data required for PERT, and software to perform the simulation is readily available.

Basically, PERT simulation assumes a statistical distribution (range between optimistic and pessimistic) for each activity duration; it then simulates the network (perhaps over 1,000 simulations) using a random number generator. The outcome is the relative probability, called a criticality index, of an activity becoming critical under the many different possible activity durations for each activity. PERT simulation also provides a list of potential critical paths and their respective probabilities of occurring. Having this information available can greatly facilitate identifying and assessing schedule risk. (See Appendix 7.1 at the end of this chapter for a more detailed description and discussion.)

7.4 Step 3: Risk Response Development

LO 7-4

Describe the five responses to managing risks.

When a risk event is identified and assessed, a decision must be made concerning which response is appropriate for the specific event. Responses to risk can be classified as mitigating, avoiding, transferring, escalating, or retaining.

Mitigating Risk

Reducing risk is usually the first alternative considered. There are basically two strategies for **mitigating risk:** (1) reduce the likelihood that the event will occur and/or (2) reduce the impact that the adverse event would have on the project. Most risk teams focus first on reducing the likelihood of risk events, since if successful this may eliminate the need to consider the potentially costly second strategy.

Testing, experimenting, and prototyping are frequently used to resolve project ambiguities and to prevent problems from escalating. An example of testing can be found in an information systems project. The project team was responsible for installing a new operating system in their parent company. Before implementing the project, the team tested the new system on a smaller, isolated network. By doing so they discovered a variety of problems and were able to come up with solutions prior to implementation. The team still encountered problems with the installation, but the number and severity were greatly reduced. Experiments can be used to test assumptions. For example, before committing to a new high-tech adhesive, a project team ran experiments with the adhesive under different conditions. Prototypes are especially useful for checking if "things fit together" and soliciting feedback from customers.

Often, identifying the root causes of an event is useful. For example, the fear that a vendor will be unable to supply customized components on time may be attributable to (1) poor vendor relationships, (2) design miscommunication, and (3) lack of motivation. As a result of this analysis, the project manager may decide to take his/her counterpart to lunch to clear the air, invite the vendor to attend design meetings, and restructure the contract to include incentives for on-time delivery.

Other examples of reducing the probability of risks occurring are scheduling outdoor work during the summer months, investing in up-front safety training, and choosing high-quality materials and equipment.

When the concerns are that duration and costs have been underestimated, managers will augment estimates to compensate for the uncertainties. It is common to use a ratio between old and new projects to adjust time or cost. The ratio typically serves as a constant. For example, if past projects have taken 10 minutes per line of computer code, a constant of 1.10 (which represents a 10 percent increase) would be used for the proposed project time estimates because the new project is more difficult than prior projects.

An alternative mitigation strategy is to reduce the impact of the risk if it occurs. For example, a bridge-building project illustrates risk reduction. A new bridge project for a coastal port was to use an innovative, continuous cement-pouring process developed by an Australian firm to save large sums of money and time. The major risk was that the continuous pouring process for each major section of the bridge could not be interrupted. Any interruption would require that the whole cement section (hundreds of cubic yards) be torn down and started over. An assessment of possible risks centered on the delivery of the cement from the cement factory. Trucks could be delayed, or the factory could break down. Such risks would result in tremendous rework costs and delays. Risk was reduced by having two additional portable cement plants built nearby on different highways within 20 miles of the bridge project in case the main factory supply was interrupted. These two portable plants carried raw materials for a whole bridge section, and extra trucks were on immediate standby each time continuous pouring was required. Similar risk reduction scenarios are apparent in system and software development projects where parallel innovation processes are used in case one fails.

In the project management lexicon, *mitigating a risk* refers to a very specific strategy of reducing the probability and/or impact of the threat. However, in any everyday language, *mitigating* refers to any action that reduces or diminishes a risk, which could include the other following responses.

Snapshot from Practice 7.3: From Dome to Dust details the steps Controlled Demolition took to minimize damage when they imploded the Seattle Kingdome.

Avoiding Risk

Avoiding risk is changing the project plan to eliminate the risk or condition. Although it is impossible to eliminate all risk events, some specific risks may be avoided before you launch the project. For example, adopting proven technology instead of experimental technology can eliminate technical failure. Choosing an Australian supplier as opposed to a Ukraine supplier would virtually eliminate the chance that political unrest would disrupt the supply of critical materials. Likewise, one could eliminate the risk of choosing the wrong software by developing web applications using both Java and PHP. Choosing to move a concert indoors would eliminate the threat of inclement weather.

Transferring Risk

Transferring risk to another party is common; this transfer does not change risk. Passing risk to another party almost always results in paying a premium for this exemption. Fixed-price contracts are the classic example of transferring risk from an owner to a contractor. The contractor understands her firm will pay for any risk event that materializes; therefore, a monetary risk factor is added to the contract bid price. Before deciding to transfer risk, the owner should decide which party can best control activities that would lead to the risk occurring. Also, is the contractor capable of absorbing the risk? Clearly identifying and documenting responsibility for absorbing risk is imperative.

Another, more obvious way to transfer risk is insurance. However, in most cases, this is impractical because defining the project risk event and conditions to an insurance broker who is unfamiliar with the project is difficult and usually expensive. Of course, low-probability and high-consequence risk events such as acts of God

SNAPSHOT FROM PRACTICE 7.3 From Dome to Dust*

On March 26, 2000, the largest concrete domed structure in the world was reduced to a pile of rubble in a dramatic implosion lasting less than 20 seconds. According to Mark Loizeaux, whose Maryland-based Controlled Demolition Inc. was hired to bring the 24-year-old Seattle Kingdome down, "We don't blow things up. We use explosives as an engine, but gravity is the catalyst that will bring it down."

Dan Levine/Getty Images

Destroying the Kingdome was the most complicated of the 7,000 demolitions Loizeaux's company had undertaken. Nearly three months of preparations were needed to implode the dome, at a total cost of $9 million. The Kingdome was considered to be one of the strongest structures in the world, containing over 25,000 tons of concrete, with each of its 40 vaulted ribs incorporating seven lengths of 2¼-inch reinforcing steel bar.

Strands of orange detonating cord—basically dynamite in a string that explodes at the lightning pace of 24,000 feet per second—connected six pielike divisions of the Kingdome to a nearby control center.

Throughout each section, Controlled Demolition workers drilled nearly 1,000 holes and packed them with high-velocity gelatin explosives the size of hot dogs. Large charges were placed about one-third of the way up each dome rib; smaller charges were put farther up the ribs. When the detonation button was pushed, blasting caps set off a chain reaction of explosions in each section, reducing the stadium to rubble.

While the actual implosion was a technical tour-de-force, risk management was a critical part of the project's success. To minimize damage to surrounding buildings, the explosive charges were wrapped in a layer of chain-link fencing covered with thick sheets of geotextile polypropylene fabric to contain flying concrete. Nearby buildings were protected in various manners depending on the structure and proximity to the Dome. Measures included sealing air-handling units, taping seams on doors and windows, covering floors and windows with plywood, and draping reinforced polyethylene sheeting around the outside.

To help absorb the impact, air-conditioning units removed from the interior were stacked with other materials to create a barrier around the perimeter of the work area.

Hundreds of police officers and security personnel were used to cordon off an area extending roughly 1,000 feet from the Dome from overzealous spectators. Traffic was closed for a larger area. Accommodations were provided for people and pets who lived within the restricted zone.

Eight water trucks, eight sweeper units, and more than 100 workers were deployed immediately after the blast to control dust and begin the cleanup.

As a side note, one-third of the concrete was crushed and used in the foundation of a new $430-million outdoor football stadium, which was built in its place. The rest of the concrete was carted away and used in roadbeds and foundations throughout the Seattle area.

**New York Times* Sunday magazine, March 19, 2000; wwwseattletimes.com, March 27, 2000.

are more easily defined and insured. Performance bonds, warranties, and guarantees are other financial instruments used to transfer risk.

On large, international construction projects like petrochemical plants and oil refineries, host countries are insisting on contracts that enforce Build-Own-Operate-Transfer (BOOT) provisions. Here the prime project organization is expected not only to build the facility but also to take over ownership until its operation capacity has been proven and all the debugging has occurred before final transfer of ownership to the client. In such cases, the host country has transferred financial risk of ownership until the project has been completed and capabilities are proven.

Escalating Risk

Escalating risk occurs when the project encounters a threat that is outside the scope of the project or the authority of the project manager. In such cases, the response should be to notify the appropriate people within the organization of the threat. For example, while working on a high-tech product, an engineer discovers through informal channels that a competitor is developing an alternative energy source. While this would not impact the current project, it may have significant implications for future products. The project manager would forward this information to the product manager and head of R&D. In another example, informal discussions with team members reveal widespread dissatisfaction with pay and benefits among staff across the company. This threat would be *escalated* to the Human Resource Department. Escalated risks are not monitored further by the project team.

Retaining Risk

Retaining risk occurs when a conscious decision is made to accept the risk of an event occurring. Some risks are so large it is not feasible to consider transferring or reducing the event (e.g., an earthquake). The project owner assumes the risk because the chance of such an event occurring is slim. In other cases, risks identified in the budget reserve can simply be absorbed if they materialize. The risk is retained by developing a contingency plan to implement if the risk materializes. In a few cases a risk event can be ignored and a cost overrun accepted, should the risk event occur.

People vary in their risk tolerance. Before deciding how to respond to a risk, one should consider the *risk appetite* of key stakeholders as well as your team.

7.5 Contingency Planning

LO 7-5

Understand the role contingency plans play in the risk management process.

A **contingency plan** is an alternative plan that will be used if a possible foreseen risk event becomes a reality. The contingency plan represents actions that will reduce or mitigate the negative impact of the risk event. A key distinction between a risk response and a contingency plan is that a response is part of the actual implementation plan and action is taken before the risk can materialize, while a contingency plan is not part of the initial implementation plan and only goes into effect after the risk is recognized.

Like all plans, the contingency plan answers the questions of what, where, when, and how much action will take place. The absence of a contingency plan, when a risk event occurs, can cause a manager to delay or postpone the decision to implement a remedy. This postponement can lead to panic and acceptance of the first remedy suggested. Such after-the-event decision making under pressure can be dangerous and costly. Contingency planning evaluates alternative remedies for possible foreseen events before the risk event occurs and selects the best plan among alternatives. This early contingency planning facilitates a smooth transition to the remedy or work-around plan. The availability of a contingency plan can significantly increase the chances for project success.

Conditions for activating the implementation of the contingency plan should be decided and clearly documented. The plan should include a cost estimate and identify the source of funding. All parties affected should agree to the contingency plan and have authority to make commitments. Because implementation of a contingency plan embodies disruption in the sequence of work, all contingency plans should be communicated to team members so that surprise and resistance are minimized.

Here is an example: A high-tech niche computer company intends to introduce a new "platform" product at a very specific target date. The project's 47 teams all agree delays will not be acceptable. Their contingency plans for two large component suppliers demonstrate how seriously risk management is viewed. One supplier's plant sits on the San Andreas Fault, which is prone to earthquakes. The contingency plan has an alternative supplier, who is constantly updated, producing a replica of the component in another plant. Another key supplier in Toronto, Canada, presents a delivery risk on their due date because of potential bad weather. This contingency plan calls for a chartered plane (already contracted to be on standby) if overland transportation presents a delay problem. To outsiders, these plans must seem a bit extreme, but in high-tech industries where time to market is king, risks of identified events are taken seriously.

Risk response matrices such as the one shown in Figure 7.8 are useful for summarizing how the project team plans to manage risks that have been identified. Again, the OS upgrade project is used to illustrate this kind of matrix. The first step is to identify whether to mitigate, avoid, transfer, escalate, or retain the risk. The team decides to reduce the chances of the system freezing by experimenting with a prototype of the system. Prototype experimentation not only allows them to identify and fix conversion "bugs" before the actual installation but also yields information that could be useful in enhancing acceptance by end users. The project team is then able to identify and document changes between the old and new systems that will be incorporated into the training the users receive. The risk of equipment malfunction is transferred by choosing a reliable supplier with a strong warranty program.

The next step is to identify contingency plans in case the risk still occurs. For example, if interface problems prove insurmountable, then the team will attempt a workaround until vendor experts arrive to help solve the problem. If the system freezes after installation, the team will first try to reinstall the software. If user dissatisfaction is high, then the Information Systems (IS) Department will provide more staff support. If the team is unable to get reliable equipment from the original supplier, then it will order a different brand from a second dealer. The team also needs to discuss and agree what would "trigger" implementation of the contingency plan. In the case of the system freezing, the trigger is not being able to unfreeze the system within one hour or, in the case of user backlash, an angry call from top management. Finally, the individual responsible for monitoring the potential risk and initiating the contingency plan needs to be assigned. Smart project managers establish protocols for contingency responses before they are needed. For an example of the importance of establishing protocols, see Snapshot from Practice 7.4: Risk Management at the Top of the World.

FIGURE 7.8 Risk Response Matrix

Risk Event	Response	Contingency Plan	Trigger	Who Is Responsible
Interface problems	Mitigate: Test prototype	Work around until help comes	Not solved within 24 hours	Nils
System freezing	Mitigate: Test prototype	Reinstall OS	Still frozen after one hour	Emmylou
User backlash	Mitigate: Prototype demonstration	Increase staff support	Call from top management	Eddie
Equipment malfunctions	Mitigate: Select reliable vendor Transfer: Warranty	Order replacement	Equipment fails	Jim

SNAPSHOT FROM PRACTICE 7.4 Risk Management at the Top of the World*

The gripping account in the 2015 film *Everest* of an ill-fated attempt to climb Mount Everest in which six climbers died provides testimony to the risks of extreme mountain climbing.

Accounts of Mount Everest expeditions provide insights into project risk management. First, most climbers spend more than three weeks acclimating their bodies to high-altitude conditions. Native Sherpas are used extensively to carry supplies and set up each of the four base camps that will be used during the final stages of the climb. To reduce the impact of hypoxia, lightheadedness, and disorientation caused by shortage of oxygen, most climbers use oxygen masks and bottles during the final ascent. If lucky enough not to be one of the first expeditions of the season, the path to the summit should be staked out and roped by previous climbers. Climbing guides receive last-minute weather reports by radio to confirm whether the weather conditions warrant the risk. Finally, for added insurance, most climbers join their Sherpas in an elaborate *puja* ritual intended to summon the divine support of the gods before beginning their ascent.

Daniel Prudek/123RF

All of these efforts pale next to the sheer physical and mental rigors of making the final climb from base camp IV to the summit. This is what climbers refer to as the "death zone" because beyond 26,000 feet the mind and body begin to quickly deteriorate despite supplemental oxygen. Under fair conditions, it takes around 18 hours to make the round-trip to the top and back to the base camp. Climbers leave as early as 1:00 a.m. in order to make it back before night falls and total exhaustion sets in.

The greatest danger in climbing Mount Everest is not in reaching the summit but in making it back to the base camp. One out of every five climbers who make it to the summit dies during their descent. The key is establishing a contingency plan in case the climbers encounter hard going or the weather changes. Guides establish a predetermined turnaround time (e.g., 2:00 p.m.) to ensure a safe return no matter how close the climbers are to the summit. Many lives have been lost by failing to adhere to the turnaround time and pushing forward to the summit. As one climber put it, "With enough determination, any bloody idiot can get to the top of the hill. The trick is to get back alive."

One climber who faced the 2:00 p.m. deadline was Goran Krupp. After cycling 8,000 miles from Stockholm to Katmandu he turned back 1,000 feet from the summit.

*B. Coburn, *Everest: Mountain without Mercy* (New York: National Geographic Society, 1997); J. Krakauer, *Into Thin Air* (New York: Doubleday, 1997), p. 190.

Some of the most common methods for handling risk are discussed in the following sections.

Technical Risks

Technical risks are problematic; they can often be the kind that cause the project to be shut down. What if the system or process does not work? Contingency plans are made for those possibilities that are foreseen. For example, Carrier Transicold was involved in developing a new Phoenix refrigeration unit for truck-trailer applications. This new unit was to use rounded panels made of bonded metals, which at the time was new technology for Transicold. Furthermore, one of its competitors had tried unsuccessfully to incorporate similar bonded metals into the products. The project team was eager to make the new technology work, but it wasn't until the very end of the project that they were able to get the new adhesives to bond adequately to complete the project. Throughout the project, the team maintained a welded-panel fabrication approach just in case they were unsuccessful. If this contingency approach had been needed, it would have increased production costs, but the project still would have been completed on time.

In addition to backup strategies, project managers need to develop methods to quickly assess whether technical uncertainties can be resolved. The use of sophisticated computer-aided design (CAD) software has greatly helped resolve design problems. At the same time, Smith and Reinertsen (1995), in their book *Developing Products in Half the Time,* argue that there is no substitute for making something and seeing how it works, feels, or looks. They suggest that one should first identify the high-risk technical areas, then build models or design experiments to resolve the risk as quickly as possible. Technology offers many methods for early testing and validation, ranging from 3-D printing and holographic imagery for model building to focus groups and early design usability testing for market testing (Thamhain, 2013). By isolating and testing the key technical questions early in a project, project feasibility can be quickly determined and necessary adjustments made, such as reworking the process or in some cases closing down the project.[3]

Schedule Risks

Often, organizations will defer the threat of a project coming in late until it surfaces. Here, contingency funds are set aside to expedite or "crash" the project to get it back on track. Crashing, or reducing project duration, is accomplished by shortening (compressing) one or more activities on the critical path. This comes with additional costs and risk. Techniques for managing this situation are discussed in Chapter 9. Some contingency plans can avoid costly procedures. For example, schedules can be altered by working activities in parallel or using start-to-start lag relationships. Also, using the best people for high-risk tasks can relieve or lessen the chance of some risk events occurring.

Cost Risks

Projects of long duration need some contingency for price changes—which are usually upward. The important point to remember when reviewing price is to avoid the trap of using one lump sum to cover price risks. For example, if inflation has been running about 3 percent, some managers add 3 percent for all resources used in the project. This lump-sum approach does not address exactly where price protection is needed and fails to provide for tracking and control. On cost-sensitive projects, price risks should be evaluated item by item. Some purchases and contracts will not change over the life of the project. Those that may change should be identified and estimates made of the magnitude of change. This approach ensures control of the contingency funds as the project is implemented.

Funding Risks

What if the funding for the project is cut by 25 percent or completion projections indicate that costs will greatly exceed available funds? What are the chances of the project

[3] This is a key principle of Agile project management, which is discussed in Chapter 15.

being canceled before completion? Seasoned project managers recognize that a complete risk assessment must include an evaluation of funding supply. This is especially true for publicly funded projects. Case in point was the ill-fated ARH-70 Arapaho helicopter being developed for the U.S. Army by Bell Aircraft. Over $300 million had been invested to develop a new-age combat and reconnaissance helicopter, when in October 2008 the Defense Department recommended that the project be canceled. The cancellation reflected a need to cut costs and a switch toward using unmanned aircraft for surveillance as well as attack missions.

Just as government projects are subject to changes in strategy and political agenda, business firms frequently undergo changes in priorities and top management. The pet projects of the new CEO replace the pet projects of the former CEO. Resources become tight, and one way to fund new projects is to cancel other projects.

Severe budget cuts or lack of adequate funding can have a devastating effect on a project. Typically when such a fate occurs, there is a need to scale back the scope of the project to what is possible. "All-or-nothing projects" are ripe targets to budget cutters. This was the case of the Arapaho helicopter once the decision was made to move away from staffed reconnaissance aircraft. Here, the "chunkability" of the project can be an advantage. For example, freeway projects can fall short of the original intentions but still add value for each mile completed.

On a much smaller scale, similar funding risks may exist for more mundane projects. For example, a building contractor may find that due to a sudden downturn in the stock market, the owners can no longer afford to build their dream house. Or, an IS consulting firm may be left empty handed when a client files for bankruptcy. In the former case, the contractor may have as a contingency selling the house on the open market, while unfortunately, the consulting firm will have to join the long line of creditors.

7.6 Opportunity Management

LO 7-6

Understand opportunity management and describe the five approaches to responding to opportunities in a project.

For the sake of brevity, this chapter has focused on negative risks—what can go wrong on a project. There is a flip side—what can go right on a project. This is commonly referred to as a positive risk or an opportunity. An **opportunity** is an event that can have a positive impact on project objectives. For example, unusually favorable weather can accelerate construction work, or a drop in fuel prices may create savings that could be used to add value to a project. Essentially the same process that is used to manage negative risks is applied to positive risks. Opportunities are identified, assessed in terms of likelihood and impact, responses are determined, and even contingency plans and funds can be established to take advantage of the opportunity if it occurs. The major exception between managing negative risks and opportunity is in the responses. The project management profession has identified five types of responses to an opportunity[4]:

Exploit. This tactic seeks to eliminate the uncertainty associated with an opportunity to ensure that it definitely happens. Examples include assigning your best personnel to a critical burst activity to reduce the time to completion and revising a design to enable a component to be purchased rather than developed internally.

Share. This strategy involves allocating some or all of the ownership of an opportunity to another party who is best able to capture the opportunity for the benefit of the project. Examples include continuous improvement incentives for external contractors and joint ventures.

[4] *Process Groups: A Practice Guide* (Newtown Square, PA: Project Management Institute, 2023), pp. 259–260.

Enhance. Enhance is the opposite of mitigate in that action is taken to increase the probability and/or the positive impact of an opportunity. Examples include choosing a site location based on favorable weather patterns and choosing raw materials that are likely to decline in price.

Escalate. Sometimes projects encounter opportunities that are outside the scope of the project or exceed the authority of the project manager. In such cases, the project manager should notify the appropriate people within the organization of the opportunity. For example, a customer is considering adapting the product to a different market and wonders whether the project manager would be interested in bidding on the work. The opportunity is passed upward to the project sponsor. Or through the course of project interactions, the project manager discovers an alternative supplier for a key component. This information would be passed on to the Procurement Department.

Accept. Accepting an opportunity is willing to take advantage of it if it occurs, but not taking action to pursue it.

While it is only natural to focus on negative risks, it is sound practice to engage in active opportunity management as well. Sometimes necessity creates a search for opportunities. For example, Ocean Fresh, a popular seafood restaurant on the Oregon Coast, like other establishments closed its doors for months during the COVID-19 pandemic. Facing dire financial difficulties, the staff launched project "Dock Box." The cooking staff would package prepared meals of popular seafood dishes and deliver them twice a week to nearby cities in Oregon. Everything was freshly cut, measured for use and with foolproof instructions. Even one of the authors was able to create a gourmet seafood dish! Meals were described and ordered online with centralized pickup spots twice a week in four Oregon locales. Customer demand exceeded expectations. Ocean Fresh went from a minimal local takeout business to selling 700+ meals every Wednesday and Friday in Oregon. Dock Box continues to be a vital part of the restaurant's business today.

7.7 Contingency Funding and Time Buffers

LO 7-7

Understand how contingency funds and time buffers are used to manage risks on a project.

Contingency funds are established to cover project risks—identified and unknown. When, where, and how much money will be spent are not known until the risk event occurs. Project "owners" are often reluctant to set up project contingency funds that seem to imply the project plan might be a poor one. Some perceive the contingency fund as an add-on slush fund. Others say they will face the risk when it materializes. Usually, such reluctance to establish reserve funds can be overcome with documented risk identification, assessment, contingency plans, and plans for when and how funds will be disbursed.

The size and amount of contingency funds depend on uncertainty inherent in the project. Uncertainty is reflected in the "newness" of the project, inaccurate time and cost estimates, technical unknowns, unstable scope, and problems not anticipated. In practice, contingencies run from 1 to 10 percent in projects similar to past projects. However, in unique and high-technology projects, it is not uncommon to find contingencies running in the 20–60 percent range. Use and rate of consumption of reserves must be closely monitored and controlled. Simply picking a percentage of the baseline—say, 5 percent—and calling it the contingency reserve is not a sound approach. Also, adding up all the identified contingency allotments and throwing them into one pot is not conducive to sound control of the reserve fund.

In practice, the contingency fund is typically divided into contingency and management reserve funds for control purposes. **Contingency reserves** are set up to cover identified risks; these reserves are allocated to specific segments or deliverables of the project. **Management reserves** are set up to cover unidentified risks and are allocated to risks associated with the total project. The risks are separated because their use requires approval from different levels of project authority. Because all risks are probabilistic, the reserves are not included in the baseline for each work package or activity; they are only activated when a risk occurs. If an identified risk does not occur and its chance of occurring is past, the fund allocated to the risk should be deducted from the contingency reserves. (This removes the temptation to use contingency reserves for other issues or problems.) Of course, if the risk does occur, funds are removed from the reserve and added to the cost baseline.

It is important that contingency allowances be independent of the original time and cost estimates. These allowances need to be clearly distinguished to avoid time and budget game playing.

Contingency Reserves

These reserves are identified for specific work packages or segments of a project found in the baseline budget or work breakdown structure. For example, a reserve amount might be added to "computer coding" to cover the risk of "testing" showing a coding problem. The reserve amount is determined by costing out the accepted contingency or recovery plan. The contingency reserves should be communicated to the project team. This openness suggests trust and encourages good cost performance. However, distributing contingency reserves should be the responsibility of both the project manager and the team members responsible for implementing the specific segment of the project. If the risk does not materialize, the funds are removed from the contingency reserves. Thus, contingency reserves decrease as the project progresses.

Management Reserves

These reserve funds are needed to cover major unforeseen risks and, hence, are applied to the total project. For example, a major scope change may appear necessary midway in the project. Because this change was not anticipated, it is covered from the management reserves. Management reserves are established *after* contingency reserves are identified and funds are established. These reserves are independent of contingency reserves and are controlled by the project manager and the "owner" of the project. The "owner" can be internal (top management) or external to the project organization. Most management reserves are set using historical data and judgments concerning the uniqueness and complexity of the project.

Placing technical contingencies in the management reserves is a special case. Identifying possible technical (functional) risks is often associated with a new, untried, innovative process or product. Because there is a chance the innovation may not work out, a fallback plan is necessary. This type of risk is beyond the control of the project manager. Hence, technical reserves are held in the management reserves and controlled by the owner or top management. The owner and project manager decide when the contingency plan will be implemented and the management reserve funds used. It is assumed there is a high probability these funds will never be used.

Table 7.1 shows the development of a budget estimate for a hypothetical project. Note how contingency and management reserves are kept separate; control is easily tracked using this format.

TABLE 7.1
Budget Estimate

Activity	Budget Baseline	Contingency Reserve	Project Budget
Design	$ 500,000	$15,000	$ 515,000
Code	900,000	80,000	980,000
Test	20,000	2,000	22,000
Subtotal	$1,420,000	$97,000	$1,517,000
Management reserve	—	—	50,000
Total	$1,420,000	$97,000	$1,567,000

Time Buffers

Just as contingency funds are established to absorb unplanned costs, managers use **time buffers** to cushion against potential delays in the project. And like contingency funds, the amount of time is dependent upon the inherent uncertainty of the project. The more uncertain the project is, the more time should be reserved for the schedule. The strategy is to assign extra time at critical moments in the project. For example, buffers are added to:

A. Activities with severe risks.

B. Merge activities that are prone to delays due to one or more preceding activities being late.

C. Noncritical activities to reduce the likelihood that they will create another critical path.

D. Activities that require scarce resources to ensure that the resources are available when needed.

In the face of overall schedule uncertainty, buffers are sometimes added to the end of the project. For example, a 300-working-day project may have a 30-day project buffer. While the extra 30 days would not appear on the schedule, they are available if needed. Like management reserves, this buffer typically requires the authorization of top management. A more systematic approach to buffer management is discussed in the Chapter 8 appendix on critical-chain project management.

7.8 Step 4: Risk Response Control

LO 7-8

Recognize the need for risk management being an ongoing activity.

Typically the results of the first three steps of the risk management process are summarized in a formal document often called the risk register. A **risk register** details all identified risks, including descriptions, category, probability of occurring, impact, responses, contingency plans, owners, and current status. The register is the backbone for the last step in the risk management process: risk control. Risk control involves executing the risk response strategy, monitoring triggering events, initiating contingency plans, and watching for new risks. Establishing a change management system to deal with events that require formal changes in the scope, budget, and/or schedule of the project is an essential element of risk control.

Project managers need to monitor risks just as they track project progress. Risk assessment and updating need to be part of every status meeting and progress report system. The project team needs to be on constant alert for new, unforeseen risks. Thamhain (2013) studied 35 major product development efforts and found that over half of the contingencies that occurred were not anticipated! Readiness to respond to the unexpected is a critical element of risk management.

Management needs to be sensitive that others may not be forthright in acknowledging new risks and problems. Admitting that there might be a bug in the design code or that different components are not compatible reflects poorly on individual performance. If the prevailing organizational culture is one where mistakes are punished severely, then it is only human nature to protect oneself. Similarly, if bad news is greeted harshly and there is a propensity to "kill the messenger," then participants will be reluctant to speak freely. The tendency to suppress bad news is compounded when individual responsibility is vague and the project team is under extreme pressure from top management to get the project done quickly and within budget.

Project managers need to establish an environment in which participants feel comfortable raising concerns and admitting mistakes (Browning & Ramasesh, 2015). The norm should be that mistakes are acceptable and hiding mistakes is intolerable. Problems should be embraced, not denied. Participants should be encouraged to identify problems and new risks. A positive attitude by the project manager toward risks is key.

On large, complex projects, it may be prudent to repeat the risk identification/assessment exercise with fresh information. Risk profiles should be reviewed to test if the original responses held true. Relevant stakeholders should be brought into the discussion and the risk register needs to be updated. While this may not be practical on an ongoing basis, project managers should touch base with them on a regular basis or hold special stakeholder meetings to review the status of risks on the project.

A second key for controlling the cost of risks is documenting responsibility. This can be problematic in projects involving multiple organizations and contractors. Responsibility for risk is frequently passed on to others with the statement "That is not my worry." This mentality is dangerous. Each identified risk should be assigned (or shared) by mutual agreement of the owner, project manager, and the contractor or person having line responsibility for the work package or segment of the project. It is best to have the line person responsible approve the use of contingency reserves and monitor their rate of usage. If management reserves are required, the line person should play an active role in estimating additional costs and funds needed to complete the project. Having line personnel participate in the process focuses attention on the management reserves, control of their rate of usage, and early warning of potential risk events. If risk management is not formalized, responsibility and responses to risk will be ignored.

The bottom line is that project managers and team members need to be vigilant in monitoring potential risks and should identify new land mines that could derail a project. Risk assessment has to be part of the working agenda of status meetings, and when new risks emerge they need to be analyzed and incorporated into the risk management process.

7.9 Change Control Management

LO 7-9

Describe the change control process.

A major element of the risk control process is change management. Not every detail of a project plan will materialize as expected. Coping with and controlling project changes present a formidable challenge for most project managers. Changes come from many sources, such as the project customer, owner, project manager, team members, and risk events. Most changes easily fall into three categories:

1. Scope changes in the form of design or additions represent big changes—for example, customer requests for a new feature or a redesign that will improve the product.
2. Implementation of contingency plans, when risk events occur, represents changes in baseline costs and schedules.
3. Improvement changes suggested by project team members represent another category.

Because change is inevitable, a well-defined change review and control process should be set up early in the project planning cycle.

Change management systems involve reporting, controlling, and recording changes to the project baseline. (Note: Some organizations consider change control systems part of configuration management.) In practice, most change management systems are designed to accomplish the following.

1. Identify proposed changes.
2. List expected effects of proposed change(s) on schedule and budget.
3. Review, evaluate, and approve or disapprove changes formally.
4. Negotiate and resolve conflicts of change, conditions, and cost.
5. Communicate changes to the parties affected.
6. Assign responsibility for implementing change.
7. Adjust the master schedule and budget.
8. Track all changes that are to be implemented.

As part of the project communication plan, stakeholders define up front the communication and decision-making process that will be used to evaluate and accept changes. The process can be captured in a flow diagram like the one in Figure 7.9. On small projects, this process may simply entail approval of a small group of stakeholders. On larger projects, more elaborate decision-making processes are established, with different processes being used for different kinds of change. For example, changes in performance requirements may require multiple sign-offs, including the project sponsor and client, while switching suppliers may be authorized by the project manager. Regardless of the nature of the project, the goal is to establish the process for introducing necessary changes in the project in a timely and effective manner.

FIGURE 7.9
Change Control Process

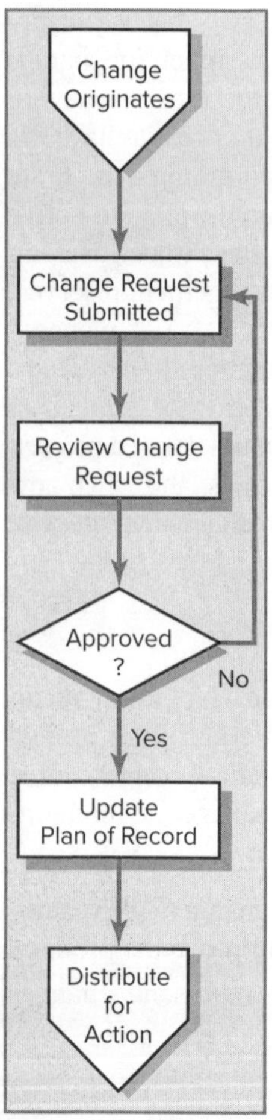

Of particular importance is assessing the impact of the change on the project. Often, solutions to immediate problems have adverse consequences on other aspects of a project. For example, self-driving software systems have been and will continue to be prototyped in order to identify anomalous driving scenarios/situations and to respond correctly to them so as to avoid accidents. It is important that the implications of changes are assessed by people with appropriate expertise and perspective. On construction projects, this is often the responsibility of the architecture firm, while "software architects" perform a similar function in software development efforts.

Organizations use change request forms and logs to track proposed changes. An example of a simplified change request form is depicted in Figure 7.10. Typically change request forms include a description of the change, the impact of not approving the change, the impact of the change on project scope/schedule/cost, and defined signature paths for review, as well as a tracking log number.

An abridged version of a change request log for a construction project is presented in Figure 7.11. These logs are used to monitor change requests. They typically summarize the status of all outstanding change requests and include such useful information as the source and date of the change, document codes for related information, cost estimates, and the current status of the request.

Every approved change must be identified and integrated into the plan of record through changes in the project WBS and baseline schedule. The plan of record is the current official plan for the project in terms of scope, budget, and schedule. The plan of record serves as a change management benchmark for future change requests as well as the baseline for evaluating project progress.

If the change control system is not integrated with the WBS and baseline, project plans and control will soon self-destruct. Thus, one of the keys to a successful change

FIGURE 7.10
Sample Change Request

Project name *Irish/Chinese culture exchange*
Project sponsor *Irish embassy*
Request number *12*
Date *June 6, 2xxx*
Originator *Jennifer McDonald*
Change requested by *Chinese culture office*

Description of requested change

1. *Request river dancers to replace a small Irish dance group.*
2. *Request one combination dance with river dancers and China ballet group.*

Reason for change

River dancers will enhance stature of event. The group is well known and loved by Chinese people.

Areas of impact of proposed change–describe each on separate sheet

- [X] Scope
- [X] Cost
- [ ] Other ________
- [ ] Schedule
- [ ] Risk

Disposition	Priority	Funding Source
[ ] Approve	[ ] Emergency	[ ] Mgmt. reserves
[X] Approve as amended	[X] Urgent	[ ] Contingency reserves
[ ] Disapprove	[ ] Low	[X] Customer
[ ] Deferred		[ ] Other

Sign-off Approvals

Project manager	*William O'Mally*	Date	*June 12, 2xxx*
Project sponsor	*Kenneth Thompson*	Date	*June 13, 2xxx*
Project customer	*Hong Lee*	Date	*June 18, 2xxx*
Other	________	Date	________

control process is document, document, document! The benefits derived from change control systems are the following.

1. Inconsequential changes are discouraged by the formal process.
2. Costs of changes are maintained in a log.
3. Integrity of the WBS and performance measures is maintained.
4. Allocation and use of contingency and management reserves are tracked.
5. Responsibility for implementation is clarified.
6. Effect of changes is visible to all parties involved.
7. Implementation of change is monitored.
8. Scope changes will be quickly reflected in baseline and performance measures.

FIGURE 7.11 Change Request Log

Owner Requested Change Status Report—Open Items							OSU—Weatherford
			Dates				
Rc#	Description	Reference Document	Date Rec'd	Date Submit	Amount	Status	Comments
51	Sewer work offset				−188,129	OPEN	FUNDING FROM OTHER SOURCE
52	Stainless Plates at restroom Shower Valves	ASI 56	1/5/2020	3/30/2020	9,308	APPROVED	
53	Waterproofing Options	ASI 77	1/13/2020		169,386	OPEN	
54	Change Electrical floor box spec change	RFI 113	12/5/2020	3/29/2020	2,544	SUBMIT	
55	VE Option for Style and rail doors	Door samples	1/14/2020		−20,000	ROM	
56	Pressure Wash C̄ tower	Owner request	3/15/2020	3/30/2020	14,861	SUBMIT	
57	Fire Lite glass in stairs	Owner request			8,000	QUOTE	ROM BASED ON FIRELITE NT
58	Cyber Café added tele /OFOI equipment	ASI 65	1/30/2020	3/29/2020	4,628	APPROVED	
59	Additional Dampers in C wing	ASI 68	2/4/2020	3/29/2020	1,085	SUBMIT	
60	Revise Corridor ceilings	ASI 72	2/13/2020	3/31/2020	−3,755	SUBMIT	

OPEN—Requires estimate
ROM—Rough order magnitude
QUOTE—Subcontractor quotes
SUBMIT—RC letter submitted
APPROVED—RC letter approved
REVISE—RC letter to be reviewed
ASI—Architect's supplemental instructions
RFI—Request for information

Clearly, change control is important and requires that someone or some group be responsible for approving changes, keeping the process updated, and communicating changes to the project team and relevant stakeholders. Project control depends heavily on keeping the change control process current. This historical record can be used for satisfying customer inquiries, identifying problems in post-project audits, and estimating future project costs.

Summary

To put the processes discussed in this chapter in proper perspective, one should recognize that the essence of project management is risk management. Every technique in this book is a risk management technique. Each in its own way tries to prevent something bad from happening. Project selection systems try to reduce the likelihood that projects will not contribute to the mission of the firm. Project scope statements, among other things, are designed to avoid costly misunderstandings and reduce scope creep. Work breakdown structures reduce the likelihood that some vital part of the project will be omitted or that the budget estimates are unrealistic. Team building reduces the likelihood of dysfunctional conflict and breakdowns in coordination. All of the techniques try to increase stakeholder satisfaction and the chances of project success.

From this perspective, managers engage in risk management activities to compensate for the uncertainty inherent in project management and that things never go according to plan. Risk management is proactive, not reactive. It reduces the number of surprises and prepares people for the unexpected.

Although many managers believe that in the final analysis, risk assessment and contingency depend on subjective judgment, some standard methods for identifying, assessing, and responding to risks should be included in all projects. The very process of identifying project risks forces some discipline at all levels of project management and improves project performance.

Contingency plans increase the chance that the project can be completed on time and within budget. Contingency plans can be simple work arounds or elaborate, detailed plans. Responsibility for risks should be clearly identified and documented. It is desirable and prudent to keep a reserve as a hedge against project risks. Contingency reserves are linked to the WBS and should be communicated to the project team. Use of contingency reserves should be closely monitored, controlled, and reviewed throughout the project life cycle. Control of management reserves should remain with the owner, project manager, and line person responsible.

Experience clearly indicates that using a formal, structured process to handle possible foreseen and unforeseen project risk events minimizes surprises, costs, delays, stress, and misunderstandings. Risk management is an iterative process that occurs throughout the lifespan of the project. When risk events occur or changes are necessary, using an effective change control process to quickly approve and record changes will facilitate measuring performance against schedule and cost. Ultimately, successful risk management requires a culture in which threats are embraced, not denied, and problems are identified, not hidden.

Key Terms

Avoiding risk, *263*
Change management system, *274*
Contingency plan, *265*
Contingency reserves, *271*
Escalate opportunity, *270*
Escalating risk, *265*
Management reserves, *271*
Mitigating risk, *262*
Opportunity, *269*
Retaining risk, *265*
Risk, *252*
Risk breakdown structure (RBS), *255*
Risk profile, *256*
Risk register, *272*
Risk severity matrix, *261*
Scenario analysis, *258*
Time buffer, *272*
Transferring risk, *263*

Review Questions

1. Project risks can/cannot be eliminated if the project is carefully planned. Explain.
2. The chances of risk events occurring and their respective costs increasing change over the project life cycle. What is the significance of this phenomenon to a project manager?
3. What is the difference between avoiding a risk and retaining a risk?
4. What is the difference between risk mitigation and contingency planning?
5. Explain the difference between contingency reserves and management reserves.
6. How are the work breakdown structure and change control connected?

7. What are the likely outcomes if a change control process is not used? Why?
8. What are the major differences between managing negative risks and managing positive risks (opportunities)?

SNAPSHOT FROM PRACTICE

Discussion Questions

7.1 *Giant Popsicle Gone Wrong*

1. Does this example support the risk event graph (Figure 7.1)? Explain.

7.2 *Terminal 5—London Heathrow Airport*

1. Why do you think British Airways decided to go fully operational on day 1?
2. How could an RBS like the one featured in Figure 7.3 have prevented the disaster from occurring?

7.3 *From Dome to Dust*

1. What do you think was the greatest risk facing this project?
2. How did Controlled Demolition Inc. respond to the risk?

7.4 *Risk Management at the Top of the World*

1. How important is it for climbers to join their Sherpas in *puja* rituals?
2. Why do climbers not turn back at the designated turnaround time?

Exercises

1. Gather a small team of students. Think of a project most students would understand; the kinds of tasks involved should also be familiar. Identify and assess major and minor risks inherent in the project. Decide on a response type. Develop a contingency plan for two to four identified risks. Estimate costs. Assign contingency reserves. How much reserve would your team estimate for the whole project? Justify your choices and estimates.
2. You have been assigned to a project risk team of five members. Because this is the first time your organization has formally set up a risk team for a project, it is hoped that your team will develop a process that can be used on all future projects. Your first team meeting is next Monday morning. Each team member has been asked to prepare for the meeting by developing, in as much detail as possible, an outline that describes how you believe the team should proceed in handling project risks. Each of the team members will hand out their proposed outline at the beginning of the meeting. Your outline should include but not be limited to the following information:
   a. Team objectives.
   b. Process for handling risk events.
   c. Team activities.
   d. Team outputs.
3. Search the Web using the key words "best practices, project management." What did you find? How might this information be useful to a project manager?

References

Atkinson, W., "Beyond the Basics," *PM Network,* May 2003, pp. 38–43.

Avery, G. *Project Management, Denial and the Death Zone* (Plantation, FL: J. Ross Publishing, 2016).

Baker, B., and R. Menon, "Politics and Project Performance: The Fourth Dimension of Project Management," *PM Network,* November 1995, pp. 16–21.

Browning, T., and R. V. Ramasesh, "Reducing Unwelcome Surprises in Project Management," *Sloan Management Review,* Spring 2015, pp. 53–62.

Carr, M. J., S. L. Konda, I. Monarch, F. C. Ulrich, and C. F. Walker, "Taxonomy-Based Risk Identification," *Technical Report CMU/SEI-93-TR 6,* Software Engineering Institute, Carnegie Mellon University, Pittsburgh, 1993.

Ford, E. C., J. Duncan, A. G. Bedeian, P. M. Ginter, M. D. Rousculp, and A. M. Adams, "Mitigating Risks, Visible Hands, Inevitable Disasters, and Soft Variables: Management Research That Matters to Managers," *Academy of Management Executive,* vol. 19, no. 4 (November 2005), pp. 24–38.

Gray, C. F., and R. Reinman, "PERT Simulation: A Dynamic Approach to the PERT Technique," *Journal of Systems Management,* March 1969, pp. 18–23.

Hamburger, D. H., "The Project Manager: Risk Taker and Contingency Planner," *Project Management Journal,* vol. 21, no. 4 (1990), pp. 11–16.

Hillson, D., "Risk Escalation," projectmanagement.com, November 1, 2016. Accessed 9/20/18.

Hulett, D. T., "Project Schedule Risk Assessment," *Project Management Journal,* vol. 26, no. 1 (1995), pp. 21–31.

Meyer, A. D., C. H. Loch, and M. T. Pich, "Managing Project Uncertainty: From Variation to Chaos," *MIT Sloan Management Review,* Winter 2002, pp. 60–67.

Orlando Sentinel, "Math Mistake Proved Fatal to Mars Orbiter," November 23, 1999.

Pavlik, A., "Project Troubleshooting: Tiger Teams for Reactive Risk Management," *Project Management Journal,* vol. 35, no. 4 (December 2004), pp. 5–14.

Pinto, J. K., *Project Management: Achieving Competitive Advantage* (Upper Saddle River, NJ: Pearson, 2007).

Project Management Institute, *A Guide to the Project Management Body of Knowledge (PMBOK Guide),* 6th edition, (Newtown Square, PA: Project Management Institute, 2017).

Project Management Institute, *Process Groups: A Practice Guide,* (Newtown Square, PA: Project Management Institute, 2023).

Schuler, J. R., "Decision Analysis in Projects: Monte Carlo Simulation," *PM Network,* January 1994, pp. 30–36.

Skelton, T., and H. Thamhain, "Managing Risk in New Product Development Projects: Beyond Analytical Methods," *Project Perspectives,* vol. 27, no. 1 (2006), pp. 12–20.

Skelton, T., and H. Thamhain, "Success Factors for Effective R&D Risk Management," *International Journal of Technology Intelligence and Planning,* vol. 3, no. 4 (2007), pp. 376–86.

Smith, P. G., and D. G. Reinertsen, *Developing Products in Half the Time* (New York: Van Nostrand Reinhold, 1995).

Snizek, J. A., and R. A. Henry, "Accuracy and Confidence in Group Judgment," *Organizational Behavior and Human Decision Processes,* vol. 4, no. 3 (1989), pp. 1–28.

Thamhain, H., "Managing Risks in Complex Projects," *Project Management Journal,* vol. 44, no. 20 (2013), pp. 20–35.

Willumsen, P. L., J. Oehmen, V. Stingl, and J. Geraldi, "Value Creation Through Project Risk Management," *International Journal of Project Management,* vol 37, no. 5 (2019), pp. 731–49.

Case 7.1

Alaska Fly-Fishing Expedition*

You are sitting around the fire at a lodge in Dillingham, Alaska, discussing a fishing expedition you are planning with your colleagues at Great Alaska Adventures (GAA). Earlier in the day you received a fax from the president of BlueNote, Inc. The president wants to reward her top management team by taking them on an all-expense-paid fly-fishing adventure in Alaska. She would like GAA to organize and lead the expedition.

You have just finished a preliminary scope statement for the project (which follows). You are now brainstorming potential risks associated with the project.

1. Brainstorm potential risks associated with this project. Try to come up with at least five different risks.
2. Use a risk assessment form similar to Figure 7.6 to analyze identified risks.
3. Develop a risk response matrix similar to Figure 7.8 to outline how you would deal with each of the risks.

PROJECT SCOPE STATEMENT

PROJECT OBJECTIVE

To organize and lead a five-day fly-fishing expedition down the Tikchik River system in Alaska from June 21 to 25 at a cost not to exceed $70,000.

DELIVERABLES

- Provide air transportation from Dillingham, Alaska, to Base I and from Base II back to Dillingham.
- Provide river transportation consisting of two eight-person drift boats with outboard motors.
- Provide three meals a day for the five days spent on the river.
- Provide four hours of fly-fishing instruction.
- Provide overnight accommodations at the Dillingham lodge plus three four-person tents with cots, bedding, and lanterns.
- Provide four experienced river guides who are also fly fishermen.
- Provide fishing licenses for all guests.

MILESTONES

1. Contract signed January 22.
2. Guests arrive in Dillingham June 20.
3. Depart by plane to Base Camp I June 21.
4. Depart by plane from Base Camp II to Dillingham June 25.

* This case was prepared with the assistance of Stuart Morigeau.

TECHNICAL REQUIREMENTS

1. Fly-in air transportation to and from base camps.
2. Boat transportation within the Tikchik River system.
3. Digital cellular communication devices.
4. Camps and fishing conforming to state of Alaska requirements.

LIMITS AND EXCLUSIONS

1. Guests are responsible for travel arrangements to and from Dillingham, Alaska.
2. Guests are responsible for their own fly-fishing equipment and clothing.
3. Local air transportation to and from base camps will be outsourced.
4. Tour guides are not responsible for the number of king salmon caught by guests.

ACCEPTANCE CRITERIA

The president of BlueNote, Inc. reviews.

Case 7.2

Silver Fiddle Construction

You are the president of Silver Fiddle Construction (SFC), which specializes in building high-quality, customized homes in the Grand Junction, Colorado, area. You have just been hired by the Czopeks to build their dream home. You operate as a general contractor and employ only a part-time bookkeeper. You subcontract work to local trade professionals. Housing construction in Grand Junction is booming. You are tentatively scheduled to complete 11 houses this year. You have promised the Czopeks that the final costs will range from $700,000 to $750,000 and that it will take five months to complete the house once groundbreaking has begun. The Czopeks are willing to have the project delayed in order to save costs.

You have just finished a preliminary scope statement for the project (which follows). You are now brainstorming potential risks associated with the project.

1. Identify potential risks associated with this project. Try to come up with at least five different risks.
2. Use a risk assessment form similar to Figure 7.6 to analyze identified risks.
3. Develop a risk response matrix similar to Figure 7.8 to outline how you would deal with each of the risks.

PROJECT SCOPE STATEMENT

PROJECT OBJECTIVE

To construct a high-quality, custom home within five months at a cost not to exceed $750,000.

DELIVERABLES

- A 2,500-square-foot, 2½-bath, 3-bedroom, finished home.
- A finished garage, insulated and sheetrocked.
- Kitchen appliances to include range, oven, microwave, and dishwasher.
- A high-efficiency gas furnace with programmable thermostat.

MILESTONES

1. Permits approved July 5.
2. Foundation poured July 12.
3. "Dry in"—framing, sheathing, plumbing, electrical, and mechanical inspections—passed September 25.
4. Final inspection November 7.

TECHNICAL REQUIREMENTS

1. Home must meet local building codes.
2. All windows and doors must pass NFRC class 40 energy ratings.
3. Exterior wall insulation must meet an "R" factor of 21.
4. Ceiling insulation must meet an "R" factor of 38.
5. Floor insulation must meet an "R" factor of 25.
6. Garage will accommodate two cars and one 28-foot-long Winnebago.
7. Structure must pass seismic stability codes.

LIMITS AND EXCLUSIONS

1. Home will be built to the specifications and design of the original blueprints provided by the customer.
2. Owner is responsible for landscaping.
3. Refrigerator is not included among kitchen appliances.
4. Air conditioning is not included, but house is prewired for it.
5. SFC reserves the right to contract out services.

ACCEPTANCE CRITERIA

"Bolo" and Izabella Czopek reviews.

Case 7.3

Trans LAN Project

Trans Systems is a small information systems consulting firm located in Meridian, Louisiana. Trans has just been hired to design and install a local area network (LAN) for the city of Meridian's social welfare agency. You are the manager for the project, which includes one Trans professional and two interns from a local university. You have just finished a preliminary scope statement for the project (which follows). You are now brainstorming potential risks associated with the project.

1. Identify potential risks associated with this project. Try to come up with at least five different risks.

2. Use a risk assessment form similar to Figure 7.6 to analyze identified risks.
3. Develop a risk response matrix similar to Figure 7.8 to outline how you would deal with each of the risks.

PROJECT SCOPE STATEMENT

PROJECT OBJECTIVE

To design and install a new local area network (LAN) within one month with a budget not to exceed $200,000 for the Meridian Social Service Agency with minimum disruption to ongoing operations.

DELIVERABLES

- Twenty workstations and 20 laptop computers.
- Two servers with 8-core processors.
- Print server with two color laser printers.
- Barracuda Firewall.
- Windows 2022 server and workstation operating system (Windows 11).
- Migration of existing databases and programs to new system.
- Four hours of introduction training for client's personnel.
- Sixteen hours of training for client network administrator.
- Fully operational LAN system.

MILESTONES

1. Hardware January 22.
2. Setting users' priority and authorization January 26.
3. In-house whole network test completed February 1.
4. Client site test completed February 2.
5. Training completed February 16.

TECHNICAL REQUIREMENTS

1. Workstations with 17-inch flat panel monitors, quad-core processors, 16 GB RAM, wireless card, Ethernet card, 500 GB SSD.
2. Laptops with 12-inch display monitor, dual-core processors, 8 GB RAM, wireless card, Ethernet card, 500 GB SSD, and weight less than 4 lbs.
3. Wireless network interface cards and Ethernet connections.
4. System must support Windows 11 platforms.
5. System must provide secure external access for field workers.

LIMITS AND EXCLUSIONS

1. On-site work to be done after 8:00 p.m. and before 7:00 a.m. Monday through Saturday.
2. System maintenance and repair only up to one month after final inspection.
3. Warranties transferred to client.
4. Only responsible for installing software designated by the client two weeks before the start of the project.
5. Client will be billed for additional training beyond that prescribed in the contract.

ACCEPTANCE CRITERIA

Director of the city of Meridian's Social Service Agency reviews.

Case 7.4

XSU Spring Concert

You are a member of the X State University (XSU) student body entertainment committee. Your committee has agreed to sponsor a spring concert. The motive behind this concert is to offer a safe alternative to Hasta Weekend. Hasta Weekend is a spring event in which students from XSU rent houseboats and engage in heavy partying. Traditionally this occurs during the last weekend in May. Unfortunately, the partying has a long history of getting out of hand, sometimes leading to fatal accidents. After one such tragedy last spring, your committee wants to offer an alternative experience for those who are eager to celebrate the change in weather and the pending end of the school year.

You have just finished a preliminary scope statement for the project (which follows). You are now brainstorming potential risks associated with the project.

1. Identify potential risks associated with this project. Try to come up with at least five different risks.
2. Use a risk assessment form similar to Figure 7.6 to analyze identified risks.
3. Develop a risk response matrix similar to Figure 7.8 to outline how you would deal with each of the risks.

PROJECT SCOPE STATEMENT

PROJECT OBJECTIVE

To organize and deliver an eight-hour concert at Wahoo Stadium at a cost not to exceed $60,000 on the last Saturday in May.

DELIVERABLES

- Local advertising.
- Concert security.
- Separate beer garden.
- Eight hours of music and entertainment.
- Food venues.
- Souvenir concert T-shirts.
- Secure all licenses and approvals.
- Secure sponsors.

MILESTONES

1. Secure all permissions and approvals by January 15.
2. Sign big-name artist by February 15.
3. Complete artist roster by April 1.
4. Secure vendor contracts by April 15.

5. Setup completed on May 27 or one day before concert starts.
6. Concert on May 28 or last Saturday in May.
7. Cleanup completed by May 31 or three days after concert is over.

TECHNICAL REQUIREMENTS

1. Professional sound stage and system.
2. At least one big-name artist.
3. At least seven performing acts.
4. Restroom facilities for 10,000 people.
5. Parking available for 1,000 cars.
6. Compliance with XSU and city requirements/ordinances.

LIMITS AND EXCLUSIONS

1. Performers are responsible for travel arrangements to and from XSU.
2. Vendors contribute a set percentage of sales.
3. Concert must be over by 11:30 p.m.

ACCEPTANCE CRITERIA

The president of XSU student body reviews.

Case 7.5

Sustaining Project Risk Management during Implementation

BACKGROUND

Bill (senior VP of product development): Carlos [project manager], we have to talk. I am concerned about the way we manage project risk here at Futuronics. I just came from an international "Future Mote Devices" meeting at UC Berkeley. [Note: A *mote* is a very small (e.g., 2- to 3-mm-square), wireless sensing pod that can be placed on land or in water to measure and communicate data.] The project management sessions receiving most attention addressed risk in product development projects. They described our management of project risk to the letter—failure to sustain risk management *after the project gets rolling*. It seems someone has to get burned before risk management is taken seriously.

Much to my surprise, almost all the project managers there admitted their firms have a problem sustaining team members' interest in managing risk after the project is on its way. The old saying "If you don't manage risk, you pay the price later" generated horror stories from a few who paid the price. We spent some time brainstorming ways to handle the problem at the project level, but there were very few concrete suggestions. The meeting gave me a wake-up call. Carlos, we need to tackle this problem or some new or known risk event could put us both out of a job. The similarities between their horror stories and some of our past mistakes are scary.

Since here at Futuronics we only develop new products that are at least seven years beyond anything on the market, the level of both "known risk events and unknown risk" is far higher than in most other organizations. Managing project risk is important to every project, but here at Futuronics every new product project is loaded with risks. Carlos, I'm willing to work with you to improve our management of project risk at Futuronics.

Carlos: Bill, I am aware of the problem. The PMI roundtables I attend also talk about the difficulty of keeping teams and other stakeholders willing to revisit risk once the project is on its way. [PMI roundtables are monthly meetings of practicing PMs across industries designed to address project management problems.] I also heard war stories at a recent project management roundtable meeting. I have some notes from the meeting right here.

It all started with the leader's question: "How many project managers actually manage risk over the complete project life cycle?"

PM 1: We all work through the risk management process well before the project begins. We have the process template of risk identification, assessment, response, control, risk register, and contingency down pat. We just don't follow through after the project begins. I think interest dies. Have you ever tried to get project stakeholders to come to a risk meeting when the project is moving relatively well?

PM 2: A recent e-mail from one of our stakeholders said, "We'll deal with it [risk] when it happens."

PM 3: I agree. Interest seems to move from future oriented to reactionary. Also, risk management seems to degenerate into issue (concerns and problems) management versus real risk management.

PM 4: I ask team members, "What is the risk of not managing risk over the life of the project?" Sometimes this question nudges a few to respond positively, especially if risks have changed or new ones are perceived. I use a failed project where a solid risk management process would have avoided the project failure. I explain all of the risk management processes that would have helped to improve the risk elements—risk identification, triggers, responsibility, transfer, accept, etc.

PM 5: Risk is not a line item in the budget or schedule. Maybe it is in the management reserve to cover "unknowns of unknowns." I have to watch that management doesn't try to squeeze out the budget for something else.

Carlos continued to share with his boss that there were many more comments, but very few gave much guidance. Carlos then shared his idea:

Carlos: Colette is our best trainer, especially in transition management, and she would be a great choice for following through on this problem. Her training classes on up-front risk management are excellent. Should we ask her to present a session?

Bill: You are right, Carlos; Colette is ideal. She is smart and a great team motivator. Ask her, but give her some kind of direction for focus.

A few days later, Carlos sent out a memo:

Colette, this is to follow up on our lunch conversation yesterday discussing sustaining risk management after the project is on its way. Given the nature of our futuristic company, we should stress the point that our product development projects carry many more inherent risks than do traditional projects. I suggest the training classes should drill down on concrete actions and policies that will encourage the interest of team members and other project stakeholders in sustaining risk management practices during project execution.

Colette, we appreciate your taking on this project. When you have developed your training session, please give me a copy so I can schedule and support your efforts.

Regards, Carlos

CHALLENGE

Divide the class into teams of three or more participants.

Colette needs your help to develop her training program. You may wish to consider the following questions to initiate ideas.

- Why do project stakeholders lose interest in project risk after the project is under way?
- What are the dangers of not keeping on top of risk management during implementation?
- What kind of business is Futuronics in?

Brainstorm specific actions that will encourage project stakeholders to continue to scan and track the project environment for risk events. Suggest three concrete actions or scenarios that will encourage project stakeholders to change their behavior and truly support risk management while projects are being implemented. The following outline headings may be helpful in developing possible actions that would improve/enhance stakeholder support.

- Improving the risk management process
- Organization actions
- Motivating participation

Case 7.6

Smart Cities Mission—Risk Assessment and Mitigation Strategies

The Smart Cities Mission, launched in 2015, aims to enhance urban living through technology-driven solutions, sustainable development, and public-private partnerships. It addresses challenges like infrastructure strain, pollution, and congestion by fostering economic growth, innovation, and inclusivity. With 7,800+ projects across 100 cities, it promotes smarter, more resilient urban spaces.

The Smart Cities Mission involves these key stakeholders—Government Bodies like Ministry of Housing and Urban Affairs (MoHUA), ULBs, and SPVs for policy and execution; Private Sector firms contributing expertise, funding, and technology via PPPs; Public Participation ensuring citizen-driven planning; and International Collaborators offering financial aid, technical expertise, and global best practices.

Each identified risk is evaluated based on its likelihood of occurrence and potential impact on the project, allowing for prioritization of the most critical risks. The assessment includes—Probability: determining the likelihood of a risk occurring (high, medium, or low); Impact: assessing its potential consequences on the project (high, medium, or low). For instance, cybersecurity threats may have both high probability and impact due to smart cities' reliance on digital infrastructure, whereas technological obsolescence might have a medium probability but a high impact due to rapid technological advancements.

RISK IDENTIFICATION

TECHNICAL RISKS AND MITIGATION STRATEGIES

Integration Challenges

Risk Assessment: Integrating new technologies with existing infrastructure can be complex and may face compatibility issues. This includes challenges in integrating IoT devices, data management systems, and legacy infrastructure. For example, integrating smart grids with traditional power systems requires significant upgrades and coordination between various stakeholders. According to a study by the National Institute of Urban Affairs (NIUA), many Indian cities face difficulties in integrating new technologies due to outdated infrastructure and lack of technical expertise.

Impact Probability Analysis: Probability: High, Impact: High

Mitigation Strategies:

- **Robust Planning:** Conducting detailed planning and feasibility studies to ensure smooth integration of new technologies with existing infrastructure. This includes pilot testing and phased implementation to identify and address potential issues early.
- **Stakeholder Coordination:** Establishing clear communication channels and coordination mechanisms among stakeholders to ensure seamless integration.
- **Technical Training:** Providing technical training and capacity building for municipal staff to handle new technologies effectively.

Cybersecurity Threats

Risk Assessment: Smart cities rely heavily on digital infrastructure, making them vulnerable to cyber-attacks. Ensuring the security of data and systems is critical to prevent breaches and protect sensitive information. Cyber threats such as malware infections, ransomware attacks, and distributed denial-of-service (DDoS) attacks can target critical infrastructure components, IoT devices, communication networks, and data repositories. A report by the Indian Computer Emergency Response Team (CERT-In) highlighted that cyber-attacks on critical infrastructure have increased by 22% in recent years.

Impact Probability Analysis: Probability: High; Impact: High

Mitigation Strategies:

- **Cybersecurity Measures:** Implementing strong cybersecurity protocols, regular audits, and continuous monitoring to protect smart systems from cyber threats. This involves using encryption, firewalls, and intrusion detection systems to safeguard data and infrastructure.
- **Incident Response Plans:** Developing and regularly updating incident response plans to quickly address and mitigate the impact of cyber-attacks.
- **Public Awareness:** Conducting cybersecurity awareness campaigns to educate citizens and stakeholders about potential threats and best practices for data protection.

Technological Obsolescence

Risk Assessment: Rapid advancements in technology can render current systems outdated. Continuous updates and upgrades are necessary to keep pace with technological changes and maintain efficiency. For example, the lifespan of IoT devices and sensors is relatively short, and they need to be replaced or upgraded regularly to ensure optimal performance. The MoHUA has emphasized the importance of adopting scalable and flexible technologies that can adapt to future advancements.

Impact Probability Analysis: Probability: Medium; Impact: High

Mitigation Strategies:

- **Technology Upgradation:** Regularly updating and upgrading technology to keep pace with advancements and avoid obsolescence. This includes investing in scalable and flexible systems that can adapt to future changes.
- **Lifecycle Management:** Implementing lifecycle management practices to plan for the timely replacement and upgrading of technological components.
- **Research and Development:** Investing in research and development to stay ahead of technological trends and innovations.

Data Privacy Concerns

Risk Assessment: With the extensive use of data in smart cities, ensuring data privacy is a significant challenge. The collection, storage, and processing of large amounts of personal data can lead to privacy breaches if not managed properly. According to a report by the Data Security Council of India (DSCI), there is a growing concern among citizens.

Impact Probability Analysis: Probability: High; Impact: High

Mitigation Strategies:

- **Data Privacy Policies:** Implementing strict data privacy policies and ensuring transparency in data handling practices to build trust among citizens.
- **Compliance with Regulations:** Ensuring compliance with data protection regulations and standards to safeguard personal information.
- **Data Minimization:** Adopting data minimization practices to collect only the necessary data and reduce the risk of privacy breaches.

Interoperability Issues

Risk Assessment: Interoperability between different systems and technologies is essential for the seamless functioning of smart cities. However, achieving interoperability can be challenging due to the use of diverse technologies and standards. For instance, different vendors may use proprietary protocols that are not compatible with each other, leading to integration issues. The Bureau of Indian Standards (BIS) has been working on developing common standards for smart city technologies to address these challenges.

Impact Probability Analysis: Probability: Medium; Impact: Medium

Mitigation Strategies:

- **Standardization:** Developing and adopting common standards for smart city technologies to ensure interoperability.
- **Vendor Collaboration:** Encouraging collaboration among vendors to develop compatible solutions and avoid proprietary lock-ins.
- **Open Architecture:** Implementing open architecture frameworks that allow for the integration of diverse technologies and systems.

OPERATIONAL RISKS AND MITIGATION STRATEGIES

Project Delays

Risk Assessment: Delays can occur due to various reasons such as land acquisition issues, regulatory approvals, and coordination among multiple stakeholders. These delays can impact project timelines and increase costs. According to a report by the MoHUA, over 30% of smart city projects have faced delays due to land acquisition and regulatory hurdles.

Impact probability Analysis: Probability: High; Impact: High

Mitigation Strategies:

- **Efficient Project Management:** Using project management tools and techniques to ensure timely completion of projects. This includes setting clear timelines, milestones, and responsibilities for all stakeholders.
- **Streamlined Approval Processes:** Simplifying and expediting regulatory approval processes to reduce delays.
- **Stakeholder Coordination:** Establishing clear communication channels and coordination mechanisms among stakeholders to ensure smooth project execution.

Resource Allocation

Risk Assessment: Inefficient allocation of resources, including financial, human, and technological resources, can lead to cost overruns and project delays. Proper planning and management are essential to optimize resource use. A study by the National Institute of Urban Affairs (NIUA) found that many smart city projects suffer from poor resource allocation, leading to inefficiencies and increased costs.

Impact Probability Analysis: Probability: Medium; Impact: High

Mitigation Strategies:

- **Resource Optimization:** Strategic allocation of resources to avoid wastage and ensure efficient use. This involves proper budgeting, manpower planning, and resource allocation for each phase of the project.
- **Capacity Building:** Investing in capacity building and training for project managers and staff to enhance their skills in resource management.
- **Regular Monitoring:** Implementing regular monitoring and evaluation mechanisms to track resource utilization and make necessary adjustments.

Maintenance Challenges

Risk Assessment: Ensuring the long-term maintenance and sustainability of smart infrastructure is crucial. This includes regular maintenance of IoT devices, data centers, and other technological systems to prevent failures and disruptions. According to the MoHUA, many cities face challenges in maintaining their smart infrastructure due to lack of technical expertise and inadequate funding.

Impact Probability Analysis: Probability: Medium; Impact: High

Mitigation Strategies:

- **Maintenance Plans:** Developing comprehensive maintenance plans to ensure the longevity of smart infrastructure. This includes regular inspections, preventive maintenance, and timely repairs to prevent failures and disruptions.
- **Technical Training:** Providing technical training and capacity building for maintenance staff to handle smart infrastructure effectively.

- **Sustainable Funding:** Securing sustainable funding sources for maintenance activities to ensure continuous operation and upkeep of smart infrastructure.

Coordination Among Stakeholders

Risk Assessment: Effective coordination among various stakeholders, including government bodies, private sector entities, and citizens, is essential for the successful implementation of smart city projects. However, achieving this coordination can be challenging due to differing priorities and interests. A report by the World Bank highlighted that lack of coordination among stakeholders is a major barrier to the successful implementation of smart city projects.

Impact Probability Analysis: Probability: High; Impact: Medium

Mitigation Strategies:

- **Stakeholder Engagement:** Conducting regular stakeholder meetings and consultations to ensure alignment of goals and priorities.
- **Clear Communication Channels:** Establishing clear communication channels to facilitate information sharing and collaboration among stakeholders.
- **Conflict Resolution Mechanisms:** Implementing conflict resolution mechanisms to address and resolve any disputes that may arise during project implementation.

Change Management

Risk Assessment: Implementing smart city projects often involves significant changes in existing processes and systems. Managing these changes effectively is essential to ensure smooth transition and adoption of new technologies. According to a study by the Indian Institute of Management (IIM), many smart city projects face resistance to change from various stakeholders, including government officials and citizens.

Impact Probability Analysis: Probability: Medium; Impact: Medium

Mitigation Strategies:

- **Change Management Strategies:** Implementing effective change management strategies, including training and capacity building, to help stakeholders adapt to new technologies and processes.
- **Stakeholder Involvement:** Involving stakeholders in the planning and implementation process to gain their buy-in and support for the changes.
- **Communication and Education:** Conducting communication and education campaigns to inform stakeholders about the benefits of the changes and address any concerns they may have.

In conclusion, the successful implementation of smart city projects in India hinges on effectively managing a range of technical, operational, financial, environmental, and social risks. By adopting robust planning, strong cybersecurity measures, efficient resource management, and inclusive development practices, stakeholders can mitigate these risks. Ensuring continuous collaboration, adaptive strategies, and proactive engagement with all stakeholders will enhance the resilience, sustainability, and inclusivity of smart cities, ultimately improving the quality of life for urban residents.

Appendix 7.1

PERT and PERT Simulation

LEARNING OBJECTIVES

After reading this appendix, you should be able to

A7-1 Calculate basic PERT simulation projections.

PERT—PROGRAM EVALUATION AND REVIEW TECHNIQUE

LO A7-1

Calculate basic PERT simulation projections.

In 1958, the Special Office of the Navy and the Booze, Allen, and Hamilton consulting firm developed PERT (program evaluation and review technique) to schedule the more than 3,300 contractors of the Polaris submarine project and to cover uncertainty of activity time estimates.

PERT is almost identical to the critical path method (CPM) technique except it assumes each activity duration has a range that follows a statistical distribution. PERT uses three time estimates for each activity. Basically this means each activity duration can range from an optimistic time to a pessimistic time, and a weighted average can be computed for each activity. Because project activities usually represent work, and because work tends to stay behind once it gets behind, the PERT developers chose an approximation of the *beta distribution* to represent activity durations. This distribution is known to be flexible and can accommodate empirical data that do not follow a normal distribution. The activity durations can be skewed more toward the high or low end of the data range. Figure A7.1A depicts a *beta distribution* for activity durations that is skewed toward the right and is representative of work that tends to stay late once it is behind. The distribution for the project duration is represented by a normal (symmetrical) distribution shown in Figure A7.1B. The project distribution represents the sum of the weighted averages of the activities on the critical path(s).

Knowing the weighted average and variances for each activity allows the project planner to compute the probability of meeting different project durations. Follow the steps described in the hypothetical example given next. (The jargon is difficult for those not familiar with statistics, but the process is relatively simple after working through a couple of examples.)

FIGURE A7.1 Activity and Project Frequency Distributions

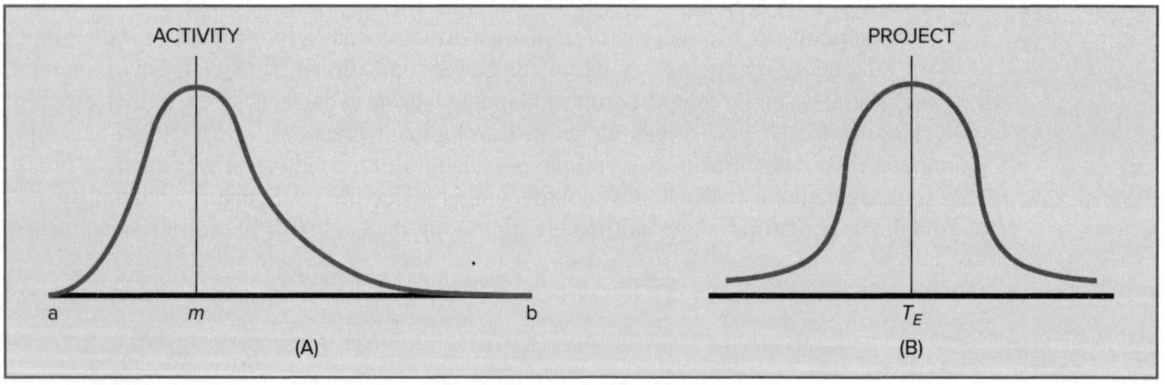

The weighted average activity time is computed by the following formula:

$$t_e = \frac{a + 4m + b}{6} \tag{7.1}$$

where

t_e = weighted average activity time
a = optimistic activity time (1 chance in 100 of completing the activity earlier under *normal* conditions)
b = pessimistic activity time (1 chance in 100 of completing the activity later under *normal* conditions)
m = most likely activity time

When the three time estimates have been specified, this equation is used to compute the weighted average duration for each activity. The average (deterministic) value is placed on the project network as in the CPM method and the early, late, slack, and project completion times are computed as they are in the CPM method.

The variability in the activity time estimates is approximated by the following equations: Equation 7.2 represents the standard deviation for the *activity*. Equation 7.3 represents the standard deviation for the *project*. Note the standard deviation of the activity is squared in Equation 7.3; this is also called variance. This summation includes only activities on the critical path(s) or path being reviewed.

$$\sigma_{t_e} = \left(\frac{b - a}{6}\right) \tag{7.2}$$

$$\sigma_{T_E} = \sqrt{\Sigma\sigma_{t_e}^2} \tag{7.3}$$

Finally, the average project duration (T_E) is the summation of all the average activity times along the critical path (summation of t_e), and it follows a normal distribution.

Knowing the average project duration and the variances of activities allows the probability of completing the project (or segment of the project) by a specific time to be computed using standard statistical tables. The following equation (Equation 7.4) is used to compute the "Z" value found in statistical tables (Z = number of standard deviations from the mean), which in turn tells the probability of completing the project in the time specified.

$$Z = \frac{T_s - T_E}{\sqrt{\Sigma\sigma_{t_e}^2}} \tag{7.4}$$

where

T_E = critical path duration
T_S = scheduled project duration
Z = probability (of meeting scheduled duration) (see statistical Table A7.2)

A HYPOTHETICAL EXAMPLE USING PERT

The activity times and variances are given in Table A7.1. The project network is presented in Figure A7.2. This figure shows the project network as AOA and AON. The AON network is presented as a reminder that PERT can use AON networks as well as AOA.

The expected project duration (T_E) is 64 time units; the critical path is 1-2-3-5-6 in AOA network. In AON, the critical path is A-B-D-F. With this information, the

TABLE A7.1
Activity Times and Variances

Node	Activity	*a*	*m*	*b*	t_e	$[(b - a)/6]^2$
1–2	A	17	29	47	30	25
2–3	B	6	12	24	13	9
2–4	C	16	19	28	20	4
3–5	D	13	16	19	16	1
4–5	E	2	5	14	6	4
5–6	F	2	5	8	5	1

FIGURE A7.2
Hypothetical Network

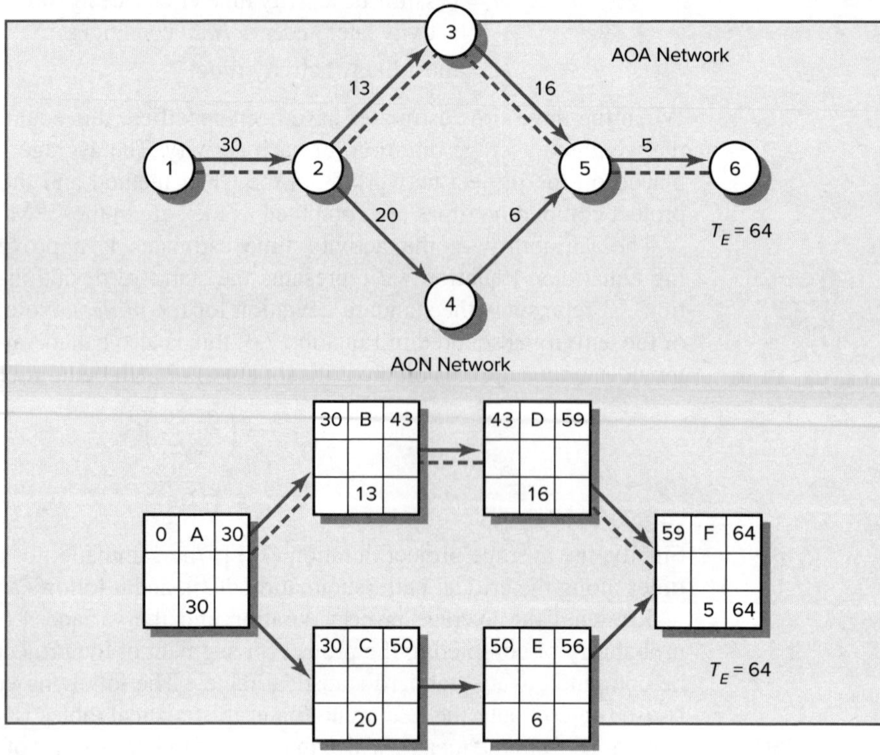

FIGURE A7.3
Possible Project Durations

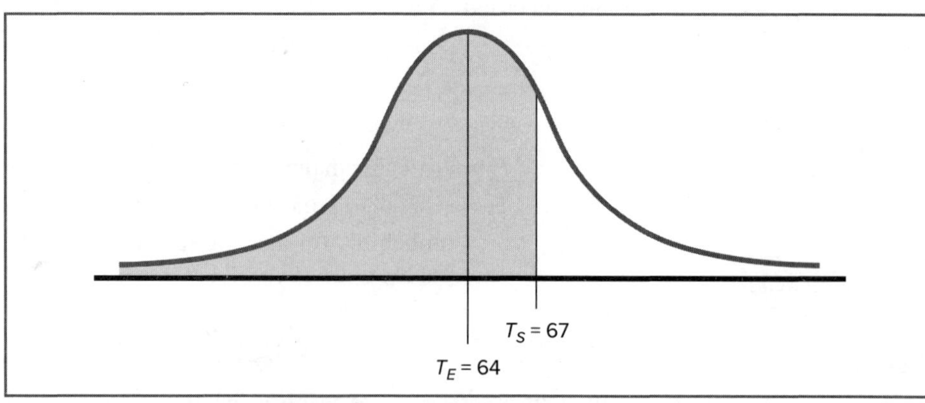

probability of completing the project by a specific date can easily be computed using standard statistical methods. For example, what is the probability the project will be completed before a scheduled time (T_S) of 67? The normal curve for the project would appear as shown in Figure A7.3.

Using the formula for the Z value, the probability can be computed as follows:

$$
\begin{aligned}
Z &= \frac{T_s - T_E}{\sqrt{\Sigma \sigma_{t_e}^2}} \\
&= \frac{67 - 64}{\sqrt{25 + 9 + 1 + 1}} \\
&= \frac{+3}{\sqrt{36}} \\
&= +0.50 \\
P &= 0.69
\end{aligned}
$$

Reading from Table A7.2, a Z value of +0.5 gives a probability of 0.69, which is interpreted to mean there is a 69 percent chance of completing the project on or before 67 time units. The probability of 0.69 for a Z value of +0.5 can be found using the linear interpolation method.

Conversely, the probability of completing the project by time period 60 is computed as follows:

$$
\begin{aligned}
Z &= \frac{60 - 64}{\sqrt{25 + 9 + 1 + 1}} \\
&= \frac{-4}{\sqrt{36}} \\
&= -0.67 \\
P &\approx 0.25
\end{aligned}
$$

From Table A7.2, a Z value of −0.67 gives an approximate probability of 0.25, which is interpreted to mean there is about a 25 percent chance of completing the project on or before 60 time units. Note that this same type of calculation can be made for any path or segment of a path in the network.

When such probabilities are available to management, trade-off decisions can be made to accept or reduce the risk associated with a particular project duration. For example, if

TABLE A7.2
Z Values and Probabilities

Z Value	Probability	*Z* Value	Probability
−3.0	.001	+0.0	.500
−2.8	.003	+0.2	.579
−2.6	.005	+0.4	.655
−2.4	.008	+0.6	.726
−2.2	.014	+0.8	.788
−2.0	.023	+1.0	.841
−1.8	.036	+1.2	.885
−1.6	.055	+1.4	.919
−1.4	.081	+1.6	.945
−1.2	.115	+1.8	.964
−1.0	.159	+2.0	.977
−0.8	.212	+2.2	.986
−0.6	.274	+2.4	.992
−0.4	.345	+2.6	.995
−0.2	.421	+2.8	.997
0.0	.500	+3.0	.999

the project manager wishes to improve the chances of completing the project by 64 time units, at least two choices are available. First, management can spend money upfront to change conditions that will reduce the duration of one or more activities on the critical path. A more prudent, second alternative would be to allocate money to a contingency fund and wait to see how the project is progressing as it is implemented.

EXERCISES

1. Given the project information in the following table, what is the probability of completing the National Holiday Toy project in 93 time units?

Act. ID	Description	Predecessor	Optm. (a)	Most likely (m)	Pess. (b)	Act time t_e	Variance $[(b-a)/6]^2$	Critical
1	Design package	None	6	12	24			
2	Design product	1	16	19	28			
3	Build package	1	4	7	10			
4	Secure patent	2	24	27	36			
5	Build product	2	17	29	47			
6	Paint	3, 4, 5	4	7	10			
7	Test market	6	13	16	19			

2. The Global Tea and Organic Juice companies have merged. The following information has been collected for the "Consolidation Project."

Activity	Description	Predecessor	a opt	m ml	b pess
1	Codify accounts	None	16	19	28
2	File articles of unification	None	30	30	30
3	Unify price and credit policy	None	60	72	90
4	Unify personnel policies	None	18	27	30
5	Unify data processing	1	17	29	47
6	Train accounting staff	1	4	7	10
7	Pilot run data processing	5	12	15	18
8	Calculate P & L and balance sheet	6, 7	6	12	24
9	Transfer real property	2	18	27	30
10	Train salesforce	3	20	35	50
11	Negotiate with unions	4	40	55	100
12	Determine capital needs	8	11	20	29
13	Explain personnel policies	11	14	23	26
14	Secure line of credit	9, 12	13	16	19
15	End	10, 13, 14	0	0	0

1. Compute the expected time for each activity.
2. Compute the variance for each activity.
3. Compute the expected project duration.
4. What is the probability of completing the project by day 112? Within 116 days?
5. What is the probability of completing "Negotiate with unions" by day 90?

3. The expected times and variances for the project activities follow. What is the probability of completing the project in 25 periods?

ID	Description	Predecessor	t_e	Variance $[(b-a)/6]^2$
1	Pilot production	None	6	3
2	Select channels of distrib.	None	7	4
3	Develop mktg. program	None	4	2
4	Test market	1	4	2
5	Patent	1	10	5
6	Full production	4	16	10
7	Ad promotion	3	3	2
8	Release	2, 5, 6, 7	2	1

Case A7.1

International Capital, Inc.—Part A

International Capital, Inc. (IC), is a small investment banking firm that specializes in securing funds for small to medium-sized firms. IC is able to use a standardized project format for each engagement. Only activity times and unusual circumstances change the standard network. Beth Brown has been assigned to this client as project manager partner and has compiled the network information and activity times for the latest client as follows:

Activity	Description	Immediate Predecessor
A	Start story draft using template	—
B	Research client firm	—
C	Create "due diligence" rough draft	A, B
D	Coordinate needs proposal with client	C
E	Estimate future demand and cash flows	C
F	Draft future plans for client company	E
G	Create and approve legal documents	C
H	Integrate all drafts into first-draft proposal	D, F, G
I	Line up potential sources of capital	G, F
J	Check, approve, and print final legal proposal	H
K	Sign contracts and transfer funds	I, J

	Time in Workdays		
Activity	Optimistic	Most Likely	Pessimistic
A	4	7	10
B	2	4	8
C	2	5	8
D	16	19	28
E	6	9	24
F	1	7	13
G	4	10	28
H	2	5	14
I	5	8	17
J	2	5	8
K	17	29	45

MANAGERIAL REPORT

Beth and other broker partners have a policy of passing their plan through a project review committee of colleagues. This committee traditionally checks that all details are covered, times are realistic, and resources are available. Beth wishes you to develop a report that presents a planned schedule and expected project completion time in workdays. Include a project network in your report. The average duration for a sourcing capital project is 70 workdays. IC partners have agreed it is good business to set up projects with a 95 percent chance of attaining the plan. How does this project stack up with the average project? What would the average have to be to ensure a 95 percent chance of completing the project in 70 workdays?

Case A7.2

Advantage Energy Technology Data Center Migration—Part B

In Chapter 6, Brian Smith, network administrator at Advanced Energy Technology (AET), was given the responsibility of implementing the migration of a large data center to a new office location.

		Time in Workdays				
	Task Name	**Optimistic Dur.**	**Most Likely Dur.**	**Pessimistic Dur.**	**Immediate Predecessor**	**Critical Path**
1	**AET DATA CENTER MIGRATION**	54	68	92		
2	Team meeting	0.5	1	1.5		✓
3	Hire contractors	6	7	8	2	
4	Network design	12	14	16	2	
5	**Ventilation system**	—	—	—	—	
6	Order ventilation system	18	21	30	2	
7	Install ventilation system	5	7	9	6	
8	**New racks**	—	—	—	—	
9	Order new racks	13	14	21	2	✓
10	Install racks	17	21	25	9	✓
11	**Power supplies and cables**	—	—	—	—	
12	Order power supplies & cables	6	7	8	2	
13	Install power supplies	5	5	11	12, 16	
14	Install cables	6	8	10	12, 16	✓
15	Renovation of data center	19	20	27	3, 4	
16	City inspection	1	2	3	3, 7, 10	✓
17	**Switchover Meetings**	—	—	—	—	
18	Facilities	7	8	9	14	
19	Operations/systems	5	7	9	14	
20	Operations/telecommunications	6	7	8	14	
21	Systems & applications	7	7	13	14	
22	Customer service	5	6	13	14	✓
23	Power check	0.5	1	1.5	13, 14, 15	✓
24	Install test servers	5	7	9	18, 19, 20, 21, 22, 23	✓
25	Management safety check	1	2	3	7, 23, 24	✓
26	Primary systems check	1.5	2	2.5	25	✓
27	Set date for move	1	1	1	26	✓
28	Complete move	1	2	3	27	✓

Careful planning was needed because AET operates in the highly competitive petroleum industry. AET is one of five national software companies that provide an accounting and business management package for oil jobbers and gasoline distributors. A few years ago, AET jumped into the "application service provider" world. Their large data center provides clients with remote access to AET's complete suite of application software systems. Traditionally one of AET's primary competitive advantages has been the company's trademark IT reliability. Due to the complexity of this project, the Executive Committee insisted that preliminary analysis of the anticipated completion date be conducted.

Brian compiled the following information, in preparation for some PERT analysis:

1. Based on these estimates and the resultant expected project duration of 69 days, the Executive Committee wants to know the probability of completing the project before a scheduled time (T_S) of 68 days.
2. The significance of this project has the Executive Committee very concerned. The committee has decided that more analysis of the duration of each activity is needed. Prior to conducting that effort, they asked Brian to calculate what the expected project duration would have to be to ensure a 93 percent chance of completion within 68 days.

ADVANTAGE ENERGY TECHNOLOGY (AET)—ACCOUNTS PAYABLE SYSTEM

The AET Sales Department has been concerned about a new start-up company that is about to release an accounts payable system. Their investigation indicates that this new package will provide features that will seriously compete with AET's current accounts payable system and in some cases exceed what AET offers.

Tom Wright, senior applications developer at AET, has been given the responsibility of analyzing, designing, developing, and delivering a new accounts payable system (A/P) for AET customers.

Complicating the issue is the concern of the Sales Department about AET's recent inability to meet promised delivery dates. They have convinced CEO (Larry Martain) that a significant marketing effort will have to be expended to convince the clients they should wait for the AET product rather than jump to a package provided by a new entry to the petroleum software business. Companion to this effort is the importance of the performance of the software development group.

Consequently, Tom has decided to take the following action: tighten up the estimating effort by his developers, incorporate some new estimating procedures, and use some PERT techniques to generate probabilities associated with his delivery dates.

Tom's planning team made a first-cut at the set of activities and associated durations:

3. Based on these estimates and the critical path, the project duration is estimated at 149 days. But an AET salesperson in the Southeast Region has discovered that the competing A/P package (with significant improvements) is scheduled for delivery in approximately 145 days. The sales force is very anxious to beat that delivery time. The Executive Committee asks Tom for an estimated probability of reducing his expected project duration by 2 days.
4. The Executive Committee is advised by Tom that after all the estimating was completed, he determined that one of his two critical systems analysts might have to move out of the area for family reasons. Tom is still very confident that with some staff rearrangements, assistance from a subcontractor, and some "hands-on" activities on his part he can still meet the original delivery date, based on 149 days.

	Task Name	Time in Workdays			Immediate Predecessor	Critical Path
		Optimistic Dur.	Most Likely Dur.	Pessimistic Dur.		
1	**ACCOUNTS PAYABLE SYSTEM**					
2	Planning meeting	1	1	2		✓
3	Team assignments	3	4	5	2	✓
4	**Program specification**					
5	Customer requirements	8	10	12	3	✓
6	Feasibility study	3	5	7	5	
7	Systems analysis	6	8	10	5	✓
8	Prelim budget & schedule	1	2	3	7	✓
9	Functional specification	3	5	7	7	✓
10	Prelim design	10	12	14	9	✓
11	Configuration & perf needs	3	4	5	10	✓
12	Hardware requirements	4	6	8	11	✓
13	System specification	5	7	9	10	
14	Detailed design	12	14	16	12, 13	✓
15	Program specification	8	10	12	14	✓
16	Programming—first phase	27	32	37	15	✓
17	Documentation	14	16	18	10	
18	**Prototype**					
19	Development	5	7	9	16	✓
20	User testing & feedback	12	14	16	19	✓
21	Programming—second phase	10	12	14	16	
22	Beta testing	18	20	22	21	
23	Final documentation pkg	9	10	11	17, 20	✓
24	Training pkg	4	5	6	21ss, 23	✓
25	Product release	3	5	7	22, 23, 24	✓

SS = start-to-start lag.

This news is very disconcerting to the committee and the sales staff. At this point, the committee decides that based on the most recent delivery performance of AET, a modified, comfortable delivery date should be communicated to AET clients—one that Tom and his staff are very likely to meet. Consequently, Tom is asked to calculate what the expected project duration would have to be to ensure a 98 percent chance of completion within 160 days—a "published, drop-dead date" that can be communicated to the clients.

CHAPTER EIGHT

8 Scheduling Resources and Costs

LEARNING OBJECTIVES

After reading this chapter you should be able to:

8-1 Understand the differences between time-constrained and resource-constrained schedules.

8-2 Identify different types of resource constraints.

8-3 Describe how the smoothing approach is used on time-constrained projects.

8-4 Describe how the leveling approach is used for resource-constrained projects.

8-5 Understand how project management software creates resource-constrained schedules.

8-6 Understand when and why splitting tasks should be avoided.

8-7 Identify general guidelines for assigning people to specific tasks.

8-8 Identify common problems with multiproject resource scheduling.

8-9 Explain why a time-phased budget baseline is needed.

8-10 Create a time-phased project budget baseline.

A8-1 Define the term *critical chain*.

A8-2 Identify the reasons projects are late even when estimates are padded.

A8-3 Describe the basic critical-chain methodology.

A8-4 Describe the differences between critical-chain scheduling and the traditional approach to scheduling.

OUTLINE

8.1 Overview of the Resource Scheduling Problem

8.2 Types of Resource Constraints

8.3 Classification of a Scheduling Problem

8.4 Resource Allocation Methods

8.5 Computer Demonstration of Resource-Constrained Scheduling

8.6 Splitting Activities

8.7 Benefits of Scheduling Resources

8.8 Assigning Project Work

8.9 Multiproject Resource Schedules

8.10 Using the Resource Schedule to Develop a Project Cost Baseline

Summary

Appendix 8.1: The Critical-Chain Approach

Appendix 8.2: MS Project Demonstration of Resource Allocation, Leveling, and Costing

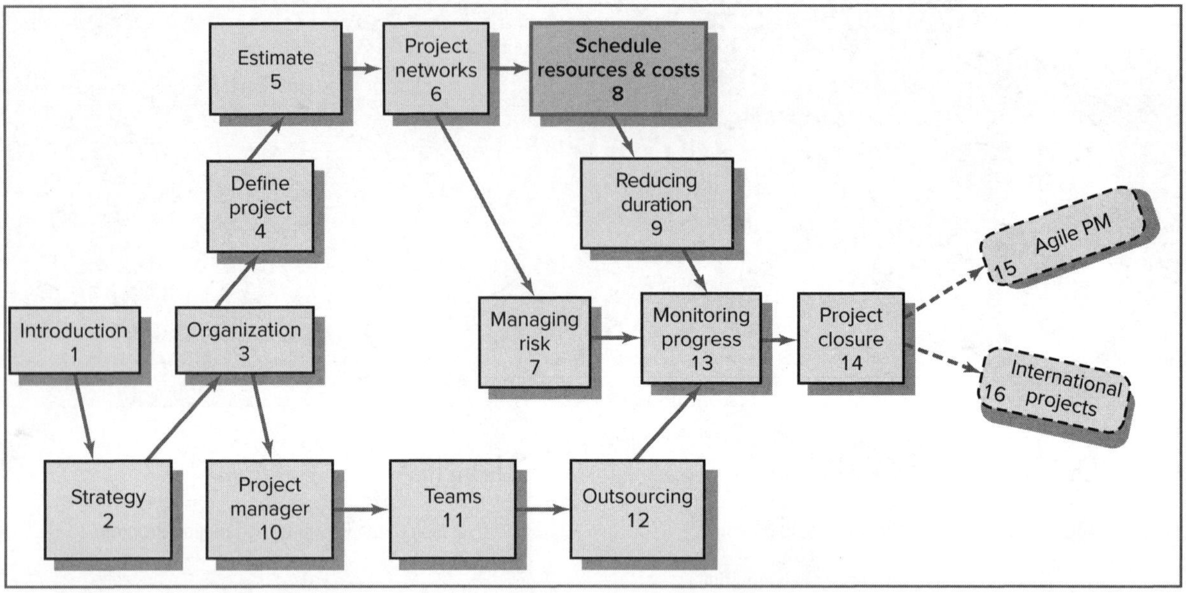

Project network times are not a schedule until resources have been assigned. Cost estimates are not a budget until they have been time-phased.

—Clifford F. Gray, Project Management educator.

We have consistently stressed that up-front planning results in big payoffs on predictable projects. For those who have diligently worked through the earlier planning processes chapters, you are nearly ready to launch your project. This chapter completes the final two planning tasks that become the master plan for your project—resource and cost scheduling (see Figure 8.1). This process uses the resource schedule to assign *time-phased* costs that provide the project budget **baseline.** Given this time-phased baseline, comparisons can be made with actual and planned schedule and costs. This chapter first discusses the process for developing the project resource schedule. This resource schedule will be used to assign the time-phased budgeted values to create a project budget baseline.

There are always more project proposals than there are available resources. The priority system needs to select projects that best contribute to the organization's objectives, within the constraints of the resources available. If all projects and their respective resources are computer scheduled, the feasibility and impact of adding a new

FIGURE 8.1
Project Planning Process

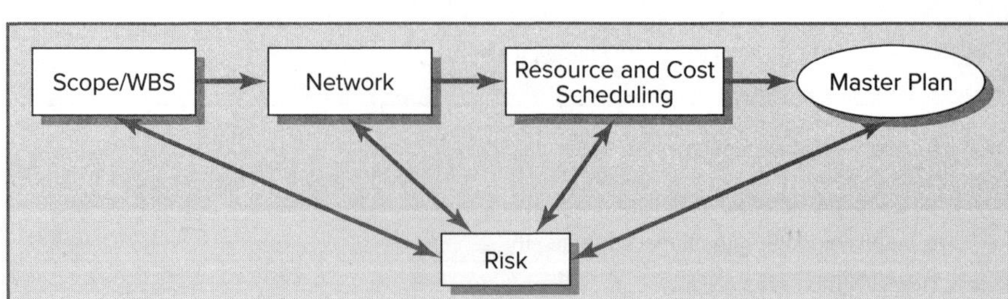

project to those in process can be quickly assessed. With this information the project priority team will add a new project only if resources are available. This chapter examines methods of scheduling resources so the team can make realistic judgments of resource availability and project durations. The project manager uses the same schedule for implementing the project. If changes occur during project implementation, the computer schedule is easily updated and the effects easily assessed.

8.1 Overview of the Resource Scheduling Problem

LO 8-1

Understand the differences between time-constrained and resource-constrained schedules.

After staff and other resources were assigned to his/her project, a project manager listed the following questions that still needed to be addressed:

- Will the assigned labor and/or equipment be adequate and available to deal with my project?
- Will outside contractors have to be used?
- Do unforeseen resource dependencies exist? Is there a new critical path?
- How much flexibility do I have in using resources?
- Is the original deadline realistic?

Clearly this project manager has a good understanding of the problems he/she is facing. Any project scheduling system should facilitate finding quick, easy answers to these questions.

The planned network and activity project duration times found in previous chapters did not take into account resource usage and availability. The time estimates for the work packages and network times were made independently with the implicit assumption that resources would be available. This may or may not be the case.

If resources are adequate but the demand varies widely over the life of the project, it may be desirable to even out resource demand by delaying noncritical activities (using slack) to lower peak demand and, thus, increase resource utilization. This process is called **resource smoothing.**

On the other hand, if resources are not adequate to meet peak demands, the late start of some activities must be delayed, and the duration of the project may be increased. This process is called **resource-constrained scheduling.**

The consequences of failing to schedule limited resources are costly and project delays usually manifest themselves midway in the project when quick corrective action is difficult. An additional consequence of failing to schedule resources is ignoring the peaks and valleys of resource usage over the duration of the project. Because project resources are usually overcommitted and because resources seldom line up by availability and need, procedures are needed to deal with these problems. This chapter addresses methods available to project managers for dealing with resource utilization and availability through resource leveling and resource-constrained scheduling.

Up to now the start and sequence of activities have been based solely on technical or logical considerations. For example, assume you are planning a wedding reception that includes four activities—(1) plan, (2) hire band, (3) decorate hall, and (4) purchase refreshments. Each activity takes one day. Activities 2, 3, and 4 could be done in parallel by different people. There is no technical reason or dependency of one on another (see Figure 8.2A). However, if one person must perform all activities, the resource constraint requires that the activities be performed in sequence or series. Clearly the consequence is a delay of these activities and a very different set of network relationships (see Figure 8.2B). Note that the resource dependency takes priority

FIGURE 8.2
Constraint Examples

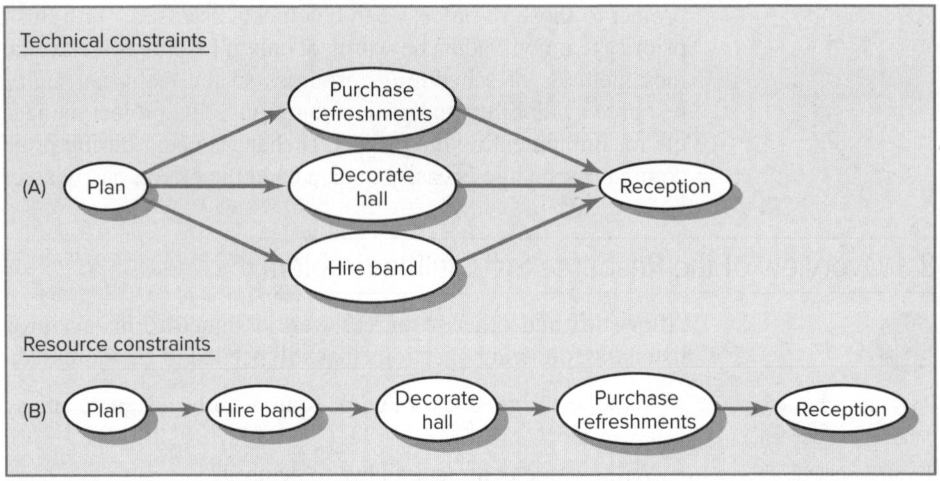

over the technological dependency but *does not violate the technological dependency;* that is, hire, decorate, and purchase may now have to take place in sequence rather than concurrently, but they must all be completed before the reception can take place.

One may ask, "Why not factor resource availability along with technical dependency when creating the original network?" First, resource availability may not be known until the initial schedule is completed. Second, even if resources are known, one could not assess the impact of resources unless a resource neutral schedule were created. For example, one would never know that the wedding could be planned in three days instead of five if three people were available instead of the assumed one. When the premise behind this simple example is applied to other, more elaborate projects, the implications can be significant.

The interrelationships and interactions among time and resource constraints are complex for even small project networks. Some effort to examine these interactions before the project begins frequently uncovers surprising problems. Project managers who do not consider resource availability in moderately complex projects usually learn of the problem when it is too late to correct. A deficit of resources can significantly alter project dependency relationships, completion dates, and project costs. Project managers must be careful to schedule resources to ensure availability in the right quantities and at the right time. Fortunately, there are computer software programs that can identify resource problems during the early project planning phase when corrective changes can be considered. These programs only require activity resource needs and availability information to schedule resources.

See Snapshot from Practice 8.1: Working in Tight Places for a third constraint that impinges on project schedules.

8.2 Types of Resource Constraints

LO 8-2

Identify different types of resource constraints.

Resources are people, equipment, and material that can be drawn on to accomplish something. In projects the availability or unavailability of resources will often influence the way projects are managed.

1. *People.* This is the most obvious and important project resource. Human resources are usually classified by the skills they bring to the project—for example,

SNAPSHOT FROM PRACTICE 8.1 Working in Tight Places

In rare situations, physical factors cause activities that would normally occur in parallel to be constrained by contractual or environmental conditions. For example, in theory the renovation of a sailboat compartment might involve four or five tasks that can be done independently. However, since space allows only one person to work at one time, all tasks have to be performed sequentially. Likewise, on a mining project it may be physically possible for only two miners to work in a shaft at a time. Another example is the erection of a communication tower and nearby groundwork. For safety considerations, the contract prohibits groundwork within 2,000 feet of the tower construction.

Andresr/iStockphoto/Getty Images

The procedures for handling physical factors are similar to those used for resource constraints.

programmer, mechanical engineer, welder, inspector, marketing director, and supervisor. In rare cases some skills are interchangeable, but usually with a loss of productivity. The many differing skills of human resources add to the complexity of scheduling projects.

2. *Materials.* Project materials cover a large spectrum—for example, chemicals for a scientific project, concrete for a road project and, survey data for a marketing project. Material availability and shortages have been blamed for the delay of many projects. When it is known that a lack of availability of materials is important and probable, materials should be included in the project network plan and schedule. For example, delivery and placement of an oil rig tower in a Siberian oil field has a very small time window during one summer month. Any delivery delay means a one-year, costly delay. Another example in which material is the major resource scheduled was the resurfacing and replacement of some structures on the Golden Gate Bridge in San Francisco. Work on the project was limited to the hours between midnight and 5:00 a.m., with a penalty of $1,000 per minute for any work taking place after 5:00 a.m. Scheduling the arrival of replacement structures was an extremely important part of managing the five-hour work-time window of the project. Scheduling materials has also become important in developing products where time-to-market can result in loss of market share.

3. *Equipment.* Equipment is usually presented by type, size, and quantity. In some cases, equipment can be interchanged to improve schedules, but this is not typical. Equipment is often overlooked as a constraint. The most common oversight is to assume the resource pool is more than adequate for the project. For example, if a project needs one earthmoving tractor six months from now and the organization owns four, it is common to assume the resource will not delay the pending project. However, when the earthmoving tractor is due on-site in six months, all four machines in the pool might be occupied on other projects. In multiproject environments it is prudent to

use a common resource pool for all projects. This approach forces a check of resource availability across all projects and reserves the equipment for specific project needs in the future. Recognition of equipment constraints before the project begins can avoid high crashing or delay costs.

8.3 Classification of a Scheduling Problem

Most of the scheduling methods available today require the project manager to classify the project as either *time constrained* or *resource constrained.* Project managers need to consult their priority matrix (see Figure 4.2) to determine which case fits their project. One simple test is to ask, "If the critical path is delayed, will resources be added to get back on schedule?" If the answer is yes, assume the project is time constrained; if no, assume the project is resource constrained.

A **time-constrained project** is one that must be completed by an imposed date. If required, resources can be added to ensure the project is completed by a specific date. Although time is the critical factor, resource usage should be no more than is necessary and sufficient.

A **resource-constrained project** is one that assumes the level of resources available cannot be exceeded. If the resources are inadequate, it will be acceptable to delay the project, but as little as possible.

In scheduling terms, *time constrained* means time (project duration) is fixed and resources are flexible, while *resource constrained* means resources are fixed and time is flexible. Methods for scheduling these projects are presented in the next section.

8.4 Resource Allocation Methods

Assumptions

Ease of demonstrating the allocation methods available requires some limiting assumptions to keep attention on the heart of the problem. The rest of the chapter depends entirely on the assumptions noted here. First, splitting activities will not be allowed. **Splitting** refers to interrupting work on one task and assigning the resources to work on a different task for a period of time, then reassigning them to work on the original task. No splitting means that once an activity is placed in the schedule, assume it will be worked on continuously until it is finished. Second, the level of resources used for an activity cannot be changed. These limiting assumptions do not exist in practice but simplify learning. It is easy for new project managers to deal with the reality of splitting activities and changing the level of resources when they meet them on the job.

LO 8-3

Describe how the smoothing approach is used on time-constrained projects.

Time-Constrained Projects: Smoothing Resource Demand

Scheduling time-constrained projects focuses on resource *utilization.* When demand for a specific resource type is erratic, it is difficult to manage, and utilization may be very poor. Practitioners have attacked the utilization problem using resource leveling techniques that balance demand for a resource. Basically all **leveling** techniques delay noncritical activities by using positive slack to reduce peak demand and fill in the valleys for the resources. An example will demonstrate the basic procedure for a time-constrained project (see Figure 8.3).

FIGURE 8.3 Botanical Garden

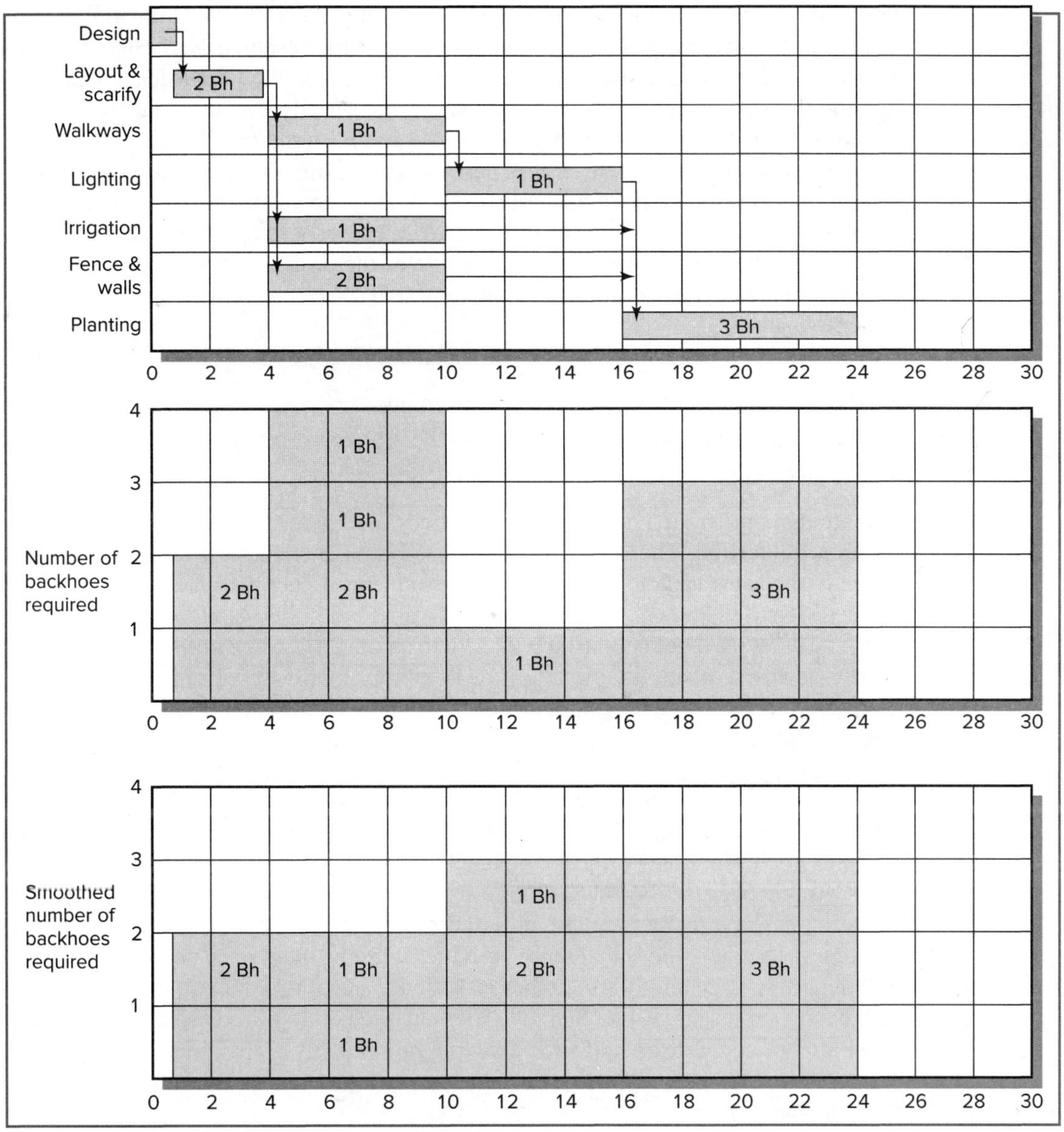

For the purpose of demonstration, the Botanical Garden project uses only one resource (backhoes); all backhoes are interchangeable. The top bar chart shows the activities on a timescale. The dependencies are shown with the vertical connecting arrows. The horizontal arrows following activities represent activity slack (for example, irrigation requires six time units to complete and has six time units of slack). The number of backhoes (Bh) needed for each task is shown in the shaded activity duration block (rectangle). After the land has been sacrificed and the plan laid out, work can begin on the walkways, irrigation, and fencing and retaining walls simultaneously. The middle chart shows the resource profile for the backhoes. For periods 4 through 10, four backhoes are needed.

Because this project is declared time constrained, the goal will be to reduce the peak requirement for the resource and thereby increase the utilization of the resource. A quick examination of the ES (early start) resource load chart suggests only two activities have slack that can be used to reduce the peak—fence and walls provide the best choice for smoothing the resource needs. Another choice could be irrigation, but it would result in an up-and-down resource profile. The choice will probably center on the activity that is perceived as having the least risk of being late. The smoothed resource loading chart (bottom chart) shows the results of delaying the fence and walls activity. Note the differences in the resource profiles. The important point is that the resources needed over the life of the project have been reduced from four to three (25 percent). In addition, the profile has been smoothed, which should be easier to manage.

The Botanical Garden project schedule reached the three goals of smoothing:

- The peak of demand for the resource was reduced.
- The number of resources over the life of the project was reduced.
- The fluctuations in resource demand were minimized.

Smoothing improves the utilization of resources. Backhoes are not easily moved from location to location. There are costs associated with changing the level of resources needed. The same analogy applies to the movement of people back and forth among projects. It is well known that people are more efficient if they can focus their effort on one project rather than multitasking their time among, say, three projects.

The downside of leveling is a loss of flexibility that occurs from reducing slack. The risk of activities delaying the project also increases because slack reduction can create more critical activities and/or near-critical activities. Pushing leveling too far for a perfectly level resource profile is risky. Every activity then becomes critical.

The Botanical Garden example gives a sense of the time-constrained problem and the smoothing approach. However, in practice the magnitude of the problem is very complex for even small projects. Manual solutions are not practical. Fortunately, the software packages available today have very good routines for leveling project resources. Typically they use activities that have the most slack to level project resources. The rationale is that those activities with the most slack pose the least risk. Although this is generally true, other risk factors such as reduction of flexibility to use reassigned resources on other activities and the nature of the activity (easy, complex) are not addressed using such a simple rationale. It is easy to experiment with many alternatives to find the one that best fits your project and minimizes the risk of delaying the project.

LO 8-4

Describe how the leveling approach is used for resource-constrained projects.

Resource-Constrained Projects

When the number of people and/or equipment is not adequate to meet peak demand requirements and it is impossible to obtain more, the project manager faces a resource-constrained problem. Something has to give. The trick is to prioritize and allocate resources to minimize project delay without exceeding the resource limit or altering the technical network relationships.

The resource scheduling problem is a large, combinatorial one. This means even a modest-sized project network with only a few resource types might have several thousand feasible solutions. A few researchers have demonstrated *optimum* mathematical solutions to the resource allocation problem but only for small networks and very few resource types (Arrow & Hurowicz, 2006; Talbot & Patterson, 1979;

Woodworth & Shanahan, 1988). The massive data requirements for larger problems make pure mathematical solutions (e.g., linear programming) impractical. An alternative approach to the problem has been the use of **heuristics** (rules of thumb) to solve large, combinatorial problems. These practical decision or priority rules have been in place for many years.

Heuristics do not always yield an optimal schedule, but they are very capable of yielding a "good" schedule for very complex networks with many types of resources. The efficiency of different rules and combinations of rules has been well documented (Davis & Patterson, 1975; Fendly, 1968). However, because each project is unique, it is wise to test several sets of heuristics on a network to determine the priority allocation rules that minimize project delay. The computer software available today makes it very easy for the project manager to create a good resource schedule for the project. A simple example of the heuristic approach is illustrated here.

Heuristics allocate resources to activities to minimize project delay; that is, heuristics prioritize which activities are allocated resources and which activities are delayed when resources are not adequate.

The parallel method is the most widely used approach to apply heuristics, which have been found to consistently minimize project delay over a large variety of projects. The parallel method is an iterative process that starts from the beginning of project time and, when the resources needed exceed the resources available, retains activities first by the priority rules:

1. Minimum slack.
2. Smallest duration.
3. Lowest activity identification number.

Those not able to be scheduled without delaying others are pushed out further in time. However, do not attempt to move activities that have already started. When considering activities not to delay, consider the resources each activity uses. In any period when two or more activities require the same resource, the priority rules are applied. For example, if in period 5 three activities are eligible to start (i.e., have the same ES) and require the same resource, the first activity placed in the schedule would be the activity with the least slack (rule 1). However, if all activities have the same slack, the next rule would be invoked (rule 2), and the activity with the smallest duration would be placed in the schedule first. In very rare cases, when all eligible activities have the same slack and the same duration, the tie is broken by the lowest activity identification number (rule 3), since each activity has a unique ID number.

When a resource limit has been reached, the early start (ES) for succeeding activities not yet in the schedule will be delayed (and all successor activities not having free slack) and their slack reduced. In subsequent periods the procedure is repeated until the project is scheduled. The procedure is demonstrated next; see Figure 8.4. The shaded areas in the resource loading chart represent the "scheduling interval" of the *time-constrained* schedule (ES through LF). You can schedule the resource anyplace *within* the interval and not delay the project. Scheduling the activity beyond the LF will delay the project.

The programmers are limited to three. Follow the actions described in Figures 8.4 and 8.5. Note how the limit of three programmers starts to delay the project.

Observe how it is necessary to update each period to reflect changes in activity early start and slack times so the heuristics can reflect changing priorities. When using

The Parallel Method:

Period	Action
	See Figure 8.4.
0–1	Only activity 1 is eligible. It requires 2 programmers.
	Load activity 1 into schedule.
1–2	No activities are eligible to be scheduled.
2–3	Activities 2, 3, and 4 are eligible to be scheduled. Activity 3 has the least slack (0)—apply rule 1.
	Load activity 3 into schedule.
	Activity 2 is next with slack of 2; however, activity 2 requires 2 programmers and only 1 is available.
	Delay activity 2. Update: ES = 3, slack = 1.
	The next eligible activity is activity 4, since it only requires 1 programmer.
	Load activity 4 into schedule.
	See Figure 8.5.
3–4	Activity 2 is eligible but exceeds limit of 3 programmers in pool.
	Delay activity 2. Update: ES = 4, slack = 0.
4–5	Activity 2 is eligible but exceeds limit of 3 programmers in pool.
	Delay activity 2. Update: ES = 5, LF = 11, slack = −1.
	Delay activity 7. Update: ES = 11, LF = 13, slack = −1.
5–6	Activity 2 is eligible but exceeds limit of 3 programmers in pool.
	Delay activity 2. Update: ES = 6, LF = 12, slack = −2.
	Delay activity 7. Update: ES = 12, LF = 14, slack = −2.
6–7	Activities 2, 5, and 6 are eligible with slack of −2, 2, and 0, respectively.
	Load activity 2 into schedule (rule 1).
	Because activity 6 has 0 slack, it is the next eligible activity.
	Load activity 6 into schedule (rule 1).
	The programmer limit of 3 is reached.
	Delay activity 5. Update: ES = 7, slack = 1.
7–8	Limit is reached. No programmers available.
	Delay activity 5. Update: ES = 8, slack = 0.
8–9	Limit is reached. No programmers available.
	Delay activity 5. Update: ES = 9, LF = 11, slack = −1.
9–10	Limit is reached. No programmers available.
	Delay activity 5. Update: ES = 10, LF = 12, slack = −2.
10–11	Activity 5 is eligible.
	Load activity 5 into schedule.
	(Note: Activity 6 does not have slack because there are no programmers available—3 maximum.)
11–12	No eligible activities.
12–13	Activity 7 is eligible.
	Load activity 7 into schedule.

the parallel scheduling method, the network in Figure 8.5 reflects the new schedule date of 14 time units, rather than the time-constrained project duration of 12 time units. The network has also been revised to reflect new start, finish, and slack times for each activity. Note that activity 6 is still critical and has a slack of 0 time units because no resources are available (they are being used on activities 2 and 5). Compare the slack for each activity found in Figures 8.4 and 8.5; slack has been reduced significantly. Note that activity 4 has only 2 units of slack rather than what appears to be

FIGURE 8.4 Resource-Constrained Schedule through Period 2–3

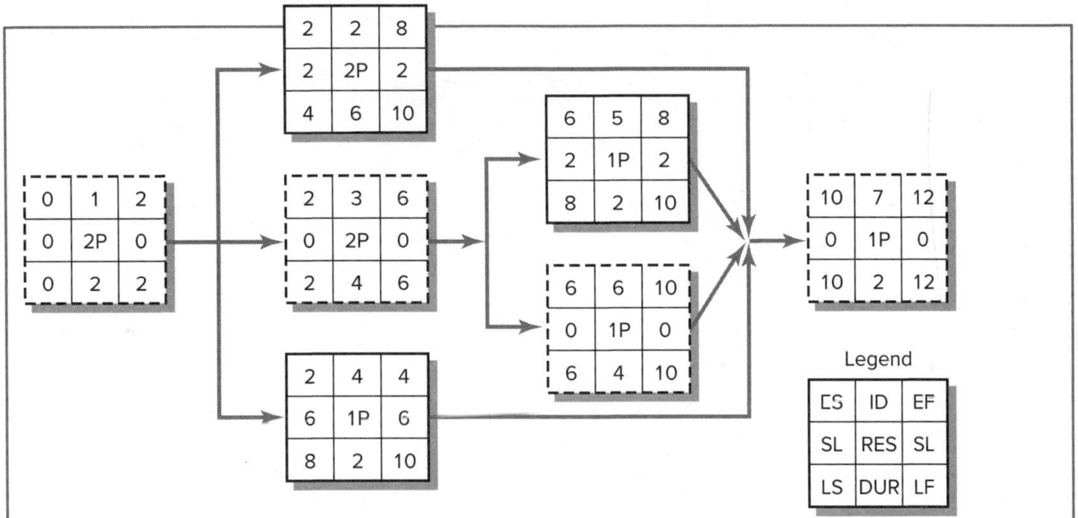

ES resource load chart

ID	RES	DUR	ES	LF	SL	0–1	1–2	2–3	3–4	4–5	5–6	6–7	7–8	8–9	9–10	10–11	11–12	12–13	13–14
1	2P	2	0	2	0	2	2												
2	2P	6	2	10	2			2	2	2	2	2	2						
3	2P	4	2	6	0			2	2	2	2								
4	1P	2	2	10	6			1	1										
5	1P	2	6	10	2							1	1						
6	1P	4	6	10	0							1	1	1	1				
7	1P	2	10	12	0											1	1		
Total resource load						2P	2P	5P	5P	4P	4P	4P	4P	1P	1P	1P	1P		

Resource-constrained schedule through period 2–3

ID	RES	DUR	ES	LF	SL	0–1	1–2	2–3	3–4	4–5	5–6	6–7	7–8	8–9	9–10	10–11	11–12	12–13	13–14
1	2P	2	0	2	0	2	2												
2	2P	6	~~2~~ 3	10	~~2~~ 1			X											
3	2P	4	2	6	0			2	2	2	2								
4	1P	2	2	10	6			1	1										
5	1P	2	6	10	2														
6	1P	4	6	10	0														
7	1P	2	10	12	0														
Total resource load						2P	2P	3P	3P	2P	2P								
Resource available						3P	3P	3P	3P	3P	3P	3P	3P	3P	3P	3P	3P		

FIGURE 8.5 Resource-Constrained Schedule through Period 5–6

Resource-constrained schedule through period 5–6

ID	RES	DUR	ES	LF	SL	0	1	2	3	4	5	6	7	8	9	10	11	12	13	14
1	2P	2	0	2	0	2	2													
2	2P	6	~~2~~ ~~3~~ ~~4~~ ~~5~~ 6	~~10~~ ~~11~~ 12	~~2~~ ~~1~~ ~~0~~ ~~-1~~ -2			X	X	X	X									
3	2P	4	2	6	0			2	2	2	2									
4	1P	2	2	10	6			1	1											
5	1P	2	6	10	2															
6	1P	4	6	10	0															
7	1P	2	~~10~~ ~~11~~ 12	~~12~~ ~~13~~ 14	~~0~~ ~~-1~~ -2											X	X			
	Total resource load					2P	2P	3P	3P	2P	2P									
	Resource available					3P	3P	3P	3P	3P	3P	3P	3P	3P	3P	3P	3P			

Final resource-constrained schedule

ID	RES	DUR	ES	LF	SL	0	1	2	3	4	5	6	7	8	9	10	11	12	13	14
1	2P	2	0	2	0	2	2													
2	2P	6	~~2~~ ~~3~~ ~~4~~ ~~5~~ 6	~~10~~ ~~11~~ 12	~~2~~ ~~1~~ ~~0~~ ~~-1~~ -2			X	X	X	X	2	2	2	2	2	2			
3	2P	4	2	6	0			2	2	2	2									
4	1P	2	2	6	~~6~~ 2			1	1	SL	SL									
5	1P	2	~~6~~ ~~7~~ ~~8~~ ~~9~~ 10	~~10~~ ~~11~~ 12	~~2~~ ~~1~~ ~~0~~ ~~-1~~ -2							X	X	X	X	1	1			
6	1P	4	6	10	0							1	1	1	1					
7	1P	2	~~10~~ ~~11~~ 12	~~12~~ ~~13~~ 14	~~0~~ ~~-1~~ -2											X	X	1	1	
	Total resource load					2P	2P	3P	3P	2P	2P	3P	3P	3P	3P	3P	3P	1P	1P	
	Resource available					3P	3P	3P	3P	3P	3P	3P	3P	3P	3P	3P	3P	3P	3P	

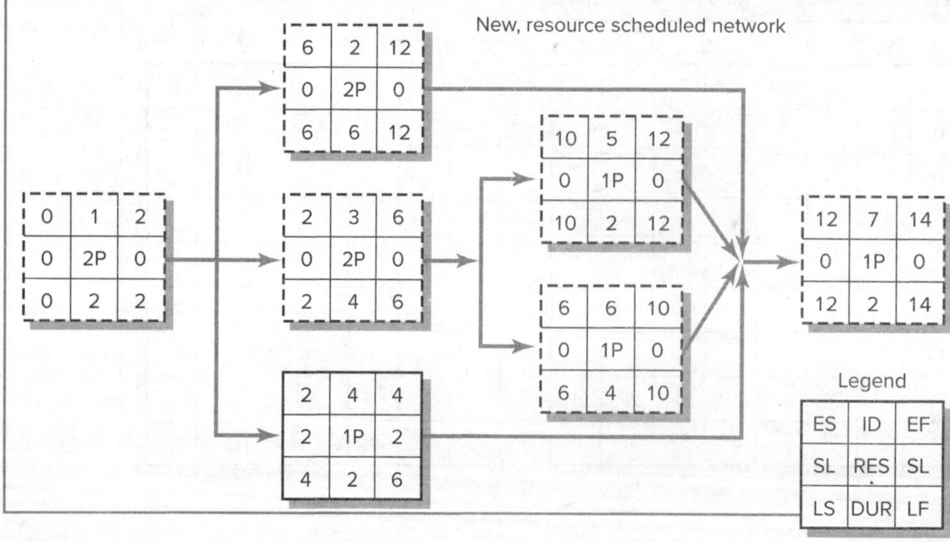

6 slack units. This occurs because only three programmers are available, and they are needed to satisfy the resource requirements of activities 2 and 5. Note that the number of critical activities (1, 2, 3, 5, 6, 7) has increased from four to six.

This small example demonstrates the scenario of scheduling resources in real projects and the resulting increase in the risk of being late. In practice this is not a trivial problem! Managers who fail to schedule resources usually encounter this scheduling risk when it is too late to work around the problem, resulting in a project delay.

Since manually using the parallel method is impractical on real-world projects because of size, project managers will depend on software programs to schedule project resources.

8.5 Computer Demonstration of Resource-Constrained Scheduling

LO 8-5

Understand how project management software creates resource-constrained schedules.

Fortunately, project management software is capable of assessing and resolving complicated resource-constrained schedules using heuristics similar to those described in the previous section. We will use the EMR project to demonstrate how this is done using MS Project. It is important to note that the software is not "managing" the project. The software is simply a tool the project manager uses to view the project from different perspectives and conditions. See Snapshot from Practice 8.2: Assessing Resource Allocation for more tips on assessing resource problems.

EMR is the name given to a hand-held electronic medical reference guide that is being developed to be used by emergency medical technicians and paramedics.

SNAPSHOT FROM PRACTICE 8.2 Assessing Resource Allocation

One of the strengths of project management software is the ability to identify and provide options for resolving resource allocation problems. One project manager who uses MS Project shared the following checklist for dealing with resource conflicts after preliminary assignment of resources.

1. Assess whether you have overallocation problems (see *Red* in the resource sheet view).
2. Identify where and when conflicts occur by examining the resource usage view.
3. Resolve the problem by
   a. Replacing overallocated resources with appropriate resources that are available. Then ask if this solves the problem.

   If not:

   b. Use the leveling tool and choose the level within slack option.
      i. Does this solve the problem? (Are resources still overallocated?)
      ii. Check the sensitivity of the network and ask if this is acceptable.

   If not:

   c. Consider splitting tasks.
      i. Make sure to readjust task durations to take into account additional start-up and shut-down time.
4. If 3 does not work, then either
   a. Use level tool default option and ask if you can live with the new completion date.

   If not:

   b. Negotiate for additional resources to complete the project. If not possible:

   c. Consider reducing project scope to meet deadline.

While this checklist makes specific references to MS Project, the same steps can be used with most project management software.

Figure 8.6 contains a time-limited network for the design phase of the project. For the purpose of this example, we assume that only design engineers are required for the tasks and that the design engineers are interchangeable. The number of engineers required to perform each task is noted in the network, where 500 percent means five design engineers are needed for the activity. For example, activity 5, feature specs, requires four design engineers (400 percent).

The project begins January 1 and ends February 14, a duration of 45 workdays. The calendar for the project has been set up to work seven days a week so the reader can trace and more easily see the results and impacts of resources—similar to manual solutions present in chapter exercises. The time-limited (constrained) bar chart for the project is shown in Figure 8.7. This bar chart incorporates the same information used to develop the project network but presents the project in the form of a bar chart along a timeline.

Finally, a resource usage chart is presented for a segment of the project—January 15 to January 23; see Figure 8.8A. Observe that the time-limited project requires 21 design engineers on January 18 and 19 (168 hrs/8 hrs per engineer = 21 engineers). This segment represents the peak requirement for design engineers for the project. However, due to the shortage of design engineers and commitments to other projects, only 8 engineers can be assigned to the project. This creates overallocation problems, more clearly detailed in Figure 8.8B, which is a resource loading chart for design engineers. Notice that the peak is 21 engineers and the limit of 8 engineers is shown by the gray shaded area.

To resolve this problem we use the "leveling" tool within the software and first try to solve the problem by leveling only within slack. This solution would preserve the original finish date. However, as expected, this does not solve all of the allocation problems. The next option is to allow the software to apply scheduling heuristics and level outside of slack. The new schedule is contained in the revised, resource-limited network chart presented in Figure 8.9. The resource-limited project network indicates the project duration has now been extended to 2/26, or 57 workdays (versus 45 days time limited). The critical path is now 2, 3, 9, 13.

Figure 8.10 presents the project bar chart and the results of leveling the project schedule to reflect the availability of only eight design engineers. The application of the heuristics can be seen in the scheduling of the internal, external, and feature specification activities. All three activities were originally scheduled to start immediately after activity 1, architectural decisions.

This is impossible, since the three activities collectively require 13 engineers. The software chooses to schedule activity 5 first because this activity is on the original critical path and has zero slack (heuristic rule # 1). Next, and concurrently, activity 4 is chosen over activity 3 because activity 4 has a shorter duration (heuristic rule # 2); internal specs, activity 3, is delayed due to the limitation of Eight design engineers. Notice that the original critical path no longer applies because of the resource dependencies created by having only eight design engineers. See Figure 8.6 for the original planned critical path.

Compare the bar chart in Figure 8.10 with the time-limited bar chart in Figure 8.7. For example, note the different start dates for activity 8 (screen). In the time-limited plan (Figure 8.7), the start date for activity 8 is 1/18, while the start date in the resource-limited schedule (Figure 8.10) is 2/16, almost a month later!

FIGURE 8.6 EMR Project Network View Schedule before Resources Leveled

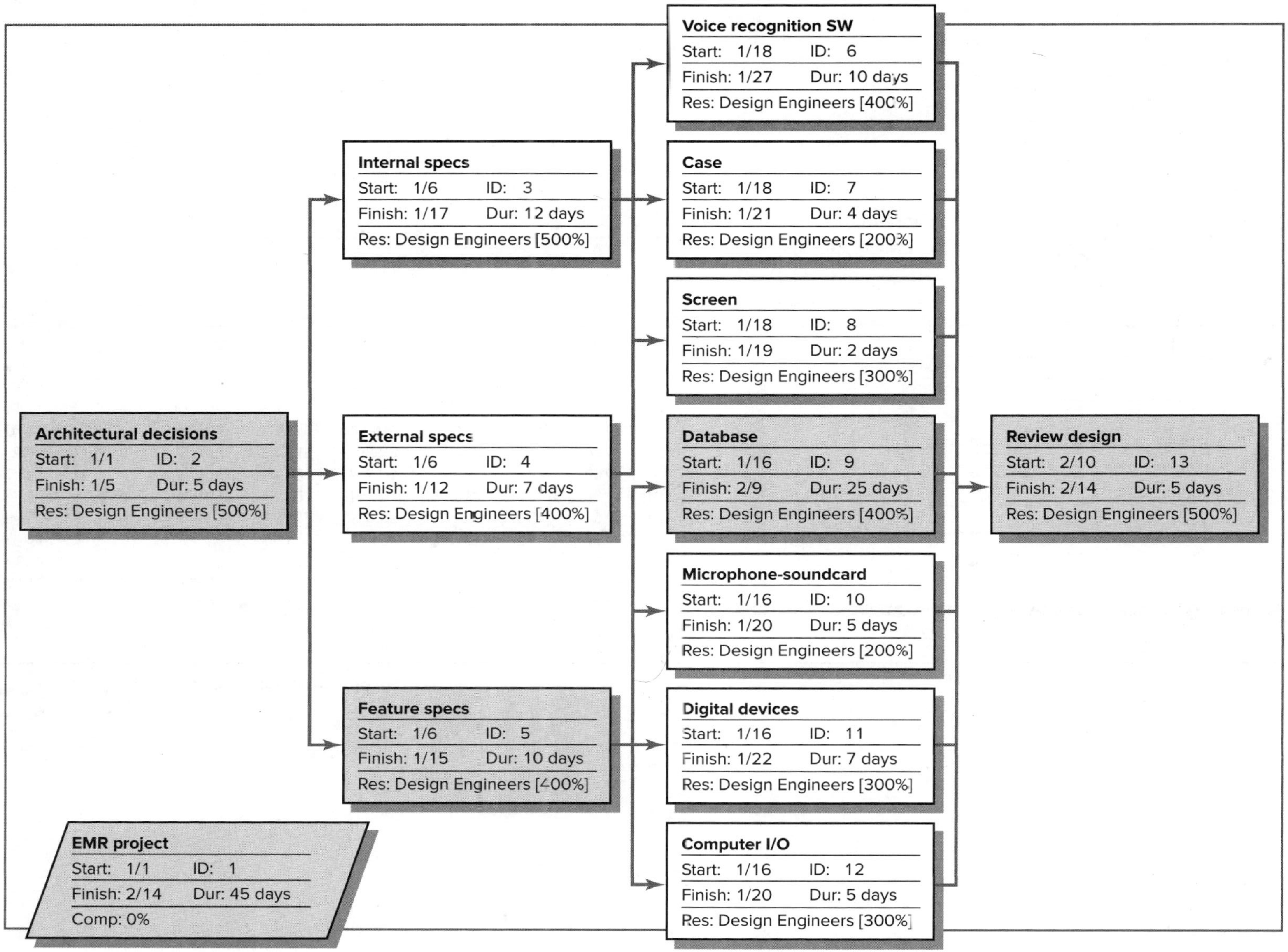

FIGURE 8.7 EMR Project before Resources Added

ID	Task Name	Start	Finish	Late Start	Late Finish	Free Slack	Total Slack
1	**EMR project**	**Tue 1/1**	**Thu 2/14**	**Tue 1/1**	**Thu 2/14**	**0 days**	**0 days**
2	Architectural decisions	Tue 1/1	Sat 1/5	Tue 1/1	Sat 1/5	0 days	0 days
3	Internal specs	Sun 1/6	Thu 1/17	Sat 1/19	Wed 1/30	0 days	13 days
4	External specs	Sun 1/6	Sat 1/12	Thu 1/24	Wed 1/30	5 days	18 days
5	Feature specs	Sun 1/6	Tue 1/15	Sun 1/6	Tue 1/15	0 days	0 days
6	Voice recognition SW	Fri 1/18	Sun 1/27	Thu 1/31	Sat 2/9	13 days	13 days
7	Case	Fri 1/18	Mon 1/21	Wed 2/6	Sat 2/9	19 days	19 days
8	Screen	Fri 1/18	Sat 1/19	Fri 2/8	Sat 2/9	21 days	21 days
9	Database	Wed 1/16	Sat 2/9	Wed 1/16	Sat 2/9	0 days	0 days
10	Microphone-soundcard	Wed 1/16	Sun 1/20	Tue 2/5	Sat 2/9	20 days	20 days
11	Digital devices	Wed 1/16	Tue 1/22	Sun 2/3	Sat 2/9	18 days	18 days
12	Computer I/O	Wed 1/16	Sun 1/20	Tue 2/5	Sat 2/9	20 days	20 days
13	Review design	Sun 2/10	Thu 2/14	Sun 2/10	Thu 2/14	0 days	0 days

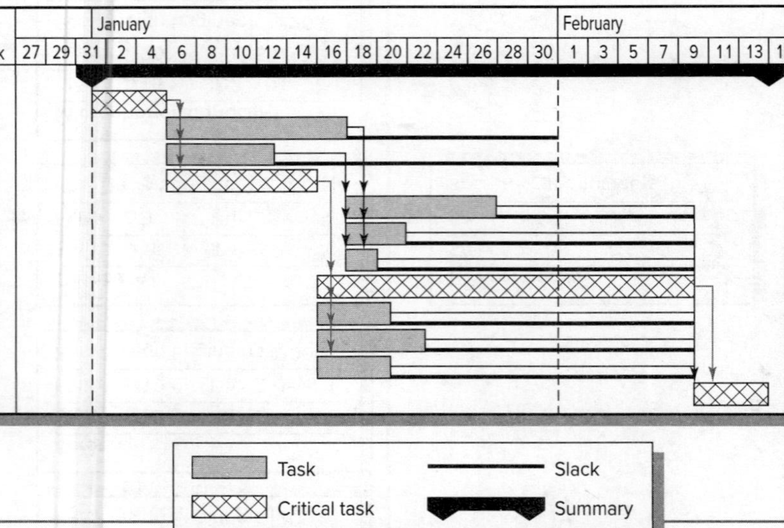

FIGURE 8.8A **EMR Project—Time-Constrained Resource Usage View, January 15–23**

Resource Name	Work	Jan 15						Jan 21		
		T	W	T	F	S	S	M	T	W
Design engineers	**3,024 hrs**	72h	136h	136h	168h	168h	144h	104h	88h	64h
Architectural decisions	200 hrs									
Internal specs	480 hrs	40h	40h	40h						
External specs	224 hrs									
Feature specs	320 hrs	32h								
Voice recognition SW	320 hrs				32h	32h	32h	32h	32h	32h
Case	64 hrs				16h	16h	16h	16h		
Screen	48 hrs				24h	24h				
Database	800 hrs		32h	32h	32h	32h	32h	32h	32h	32h
Microphone-soundcard	80 hrs		16h	16h	16h	16h	16h			
Digital devices	168 hrs		24h	24h	24h	24h	24h	24h	24h	
Computer I/O	120 hrs		24h	24h	24h	24h	24h			
Review design	200 hrs									

FIGURE 8.8B **Resource Loading Chart for EMR Project, January 15–23**

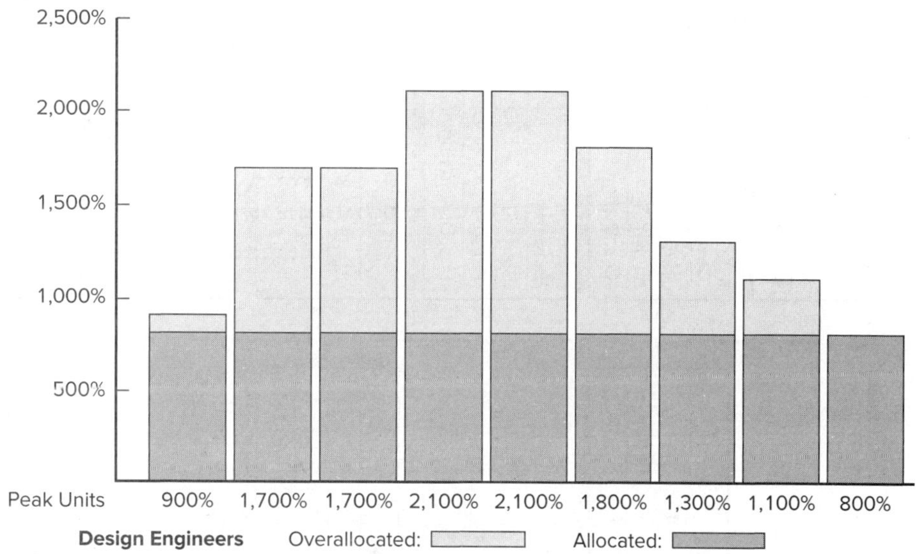

While resource bar graphs are commonly used to illustrate overallocation problems, we prefer to view resource usage tables like the one presented in Figure 8.8A. This table tells you when you have an overallocation problem and identifies activities that are causing the overallocation.

The Impacts of Resource-Constrained Scheduling

Like leveling schedules, the limited resource schedule usually reduces slack, reduces flexibility by using slack to ensure delay is minimized, and increases the number of critical and near-critical activities. Scheduling complexity is increased because resource constraints are added to technical constraints; start times may now have two constraints. The traditional critical path concept of sequential activities from the start to the end of the project is no longer meaningful. The resource constraints can break the sequence and leave the network with a set of disjointed critical activities.[1]

[1] See the appendix at the end of this chapter for more on how resource constraints affect project schedule.

FIGURE 8.9 EMR Project Network View Schedule after Resources Leveled

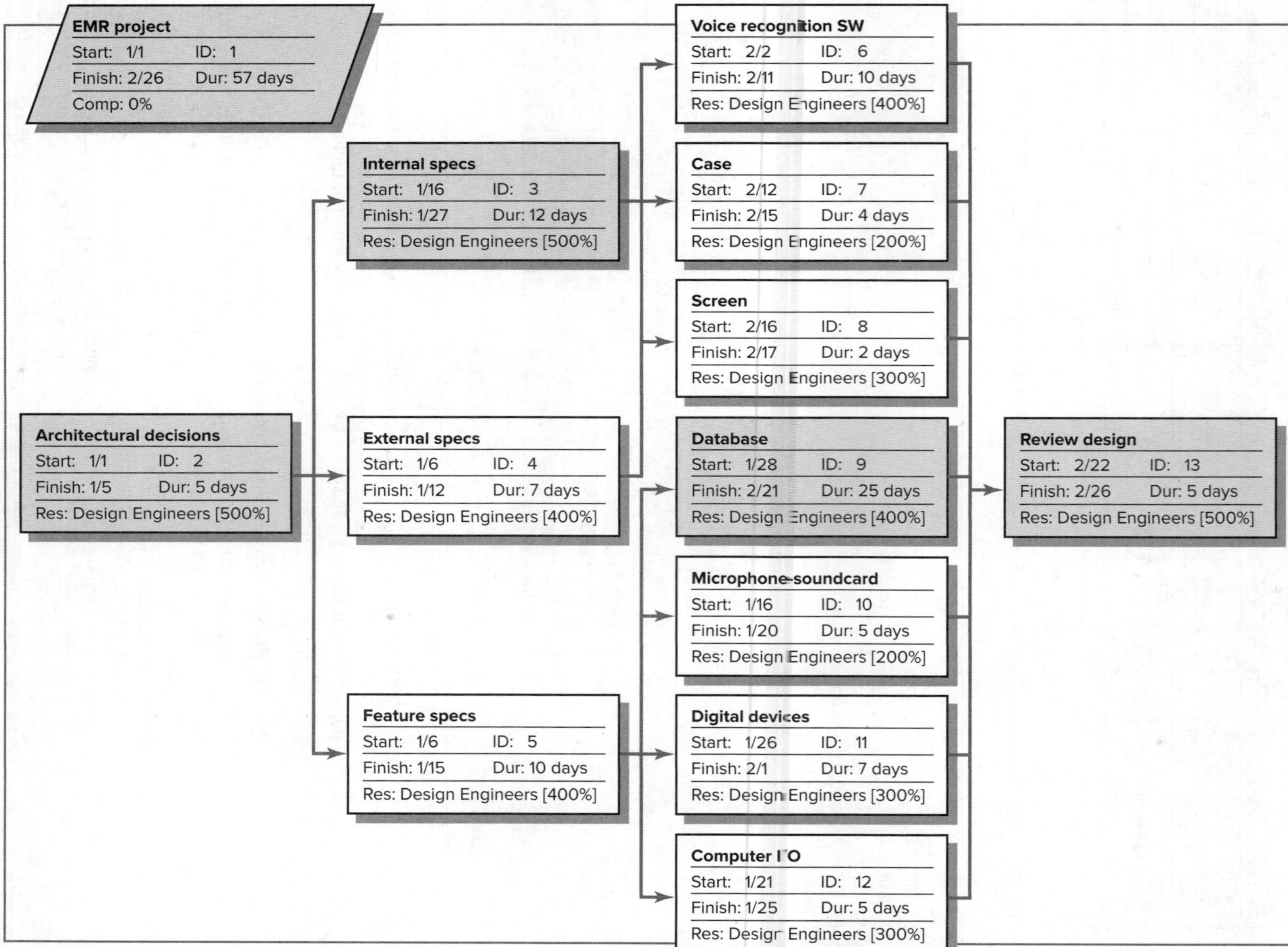

FIGURE 8.10 EMR Project Resources Leveled

ID	Task Name	Start	Finish	Late Start	Late Finish	Free Slack	Total Slack
1	**EMR project**	**Tue 1/1**	**Thu 2/26**	**Tue 1/1**	**Tue 2/26**	**0 days**	**0 days**
2	Architectural decisions	Tue 1/1	Sat 1/5	Tue 1/1	Sat 1/5	0 days	0 days
3	Internal specs	Wed 1/16	Sun 1/27	Sun 1/20	Thu 1/31	0 days	4 days
4	External specs	Sun 1/6	Sat 1/12	Fri 1/25	Thu 1/31	15 days	19 days
5	Feature specs	Sun 1/6	Tue 1/15	Sun 1/6	Tue 1/15	0 days	0 days
6	Voice recognition SW	Sat 2/2	Mon 2/11	Tue 2/12	Thu 2/21	10 days	10 days
7	Case	Tue 2/12	Fri 2/15	Mon 2/18	Thu 2/21	6 days	6 days
8	Screen	Sat 2/16	Sun 2/17	Wed 2/20	Thu 2/21	4 days	4 days
9	Database	Mon 1/28	Thu 2/21	Mon 1/28	Thu 2/21	0 days	0 days
10	Microphone-soundcard	Wed 1/16	Sun 1/20	Sun 2/17	Thu 2/21	32 days	32 days
11	Digital devices	Sat 1/26	Fri 2/1	Fri 2/15	Thu 2/21	20 days	20 days
12	Computer I/O	Mon 1/21	Fri 1/25	Sun 2/17	Thu 2/21	27 days	27 days
13	Review design	Fri 2/22	Tue 2/26	Fri 2/22	Tue 2/26	0 days	0 days

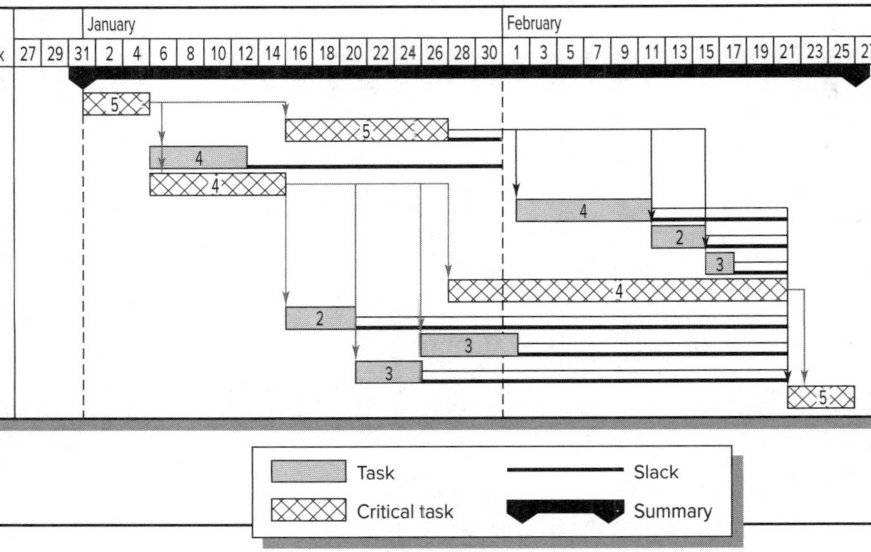

Conversely, parallel activities can become sequential. Activities with slack on a time-constrained network can change from critical to noncritical.

8.6 Splitting Activities

LO 8-6

Understand when and why splitting tasks should be avoided.

Splitting tasks is a scheduling technique used to get a better project schedule and/or to increase resource utilization. A planner splits the continuous work included in an activity by interrupting the work and sending the resource to another activity for a period of time and then having the resource resume work on the original activity. Splitting can be a useful tool if the work involved does not include large start-up or shutdown costs—for example, moving equipment from one activity location to another. Conversely, painting a house involves significant set-up and clean-up work.

One of the most common errors is to interrupt "people work," where there are high conceptual start-up and shutdown costs. For example, having a bridge designer take time off to work on the design problem of another project may cause this individual to lose four days shifting conceptual gears in and out of two activities. The cost may be hidden, but it is real. Figure 8.11 depicts the nature of the splitting problem. The original activity has been split into three separate activities: A, B, and C. The shutdown and start-up times lengthen the time for the original activity. One study reported that task switching can cost from 20 percent to 40 percent loss in efficiency (Rubinstein, Meyer, & Evans, 2001).

Some have argued that the propensity to deal with resource shortages by splitting is a major reason projects fail to meet schedule (c.f., Goldratt, 1997). We agree. Planners should avoid the use of splitting as much as possible, except in situations where splitting costs are known to be small or when there is no alternative for resolving the resource problem. Likewise, project managers need to protect against unnecessary interruptions and avoid the temptation to switch people for expediency's sake. Computer software offers the splitting option for each activity; use it sparingly.

FIGURE 8.11
Splitting Activities

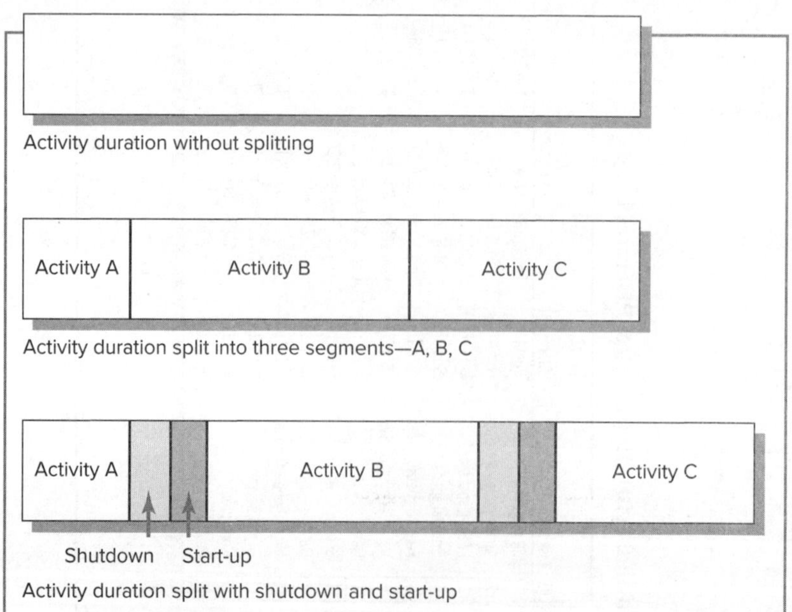

8.7 Benefits of Scheduling Resources

It is important to remember that if resources are truly limited and activity time estimates are accurate, the resource-constrained schedule *will* materialize as the project is implemented—*not* the time-constrained schedule! Therefore, failure to schedule limited resources can lead to serious problems for a project manager. The benefit of creating this schedule *before* the project begins leaves time for considering reasonable alternatives. If the scheduled delay is unacceptable or the risk of being delayed too high, the assumption of being resource constrained can be reassessed. Cost-time trade-offs can be considered. In some cases priorities may be changed. See Snapshot from Practice 8.3: U.S. Forest Service Resource Shortage.

Resource schedules provide the information needed to prepare time-phased work package budgets with dates. Once established, they provide a quick means for a project manager to gauge the impact of unforeseen events such as turnover, equipment breakdowns, or transfer of project personnel. Resource schedules also allow project managers to assess how much flexibility they have over certain resources. This is useful when they receive requests from other managers to borrow or share resources. Honoring such requests creates goodwill and an "IOU" that can be cashed in during a time of need.

SNAPSHOT FROM PRACTICE 8.3 U.S. Forest Service Resource Shortage

Darinburt/iStock/Getty Images

A major segment of work in managing U.S. Forest Service (USFS) forests is selling mature timber to logging companies that harvest the timber under contract conditions monitored by the service. The proceeds are returned to the federal government. The budget allocated to each forest depends on the two-year plan submitted to the U.S. Department of Agriculture.

Olympic Forest headquarters in Olympia, Washington, was developing a two-year plan as a basis for funding. All of the districts in the forest submitted their timber sale projects (numbering more than 50) to headquarters, where they were compiled and aggregated into a project plan for the whole forest. The first computer run was reviewed by a small group of senior managers to determine if the plan was reasonable and "doable." Management was pleased and relieved to note all projects appeared to be doable in the two-year time frame until a question was raised concerning the computer printout. "Why are all the columns in these projects labeled 'RESOURCE' blank?" The response from an engineer was "We don't use that part of the program."

The discussion that ensued recognized the importance of resources in completing the two-year plan and ended with a request to "try the program with resources included." The new output was startling. The two-year program turned into a three-and-a-half-year plan because of the shortage of specific labor skills such as road engineer and environmental impact specialist. Analysis showed that adding only three skilled people would allow the two-year plan to be completed on time. In addition, further analysis showed hiring only a few more skilled people, beyond the three, would allow an extra year of projects to also be compressed into the two-year plan. This would result in additional revenue of more than $3 million. The Department of Agriculture quickly approved the requested extra dollars for additional staff to generate the extra revenue.

8.8 Assigning Project Work

LO 8-7

Identify general guidelines for assigning people to specific tasks.

When making individual assignments, project managers should match, as best they can, the demands and requirements of specific work with the qualifications and experience of available participants. In doing so, there is a natural tendency to assign the best people the most difficult tasks. Project managers need to be careful not to overdo this. Over time these people may grow to resent the fact that they are always given the toughest assignments. At the same time, less experienced participants may resent the fact that they are never given the opportunity to expand their skill/knowledge base. Project managers need to balance task performance with the need to develop the talents of people assigned to the project.

Project managers need to decide not only who does what but also who works with whom. A number of factors need to be considered in deciding who should work together. First, to minimize unnecessary tension, managers should pick people with compatible work habits and personalities but who complement each other (i.e., one person's weakness is the other person's strength). For example, one person may be brilliant at solving complex problems but sloppy at documenting his/her progress. It would be wise to pair this person with an individual who is good at paying attention to details. Experience is another factor. Veterans should be teamed up with new hires—not only so they can share their experience but also to help socialize the newcomers to the customs and norms of the organization. Finally, future needs should be considered. If managers have some people who have never worked together before but who have to later on in the project, they may be wise to take advantage of opportunities to have these people work together early on so that they can become familiar with each other. Finally, see Snapshot from Practice 8.4: Managing Geeks for some interesting thoughts from the former CEO of Google on how to put together teams.

SNAPSHOT FROM PRACTICE 8.4 Managing Geeks*

Eric Schmidt, after a successful career at Sun Microsystems, took over struggling Novell, Inc., and helped turn it around within two years. Four years later he became the CEO of Google. One of the keys to his success is his ability to manage the technical wizards who develop the sophisticated systems, hardware, and software that are the backbone of electronically driven companies. He uses the term "geek" (and he can, since he is one, with a Ph.D. in computer science) to describe this group of technologists who rule the cyberworld.

Schmidt has some interesting ideas about assigning geeks to projects. He believes that putting geeks together in project teams with other geeks creates productive peer pressure. Geeks care a great deal about how other geeks perceive them. They are good at judging the quality of technical work and are quick to praise as well as criticize each other's work. Some geeks can be unbearably arrogant, but Schmidt claims that having them work together on projects is the best way to control them—by letting them control each other.

At the same time, Schmidt argues that too many geeks spoil the soup. By this he means that when there are too many geeks on a development team, there is a tendency for intense technical navel gazing. Members lose sight of deadlines, and delays are inevitable. To combat this tendency, he recommends using geeks only in small groups. He urges breaking up large projects into smaller, more manageable projects so that small teams of geeks can be assigned to them. This keeps the project on time and makes the teams responsible to each other.

*R. Mitchel, "How to Manage Geeks," *Fast Company,* May 31, 1999, pp. 175–80.

8.9 Multiproject Resource Schedules

LO 8-8

Identify common problems with multiproject resource scheduling.

For clarity we have discussed key resource allocation issues within the context of a single project. In reality resource allocation generally occurs in a multiproject environment where the demands of one project have to be reconciled with the needs of other projects. Organizations must develop and manage systems for efficiently allocating and scheduling resources across several projects with different priorities, resource requirements, sets of activities, and risks. The system must be dynamic and capable of accommodating new projects as well as reallocating resources once project work is completed. While the same resource issues and principles that apply to a single project also apply to this multiproject environment, application and solutions are more complex, given the interdependency among projects.

The following are three of the more common problems encountered in managing multiproject resource schedules. Note that these are macro manifestations of single-project problems that are now magnified in a multiproject environment.

1. **Overall schedule slippage.** Because projects often share resources, delays in one project can have a ripple effect and delay other projects. For example, work on one software development project can grind to a halt because the coders scheduled for the next critical task are late in completing their work on another development project.
2. **Inefficient resource utilization.** Because projects have different schedules and requirements, there are peaks and valleys in overall resource demands. For example, a firm may have a staff of 10 electricians to meet peak demands when, under normal conditions, only 5 electricians are required.
3. **Resource bottlenecks.** Delays and schedules are extended as a result of shortages of critical resources that are required by multiple projects. For example, at one Lattice Semiconductor facility, project schedules were delayed because of competition over access to test the equipment necessary to debug programs. Likewise, several projects at a U.S. forest area were extended because there was only one silviculturist on the staff.

To deal with these problems, more and more companies are creating project offices or departments to oversee the scheduling of resources across multiple projects. One approach to multiple project resource scheduling is to use a first come–first served rule. A project queue system is created in which projects currently under way take precedence over new projects. New project schedules are based on the projected availability of resources. This queuing tends to lead to more reliable completion estimates and is preferred on contracted projects that have stiff penalties for being late. The disadvantages of this deceptively simple approach are that it does not optimally utilize resources or take into account the priority of the project. See Snapshot from Practice 8.5: Multiple Project Resource Scheduling.

Many companies utilize more elaborate processes for scheduling resources to increase the capacity of the organization to initiate projects. Most of these methods approach the problem by treating individual projects as part of one big project and adapting the scheduling heuristics previously introduced to this "mega project." Project schedulers monitor resource usage and provide updated schedules based on progress and resource availability across all projects. One major improvement in project management software in recent years is the ability to prioritize resource allocation to specific projects. Projects can be prioritized in ascending order (e.g., 1, 2, 3, 4, . . .), and these priorities will override scheduling heuristics so that resources go to the project highest on the priority list. (Note: This improvement fits perfectly with organizations that use project priority models similar to those described in Chapter 2.) Centralized project scheduling also makes it easier to identify resource bottlenecks

SNAPSHOT FROM PRACTICE 8.5 Multiple Project Resource Scheduling

The case for a central source to oversee project resource scheduling is well known by practitioners. Here is a synopsis of a conversation with one middle manager.

Interviewer: Congratulations on acceptance of your multiproject scheduling proposal. Everyone tells me you were very convincing.

Middle Manager: Thanks. Gaining acceptance was easy this time. The board quickly recognized we have no choice if we are to keep ahead of competition by placing our resources on the right projects.

Interviewer: Have you presented this to the board before?

Middle Manager: Yes, but not this company. I presented the same spiel to the firm I worked for two years ago. For their annual review meeting I was charged to present a proposal suggesting the need and benefits of central capacity resource planning for managing the projects of the firm.

I tried to build a case for bringing projects under one umbrella to standardize practices and to forecast and assign key people to mission critical projects. I explained how benefits such as resource demands would be aligned with mission critical projects, proactive resource planning, and a tool for catching resource bottlenecks and resolving conflicts.

Almost everyone agreed the idea was a good one. I felt good about the presentation and felt confident something was going to happen. But the idea never really got off the ground; it just faded into the sunset.

With hindsight, managers really did not trust colleagues in other departments, so they only gave half-hearted support to central resource planning. Managers wanted to protect their turf and ensure that they would not have to give up power. The culture there was simply too inflexible for the world we live in today. They are still struggling with constant conflicts among projects.

I'm glad I made the switch to this firm. The culture here is much more team-oriented. Management is committed to improving performance.

that stifle progress on projects. Once bottlenecks have been identified, their impact can be documented and used to justify acquiring additional equipment, recruiting critical personnel, or delaying the project.

Finally, many companies are using outsourcing as a means of dealing with their resource allocation problems. In some cases, a company will reduce the number of projects they have to manage internally to only core projects and outsource noncritical projects to contractors and consulting firms. In other cases, specific segments of projects are outsourced to overcome resource deficiencies and scheduling problems. Companies may hire temporary workers to expedite certain activities that are falling behind schedule or contract project work during peak periods when there are insufficient internal resources to meet the demands of all projects. The ability to more efficiently manage the ebbs and flows of project work is one of the major driving forces behind outsourcing today, which is the subject of Chapter 12.

8.10 Using the Resource Schedule to Develop a Project Cost Baseline

LO 8-9

Explain why a time-phased budget baseline is needed.

Once resource assignments have been finalized, you are able to develop a baseline budget schedule for the project. Using your project schedule, you can *time-phase* work packages and assign them to their respective scheduled activities to develop a budget schedule over the life of your project. Understanding the reason for time-phasing your budget is very important. Without a time-phased budget, a good project schedule and cost control are impossible.

Why a Time-Phased Budget Baseline Is Needed

The need for a **time-phased budget baseline** is demonstrated in the following scenario. The development of a new product is to be completed in 10 weeks at an estimated cost of $400,000 per week, for a total cost of $4 million. Management wants a status report at the end of five weeks. The following information has been collected:

- Planned costs for the first five weeks are $2,000,000.
- Actual costs for the first five weeks are $2,400,000.

How are we doing? It would be easy to draw the conclusion there is a $400,000 cost overrun. But we really have no way of knowing. The $400,000 may represent money spent to move the project ahead of schedule. Assume another set of data at the end of Five weeks:

- Planned costs for the first five weeks are $2,000,000.
- Actual costs for the first five weeks are $1,700,000.

Is the project costing $300,000 less than we expected? Perhaps. But the $300,000 may represent the fact that the project is behind schedule and work has not started. Could it be the project is behind schedule and over cost? We cannot tell from these data. The many systems found in the real world that use only planned funds (a constant burn rate) and actual costs can provide false and misleading information. There is no way to be certain how much of the physical work has been accomplished. *These systems do not measure how much work was accomplished for the money spent! Hence, without time-phasing cost to match your project schedule, it is impossible to have reliable information for control purposes.*

Creating a Time-Phased Budget

LO 8-10

Create a time-phased project budget baseline.

By using information from your WBS and resource schedule, you can create a time-phased cost baseline. Remember from the WBS for the E-Slim Tablet Project in Chapter 4 that we integrated the WBS and OBS organization breakdown structure so the work packages could be tracked by deliverable and organization responsible. See Figure 8.12 for an example of a similar prototype project arranged by deliverable and organization unit responsible. For each intersection point of the WBS/OBS matrix, you see work package budgets and the total cost. The total cost at each intersection is called a cost or control account. For example, at the intersection of the Read/write head deliverable and the Production Department we see there are three work packages with a total budget of $200,000. The sum of all cost accounts in a column should represent the total costs for the deliverable. Conversely, the sum of the cost accounts in a row should represent the costs or budget for the organization unit responsible for accomplishing the work. You can continue to "roll up" costs on the WBS/OBS to total project costs. This WBS provides the information you can use to time-phase work packages and assign them to their respective scheduled activities over the life of the project.

Recall, from the development of your work breakdown structure for each work package, the following information needed to be developed:

1. Define work (what).
2. Identify time to complete a work package (how long).
3. Identify a time-phased budget to complete a work package (cost).
4. Identify resources needed to complete a work package (how much).
5. Identify a single person responsible for units of work (who).
6. Identify monitoring points for measuring progress (how well).

Number three, time-phasing the work package, is critical for the final step of creating your budget baseline. The process of time-phasing work packages, which is illustrated next, is demonstrated in Figure 8.13. The work package has a duration of three weeks. Assuming labor, materials, and equipment are tracked separately, the work package costs

FIGURE 8.12 Direct Labor Budget Rollup ($000)

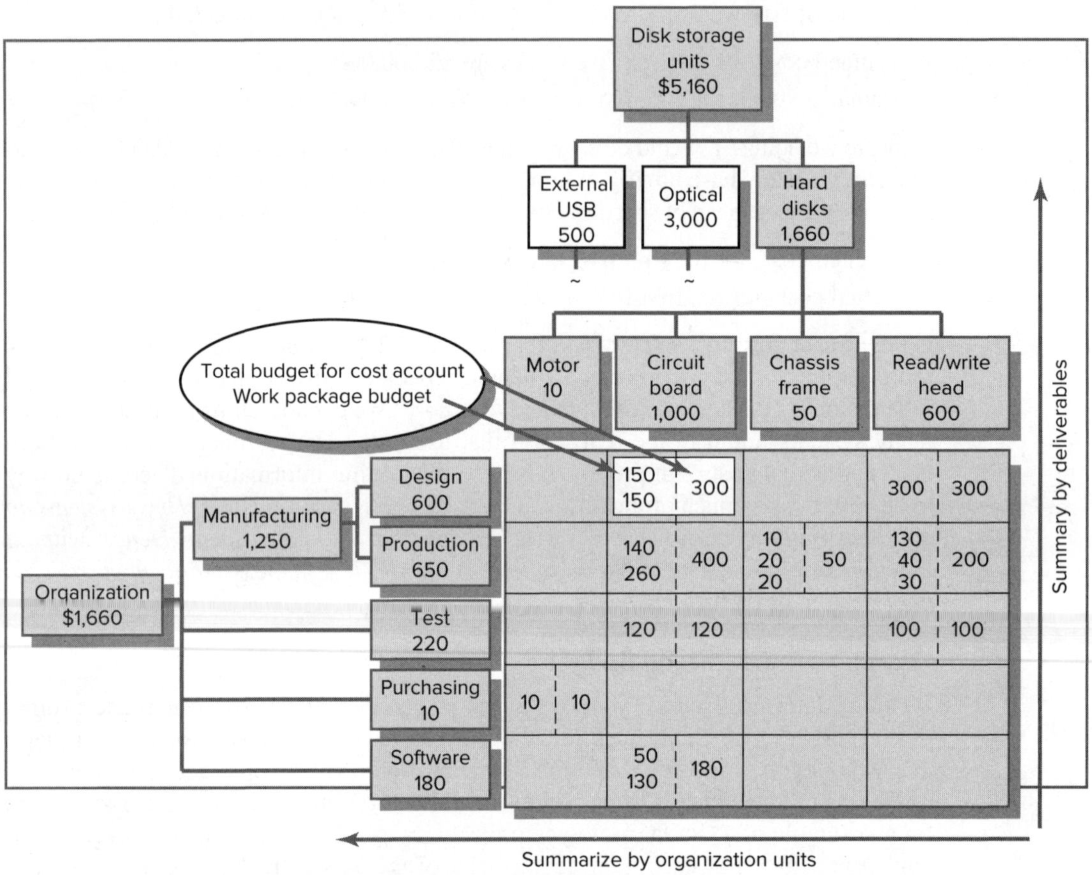

FIGURE 8.13 Time-Phased Work Package Budget (labor cost only)

Time-Phased Work Package Budget
Labor cost only

Work Package Description *Test* | Page *1* of *1*

Work Package ID ***1.1.3.2.3*** | Project *PC Prototype*

Deliverable *Circuit board* | Date *3/24/xx*

Responsible organization unit *Test* | Estimator *CEG*

Work Package Duration *3* weeks | Total labor cost *$120,000*

Time-Phased Labor Budget ($000)

Work Package	Resource	Labor rate	Work Periods–Weeks					
			1	2	3	4	5	Total
Code ***1.1.3.2.3***	Quality testers	$xxxx/ week	$40	$30	$50			$120

for labor are distributed over the three weeks as they are expected to occur—$40,000, $30,000, and $50,000 for each week, respectively. When the three-week work package is placed in the network schedule, the costs are distributed to the time-phased budget for the same three scheduled weeks. Fortunately, most single WPs become an activity and

FIGURE 8.14
Two Time-Phased Work Packages (labor cost only)

Time-Phased Work Package Budget
Labor cost only

Work Package Description *Software*
Page *1* of *1*
Work Package ID ***1.1.3.2.4.1 and 1.1.3.2.4.2***
Project *PC Prototype*
Deliverable *Circuit board*
Date *3/24/xx*
Responsible organization unit *Software*
Estimator *LGG*
Work Package Duration *4* weeks
Total labor cost *$180,000*

Time-Phased Labor Budget ($000)

Work Package	Resource	Labor rate	Work Periods–Weeks 1	2	3	4	5	Total
Code ***1.1.3.2.4.1***	Program'rs	$2,000/ week	$20	$15	$15			$50
Integration ***1.1.3.2.4.2***	System/ program'rs	$2,500/ week			$60	$70		$130
Total			$20	$15	$75	$70		$180

the process of distributing costs is relatively simple. That is, the relationship is one-for-one. Such budget timing is directly from the work package to the activity.

In a few instances an activity will include more than one work package, where the packages are assigned to *one responsible person or department and deliverable.* In this case the work packages are consolidated into one activity. As seen in Figure 8.14, this activity includes two WPs. The first, WP-1.1.3.2.4.1 (Code), is distributed over the first three weeks. The second, WP-1.1.3.2.4.2 (Integration), is sequenced over weeks 3 and 4. The activity duration is four weeks. When the activity is placed in the schedule, the costs are distributed starting with the schedule start—$20,000, $15,000, $75,000, and $70,000, respectively.

These time-phased budgets for work packages are lifted from your WBS and are placed in your project schedule as they are expected to occur over the life of the project. The outcome of these budget allocations is the project *cost* baseline (also called **planned value—PV**), which is used to determine cost and schedule variances as the project is implemented.

Figure 8.15 shows the Patient Entry project network schedule, which is used to place the time-phased work packages' budgets in the baseline. Figure 8.16 presents the project time-phased budget for the Patient Entry project and the cumulative graph of the project budget baseline. In this figure, you can see how the time-phased work package costs were placed into the network and how the cumulative project budget graph for a project is developed. Notice that costs do not have to be distributed linearly, but the costs should be placed as you expect them to occur.

You have now developed complete time and cost plans for your project. These project baselines will be used to compare planned schedule and costs using an integrative system called *earned value.* The application and use of project baselines to measure performance are discussed in detail in Chapter 13. With your project budget baseline established, you are also able to generate cash flow statements for your project, like the one presented in Figure 8.17. Such statements prepare the firm to cover costs over the lifespan of the project. Finally, with resource assignments finalized, you are able to generate resource usage schedules for your project (see Figure 8.18). These schedules map out the full deployment of personnel and equipment and can be used to generate individual work schedules.

FIGURE 8.15 Patient Entry Project Network

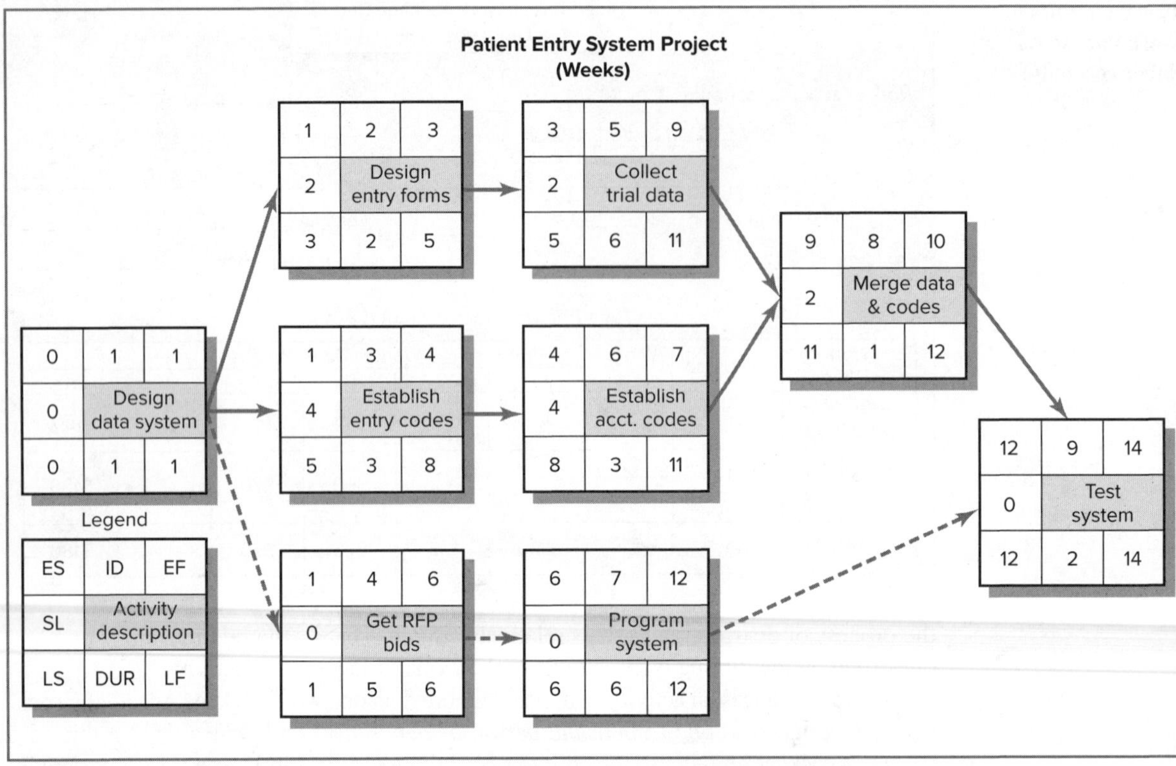

FIGURE 8.16 Patient Entry Time-Phased Work Packages Assigned

($000) Week

ID	Dur.	Task	Budget	1	2	3	4	5	6	7	8	9	10	11	12	13	14
1	1	Design data system	5	5													
2	2	Design entry forms	4		2	2											
3	3	Establish entry codes	6		2	2	2										
4	5	Get RFP bids	3		2				1								
5	6	Collect trial data	6				1	1	1	1	1	1					
6	3	Establish account codes	5					2	2	1							
7	6	Program system	12							2		4	2		4		
8	1	Merge data & codes	4										4				
9	2	Test system	7													4	3
		Week total	52	5	6	4	3	3	4	4	1	5	6	0	4	4	3
		Cumulative		5	11	15	18	21	25	29	30	35	41	41	45	49	52

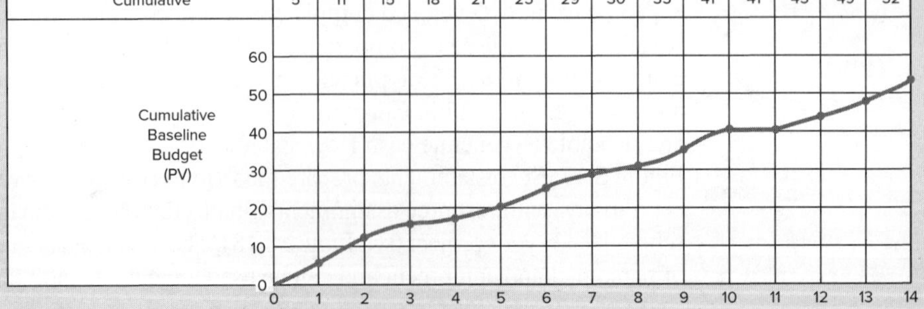

FIGURE 8.17
Project Monthly Cash Flow Statement

	January	February	March	April	May	June	July
Project							
Hardware							
Hardware specifications	$11,480.00	$24,840.00	$3,360.00				
Hardware design			$23,120.00	$29,920.00	$14,960.00		
Hardware documentation					$14,080.00	$24,320.00	
Prototypes							
Order GXs							
Assemble preproduction models							
Operating system							
Kernel specifications	$5,320.00	$9,880.00					
Drivers							
OC drivers				$3,360.00	$12,320.00	$11,760.00	$12,880.00
Serial VO drivers							
Memory management							
Operating system documentation		$10,240.00	$21,760.00				
Network interface							
Utilities							
Utilities specifications				$8,400.00			
Routine utilities				$5,760.00	$21,120.00	$20,160.00	$10,560.00
Complex utilities							
Utilities documentation				$7,680.00	$17,920.00		
Shell							
System integration							
Architectural decisions	$20,400.00						
Integration first phase							
System H/S test							
Project documentation							
Integration acceptance test							
Total	$37,200.00	$44,960.00	$48,240.00	$55,120.00	$80,400.00	$56,240.00	$23,440.00

FIGURE 8.18
Project Weekly Resource Usage Schedule

	12/30	1/6	1/13	1/20	1/27	2/03
I. Suzuki	24 hrs	40 hrs	40 hrs	40 hrs	40 hrs	40 hrs
Hardware specifications				24 hrs	40 hrs	40 hrs
Hardware design						
Hardware documentation						
Operating system documentation						
Utilities documentation						
Architectural decisions	24 hrs	40 hrs	40 hrs	16 hrs		
J. Lopez	24 hrs	40 hrs	40 hrs	40 hrs	40 hrs	40 hrs
Hardware specifications				12 hrs	20 hrs	20 hrs
Hardware design						
Prototypes						
Kernel specifications				12 hrs	20 hrs	20 hrs
Utilities specifications						
Architectural decisions	24 hrs	40 hrs	40 hrs	16 hrs		
Integration first phase						
J.J. Putz				24 hrs	40 hrs	40 hrs
Hardware documentation						
Kernel specifications				24 hrs	40 hrs	40 hrs
Operating system documentation						
Utilities documentation						
Project documentation						
R. Sexon				24 hrs	40 hrs	40 hrs
Hardware specifications				24 hrs	40 hrs	40 hrs
Prototypes						
Assemble preproduction models						
OC drivers						
Complex utilities						
Integration first phase						
System H/S test						
Integration acceptance test						

SNAPSHOT FROM PRACTICE 8.6 Indian Telecom Company – PMO for Scheduling Resources and Costs

A Project Management Office (PMO) centralizes and coordinates project management activities, ensuring standardization, governance, and smooth execution. Its key objectives include:

- Streamlining and standardizing project processes
- Enforcing governance rules and procedures for project delivery
- Monitoring and controlling execution
- Managing project knowledge and developing team skills
- Advising senior management on resource allocation

KEY STAKEHOLDERS

- Customer
- Project Manager
- Project Office
- Project Team (Subject Matter Experts, Team Leads, Technical Team, Documenters, QA/QC, etc.)
- Client Partner
- Sales Director

Project Implementation Process

The project implementation process consists of three phases:

- Pre-delivery
- Delivery
- Post-delivery

It begins with receiving the Letter of Award (LOA) from the customer, which sets the terms and conditions of service engagement. Following this, the project scope confirmation ensures alignment with the initial proposal, often using a Requirement Traceability Matrix. Given the extended duration of tendering, adjustments to scope may be necessary due to evolving requirements or technological changes.

CONTRACT PREPARATION

Once the scope is confirmed, contract preparation begins, formalizing agreements through:

- **Main Contract:** Signed between the customer and the vendor.
- **Sub-Contracts:** Signed between the vendor and third-party partners, linked to the Main Contract.

PROJECT DELIVERY PHASE

This phase integrates Project Management and Financial Management to ensure smooth execution while maintaining budgetary control. The delivery phase involves:

- **Project Initiation:** Conducting a formal kick-off meeting to establish strategies, milestones, timelines, deliverables, and stakeholder expectations.
- **Planning:** The Project Manager works with team leads and vendors to create a detailed timeline, defining start and end dates for each task.

Execution & Resource Management: Managing activities per the detailed plan, ensuring effective communication with all stakeholders, and reporting progress to the customer.

MONITORING & CONTROLLING

- **Timeline Management:** Tracking dependencies and detecting delays using tools like timesheets and scheduling systems.
- **Risk & Issue Management:** Conducting weekly risk assessments and logging resolutions. If an issue affects the timeline, mitigation plans are implemented with necessary approvals.

By employing a structured PMO framework, telecom projects benefit from standardization, risk mitigation, and quality assurance, leading to improved stakeholder engagement, detailed planning, and efficient resource management. Tools like the Requirement Traceability Matrix and Change Control Board ensure minimal disruptions, keeping deliverables aligned with client expectations.

Summary

A project schedule is not a schedule until resources have been assigned. If resources are inadequate then task sequences are likely to be impacted and the schedule extended. If resources are adequate it may be advantageous to "smooth" resources to improve their utilization. The results after resource scheduling are frequently significantly different from the results of the standard CPM method.

With the rapid changes in technology and emphasis on time-to-market, catching resource usage and availability problems before the project starts can save the costs of crashing (reducing) project activities later. Any resource deviations from plan and schedule that occur when the project is being implemented can be quickly recorded and the effect noted. Without this immediate update capability, the real negative effect of a change may not be known until it happens. Tying resource availability to a multiproject, multiresource system supports a project priority process that selects projects by their contribution to the organization's objectives and strategic plan.

Assignment of individuals to projects may not fit well with those assigned by computer software routines. In these cases, overriding the computer solution to accommodate individual differences and skills is almost always the best choice.

The project resource schedule is important because it serves as your time baseline, which is used for measuring time differences between plan and actual. The resource schedule serves as the basis for developing your time-phased project cost budget baseline. The baseline (planned value, PV) is the sum of the cost accounts, and each cost account is the sum of the work packages in the cost account. Remember, if your budgeted costs are not time-phased, you have no reliable way to measure performance. Although there are several types of project costs, the cost baseline is usually limited to direct costs (such as labor, materials, and equipment) that are under the control of the project manager; other, indirect costs can be added to project costs separately.

Key Terms

Baseline, *302*
Heuristics, *309*
Leveling, *306*
Planned value—(PV), *327*
Resource-constrained project, *306*
Resource-constrained scheduling, *303*
Resource smoothing, *303*
Splitting, *306*
Time-constrained project, *306*
Time-phased budget baseline, *324*

Review Questions

1. How does resource scheduling tie to project priority?
2. How does resource scheduling reduce flexibility in managing projects?
3. Present six reasons scheduling resources is an important task.
4. How can outsourcing project work alleviate the three most common problems associated with multiproject resource scheduling?
5. Explain the risks associated with leveling resources, compressing or crashing projects, and imposed durations or "catch-up" as the project is being implemented.
6. Why is it critical to develop a time-phased baseline?

SNAPSHOT FROM PRACTICE

Discussion Questions

8.1 *Working in Tight Places*

1. Can you think of other examples where the physical environment constrains project work?

8.3 *U.S. Forest Service Resource Shortage*

1. What do you think would have happened if the Washington Forest Service did not assess the impact of resources on their two-year plan?

8.4 *Managing Geeks*

1. Do you agree that geeks are different from other workers?

8.5 *Multiple Project Resource Scheduling*

1. Why would people resist a multiproject resource scheduling system?

Exercises

1. Consider a project with the accompanying Gantt chart. Stella is your only electrical engineer and she is responsible for activities 3 and 4, which overlap. Level the project so that Stella is only working a maximum of eight hours each day. What would the new Gantt chart look like? What would be the new project completion date?

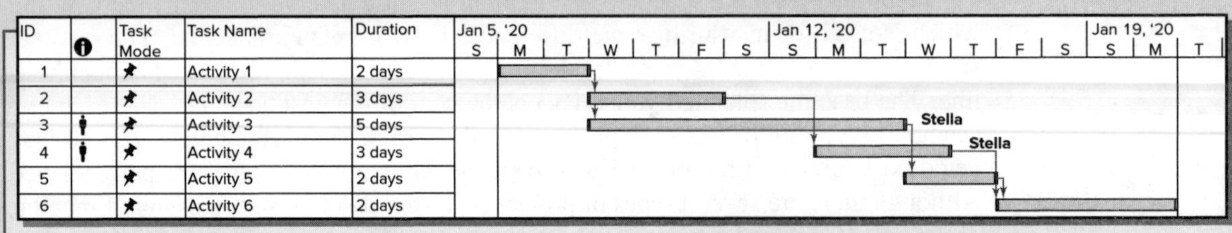

Consider a project with the following Gantt chart to answer exercises 2 and 3.

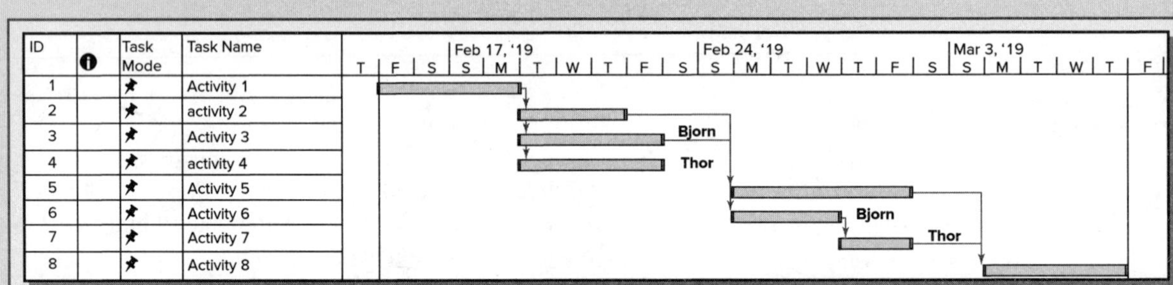

2. Bjorn and Thor are plumbers who have been scheduled to work on the construction of a new school building. Just before the start of the project, Bjorn broke his arm and cannot work on the project. Now Thor has to handle his own activities as well as Bjorn's. Level the project Gantt chart so that Thor is responsible for activities 3, 4, 6, and 7. What is the new estimated completion date for the project?
3. Suppose instead of assigning Bjorn's work to Thor, you have the opportunity to hire two new plumbers to perform Bjorn tasks (shortening them by 50 percent). What would the new project estimated completion date be? Show your work.

4. Given the network plan that follows, compute the early, late, and slack times. What is the project duration? Using any approach you wish (e.g., trial and error), develop a loading chart for resource, electrical engineers (EE), and resource, mechanical engineers (ME). Assume only one of each resource exists. Given your resource schedule, compute the early, late, and slack times for your project. Which activities are now critical? What is the project duration now? Could something like this happen in real projects?

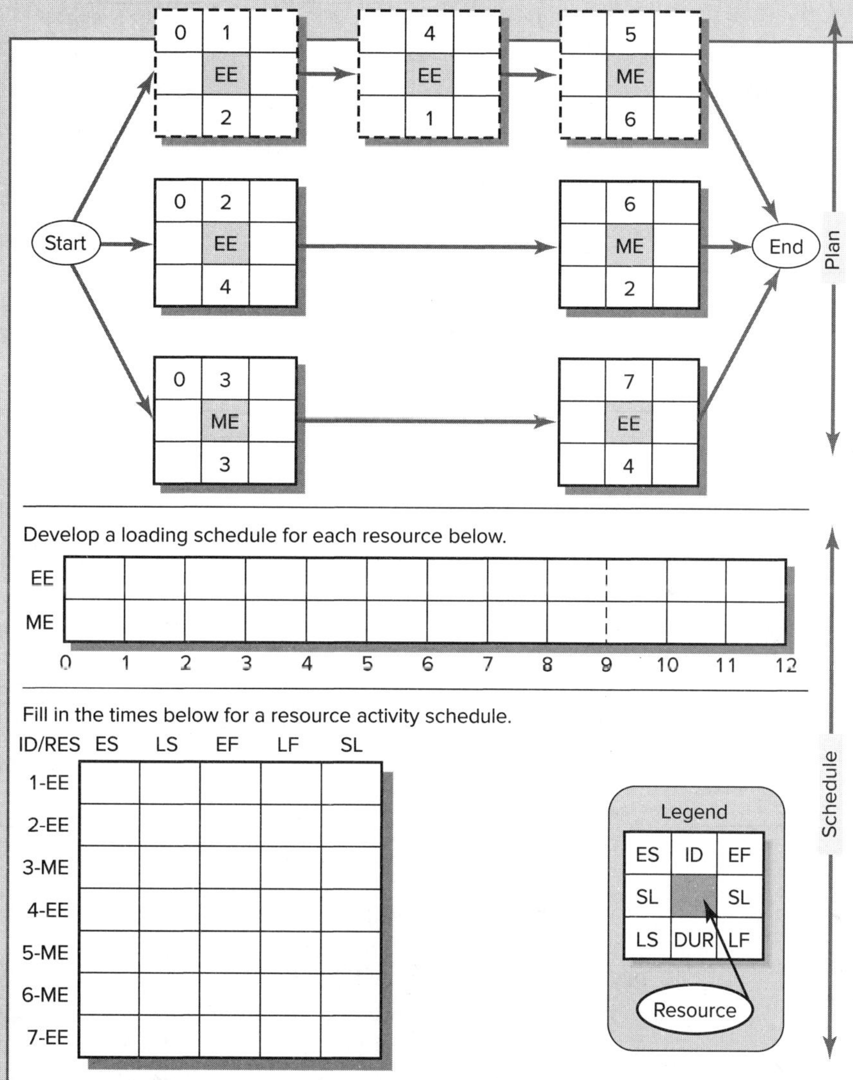

5. Given the network plan that follows, compute the early, late, and slack times. What is the project duration? Using any approach you wish (e.g., trial and error), develop a loading chart for resources carpenters (C) and electricians (E). Assume only one carpenter is available and two electricians are available. Given your

resource schedule, compute the early, late, and slack times for your project. Which activities are now critical? What is the project duration now?

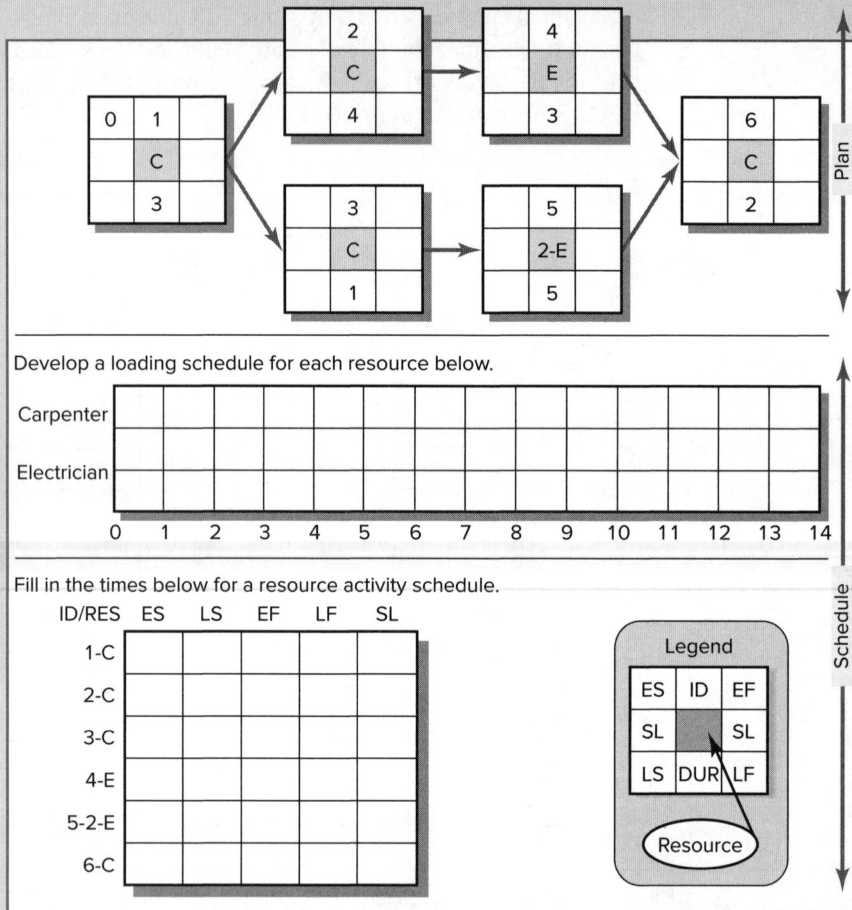

6. Compute the early, late, and slack times for the activities in the network that follows, assuming a time-constrained network. Which activities are critical? What is the time-constrained project duration?

   Note: Recall that in the schedule resource load chart the *time-constrained* scheduling interval (ES through LF) has been shaded. Any resource scheduled beyond the shaded area will delay the project.

   Assume you have only three resources and you are using software that schedules projects by the parallel method and following heuristics. Schedule only one period at a time!

   Minimum slack

   Smallest duration

   Lowest identification number

   Keep a log of each activity change and update you make each period—for example, period 0–1, 1–2, 2–3, etc. (Use a format similar to the one on page 274)

The log should include any changes or updates in ES, LF, and slack times each period, activities scheduled, and activities delayed. (Hint: Remember to maintain the technical dependencies of the network.) Use the resource load chart to assist you in scheduling (see Figures 8.4 and 8.5).

List the order in which you scheduled the activities of the project. Which activities of your schedule are now critical?

Recompute your slack for each activity, given your new schedule. What is the slack for activity 1? 4? 5?

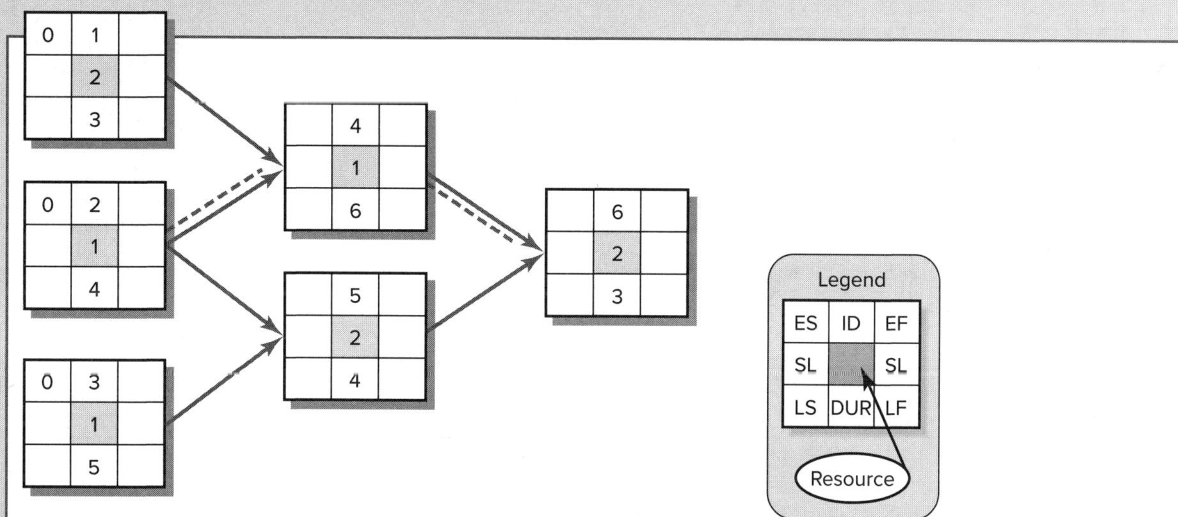

Scheduled resource load chart with ES and slack updates

Time scale: 0 1 2 3 4 5 6 7 8 9 10 11 12 13 14 15

ID	RES	DUR	ES	LF	SL															
1	2	3	0	4	1															
2	1	4	0	4	0															
3	1	5	0	6	1															
4	1	6	4	10	0															
5	2	4	5	10	1															
6	2	3	10	13	0															
Resources scheduled																				
Resources available						3	3	3	3	3	3	3	3	3	3	3	3	3	3	3

7. You have prepared the following schedule for a project in which the key resource is a tractor(s).* There are three tractors available to the project. Activities A and D require one tractor to complete, while activities B, C, E, and F require two tractors.

* The solution to this exercise can be found in Appendix One.

Develop a resource-constrained schedule in the loading chart that follows. Use the parallel method and heuristics given. Be sure to update each period as the computer would do. Record the early start (ES), late finish (LF), and slack (SL) for the new schedule.

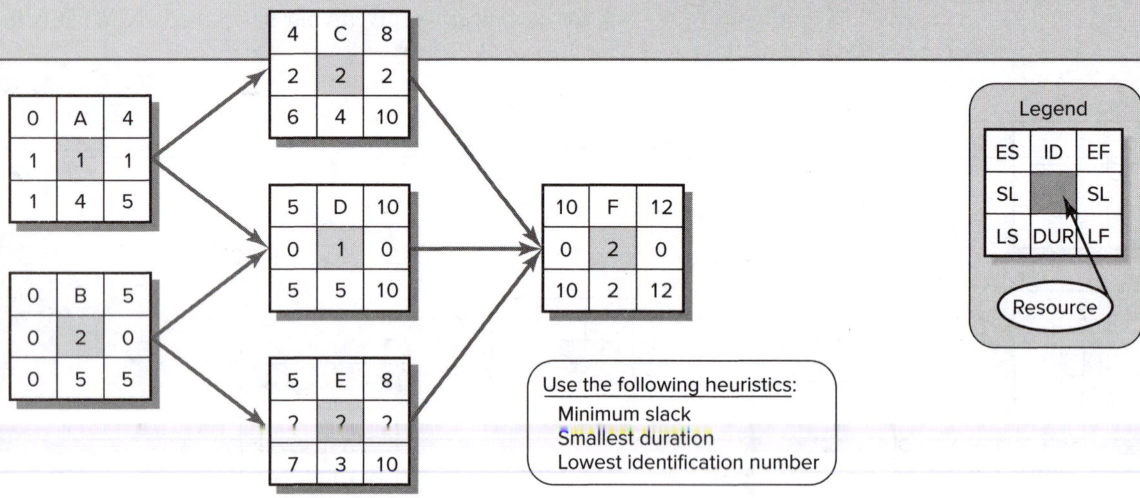

ID	RES	DUR	ES	LF	SL	0–1	1–2	2–3	3–4	4–5	5–6	6–7	7–8	8–9	9–10	10–11	11–12	12–13	13–14	14–15
A	1	4																		
B	2	5																		
C	2	4																		
D	1	5																		
E	2	3																		
F	2	2																		
Resources scheduled																				
Resources available						3	3	3	3	3	3	3	3	3	3	3	3	3	3	3

8. Develop a resource schedule in the loading chart that follows. Use the parallel method and heuristics given. Be sure to update each period as the computer would do. Note: Activities 2, 3, 5, and 6 use two of the resource skills. Three of the resource skills are available. How has slack changed for each activity? Has the risk of being late changed? How?

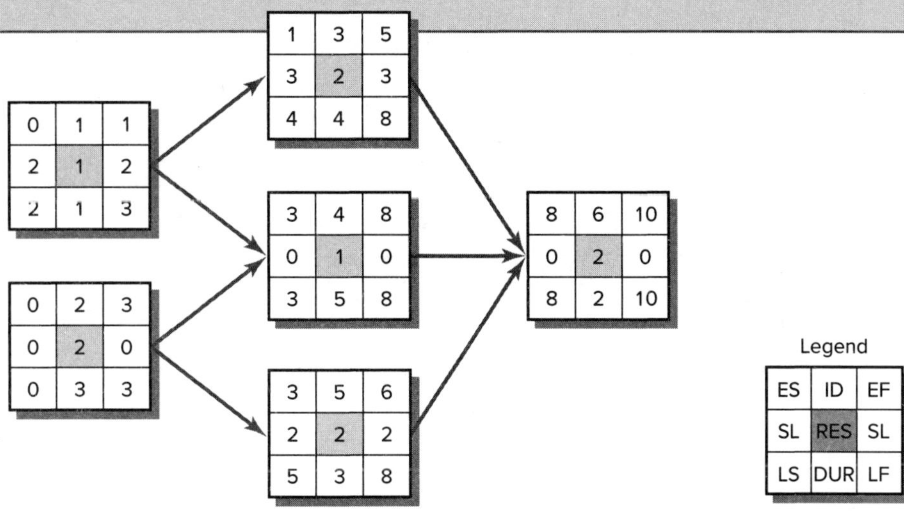

Use the following heuristics:
- Minimum slack
- Smallest duration
- Lowest identification number

List the order in which your activities are scheduled

/______/______/______/

/______/______/______/

ID	RES	DUR	ES	LF	SL	0	1	2	3	4	5	6	7	8	9	10	11	12
1	1	1	0	3														
2	2	3	0	3														
3	2	4	1	8														
4	1	5	3	8														
5	2	3																
6	2	2																
	Resources scheduled																	
	Resources available					3	3	3	3	3	3	3	3	3	3	3	3	3

What is the schedule slack for 1_____, 3_____, and 4______?
Which activities are critical now? ______________________

9. You have prepared the following schedule for a project in which the key resource is a backhoe(s). This schedule is contingent on having three backhoes. You receive a call from your partner, Brooker, who desperately needs one of your backhoes.

You tell Brooker you are willing to let him have the backhoe if you are still able to complete your project in 11 months.

Develop a resource schedule in the loading chart that follows to see if it is possible to complete the project in 11 months with only two backhoes. Be sure to record the order in which you schedule the activities using scheduling heuristics. Activities 5 and 6 require two backhoes, while activities 1, 2, 3, and 4 require one backhoe. No splitting of activities is possible. Can you say yes to Brooker's request?

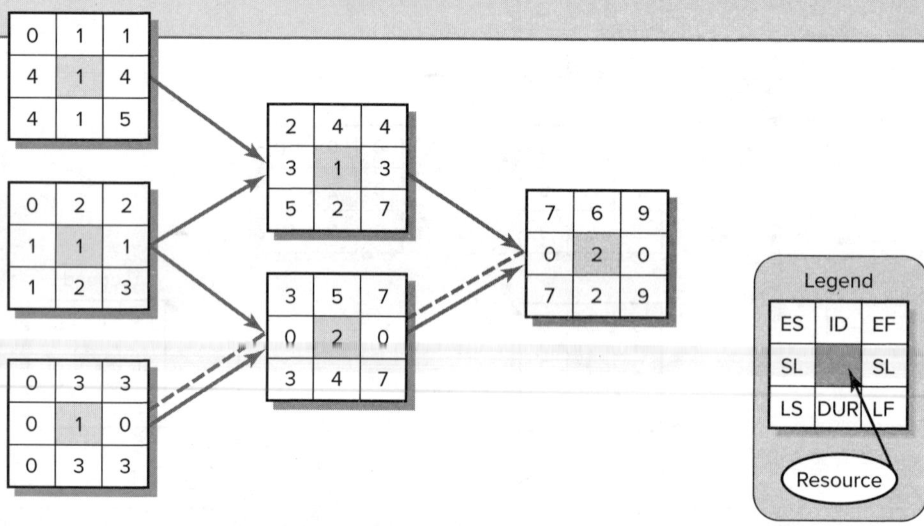

Schedule the resource load chart with ES and slack updates

ID	RES	DUR	ES	LF	SL	0	1	2	3	4	5	6	7	8	9	10	11	12
1	1	1	0	5	4													
2	1	2	0	3	1													
3	1	3	0	3	0													
4	1	2	2	7	3													
5	2	4	3	7	0													
6	2	2	7	9	0													
Resources scheduled																		
Resources available						2	2	2	2	2	2	2	2	2	2	2	2	2

10. You are one of three carpenters assigned to complete a short construction project.* Right before the start of the project, one of your fellow carpenters is hospitalized and will not be available to work on the project.

    Develop a resource-constrained schedule in the loading chart that follows to see how long the project will take with only two carpenters. Be sure to record the

* The solution to this exercise can be found in Appendix One.

order in which you schedule the activities using the scheduling heuristics. Activities A, B, C, D, E, G, and H require two carpenters to complete. Activity F requires only one carpenter. No splitting of activities is possible.

You will receive a bonus if the project is completed within 15 days. Should you start planning how you will spend your bonus?

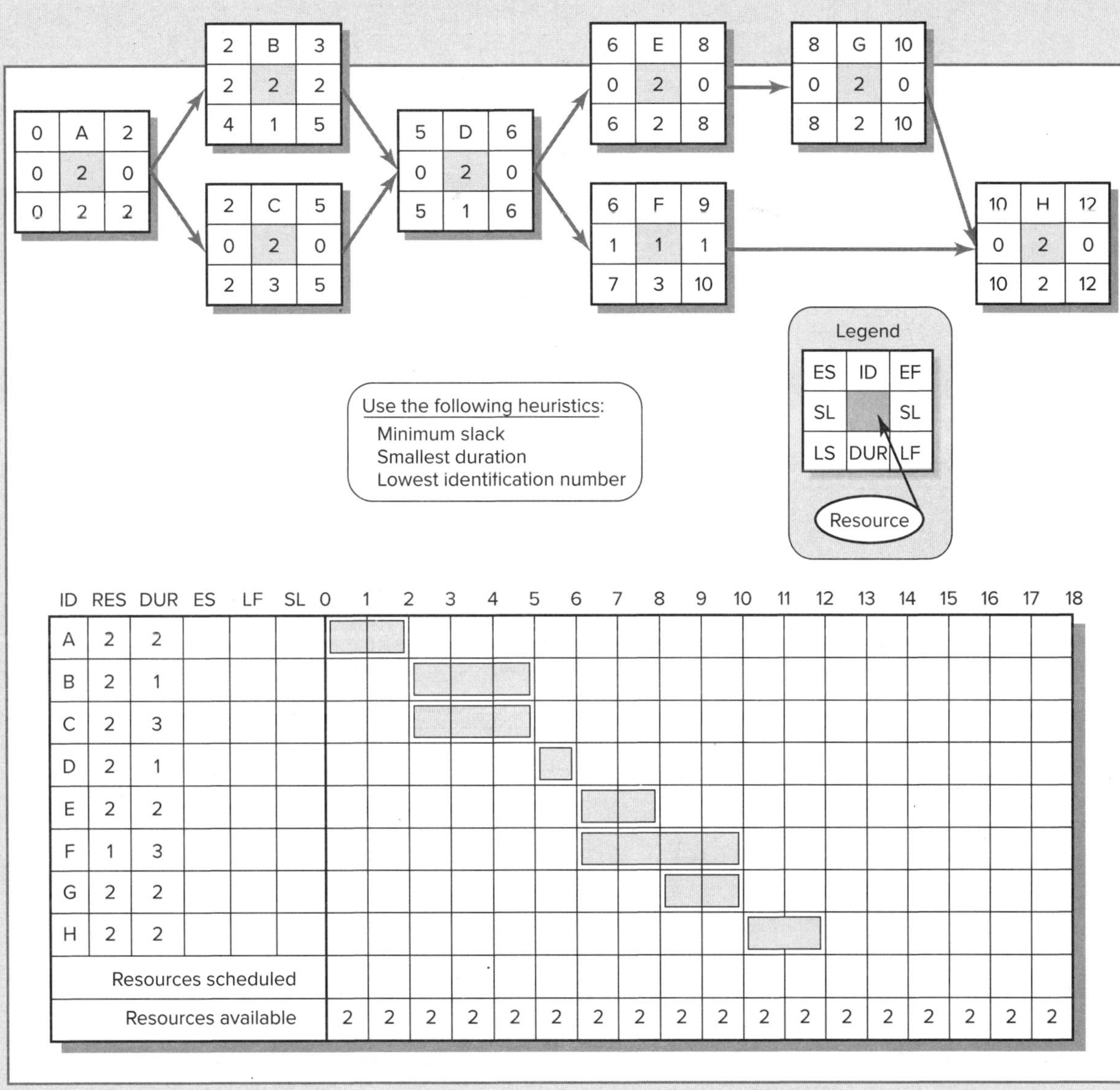

11. Given the time-phased work packages, complete the baseline budget form for the project.

Time-phased budget ($ 000)

Task	Budget	Week 1	2	3	4	5	6	7	8	9	10
Activity 1	4	4									
Activity 2	6		1	3	2						
Activity 3	10		2	4	2	2					
Activity 4	8						2	3	3		
Activity 5	3									2	1
Total	31										
Cumulative											

12. Given the time-phased work packages and network, complete the baseline budget form for the project.

Market Survey Project

WBS Work Package Cost by Week

WP Design	4	5	2			
WP Survey	2	2	4	4	4	5
WP Report	3	3	2			

Project Network

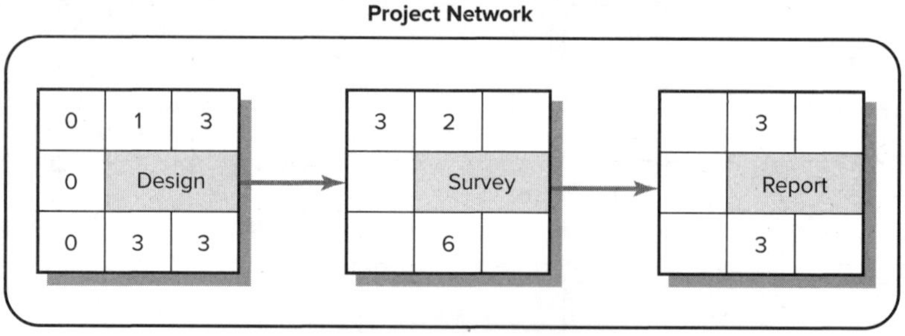

Time-Phased Budget

Task	Budget	Week 1	2	3	4	5	6	7	8	9	10	11	12
Design	11	4	5	2									
Survey	21												
Report	8												
Total	40												
Cumulative													

13. Given the time-phased work packages and network, complete the baseline budget form for the project.*

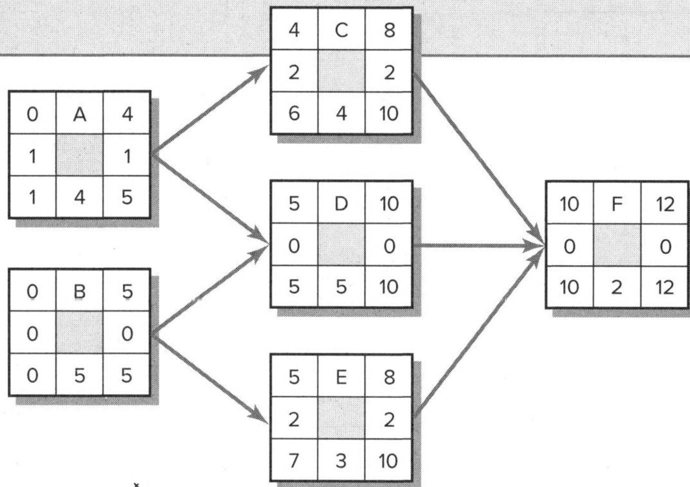

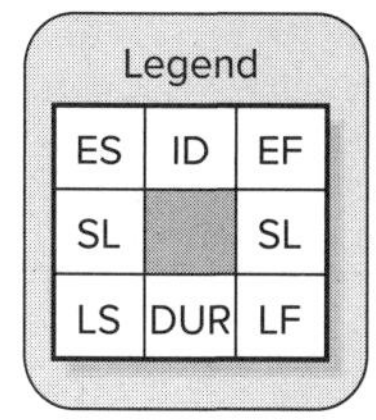

Cost by Week

A	10	10	10	10	
B	8	4	8	4	8
C	12	12	12	12	
D	6	2	2	2	6
E	8	8	12		
F	20	20			

ID	Budget	0	1	2	3	4	5	6	7	8	9	10	11	12
A	40													
B	32													
C	48													
D	18													
E	28													
F	40													
Total	206													
Cumulative														

* The solution to this exercise can be found in Appendix One.

14. Given the time-phased work packages and network, complete the baseline budget form for the project.

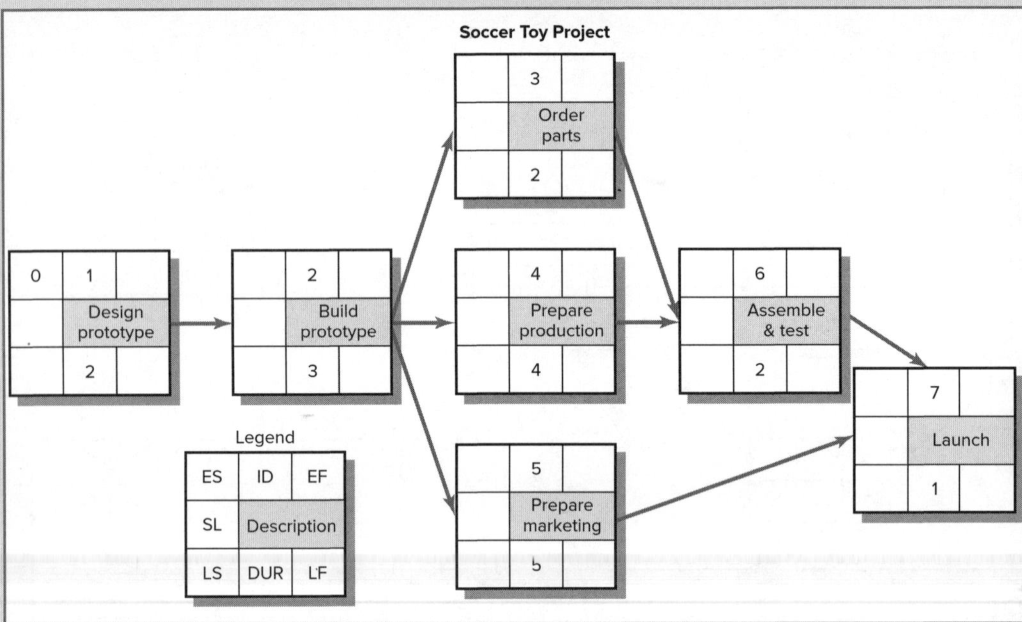

Soccer Toy Project

Cost by Week ($000)

	←1	←2	←3	←4	←5
Design prototype	12	12			
Build prototype	10	10	10		
Order parts	5	5			
Prepare production	16	10	22	16	
Prepare marketing	6	6	0	6	12
Assemble & test	18	18			
Launch	12				

Time-phased Budget ($000)

Week

	Budget / 0	1	2	3	4	5	6	7	8	9	10	11	12	13
Design prototype	24													
Build prototype	30													
Order parts	10													
Prepare prod'n	64													
Prepare market'g	30													
Assemble & test	36													
Launch	12													
Total	206													
Cumulative														

15. The National Oceanic Research Institute is planning a research study on global warming in Antarctica. The 16-month network schedule is presented below. It is followed by budgets for each activity. Create a time-phased budget for the research project in the form provided.

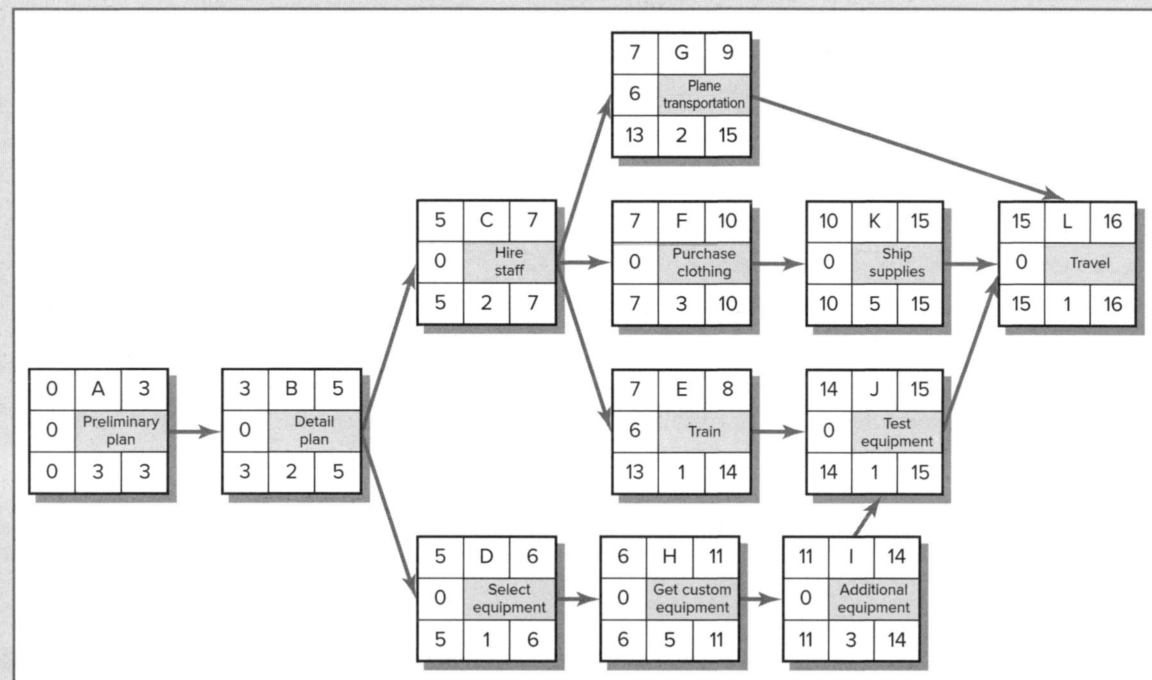

Global Warming Antarctic Research Project
Activity Time-Phased Work Packages by Month ($000)

	Task	Duration	Budget	0	1	2	3	4	5	6
A	Preliminary plan	3	3	1	1	1				
B	Detail plan	2	2	1	1					
C	Hire staff	2	4	4						
D	Select equipment	1	5	5						
E	Train	1	3	3						
F	Purchase clothing	3	9	3	0	6				
G	Plane transportation	2	60	5	55					
H	Get custom equipment	5	36	5	5	10	10	6		
I	Additional equipment	3	20	10	5	5				
J	Test equipment	1	6	6						
K	Ship all supplies	5	15	3	3	0	0	9		
L	Travel	1	9	9						
	Total budget		172							

References

Arrow, K. J., and L. Hurowicz, *Studies in Resource Allocation Process* (New York: Cambridge University Press, 2006).

Brucker, P., A. Drexl, R. Mohring, L. Newmann, and E. Pesch, "Resource-Constrained Project Scheduling: Notation, Classification, Models and Methods," *European Journal of Operational Research,* vol. 112 (1999), pp. 3–42.

Burgess, A. R., and J. B. Kellebrew, "Variations in Activity Level on Cyclical Arrow Diagrams," *Journal of Industrial Engineering,* vol. 13 (March/April 1962), pp. 76–83.

Charnes, A., and W. W. Cooper, "A Network Interpretation and Direct Sub Dual Algorithm for Critical Path Scheduling," *Journal of Industrial Engineering* (July/August 1962).

Davis, E. W., and J. Patterson, "A Comparison of Heuristic and Optimum Solutions in Resource-Constrained Project Scheduling," *Management Science,* April 1975, pp. 944–55.

Demeulemeester, E. L., and W. S. Herroelen, *Project Scheduling: A Research Handbook* (Norwell, MA: Kluwer Academic Publishers, 2002).

Fendly, L. G., "Towards the Development of a Complete Multi Project Scheduling System," *Journal of Industrial Engineering,* vol. 19 (1968), pp. 505–15.

Goldratt, E., *Critical Chain* (Great Barrington, MA: North River Press, 1997).

Kurtulus, I., and E. W. Davis, "Multi-project Scheduling: Categorization of Heuristic Rules Performance," *Management Science* (February 1982), pp. 161–72.

Reinersten, D., "Is It Always a Bad Idea to Add Resources to a Late Project?" *Electric Design,* October 30, 2000, pp. 17–18.

Rubinstein, J., D. Meyer, and J. Evans, "Executive Control of Cognitive Processes in Task Switching," *Journal of Experimental Psychology: Human Perception and Performance,* vol. 27, no. 4 (2001), pp. 763–97.

Talbot, B. F., and J. H. Patterson, "Optimal Methods for Scheduling under Resource Constraints," *Project Management Journal* (December 1979).

Wiest, J. D., "A Heuristic Model for Scheduling Large Projects with Unlimited Resources," *Management Science,* vol. 18 (February 1967), pp. 359–77.

Woodworth, B. M., and C. J. Willie, "A Heuristic Algorithm for Resource Leveling in Multiproject, Multiresource Scheduling," *Decision Sciences,* vol. 6 (July 1975), pp. 525–40.

Woodworth, B. M., and S. Shanahan, "Identifying the Critical Sequence in a Resource Constrained Project," *International Journal of Project Management,* vol. 6 (1988), pp. 89–96.

Case 8.1

Blue Mountain Cabin

Jack and Jill Smith have just retired and want to build a small, basic cabin in the Blue Mountains of Vermont. They have hired Daryl Hannah as the general contractor for the project. She has assembled a team of three workers to complete the project: Tom, Dick, and Harry. Daryl has negotiated a cost-plus contract with the Smiths whereby she will receive 15 percent beyond the cost of labor and materials.

Before they sign the contract the Smiths want an estimate of how much the project is likely to cost and how long it will take.

Daryl has estimated that the cost for materials, permits, etc., will total $80,000. She wants to determine labor costs as well as how long the project will take. This is one of several projects Daryl is managing, and other than occasionally helping out, her role is strictly limited to supervising. She has devised the following master plan and assignments.

Note that Dick is the only skilled plumber in the group, while Harry is the only skilled electrician. Tom is a general carpenter and can assist them with their work. Dick and Harry each get paid $600 a day, while Tom gets paid $400 per day.

Daryl has negotiated a 10 percent management reserve to deal with unexpected problems. Unused funds will be returned to the Smiths.

ID	Task	Predecessor	Time (days)	Assignment
A	Prepare Site	none	2	Tom, Dick, Harry
B	Pour Foundation	A	2	Tom, Dick, Harry
C	Erect Frame	B	4	Tom, Dick, Harry
D	Roof	C	3	Tom, Dick, Harry
E	Windows/Doors	D	2	Tom, Dick
F	Electrical	D	2	Harry, Tom
G	Plumbing	D	2	Dick, Tom
H	Rough-in Frame	E, F, G	2	Tom, Dick, Harry
I	Clean Up	H	1	Tom, Dick, Harry

Prepare a short proposal for the Smiths that includes a Gantt chart with resources assigned and cost estimates if the project starts on 8/1/24. Did resource limitations affect the final schedule? If so, how? What financial risks does this project face? What can the Smiths do to protect themselves against those risks?

Case 8.2

Power Train, Ltd.

Memo: Power Train Management Team

We have great information systems for reporting, tracking, and controlling costs on design projects. Our planning of projects is better than any I have seen at other companies. Our scheduling seemed to serve us well when we were small and we had only a few projects. Now that we have many more projects and schedule using multiproject software, there are too many occasions when the right people are not assigned to the projects deemed important to our success. This situation is costing us big money, headaches, and stress!

Claude Jones, VP, Design and Operations

HISTORY

Power Train (PT), Ltd., was founded in 1970 by Daniel Gage, a skilled mechanical engineer and machinist. Prior to founding PT he worked for three years as design engineer for a company that designed and built transmissions for military tanks and trucks. It was a natural transition for Dan to start a company designing and building power trains for farm tractor companies. Today Dan is no longer active in the management of PT but is still revered as its founder. He and his family still own 25 percent of the company, which went public in 1998. PT has been growing at a 6 percent clip for the last five years but expects industry growth to level off as supply exceeds demand.

Today PT continues its proud tradition of designing and building the best-quality power trains for manufacturers of farm tractors and equipment. The company employs 178 design engineers and has about 1,800 production and support staff. Contract design projects for tractor manufacturers represent a major portion of PT's revenue. At any given time, about 45 to 60 design projects are going on concurrently. A small portion of their design work is for military vehicles. PT only accepts military contracts that involve very advanced, new technology and are cost plus.

A new phenomenon has attracted the management of PT to look into a larger market. Last year a large Swedish truck manufacturer approached PT to consider designing power trains for its trucks. As the industry consolidates, the opportunities for PT should increase because these large firms are moving to more outsourcing to cut infrastructure costs and stay very flexible. Only last week a PT design engineer spoke to a German truck manufacturing manager at a conference. The German manager was already exploring outsourcing of drive trains to Porsche and was very pleased to be reminded of PT's expertise in the area. A meeting is set up for next month.

CLAUDE JONES

Claude Jones joined PT in 1999 as a new MBA from the University of Edinburgh. He worked as a mechanical engineer for U.K. Hydraulics for five years prior to returning to school for the MBA. "I just wanted to be part of the management team and where the action is." Claude moved quickly through the ranks. Today he is the vice president of design and operations. Sitting at his desk, Claude is pondering the conflicts and confusion that seem to be increasing in scheduling people to projects. He gets a real rush at the thought of designing power trains for large trucks; however, given their current project scheduling problems, a large increase in business would only compound their problems. Somehow these conflicts in scheduling have to be resolved before any serious thought can be given to expanding into the design of power transmissions for truck manufacturers.

Claude is thinking of the problems PT had in the last year. The MF project is the first to come to mind. The project was not terribly complex and did not require their best design engineers. Unfortunately, the scheduling software assigned one of the most creative and expensive engineers to the MF project. A similar situation, but reversed, happened on the Deer project. This project involved a big customer and new hydrostatic technology for small tractors. In this project the scheduling software assigned engineers who were not familiar with small tractor transmissions. Somehow, thinks Claude, the right people need to be scheduled to the right projects. Upon reflection, this problem with scheduling has been increasing since PT went to multiproject scheduling. Maybe a project office is needed to keep on top of these problems.

A meeting with the information technology team and software vendors was positive but not very helpful because these people are not really into detailed scheduling problems. The vendors provided all sorts of evidence suggesting the heuristics used—least slack, shortest duration, and identification number—are absolutely efficient in scheduling people and minimizing project delays. One project software vendor, Lauren, kept saying their software would allow PT to customize the scheduling of projects and people to almost any variation selected. Lauren repeated over and over, "If the standard heuristics do not meet your requirements, create your own heuristics that do." Lauren even volunteered to assist in setting up the system. But she is not willing to spend time on the problem until PT can describe to her exactly what criteria will be used (and their sequence) to select and schedule people to projects.

WHAT NEXT?

Potential expansion into the truck power train business is not feasible until the confusion in project scheduling is solved or reduced significantly. Claude is ready to tackle this problem, but he is not sure where to start. What criteria should he consider? What should be the sequence for selecting and assigning people to projects?

Case 8.3

Tham Luang Cave Rescue

On June 23, 2018, in Thailand, a group of 12 boys aged between 11 and 17 from the local football team, named the *Wild Boars,* and their 23-year-old assistant coach entered the Tham Luang cave. Tham Luang is a large cave complex in northern Thailand along the border with Myanmar. The cavern was popular with locals and the boys had visited Tham Luang before. Tham Luang cave is isolated—there is no GPS, Wi-Fi, or cell phone service. The last known survey was conducted in the 1980s by a French caving society, but many of the deeper recesses remain unmapped.

The boys had little difficulty getting fairly far into the cave, crawling through a couple of choke points to open spaces. They did not anticipate any problems getting back. The monsoon rains weren't expected until the next week, and the year before, the cave did not begin to flood until the middle of July. The team took no food with them, because this was going to be a brief field trip. They planned to stay for perhaps an hour, then return home to their parents.

However, nature had different plans. Heavy monsoon rain began to fall. The Wild Boars didn't know about the rain at first. There was a thousand feet of rock above them and they were more than a mile from the open forest. Heavy rains gathered in streams that disappeared into sinks, rushing through limestone into the cavern. Water rose suddenly and quickly, forcing the team to retreat farther and farther into the cave. The interior of the cave is not level but rather rises and falls as it burrows into the mountain. The team scrambled for higher ground as the water continued to rise. Finally, they settled on a mud slope and waited to see if the water would continue to rise. It didn't.

A mother of one of the boys contacted the police when her child failed to come home. A teammate who had missed practice that day told people that the team had planned to visit the cave after practice. Parents rushed to the cave, only to find their children's bikes and cleats at the entrance and the cave flooded.

A contingent of Thai Navy SEAL divers arrived the next day and began pushing their way into the flooded cave. This was no easy task. The Thai frogmen were accustomed to tropical open water, not the dark, cold currents racing through the cave.

They lacked equipment, much less expertise needed for caves, where divers cannot just rise to the surface if something goes wrong.

The plight of the Wild Boars drew international attention overnight. Soon skilled cave divers from around the world, including Finland, Britain, China, Australia, and the United States, volunteered their services. At first the foreign divers were not met with open arms by the Thai military in charge of the rescue. Many of the Thai divers bristled at the idea of needing foreign assistance. The divers were not even allowed into the cave. After much political haggling, the Thai Ministry of Foreign Affairs told the military chiefs to let the foreign divers go.

Even the experienced cave divers found the conditions extremely difficult. "It was like walking into a strong waterfall and feeling the water rushing at you," one diver said. "It was a horizontal climb against water with every move."

The divers painstakingly penetrated the cave, securing guidelines needed to ensure safety. Visibility at times was negligible. "If you put your hand in front of you, it just disappeared," said one diver. "You couldn't see anything."

Meanwhile, on the surface, policemen with sniffer dogs searched for shaft openings that could provide an alternative entrance to the cave system. The search was augmented by hundreds of volunteers dressed in lemon-yellow shirts and sky-blue caps, searching for hidden cracks in the limestone that might reveal an opening to the cave. Drones were also used, but no technology existed to scan for humans deep underground. Local holy men created a shrine at the mouth of the cave, where they chanted and communed with the spirit of the cave, "Jao Mae Tham." Several times the search had to be suspended due to heavy rains.

After the team had spent 10 days of captivity without real food or water, there was little hope among the rescuers of discovering the boys alive. Two of the British divers asked to book flights home.

On the 11th day, a pair of British divers working to extend the guide ropes popped up near a narrow ledge. First they smelled, and then they saw, 13 emaciated people perched in the dark. The Wild Boars had run out of food and light but had survived by sipping the condensation from the cave walls. Later it was reported that the assistant coach, a Buddhist, had led the boys in meditation to relax and conserve energy. The ledge where they were found was about 2.5 miles from the cave mouth.

The next day Thai SEALs ferried food, water, and blankets to the Wild Boars. Four divers, including a doctor, would stay with them until their rescue. Thai officials reported that the rescuers were providing health checks, keeping the boys entertained, and none of the boys were in serious condition.

Thai officials released a video made by the rescuers and shared to the world. The video showed all 12 boys and their coach introducing themselves and stating their ages. Wrapped in emergency blankets and appearing frail, each boy said hello to the outside world, "*Sawasdee krub,*" with his palms together in *wai,* the traditional Thai greeting. The video went viral. Soon all the major newscasts across the world were covering the story. The big question then became, now that the boys had been found, how could they be gotten out alive?

A rescue camp was set up at the cave entrance, accommodating the volunteers and journalists in addition to the rescue workers. The camp was divided into zones: restricted areas for the Thai Navy SEALs, other military personnel, and civilian rescuers; an area for relatives to wait in privacy; and areas for the press and general public.

An estimated 10,000 people contributed to the rescue effort, including more than 100 divers, 900 police officers, 2,000 soldiers, and numerous volunteers. Equipment included 10 police helicopters, seven ambulances, and more than 700 diving cylinders, of which more than 500 were in the cave at any time while another 200 were in queue to be refilled.

The plight of the Wild Boars caught the attention of Elon Musk of Tesla and Space X fame. He tasked engineers to build a kid-size submarine that could be used to transport the boys out of the cave. Within days an actual submarine was sent to Tham Luang. Thai officials praised the effort but concluded it was not practical, given the narrow passages in the cavern.

The journey through the cave to the team took six hours against current and five hours to exit with the current. The route had several flooded sections, some with strong currents and zero visibility, and some extremely narrow parts, the smallest measuring only 15 by 28 inches. The boys were perched on a ledge 400 yards from Pattaya beach chamber, named after an above-ground beach in Thailand. Chamber 3, which was dry, would be used as rescue base.

Pumps were brought in to remove water from the cave. Although not a solution, efforts at draining the cave began to produce results. Crags and outcroppings emerged from the murk. The most challenging passage, which had taken five hours to navigate early on, could now be traversed in two hours with the help of guide ropes.

As the crisis unfolded, rescuers considered several different methods to save the team. The principal options included

- Wait until the end of the monsoon season, with divers providing food and water.
- Find an alternative entrance to the cave that would allow for an easier escape.
- Drill a rescue shaft.
- Teach the group basic diving skills and have them swim out with the divers.

Waiting until the monsoons ended in November and the water drained was the simplest solution. The boys could walk out on their own. However, the logistics did not make sense. Feeding 13 people, three times a day, for even 60 days is more than 2,750 meals. Every meal would have to be ferried in by a team of divers, flirting with death each time they went under.

This was a growing concern. Four days after the boys were found, retired Navy SEAL diver Saman Kunan lost consciousness while returning from dropping off three air tanks. His dive buddy attempted CPR without success. Kunan had left his airport security job to volunteer for the rescue mission. Before that fatality, three divers were lost for over three hours in the dark cave, and rescue efforts had to be redirected to find them.

From the beginning, hundreds of volunteers crawled over the hillside in search of hidden openings. People knew the odds were slim to none, given the depth of the cave, but it was worth a try.

Drilling through a couple thousand feet of rock would require extensive infrastructure work and take too long. Besides, there was significant uncertainty as to where to drill.

That left the fourth option. None of the boys or the coach knew how to dive. Even if they could master the basics, cave diving is not the same as a practice run at a resort swimming pool. A weakened child submerged in darkness and breathing unnaturally through a regulator is likely to panic. Yet through long stretches of the cave, he wouldn't be able to surface and regain his composure—he would be in a flooded tunnel.

Privately experts thought maybe half the boys would survive the journey. But pulling it off 13 times in a row would take a miracle.

While plans were being developed, two alarming events occurred. First, the oxygen levels in the cave began to drop faster than anticipated. This raised fears that the boys could develop hypoxia if they remained for a prolonged time. By July 7, the oxygen level was measured to be 15 percent. The level needed to maintain normal functions for humans is between 19.5 percent and 23.5 percent. Thai engineers' attempts to install an air supply line to the boys failed.

The second development was the weather forecast. Monsoon rains were predicted for later in the week, which could flood the cave until November.

The Thai Navy SEALs, with the support of U.S. Air Force rescue experts, devised a plan approved by the Thai Minister of the Interior. Rescuers initially wanted to teach the boys basic diving skills to enable them to make the journey. Organizers even built a mockup of a tight passage with chairs and had divers practice with local boys in a nearby school swimming pool. Eventually it was decided that the boys were too weak to swim, and the plan was revised to have divers bring the boys out. The breakthrough came when planners considered medicating the boys so as they would become sedated.

On July 8, the rescue attempt was initiated. For the first part of the mission, 18 divers were sent into the caves to retrieve the boys, with one diver to accompany each boy on the dive out. The boys were dressed in a wetsuit, a buoyancy jacket, and a harness. Instead of sticking a regulator in each boy's mouth, they were given a full face mask that allowed them to breathe naturally. An oxygen cylinder was clipped to their front, a handle was attached to their back, and they were tethered to a diver in case they were lost in poor visibility.

Panic was a chief concern. The SEAL doctor administered an anesthetic to the boys before the journey, rendering them unconscious to prevent them from panicking on the escape and risking the lives of their rescuers.[1] The anesthetic lasted about 50 minutes, requiring the divers, whom the doctor had trained, to re-sedate their bodies during the three-hour-plus journey.

There was discussion about which boy should go first—the weakest, the youngest, the strongest—but in the end it came to a boy who volunteered. The boys were maneuvered out by the divers holding on to their back or chest, with each boy on the left or right depending upon the guideline. In very narrow spots, the divers had to push the boys from behind. The divers kept their heads higher than the boys so that in poor visibility the divers would hit their heads first against the rocks. After a short dive to a dry section of cave, the divers and boys were met by three divers, and the boys' dive gear was removed. A drag stretcher was used to transport the boys up over a 200-meter stretch of rocks and sandy hills. The dive gear was put back on before entering the next submerged section. The duo negotiated the narrow, underwater at times, passage way to chamber 2.

After being delivered by the divers into the rescue base in chamber 3, the boys were then passed along a "daisy chain" of hundreds of workers stationed along the treacherous path out of the cave. The boys were alternately carried, slid, and zip-lined over a complex network of pulleys installed by rock climbers. The path out of the chamber contained many areas still partially submerged, and the boys had to be transported over slippery rocks and through muddy waters. The journey out of chamber 3 took about four to five hours initially, less later as a result of drainage.

Soon after 7 p.m. local officials announced that two boys had been rescued. Shortly later, two more boys appeared out of the cave. On July 9, four more boys were rescued. On July 10, the last four boys and their coach were rescued.

The four Thai Navy SEALs, including the doctor who had stayed with the boys the entire time, were the last to dive out. When they got to chamber 3, a water pipe burst, and the main pump stopped working. All of a sudden, the water began to rise rapidly. This forced the SEALs and 100 of the rescuers still a mile inside the cave to abandon the rescue equipment and scramble out of the cave.

[1] The Thai government provided the SEAL doctor with diplomatic immunity if something went wrong.

Upon reaching the surface the boys were quarantined while health workers determined whether they had caught any infectious diseases. The boys were on a fixed rice porridge diet for the first 10 days. Parents initially visited their children looking through a window, but once the laboratory results proved negative, they were allowed to visit in person while wearing a medical gown, face mask, and hair cap.

During their 11-day ordeal, the assistant coach was confident they were going to be rescued and encouraged the boys not to be worried or scared. He led the boys in meditation to relax and conserve energy. The boys chanted "su-su" which is Thai for "fight on." Chanin Viboonrungruang, the youngest team member told reporters, "We felt dizzy and hungry. . . we tried not to think of food, like fried rice, because it would make us hungrier."

After the rescue, the boys' families, officials, and thousands of volunteers gathered at the cave entrance. The group gave thanks for the lives saved and asked forgiveness from the cave goddess, "Jao Mae Tham," for the intrusion of pumps, ropes, and people during the rescue.

The world rejoiced with the news of the successful rescue. The head of the rescue mission said that the cave system would eventually be turned into a living museum to highlight how the operation unfolded. As a result of the incident, Thailand's Navy SEALs will include cave diving in their training programs.

On September 7, 2018, the Royal Thai government hosted a reception for all Thai and foreign officials and personnel involved in the rescue. His Majesty the King granted a royal decoration, *The Most Admirable Order of the Direkgunabhorn,* to those who were involved in the rescue of the football team—114 foreigners and 74 Thais. The order is bestowed upon those who render devotional service to the Kingdom of Thailand. The title *Direkgunabhorn* roughly translates as "Noble order of abundance and quality."

Three months after being rescued, the entire Wild Boars team and coach appeared on the U.S. day-time talk show *Ellen.* Speaking through a translator, the team revealed that four of the boys had had birthdays while trapped in the cave. The team and coach were stunned when their football hero, Zlatan Ibrahimović, who now plays for the LA Galaxy, made a surprise appearance on the show to meet them. The Swedish star high-fived each member. "These kids, this team is braver than me and they showed their collective teamwork and had patience, faith," Ibrahimović said. "This is probably the best team in the world."

1. How did the physical environment of the cave affect the rescue plan?
2. How did the rescue team respond to the risks of the project?
3. Some have called the rescue a miracle and that luck was the decisive factor. Do you agree?

Sources

ABC News, "It Was Utter Chaos: Inside the Thai Cave Rescue That Nearly Didn't Happen," December 1, 2018. www.abc.net.au. Accessed 2/8/19.

ABC News, "Thai Cave Rescue: Elon Musk Hits Out at Mission Chief Who Turned Down Mini-submarine Offer," July 11, 2018. www.abc.net.au. Accessed 2/8/19.

Beech, H., R. C. Paddock, and M. Suhartono, "Still Can't Believe It Worked: The Story of the Thailand Cave Rescue," *New York Times,* July 12, 2018. www.nytimes.com. Accessed 2/9/19.

Ellis-Petersen, H., "Thai Cave Rescue Boys Meet Hero Zlatan during *Ellen* Interview," *The Guardian,* October 17, 2018. www.theguardian.com. Accessed 2/12/19.

Flynn, S., "Miracle at Tham Luang," *GQ,* December 3, 2018. www.gq.com. Accessed 2/10/19.

Case 8.4

Midnight Sun II Project

Elena Acosta was excited; she was about to begin working on Pacific Tech University's "Midnight Sun II Project." Elena was enrolled in PhD program in Geographic Sciences and had just completed her course work. She just started working as a Research Assistant for Professor Jing Zhão.

Professor Zhão is the lead investigator on a five-year study of the effects of climate change on fauna and vegetation in the Arctic Circle. There are six scientists (resources) on the team. Due to academic commitments and daylight restrictions in the Arctic, the project is scheduled to take 14 weeks beginning May 15 and ending August 31. Zhão and a team of scientists completed Midnight Sun I last summer. When they got back to Vancouver, the team spent two days conducting a post-project retrospective.[1] The candid discussions yielded many valuable lessons that should improve the performance on Midnight Sun II.

Given inflation, and the spike in airfare to the Arctic basecamp, Professor Zhão knew she had to find ways to cut costs to make up for the deficit in the research grant budget. Both the budget and the project schedule were constrained, and Zhão didn't want to scale back on the project.

Elena was hand-picked by Professor Zhão because of her engineering project management background. Elena used her undergrad engineering degree to work six years for the City of Vancouver on a wide range of projects. She split her time between field and planning work. Over time she became proficient in the use of MS Project to manage projects. This was a scarce skill in Zhão's team. MS Project was required by the Canadian Science Foundation in an effort to control costs and better manage projects. Zhão's team struggled with using MS Project for the first time. Professor Zhão was counting on Elena to play a key role in planning the project and more fully utilizing the capabilities of the project management software.

Project Midnight Sun II consisted of a battery of experiments conducted at basecamp and the two satellite mini camps. The project included 11 experiments, ranging in duration from 2 to 12 weeks. Some experiments were independent while others had to wait for results of previous experiment(s) before starting.

Elena was given the Master schedule that included manpower requirements for each of the experiments. The schedule consisted of a network of experiments with the critical path being 14 weeks. One of the issues that surfaced during Midnight Sun I project retrospective was some of the participants felt that maybe there was too much downtime between experiments they were assigned to. They reported using the majority of this time working on their own research. Elena was to use her expertise to explore the ramifications.

The table below contains the 14-week experiment schedule for the Midnight Sun II project. Each experiment requires two scientists and cannot be interrupted. Utilize the information in the table to determine the original resource demands for the project over time (i.e., resource demand graph) and assess whether it is possible to reduce the number of scientists required to complete the project within 14 weeks. Submit a brief document to Professor Zhão documenting your recommendation.

[1] A project retrospective is when project team reviews the finished project and identify lessons learned as well as other relevant issues (discussed in Chapter 14).

Experiment Schedule for Midnight Sun II Project

ID	Experiment	Duration (weeks)	Predecessor	Resources
1	A	4	-	2
2	B	4	-	2
3	C	2	-	2
4	D	4	-	2
5	E	2	B	2
6	F	4	B	2
7	G	4	C, D	2
8	H	2	D	2
9	I	2	E, F	2
10	J	4	F, G	2
11	K	2	A, I, J, H	2

Appendix 8.1

The Critical-Chain Approach

LEARNING OBJECTIVES

After reading this appendix you should be able to:

A8-1 Define the term *critical chain.*

A8-2 Identify the reasons projects are late even when estimates are padded.

A8-3 Describe the basic critical-chain methodology.

A8-4 Describe the differences between critical-chain scheduling and the traditional approach to scheduling.

In practice, project managers carefully manage slack on sensitive resource-limited projects. If possible, they will add slack at the end of the project by committing to a completion date that goes beyond the scheduled date. For example, the plans say the project should be completed on April 1, although the official completion date is May 1. Other managers take a more aggressive approach to managing slack within the schedule. They use an early start schedule and prohibit use of slack on any activity or work package to be used unless authorized by the project manager. Progress by percent complete and by remaining time is carefully monitored. Activities that are beating estimated completion times are reported so that succeeding activities can start ahead of schedule. This ensures that the time gained is used to start a succeeding activity earlier and time is not wasted. The overall intent is to create and save slack as a time buffer to complete the project early or to cover delay problems that may creep up on critical activities or paths.

LO A8-1 Define the term *critical chain.*

Eliyahu Goldratt, who championed the "theory of constraints" in his popular book *The Goal,* advocates an alternative approach to managing slack.[1] He has coined the term *critical chain* to recognize that the project network may be constrained by both resource and technical dependencies. Each type of constraint can create task dependencies, and in

[1] Goldratt, E., *The Goal* (Great Barrington, MA: North River Press, 1997).

the case of resource constraints, new task dependencies can be created! Remember how resource constraints shifted the critical path? If not, visit Figure 8.5 again. The critical chain is the longest string of dependencies that exist on the project. *Chain* is used instead of *path,* since the latter tends to be associated with just technical dependencies, not resource dependencies. Goldratt uses the critical-chain concept to develop strategies for accelerating the completion of projects. These strategies are based on his observations about time estimates of individual activities.

TIME ESTIMATES

LO A8-2

Identify the reasons projects are late even when estimates are padded.

Goldratt argues that there is a natural tendency for people to add safety (just-in-case) time to their estimations. It is believed that those who estimate activity times provide an estimate that has about an 80 to 90 percent chance of being completed on or before the estimated time. Hence, the median time (50/50 chance) is overestimated by approximately 30 to 40 percent. For example, a programmer may estimate that there is a 50/50 chance that he can complete an activity in six days. However, to ensure success and to protect against potential problems, he adds three days of safety time and reports that it will take nine days to complete the task. In this case, the median (50/50) time is overestimated by approximately 50 percent. He now has a 50/50 chance of completing the project three days ahead of schedule. If this hidden contingency is pervasive across a project, then most activities in theory should be completed ahead of schedule.

Not only do workers add safety, but project managers like to add safety to ensure that they will be able to bring the project in ahead of schedule. They will add a month to a nine-month project to cover any delays or risks that might spring up. This situation raises an interesting paradox:

Why, if there is a tendency to overestimate activity durations, and add safety to the end of a project, do so many projects come in behind schedule?

Critical-Chain Project Management (CCPM) offers several explanations:

- **Parkinson's law.** Work fills the time available. Why hustle to complete a task today when it isn't due until tomorrow? Not only will the pace of work be dictated by deadline, but workers will take advantage of perceived free time to catch up on other things. This is especially true in matrix environments where workers will use this time to clear work backlog on other projects and duties.
- **Self-protection.** Participants fail to report early finishes out of fear that management will adjust their future standards and demand more next time. For example, if a team member estimates that a task will take seven days and delivers it in five, the next time she is asked for an estimate, the project manager may want to trim the estimate based on past performance. Peer pressure may also be a factor here: to avoid being labeled a "rate buster," members might not report early finishes.
- **Dropped baton.** Goldratt uses the metaphor of project as relay race to illustrate the impact of poor coordination. Just as a runner's time is lost if the next runner is not ready to receive the baton, so is the time gained from completing a task early lost if the next group of people are not ready to receive the project work. Poor communication and inflexible resource schedules prevent progress from occurring.
- **Excessive multitasking.** The norm in most organizations is to have project personnel work on several projects, activities, or assignments at the same time. This leads to costly interruptions and excessive task splitting. As pointed out in our discussion of splitting tasks, this adds time to each activity. When looked at in isolation the time loss may seem minimal, but when taken as a whole the transition costs can be staggering.

- **Resource bottlenecks.** In multiproject organizations, projects are frequently delayed because test equipment or other necessary resources are tied up on other project work.
- **Student syndrome (procrastination).** Goldratt asserts that just as students delay writing a term paper until the last minute, workers delay starting tasks when they perceive that they have more than enough time to complete the task. The problem with delaying the start of a task is that obstacles are often not detected until the task is under way. When the start of the task is postponed, the opportunity to cope with these obstacles and complete the task on time is compromised.

LO A8-3

Describe the basic critical-chain methodology.

Critical Chain in Action

CCPM's solution to reducing project time overruns is to insist on people using the "true 50/50" activity time estimates (rather than estimates that have an 80 to 90 percent chance of being completed before the estimated time); the 50/50 estimates result in a project duration about one-half the low risk of 80–90 percent estimates. This requires a corporate culture that values accurate estimates and refrains from blaming people for not meeting deadlines. According to CCPM, using 50/50 estimates will discourage Parkinson's law, the student syndrome, and self-protection from coming into play because there is less "free time" available. Productivity will be increased as individuals try to meet tighter deadlines. Similarly, the compressed time schedule reduces the likelihood of the dropped baton effect.

CCPM recommends inserting time buffers into the schedule to act as "shock absorbers" to protect the project completion date against task durations taking longer than the 50/50 estimate. The rationale is that by using 50/50 estimates you are in essence taking out all of the "safety" in individual tasks. CCPM also recommends using portions of this collective safety strategically by inserting time buffers where potential problems are likely to occur. There are three kinds of buffers in CCPM:

- **Project buffer.** First, since all activities along the critical chain have inherent *uncertainty* that is difficult to predict, project duration is uncertain. Therefore, a project time buffer is added to the expected *project duration.* CCPM recommends using roughly 50 percent of the aggregate safety. For example, if the modified schedule reduces the project duration by 20 days from 50 to 30, then a 10-day project buffer would be used.
- **Feeder buffers.** Buffers are added to the network where noncritical paths merge with the critical chain. These buffers protect the critical chain from being delayed.
- **Resource buffers.** Time buffers are inserted where scarce resources are needed for an activity. Resource time buffers come in at least two forms. One form is a time buffer attached to a critical resource to ensure that the resource is on call and available when needed. This preserves the relay race. The second form of time buffer is added to activities preceding the work of a scarce resource. This kind of buffer protects against resource bottlenecks by increasing the likelihood that the preceding activity will be completed when the resource is available.

All buffers reduce the risk of the project duration being late and increase the chance of early project completion.[2] See Snapshot from Practice A8.1: Critical Chain Applied to Airplane Part Arrivals.

[2] For more information on buffers, see: Leach, L. P., "Critical Chain Project Management Improves Project Performance," *Project Management Journal,* vol. 30, no. 2 (1999), pp. 39–51.

SNAPSHOT FROM PRACTICE A8.1 Critical Chain Applied to Airplane Part Arrivals*

In the past Spirit Aero Systems, manufacturer of airplane parts, was forced to delay product development projects as a result of missing parts for assemblies. Spirit management cycled through several approaches, such as lean, value chain, cycle time reduction, and knowledge-based engineering, to reduce the problem. Although each yielded minor improvements, the impacts were not substantial. Rework, overtime, delay costs, and vendor expediting costs continued to have significant impact on costs, meeting commitments, and reputation. Spirit turned to critical-chain management methodology in a pilot project.

Joseph Zenisek, the critical-chain manager, said the choice of critical chain was "a game changer for us." Spirit applied the critical-chain approach to assembly of newly designed pylons (brackets) used for failure destruction testing of casings for a jet engine project. Zenisek credited success to three key factors:

- Creating a rule to never start a work package until all parts and staff are available.
- Ensuring part buffers to cover work packages by vigilantly monitoring assembly parts that use a large number of parts or where rate or number used is high.
- Developing a small engineering team to manage vendors and buffers to ensure that delivery of over 300 parts arrived on time.

The critical-chain program led to impressive results. The parts and staffing rule cut down on late deliveries and rework on partially completed work packages caused by missing parts. The result was a reduction of 50 percent in overtime. Reducing delays reduced assembly cycle time by 18 percent. Work in process and work packages were also reduced since availability of buffer parts avoided delays. The critical-chain method led to better resource management and reduced stress.

Given the success of the critical-chain program, Spirit intends to expand the application of the critical-chain method to new product development projects for their clients.

*P. Fretty, "E Is in the Air," *PM Network*, February 2012, pp. 50–56.

LO A8-4

Describe the differences between critical-chain scheduling and the traditional approach to scheduling.

Critical-Chain versus Traditional Scheduling Approach

To illustrate how CCPM affects scheduling, let's compare it with the traditional approach to project scheduling. We will first resolve resource problems in the way described in Chapter 8 and then using the CCPM method. Figure A8.1A shows the *planned* Air Control project network without any concern for resources. That is, activities are assumed to be independent and resources will be made available and/or are interchangeable.

Figure A8.1B depicts the bar chart for the project. The dark blue bars represent the durations of critical activities; the light blue bars represent the durations of noncritical activities; the gray bars represent slack. Note that the duration is 45 days and the critical path is represented by activities 1, 4, 6, 7, and 8.

Parallel activities hold potential for resource conflicts. This is the case in this project. Ryan is the resource for activities 3 and 6. If you insert Ryan into the bar chart in Figure A8.1B for activities 3 and 6, you can see activity 3 overlaps activity 6 by five days—an impossible situation. Because Ryan cannot work two activities simultaneously and no other person can take his place, a resource dependency exists. The result is that two activities (3 and 6) that were assumed to be independent now become dependent. Something has to give! Figure A8.2A shows the Air Control project network with the resources included. A pseudo-dashed arrow has been added to the network to indicate the resource dependency. The bar chart in Figure A8.2B reflects the revised schedule resolving the overallocation of Ryan. Given the new schedule, slack

FIGURE A8.1A **Air Control Project: Time Plan without Resources**

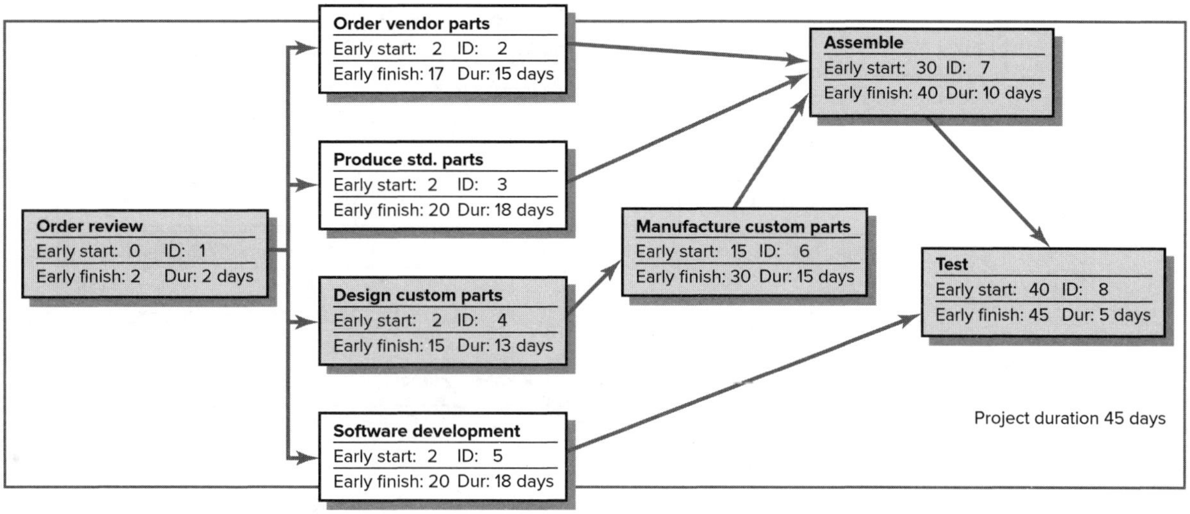

FIGURE A8.1B
Air Control Project: Schedule without Resources

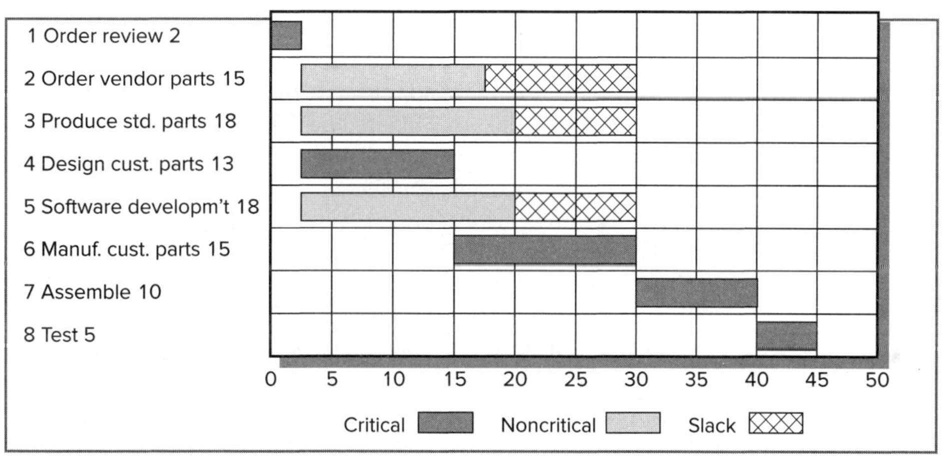

FIGURE A8.2A **Air Control Project: Time Plan with Resources Limited**

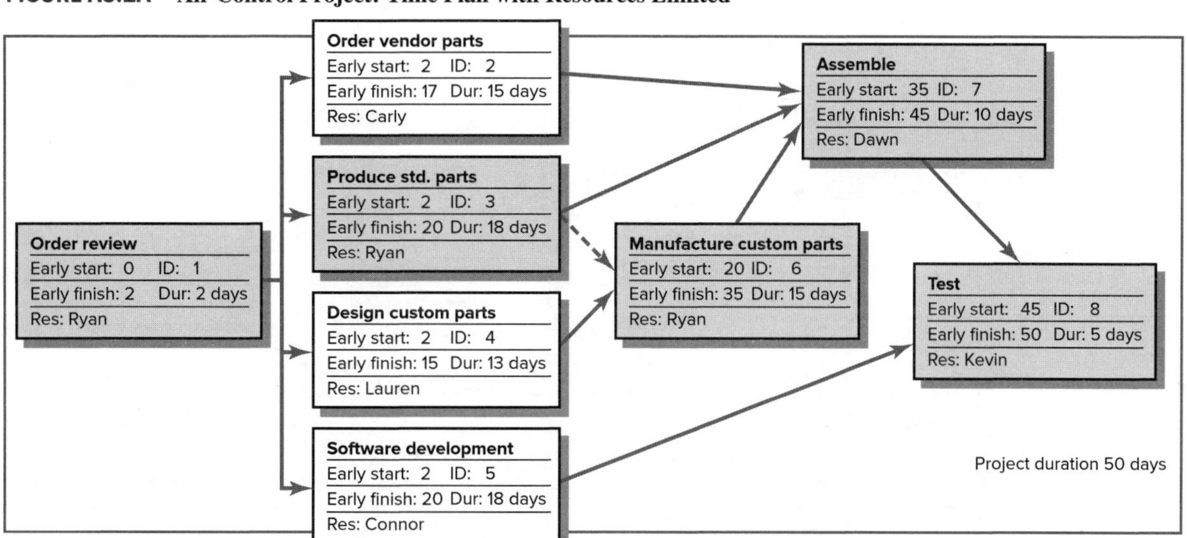

FIGURE A8.2B Air Control Project: Schedule with Resources Limited

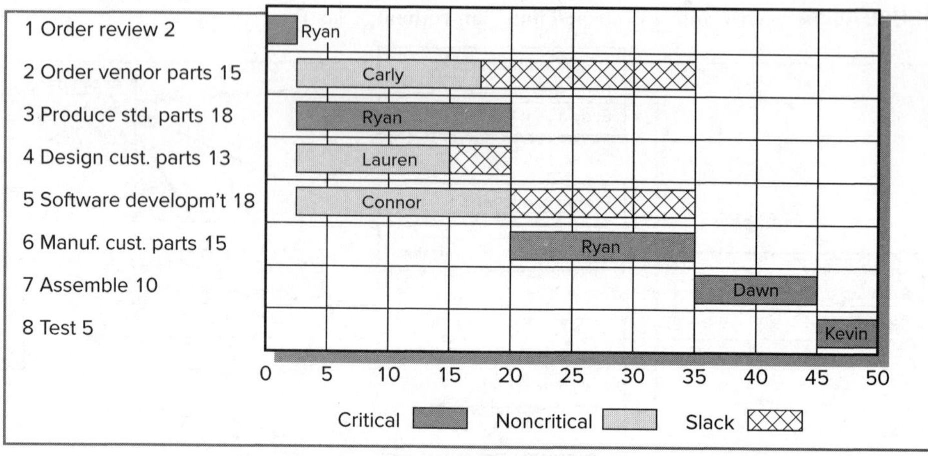

for some activities has changed. More importantly, the critical path has changed. It is now 1, 3, 6, 7, 8. The resource schedule shows the new project duration to be 50 days rather than 45 days.

Now let's apply the CCPM approach to the Air Control project. Figure A8.3 details many of the changes. First, notice that task estimates now represent approximations of the 50/50 rule. Second, observe that not all of the activities on the critical chain are technically linked. Manufacture custom parts is included because of previously defined resource dependency. Third, a project time buffer is added at the end of schedule. Finally, feeder buffers are inserted at each point where a noncritical activity merges with the critical chain.

The impact the CCPM approach has on the project schedule can best be seen in the Gantt chart presented in Figure A8.4. Notice first the late start times for each of the three noncritical activities. For example, under the critical path method, Order vendor parts and Software development would be scheduled to begin immediately after the Order review. Instead they are scheduled later in the project. Three-day feeder buffers have been added to each of these activities to absorb any delays that might occur in these activities. Finally, instead of taking 50 days, the project is now estimated to take only 27 days with a 10-day project buffer!

FIGURE A8.3 Air Control Project: CCPM Network

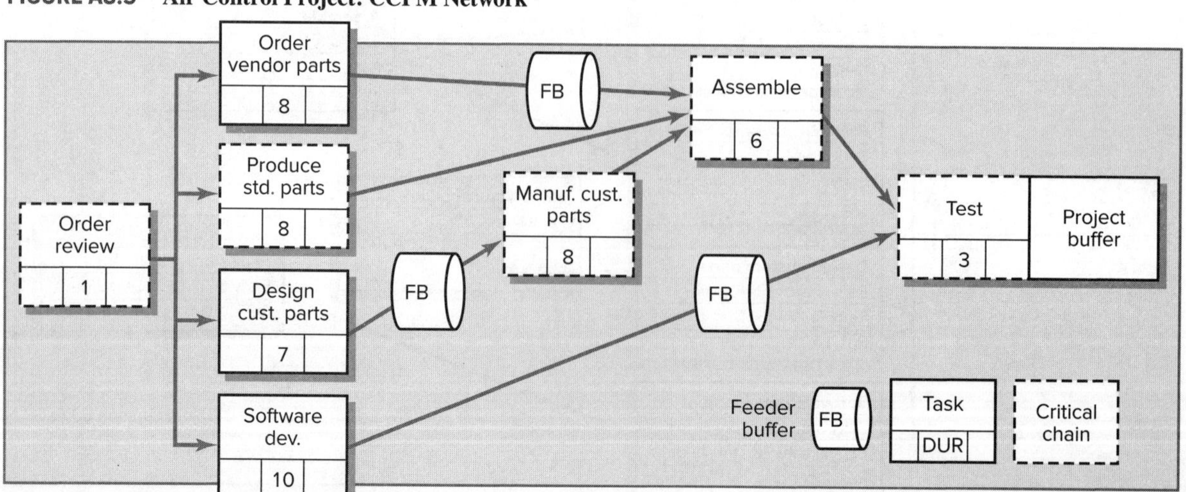

FIGURE A8.4
Air Control Project Gantt Chart: CCPM Network

Activity	DUR	LS	LF	Buffer
1. Order review	1	0	1	0
2. Order vendor parts	8	7	15	3
3. Produce std. parts	8	1	9	0
4. Design cust. parts	7	1	8	3
5. Software dev.	10	11	21	3
6. Manuf. cust. parts	8	11	19	0
7. Assemble	6	18	24	0
8. Test	3	24	27	12

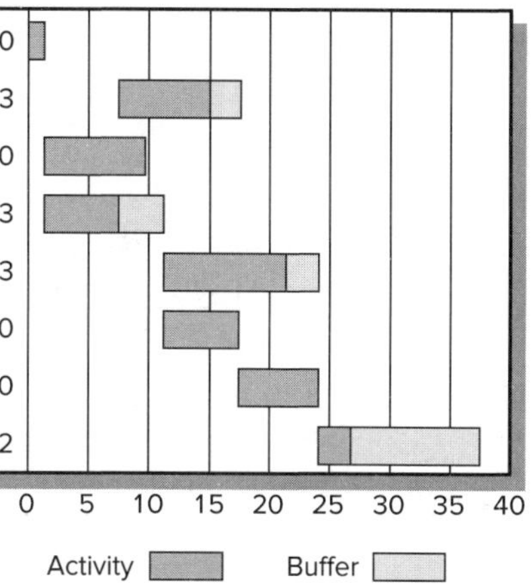

This example provides an opportunity for explaining the differences between buffers and slack. Slack is spare time inherent in the schedule of noncritical activities and can be determined by differences between the early start and late start of a specific activity. Buffers, on the other hand, are dedicated time blocks reserved to cover most likely contingencies and are monitored closely so, if they are not needed, subsequent activities can proceed on schedule. Buffers are needed in part because the estimates are based on 50/50 approximations, and therefore roughly half of the activities will take longer than planned. To protect against these extended activity durations, buffers are inserted to minimize the impact on the schedule. Buffers are not part of the project schedule and are used only when sound management dictates it.

While not depicted in the figures, an example of a resource buffer would be to add six days to Ryan's schedule (remember, he is the critical resource that caused the schedule to be extended). This would ensure that he could continue to work on the project beyond the 18th day in case either Produce standard parts or Manufacture custom parts takes longer than planned. Progress on these two tasks would be monitored closely, and his schedule would be adjusted accordingly.

CCPM and Splitting Tasks

Buffers do not address the insidious effects of pervasive task splitting, especially in a multiproject environment where workers are juggling different project assignments. CCPM has three recommendations that will help reduce the impact of splitting activities:

1. Reduce the number of projects so people are not assigned to as many projects concurrently.
2. Control start dates of projects to accommodate resource shortages. Don't start projects until sufficient resources are available to work full time on the project.
3. Contract (lock in) for resources *before* the project begins.

Monitoring Project Performance

The CCPM method uses buffers to monitor project time performance. Remember that as shown in Figure A8.3 a project buffer is used to insulate the project against delays along the critical chain. For monitoring purposes, this buffer is typically divided into three zones—OK, Watch & Plan, and Act, respectively (see Figure A8.5). As the buffer begins to decrease and moves into the second zone, alarms are set off to seek corrective action. To be truly effective, buffer management requires comparing buffer

FIGURE A8.5
Project Control—Buffer Management

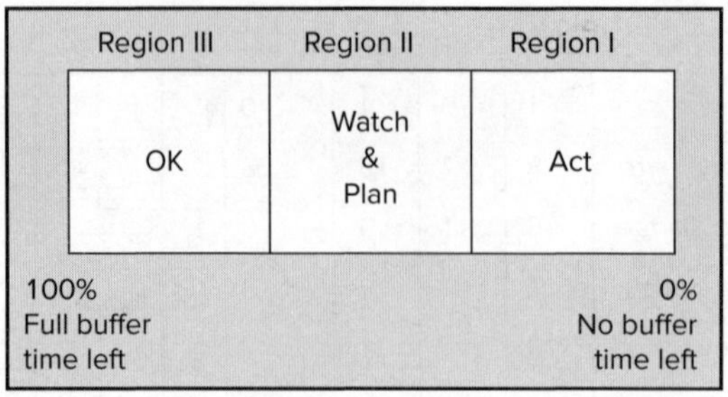

usage with actual progress on the project. For example, if the project is 75 percent complete and you have only used 50 percent of the project buffer, then the project is in pretty good shape. Conversely, if the project is only 25 percent complete and 50 percent of the buffer has already been used, you are in trouble and corrective action is needed. A method for estimating percentage complete is described in Chapter 13.

Success with the CCPM Method

CCPM has generated considerable debate within the project management community. While sound in theory, support at this time is limited but growing. For example, Harris Semiconductor was able to build a new automated wafer fabrication facility within 13 months using CCPM methods when the industry standard for such a facility was 26–36 months. The Israeli aircraft industry has used CCPM techniques to reduce average maintenance work on aircraft from two months to two weeks. The U.S. Air Force and Navy as well as Boeing, Lucent Technologies, Intel, GM, and 3M are applying critical-chain principles to their multiproject environments.[3]

CCPM is not without critics. First, CCPM does not address the biggest cause of project delays, which is an ill-defined and unstable project scope. Second, some critics challenge Goldratt's assumptions about human behavior. They question the tendency of experts to pad estimates and the fact that employees act deliberately against the organization for their own interest and benefit (c.f., Button, 2011; Pinto, 1999). Critics also object to the insinuation that trained professionals would exhibit the student syndrome habits (Zalmanson, 2001). Third, evidence of success is almost exclusively anecdotal and based on single case studies or on computer modeling. The lack of systematic evidence raises questions about generalizability of application. CCPM may prove to work best for only certain kinds of projects (Raz, Barnes, & Dvir, 2003).

One of the keys to implementing CCPM is the culture of the organization. If the organization honors noble efforts that fail to meet estimates as it does efforts that do meet estimates, then greater acceptance will occur. Conversely, if management treats honest failure differently than success, then resistance will be high. Organizations adopting the CCPM approach have to invest significant energy in obtaining "buy-in" on the part of all participants to its core principles and allaying the fears that this system may generate.

Appendix Summary

Regardless of where one stands in the debate, the CCPM approach deserves credit for bringing resource dependency to the forefront, highlighting the modern ills of multitasking, and forcing us to rethink conventional methods of project scheduling.

[3] Cited in materials developed by the Eliyahu Goldratt Institute (New Haven, CT) for a workshop attended by one of the authors entitled "Project Management the TOC Way," 1998.

Appendix Review Questions

1. Explain how time is wasted in the management of projects.
2. Distinguish between project and feeder buffers.
3. Buffers are not the same as slack. Explain.

Appendix Exercises

1. Check out the Goldratt Institute's homepage at http://www.goldratt.com for current information on the application of critical-chain techniques to project management.
2. Apply critical-chain scheduling principles to the Print Software, Inc., project (Exercise 10) presented in Chapter 6. Revise the estimated time durations by 50 percent, except round up the odd time durations (e.g., 3 becomes 4). Draw a CCPM network diagram similar to the one contained in Figure A8.3 for the Print Software project, as well as a Gantt chart similar to Figure A8.4. How would these diagrams differ from the ones generated using the traditional scheduling technique?

Appendix References

Budd, C. S., and M. J. Cooper, "Improving On-time Service Delivery: The Case of Project as Product," *Human Systems Management,* vol. 24, no. 1 (2005), pp. 67–81.

Button, S., "A Critical Look at Critical Chain," EM 540 research paper, March 2011.

Goldratt, E., *The Goal* (Great Barrington, MA: North River Press, 1997).

Herroelen, W., R. Leus, and E. Demeulemeester, "Critical Chain Project Scheduling: Do Not Oversimplify," *Project Management Journal,* vol. 33, no. 4 (2002), pp. 48–60.

Leach, L. P., "Critical Chain Project Management," *Proceedings of 29th Annual Project Management Institute, 1998, Seminars and Symposium* (Newtown, PA: Project Management Institute, 1998), pp. 1239–44.

Levine, H. A., "Shared Contingency: Exploring the Critical Chain," *PM Network,* October 1999, pp. 35–38.

Newbold, R. C., *Project Management in the Fast Lane: Applying the Theory of Constraints* (Boca Raton, FL: St. Lucie Press, 1998).

Noreen, E., D. Smith, and J. Mackey, *The Theory of Constraints and Its Implication for Management Accounting* (Great Barrington, MA: North River Press, 1995).

Ordonez, R. E., M. Vanhoucke, J. Coelho, R. Anholon, and O. Novaski, "A Study of the Critical Chain Project Management Method Applied to a Multiproject System," *Project Management Journal,* vol. 50, no. 1 (2019), pp. 322–34.

Pinto, J., "Some Constraints on the Theory of Constraints: Taking a Critical Look at Critical Chain," *PM Network,* 1999, pp. 49–51.

Raz, T., R. Barnes, and D. Dvir, "A Critical Look at Critical Chain Project Management," *Project Management Journal* (December 2003), pp. 24–32.

Sood, S., "Taming Uncertainty: Critical-Chain Buffer Management Helps Minimize Risk in the Project Equation," *PM Network,* March 2003, pp. 57–59.

Steyn, H., "An Investigation into the Fundamentals of Critical Chain Scheduling," *International Journal of Project Management,* vol., no. 6 (2001), pp. 363–69.

Zalmanson, E., "Readers Feedback," *PM Network,* 2001, p. 4.

Case A8.1

The CCPM Dilemma

Achara worked in the IT Department of a diversified IT firm. She was describing the firm's early encounters with critical-chain scheduling to a friend in another IT firm.

Three years ago management decided to add 10 percent time to all activity estimates because almost all projects were coming in late. One thought was people were simply working too hard and needed some relief. This approach did not work! Projects still came in late. Next, management decided to take away the extra time for activities and add 10 percent for project estimates to ensure project durations would be met. Again, nothing improved and projects continued to come in late. Recently, the firm hired a consultant who promoted critical-chain scheduling, which was implemented for all projects in her division. Almost all failed to perform.

Achara explained, "The estimates were basically impossible. The activity durations got squeezed down to less than the 50 percent guideline. We were late on nearly every task. In addition, I was not allowed to put in a big enough project buffer, which only added to projects being late. One colleague who was working on six projects gave up and quit; he said he was killing himself and saw no hope of things getting better. My projects are not the only ones having big problems. Some people had no idea why anyone would use CCPM scheduling. To quote one of my best programmers: "They ask for an estimate and then they cut it 50 percent or more. What kind of game is this? Apparently they don't trust us."

A week later, to Achara's surprise, she was called to the IT manager's office. Achara imagined numerous bad scenarios of how the meeting would go—even to the remote possibility of being fired! The manager wanted the division to straighten out their project management practices and stop this business of nearly all IT projects being late. There were rumors of cleaning house or outsourcing IT work.

The manager believed that Achara, who passed the PMP exam, had the best chance of turning things around. She said, "Achara, I'm nearing the desperate level; top management is reaching the end of the rope with our division. We need to turn this around for both our sakes. Give me a plan that I can sponsor within the week."

Achara explained to her friend a few of her ideas—like squeezing estimates too far. But she said she would take any ideas she could get from anyone.

Give Achara a report that identifies the key problems and a plan of action she can present to her sponsor. Limit your report to 800 words or less.

Appendix 8.2

LEARNING OBJECTIVES

After reading this appendix you should be able to:

LO A8.2-1 Observe Hands-on demonstration of Example 1: Table 6.2 in MS Project on Resource Allocation and Leveling and Costing

LO A8.2-1

Observe Hands-on demonstration of Example 1: Table 6.2 in MS Project on Resource Allocation and Leveling and Costing

MS Project Demonstration of Resource Allocation, Leveling, and Costing

This exercise is in continuation to Appendix 6.1: Chapter 6, where through Example 1: Table 6.2, we learnt step-by-step process of initiation of the project, tasks, predecessor relationship among the tasks, assigning time duration, identification of Critical time, slack time, and the overall project duration using MS Project in Step 1 – Step 7. Now we are proceeding with our exercise with Resource Assignment to the assigned tasks and based on the constraints (time or resource) we will use MS Project to optimize the resources utilization. Also, MS Project would help us in calculation of the overall cost of the project.

For a Quick Review Let Us Revisit Step 7

Step 7: We got the total project time. Add a row on the top of the given tasks. Select all the below tasks and get these right indented. The right indent groups the activities under one heading, which is Automated Warehouse in our case.

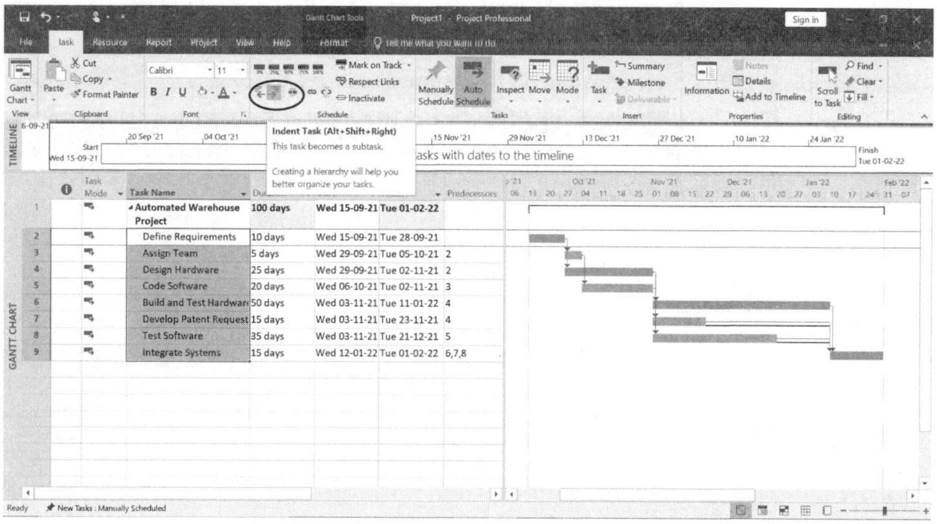

We matched the software result with the manual result as depicted in Figure 6.8, where the dashed activities show the Critical path. Here activity A, C, E, and H are represented by 1, 3, 5, 8. Delay in any of these activities would have direct implications on the overall project duration which is 100 days.

Step 8: Once tasks are entered into a schedule, resources are assigned to work on them. For assigning the resources we have to first have the pool of resources. For entering the pool of resources, you have to create the resource sheet. Click the Gantt chart drop-down list and select resource sheet.

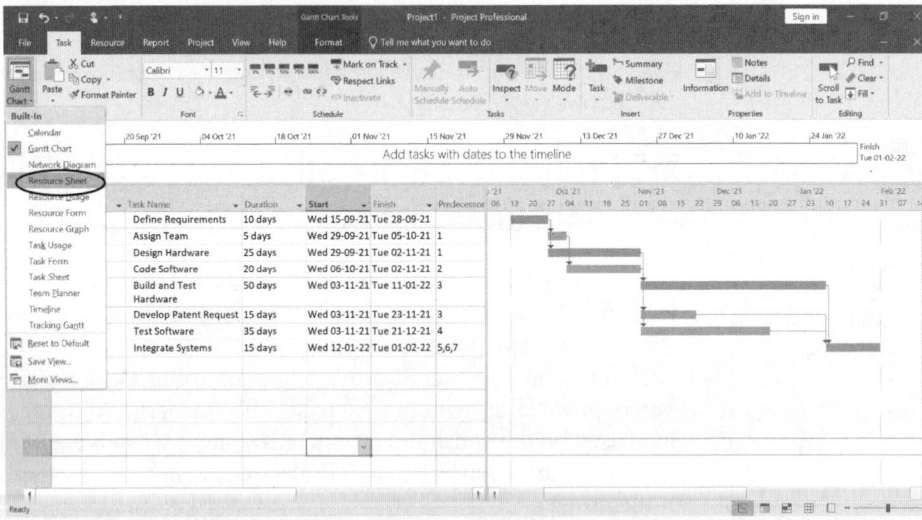

There are three types of resources we can add in MS Project – Work, Cost, Material. Work resource is used for people, Cost is used when the services of the resource are used, like travel, rent, training,and when the resource is material/material.

As no resource has been added to the project we don't see any names on the list. We have to enter a new name in the column or add resources to your project before assigning them to work on tasks.

Step 9: We need to assign resources.

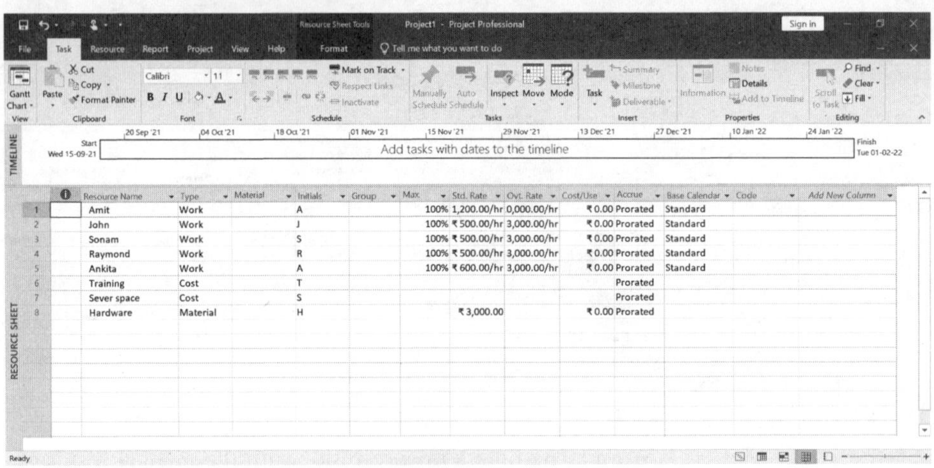

Work resources will require a resource name, like we added Amit, John, Sonam, etc., and, additional information may be entered, such as resource initials, standard rates, group/department, accounting code, maximum resource utilization and so on. We can enter maximum units as a percentage (50%, 100%, 300%). The default resource type is Work, and we can change the drop-down list. A work resource is generally thought of as a person usually name or role the person is playing.

Material resources require a material label such as cost per unit, cost per use value. For example, hardware or coffee can be a material resource. Because it is priced per pound, coffee would have a label of Kg and the cost would be Rs. 300. To create a material resource, set the type for the resource to "Material."

Cost resources need a name and the resource type set to "Cost." For example, a cost resource could be Training, Renting a vehicle.

Step 10: Assign the resources to the task by drop-down list.

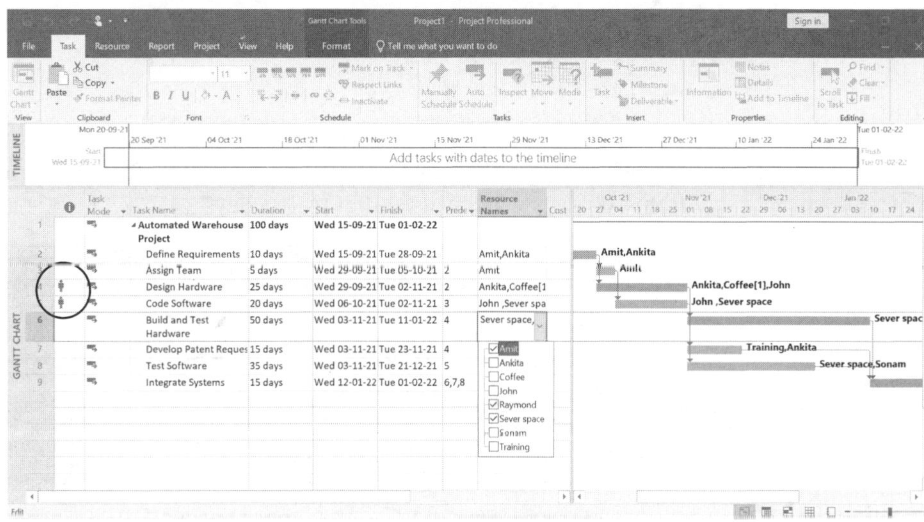

Once all the tasks are assigned as per the requirement, the assigned resources are visible in the Gantt chart too for a quick reference.

Now all the tasks are allotted with respective resources. We can see two red soldiers (flags) depicting resource over allocation. We need to resolve this resource allocation issue with the Resource Leveling method.

Step 11: Resource leveling

MS Project computes resource leveling to resolve resource over allocation in tasks. As we have resource constraints, we have an assumption here that says one person can't work on two tasks simultaneously. So, MS Project adjusts the start and finish date depending upon resource limitation to balance resource requirements. So, when specific tasks are required, the best option is to reschedule them assuming time is not the constraint.

For Resource Leveling go to tab Resource > Level Resource

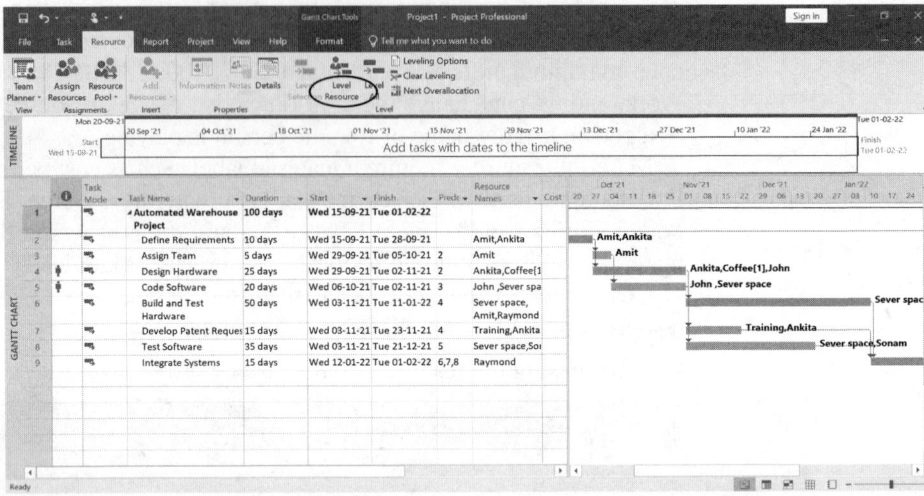

The Project will level tasks that are unlevelled or over assigned. Here is a caution that while we choose automatic leveling of resources, the project duration increased from 100 days which was earlier to 105 days.

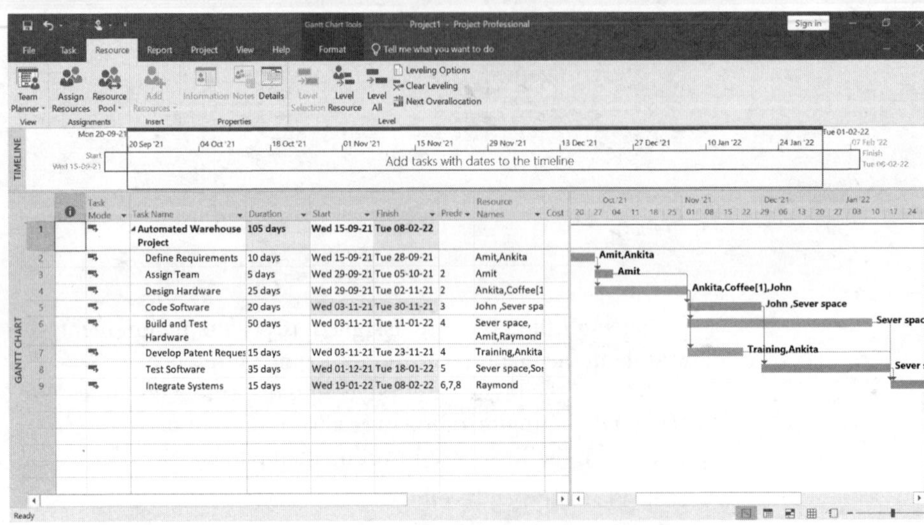

Step 12: Project cost calculation

Once the resources are leveled for the entire project and no more resource conflict exists, we can find total completion days and Project cost.

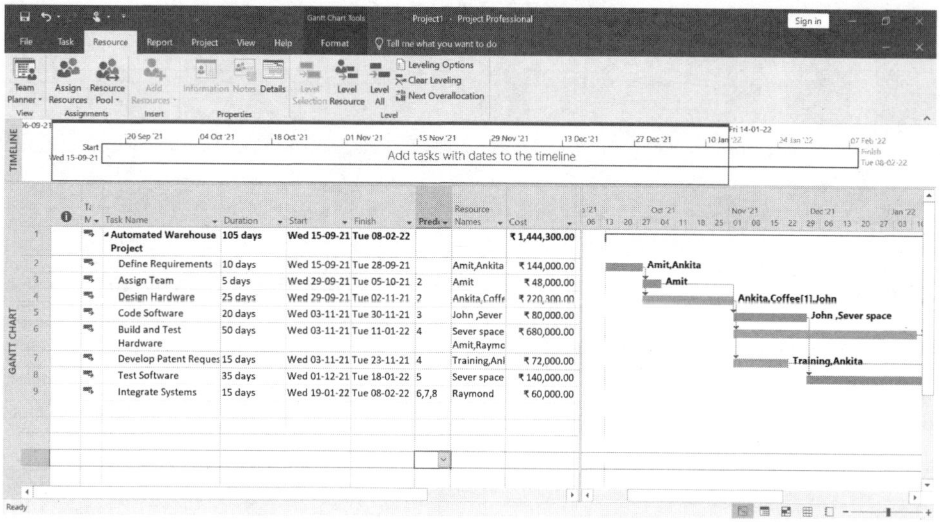

	Task Name	Duration	Start	Finish	Predecessors	Resource Names	Cost
1	**Automated Warehouse Project**	**105 days**	**Wed 15-09-21**	**Tue 08-02-22**			**₹1,444,300.00**
2	Define Requirements	10 days	Wed 15-09-21	Tue 28-09-21		Amit,Ankita	₹144,000.00
3	Assign Team	5 days	Wed 29-09-21	Tue 05-10-21	2	Amit	₹48,000.00
4	Design Hardware	25 days	Wed 29-09-21	Tue 02-11-21	2	Ankita,Coffe	₹220,300.00
5	Code Software	20 days	Wed 03-11-21	Tue 30-11-21	3	John ,Sever	₹80,000.00
6	Build and Test Hardware	50 days	Wed 03-11-21	Tue 11-01-22	4	Sever space Amit,Raymc	₹680,000.00
7	Develop Patent Reques	15 days	Wed 03-11-21	Tue 23-11-21	4	Training,Anl	₹72,000.00
8	Test Software	35 days	Wed 01-12-21	Tue 18-01-22	5	Sever space	₹140,000.00
9	Integrate Systems	15 days	Wed 19-01-22	Tue 08-02-22	6,7,8	Raymond	₹60,000.00

We add a new column named Cost by selecting from drop-down list, and the project total cost is presented (₹1,444,300.00). We can also calculate how much each activity and resource is costing the project.

Design elements: Snapshot from Practice, Highlight box, Case icon: Sky Designs/Shutterstock

CHAPTER NINE

9 Reducing Project Duration

LEARNING OBJECTIVES

After reading this chapter you should be able to:

9-1 Understand the different reasons for crashing a project.

9-2 Identify the different options for crashing an activity when resources are not constrained.

9-3 Identify the different options for crashing an activity when resources are constrained.

9-4 Determine the optimum cost-time point in a project network.

9-5 Understand the risks associated with compressing or crashing a project.

9-6 Identify different options for reducing the costs of a project.

OUTLINE

9.1 Rationale for Reducing Project Duration

9.2 Options for Accelerating Project Completion

9.3 Project Cost-Duration Graph

9.4 Constructing a Project Cost-Duration Graph

9.5 Practical Considerations

9.6 What If Cost, Not Time, Is the Issue?

Summary

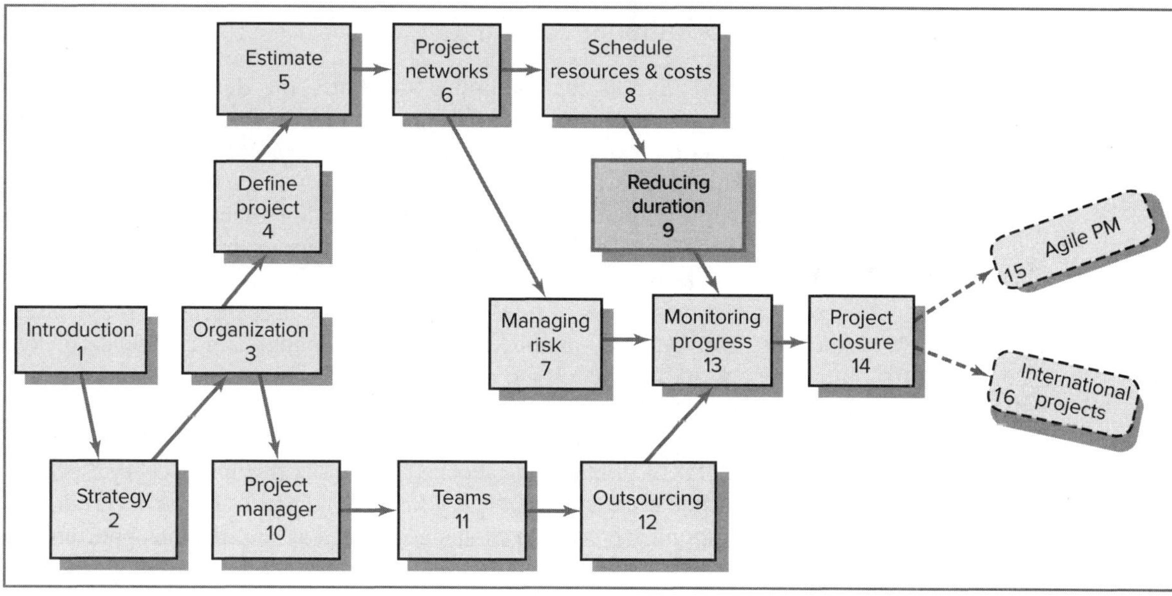

Speed is the ultimate weapon in business. All else being equal, the fastest company in any market will win.

—Dave Girouard, CEO and co-founder of Upstart Holdings Inc.

Imagine the following scenarios:

—After finalizing your project schedule, you realize the estimated completion date is two months beyond what your boss publicly promised an important customer.

—Five months into the project, you realize that you are already three weeks behind the drop-dead date for the project.

—Four months into a project, top management changes its priorities and now tells you that money is not an issue. Complete the project ASAP!

What do you do?

This chapter addresses strategies for reducing project duration either prior to setting the baseline for the project or in the midst of project execution. Choice of options is based on the constraints surrounding the project. Here the project priority matrix introduced in Chapter 4 comes into play. For example, there are many more options available for reducing project time if you are not resource constrained than if you cannot spend more than your original budget. We will begin by examining the reasons for reducing project duration, followed by a discussion of different options for accelerating project completion. The chapter will conclude with the classic time-cost framework for selecting which activities to "crash." **Crash** is a term that has emerged in the project management lexicon for shortening the duration of an activity or a project beyond when it can be normally done.

9.1 Rationale for Reducing Project Duration

LO 9-1

Understand the different reasons for crashing a project.

There are many good reasons for attempting to reduce the duration of a project. One of the more important reasons today is time-to-market. Intense global competition and rapid technological advances have made speed a competitive advantage. To succeed, companies have to spot new opportunities, launch project teams, and bring new products or services to the marketplace in a flash. Perhaps in no other industry does speed matter as much as in high-tech industries. For example, a rule of thumb for moderate- to high-technology firms is that a six-month delay in bringing a product to market can result in a loss of market share of about 35 percent. In these cases, high-technology firms typically assume that the time savings and avoidance of lost profits are worth any additional costs to reduce time without any formal analysis. See Snapshot from Practice 9.1: Smartphone Wars for more on this.

Business survival depends not only on rapid innovation but also on the ability to adapt quickly. The COVID-19 pandemic shocked the world, disrupting every aspect of work and daily life. Agile became the battle cry for responding to shifting uncertainties. Organizations that responded quickly to challenges as well as seized upon opportunities were able to ride the waves of emerging COVID-19 information and predictions. This required not only project management but also the ability to adapt quickly.

Another common reason for reducing project time occurs when unforeseen delays for example, adverse weather, design flaws, and equipment breakdown—cause

SNAPSHOT FROM PRACTICE 9.1 Smartphone Wars*

Speed has been critical in business ever since the California Gold Rush. The smartphone industry is a good example of an intensely competitive business that places a premium on speed and innovation. Analysts forecast over 15 different new smartphones on the market in 2025 with artificial intelligence playing a key role.

Among the new features in development include ability to project holographic images, flexible frames that allow the phone to be folded, eco-friendly devices, and advanced video imaging. Artificial intelligence (AI) will continue to be a driving force behind friction-less identification, as one's smartphone becomes more trusted than other credential like credit cards and even passports. The personal health, entertainment, financial, and communication possibilities are endless.

In order to survive, Samsung, Apple, Xiaomi, and other smartphone manufacturers have become masters at project management. They have been able to cut the market release time of new phones from 12–18 months to 6–9 months. What is at stake is over $1 billion in forecasted sales of new smartphones.

Robert Churchill/Rawpixel Ltd./123RF

*A. Jackson, "Future of Mobile Phones in 2025," the-next-tech.com. Accessed 5/18/22.

substantial delays midway in the project. Getting back on schedule usually requires compressing the time on some of the remaining critical activities. The additional costs of getting back on schedule need to be compared with the consequences of being late. This is especially true when time is a top priority.

Incentive contracts can make the reduction of project time rewarding—usually for both the project contractor and the owner. For example, a contractor finished a bridge across a lake 18 months early and received more than $6 million for the early completion. The availability of the bridge to the surrounding community 18 months early to reduce traffic gridlock made the incentive cost to the community seem small to users. In another example, in a continuous improvement arrangement, the joint effort of the owner and contractor resulted in early completion of a river lock and a 50/50 split of the savings to the owner and contractor. See Snapshot from Practice 9.2: Responding to the Northridge Earthquake for a classic example of a contractor who went to great lengths to quickly complete a project with a big payoff.

"Imposed deadlines" is another reason for accelerating project completion. For example, a politician makes a public statement that a new law building will be available in two years. Or the president of a software company remarks in a speech that new advanced software will be available on January 22. Such statements too often become project objectives without any consideration of the problems or cost of meeting such a date. The project duration time is set while the project is in its "concept" phase before or without any detailed scheduling of all the activities in the project. This phenomenon occurs frequently in practice! Unfortunately, this practice almost always leads to a higher-cost project than one that is planned using low-cost and detailed planning. In addition, quality is sometimes compromised to meet deadlines.

Sometimes very high overhead costs are recognized before the project begins. For example, it may cost $80,000 per day to simply house and feed a construction crew in the farthest reaches of northern Alaska. In these cases, it is prudent to examine the direct costs of shortening the critical path versus the overhead cost savings. Usually there are opportunities to shorten a few critical activities at less than the daily overhead rate.

Finally, there are times when it is important to reassign key equipment and/or people to new projects. Under these circumstances, the cost of compressing the project can be compared with the opportunity costs of not releasing key equipment or people.

9.2 Options for Accelerating Project Completion

LO 9-2

Identify the different options for crashing an activity when resources are not constrained.

Managers have several effective methods for crashing specific project activities when resources are not constrained. Several of these are summarized in this section.

Options When Resources Are Not Constrained

Adding Resources

The most common method for shortening project time is to assign additional staff and equipment to activities. There are limits, however, as to how much speed can be gained by adding staff. Doubling the size of the workforce will not necessarily reduce completion time by half. The relationship is correct only when tasks can be partitioned so minimal communication is needed between workers, as in harvesting a crop by hand or repaving a highway. Most projects are not set up that way; additional workers increase the communication requirements to coordinate their efforts. For example, doubling a team by adding two workers requires six times as much pairwise intercommunication than is required in the original two-person team. Not only is more time needed to coordinate and manage a larger team but also there is the additional delay of training the

SNAPSHOT FROM PRACTICE 9.2 Responding to the Northridge Earthquake*

Robert A. Eplett/FEMA

On January 17, 1994, a 6.8-magnitude earthquake struck the Los Angeles basin, near suburban Northridge, causing 60 deaths, thousands of injuries, and billions of dollars in property damage. Nowhere was the destructive power of nature more evident than in the collapsed sections of the freeway system, disrupting the daily commute of an estimated 1 million Los Angelenos.

The Northridge earthquake posed one of the greatest challenges to the California Department of Transportation (CalTrans) in its nearly 100-year history. To expedite the recovery process, Governor Pete Wilson signed an emergency declaration allowing CalTrans to streamline contracting procedures and offer attractive incentives for completing work ahead of schedule. For each day that the schedule was beaten, a sizable bonus was to be awarded. Conversely, for each day over the deadline, the contractor would be penalized the same amount. The amount ($50,000 to $200,000) varied depending on the importance of the work.

The incentive scheme proved to be a powerful motivator for the freeway reconstruction contractors. C. C. Myers, Inc., of Rancho Cordova, California, won the contract for the reconstruction of the Interstate 10 bridges. Myers pulled out all the stops to finish the project in a blistering 66 days—a whopping 74 days ahead of schedule—and earning a $14.8 million bonus! Myers took every opportunity to save time and streamline operations. They greatly expanded the workforce. For example, 134 iron-workers were employed instead of the normal 15. Special lighting equipment was set up so that work could be performed around the clock. Likewise, the sites were prepared and special materials were used so that work could continue despite inclement weather that would normally shut down construction. The work was scheduled much like an assembly line so that critical activities were followed by the next critical activity. A generous incentive scheme was devised to reward teamwork and reach milestones early. Carpenters and iron-workers competed as teams against each other to see who could finish first.

Although C. C. Myers received a substantial bonus for finishing early, they spent a lot of money on overtime, bonuses, special equipment, and other premiums to keep the job rolling along. CalTrans supported Myers's efforts. With reconstruction work going on 24 hours a day, including jackhammering and pile-driving, CalTrans temporarily housed many families in local motels. CalTrans even erected a temporary plastic soundwall to help reduce the construction noise traveling to a nearby apartment complex. The double-layer curtain, 450 feet long and 20 feet high, was designed to reduce construction noise by 10 decibels.

Despite the difficulties and expense incurred by around-the-clock freeway building, most of Los Angeles cheered CalTrans's quake recovery efforts. The Governor's Office of Planning and Research issued a report concluding that for every day the Santa Monica Freeway was closed, it cost the local economy more than $1 million.

*J. B. Baxter, "Responding to the Northridge Earthquake," *PM Network*, November 1994, pp. 13–22.

new people and getting them up to speed on the project. The end result is captured in Brooks's law: *adding manpower to a late software project makes it later.*[1]

Frederick Brooks formulated this principle based on his experience as a project manager for IBM's System/360 software project during the early 1960s. Although subsequent research confirmed Brooks's prediction, it also discovered that adding more people to a late project does not always cause the project to be later.[2] The key

[1] Brooks's *The Mythical Man-Month* (Reading, MA: Addison-Wesley, 1994) is considered a classic on software project management.

[2] Gordon, R. L., and J. C. Lamb, "A Close Look at Brooks' Law," *Datamation*, June 1977, pp. 81–86.

is whether the new staff is added early so there is sufficient time to make up for lost ground once the new members have been fully assimilated.

Outsourcing Project Work

A common method for shortening project time is to subcontract an activity. The subcontractor may have access to superior technology or expertise that will accelerate the completion of the activity. For example, contracting for a backhoe can accomplish in two hours what it can take a team of laborers two days to do. Likewise, by hiring a consulting firm that specializes in Active Directory Service Interfaces (ADSI) programming, a firm may be able to cut in half the time it would take for less experienced, internal programmers to do the work. Subcontracting also frees up resources that can be assigned to a critical activity and will ideally result in a shorter project duration. See Snapshot from Practice 9.3: Outsourcing in Bio-Tech Picks Up Speed. Outsourcing will be addressed more fully in Chapter 12.

Scheduling Overtime

The easiest way to add more labor to a project is not to add more people but to schedule overtime. If a team works 50 hours a week instead of 40, it might accomplish 20 percent more. By scheduling overtime, you avoid the additional costs of coordination and communication encountered when new people are added. If people involved are salaried workers, there may be no additional cost for the extra work. Another advantage is that there are fewer distractions when people work outside normal hours.

Overtime has disadvantages. First, hourly workers are typically paid time and a half for overtime and double time for weekends and holidays. Sustained overtime work by salaried employees may incur intangible costs such as divorce, burnout, and turnover. Turnover is a key organizational concern when there is a shortage of workers. Furthermore, it is an oversimplification to assume that over an extended period of time a person is as productive during her eleventh hour at work as during her third hour of work. There are natural limits to what is humanly possible, and extended overtime may actually lead to an overall decline in productivity when fatigue sets in (DeMarco, 2002).

SNAPSHOT FROM PRACTICE 9.3 Outsourcing in Bio-Tech Picks Up Speed*

In the face of increasing time-to-market pressures, many bio-tech firms are turning to outsourcing to expedite the drug development process. Panos Kalaritis, vice president of operations for Irix Pharmaceuticals, says that outsourcing process development can accelerate a drug's evolution by allowing a pharmaceutical company to continue research while a contractor works on process optimization. Susan Dexter of Lonza Biologics identified different types of outsourcing contracts including agreements for product development, clinical trial supplies, in-market or commercial supplies, and technology transfer. Often, she said, a given project can encompass more than one of the above stages over a period of several years.

Using a contractor, said Paul Henricks, business manager for Patheon Inc., gives the client company access to specialized knowledge and infrastructure as well as flexible resources and capacity. The sponsoring company can also manage risks by sharing responsibilities through outsourcing.

"Communication is key to a successful outsourcing relationship," said Dan Gold, vice president of process development for Covance, which was formerly Corning Bio. "Contractors and sponsors should both assign project managers, and the two must work together to maintain, track, and document project completion. There must be a concerted effort on the part of both parties to work as partners to complete the project."

*M. Lerner, "Outsourcing in Bio-Technology Picks Up Speed," *Chemical Market Reporter,* vol. 251, no. 14 (2002), p. 17.

Working overtime and longer hours is the preferred choice for accelerating project completion, especially when the project team is salaried. The key is to use overtime judiciously. Remember, a project is a marathon, not a sprint! You do not want to run out of energy before the finish line.

Establish a Core Project Team

As discussed in Chapter 3, one of the advantages of creating a dedicated core team to complete a project is speed. Assigning professionals full time to a project avoids the hidden cost of multitasking in which people are forced to juggle the demands of multiple projects. Professionals are allowed to devote their undivided attention to a specific project. This singular focus creates a shared goal that can bind a diverse set of professionals into a highly cohesive team capable of accelerating project completion. Factors that contribute to the emergence of high-performing project teams will be discussed in detail in Chapter 11.

Do It Twice—Fast and Correctly

If you are in a hurry, try building a "quick and dirty" short-term solution; then go back and do it the right way. For example, pontoon bridges are used as temporary solutions to damaged bridges in combat. In business, software companies are notorious for releasing version 1.0 of products that are not completely finished and tested. Subsequent versions 1.1 . . . x correct bugs and add intended functionality to the product. The additional costs of doing it twice are often more than compensated for by the benefits of satisfying the deadline.

Options When Resources Are Constrained

LO 9-3

Identify the different options for crashing an activity when resources are constrained.

A project manager has fewer options for accelerating project completion when additional resources are not available or the budget is severely constrained. This is especially true once the schedule has been established. This section discusses some of these options, which are also available when resources are not constrained.

Improve the Efficiency of the Project Team

The project team may be able to improve productivity by implementing more efficient ways to do their work. This can be achieved by improving the planning and organization of the project or eliminating barriers to productivity such as excessive bureaucratic interference and red tape.

Fast Tracking

Sometimes it is possible to rearrange the logic of the project network so that critical activities are done in parallel (concurrently) rather than sequentially. This alternative is commonly referred to as **fast tracking** and is a good one if the project situation is right. When this alternative is given serious attention, it is amazing to observe how creative project team members can be in finding ways to restructure sequential activities in parallel. As noted in Chapter 6, one of the most common methods for restructuring activities is to change a finish-to-start relationship to a start-to-start relationship. For example, instead of waiting for the final design to be approved, manufacturing engineers can begin building the production line as soon as key specifications have been established. Changing activities from sequential to parallel is not without risk, however. Late design changes can produce wasted effort and rework. Fast tracking requires close coordination among those responsible for the activities affected and confidence in the work that has been completed.

Use Critical-Chain Management

Critical-Chain Project Management (CCPM) is designed to accelerate project completion. As discussed in Appendix 8.1, it would be difficult to apply CCPM midstream in a project. CCPM requires considerable training and a shift in habits and perspectives that takes time to adopt. Although there have been reports of immediate gains, especially in terms of completion times, a long-term management commitment is probably necessary to reap full benefits. See Snapshot from Practice 9.4: The Fastest House in the World for an extreme example of CCPM application.

SNAPSHOT FROM PRACTICE 9.4 The Fastest House in the World*

Ariel Skelley/Blend Images/the Agency Collection/Getty Images

December 17, 2002—after revving up their power tools and lining up volunteers, Shelby County Habitat for Humanity broke the world record for the fastest house ever built, clocking in at 3 hours, 26 minutes, and 34 seconds. Former record holder, New Zealand's Habitat Affiliate Mannakau, held the record for three years at 3 hours, 44 minutes, and 59 seconds. The Alabama project beat the New Zealand record by 18 minutes.

"This was different than any construction project that I've ever been a part of," said Project Manager Chad Calhoun. "The minute-by-minute schedule, the planning of each precise movement, the organization of all the teams and materials, could not have gone more smoothly on build day. All the long hours of planning definitely paid off."

In preparation for the build, Habitat volunteers put the foundation in place and constructed prefabricated wall panels. Once the whistle blew at 11:00 a.m. on December 17, the exterior wall panels were raised into place, followed by the interior panel, which took only 16 minutes. Special color-coded teams of workers connected the wiring and plumbing, put in insulation, installed appliances, laid carpet and tile, installed light fixtures, painted the house inside, applied vinyl siding outside, and attached assembled front and back porches.

At the same time, the roof was constructed on the ground next to the house. Once the roof was completed—approximately 1½ hours later—a Steel City crane lifted the 14,000-pound roof assembly into place. Crews attached the roof while others completed the interior work. There was even time to lay sod, plant shrubbery, and decorate a Christmas tree in the front yard—all within the official build time of 3 hours, 26 minutes, and 34 seconds.

The recipient of this wonderful holiday gift was Bonnie Lilly, a single mother and nursing technician who had applied to Habitat for Humanity three times before she was selected to receive the three-bedroom, two-bath home. "It's amazing," Lilly said. "Who am I to have this happen for me? A world record, hundreds of people coming together to build my house—I still can't believe it."

Habitat for Humanity is an international charitable organization that builds simple, affordable houses and sells them on a no-interest, no-profit basis to needy families.

*E. Drummond, "The House That Love Built, Really FAST—and Just in Time for Christmas Kicker: Habitat for Humanity Breaks World Record Set by New Zealand," www.csre.com; "Shelby County, Ala. Builds Fastest Habitat House in Three and a Half Hours," www.habitat.org/newsroom/2002archive.

Reduce Project Scope

Probably the most common response to meeting unattainable deadlines is to reduce the scope of the project. This invariably leads to a reduction in the functionality of the project. For example, a new car will average only 25 mpg instead of 30, or a software product will have fewer features than originally planned. While scaling back the scope of the project can lead to big savings in both time and money, it may come at a cost of reducing the value of the project. If the car gets lower gas mileage, will it stand up to competitive models? Will customers still want the software minus the features?

The key to reducing project scope without reducing value is to reassess the true specifications of the project. Often requirements are added under best-case, blue-sky scenarios and represent desirables, but not essentials. Here it is important to talk to the customer and/or project sponsors and explain the situation—"you can get it your way but not until February." This may force them to accept an extension or to add money to expedite the project. If not, then a healthy discussion of what the essential requirements are and what items can be compromised in order to meet the deadline needs to take place. More intense reexamination of requirements may actually improve the value of the project by getting it done more quickly and for a lower cost.

Compromise Quality

Reducing quality is always an option, but it is rarely acceptable or used. Sacrificing quality may reduce the time of an activity on the critical path.

In practice the methods most commonly used to crash projects are scheduling overtime, outsourcing, and adding resources. Each of these maintains the essence of the original plan. Options that depart from the original project plan include do it twice and fast tracking. Rethinking of project scope, customer needs, and timing become major considerations for these techniques.

See Snapshot from Practice: Operation Warp Speed for an account of the U.S. government efforts to develop a COVID-19 vaccine as quickly as possible.

9.3 Project Cost-Duration Graph

LO 9-4

Determine the optimum cost-time point in a project network.

Nothing on the horizon suggests that the need to shorten project time will change. In fact, if anything, the pressure to get projects done quicker and sooner is likely to increase in importance. The challenge for the project manager is to use a quick, logical method to compare the benefits of reducing project time with the costs involved. Without sound, logical methods, it is difficult to isolate those activities that will have the greatest impact on reducing project time at least cost. This section describes a procedure for identifying the costs of reducing project time so that comparisons can be made with the benefits of getting the project completed sooner. The method requires gathering direct and indirect costs for specific project durations. Critical activities are searched to find the lowest direct-cost activities that will shorten the project duration. Total costs for specific project durations are computed and then compared with the benefits of reducing project time—before the project begins or while it is in progress.

Explanation of Project Costs

The general nature of project costs is illustrated in Figure 9.1, which shows a **project cost-duration graph.** The total cost for each duration is the sum of the indirect and direct costs. Indirect costs continue for the life of the project. Hence, any reduction in project duration means a reduction in indirect costs. Direct costs on the graph grow

SNAPSHOT FROM PRACTICE Operation Warp Speed*

On May 15, 2020, the Trump administration launched Operation Warp Speed to develop vaccines against the deadly COVID-19. The name was inspired by terminology for faster-than-light travel used in the Star Trek fictional universe, evoking a sense of rapid progress. Operation Warp Speed was formed to encourage private and public partnerships to enable faster approval and production of vaccines during the COVID-19 pandemic.

Specific targets, as outlined in various media, included:

1. Support pharmaceutical companies for R&D of seven different vaccine candidates simultaneously and certain therapeutic compounds.
2. Support several vaccine manufacturers for rapid scale-up of manufacturing capacity.
3. Support organization and facilitate simultaneous Food and Drug Administration (FDA) review of Phase I–III clinical trials on several of the most promising vaccine candidates.
4. Facilitate manufacturing vaccine candidates while they remain pre-approved during prefinal clinical research to prepare for rapid deployment, if proven to be safe and effective.
5. Coordinate with the Department of Defense for vaccine supply, production, and deployment around the United States, and track every vaccine vial and the injection schedule for each American receiving a vaccination.

According to the Department of Health and Human Services' fact sheet, the main stated goal of Operation Warp Speed was to "produce and deliver 300 million doses of safe and effective vaccines with the initial doses available by January 2021."

Clearly cost was not a priority. The U.S. congress quickly authorized billions of dollars be spent on supporting joint efforts by government and businesses to rapidly deliver a viable vaccine to the public. The funds not only dramatically increased the number of people searching for solutions but also allow firms to broaden their search for solutions not normally considered. Hoping to strike a "gold." At one time over 145 different vaccines were being tested worldwide.

FDA streamlined the approval process by initiating Emergency Use Authorization (EUA) procedures. Both Pfizer and Moderna were issued EUAs in December 2020 that accelerated their approval deadlines.

On June 30, 2020, the FDA announced that a vaccine would need to be at least 50% effective for diminishing the severity of COVID-19 symptoms to obtain regulatory and marketing approval. It should be noted that normal flu vaccines have 40–60% efficacy.

Investments extended beyond pharmaceutical firms to include the entire network of business required to manufacture and deliver vaccines including both UPS and FedEx. Fast tracking (aka, Start to Start lags) were used to shorten delivery times by building manufacturing and distribution systems before vaccine approval.

While Operation Warp Speed fell short of its January 2021 target, it did pave the way for the rapid distribution of vaccines to American public. Future retrospectives will ultimately assess the efficacy of the operation in general and the projects that were attempted. More critical will be the lessons learned developed by people at all levels of operations.

*P. Hall, "The Lightning-Fast Quest for COVID Vaccines – and What It Means for Other Diseases," www.nature.com, December 18, 2020. Accessed 6/5/2022.

at an increasing rate as the project duration is reduced from its originally planned duration. With the information from a graph such as this for a project, managers can quickly judge any alternative such as meeting a time-to-market deadline. Further discussion of indirect and direct costs is necessary before demonstrating a procedure for developing the information for a graph similar to the one in Figure 9.1.

Project Indirect Costs

Indirect costs generally represent overhead costs such as supervision, administration, consultants, and interest. Indirect costs cannot be associated with any particular work

FIGURE 9.1
Typical Project Cost-Duration Graph

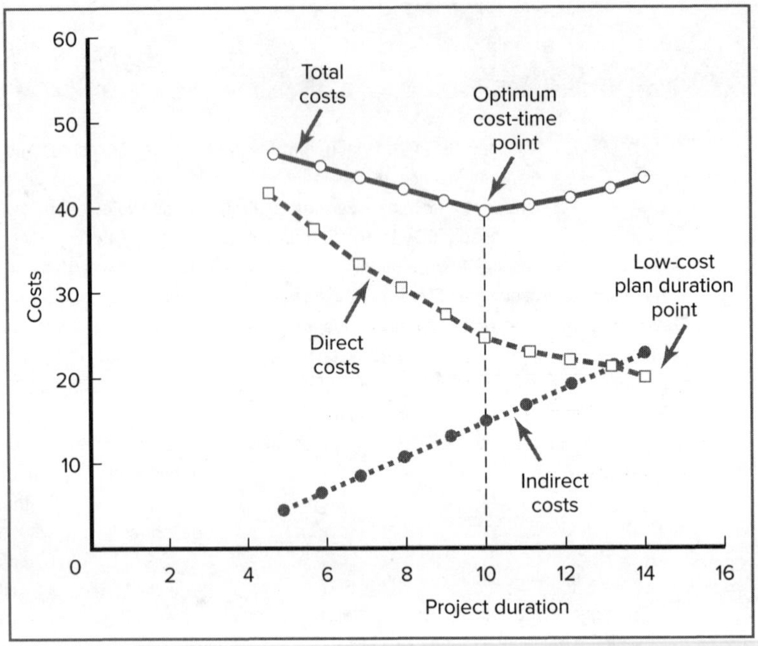

package or activity, hence the term. Indirect costs vary directly with time. That is, any reduction in time should result in a reduction of indirect costs. For example, if the daily costs of supervision, administration, and consultants are $2,000, any reduction in project duration would represent a savings of $2,000 per day. If indirect costs are a significant percentage of total project costs, reductions in project time can represent very real savings (assuming the indirect resources can be utilized elsewhere).

Project Direct Costs

Direct costs commonly represent labor, materials, equipment, and sometimes subcontractors. Direct costs are assigned directly to a work package and activity, hence the term. The ideal assumption is that direct costs for an activity time represent normal costs, which typically mean low-cost, efficient methods for a normal time. When project durations are imposed, direct costs may no longer represent low-cost, efficient methods. Costs for the imposed duration date will be higher than for a project duration developed from ideal normal times for activities. Because direct costs are assumed to be developed from normal methods and time, any reduction in activity time should add to the costs of the activity. The sum of the costs of all the work packages or activities represents the total direct costs for the project.

The major challenge faced in creating the information for a graph similar to Figure 9.1 is computing the direct cost of shortening individual critical activities and then finding the total direct cost for each project duration as project time is compressed; the process requires selecting those critical activities that cost the least to shorten. (Note: The graph implies that there is always an optimum cost-time point. This is only true if shortening a schedule has incremental indirect cost savings exceeding the incremental direct cost incurred. However, in practice there are almost always several activities in which the direct costs of shortening are less than the indirect costs.)

9.4 Constructing a Project Cost-Duration Graph

Three major steps are required to construct a project cost-duration graph:

1. Find total direct costs for selected project durations.
2. Find total indirect costs for selected project durations.
3. Sum direct and indirect costs for these selected durations.

The graph is then used to compare additional cost alternatives for benefits. Details of these steps are presented here.

Determining the Activities to Shorten

The most difficult task in constructing a cost-duration graph is finding the total direct costs for specific project durations over a relevant range. The central task is to decide which activities to shorten and how far to carry the shortening process. Basically managers need to look for critical activities that can be shortened with the *smallest increase in cost per unit of time.* The rationale for selecting critical activities depends on identifying the activity's normal and crash times and corresponding costs. *Normal time* for an activity represents low-cost, realistic, efficient methods for completing the activity under normal conditions. The shortest possible time in which an activity can realistically be completed is called its **crash time.** The direct cost for completing an activity in its crash time is called *crash cost.* Both normal and crash times and costs are collected from the personnel most familiar with completing the activity. Figure 9.2 depicts a hypothetical cost-duration graph for an activity.

The normal time for the activity in Figure 9.2 is 10 time units, and the corresponding cost is \$400. The crash time for the activity is five time units and \$800.

FIGURE 9.2
Activity Graph

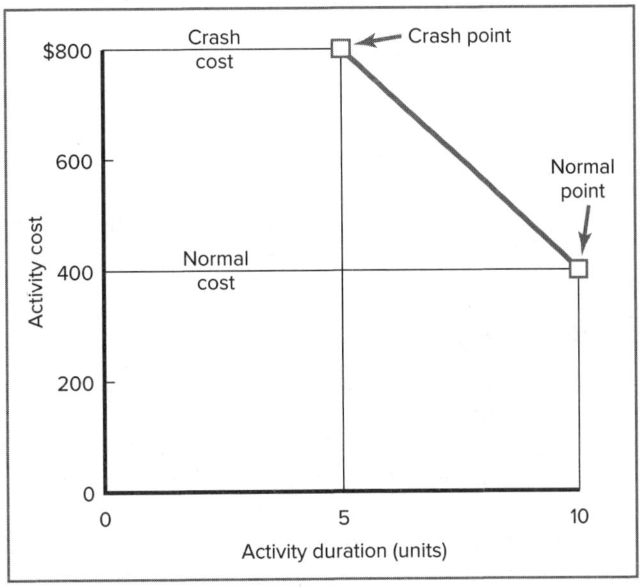

The intersection of the normal time and cost represents the original low-cost, early-start schedule. The **crash point** represents the maximum time an activity can be compressed. The heavy line connecting the normal and crash points represents the slope, which assumes that the cost of reducing the time of the activity is constant *per unit of time.* The assumptions underlying the use of this graph are as follows:

1. The cost-time relationship is linear.
2. Normal time assumes low-cost, efficient methods to complete the activity.
3. Crash time represents a limit—the greatest time reduction possible under realistic conditions.
4. Slope represents cost per unit of time.
5. All accelerations must occur within the normal and crash times.

Knowing the slope of activities allows managers to compare which critical activities to shorten. The less steep the cost slope of an activity, the less it costs to shorten one time period; a steeper slope means it will cost more to shorten one time unit. The cost per unit of time or slope for any activity is computed by the following equation:

$$\text{Cost slope} = \frac{\text{Rise}}{\text{Run}} = \frac{\text{Crash cost} - \text{Normal cost}}{\text{Normal time} - \text{Crash time}}$$

$$= \frac{CC - NC}{NT - CT} = \frac{\$800 - \$400}{10 - 5}$$

$$= \frac{\$400}{5} = \$80 \text{ per unit of time}$$

In Figure 9.2, the rise is the *y*-axis (cost) and the run is the *x*-axis (duration). The slope of the cost line is $80 for each time unit the activity is reduced; the limit reduction of the activity time is five time units. Comparison of the slopes of all critical activities allows us to determine which activity(ies) to shorten to minimize total direct cost. Given the preliminary project schedule (or one in progress) with all activities set to their early-start times, the process of searching critical activities as candidates for reduction can begin. The total direct cost for each specific compressed project duration must be found.

A Simplified Example

Figure 9.3A presents normal and crash times and costs for each activity, the computed slope and time reduction limit, the total direct cost, and the project network with a duration of 25 time units. Note that the total direct cost for the 25-period duration is $450. This is an anchor point to begin the procedure of shortening the critical path(s) and finding the total direct costs for each specific duration less than 25 time units. The maximum time reduction of an activity is simply the difference between the normal and crash times for an activity. For example, activity D can be reduced from a normal time of 11 time units to a crash time of 7 time units, or a maximum of 4 time units. The positive slope for activity D is computed as follows:

$$\text{Slope} = \frac{\text{Crash cost} - \text{Normal cost}}{\text{Normal time} - \text{Crash time}} = \frac{\$150 - \$50}{11 - 7}$$

$$= \frac{\$100}{4} = \$25 \text{ per period reduced}$$

The network shows the critical path to be activities A, D, F, G. Because it is impossible to shorten activity G ("x" is used to indicate this), activity A is circled because it is the least-cost candidate; that is, its slope ($20) is less than the slopes for activities D and F ($25 and $30). Reducing activity A 1 time unit cuts the project duration to 24 time units

FIGURE 9.3
Cost-Duration Trade-off Example

Activity ID	Slope	Maximum crash time	Direct costs: Normal Time	Normal Cost	Crash Time	Crash Cost
A	*$20*	*1*	3	$50	2	$70
B	*40*	*2*	6	80	4	160
C	*30*	*1*	10	60	9	90
D	*25*	*4*	11	50	7	150
E	*30*	*2*	8	100	6	160
F	*30*	*1*	5	40	4	70
G	*0*	*0*	6	70	6	70

Total direct cost *$450*

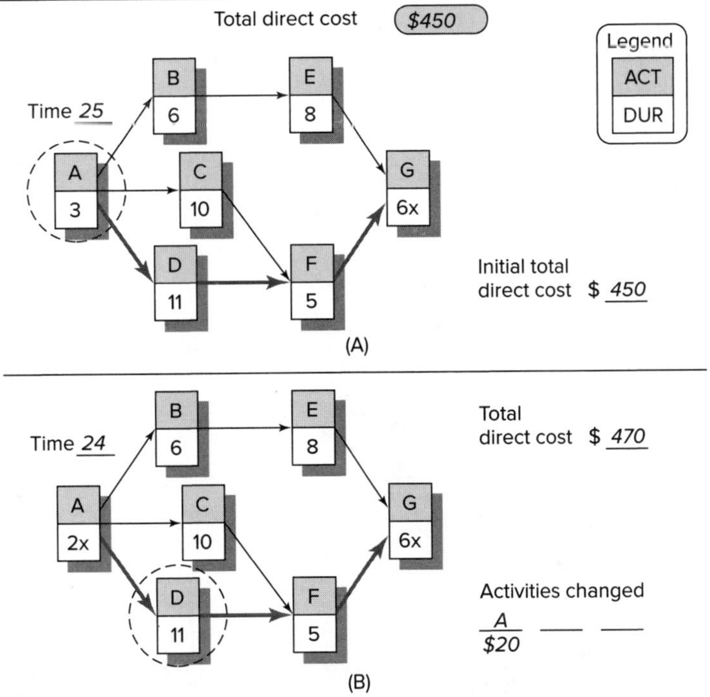

but increases the total direct costs to \$470 (\$450 + \$20 = \$470). Figure 9.3B reflects these changes. The duration of activity A has been reduced to 2 time units; the "x" indicates the activity cannot be reduced any further. Activity D is circled because it costs the least (\$25) to shorten the project to 23 time units. Compare the cost of activity F. The total direct cost for a project duration of 23 time units is \$495 (see Figure 9.4A).

Observe that the project network in Figure 9.4A now has two critical paths—A, C, F, G and A, D, F, G. Reducing the project to 22 time units will require that activity F be reduced; thus, it is circled. This change is reflected in Figure 9.4B. The total direct cost for 22 time units is \$525. This reduction has created a third critical path—A, B, E, G; all activities are critical. Note that we can also reduce the project duration from 23 time units to 22 time units by crashing activities C and D together. We do not select this alternate because it costs more to reduce activities C and D than to reduce activity F only. Reducing activities C and D will cost \$55 (\$30 + \$25) while reducing activity F costs \$30 only.

The least-cost method for reducing the project duration to 21 time units is the combination of the circled activities C, D, E—which cost \$30, \$25, \$30, respectively—and increase total direct costs to \$610. The results of these changes are depicted in

FIGURE 9.4
Cost-Duration Trade-off Example

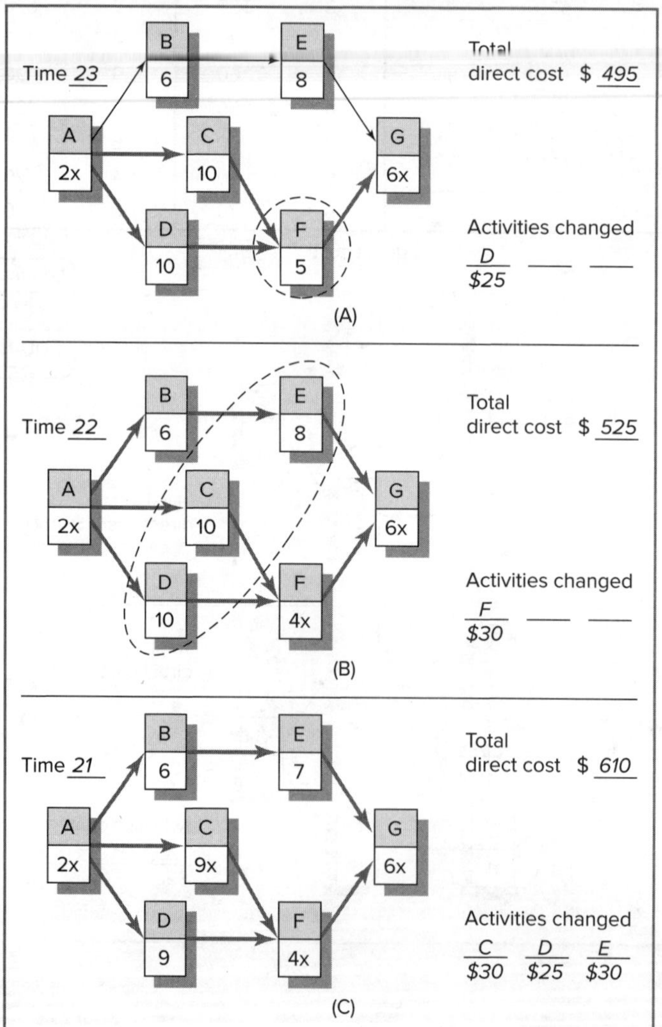

FIGURE 9.5
Summary Costs by Duration

Project duration	Direct costs	+	Indirect costs	=	Total costs
25	*450*		400		*$850*
24	*470*		350		*820*
23	*495*		300		*795*
22	*525*		250		*775*
21	*610*		200		*810*

FIGURE 9.6
Project Cost-Duration Graph

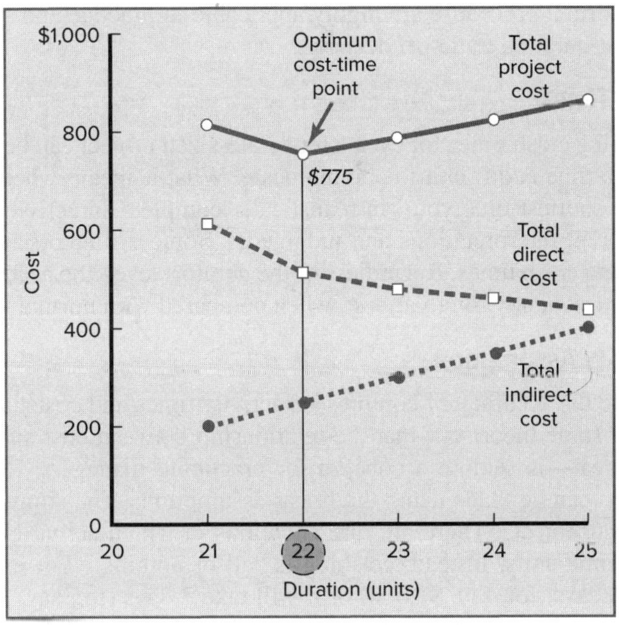

Figure 9.4C. Although some activities can still be reduced (those without the "x" next to the activity time), no activity or combination of activities will result in a reduction in the project duration.

With the total direct costs for the array of specific project durations found, the next step is to collect the indirect costs for the same durations. These costs are typically a rate per day and are easily obtained from the Accounting Department. Figure 9.5 presents the total direct costs, total indirect costs, and total project costs. The same costs are plotted in Figure 9.6. This graph shows that the optimum cost-time duration is 22 time units and $775. Assuming the project will actually materialize as planned, any movement away from this time duration will increase project costs. The movement from 25 to 22 time units occurs because, in this range, the absolute slopes of the indirect costs are greater than the direct-cost slopes.

9.5 Practical Considerations

Using the Project Cost-Duration Graph

The project cost-duration graph, as presented in Figures 9.1 and 9.6, is valuable in comparing any proposed alternative or change with the optimum cost and time. More importantly the creation of such a graph keeps the importance of indirect costs in the forefront of decision making. Indirect costs are frequently forgotten in the field when the pressure for action is intense. Finally, such a graph can be used before the project begins or while the project is in progress.

Creating the graph in the pre-project planning phase without an imposed duration is the first choice because normal time is more meaningful. Creating the graph in the project planning phase with an imposed duration is less desirable because normal time is made to fit the imposed date and is probably not low cost. Creating the graph after the project has started is the least desirable because some alternatives may be ruled out of the decision process. Managers may choose not to use the formal procedure demonstrated. However, regardless of the method used, the principles and concepts inherent in the formal procedure are highly applicable in practice and should be considered in any cost-duration trade-off decision.

Crash Times

Collecting crash times for even a moderate-sized project can be difficult. The meaning of crash time is difficult to communicate. What is meant when you define crash time as "the shortest time you can realistically complete an activity"? Crash time is open to different interpretations and judgments. Some estimators feel very uncomfortable providing crash times. Regardless of the comfort level, the accuracy of crash times and costs is frequently rough at best, when compared with normal time and cost.

Linearity Assumption

Because the accuracy of compressed activity times and costs is questionable, the concern of some theorists—that the relationship between cost and time is not linear but curvilinear—is seldom a concern for practicing managers. Reasonable, quick comparisons can be made using the linear assumption.[3] The simple approach is adequate for most projects. There are rare situations in which activities cannot be crashed by single time units. Instead, crashing is "all or nothing." For example, activity A will take 10 days (for, say, $1,000) or it will take 7 days (for, say, $1,500), but no options exist in which activity A will take 8 or 9 days to complete. In a few, rare cases of very large, complex, long-duration projects, present value techniques may be useful; such techniques are beyond the scope of this text.

Choice of Activities to Crash Revisited

LO 9-5

Understand the risks associated with compressing or crashing a project.

The cost-time crashing method relies on choosing the cheapest method for reducing the duration of the project. There are other factors that should be assessed beyond simply cost. First, the inherent risks involved in crashing particular activities need to be considered. Some activities are riskier to crash than others. For example, accelerating the completion of a software design code may not be wise if it increases the likelihood of errors surfacing downstream. Conversely, crashing a more expensive activity may be wise if fewer inherent risks are involved.

Second, the timing of activities needs to be considered. Crashing an early activity may be prudent if there is concern that subsequent activities are likely to be delayed, and absorb the time gained. Then the manager would still have the option of crashing final activities to get back on schedule.

Third, crashing frequently results in overallocation of resources. The resources required to accelerate a cheaper activity may suddenly not be available. Resource availability, not cost, may dictate which activities are crashed.

[3] Linearity assumes that the cost for crashing each time unit is constant.

Finally, the impact of crashing would have on the morale and motivation of the project team needs to be assessed. If the least-cost method repeatedly signals a subgroup to accelerate progress, fatigue and resentment may set in. Conversely, if overtime pay is involved, other team members may resent not having access to this benefit. This situation can lead to tension within the entire project team. Good project managers gauge the response that crashing activities will have on the entire project team. See Snapshot from Practice 9.5: I'll Bet You . . . for a novel approach to motivating employees to work faster.

SNAPSHOT FROM PRACTICE 9.5 I'll Bet You . . .

The focus of this chapter has been on how project managers crash activities by typically assigning additional manpower and equipment to cut significant time off of scheduled tasks. Project managers often encounter situations in which they need to motivate individuals to accelerate the completion of a specific, critical task. Imagine the following scenario.

Bruce Young just received a priority assignment from corporate headquarters. The preliminary engineering sketches that were due tomorrow need to be e-mailed to the West Coast by 4:00 p.m. today so that the model shop can begin construction of a prototype to present to top management. Bruce approaches Danny Whitten, the draftsman responsible for the task, whose initial response is "That's impossible!" While Bruce agrees that it would be very difficult, he does not believe that it is as impossible as Danny suggests or that Danny truly believes that. What should he do?

He tells Danny that he knows this is going to be a rush job but he is confident that he can do it. When Danny balks, he responds, "I tell you what, I'll make a bet with you. If you are able to finish the design by 4:00, I'll make sure you get two of the company's tickets to tomorrow night's Celtics-Knicks basketball game." Danny accepts the challenge, works feverishly to complete the assignment, and is able to take his daughter to her first professional basketball game.

Conversations with project managers reveal that many use bets like this one to motivate extraordinary performance. These bets range from tickets to sporting and entertainment events to gift certificates at high-class restaurants to a well-deserved afternoon off. For bets to work, they need to adhere to the principles of expectancy theory of motivation.* Boiled down to simple terms, expectancy theory rests on three key questions:

1. Can I do it (is it possible to meet the challenge)?
2. Will I get it (can I demonstrate that I met the challenge and can I trust the project manager will deliver his/her end of the bargain)?
3. Is it worth it (is the payoff of sufficient personal value to warrant the risk and extra effort)?

If in the mind of the participant the answer to any of these three questions is no, then the person is unlikely to accept the challenge. However, when the answers are affirmative, then the individual is likely to accept the challenge.

Bets can be effective motivational tools and add an element of excitement and fun to project work. But the following practical advice should be heeded:

1. The bet has greater significance if it also benefits family members or significant others. Being able to take a son or daughter to a professional basketball game allows that individual to "score points" at home through work. These bets also recognize and reward the support project members receive from their families and reinforces the importance of their work to loved ones.
2. Bets should be used sparingly; otherwise, everything can become negotiable. They should be used only under special circumstances that require extraordinary effort.
3. Individual bets should involve clearly recognizable individual effort; otherwise, others may become jealous and discord may occur. As long as others see it as requiring truly remarkable, "beyond the call of duty" effort, they will consider it fair and warranted.

*Expectancy theory is considered one of the major theories of human motivation and was first developed by V. H. Vroom in Work and Motivation (New York: John Wiley & Sons, 1964).

Time Reduction Decisions and Sensitivity

Should the project owner or project manager go for the optimum cost-time? The answer is "It depends." Risk must be considered. Recall from our example that the optimum project time point represented a reduced project cost and was less than the original normal project time (review Figure 9.6). The project direct-cost line near the normal point is usually relatively flat. Because indirect costs for the project are usually greater in the same range, the optimum cost-time point is less than the normal time point. Logic of the cost-time procedure suggests managers should reduce the project duration to the lowest total cost point and duration.

How far to reduce the project time from the normal time toward the optimum depends on the *sensitivity* of the project network. A network is sensitive if it has several critical or near-critical paths. In our example, project movement toward the optimum time requires spending money to reduce critical activities, resulting in slack reduction and/or more critical paths and activities. Slack reduction in a project with several near-critical paths increases the risk of being late. The practical outcome can be a higher total project cost if some near-critical activities are delayed and become critical; the money spent reducing activities on the original critical path would be wasted. Sensitive networks require careful analysis. The bottom line is that the compression of projects with several near-critical paths reduces scheduling flexibility and increases the risk of delaying the project. The outcome of such analysis will probably suggest only a partial movement from the normal time toward the optimum time.

There is a positive situation where moving toward the optimum time can result in large savings—this occurs when the network is *insensitive*. A project network is insensitive if it has a dominant critical path, that is, no near-critical paths. In this project circumstance, movement from the normal time point toward the optimum time will *not* create new or near-critical activities. The bottom line here is that the reduction of the slack of noncritical activities increases the risk of their becoming critical only slightly when compared with the effect in a sensitive network. Insensitive networks hold the greatest potential for real, sometimes large, savings in total project costs with a minimum risk of noncritical activities becoming critical.

Insensitive networks are not a rarity in practice; they occur in perhaps 25 percent of all projects. For example, a light rail project team observed from their network a dominant critical path and relatively high indirect costs. It soon became clear that by spending some dollars on a few critical activities, very large savings of indirect costs could be realized. Savings of several million dollars were spent extending the rail line and adding another station. The logic found in this example is just as applicable to small projects as to large ones. Insensitive networks with high indirect costs can produce large savings.

Ultimately, deciding if and which activities to crash is a judgment call requiring careful consideration of the options available, the costs and risks involved, and the importance of meeting a deadline.

9.6 What If Cost, Not Time, Is the Issue?

LO 9-6

Identify different options for reducing the costs of a project.

In today's fast-paced world, there appears to be a greater emphasis on getting things done quickly. Still, organizations are always looking for ways to get things done cheaply. This is especially true for fixed-bid projects, where profit margin is derived from the difference between the bid and the actual cost of the project. Every dollar saved is a dollar in your pocket. Sometimes, in order to secure a contract, bids are tight, which puts added pressure on cost containment. In other cases, there are financial incentives tied to cost containment.

Even in situations where cost is transferred to customers, there is pressure to reduce cost. Cost overruns make for unhappy customers and can damage future business opportunities. Budgets can be fixed or cut, and when contingency funds are exhausted, cost overruns have to be made up with remaining activities.

As discussed earlier, shortening project duration may come at the expense of working overtime, adding additional personnel, and using more expensive equipment and/or materials. Conversely, sometimes cost savings can be generated by extending the duration of a project. This may allow for a smaller workforce, less-skilled (expensive) labor, and even cheaper equipment and materials to be used. Discussed in this section are some of the more commonly used options for cutting costs.

Reduce Project Scope

Just as scaling back the scope of the project can gain time, delivering less than what was originally planned also produces significant savings. Again, calculating the savings of a reduced project scope begins with the work breakdown structure. However, since time is not the issue, you do not need to focus on critical activities. For example, on over-budget movie projects it is not uncommon to replace location shots with stock footage to cut costs.

Have Owner Take on More Responsibility

One way of reducing project costs is identifying tasks that customers can do themselves. Homeowners frequently use this method to reduce costs on home improvement projects. For example, to reduce the cost of a bathroom remodel, a homeowner may agree to paint the room instead of paying the contractor to do it. On IS projects, a customer may agree to take on some of the responsibility for testing equipment or providing in-house training. Naturally this arrangement is best negotiated before the project begins. Customers are less receptive to this idea if you suddenly spring it on them. An advantage of this method is that, while costs are lowered, the original scope is retained. Clearly this option is limited to areas in which the customer has the expertise and capability to pick up the tasks.

Outsource Project Activities or Even the Entire Project

When estimates exceed budget, it makes sense to not only re-examine the scope but also search for cheaper ways to complete the project. Perhaps instead of relying on internal resources, it would be more cost-effective to outsource segments or even the entire project, opening up work to external price competition. Specialized subcontractors often enjoy unique advantages, such as material discounts for large quantities, as well as equipment that gets the work done not only more quickly but also less expensively. They may have lower overhead and labor costs. For example, to reduce costs of software projects, many American firms outsource work to firms overseas where the salary of a software engineer is one-third that of an American software engineer. However, outsourcing means you have less control over the project and will need to have clearly definable deliverables.

Brainstorm Cost Savings Options

Just as project team members can be a rich source of ideas for accelerating project activities, they can offer tangible ways for reducing project costs. For example, one project manager reported that his/her team was able to come up with over $75,000 worth of cost-saving suggestions without jeopardizing the scope of the project. Project managers should not underestimate the value of simply asking if there is a cheaper, better way.

Summary

The need for reducing the project duration occurs for many reasons such as imposed deadlines, time-to-market considerations, incentive contracts, key resource needs, high overhead costs, or simply unforeseen delays. These situations are very common in practice and are known as cost-time trade-off decisions. This chapter presented a logical, formal process for assessing the implications of situations that involve shortening the project duration. Crashing the project duration increases the *risk* of being late. How far to reduce the project duration from the normal time toward the optimum depends on the sensitivity of the project network. A sensitive network is one that has several critical or near-critical paths. Great care should be taken when shortening sensitive networks to avoid increasing project risks. Conversely, insensitive networks represent opportunities for potentially large project cost savings by eliminating some overhead costs with little downside risk.

Alternative strategies for reducing project time were discussed within the context of whether or not the project is resource limited. Project acceleration typically comes at a cost of either spending money for more resources or compromising the scope of the project. If the latter is the case, then it is essential that all relevant stakeholders be consulted so that everyone accepts the changes that have to be made. One other key point is the difference in implementing time-reducing activities in the midst of project execution versus incorporating them into the project plan. You typically have far fewer options once the project is under way than before it begins. This is especially true if you want to take advantage of the new scheduling methodologies such as fast tracking and critical chain. Time spent up front considering alternatives and developing contingency plans will lead to time savings in the end.

Key Terms

Crash, *369*
Crash point, *380*
Crash time, *379*
Direct costs, *378*
Fast tracking, *374*
Indirect costs, *377*
Project cost-duration graph, *376*

Review Questions

1. What are five common reasons for crashing a project?
2. What are the advantages and disadvantages of reducing project scope to accelerate a project? What can be done to reduce the disadvantages?
3. Why is scheduling overtime a popular choice for getting projects back on schedule? What are the potential problems of relying on this option?
4. Identify four indirect costs you might find on a moderately complex project. Why are these costs classified as indirect?
5. How can a cost-duration graph be used by the project manager? Explain.
6. Reducing the project duration increases the risk of being late. Explain.
7. It is possible to shorten the critical path and save money. Explain how.

SNAPSHOT FROM PRACTICE

Discussion Questions

9.1 *Smartphone Wars*

1. Can you think of another product like smartphones that have rapid new-product releases?
2. What do you think would have happened if for some reason it took Samsung three years to release its next-generation smartphone?

9.2 *Responding to the Northridge Earthquake*

1. What options for accelerating project completion did C. C. Myers use on the Northridge Earthquake project?
2. If you were Governor Pete Wilson, how would you respond to criticism that C. C. Myers made too much profit from the project?

9.3 *Outsourcing in Bio-Tech Picks Up Speed*

1. What benefits do small pharma firms accrue through outsourcing project work?
2. What do you think Dan Gold is referring to when he argues that all parties must make a concerted effort to work as *partners*?

9.4 *The Fastest House in the World.*

Watch the YouTube video "World Record: Fastest House Built."
www.youtubc.com/watch?v=AwEcW6hH-B8

1. What options did Habitat for Humanity (H4H) use to complete the house so quickly?
2. How did H4H reduce the chances of human error on the project?

9.5 *I'll Bet You . . .*

1. Have you ever used bets to motivate someone? How effective was it?
2. Have you ever responded to a bet? How effective was it?

Operation Warp Speed

1. What options were used to develop vaccines as quickly as possible?
2. Why is conducting COVID-19 post-project retrospectives important?

Exercises

1. Use the following information to compress one time unit per move using the least-cost method. Reduce the schedule until you reach the crash point of the network. For each move identify what activity or activities were crashed and the adjusted total cost.

   Note: The correct normal project duration, critical path, and total direct cost are provided.

Act.	Crash Cost (slope)	Maximum Crash Time	Normal Time	Normal Cost
A	50	1	3	150
B	100	1	3	100
C	60	2	4	200
D	60	2	3	200
E	70	1	4	200
F	0	0	1	150

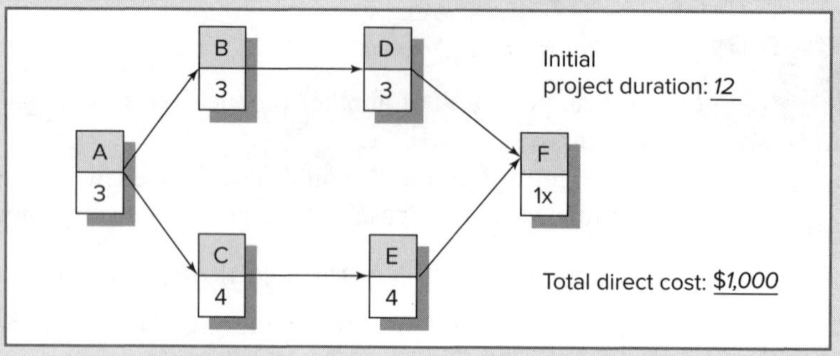

2. Use the following information to compress one time unit per move using the least-cost method.* Reduce the schedule until you reach the crash point of the network. For each move identify what activity or activities were crashed and the adjusted total cost.

   Note: Choose B instead of C and E (equal costs) because it is usually smarter to crash early rather than late AND one activity instead of two activities

Act.	Crash Cost (slope)	Maximum Crash Time	Normal Time	Normal Cost
A	0	0	2	150
B	100	1	3	100
C	50	2	6	200
D	40	1	4	200
E	50	1	3	200
F	0	0	1	150

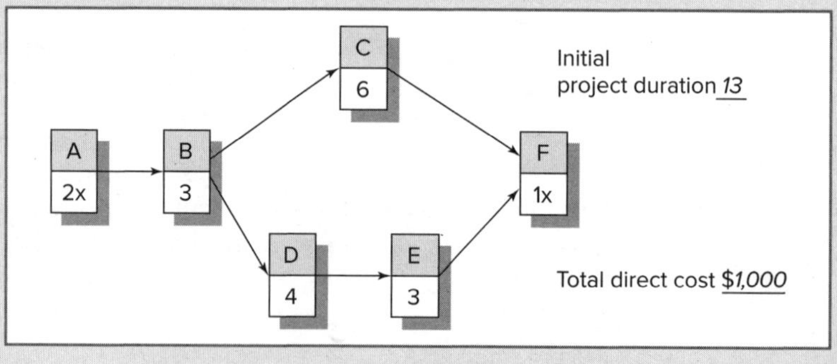

3. Use the following information to compress one time unit per move using the least-cost method. Reduce the schedule until you reach the crash point of the network. For each move, identify what activity or activities were crashed and the adjusted total cost.

* The solution to this exercise can be found in Appendix One.

Act.	Crash Cost (slope)	Maximum Crash Time	Normal Time	Normal Cost
A	100	1	2	150
B	80	1	3	100
C	60	1	2	200
D	40	1	5	200
E	40	2	5	200
F	40	2	3	150
G	20	1	5	200
H	0	0	1	200

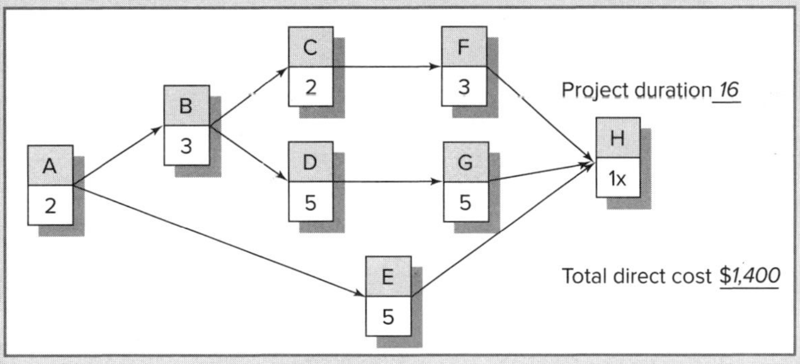

4. Given the data and information that follow, compute the total direct cost for each project duration. If the indirect costs for each project duration are $90 (15 time units), $70 (14), $50 (13), $40 (12), and $30 (11), compute the total project cost for each duration. What is the optimum cost-time schedule for the project? What is this cost?

Act.	Crash Cost (slope)	Maximum Crash Time	Normal Time	Normal Cost
A	30	1	5	50
B	60	2	3	60
C	0	0	4	70
D	10	1	2	50
E	60	3	5	100
F	100	1	2	90
G	30	1	5	50
H	0	0	2	60
I	200	1	3	200
				$730

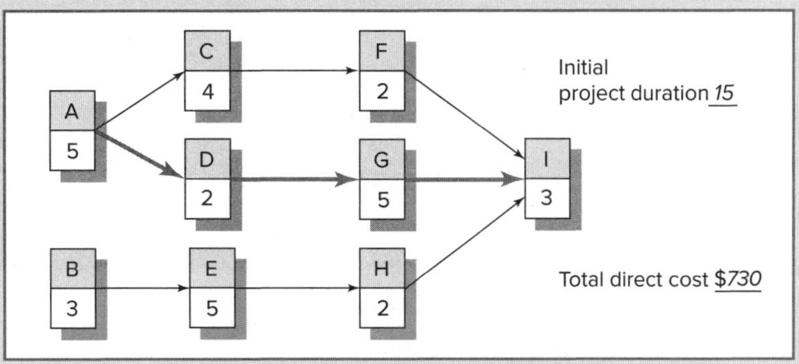

5. Use the following information to compress one time unit per move using the least-cost method. Assume the total indirect cost for the project is $700 and there is a savings of $50 per time unit reduced. Record the total direct, indirect, and project costs for each duration. What is the optimum cost-time schedule for the project? What is the cost?
Note: The correct normal project duration and total direct cost are provided.

Act.	Crash Cost (slope)	Maximum Crash Time	Normal Time	Normal Cost
A	0	0	2	100
B	100	1	3	200
C	40	1	5	200
D	60	2	3	200
E	20	1	5	200
F	40	1	4	150
G	0	0	2	150

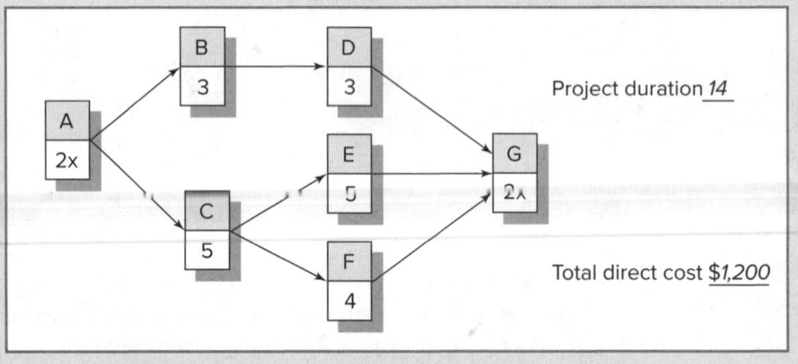

6. If the indirect costs for each duration are $300 for 27 days, $240 for 26 days, $180 for 25 days, $120 for 24 days, $60 for 23 days, and $50 for 22 days, compute the direct, indirect, and total costs for each duration. What is the optimum cost-time schedule? The customer offers you $10 for every day you shorten the project from your original network. Would you take it? If so for how many days?

Act.	Crash Cost (slope)	Maximum Crash Time (days)	Normal Time (days)	Normal Cost
A	80	2	10	40
B	30	3	8	10
C	40	1	5	80
D	50	2	11	50
E	100	4	15	100
F	30	1	6	20
				$300

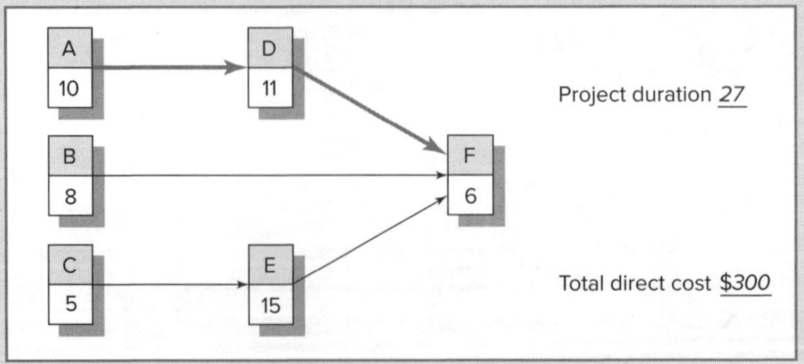

7. Use the following information to compress one time unit per move using the least-cost method. Assume the total indirect cost for the project is $2,000 and there is a savings of $100 per time unit reduced. Calculate the total direct, indirect, and project costs for each duration. Plot these costs on a graph. What is the optimum cost-time schedule for the project?

   Note: The correct normal project duration and total direct cost are provided.

Act.	Crash Cost (slope)	Maximum Crash Time	Normal Time	Normal Cost
A	0	0	2	200
B	50	1	4	1,000
C	200	2	5	800
D	200	2	5	1,000
E	100	1	3	800
F	40	1	5	1,000
G	40	1	4	1,000
H	0	0	1	200

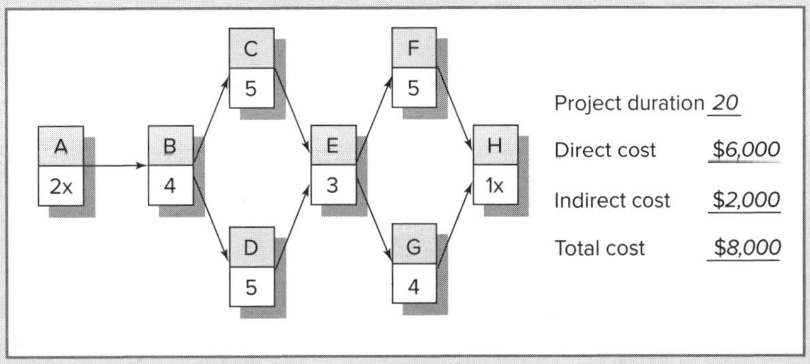

8. Use the following information to compress one time unit per move using the least-cost method.* Reduce the schedule until you reach the crash point of the network. For each move, identify what activity or activities were crashed and the adjusted total cost, and explain your choice if you have to choose between activities that cost the same.

   If the indirect cost for each duration is $1,500 for 17 weeks, $1,450 for 16 weeks, $1,400 for 15 weeks, $1,350 for 14 weeks, $1,300 for 13 weeks, $1,250 for 12 weeks, $1,200 for 11 weeks, and $1,150 for 10 weeks, what is the optimum cost-time schedule for the project? What is the cost?

Act.	Crash Cost (slope)	Maximum Crash Time (weeks)	Normal Time (weeks)	Normal Cost
A	0	0	3	150
B	100	1	4	200
C	60	1	3	250
D	40	1	4	200
E	0	0	2	250
F	30	2	3	200
G	20	1	2	250
H	60	2	4	300
I	200	1	2	200

* The solution to this exercise can be found in Appendix One.

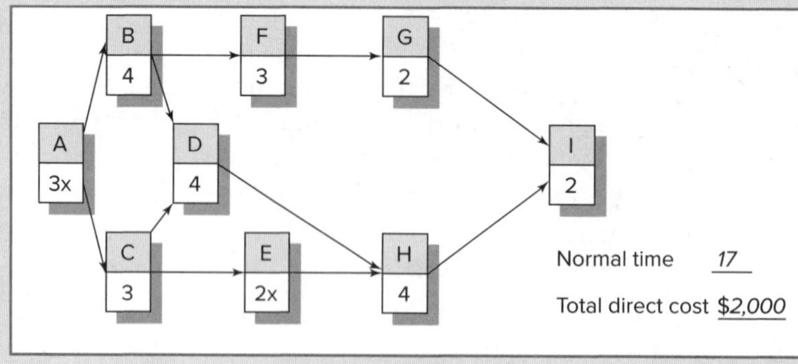

References

Abdel-Hamid, T., and S. Madnick, *Software Project Dynamics: An Integrated Approach* (Englewood Cliffs, NJ: Prentice Hall, 1991).

Baker, B. M., "Cost/Time Trade-off Analysis for the Critical Path Method," *Journal of the Operational Research Society,* vol. 48, no. 12 (1997), pp. 1241–44.

Brooks, F. P., Jr., *The Mythical Man-Month: Essays on Software Engineering Anniversary Edition* (Reading, MA: Addison-Wesley Longman, Inc., 1994), pp. 15–26.

DeMarco, T., *Slack: Getting Past Burnout, Busywork, and the Myth of Total Efficiency* (New York: Broadway, 2002).

Gordon, R. I., and J. C. Lamb, "A Closer Look at Brooks's Law," *Datamation,* June 1977, pp. 81–86.

Ibbs, C. W., S. A. Lee, and M. I. Li, "Fast-Tracking's Impact on Project Change," *Project Management Journal,* vol. 29, no. 4 (1998), pp. 35–42.

Khang, D. B., and M. Yin, "Time, Cost, and Quality Trade-off in Project Management," *International Journal of Project Management,* vol. 17, no. 4 (1999), pp. 249–56.

Perrow, L. A., *Finding Time: How Corporations, Individuals, and Families Can Benefit from New Work Practices* (Ithaca, NY: Cornell University Press, 1997).

Roemer, T. R., R. Ahmadi, and R. Wang, "Time-Cost Trade-offs in Overlapped Product Development," *Operations Research,* vol. 48, no. 6 (2000), pp. 858–65.

Smith, P. G., and D. G. Reinersten, *Developing Products in Half the Time,* 2nd ed. (New York: Van Nostrand Reinhold, 1997).

Verzuh, E., *The Fast Forward MBA in Project Management,* 4th ed. (New York: John Wiley, 2015).

Vroom, V. H., *Work and Motivation* (New York: John Wiley & Sons, 1964).

Case 9.1

International Capital, Inc.—Part B

Given the project network derived in Part A of the case from Chapter 7, Appendix 7.1, Beth also wants to be prepared to answer any questions concerning compressing the project duration. This question will almost always be entertained by the Accounting Department, the review committee, and the client. To be ready for the compression question, Beth has prepared the following data in case it is necessary to crash the project. (Use your weighted average times [t_e] computed in Part A of the International Capital case found in Chapter 7.)

Activity	Normal Cost	Maximum Crash Time	Crash Cost/Day
A	$ 3,000	3	$ 500
B	5,000	2	1,000
C	6,000	0	—
D	20,000	3	3,000
E	10,000	2	1,000
F	7,000	1	1,000
G	20,000	2	3,000
H	8,000	1	2,000
I	5,000	1	2,000
J	7,000	1	1,000
K	12,000	6	1,000
Total normal costs =	$103,000		

Using the data provided, determine the activity crashing decisions and best time-cost project duration. Given the information you have developed, what suggestions would you give Beth to ensure she is well prepared for the project review committee? Assume the overhead costs for this project are $700 per workday. Will this alter your suggestions?

Case 9.2

Ventura Baseball Stadium—Part B

This case is based on a case introduced at the end of Chapter 6. You will need to use the project plan created in the Ventura Baseball Stadium case to complete this assignment.

Ventura Baseball Stadium is a 47,000-seat professional baseball stadium. G&E Company began construction on June 10, 2019, and will complete it on February 23, 2022. The stadium must be ready for the opening of the 2022 regular season. G&E would accrue a $500,000-per-day penalty for not meeting the April 3, 2022, deadline.

The project started on time and was progressing well until an accident occurred during the pouring of the lower bowl. Two workers were seriously injured, and the activity was delayed four weeks while the cause of the accident was investigated and the site cleared to proceed.

The president of G&E Company, Percival Young, is concerned about the delay of the project. The project began with roughly six weeks of cushion between expected completion deadline and imposed deadline of April 3 (opening day). Now there is only a two-week cushion with over a year's worth of work still to be completed. He has asked you to consider the following options to reduce the duration of the project and restore some of the time buffer that has been lost.

A. Assign overtime to complete the installation of seats in 120 days, not 140 days.
B. Assign overtime to complete the infrastructure in 100 days, not 120 days.
C. Introduce a start-to-start lag whereby construction of the roof begins 70 days after the start of building roof supports.
D. Introduce a start-to-start lag whereby installing the scoreboard can start 100 days after the start of construction of the upper steel bowl.
E. Introduce a start-to-start lag whereby installing seats can start 100 days after the start of both pouring the main concourse and constructing the upper steel bowl.

Write a short memo to Young, detailing your recommendation and rationale.

Case 9.3

Whitbread World Sailboat Race

Each year countries enter their sailing vessels in the nine-month Round the World Whitbread Sailboat Race. In recent years about 14 countries entered sailboats in the race. Each year's sailboat entries represent the latest technologies and human skills each country can muster.

Bjorn Ericksen has been selected as a project manager because of his past experience as a master helmsman and because of his recent fame as the "best designer of racing sailboats in the world." Bjorn is pleased and proud to have the opportunity to design, build, test, and train the crew for next year's Whitbread entry for his country. Bjorn has picked Karin Knutsen (as chief design engineer) and Trygve Wallvik (as master helmsman) to be team leaders responsible for getting next year's entry ready for the traditional parade of all entries on the Thames River in the United Kingdom, which signals the start of the race.

As Bjorn begins to think of a project plan, he sees two parallel paths running through the project—design and construction and crew training. Last year's boat will be used for training until the new entry can have the crew on board to learn maintenance tasks. Bjorn calls Karin and Trygve together to develop a project plan. All three agree the major goal is to have a winning boat and crew ready to compete in next year's competition at a cost of $3.2 million. A check of Bjorn's calendar indicates he has 45 weeks before next year's vessel must leave port for the United Kingdom to start the race.

THE KICKOFF MEETING

Bjorn asks Karin to begin by describing the major activities and the sequence required to design, construct, and test the boat. Karin starts by noting that design of the hull, deck, mast, and accessories should only take 6 weeks—given the design prints from past race entries and a few prints from other countries' entries. After the design is complete, the hull can be constructed, mast ordered, sails ordered, and accessories ordered. The hull will require 12 weeks to complete. The mast can be ordered and will require a lead time of 8 weeks; the seven sails can be ordered and will take 6 weeks to get; accessories can be ordered and will take 15 weeks to receive. As soon as the hull is finished, the ballast tanks can be installed, requiring 2 weeks. Then the deck can be built, which will require 5 weeks. Concurrently the hull can be treated with special sealant and friction-resistance coating, taking 3 weeks. When the deck is completed and mast and accessories received, the mast and sails can be installed, requiring 2 weeks; the accessories can be installed, which will take 6 weeks. When all of these activities have been completed, the ship can be sea-tested, which should take 5 weeks. Karin believes she can have firm cost estimates for the boat in about 2 weeks.

Trygve believes he can start selecting the 12-man or woman crew and securing their housing immediately. He believes it will take 6 weeks to get a committed crew on-site and 3 weeks to secure housing for the crew members. Trygve reminds Bjorn that last year's vessel must be ready to use for training the moment the crew is on-site until the new vessel is ready for testing. Keeping the old vessel operating will cost $4,000 per week as long as it is used. Once the crew is on-site and housed, they can develop and implement a routine sailing and maintenance training program, which will take 15 weeks (using the old vessel). Also, once the crew is selected and on-site, crew equipment can be selected, taking only 2 weeks. Then crew equipment can be ordered; it will take 5 weeks to arrive. When the crew equipment and maintenance training program are complete, crew maintenance on the new vessel can begin; this should take 10 weeks. But crew maintenance on the new vessel cannot begin until the deck is complete and the mast, sails, and accessories have arrived. Once crew maintenance on the new vessel begins, the new vessel will cost $6,000 per week until sea training is complete. After the new ship maintenance is complete and while the boat is being tested, initial sailing training can be implemented; training should take 7 weeks. Finally, after the boat is tested and initial training is complete, regular sea training can be implemented—weather permitting; regular sea training requires 8 weeks. Trygve believes he can put the cost estimates together in a week, given last year's expenses.

Bjorn is pleased with the expertise displayed by his team leaders. But he believes they need to have someone develop one of those critical path networks to see if they can safely meet the start deadline for the race. Karin and Trygve agree. Karin suggests

FIGURE C9.1
Project Priority Matrix: Whitbread Project

	Time	Performance	Cost
Constrain			
Enhance			
Accept			

the cost estimates should also include crash costs for any activities that can be compressed and the resultant costs for crashing. Karin also suggests the team complete the priority matrix shown in Figure C9.1 for project decision making.

TWO WEEKS LATER

Karin and Trygve submit the following cost estimates for each activity and corresponding crash costs to Bjorn (costs are in thousands of dollars):

	Activity	Normal Time	Normal Cost	Crash Time	Crash Cost	Slope
A	Design	6	$ 40	4	$ 160	60
B	Build hull	12	1,000	10	1,400	200
C	Install ballast tanks	2	100	2	100	—
D	Order mast	8	100	7	140	40
E	Order sails	6	40	6	40	—
F	Order accessories	15	600	13	800	100
G	Build deck	5	200	5	200	—
H	Coat hull	3	40	3	40	—
I	Install accessories	6	300	5	400	100
J	Install mast and sails	2	40	1	80	40
K	Test	5	60	4	10	40
L	Sea trials	8	200	7	45	250
M	Select crew	6	10	5	20	10
N	Secure housing	3	30	3	30	—
O	Select crew equipment	2	10	2	10	—
P	Order crew equipment	5	30	5	30	—
Q	Routine sail/maintenance	15	40	12	130	30
R	Crew maintenance train	10	100	9	340	240
S	Initial sail training	7	50	5	350	150
	Total direct cost		**$2,990**			

Bjorn reviews the materials and wonders if the project will come in within the budget of $3.2 million and in 45 weeks. Advise the Whitbread team of their situation.

Case 9.4

Nightingale Project—Part A

You are the assistant project manager to Rassy Brown, who is in charge of the Nightingale project. Nightingale was the code name given to the development of a handheld electronic medical reference guide. Nightingale would be designed for emergency medical technicians and paramedics who need a quick reference guide to use in emergency situations.

Rassy and her project team were developing a project plan aimed at producing 30 working models in time for MedCON, the biggest medical equipment trade show each year. Meeting the MedCON October 25 deadline was critical to success. All the major medical equipment manufacturers demonstrated and took orders for new products at MedCON. Rassy had also heard rumors that competitors were considering developing a similar product, and she knew that being first to market would have a significant sales advantage. Besides, top management made funding contingent upon developing a workable plan for meeting the MedCON deadline.

The project team spent the morning working on the schedule for Nightingale. They started with the WBS and developed the information for a network, adding activities when needed. Then the team added the time estimates they had collected for each activity. Following is the preliminary information for activities with duration time and predecessors.

Activity	Description	Duration	Predecessor
1	Architectural decisions	10	None
2	Internal specifications	20	1
3	External specifications	18	1
4	Feature specifications	15	1
5	Voice recognition	15	2, 3
6	Case	4	2, 3
7	Screen	2	2, 3
8	Speaker output jacks	2	2, 3
9	Tape mechanism	2	2, 3
10	Database	40	4
11	Microphone/soundcard	5	4
12	Pager	4	4
13	Barcode reader	3	4
14	Alarm clock	4	4
15	Computer I/O	5	4
16	Review design	10	5, 6, 7, 8, 9, 10, 11, 12, 13, 14, 15
17	Price components	5	5, 6, 7, 8, 9, 10, 11, 12, 13, 14, 15
18	Integration	15	16, 17
19	Document design	35	16
20	Procure prototype components	20	18
21	Assemble prototypes	10	20
22	Lab test prototypes	20	21
23	Field test prototypes	20	19, 22
24	Adjust design	20	23
25	Order stock parts	15	24
26	Order custom parts	2	24
27	Assemble first production unit	10	25, FS—8 time units 26, FS—13 time units
28	Test unit	10	27
29	Produce 30 units	15	28
30	Train sales representatives	10	29

Use any project network computer program available to you to develop the schedule for activities (see the case appendix following Case 9.5 for further instructions)—noting late and early times, the critical path, and estimated completion for the project.

Prepare a short memo that addresses the following questions:

1. Will the project as planned meet the October 25 deadline?
2. What activities lie on the critical path?
3. How sensitive is this network?

Case 9.5

Nightingale Project—Part B

Rassy and the team were concerned with the results of your analysis. They spent the afternoon brainstorming alternative ways for shortening the project duration. They rejected outsourcing activities because most of the work was developmental in nature and could only be done in-house. They considered altering the scope of the project by eliminating some of the proposed product features. After much debate, they felt they could not compromise any of the core features and be successful in the marketplace. They then turned their attention to accelerating the completion of activities through overtime and adding additional technical manpower. Rassy had built into her proposal a discretionary fund of $200,000. She was willing to invest up to half of this fund to accelerate the project but wanted to hold on to at least $100,000 to deal with unexpected problems. After a lengthy discussion, her team concluded that the following activities could be reduced at the specified cost:

- Development of voice recognition system could be reduced from 15 days to 10 days at a cost of $15,000.
- Creation of database could be reduced from 40 days to 35 days at a cost of $35,000.
- Document design could be reduced from 35 days to 30 days at a cost of $25,000.
- External specifications could be reduced from 18 days to 12 days at a cost of $20,000.
- Procure prototype components could be reduced from 20 days to 15 days at a cost of $30,000.
- Order stock parts could be reduced from 15 days to 10 days at a cost of $20,000.

Ken Clark, a development engineer, pointed out that the network contained only finish-to-start relationships and that it might be possible to reduce project duration by creating start-to-start lags. For example, he said that his people would not have to wait for all of the field tests to be completed to begin making final adjustments in the design. They could start making adjustments after the first 15 days of testing. The project team spent the remainder of the day analyzing how they could introduce lags into the network to shorten the project. They concluded that the following finish-to-start relationships could be converted into lags:

- Document design could begin 5 days after the start of the review design.
- Adjust design could begin 15 days after the start of field test prototypes.
- Order stock parts could begin 5 days after the start of adjust design.
- Order custom parts could begin 5 days after the start of adjust design.
- Training sales representatives could begin 5 days after the start of test unit and completed 5 days after the production of 30 units.

As the meeting adjourns, Rassy turns to you and tells you to assess the options presented and try to develop a schedule that will meet the October 25 deadline. You are to prepare a report to be presented to the project team that answers the following questions:

1. Is it possible to meet the deadline?
2. If so, how would you recommend changing the original schedule (Part A) and why? Assess the relative impact of crashing activities versus introducing lags to shorten project duration.
3. What would the new schedule look like?
4. What other factors should be considered before finalizing the schedule?

CASE APPENDIX: TECHNICAL DETAILS

Create your project schedule and assess your options based on the following information:

1. The project will begin the first working day in January.
2. The following holidays are observed: January 1, Memorial Day (last Monday in May), July 4, Labor Day (first Monday in September), Thanksgiving Day (fourth Thursday in November), December 25 and 26.
3. If a holiday falls on a Saturday, then Friday will be given as an extra day off; if it falls on a Sunday, then Monday will be given as a day off.
4. The project team works Monday through Friday, 8-hour days.
5. If you choose to reduce the duration of any one of the activities mentioned, then it must be for the specified time and cost (e.g., you cannot choose to reduce database to 37 days at a reduced cost; you can only reduce it to 35 days at a cost of $35,000).
6. You can only spend up to $100,000 to reduce project activities; lags do not contain any additional costs.

Case 9.6

The "Now" Wedding—Part A*

On December 31 of last year, Lauren burst into the family living room and announced that she and Connor (her college boyfriend) were going to be married. After recovering from the shock, her mother hugged her and asked, "When?" The following conversation resulted:

Lauren: January 21.

Mom: What?

Dad: The Now Wedding will be the social hit of the year. Wait a minute. Why so soon?

Lauren: Because on January 30 Connor, who is in the National Guard, will be shipping out overseas. We want a week for a honeymoon.

Mom: But, Honey, we can't possibly finish all the things that need to be done by then. Remember all the details that were involved in your sister's wedding? Even if we start tomorrow, it takes a day to reserve the church and reception hall, and they need at least 14 days' notice. That has to be done before we can start decorating, which takes 3 days. An extra $200 on Sunday would probably cut that 14-day notice to 7 days, though.

Dad: Oh, boy!

Lauren: I want Jane Summers to be my maid of honor.

Dad: But she's in the Peace Corps in Guatemala, isn't she? It would take her 10 days to get ready and drive up here.

Lauren: But we could fly her up in 2 days and it would only cost $1,000.

Dad: Oh, boy!

Mom: And catering! It takes 2 days to choose the cake and decorations, and Jack's Catering wants at least 5 days' notice. Besides, we'd have to have those things before we could start decorating.

Lauren: Can I wear your wedding dress, Mom?

Mom: Well, we'd have to replace some lace, but you could wear it, yes. We could order the lace from New York when we order the material for the bridesmaids' dresses. It takes 8 days to order and receive the material. The pattern needs to be chosen first, and that would take 3 days.

Dad: We could get the material here in 5 days if we paid an extra $20 to airfreight it. Oh, boy!

Lauren: I want Mrs. Jacks to work on the dresses.

Mom: But she charges $48 a day.

Dad: Oh, boy!

Mom: If we did all the sewing we could finish the dresses in 11 days. If Mrs. Jacks helped we could cut that down to 6 days at a cost of $48 for each day less than 11 days. She is very good, too.

Lauren: I don't want anyone but her.

* This case was adapted from a case originally written by Professor D. Clay Whybark, University of North Carolina, Chapel Hill, N.C.

Mom: It would take another 2 days to do the final fitting and 2 more days to clean and press the dresses. They would have to be ready by rehearsal night. We must have rehearsal the night before the wedding.

Dad: Everything should be ready rehearsal night.

Mom: We've forgotten something. The invitations!

Dad: We should order the invitations from Bob's Printing Shop, and that usually takes 7 days. I'll bet he would do it in 6 days if we slipped him an extra $20!

Mom: It would take us 2 days to choose the invitation style before we could order them and we want the envelopes printed with our return address.

Lauren: Oh! That will be elegant.

Mom: The invitations should go out at least 10 days before the wedding. If we let them go any later, some of the relatives would get theirs too late to come and that would make them mad. I'll bet that if we didn't get them out until 8 days before the wedding, Aunt Ethel couldn't make it and she would reduce her wedding gift by $200.

Dad: Oh, boy!!

Mom: We'll have to take them to the Post Office to mail them and that takes a day. Addressing would take 3 days unless we hired some part-time girls and we can't start until the printer is finished. If we hired the girls we could probably save 2 days by spending $40 for each day saved.

Lauren: We need to get gifts for the bridesmaids. I could spend a day and do that.

Mom: Before we can even start to write out those invitations we need a guest list. Heavens, that will take 4 days to get in order and only I can understand our address file.

Lauren: Oh, Mom, I'm so excited. We can start each of the relatives on a different job.

Mom: Honey, I don't see how we can do it. Why, I've got to choose the invitations and patterns and reserve the church and . . .

Dad: Why don't you just take $3,000 and elope? Your sister's wedding cost me $2,400 and she didn't have to fly people up from Guatemala, hire extra girls and Mrs. Jacks, use airfreight, or anything like that.

1. Using the yellow sticky approach shown in Snapshot from Practice 6.1, develop a project network for the "Now" wedding.
2. Create a schedule for the wedding using MS Project. Can you reach the deadline of January 21 for the "Now" wedding? If you cannot, what would it cost to make the January 21 deadline and which activities would you change?

Case 9.7

The "Now" Wedding—Part B

Several complications arose during the course of trying to meet the deadline of January 20 for the "Now" wedding rehearsal. Since Lauren was adamant on having the wedding on January 21 (as was Connor for obvious reasons), the implications of each of these complications had to be assessed.

1. On January 1, the chairman of the Vestry Committee of the church was left unimpressed by the added donation and said he wouldn't reduce the notice period from 14 to 7 days.
2. Mother came down with the 3-day flu as she started working on the guest list January 2.
3. Bob's Printing Shop press was down for 1 day on January 5 in order to replace faulty brushes in the electric motor.
4. The lace and dress material were lost in transit. Notice of the loss was received on January 10.

Could the wedding still take place on January 21? If not, what options were available?

Case 9.8

Chandrayaan Mission

BACKGROUND AND CONTEXT

The Chandrayaan mission is a series of lunar exploration missions that the Indian Space Research Organisation (ISRO) has planned to expand India's involvement in space research. The core objectives of the Chandrayaan programme are lunar surface exploration, investigation of soil composition and water presence, and material contribution to universal scientific research. The project was subject to extreme time and resource constraints because of its complex design and high-value outcomes. Shortening the project duration was crucial to meet launch windows and prevent delays that could increase costs or reduce the mission's value, particularly in coordinating with international partners.

CHANDRAYAAN-1

Launch Date: 22 October, 2008
Budget: ₹386 crore (approx. $54 million)
Objectives: Orbital reconnaissance of the Moon to generate high-resolution imaging for soil analysis and search for water ice.
Duration: It was programmed for a duration of two years but was operational for about 312 days.
Stakeholders: NASA (instrument collaboration), ISRO, EADS Astrium (satellite bus).

CHANDRAYAAN-2

Launch Date: 22 July, 2019
Budget: ₹978 crore (approx. $141 million)
Objectives: In-situ analysis of the lunar surface composition, soft landing on the Moon's south pole, and deployment of a rover for surface exploration.
Duration: The planned life of one year for the orbiter; the lander's communication was lost shortly after the soft landing attempt.
Stakeholders: ISRO, NASA (tracking support), and various private vendors for the manufacture of subsystems.

PROJECT SCOPE AND OBJECTIVES

SCOPE

The scope of the project involved designing, testing, and launching the Chandrayaan mission within the curtailed time frame. Any compromise to safety, data accuracy, or technological reliability was ruled out during the process.

PROJECT OBJECTIVES

1. To simplify project completion time to align with the narrow launch time frames.
2. To enhance the collaborative efficiency among government-body-turned-private-vendor.
3. To enhance several processes during design, manufacture and testing without delay.
4. To ensure Chandrayaan was launched long before the chosen time frame.

PROJECT MANAGEMENT FRAMEWORK

PROJECT INITIATION

Feasibility Studies: A thorough feasibility analysis was carried out to assess the technical challenges, resource requirements, and risk factors involved in the lunar missions. Feasibility studies were at high stake because they included testing technological capabilities, calculation of lunar distances, and assessments of the launch windows.

Approvals and Clearances: Approvals were sought from ISRO, the Government of India, and all applicable regulatory authorities. Some key clearances include budgetary approvals, environmental considerations at launch sites, and quality standards for spacecraft parts.

PROJECT PLANNING

WBS or **Work Breakdown Structure:** The mission was broken down into large components like design, engineering, assembly, testing, and launch operations, each with its own subcomponents. Each phase involved tasks like fabrication, software testing, and satellite integration, which helped ISRO understand the steps required to complete the mission.

WBS Level	Task/ Component	Chandrayaan-1 (2008)	Chandrayaan-2 (2019)	Dependency	Duration
1	Mission Planning	Mission Design, Timelines, Budget	Mission Design, Timelines, Budget	None	12 months
2	Launch Vehicle	PSLV-C11 for Launch	GSLV Mk III for Launch	Mission Planning	6 months
3	Orbiter Development	Development of Orbiter Payloads	Development of Orbiter Payloads	Mission Planning	24 months
4	Payload Design	CxB, Moon Impact Probe (MIP)	Vikram Lander, Pragyan Rover	Mission Planning, Orbiter Development	18 months

WBS Level	Task/ Component	Chandrayaan-1 (2008)	Chandrayaan-2 (2019)	Dependency	Duration
5	Science Instruments	Moon Mineralogy Mapper (M3), Terrain Mapping Camera (TMC)	Dual Frequency Synthetic Aperture Radar (DFSAR), Imaging IR Spectrometer (IIRS)	Payload Design	18 months
6	Spacecraft Integration	Integration of Payload and Orbiter	Integration of Payload and Orbiter	Orbiter Development, Payload Design	6 months
7	Launch Preparation	Vehicle Integration, Pre-Launch Testing	Vehicle Integration, Pre-Launch Testing	Spacecraft Integration	6 months
8	Launch Execution	Launch on October 22, 2008	Launch on July 22, 2019	Launch Preparation	1 day
9	Orbital Operations	Lunar Orbit Insertion, Scientific Data Collection	Lunar Orbit Insertion, Scientific Data Collection	Launch Execution	12 months
10	Lander Operations	N/A	Vikram Lander Descent, Soft Landing Attempt	Orbital Operations	1 week
11	Rover Operations	N/A	Pragyan Rover Deployment, Surface Operations	Orbital Operations, Lander Operations	14 days
12	Communication & Data Transmission	Communication via DSN (Deep Space Network)	Communication via DSN (Deep Space Network)	Orbital Operations	Ongoing (Throughout Mission)
13	Mission Achievements	Successful insertion into lunar orbit, Moon Impact	Orbiter Success, Rover Deployment, Lander Operations	Orbital Operations, Lander Operations	12 months
14	Post-Mission Analysis	Data Analysis, Review of Data from M3 and TMC	Data Analysis from Orbiter, Partial Lander Data	Mission Achievements	12 months
15	Conclusion & Future Learnings	Data Dissemination, Scientific Publication	Data Dissemination, Ongoing Analysis	Post-Mission Analysis	6 months

Resource Allocation: ISRO carefully allocated resources such as specialized manpower, advanced materials, and a carefully planned budget. Coordination among various departments ensured efficient utilization of scientific expertise and technological resources.

Gantt Chart for Chandrayaan-1 (2004–2009)

Mission Phase	2004	2005	2006	2007	2008	2009
Project Initiation	■	■				
Feasibility Studies	■					
Approvals and Funding		■				
Project Planning			■	■		
WBS & Resource Allocation			■			
Risk Analysis & Contingency				■		
Execution						
Subsystem Design					■	■
Testing & Integration					■	■
Launch Preparation					■	
Payload Assembly & Check					■	
Launch					■	
Mission Operations					■	■

Gantt Chart for Chandrayaan-2 (2008–2020+)

Mission Phase	2008	2009	2010	2011	2012	2013	2014	2015	2016	2017	2018	2019	2020+
Project Initiation	■	■											
Feasibility Studies	■												
Approvals and Funding		■											
Project Planning			■	■									
WBS & Resource Allocation			■										
Risk Analysis & Contingency				■									
Execution					■	■	■	■	■	■	■	■	
Subsystem Design			■	■									
Testing & Integration				■	■	■	■	■	■	■			
Launch Preparation										■			
Payload Assembly & Check										■			
Launch											■		
Mission Operations											■	■	■

Critical Path: Project Initiation → Project Planning → Execution → Launch Preparation → Launch → Mission Operations

Total Duration: Approximately 57 months (or 4 years and 9 months) from initiation to mission closure

PROJECT CHALLENGES AND ISSUES

Technical Challenges

- **Engineering or Design Problems:** Designing a reliable and efficient lunar mission within a reduced time frame posed significant engineering challenges. Each component had to be lightweight yet robust to withstand space conditions. Complexities in spacecraft design and integration demanded extensive testing to ensure functionality under extreme lunar conditions.
- **Newer Technology Acceptance:** ISRO accepted high-advanced lunar imaging and communication technologies that needed stringent calibration and validation. The short testing and validation time, however, also introduced complexity because when one of these new technologies fails, the whole mission could be at risk.

Operational Challenges

- **Delays and Cost Overruns:** Executing the mission within a tight schedule posed operational challenges, especially in the synchronization of critical component delivery with the timeline. Procurement delays and unforeseen testing problems resulted in spurts of overrun timelines, which put pressure on budgeting.
- **Manpower Crisis:** Considering the heavy task that had to be accomplished, ISRO personnel were under significant stress to present with no margin for error. At times, this requirement of maintaining sustained productivity levels caused teamwork and work-life balance-related issues for the personnel.

Environmental and Social Issues

- **Impact on Communities:** While the Chandrayaan programme did not directly impact surrounding communities, its success had broader national and scientific significance. ISRO maintained transparency to inform and engage the public, fostering a sense of collective pride and awareness.
- **Measures for Sustainable Development:** ISRO adopted eco-friendly practices at the launch sites and minimized space debris. The sustainability of this project was aligned with the environment commitments of India and met various international standards.

Completion

- **Results and Initial Aims:** The Chandrayaan programme accomplished its prime objectives of visiting the lunar surface, the detection of water, and mineral analysis. Despite the tight timeline, the launch schedule was met, and the scientific data has been highly productive, demonstrating India's capabilities in space exploration.
- **Hand-over and Execution:** The mission transitioned well into operation with the satellite deployed for lunar observation. Data from the mission has since been handed over to ISRO's research and analysis teams for further studies and global sharing.

LESSONS LEARNT

- **What Went Right**. Planning of the project was quite efficient, and timelines were strictly followed to make the mission a success. The use of advanced technologies, careful testing, and robust communication between teams and stakeholders were key factors in the success.

- **What Could Have Been Done Better:** Early-stage component procurement and testing could have been more streamlined to prevent last-minute delays. Additionally, enhancing risk management strategies could have further mitigated timeline variances.
- **Future Opportunity for Similar Projects:** ISRO must think of making pre-vetted supplier alliances in the future to reduce procurement timelines and invest in backup technologies for critical mission parts. The level of assessments toward risk, particularly at the earliest possible stages, with the right stakeholder alignment at early stages to ensure schedule integrity is recommended.

REFERENCES

1. ISRO Official Website: Comprehensive details about Chandrayaan-1 and Chandrayaan-2 missions, including objectives, timelines, and technological advancements.
2. Press Information Bureau (PIB), Government of India: Official announcements, updates, and achievements related to Chandrayaan missions.
3. Mylswamy Annadurai, S. N. Om Prakash. Chandrayaan-1: India's First Mission to the Moon – Scientific Objectives and Results. Current Science Journal, Volume 96, Issue 4.
4. Supriya Chakraborty. India's Chandrayaan-2 Mission: Engineering Challenges and Achievements. Advances in Space Research, 2020.
5. C. Sivaram. Chandrayaan-1 and its Impact on Space Exploration in India. Indian Journal of Physics, 2019.
6. KPMG Report on India's Space Economy: Insights into how Chandrayaan and other ISRO missions have contributed to India's space economy and global standing.
7. Deloitte's Space Sector in India – Growing Beyond Earth: Discusses the technological and economic impacts of India's space missions, including Chandrayaan.

CHAPTER TEN

10 Being an Effective Project Manager

LEARNING OBJECTIVES

After reading this chapter you should be able to:

10-1 Understand the difference between managing and leading a project.

10-2 Understand the need to engage project stakeholders.

10-3 Identify and apply different "influence currencies" to build positive relations with others.

10-4 Create a stakeholder map and develop strategies for managing project dependencies.

10-5 Understand the need for a highly interactive management style on projects.

10-6 More effectively manage project expectations.

10-7 Develop strategies for managing upward relations.

10-8 Understand the importance of building trust and acting in an ethical manner while working on a project.

10-9 Identify the qualities of an effective project manager.

OUTLINE

10.1 Managing versus Leading a Project

10.2 Engaging Project Stakeholders

10.3 Influence as Exchange

10.4 Social Network Building

10.5 Ethics and Project Management

10.6 Building Trust: The Key to Exercising Influence

10.7 Qualities of an Effective Project Manager

Summary

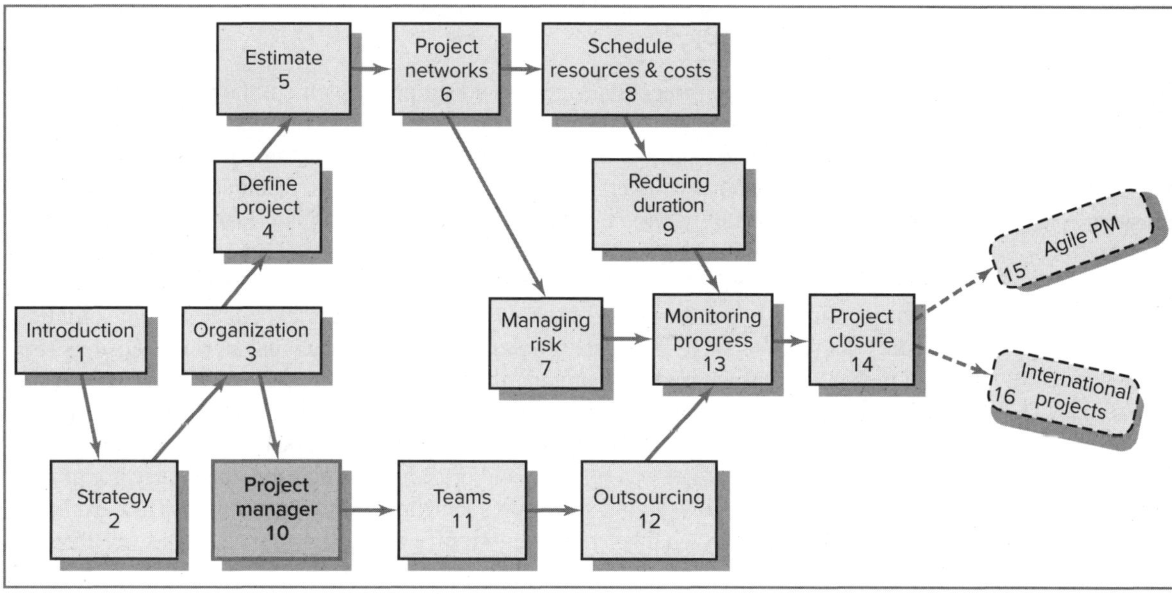

I couldn't wait to be the manager of my own project and run the project the way I thought it should be done. Boy, did I have a lot to learn!

—First-time project manager

This chapter is based on the premise that one of the keys to being an effective project manager is building cooperative relationships among different groups of people to complete projects. Project success does not just depend on the performance of the project team. Success or failure often depends on the contributions of top management, functional managers, customers, suppliers, contractors, and others.

The chapter begins with a brief discussion of the differences between managing and leading a project. The importance of engaging project stakeholders is then introduced. Managers require a broad influence base to be effective in this area. Different sources of influence are discussed and are used to describe how project managers build social capital. This management style necessitates constant interacting with different groups of people whom project managers depend on. Special attention is devoted to managing the critical relationship with top management and the importance of leading by example. The importance of gaining cooperation in ways that build and sustain the trust of others is emphasized. The chapter concludes by identifying personal attributes associated with being an effective project manager. Subsequent chapters will expand on these ideas in a discussion of managing the project team and working with people outside the organization. It should be noted that the material presented in this chapter is from the point of view of a project manager assigned to a traditional, plan-driven project, although many of the ideas would apply to those leading agile projects. Applications will be addressed in Chapter 15.

10.1 Managing versus Leading a Project

LO 10-1

Understand the difference between managing and leading a project.

In a perfect world, the project manager would simply implement the project plan and the project would be completed. The project manager would work with others to formulate a schedule, organize a project team, keep track of progress, and announce what needs to be done next, and then everyone would charge along. Of course, no one lives in a perfect world, and rarely does everything go according to plan. Project participants get testy; they fail to get along with each other; other departments are unable to fulfill their commitments; technical glitches arise; work takes longer than expected. The project manager's job is to get the project back on track. A manager expedites certain activities; figures out ways to solve technical problems; serves as peacemaker when tensions rise; and makes appropriate trade-offs among the time, cost, and scope of the project.

However, project managers often do more than put out fires and keep the project on track. They also innovate and adapt to ever-changing circumstances. They sometimes have to deviate from what was planned and introduce significant changes in the project scope and schedule to respond to unforeseen threats or opportunities. For example, customers' needs may change, requiring significant design changes midway through the project. Competitors may release new products that dictate crashing project deadlines. Working relationships among project participants may break down, requiring a reformulation of the project team. Ultimately, what was planned or expected in the beginning may be very different from what was accomplished by the end of the project.

Project managers are responsible for integrating assigned resources to complete the project according to plan. At the same time they need to initiate changes in plans and schedules as persistent problems make plans unworkable. In other words, managers want to keep the project going while making necessary adjustments along the way. According to Kotter (1990) these two different activities represent the distinction between management and leadership. Management is about coping with complexity, while leadership is about coping with change.

Good management brings about order and stability by formulating plans and objectives, designing structures and procedures, monitoring results against plans, and taking corrective action when necessary. Leadership involves recognizing and articulating the need to significantly alter the direction and operation of the project, aligning people to the new direction, and motivating them to work together to overcome hurdles produced by the change and to realize new objectives.

Strong leadership, while usually desirable, is not always necessary to successfully complete a project. Well-defined projects that encounter no significant surprises require little leadership, as might be the case in constructing a conventional apartment building in which the project manager simply administrates the project plan. Conversely, the higher the degree of uncertainty encountered on a project—whether in terms of changes in project scope, technological stalemates, or breakdowns in coordination between people—the more leadership is required. For example, strong leadership would be needed for a software development project in which the parameters are always changing to meet developments in the industry. Sometime external events demand leadership like the COVID-19 pandemic or a tragic accident.

It takes a special person to perform both roles well. Some individuals are great visionaries who are good at exciting people about change. Often though, these people lack the discipline or patience to deal with the day-to-day drudgeries of managing. Likewise, there are individuals who are very well organized and methodical but lack the ability to inspire others.

Strong leaders can compensate for their managerial weaknesses by having trusted assistants who oversee and manage the details of the project. Conversely, a weak leader can complement his strengths by having assistants who are good at sensing the need to change and rallying project participants. Still, one of the things that make good project managers so valuable to an organization is that they have the ability to both manage and lead a project. In doing so, they recognize the need to create a social network that allows them to find out what needs to be done and obtain the cooperation necessary to achieve it.

10.2 Engaging Project Stakeholders

LO 10-2

Understand the need to engage project stakeholders.

First-time project managers are eager to implement their own ideas and manage their people to successfully complete their project. What they soon find out is that project success depends on the cooperation of a wide range of individuals, many of whom do not directly report to them. For example, during the course of a system integration project, a project manager was surprised by how much time s/he was spending negotiating and working with vendors, consultants, technical specialists, and other functional managers:

> Instead of working with my people to complete the project, I found myself being constantly pulled and tugged by demands of different groups of people who were not directly involved in the project but had a vested interest in the outcome.

Often when new project managers do find time to work directly on the project, they adopt a hands-on approach to managing the project. They choose this style not because they are power-hungry egomaniacs but because they are eager to achieve results. They become quickly frustrated by how slowly things operate, the number of people that have to be brought on board, and the difficulty of gaining cooperation. Unfortunately, as this frustration builds, the natural temptation is to exert more pressure and get more heavily involved in the project. These project managers quickly earn the reputation of "micro managing" and begin to lose sight of the real role they play on guiding a project.

Some new managers never break out of this vicious cycle. Others soon realize that authority does not equal influence and that being an effective project manager involves managing a much more complex set of stakeholders than they had anticipated. They encounter a web of relationships that requires a much broader spectrum of influence than they felt was necessary or even possible.

For example, a significant project, whether it involves renovating a bridge, creating a new product, or installing a new information system, will likely involve, in one way or another, working with a number of different groups of stakeholders. First, there is the core group of specialists assigned to complete the project. This group is likely to be supplemented at different times by professionals who work on specific segments of the project. Second, there are groups of people within the performing organization who are either directly or indirectly involved with the project. The most notable is top management, to whom the project manager is accountable. There are also other managers, who provide resources and/or may be responsible for specific segments of the project, and administrative support services such as Human Resources, Finance, and so on. Depending on the nature of the project, a number of groups outside the organization influence the success of the project. They include vendors and contractors as well as the most important one—the customer for which the project is designed (see Figure 10.1).

FIGURE 10.1
Network of Stakeholders

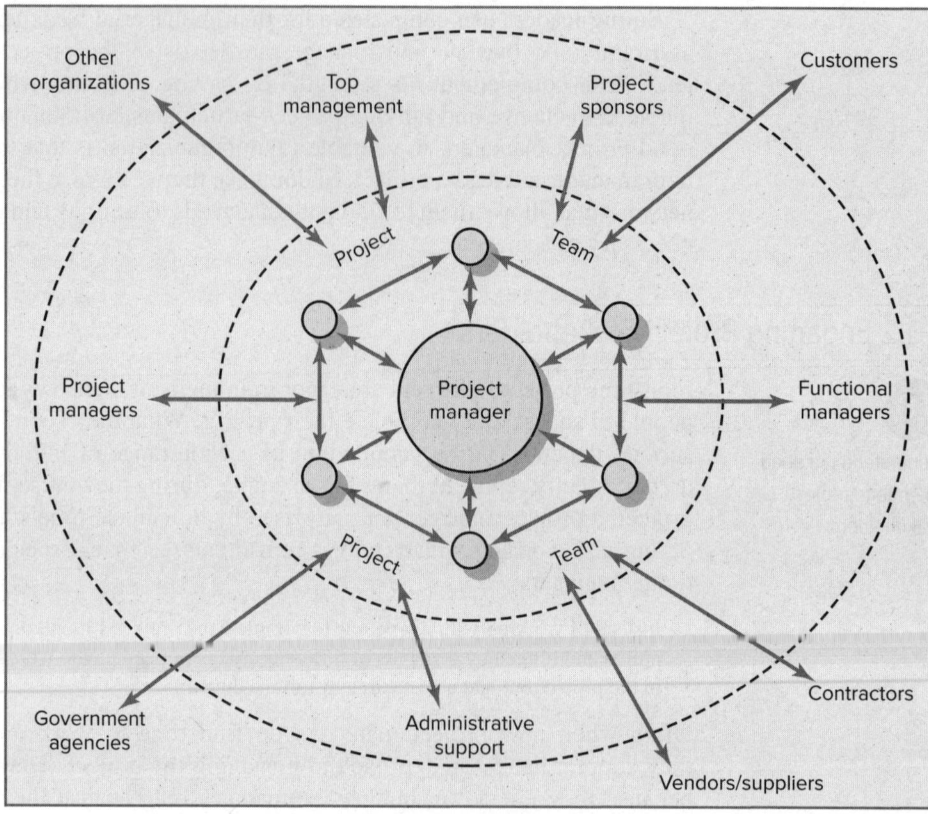

Each of these groups of stakeholders brings different expertise, standards, priorities, and agendas to the project. **Stakeholders** are people and organizations that are actively involved in the project or whose interests may be positively or negatively affected by the project (Project Management Institute, 2017). The sheer breadth and complexity of stakeholder relationships distinguish project management from regular management. To be effective, a project manager must understand how stakeholders can affect the project and develop methods for managing the dependency. The nature of these dependencies is identified here:

- The *project team* manages and completes project work. Most participants want to do a good job, but they are also concerned with their other obligations and how their involvement on the project will contribute to their personal goals and aspirations.
- *Project managers* naturally compete with each other for resources and the support of top management. At the same time they often have to share resources and exchange information.
- *Administrative support* groups, such as human resources, information systems, purchasing agents, and maintenance, provide valuable support services. At the same time they impose constraints and requirements on the project such as the documentation of expenditures and the timely and accurate delivery of information.
- *Functional managers,* depending on how the project is organized, can play a minor or major role in project success. In matrix arrangements, they may be responsible for assigning project personnel, resolving technical dilemmas, and overseeing the completion of significant segments of the project work. Even in dedicated project

teams, the technical input from functional managers may be useful, and acceptance of completed project work may be critical to in-house projects. Functional managers want to cooperate up to a point, but only up to a certain point. They are also concerned with preserving their status within the organization and minimizing the disruptions the project may have on their own operations.

- *Top management* approves funding of the project and establishes priorities within the organization. They define success and adjudicate rewards for accomplishments. Significant adjustments in budget, scope, and schedule typically need their approval. They have a natural vested interest in the success of the project but, at the same time, have to be responsive to what is best for the entire organization.
- *Project sponsors* champion the project and use their influence to gain approval of the project. Their reputation is tied to the success of the project, and they need to be kept informed of any major developments. They defend the project when it comes under attack and are a key project ally.
- *Contractors* may do all the actual work—in some cases, with the project team merely coordinating their contributions. In other cases, they are responsible for ancillary segments of the project scope. Poor work and schedule slips can affect the work of the core project team. While contractors' reputations rest with doing good work, they must balance their contributions with their own profit margins and their commitments to other clients.
- *Government agencies* regulate project work. Permits need to be secured. Construction work has to be built to code. New drugs have to pass a rigorous battery of U.S. Food and Drug Administration tests. Other products have to meet safety standards, for example, Occupational Safety and Health Administration standards.
- *Vendors/suppliers* provide the necessary resources for the completion of project work. Delays, shortages, and poor quality can bring a project to a standstill.
- *Other organizations,* depending on the nature of the project, may directly or indirectly affect the project. For example, environmental groups may challenge or even block project work. Public interest groups may apply pressure on government agencies. Customers often hire consultants and auditors to protect their interests on a project.
- *Customers* define the scope of the project, and ultimate project success rests in their satisfaction. Project managers need to be responsive to changing customer needs and requirements and to meeting their expectations. Customers are primarily concerned with getting a *good deal* and, as will be elaborated in Chapter 11, this naturally breeds tension with the project manager.

These relationships are interdependent in that a project manager's ability to work effectively with one group will affect his or her ability to engage other groups. For example, functional managers are likely to be less cooperative if they perceive that top management's commitment to the project is waning. Conversely, the ability of the project manager to buffer the team from excessive interference from a client is likely to increase his or her standing with the project team.

The project management structure being used will influence the number and degree of external dependencies that need to be engaged. One major advantage of creating a dedicated project team is that it reduces dependencies, especially within the organization, because most of the resources are assigned to the project. Conversely, a functional matrix structure increases dependencies, with the result that the project manager is much more reliant upon functional colleagues for work and staff.

The old-fashioned view of managing projects emphasized planning and directing the project team; the new perspective emphasizes engaging project stakeholders and anticipating change as the most important jobs. Project managers need to be able to assuage the concerns of customers, sustain support for the project at higher levels of the organization, and quickly identify problems that threaten project work. They do so while defending the integrity of the project and the interests of the project participants.[1]

Within this web of relationships, the project manager must find out what needs to be done to achieve the goals of the project and build a cooperative network to accomplish it. Project managers must do so without the requisite authority to expect or demand cooperation. Doing so requires sound communication skills, political savvy, and a broad influence base. See Snapshot from Practice 10.1: The Project Manager as Conductor for more on what makes project managers special.

SNAPSHOT FROM PRACTICE 10.1 The Project Manager as Conductor

Metaphors convey meaning beyond words. For example, a meeting can be described as being difficult or "like wading through molasses." A popular metaphor for the role of a project manager is that of *conductor.*

Jamie Grill/JGI/Blend Images

The conductor of an orchestra integrates the divergent sounds of different instruments to perform a given composition and make beautiful music. Similarly, the project manager integrates the talents and contributions of different specialists to complete the project. Many consider coordinating and integrating the work of others as the primary role of project managers (Project Management Institute, 2017).

Both a conductor and a project manager have to be good at understanding how the different players contribute to the performance of the whole. Both are almost entirely dependent upon the expertise and know-how of the players. The conductor does not have command of all the musical instruments. Likewise, the project manager usually possesses only a small proportion of the technical knowledge to make decisions. As such, the conductor and project manager both facilitate the performance of others rather than actually perform.

Conductors use their arms, baton, and other nonverbal gestures to influence the pace, intensity, and involvement of different musicians. Likewise, project managers orchestrate the completion of the project by managing the involvement and attention of project members. Project managers balance time and process and induce participants to make the right decisions at the right time, just as the conductor induces the wind instruments to perform at the right moment in a movement. Each controls the rhythm and intensity of work by managing the tempo and involvement of the players.

Finally, each has a vision that transcends the music score or project plan. To be successful, they must both earn the confidence, respect, and trust of their players.

[1] For a systematic treatise on stakeholder engagement, see: Bourne, L., *Stakeholder Relationship Management* (Farnham, England: Gower Publishing Ltd., 2009).

10.3 Influence as Exchange

LO 10-3

Identify and apply different "influence currencies" to build positive relations with others.

To successfully manage a project, a manager must adroitly build a cooperative network among divergent allies. Networks are mutually beneficial alliances that are generally governed by the **law of reciprocity** (Grant, 2013; Kaplan, 1984). The basic principle is that "one good deed deserves another, and likewise one bad deed deserves another." The primary way to gain cooperation is to provide resources and services for others in exchange for future resources and services. This is the age-old maxim "Quid pro quo (something for something)" or, in today's vernacular, "You scratch my back, I'll scratch yours."

Cohen and Bradford (1990) described the exchange view of influence as "currencies." If you want to do business in a given country, you have to be prepared to use the appropriate currency, and the exchange rates can change over time as conditions change. In the same way, what is valued by a marketing manager may be different from what is valued by a veteran project engineer, and you are likely to need to use different influence currency to obtain the cooperation of each individual. Although this analogy is a bit of an oversimplification, the key premise holds true that in the long run, "debit" and "credit" accounts must be balanced for cooperative relationships to work. See Research Highlight 10.1: Give and Take for an interesting finding regarding this concept. Table 10.1 presents the commonly traded organizational currencies identified by Cohen and Bradford; they are then discussed in more detail in the following sections.

TABLE 10.1
Commonly Traded Organizational Currencies

Task-related currencies	
Resources	Lending or giving money, budget increases, personnel, etc.
Assistance	Helping with existing projects or undertaking unwanted tasks.
Cooperation	Giving task support, providing quicker response time, or aiding implementation.
Information	Providing organizational as well as technical knowledge.
Position-related currencies	
Advancement	Giving a task or assignment that can result in promotion.
Recognition	Acknowledging effort, accomplishments, or abilities.
Visibility	Providing a chance to be known by higher-ups or significant others in the organization.
Network/contacts	Providing opportunities for linking with others.
Inspiration-related currencies	
Vision	Being involved in a task that has larger significance for the unit, organization, customer, or society.
Excellence	Having a chance to do important things really well.
Ethical correctness	Doing what is "right" by a higher standard than efficiency.
Relationship-related currencies	
Acceptance	Providing closeness and friendship.
Personal support	Giving personal and emotional backing.
Understanding	Listening to others' concerns and issues.
Personal-related currencies	
Challenge/learning	Sharing tasks that increase skills and abilities.
Ownership/involvement	Letting others have ownership and influence.
Gratitude	Expressing appreciation.

Source: Adapted from Cohen, A. R., and D. L. Bradford, *Influence without Authority* (New York: John Wiley & Sons, 1990).

SNAPSHOT FROM PRACTICE 10.2 Organizational Strategy for Dedicated Freight Corridors (DFC)

A successful Project Manager plays a critical role in executing large-scale infrastructure projects like the Dedicated Freight Corridor (DFC) by aligning project goals with organizational strategy, ensuring efficient execution, and mitigating risks. The DFC initiative by the Indian Railways is a transformative project aimed at creating a sustainable, high-capacity freight transportation network that will enhance India's economic growth and global competitiveness. An effective Project Manager must integrate strategic vision with meticulous execution, balancing efficiency, sustainability, and technological innovation.

The vision of the DFC project is to position Indian Railways as a key enabler of economic growth by developing a modern freight transportation network. The mission focuses on improving capacity, speed, and reliability while reducing congestion and enhancing overall logistics efficiency. A Project Manager ensures that each phase of the project—from planning to execution—stays aligned with this broader vision and mission by implementing structured project management frameworks and best practices.

STRATEGIC OBJECTIVES: THE PROJECT MANAGER'S ROLE

An effective Project Manager must address key strategic objectives while ensuring seamless project execution:

- **Enhancing Freight Efficiency:** The Project Manager oversees the creation of dedicated freight corridors, minimizing delays caused by passenger train traffic.
- **Maximizing Capacity Utilization:** By leveraging modern project management tools, the manager ensures that high-capacity corridors are designed efficiently and optimized for freight movement.
- **Promoting Economic Growth:** Through proactive stakeholder management, the Project Manager fosters industrial growth by facilitating reliable, faster market access and improving supply chain efficiency.
- **Ensuring Sustainability:** The Project Manager integrates green technologies, electrification, and renewable energy sources to minimize the project's environmental impact.
- **Embracing Technological Advancements:** The implementation of AI, automation, and predictive analytics under the guidance of a Project Manager ensures operational efficiency and risk mitigation.

An effective Project Manager ensures successful execution by focusing on the following key areas:

- **Infrastructure Development:** Managing the construction of dedicated freight corridors, electrified tracks, and freight terminals while ensuring smooth integration with logistics hubs.
- **Technological Integration:** Overseeing the deployment of GPS, IoT, and AI-based real-time tracking for freight management and supply chain transparency.
- **Sustainability Initiatives:** Ensuring the project prioritizes full electrification and explores alternative fuels like LNG and hydrogen.
- **Human Resource Development:** Leading training initiatives to upskill personnel in automated systems, safety protocols, and new-age railway operations.

PHASED IMPLEMENTATION: A PROJECT MANAGER'S ROADMAP

A well-defined roadmap is essential for structured project execution. A Project Manager ensures each phase progresses as planned, addressing challenges proactively:

- **Phase 1 (Year 1) – Planning & Design:** Conducting feasibility studies, finalizing routes, and securing approvals, much like NASA's Work Breakdown Structure (WBS) approach for complex projects.
- **Phase 2 (Years 2-5) – Construction & Development:** Supervising infrastructure development and ensuring the seamless integration of technology.
- **Phase 3 (Years 5-7) – Testing & Launch:** Overseeing pilot runs, refining operations, and ensuring project readiness for full-scale freight operations.
- **Phase 4 (Years 8-15) – Expansion & Optimization:** Managing the expansion of corridors and leveraging data analytics for continuous improvements and performance tracking.

RISK MANAGEMENT: THE PROJECT MANAGER'S APPROACH

Risk mitigation is a fundamental responsibility of a Project Manager in large-scale infrastructure projects. Key risks and mitigation strategies include:

- **Land Acquisition Challenges:** Coordinating with government agencies to ensure smooth acquisition processes.
- **Cost Control:** Implementing budget tracking mechanisms, contingency planning, and financial oversight.
- **Technological Risks:** Conducting rigorous testing, training skilled personnel, and ensuring system redundancies to prevent failures.
- For instance, Microsoft's use of dashboards to track KPIs can be applied to DFC, enabling real-time project tracking and decision-making.

PERFORMANCE METRICS: MEASURING PROJECT SUCCESS

Project Manager ensures the success of DFC by monitoring key performance indicators (KPIs):

- **Freight Turnaround Time:** Measuring improvements in delivery speed compared to conventional routes.
- **Capacity Utilization:** Ensuring freight corridors operate at optimal efficiency.
- **Environmental Impact:** Tracking reductions in emissions and energy usage.
- **Customer Satisfaction:** Regularly assessing feedback on service reliability, quality, and cost-effectiveness.

The success of the Dedicated Freight Corridor hinges on an effective Project Manager's ability to integrate meticulous planning, proactive risk management, and strategic execution. By focusing on efficiency, technological integration, and sustainability, a Project Manager ensures that DFC not only enhances India's freight transportation infrastructure but also strengthens the country's position as a global trade hub. Through structured project management methodologies, continuous monitoring, and strategic foresight, organizations can achieve long-term project success.

Task-Related Currencies

Task-related currencies come in different forms and are based on the project manager's ability to contribute to others' accomplishing their work. Probably the most significant form of this currency is the ability to respond to subordinates' requests for additional manpower, money, or time to complete a segment of a project. This kind of currency is also evident in sharing resources with another project manager who is in need. At a more personal level, it may simply mean providing direct assistance to a colleague in solving a technical problem.

Providing a good word for a colleague's proposal or recommendation is another form of this currency. Because most work of significance is likely to generate some form of opposition, the person who is trying to gain approval for a plan or proposal can be greatly aided by having a "friend in court."

Another form of this currency includes extraordinary effort. For example, fulfilling an emergency request to complete a design document in two days instead of the normal four days is likely to engender gratitude. Finally, sharing valuable information that would be useful to other managers is another form of this currency.

Research Highlight 10.1

Give and Take*

Adam Grant from the University of Pennsylvania identifies three fundamental styles of social interaction with regard to the law of reciprocity:

Takers—like to get more than give and put their own interests ahead of others.

Givers—prefer to give more than they get and pay more attention to what others need.

Matchers—strive to preserve an equal balance between giving and getting and operate on the principle of fairness.

While Grant admits that people will shift from one style to another, he cites research that indicates that most people develop a primary interaction style. He goes on to review research on the relationship between interaction style and professional success. Not surprisingly, he found *Givers* tend to sink to the bottom of the success ladder. They make others better off but sacrifice their own success in the process.

Guess who is at the very top of the success ladder? It is *Givers* again! Grant goes on to explain this paradox by arguing that while it is true that many *Givers* are too caring and too timid, there are other *Givers* who are willing to give more than they receive and still keep their own interests in sight, using them as a guide for choosing when, how, and to whom to give. These kind of *Givers* are able to create much bigger and more powerful social networks than *Takers* and *Matchers*. The goodwill they are able to generate is a major factor behind the success of this kind of *Givers*.

Grant claims that Abraham Lincoln is a perfect example of a *Giver* who climbed to the top. When he won the presidency in 1860, he recruited bitter competitors whom he had earlier defeated to join his management team (Cabinet) in key positions. Grant predicts a *Taker* would have protected his ego and invited only "yes men," and a *Matcher* would have offered appointments to allies. Lincoln reported he needed the best men possible to run the country, and by always focusing on what was best for the country he was able to forge an effective management team.

Effective project managers, like Lincoln, make decisions based on what is best for the project/organization, not personal interests. They go out of their way to help others and build social capital. They are not timid, but proactive in building connections with key people both within and outside their organization. They value dissent and encourage healthy discussions.

*A. Grant, *Give and Take: A Revolutionary Approach to Success* (New York: Viking Press, 2013).

Position-Related Currencies

Position-related currencies stem from the manager's ability to enhance others' positions within their organization. A project manager can do this by giving someone a challenging assignment that can aid his or her advancement by developing his or her skills and abilities. Being given a chance to prove yourself naturally generates a strong sense of gratitude. Sharing the glory and bringing to the attention of higher-ups the efforts and accomplishments of others generate goodwill.

Project managers confide that a useful strategy for gaining the cooperation of professionals in other departments/organizations is figuring out how to make these people look good to their bosses. For example, a project manager worked with a subcontractor whose organization was heavily committed to total quality management (TQM). The project manager made it a point in top-level briefing meetings to point out how quality improvement processes initiated by the contractor contributed to cost control and problem prevention.

Another variation of recognition is enhancing the reputation of others within the firm. "Good press" can pave the way for lots of opportunities, while "bad press" can quickly shut a person off and make it difficult to perform. This currency is also evident in helping to preserve someone's reputation by coming to the defense of someone unjustly blamed for project setbacks.

Finally, one of the strongest forms of this currency is sharing contacts with other people. Helping individuals expand their own networks by introducing them to key people naturally engenders gratitude. For example, suggesting to functional managers that they should contact a particular person or party if they want to get a request expedited is likely to engender a sense of indebtedness.

Inspiration-Related Currencies

Inspiration-related currencies are perhaps the most powerful form of influence. Most sources of inspiration derive from people's burning desire to make a difference and add meaning to their lives. Creating an exciting, bold vision for a project can elicit extraordinary commitment. For example, many of the technological breakthroughs associated with the introduction of the original Macintosh computer were attributed to the feeling that the project members had a chance to change the way people approached computers. A variant form of vision is providing an opportunity to do something really well. Being able to take pride in your work often drives many people.

Often the very nature of the project provides a source of inspiration. Discovering a cure for a devastating disease, introducing a new social program that will help those in need, or simply building a bridge that will reduce a major traffic bottleneck can provide opportunities for people to feel good about what they are doing and to feel that they are making a difference. Inspiration operates as a magnet—pulling people as opposed to pushing people toward doing something.

Relationship-Related Currencies

Relationship-related currencies have more to do with strengthening the relationship with someone than directly accomplishing the project tasks. The essence of this form of influence is forming a relationship that transcends normal professional boundaries and extends into the realm of friendship. Such relationships develop by giving personal and emotional backing. Picking people up when they are feeling down, boosting their confidence, and providing encouragement naturally breed goodwill. Sharing a sense of humor and making difficult times fun is another form of this currency. Similarly, engaging in non–work-related activities such as sports and family outings is another way relationships are naturally enhanced.

Perhaps the most basic form of this currency is simply listening to other people. Psychologists suggest that most people have a strong desire to be understood and that relationships break down because the parties stop listening to each other. Sharing personal secrets/ambitions and being a wise confidant also creates a special bond between individuals.

Personal-Related Currencies

Personal-related currencies deal with individual needs and an overriding sense of self-esteem. Some argue that self-esteem is a primary psychological need; the extent to which you can help others feel a sense of importance and personal worth will naturally generate goodwill. A project manager can enhance a colleague's sense of worth by asking for help and seeking opinions, delegating authority over work, and allowing individuals to feel comfortable stretching their abilities. This form of currency can also be seen in sincere expressions of gratitude for the contributions of others. Care, though, must be exercised in expressing gratitude, since it is easily devalued when overused. That is, the first *thank you* is likely to be more valued than the fiftieth.

The bottom line is that project managers will be influential only insofar as they can offer something that others value. Furthermore, given the diverse cast of people project managers depend on, it is important that they be able to acquire and exercise different influence currencies. The ability to do so will be constrained in part by the nature of the project and how it is organized. For example, a project manager who is in charge of a dedicated team has considerably more to offer team members than a manager who is given the responsibility of coordinating the activities of different professionals across different departments and organizations. In such cases, that manager will probably have to rely more heavily on personal and relational bases of influence to gain the cooperation of others.

10.4 Social Network Building

LO 10-4

Create a stakeholder map and develop strategies for managing project dependencies.

Mapping Stakeholder Dependencies

The first step to **social network building** is identifying those stakeholders on whom the project depends for success. The project managers and their key assistants need to ask the following questions:

- Whose cooperation will we need?
- Whose agreement or approval will we need?
- Whose opposition would keep us from accomplishing the project?

Many project managers find it helpful to draw a map of these dependencies. For example, Figure 10.2 contains the dependencies identified by a project manager responsible for installing a new financial software system in his or her company.

It is always better to overestimate rather than underestimate dependencies. All too often, otherwise talented and successful project managers have been derailed because they were blindsided by someone whose position or power they had not anticipated. After identifying the stakeholders associated with your project, it is important to assess their significance. Here the power/interest matrix introduced in Chapter 3 becomes useful. Those individuals with the most power over and interest in the project are the most significant stakeholders and deserve the greatest attention. In particular, you need to "step into their shoes" and see the project from their perspective by asking the following questions:

- What differences exist between myself and the people on whom I depend (goals, values, pressures, working styles, risks)?

FIGURE 10.2
Stakeholder Map for Financial Software Installation Project

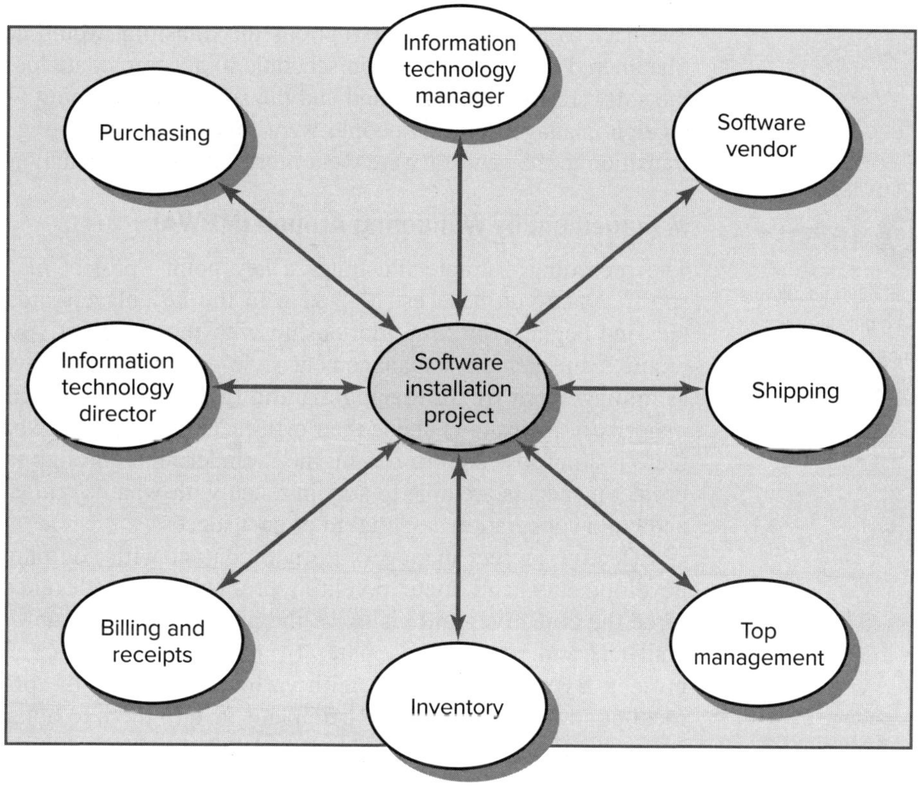

- How do these different people view the project (supporters, indifferents, antagonists)?
- What is the current status of the relationship I have with the people I depend on?
- What sources of influence do I have relative to those on whom I depend?

Once you start this analysis, you can begin to appreciate what others value and what currencies you might have to offer as a basis on which to build a working relationship. You begin to realize where potential problems lie—relationships in which you have a current debit or no convertible currency. Furthermore, diagnosing others' points of view as well as the basis for their positions will help you anticipate their reactions and feelings about your decisions and actions. This information is vital for selecting the appropriate influence strategy and tactics and producing win/win solutions.

For example, after mapping her dependency network, the project manager who was in charge of installing the software system realized that she was likely to have serious problems with the manager of the Receipts Department, who would be one of the primary users of the software. She had no previous history of working with this individual but had heard through the grapevine that the manager was upset with the choice of software and that he considered this project to be another unnecessary disruption of his department's operation.

Prior to project initiation the project manager arranged to have lunch with the manager, where she sat patiently and listened to his concerns. She later invested additional time and attention to educate him and his staff about the benefits of the new software.

She tried to minimize the disruptions the transition would cause in his department. She altered the implementation schedule to accommodate his preferences as to when the software would be installed and the subsequent training would occur. In turn, the receipts manager and his people were much more accepting of the change, and the transition to the new software went more smoothly than anticipated.

LO 10-5

Understand the need for a highly interactive management style on projects.

Management by Wandering Around (MBWA)

The preceding example illustrates a key point—project management is a "contact sport." Once you have established who the key players are, then you initiate contact and begin to build a relationship with those players. Building this relationship requires an interactive management style employees at Hewlett Packard referred to as **management by wandering around (MBWA)** to reflect that managers spend the majority of their time outside their offices. MBWA is somewhat of a misnomer in that there is a purpose/pattern behind the "wandering." Through face-to-face interactions, project managers are able to stay in touch with what is really going on in the project and build cooperation essential to project success.

Effective project managers initiate contact with key players to keep abreast of developments, anticipate potential problems, provide encouragement, and reinforce the objectives and vision of the project. They are able to intervene to resolve conflicts and prevent stalemates from occurring. In essence, they "manage" the project. By staying in touch with various aspects of the project, they become the focal point for information. Participants turn to them to obtain the most current and comprehensive information about the project, which reinforces their central role as project manager.

We have also observed less effective project managers who eschew MBWA and attempt to manage projects from their offices and computer terminals. Such managers proudly announce an open-door policy and encourage others to see them when a problem or an issue comes up. To them, no news is good news. This allows their contacts to be determined by the relative aggressiveness of others. Those who take the initiative and seek out the project manager get too high a proportion of the project manager's attention. Those people less readily available (physically removed) or more passive get ignored. This behavior contributes to the adage "Only the squeaky wheel gets greased," which breeds resentment within the project team.

LO 10-6

More effectively manage project expectations.

Effective project managers also find the time to interact regularly with more distal stakeholders. They keep in touch with suppliers, vendors, top management, and other functional managers. In doing so, they maintain familiarity with different parties, sustain friendships, discover opportunities to do favors, and understand the motives and needs of others. They remind people of commitments and champion the cause of their project. They also shape people's expectations (see Snapshot from Practice 10.3: Managing Expectations). Through frequent communication they alleviate people's concerns about the project, dispel rumors, warn people of potential problems, and lay the groundwork for dealing with setbacks in a more effective manner.

Project managers have adapted the principles of MBWA to the new post pandemic, virtual business world. While in-person interactions are preferred, teleconferencing has evolved into a worthy substitute. "Face-to-face" communications increase the richness of the interaction and identification with the other individuals. Video conferencing provides an efficient means for staying in touch with people regardless of where they are located. However, there may be a hidden cost to relying too much on video conferencing (see Snapshot from Practice: Fighting Zoom Fatigue).

SNAPSHOT FROM PRACTICE 10.3 Managing Expectations*

Dorothy Kirk, a project management consultant and program manager with Financial Solutions Group of Mynd, offers several keen insights into the art of managing stakeholder expectations:

> . . . expectations are hardy. All they need to take root is the absence of evidence to the contrary. Once rooted, the unspoken word encourages growth. They can develop and thrive without being grounded in reality. For this reason, project managers do daily battle with unrealistic expectations.

She goes on to offer several tips for managing expectations:

- The way you present information can either clarify or muddy expectations. For example, if you estimate that a task will take 317 hours, you are setting high expectations by your precision. The stakeholder is likely to be unhappy if it takes 323 hours. The stakeholder will not be unhappy with 323 hours if you quoted an estimate of 300–325 hours.
- Recognize that it is only human nature to interpret a situation in one's best interest. For example, if you tell someone it will be done by January, you are inclined to interpret it to your advantage and assume you have to the end of January, while the other person believes it will be done January 1st.
- Seize every opportunity to realign expectations with reality. Too often we avoid opportunities to adjust expectations because we hold on to a false hope that things will somehow work out.
- Do not ask for stakeholder suggestions for improvement if you do not intend to do something with their input. Asking for their input raises expectations.
- State the obvious. What is obvious to you may be obscure to others.
- Don't avoid delivering bad news. Communicate openly and in person. Expect some anger and frustration. Do not get defensive in return. Be prepared to explain the impact of the problems. For example, never say the project is going to be late without being able to give a new date. Explain what you are doing to see that this does not continue to happen.

All stakeholders have expectations about the schedule, cost, and project benefits. Project managers need to listen for, understand, and manage these expectations.

*D. Kirk, "Managing Expectations," *PM Network*, August 2000, pp. 59–62.

Unless project managers take the initiative to build a supportive network up front, they are likely to see a manager (or other stakeholder) only when there is bad news or when they need a favor (e.g., they don't have the data they promised or the project has slipped behind schedule). Without prior, frequent, easy give-and-take interactions around nondecisive issues, the encounter prompted by the problem is likely to provoke excess tension. The parties are more likely to act defensively, interrupt each other, and lose sight of the common goal.

Experienced project managers recognize the need to build relationships before they need them. They initiate contact with the key stakeholders at times when there are no outstanding issues or problems and therefore no anxieties and suspicions. On these social occasions, they naturally engage in small talk and responsive banter. They respond to others' requests for aid, provide supportive counsel, and exchange information. In doing so, they establish good feelings which will allow them to deal with more serious problems down the road. When one person views another as pleasant, credible, and helpful based on past contact, s/he is much more likely to be responsive to requests for help and less confrontational when problems arise.[2]

[2] This discussion is based on Sayles, L. R., *Leadership: Managing in Real Organizations* (New York: McGraw-Hill, 1989), pp. 70–78.

SNAPSHOT FROM PRACTICE Fighting Zoom Fatigue*

The COVID-19 pandemic created a transition from offices to homes where there were fewer people to come in close contact with. Zoom, Microsoft Teams, Google Hangouts, and other conferencing systems emerged as the dominate methods of communication. These programs did an extraordinary job of linking people together visually. But, soon people all over the planet were experiencing "zoom fatigue." Zoom fatigue describes the tiredness, weariness, worry, and burnout that accompanies overuse of these virtual communications platforms.

Why do video conversations become so tiring? Scientists have found that video conferencing affects different kinds of brain processes. Among other things, it (1) mutes echo neurons (that help humans to understand and empathize with others) and (2) confounds our Global Positioning System (GPS) neurons (which encode our location). Confounded GPS neurons cause exhaustion and confusion by positioning the Zoomer simultaneously in one physical place and another—perhaps very distant—virtual place. Related effects include:

1. **Cerebral overload.** The thinking overload refers to the extent of cognition we have to put into a task, in terms of intensity and duration. A dialogue or discussion is usually easy for humans, but with Zoom in the middle, it entails more focused intensity. This is because we normally rely on hand gestures and body language. But when we can only see one another's heads, we tend to make our facial expressions more pronounced to make sure the recipient get the message. We must also focus harder to understand the body language of those participating in the Zoom meeting.
2. **Excessive eye contact.** The number of people looking at you and the size of the faces on the screen are abnormal in a video conference call. So much eye contact with your fellow attendees would not occur in a face-to-face meeting. In an ordinary face-to-face meeting, participants gaze at the speaker, around the room, and at their electronic devices. By contrast, everyone is always observing each other in Zoom meetings. Further, the large size of their faces on-screen creates the false feeling of being near to them. Because our minds interpret physical closeness as being in stressful circumstances, we feel increased fatigue.
3. **All-day mirror.** Visualize staring at yourself with a mirror in front of you for eight hours a day. It's bizarre, yes; however, that is exactly what self-view within most conferencing systems do. This may not bother some people, but for others, who may be insecure, this can be nerve-racking.

HOW TO COMBAT ZOOM FATIGUE?

Shorten and, when possible, curtail Zoom meetings. Virtual meetings conducted using conferencing systems require a meeting facilitator who keeps the participants on task with a targeted termination time. A prepared agenda distributed in advance of the meeting is critical. Let everyone know that the meeting will not last beyond a specified time.

Prevent multi-tasking. It is tempting to take advantage of being visible only from the head up and to engage in multi-tasking during Zoom meetings. This might entail use of your smartphone, tablet, or notebook computer. These distractions interfere with your tracking the meeting and lead to further stress and fatigue.

Shrink the screen stimuli. Some experts suggest conducting Zoom meetings with a backdrop that is plain and uninteresting; otherwise, attendees will focus on trying to read your background, that is, straining to read the titles of books on bookshelves behind you in your background. Such attention to things other than the issue being addressed by the Zoom meeting are distracting and contribute to stress and fatigue.

Disable self-view. Researchers have discovered that many video conference participants spend most of the time gazing at their own faces. Knowing that your video is transmitted to others increases your cognizance of being seen. Such self-awareness can induce apprehension and make it difficult to concentrate on the issue at hand.

Integrate "eye" breaks. An optometrist suggested something called the 20-20-20 rule. For every 20 minutes spent looking at a display monitor, take 20 seconds to look at a building or other object across the street that is 20 or more feet away. This practice can help rest the eye muscles.

* E. Eatough, "Zoom Fatigue is Real: How to Make It Stop," www.betterup.com, July 13, 2021. Accessed 5/5/23; J. N. Bailenson, "Nonverbal Overload: A Theoretical Argument for the Causes of Zoom Fatigue," *Technology, Mind, and Behavior*, vol. 2, no. 1 (2021).

LO 10-7

Develop strategies for managing upward relations.

Managing Upward Relations

Research consistently points out that project success is strongly affected by the degree to which a project has the support of top management.[3] Such support is reflected in an appropriate budget, responsiveness to unexpected needs, and a clear signal to others in the organization of the importance of the project and the need to cooperate.

Visible top management support is not only critical for securing the support of other managers within an organization but also key in the project manager's ability to motivate the project team. Nothing establishes a manager's right to lead more than his or her ability to defend. To win the loyalty of team members, project managers have to be effective advocates for their projects. They have to be able to get top management to rescind unreasonable demands, provide additional resources, and recognize the accomplishments of team members. This is more easily said than done.

Working relationships with upper management are a common source of consternation. Laments like the following are often made by project managers about upper management:

They don't know how much it sets us back losing Neil to another project.

I would like to see them get this project done with the budget they gave us.

I just wish they would make up their minds as to what is really important.

While it may seem counterintuitive for a subordinate to "manage" a superior, smart project managers devote considerable time and attention to influencing and garnering the support of top management. Project managers have to accept profound differences in perspective and become skilled at the art of persuading superiors.

Many of the tensions that arise between upper management and project managers are a result of differences in perspective. Project managers become naturally absorbed with what is best for their project. To them the most important thing in the world is their project. Top management should have a different set of priorities. They are concerned with what is best for the entire organization. "Your project" is just one of many concerns they are dealing with. It is only natural for these two interests to conflict at times. For example, a project manager may lobby intensively for additional personnel, only to be turned down because top management believes that the other departments cannot afford a reduction in staff. Although frequent communication can minimize differences, the project manager has to accept the fact that top management is inevitably going to see the world differently.

FIGURE 10.3 Significance of a Project Sponsor

Once project managers accept that disagreements with superiors are more a question of perspective than substance, they can focus more of their energy on the art of persuading upper management. But before they can persuade superiors, they should first prove loyalty (Sayles, 1989). Loyalty in this context simply means that most of the time project managers consistently follow through on requests and adhere to the parameters established by top management without a great deal of grumbling or fuss. Once managers have proven loyalty to upper management, senior management is much more receptive to their challenges and requests.

Project managers have to cultivate strong ties with upper managers who are sponsoring the project. As noted earlier, these are high-ranking officials who have championed approval and funding of the project; as such, their reputations are aligned with the project. Sponsors are also the ones who defend the project when it is under attack in upper circles of management. They shelter the project from excessive interference (see Figure 10.3). Project managers should *always* keep such people informed of any

[3] See, for example: Pinto, J. L., and S. K. Mantel, "The Causes of Project Failure," *IEEE Transactions in Engineering Management*, vol. 37, no. 4 (1990), pp. 269–76.

problems that may cause embarrassment or disappointment. For example, if costs are beginning to outrun the budget or a technical glitch is threatening to delay the completion of the project, managers make sure that the sponsors are the first to know.

Timing is everything. Asking for additional budget the day after disappointing third-quarter earnings are reported is going to be much more difficult than making a similar request four weeks later. Good project managers pick the optimum time to appeal to top management. They enlist their project sponsors to lobby their cause. They also realize there are limits to top management's accommodations. Here, the Lone Ranger analogy is appropriate—you have only so many silver bullets, so use them wisely.

Project managers need to adapt their communication pattern to that of the senior group. For example, one project manager recognized that top management had a tendency to use sports metaphors to describe business situations, so s/he framed a recent slip in schedule by admitting that "we lost five yards, but we still have two plays to make a first down." Smart project managers learn the language of top management and use it to their advantage.

Finally, a few project managers admit ignoring chains of command. If they are confident that top management will reject an important request and that what they want to do will benefit the project, they do it without asking permission. While acknowledging that this is very risky, they claim that bosses typically won't argue with success.

Leading by Example

A highly visible, interactive management style not only is essential to building and sustaining cooperative relationships but also allows project managers to utilize their most powerful leadership tool—their own behavior (Kouzes & Posner, 2012; Peters, 1988). Often, when faced with uncertainty, people look to others for cues as to how to respond and demonstrate a propensity to mimic the behavior of people they respect. A project manager's behavior symbolizes how other people should work on the project. Through their behavior, project managers can influence how others act and respond to a variety of issues related to the project. (See Snapshot from Practice 10.4: Leading at the Edge for a dramatic example of this.)

To be effective, project managers must "walk the talk" (see Figure 10.4). Six aspects of leading by example are discussed next.

FIGURE 10.4
Leading by Example

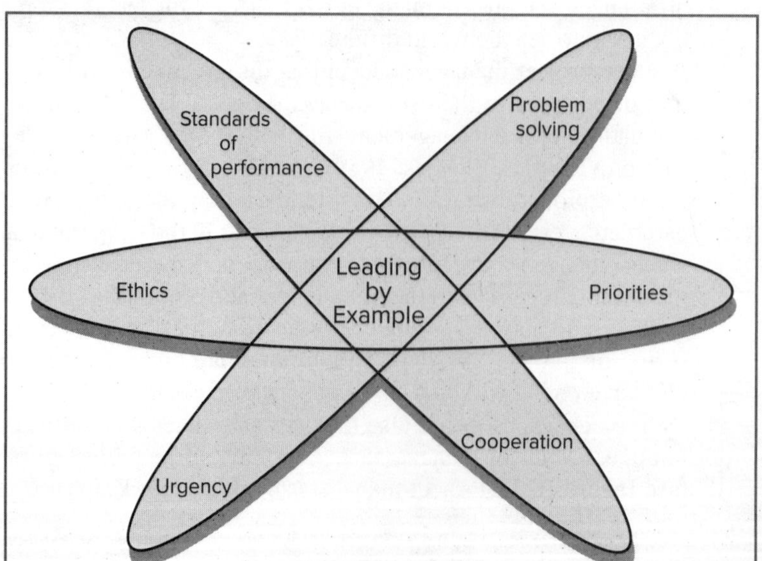

SNAPSHOT FROM PRACTICE 10.4 Leading at the Edge*

In 1914, the intrepid explorer Ernest Shackleton embarked on the *Endurance* with his team of seamen and scientists, intent upon crossing the unexplored Antarctic continent. What happened in the two years between their departure and their ultimate, incredible rescue has rarely been matched in the annals of survival: a ship crushed by expanding ice pack; a crew stranded on the floes of the frozen Weddell Sea; two perilous treks in open boats across a raging Southern Ocean; and a team marooned on wild, forlorn Elephant Island, stretched to the limits of human endurance.

Library of Congress, Prints & Photographs Division, LC-USZ62-17180

This adventure provided the basis for the book *Leading at the Edge: Leadership Lessons from the Extraordinary Saga of Shackleton's Antarctic Expedition,* written by Dennis Perkins. Perkins provides numerous incidents of how Shackleton's personal example influenced the behavior of his beleaguered crew. For example, from the beginning of the Trans-Atlantic expedition to its end, Shackleton consistently encouraged behavior that emphasized caring and respect:

> After the destruction of the *Endurance* Shackleton heated hot milk for the crew and went from tent to tent with the "life giving" drink. After the sail to the island of South Georgia, when the exhausted crew had landed, Shackleton took the first watch, which he kept for three hours instead of the usual one.

Crew members emulated the caring behaviors that Shackleton modeled. A good example of this occurred during one of the most dramatic moments in the *Endurance* saga. The food supply had dwindled to perilously low levels. Less than a week's supply remained, and the tiny ration of seal steak usually served at breakfast was eliminated. The waste meat generally used to feed the dogs was inspected for edible scraps.

Under these wretched conditions, and after a wet, sleepless night, an argument broke out among some of the team members. Caught in the middle, one crew member (Greenstreet) spilled his tiny ration of powdered milk and shouted at the biologist (Clark). Alfred Lansing described what happened next:

> Greenstreet paused to get his breath, and in that instant his anger was spent and he suddenly fell silent. Everyone else in the tent became quiet, too, and looked at Greenstreet, shaggy-haired, bearded, and filthy with blubber soot, holding his empty mug in his hand and looking helplessly down into the snow that had thirstily soaked up his precious milk. The loss was so tragic he seemed almost on the point of weeping. Without speaking, Clark reached out and poured some milk into Greenstreet's mug. Then Worsely, then Macklin, and Rickerson and Kerr, Orde-Lees, and finally Blackborrow. They finished in silence.

* Adapted from D. N. T. Perkins, *Leading at the Edge: Leadership Lessons from the Extraordinary Saga of Shackleton's Antarctica Expedition* (New York: AMACOM Press, 2000), pp. 94–95; A. Lansing, Endurance: *Shackleton's Incredible Voyage* (New York: Carroll & Graf, 1998), p. 127.

Priorities

Actions speak louder than words. Subordinates and others discern project managers' priorities by how they spend their time. If a project manager claims that this project is critical and then is perceived as devoting more time to other projects, then all her verbal reassurances are likely to fall on deaf ears. Conversely a project manager who takes the time to observe a critical test instead of simply waiting for a report affirms the importance of the testers and their work. Likewise, the types of questions project managers pose communicate priorities. By repeatedly asking how specific issues relate to satisfying the customer, a project manager can reinforce the importance of customer satisfaction.

Urgency

Through their actions, project managers can convey a sense of urgency, which can permeate project activities. This urgency in part can be conveyed through stringent deadlines, frequent status report meetings, and aggressive solutions for expediting the project. The project manager uses these tools like a metronome to pick up the beat of the project. At the same time, such devices will be ineffective if there is not also a corresponding change in the project manager's behavior. If project managers want others to work faster and solve problems quicker, then they need to work faster. They need to hasten the pace of their own behavior. They should accelerate the frequency of their interactions, talk and walk more quickly, get to work sooner, and leave work later. By simply increasing the pace of their daily interaction patterns, project managers can reinforce a sense of urgency in others.

Problem Solving

How project managers respond to problems sets the tone for how others tackle problems. If bad news is greeted by verbal attacks, then others will be reluctant to be forthcoming.[4] If the project manager is more concerned with finding out who is to blame instead of how to prevent problems from happening again, then others will tend to cover their tracks and cast the blame elsewhere. If, on the other hand, project managers focus more on how they can turn a problem into an opportunity or what can be learned from a mistake, then others are more likely to adopt a more proactive approach to problem solving.

Cooperation

How project managers act toward outsiders influences how team members interact with outsiders. If a project manager makes disparaging remarks about the "idiots" in the Marketing Department, then this oftentimes becomes the shared view of the entire team. If project managers set the norm of treating outsiders with respect and being responsive to their needs, then others will more likely follow suit.

Standards of Performance

Veteran project managers recognize that if they want participants to exceed project expectations, then they have to exceed others' expectations of a good project manager. They establish a high standard for project performance through the quality of their daily interactions. They respond quickly to the needs of others, carefully prepare and run crisp meetings, stay on top of all the critical issues, facilitate effective problem solving, and stand firm on important matters.

Ethics

How others respond to ethical dilemmas that arise in the course of a project will be influenced by how the project manager has responded to similar dilemmas.

[4] This is the classic "kill the messenger" syndrome. This and other forces that contribute to distorting information can be found in Larson, E., and J. King, "The Systemic Distortion of Information: An On-going Management Challenge," *Organizational Dynamics*, Winter 1996, pp. 49–62.

In many cases, team members base their actions on how they think the project manager would act. If project managers deliberately distort or withhold vital information from customers or top management, then they are signaling to others that this kind of behavior is acceptable. Project management invariably creates a variety of ethical dilemmas; this would be an appropriate time to delve into this topic in more detail.

10.5 Ethics and Project Management

LO 10-8

Understand the importance of building trust and acting in an ethical manner while working on a project.

Questions of ethics have already arisen in previous chapters that discussed padding of cost and time estimations, exaggerating pay-offs of project proposals, and so forth. Ethical dilemmas involve situations where it is difficult to determine whether conduct is right or wrong.

In a survey of project managers, 81 percent reported that they encounter ethical issues in their work.[5] These dilemmas include being pressured to alter status reports, backdate signatures, compromising safety standards to accelerate progress, and approving shoddy work. The work of Müller and colleagues suggests that the most common dilemma project managers face involves *transparency* issues related to project performance (Müller et al., 2013, 2014). For example, is it acceptable to falsely assure customers that everything is on track when in reality you are doing so to prevent them from panicking and making matters even worse?

Project management is complicated work, and, as such, ethics invariably involve gray areas of judgment and interpretation. For example, it is difficult to distinguish deliberate falsification of estimates from genuine mistakes or the willful exaggeration of project payoffs from genuine optimism. It becomes problematic to determine whether unfulfilled promises were deliberate deception or an appropriate response to changing circumstances.

To provide greater clarity to business ethics, many companies and professional groups publish a code of conduct. Cynics see these documents as simply window dressing, while advocates argue that they are important, albeit limited, first steps. In practice, personal ethics do not lie in formal statutes but at the intersection of one's work, family, education, profession, religious beliefs, and daily interactions. Most project managers report that they rely on their own private sense of right and wrong—what one project manager called his "internal compass." One common rule of thumb for testing whether a response is ethical is to ask, "Imagine that whatever you did was going to be reported on the front page of your local newspaper. How would you like that? Would you be comfortable?"

Unfortunately, scandals at Wells Fargo, Enron, WorldCom, and Arthur Andersen have demonstrated the willingness of highly trained professionals to abdicate personal responsibility for illegal actions and to obey the directives of superiors (see Snapshot from Practice 10.5: The Collapse of Arthur Andersen). Top management and the culture of an organization play a decisive role in shaping members' beliefs of what is right and wrong. Many organizations encourage ethical transgressions by creating a "win at all cost" mentality. The pressures to succeed obscure the consideration of whether the

[5] While this survey is a bit old, our conversations with project managers suggest that the results hold true today: (Cabanis, J., "A Question of Ethics: The Issues Project Managers Face and How They Resolve Them," *PM Network*, December 1996, pp. 8–28).

SNAPSHOT FROM PRACTICE 10.5 The Collapse of Arthur Andersen*

"Think straight and talk straight" was the principle on which Arthur E. Andersen built his accounting firm in the early 1900s. It was a phrase his mother taught him and became the firm's motto. The commitment to integrity and a systematic, planned approach to work were instrumental in Arthur Andersen becoming one of the largest and best-known accounting firms in the world.

According to the book *Inside Arthur Anderson* by Susan Squires and colleagues,

> Working for Arthur Andersen was not for everyone. It could be a tough culture. It was much too hierarchical and top down for the more free spirited. Many people left after less than two years, believing the rewards did not warrant the demands that were made on them. Others learned to play by the rules and some even thrived. To remain in the firm, staff members were expected to work hard, respect authority of rank, and maintain a high level of conformity. In return they were rewarded with support, promotion, and the possibility of making partner. Those individuals who made a career with the firm grew old together, professionally and personally, and most had never worked anywhere else. To these survivors, Andersen was their second family, and they developed strong loyalties to the firm and its culture. (p. 133)

On October 23, 2001, David Duncan told his Houston-based Enron project team that they needed to start complying with Andersen's new policy on handling audit documents. The policy had been instituted to make sure that the firm's extraneous paperwork could not be used in court cases. Although the document retention policy required that papers supporting the firm's opinions and audit be retained, it allowed a broad category of secondary documents to be destroyed. The team reacted with stunned silence to Duncan's directive. Then everyone got up and began racing to do what they had been told to do. No one asked Duncan to explain further. None asked whether what they were doing was wrong. No one questioned whether what he or she were doing might be illegal. Andersen's Houston staff just reacted, following orders without question.

plamens art/Shutterstock

On November 9, 2001, the day after the Securities Exchange Commission (SEC) issued a subpoena to Andersen, the shredding stopped. More than one ton of documents had been destroyed and 30,000 e-mails and Enron-related computer files erased. According to Andersen's legal defense team, the shredding was business as usual. The lawyers claimed that the shredding was standard practice for eliminating unnecessary files. To the SEC, it appeared to be the start of a deep cover-up operation. Subsequently one of the most respected accounting firms in the world closed its doors.

* S. E. Squires, C. J. Smith, L. McDougall, and W. R. Yeak, *Inside Arthur Andersen: Shifting Values, Unexpected Consequences* (Upper Saddle River, NJ: Prentice Hall, 2004).

ends justify the means. Other organizations place a premium on "fair play" and command a market position by virtue of being trustworthy and reliable.[6]

Many project managers claim that ethical behavior is its own reward. By following your own internal compass, your behavior expresses your personal values. Others suggest that ethical behavior is doubly rewarding. You not only are able to fall asleep at night but also develop a sound and admirable reputation. As will be explored in the next section, such a reputation is essential to establishing the trust necessary to exercise influence effectively.

[6] For a more in-depth discussion of ethics, see: Trevino, L., and K. Nelson, *Managing Business Ethics: Straight Talk about How to Do It Right,* 5th ed. (Hoboken, NJ: John Wiley & Sons, 2011).

10.6 Building Trust: The Key to Exercising Influence

The significance of trust can be discerned by its absence. Imagine how different a working relationship is when you distrust the other party as opposed to trusting them. Here is what one line manager had to say about how she reacted to a project manager she did not trust:

> Whenever Jim approached me about something, I found myself trying to read between the lines to figure what was really going on. When he made a request, my initial reaction was "no" until he proved it.

Conversely trust is the "lubricant" that maintains smooth and efficient interactions. For example, here is what a functional manager had to say about how he dealt with a project manager he trusted:

> If Sally said she needed something, no questions were asked. I knew it was important or she wouldn't have asked. Likewise, if I needed something, I knew she would come through for me if she could.

Trust is an elusive concept. It is hard to nail down in precise terms why some project managers are trusted and others are not. One popular way to understand trust is to see it as a function of character and competence. Character focuses on personal motives (e.g., does he or she want to do the right thing?), while competence focuses on skills necessary to realize motives (e.g., does he or she know the right things to do?).

Stephen Covey resurrected the significance of character in the leadership literature in his best-selling *Seven Habits of Highly Effective People.* Covey criticized popular management literature as focusing too much on shallow human relations skills and manipulative techniques, which he labeled the *personality ethic.* He argues that at the core of highly effective people is a *character ethic* that is deeply rooted in personal values and principles such as dignity, service, fairness, the pursuit of truth, and respect.

One of the distinguishing traits of character is consistency. When people are guided by a core set of principles, they are naturally more predictable because their actions are consistent with these principles. Another feature of character is openness. When people have a clear sense of who they are and what they value, they are more receptive to others. This trait provides them with the capacity to empathize and the talent to build consensus among divergent people. Finally, another quality of character is a sense of purpose. Managers with character are driven not only by personal ambitions but also for the common good. Their primary concern is what is best for their organization and the project, not what is best for themselves. This willingness to subordinate personal interests to a higher purpose garners the respect, loyalty, and trust of others.

The significance of character is summarized by the comments made by two team members about two very different project managers:

> At first everyone liked Joe and was excited about the project. But after a while, people became suspicious of his motives. He had a tendency to say different things to different people. People began to feel manipulated. He spent too much time with top management. People began to believe that he was only looking out for himself. It was HIS project. When the project began to slip he jumped ship and left us holding the bag. I'll never work for that guy again.
>
> My first impression of Jack was nothing special. He had a quiet, unassuming management style. Over time I learned to respect his judgment and his ability to get people to work together. When you went to him with a problem or a request, he always listened carefully. If he couldn't do what you wanted him to do, he would take the time to explain why. When disagreements arose he always thought of what was best for the project. He treated everyone by the same rules; no one got special treatment. I'd jump at the opportunity to work on a project with him again.

Character alone will not engender trust. We must also have confidence in the competency of individuals before we really trust them (Kanter, 1979). We all know well-intended managers whom we like but do not trust because they have a history of coming up short on their promises. Although we may befriend these managers, we don't like to work with or for them.

Competence is reflected at a number of different levels. First, there is task-related knowledge and skills reflected in the ability to answer questions, solve technical problems, and excel in certain kinds of work. Second, there is competence at an interpersonal level demonstrated in being able to listen effectively, communicate clearly, resolve arguments, provide encouragement, and so forth. Finally, there is organizational competence. This includes being able to run effective meetings, set meaningful objectives, reduce inefficiencies, and build a social network. Often young engineers and other professionals tend to place too much value on task or technical competence. They underestimate the significance of organizational skills. Veteran professionals, on the other hand, recognize the importance of management and place a greater value on organizational and interpersonal skills.

One problem new project managers experience is that it takes time to establish a sense of character and competency. Character and competency are often demonstrated when they are tested, such as when a tough call has to be made or when difficult problems have to be solved. Veteran project managers have the advantage of reputation and an established track record of success. Although endorsements from credible sponsors can help young project managers create a favorable first impression, ultimately their behavior will determine whether they can be trusted. Recent research suggests that the first step in building trust is connecting. Instead of starting off emphasizing your competency, focus on exhibiting warmth and concern.[7] In doing so, you demonstrate to others that you hear them, understand them, and can be trusted by them (Cuddy, Kohu, & Neffinger, 2013).

So far this chapter has addressed the importance of building a network of relationships to complete a project based on trust and reciprocity. The next section examines the nature of project management work and the personal qualities needed to excel at it.

10.7 Qualities of an Effective Project Manager

LO 10-9

Identify the qualities of an effective project manager.

Project management is, at first glance, a misleading discipline in that there is an inherent logic to the process. There is a natural progression from formulating a project scope statement to creating a WBS, developing a network, adding resources, finalizing a plan, and reaching milestones. However, when it comes to actually implementing and completing projects, this logic can quickly disappear. Project managers often encounter a much messier world, filled with inconsistencies and paradoxes. Effective project managers have to be able to deal with the contradictory nature of their work. Some of those contradictions are listed here:

- **Innovate and maintain stability.** Project managers have to put out fires, restore order, and get the project back on track. At the same time they often need to be innovative and develop new, better ways of doing things. Innovations upset routines and may spark new disturbances that have to be dealt with.

[7] Warmth is reflected nonverbally in terms of smiling, appropriate eye contact, and gestures as well as verbally in questions asked and empathetic listening.

- **See the big picture while getting their hands dirty.** Project managers have to see the big picture and how their project fits within the larger strategy of their firm. There are also times when they must get deeply involved in project work and technology. If they don't worry about the details, who will?
- **Encourage individuals but stress the team.** Project managers have to motivate, cajole, and entice individual performers while maintaining teamwork. They have to be careful that they are considered fair and consistent in their treatment of team members while treating each member as a special individual.
- **Be hands-off/hands-on.** Project managers have to intervene, resolve stalemates, solve technical problems, and insist on different approaches. At the same time they have to recognize when it is appropriate to sit on the sidelines and let other people figure out what to do.
- **Be flexible but firm.** Project managers have to be adaptable and responsive to events and outcomes that occur on the project. At the same time they have to hold the line at times and tough it out when everyone else wants to give up.
- **Manage team versus organizational loyalties.** Project managers need to forge a unified project team whose members stimulate one another to extraordinary performance. But at the same time they have to counter the excesses of cohesion and the team's resistance to outside ideas. They have to cultivate loyalties to both the team and the parent organization.

Managing these and other contradictions requires finesse and balance. Finesse involves the skillful movement back and forth between opposing behavioral patterns (Sayles, 1989). For example, most of the time project managers actively involve others, move by increment, and seek consensus. There are other times when project managers must act as autocrats and take decisive, unilateral action. Balance involves recognizing the danger of extremes and that too much of a good thing invariably becomes harmful. For example, many managers have a tendency to always delegate the most stressful, difficult assignments to their best team members. This habit often breeds resentment among those chosen ("why am I always the one who gets the tough work?") and never allows the weaker members to develop their talents further.

There is no one management style or formula for being an effective project manager. The world of project management is too complicated for formulas. Successful project managers have a knack for tailoring styles to specific circumstances of the situation.

So what should one look for in an effective project manager? Many authors have addressed this question and have generated list after list of skills and attributes associated with being an effective manager (Posner, 1987; Shenhar & Nofziner, 1997; Turner & Müller, 2005). When reviewing these lists, one sometimes gets the impression that to be a successful project manager requires someone with superhuman powers. While not everyone has the right stuff to be an effective project manager, there are some core traits and skills that can be developed to successfully perform the job. The following are eight of these traits.

1. **Effective communication skills.** Communication is critical to project success. Project managers need to speak the language of different stakeholders and be empathetic listeners.
2. **Systems thinking.** Project managers must be able to take a holistic rather than a reductionist approach to projects. Instead of breaking up a project into individual pieces (planning, budget) and managing it by understanding each part, a systems perspective focuses on trying to understand how relevant project factors collectively

Research Highlight 10.2

Emotional Intelligence*

Emotional intelligence (EQ) is the ability or skill to perceive, assess, and manage the emotions of oneself and others. Although the notion of EQ emerged in the 1920s, it was not until Daniel Goleman published his book *Emotional Intelligence* that the concept captured the attention of business people and the public alike.

Goleman divided EQ into the following five emotional competencies:

- **Self-awareness**—knowing your emotions, recognizing feelings as they occur, and understanding the link between your emotions and your behavior. Self-awareness is reflected in confidence, a realistic assessment of personal strengths/weaknesses, and an ability to make fun of oneself.
- **Self-regulation**—being able to control disruptive impulses and moods and respond appropriately to situations. Self-regulation is reflected in trustworthiness and openness to change.
- **Self-motivation**—being able to gather up your feelings and pursue goals with energy, passion, and persistence. The hallmarks of self-motivation include a strong desire to achieve and internal optimism.
- **Empathy**—being able to recognize the feelings of others and tuning in to their verbal and nonverbal cues. Empathy is reflected in the ability to sustain relationships and in cross-cultural sensitivity.
- **Social skills**—being able to build social networks and rapport with different kinds of people. Social skills include being able to lead change, resolve conflicts, and build effective teams.

Not much imagination is needed to see how EQ would contribute to being an effective project manager.

In Goleman's view, these competences build on each other in a hierarchy. At the bottom of his hierarchy is self-awareness. Some level of self-awareness is needed to move to self-regulation. Ultimately, social skills require all four of the other competencies in order to begin to be proficient at leading others. Experts believe that most people can learn to significantly increase their EQ. Numerous training programs and materials have emerged to help individuals realize their EQ potential.

* T. Bradberry, and J. Graves, *The Emotional Intelligence Quick Book: How to Put Your EQ to Work* (New York: Simon & Schuster, 2005); R. Maqbool, Y. Sudong, N. Manzoor, and Y. Rashid, "The Impact of Emotional Intelligence, Project Manager's Competencies, and Transformational Leadership on Project Success," *Project Management Journal,* vol. 48, no. 3 (2017), pp. 58–75.

interact to produce project outcomes. The key to success then becomes managing the interaction between different parts and not the parts themselves.[8]

3. **Personal integrity.** Before you can lead and manage others, you have to be able to lead and manage yourself (Bennis, 1989). Begin by establishing a firm sense of who you are, what you stand for, and how you should behave. This inner strength provides the buoyancy to endure the ups and downs of the project life cycle and the credibility essential to sustaining the trust of others.
4. **Proactivity.** Good project managers take action before it is needed to prevent small concerns from escalating into major problems. They spend the majority of their time working within their sphere of influence to solve problems and not dwelling on things they have little control over. Project managers can't be whiners.[9]
5. **High emotional intelligence (EQ).** Project management is not for the meek. Project managers have to have command of their emotions and be able to respond constructively to others when things get a bit out of control. See Research Highlight 10.2: Emotional Intelligence to read more about this quality.

[8] For a practical elaboration on what it means to be a systems thinker, see: Senge, P. M., *The Fifth Discipline* (New York: Doubleday, 1990).

[9] For a more extensive discussion of the habit of being proactive, see: Covey, S., *The Seven Habits of Highly Effective People* (New York: Simon & Schuster, 1989), pp. 65–94.

6. **General business perspective.** Because the primary role of a project manager is to integrate the contributions of different business and technical disciplines, it is important that a manager have a general grasp of business fundamentals and how the different functional disciplines interact to contribute to a successful business.
7. **Effective time management.** Time is a manager's scarcest resource. Project managers have to be able to budget their time wisely and quickly adjust their priorities. They need to balance their interactions so no one feels ignored.
8. **Optimism.** Project managers have to display a can-do attitude. They have to be able to find rays of sunlight in a dismal day and keep people's attention positive. A good sense of humor and a playful attitude are often a project manager's greatest strengths.

So how does one develop these traits? Workshops, self-study, and courses can upgrade one's general business perspective and capacity for systems thinking. Training programs can improve emotional intelligence and communication skills. People can also be taught stress and time management techniques. However, we know of no workshop or magic potion that can transform a pessimist into an optimist or provide a sense of purpose when there is not one. These qualities get at the very soul or being of a person. Optimism, integrity, and even proactivity are not easily developed if there is not already a predisposition to display them.

Summary

To be successful, project managers must build a cooperative network among a diverse set of allies. They begin by identifying the key stakeholders on a project, then diagnose the nature of the relationships and the basis for exercising influence. Effective project managers are skilled at acquiring and exercising a wide range of influence. They use this influence and a highly interactive management style to monitor project performance and initiate appropriate changes in project plans and direction. They do so in a manner that generates trust, which is ultimately based on others' perceptions of their character and competence.

Project managers are encouraged to keep in mind the following suggestions.

- *Relationships should be built before they are needed.* Identify key players and what you can do to help them before you need their assistance. It is always easier to receive a favor after you have granted one. This requires the project manager to see the project in systems terms and to appreciate how it affects other activities and agendas inside and outside the organization. From this perspective they can identify opportunities to do good deeds and garner the support of others.
- *Trust is sustained through frequent face-to-face contact.* Trust withers through neglect. This is particularly true under conditions of rapid change and uncertainty that naturally engender doubt, suspicion, and even momentary bouts of paranoia. Project managers must maintain frequent contact with key stakeholders to keep abreast of developments, assuage concerns, engage in reality testing, and focus attention on the project. Frequent face-to-face interactions either directly or by teleconferencing affirm mutual respect and trust in each other.

Ultimately, exercising influence in an effective and ethical manner begins and ends with how you view the other parties. Do you view them as potential partners or obstacles to your goals? If obstacles, then you wield your influence to manipulate and gain compliance and cooperation. If partners, you exercise influence to gain their commitment and support. People who view social network building as building partnerships see every interaction with two goals: resolving the immediate problem/concern and improving the working relationship so that next time it will be even more effective. Experienced project managers realize that "what goes around comes around" and try at all cost to avoid antagonizing players for quick success.

Key Terms

Emotional intelligence (EQ), *436*
Inspiration-related currencies, *421*
Law of reciprocity, *417*
Management by wandering around (MBWA), *424*
Personal integrity, *436*
Personal-related currencies, *421*
Position-related currencies, *420*
Relationship-related currencies, *421*
Social network building, *422*
Stakeholders, *414*
Systems thinking, *435*
Task-related currencies, *419*

Review Questions

1. What is the difference between managing and leading a project?
2. What does the exchange model of influence suggest you do to build cooperative relationships to complete a project?
3. What differences would you expect to see between the kinds of influence currencies that a project manager in a functional matrix would use and the influence a project manager of a dedicated project team would use?
4. Why is it important to build a relationship before you need it?
5. Why is it critical to keep the project sponsor informed?
6. Why is trust a function of both character and competence?
7. Which of the eight traits/skills associated with being an effective project manager is the most important? The least important? Why?

SNAPSHOT FROM PRACTICE

Discussion Questions

10.1 *The Project Manager as Conductor*

1. Why is a conductor of an orchestra an appropriate metaphor for a project manager?
2. What aspects of being a project manager are not reflected in this metaphor?
3. Can you think of other metaphors that would be appropriate?

10.3 *Leading at the Edge*

1. How important is leading by example on a project?
2. What do you think would have happened to the crew of the *Endurance* if Shackleton had not led by example?

10.4 *The Collapse of Arthur Andersen*

1. It seems like every 5–10 years a scandal damages, if not brings down, a well-known business. Is this inevitable, given the competitive nature of business?
2. What aspects of the Arthur Andersen culture contributed to the scandal?

Fighting Zoom Fatigue

1. Have you heard of "Zoom fatigue"? Have you experienced it? What was it like?

Exercises

1. Do an Internet search for the Keirsey Temperament Sorter Questionnaire and find a site that appears to have a reputable self-assessment questionnaire. Respond to the questionnaire to identify your temperament type. Read supportive documents associated with your type. What does this material suggest are the kinds of projects that would best suit you? What does it suggest your strengths and weaknesses are as a project manager? How can you compensate for your weaknesses?
2. Access the Project Management Institute website and review the standards contained in the PMI Member Ethical Standards section. How useful is the information for helping someone decide what behavior is appropriate and inappropriate?
3. You are organizing a benefit concert in your hometown that will feature local heavy metal rock groups and guest speakers. Draw a dependency map identifying the major groups of people that are likely to affect the success of this project. Who do you think will be most cooperative? Who do you think will be least cooperative? Why?
4. You are the project manager responsible for the overall construction of a new international airport. Draw a dependency map identifying the major groups of people that are likely to affect the success of this project. Who do you think will be most cooperative? Who do you think will be least cooperative? Why?
5. Identify an important relationship (co-worker, boss, friend) in which you are having trouble gaining cooperation. Assess this relationship in terms of the influence currency model. What kinds of influence currency have you been exchanging in this relationship? Is the "bank account" for this relationship in the "red" or the "black"? What kinds of influence would be appropriate for building a stronger relationship with that person?
6. The following seven mini-case scenarios involve ethical dilemmas associated with project management. How would you respond to each situation and why?

Jack Nietzche

You returned from a project staffing meeting in which future project assignments were finalized. Despite your best efforts, you were unable to persuade the director of project management to promote one of your best assistants, Jack Nietzche, to a project manager position. You feel a bit guilty because you dangled the prospect of this promotion to motivate Jack. Jack responded by putting in extra hours to ensure that his segments of the project were completed on time. You wonder how Jack will react to this disappointment. More importantly, you wonder how his reaction might affect your project. You have five days remaining to meet a critical deadline for a very important customer. While it won't be easy, you believed you would be able to complete the project on time. Now you're not so sure. Jack is halfway through completing the documentation phase, which is the last critical activity. Jack can be pretty emotional at times, and you are worried that he will blow up once he finds he didn't get the promotion. As you return to your office, you wonder what you should do. Should you tell Jack that he isn't going to be promoted? What should you say if he asks about whether the new assignments were made?

Seaburst Construction Project

You are the project manager for the Seaburst construction project. So far the project is progressing ahead of schedule and below budget. You attribute this in part to the good working relationship you have with the carpenters, plumbers, electricians, and machine operators who work for your organization. More than once you have asked them to give 110 percent, and they have responded.

One Sunday afternoon you decide to drive by the site and show it to your son. As you point out various parts of the project to your son, you discover that several pieces of valuable equipment are missing from the storage shed. When you start work again on Monday, you are about to discuss this matter with a supervisor when you realize that all the missing equipment is back in the shed. What should you do? Why?

The Project Status Report Meeting

You are driving to a project status report meeting with your client. You encountered a significant technical problem on the project that has put your project behind schedule. This is not good news because completion time is the number one priority for the project. You are confident that your team can solve the problem if they are free to give their undivided attention to it and that with hard work you can get back on schedule. You also believe if you tell the client about the problem, she will demand a meeting with your team to discuss the implications of the problem. You can also expect her to send some of her personnel to oversee the solution to the problem. These interruptions will likely further delay the project. What should you tell your client about the current status of the project?

Gold Star LAN Project

You work for a large consulting firm and were assigned to the Gold Star LAN project. Work on the project is nearly completed and your clients at Gold Star appear to be pleased with your performance. During the course of the project, changes in the original scope had to be made to accommodate specific needs of managers at Gold Star. The costs of these changes were documented as well as overhead and submitted to the centralized Accounting Department. They processed the information and submitted a change order bill for your signature. You are surprised to see the bill is 10 percent higher than what you submitted. You contact Jim Messina in the accounting office and ask if a mistake has been made. He curtly replies that no mistake was made and that management adjusted the bill. He recommends that you sign the document. You talk to another project manager about this and she tells you off the record that overcharging clients on change orders is common practice in your firm. Would you sign the document? Why? Why not?

Cape Town Bio-Tech

You are responsible for installing the new Double E production line. Your team has collected estimates and used the WBS to generate a project schedule. You have confidence in the schedule and the work your team has done. You report to top management that you believe the project will take 110 days and be completed by March 5. The news is greeted positively. In fact, the project sponsor confides that orders do not have to be shipped until April 1. You leave the meeting wondering whether you should share this information with the project team or not?

Ryman Pharmaceuticals

You are a test engineer on the Bridge project at Ryman Pharmaceuticals. You have just completed conductivity tests of a new electrochemical compound. The results exceeded expectations. This new compound should revolutionize the industry. You are wondering whether to call your stockbroker and ask him to buy $20,000 worth of Ryman stock before everyone else finds out about the results. What would you do and why?

Princeton Landing

You are managing the renovation of the Old Princeton Landing Bar and Grill. The project is on schedule despite receiving a late shipment of paint. The paint was supposed to arrive on 1/30 but instead arrived on 2/1. The assistant store manager apologizes profusely for the delay and asks if you would be willing to sign the acceptance form and backdate it to 1/30. He says he won't qualify for a bonus that he has worked hard to meet for the past month if the shipment is reported late. He promises to make it up to you on future projects. What would you do and why?

References

Anand, V., B. E. Ashforth, and M. Joshi, "Business as Usual: The Acceptance and Perpetuation of Corruption in Organizations," *Academy of Management Executive,* vol. 19, no. 4 (2005), pp. 9–23.

Ancona, D. G., and D. Caldwell, "Improving the Performance of New-Product Teams," *Research Technology Management,* vol. 33, no. 2 (March/April 1990), pp. 25–29.

Badaracco, J. L., Jr., and A. P. Webb, "Business Ethics: A View from the Trenches," *California Management Review,* vol. 37, no. 2 (Winter 1995), pp. 8–28.

Baker, W. E., *Network Smart: How to Build Relationships for Personal and Organizational Success* (New York: McGraw-Hill, 1994).

Bennis, W., *On Becoming a Leader* (Reading, MA: Addison-Wesley, 1989).

Bertsche, R., "Seven Steps to Stronger Relationships between Project Managers and Sponsors," *PM Network,* September 2014, pp. 50–55.

Bourne, L., *Stakeholder Relationship Management* (Farnham, England: Gower Publishing Ltd., 2009).

Brownlee, D., "Here's How the Best Project Managers Build a Candid Team Culture. You Can Too." Forbes.com, October 27, 2021. Accessed 3/31/23.

Cabanis-Brewin, J., "The Human Task of a Project Leader: Daniel Goleman on the Value of High EQ," *PM Network,* November 1999, pp. 38–42.

Cohen, A. R., and D. L. Bradford, *Influence without Authority* (New York: John Wiley & Sons, 1990).

Cuddy, J. A., M. Kohu, and J. Neffinger, "Connect Then Lead," *Harvard Business Review,* vol. 91, no. 7/8 (July/August 2013), pp. 54–61.

Dinsmore, P. C., "Will the Real Stakeholders Please Stand Up?" *PM Network,* December 1995, pp. 9–10.

Einsiedel, A. A., "Profile of Effective Project Managers," *Project Management Journal,* vol. 31, no. 3 (1987), pp. 51–56.

Ferrazzi, K., *Never Eat Alone and Other Secrets to Success One Relationship at a Time* (New York: Crown Publishers, 2005).

Gabarro, S. J., *The Dynamics of Taking Charge* (Boston: Harvard Business School Press, 1987).

Grant, A., *Give and Take: A Revolutionary Approach to Success* (New York: Viking Press, 2013).

Hill, L. A., *Becoming a Manager: Mastery of a New Identity* (Boston: Harvard Business School Press, 1992).

Kanter, R. M., "Power Failures in Management Circuits," *Harvard Business Review* (July/August 1979), pp. 65–79.

Kaplan, R. E., "Trade Routes: The Manager's Network of Relationships," *Organizational Dynamics,* vol. 12, no. 4 (Spring 1984), pp. 37–52.

Kotter, J. P., "What Leaders Really Do," *Harvard Business Review,* vol. 68, no. 3 (May/June 1990), pp. 103–11.

Kouzes, J. M., and B. Z. Posner, *Credibility: How Leaders Gain and Lose It, Why People Demand It* (San Francisco: Jossey-Bass, 1993).

Kouzes, J. M., and B. Z. Posner, *The Leadership Challenge,* 5th ed. (San Francisco: Jossey-Bass, 2012).

Lewis, M. W., M. A. Welsh, G. E. Dehler, and S. G. Green, "Product Development Tensions: Exploring Contrasting Styles of Project Management," *Academy of Management Journal,* vol. 45, no. 3 (2002), pp. 546–64.

Müller, R., E. S. Andersen, Ø. Kvalnes, J. Shao, S. Sankaran, J. R. Turner, C. Biesenthal, D. Walker, and S. Gudergan, "The Interrelationship of Governance, Trust, and Ethics in Temporary Organizations,"*Project Management Journal,* vol. 44, no. 4 (August 2013), pp. 26–44.

Müller, R., and R. Turner, "Leadership Competency Profiles of Successful Project Managers," *International Journal of Project Management,* vol. 28, no. 5 (July 2010), pp. 437–48.

Müller, R., R. Turner, E. S. Andersen, J. Shao, and O. Kvalnes, "Ethics, Trust, and Goverance in Temporary Organizations," *Project Management Journal,* vol. 45, no. 4 (August/September 2014), pp. 39–54.

Peters, L. H., "A Good Man in a Storm: An Interview with Tom West," *Academy of Management Executive,* vol. 16, no. 4 (2002), pp. 53–63.

Peters, L. H., "Soulful Ramblings: An Interview with Tracy Kidder," *Academy of Management Executive,* vol. 16, no. 4 (2002), pp. 45–52.

Peters, T., *Thriving on Chaos: Handbook for a Management Revolution* (New York: Alfred A. Knopf, 1988).

Pinto, J. K., and D. P. Slevin, "Critical Success Factors in Successful Project Implementation," *IEEE Transactions in Engineering Management,* vol. 34, no. 1 (1987), pp. 22–27.

Posner, B. Z., "What It Takes to Be an Effective Project Manager," *Project Management Journal* (March 1987), pp. 51–55.

Project Management Institute, *PMBOK Guide,* 6th ed. (Newtown Square, PA: Project Management Institute, 2017).

Robb, D. J., "Ethics in Project Management: Issues, Practice, and Motive," *PM Network,* December 1996, pp. 13–18.

Shenhar, A. J., and B. Nofziner, "A New Model for Training Project Managers," *Proceedings of the 28th Annual Project Management Institute Symposium,* 1997, pp. 301–6.

Turner, J. R., and R. Müller, "The Project Manager Leadership Style as a Success Factor on Projects: A Literature Review," *Project Management Journal,* vol. 36, no. 2 (2005), pp. 49–61.

Case 10.1

The Blue Sky Project*

Garth Hudson was a 29-year-old graduate of Eastern State University (ESU) with a BS degree in management information systems. After graduation, he worked for seven years at Bluegrass Systems in Louisville, Kentucky. While at ESU he worked part time for an oceanography professor, Ahmet Green, creating a customized database for a research project he was conducting. Green was recently appointed director of Eastern Oceanography Institute (EOI), and Garth was confident that this prior experience was instrumental in his getting the job as information services (IS) director at the institute. Although he took a significant pay cut, he jumped at the opportunity to return to his alma mater. His job at Bluegrass Systems had been very demanding. The long hours and extensive traveling had created tension in his marriage. He was looking forward to a normal job with reasonable hours. Besides, Jenna, his wife, would be busy pursuing her MBA at Eastern State University. While at Bluegrass, Garth worked on a wide range of IS projects. He was confident that he had the requisite technical expertise to excel at his new job.

Eastern Oceanography Institute was an independently funded research facility aligned with Eastern State University. Approximately 50 full- and part-time staff worked at the institute. They worked on research grants funded by the National Science Foundation (NSF) and the United Nations (UN), as well as research financed by private industry. There were typically 7 to 9 major research projects under way at any one time, as well as 20 to 25 smaller projects. One-third of the institute's scientists had part-time teaching assignments at ESU and used the institute to conduct their own basic research.

FIRST YEAR AT EOI

Garth made a point of introducing himself to the various groups of people upon his arrival at the institute. Still, his contact with the staff was limited. He spent most of his time becoming familiar with EOI's information system, training his staff, responding to unexpected problems, and working on various projects. Garth suffered from food allergies and refrained from informal staff lunches at nearby restaurants. He stopped regularly attending the biweekly staff meetings in order to devote more time to his work. He only attended the meetings when there was a specific agenda item regarding his operation.

The IS staff at EOI consisted of two full-time assistants, Tom Jackson and Celeste Jackson. They were supported by five part-time student assistants from the Computer Science Department. Celeste Jackson was assigned full-time to a large five-year NSF grant aimed at creating a virtual library of oceanographic research. Celeste worked out of the project leader's office and had very little interaction with Garth or Tom. Garth's relationship with Tom was awkward from the start. He found out, after the fact, that Tom thought he would get the job as director. They never talked about it, but he sensed tension the first couple of months on the job. One of the problems was that he and Tom were totally different personalities. Tom was gregarious and very talkative. He had a habit of walking around the institute after lunch, talking to different scientists and researchers. Often this led to useful information. Garth, on the other hand, preferred to stay in his office, working on various assignments, and ventured out only when called

*Prepared by E. W. Larson and V. T. Raja, senior instructor at the College of Business, Oregon State University.

upon. While Garth felt Tom was not on top of the latest developments, as he was, he respected Tom's work.

Last month the system was corrupted by a virus introduced over the Internet. Garth devoted an entire weekend to restoring the system to operation. A recurring headache was one of the servers, code-named "Poncho," that would occasionally shut down for no apparent reason. Instead of replacing it, he decided to nurse Poncho along until it could be replaced. His work was frequently interrupted by frantic calls from staff researchers who needed immediate help on a variety of computer-related problems. He was shocked at how computer illiterate some of the researchers were and how he had to guide them through some of the basics of e-mail management and database configuration. He did find time to help Assistant Professor Amanda Johnson on a project. Amanda was the only researcher to respond to Garth's e-mail announcing that the IS staff was available to help on projects. Garth created a virtual project office on the Internet so that Amanda could collaborate with colleagues from institutes in Italy and Thailand on a UN research grant. He looked forward to the day when he could spend more time on fun projects like that.

THE BLUE SKY CONVERSION PROJECT

The "Blue Sky" conversion project began in earnest four months ago. Ahmet Green returned from Washington, D.C., with grim news. The economic downturn was going to lead to a dramatic reduction in funding. He anticipated as much as a 25 percent reduction in annual budget over the next three to five years. This would lead to staff reductions and cutting of operating costs. One cost-cutting measure was moving IT operations to the "cloud." Ahmet had first proposed the idea to Garth after attending a meeting with several directors of other institutes who faced similar financial challenges.

The basic strategy was to move all of the institute's databases, software, and even hardware to a "private cloud." Staff would use their current PCs to simply access more powerful machines over the Internet. These powerful machines could be partitioned and configured differently according to the needs of research staff, giving each staff member his or her own virtual machine (VM). Staff could also access, use, and share virtual servers over the Internet as needed. Garth worked with the institute's accountant on a cost/benefit analysis. From their standpoint it made perfect sense. First, the institute would not have to replace or upgrade aging computers and servers. Second, the institute would enjoy significant IT savings, since they would pay for only IT resources actually used. They would not have to make any major IT capital expenditures. Third, cloud computing would provide the scientists greater flexibility by accessing desired resources or software from anywhere at any time. And finally, once the system was up and running, the institute would no longer need the services of at least one full-time IT worker. Ahmet decided to name the project "Blue Sky" to put a positive spin on the conversion.

At first the associate directors balked at the idea. Some had a hard time conceptualizing what cloud computing meant. Others were worried about security and reliability. In the end they reluctantly signed off on the project when given alternative cost-cutting initiatives. Garth assured them that cloud computing was the wave of the future and setting up or accessing virtual machines on the "cloud" was as simple as setting up or accessing their G-mail account.

The conversion project would be completed in stages. The first stage was selecting a provider. The next stage was migrating non-mission critical information to the cloud.

The next stages would entail migrating each of the six big grant projects in waves to the cloud. The final stage would focus on the remaining smaller projects. Training would be an integral part of each stage. The institute would maintain a back-up for all the data until six months after complete conversion. After that the cloud service provider would be responsible for backing up the data.

At first Tom was excited about the project. He was savvy enough to realize that this was the future of computing and he was intrigued with how the whole system would work. His feelings soon changed when he started thinking about the potential ramifications for his job. He asked Garth more than once what the department would look like after the conversion. Garth replied vaguely that they would figure it out once the system was up and running.

A task force was formed, headed by Garth, to select a cloud service provider. Garth was surprised by how many choices there were. Plans and cost structures varied considerably. After much deliberation the committee narrowed the choices to three. The first two were among the bigger providers in the industry, VMWARE and Microsoft. The third choice was a relatively new company, OpenRange, which offered a cheaper solution. Tom argued that even though the bigger providers would cost more, they were a much safer bet. Garth responded that he had confidence in OpenRange and cutting costs was the primary goal behind the project. In the end, Garth persuaded the committee to choose OpenRange. Not only would cost be significantly cheaper, but OpenRange would help in training the personnel. Garth liked this idea; training was not his strength, and he wasn't looking forward to holding senior scientists' hands through the process.

It took Garth and Tom six weeks to identify noncritical data. Garth worked on the back end while Tom met with staff to identify noncritical information. The motto was when in doubt, leave it out. The actual migration only took a couple of days. Training proved to be more problematic. The staff sent by OpenRange appeared to be straight out of college. While enthusiastic, they were inexperienced in the art of getting older staff to accept and use new technology. Many trainers had the habit of simply doing things for the staff instead of showing them how to do it themselves. It all came to a head when a power outage at the OpenRange storage system shut down and disrupted operations at the institute for 36 hours.

Ahmet held an emergency meeting. Garth reported that the power outage occurred in North East India and that OpenRange was expanding their back-up systems. Several members argued that the institute should switch to one of the bigger providers. When this came up, Garth looked at Tom and was relieved when he remained silent. In the end, Ahmet announced that it would be too costly to switch providers and Garth and his staff would have to make the conversion work. Tom stepped forward and volunteered to manage the training. Everyone agreed that the institute should hire three more part-time assistants to help the staff with the transition.

Garth worked behind the scenes, coordinating with his counterparts at OpenRange and planning the conversion of the next segment of the project. Tom worked closely with the OpenRange trainers and refocused their attention on teaching. Resistance was pretty high at first. Tom used his personal contacts within the institute to rally support for the change. He persuaded Garth to change the conversion schedule to begin with those projects in which the leads were most supportive of the change. Training improved and Tom created some useful training materials, including short videos on how to access the virtual machines.

One problem that occurred early in the process involved a graduate research assistant who mistakenly hit the wrong commands and terminated her virtual machine instead of logging off. This resulted in complete loss of that machine's data in the cloud. Fortunately, the institute had back-up and Tom was able to recover the work. Collaborating with some programmers at OpenRange, Tom wrote a program that triggered a pop-up message on the screen, warning users not to terminate their virtual machine when logging off.

CLOSING OUT THE BLUE SKY PROJECT

It took almost a year to complete the Blue Sky project. After the rocky beginning things went relatively smoothly. Acceptance was slow, but Tom and his staff worked with the staff to demonstrate how the new system would make their work easier. Two student assistants were always on call to address any problem or question. Garth spent most of his time interacting with the OpenRange counterparts and rarely ventured out of his office. He had his student assistants collect information from staff so he could configure the new virtual machines to exactly match staff needs. He put in long hours so that customized databases would work in the new environment. This proved to be a very difficult task and he was quite pleased with his work. Twice OpenRange experienced momentary power shortages at their server facility, which disrupted work at the institute. Garth was happy to report that OpenRange was breaking ground on an alternative server system in Ukraine.

When the institute conducted a retrospective (project review) on the Blue Sky project, some still questioned the choice of OpenRange as a cloud service provider but praised Tom's work on helping the staff make the transition. Despite the criticism over the choice of OpenRange, Garth felt good about the project. The system was up and running and the staff was beginning to enjoy the flexibility it provided. Besides, the institute would achieve real savings from the new system.

Soon after the retrospective, Garth was surprised when Ahmet walked into his office and closed the door. Ahmet began by thanking Garth for his work on the project. He then cleared his throat and said, "You know, Garth, one of the consequences of Blue Sky is reducing our IT staff. Celeste is needed for the data library project. So it comes down to you or Tom. Frankly, there is general agreement among the associate directors that Tom is essential to the institute. I know this might come as a surprise to you, and before I make a decision I want to give you a chance to change my mind."

1. If you were Garth, how would you respond to the director?
2. What mistakes did Garth make?
3. What are the lessons to be learned from this case?

Case 10.2

Tom Bray

Tom Bray was mulling over today's work schedule as he looked across the bay at the storm that was rolling in. It was the second official day of the Pegasus project and now the real work was about to begin.

Pegasus was a two-month renovation project for AtlantiCorp, a major financial institution headquartered in Boston, Massachusetts. Tom's group was responsible for installing the furniture and equipment in the newly renovated Accounts Receivable

Department on the third floor. The Pegasus project was a dedicated project team formed out of AtlantiCorp's Facilities Department, with Tom as the project lead.

Tom was excited because this was his first *major league* project and he was looking forward to practicing a new management style—management by wandering around (MBWA). He had been exposed to MBWA in a business class in college, but it wasn't until he attended an AtlantiCorp leadership training seminar that he decided to change how he managed people. The trainer was a devout MBWA champion ("You can't manage people from a computer!"). Furthermore, the testimonies from his peers reinforced the difference that MBWA can make when it comes to working on projects.

Tom had joined the facilities group at AtlantiCorp five years earlier after working for Electronic Data Systems for six years. He quickly demonstrated technical competencies and good work habits. He was encouraged to take all the internal project management workshops offered by AtlantiCorp. On his last two projects he served as assistant project manager responsible for procurement and contract management.

He had read books about the soft side of project management, and MBWA made sense—after all, people, not tools, get projects done. His boss had told him he needed to refine his people skills and work on developing rapport with team members. MBWA seemed like a perfect solution.

Tom reviewed the list of team member names; some of the foreign names were real tongue twisters. For example, one of his better workers was from Thailand and her name was Penphim Bhatravidhya. He practiced saying "Pen-pim Phat-tha-ra-vit." He got up, tucked in his shirt, and walked out of his office and down to the floor where his team was busy unloading equipment.

Tom said "Hi" to the first few workers he met until he encountered Jack and three other workers. Jack was busy pulling hardware out of a box while his teammates were standing around, talking. Tom blurted, "Come on, guys, we've got work to do." They quickly separated and began unloading boxes.

The rest of the visit seemed to go well. He helped Steve unload a heavy box and managed to get an appreciative grin from Penphim when he almost correctly pronounced her name. Satisfied, Tom went back up to his office, thinking that MBWA wouldn't be that tough to do.

After responding to e-mails and calling some vendors, Tom ventured back out to see how things were going downstairs. When he got there, the floor was weirdly quiet. People were busy doing their work, and his attempts at generating conversation elicited stiff responses. He left thinking that maybe MBWA is going to be tougher than he thought.

1. What do you think is going on at the end of this case?
2. What should Tom do next and why?
3. What can be learned from this case?

Case 10.3

Cerberus Corporation*

Cerberus is a successful producer of specialty chemicals. It operates nine large campus sites in the United States, with a number of different business units on each site. These business units operate independently, with direct reporting to corporate headquarters.

* Courtesy of John Sloan, Oregon State University.

Site functions such as safety, environmental, and facilities management report to a host organization—typically the business unit that is the largest user of their services.

SUSAN STEELE

Susan Steele has worked in the facilities group at the Cerberus Richmond site for the last two years. The facilities manager, Tom Stern, reports to the general manager of the largest business unit on-site, the highly profitable Adhesives and Sealants Division. Susan started with Cerberus when she graduated with her business degree from Awsum University. She was excited about her new assignment—leading a project for the first time. She remembered Tom saying, "We've got office furniture dating back to the '80s. There are those ugly green-top desks that look like they came from military surplus! I'm especially concerned about computer workstation ergonomics—it's a major issue that we absolutely must fix! I want you to lead a project to transition our office furniture to the new corporate standard."

Susan assembled her project team: Jeff, the site safety/ergonomics engineer; Gretchen, the space planner; Cindy, the move coordinator; and Kari, the accounting liaison for Facilities. At their first meeting, everyone agreed that ergonomics was the most urgent concern. All five business units responded to a workstation survey that identified injury-causing ergonomics. The team was developing a plan to replace old desks with new, ergo-adjustable furniture by the end of the year. Susan asked Kari about the budget, and Kari responded, "Facilities should not pay for this. We want the individual business units to pay so that the costs will show where they are incurred."

Gretchen spoke up: "You know, we've got lots of department moves going on constantly. Everybody is always jockeying for space and location as their business needs change. Besides the ergonomics, could we say that only corporate standard furniture gets moved? That would force changing some of the stuff that's just plain ugly." Everyone agreed that this was a great idea.

Susan presented the project plan to Tom and got a green light to proceed.

JON WOOD

Jon Wood is a planning manager, with 22 years' experience at Cerberus. His business unit, Photographic Chemicals Division (PCD), is losing money. Digital photography is continuing to reduce the size of the market, and PCD is having trouble matching the competition's relentless price-cutting. Jon recently transferred to Richmond from corporate headquarters, where he ran the economic forecasting group. He is considered a new broom, and he is determined to sweep clean.

One of Jon's early actions was to negotiate with his general manager for a department move. Money was tight, and the site facilities function charged an arm and a leg for moves (covering all their fixed overhead, the operations people groused). However, Jon felt it was important to move from Building 4, where they were next to Production, to Building 6, where they could be close to Marketing, Forecasting, and Accounting. His general manager agreed, and there was lots of excitement in his team about their upcoming move. Jon assigned one of his planners, Richard, to work with the facilities team on the layout and move plan for the group. Things seemed to be going fine—Jon saw Richard sitting down with the move coordinator, and they seemed to be on track.

The day before the move, Jon hung up the phone from a particularly tense teleconference with a Canadian subcontractor. Production was not going well, and product availability would be tight for the rest of the quarter. Clustered around his desk were Richard, Cindy, and a person he hadn't met yet, Susan. After hurried introductions,

Susan told Jon that his filing cabinets could not be moved. The cabinets are large lateral files, 5 feet wide and 2 feet deep, a combination of both filing cabinets and bookshelves. Jon brought them with him from corporate headquarters because he thought they looked nice with their dark grey steel sides and wood veneer tops. Susan told him that he would have to replace them with new corporate standard cabinets, virtually the same size. Jon said, "You mean you want me to throw away perfectly good filing cabinets and spend another $2,000 on new ones, just so they match? I won't do it!"

Susan replied, "Then I won't authorize the movement of the old cabinets."

Jon said, "You're joking—these cabinets are grey, the new ones are grey—the only difference is the wood top! You'd throw away $2,000 for nothing?"

Susan replied stiffly, "I'm sorry, that's the policy."

Jon said, "I don't care what the policy is. If I have to move them myself, those cabinets are not going to the dump. My division is losing money and I'm not going to throw money away. If you don't like it, you're going to have to get your general manager to convince my general manager to make me do it. Now would you please leave so I can get some work done."

1. If you were Susan, what would you do?
2. What, if anything, could Susan have done differently to avoid this problem?
3. What could the management of Cerberus do to more effectively manage situations like this?

Case 10.4

Navigating Communication Challenges in Global Remote Teams

In the wake of Covid-19, the project teams at XYZ Digital (an in-house IT and Digital Solutions subsidiary) were not only restricted from meeting their stakeholders around the globe but also each other. A high visibility project to automate the global marketing process from end-to-end was well underway when all teams were restricted to their home offices. The business stakeholders were based in Paris, France, and Boston, USA. The development team was based in Lisbon, Portugal. The PMO was based in Bangalore, India. The team, however, viewed this interruption as another curve ball that Agile Development Method was designed to tackle. While the work was challenging as it required the teams to communicate with each other at odd hours (owing to the time zones) on almost a daily basis, it soon settled into a routine that worked well for the project teams all around.

A pace was set up to interact with different stakeholders everyday or every week based on their priority and involvement. There were weekly and biweekly touchpoints set up for all stakeholders to align on the progress and roadmap internally. Daily standups were used to discuss the objectives and responsibility for each day. Sprints were kept short and were often followed by a demo as well as a testing period for all stakeholders. This hands-on approach kept the whole team invested and the final delivery had no surprises for anyone. It was a deliberate success that was achieved by persistent and effective communication that helped the team overcome the obstacles of remote working.

Case 10.5

Poor Communication Leads to Loss of Customer

HiltopFilters Pvt Ltd. is one of the leading filter manufacturers in India with OEM customers. The company got one project from one of the leading compressor manufacturers in the USA with some unique requirements of assembly for compressor external exhaust. The assigned team was based in Pune and the entire communication was conducted over the calls and emails. The first phase regarding report submission and product design approval was done without any difficulties.

The customer's design team was connected with the project manager to incorporate timely changes in the product as per new requirements. Later during manufacturing, continuous defects were received while testing the parts. There was no direct communication between the production head and customer's design team head, which led to the production head having to approach the project manager and then the project manager had to convey the same to the customer while doing any changes in the production process. Due to a lack of knowledge about design parameters, production process and machinery, the project manager was not able to convey the exact requirements to the production head. So, after so many trials of product testing, the company was not able to deliver the expected filtration ratio for that product and the customer rejected the further orders which turned out to be a loss of a potential customer in the global market.

Design elements: Snapshot from Practice, Highlight box, Case icon: Sky Designs/Shutterstock

CHAPTER ELEVEN

11 Managing Project Teams

LEARNING OBJECTIVES

After reading this chapter you should be able to:

11-1 Identify key characteristics of a high-performance project team.

11-2 Distinguish the different stages of team development.

11-3 Understand the impact situational factors have on project team development.

11-4 Identify strategies for developing a high-performance project team.

11-5 Distinguish functional conflict from dysfunctional conflict, and describe strategies for encouraging functional conflict and discouraging dysfunctional conflict.

11-6 Understand the challenges of managing virtual project teams.

11-7 Recognize the different pitfalls that can occur in a project team.

OUTLINE

11.1 The Five-Stage Team Development Model

11.2 Situational Factors Affecting Team Development

11.3 Building High-Performance Project Teams

11.4 Managing Virtual Project Teams

11.5 Project Team Pitfalls

Summary

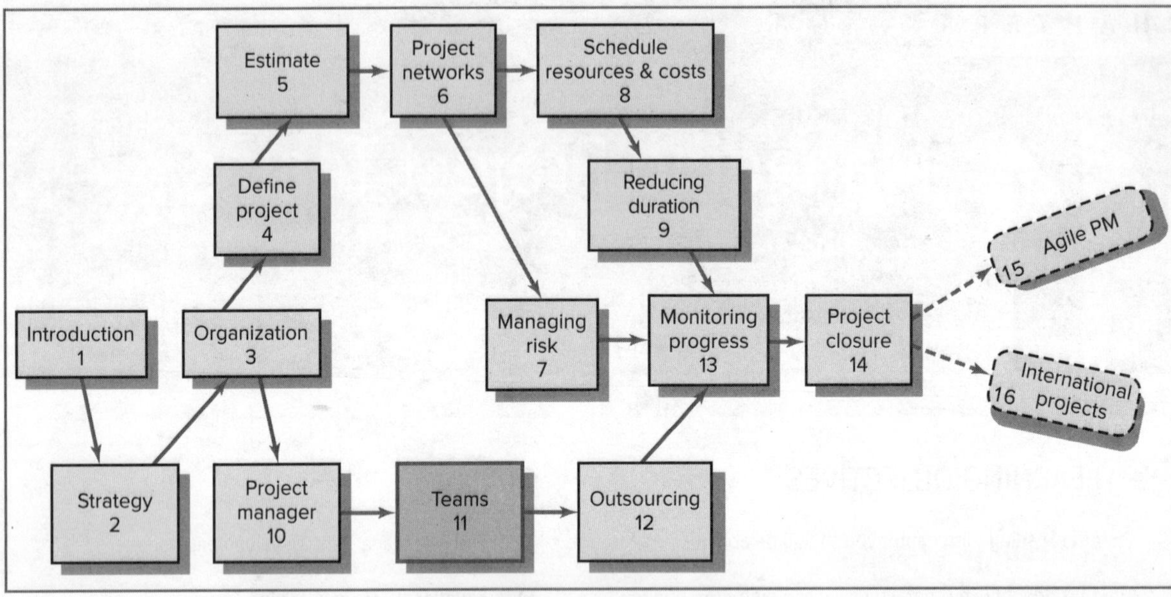

Coming together is a beginning. Keeping together is progress. Working together is success.

—Henry Ford, founder of the Ford Motor Co.

LO 11-1

Identify key characteristics of a high-performance project team.

The magic and power of teams are captured in the term *synergy,* which is derived from the Greek word *sunergos:* "working together." There is positive and negative synergy. The essence of positive synergy can be found in the statement "The whole is greater than the sum of the parts." Conversely, negative synergy occurs when the whole is less than the sum of the parts. Mathematically, these two states can be symbolized by the following equations:

$$\text{Positive Synergy } 1 + 1 + 1 + 1 + 1 = 10$$

$$\text{Negative Synergy } 1 + 1 + 1 + 1 + 1 = 2 \text{ (or even} -2)$$

Synergy perhaps can best be seen on a basketball court, a soccer pitch, or a football field where teammates play as one to defeat a superior foe (see Snapshot from Practice 11.1: The 2008 Olympic Redeem Team).

Although less visible than in team sports, positive and negative synergy can also be observed and felt in the daily operations of project teams. Here is a description from one team member:

> Instead of operating as one big team we fractionalized into a series of subgroups. The marketing people stuck together as well as the systems guys. A lot of time was wasted gossiping and complaining about each other. When the project started slipping behind schedule, everyone started covering their tracks and trying to pass the blame on to others. After a while we avoided direct conversation and resorted to e-mail. Management finally pulled the plug and brought in another team to salvage the project. It was one of the worst project management experiences in my life.

SNAPSHOT FROM PRACTICE 11.1 The 2008 Olympic Redeem Team*

In the 2004 Olympics in Athens, 12 years after Magic Johnson and Michael Jordan led the U.S. Dream Team to Olympic gold in Barcelona, the U.S. Basketball Team, composed of NBA stars, lost not once but three times to international competition. For the first time in Olympic history, the United States settled for a bronze medal in men's basketball. Basketball was no longer America's game.

An autopsy of the debacle in Athens turned up a severe case of negative synergy. The causes were many. The team featured only three holdovers from the group that had qualified the previous summer. Seven of the original invitees withdrew. In the end, 14 players turned down Uncle Sam, invoking excuses from family obligations to nagging injuries to the security situation in Greece. As a result, coach Larry Brown took charge of a team with an average age of 23 years, and it showed. Behind the scenes, problems of dress and punctuality festered and, on the eve of the games, Brown wanted to send several players home. The million-dollar players were overconfident and assumed that their individual brilliance would prevail. An over-reliance on one-on-one basketball and poor team defense doomed them as they lost games to Puerto Rico, Lithuania, and Argentina.

Enter Jerry Colangelo, 68, former coach, player, and president of the Phoenix Suns. "The way they conducted themselves left a lot to be desired," he says of the 2004 team. "Watching and listening to how people reacted to our players, I knew we'd hit bottom." Colangelo told NBA commissioner David Stern that he would only assume duties as managing director if he was given complete control. As a measure of how abysmal the situation was, he immediately got what he asked for.

In 2005 Colangelo met face-to-face with every prospective national player, to hear in their own words why they wanted to represent their country. The few good men to set things right wouldn't be paid or guaranteed playing time, much less a starting spot. A key recruit was superstar LeBron James, who had been tagged "LeBronze" after his performance on the disappointing 2004 team. Colangelo says, "I got buy-in. Halfway through my talk with him, LeBron said, I'm in." Kobe Bryant soon followed and all but 2 of the 30 top NBA stars accepted Colangelo's offer.

Mike Krzyzewski, the college coach at Duke, was hired with one project objective in mind—win the gold medal. To do so he had to change the attitude of team USA. They had to subordinate their superstar egos and buy in to the concept of team ball. A blessing in disguise was being knocked out of the 2006 world championship by a Greek team. The players came away from that disappointment committed to team ball as extra passes became the staple in practices. The change in attitude was evident in more subtle ways. The USA on the uniforms was bright red, while the players' names were muted blue. The players no longer referred to hoops as "our game" and spoke about how it had become the world's game. Even the team's official slogan (United We Rise) and unofficial nickname (the Redeem Team) implied room for improvement.

Sipa/Shutterstock

The team bought into a common objective. Team USA marched to the final gold medal game by beating opponents by an average margin of 30+ points. Experts marveled not so much at the victory margin but at how well they played as a team. "Our goal is to win a gold medal and be humble about it," said Jason Kidd, six-time all-pro point guard, "and if we do it by 50, to make sure it's because we're playing the right way." Nothing exemplified the right way more than a moment in the final, in which flawless ball movement from the Redeemers for 16 seconds, without a dribble being taken, culminated with Dwight Howard receiving a perfect pass for an uncontested dunk.

In the end, they didn't dominate the gold medal game. Spain proved to be inspired opponents. They simply closed the game out and for the first time since NBA players have gone to the Olympics, the USA played as a team rather than showboating individuals.

*A. Wolff, "The Redeem Team: New Nickname, New Outlook for U.S. at Olympics," si.com, July 22, 2008. Accessed 5/12/23; "Top Facts about the U.S. Stars of 'The Redeem Team'," www.olympics.com, January 25, 2023. Accessed 5/13/23.

Fortunately, the same individual was also able to recount a more positive experience:

> There was a contagious excitement within the team. Sure, we had our share of problems and setbacks, but we dealt with them straight on and, at times, were able to do the impossible. We all cared about the project and looked out for each other. At the same time we challenged each other to do better. It was one of the most exciting times in my life.

The following is a set of characteristics commonly associated with high-performing teams that exhibit **positive synergy**[1]**:**

1. The team shares a sense of common purpose, and each member is willing to work toward achieving project objectives.
2. The team identifies individual talents and expertise and uses them, depending on the project's needs at any given time. At these times, the team willingly accepts the influence and leadership of the members whose skills are relevant to the immediate task.
3. Roles are balanced and shared to facilitate both the accomplishment of tasks and feelings of group cohesion and morale.
4. The team exerts energy toward problem solving rather than allowing itself to be drained by interpersonal issues or competitive struggles.
5. Differences of opinion are encouraged and freely expressed.
6. To encourage risk taking and creativity, mistakes are treated as opportunities for learning rather than reasons for punishment.
7. Members set high personal standards of performance and encourage each other to realize the objectives of the project.
8. Members identify with the team and consider it an important source of both professional and personal growth.

High-performing teams become champions, create breakthrough products, exceed customer expectations, and overcome project obstacles. They are bonded together by mutual interdependency and a common goal or vision. They trust each other and exhibit a high level of collaboration.

11.1 The Five-Stage Team Development Model

LO 11-2

Distinguish the different stages of team development.

Many experts argue that just as infants develop in certain ways during their first months of life, groups develop in a predictable manner. One of the most popular models identifies five stages (see Figure 11.1) through which groups develop into effective teams (Tuckman, 1965; Tuckman & Jensen, 1977):

1. **Forming.** During this initial stage, the members get acquainted with each other and understand the scope of the project. They begin to establish ground rules by trying to find out what behaviors are acceptable with respect to both the project (what role they will play, what performance expectations are) and interpersonal relations (who's really in charge). This stage is completed once members begin to think of themselves as part of a group.
2. **Storming.** As the name suggests, this stage is marked by a high degree of internal conflict. Members accept that they are part of a project group but resist the

[1] See, Schein, E. H., *Process Consultation,* 2nd ed. (Reading, MA: Addison-Wesley, 1988), pp. 42–43; Likert, R., *New Patterns of Management* (New York: McGraw-Hill, 1961), pp. 162–77.

FIGURE 11.1
The Five-Stage Team Development Model

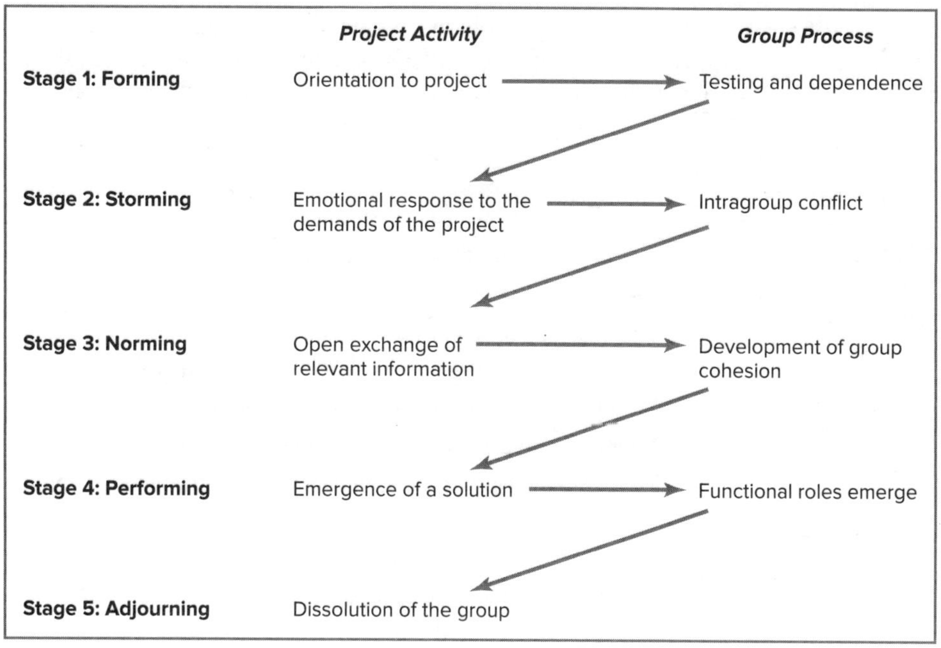

constraints that the project and group put on their individuality. There is conflict over who will control the group and how decisions will be made. As these conflicts are resolved, the project manager's leadership becomes accepted, and the group moves to the next stage.

3. **Norming.** The third stage is one in which close relationships develop and the group demonstrates cohesiveness. Feelings of camaraderie and shared responsibility for the project are heightened. The norming phase is complete when the group structure solidifies and the group establishes a common set of expectations about how members should work together.
4. **Performing.** The team operating structure at this point is fully functional and accepted. Group energy has moved from getting to know each other and how the group will work together to accomplishing the project goals.
5. **Adjourning.** For conventional work groups, performing is the last stage of their development. However, for project teams, there is a completion phase. During this stage, the team prepares for its own disbandment. High performance is no longer a top priority. Instead, attention is devoted to wrapping up the project. The members' responses vary in this stage. Some members are upbeat, basking in the project team's accomplishments. Others may be depressed over the loss of camaraderie and friendships gained during the project's life.

This model has several implications for those working on project teams. The first is that the model provides a framework for the group to understand its own development. Project managers have found it useful to share the model with their teams. It helps members accept the tensions of the storming phase, and it directs their focus to move toward the more productive phases. Another implication is that it stresses the importance of the norming phase, which contributes significantly to the level of productivity experienced during the performing phase. Project managers, as we will see, have to take an active role in shaping group norms that will contribute to ultimate project success. For an alternative model of group development see Research Highlight 11.1: The Punctuated Equilibrium Model of Group Development.

11.2 Situational Factors Affecting Team Development

LO 11-3

Understand the impact situational factors have on project team development.

Experience and research indicate that high-performance project teams are much more likely to develop under the following conditions.[2]

- There are 10 or fewer members per team.
- Members volunteer to serve on the project team.
- Members serve on the project from beginning to end.
- Members are assigned to the project full time.
- Members are part of an organizational culture that fosters cooperation and trust.
- Members report solely to the project manager.
- All relevant functional areas are represented on the team.
- The project involves a compelling objective.
- Members are located within conversational distance of each other.

In reality, it is rare that a project manager is assigned a project that meets all of these conditions. For example, many projects' requirements dictate the active involvement of more than 10 members and may consist of a complex set of interlocking teams comprising more than 100 professionals. In many organizations, functional managers or central manpower offices assign project members with little input from the project manager. To optimize resource utilization, team member involvement may be part time, and/or participants may move into and out of the project team on an as-needed basis. In the case of ad hoc task forces, no member of the team works full time on the project. In many corporations, an NIH (not invented here) culture discourages collaboration across functional boundaries.

Team members often report to different managers, and in some cases, the project manager has no direct input over performance appraisals and advancement opportunities of team members. Key functional areas may not be represented during the entire duration of the project but may only be involved in a sequential manner. Not all projects have a compelling objective. It can be hard to get members excited about mundane projects such as a simple product extension or a conventional apartment complex. Finally, team members are often scattered across different corporate offices and buildings or, across the entire globe.

It is important for project managers and team members to recognize the situational constraints they are operating under and do the best they can. It is naive to believe that every project team has the same potential to evolve into a high-performance team. Under less-than-ideal conditions, it may be a struggle just to meet project objectives. Ingenuity, discipline, and sensitivity to team dynamics are essential to maximizing the performance of a project team.

[2] See, for example: Homans, G. C., *Social Behavior: Its Elementary Forms* (New York: Harcourt Brace Jovanovich, 1961); Sherif, M., *Group Conflict and Cooperation: Their Social Psychology* (Chicago: Aldine, 1967); Seta, J. J., P. B. Paulus, and J. Schkade, "Effects of Group Size and Proximity under Cooperative and Competitive Conditions," *Journal of Personality and Social Psychology,* vol. 98, no. 2 (1976), pp. 47–53; Zander, A., *Making Groups Effective* (San Francisco: Jossey-Bass, 1994).

Research Highlight 11.1

The Punctuated Equilibrium Model of Group Development*

Connie Gersick's research suggests that groups don't develop in a universal sequence of stages, as suggested by the five-phase model. Her research, which is based on the systems concept of *punctuated equilibrium,* found that the *timing* of when groups form and actually change the way they work is highly consistent. What makes this research appealing is that it is based on studies of more than a dozen field and laboratory task forces assigned to complete a specific project.

Gersick's research reveals that each group begins with a unique approach to accomplishing its project, which is set in its first meeting and includes the behavior and roles that dominate phase I. Phase I continues until one-half of the allotted time for project completion has expired (regardless of actual amount of time). At this midpoint, a major transition occurs that includes the dropping of the group's old norms and behavior patterns and the emergence of new behavior and working relationships that contribute to increased progress toward completing the project. The last meeting is marked by accelerated activity to complete the project. These findings are summarized in Figure 11.2.

The remarkable discovery in these studies was that each group experienced its transition at the same point in its calendar—roughly halfway between the first meeting and the completion deadline—despite the fact that some groups spent as little as an hour on their project, while others spent six months. It was as if the groups universally experienced a midlife crisis at this point. The midpoint appeared to work like an alarm clock, heightening members' awareness that time was limited and they needed to get moving. Within the context of the five-stage model, it suggests that groups begin by combining the forming and norming stages, then go through a period of low performing, followed by storming, then a period of high performing, and finally adjourning.

Gersick's findings suggest that there are natural transition points during the life of teams in which the group is receptive to change and that such a moment naturally occurs at the midpoint of a project. However, a manager does not want to have to wait 6 months on a complicated 12-month project for a team to get its act together! Here it is important to note that Gersick's groups were working on relatively small-scale projects, such as a 4-person bank task force in charge of designing a new bank account in 1 month and a 12-person medical task force in charge of reorganizing two units of a treatment facility. In most cases, no formal project plan was established.

The results point to the importance of good project management and the need to establish deadlines and milestones. By imposing a series of deadlines associated with important milestones, it is possible to create multiple transition points for natural group development. For example, a 12-month construction project can be broken down into six to eight significant milestones with the challenge of meeting each deadline producing the prerequisite tension for elevating team performance.

*C. J. Gersick, "Time and Transition in Work Teams: Toward a New Model of Group Development," *Academy of Management Journal,* vol. 31, no. 1 (March 1988), pp. 9–41; C. J. Gersick, "Making Time Predictable Transitions in Task Groups," *Academy of Management Journal,* vol. 32, no. 2 (June 1989), pp. 274–309.

FIGURE 11.2 The Punctuated Equilibrium Model of Group Development

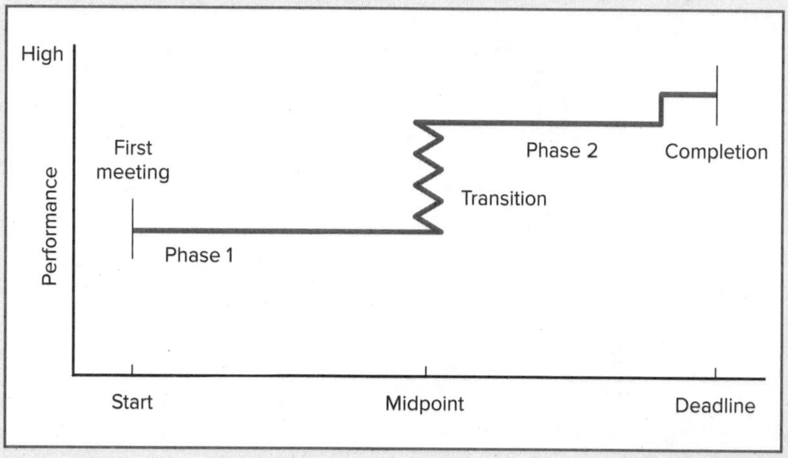

11.3 Building High-Performance Project Teams

LO 11-4

Identify strategies for developing a high-performance project team.

Project managers play a key role in developing high-performance project teams. They recruit members, conduct meetings, establish a team identity, create a common sense of purpose or a shared vision, manage a reward system that encourages teamwork, orchestrate decision making, resolve conflicts that emerge within the team, and rejuvenate the team when energy wanes (see Figure 11.3). Project managers take advantage of situational factors that naturally contribute to team development while improvising around those factors that inhibit team development. In doing so they exhibit a highly interactive management style that exemplifies teamwork and, as discussed in Chapter 10, manage the interface between the team and the rest of the organization.

Recruiting Project Members

The process of selecting and recruiting project members will vary across organizations. Two important factors affecting recruitment are the importance of the project and the management structure being used to complete the project. Often for high-priority projects that are critical to the future of the organization, the project managers will be given virtual carte blanche to select whomever they deem necessary. For less significant projects, personnel will simply be assigned to the project.

In many matrix structures, the functional manager controls who is assigned to the project; the project manager will have to work with the functional manager to obtain the necessary personnel. Even in a project team where members are selected and assigned full time to the project, the project manager has to be sensitive to the needs of others. There is no better way to create enemies within an organization than to be perceived as unnecessarily robbing other departments of essential personnel.

Experienced project managers stress the importance of asking for volunteers. However, this desirable step often is outside the manager's control. Still, the value of having team members volunteer for the project as opposed to being assigned cannot be overlooked. Agreeing to work on the project is the first step toward building personal commitment to the project. Such commitment will be essential to maintain motivation when the project hits hard times and extra effort is required.

FIGURE 11.3
Creating a High-Performance Project Team

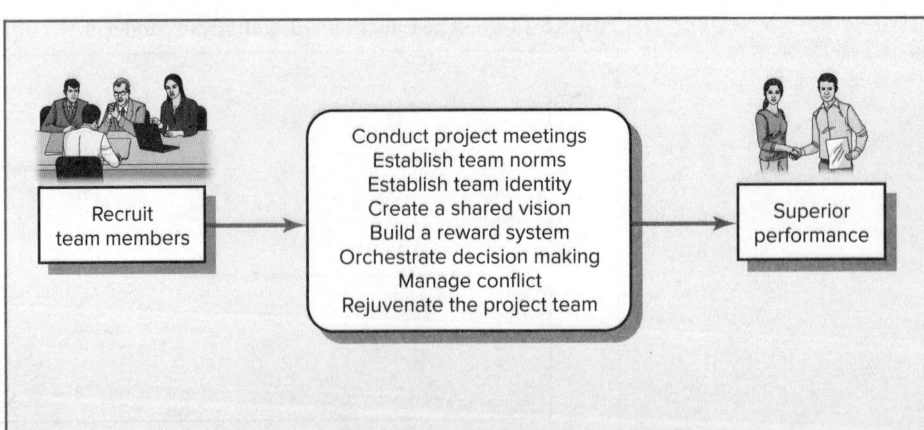

When selecting and recruiting team members, project managers naturally look for individuals with the necessary experience and knowledge/technical skills critical for project completion. At the same time, there are less obvious considerations that need to be factored into the recruitment process:

- **Problem-solving ability.** If the project is complex and fuzzy, then a manager wants people who are good at working under uncertainty and have strong problem-identification and problem-solving skills. These people are likely to be bored and less productive working on straightforward projects that go by the book.
- **Availability.** Sometimes the people who are most available are not the ones wanted for the team. Conversely, if members recruited are already overcommitted, they may not be able to offer much.
- **Technological expertise.** Managers should be wary of people who know too much about a specific technology. They may be technology buffs who like to study but have a hard time doing the work.
- **Credibility.** The credibility of the project is enhanced by the reputation of the people involved in it. Recruiting a sufficient number of "winners" lends confidence to the project.
- **Political connections.** Managers are wise to recruit individuals who already have a good working relationship with key stakeholders. This is particularly true for projects operating in a matrix environment in which a significant portion of the work will be under the domain of a specific functional department and not the core project team.
- **Ambition, initiative, and energy.** These qualities can make up for a lot of shortcomings in other areas and should not be underestimated.
- **Familiarity.** Research suggests that repeat collaboration stifles creativity and innovation. On challenging, breakthrough projects it is wise to interject the team with experts who have little previous working experience with others (Skilton & Dooley, 2010).

After reviewing the needed skills, the manager should try to find out through the corporate grapevine who is good, who is available, and who might want to work on the project. Some organizations may allow direct interviews. Often a manager will have to expend political capital to get highly prized people assigned to the project.

In matrix environments, the project manager will have to request appointments with functional managers to discuss the project requirements for staffing. The following documents should be available at these discussions: an overall project scope statement, endorsements of top management, and a description of the tasks and general schedule that pertain to the people from their departments. Managers need to be precise as to what attributes they are seeking and why they are important.

Conducting Project Meetings

The First Project Team Meeting Research on team development confirms what project managers have stated: the **project kick-off meeting** is critical to the early functioning of the project team. According to one veteran project manager,

> The first team meeting sets the tone for how the team will work together. If it is disorganized, or becomes bogged down with little sense of closure, then this can often become a self- fulfilling prophecy for subsequent group work. On the other hand, if it is crisply run, focusing on real issues and concerns in an honest and straightforward manner, members come away excited about being part of the project team.

There are typically three objectives project managers try to achieve during the first meeting of the project team. The first is to provide an overview of the project, including the scope and objectives, general schedule, method, and procedures. The second is to begin to address some of the interpersonal concerns captured in the team development model: Who are the other team members? How will I fit in? Will I be able to work with these people? The third and most important objective is to begin to model how the team is going to work together to complete the project. Project managers need to recognize that first impressions are important; their behavior will be carefully monitored and interpreted by team members. This meeting should serve as an exemplary role model for subsequent meetings and reflect the leader's style.

The meeting itself takes a variety of forms. It is not uncommon in major projects for the kick-off meeting to involve one or two days, often at a remote site away from interruptions. This retreat provides sufficient time to complete a preliminary introduction, to begin to establish ground rules, and to define the structure of the project. One advantage of off-site kick-off meetings is that they provide ample opportunity for informal interaction among members during breaks, meals, and evening activities; such informal interactions are critical to forming relationships.

However, many organizations do not have the luxury of holding elaborate retreats. In other cases, the scope of a project does not warrant such an investment of time. In these cases, the key operating principle should be KISS (keep it simple, stupid!). Too often when constrained by time, project managers try to accomplish too much during the first meeting; in such instances, issues do not get fully resolved, and members come away with an information headache.

The project manager needs to remember that the primary goal is to run a productive meeting, and objectives should be realistic, given the time available. If the meeting is only one hour, then the project manager should simply review the scope of the project, discuss how the team was formed, and provide an opportunity for members to introduce themselves to the team.

Establishing Ground Rules Whether as part of an elaborate first meeting or during follow-up meetings, the project manager must quickly begin to establish operational ground rules for how the team will work together. These ground rules involve not only organizational and procedural issues but also normative issues on how the team will interact with each other. Although specific procedures will vary across organizations and projects, some of the major issues that need to be addressed include the following:

Planning Decisions

- How will the project plan be developed?
- Will a specific project management software package be used? If so, which one?
- What are the specific roles and responsibilities of all the participants?
- Who needs to be informed of decisions? How will they be kept informed?
- What is the relative importance of cost, time, and performance?
- What are the deliverables of the project planning process?
- Who will approve and sign off at the completion of each deliverable?
- Who receives each deliverable?

Tracking Decisions

- How will progress be assessed?
- At what level of detail will the project be tracked?
- How will team members get data from each other?
- How often will they get these data?
- Who will generate and distribute reports?
- Who needs to be kept informed about project progress, and how will they be informed?
- What content/format is appropriate for each audience?
- Meetings
  - Where will meetings be located?
  - What kind of meetings will be held?
  - Who will run these meetings?
  - How will agendas be produced?
  - How will information be recorded?

Managing Change Decisions

- How will changes be instituted?
- Who will have change approval authority?
- How will plan changes be documented and evaluated?

Relationship Decisions

- What department or organizations will the team need to interact with during the project?
- What are the roles and responsibilities of each organization (reviewer, approver, creator, user)?
- How will all involved parties be kept informed of deliverables, schedule dates, expectations, etc.?
- How will the team members communicate among themselves?
- What information will and won't be exchanged?

Checklists like these are only a guide; items should be added or deleted as needed. Many of these procedures will have already been established by precedent and will only have to be briefly reviewed. For example, Microsoft Project or Primavera may be the standard software for planning and tracking. Likewise, a firm is likely to have an established format for reporting status information. How to deal with other issues will have to be determined by the project team. When appropriate, the project manager should actively solicit input from the project team members and draw upon their experience and preferred work habits. This process also contributes to their buying into the operational decisions. Decisions should be recorded and circulated to all members.

Establishing Team Norms

During the course of establishing these operational procedures, the project manager, through word and deed, should begin working with members to establish the norms for team interaction. Following are examples of some of the norms researchers have found to be associated with high-performance teams.[3]

- Confidentiality is maintained; no information is shared outside the team unless all agree to it.
- It is acceptable to be in trouble, but it is not acceptable to surprise others. Tell others immediately when deadlines or milestones will not be reached.
- There is zero tolerance for bullying a way through a problem or an issue.
- Agree to disagree, but when a decision has been made, regardless of personal feelings, move forward.
- Respect outsiders, and do not flaunt one's position on the project team.
- Hard work does not get in the way of having fun.

One way of making these norms more tangible is by creating a team charter that goes beyond the scope statement of the project and states in explicit terms the norms and values of the team. This charter should be a collaborative effort on the part of the core team. Project managers can lead by proposing certain tenets, but they need to be open to suggestions from the team. Once there is general agreement to the rules of conduct, each member signs the final document to symbolize commitment to the principles it contains.

Unfortunately, in some cases creating a charter becomes a meaningless ritual because the charter is signed and filed away, never to be discussed again. To have a lasting effect, the charter has to be a legitimate part of the project monitoring system. Just as the team reviews progress toward project objectives, the team assesses the extent to which members are adhering to the principles in the charter.

Project managers play a major role in establishing team norms through personal example. If they freely admit mistakes and share what they have learned from them, other team members will do the same. At the same time, project managers need to intervene when they believe such norms are being violated. They should talk to offenders privately and clearly state their expectations. The amazing thing about groups is that once a group is cohesive, with well-established norms, the members will police themselves so that the manager doesn't have to be the heavy. For example, one project manager confided that the project team had a practice of having a small bean bag present at every meeting. If any one member felt that a colleague was shading the truth, s/he was obligated to toss the bean bag at the speaker. See Snapshot from Practice 11.2: Putting Ford on Fast Forward for examples of norms that encourage innovation.

Managing Subsequent Project Meetings The project kick-off meeting is one of several kinds of meetings required to complete a project. Others are status report meetings, problem-solving meetings, and audit meetings. Issues unique to these meetings will be discussed in subsequent chapters. For now, here are some general guidelines for running effective meetings; they speak directly to the person chairing the meeting.

- Start meetings on time regardless of whether everyone is present.
- Prepare and distribute an agenda prior to the meeting.

[3] See, Katzenbach, J. R., and D. K. Smith, *The Wisdom of Teams* (Boston: Harvard Business School Press, 1993); Bolman, L. G., and T. E. Deal, "What Makes Teams Work," *Organizational Dynamics*, vol. 21, no. 2 (1992), pp. 34–45; Katz, R., "How a Team at Digital Equipment Designed the 'Alpha' Chips," in R. Katz (ed.), *The Human Side of Managing Technological Innovation* (New York: Oxford Press, 1997), pp. 137–48.

SNAPSHOT FROM PRACTICE 11.2 Putting Ford on Fast Forward*

Adam Gryglak was given mission impossible: deliver an all-new Ford diesel engine in less than 36 months. The challenge was all the more daunting in that in the past Ford had outsourced the design and manufacture of diesel engines to Navistar. Not only did he have to meet a ridiculous deadline, but he also had to build an in-house engine from scratch. Gryglak, the chief diesel engineer, knew that success depended on short-circuiting the design process at Ford. So he put together a team of hungry engineers, moved off-site, and shielded the team from anxious top management. He called the project Scorpion after the heavy metal band the Scorpions.

Progress was immediate. Specialists who were used to working only with their own kind became familiar with what the other engineers were up to. "We saved months by knowing hourly what the other guys were thinking and what their problems were," says Pat Morgan, a veteran Ford engineer. "The result was that the engine fit into the truck perfectly the first time, and that almost never happens."

Gryglak also realized that engineers work harder and smarter when they are having fun. To relieve pressure, the engineers played jokes on each other, building full-size snowmen decorated with machine parts on each other's desks. Gryglak encouraged friendly competition. After hitting a critical design milestone the team organized a Pinewood Derby contest. Pinewood Derby is a famous Cub Scout event where young boys whittle toy cars out of wood and race them down a ramp. These were engineers, not Cub Scouts, so instead of wooden cars, the engineers milled cars out of aluminum. Some of the cars even had remote controls and engines.

The fun culture paid off. The new Ford diesel engine was completed on time to critical acclaim. The engine was the first of its kind to use state-of-the-art antipollution technology that met new federal standards. It also had the best fuel economy in its category and wouldn't need significant maintenance for 300,000 miles. The engine was featured in the best-selling F-150 line of trucks and was considered one of the keys to Ford's comeback.

*"Putting Ford on Fast Forward," *BusinessWeek*, October 26, 2009, pp. 58–59.

- Identify an adjournment time.
- Periodically take time to review how effective previous meetings have been.
- Solicit recommendations and implement changes.
- Assign good recordkeeping.
- Review the agenda before beginning, and tentatively allocate time for each item.
- Prioritize issues so that adjustments can be made, given time constraints.
- Encourage active participation of all members by asking questions instead of making statements.
- Summarize decisions, and review assignments for the next meeting.
- Prepare and distribute a summary of the meeting to the appropriate people.
- Recognize accomplishments and positive behavior.

Meetings are often considered anathema to productivity, but this does not have to be the case. The most common complaint is that meetings last too long. Establishing an agenda and adjournment time helps participants budget discussion time and provides a basis for expediting the proceedings. Recordkeeping can be an unwelcome, tedious task. Utilizing laptop computers to record decisions and information in real time can facilitate the communication process. Careful preparation and consistent application of these guidelines can make meetings a vital part of projects.

Establishing a Team Identity

One of the challenges project managers often face in building a team is the lack of full-time involvement of team members. Specialists work on different phases of the project and spend the majority of their time and energy elsewhere. They are often members of multiple teams, each competing for their time and allegiance. Project expert J. D. Frame (1995) points out that for many of these specialists, a specific project is an abstraction; as a consequence, their level of motivation suffers. Project managers need to make the project team as tangible as possible to the participants by developing a unique team identity to which participants can become emotionally attached. Team meetings, co-location of team members, team names, and **team rituals** are common vehicles for doing so.

- **Effective use of meetings.** Periodic team meetings provide an important forum for communicating project information. A less obvious function of project meetings is to help establish a concrete team identity. During project meetings, members see that they are not working alone. They are part of a larger project team, and project success depends on the collective efforts of all the team members. Timely gatherings of all the project participants help define team membership and reinforce a collective identity.
- **Co-location of team members.** The most obvious way to make the project team tangible is to have members work together in a common space. This is not always possible in matrix environments where involvement is part time and members are working on other projects and activities. A worthwhile substitute for co-location is the creation of a project office, sometimes referred to as the project war room or clubhouse. Such rooms are the common meeting place and contain the most significant project documentation. Frequently, their walls are covered with Gantt charts, cost graphs, and other outputs associated with project planning and control. These rooms serve as a tangible sign of project effort.
- **Creation of project team name.** The development of a team name such as the "A-Team" or "Casey's Crusaders" is a common device for making a team more tangible. Frequently an associated team logo is also created. Again, the project manager should rely on the collective ingenuity of the team to come up with the appropriate name and logo. Such symbols then can be affixed to stationery, T-shirts, coffee mugs, and so on to help signify team membership.
- **Get the team to build or do something together early on.** Nothing reinforces a sense of a team more than working on something together. In the case of one international project, the manager simply hosted a potluck dinner where the members brought dishes their countries were famous for.
- **Team rituals.** Just as corporate rituals help establish the unique identity of a firm, similar symbolic actions at the project level can contribute to a unique team subculture. For example, on one project, members were given ties with stripes that corresponded to the number of milestones on the project. After reaching each milestone, the members gathered and cut the next stripe off their ties to signify progress.[4] Katz (2004) reports it was common practice for Digital Equipment's alpha chip design team to recognize people who found a bug in the design by giving them a phosphorescent toy roach. The bigger the bug that was discovered, the bigger the toy roach received. Such rituals help set project work apart from mainstream operations and reinforce a special status.

[4] This anecdote was provided by Dr. Frances Hartman, University of Calgary, Alberta.

[5] Quoted in Senge, P., *The Fifth Discipline*(New York: Doubleday, 1990), p. 209.

Creating a Shared Vision

Unlike project scope statements, which include specific cost, completion dates, and performance requirements, a **project vision** involves the less tangible aspects of project performance. A project vision is an image project team members hold in common about how the project will look upon completion, how they will work together, and/or how customers will accept the project. At its simplest level, a shared vision is the answer to the question "What do we want to create?" Not everyone will have the same vision, but the images should be similar. Visions come in a variety of forms; they can be captured in a slogan or symbol or can be written as a formal vision statement.

What a vision is, is not as important as what it does. A vision inspires members to give their best effort. (See Snapshot from Practice 11.3: A Good Man in a Storm.) Moreover, a shared vision unites professionals with different backgrounds and agendas to a common aspiration. It helps motivate members to subordinate their individual agendas and do what is best for the project. As psychologist Robert Fritz puts it, "In the presence of greatness, pettiness disappears."[5] Visions also provide focus and help communicate less tangible priorities, helping members make appropriate judgment calls. Finally, a shared vision for a project fosters commitment to the long term and discourages expedient responses that collectively dilute the quality of the project.

Visions can be surprisingly simple. For example, the vision for a new car could be expressed as a "pocket rocket." Compare this vision with the more traditional product description—"a sports car in the midprice range." The "pocket rocket" vision provides a much clearer picture of what the final product should be. Design engineers would immediately understand that the car will be both small and fast and that the car should be quick at the getaway, nimble in the turns, and very fast in the straightaways (Bowen et al., 1994). Alternatively, visions can be more concrete: "The Helpdesk Automated Site (HASS) Version 4.5 will address the top 10 customer complaints across the university without any negative impact on average performance, reliability or response time across the system."[6]

There appear to be four essential qualities of an effective vision (see Figure 11.4). First, its essential qualities must be able to be communicated. A vision is worthless if it only resides in someone's head. The use of concrete, image-based language, such as "pocket rocket," is critical (Murphy & Clark, 2016). Second, visions have to be not only challenging but also realistic. For example, a task force directed at overhauling the curriculum at the college of business at a state university is likely to roll its collective eyes if the dean announces that their vision is to compete against the Harvard Business School. Conversely, developing the best undergraduate business program in that state may be a realistic vision for that task force. Third, the project manager has to believe in the vision. Passion for the vision is an essential element of an effective vision. Finally, it should be a source of inspiration to others. Just like not all projects require strong leadership, not all projects need a "vision" to be successfully managed. These would include plan driven, do it by the numbers projects like assembling a production line or building a bridge. Likewise, visions are less likely to be important when the project objectives are a clear source of inspiration like rescue efforts or solving a crucial problem.

Once a project manager accepts the importance of building a shared vision, the next question is how to get a vision for a particular project. First, project managers don't get visions. They act as catalysts and midwives for the formation of a shared vision of a

[6] Berkun, S., *The Art of Project Management* (Sebastopol, CA: O'Reilly, 2005), p. 79.

SNAPSHOT FROM PRACTICE 11.3 A Good Man in a Storm*

Once upon a time, back in 1976, Data General (DG) Corporation needed to come up quickly with a fast, reasonably priced, 32-bit mini-computer to compete with Digital Equipment Corporation's VAX. Data General CEO Edson de Castro launched the Fountainhead project and gave it the best people and ample resources to complete the 32-bit initiative. As a backup to the Fountainhead project, DG created the Eagle project within the Eclipse group under the leadership of Tom West. Work on both projects began in 1978.

In 1980 Data General announced its new computer, featuring simplicity, power, and low cost. This computer was not the Fountainhead from the well-funded "best" DG group but the Eagle from Tom West's underfunded Eclipse team. Tracy Kidder saw all this happen and told the story in *The Soul of a New Machine*, which won a Pulitzer Prize in 1982. This book, which Kidder thought might be of interest to a handful of computer scientists, has become a project management classic.

In the beginning of his book, Kidder introduces the book's protagonist, Tom West, by telling the story of him sailing a yacht across rough seas off the coast of New England. Kidder's title for the prologue was "A Good Man in a Storm."

Twenty years after Kidder's book was published, Tom West was interviewed by Lawrence Peters for the *Academy of Management Executive*. The following are some excerpts that capture West's views on managing innovative projects.

On selecting team members:

> You explain to a guy what the challenge was, and then see if his eyes light up.

On motivating team members:

> Challenge was everything. People, especially creative technical people who really want to make a difference, will do whatever is possible or whatever is necessary. I've done this more than once, and I've repeated it over and over. It seems to work.

On the importance of having a vision:

> You've got to find a rallying cry. You need to have something that can be described very simply and has that sort of ring of truth to an engineer that says "yes that's the thing to be doing right now." Otherwise you're going to be rolling rocks up hill all the time.

On the role of being a project manager:

> You have to act as a cheerleader. You have to act as the instructor. You have to constantly bring to mind what the purpose is and what's moving the ball towards the goal post, and what's running sideways, and you have to take up a lot of battles for them. I mean you really don't want your design engineer arguing with the guy in the drafting shop about why he ought to do it the designer's way. I can do that, and I can pull rank too, and sometimes I did just that.

*T. Kidder, *The Soul of a New Machine* (New York: Avon Books, 1981); L. H. Peters, "'A Good Man in a Storm': An Interview with Tom West," *Academy of Management Executive*, vol. 16, no. 4 (2002), pp. 42–43.

FIGURE 11.4
Requirements for an Effective Project Vision

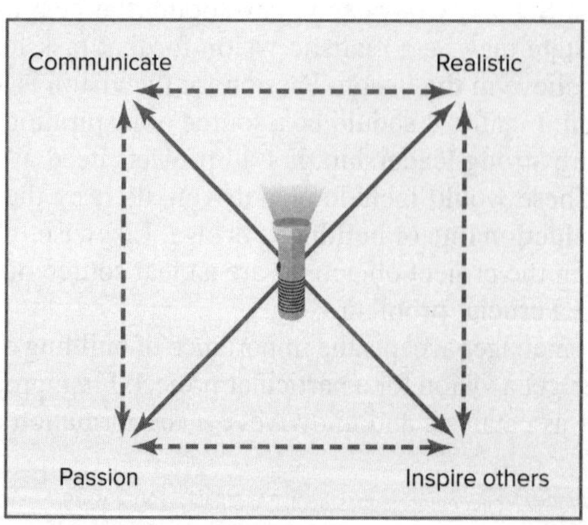

project team (Smith, 1994). In many cases, visions are inherent in the scope and objectives of the project. People get naturally excited about being the first ones to bring a new technology to the market or solving a problem that is threatening their organization. Even with mundane projects, there are often ample opportunities for establishing a compelling vision. One way is to talk to various people involved in the project and find out early on what gets them excited about the project. For some, it may be doing a better job than on the last project or the satisfaction in the eyes of the customers when the project is over. Many visions evolve reactively in response to competition—for example, Google engineers trying to develop a next-generation smartphone that critics will proclaim superior to the iPhone.

Some experts advocate engaging in formal vision-building meetings. These meetings generally involve several steps, beginning with members identifying different aspects of the project and generating ideal scenarios for each aspect. For example, on a construction project, the scenarios may include "no accidents," "no lawsuits," "winning a prize," or "how we are going to spend our bonus for completing the project ahead of schedule." The group reviews and chooses the scenarios that are most appealing and translates them into vision statements for the project. The next step is to identify strategies for achieving the vision statements. For example, if one of the vision statements is that there will be no lawsuits, members will identify how they will have to work with the owner and subcontractors to avoid litigation. Next, members volunteer to be responsible for each statement. The vision, strategies, and name of the responsible team member are published and distributed to relevant stakeholders.

In more cases than not, shared visions emerge informally. Project managers collect information about what excites participants about the project. They test bits of their working vision in their conversations with team members to gauge the level of excitement the early ideas elicit in others. To some extent, they engage in basic market research. They seize opportunities to galvanize the team, such as a disparaging remark by an executive that the project will never get done on time or the threat of a competing firm launching a similar project. Consensus in the beginning is not essential. What is essential is a core group of at least one-third of the project team that is genuinely committed to the vision. They will provide the critical mass to draw others aboard. Once the language has been formulated to communicate the vision, the statement needs to be a staple part of every working agenda, and the project manager should be prepared to deliver a "stump" speech at a moment's notice. When problems or disagreements emerge, all responses should be consistent with the vision.

Much has been written about visions and leadership. Critics argue that vision is a glorified substitute for shared goals. Others argue that it is one of the things that separate leaders from managers. The key is discovering what excites people about a project, being able to articulate this source of excitement in an appealing manner, and protecting and nurturing this source of excitement throughout the project.

Managing Project Reward Systems

Project managers are responsible for managing the reward system that encourages team performance and extra effort. One advantage they have is that often project work is inherently satisfying, whether it is manifested in an inspiring vision or a simple sense of accomplishment. Projects provide participants with a change in scenery, a chance to learn new skills, and an opportunity to break out of their departmental cocoon. Another inherent reward is what has been referred to as "pinball"—project success typically gives team members an option to play another exciting game.[7]

Still, many projects are underappreciated and boring; interfere with other, more significant priorities; and are considered an extra burden. In some of these cases, the biggest reward is finishing the project so that team members can go back to what they really enjoy doing and what will yield the biggest personal payoffs. Unfortunately, when this attitude is the primary incentive, project quality is likely to suffer. In these circumstances, external rewards play a more important role in motivating team performance.

Most project managers we talk to advocate the use of group rewards. Because most project work is a collaborative effort, it only makes sense that the reward system would encourage teamwork. Recognizing individual members regardless of their accomplishments can distract from team unity. Project work is highly interdependent, so it can become problematic to distinguish who truly deserves additional credit. Cash bonuses and incentives need to be linked to project priorities. It makes no sense to reward a team for completing their work early if controlling cost was the number one priority.

One of the limitations of lump-sum cash bonuses is that all too often they are consumed by the household budget to pay the dentist or mechanic. To have more value, rewards need to have lasting significance (Smith & Reinertsen, 1997). Many companies convert cash into vacation rewards, sometimes with corresponding time off. For example, one firm rewarded a project team for getting the job done ahead of schedule with a four-day, all-expenses-paid trip to Walt Disney World for the members' entire families. That vacation not only will be remembered for years but also recognizes spouses and children, who, in a sense, also contributed to the project's success. Similarly, other firms have been known to give members home computers and entertainment centers. Wise project managers negotiate a discretionary budget so that they can reward teams' surpassing milestones with gift certificates to popular restaurants or tickets to sporting events. Impromptu pizza parties and barbecues are also used to celebrate key accomplishments.

Sometimes project managers have to use negative reinforcement to motivate project performance. For example, Ritti and Levy recount the story of one project manager who was in charge of the construction of a new, state-of-the-art manufacturing plant. His project team was working with a number of different contracting firms. The project was slipping behind schedule, mostly because of a lack of cooperation among the different players. The project manager did not have direct authority over many key people, especially the contractors from the other companies. He did, however, have the freedom to convene meetings at his convenience. So the project manager instituted daily "coordination meetings," which were required of all the principals involved, at 6:00 a.m. The meetings continued for about two weeks until the project got back on schedule. At that time, the project manager announced that the next meeting was canceled, and no further sunrise meetings were ever scheduled.[8]

While project managers tend to focus on group rewards, there are times when they need to reward individual performance. This is done not only to compensate extraordinary effort but also to signal to the others what exemplary behavior is. Examples of this kind of reward include

[7] Kidder, T., *The Soul of a New Machine* (New York: Avon Books, 1981), pp. 221–22.

[8] Ritti, R. R., and S. L. Levy, *The Ropes to Skip and Ropes to Know: Studies in Organizational Theory and Behavior* (New York: Wiley, 2009), pp. 93–94.

- **Letters of commendation.** While project managers may not have responsibility for their team members' performance appraisals, they can write letters commending their project performance. These letters can be sent to the workers' supervisors to be placed in their personnel files.
- **Public recognition for outstanding work.** Superlative workers should be publicly recognized for their efforts. Some project managers begin each status review meeting with a brief mention of project workers who have exceeded their project goals.
- **Job assignments.** Good project managers recognize that while they may not have much budgetary authority, they do have substantial control over who does what, with whom, when, and where. Good work should be rewarded with desirable job assignments. Managers should be aware of member preferences and, when appropriate, accommodate them.
- **Flexibility.** Being willing to make exceptions to rules, if done judiciously, can be a powerful reward. Allowing members to work at home when a child is sick or excusing a minor indiscretion can engender long-lasting loyalty.

Individual rewards should be used judiciously, and under extraordinary circumstances. Nothing undermines the cohesiveness of a team more than members beginning to feel that others are getting special treatment or that they are being treated unfairly. Camaraderie and collaboration can quickly vanish, only to be replaced by bickering and obsessive preoccupation with group politics. Such distractions can absorb energy that otherwise would be directed toward completing the project. Individual rewards typically should be used only when everyone in the team recognizes that a member is deserving of special recognition.

Orchestrating the Decision-Making Process

Most decisions on a project do not require a formal meeting to discuss alternatives and determine solutions. Instead, decisions are made in real time as part of the daily interactions among project managers, stakeholders, and team members. For example, as a result of a routine "How's it going?" question, a project manager discovers that a mechanical engineer is stuck trying to meet the performance criteria for a prototype she is responsible for building. The project manager and engineer go down the hallway to talk to the designers, explain the problem, and ask what, if anything, can be done. The designers distinguish which criteria are essential and which ones they think can be compromised. The project manager then checks with the marketing group to make sure the modifications are acceptable. They agree with all but two of the modifications. The project manager goes back to the mechanical engineer and asks whether the proposed changes would help solve the problem. The engineer agrees. Before authorizing the changes he calls the project sponsor, reviews the events, and gets the sponsor to sign off on the changes. This is an example of how, by practicing MBWA (management by wandering around), project managers consult team members, solicit ideas, determine optimum solutions, and create a sense of involvement that builds trust and commitment to decisions.

Still, projects encounter problems and decisions that require the collective wisdom of team members, as well as relevant stakeholders. Group decision making should be used when it will improve the quality of important decisions (Vroom & Jago, 1988). This is often the case with complex problems that require the input of various specialists. Group decision making should also be used when strong commitment to the decision is needed and there is a low probability of acceptance if only one person makes the decision. Participation is used to reduce resistance and secure support for the decision. Guidelines for managing group decision making are provided in the following section.

Facilitating Group Decision Making Project managers play a pivotal role in guiding the group decision-making process. They must remind themselves that their job is not to make a decision but to facilitate the discussion within the group so that the team reaches a consensus on the best possible solution. Consensus within this context does not mean that everyone supports the decision 100 percent but that they all agree what the best solution is under the circumstances. Facilitating group decision making essentially involves four major steps.[9]

1. **Identifying problems.** The project manager needs to be careful not to state the problem in terms of choices (e.g., "Should we do X or Y?"). Rather, the project manager should identify the underlying problem to which these alternatives and probably others are potential solutions. This allows group members to generate alternatives, not just choose among them. One useful way of defining problems is to consider the gap between where a project is (the present state) and where it should be (desired state). For example, the project may be four days behind schedule or the prototype weighs two pounds more than the specifications. Whether the gap is small or large, the purpose is to eliminate it. The group must find one or more courses of action that will change the existing state into the desired one.

   If defensive posturing is detected during the problem-identification discussion, then it may be wise to postpone the problem-solving step if possible. This allows for emotions to subside and members to gain a fresh perspective on the issues involved.
2. **Generating alternatives.** Once there is general agreement on the nature of the problem(s), the next step is to generate alternative solutions. If the problem requires creativity, then **brainstorming** is commonly recommended. Here, the team generates a list of possible solutions on a flipchart or blackboard. During that time, the project manager establishes a moratorium on criticizing or evaluating ideas. Members are encouraged to "piggyback" on others' ideas by extending them or combining ideas into a new idea. The object is to create as many alternatives as possible, no matter how outlandish they appear to be. Some project managers report that for really tough problems they have found it beneficial to conduct such sessions away from the normal work environment; the change in scenery stimulates creativity.
3. **Reaching a decision.** The next step is to evaluate the merits of alternative solutions. During this phase, it is useful to have a set of criteria for this process. In many cases, the project manager can draw upon the priorities for the project and have the group assess each alternative in terms of its impact on cost, schedule, and performance as well as reducing the problem gap. For example, if time is critical, then the solution that solves the problem as quickly as possible would be chosen.

   During the course of the discussion, the project manager attempts to build consensus among the group. This can be a complicated process. Project managers need to provide periodic summaries to help the group keep track of its progress. They must protect those members who represent the minority view and ensure that such views get a fair hearing. They need to guarantee that everyone has an opportunity to share opinions and no one individual or group dominates the conversation. It may

[9] This discussion is based on the classic work of Maier, N. R. F.: *Problem-Solving Discussion and Conferences* (New York: McGraw-Hill, 1963) and *Problem Solving and Creativity in Individuals and Groups* (Belmont, CA: Brooks-Cole, 1970).

be useful to regulate the use of air time with a two-minute timer. When conflicts occur, managers need to apply some of the ideas and techniques discussed in the next section.

Project managers need to engage in consensus testing to determine what points the group agrees on and what are still sources of contention. They are careful not to interpret silence as agreement; they confirm agreement by asking questions. Ultimately, through thoughtful interaction, the team reaches a "meeting of the minds" as to what solution is best for the project.

4. **Following up.** Once the decision has been made and implemented, it is important for the team to find the time to evaluate the effectiveness of the decision. If the decision failed to provide the anticipated solution, then the reasons should be explored and the lessons learned added to the collective memory bank of the project team.

Managing Conflict within the Project

LO 11-5

Distinguish functional conflict from dysfunctional conflict, and describe strategies for encouraging functional conflict and discouraging dysfunctional conflict.

Disagreements and conflicts naturally emerge within a project team during the life of the project. Participants will disagree over priorities, the allocation of resources, the quality of specific work, solutions to discovered problems, and so forth (see Snapshot from Practice 11.4: Managing Low-Priority Projects). Some conflicts support the goals of the group and improve project performance. For example, two members may be locked in a debate over a design trade-off decision involving different features of a product. They argue that their preferred feature is what the primary customer truly wants. This disagreement may force them to get more information from the customer, with the result that they realize neither feature is highly valued and the customer wants something else instead. On the other hand, conflicts can also hinder group performance. Initial disagreements can escalate into heated arguments with both parties refusing to work together.

Sources of conflict are likely to change as projects progress along the project life cycle (Adams & Brandt, 1988; Posner, 1986; Thamhain & Wilemon, 1975). Figure 11.5 summarizes the major sources of conflict in each phase.

During project definition, the most significant sources of conflict are priorities, administrative procedures, and schedule. Disputes occur over the relative importance of the project compared with other activities, which project management structure to use (especially how much control the project manager should have), the personnel to be assigned, and the scheduling of the project into existing workloads.

FIGURE 11.5
Sources of Conflict over the Project Life Cycle

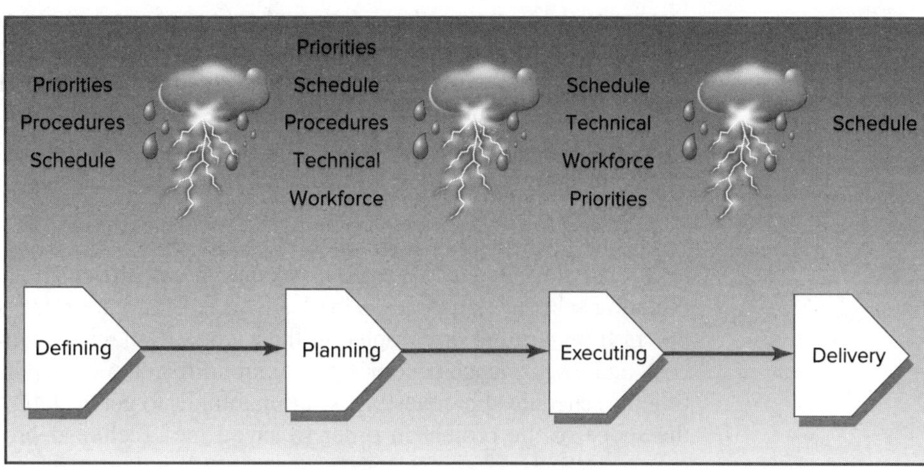

SNAPSHOT FROM PRACTICE 11.4 Managing Low-Priority Projects

So far the discussion of team building has been directed primarily to significant projects that command the attention of assigned members. But what about projects that have low priority for team members: the perfunctory task forces that members begrudgingly join? The committee work people get assigned to do? The part-time projects that pull members away from the critical work they would rather be doing? The projects that cause members to privately question why they are doing this.

There is no magic wand available that transforms mildly interested, part-time project teams into high-performance teams. We interviewed several project managers about such project scenarios. They all agreed that these can be very difficult and frustrating assignments and that there are limits to what is possible. Still, they offered tips and advice for making the best of the situation. Most of these tips focused on building commitment to the project when it does not naturally exist.

One project manager advocated orchestrating a large "time" investment up front on such projects—in the form of either a lengthy meeting or a significant early assignment. He viewed this as a form of down payment that members would forfeit if they didn't carry the project to completion.

Others emphasized interjecting as much fun into activities as possible. Here rituals for building team identity come into play. People become committed because they enjoy working together on the project. One project manager even confided that the perfect attendance at her project meetings was due primarily to the quality of the doughnuts she provided.

Another strategy is to make the benefits of the project as real to the team members as possible. One project manager escalated commitment to a mandated accidents prevention task force by bringing accident victims to a project meeting. Another project manager brought the high-ranking project sponsor to recharge the team by reinforcing the importance of the project to the company.

Most of the project managers emphasized the importance of building a strong personal relationship with each of the team members. When this connection occurs, members work hard not so much because they really care about the project but because they don't want to let the project manager down. Although not couched in influence currency terms, these managers talked about getting to know each member, sharing contacts, offering encouragement, and extending a helping hand when needed.

Finally, all the project managers cautioned that nothing should be taken for granted on low-priority projects. They recommended reminding people about meetings and bringing extra copies of materials to meetings for those who have forgotten them or can't find them. Project managers should remain in frequent contact with team members and remind them of their assignments. One manager summed it up best when he said, "Sometimes it all boils down to just being a good nag."

During the planning phase, the chief source of conflict remains priorities, followed by schedules, procedures, and technical requirements. This is the phase when the project moves from a general concept to a detailed set of plans. The relative importance of the project still must be established, as well as project priorities (time, cost, scope). Disagreements often emerge over the final schedule, the assignment of resources, communication and decision-making procedures, and the technical requirements for the project.

During the execution phase, friction arises over schedule slippage, technical problems, and staff issues. Milestones become more difficult to meet because of accumulating schedule slippages. This leads to tension within the team as delays prevent others from starting or completing their work. Managing the trade-offs among time, cost, and performance becomes paramount. Project managers must decide among letting the schedule slip, investing additional funds to get back on track, and scaling back the scope of the project in order to save time. Technical problems involve finding solutions to unexpected problems and integrating the contributions of various people. The strain of the project may be expressed in interpersonal conflicts as well as pressures to use resources more effectively.

During the delivery phase, the level of conflict tends to subside. On troubled projects, schedules continue to be the biggest source of conflict as schedule slippages make it more difficult to meet target completion dates. Pressures to meet objectives coupled with growing anxiety over future assignments increase interpersonal tensions. Technical problems are rare, since most of them have been worked out during the earlier phases.

Encouraging Functional Conflict The demarcation between **functional** and **dysfunctional conflict** is neither clear nor precise. In one team, members may exchange a diatribe of four-letter expletives and eventually resolve their differences. Yet in another project team, such behavior would create irreconcilable divisions and would prohibit the parties from ever working together productively again. The distinguishing criterion is how the conflict affects project performance, not how individuals feel. Members can be upset and dissatisfied with the interchange, but as long as the disagreement furthers the objectives of the project, the conflict is functional. Project managers should recognize that conflict is an inevitable and even a desirable part of project work; the key is to encourage functional conflict and manage dysfunctional conflict.

A shared vision can transcend the incongruities of a project and establish a common purpose to channel debate in a constructive manner. Without shared goals, there is no common ground for working out differences. In the previous example involving the design trade-off decision, when both parties agreed that the primary goal was to satisfy the customer, there was a basis for more objectively resolving the dispute. Therefore, agreeing in advance which priority is most important—cost, schedule, or scope—can help a project team decide what response is most appropriate.

Sometimes it's not the presence of conflict but the absence of conflict that is the problem. Often as a result of compressed time pressures, self doubt, and the desire to preserve team harmony, members are reluctant to voice objections. This hesitation robs the team of useful information that might lead to better solutions and the avoidance of critical mistakes. Project managers need to encourage healthy dissent in order to improve problem solving and innovation. They can demonstrate this process by asking tough questions and challenging the rationale behind recommendations. They can also orchestrate healthy conflict by bringing people with different points of view to critical meetings.

Project managers can legitimize dissent within the team by designating someone to play the role of devil's advocate or by asking the group to take 15 minutes to come up with all the reasons the team should not pursue a course of action. Functional conflict plays a critical role in obtaining a deeper understanding of the issues and coming up with the best decisions possible.

One of the most important things project managers can do is model an appropriate response when someone disagrees or challenges their ideas. They need to avoid acting defensively and instead encourage critical debate. They should exhibit effective listening skills and summarize the key issues before responding. They should check to see if others agree with the opposing point of view. Finally, project managers should value and protect dissenters. Organizations have a tendency to create too many yes-men, and the emperor needs to be told when he doesn't have any clothes on.

Managing Dysfunctional Conflict Managing dysfunctional conflict is a much more challenging task than encouraging functional conflict. First, dysfunctional conflict is hard to identify. A manager might have two highly talented professionals who hate each other but in the heat of competition produce meritorious results. Is this a pleasant situation? No. Is it functional? Yes, as long as it contributes to project performance. Conversely, sometimes functional conflict degenerates into dysfunctional conflict. This change occurs when technical disagreements evolve into irrational personality clashes or when failure to resolve an issue causes unnecessary delays in critical project work.

The second major difficulty managers face is that there is often no easy solution to dysfunctional conflict. Project managers have to choose from among a number of strategies to manage it; the following are five possibilities.

1. **Mediate the conflict.** The manager intervenes and tries to negotiate a resolution by using reasoning and persuasion, suggesting alternatives and the like. One of the keys is trying to find common ground. In some cases the project manager can make the argument that the win/lose interchange has escalated to the point that it has become lose/lose for everyone and now is the time to make concessions.
2. **Arbitrate the conflict.** The manager imposes a solution to the conflict after listening to each party. The goal is not to decide who wins but to have the project win. In doing so, it is important to seek a solution that allows each party to save face; otherwise, the decision may provide only momentary relief. One project manager admits that she has had great success using a King Solomon approach to resolving conflict. She announces a solution that neither party will like and gives the opponents two hours to come up with a better solution they can both agree on.
3. **Control the conflict.** Reducing the intensity of the conflict by smoothing over differences or interjecting humor is an effective strategy. If feelings are escalating, the manager can adjourn the interaction and hope cooler heads prevail the next day. If the conflict continues to escalate, project assignments may need to be rearranged if possible so that the two parties don't have to work together.
4. **Accept the conflict.** In some cases the conflict will outlive the project and, though a distraction, it is one the manager has to live with.
5. **Eliminate the conflict.** Sometimes the conflict has escalated to the point that it is no longer tolerable. If there is a clear villain, then only that person should be removed. If, as is often the case, both parties are at fault, then it is wise, if possible, to eliminate both individuals. Their removal gives a clear signal to the others on the team that this kind of behavior is unacceptable.

In summary, project managers create the foundation for functional conflict by establishing clear roles and responsibilities, developing common goals or a shared vision, and using group incentives that reward collaboration. Project managers have to be adroit at reading body language to identify unspoken disagreement. They also have to keep in touch with what is going on in a project to identify small problems that might escalate into big conflicts. Using well-timed humor and redirecting the focus to what is best for the project can alleviate the interpersonal tensions that are likely to flare up on a project team.

Rejuvenating the Project Team

Over the course of a long project, a team sometimes drifts off track and loses momentum. The project manager needs to swing into action to realign the team with the project objectives. There are both formal and informal ways of doing this. Informally, the project manager can institute new rituals, like the "toy roaches," to re-energize the team. On one project that was experiencing rough going, the project manager stopped work and took the team bowling to relieve frustrations. On another project, a manager showed the team the movie *The Shawshank Redemption* to rekindle hope and commitment to success.

Another option is to have the project sponsor give a pep talk to the "troops." In other cases, a friendly challenge can reinvigorate a team. For example, one project sponsor offered to cook a five-course meal if the project got back on track and hit the next milestone.

Sometimes more formal action needs to be taken. The project manager may recognize the need for a team-building session devoted to improving the work processes of the team. This meeting is particularly appropriate if the project manager senses that the team is approaching a transition point in its development. The goal of such a session is to improve the project team's effectiveness through better management of project demands and group processes. It is the team's inward look at its own performance, behavior, and culture to eliminate dysfunctional behaviors and strengthen functional ones. The project team critiques its performance, analyzes its way of doing things, and attempts to develop strategies to improve its operation.

Often an external consultant is hired or an internal staff specialist is assigned to facilitate the session. This process brings a more objective, outside perspective to the table, frees the project manager to be part of the process, and provides a specialist trained in group dynamics. Furthermore, if preliminary information is to be collected, team members may be more candid with and open to an outsider.

One caveat about using outside consultants is that too often managers resort to this as a method for dealing with a problem that they have been unable or unwilling to deal with. The marching order to the consultant is "Fix my team for me." What the managers fail to recognize is that one of the keys to fixing the team is improving the working relationship between themselves and the remainder of the team. For such sessions to be effective, project managers must be willing to have their own role scrutinized and be receptive to changing their own behavior and work habits based on the team's comments and suggestions.

Consultants use a wide variety of **team-building** techniques to elevate team performance. Here is a brief description of one of the more common approaches. The first step is to gather information and make a preliminary diagnosis of team performance. Whether through individual interviews or in a group forum, the consultant asks general questions about the project team performance, that is, what obstacles are getting in the way of the team being able to perform better? This information is summarized in terms of themes. When everyone has understood the themes, the group ranks them in terms of both their importance and the extent the team has ownership over them. This last dimension is critical. *Ownership* refers to whether the team has direct influence over the issue. For example, a team probably has little influence over the delivery of contracted supplies, but team members do control how quickly they inform each other of sudden changes in plans.

If the group becomes preoccupied with issues outside its control, the meeting can quickly evolve into a demoralizing gripe session. Therefore, the most important issues they have direct control over become the subjects of the agenda. During the meeting, much interpersonal and group process information will be generated, and that is examined too. Thus, the group works on two sets of items: the agenda items and the items that emerge from the interaction of the participants. This is where the expertise of the external facilitator becomes critical for identifying interaction patterns and their implications for team performance.

As important problems are discussed, alternatives for action are developed. The team-building session concludes by deciding on specific action steps for remedying problems and setting target dates for who will do what, and when. These assignments can be reviewed at project status meetings or at a follow-up session.

It has become fashionable to link team-building activities with outdoor experiences. The outdoor experience—such as whitewater rafting down the Rogue River in Oregon or rock climbing in Colorado—places group members in a variety of physically challenging situations that must be mastered through teamwork, not individual effort. By having to work together to overcome difficult obstacles, team members are supposed to experience increased self-confidence, more respect for one another's capabilities, and a greater commitment to teamwork. No empirical data are available to support such exotic endeavors other than the enthusiastic support of the participants. Such activities are likely to provide an intense common experience that may accelerate the social development of the team. Such an investment of time and money communicates the importance of teamwork and is considered by some a perk for being on the project. At the same time, unless the lessons from these experiences can be immediately transferred to actual project work, their significance is likely to vanish.

11.4 Managing Virtual Project Teams

LO 11-6

Understand the challenges of managing virtual project teams.

The COVID-19 Pandemic forced people to work from home and changed the nature of work forever. A 2022 Gallup survey found that 8 out of 10 people are working at least part-time from home (Wigert & Agrawal, 2022). Houses and apartments are being renovated to create a workspace around a home computer. Global industries have a history of advancing electronic forms of communication to link people across the globe on projects. This provided companies access to greater expertise and the ability to work 24/7 on projects (see Snapshot for Practice 11.5: Managing Virtual Global Teams).

One way to characterize this new "virtual" world in terms of projects is to consider four types of working conditions:

- The traditional project team where everybody comes to work each day and can interact in person.
- The virtual project team in which the team is spatially separated and relies primarily on electronic forms of communication to interact with each other.
- Mixed project teams where most of the team are able to work together in person, but there are significant other members who can only communicate electronically with the team.
- Hybrid project teams where team members are centrally located. Team members spend part of their time at the "office" where they can interact with each other and part of their time working on projects at home. Some say this will be the new norm of work (Bloom, 2020).

Lessons learned from the creation of virtual project teams (aka virtual project) will be discussed first, and followed by their ramifications for managing mixed and hybrid teams.

Two of the biggest challenges involved in managing a virtual project team are establishing trust and developing effective patterns of communication (Lipsinger & DeRosa, 2010). Trust is difficult to establish in a virtual work environment. Unlike working as a traditional team, where members can see whether someone has done what s/he says s/he

SNAPSHOT FROM PRACTICE 11.5 Managing Virtual Global Teams*

Carl A. Singer, a senior program manager at IBM Global Services, described how global time zones were used to complete a time-intensive project. The project required subject matter experts (SMEs) to document existing best practices in the maintenance domain and to port these into a knowledge management tool. The most proficient SMEs available were on opposite sides of the globe—Australia and Scotland. Review and control of the project were from the United States.

Ariel Skelley/Blend Images/Getty Images

Management realized that just working harder and smarter was not going to meet the time and quality targets. For this project, they used the dimension of time to their benefit. Applying sound management principles as well as taking advantage of electronic communication systems, the team was able to create a virtual 24-hour workday for quick responses and accelerated reviews.

Each team consisted of veteran professionals familiar with the rigors of time-pressured consulting projects. A local point person was identified for each team, and mutually agreed-upon targets, terminology, and processes were established.

An all-hands kick-off meeting was organized in which participants were able to socialize, understand local and project-wide constraints, and finalize an agreed-upon plan. The meeting was held at a corporate hotel with dining accommodations. The facility was considered an "assisted living community for IBM consultants." This hastened recovery from jet lag and provided an interruption-free work environment.

Upon returning to their home bases, each team created the majority of their deliverables independently with periodic three-way conference calls to maintain coordination. A project control book was established electronically so that all participants had access to the latest project documents.

The final phase of the project required intense interfacing and reviews between the teams. These reviews necessitated changes to deal with concerns, differences among subprojects, and other issues. It was here that the worldwide nature of the project was leveraged. Using a "dry cleaning approach" (in by 5 p.m. out by 9 a.m.), team members in Australia and Scotland were able to address issues generated during the U.S.-based external reviews and provide concrete responses by the beginning of the next business day. Conference calls at 6:00 a.m. (U.S. EST) were used to coordinate responses and resolve issues. Conference calls at the end of the U.S. workday were used to finalize issues and assignments. Figure 11.6 depicts the 24-hour clock used to align communication schedules.

Telephone conferencing was used instead of videoconferencing due to the setup lead time and because it would force participants to leave their offices. E-mail was used extensively for general communication. An electronic repository of project work was used to coordinate global involvement. In practice, a participant could draft a document and deposit it electronically, only to wake up the next day to find the document annotated with suggested revisions. Likewise, one could start the day by checking an in-basket populated with documents to review and issues to address. Over time, "G'day" and "Cheers" crept into the U.S. speech—a clear indicator of team cohesion.

Singer identified a number of lessons learned from the project:

- The all-hands kick-off meeting was critical for establishing goals and procedures as well as "rules of courtesy."
- Loosen the reins—establish clear deliverables and then step out of the way and let the professionals do their work.

FIGURE 11.6 24-Hour Global Clock

United States (East Coast)	Australia	Scotland	Comments
12 midnight	2 PM	5 AM	
1 AM	3 PM	6 AM	
2 AM	4 PM	7 AM	
3 AM	5 PM	8 AM	
4 AM	6 PM	9 AM	Australia handoff for off-shift review
5 AM	7 PM	10 AM	
6 AM	8 PM	11 AM	3-way conferencing window (primary)
7 AM	9 PM	12 noon	3-way conferencing window (primary)
8 AM	10 PM	1 PM	3-way conferencing window (primary)
9 AM	11 PM	2 PM	
10 AM	12 midnight	3 PM	
11 AM	1 AM	4 PM	
12 noon	2 AM	5 PM	Scotland handoff for off-shift review
1 PM	3 AM	6 PM	
2 PM	4 AM	7 PM	
3 PM	5 AM	8 PM	
4 PM	6 AM	9 PM	3-way conferencing window (secondary)
5 PM	7 AM	10 PM	3-way conferencing window (secondary)
6 PM	8 AM	11 PM	U.S. handoff for off-shift review
7 PM	9 AM	12 midnight	
8 PM	10 AM	1 AM	
9 PM	11 AM	2 AM	
10 PM	12 noon	3 AM	
11 PM	1 PM	4 AM	
12 midnight	2 PM	5 AM	

Prime time   Secondary time   Downtime

- Establish and enforce agreed-upon quality standards and deliverable templates.
- Maintain a regular schedule of conference calls, even if only to say, "Hello, we have nothing to talk about today." Conference calls should be guided by pre-established agendas, note-taking procedures, and reviews.

*C. A. Singer, "Leveraging a Worldwide Project Team," *PM Network*, April 2001, pp. 36–40.

has done, virtual team members depend on the word of distant members. At the same time, it can be difficult to trust someone you may have met only one or two times or not at all. Geographical separation also prohibits the informal social interactions that are often essential to building camaraderie among team members. As one virtual team member put it, "You can't have a beer together over the Internet."

So how can a project manager facilitate the development of trust within a virtual team? First, if it is impossible to hold a face-to-face meeting in the beginning, managers need to orchestrate the exchange of social information—who everyone is and some personal background information during the initial electronic interchange. Second, they need to set clear roles for each team member. Ideally, specific tasks should be assigned to each member so that s/he can make an immediate contribution to the project. Third, project managers should have the team work on a mini-project so they can get used to working together. Trust in virtual projects grows through team member reliability, consistency, and responsiveness (Coutu, 1998). Finally, if possible, teams should be seeded with people who have already worked effectively together on projects.

The second major challenge for managing a virtual project team is to establish effective patterns of communication. E-mail and faxes are great for communicating facts—but not the feelings behind the facts; nor do they allow for real-time communication. Conference calls and project chat rooms can help, but they also have their limitations. Videoconferencing is a significant improvement over nonvisual electronic forms of communication. Still, videoconferencing is not always available or is of such poor quality to be a distraction in many parts of the world. The maxim is "Match technology to the communication need." The following are some guidelines developed by 3M for use on their distributed projects.[10]

- **When to e-mail.** Use e-mail to distribute important information and news in a one-to-one or one-to-many frame of reference.
- **When to use electronic bulletin boards.** Use electronic bulletin boards to encourage discussion and flush out the diversity of opinion on issues.
- **When to videoconference.** Videoconference when you need to see each other's faces and expressions. This is important during the early phases of a project, when you are building relationships and developing a common understanding of what needs to be done. Use it, again, when working on critical decisions and/or contentious issues.
- **When to use conference calls.** Use conference calls when people in different locations are working with common documents, presentations, sketches, and models. In addition, use them for status report meetings and to sustain social camaraderie.
- **When to fly/meet.** Fly to build or repair trust. Use the travel budget to get all the key players together early on to instill commitment to the goals of the project and engage in team building activities. Meet when the different talents and expertise of team members are needed to innovate and problem solve. More than one project manager has reported dissatisfaction with videoconferencing as a means to collectively solving difficult problems.

Even with the best communication system, managers have to overcome the problems of working within time zone differences, working with cultural nuances, and finding a convenient time for people to conference.

Following are some additional tips for alleviating communication problems and enhancing the performance of working in virtual environments:

1. **Don't let team members vanish.** Virtual teams often experience problems getting in touch with each other. Use Internet scheduling software to store members' calendars. Check in with team members on a regular basis.
2. **Establish a code of conduct to avoid delays.** Team members need to agree not only on what, when, and how the information will be shared but also on how and when they will respond to it. Develop a priority system to distinguish messages that require an immediate response from those with longer time frames. Recognize differences between how a person communicates via e-mail (written) versus face to face (verbal). Use the means most effective for that person and ask follow-up questions on inadequately written communiques.

[10] "3M Meeting Network," www.3M.com/meetings. Accessed 6/6/02.

3. **Establish clear norms and protocols for surfacing assumptions and conflicts.** Because most communication is nonvisual, project managers cannot watch body language and facial expressions to develop a sense of what is going on. They need to probe deeper when communicating to force members to explain their viewpoints, actions, and concerns more clearly; they must double-check comprehension.
4. **Use electronic video technology to verify work.** Instead of relying on others' judgment, have members "show" work that has been done via Internet video. This can avoid costly misunderstanding and provide useful feedback.
5. **Share the pain.** Do not require everyone to conform to your time zone and preferences. Rotate meeting times so that all team members have a turn working according to their clock.

Mixed Project Teams

In many cases, a core group of a project team is centrally located while other key members live in separate locales. For example, a core group of coders work in Austin, Texas, while the testers live in Sioux Falls, South Dakota, and Fayetteville, Arkansas, while customer focus groups are being conducted in Athens, Georgia, Worcester, Massachusetts, and Provo, Utah. One of the biggest threats to mixed project team performance is subgrouping, that instead of working together as one team, smaller groups form around their common location.

Mixed project teams are particularly susceptible to subgrouping, given that some members share a much richer interaction experience with their immediate colleagues than those more distal team members. Here it is important for project managers not let one group dominate discussions and they should go out of their way to solicit opinions from more isolated members. Often times, the isolated team member's accomplishments are invisible to others. It is vital for the project manager to draw attention to the contributions of less visible team members so that they feel a part of the team.

Hybrid Project Teams

Now that people experienced the benefits of working at home (fewer disruptions, flexible daily schedule, no commute, etc.), there will be greater demands on accommodating home/work project schedules. This is in part due to greater reliance on electronic forms of business communication and that one can replicate the office workstation at home.

It is only natural for many to wish to do as much work at home as possible, especially those with challenging commutes. This personal preference should not take precedent over the requirements of the work being performed and the need to work directly with others. The project managers need to oversee communication patterns within the team and make sure people are interacting face to face when needed. They should be on the look-out for team members avoiding direct contact with people who disagree with them or have had unpleasant exchanges in the past. It is only natural to avoid unpleasant encounters and try to rely on e-mail to solve problems.

Not all people respond the same to working at home on projects. Here the introvert/extrovert personality dimension is likely to be a key factor. **Extroverts** tend to be talkative, outgoing, and enjoy social interaction. **Introverts,** on the other hand, are more reserved and like alone time to engage in more reflective thinking. Introverts and extroverts seek energy in different ways. Introverts require fewer stimuli and social interaction while extroverts enjoy more stimulation and become more energized in social settings. This is not an either–or question. People will vary on the introvert/extrovert spectrum. Introverts are likely to prefer and excel at working at home while extroverts may struggle with a lack of social interaction. Strong extroverts' performance actually may improve by spending less time at home than at work office.

To some extent managing a virtual, mixed, or hybrid project team is no different from managing a regular project team. The key is working within the constraints of the situation to develop effective ways for team members to interact and combine their talents to complete the project.

11.5 Project Team Pitfalls

LO 17-1

Recognize the different pitfalls that can occur in a project team.

High-performance project teams can produce dramatic results. However, like any good thing, there is a dark side to project teams that managers need to be aware of. In this section, we examine some of the pathologies that high-performance project teams can succumb to and highlight what project managers can do to reduce the likelihood of these problems occurring.

Groupthink

Janis (1982) first identified **groupthink** as a factor that influenced the misguided 1961 Bay of Pigs invasion of Cuba. His term refers to the tendency of members in highly cohesive groups to lose their critical evaluative capabilities. This malady appears when pressures for conformity are combined with an illusion of invincibility to suspend critical discussion of decisions. As a result, decisions are made quickly with little consideration of alternatives; often the practice leads to fiascoes that, after the fact, appear totally improbable. Some of the symptoms of groupthink include the following:

- **Illusion of invulnerability.** The team feels invincible. It is marked by a high degree of esprit de corps, an implicit faith in its own wisdom, and an inordinate optimism that allows group members to feel complacent about the quality of their decisions.
- **Whitewash of critical thinking.** The group members discuss only a few solutions, ignoring alternatives; they fail to examine the adverse consequences that could follow their preferred course of action; and they too quickly dismiss any alternatives that, on the surface, appear to be unsatisfactory.
- **Negative stereotypes of outsiders.** "Good guy/bad guy" stereotypes emerge in which the group considers any outsiders who oppose their decisions as the "bad guys," who are perceived as incompetent and malicious and whose points are unworthy of serious consideration.
- **Direct pressure.** When a team member does speak out or question the direction in which the team is headed, direct pressure is applied to the dissenter. The individual is reminded that speed is important and that the aim is agreement, not argument.

Bureaucratic Bypass Syndrome

Project teams are often licensed to get things done without having to go through the normal protocols of the parent organization. Bypassing bureaucratic channels is appealing and invigorating. However, if bypassing becomes a way of life, it results in the rejection of bureaucratic policies and procedures, which provide the glue for the overall organization. A team that operates outside the organization may alienate other

SNAPSHOT FROM PRACTICE 11.6 Nominal Group Technique*

GE Appliances, Marriott Corp., and Hewlett Packard are among the many firms that use the **nominal group technique (NGT)** to guide decisions on projects. The NGT begins by gathering project team members and/or stakeholders around a table and identifying the project problem at hand. Each member then writes his or her solutions. Next, each member presents his or her solution to the group, and the leader writes these solutions on a chart. No criticism is allowed. This process continues until all the ideas have been expressed. Each solution then is discussed and clarified by the group. After all the ideas have been discussed, the group members privately rank-order their preferred solutions. The balloting is tallied to create a rank-ordering of each solution. These steps are repeated if necessary to refine the list further in order to get the most preferred solution.

NGT provides an orderly process for dealing with potentially inflammatory problems. It also prevents groupthink from occurring. NGT discourages any pressure to conform to the wishes of a high-status, powerful group member, since all ideas are discussed and all preferences are expressed privately. Creativity should be enhanced, since members are able to offer a solution based on their expertise and viewpoint. Finally, important decisions can be made in a relatively timely manner. NGT works best when there is a well-defined problem.

*A. Delbeeq, A. H. Van de Ven, and D. H. Gustafson, *Group Techniques for Program Planning* (Glenview, Il: Scott, Foresman, 1975).

workers, who are constrained by the norms and procedures of the organization; eventually, these outside bureaucrats will find ways to put up roadblocks and thwart the project team (Johansen et al., 1991).

Team Spirit Becomes Team Infatuation

High-performance project teams can be a tremendous source of personal satisfaction. The excitement, chaos, and joy generated by working on a challenging project can be an invigorating experience. Leavitt and Lipman-Blumen (1995) even go so far as to say that team members behave like people in love. They become infatuated with the challenge of the project and the talent around them. This total preoccupation with the project and the project team, while contributing greatly to the remarkable success of the project, can leave in its wake a string of broken professional and personal relationships that contribute to burnout and disorientation upon completion of the project.

Going Local

Going local is a phrase used to describe employees who assume the customs, values, and prerogatives of their foreign country assignment.[11] They no longer represent the interests of the company that sent them but rather those of the local people, culture, or government.

This phenomenon can occur in project teams working abroad or in those who become closely identified with their customers. In essence, the customer's interests take precedence over the parent organization's interests. This change in viewpoint can lead to excessive scope creep and open defiance of corporate policy and interests.

Dealing with going local and other maladies is problematic because, in most cases, they are a distortion of a good thing, rather than a simple evil.

[11] Movie examples of this include *Avatar* (2010), *The Sleeping Dictionary* (2003), and *Lawrence of Arabia* (1962).

Awareness is the first step in prevention. The next step is to take preemptive action to reduce the likelihood of these pitfalls occurring. For example, managers can reduce the isolation of the project team by creating work-related connections outside the project team. These interactions naturally occur in a matrix environment where members work on multiple projects and maintain ties to their home department. Likewise, the isolation of dedicated project teams can be reduced by the timely involvement of external specialists.

In either case, the active involvement of relevant members of the parent organization at project status meetings can help maintain the link between the project and the rest of the organization. If the team appears to be suffering from groupthink, then the project manager can encourage functional conflict by playing a devil's advocate role to encourage dissent or using a structured problem-solving approach like the nominal group technique (see Snapshot from Practice 11.6: Nominal Group Technique). Finally, formal team-building sessions may reveal dysfunctional norms and refocus the team's attention on project objectives.

Summary

Project managers often work under less-than-ideal conditions to develop a cohesive team committed to working together and completing the project to the best of their abilities. They have to recruit personnel from other departments and manage the temporary involvement of team members. They often have to bring strangers together and quickly establish a set of operational procedures that unite their efforts and contributions. They have to be skilled at managing meetings so that they do not become a burden but, rather, a vehicle for progress. Project managers need to forge a team identity and a shared vision that command the attention and allegiance of participants. They often have to manage team members they have little or no direct contact with. Project managers have to encourage functional conflict that contributes to superior solutions while being on guard against dysfunctional conflict that can break a team apart. In doing these things, they have to avoid the pitfalls of excessive group cohesion.

While agendas, charters, visions, rewards, and so forth are important tools and techniques, it was emphasized both in this chapter and in Chapter 10 that the most important tool a project manager has to build an effective project team is his or her own behavior. Just as the founding members of an organization shape the culture of the organization, the project manager shapes and influences the internal culture of the project team. A positive example can define how team members respond to changes, how they handle new tasks, and how they relate to one another and the rest of the organization. There is no easy way to lead by example. It requires personal conviction, discipline, sensitivity to team dynamics, and a constant awareness of how personal actions are perceived by others.

Key Terms

Brainstorming, *470*
Dysfunctional conflict, *473*
Extrovert, *480*
Functional conflict, *473*
Groupthink, *481*
Introvert, *480*
Nominal group technique (NGT), *482*
Positive synergy, *454*
Project kick-off meeting, *459*
Project vision, *465*
Team building, *475*
Team rituals, *464*

Review Questions

1. What are the differences between the five-stage model of team development and the punctuated equilibrium model?
2. What are the elements of an effective project vision? Why are they important?
3. Why should a project manager emphasize group rewards over individual rewards?
4. What is the difference between functional and dysfunctional conflict on a project?
5. When would it be appropriate to hold a formal team-building session on a project?
6. What are the unique challenges of managing a virtual project team?
7. What can a project manager do to avoid some of the pitfalls of a highly cohesive project team?
8. "Trust can actually encourage disagreement and conflict among team members." Explain why this would be the case.

SNAPSHOT FROM PRACTICE

Discussion Questions

11.1 *The 2008 Olympic Redeem Team*

1. Which of the eight characteristics associated with positive synergy were evident in the case of the Redeem team?
2. Which of the eight characteristics associated with positive synergy were not evident in the 2004 team that lost in the Olympics in Athens?

11.2 *Putting Ford on Fast Forward*

1. How important is a fun culture for innovation?
2. What similarities do you see between the Ford Diesel team and the Mac team at Apple and the Skunk Works at Lockheed?

11.3A *Good Man in a Storm*

1. How easy do you think it is to identify people who respond to challenges?
2. In addition to acting as a cheerleader, what other important roles does Tom West suggest a project manager play?

11.4 *Managing Low-Priority Projects*

1. Looking back on your experience working on low-priority projects, did any of these strategies work?

11.5 *Managing Virtual Global Teams*

1. How did Singer enhance trust on his project?
2. How did Singer establish effective patterns of communication?
3. What do you think would have happened if the work had been completed in Japan instead of Australia?

11.6 *Nominal Group Technique*

1. How does the nominal group technique prevent groupthink from occurring on a project?

Exercises

1. The following activities are based on a recently completed group project that you were involved in. This project may have been a student project, a work project, or an extracurricular project.
   a. Analyze the development of the team in terms of the five-stage model and the punctuated equilibrium model. Which model does the best job of describing how the team evolved?
   b. Analyze the group in terms of the nine situational factors that influence team development. What factors positively contributed to group performance? What factors negatively contributed to group performance? How did the

group try to overcome the negative factors? What could you have done differently to overcome these negative factors?

c. Analyze how effectively the group managed meetings. What did the group do well? What didn't the group do well? If the group were formed again, what specific recommendations would you make about how the group should manage meetings?

2. Assume that you have the following decision-making options: (1) make decisions on your own with available information, (2) consult others before making a decision, and (3) call a meeting and reach a consensus, seeking to arrive at a final decision everyone can agree on. Which approach would you use to make each of the following decisions and why?
   a. You were the project leader for Casino Night on campus, a charitable event organized by your group to raise money for the homeless. The event was a big success, garnering a net profit of $8,500. Before the event, your team researched nearby organizations that support the homeless and to whom the money could be given. You narrowed the choices to the Chunk of Coal House and St. Mary's Soup Kitchen. Eventually, your group decided that the funds should be given to Chunk of Coal House. You are about to write a check to its director when you read in the local newspaper that the Chunk of Coal House has terminated operations. What should you do with the money?
   b. You are a golf course designer hired by Trysting Tree Golf Club to renovate their golf course. You have worked closely with the board of directors of the club to develop a new layout that is both challenging and aesthetically pleasing. Everyone is excited about the changes. The project is nearly 75 percent complete when you encounter problems on the 13th hole. The 13th hole at Trysting Tree is a 125-yard par three in which golfers have to hit their tee shots over a lake to a modulated green. During the construction of the new tee box, workers discovered that an underground spring runs beneath the box to the lake. You inspected the site and agreed with the construction supervisor that this could create serious problems, especially during the rainy winter months. After surveying the area, you believe the only viable option would be to extend the hole to 170 yards and create elevated tees on the adjacent hillside. Which of the three decision-making options should you use to make a decision about Hole 13?
   c. You are the leader of a new-product development project. Your team has worked hard on developing a third-generation product that incorporates new technology and meets customer demands. The project is roughly 50 percent complete. You have just received a report from the Marketing Department detailing a similar product that is about to be released by a competitor. The product appears to utilize radical new design principles that expand the functionality of the product. This poses a serious threat to the success of your project. Top management is considering canceling your project and starting over again. They want you to make a recommendation.

3. The following activities are based on a current or recently completed group project that you are (were) involved in. This project may be a student project, a work project, or an extracurricular project.
   a. How strong is the team identity on this project and why?
   b. What could participants do to strengthen team identity?
   c. What kind of informal activities could be used to rejuvenate the team? Why would these activities work?

References

Adams, J. R., and S. E. Brandt, "Behavioral Implications of the Project Lifecyle," in D. I. Cleland and W. R. King (eds.), *Project Management Handbook,* 2nd ed. (New York: Van Nostrand Reinhold, 1988), pp. 206–30.

Bloom, N., "How Working from Home Works Out," Stanford Institute for Economic Policy Research, siper.standford.edu/publications, June 2020. Accessed 5/12/23.

Bowen, K. H., K. B. Clark, C. A. Holloway, and S. C. Wheelwright, *The Perpetual Enterprise Machine* (New York: Oxford Press, 1994).

Cleland, D. I., "Team Building: The New Strategic Weapon," *PM Network,* January 1997, pp. 29–31.

Coutu, D. L., "Organization Trust in Virtual Teams," *Harvard Business Review,* vol. 76, no. 3 (1998), pp. 20–21.

DeMarco, T., and T. Lister, *Peopleware: Productive Projects and Teams,* 2nd ed. (New York: Dorsett House, 1999).

Ericksen, J., and L. Dyer, "Right from the Start: Exploring the Effects of Early Team Events on Subsequent Project Team Performance," *Administrative Science Quarterly,* vol. 49, no. 3 (2004), pp. 438–71.

Frame, J. D., *Managing Projects in Organizations* (San Francisco: Jossey-Bass, 1995).

Hackman, J. R., *Leading Teams: Setting the Stage for Great Performances* (Cambridge, MA: Harvard Business School Press, 2002).

Hoegl, M., and K. P. Parboteeah, "Goal Setting and Team Performance on Innovative Projects: On the Moderating Role of Teamwork Quality," *Small Group Research,* vol. 34 (2003), pp. 3–19.

Janis, I. L., *Groupthink* (Boston: Houghton Mifflin, 1982).

Johansen, R., D. Sibbett, S. Benson, A. Martin, R. Mittman, and P. Saffo, *Leading Business Teams: How Teams Can Use Technology and Group Process Tools to Enhance Performance* (Reading, MA: Addison-Wesley, 1991).

Katz, R., "How a Team at Digital Equipment Designed the 'Alpha' Chip," in Ralph Katz (ed.), *The Human Side of Managing Technological Innovation,* 2nd ed. (New York: Oxford University Press, 2004), pp. 121–33.

Kirkman, B. L., B. Rosen, C. B. Gibson, P. E. Tesluk, and S. O. McPherson, "Five Challenges to Virtual Team Success: Lessons from Sabre, INC.," *Academy of Management Executive,* vol. 16, no. 2 (2002), pp. 67–79.

Kuruppuarachchi, P., "Virtual Team Concepts in Projects: A Case Study," *Project Management Journal,* vol. 40, no. 2 (June 2009), pp. 19–33.

Leavitt, H. J., and J. Lipman-Blumen, "Hot Groups," *Harvard Business Review,* vol. 73 (July–August 1995), pp. 109–16.

Lipsinger, R., and D. DeRosa, *Virtual Team Success: A Practical Guide for Working and Leading from a Distance* (San Francisco: Jossey-Bass, 2010).

Malhotra, A., A. Majchrzak, and B. Rosen, "Leading Virtual Teams," *Academy of Management Perspectives,* vol. 21, no. 1 (2007), pp. 60–70.

Maznevski, M. L., and K. M. Chudoba, "Bridging Space over Time: Global Virtual Team Dynamics and Effectiveness," *Organization Science,* vol. 11. no. 5 (September/October 2000), pp. 473–92.

McComb, S. A., and S. G. Green, "Project Goals, Performance, and Shared Understanding," *Engineering Management Journal,* vol. 11, no. 3 (1999), pp. 7–12.

Murphy, C., and J. Clark, "Picture This: How the Language of Leaders Drives Performance," *Organizational Dynamics,* vol. 45, no. 2 (March 2016), pp. 139–46.

Peters, T., *Thriving on Chaos: Handbook for a Management Revolution* (New York: Knopf, 1988).

Posner, B. Z., "What's All the Fighting About? Conflicts in Project Management," *IEEE Transactions in Engineering Management,* EM-33, 1986, pp. 207–11.

Siebdrat, F., M. Hoegl, and H. Ernst, "How to Manage Virtual Teams," *MIT Sloan Management Review,* http://sloanreview.mit.edu/the-magazine/2009-summer/50412/how-to-manage-virtual teams/2009.

Skilton, P. F., and K. J. Dooley, "The Effects of Repeat Collaboration on Creative Abrasion," *Academy of Management Review,* vol. 35, no. 1 (2010), pp. 118–34.

Smith, B. J., "Building Shared Visions: How to Begin," in P. M. Senge, C. Roberts, R. B. Ross, B. J. Smith, and A. Kleiner (eds.), *The Fifth Discipline Fieldbook: Strategies and Tools for Building a Learning Organization* (New York: Doubleday, 1994), pp. 312–27.

Smith, P. G., and D. G. Reinertsen, *Developing Products in Half the Time,* 2nd ed. (New York: Wiley, 1997).

Thamhain, H. J., and D. L. Wilemon, "Conflict Management in Project Life Cycle," *Sloan Management Review,* vol. 16, no. 3 (1975), pp. 31–41.

Thoms, P., "Creating a Shared Vision with a Project Team," *PM Network,* January 1997, pp. 33–35.

3M, "Leading a Distributed Team," www.3m.com/meetingnetwork/readingroom/meetingguide_distribteam.html. Accessed 6/6/06.

Tippet, D. D., and J. F. Peters, "Team Building and Project Management: How Are We Doing?" *Project Management Journal,* vol. 26, no. 4 (1995), pp. 29–37.

Tuckman, B. W., "Development Sequence of Small-Groups," *Psychological Bulletin,* vol. 63 (1965), pp. 384–99.

Tuckman, B. W., and M. C. Jensen, "Stages of Small-Group Development Revisited," *Group & Organization Studies,* vol. 2, no. 4 (December 1977), pp. 419–27.

Vroom, V. H., and A. G. Jago, *The New Leadership* (Englewood Cliffs, NJ: Prentice Hall, 1988).

Wigert, B., and S. Agrawal, "Returning to the Office: The Current, Preferred and Future State of Remote Work," gallup.com, August 31, 2022. Accessed 5/1/23.

Case 11.1

Kerzner Office Equipment

Amber Briggs looked nervously at her watch as she sat at the front of a large table in the cafeteria at Kerzner Office Equipment. It was now 10 minutes after 3:00 and only 10 of the 14 members had arrived for the first meeting of the Kerzner anniversary task force. Just then two more members hurriedly sat down and mumbled apologies for being late. Briggs cleared her throat and started the meeting.

KERZNER OFFICE EQUIPMENT

Kerzner Office Equipment is located in Charleston, South Carolina. It specializes in the manufacture and sales of high-end office furniture and equipment. Kerzner enjoyed steady growth during its first five years of existence with a high-water employment mark of more than 1,400 workers. Then a national recession struck, forcing Kerzner to lay off 25 percent of its employees. This was a traumatic period for the company. Justin Tubbs was brought in as the new CEO, and things began to slowly turn around. Tubbs was committed to employee participation and redesigned operations around the concept of self-managing teams. The company soon introduced an innovative line of ergonomic furniture designed to reduce back strain and carpal tunnel. This line of equipment proved to be a resounding success, and Kerzner became known as a leader in the industry. The company currently employs 1,100 workers and has just been selected for the second straight time by the *Charleston Post and Courier* as one of the 10 best local firms to work for in South Carolina.

AMBER BRIGGS

Amber Briggs is a 42-year-old human resource specialist who has worked for Kerzner for the past five years. During this time, she has performed a variety of activities involving recruitment, training, compensation, and team building. David Brown, vice president of human resources, assigned Briggs the responsibility for organizing Kerzner's 10th-anniversary celebration. She was excited about the project because she would report directly to top management.

CEO Tubbs briefed her as to the purpose and objectives of the celebration. Tubbs stressed that this should be a memorable event and that it was important to celebrate Kerzner's success since the dark days of the layoffs. Moreover, he confided that he had just read a book on corporate cultures and believed that such events were important for conveying the values at Kerzner. He went on to say that he wanted this to be an employee celebration—not a celebration conjured up by top management. As such, she would be assigned a task force of 14 employees from each of the major departments to organize and plan the event. Her team was to present a preliminary plan and budget for the event to top management within three months. When discussing budgets, Tubbs revealed that he felt the total cost should be somewhere in the $250,000 range. He concluded the meeting by offering to help Briggs in any way he could to make the event a success.

Soon thereafter Briggs received the list of the names of the task force members, and she contacted them by either phone or e-mail to arrange today's meeting. She had to scramble to find a meeting place. Her cubicle in Human Resources was too small to accommodate such a group, and all the meeting rooms at Kerzner were booked or being refurbished. She settled on the cafeteria because it was usually deserted in the late afternoon. Prior to

FIGURE C11.1
Celebration Task Force

Agenda

3:00	Introductions
3:15	Project overview
3:30	Ground rules
3:45	Meeting times
4:00	Adjourn

the meeting, she posted the agenda on a flipchart (see Figure C11.1) adjacent to the table. Given everyone's busy schedules, the meeting was limited to just one hour.

THE FIRST MEETING

Briggs began the meeting by saying, "Greetings. For those who don't know me, I'm Amber Briggs from Human Resources and I've been assigned to manage the 10th-anniversary celebration at Kerzner. Top management wants this to be a special event—at the same time, they want it to be our event. This is why you are here. Each of you represents one of the major departments, and together our job is to plan and organize the celebration." She then reviewed the agenda and asked each member to introduce him/herself. The tall, red-haired woman to the right of Briggs broke the momentary silence by saying, "Hi, I'm Cara Miller from Plastics. I guess my boss picked me for this task force because I have a reputation for throwing great parties."

In turn, each member followed suit. Following is a sampling of their introductions:

> "Hi, I'm Mike Wales from Maintenance. I'm not sure why I'm here. Things have been a little slow in our department, so my boss told me to come to this meeting."
>
> "I'm Megan Plinski from Domestic Sales. I actually volunteered for this assignment. I think it will be a lot of fun to plan a big party."
>
> "Yo, my name is Nick Psias from Accounting. My boss said one of us had to join this task force, and I guess it was my turn."
>
> "Hi, I'm Rick Fennah. I'm the only one from Purchasing who has been here since the beginning. We've been through some rough times, and I think it is important to take time and celebrate what we've accomplished."
>
> "Hi, I'm Ingrid Hedstrom from International Sales. I think this is a great idea, but I should warn you that I will be out of the country for most of the next month."
>
> "I'm Abby Bell from Engineering. Sorry for being late, but things are a bit crazy in my department."

Briggs circled the names of the two people who were absent and circulated a roster so that everyone could check to see if his or her phone number and e-mail address were correct. She then summarized her meeting with Tubbs and told the group that he expected them to make a formal presentation to top management within 10 weeks. She acknowledged that they were all busy people and that it was her job to manage the project as efficiently as possible. At the same time, she reiterated the importance of the project and that this would be a very public event: "If we screw up, everyone will know about it."

Briggs went over the ground rules and emphasized that from now on meetings would start on time and that she expected to be notified in advance if someone was going to be absent. She summarized the first part of the project as centering on five key questions: when, where, what, who, and how much. She created a stir in the group when she responded to a question about cost by informing them that top management was willing to pay up to $250,000 for the event. Megan quipped, "This is going to be one hell of a party."

Briggs then turned the group's attention to identifying a common meeting time. After jousting for 15 minutes, she terminated the discussion by requesting that each member submit a schedule of free time over the next month by Friday. She would use this information and a new planning software to identify optimal times. She ended the meeting by thanking the members for coming and asking them to begin soliciting ideas from co-workers about how this event should be celebrated. She announced that she would meet individually with each of them to discuss their roles on the project. The meeting was adjourned at 4:00 p.m.

1. Critique Briggs's management of the first meeting. What, if anything, should she have done differently?
2. What barriers is she likely to encounter in completing this project?
3. What can she do to overcome these barriers?
4. What should she do between now and the next meeting?

Case 11.2

Ajax Project

Tran was taking his dog, Callie, on her evening walk as the sun began to set over the coastal range. He looked forward to this time of the day. It was an opportunity to enjoy some peace and quiet. It was also a time to review events on the Ajax project and plot his next moves.

Ajax is the code name given by CEBEX to a high-tech security system project funded by the U.S. Department of Defense (DOD). Tran is the project manager, and his core team consists of 30 full-time hardware and software engineers.

Tran and his family fled Cambodia when he was 4 years old. He joined the U.S. Air Force when he was 18 and used the education stipend to attend Washington State University. He joined CEBEX upon graduating with a dual degree in mechanical and electrical engineering. After working on a variety of projects for 10 years, Tran decided he wanted to enter management. He went to night school at the University of Washington to earn an MBA.

Tran became a project manager for the money. He also thought he was good at it. He enjoyed working with people and making the right things happen. This was his fifth project and up to now he was batting .500, with half of his projects being completed ahead of schedule. Tran was proud that he could now afford to send his oldest child to Stanford University.

Ajax was one of many defense projects the CEBEX Corporation had under contract with DOD. CEBEX is a huge defense company with annual sales in excess of $45 billion and more than 120,000 employees worldwide. CEBEX's five major business areas are Aeronautics, Electronic Systems, Information & Technology Services, Integrated Systems & Solutions, and Space Systems. Ajax was one of several new projects sponsored by the Integrated Systems & Solutions Division aimed at the homeland security business. CEBEX was confident that it could leverage its technical expertise and political connections to become a major player in this growing market. Ajax is directed at designing, developing, and installing a security system at an important government installation.

Tran had two major concerns when he started the Ajax project. The first was the technical risks inherent in the project. In theory, the design principles made sense and the project used proven technology. Still, the technology had never been applied in the field in this matter. From experience, Tran knew there was a big difference between the laboratory and the real world. He also knew that integrating the audio, optical, tactile, and laser subsystems would test the patience and ingenuity of his team.

The second concern involved his team. The team is pretty much split down the middle between hardware and electrical engineers. Not only do these engineers have different skill sets and tend to look at problems differently, but generational differences between the two groups are evident as well. The hardware engineers are almost all former military with conservative attire and beliefs. The electrical engineers are a much motlier crew; most are young, single, and at times very cocky. While the hardware engineers talk about raising teenagers and going to Palm Desert to play golf, the electrical engineers talk about Vapor, the latest concert at the Gorge amphitheater, and mountain biking in Peru.

To make matters worse, tension between these two groups within CEBEX festers around salary issues. Electrical engineers were at a premium, and the hardware engineers resented the new hires' salary packages, which were comparable to what they were earning after 20 years of working for CEBEX. Still, the real money was to be made from the incentives associated with project performance. These were all contingent on meeting project milestones and the final completion date.

Before actual work started on the project, Tran arranged a two-day team-building retreat at a lodge on the Olympic peninsula for his entire team as well as key staff from the government installation. He used this time to go over the major objectives of the project and unveil the basic project plan. An internal consultant facilitated several team-building activities that made light of cross-generational issues. Tran felt a real sense of camaraderie within the team.

The good feelings generated from the retreat carried over to the beginning of the project. The entire team bought into the mission of the project and the technical challenges it represented. Hardware and electrical engineers worked side by side to solve problems and build subsystems.

The project plan was built around a series of five tests, with each test being a more rigorous verification of total system performance. Passing each test represented a key milestone for the project. The team was excited about conducting the first Alpha test one week early—only to be disappointed by a series of minor technical glitches that took two weeks to resolve. The team worked extra hard to make up for the lost time. Tran was proud of the team and how hard the members had worked together.

The Alpha II test was conducted on schedule, but once again the system failed to perform. This time three weeks of debugging was needed before the team received the green light to move to the next phase of the project. By this time, team goodwill had been tested, and emotions were a bit frayed. A cloud of disappointment descended over the team as hopes of bonuses disappeared with the project falling further behind schedule. This was augmented by cynics who felt that the original schedule was unfair, and the deadlines were impossible to begin with.

Tran responded by starting each day with a status meeting, where the team reviewed what they had accomplished the previous day and set new objectives for that day. He believed these meetings were helpful in establishing positive momentum and reinforcing a team identity among the engineers. He also went out of his way to spend more time with the "troops," helping them solve problems, offering encouragement, and giving a sincere pat on the back when one was deserved.

He was cautiously optimistic when the time came to conduct the Alpha III test. It was the end of the day when the switch was turned on, but nothing happened. Within minutes the entire team heard the news. Screams could be heard down the hallway. Perhaps the most telling moment was when Tran looked down at the company's parking lot and saw most of his project team walking by themselves to their cars.

As his dog, Callie, chased some wild bunnies, Tran pondered what he should do next.

1. How effective has Tran been as a project manager? Explain.
2. What problem(s) does Tran face?
3. How would you go about solving them? Why?

Case 11.3

Franklin Equipment, Ltd.*

Franklin Equipment, Ltd. (FEL), with headquarters and main fabrication facilities in Saint John, New Brunswick, was founded 75 years ago to fabricate custom-designed, large machines for construction businesses in the Maritime Provinces. Over the years its product lines became strategically focused on creating rock-crushing equipment for dam and highway construction and for a few other markets that require the processing of aggregate. FEL now designs, fabricates, and assembles stationary and portable rock-crushing plants and services its own products and those of its competitors.

In the 1970s, FEL began to expand its market from the Maritime Provinces to the rest of Canada. FEL currently has several offices and fabrication facilities throughout the country. More recently, FEL has made a concerted effort to market its products internationally.

Last month, FEL signed a contract to design and fabricate a rock-crushing plant for a Middle East construction project, called Project Abu Dhabi. Charles Gatenby secured this contract and has been assigned as project manager. This project is viewed as a coup because FEL has wanted to open up markets in this area for a long time and has had difficulty getting prospective customers to realize that FEL is a Canadian firm and not from the United States. Somehow these customers view all North American vendors as the same and are reluctant to employ any of them because of international political considerations.

A project of this scope typically starts with the selection of a team of managers responsible for various aspects of the design, fabrication, delivery, and installation of the product. Manager selection is important because the product design and fabrication vary with the unique needs of each customer. For example, the terrain, rock characteristics, weather conditions, and logistical concerns create special problems for all phases of plant design and operations. In addition, environmental concerns and labor conditions vary from customer to customer and from region to region.

In addition to the project manager, all projects include a design engineer; an operations manager, who oversees fabrication and on-site assembly; and a cost accountant, who oversees all project financial and cost reporting matters. Each of these people must work closely together if a well-running plant is to be delivered on time and within cost constraints. Because international contracts often require FEL to employ host nationals for plant assembly and to train them for operations, a human resource manager is also assigned to the project team. In such cases, the human resource manager needs to understand the particulars of the plant specifications and then use this knowledge to design selection procedures and assess particular training needs. The human resource manager also needs to learn the relevant labor laws of the customer's country.

FEL assigns managers to project teams based on their expertise and their availability to work on a particular project, given their other commitments. This typically means that managers without heavy current project commitments will be assigned to new projects. For instance, a manager finishing one project will likely be assigned a management position on a new project team. The project manager typically has little to say about who is assigned to his or her team.

Because he secured Project Abu Dhabi and has established positive working relationships with the Abu Dhabi customer, Gatenby was assigned to be project manager.

* Courtesy of John A. Drexler, Jr., Oregon State University.

Gatenby has successfully managed similar projects. The other managers assigned to Project Abu Dhabi are Bill Rankins, a brilliant design engineer; Rob Perry, operations manager, with responsibility for fabrication and installation; Elaine Bruder, finance and cost accounting manager; and Sam Stonebreaker, human resource manager. Each of these managers has worked with the others on numerous past projects.

A few years ago, FEL began contracting for team facilitator services from several consulting firms to help new project teams operate effectively. Last month, FEL recruited Carl Jobe from one of these consulting firms to be a full-time internal consultant. A number of managers, including Gatenby, were so impressed with Jobe's skills that they convinced FEL top management of the need to hire a permanent internal facilitator; Jobe was the obvious choice.

Because Gatenby was instrumental in hiring Jobe at FEL, he was excited at the prospect of using Jobe to facilitate team building among Project Abu Dhabi team members. Gatenby was very proud of having secured this project and had expected to be appointed project manager. He knew that this project's success would be instrumental in advancing his own career.

Gatenby told Jobe, "This project is really important to FEL and to me personally. I really need for you to help us develop into a team that works well together to achieve the project's goals within budget. I've observed your success in developing teams on other projects, and I expect you'll do the same for Project Abu Dhabi. I'll take care of you if you help me make this work."

Jobe outlined for Gatenby how he would proceed. Jobe would begin by interviewing team members individually to learn their perceptions of each other and of the promises and pitfalls of being involved in this project. Meetings of the entire team would follow these interviews using the information he collected to help establish a team identity and a shared vision.

Jobe interviewed Bruder first. She expressed skepticism about whether the project could succeed. During the interview, Bruder appeared to be distant, and Jobe could not figure out why he had not established a good rapport with her. Bruder intimated that she expected a lot of cost overruns and a lot of missed production deadlines. But not knowing Jobe well, Bruder was reluctant to identify any specific barriers to the project's success. While she would not directly say so, it was clear to Jobe that Bruder did not want to be a part of Project Abu Dhabi. Jobe left this interview confused and wondering what was going on.

Jobe's next interview was with Perry, the operations manager. Perry has worked at FEL for 15 years, and he immediately came to the point: "This project is not going to work. I cannot understand why upper management keeps assigning me to work on projects with Rankins. We simply cannot work together, and we don't get along. I've disliked him from day one. He keeps dropping the fact that he has earned all these advanced degrees from Purdue. And he keeps telling us how things are done there. I know he's better educated than I am, and he's really smart. But I'm smart, too, and am good at what I do. There's no need for Rankins to make me feel like an idiot because I don't have a degree. Jobe, I'll be honest with you. Rankins has only been here for five years, but I hold him personally responsible for my problem with alcohol, and for its resulting effect on my marriage. I got divorced last year, and it's Rankins's fault."

Jobe next talked with Rankins, who said, "I don't care what you do. Perry and I simply can't work closely together for the nine months it will take to get it done. One of us will kill the other. Ever since I arrived at FEL, Perry has hated my guts and does everything he can to sabotage my designs. We usually worry about customers creating change orders; here it's the fabrication and operations manager who is responsible for them. Perry second-guesses everything I do and makes design changes on his own, and these are always bad decisions. He is out of control. I swear he stays awake at nights, thinking up ways to ruin my designs. I don't have this problem with any other manager."

Jobe left these interviews thoroughly discouraged and could not imagine what would come up in his interview with Stonebreaker. But Stonebreaker was quite positive: "I enjoy these international projects where I get to travel abroad and learn about different cultures. I can't wait to get started on this."

Jobe asked Stonebreaker about the ability of various team members to work together. Stonebreaker replied, "No problem! We've all worked together before and have had no problems. Sure, there have been ruffled feathers and hurt feelings between Rankins and Perry. Rankins can be arrogant and Perry stubborn, but it's never been anything that we couldn't work around. Besides, both of them are good at what they do—both professionals. They'll keep their heads on straight."

Jobe was even more bewildered. Gatenby says this project's success rides on Jobe's facilitation skills. The finance manager appears to want off this project team. The design engineer and operations manager admit they detest each other and cannot work together. And the human resource manager, having worked on projects with Perry and Rankins before, expects a rosy working relationship and anticipates no problems.

Jobe had a second meeting with Gatenby. Before discussing the design of the team-building sessions, he asked questions to learn what Gatenby thought about the ability of team members to work together. Gatenby admitted that there has been very bad blood between Perry and Rankins but added, "That's why we hired you. It's your job to make sure that the history between those two doesn't interfere with Project Abu Dhabi's success. It's your job to get them to work well together. Get it done."

Their dialogue toward the end of this meeting progressed as follows:

Jobe: "Why do you expect Rankins and Perry to work well together, given their history? What incentives do they have to do so?"

Gatenby: "As you should know, FEL requires formal goal setting between project managers and functional managers at the beginning of each project. I've already done this with Bruder, Stonebreaker, Perry, and Rankins. Perry and Rankins have explicit goals stating they must work well together and cooperate with each other."

Jobe: "What happens if they do not meet these goals?"

Gatenby: "I've already discussed this with top management. If it appears to me after two months that things are not working out between Perry and Rankins, FEL will fire Rankins."

Jobe: "Does Perry know this?"

Gatenby: "Yes."

1. Evaluate the criteria FEL uses to assign managers to project teams. What efficiencies do these criteria create? What are the resulting problems?
2. Why is it even more important that project team members work well together on international projects such as Project Abu Dhabi?
3. Discuss the dilemma that Jobe now faces.
4. What should Jobe recommend to Gatenby?

Case 11.4

L&T-IBM Collaboration: Pioneering India's Semiconductor Revolution

INTRODUCTION

The partnership between L&T Semiconductor Technologies Ltd. (LTSCT) and IBM represents a pivotal moment in India's efforts to become self-reliant in advanced semiconductor technologies. As global industries increasingly rely on connected devices, IoT, and electric vehicles, the need for high-performance, energy-efficient processors has grown exponentially. Recognizing this, LTSCT and IBM launched a groundbreaking collaboration to design processors tailored for critical sectors such as automotive, renewable energy, and industrial automation. This project not only aimed to address India's reliance on imported semiconductors but also to bolster its position as a key player in the global semiconductor ecosystem. The increasing need for high-performance, energy-efficient processors designed for vital industries, including industrial automation, renewable energy, and the automotive industry, prompted the start of this project.

Global Context

The global semiconductor industry has become increasingly critical due to the proliferation of connected devices, IoT applications, and electric vehicles. However, geopolitical tensions and supply chain disruptions have highlighted vulnerabilities in semiconductor supply, pushing countries, including India, to invest in domestic innovation and manufacturing.

Indian Context

Due to its reliance on imports for around 80% of its demand, India is vulnerable to supply chain risks worldwide. The Indian government has approved the Semicon India programme, where the Indian government's Production Linked Incentive scheme for semiconductors, launched in December 2021 with an outlay of INR 76,000 crore, aims to boost domestic manufacturing and attract investment in the semiconductor industry, encompassing design, manufacturing, packaging, and testing. This national strategy to support advanced semiconductor technology and strengthen India's position in the international market is in line with the L&T-IBM partnership.

WHAT IS THE PROJECT ABOUT?

The project aims to develop next-generation processors optimized for three primary applications:

1. **Automotive:** Processors for Advanced Driver Assistance Systems (ADAS) and Electric Vehicle (EV) control systems.
2. **Energy Applications:** High-performance processors for managing renewable energy grids and smart meters to optimize energy distribution.
3. **Industrial Automation:** AI-integrated processors for robotics, factory automation, and predictive maintenance.

The partnership will create a synergy for innovation by fusing L&T's engineering and production skills with IBM's knowledge of semiconductor design and AI-driven processor technologies.

RATIONALE FOR PROJECT INITIATION

The project was initiated to address several key challenges:

- **Technological Gaps:** The lack of specialized processors for applications unique to India, like complicated grid management in renewable energy or extremely high temperatures in industrial settings.
- **Energy Efficiency Needs:** The need to reduce energy consumption across sectors while maintaining high computing power.
- **Global Supply Chain Issues:** To improve India's semiconductor ecosystem and lessen reliance on imports.
- **Economic Opportunity:** Use industry alliances and government incentives to establish India as a global center for semiconductor innovation.

KEY STAKEHOLDERS

The project involves a diverse range of stakeholders:

Government Bodies

Ministry of Electronics and Information Technology (MeitY): Supplying regulatory assistance and financial incentives through the Semiconductor PLI Scheme.

Automotive Testing and R&D Bodies: Guaranteeing adherence to automotive performance and safety requirements.

Private Sector

- **L&T Semiconductor Technologies Ltd. (LTSCT):** Leading the design and manufacturing efforts.
- **IBM:** Offering cutting-edge research skills in computing power optimization and AI-driven processor design.

Public Sector and End Users

- **Automotive OEMs:** Early adopters of driving assistance systems and electric car processors.
- **Industrial Enterprises:** Implementing the processors in factory automation systems.

Academic and Research Institutions

Offering expertise and carrying out trial projects to evaluate processor performance.

PROJECT SCOPE AND OBJECTIVES

Scope

The project focuses on the design, development, testing, and deployment of specialized processors for applications in the automotive, energy, and industrial automation sectors. These processors must meet stringent performance, reliability, and scalability requirements.

Objectives

- **Technical Innovation:** Develop processors that are 20% more energy-efficient and 30% faster than current solutions. Integrate AI capabilities for predictive analysis and real-time decision-making.

- **Cost Optimization:** Achieve a 15–20% reduction in manufacturing costs through advanced fabrication techniques.
- **Scalability:** Design modular architectures that can be adapted for different industry-specific use cases.
- **Sustainability:** Incorporate eco-friendly manufacturing practices and reduce the carbon footprint of semiconductor production.

Key Deliverables

- **Processor Architecture:** A scalable design tailored to automotive, energy, and industrial automation sectors.
- **Prototypes:** Functional prototypes for testing in real-world environments within 18 months.
- **Pilot Production:** Small-scale production for industry feedback by the end of the second year.
- **Mass Production:** Full-scale production within three years, targeting domestic and global markets.

PROJECT EXECUTION AND RESOURCE MANAGEMENT

RESOURCE MANAGEMENT

During the L&T Semiconductor Technologies and IBM collaboration, effective resource management played a pivotal role in the successful execution of the project. The resources were allocated and managed strategically to optimize efficiency and meet the project milestones:

Manpower Management

Team Structure:

- L&T contributed 100 engineers specializing in semiconductor manufacturing, and IBM provided 60 experts focusing on AI and processor architecture.
- External collaborations with academic institutions brought in niche expertise for specific R&D challenges.

Training:

- Conducted joint training programs for L&T engineers to familiarize them with IBM's advanced technologies.
- Hosted regular workshops to align team members on objectives, tools, and methodologies.

Material and Infrastructure Management

Procurement:

- Secured high-quality silicon wafers and raw materials under the Make in India initiative to ensure local sourcing and minimize import dependencies.
- IBM's advanced foundries were leveraged for prototype fabrication and testing.

Contingency Planning:

- Buffer inventories were maintained to counteract supply chain disruptions.
- Alternative suppliers were identified to mitigate risks.

Budget Management

- Periodic audits ensured adherence to the allocated ₹500 crore budget.
- Budget overruns were addressed by reallocating resources from less critical tasks.

Challenges in Procurement, Manpower, or Technology

Procurement Challenges

- Global Supply Chain Disruptions: Shortages of critical raw materials like silicon wafers due to geopolitical and economic factors.

Resolution:

- Partnered with local suppliers to reduce dependency on imports.
- Established long-term contracts with global suppliers to ensure availability.

Manpower Challenges

- Coordination Across Teams: Managing cross-functional teams from two global organizations with different work cultures.

Resolution:

- Implemented SCRUM methodologies to facilitate daily stand-ups and improve communication.
- Assigned dedicated project leads to streamline interactions between L&T and IBM teams.

Technological Challenges

- Integration with Legacy Systems: Compatibility issues between new processor technologies and existing automotive/industrial systems.

Resolution:

- Conducted early-stage integration tests to identify and address compatibility issues.
- Leveraged IBM's expertise in middleware development for seamless integration.

PROJECT MONITORING AND CONTROL

TECHNIQUES FOR TRACKING PROGRESS

Key Performance Indicators (KPIs)

- Progress was tracked using specific KPIs for each phase:
- Design Phase: Number of completed architecture designs.
- Prototyping Phase: Number of prototypes passing functional tests.
- Deployment Phase: Percentage of successful integrations in pilot trials.

Earned Value Management (EVM)

- Schedule Performance Index (SPI): Measured adherence to timelines.
- Cost Performance Index (CPI): Tracked budget utilization and cost efficiency.

Agile Methodologies

- Agile sprints ensured incremental progress and timely delivery of prototypes and updates.
- Adaptive planning allowed teams to respond to changes dynamically.

PROJECT CHALLENGES

The ambitious collaboration between L&T Semiconductor Technologies Ltd. and IBM was not without its challenges. These hurdles spanned technical complexities, operational obstacles, and environmental and social considerations. Addressing these challenges was crucial for the project's success and provided valuable lessons for future initiatives.

TECHNICAL CHALLENGES

Engineering and Design Problems

Despite the combined expertise of L&T and IBM, the development of next-generation processors presented significant engineering hurdles:

- **Advanced Processor Architecture:** Designing processors that were 20% more energy-efficient and 30% faster required pushing the boundaries of existing semiconductor technology. This involved innovating new architectures that could handle increased computational loads without compromising on energy consumption.
- **Miniaturization Limitations:** As processors become smaller, issues like heat dissipation and quantum tunneling become more pronounced. Overcoming these required advanced materials and cooling solutions, which were still in developmental stages.
- **Integration of AI Capabilities:** Embedding AI functionalities into processors for real-time decision-making added layers of complexity to the design. Ensuring that these processors could perform AI computations efficiently without additional power consumption was a significant challenge.

Adoption of New Technology

- **Advanced Fabrication Techniques:** Implementing cutting-edge fabrication methods, such as Extreme Ultraviolet Lithography (EUVL), was necessary to achieve the desired processor specifications. However, this technology was relatively new and required substantial investment in equipment and training.
- **Compatibility with Existing Systems:** Ensuring that the new processors could seamlessly integrate with existing automotive, energy, and industrial systems was critical. This required extensive testing and the development of custom interfaces or middleware solutions.
- **Intellectual Property (IP) Concerns:** Navigating the complexities of IP rights, especially when using proprietary technologies from both L&T and IBM, required careful legal considerations to protect both parties' interests.

OPERATIONAL CHALLENGES

Delays

- **Schedule Variance**:

  Issue: A 2-month delay in the prototyping phase due to supply chain disruptions.

  Resolution: Reallocated resources from the testing phase to expedite prototype completion and established agreements with alternative suppliers.

- **Supply Chain Disruptions:** Global shortages of semiconductor materials, exacerbated by geopolitical tensions and the pandemic, led to delays in procuring critical components like silicon wafers.
- **Regulatory Approvals:** Obtaining certifications and meeting compliance standards in multiple sectors (automotive, energy, industrial) extended timelines beyond initial projections.
- **Performance Variance:**

  Issue: Initial prototypes underperformed in energy efficiency metrics.

  Resolution: IBM's AI-driven optimization tools were employed to redesign and fine-tune the processors.

Cost Overruns

- **Cost Variance:**

  Issue: A 10% budget overrun during pilot production due to unexpected testing costs.

  Resolution: Reduced discretionary spending and optimized resource allocation to balance the budget.
- **Unexpected R&D Expenses:** The need for additional research to overcome technical challenges led to budget overruns. For instance, more resources had to be allocated for developing new cooling solutions for processors
- **Investment in Training:** Additional funds were required to upskill the workforce, particularly in handling new fabrication equipment and advanced design software.

Workforce Issues

- **Talent Shortage:** There was a scarcity of engineers specialized in advanced semiconductor technologies and AI integration. Competing with global tech giants for talent posed a significant challenge.
- **Cultural Differences:** Integrating teams from L&T and IBM, each with distinct corporate cultures and working styles, required effort to ensure smooth collaboration. Misalignments occasionally led to miscommunication and inefficiencies.
- **Remote Collaboration:** The pandemic necessitated remote work arrangements, which impacted coordination, especially during critical phases like prototyping and testing that traditionally rely on in-person collaboration.

Environmental and Social Issues

(a) Impact on Communities

- **Environmental Footprint:** Semiconductor manufacturing is resource-intensive, consuming significant amounts of water and energy, and producing hazardous waste. Local communities expressed concerns about the potential environmental impact of the new manufacturing facilities.
- **Land Use and Displacement:** Establishing new manufacturing units required land acquisition, which risked displacing local populations and affecting livelihoods, leading to social unrest.

(b) Measures for Sustainable Development

- **Eco-Friendly Manufacturing Practices:** The project incorporated sustainable practices such as:

  - **Water Recycling Systems:** Implementing advanced systems to recycle and reuse water within the manufacturing process reduced freshwater consumption by 50%.
  - **Renewable Energy Usage:** Committed to sourcing at least 30% of the facility's energy needs from renewable sources like solar and wind power.
  - **Waste Management:** Established protocols for the safe disposal and treatment of hazardous waste, including partnerships with certified waste management companies.

(c) Community Engagement Initiatives

- **Stakeholder Consultations:** Regular meetings with local communities to address concerns and incorporate feedback into project planning.
- **Corporate Social Responsibility (CSR) Programs:** Investments in local infrastructure, education, and healthcare facilities to improve community well-being.
- **Employment Opportunities:** Prioritized hiring from the local population, providing training programs to develop necessary skills, thereby boosting local employment rates.

(d) Compliance with Environmental Regulations

- **Regulatory Adherence:** Ensured full compliance with national and international environmental standards, including the **Environmental Impact Assessment (EIA)** requirements.
- **Third-Party Audits:** Engaged independent auditors to assess environmental performance and suggest improvements, enhancing transparency and accountability.

ADDRESSING THE CHALLENGES

The project team adopted a proactive approach to overcome these challenges:

- **Collaborative Problem-Solving:** Joint task forces comprising experts from both L&T and IBM were formed to tackle specific technical issues, fostering innovation through diverse perspectives.
- **Flexible Project Management:** Employed agile methodologies to adapt to changes swiftly, reallocating resources and adjusting timelines as needed.
- **Investment in R&D:** Increased funding for research initiatives, particularly in areas like advanced materials and AI integration, to find viable solutions to technical roadblocks.
- **Enhanced Communication Strategies:** Implemented regular cross-functional meetings and used collaborative tools to bridge communication gaps between teams.
- **Sustainability as a Core Principle:** Recognized that environmental stewardship was not just a compliance requirement but also a competitive advantage, leading to the integration of sustainable practices into every aspect of the project.

OUTCOMES AND LEARNINGS

By effectively navigating these challenges, the project achieved significant milestones:

- **Technical Innovations:** Successfully developed processors that met the desired energy efficiency and performance metrics, with several patents filed for new technologies developed during the project.

- **Operational Efficiency:** Despite initial delays and cost overruns, the project was realigned to meet critical deadlines without compromising on quality, demonstrating the effectiveness of adaptive project management strategies.
- **Positive Community Impact:** The measures taken for sustainable development not only mitigated environmental and social risks but also enhanced the company's reputation, fostering goodwill and support from local communities.

REFERENCES

- Ministry of Electronics and Information Technology (MeitY): Semiconductor Manufacturing Incentive Scheme Guidelines. Available at: https://www.meity.gov.in/
- National Policy on Electronics, 2019. Available at: https://www.meity.gov.in/npe-2019
- McKinsey & Company: The Semiconductor Industry's Impact on the Global Economy. Available at: https://www.mckinsey.com/
- Deloitte Insights: 2023 Semiconductor Industry Outlook. Available at: https://www2.deloitte.com/
- SEMI: Global Semiconductor Market Trends and Projections. Available at: https://www.semi.org/
- Business Standard: L&T Semiconductor Technologies, IBM Ink Pact to Develop Advanced Processors. Available at: https://www.business-standard.com/
- Inc42: L&T Semiconductor Partners with IBM to Design Processors. Available at: https://inc42.com/
- IEEE Xplore: AI-Driven Processor Architectures for Automotive and Industrial Applications. Available at: https://ieeexplore.ieee.org/
- ACM Digital Library: Challenges and Opportunities in Advanced Semiconductor Fabrication. Available at: https://dl.acm.org/
- L&T Semiconductor Technologies Ltd: Company Announcements and Project Updates. Available at: https://www.larsentoubro.com/
- IBM Research: Semiconductor Innovations and AI Integration. Available at: https://www.ibm.com/research/
- UN Sustainable Development Goals (SDGs): Guidelines for Sustainable Manufacturing. Available at: https://sdgs.un.org/
- Environmental Impact Assessment (EIA) Reports: Indian Regulatory Frameworks for High-Tech Projects.

CHAPTER TWELVE

12 Outsourcing: Managing Interorganizational Relations

LEARNING OBJECTIVES

After reading this chapter you should be able to:

12-1 Understand the advantages and disadvantages of outsourcing project work.

12-2 Describe the basic elements of a Request for Proposal (RFP)

12-3 Identify best practices for outsourcing project work.

12-4 Practice principled negotiation.

12-5 Describe the met-expectations model of customer satisfaction and its implications for working with customers on projects.

A12-1 Describe the procurement management process.

A12-2 Describe the differences between fixed-price and cost-plus contracts and their advantages and disadvantages.

OUTLINE

12.1 Outsourcing Project Work

12.2 Request for Proposal (RFP)

12.3 Best Practices in Outsourcing Project Work

12.4 The Art of Negotiating

12.5 A Note on Managing Customer Relations

Summary

Appendix 12.1: Contract Management

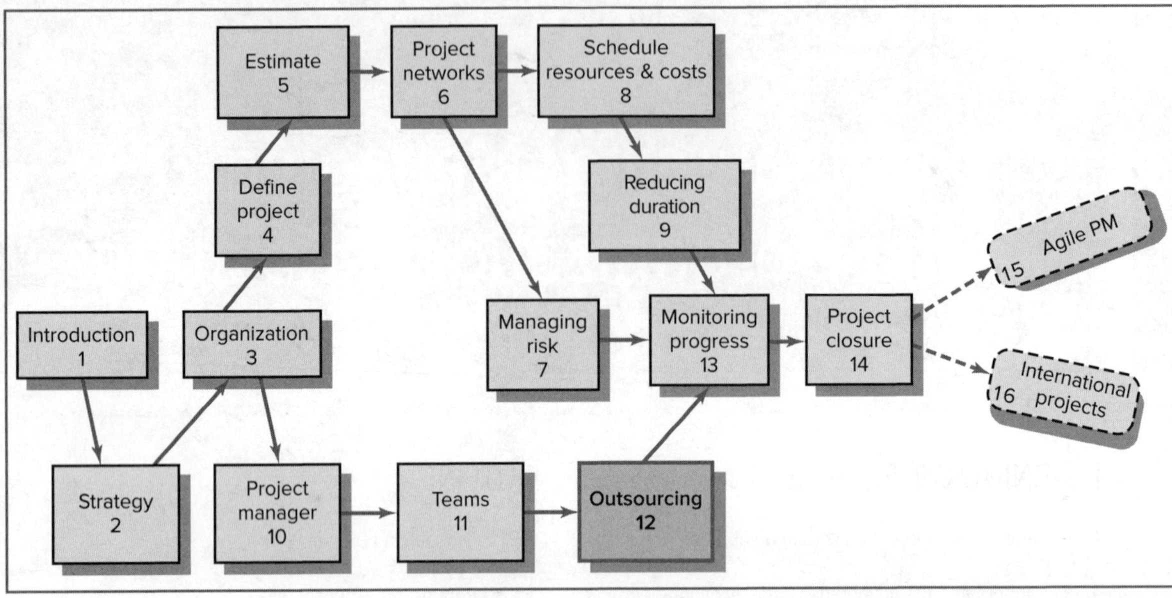

. . . being a good partner has become a key corporate asset. I call it a company's collaborative advantage. In the global economy, a well-developed ability to create and sustain fruitful collaborations gives companies a significant competitive leg up.

—Rosabeth Moss Kanter, Harvard Business School professor

It is rare in today's flat world to find important projects that are being completed totally in-house. Outsourcing, or contracting significant segments of project work to other companies, is commonplace. For example, small high-tech businesses hire marketing firms to research what features customers value in new products they are creating. Even industry giants such as Microsoft and Intel commonly hire independent firms to test new products they are developing.

Contracting project work has long been the norm in the construction industry, where firms hire general contractors who, in turn, hire and manage cadres of subcontractors to create new buildings and structures. For example, the Chunnel project, which created a transportation tunnel between France and England, involved more than 250 organizations. Contracting is not limited to large projects. For example, an insurance company worked with an outside contractor to develop an answering service that directs customers to specific departments and employees. The trend for the future suggests that more and more projects will involve working with people from different organizations.

This chapter extends the previous two chapters' discussion of building and managing relations by focusing specifically on issues surrounding working on projects with people from other organizations. First, the advantages and disadvantages of outsourcing project work are introduced. This is followed by a discussion of Request for Proposals (RFPs) and the solicitation process. Best practices used by firms to outsource and collaborate with each other are discussed next. The focus then shifts to the art of negotiating, which is at the heart of effective collaboration. Negotiating skills and techniques for resolving disagreements and reaching optimal solutions are then presented. The chapter closes with a brief, but important, note on managing customer relations. In addition, an appendix on contract management is included to augment our discussion of how organizations work together on projects.

12.1 Outsourcing Project Work

LO 12-1

Understand the advantages and disadvantages of outsourcing project work.

The term **outsourcing** has traditionally been applied to the transferring of business functions or processes (e.g., customer support, IT, accounting) to other, often foreign companies. For example, when you call your Internet provider to solve a technical problem you are likely to talk to a technician in Bangalore, India, or Bucharest, Romania. Outsourcing is now being applied to contracting significant chunks of project work. For example, Apple and Motorola work closely with manufacturers in China to develop next-generation smartphones. Toyota and DaimlerChrysler collaborate with suppliers to develop new automobile platforms.

The shift toward outsourcing is readily apparent in the film industry. During the golden era of Hollywood, huge, vertically integrated corporations made movies. Studios such as MGM, Warner Brothers, and 20th Century Fox owned large movie lots and employed thousands of full-time specialists—set designers, camera people, film editors, and directors. Star actors like Humphrey Bogart and Marilyn Monroe were signed to exclusive studio contracts for a set number of films (e.g., six films over three years). Today, most movies are made by a collection of individuals and small companies who come together to make films project by project. This structure allows risks to be shared and each project to be staffed with the best available talent rather than only studio employees. This same approach is being applied to the creation of new products and services. For example, see Figure 12.1.

Figure 12.1 depicts a situation in which a zero-gravity reclining chair is being developed. The genesis for the chair comes from a mechanical engineer who developed the

FIGURE 12.1
Reclining Chair Project

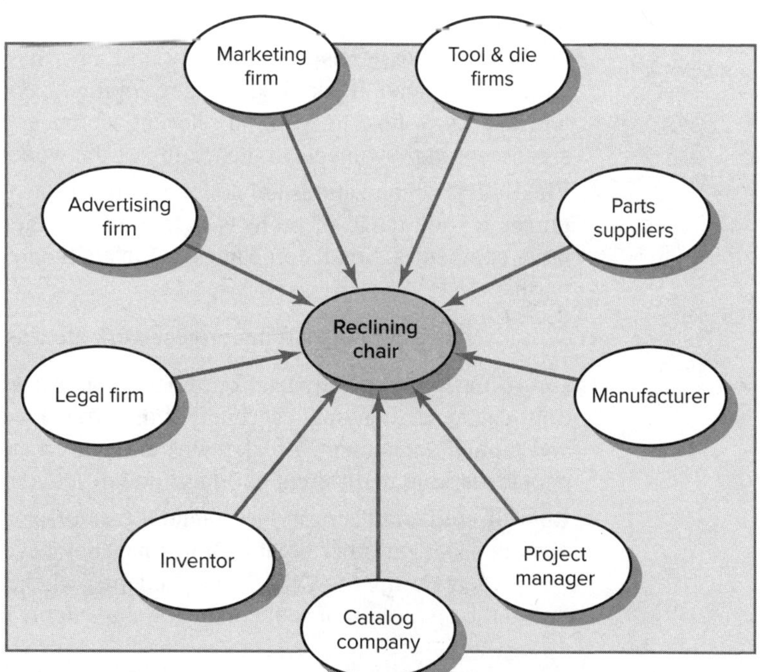

idea in her garage. The inventor negotiates a contract with a catalog firm to develop and manufacture the chair. The catalog company in turn creates a project team of manufacturers, suppliers, and marketing firms to create the new chair. Each participant adds requisite expertise to the project. The catalog firm brings its brand name and distribution channels to the project. Tool and die firms provide customized parts, which are delivered to a manufacturing firm that will produce the chair. Marketing firms refine the design, develop packaging, and test market potential names. A project manager is assigned by the catalog firm to work with the inventor and the other parties to complete the project.

Many outsourced projects operate in a virtual environment in which people are linked by computers, faxes, computer-aided design systems, and video teleconferencing. They rarely, if ever, see one another face-to-face. On other projects, participants from different organizations work closely together, for example, at a construction site or in shared office space. In either case, people come and go as services are needed, much as in a matrix structure, but they are not formal members of one organization, just technical experts who form a temporary alliance with an organization, fulfill their contractual obligations, and then move on to the next project.

The advantages of outsourcing project work are many:

1. **Cost reduction.** Companies can secure competitive prices for contracted services, especially if the work can be outsourced offshore. Furthermore, overhead costs are dramatically cut, since the company no longer has to internally maintain the contracted services.
2. **Faster project completion.** Not only can work be done more cheaply, but it can also be done faster. Competitive pricing means more resources for the dollar. For example, three Indian software engineers can be hired for the price of one American software engineer. Furthermore, outsourcing can provide access to equipment that can accelerate the completion of project tasks. For example, by contracting a backhoe operator you are able to accomplish in four hours what it would take a landscaping crew four days to complete.
3. **High level of expertise.** A company no longer has to keep up with technological advances. Instead, it can focus on developing its core competencies and hire firms with the know-how to work on relevant segments of the project. This can lead to significant improvements in the quality of the work performed.
4. **Flexibility.** Organizations are no longer constrained by their own resources but can pursue a wide range of projects by combining their resources with the talents of other companies. Small companies can instantly go global by working with foreign partners.

The disadvantages of outsourcing project work are less well documented:

1. **Coordination breakdowns.** Coordination of professionals from different organizations can be challenging, especially if the project work requires close collaboration and mutual adjustment. Breakdowns are exacerbated by physical separation with people working in different buildings and different cities, if not different countries.
2. **Loss of control.** There is the potential loss of control over the project. The core team depends on other organizations that they have no direct authority over. This was evident during the COVID-19 pandemic when so many projects came to a halt due to the disruption of semiconductor chip supply chain.

3. **Conflict.** Projects are more prone to interpersonal conflict, since the different participants do not share the same values, priorities, and culture. Trust, which is essential to project success, can be difficult to forge when interactions are limited and people come from different organizations.
4. **Security issues.** Depending on the nature of the project, trade and business secrets may be revealed. This can be problematic if the contractor also works for your competitor. Confidentiality is another concern and companies have to be very careful when outsourcing processes like payroll, medical transcriptions, and insurance information.
5. **Political hot potato.** Foreign outsourcing of work is perceived as a major cause of underemployment and U.S. companies are under increased pressure to keep jobs local. Furthermore, several U.S. firms have been criticized for the oppressive labor practices of some of their suppliers in China.

Few people disagree that reducing costs is one, if not, the primary motive behind outsourcing project work. However, there are limits to outsourcing (see Snapshot from Practice 12.1: The Boeing 787 Dreamliner), and there appears to be a shift away from

SNAPSHOT FROM PRACTICE 12.1 The Boeing 787 Dreamliner*

BACKGROUND

In 2002 the basic design and plans for Boeing's 787 Dreamliner were accepted and given the charter to "Go." The Dreamliner boasted the latest design and revolutionary technology in the history of commercial air travel. But the project met bumpy weather. The first 787 aircraft, scheduled to be tested in July 2007, was delayed until December 2009. Orders for the advanced 787 grew quickly to over 800 planes. This rosy picture presented Boeing with a giant-sized headache. For various reasons (such as design, outsourcing, and labor issues) delivery dates slipped behind three years or more and costs ballooned to several billion dollars. Many analysts blame outsourcing work to foreign suppliers for a majority of the cost and schedule overruns.

MO:SE/Alamy Stock Photo

KEY FACTORS INFLUENCING OUTSOURCING DECISION

The Dreamliner outsourcing decision that gave 70 percent of plane content to outside suppliers included 30 percent to foreign suppliers. These percentages were greater than any previous commercial plane built by Boeing. Boeing's outsourcing rationale was based on typical economic considerations of cost, sales, and risk. In Boeing's case, this meant

Cost. Establishing partnerships with suppliers to lower risks and development costs, along with gaining some valuable expertise and process innovation.
Sales. Farming out numerous designs and components to foreign countries (e.g., Sweden, Italy, South Korea, and China) with the expectation that these countries will buy planes from Boeing in the future.
Risk. Recognizing the need to balance the risk of outsourcing at the organizational and operational levels is crucial. The different levels are co-dependent.

Clearly, the outsourcing decision ricocheted. Costs are over budget, some sales have been rescinded, customers are seeking compensation for delays, and potential ROI is reduced.

IMPACTS

Boeing's brand has been seriously tarnished by delays and mismanagement. The process to manage the logistics of outsourcing was not able to handle the volume of logistical problems and change management issues. Chronic delays of a few nonperforming partners induced Boeing to buy out or support partners and consumed cash. Wall Street estimates cost overruns range between $12 and $18 billion over the original planned investment of $5 billion. Lessons learned from outsourcing of the 787 Dreamliner can point the way to bring back the shine to Boeing's reputation as the leader in design, technology, and integration.

LESSONS LEARNED

The lessons learned in the Dreamliner launch have been well documented. A few obvious relevant lessons are noted in suggestion form here:

- Identify and analyze all risks of outsourcing at organization *and* component levels. For example, assess the risks and implications of farming out large portions (30 percent) of the design and manufacture of crucial components to foreign suppliers. Outsourcing tends to work better in noncore areas.
- Thoroughly investigate partnership capabilities and resources. Due diligence reduces problems.
- Develop processes for quickly addressing issues and problems. Increase liaison and supervision of supply chain logistics with outsource partners.
- Reconsider seriously the implications of farming out key expertise. This runs the risk of becoming fully reliant on suppliers and transferring unique intellectual property. Partners get risk-free technical know-how, high-margin markets for component parts over the life of the plane, and perhaps the ability to become a future competitor.
- The risk of outsourcing complex high-technology components carries the burden of careful coordination and liaison.

Boeing executives have acknowledged the problems associated with outsourcing large portions of the 787 Dreamliner. For example, Boeing's commercial airplanes chief, Jim Albaugh, expressed to students at Seattle University, "We spent a lot more money in trying to recover [the project] than we ever would have spent if we'd tried to keep the key technologies closer to home. The pendulum swung too far." He added that, in part, chasing the financial measure of return on assets led Boeing astray. Boeing CEO Jim McNerney noted that the 787 game plan may have been overly ambitious, incorporating too many firsts all at once.

THE FUTURE

Although Boeing's 787 outsourcing experience was very costly, outsourcing will continue and evolve. Lessons learned will prompt aircraft builders to reevaluate future outsourcing and move on. Expect to see emphasis on risk- and cost-sharing partnerships.

The major short-term challenge for Boeing is to ramp up production to satisfy the hundreds of waiting orders. Boeing can recoup by adjusting their integrative outsourcing and logistics model as a top priority.

*http://seattletimes.nwsource.com/html/sundaybuzz/2014125414_sundaybuzz06.html; http://atwonline.com/aircraft-engines-components/news/boeing-commercial-airplanes-ceo-concedes-787-outsourcingbackfired. Accessed 1/12/13.

simply nailing the best low-cost deal to securing services from companies that provide the best value in terms of both cost and performance. Performance is not limited to simply the quality of specific work but also includes the ability to collaborate and work together. Companies are doing their homework to determine "Can we work with these people?"

12.2 Request for Proposal (RFP)

LO 12-2

Describe the basic elements of a Request for Proposal (RFP).

Once an organization decides to outsource project work, the customer or project manager is frequently responsible for developing a **Request for Proposal (RFP).**

The responsible project manager will require input from all stakeholders connected to the activities covered in the RFP. The RFP will be announced to external contractors/vendors with adequate experience to implement the project. For example, government projects frequently advertise with a "request for proposal" to outside contractors for roads, buildings, airports, military hardware, and space vehicles. Similarly, businesses use RFPs to solicit bids for building a clean room, developing a new manufacturing process, delivering software for insurance billing, and conducting a market survey. In all these examples, requirements and features should be in enough detail that contractors have a clear description of the final deliverable that will meet the customer's needs.

RFPs are important. In practice, the most common error is to offer an RFP that lacks sufficient detail. This lack of detail typically results in conflict issues, misunderstandings, often legal claims between the contractor and owner, and ultimately a dissatisfied customer. All RFPs are different, but the outline in Figure 12.2 is a good starting point for the development of a detailed RFP. Each step is briefly described next.

1. **Summary of needs and request for action.** The background and a simple description of the final project deliverable are given first. For example, through simulated war games, the U.S. Navy has found their giant warships of the past are too vulnerable against today's technology (an example is the Silkworm antiship missiles). In addition, the Navy's mission has shifted to supporting ground forces and peacekeeping missions, which require getting closer to shore. As a result, the Navy is revamping ships for near-shore duty. The Navy will select three designs for further refinement from the responses to its RFP. In general, it is expected that the new ship will be capable of at least 55 knots, measure between 80 and 250 feet in length, and be fitted with radar absorbing panels to thwart guided missiles.
2. **Statement of work (SOW) detailing the scope and major deliverables.** For example, if the project involves a market research survey, the major deliverables could be design, data collection, data analysis, and providing recommendations by February 21, 2024, for a cost not to exceed $300,000.
3. **Deliverable specifications/requirements, features, and tasks.** This step should be very comprehensive so bid proposals from contractors can be validated and later used for control. Typical specifications cover physical features such as size,

FIGURE 12.2
Request for Proposal

1. Summary of needs and request for action
2. Statement of work (SOW) detailing the scope and major deliverables
3. Deliverable specifications/requirements, features, and tasks
4. Responsibilities—vendor and customer
5. Project schedule
6. Costs and payment schedule
7. Type of contract
8. Experience and staffing
9. Evaluation criteria

quantity, materials, speed, and color. For example, an IT project might specify requirements for hardware, software, and training in great detail. Tasks required to complete deliverables can be included if they are known.

4. **Responsibilities—vendor and customer.** Failing to spell out the responsibilities for both parties is notorious for leading to serious problems when the contractor implements the project. For example, who pays for what? (If the contractor is to be on-site, will the contractor be required to pay for office space?) What are the limits and exclusions for the contractor? (For example, who will supply test equipment?) What communication plan will be used by the contractor and owner? If escalation of an issue becomes necessary, what process will be used? How will progress be evaluated? Well-defined responsibilities will avoid many unforeseen problems later.
5. **Project schedule.** This step is concerned with getting a "hard" schedule that can be used for control and evaluating progress. Owners are usually very demanding in meeting the project schedule. In today's business environment, time-to-market is a major "hot button" that influences market share, costs, and profits. The schedule should spell out what, who, and when.
6. **Costs and payment schedule.** The RFP needs to set out very clearly how, when, and the process for determining costs and conditions for progress payments.
7. **Type of contract.** Essentially there are two types of contracts—fixed-price and cost-plus. Fixed-price contracts agree on a price or lump sum in advance, and it remains as long as there are no changes to the scope provisions of the agreement. This type is preferred in projects that are well defined with predictable costs and minimal risks. The contractor must exercise care in estimating cost because any underestimating of costs will cause the contractor's profit to be reduced. In cost-plus contracts, the contractor is reimbursed for all or some of the expenses incurred during the performance of the contract. This fee is negotiated in advance and usually involves a percent of total costs. "Time and materials" plus a profit factor are typical of cost-plus contracts. Both types of contracts can include incentive clauses for superior performance in time and cost, or in some cases penalties—for example, missing the opening date of a new sports stadium. Appendix 12.1 elaborates further on contract management.
8. **Experience and staffing.** The ability of the contractor to implement the project may depend on specific skills; this necessary experience should be specified, along with assurance such staff will be available for this project.
9. **Evaluation criteria.** The criteria for evaluating and awarding the project contract should be specified. For example, selection criteria frequently include methodology, price, schedule, and experience; in some cases, these criteria are weighted. Use of the outline in Figure 12.2 will help to ensure key items in the proposal are not omitted. A well-prepared RFP will provide contractors with sufficient guidelines to prepare a proposal that clearly meets the project and customer's needs.

Selection of Contractor from Bid Proposals

Interested contractors respond to project RFPs with a written bid proposal. It is likely that several contractors will submit bid proposals to the customer.

The final step in the RFP process is to select the contractor who best meets the requirements requested in the RFP. The selection criteria given in the RFP are used to evaluate which contractor is awarded the contract to implement the project. Losing contractors should be given an explanation of the key factors that led to the selection

FIGURE 12.3 Contractor Evaluation Template

Contractor Evaluation Template	Maximum Weight	Proposal 1	Proposal 2	Proposal 3	Proposal 4
Contractor qualifications	Weight = 10				
Technical skills available	Weight = 20				
Understanding of contract and conditions	Weight = 5				
Financial strength to implement project	Weight = 15				
Understanding of proposal specifications	Weight = 10				
Innovativeness and originality of proposal	Weight = 5				
Reputation for delivering on time and budget	Weight = 15				
Price	Weight = 20				
Total	**100**				

of the winning contractor/vendor; appreciation for their participation and effort should be acknowledged. See Figure 12.3, Contractor Evaluation Template, adapted from one used in practice.

12.3 Best Practices in Outsourcing Project Work

LO 12-3

Identify best practices for outsourcing project work.

This section describes some of the best practices we have observed being used by firms that excel in project management (see Figure 12.4). Although the list is by no means comprehensive, it reflects strategies used by organizations with extensive outsourcing experience. These practices reveal an underlying theme in how firms approach contracted work on projects. Instead of the traditional master–slave relationship between owner and provider or buyer and seller, all parties work together as partners sharing the ultimate goal of a successful project.

Differences between the traditional approach and the partnering approach to managing contracted relationships are summarized in Table 12.1.[1] Partnering requires more than a simple handshake. It typically entails a significant commitment of time and energy to forge and sustain collaborative relations among all parties. This commitment is reflected in the seven best practices that will be discussed next.

FIGURE 12.4 Best Practices in Outsourcing Project Work

- Well-defined requirements and procedures.
- Extensive training and team-building activities.
- Well-established conflict management processes in place.
- Frequent review and status updates.
- Co-location when needed.
- Fair and incentive-laden contracts.
- Long-term outsourcing relationships.

Well-Defined Requirements and Procedures

Convincing people from different professions, organizations, and cultures to work together is difficult. If expectations and requirements are fuzzy or open to debate, this is even harder. Successful firms are very careful in selecting the work to be outsourced. They often choose to contract only work with clearly defined deliverables with

[1] Cowan, C., C. F. Gray, and E. W. Larson, "Project Partnering," *Project Management Journal,* vol. 12, no. 4 (December 1992), pp. 5–15.

TABLE 12.1
Key Differences between Partnering and Traditional Approaches to Managing Contracted Relationships

Partnering Approach	Traditional Approach
Mutual trust forms the basis for strong working relationships.	Suspicion and distrust; each party is wary of the motives for actions by the other.
Shared goals and objectives ensure common direction.	Each party's goals and objectives, although similar, are geared to what is best for that party.
Joint project team exists with high level of interaction.	Independent project teams; teams are spatially separated with managed interactions.
Open communications avoid misdirection and bolster effective working relationships.	Communications are structured and guarded.
Long-term commitment provides the opportunity to attain continuous improvement.	Single project contracting is normal.
Objective critique is geared to candid assessment of performance.	Objectivity is limited due to fear of reprisal and lack of continuous improvement opportunity.
Access to each other's organization resources is available.	Access is limited with structured procedures and self-preservation taking priority over total optimization.
Total company involvement requires commitment from CEO to team members.	Involvement is normally limited to project-level personnel.
Integration of administrative systems equipment takes place.	Duplication and/or translation takes place with attendant costs and delays.
Risk is shared jointly among the partners, which encourages innovation and continuous improvement.	Risk is transferred to the other party.

measurable outcomes. For example, contractors hire electric firms to install heating and air-conditioning systems, electronic firms use design firms to fabricate enclosures for their products, and software development teams outsource the testing of versions of their programs. In all of these cases, the technical requirements are spelled out in detail. Even so, communicating requirements can be troublesome, especially with foreign providers (see Snapshot from Practice 12.2: Four Strategies for Communicating with Outsourcers), and extra care has to be taken to ensure that expectations are understood.

Not only do requirements have to be spelled out, but the different firms' project management systems need to be integrated. Common procedures and terminology need to be established so that different parties can work together. This can be problematic when you have firms with more advanced project management systems working with less developed organizations. Surprisingly, this often is the case when U.S. firms outsource software work to India. We have heard reports that Indian providers are shocked at how unsystematic their U.S. counterparts are in their approach to managing software projects.

The best companies address this issue up front instead of waiting for problems to emerge. First, they assess "fit" between providers' project management methods and their own project management system. This is a prime consideration in choosing vendors. Work requirements and deliverables are spelled out in detail in the procurement process. They invest significant time and energy in establishing project communication systems to support effective collaboration.

Finally, whenever you work with other organizations on projects, security is an important issue. Security extends beyond competitive secrets and technology to include access to information systems. Firms have to establish robust safeguards to prevent information access and the introduction of viruses due to less secure provider systems. Information technology security is an additional cost and risk that needs to be addressed up front before outsourcing project work.

SNAPSHOT FROM PRACTICE 12.2 Four Strategies for Communicating with Outsourcers*

Dr. Adam Kolawa offers four strategies for overcoming poor communication with offshore project partners.

STRATEGY 1: RECOGNIZE CULTURAL DIFFERENCES

Realize that not everyone you communicate with shares your assumptions. What is obvious to you is not necessarily obvious to your partner. This is especially true with foreign outsourcers. As an American, you likely assume that laws are generally obeyed. Believe it or not, that's generally not true in most of the world, where laws are guidelines that are not necessarily followed. This can lead to major communication problems! You think that if you write a contract, everybody is going to adhere to it. For many people, a contract is merely a suggestion.

STRATEGY 2: CHOOSE THE RIGHT WORDS

When you explain your requirements to an outsourcer, word choice is critical. For many outsourcers, English is still a foreign language—even in India, where both outsourcing and the English language are common. No matter how prevalent English has become, your outsourcer might have a basic understanding of each word you utter yet be not completely clear on the exact meaning of the message you're trying to convey. This is why you should speak in a direct manner using short sentences made of basic, simple words.

STRATEGY 3: CONFIRM YOUR REQUIREMENTS

You should take the following steps to confirm that the outsourcer thoroughly understands your requirements:

1. *Document your requirements.* Follow up your conversations in writing. Commit your requirements to paper for the outsourcer. Many people understand written language better than spoken language, probably because they have more time to process the message.
2. *Insist your outsourcer re-document your requirements.* Leave nothing to chance. Require outsourcers to write the requirements in their own words. If outsourcers cannot relay to you what you explained to them, then they didn't understand.
3. *Request a prototype.* After the requirements are written, ask the outsourcer to create a prototype for you. This is a safety net to ensure that your wants and needs are positively understood. Ask the provider to sketch what you want your final product to look like or build a quick, simple program that reflects how the final product will look.

STRATEGY 4: SET DEADLINES

Another important cultural difference relates to schedules and deadlines. To most Americans, a deadline is a set completion date. In many other cultures, a deadline is a suggestion that maybe something will be finished by that indicated date. To ensure that outsourced work is completed on time it is imperative to add a penalty clause to your contract or enforce late fees.

Although these strategies were directed toward working with foreign outsourcers, you would be surprised to find how many project managers use them when working with their American counterparts!

*A. Kolawa, "Four Strategies for Communicating with Outsourcers," *Enterprise Systems Journal*, www.esj.com. Accessed 9/12/05.

Extensive Training and Team-Building Activities

Too often managers become preoccupied with the plans and technical challenges of the project and assume that people's issues will work themselves out over time. Smart firms recognize that people issues are as important, if not more important, than technical issues. They train their personnel to work effectively with people from other organizations and countries. This training is pervasive. It is not limited to management but involves all the people, at all levels, who interact with and are dependent upon outsourcers. Whether in a general class on negotiation or a specific one on working with Chinese programmers, team members are provided with a theoretical understanding of the barriers to collaboration as well as the skills and procedures to be successful.

The training is augmented by interorganizational team-building sessions designed to forge healthy relationships before the project begins. Team-building workshops involve the key players from the different firms, for example, engineers, architects, lawyers, specialists, and other staff. In many cases, firms find it useful to hire an outside consultant to design and facilitate the sessions. Such a consultant is typically well versed in interorganizational team building and can provide an impartial perspective to the workshop.

The length and design of the team-building sessions will depend on the experience, commitment, and skill level of the participants. For example, one project, in which the owner and the contractors were relatively inexperienced at working together, utilized a two-day workshop. The first day was devoted to ice-breaking activities and establishing the rationale behind partnering. The conceptual foundation was supported by exercises and mini-lectures on teamwork, synergy, win/win, and constructive feedback. The second day began by examining the problems and barriers that prevented collaboration in the past. Representatives from the different organizations were separated and each asked the following:

- What actions do the other groups engage in that create problems for us?
- What actions do we engage in that we think create problems for them?
- What recommendations would we make to improve the situation?

The groups shared their responses and asked questions on points needing clarification. Agreements and disparities in the lists were noted and specific problems were identified. Once problem areas were noted, each group was assigned the task of identifying its specific interests and goals for the project. Goals were shared across groups, and special attention was devoted to establishing what goals they had in common. Recognition of shared goals is critical for transforming different groups into a cohesive team.

Team-building sessions often culminate with the creation of a **partnering charter** signed by all of the participants. This charter states their common goals for the project as well as the procedures that will be used to achieve these goals (see Figure 12.5 for an example of the first page of a project charter).

Well-Established Conflict Management Processes in Place

Conflict is inevitable on a project and, as pointed out in Chapter 11, disagreements handled effectively can elevate performance. Dysfunctional conflict, however, can catch fire and severely undermine project success. Outsourced projects are susceptible to conflicts, since people are unaccustomed to working together and have different values and perspectives. Successful firms invest significant time and energy up front in establishing the "rules of engagement" so that disagreements are handled constructively.

Escalation is the primary control mechanism for dealing with and resolving problems. The basic principle is that problems should be resolved at the lowest level within a set time limit (say, 24 hours), or they are "escalated" to the next level of management. If so, the principals have the same time limit to resolve the problem, or it gets passed on to the next higher level. No action is not an option. Nor can one participant force concessions from the other by simply delaying the decision. There is no shame in pushing significant problems up the hierarchy; at the same time, managers should be quick to point out to subordinates those problems or questions that they should have been able to resolve on their own.

If possible, key personnel from the respective organizations are brought together to discuss potential problems and responses. This is usually part of the coordinated series of team-building activities discussed earlier. Particular attention is devoted to

FIGURE 12.5 Project Partnering Charter

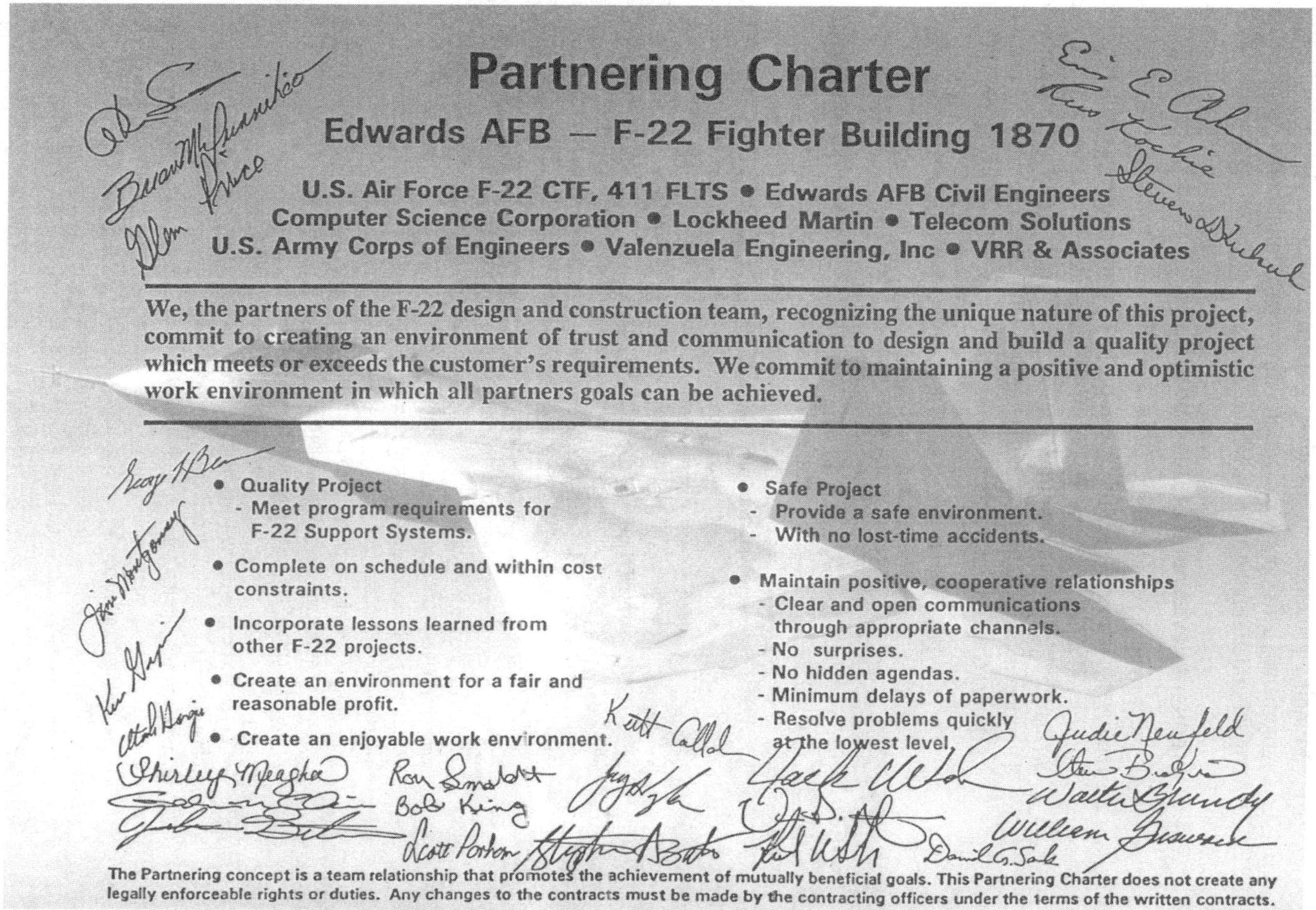

Partnering Charter

Edwards AFB — F-22 Fighter Building 1870

U.S. Air Force F-22 CTF, 411 FLTS • Edwards AFB Civil Engineers
Computer Science Corporation • Lockheed Martin • Telecom Solutions
U.S. Army Corps of Engineers • Valenzuela Engineering, Inc • VRR & Associates

We, the partners of the F-22 design and construction team, recognizing the unique nature of this project, commit to creating an environment of trust and communication to design and build a quality project which meets or exceeds the customer's requirements. We commit to maintaining a positive and optimistic work environment in which all partners goals can be achieved.

- Quality Project
  - Meet program requirements for F-22 Support Systems.
- Complete on schedule and within cost constraints.
- Incorporate lessons learned from other F-22 projects.
- Create an environment for a fair and reasonable profit.
- Create an enjoyable work environment.
- Safe Project
  - Provide a safe environment.
  - With no lost-time accidents.
- Maintain positive, cooperative relationships
  - Clear and open communications through appropriate channels.
  - No surprises.
  - No hidden agendas.
  - Minimum delays of paperwork.
  - Resolve problems quickly at the lowest level.

The Partnering concept is a team relationship that promotes the achievement of mutually beneficial goals. This Partnering Charter does not create any legally enforceable rights or duties. Any changes to the contracts must be made by the contracting officers under the terms of the written contracts.

establishing the change management control system where problems often erupt. People who are dependent on each other try to identify potential problems that may occur and agree in advance how they should be resolved. See Snapshot from Practice 12.3: "Partnering" a Flu Shot for Projects for the benefits of doing this.

Finally, principled negotiation is the norm for resolving problems and reaching agreements. This approach, which emphasizes collaborative problem solving, is discussed in detail later in this chapter.

Frequent Review and Status Updates

Project managers and other key personnel from all involved organizations meet on a regular basis to review and assess project performance. Collaborating as partners is considered a legitimate project priority and is assessed along with time, cost, and performance. Teamwork, communication, and timely problem resolution are evaluated. This provides a forum for identifying problems not only with the project but also with working relationships so that they can be resolved quickly and appropriately.

SNAPSHOT FROM PRACTICE 12.3 "Partnering" a Flu Shot for Projects*

Before starting a bond-financed school construction project, Ohio does what a theater company does before opening night—it holds a dress rehearsal. Led by Cleveland-based Project Management Consultants, state and local school officials, construction managers, and architects get together before building begins to figure out how to talk to each other and how to handle problems. Each party discusses problems that have occurred in the past and collectively they problem solve ways for preventing them from occurring in the current project. Consultants help participants develop a set of guidelines for working together.

Just as a theatrical dress rehearsal can allow a company to find and fix glitches before they ruin a show, preconstruction partnering can find early solutions to problems before they become lawsuits. For example, during the discussions it becomes apparent that different parties are interpreting a key requirement differently. Instead of waiting for this difference to escalate into a major problem, the parties reach a shared understanding before work begins.

"This works because traditionally everyone does their own work on a project, behind their own walls," said Jeffrey Applebaum, a construction lawyer and managing director of Project Management Consultants, a wholly owned subsidiary of the law firm of Thompson, Hine, & Flory. "We're taking down the walls. This is more efficient."

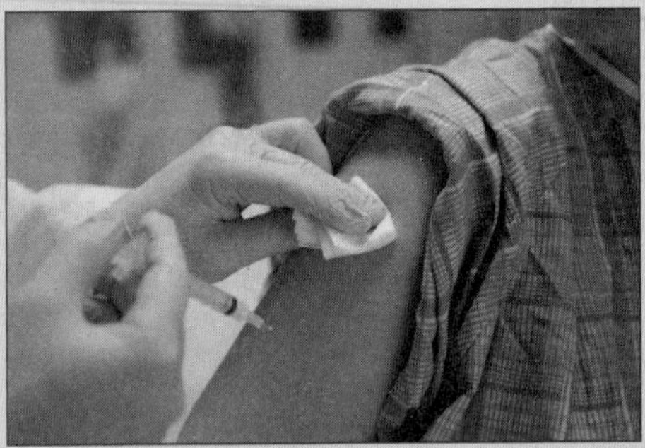

PhotoAlto/Alamy Stock Photo

"We couldn't be more pleased with this process," said Randy Fischer, executive director of the Ohio School Facilities Commission, which distributes state money to school construction projects. "We are currently administering $3 billion of construction, and we don't have any major disputes."

Crystal Canan, chief of contract administration for the commission, offered a medical metaphor, comparing partnering to a "flu shot" that will prevent the debilitating effects of litigation, work stoppages, and communication breakdowns. "Every building construction project is a candidate for the flu," Canan said. "We see partnering as a vaccination."

*M. Wisneiski, "Partnering Used to Curb Costs in Ohio School Construction," *Bond Buyer*, Accessed 11/22/2000, 334 (31023) 3/4p, 2bw.

More and more companies are using online surveys to collect data from all project participants about the quality of working relations (see Figure 12.6 for a partial example). With this data, one can gauge the "pulse" of the project and identify issues that need to be addressed. Comparison of survey responses period by period permits tracking areas of improvement and potential problems. In some cases, follow-up team-building sessions are used to focus on specific problems and recharge collaboration.

Finally, when the time to celebrate a significant milestone arrives, no matter who is responsible, all parties gather if possible to celebrate the success. This reinforces a common purpose and project identity. It also establishes positive momentum going into the next phase of the project.

Co-location When Needed

One of the best ways to overcome interorganizational friction is to have people from each organization working side by side on the project. Smart companies rent or make available the necessary accommodations so that all key project personnel can work collectively together. This allows the high degree of face-to-face interaction needed to coordinate activities, solve difficult problems, and form a common bond. This is especially relevant for complex projects in which close collaboration from different parties is required to be successful. For example, the U.S. government provides housing and common office space for all key contractors responsible for developing disaster response plans.

FIGURE 12.6
Sample Online Survey

Evaluation of partnering process: attitudes, teamwork, process.
(Collected separately from owner and contractor participants, compared, and aggregated.)

1. Communications between the owner/contractor personnel are

1	2	3	4	5
Difficult, guarded				Easy, open, up front

2. Top management support of partnering process is

1	2	3	4	5
Not evident or inconsistent				Obvious and consistent

3. Problems, issues, or concerns are

1	2	3	4	5
Ignored				Attacked promptly

4. Cooperation between owner and contractor personnel is

1	2	3	4	5
Cool, detached, unresponsive, removed				Genuine, unreserved, complete

5. Responses to problems, issues, or concerns frequently become

1	2	3	4	5
Personal issues				Treated as project problems

Our experience tells us that co-location is critical and well worth the added expense and inconvenience. When creating this is not practically possible, the travel budget for the project should contain ample funds to support timely travel to different organizations.

Co-location is less relevant for independent work that does not require ongoing coordination between professionals from different organizations. This would be the case if you were outsourcing discrete, independent deliverables, like beta testing or a marketing campaign. Here normal channels of communication could handle the coordination issues.

Fair and Incentive-Laden Contracts

When negotiating contracts, the goal is to reach a fair deal for all involved. Managers recognize that cohesion and cooperation are undermined if one party feels s/he is being unfairly treated by others. They also realize that negotiating the best deal in terms of price can come back to haunt them with shoddy work and change order gouging.

Performance-based contracts, in which significant incentives are established based on the priorities of the project, are becoming increasingly popular. For example, if time is critical, then contractors accrue payoffs for beating deadlines; if the scope is critical, then bonuses are issued for exceeding performance expectations. At the same time, contractors are held accountable with penalty clauses for failure to perform up to standard, meet deadlines, and/or control costs. More specific information about different types of contracts is presented in this chapter's appendix on contract management.

Companies recognize that contracts can discourage continuous improvement and innovation. Instead of trying some new, promising technique that may reduce costs, contractors will avoid the risks and apply tried-and-true methods to meet contracted requirements. Companies that treat contractors as partners consider continuous improvement as a joint effort to eliminate waste and pursue opportunities for cost savings. Risks as well as benefits are typically shared 50/50 between the principals, with the owner adhering to a fast-track review of proposed changes.

How the U.S. Department of Defense reaps the benefits of continuous improvement through value engineering is highlighted in Snapshot from Practice 12.4: U.S. Department of Defense's Value Engineering Awards.

Long-Term Outsourcing Relationships

Many companies recognize that major benefits can be enjoyed when outsourcing arrangements extend across multiple projects and are long term. For example, Corning and Toyota are among the many firms that have forged a network of long-term strategic partnerships with their suppliers. The average large corporation is involved in around 30 alliances today versus fewer than 3 in the early 1990s. Among the many advantages for establishing a long-term partnership are the following:

- **Reduced administrative costs.** The costs associated with bidding and selecting a contractor are eliminated. Contract administration costs are reduced as partners become knowledgeable of their counterpart's legal concerns.
- **More efficient utilization of resources.** Contractors have a known forecast of work, while owners are able to concentrate their workforce on core businesses and avoid the demanding swings of project support.
- **Improved communication.** As partners gain experience with each other, they develop a common language and perspective, which reduces misunderstanding and enhances collaboration.

SNAPSHOT FROM PRACTICE 12.4 U.S. Department of Defense's Value Engineering Awards*

As part of an effort to cut costs, the U.S. Department of Defense (DoD) issues annual Value Engineering Awards. Value engineering is a systematic process to analyze functions to identify actions to reduce cost, increase quality, and improve mission capabilities across the entire spectrum of DoD systems, processes, and organizations. The Value Engineering Awards Program is an acknowledgment of outstanding achievements and encourages additional projects to improve in-house and contractor productivity.

In 2018, 36 individuals and project teams received recognition from the DoD, reporting over $6 billion in savings and cost reductions.

Marc Dalangin received the award for his work on the M151 Spotting Scope Upgrade project. The M151 Spotting Scope is a compact, light, high-power optical device that allows the identification and recognition of targets at long distances (1,000+ yards). The scope is weather-resistant and fog proof. The M151 has been used for many years by U.S. Army snipers to identify and confirm targets. Given recent developments, the M151 was deemed no longer compatible with current weapons and the operational mode it was intended to support.

Dalangin was part of a project team charged with replacing the M151. Dalangin, on his own, worked closely with the sniper community at Ft. Benning, Georgia, to come up with a novel solution. Instead of replacing the scope, he developed and designed a Mil-Grid reticle that improved the performance of the M151 scope. What, you may ask, is a reticle? A reticle is a series of fine lines in the eyepiece of a scope, used as a measuring scale for locating objects.

The army accepted Dalangin's proposal to upgrade the spotting scope with the Mil-Grid reticle as well as other minor upgrades. The Value Engineering effort resulted in cost avoidance of over $4.5 million during fiscal 2017 and 2018. Not only were there significant cost savings, but the new scope contributed to army operational readiness by enhancing the army's sniper capability for deploying soldiers.

*www.acq.osd.mil/se/docs/FY17-VE-Honorees.pdf. Accessed 9/20/18.

- **Improved innovation.** The partners are able to discuss innovation and associated risks in a more open manner and share risks and rewards fairly.
- **Improved performance.** Over time partners become more familiar with each other's standards and expectations and are able to apply lessons learned from previous projects to current projects.

Working as partners is a conscious effort on the part of management to form collaborative relationships with personnel from different organizations to complete a project. For outsourcing to work, the individuals involved need to be effective negotiators capable of merging interests and discovering solutions to problems that contribute to the project. The next section addresses some of the key skills and techniques associated with effective negotiation.

12.4 The Art of Negotiating

LO 12-4

Practice principled negotiation.

Effective negotiating is critical to successful collaboration. All it takes is one key problem to explode to convert a sense of "we" into "us versus them." At the same time, negotiating is pervasive through all aspects of project management work. Project managers must negotiate support and funding from top management. They must negotiate staff and technical input from functional managers. They must coordinate with other project managers and negotiate project priorities and commitments. They must negotiate within their project team to determine assignments, deadlines, standards, and priorities. Project managers must negotiate prices and standards with vendors and suppliers. A firm understanding of the negotiating process, skills, and tactics is essential to project success.

Many people approach negotiating as if it were a competitive contest. Negotiators are out to win as much as they can for their side. Success is measured by how much is gained compared with the other party. While this may be applicable when negotiating the sale of a house, it is not true for project management. *Project management is not a contest!* First, the people working on the project, whether they represent different companies or departments within the same organization, are not enemies or competitors but, rather, allies or partners. They have formed a temporary alliance to complete a project. For this alliance to work requires a certain degree of trust, cooperation, and honesty.

Second, if conflicts escalate to the point where negotiations break down and the project comes to a halt, then everyone loses. Third, unlike bartering with a street vendor, the people involved on project work have to continue to work together. Therefore, it behooves them to resolve disagreements in a way that contributes to healthy working relationships. Finally, as pointed out in Chapter 11, conflict on a project can be good. When dealt with effectively, it can lead to innovation, better decisions, and more creative problem solving.

Project managers accept this noncompetitive view of negotiation and realize that negotiation is essentially a two-part process: the first part deals with reaching an agreement; the second part is the implementation of that agreement. It is the implementation phase, not the agreement itself, that determines the success of negotiations. All too often, managers reach an agreement with someone, only to find out later that he failed to do what he agreed to do or that his actual response fell far short of expectations. Experienced project managers recognize that implementation is based on satisfaction not only with the outcome but also with the process by which the agreement was reached. If someone feels bullied or tricked into doing something, this feeling will invariably be reflected by half-hearted performance.

Veteran project managers do the best they can to merge individual interests with what is best for the project and come up with effective solutions to problems. Fisher and Ury from the Harvard Negotiation Project champion an approach to negotiating that embodies these goals.[2] It emphasizes developing win/win solutions while protecting yourself against those who would take advantage of your forthrightness. Their approach is called **principled negotiation** and is based on four key points, which are listed in Table 12.2 and discussed in the following sections.

1. Separate the People from the Problem

Too often personal relations become entangled with the substantive issues under consideration. Instead of attacking the problem(s), people attack each other. Once people feel attacked or threatened, their energy naturally goes to defending themselves, not to solving the problem. The key, then, is to focus on the problem—not the other person—during negotiation. Avoid personalizing the negotiation and framing the negotiation as

TABLE 12.2
Principled Negotiation

1. Separate the people from the problem.
2. Focus on interests, not positions.
3. Invent options for mutual gain.
4. When possible, use objective criteria.

[2] Fisher, R., and W. Ury, Getting to Yes: *Negotiating Agreement without Giving In,* 2nd ed. (New York: Penguin Books, 1991).

a contest. Instead, try to keep the focus on the problem to be resolved. In Fisher and Ury's words, *be hard on the problem, soft on the people.*

By keeping the focus on the issues and not the personalities, negotiators are better able to let the other person blow off steam. On important problems, it is not uncommon for people to become upset, frustrated, and angry. However, one angry attack produces an angry counterattack and the discussion quickly escalates into a heated argument, an emotional chain reaction.

In some cases, people use anger as a means of intimidating and forcing concessions because the other person wishes to preserve the relationship. When people become emotional, negotiators should keep a cool head and remember the old German proverb "Let anger fly out the window."[3] In other words, in the face of an emotional outburst, imagine opening a window and letting the heat of the anger out the window. Avoid taking things personally, and redirect personal attacks back to the question at hand. Don't react to the emotional outburst, but try to find the issues that triggered it. Skilled negotiators keep their cool under stressful times and, at the same time, build a bond with others by empathizing and acknowledging common sources of frustration and anger.

While it is important to separate the people from the problem during actual negotiations, it is beneficial to have a friendly rapport with the other person prior to negotiating. Friendly rapport is consistent with the social network tenet, introduced in Chapter 10, of building a relationship before you need it. If, in the past, the relationship has been marked by healthy give-and-take, in which both parties have demonstrated a willingness to accommodate the interests of the other, then neither individual is likely to adopt an immediate win/lose perspective. Furthermore, a positive relationship adds a common interest beyond the specific points of contention. Not only do both parties want to reach an agreement that suits their individual interests, but they also want to do so in a manner that preserves their relationship. Each is therefore more likely to seek solutions that are mutually beneficial.

2. Focus on Interests, Not Positions

Negotiations often stall when people focus on positions:

I'm willing to pay $10,000. No, it will cost $15,000.

I need it done by Monday. That's impossible, we can't have it ready until Wednesday.

While such interchanges are common during preliminary discussions, managers must prevent this initial posturing from becoming polarized. When such positions are stated, attacked, and then defended, each party figuratively begins to draw a line s/he will not cross. This line creates a win/lose scenario in which someone has to lose by crossing the line in order to reach an agreement. As such, the negotiations can become a war of wills, with concessions being seen as a loss of face.

The key is to focus on the interests behind your positions (what you are trying to achieve) and separate these goals from your ego as best you can. Not only should you be driven by your interests, but you should try to identify the interests of the other party. Ask why it will cost so much or why it can't be done by Monday. At the same time, make your own interests come alive. Don't just say that it is critical that it be done by Monday; explain what will happen if it isn't done by Monday.

Sometimes when the true interests of both parties are revealed, there is no basis for conflict. Take, for example, the Monday versus Wednesday argument. This argument

[3] Ibid.

could apply to a scenario involving a project manager and the production manager of a small, local firm that was contracted to produce prototypes of a new generation of computer mouse. The project manager needs the prototypes on Monday to demonstrate to a user's focus group. The production manager said it would be impossible. The project manager said this would be embarrassing because Marketing had spent a lot of time and effort setting up this demonstration. The production manager again denied the request and added that he had already had to schedule overtime to meet the Wednesday delivery date. However, when the project manager revealed that the purpose of the focus group was to gauge consumers' reactions to the color and shape of the new devices, not the finished product, the conflict disappeared. The production manager told the project manager that s/he could pick up the samples today if s/he wanted because production had an excess supply of shells.

When focusing on interests, it is important to practice the following communication habit: *seek first to understand, then to be understood.* This involves what Stephen Covey calls empathetic listening, which allows a person to fully understand another person's frame of reference—not only what that person is saying but also how s/he feels. Covey asserts that people have an inherent need to be understood. He goes on to observe that satisfied needs do not motivate human behavior; only unsatisfied needs do. People try to go to sleep when they are tired, not when they are rested. The key point is that until people believe they are being understood, they will repeat their points and reformulate their arguments.[4] If, on the other hand, you satisfy this need by seeking first to understand, then the other party is free to understand your interests and focus directly on the issues at hand. Seeking to understand requires discipline and compassion. Instead of responding to the other person by asserting your agenda, respond by summarizing both the facts and the feelings behind what the other person has said and checking the accuracy of comprehension.

3. Invent Options for Mutual Gain

Once the individuals involved have identified their interests, then they can explore options for mutual gain. This is not easy. Stressful negotiations inhibit creativity and free exchange. What is required is collaborative brainstorming in which people work together to solve the problem in a way that will lead to a win/win scenario. The key to brainstorming is separating the inventing from the deciding. Begin by taking 15 minutes to generate as many options as possible. No matter how outlandish any option is, it should not be subject to criticism or immediate rejection. People should feed off the ideas of others to generate new ideas. When all the possible options are exhausted, they should then sort through the ideas that were generated to focus on those with the greatest possibilities.

Clarifying interests and exploring mutual options create the opportunity for dovetailing interests. Dovetailing means one person identifies options that are of low cost to him or her but of high interest to the other party. This is only possible if each party knows what the other's needs are. For example, in negotiating price with a parts supplier, a project manager learned from the discussion that the supplier was in a cash flow squeeze after purchasing a very expensive fabrication machine. Needed cash was the primary reason the supplier had taken such a rigid position on price. During the brainstorming session, one of the options presented was to prepay for the order instead of the usual payment on delivery arrangement. Both parties seized on this option and reached an amicable agreement in which the project manager would pay the supplier

[4] Covey, S. R., *The Seven Habits of Highly Effective People* (New York: Simon and Schuster, 1990).

for the entire job in advance in exchange for a faster turnaround time and a significant price reduction. Such opportunities for win/win agreements are often overlooked because the negotiators become fixated on solving their problems and not on opportunities to solve the other person's problems.

4. When Possible, Use Objective Criteria

Most established industries and professions have developed standards and rules to help them deal with common areas of dispute. For example, both buyers and sellers rely on the blue book to establish price parameters for a used car. The construction industry has building codes and fair practice policies to resolve proof of quality and safe work procedures. The legal profession uses precedents to adjudicate claims of wrongdoing.

Whenever possible, you should insist on using external, objective criteria to settle disagreements. For example, a disagreement arose between a regional airlines firm and the independent accounting team entrusted with preparing the annual financial statement. The airline firm had made a significant investment by leasing several used airplanes from a larger airline. The dispute involved whether this lease should be classified as an operating or capital lease. This was important to the airline because if the purchase was classified as an operating lease, then the associated debt would not have to be recorded in the financial statement. However, if the purchase was classified as a capital lease, then the debt would be factored into the financial statement and the debt/equity ratio would be much less attractive to stockholders and would-be investors. The two parties resolved this dispute by deferring to formulas established by the Financial Accounting Standards Board. As it turned out, the accounting team was correct, but, by deferring to objective standards, they were able to deflect the disappointment of the airline managers away from the accounting team and preserve a professional relationship with that firm.

Dealing with Unreasonable People

Most people working on projects realize that in the long run, it is beneficial to work toward mutually satisfying solutions. Still, occasionally you encounter someone who has a dominant win/lose attitude about life and will be difficult to deal with. Fisher and Ury recommend that you use negotiation jujitsu when dealing with such a person. That is, when the other person begins to push, don't push back. As in the martial arts, avoid pitting your strengths against another's directly; instead, use your skill to step aside and turn that person's strength to your ends. When someone adamantly sets forth a position, neither reject it nor accept it. Treat it as a possible option and then look for the interests behind it. Instead of defending your ideas, invite criticism and advice. Ask why it's a bad idea and discover the other's underlying interest.

Those who use negotiation jujitsu rely on two primary weapons. They ask questions instead of making statements. Questions allow for interests to surface and do not provide the opponent with something to attack. The second weapon is silence. If the other person makes an unreasonable proposal or attacks you personally, just sit there and don't say a word. Wait for the other party to break the stalemate by answering your question or coming up with a new suggestion.

The best defense against unreasonable, win/lose negotiators is having what Fisher and Ury call a strong **best alternative to a negotiated agreement (BATNA).** They point out that people try to reach an agreement to produce something better than the result of not negotiating with that person. What those results would be is the true benchmark for determining whether you should accept an agreement. A strong

BATNA gives you the power to walk away and say, "No deal unless we work toward a win/win scenario."

Your BATNA reflects how dependent you are on the other party. If you are negotiating price and delivery dates and can choose from a number of reputable suppliers, then you have a strong BATNA. If, on the other hand, there is only one vendor who can supply you with specific, critical material on time, then you have a weak BATNA. Under these circumstances, you may be forced to concede to the vendor's demands. At the same time, you should begin to explore ways of increasing your BATNA for future negotiations. This can be done by reducing your dependency on that supplier. You could begin to find substitutable material or negotiate better lead times with other vendors.

Negotiating is an art. There are many intangibles involved. This section has reviewed some time-tested principles of effective negotiating based on the groundbreaking work of Fisher and Ury. Given the significance of negotiating, you are encouraged to read their book as well as others on negotiating. In addition, attending training workshops can provide an opportunity to practice these skills. You should also take advantage of day-to-day interactions to sharpen your negotiating acumen.

12.5 A Note on Managing Customer Relations

LO 12-5

Describe the met-expectations model of customer satisfaction and its implications for working with customers on projects.

In Chapter 4 it was emphasized that ultimate success is not determined by whether the project was completed on time, within budget, or according to specifications but on whether the customer is satisfied with what has been accomplished. Customer satisfaction is the bottom line. Bad news travels faster and farther than good news. For every happy customer who shares his or her satisfaction regarding a particular product or service with another person, a dissatisfied customer is likely to share his or her dissatisfaction with eight other people. Project managers need to cultivate positive working relations with clients to preserve their reputations.

Customer satisfaction is a complex phenomenon. One simple but useful way of viewing customer satisfaction is in terms of **met expectations.** According to this model, customer satisfaction is a function of the extent to which perceived performance (or outcome) exceeds expectations. Mathematically, this relationship can be represented as the ratio between perceived performance and expected performance (see Figure 12.7). When performance falls short of expectations (ratio < 1), the customer is dissatisfied. If the performance matches expectations (ratio = 1), the customer is satisfied. If the performance exceeds expectations (ratio > 1), the customer is very satisfied or even delighted.

High customer satisfaction is the goal of most projects. However, profitability is another major concern. Exceeding expectations typically entails additional costs. For example, completing a construction project two weeks ahead of schedule may involve significant overtime expenses. Similarly, exceeding reliability requirements for a new electronic component may involve considerably more design and debugging effort. Under most circumstances, the most profitable arrangement occurs when the customer's expectations are only slightly exceeded. Returning to the mathematical model, with all other things being equal, one should strive for a satisfaction ratio of 1.05, not 1.5!

FIGURE 12.7
The Met-Expectations Model of Customer Satisfaction

$$\underset{\text{Dissatisfied}}{0.90} \leftarrow \frac{\text{Perceived performance}}{\text{Expected performance}} \rightarrow \underset{\text{Very satisfied}}{1.10}$$

The met-expectations model of customer satisfaction highlights the point that whether a client is dissatisfied or delighted with a project is not based on hard facts and objective data but on perceptions and expectations. For example, a customer may be dissatisfied with a project that was completed ahead of schedule and under budget if he thought the work was poor quality and that his fears and concerns were not adequately addressed. Conversely, a customer may be very satisfied with a project that was over budget and behind schedule if s/he felt the project team protected his or her interests and did the best job possible under adverse circumstances.

Project managers must be skilled at managing customer expectations and perceptions. Too often they deal with these expectations after the fact when they try to alleviate a client's dissatisfaction by carefully explaining why the project cost more or took longer than planned. A more proactive approach is to begin to shape the proper expectations up front and accept that this is an ongoing process throughout the life of a project. Project managers need to direct their attention both to the customer's base expectations, the standard by which perceived performance will be evaluated, and to the customer's perceptions of actual performance. The ultimate goal is to educate clients so that they can make a valid judgment as to project performance.

Managing customer expectations begins during the preliminary project approval phase of negotiations. It is important to avoid the temptation to oversell the virtues of a project to win approval because this may create unrealistic expectations that may be too difficult, if not impossible, to achieve. At the same time, project proponents have been known to lower customer expectations by underselling projects. If the estimated completion time is 10 to 12 weeks, they will promise to have the project completed within 12 to 14 weeks, therefore increasing the chances of exceeding customer expectations by getting the project completed early.

Once the project is authorized, the project manager and team need to work closely with the client organization to develop a well-defined project scope statement that clearly states the objectives, parameters, and limits of the project work. The project scope statement is essential to establishing customer expectations regarding the project. It is critical that all parties are in agreement as to what is to be accomplished. It is also important to share significant risks that might disrupt project execution. Customers do not like surprises, and if they are aware in advance of potential problems they are much more likely to be accepting of the consequences.

Once the project is initiated it is important to keep customers abreast of project progress. No longer do project managers simply take orders from customers and tell them to return when the project is done. More and more organizations and their project managers are treating their customers as de facto members of the project team and are actively involving them in key aspects of project work. In the case of consulting assignments, project managers sometimes morph into members of the client organization (see Research Highlight 12.1: IT Project Managers).

Project managers need to keep customers informed of project developments so that customers can make adjustments in their own plans. When circumstances dictate changing the scope or priorities of the project, project managers need to be quick to spell out as best they can the implications of these changes to the customers so that they can make an informed choice. Active customer involvement allows customers to naturally adjust their expectations in accordance with the decisions and events that transpire on a project while the customer's presence keeps the project team focused on the customer's objectives for the project.

Active customer involvement also provides a firmer basis for assessing project performance. The customer not only sees the results of the project but also acquires

Research Highlight 12.1

IT Project Managers Doubling as Client Account Executives*

Webber and Torti studied the multiple roles project managers play on IT projects. Based on a comprehensive set of interviews with project managers and clients in three different information-technology service organizations, they identified five key roles critical to successfully implement IT projects in client organizations: entrepreneur, politician, friend, marketer, and coach. They are described in part in Table 12.3.

Webber and Torti observed that instead of maintaining a clearly defined relationship with the client, project managers become part of the client organization. They reported that project managers attempt to "dress like the client, act like the client, and participate in the client organization's activities (i.e., social gatherings, blood drives, etc.)." They become such an integral part of their existence that many client employees, over the course of time, forget that the project manager is not an employee of the client organization. This helps establish a degree of trust essential to effective collaboration.

* S. S. Webber and M. T. Torti, "Project Managers Doubling as Client Account Executives," *Academy of Management Executive*, vol. 18, no. 1 (2004), pp. 60–71.

TABLE 12.3 Project Roles, Challenges, and Strategies

Project Manager Roles	Challenges	Strategies
Entrepreneur	Navigate unfamiliar surroundings	Use persuasion to influence others
Politician	Understand two diverse cultures (parent and client organization)	Align with the powerful individuals
Friend	Determine the important relationships to build and sustain outside the team itself	Identify common interests and experiences to bridge a friendship with the client
Marketer	Understand the strategic objectives of the client organization	Align new ideas/proposals with the strategic objectives of the client organization
Coach	Motivate client team members without formal authority	Provide challenging tasks to build the skills of the team members

glimpses of the effort and actions that produced those results. Naturally, project managers want to make sure these glimpses reflect favorably on their project teams, so they exercise extra care that customer interactions are handled in a competent and professional manner. In some respects, customer perceptions of performance are shaped more by how well the project team deals with adversity than by actual performance. Project managers can impress customers with how diligently they deal with unexpected problems and setbacks. Likewise, industry analysts have noted that customer dissatisfaction can be transformed into customer satisfaction by quickly correcting mistakes and being extremely responsive to customer concerns.

Managing customer relations on a project is a broad topic; we have only highlighted some of the central issues involved. This brief segment concludes with two words of advice passed on by veteran project managers:

Speak with one voice. Nothing erodes confidence in a project more than for a customer to receive conflicting messages from different project members. The project manager should remind team members of this fact and work with them to ensure that appropriate information is shared with customers.

Speak the language of the customer. Too often project members respond to customer inquiries with technical jargon that exceeds the customer's vocabulary. Project managers and members need to describe problems, trade-offs, and solutions in ways that the customer can understand.

Summary

Outsourcing has become an integral part of project management. The disruption of global supply chains by the COVID-19 pandemic has caused leaders to rethink being so dependent upon foreign suppliers, contractors, etc. Still, companies need to collaborate with each other on projects to compete in today's business world. The advantages of outsourcing include cost reduction, quicker completion times, greater flexibility, and higher level of expertise. Disadvantages include coordination problems, loss of control, conflicts, security issues, and political fallout.

A number of proactive best practices have emerged among firms that have mastered the outsourcing process. These practices include establishing well-defined requirements and procedures and utilizing fair and incentive-laden contracts. Team-building sessions are held before the project begins in order to forge relationships between personnel from different organizations. Escalation guidelines for resolving conflicts are established, as are provisions for process improvement and risk sharing. On highly critical work, arrangements are made so that key personnel work together, face to face. Joint assessments of how well people are collaborating are the norm during status report briefings. Finally, many companies are realizing the benefits of forming long-term alliances with each other on projects. The ultimate goal is to work together as partners.

Effective negotiating skills are essential to working on projects as partners. People need to resolve differences at the lowest level possible in order to keep the project on track. Veteran project managers realize that negotiating is not a competitive game and work toward collaborative solutions to problems. They accomplish this by separating people from the problem, focusing on interests and not positions, inventing options for mutual gain, and relying on objective criteria whenever possible to resolve disagreements. They also recognize the importance of developing a strong BATNA, which provides them with the leverage necessary to seek collaborative solutions.

Customer satisfaction is the litmus test for project success. Project managers need to take a proactive approach to manage customer expectations and perceptions. They need to actively involve customers in key decisions and keep them abreast of important developments. Active customer involvement keeps the project team focused on the objectives of the project and reduces misunderstandings and dissatisfaction.

Key Terms

Best alternative to a negotiated agreement (BATNA), *523*
Co-location, *518*
Escalation, *514*
Met expectations, *524*
Outsourcing, *505*
Partnering charter, *514*
Principled negotiation, *520*
Request for Proposal (RFP), *509*

Review Questions

1. Why do firms outsource project work?
2. How can outsourcing increase the quality of work performed?
3. What are the best practices used by firms to outsource project work?
4. What does the term *escalate* refer to and why is it essential to project success?
5. Why is the principled negotiation approach recommended for negotiating agreements on projects?
6. What does the acronym BATNA refer to and why is it important to being a successful negotiator?
7. How can a project manager influence customer expectations and perceptions?

SNAPSHOT FROM PRACTICE

Discussion Questions

12.1 *The Boeing 787 Dreamliner*

1. What disadvantages of outsourcing were evident in the Boeing 787 project?
2. What does this project say about the importance of taking a socio-technical approach to projects?

12.2 *Four Strategies for Communicating with Outsourcers*

1. Has anyone used these strategies when dealing with foreigners? Or wish he or she had?

12.3 *"Partnering" a Flu Shot for Projects*

1. What best practices are evident in this snapshot?
2. Does partnering only work on construction projects?

Exercises

1. Break into groups of four or five students. Assign half of the groups the role of owner and the other half the role of contractor.

   Owners: After saving for many years you are about to hire a contractor to build your "dream home." What are your objectives for this project? What concerns or issues do you have about working with a general contractor to build your home?

   Contractors: You specialize in building customized homes. You are about to meet with prospective owners to begin to negotiate a contract for building their "dream home." What are your objectives for this project? What concerns or issues do you have about working with the owners to build their home?

   Each owner group meets with a contractor group and shares their objectives, concerns, and issues.

   Identify what objectives, issues, and concerns you have in common and which ones are unique. Discuss how you could work together to realize your objectives. What would be the keys to working as partners on this project?
2. Enter "outsourcing" in an Internet search engine and browse different websites. Who appears to be interested in outsourcing? What are the advantages of outsourcing? What are the disadvantages? Does outsourcing mean the same thing to different people? What are future trends in outsourcing?
3. Break into four groups and review the instructions for a "Get the most you can" exercise provided by your teacher. Complete the exercise. What was your initial strategy? Did it change? If so, why? What does this exercise tell you about our ability to collaborate with each other?
4. Review the network of stakeholders found in Figure 10.1. Choose five different stakeholders and provide examples of why a project manager would need to negotiate with that stakeholder.

References

Bygballe, L. E., and A. Sward, "Collaborative Project Delivery Models and the Role of Routines in Institutionalizing Partnering," *Project Management Journal,* vol. 50, no. 2 (2019), pp. 161–76.

DiDonato, L. S., "Contract Disputes: Alternatives for Dispute Resolution (Part 1)," *PM Network,* May 1993, pp. 19–23.

Drexler, J. A., and E. W. Larson, "Partnering: Why Project Owner-Contractor Relationships Change," *Journal of Construction Engineering and Management,* vol. 126, no. 4 (July/August 2000), pp. 293–97.

Dyer, S., *Partner Your Project* (Warwickshire, UK: Pendulum, 1997).

Economy, P., *Business Negotiating Basics* (Burr Ridge, IL: Irwin Professional Publishing, 1994).

Hedberg, B., G. Dahlgren, J. Hansson, and N. Olve, *Virtual Organizations and Beyond* (New York: Wiley, 1997).

Hoang, H., and F. T. Rothaermel, "The Effect of General and Partner-Specific Alliance Experience on Joint R&D Project Performance," *Academy of Management Journal,* vol. 48, no. 2 (2005), pp. 332–45.

Kanter, R. M., "Collaborative Advantage: The Art of Alliances," *Harvard Business Review,* July/August 1994, pp. 92–113.

Larson, E. W., "Partnering on Construction Projects: A Study of the Relationship between Partnering Activities and Project Success," *IEEE Transactions in Engineering Management,* vol. 44, no. 2 (May 1997), pp. 188–95.

Larson, E. W., "Project Partnering: Results of a Study of 280 Construction Projects," *Journal of Management Engineering,* vol. 11, no. 2 (March/April 1995), pp. 30–35.

Larson, E. W., and J. A. Drexler, "Barriers to Project Partnering: Report from the Firing Line," *Project Management Journal,* vol. 28, no. 1 (March 1997), pp. 46–52.

Magenau, J. M., and J. K. Pinto, "Power, Influence, and Negotiation in Project Management," in P. W. G. Morris and J. K. Pinto (eds.), *The Wiley Guide to Managing Projects* (New York: Wiley, 2004), pp. 1033–60.

Maurer, I., "How to Build Trust in Inter-organizational Projects: The Impact of Project Staffing and Project Rewards on the Formation of Trust, Knowledge Acquisition, and Product Innovation," *International Journal of Project Management,* vol. 28, no. 7 (2010), pp. 629–37.

Nambisan, S., "Designing Virtual Customer Environments for New Product Development: Toward a Theory," *Academy of Management Review,* vol. 27, no. 3 (2002), pp. 392–413.

Nevstad, K., S. Børve, A. T. Karlsen, and W. Aarseth, "Understanding How to Succeed with Project Partnering," *International Journal of Managing Projects in Business,* vol. 11, no. 4 (2018), pp. 1044–65.

Nissen, M. E., "Procurement: Process Overview and Emerging Project Management Techniques," in P. W. G. Morris and J. K. Pinto (eds.), *The Wiley Guide to Managing Projects* (New York: Wiley, 2004), pp. 643–54.

Quinn, R. E., S. R. Faerman, M. P. Thompson, and M. R. McGrath, *Becoming a Master Manager: A Competency Framework* (New York: Wiley, 1990).

Schultzel, H. J., and V. P. Unruh, *Successful Partnering: Fundamentals for Project Owners and Contractors* (New York: Wiley, 1996).

Shell, G. R., *Bargaining for Advantage: Negotiation Strategies for Reasonable People* (New York: Penguin, 2000).

Case 12.1

Shell Case Fabricators

BACKGROUND

Shell Case Fabricators (SCF) designs and builds shell casings that enclose electronic products such as calculators, cell phones, and modems. Typically the cases are plastic or plastic compounds. SCF has six different production lines that cover different types of products. For example, the largest high-volume production line for modems can produce three different colors and two models (vertical and flat). Air Connection Links (ACL) is the biggest customer that buys product from this line. This high-output line now runs at full capacity on an eight-hour shift. The other five lines run smaller quantities and tend to meet the needs of other specialty products manufactured by different, smaller firms.

Ninety-five percent of SCF's product casings line is designed by the original hardware manufacturer. Getting a casing to the production stage requires a great deal of collaboration and interaction between the original hardware and case design manufacturer (e.g., ACL) and SCF's shell design engineers and Production Department. The latest new product of ACL is a modem designed to be used for monitoring water activity in bays, such as ship traffic, pollution, and floating debris. Because of the product's high functionality and low cost, potential demand for the new product is out of sight. It seems every country with small bays used for shipping wants enough underwater modems to cover its respective bays.

THE UNDERWATER MODEM PROJECT

At SCF each new product is assigned a project manager to coordinate and manage the shell design, budgets, and manufacturing start-up. Songsee is SCF's star project manager and is the project manager of the shell for the new short-range, underwater acoustical modem. The shell casing for the underwater modem required special design and materials, custom equipment, and a seal to withstand pressure to 50 meters. Air Connection Links, the product owner, needs 60,000 modems in 91 days (next January 15) for the Estuary Control Institute meeting in Hong Kong.

CLIENT CHANGE REQUEST

Songsee has felt the project was moving along smoothly, with the exception of being two weeks behind schedule. She feels she can "lean on" the Design Department to put the project on top priority and make up the two weeks. Yesterday ACL's project manager, Sabin, came in with a "*simple* change": change the outer shell shape from rectangular to dome shape; it will improve performance by 2 percent. Songsee couldn't believe Sabin. He knows better. He knows the engineering implications, and it is NOT simple! Yet Sabin tells Songsee, "It shouldn't cost much." Songsee imagined a sharp retort, but she counted to five and aborted. At this late stage of the game, changes and schedule compression cost big money! Songsee said she would get together with her team and start on a new time and cost estimate that day. She told Sabin he would have to give her a written change request of the new requirements by the next day. Sabin appeared disappointed: "Why don't we just add €100,000 to the price and get on with it? We have been doing business with SCF for six years. With expected demand out of sight, SCF will break even quickly and have a great profit on the production side." Songsee sighed. "Let's proceed with the change order process. I will take your request to the change order governance committee."

Songsee's meeting with her team about the change went about as expected. Every department moaned about changing at this late date. The guesstimate cost and time estimates were over triple Sabin's idea of €100,000. For example, designing a new seal for a dome-style modem will require a new custom water sealing approach, possibly an untested different sealant, and new molds. Has ACL frozen the design of the new style modem? Songsee asked the team to come in with a more detailed estimate by tomorrow afternoon, before her meeting with the change order governance committee.

THE NEXT DAY (FRIDAY)

Sabin called from ACL at midmorning the next day: "Our senior management is upset that we have to be so formal for such a small change. They just want to get on with the project and meet the time-to-market launch date. €100,000 seems like a fair price. They believe you need to talk to your management. They want a response by Monday."

The team estimates came close to yesterday's guesstimate (€391,000)—not good news. Songsee knew the answer of the change committee would be to hold for the full amount. She was right. The change committee believed the costs are there and need to be covered to meet the launch date. The committee was also concerned that priorities and resource scheduling would have to change for SCF's Design and Production Departments. In three hours, she would meet with senior management to decide whether to accept the client's request at their price or come up with an alternate plan. Songsee realized she should have several options for senior management to consider, along with a recommendation.

1. Should SCF accept or reject ACL's request? Which option would you select? What risks are involved?
2. How should SCF negotiate with ACL? How can SCF and ACL develop a positive, long-range relationship? Give some specifics.

Case 12.2

The Accounting Software Installation Project

Sitting in her office, Karin Chung is reviewing the past four months of the large corporate accounting software installation project she has been managing. Everything seemed so well planned before the project started. Each company division had a task force that provided input into the proposed installation along with potential problems. Each of the divisions had been trained and briefed on exactly how that division would interface with and use the forthcoming accounting software. All six contractors, which included one of the Big Four consulting companies, assisted in developing the work breakdown structure—costs, specifications, and time.

Karin hired a consultant to conduct a one-day "partnering" workshop attended by the major accounting heads, a member of each task force group, and key representatives from each of the contractors. During the workshop, several different team-building exercises were used to illustrate the importance of collaboration and effective communication. Everyone laughed when Karin fell into an imaginary acid pit during a human bridge–building exercise. The workshop ended on an upbeat note with everyone signing a partnering charter that expressed their commitment to working together as partners to complete the project.

TWO MONTHS LATER

One task force member came to Karin to complain that the contractor dealing with billing would not listen to his concerns about problems that could occur in the Virginia division when billings were consolidated. The contractor had told him, the task force member, he had bigger problems than consolidation of billing in the Virginia division. Karin replied, "You can settle the problem with the contractor. Go to him and explain how serious your problem is and that it will have to be settled before the project is completed."

Later in the week in the lunchroom, she overheard one consulting contractor badmouthing the work of another—"never on time, interface coding not tested." In the hallway the same day an Accounting Department supervisor told her that tests showed the new software will never be compatible with the Georgia division's accounting practices.

While concerned, Karin considered these problems typical of the kind she had encountered on other, smaller software projects.

FOUR MONTHS LATER

The project seemed to be falling apart. What had happened to the positive attitude fostered at the team-building workshop? One contractor wrote a formal letter complaining that another contractor was sitting on a coding decision that was delaying their work. "We cannot be held responsible or liable for delays caused by others." The project was already two months behind, so problems were becoming very serious. Karin finally decided to call a meeting of all parties to the project and partnering agreement.

She began by asking about problems people were encountering while working on the project. Although participants were reluctant to be first for fear of being perceived as a complainer, it was not long before accusations and tempers flared out of control. It was always some group complaining about another group. Several participants complained that others were sitting on decisions that resulted in their work being held up. One consultant said, "It is impossible to tell who's in charge of what." Another participant complained that although the group met separately on small problems, it never met as a total group to assess new risk situations that developed.

Karin felt the meeting had degenerated into an unrecoverable situation. Commitment to the project and partnering appeared to be waning. She quickly decided to stop the meeting and cool things down. She spoke to the project stakeholders: "It is clear that we have some serious problems and the project is in jeopardy. The project must get back on track, and the backbiting must stop. I want each of us to come to a meeting Friday morning with concrete suggestions of what it will take to get the project back on track and specific actions of how we can make it happen. We need to recognize our mutual interdependence and bring our relationships with each other back to a win/win environment. When we do get things back on track, we need to figure out how to stay on track."

1. Why does this attempt at project partnering appear to be failing?
2. If you were Karin, what would you do to get this project back on track?
3. What action would you take to keep the project on track?

Case 12.3

Buxton Hall

Chad Cromwell, head of university housing, gazed up at the tower at Buxton Hall and smiled as he walked toward the landmark building. Buxton Hall was built in 1927 as a residential complex for over 350 students at Pacifica State University. At the time, Buxton was the tallest building on campus, and its tower had a panoramic view of the athletic fields and coastal range. Buxton quickly became a focal point at Pacifica State. Students perched on the tower dominated the campus during the annual spring water fight with their huge slingshots and catapults. The first intranet on the Pacific coast was created at Buxton that linked students' computers and allowed them to share printers. Around the 1970s, some student artists began the tradition of painting their room doors. Whether a Rolling Stones logo or Bugs Bunny on a skateboard, these colorful doors were an artistic legacy that caught the attention of students and faculty.

Buxton Hall served as a residence hall for the university for many years, but time was not kind to the stately building. Leaks destroyed plaster in the interior. Wiring and plumbing became outdated and so dangerous that the building was deemed unsafe. Buxton Hall's doors were closed to students and windows boarded up at the end of the 2010 spring quarter. For 10 years Buxton sat silent and over time became a symbol of the general decline of Pacifica State. Now thanks to state bonds and generous contributions, Buxton Hall was about to be reopened after a $20 million renovation.

18 MONTHS AGO

Chad and key representatives from university facilities were engaged in the second of a two-day partnering workshop. Also in attendance were managers from Crawford Construction, the chief contractor for the Buxton renovation project, as well as several key subcontractors and architects from the firm of Legacy West. During the first day, a consultant ran them through a series of team-building and communication exercises that accentuated the importance of open communication, principle negotiation, and win/win thinking. The second day began with the "project from hell" exercise, with each group describing the worst project they had ever worked on. Chad was surprised that the Crawford and Legacy West descriptions were very similar to his own. For example, each group talked about how frustrating it was when changes were made without proper consultation or costs were hidden until it was too late to do anything about them. This was followed by a discussion of the best project they had ever worked on. The consultant then asked the groups which of the two they wanted the Buxton project to be. A genuine sense of common purpose emerged, and everyone became actively engaged in spelling out in specific terms how they wanted to work together. The session concluded with all of the participants signing a partnering charter, followed by a picnic and a friendly softball game.

12 MONTHS AGO

Chad was on his way, with Nick Bolas, to meet Dat Nguyen, the Crawford project manager, on the third floor at Buxton Hall. Dat had contacted him to discuss a problem with the tile work in one of the communal bathrooms. Dat's people had completed the work, but Nick, who was a Pacifica facilities manager, refused to sign off on it, claiming that it was not up to spec. After a 24-hour impasse, the Crawford foreman exercised the escalation clause in the partnering agreement and passed the issue up to management's level to be resolved. Dat and Chad inspected the work. While both agreed that the job could have been prettier, it did meet specifications, and Chad told Nick to sign off on it.

Chad met Dat again later in the day at the weekly Buxton status report meeting. The meeting kicked off with a brief review of what had been accomplished during the past week. Discussion centered on the removal of elm trees. Alternative strategies for dealing with the city inspector, who had a reputation for being a stickler for details, were considered. The project was two weeks behind schedule, which was an important issue, since it was imperative that the building be ready for students to move in at the 2025 fall term. The project was also on a very tight budget, and the management reserves had to be carefully administered. Renovation of existing buildings was always a bit of a gamble, since you never knew what you would find once you began tearing down walls. Fortunately, only small amounts of asbestos were found, but rot was much more severe than anticipated.

The meeting included a partnering assessment. The results of an online survey filled out by all the principals were distributed. The results revealed a dip in the ratings between the Crawford foremen and university officials regarding timely collaboration and effective problem solving. One of Chad's people said that the primary source of frustration was Crawford foremen failing to respond to email and telephone messages. Dat asked for the names of his people and said he would talk to each of them. The Crawford foremen complained that the university officials were being too nit-picky. "We don't have the time or money to do A+ work on everything," argued a foreman. Chad told Dat and his people that he would talk to the facilities workers and ask them to focus on what was really important.

6 MONTHS AGO

The project status report meeting started on time. Crawford had been able to make up for lost time, and it now looked like the building would open on time. Chad was glad to see that the partnering assessment had been positive and steady over the past month. The big issue was the surge in costs consuming all but $90,000 of management reserves. With six months to go, everyone knew that this would not cover all the change orders needed to have the building ready. After all, there was already $54,000 worth of change orders pending.

Chad looked across the table and saw nothing but grim faces. Then one of the Crawford foremen proposed postponing treating all of the exterior walls: "Instead of cleaning and preserving the entire brick building, let's only do the front entrance and the north and south walls that the public sees. We can just refurbish the interior court walls as well as the west side. This would be adequate for at least eight years, in which time money should be available to complete the job."

At first Chad didn't like this idea, but eventually, he realized that this was the only way they could have the building ready for the students. Friendly arguments broke out over which exterior segments needed the full treatment and which ones didn't. The whole team ended up touring the outside of the building, identifying what kind of work needed to be done. In the end, only 70 percent of the exterior brick walls were reconditioned according to plan, with savings of over $450,000. While this boost to the reserve would still make things tight, everyone felt that they now had a fighting chance to complete the project on time.

TODAY

As Chad mingled, with a glass of champagne, no one talked about the walls that still needed to be refurbished—tonight was a night to celebrate. All of the major participants and their spouses were at the party, and the university was hosting a five-course meal at the top of the tower. During the toasts, jokes were exchanged and stories were told about the ghosts in the west wing and the discovery of a dead skunk in the south basement. Everyone talked about how proud he or she felt about bringing the grand old building back to life. More than one person mentioned that this was much more satisfying than tearing down an old relic and constructing a new building. The president of the university concluded the festivities by thanking everyone for all the hard work and proclaiming that Buxton would become a bright, shining icon for Pacifica State.

1. How successful was this project?
2. What best practices were evident in the case? How did they contribute to project objectives?

Case 12.4

Goldrush Electronics Negotiation Exercise

OBJECTIVE

The purpose of this case is to provide you with an opportunity to practice negotiations.

PROCEDURE

STEP 1

The class is divided into four groups, each comprising the project management group for one of four projects at Goldrush Electronics.

STEP 2

Read the Goldrush Electronics background information in the following section. Then read the instructions for the project you represent. Soon you will meet with the management of the other projects to exchange personnel. Plan how you want to conduct those meetings.

BACKGROUND INFORMATION

Goldrush Electronics (GE) produces a range of electronic products. GE has a strong commitment to project management. GE operates as a projectized organization, with each project organized as a fully dedicated team. The compensation system is based on a 40 + 30 + 30 formula. Forty percent is based on your base salary, 30 percent on your project performance, and 30 percent on the overall performance of the firm.

Four new product development projects have been authorized. They are code named Alpha, Beta, Theta, and Zeta. The preliminary personnel assignments are listed in the following table. You are assigned to represent the management of one of these projects. The policy at GE is that once preliminary assignments are made, project managers are free to exchange personnel as long as both parties agree to the transaction. Personnel may be traded for one or more other personnel. You will have the opportunity to adjust your team by negotiating with other project managers.

	Alpha Project	
Software Engineer	**Hardware Engineer**	**Design Engineer**
Jill	Cameron	Mitch
John	Chandra	Marsha

	Beta Project	
Software Engineer	**Hardware Engineer**	**Design Engineer**
Jake	Casey	Mike
Jennifer	Craig	Maria

	Theta Project	
Software Engineer	**Hardware Engineer**	**Design Engineer**
Jack	Chuck	Monika
Johan	Cheryl	Mark

	Zeta Project	
Software Engineer	**Hardware Engineer**	**Design Engineer**
Jeff	Carlos	Max
Juwoo	Chad	Maile

STEP 3

Meet and negotiate with the other project managers.

STEP 4

Individual project scores are totaled and posted.

STEP 5

Discussion questions

1. What was your initial strategy before starting the actual negotiations? How did you view the other groups?
2. Did your initial strategy change once negotiations began? If so, how and why?
3. What could top management at GE have done to make it easier to reach agreement with the other groups?

Case 12.5

Umdanso Project

Hannah just tried calling her supplier in Guangzhou for the third time and still no response. Hannah is the assistant project manager working on the Umdanso project for the Apollo electronics firm. Apollo is a small, high-end boutique developer and manufacturer of stereo music electronics. The Umdanso project is named after the Zulu word for Dance. The project objective is to create the next-generation analog/digital conversion device that allows users to listen to high-fidelity music from their vinyl record players through their wireless music system. The popularity of vinyl record sales and the growing segment market of audiophiles with disposable income has led to a boom in Apollo's business and Umdanso is seen as a flagship product.

The project progressed successfully to the prototype stage. So far the tests have exceeded expectations, and everyone was excited to hear the prototype. The Umdanso device relied on two chip suppliers from mainland China. One was in Shenzhen and the other was in Guangzhou.

Hannah has a long-distance working relationship with her counterparts in Shenzhen. They had been supplying Apollo with chips from the beginning. While there were some communication problems early on, over time they had been resolved, and both firms seemed pleased with working arrangement. In fact, Stoffel Theron, the CEO of Apollo, hosted the Shenzhen VP of operations and his family at his ranch last summer.

The chip supplier in Guangzhou was a different story. This was a new contract. The firm was a new manufacturer and was chosen based on price. Hannah had a virtual meeting via Zoom with her Guangzhou counterparts, and they appeared stiff but competent. That was until the COVID-19 virus struck China and government restrictions began to be put into place.

Hannah woke up early that morning with the news that the Chinese government was considering travel restrictions in face of the COVID 19 virus threat. Hannah first called Shenzhen. Shenzhen confirmed her fears that this was going to be a long-term problem. The Shenzhen manager assured her that they would expedite shipping the chips to Apollo. Hannah checked her email and tried calling Guangzhou again with no response.

1. What should Hannah do right now?
2. What should her long-term strategy be?
3. What does the case say about the risks working with foreign suppliers?

Appendix 12.1

Contract Management

LEARNING OBJECTIVES

After reading this appendix you should be able to:

LO A12-1 Describe the procurement management process.

LO A12-2 Describe the differences between fixed-price and cost-plus contracts and their advantages and disadvantages.

LO A12-1

Describe the procurement management process.

Since most outsourced work on projects is contractual, this appendix discusses the different kinds of contracts that are used, their strengths and weaknesses, and how contracts shape the motives and expectations of different participants. Contract management is a key element of any project procurement management system. It is beyond the scope of this book to describe this system. However, the basic processes are listed here to put contract management and related topics like Request for Proposal (RFP) in perspective. Procurement management consists of six main steps:

- **Planning purchases and acquisitions** involves determining what to procure, when, and how. This entails the classic build-versus-buy analysis as well as determination of the type of contract to use.
- **Planning contracting** involves describing the requirements for products or services desired from outsourcing and identifying potential suppliers or sellers. Outputs include procurement documents such as an RFP as well as selection criteria.
- **Requesting seller responses** involves obtaining information, quotes, bids, or proposals from sellers and providers. The main outputs of this process include a qualified sellers list and specific proposals.
- **Selecting sellers** involves choosing from potential suppliers through a process of evaluating potential providers and negotiating a contract.
- **Administering the contract** involves managing the relationship with the selected seller or provider.
- **Closing the contract** involves completion and settlement of the contract.

Most companies have Purchasing Departments that specialize in procurement. Often purchasing agents will be assigned to project teams and they work with other team members to come up with optimum solutions for the project. Even if project teams are not directly involved in contract negotiations and the decision to outsource project work, it is important that the team understand the procurement process and the nature of different kinds of contracts.

LO A12-2

Describe the differences between fixed-price and cost-plus contracts and their advantages and disadvantages.

CONTRACTS

A contract is a formal agreement between two parties wherein one party (the contractor) obligates itself to perform a service and the other party (the client) obligates itself to do something in return, usually in the form of a payment to the contractor. For example, an insurance firm contracted with a consulting firm to reprogram segments of their information system to conform to the latest operating system.

A contract is more than just an agreement between parties. A contract is a codification of the private law, which governs the relationship between the parties to it. It defines the responsibilities, spells out the conditions of its operations, defines the rights of the parties in relationship to each other, and grants remedies to a party if the other party breaches its obligations. A contract attempts to spell out in specific terms the transactional obligations of the parties involved as well as contingencies associated with the execution of the contract. An ambiguous or inconsistent contract is difficult to understand and enforce.

There are essentially two kinds of contracts. The first is the "fixed-price" contract, in which a price is agreed upon in advance and remains fixed as long as there are no changes to the scope or provisions of the agreement. The second is a "cost-plus" contract, in which the contractor is reimbursed for all or some of the expenses incurred during the performance of the contract. Unlike in a fixed-price contract, the final price is not known until the project is completed. Within these two types of contracts, several variations exist.

FIXED-PRICE CONTRACTS

Under a fixed-price (FP), or lump-sum, agreement, the contractor agrees to perform all work specified in the contract at a fixed price. Clients are able to get a minimum price by putting out the contract to competitive bid. Advertising an invitation for bid (IFB) that lists customer requirements usually results in low bids. Prospective contractors can obtain IFB notices through various channels. In the case of large business organizations and government agencies, potential contractors can request to be included on the bidder's list in the area of interest. In other cases, IFBs can be found by scanning appropriate industry media such as newspapers, trade journals, and websites. In many cases, the owner can put restrictions on potential bidders, such as requiring that they be ISO 9000 certified.

With fixed-price contract bids, the contractor has to be very careful in estimating target cost and completion schedule because once agreed upon, the price cannot be adjusted. If contractors overestimate the target cost in the bidding stage, they may lose the contract to a lower-priced competitor; if the estimate is too low, they may win the job but make little or no profit.

Fixed-price contracts are preferred by both owners and contractors when the scope of the project is well defined with predictable costs and low implementation risks. Such might be the case for producing parts or components to specifications, executing training programs, or orchestrating a banquet. With fixed-price contracts, clients do not have to be concerned with project costs and can focus on monitoring work progress and performance specifications. Likewise, contractors prefer fixed-price contracts because the client is less likely to request changes or additions to the contract. Fewer potential changes reduce project uncertainty and allow the contractors to more efficiently manage their resources across multiple projects.

The disadvantage of a fixed-price contract for owners is that it is more difficult and more costly to prepare. To be effective, design specifications need to be spelled out in sufficient detail to leave little doubt as to what is to be achieved. Because the contractor's profit is determined by the difference between the bid and the actual costs, there is some incentive for contractors to use cheaper-quality materials, perform marginal workmanship, or extend the completion date to reduce costs. The client can counteract these by stipulating rigid end-item specifications and completion date and by supervising work. In many cases, the client will hire a consultant who is an expert in the field to oversee the contractor's work and protect the client's interest.

The primary disadvantage of a fixed-price contract for contractors is that they run the risk of underestimating. If the project gets into serious trouble, cost overruns may make the project unprofitable and, in some cases, may lead to bankruptcy. To avoid this, contractors have to invest significant time and money to ensure that their estimates are accurate.

Contracts with long lead times such as construction and production projects may include escalation provisions that protect the contractor against external cost increases in materials, labor rates, or overhead expenses. For example, the price may be tied to an inflation index, so it can be adjusted to sudden increases in labor and material prices, or it may be redetermined as costs become known. A variety of redetermination contracts are used. Some establish a ceiling price for a contract and permit only downward adjustments; others permit upward and downward adjustments. Some establish one readjustment period at the end of the project; others use more than one period. Redetermination contracts are appropriate where engineering and design efforts are difficult to estimate or when final price cannot be estimated for lack of accurate cost data.

While, in principle, redetermination contracts are used to make appropriate adjustments in cost uncertainties, they are prone to abuse. A contractor may win an initial low bid contract, initiate the contracted work, and then "discover" that the costs are much higher than expected. The contractor can take advantage of redetermination provisions and a client's ignorance to justify increasing the actual cost of the contract. The contract evolves into a cost-plus contract.

To alleviate some of the disadvantages of a fixed-price contract while maintaining some certainty as to final cost, many fixed-price contracts contain incentive clauses designed to motivate contractors to reduce costs and improve efficiency. For example, a contractor negotiates to perform the work for a target price based on a target cost and a target profit. A maximum price and maximum profit are also established. If the total cost ends up being less than the target cost, the contractor makes a higher profit up to the profit maximum. If there is a cost overrun, the contractor absorbs some of the overrun until a profit floor is reached.

Profit is determined according to a formula based on a cost-sharing ratio (CSR). A CSR of 75/25, for example, indicates that for every dollar spent above target costs, the client pays 75 cents and the contractor pays 25 cents. This provision motivates contractors to keep costs low, since they pay 25 cents on every dollar spent above the expected cost and earn 25 cents more on every dollar saved below the expected cost. Fixed-price incentive contracts tend to be used for long-duration projects with fairly predictable cost estimates. The key is being able to negotiate a reasonable target cost estimate. Unscrupulous contractors have been known to take advantage of the ignorance of the client to negotiate an unrealistically high target cost and use performance incentives to achieve excessive profits.

COST-PLUS CONTRACTS

Under a cost-plus contract the contractor is reimbursed for all direct allowable costs (materials, labor, travel) plus an additional fee to cover overhead and profit. This fee is negotiated in advance and usually involves a percentage of the total costs. On small projects this kind of contract comes under the rubric "time and materials contract," in which the client agrees to reimburse the contractor for labor cost and materials. Labor costs are based on an hourly or daily rate, which includes direct and indirect costs as well as profit. The contractor is responsible for documenting labor and materials costs.

Unlike fixed-price contracts, cost-plus contracts put the burden of risk on the client. The contract does not indicate what the project is going to cost until the end of the project. Contractors are supposed to make the best effort to fulfill the specific technical requirements of the contract but cannot be held liable, in spite of their best efforts, if the work is not produced within the estimated cost and time frame. These contracts are often criticized because there is little formal incentive for the contractors to control costs or finish on time because they get paid regardless of the final cost. The major factor motivating contractors to control costs and schedule is the effect overruns have on their reputation and their ability to secure future business.

The inherent weakness of cost-plus contracts has been compensated for by a variety of incentive clauses directed at providing incentives to contractors to control costs, maintain performance, and avoid schedule overruns. Contractors are reimbursed for costs, but instead of the fee being fixed, it is based on an incentive formula and subject to additional provisions. This is very similar to fixed-price incentive contracts, but instead of being based on a target cost, the fee is based on actual cost, using a cost-sharing formula.

Most contracts are concerned with the negotiated cost of the project. However, given the importance of speed and timing in today's business world, more and more contracts involve clauses concerning completion dates. To some extent, schedule incentives provide some cost-control measures because schedule slippage typically, but not always, involves cost overruns. Schedule incentives/penalties are stipulated depending on the significance

FIGURE A12.1
Contract Type versus Risk

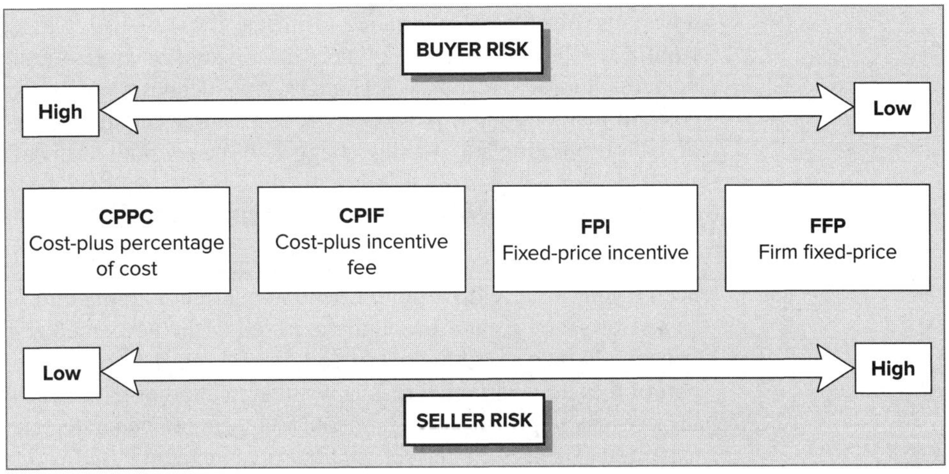

of time to completion for the owner. For example, the contract involving the construction of a new baseball stadium is likely to contain stiff penalties if the stadium is not ready for opening day of the season. Conversely, time-constrained projects in which the number one priority is getting the project completed as soon as possible are likely to include attractive incentives for completing the project early.

A good example of this can be seen in Snapshot from Practice 9.2: Responding to the Northridge Earthquake, in which the construction firm pulled out all the stops to restore the damaged highway system 74 days ahead of schedule. The firm received a $14.8 million bonus for these efforts!

Figure A12.1 summarizes the spectrum of risk to the buyer and supplier for different kinds of contracts. Buyers have the lowest risk with firm fixed-price contracts because they know exactly what they will need to pay the supplier. Buyers have the most risk with cost-plus percentage of cost contracts because they do not know in advance what the suppliers' costs will be and suppliers may be motivated to increase costs. From the suppliers' perspective, the cost-plus contract offers the least risk and the firm fixed-price contract entails the most risk.

CONTRACT CHANGE CONTROL SYSTEM

A contract change control system defines the process by which the contract may be modified. It includes the paperwork, tracking systems, dispute resolution procedures, and approval levels necessary for authorizing changes. There are a number of reasons a contract may need to be changed. Clients may wish to alter the original design or scope of the project once the project is initiated. This is quite common as the project moves from concept to reality. For example, an owner may wish to add windows after inspecting the partially completed homesite. Market changes may dictate adding new features or increasing the performance requirements of equipment. Declining financial resources may dictate that the owner cut back on the scope of the project. The contractor may initiate changes in the contract in response to unforeseen legitimate problems. A building contractor may need to renegotiate the contract in the face of excessive groundwater or the lack of availability of specified materials. In some cases, external forces may dictate contract changes, such as a need to comply with new safety standards mandated by the federal government.

There need to be formal, agreed-upon procedures for initiating changes in the original contract. Contract change orders are subject to abuse. Contractors sometimes take advantage of owners' ignorance to inflate the costs of changes to recoup profit lost from a low bid. Conversely, owners have been known to "get back" at contractors by delaying approval of contract changes, thus delaying project work and increasing the costs to the contractor. All parties need to agree, in advance, on the rules and procedures for initiating and making changes to the original terms of the contract.

CONTRACT MANAGEMENT IN PERSPECTIVE

Contract management is not an exact science. For decades the federal government has been trying to develop a more effective contract administration system. Despite their best efforts, abuses are repeatedly exposed in the news media. The situation is similar to trying to take a wrinkle out of an Oriental rug. Efforts to eliminate a wrinkle in one part of the rug invariably create a wrinkle in another part. Likewise, each new revision in government procurement procedures appears to generate a new loophole that can be exploited. There is no perfect contract management system. Given the inherent uncertainty involved in most project work, no contract can handle all the issues that emerge. Formal contracts cannot replace or eliminate the need to develop effective working relationships between the parties involved that are based on mutual goals, trust, and cooperation. For this reason, the earlier discussion of best practices in outsourcing and effective negotiating is very important.

APPENDIX REVIEW QUESTIONS

1. What are the fundamental differences between fixed-price and cost-plus contracts?
2. For what kinds of projects would you recommend that a fixed-price contract be used? For what kinds of projects would you recommend that a cost-plus contract be used?

APPENDIX REFERENCES

Angus, R. B., N. A. Gundersen, and T. P. Cullinane, *Planning, Performing, and Controlling Projects* (Upper Saddle River, NJ: Prentice Hall, 2003).

Cavendish, J., and M. Martin, *Negotiating and Contracting for Project Management* (Upper Darby, PA: Project Management Institute, 1982).

Fleming, Q. W., *Project Procurement Management: Contracting, Subcontracting, Teaming* (Tustin, CA: FMC Press, 2003).

Fraser, J., *Professional Project Proposals* (Aldershot, UK: Gower/Ashgate, 1995).

Lowe, D., "Contract Management" in P. W. G. Morris and J. K. Pinto (eds.), *The Wiley Guide to Managing Projects* (New York: Wiley, 2004), pp. 678–707.

Schwalbe, K., *Information Technology Project Management,* 4th ed. (Boston: Thomson Course Technology, 2006).

Worthington, M. M., and L. P. Goldsman, *Contracting with the Federal Government,* 4th ed. (New York: Wiley, 1998).

CHAPTER THIRTEEN

13 Progress and Performance Measurement and Evaluation

LEARNING OBJECTIVES

After reading this chapter you should be able to:

13-1 Identify the four steps for controlling a project.

13-2 Utilize a tracking Gantt chart to monitor time performance.

13-3 Understand and appreciate the significance of earned value management.

13-4 Calculate and interpret cost and schedule variance.

13-5 Calculate and interpret performance and percent indexes.

13-6 Forecast final project cost.

13-7 Identify and manage scope creep.

A13.1-1 Apply pseudo-earned value rules to measure progress on a project.

OUTLINE

13.1 Structure of a Project Monitoring Information System

13.2 The Project Control Process

13.3 Monitoring Time Performance

13.4 Earned Value Management (EVM)

13.5 Developing a Status Report: A Hypothetical Example

13.6 Indexes to Monitor Progress

13.7 Forecasting Final Project Cost

13.8 Other Control Issues

Summary

Appendix 13.1: The Application of Additional Earned Value Rules

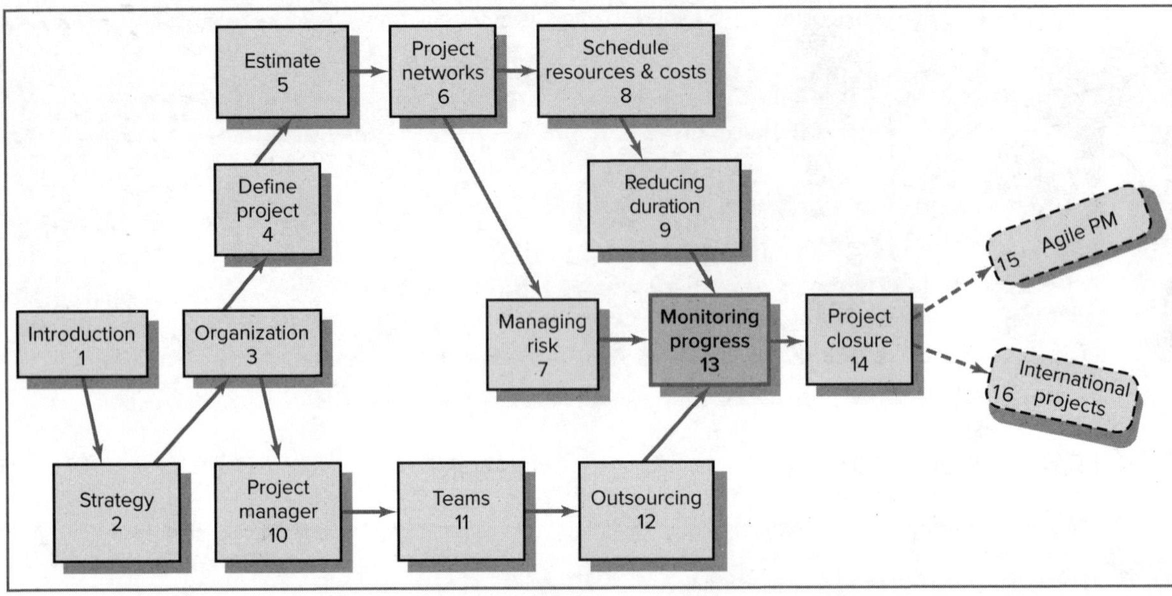

How does a project get one year late?

. . . One day at a time.

—Frederick P. Brooks, The Mythical Man-Month, p. 153

Nothing ever goes completely according to plan. Once a project is launched, management needs an information and control system to make adjustments and steer the project toward its objectives. On time-sensitive projects, project managers need to be able to track progress and know when to speed things up. On set budget projects, project managers need to be able to monitor costs and know when it is necessary to cut costs. Not only are you interested in whether the project is on schedule and budget, but management and customers want to know when the project is likely to be completed and at what cost.

This chapter begins by describing the structure and process of project control systems. Indicators used to assess meeting schedule are discussed next, followed by an introduction to earned value management (EVM). Earned value is a key concept. It will be used both to assess current performance and to predict final costs and completion dates. Be forewarned this is not an easy chapter. Measuring progress can seem complicated quickly and you may find yourself overwhelmed by terminology and indices. However, if you master these concepts, you will have a distinct advantage.

13.1 Structure of a Project Monitoring Information System

A project monitoring system involves *determining what* data to collect; *how, when,* and *who* will collect the data; *analysis* of the data; and *reporting* current progress.

What Data Are Collected?

Data collected are determined by *which* metrics will be used for project control. Typical key data collected are actual activity duration times, resource usage and rates, and actual costs, which are compared against planned times, resources, and budgets. Since a major portion of the monitoring system focuses on cost/schedule concerns, it is crucial to provide the project manager and stakeholders with data to answer questions such as

- What is the current status of the project in terms of schedule and cost?
- How much will it cost to complete the project?
- When will the project be completed?
- Are there potential problems that need to be addressed now?
- What, who, and where are the causes for cost or schedule overruns?
- If there is a cost overrun midway in the project, can we forecast the overrun at completion?

The performance metrics you need to collect should support answering these questions. Examples of specific metrics and tools for collecting data will be discussed in detail later in this chapter.

Collecting Data and Analysis

With the determination of what data are collected, the next step is to establish who, when, and how the data will be assembled. Will the data be collected by the project team, contractor, independent cost engineers, and project manager? Or will the data be derived electronically from some form of surrogate data such as cash flow, machine hours, labor hours, or materials in place? Should the reporting period be one hour, one day, one week, or what? Is there a central repository for the data collected and is someone responsible for its dissemination?

Electronic means of collecting data have vastly improved data assembly, analysis, and dissemination. Numerous software vendors have programs and tools to analyze customized collected data and present it in a form that facilitates monitoring the project, identifying sources of problems, and updating the plan.

Reports and Reporting

First, who gets the progress reports? We have already suggested that different stakeholders and levels of management need different kinds of project information. Senior management's major interests are usually "Are we on time and within budget? If not, what corrective action is taking place?" Likewise, IT managers working on the project are concerned primarily about their deliverable and specific work packages. The reports should be designed for the right audience.

Typically project progress reports are designed and communicated in written or oral form. A common topic format for progress reports follows:

- Progress since last report
- Current status of project
    1. Schedule
    2. Cost
    3. Scope
- Cumulative trends
- Problems and issues since last report
    1. Actions and resolution of earlier problems
    2. New variances and problems identified
- Corrective action planned

Given the structure of your information system and the nature of its outputs, you can use the system to interface and facilitate the project control process. These interfaces need to be relevant and seamless if control is to be effective.

13.2 The Project Control Process

LO 13-1

Identify the four steps for controlling a project.

Control is the process of comparing actual performance against the plan to identify deviations, evaluate possible alternative courses of actions, and take appropriate corrective action. The project control steps for measuring and evaluating project performance are

1. Setting a baseline plan.
2. Measuring progress and performance.
3. Comparing plan against actual.
4. Taking action.

Each of the control steps is described in the following paragraphs.

Step 1: Setting a Baseline Plan

The baseline plan provides the elements for measuring performance. The baseline is derived from the cost and duration information found in the work breakdown structure (WBS) database and time-sequence data from the network and resource scheduling decisions. From the WBS the project resource schedule is used to time-phase all work, resources, and budgets into a baseline plan. See Chapter 8.

Step 2: Measuring Progress and Performance

Time and budgets are quantitative measures of performance that readily fit into the integrated information system. Qualitative measures such as meeting customer technical specifications and product function are most frequently determined by on-site inspection or actual use. This chapter is limited to quantitative measures of time and budget. Measurement of time performance is relatively easy and obvious. That is, is the critical path early, on schedule, or late; is the slack of near-critical paths decreasing to cause new critical activities? Measuring performance against budget (e.g., money, units in place, labor hours) is more difficult and is *not* simply a case of comparing actual versus budget. Earned value is necessary to provide a realistic estimate of performance against a time-phased budget. **Earned value (EV)** is the budgeted cost of the work performed.

Step 3: Comparing Plan against Actual

Because plans seldom materialize as expected, it becomes imperative to measure deviations from plan to determine if action is necessary. Periodic monitoring and measuring the status of the project allow for comparisons of actual versus expected plans. It is important that the timing of status reports be frequent enough to allow for early detection of variations from plan and early correction of causes. Usually, status reports should take place every one to four weeks to be useful and allow for proactive correction.

Step 4: Taking Action

If deviations from plans are significant, corrective action will be needed to bring the project back in line with the original or revised plan. For example, if the project is behind schedule, overtime may be authorized to get back on schedule. In some cases, conditions or scope can change, which in turn will require a change in the baseline plan to recognize new information.

The remainder of this chapter describes and illustrates monitoring systems, tools, and components to support managing and controlling projects. Several of the tools you developed in the planning and scheduling chapters now serve as input to your information system for monitoring performance. Monitoring time performance is discussed first, followed by cost performance.

13.3 Monitoring Time Performance

A major goal of progress reporting is to catch any negative variances from plan as early as possible to determine if corrective action is necessary. Fortunately, monitoring schedule performance is relatively easy. The project network schedule, derived from the WBS/OBS, serves as the baseline to compare against actual performance.

Gantt charts (bar charts), control charts, and milestone schedules are the typical tools used for communicating project schedule status. As suggested in Chapter 6, the Gantt chart is the most favored, used, and understandable. This kind of chart is commonly referred to as a **tracking Gantt** chart. Adding actual and revised time estimates to the Gantt chart gives a quick overview of project status on the report date.

Tracking Gantt Chart

LO 13-2

Utilize a tracking Gantt chart to monitor time performance.

Figure 13.1 presents a baseline Gantt chart and a tracking Gantt chart for a project at the end of period 6. The solid bar below the original schedule bar represents the actual start and finish times for completed activities or any portion of an activity completed (see activities A, B, C, D, and E). For example, the actual start time for activity C is period 2; the actual finish time is period 5; the actual duration is three time units, rather than four scheduled time periods. Activities in process show the actual start time; the extended bar represents the expected remaining duration (see activities D and E). The remaining duration for activities D and E is shown with the hatched bar. Activity F, which has not started, shows a revised estimated actual start (9) and finish time (13).

Note how activities can have durations that differ from the original schedule, as in activities C, D, and E. Either the activity is complete and the actual is known, or new information suggests the estimate of time be revised and reflected in the status report. Activity D's revised duration results in an expected delay in the start of activity F. The project is now estimated to be completed one period later than planned. Although sometimes the Gantt chart does not show dependencies, when it is used with a network, the dependencies are easily identified if tracing is needed.

Control Chart

A **control chart** is another tool used to monitor past project schedule performance and current performance and to estimate future schedule trends. Figure 13.2 depicts a project control chart. The chart is used to plot the difference between the scheduled and actual times on the critical path at a given point on the project. Although Figure 13.2 shows the project was behind early in the project, the plot suggests corrective action brought the project back on track. If the trend is sustained, the project will come in ahead of schedule. Because the activity scheduled times represent average durations, four observations trending in one direction indicate there is a very high probability that there is an identifiable cause. The cause should be located and action taken if necessary. Control chart trends are very useful for warning of potential problems so appropriate action can be taken if necessary.

FIGURE 13.1
Baseline and Tracking Gantt Charts

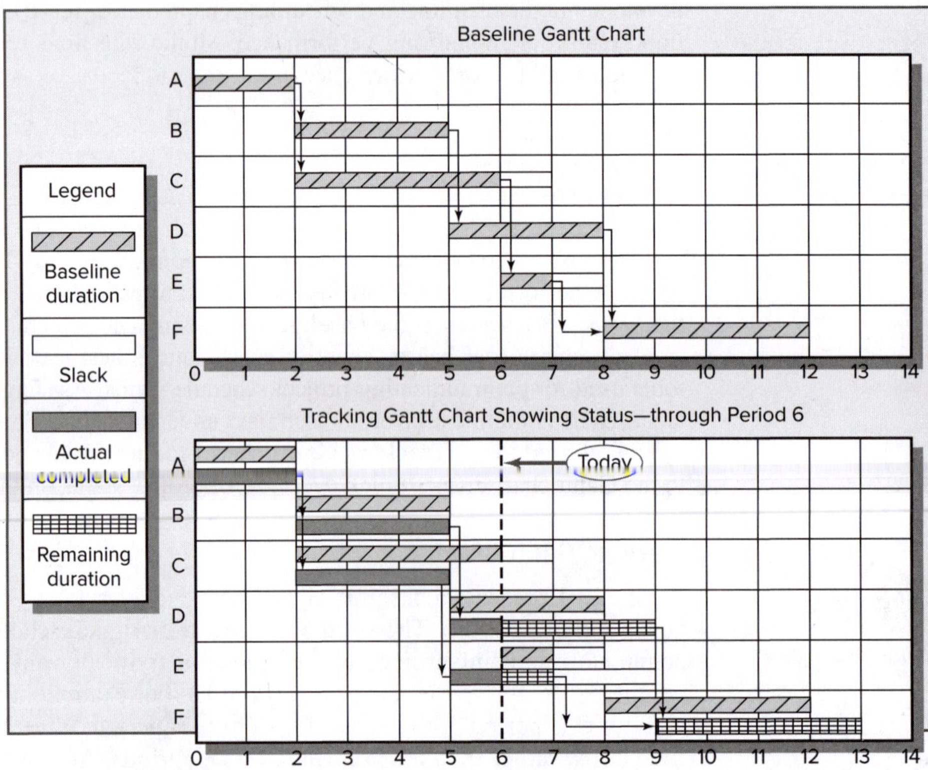

FIGURE 13.2
Project Schedule Control Chart

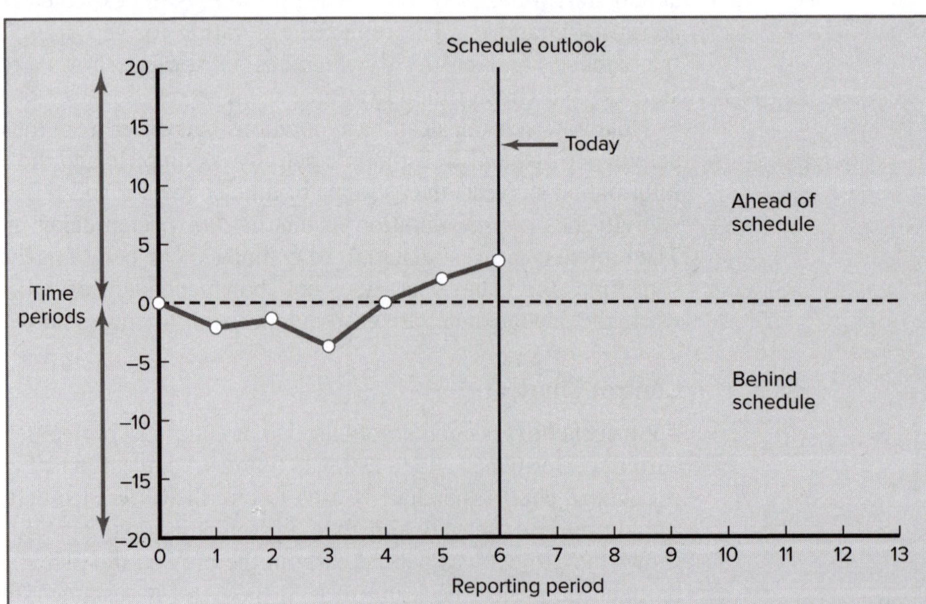

Milestone Schedules

Milestone schedules are often used to keep more distal stakeholders informed on the progress of a project. Such stakeholders, whether it is senior management, the owner, or regulatory agencies, often neither need nor desire a detailed accounting of project progress. Instead, their interests can be satisfied by reporting progress toward major project milestones. Remember from Chapter 4 that milestones are significant project events that mark major accomplishments. Table 13.1 is the milestone schedule used to keep the president of a university and his/her cabinet informed on the construction of a new College of Business building.

Project managers recognize the need to use a more macro schedule of significant deliverables to keep external stakeholders informed and a more detailed milestone-driven schedule to manage and motivate the project team to achieve those deliverables. For more on the latter, see Snapshot from Practice 13.1: Guidelines for Setting Milestones.

13.4 Earned Value Management (EVM)

LO 13-3

Understand and appreciate the significance of earned value management.

The Need for Earned Value Management

Earned value management (EVM) is a methodology that combines scope, schedule, and resource measurements to assess project performance and progress. To understand the value of EVM, imagine you are a project manager for a large painting company that has secured the contract with a local developer to paint 10 identical condos. It is estimated that it will take your team 2 weeks to paint each condo at a cost of $10,000. You expect to complete the project in 20 weeks at a total cost of $100,000.

After 10 weeks management asks for a status report. You report you have spent $50,000. Management might conclude the following: good, you spent as much as you were supposed to spend, and everything is going according to plan. This might be correct, but it might not be. It is also possible that after 10 weeks due to unusually warm weather you were able to paint 6 condos at a cost of only $50,000. Conversely, due to inclement weather you may have been able to paint only 4 condos at a cost of $50,000. What is true?

TABLE 13.1
College of Business Milestone Schedule, Planned, and Actual

Components	Milestone	Planned	Actual Days +/–
Schematic Design	January 15, 2022	January 21, 2022	–6
Design Development	August 31, 2022	August 31, 2022	0
Construction Document	January 15, 2023	January 19, 2023	–4
Historic Review	October 31, 2022	October 21, 2022	+10
1% for Art Selection	May 31, 2023	May 28, 2023	+3
Bid and Permit	March 31, 2023		
Furnishings Selections	November 30, 2023		
Construction	August 31, 2024		
Programming	August 31, 2024		
Occupancy	September 7, 2024		

SNAPSHOT FROM PRACTICE 13.1 Guidelines for Setting Milestones

Erik Larson

In medieval times, mounds of stones were used to mark the distance traveled along a path or road. Travelers used these rock formations to gauge their progress and adjust their plans. In modern times, milestones are distinct events along the project timeline that are used to gauge progress and adjust plans. Milestones are building blocks for the project's schedule and often create positive momentum to propel the project along to completion. To be effective, milestones need to be concrete, specific, measurable events.

Here are some guidelines for setting milestones gleaned from conversations with veteran project managers:

Avoid the temptation to overuse milestones as a motivational tool by labeling every task a milestone. Only important deliverables or achievements should be used as milestones.

Timing of milestones is important. Milestones that are placed too far apart will not generate momentum. Conversely, milestones placed too close together quickly lose their distinctiveness.

Critical merge and burst activities are often useful milestones, since they indicate significant work has been or is about to be accomplished. Here it is important to remember that milestones are events, not tasks, and the start of a merge activity (e.g., patent application submitted) or the completion of a burst activity (e.g., building permit approved) should be used.

Significant accomplishments are always good milestones and are opportunities to celebrate progress. Completion of the roof on construction projects is typically celebrated across the world. Note this is most likely a burst activity.

Rates of completion can be used on projects involving repetition and not sequential advancement. For example, on a training project, milestones could be set as percentages of employees fully trained and certified, such as 25 percent, 50 percent, 75 percent, and 100 percent.

Completing a high-anxiety, high-risk task is always worthy of milestone consideration. For example, gaining foreign approval or completing dangerous work like transporting volatile chemicals or crossing a treacherous part of mountain trek.

Judicious use of milestones helps motivate and keep the project team focused.

From this example, it is easy to understand why using only actual and planned costs can mislead management and customers in evaluating project performance. Cost variance of budget-to-actual alone is inadequate. It does not measure how much work was accomplished for the money spent.

Enter the concept of earned value (EV). Earned value is the budgeted cost of the work you have actually accomplished to date. Let's return to the previous examples and include EV in the analysis.

Management thank you for cost information but want to know how much work has been accomplished. You survey the work site and report that 4½ condos have been painted. According to the budget, 4½ condos should have cost $45,000. You *earn the value* of the work that has been completed.

Earned value for the first 10 weeks is $45,000.

Actual costs for the first 10 weeks are $50,000.

Planned budget costs for the first 10 weeks are $50,000.

We can now infer with confidence that the project is (1) behind schedule—we have accomplished \$5,000 (one-half a condo) less than planned and (2) overbudget—we spent \$50,000 to accomplish \$45,000 worth of work.

Now let's assume you survey the site and instead of finding 4½ condos painted, you are happy to report that 6 have been painted. You *earn the value* of the work that has been accomplished (6 × \$10,000) = \$60,000. Now you can report that the project is both (1) ahead of schedule—we have accomplished \$10,000 (one condo) worth of work more than planned and (2) under budget—we were able to paint 6 condos for only \$50,000 instead of the estimated \$60,000.

Earned value is not new. The original earned value cost/schedule system was pioneered by the U.S. Department of Defense (DoD) in the 1960s. Cost overruns and public outcry motivated the DoD to search for a more effective system to track schedule and cost in large project contracts. The private sector was quick to recognize the worth of EVM. It is probably safe to say project managers in every major country are using some form of EVM. It is not limited to construction or contracts. EVM is being used on internal projects in the manufacturing, pharmaceutical, and high-tech industries. For example, organizations such as EDS, NCR, Levi Strauss, Tektronics, and Disney have used earned value systems to track projects. More recently one of the authors used his expertise in EVM to help the College of Oceanography (CoO) at Oregon State University secure a multimillion-dollar National Science Foundation (NSF) grant to design and build the next generation of off-shore research vessels. This was the first time CoO encountered an NSF grant application that required an EVM system.

The earned value system starts with the time-phased costs that provide the project budget **baseline,** which is called the planned budgeted value of the work scheduled (PV). Given this time-phased baseline, comparisons can be made with actual and planned schedule and costs using a concept called earned value. The earned value system uses data developed from the work breakdown structure, project network, and schedule. This integrated cost/schedule system provides schedule and cost variance and can be used to forecast the remaining costs for the in-process project. The earned value approach provides the missing links not found in conventional cost-budget systems. At any point in time, a status report can be developed for the project. The development of an integrated cost/schedule system is discussed next.

EVM uses several acronyms and equations for analysis. Table 13.2 presents a glossary of these acronyms. You will need this glossary as a reference. In recent years acronyms have been shortened to be more phonetically friendly. This movement is reflected in material from the Project Management Institute, in project management software, and by most practitioners. This text edition follows the recent trend. The acronyms found in brackets represent the older acronyms, which are often found in software programs. To the uninitiated, the terms used in practice appear horrendous and intimidating. However, once a few basic terms are understood, the intimidation index will evaporate.

Carefully following five steps ensures that the cost/schedule system is integrated. These steps are outlined here. Steps 1, 2, and 3 are accomplished in the planning stage. Steps 4 and 5 are sequentially accomplished during the execution stage of the project.

1. Define the work using a WBS/OBS. This step involves developing documents that include the following information (see Chapters 4 and 5):
   a. Scope.
   b. Work packages.
   c. Deliverables.

TABLE 13.2
Glossary of Terms

Term	Definition
EV	Earned value for a task is the budgeted value of the work accomplished. Work accomplished is often measured in terms of percentages (e.g., 25% complete) in which case, EV is simply percent complete times its original budget. [The older acronym for this value was BCWP—budgeted cost of the work performed.]
PV	The planned time-phased baseline of the value of the work scheduled. An approved cost estimate of the resources scheduled in a time-phased cumulative baseline [BCWS—budgeted cost of the work scheduled].
AC	Actual cost of the work completed. The sum of the costs incurred in accomplishing work [ACWP—actual cost of the work performed].
CV	Cost variance is the difference between the earned value and the actual costs for the work completed to date where CV = EV – AC.
SV	Schedule variance is the difference between the earned value and the baseline to date where SV = EV – PV.
BAC	Budgeted cost at completion. The total budgeted cost of the baseline or project cost accounts.
EAC	Estimated cost at completion
ETC	Estimated cost to complete remaining work
VAC	Cost variance at completion. VAC indicates expected actual over- or underrun cost at completion.

   d. Organization units.
   e. Resources.
   f. Budgets for each work package.
2. Develop work and resource schedule.
   a. Schedule resources to activities (see Chapter 8).
   b. Time-phase work packages into a network.
3. Develop a time-phased budget using work packages included in an activity. The cumulative values of these budgets will become the baseline and will be called the planned budgeted cost of the work scheduled (PV). The sum should equal the budgeted amounts for all the work packages in the cost accounts (see Chapter 8).
4. At the work package level, collect the actual costs for the work performed. These costs will be called the actual cost of the work completed (AC). Collect percent complete and multiply this times the original budget amount for the value of the work actually completed. These values will be called earned value (EV).
5. Compute the **schedule variance (SV)** (SV = EV – PV) and **cost variance (CV)** (CV = EV – AC). Prepare hierarchical status reports for each level of management—from work package manager to customer or project manager. The reports should also include project rollups by organization unit and deliverables. In addition, actual time performance should be checked against the project network schedule.

Figure 13.3 presents a schematic overview of the integrated information system, which includes the techniques and systems presented in earlier chapters. Those who have tenaciously labored through the early chapters can smile! Steps 1 and 2 are already carefully developed. Observe that control data can be traced backward to specific deliverables and organization unit responsible.

The major reasons for creating a baseline are to monitor and report progress and to estimate cash flow. Therefore, it is crucial to integrate the baseline with the performance measurement system. Costs are placed (time-phased) in the baseline exactly as managers expect them to be "earned." This approach facilitates tracking costs to their

FIGURE 13.3
Project Management Information System Overview

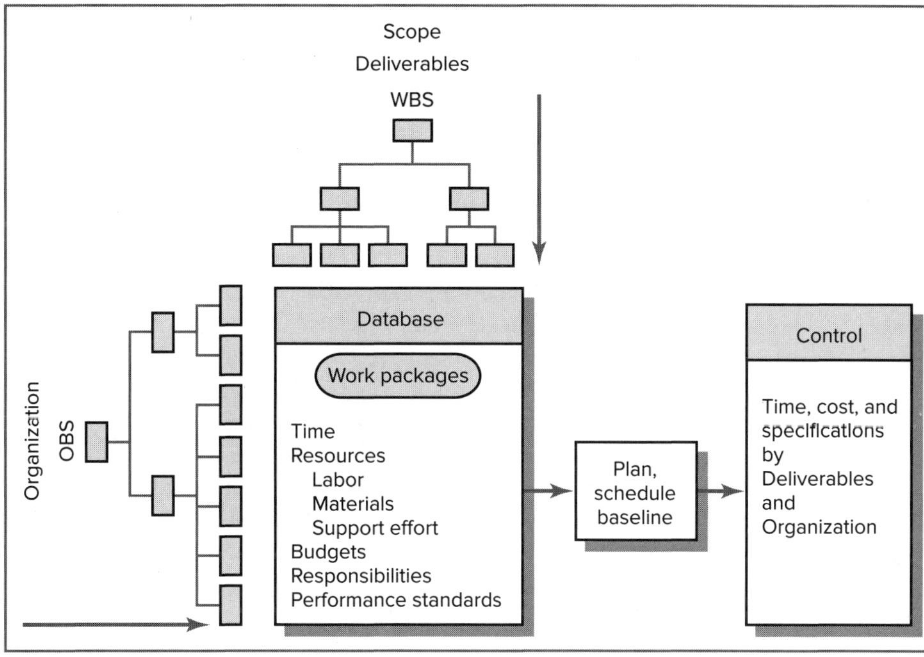

point of origin. In practice, the integration is accomplished by using the same rules in assigning costs to the baseline as those used to measure progress using earned value. You may find several rules in practice, but percent complete is the workhorse most commonly used. Someone familiar with each task estimates what percent of the task has been completed or how much of the task remains.

Percent Complete Rule

This rule is the heart of any earned value system. The best method for assigning costs to the baseline under this rule is to establish frequent checkpoints over the duration of the work package and assign completion percentages in dollar terms. For example, units completed could be used to assign baseline costs and later to measure progress. Units might be lines of code, hours, drawings completed, cubic yards of concrete in place, workdays, prototypes complete, and so on. This approach to percent complete adds "objectivity" to the subjective observation approaches often used. When measuring percent complete in the monitoring phase of the project, it is common to limit the amount earned to 80 or 90 percent until the work package is 100 percent complete.

What Costs Are Included in Baselines?

The baseline (PV) is the sum of the cost accounts, and each cost account is the sum of the work packages in the cost account. Three direct costs are typically included in baselines—labor, equipment, and materials—because these are direct costs the project manager can control. Overhead costs and profit are typically added later by accounting processes. Most work packages should be discrete and of a short time span and have measurable outputs. If materials and equipment are a significant portion of the cost of work packages, they can be budgeted in separate work packages and cost accounts.

Methods of Variance Analysis

LO 13-4

Calculate and interpret cost and schedule variance.

Generally the method for measuring accomplishments centers on two key computations:

1. Comparing earned value with the expected schedule value.
2. Comparing earned value with the actual costs.

These comparisons can be made at the project level or down to the cost account level. Project status can be determined for the latest period, all periods to date, and estimated to the end of the project.

Assessing the current status of a project using the earned value cost/schedule system requires three data elements—planned cost of the work scheduled (PV), budgeted cost of the work completed (EV), and actual cost of the work completed (AC). From these data, the schedule variance (SV) and cost variance (CV) are computed each reporting period. *A positive variance indicates a desirable condition, while a negative variance suggests problems or changes that have taken place.*

Cost variance tells us if the work accomplished costs more or less than was planned at any point over the life of the project. If labor and materials have not been separated, cost variance should be reviewed carefully to isolate the cause to either labor or materials—or to both.

Schedule variance presents an overall assessment of *all* work packages in the project scheduled to date. It is important to note schedule variance contains *no* critical path information. Critical and noncritical activities are combined in the calculation. Schedule variance measures progress in dollars rather than time units. Therefore, it is unlikely that any translation of dollars to time will yield accurate information telling if any milestone or critical path is early, on time, or late (even if the project occurs exactly as planned). *The only accurate method for determining the true time progress of the project is to compare the project network schedule against the actual network schedule to measure if the project is on time* (refer to Figure 13.1). However, SV is very useful in assessing the direction all the work in the project is taking—after 20 or more percent of the project has been completed.

Figure 13.4 presents a sample cost/schedule graph with variances identified for a project at the current status report date. Note the graph also focuses on what remains to be accomplished and any favorable or unfavorable trends. The "today" label marks the report date (time period 25) of where the project has been and where it is going. Because our system is hierarchical, graphs of the same form can be developed for different levels of management. In Figure 13.4 the top line represents the actual costs (AC) incurred for the project work to date. The middle line is the baseline (PV) and ends at the scheduled project duration (45). The bottom line is the budgeted value of the work actually completed to date (EV), or the earned value. The dotted line extending the actual costs from the report date to the new estimated completion date represents revised estimates of *expected* actual costs; that is, additional information suggests the costs at completion of the project will differ from what was planned. Note that the project duration has been extended and the **variance at completion (VAC)** is negative (BAC – EAC).

Another interpretation of the graph uses percentages. At the end of period 25, 75 percent of the work was scheduled to be accomplished. At the end of period 25, the value of the work accomplished is 50 percent. The actual cost of the work completed to date is $340, or 85 percent of the total project budget. The graph suggests the project will have about an 18 percent cost overrun and be five time units late. The current status of the project shows the cost variance (CV) to be over budget by \$140 (EV − AC = 200 − 340 = −140). The schedule variance (SV) is negative \$100 (EV − PV = 200 − 300 = −100), which suggests the project is behind schedule. Before moving to an example, consult Figure 13.5 to practice interpreting the outcomes of cost/schedule graphs. Remember, PV is your baseline and anchor point.

FIGURE 13.4
Cost/Schedule Graph

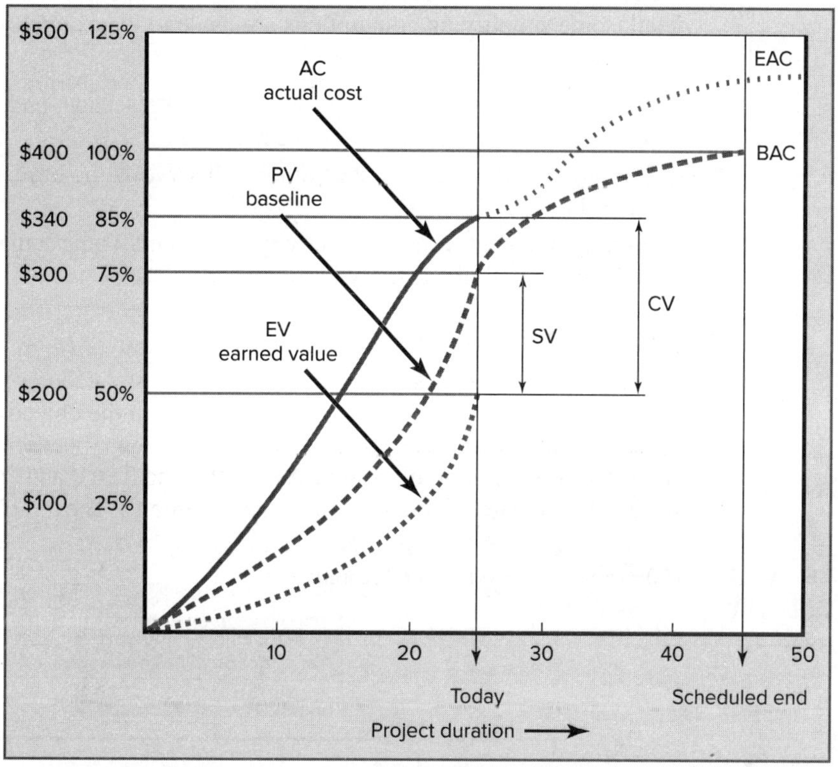

FIGURE 13.5
Earned Value Review Exercise

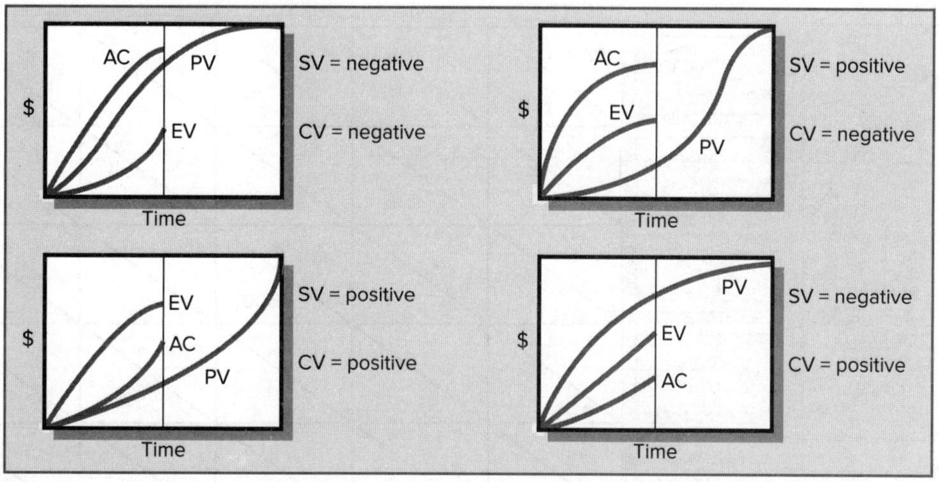

13.5 Developing a Status Report: A Hypothetical Example

Working through an example demonstrates how the baseline serves as the anchor from which the project can be monitored using earned value techniques.

Assumptions

Because the process becomes geometrically complex with the addition of project detail, some simplifying assumptions are made in the example to more easily demonstrate the process:

1. Assume each cost account has only one work package, and each cost account will be represented as an activity on the network.
2. The project network early start times will serve as the basis for assigning the baseline values.
3. From the moment work on an activity task begins, some actual costs will be incurred each period until the activity is completed.

Baseline Development

Figure 13.6 (Work Breakdown Structure with Cost Accounts) depicts a simple work breakdown structure (WBS/OBS) for a project with the objective of developing a new digital camera. There are six deliverables (Design Specifications, Shell & Power, Memory/Software, Zoom System, Assemble, and Test), and five responsible departments (Design, Shell, Storage, Zoom, and Assembly). The total for all the cost accounts

FIGURE 13.6 **Work Breakdown Structure with Cost Accounts**

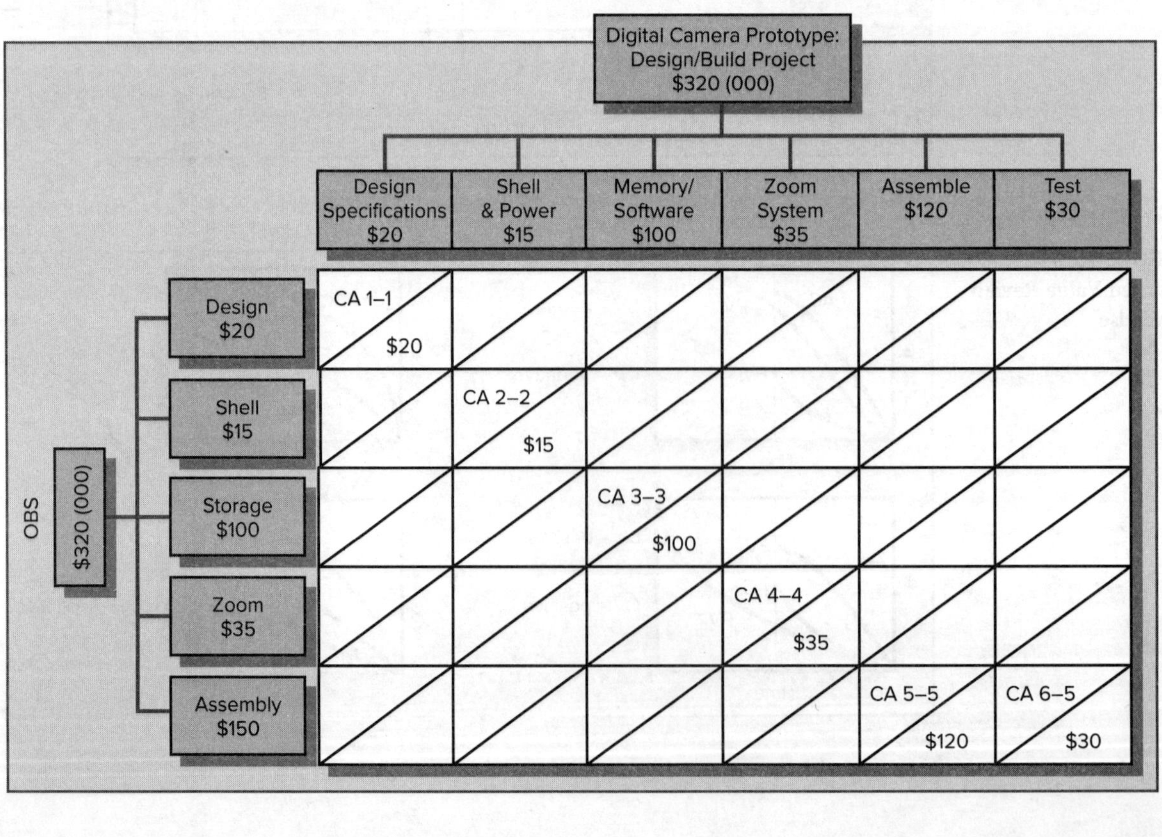

(CA) is \$320,000, which represents the total project cost. Figure 13.7, derived from the WBS, presents a planning Gantt chart for the Digital Camera project. The planned project duration is 11 time units. This project information is used to time-phase the project budget baseline. Figure 13.8 (project baseline budget) presents a worksheet with an early start baseline developed with costs assigned. They are assigned "exactly" as managers plan to monitor and measure schedule and cost performance.

Development of the Status Report

A status report is analogous to a camera snapshot of a project at a specific point in time. The status report uses earned value to measure schedule and cost performance. Measuring earned value begins at the work package level. Work packages are in one of three conditions on a report date:

1. Not yet started.
2. Finished.
3. In process or partially complete.

Earned values for the first two conditions present no difficulties. Work packages that are not yet started earn zero percent of the PV (budget). Packages that are completed earn 100 percent of their PV. In-process packages apply the percent complete rule to the PV baseline to measure earned value (EV). In our camera example, we will only use the percent complete rule to measure progress.

Table 13.3 presents the completed, separate status reports of the Digital Camera Prototype project for periods 1 through 7. Each period percent complete and actual cost

FIGURE 13.7
Digital Camera Prototype Project Baseline Gantt Chart

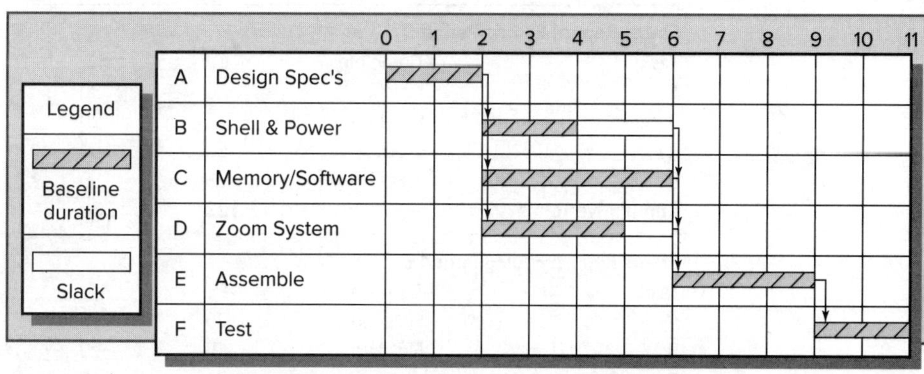

FIGURE 13.8
Digital Camera Prototype Project Baseline Budget (\$000)

Schedule information						Baseline budget needs										
						Time period										
ACT/WP	DUR	ES	LF	SL	Total PV	1	2	3	4	5	6	7	8	9	10	11
A	2	0	2	0	20	10	10									
B	2	2	6	2	15			5	10							
C	4	2	6	0	100			20	30	30	20					
D	3	2	6	1	35			15	10	10						
E	3	6	9	0	120							30	40	50		
F	2	9	11	0	30										10	20
Total PV by period						10	10	40	50	40	20	30	40	50	10	20
Cumulative PV by period						10	20	60	110	150	170	200	240	290	300	320

TABLE 13.3 Digital Camera Prototype Status Reports: Periods 1–7 ($000)

Cost Variance CV = EV − AC
Schedule Variance SV = EV − PV

Status Report: Ending Period 1

Task	%Complete	EV	AC	PV	CV	SV
A	50%	10	10	10	0	0
Cumulative Totals		**10**	**10**	**10**	**0**	**0**

Status Report: Ending Period 2

Task	%Complete	EV	AC	PV	CV	SV
A	Finished	20	30	20	−10	0
Cumulative Totals		**20**	**30**	**20**	**−10**	**0**

Status Report: Ending Period 3

Task	%Complete	EV	AC	PV	CV	SV
A	Finished	20	30	20	−10	0
B	33%	5	10	5	−5	0
C	20%	20	30	20	−10	0
D	60%	21	20	15	+1	+6
Cumulative Totals		**66**	**90**	**60**	**−24**	**+6**

Status Report: Ending Period 4

Task	%Complete	EV	AC	PV	CV	SV
A	Finished	20	30	20	−10	0
B	Finished	15	20	15	−5	0
C	50%	50	70	50	−20	0
D	80%	28	30	25	−2	+3
Cumulative Totals		**113**	**150**	**110**	**−37**	**+3**

Status Report: Ending Period 5

Task	%Complete	EV	AC	PV	CV	SV
A	Finished	20	30	20	−10	0
B	Finished	15	20	15	−5	0
C	60%	60	100	80	−40	−20
D	80%	28	50	35	−22	−7
Cumulative Totals		**123**	**200**	**150**	**−77**	**−27**

Status Report: Ending Period 6

Task	%Complete	EV	AC	PV	CV	SV
A	Finished	20	30	20	−10	0
B	Finished	15	20	15	−5	0
C	80%	80	110	100	−30	−20
D	Finished	35	60	35	−25	0
Cumulative Totals		**150**	**220**	**170**	**−70**	**−20**

Status Report: Ending Period 7

Task	%Complete	EV	AC	PV	CV	SV
A	Finished	20	30	20	−10	0
B	Finished	15	20	15	−5	0
C	90%	90	120	100	−30	−10
D	Finished	35	60	35	−25	0
E	0%	0	0	30	0	−30
F	0%	0	0	0	0	0
Cumulative Totals		**160**	**230**	**200**	**−70**	**−40**

were gathered for each task from staff in the field. The schedule and cost variance are computed for each task and the project to date. For example, the status in period 1 shows only Task A (Design Specifications) is in process and it is 50 percent complete, and the actual cost for the task is 10. The planned value at the end of period 1 for Task A is 10 (see Figure 13.8). The cost and schedule variance are both zero, which indicates the project is on budget and schedule. By the end of period 3, Task A is finished; Task B (Shell & Power) is 33 percent complete and AC is 10; Task C is 20 percent complete and AC is 30; and Task D is 60 percent complete and AC is 20. Again, from Figure 13.8 *at the end of period 3,* we can see that the PV for Task A is 20 (10 + 10 = 20), for Task B is 5, for Task C is 20, and for Task D is 15. At the end of period 3 it is becoming clear the actual cost (AC) is exceeding the value of the work completed (EV). The cost variance (see Table 13.3) for the project at the end of period 3 is negative 24. Schedule variance is positive 6, which suggests the project may be ahead of schedule.

It is important to note that since earned values are computed from costs (or sometimes labor hours or other metrics), the relationship of costs to time is not one-for-one. For example, it is possible to have a negative SV variance when the project is actually ahead on the critical path. This occurs when delays in noncritical activities outweigh progress on the critical path. Therefore, it is important to remember that SV is in dollars and is not an accurate measure of time; however, it is a fairly good indicator of the status of the whole project in terms of being ahead or behind schedule after the project is over 20 percent complete. Only the project network, or tracking Gantt chart, and actual work completed can give an accurate assessment of schedule performance down to the work package level.

By studying the separate status reports for periods 5 through 7, you can see the project will be over budget and behind schedule. By period 7, Tasks A, B, and D are finished, but all are over budget—negative 10, 5, and 25. Task C (Memory/Software) is 90 percent complete. Task E is late and hasn't started because Task C is not yet completed. The result is that, at the end of period 7, the Digital Camera project is over budget $70,000, with a schedule budget over $40,000.

Figure 13.9 shows the graphed results of all the status reports through period 7. This graph represents the data from Table 13.3. The cumulative actual costs (AC) to

FIGURE 13.9
Digital Camera Prototype Summary Graph ($000)

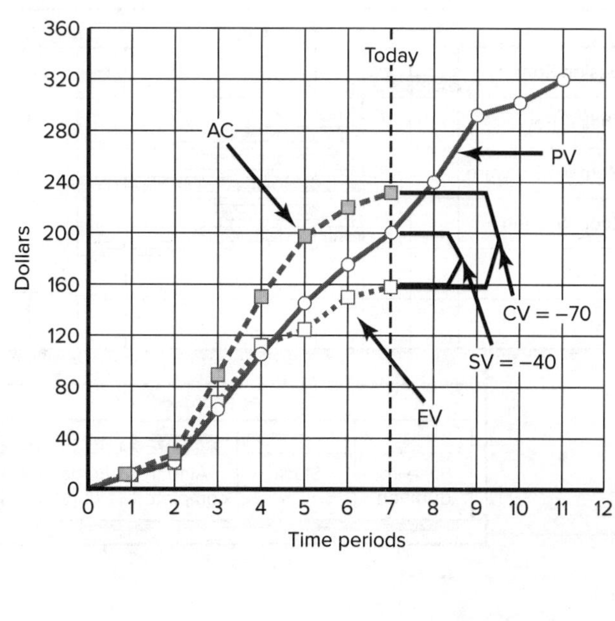

date and the earned value budgeted costs to date (EV) are plotted against the original project baseline (PV). The cumulative AC to date is $230,000; the cumulative EV to date is $160,000. Given these cumulative values, the cost variance (CV = EV – AC) is negative $70,000 (160,000 – 230,000 = –70,000). The schedule variance (SV = EV – PV) is negative $40,000 (160,000 – 200,000 = –40,000). Again, recall that only the project network or tracking Gantt chart can give an accurate assessment of schedule performance down to the work package level.

A tracking Gantt bar chart for the Digital Camera Prototype is shown in Figure 13.10. From this figure you can see Task C (Memory/Software), which had an original duration of four time units, now is expected to require six time units. This delay of two time units for Task C will also delay Tasks E and F two time units and result in the project being late for two time periods.

Figure 13.11 shows an oversimplified project rollup at the end of period 7. The rollup is by deliverables and organization units. For example, the Memory/Software deliverable has an SV of $–10,000 and a CV of $–30,000. The responsible "Storage" Department should have an explanation for these variances. Similarly, the Assembly Department, which is responsible for the Assemble and Test deliverables, has an SV of $–30,000 due to the delay of Task C (see Figure 13.10). Most deliverables look unfavorable on schedule and cost variance.

In more complex projects, the crosstabs of cost accounts by deliverables and organization units can be very revealing and more profound. This example contains the basics for developing a status report, developing baselines, and measuring schedule and cost variance. In our example, performance analysis had only one level above the cost account level. Because all data are derived from the detailed database, it is relatively easy to determine the progress status at all levels of the work and organization breakdown structures. Fortunately, this same current database can provide additional views of the current status of the project and forecast costs at the completion of the project. Approaches for deriving additional information from the database are presented next.

To the uninitiated, a caveat is in order. In practice, budgets may not be expressed in total dollars for an activity. Frequently budgets are time-phased for materials and labor separately for more effective control over costs. Another common approach is to use labor hours in place of dollars in the earned value system. Later, labor hours are

FIGURE 13.10
Digital Camera Project-Tracking Gantt Chart Showing Status—through Period 7

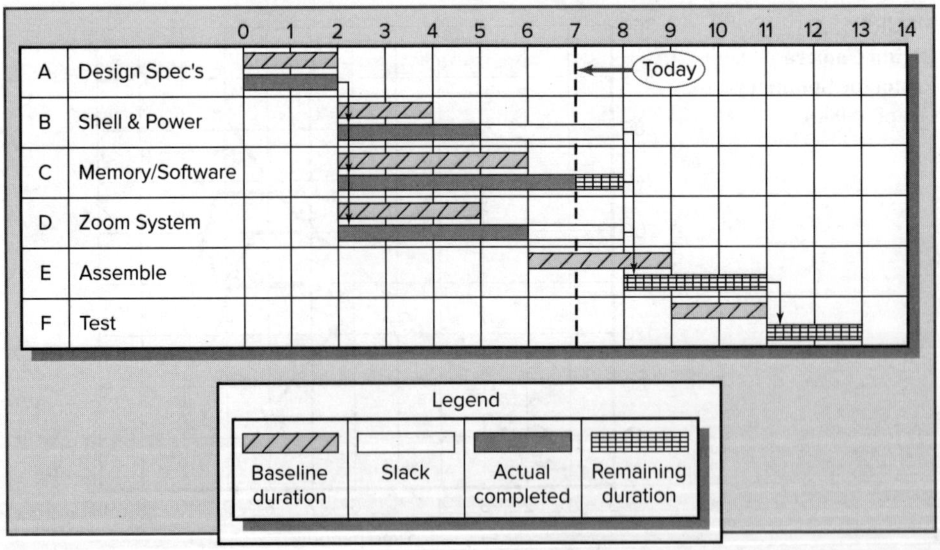

FIGURE 13.11 Digital Camera Project Rollup End Period 7 ($000)

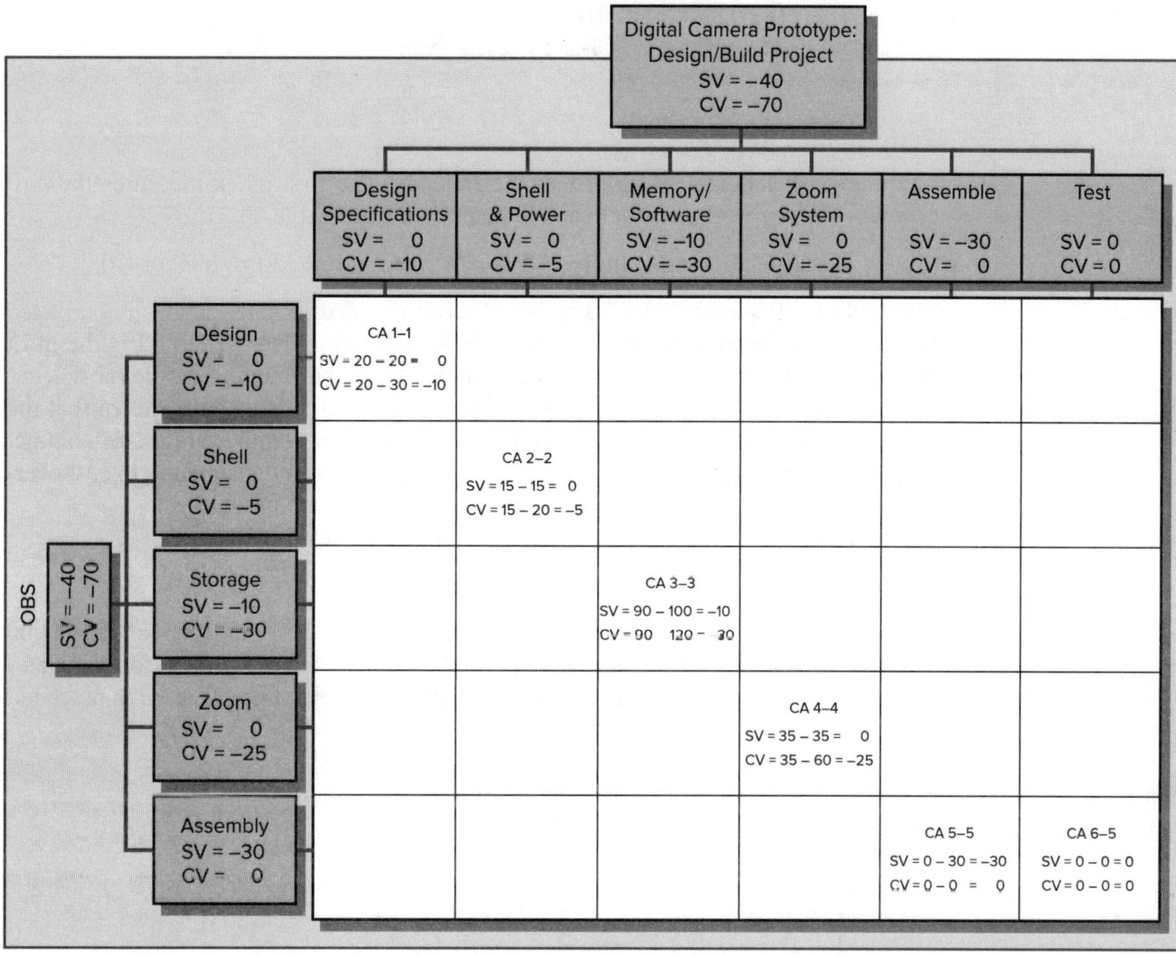

converted to dollars. The use of labor hours in the earned value system is the *modus operandi* for most construction work. Labor hours are easy to understand and are often the way many time and cost estimates are developed. Most earned value software easily accommodates the use of labor hours for the development of cost estimates.

13.6 Indexes to Monitor Progress

LO 13-5

Calculate and interpret performance and percent indexes.

Practitioners sometimes prefer to use schedule and cost indexes over the absolute values of SV and CV, because indexes can be considered efficiency ratios. Graphed indexes over the project life cycle can be very illuminating and useful. The trends are easily identified for deliverables and the whole project.

Indexes are typically used at the cost account level and above. In practice, the database is also used to develop indexes that allow the project manager and customer to view progress from several angles. An index of 1.00 (100 percent) indicates progress is as planned. An index greater than 1.00 shows progress is better than expected. An index less than 1.00 suggests progress is poorer than planned and deserves attention. Table 13.4 presents the interpretation of the indexes.

TABLE 13.4
Interpretation of Indexes

Index	Cost (CPI)	Schedule (SPI)
>1.00	Under cost	Ahead of schedule
=1.00	On cost	On schedule
<1.00	Over cost	Behind schedule

Performance Indexes

There are two indexes of performance efficiency. The first index measures the *cost* efficiency of the work accomplished to date (data from Table 13.3):

Cost performance index (CPI) = EV/AC = 160/230 = .696, or .70

The CPI of .70 shows that $.70 worth of work planned to date has been completed for each $1.00 actually spent—an unfavorable situation indeed. The CPI is the most accepted and used index. It has been tested over time and found to be the most accurate, reliable, and stable. For example, U.S. government studies have shown that the CPI is stable from as early as the 20 percent completion point regardless of contract type, program, or service. The CPI can provide an early warning signal as to cost overruns so that adjustments can be made to the budget or scope of a project.[1]

The second index is a measure of scheduling efficiency to date:

Scheduling performance index (SPI) = EV/PV = 160/200 = .80

The schedule index indicates $.80 worth of work has been accomplished for each $1.00 worth of scheduled work to date. Figure 13.12 shows the indexes plotted for our example project through period 7. This figure is another example of graphs used in practice.

FIGURE 13.12
Indexes Periods 1–7

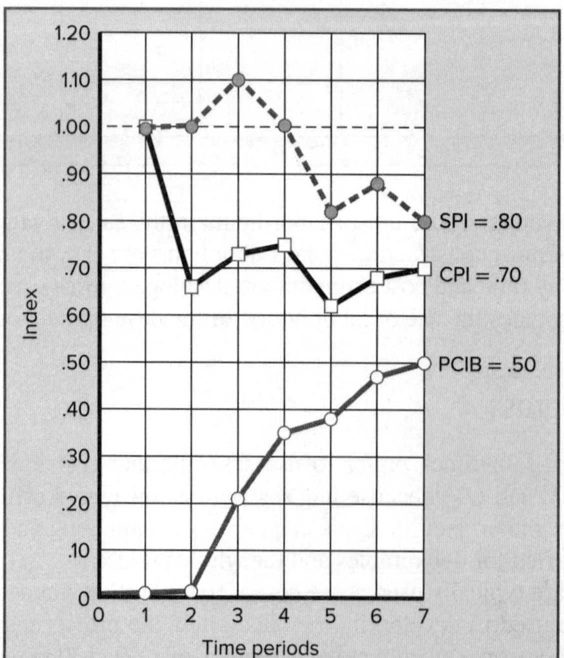

[1] Cited by Fleming, Q. W., and J. M. Koppleman, *Earned Value Project Management* (Newton Square, PA: Project Management Institute, 2010), pp. 39–42.

Project Percent Complete Indexes

Two project percent complete indexes are used, depending on your judgment of which one is most representative of your project. The first index assumes the original budget of work complete is the most reliable information to measure project percent complete. The second index assumes the actual costs-to-date and expected cost at completion are the most reliable for measuring project percent complete. These indexes compare the to-date progress to the end of the project. The implications underlying the use of these indexes are that conditions will not change, no improvement or action will be taken, and the information in the database is accurate. The first index looks at percent complete in terms of *budget* amounts:

Percent complete index budgeted costs

PCIB = EV/BAC = 160/320 = .50 (50%)

This PCIB indicates the work accomplished represents 50 percent of the total budgeted (BAC) dollars to date. Observe that this calculation does not include actual costs incurred. Because actual dollars spent do not guarantee project progress, this index is favored by many project managers when there is a high level of confidence in the original budget estimates.

The second index views percent complete in terms of *actual* dollars spent to accomplish the work to date and the actual expected dollars for the completed project (EAC). For example, at the end of period 7, the staff re-estimates that the EAC will be 575 instead of 320. The application of this view is written as

Percent complete index actual costs

PCIC = AC/EAC = 230/575 = .40(40%)

Some managers favor this index because it contains actual and revised estimates that include newer, more complete information.

These two views of percent complete present alternative views of the "real" percent complete. These percents may be quite different, as shown. (Note: The PCIC index was not plotted in Figure 13.12. The new figures for EAC would be derived each period by estimators in the field.)

A third percent index that is popular in the construction industry reflects the amount of management reserves that have been absorbed by cost overruns. Remember that management reserves are funds set aside to cover unforeseen events (see Chapter 7). Let's assume that $40 was reserved for the Digital Camera project:

Management reserve index

MRI = CV/MR = The percentage of 140/40 = 3.50 (350%)

The project has already spent 3 and half times the total funds set aside as management reserve. Clearly, this project is in trouble and changes in either the scope or the budget are required. Many managers assess cost overruns in terms of management reserves rather than simply cost variance, since it reflects how much one can afford to spend on the project.

Software for Project Cost/Schedule Systems

Software developers have created sophisticated schedule/cost systems for projects that track and report budget, actual, earned, committed, and index values. These values can be labor hours, materials, and/or dollars. This information supports cost and schedule progress, performance measurements, and cash flow management. Recall from Chapter 5 that budget, actual, and committed dollars usually run in different time frames (see Figure 5.6). A typical computer-generated status report includes the following information outputs:

1. Schedule variance (EV – PV) by cost account and WBS and OBS.
2. Cost variance (EV – AC) by cost account and WBS and OBS.
3. Indexes—total percent complete and performance index.
4. Cumulative actual total cost to date (AC).
5. Expected costs at completion (EAC).
6. Paid and unpaid commitments.

The variety of software packages, with their features and constant updating, is too extensive for inclusion in this text. Software developers and vendors have done a superb job of providing software to meet the information needs of most project managers. Differences among software in the last decade have centered on improving "friendliness" and output that is clear and easy to understand. Anyone who understands the concepts and tools presented in Chapters 4, 5, 6, 8, and 13 should have little trouble understanding the output of any of the popular project management software packages.

Additional Earned Value Rules

Although the percent complete rule is the most-used method of assigning budgets to baselines and for cost control, there are additional rules that are very useful for reducing the overhead costs of collecting detailed data on percent complete of individual work packages. (An additional advantage of these rules, of course, is that they remove the often subjective judgments of the contractors or estimators as to how much work has actually been completed.) The first two rules are typically used for short-duration activities and/or small-cost activities. The third rule uses gates before the total budgeted value of an activity can be claimed.

- **0/100 rule.** This rule assumes credit is earned for having performed the work once it is completed. Hence, 100 percent of the budget is earned when the work package is completed. This rule is used for work packages having very short durations.
- **50/50 rule.** This approach allows 50 percent of the value of the work package budget to be earned when it is started and 50 percent to be earned when the package is completed. This rule is popular for work packages of short duration and small total costs.
- **Percent complete with weighted monitoring gates.** This more recent rule uses subjective estimated percent complete in combination with hard, tangible monitoring points. This method works well on long-duration activities that can be broken into short, discrete work packages of no more than one or two report periods. These discrete packages limit the subjective estimated values. For example, assume a long-duration activity with a total budget of $500. The activity is cut into three sequentially discrete packages with monitoring gates representing 30, 50, and 100 percent of the total budget. The earned amount at each monitoring gate cannot exceed $150, $250, and $500. These hard monitoring points serve as a check on overly optimistic estimates.

Notice the only information needed for the first two rules is that the work package has started and the package has been completed. Appendix 13.1 presents two exercises that apply these rules along with the percent complete rule.

The third rule is frequently used to authorize progress payments to contractors. This rule supports careful tracking and control of payments; it discourages payment to contractors for work not yet completed.

13.7 Forecasting Final Project Cost

LO 13-6

Forecast final project cost.

There are basically two methods used to revise estimates of future project costs. In many cases, both methods are used on specific segments of the project. The result is confusion of terms in texts, in software, and among practitioners in the field. We have chosen to note the differences between the methods.

The first method allows experts in the field to change original baseline durations and costs because new information tells them the original estimates are not accurate. We have used EAC_{re} to represent revisions made by experts and practitioners associated with the project. The revisions from project experts are almost always used on smaller projects.

The equation for calculating revised estimated cost at completion (EAC_{re}) is as follows:

$$EAC_{re} = AC + ETC_{re}$$

where $\mathbf{EAC_{re}}$ **= revised estimated cost at completion.**

AC = cumulative actual cost of work completed to date.

ETC_{re} = revised estimated cost to complete remaining work.

A second method is used in large projects where the original budget is reliable. This method uses the actual costs to date plus an efficiency index (CPI = EV/AC) applied to the remaining project work. When the estimate for completion uses the CPI as the basis for forecasting cost at completion, we use the acronym EAC_f. The equation for this forecasting model (EAC_f) is as follows:

$$EAC_f = ETC + AC$$

$$ETC = \frac{\text{Work remaining}}{\text{CPI}} = \frac{BAC - EV}{EV/AC}$$

where $\mathbf{EAC_f}$ **= forecasted total cost at completion.**

ETC = estimated cost to complete remaining work.

AC = cumulative actual cost of work completed to date.

CPI = cumulative cost index to date.

BAC = total budget of the baseline.

EV = cumulative budgeted cost of work completed to date.

The following information is available from our earlier example; the estimated cost at completion (EAC_f) is computed as follows:

	in $000
Total baseline budget (BAC) for the project	$320
Cumulative earned value (EV) to date	$160
Cumulative actual cost (AC) to date	$230

$$EAC_f = \frac{320 - 160}{160/230} + 230 = \frac{160}{.7} + 230 = 229 + 230$$

$$EAC_f = 459$$

The final project projected cost forecast is $459,000 versus $320,000 originally planned.

Another popular index is the **To complete performance index (TCPI),** which is useful as a supplement to the estimate at complete (EAC_f) computation. This ratio measures the amount of value each *remaining* dollar in the budget must earn to stay within the budget. The index is computed for the Digital Camera project at the end of period 7:

$$\textbf{TCPI} = \frac{\text{BAC} - \text{EV}}{\text{BAC} - \text{AC}} = \frac{320 - 160}{320 - 230} = \frac{160}{90} = 1.78$$

The index of 1.78 indicates that each remaining dollar in the budget must earn $1.78 in value in order for the project to stay within budget. There is more work to be done than there is budget left. Clearly, it would be tough to increase productivity that much to make budget. The work to be done will have to be reduced, or you will have to accept running over budget. If the TCPI is less than 1.00, you should be able to complete the project without using all of the remaining budget. A ratio of less than 1.00 opens the possibility of other opportunities such as improving quality, increasing profit, or expanding scope.

Research data indicate that on large projects that are more than 15 percent complete, the model performs well with an error of less than 10 percent (Christensen, 1998; Fleming & Koppleman, 2010). This model can also be used for WBS and OBS cost accounts that have been used to forecast remaining and total costs. It is important to note that this model assumes conditions will not change, the cost database is reliable, EV and AC are cumulative, and past project progress is representative of future progress. This objective forecast represents a good starting point or benchmark that management can use to compare other forecasts that include other conditions and subjective judgments.

Exhibit 13.1 presents an abridged monthly status report similar to one used by a project organization. The form is used for all projects in their project portfolio.

EXHIBIT 13.1
Monthly Status Report

Project: Red Octopus (#72) **Project manager:** Xavier Hart

Project priority now: 4

Status as of: April 1

Earned value figures:

PV	EV	AC	SV	CV	BAC
588,240	566,064	596,800	−22,176	−30,736	1,051,200
EAC	**VAC**	**EAC_f**	**CPI**	**PCIB**	**PCIC**
1,090,640	−39,440	1,107,469	.95	.538	.547

Project description: A computer-controlled conveyor belt that will move and position items on the belt with accuracy of less than one millimeter.

Status summary: The project is approximately 25 days behind schedule and $30,736 over budget.

Explanations: The schedule variance has moved from noncritical activities to those on the critical path. Integration first phase, scheduled to start 3/26, is now expected to start 4/19, which means it is approximately 25 days behind schedule. This delay is traced to the loss of the second design team, which made it impossible to start utilities documentation on 2/27 as planned. The cost variance to date is largely due to a design change that cost $21,000.

Major changes since last report: The major change was loss of one design team to the project.

Total cost of approved design changes: $21,000. Most of this amount is attributed to the improved design of the serial I/O drivers.

Projected cost at completion: EAC_f is estimated to be $1,107,469. This represents an overrun of $56,269, given a CPI of .95.

Forecasted completion date: October 23.

Risk watch: Five team members were stricken with flu.

SNAPSHOT FROM PRACTICE 13.2 Trojan Decommissioning Project

Portland General Electric Company has been charged with decommissioning the Trojan Nuclear Plant. This is a long and complex project extending over two decades. The first segment of the project of moving the used reactors to a storage location is complete and was awarded the Project of the Year, 2000, by the Project Management Institute (PMI). The remainder of the project—decontamination of the remaining structures and waste—is ongoing.

Exhibit 13.2 shows the company's earned value status report. This report measures schedule and cost performance for monitoring the project. The report also serves as a basis for funding for rate filings with the Public Utilities Commission.

Ingram Publishing/SuperStock

(Note that the schedule variance of −$22,176 does not translate directly to days. The 25 days were derived from the network schedule.)

Another summary report is shown in Snapshot from Practice 13.2: Trojan Decommissioning Project. Compare the differences in format. Software companies are developing electronic **dashboards** that show project progress against key performance measures of the projects. The dashboards use tables and colored graphics to display project performance data like percentage complete, budget consumption, CPI, workloads, etc.

13.8 Other Control Issues

Technical Performance Measurement

Measuring technical performance is as important as, if not more important than, measuring schedule and cost performance. After all, who cares if the project is under budget or ahead of schedule if the deliverable doesn't work? The ramifications of poor technical performance frequently are profound—re-work, dissatisfied customers, and tarnished reputation.

Assessing technical performance of a system, facility, or product is often accomplished by examining the requirements found in the scope statement and/or work packages. Requirements should specify criteria and tolerance limits against which performance can be measured. For example, the technical performance of a software project suffered because the feature of "drag and drop" was deleted in the final product. Conversely, the prototype of an experimental car exceeded the miles per gallon technical specification and, thus, its technical performance. Frequently tests and inspections are conducted on different performance dimensions. These tests become an integral part of the project schedule.

It is difficult to specify how to measure technical performance because it depends on the nature of the project. For example, a marketing project might use the number of

EXHIBIT 13.2

Cost/Budget Performance			Decommissioning Cumulative Costs				Nominal Year Dollars			
Portland General Electric Co.-Trojan Nuclear Plant			Report Run: 23-Jan-01			Report Number: DECT005		Page:		1 of 1
				Year-to-Date			YTD			
Description	PV	EV	AC	PV	EV	AC	Variance EV–AC	PV	CPI = EV/AC	SPI = EV/PV
ISFSI	193,014	182,573	162,579	3,655,677	3,586,411	3,263,995	322,416	3,655,677	1.10	0.98
RVAIR	0	0	0	0	0	399	(399)	0	0.00	0.00
Equip removal—AB/FB	79,083	79,649	73,899	497,197	504,975	308,461	196,514	497,197	1.64	1.02
Equip removal—other	0	0	0	0	(36,822)	519	(37,341)	0	0.00	0.00
Embed piping—AB/FB	3,884	0	2,118	532,275	540,232	515,235	24,997	532,275	1.05	1.01
Embed piping—other	0	0	3,439	175,401	210,875	79,235	131,640	175,401	2.66	1.20
Surface decon—AB/FB	29,935	23,274	21,456	1,266,685	1,293,315	1,171,712	121,603	1,266,665	1.10	1.02
Surface decon—other	2,875	2	11,005	308,085	199,853	251,265	(51,412)	308,085	0.80	0.65
Surface decon—containment	680,502	435,657	474,427	5,271,889	4,950,528	4,823,338	127,190	5,271,889	1.03	0.94
Radwaste disposal	884,873	453,032	(28,675)	10,680,118	8,276,616	10,807,916	(2,531,300)	10,880,118	0.77	0.77
Final survey	58,238	57,985	27,091	780,990	780,990	700,942	80,048	780,990	1.11	1.00
Nonradiological areas	92,837	91,956	58,538	2,471,281	2,376,123	834,643	1,541,480	2,471,281	2.85	0.96
Staffing	714,806	714,509	468,858	9,947,775	9,947,775	8,241,383	1,706,392	9,947,775	1.21	1.00
ISFSI—Long-term ops	85,026	85,028	19,173	2,004,398	2,004,398	337,206	1,667,192	2,004,398	5.94	1.00
Labor loadings	258,289	258,289	240,229	3,216,194	3,216,194	2,755,604	460,590	3,216,194	1.17	1.00
Material loadings	17,910	17,910	(95,128)	211,454	211,454	136,973	74,481	211,454	1.54	1.00
Corporate governance	153,689	228,499	228,521	1,814,523	1,814,523	1,814,520	3	1,814,523	1.00	1.00
Undistributable costs	431,840	401,720	242,724	5,541,679	5,575,879	4,007,732	1,567,947	5,541,679	1.39	1.01
Total decommissioning	3,688,481	3,008,081	1,905,084	48,375,399	45,453,119	40,051,079	5,402,040	48,375,399	1.13	0.94
Total (less ISFSI and RVAIR)	3,493,467	2,845,508	1,743,485	44,719,720	41,886,710	36,788,680	5,080,024	44,719,720	1.14	0.94

"likes" at their Facebook site as an indicator of performance. Alternatively, a software project may rely on frequency of bugs (errors) discovered as an indicator of technical performance. Technical performance is frequently where quality control processes are needed and used. Here quality tools like histograms, scatter diagrams, and Pareto charts are used to identify the root causes of the problems.

Scope Creep

LO 13-7

Identify and manage scope creep.

Large changes in scope are easily identified. It is the "minor refinements" that eventually build to be major scope changes that can cause problems. These small refinements are known in the field as **scope creep.** For example, the customer of a software developer requested small changes in the development of a custom accounting software package. After several minor refinements, it became apparent the changes represented a significant enlargement of the original project scope. The result was an unhappy customer and a development firm that lost money and reputation.

Although scope changes are usually viewed negatively, there are situations when scope changes result in positive rewards. Scope changes can represent significant opportunities.[2] In product development environments, adding a small feature to a product can result in a huge competitive advantage. A small change in the production process may get the product to market one month early or reduce product cost.

Scope creep is common early in projects—especially in new-product development projects. Customer requirements for additional features, new technology, poor design assumptions, and so on, all manifest pressures for scope changes. Frequently these changes are small and go unnoticed until time delays or cost overruns are observed. Scope creep affects the organization, project team, and project suppliers. Scope changes alter the organization's cash flow requirements in the form of fewer or additional resources, which may also affect other projects. Frequent changes eventually wear down team motivation and cohesiveness. Clear team goals are altered, become less focused, and cease being the focal point for team action. Starting over again is annoying and demoralizing to the project team because it disrupts project rhythm and lowers productivity. Project suppliers resent frequent changes because they represent higher costs and have the same effect on their team as on the project team.

The key to managing scope creep is change management. Many project managers report that scope creep was the biggest risk their firm faced in projects. The best defense against scope creep is a well-defined scope statement and communication. Poor scope statements are one of the major causes of scope creep.

A second defense against scope creep is stating what the project is not, which can avoid misinterpretations later. (Chapter 7 discusses the change control process. See Figure 7.9 to review key variables to document in project changes.) First, the original baseline must be well defined and agreed upon with the project customer. Before the project begins, it is imperative that clear procedures be in place for authorizing and documenting scope changes by the customer or project team. If a scope change is necessary, the impact on the baseline should be clearly documented—for example, cost, time, dependencies, specifications, or responsibilities. Finally, the scope change must be quickly added to the original baseline to reflect the change in budget and schedule; these changes and their impacts need to be communicated to all project stakeholders.

[2] See, Keifer, S. "Scope Creep . . . Not Necessarily a Bad Thing," *PM Network*, May 1996, pp. 33–35.

Baseline Changes

Changes during the life cycle of projects are inevitable. Some changes can be very beneficial to project outcomes; changes having a negative impact are the ones we wish to avoid. Careful project definition can minimize the need for changes. The price for poor project definition can change that result in cost overruns, late schedules, low morale, and loss of control. Change comes from external sources or from within. Externally, for example, the customer may request changes that were not included in the original scope statement and that will require significant changes to the project and thus to the baseline. Or the government may render requirements that were not a part of the original plan and that require a revision of the project scope. Internally, stakeholders may identify unforeseen problems or improvements that change the scope of the project.

Force majeure, or acts of nature, such as hurricanes or floods can disrupt plans and force resetting a baseline. Imagine how many baselines were made meaningless by the COVID-19 virus! Given the recovery uncertainty, it made no sense to try to reset a baseline. Many projects were postponed or canceled. Other companies used agile methods (see Chapter 15) to navigate the project until things cleared and the project could be planned with some degree of certainty again. See Snapshot from Practice: Oregon State University's RCRV Project that had to reformulate its baseline three times and used EVM to manage the project.

SNAPSHOT FROM PRACTICE — Oregon State University's Regional Coastal Research Vessels (RCRV) Project*

In 2019 Oregon State University (OSU) and its College of Earth, Ocean, and Atmospheric Sciences (CEOAS), on behalf of the National Science Foundation (NSF), began construction of three, "next generation," regional coastal research vessels (RCRV). The price tag for the entire project was $354M for the multi-year project. The new vessels would be equipped with a state-of-the-art sensor suite capable of making measurements from below the ocean bottom to the top of the atmosphere and to relay those measurements in real time, to researchers around the world. To help with that, the vessels will also have dynamic positioning that will help them stay in place in rugged seas. This is needed to launch and retrieve gliders and other remotely operated vehicles as well as to conduct precise mapping of the ocean floor.

Oregon State University

One of the new requirements imposed by NSF in the grant application was a commitment to using earned value management (EVM) to monitor costs and schedules. Demian Bailey, the OSU project manager, had limited experience with earned value and most of the research scientists at CEOAS had never heard of the concept. Some may have thought EVM was another "bureaucratic control" that would get in the way of getting the project done. CEOAS drew upon the project management expertise of the College of Business at OSU in their grant submission.

The RCRV project's journey to date has been a rough one. Among the major obstacles, Bailey and his team encountered included the original shipyard being acquired, the COVID-19 pandemic, and Hurricane Ida—which disrupted shipbuilding. These forced three major revisions of the baseline plan. The estimated completion date has been extended from mid 2023 to early 2026. Bailey estimated that there have been over 300 days of downtime due to these and other events outside their control.

How about EVM?

In 2023, NSF scheduled a self-assessment of the RCRV earned value management system:

> Does the use of EVM by the project, as described in the OSU self-assessment, provide effective evaluation of progress against the baseline plan, adequate information on cost and schedule performance, and is EVM being used to inform timely management decisions?

So how did first-time users of EVM assess the value of using EVM despite the hardships they experienced?

Bailey and his team concluded that EVM was critical to overcoming the obstacles they encountered and getting the project back on track:

> "The RCRV has built its entire project management structure around its EVM system. The system serves as a vibrant, relevant, and useful tool to provide insights into project performance. But, beyond those insights, it provides control of the baseline and provides a flexible structure for project leaders to manage their scope and, frankly, do their jobs."
>
> Conclusion: RCRV Self-Assessment

The report contained specific examples of how EVM has been used to manage the RCRV project. For example, in response to Hurricane Ida, management was able to use EVM to quickly distinguish delays and to what extent they occur. This allowed management to quickly establish a robust and defensible Management Reserve request. EVM was critical in justifying the request and the eventual distribution of $17 million in the budget. If EVM system had not been established before the hurricane event, OSU would have had to spend a lot of time creating justifications for additional hurricane-attributable costs. Cost estimates were linked directly to the EVM system, so it was a simple matter to forecast Ida's impacts.

Another example was how EVM has helped OSU manage the Shipyard.

Shipbuilder X (SBX) presented a six-month schedule wherein they claimed they could, through various schedule crashing techniques, meet ambitious milestones. OSU pushed back, using earned value (EV) data to date, to illustrate that their plan was likely unachievable. In one case, OSU's deputy Shipyard Manager, an experienced shipbuilder with deep EVM understanding, used the historical metric of earned value percent of total per month earned. He showed that today, SBX has never earned more than 1% per month whereas their plan indicated. They would need to earn at least 3 times that to meet their milestones.

The EVM analysis revealed SBX losing roughly one week per month on the critical path. OSU was able to inform stakeholders that the delivery of Vessel 1 has slipped 4 months to January 2024. The project could now plan accordingly due to this proactive decision based on EVM data. For example, certain aggressive procurement timelines could be relaxed. The OSU crew could be sent out in a relief capacity throughout the Academic Research Fleet for a longer window of time. This example additionally shows the integration of EVM data decision making between control accounts.

Examples of EVM Reporting System

Below are examples of how EV data are reported in status reports. Table 13.5 features segments of the Top Level Earned Value table used in an RCRV project for all three vessels. It includes data for the first six quarters, after the Hurricane Ida re-plan. Note, in addition to traditional EV indicators, the report tracks remaining contingency and funding from NSF to-date.

Figure 13.13 contains the Cost/Schedule graph rolling up 15,000 activities for the project and Figure 13.14 reports the Schedule Performance (SPI) and Cost Performance (CPI) since the Ida re-plan. Notice the progress made in getting back on schedule after falling behind the first three months.

TABLE 13.5 RCRV EVM Status Summary Table

RCRV Status	$M
EVM as of:	Oct-22
Total Project Cost (Three vessels)	$391.5
Planned Value	$190.6
Earned Value	$184.1
Actual Cost	$183.0
CPI	1.01
SPI	0.97
Funding To-Date (MREFC)	$391.5
% Complete	50.50%
% Spent	50.20%
Budget at Completion (BAC)	$364.5
Estimate at Completion (EAC)	$363.4
EAC = AC+BAC-EV	$363.4
EAC = AC+((BAC-EV)/(CPI*SPI))	$367.2
Cost Variance (CV)	$1.1
Schedule Variance (SV)	–$6.5
Contingency Balance against Allocated	$27.0
Contingency Balance against Budget	$27.0
Estimate to Complete (ETC)	$180.4
Contingency % of Estimate to Complete (ETC)	14.96%

*Information provided by Demian Bailey, project manager, Oregon State University, RCRV project.

FIGURE 13.13 RCRV Cost/Schedule Graph

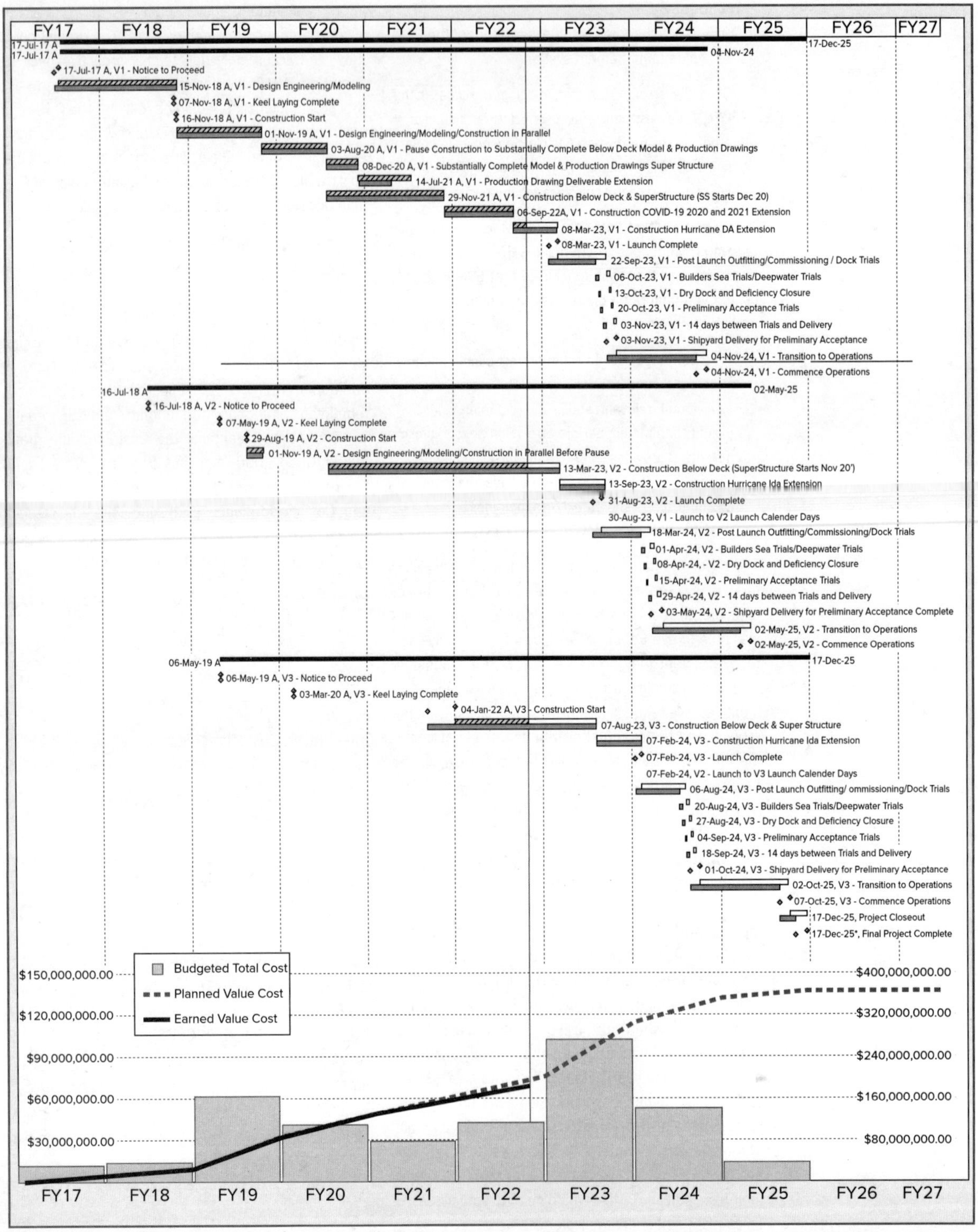

FIGURE 13.14 RCRV SPI and CPI

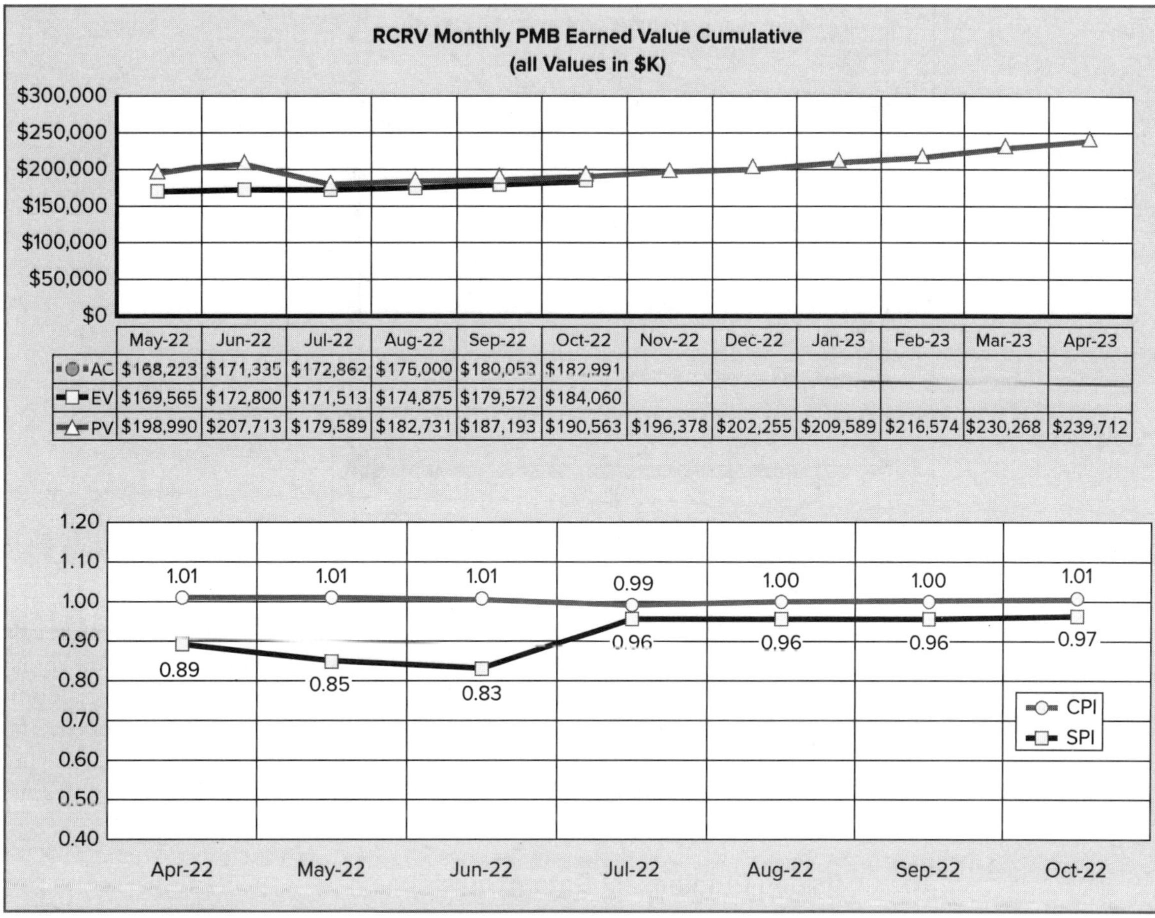

	May-22	Jun-22	Jul-22	Aug-22	Sep-22	Oct-22	Nov-22	Dec-22	Jan-23	Feb-23	Mar-23	Apr-23
AC	$168,223	$171,335	$172,862	$175,000	$180,053	$182,991						
EV	$169,565	$172,800	$171,513	$174,875	$179,572	$184,060						
PV	$198,990	$207,713	$179,589	$182,731	$187,193	$190,563	$196,378	$202,255	$209,589	$216,574	$230,268	$239,712

Generally, project managers monitor scope changes very carefully. They should allow scope changes only if it is clear that the project will fail without the change, the project will be improved significantly with the change, or the customer wants it and will pay for it. This statement is an exaggeration, but it sets the tone for approaching baseline changes. The effect of the change on the scope and baseline should be accepted and signed off by the project customer. Figure 13.15 depicts the cost impact of a scope change on the baseline at a point in time—"today." New baseline A represents a scope change that results in an increase in cost. New baseline B represents a scope change that decreases cost. Quickly recording scope changes to the baseline keeps the computed earned values valid. Failure to do so results in misleading cost and schedule variances.

Care should be taken to not use baseline changes to disguise poor performance on past or current work. A common signal of this type of baseline change is a constantly revised baseline that seems to match results. Practitioners call this a "rubber baseline" because it stretches to match results. Most changes will not result in

FIGURE 13.15
Scope Changes to a Baseline

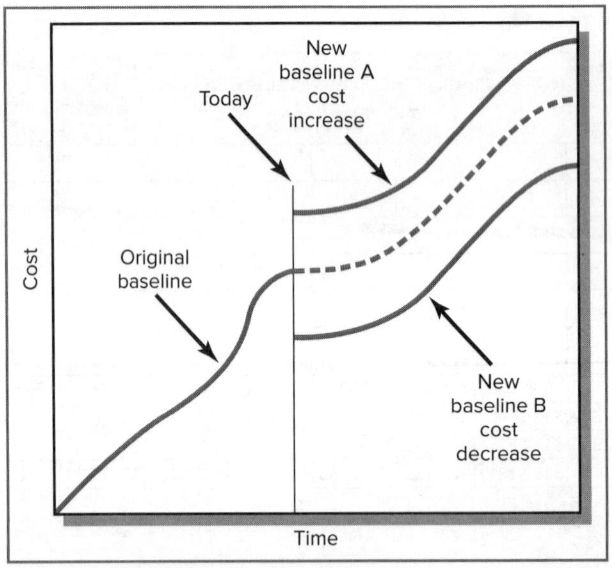

serious scope changes and should be absorbed as positive or negative variances. Retroactive changes for work already accomplished should not be allowed. Transfer of money among cost accounts should not be allowed after the work is complete. Unforeseen changes can be handled through the contingency reserve. The project manager typically makes this decision. In some large projects, a partnering "change review team," made up of members of the project and customer teams, makes all decisions on project changes.

The Costs and Problems of Data Acquisition

Data acquisition is time consuming and costly. Snapshot from Practice 13.3: A Pseudo-Earned Value Percent Complete Approach captures some of the frequent issues surrounding resistance to data collection of percent complete for earned value systems. Similar pseudo-percent complete systems have been used by others. Such pseudo-percent complete approaches appear to work well in multiproject environments that include several small- and medium-sized projects. Assuming a one-week reporting period, care needs to be taken to develop work packages with a duration of about one week long so problems are identified quickly. For large projects, there is no substitute for using a percent complete system that depends on data collected through observation at clearly defined monitoring points.

In some cases, data exist but are not sent to the stakeholders who need information relating to project progress. Clearly, if the information does not reach the right people in a timely manner, you can expect serious problems. Your communication plan developed in the project planning stage can greatly mitigate this problem by mapping out the flow of information and keeping stakeholders informed on all aspects of project progress and issues. See Figure 13.16 for an internal communication plan for a WiFi project. The information developed in this chapter contributes significant data to support your communication plan and ensures correct dissemination of the data.

SNAPSHOT FROM PRACTICE 13.3 A Pseudo-Earned Value Percent Complete Approach

A consultant for the U.S. Forest Service suggested the use of earned value to monitor the 50-plus timber sale projects taking place concurrently in the district. As projects were completed, new ones were started. Earned value was tried for approximately nine months. After a nine-month trial, the process was to be reviewed by a task force. The task force concluded the earned value system provided good information for monitoring and forecasting project progress; however, the costs and problems of collecting timely percent complete data were unacceptable because there were no funds available to collect such data.

The level of detail dilemma was discussed, but no suggestions satisfied the problem. The discussion recognized that too little data fail to offer good control, while excessive reporting requires paperwork and people, which are costly. The task force concluded progress and performance could be measured using a pseudo-version of percent complete while not giving up much accuracy for the total project. This modified approach to percent complete required that very large work packages (about 3 to 5 percent of all work packages in a project) be divided into smaller work packages for closer control and identification of problems sooner. It was decided work packages of about a week's duration would be ideal. The pseudo-version required only a telephone call and yes/no answers to one of the following questions to assign percent complete:

Has work on the work package started?	No = 0%
Working on the package?	Yes = 50%
Is the work package completed?	Yes = 100%

Data for the pseudo-earned value percent complete system were collected for all 50-plus projects by an intern working fewer than eight hours each week.

The pseudo-earned value method turned out to be a success. It provided sufficient performance information to monitor more than 50 projects. The key was limiting all work packages to one week whenever possible. This enabled management to keep track of costs and schedule despite the crude reporting method.

FIGURE 13.16
Conference Center WiFi Project Communication Plan

What Information?	When?	Mode?	Responsible?	Recipient?
Milestone report	Bimonthly	E-mail	Project office	Senior management
Time/cost report	Weekly	E-mail	Project office	Staff and customer
Risk report	Weekly	E-mail	Project office	Staff and customer
Issues	Weekly	E-mail	Anyone	Staff and customer
Team meeting times	Weekly	Meeting	Project manager	Staff and customer
Outsourcing performance	Bimonthly	Meeting	Project manager	Project office, staff, and customer
Change requests	Anytime	Document	Project manager, customer, design	Project office, staff, and customer
Stage gate decisions	Monthly	Meeting	Project office	Senior management

Summary

The best information system does not result in good control. Control requires the project manager to *use* the information to steer the project through rough waters. Control and Gantt charts are useful vehicles for monitoring time performance. Earned value management (EVM) allows the manager to have a positive influence on cost and schedule in a timely manner. The ability to influence cost decreases with time; therefore, timely reports identifying adverse cost trends can greatly assist the project manager in getting back on budget and schedule. EVM provides the project manager and other stakeholders with a snapshot of the current and future status of the project. The benefits of EVM are as follows:

1. Measures accomplishments against plan and deliverables.
2. Provides a method for tracking directly to a problem work package and organization unit responsible.
3. Alerts all stakeholders to early identification of problems and allows for quick, proactive corrective action.
4. Improves communication because all stakeholders are using the same database.
5. Keeps customers informed of progress and encourages customer confidence that the money spent is resulting in the expected progress.
6. Provides for accountability over individual portions of the overall budget for each organization unit.

These benefits are significant, but one must remember that EVM systems focus on costs and time and assume technical performance. Project managers need to monitor and make technical performance a key agenda item.

Key Terms

Baseline, *551*
Budget at completion (BAC), *552*
Control chart, *547*
Cost performance index (CPI), *562*
Cost variance (CV), *552*
Dashboard, *567*
Earned value (EV), *546*
Earned Value Management (EVM), *549*
Force majeure, *570*
Forecasted total cost at completion (EAC_f), *565*
Management reserve index (MRI), *563*
Percent complete index actual costs (PCIC), *563*
Percent complete index budgeted costs (PCIB), *563*
Revised estimated cost at completion (EAC_{re}), *565*
Schedule variance (SV), *552*
Scheduling performance index (SPI), *562*
Scope creep, *569*
To complete performance index (TCPI), *566*
Tracking Gantt chart, *547*
Variance at completion (VAC), *554*

Review Questions

1. How does a tracking Gantt chart help communicate project progress?
2. How does earned value give a clearer picture of project schedule and cost status than a simple plan versus actual system?
3. Schedule variance (SV) is in dollars and does not directly represent time. Why is it still useful?
4. How would a project manager use the CPI?
5. What are the differences between BAC and EAC?
6. Why is it important for project managers to resist changes to the project baseline? Under what conditions would a project manager make changes to a baseline? When would a project manager not allow changes to a baseline?

SNAPSHOT FROM PRACTICE

Discussion Questions

13.1 *Guidelines for Setting Milestones*

1. Why should a milestone be a concrete, specific, measurable event?
2. Should milestones only be on the critical path?

13.2 *Trojan Decommissioning Project*

1. Based on the information provided in Exhibit 13.2, how well is the Decommissioning project doing in terms of cost and schedule?
2. What additional information would you like to have in order to assess performance on the project?

13.3 *A Pseudo-Earned Value Percent Complete Approach*

1. How did limiting work packages to one week help management identify problems sooner?
2. Why do organizations use the percent complete instead of the cheaper, easier pseudo-earned value percent approach?

Oregon State University's Regional Coastal Research Vessels (RCRV) Project

1. Is the project currently over or under budget?
2. What does NSF hope to gain by requiring funded projects to use EVM?

Exercises

1. In month 9 the following project information is available: actual cost is $2,000, earned value is $2,100, and planned cost is $2,400. Compute the SV and CV for the project.
2. On day 51 a project has an earned value of $600, an actual cost of $650, and a planned cost of $560. Compute the SV, CV, and CPI for the project. What is your assessment of the project on day 51?
3. Given the following project network and baseline information, complete the form to develop a status report for the project at the end of period 4 and the end of period 8. From the data you have collected and computed for periods 4 and 8, what information are you prepared to tell the customer about the status of the project at the end of period 8?

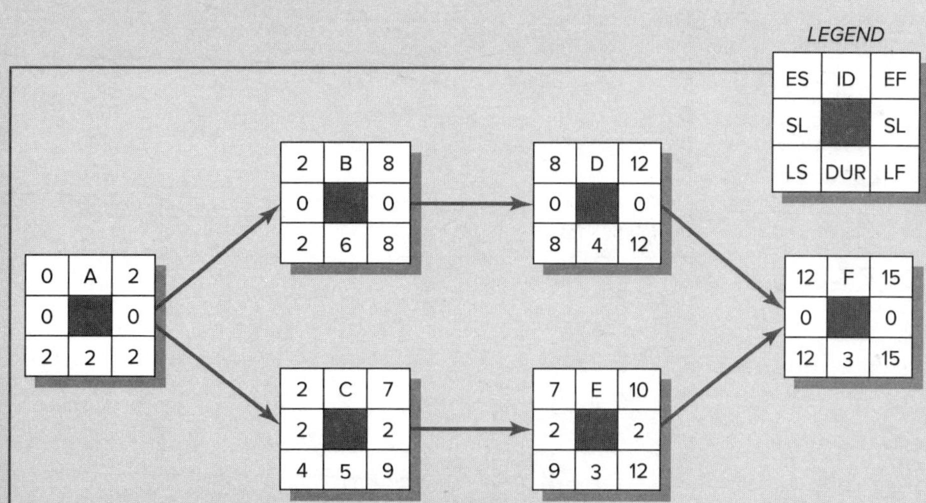

Project baseline (PV) (in $)

Task	DUR	ES	LF	SL	Budget (PV)	1	2	3	4	5	6	7	8	9	10	11	12	13	14	15
A	2	0	2	0	400	200	200													
B	6	2	8	0	2400			200	600	200	600	200	600							
C	5	2	9	2	1500			200	400	500	100	300								
D	4	8	12	0	1600									400	400	400	400			
E	3	7	12	2	900								300	400	200					
F	3	12	15	0	600													200	100	300
					Period PV total	200	200	400	1000	700	700	500	900	800	600	400	400	200	100	300
					Cumulative PV total	200	400	800	1800	2500	3200	3700	4600	5400	6000	6400	6800	7000	7100	7400

End of Period 4

Task	Actual % Complete	EV	AC	PV	CV	SV
A	Finished	—	300	400	—	—
B	50%	—	1000	800	—	—
C	33%	—	500	600	—	—
D	0%	—	0	—	—	—
E	0%	—	—	—	—	—
Cumulative Totals		—	—	—	—	—

End of Period 8

Task	Actual % Complete	EV	AC	PV	CV	SV
A	Finished	—	300	400	—	—
B	Finished	—	2200	2400	—	—
C	Finished	—	1500	1500	—	—
D	25%	—	300	0	—	—
E	33%	—	300	—	—	—
F	0%	—	0	—	—	—
Cumulative Totals		—	—	—	—	—

4. Given the following project network, baseline, and status information, develop status reports for periods 2, 4, 6, 8 and complete the performance indexes table. Calculate the EAC_f and the VAC_f. Based on your data, what is your assessment of the current status of the project? At completion?

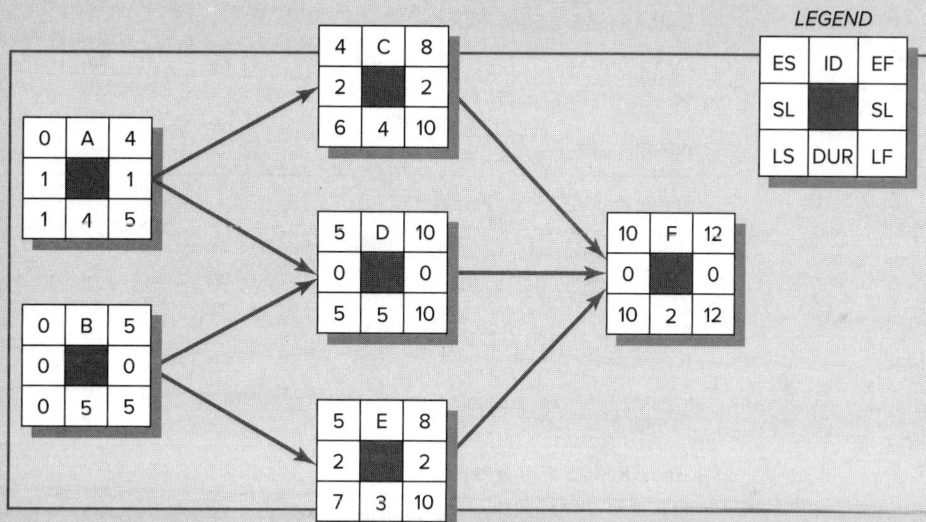

ID	Budget ($000) 0	1	2	3	4	5	6	7	8	9	10	11	12
A	40	10	10	10	10								
B	32	8	4	8	4	8							
C	48					12	12	12	12				
D	18						6	2	2	2	6		
E	28						8	8	12				
F	40											20	20
Total	206	18	14	18	14	20	26	22	26	2	6	20	20
Cumulative		18	32	50	64	84	110	132	158	160	166	186	206

Status Report: Ending Period 2 ($000)

Task	% Complete	EV	AC	PV	CV	SV
A	75%	—	25	—	—	—
B	50%	—	12	—	—	—
Cumulative Totals		—	**37**	—	—	—

Status Report: Ending Period 4 ($000)

Task	% Complete	EV	AC	PV	CV	SV
A	100%	—	35	—	—	—
B	100%	—	24	—	—	—
Cumulative Totals		—	**59**	—	—	—

Status Report: Ending Period 6 ($000)

Task	% Complete	EV	AC	PV	CV	SV
A	100%	—	35	—	—	—
B	100%	—	24	—	—	—
C	75%	—	24	—	—	—
D	0%	—	0	—	—	—
E	50%	—	10	—	—	—
Cumulative Totals		—	**93**	—	—	—

Status Report: Ending Period 8 ($000)

Task	% Complete	EV	AC	PV	CV	SV
A	100%	—	35	—	—	—
B	100%	—	24	—	—	—
C	100%	—	32	—	—	—
D	33%	—	20	—	—	—
E	100%	—	20	—	—	—
Cumulative Totals		—	**131**	—	—	—

Performance Indexes Summary

Period	EV	AC	PV	SPI	CPI	PCIB
2	—	—	—	—	—	—
4	—	—	—	—	—	—
6	—	—	—	—	—	—
8	—	—	—	—	—	—

EAC_f = ______ VAC_f = ______

5. Given the following project network, baseline, and status information, develop status reports for periods 1–4 and complete the project summary graph (or a similar one). Report the final SV, CV, CPI, and PCIB. Based on your data, what is your assessment of the current status of the project? At completion?

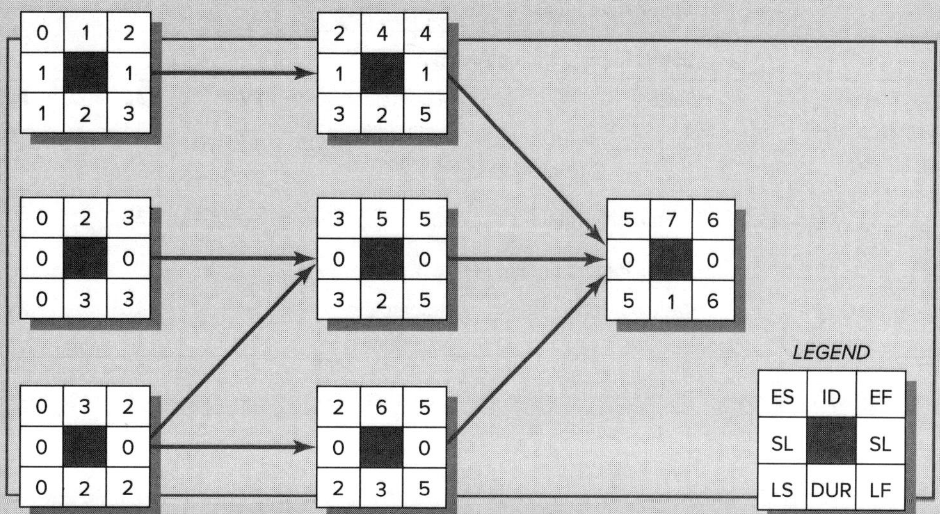

Schedule information						Baseline budget needs ($000)					
						Time period					
ACT/WP	DUR	ES	LF	SL	Total PV	1	2	3	4	5	6
1	2	0	3	1	12	4	8				
2	3	0	3	0	15	3	7	5			
3	2	0	2	0	8	4	4				
4	2	2	5	1	6			3	3		
5	2	3	5	0	10				6	4	
6	3	2	5	0	9			3	3	3	
7	1	5	6	0	5						5
Total PV by period						11	19	11	12	7	5
Cumulative PV by period						11	30	41	53	60	65

Status Report: Ending Period 1 ($000)

Task	%Complete	EV	AC	PV	CV	SV
1	50%	—	6	4	—	—
2	40%	—	8	3	—	—
3	25%	—	3	—	—	—
Cumulative Totals		—	**17**	—	—	—

Status Report: Ending Period 2 ($000)

Task	%Complete	EV	AC	PV	CV	SV
1	Finished	—	13	—	—	—
2	80%	—	14	—	—	—
3	75%	—	8	—	—	—
Cumulative Totals		—	**35**	—	—	—

Status Report: Ending Period 3 ($000)

Task	%Complete	EV	AC	PV	CV	SV
1	Finished	12	13	—	—	—
2	80%	—	15	—	—	—
3	Finished	—	10	—	—	—
4	50%	—	4	—	—	—
5	0%	—	0	—	—	—
6	33.3%	—	4	—	—	—
Cumulative Totals		—	—	—	—	—

Status Report: Ending Period 4 ($000)

Task	%Complete	EV	AC	PV	CV	SV
1	Finished	12	13	—	—	—
2	Finished	15	18	—	—	—
3	Finished	—	10	—	—	—
4	Finished	—	8	—	—	—
5	30%	—	3	—	—	—
6	66.7%	—	8	—	—	—
7	0%	—	0	—	—	—
Cumulative Totals		—	—	—	—	—

Summary Graph

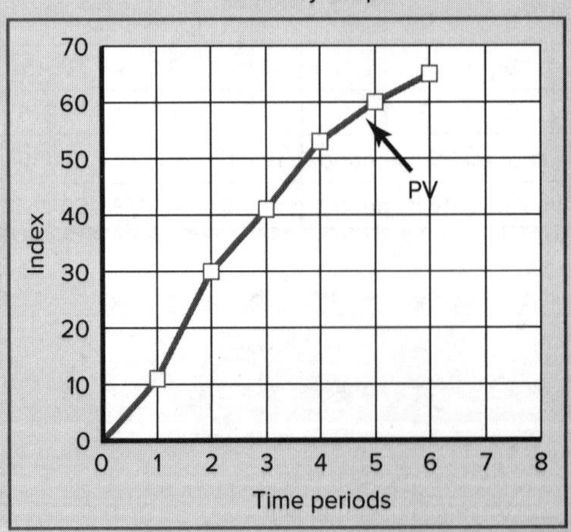

6. The following labor hours data have been collected for a nanotechnology project for periods 1 through 6. Compute the SV, CV, SPI, and CPI for each period. Plot the EV and the AC on the summary graph provided (or a similar one). Plot the SPI, CPI, and PCIB on the index graph provided (or a similar one). What is your assessment of the project at the end of period 6?

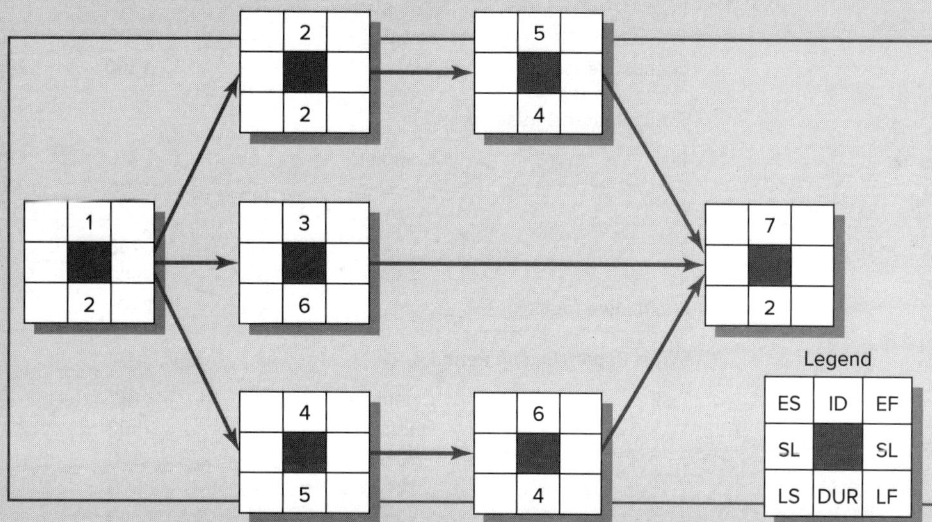

Schedule information						Baseline budget needs—labor hours (00)													
ACT/ WP	DUR	ES	LF	SL	Total PV	Time period 0 1	2	3	4	5	6	7	8	9	10	11	12	13	14
1	2	0	2	0	20	10	10												
2	2	2	7	3	24			16	8										
3	6	2	11	3	30			5	5	10	3	2	5						
4	5	2	7	0	25			10	10	2	2	1							
5	4	4	11	3	16					4	4	4	4						
6	4	7	11	0	20								5	5	6	4			
7	2	11	13	0	10												5	5	
					Total PV by period	10	10	31	23	16	9	7	14	5	6	4	5	5	
					Cumulative PV by period	10	20	51	74	90	99	106	120	125	131	135	140	145	

Status Report: Ending Period 1

Task	%Complete	EV	AC	PV	CV	SV
1	50%	—	500	1000	—	—
Cumulative Totals		—	**500**	**1000**	—	—

Status Report: Ending Period 2

Task	%Complete	EV	AC	PV	CV	SV
1	Finished	—	1500	2000	—	—
Cumulative Totals		—	**1500**	**2000**	—	—

Status Report: Ending Period 3

Task	%Complete	EV	AC	PV	CV	SV
1	Finished	2000	1500	2000	—	—
2	0%	—	0	—	—	—
3	10%	—	200	—	—	—
4	20%	—	500	—	—	—
Cumulative Totals		—	**2200**	—	—	—

Status Report: Ending Period 4

Task	%Complete	EV	AC	PV	CV	SV
1	Finished	2000	1500	2000	—	—
2	50%	—	1000	—	—	—
3	30%	—	800	—	—	—
4	40%	—	1500	—	—	—
Cumulative Totals		—	**4800**	—	—	—

Status Report: Ending Period 5

Task	%Complete	EV	AC	PV	CV	SV
1	Finished	2000	1500	2000	—	—
2	Finished	—	2000	—	—	—
3	50%	—	800	—	—	—
4	60%	—	1500	—	—	—
5	25%	—	400	—	—	—
Cumulative Totals		—	**6200**	—	—	—

Status Report: Ending Period 6

Task	%Complete	EV	AC	PV	CV	SV
1	Finished	2000	1500	2000	—	—
2	Finished	—	2000	—	—	—
3	80%	—	2100	—	—	—
4	80%	—	1800	—	—	—
5	50%	—	600	—	—	—
Cumulative Totals		—	**8000**	—	—	—

Period	SPI	CPI	PCIB
1	—	—	—
2	—	—	—
3	—	—	—
4	—	—	—
5	—	—	—
6	—	—	—

SPI = EV/AC
CPI = EV/AC
PCIB = EV/BAC

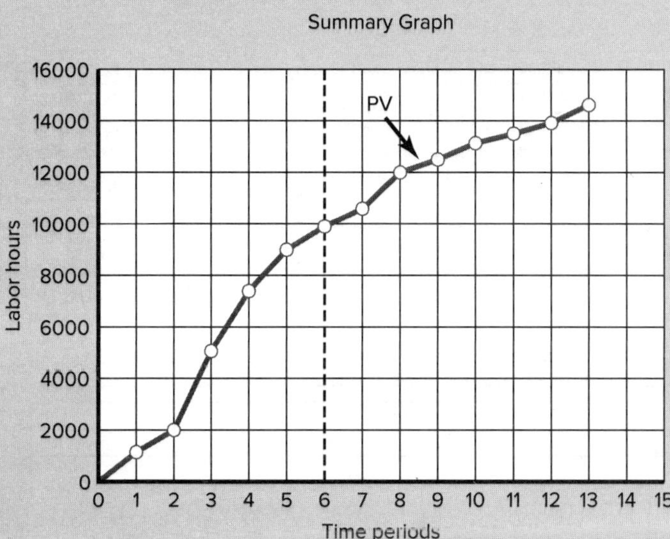

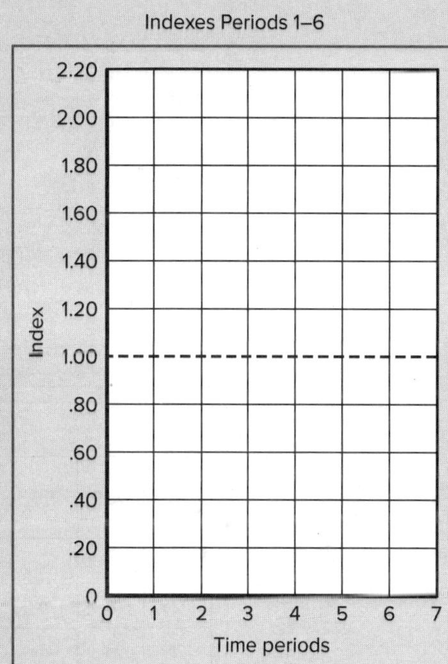

7. The following data have been collected for a British healthcare IT project for two-week reporting periods 2 through 12. Compute the SV, CV, SPI, and CPI for each period. Plot the EV and the AC on the summary graph provided. Plot the SPI, CPI, and PCIB on the index graph provided. (You may use your own graphs.) What is your assessment of the project at the end of period 12?

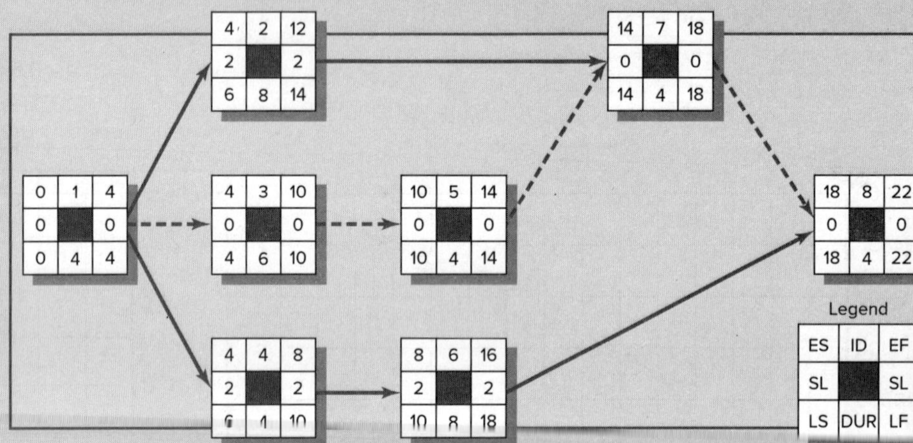

Baseline (PV) ($00)																
Task	DUR	ES	LF	SL	PV ($00)	0–2	2–4	4–6	6–8	8–10	10–12	12–14	14–16	16–18	18–20	20–22
1	4	0	4	0	8	4	4									
2	8	4	14	2	40			10	10	10	10					
3	6	4	10	0	30			10	15	5						
4	4	4	10	2	20			10	10							
5	4	10	14	0	40						20	20				
6	8	8	18	2	60					20	20	10	10			
7	4	14	18	0	20								10	10		
8	4	18	22	0	30										20	10
					Period PV total	4	4	30	35	35	50	30	20	10	20	10
					Cumulative PV total	4	8	38	73	108	158	188	208	218	238	248

Status Report: Ending Period 2						**($00)**
Task	**%Complete**	**EV**	**AC**	**PV**	**CV**	**SV**
1	50%	—	4	—	—	—
Cumulative Totals		—	**4**	—	—	—

Status Report: Ending Period 4 **($00)**

Task	%Complete	EV	AC	PV	CV	SV
1	Finished	—	10	—	—	—
Cumulative Totals		—	**10**	—	—	—

Status Report: Ending Period 6 **($00)**

Task	%Complete	EV	AC	PV	CV	SV
1	Finished	—	10	—	—	—
2	25%	—	15	—	—	—
3	33%	—	12	—	—	—
4	0%	—	0	—	—	—
Cumulative Totals		—	**37**	—	—	—

Status Report: Ending Period 8 **($00)**

Task	%Complete	EV	AC	PV	CV	SV
1	Finished	—	10	—	—	—
2	30%	—	20	—	—	—
3	60%	—	25	—	—	—
4	0%	—	0	—	—	—
Cumulative Totals		—	**55**	—	—	—

Status Report: Ending Period 10 **($00)**

Task	%Complete	EV	AC	PV	CV	SV
1	Finished	—	10	—	—	—
2	60%	—	30	—	—	—
3	Finished	—	40	—	—	—
4	50%	—	20	—	—	—
5	0%	—	0	—	—	—
6	30%	—	24	—	—	—
Cumulative Totals		—	**124**	—	—	—

Status Report: Ending Period 12 **($00)**

Task	%Complete	EV	AC	PV	CV	SV
1	Finished	—	10	—	—	—
2	Finished	—	50	—	—	—
3	Finished	—	40	—	—	—
4	Finished	—	40	—	—	—
5	50%	—	30	—	—	—
6	50%	—	40	—	—	—
Cumulative Totals		—	**210**	—	—	—

Period	SPI	CPI	PCIB
2	—	—	—
4	—	—	—
6	—	—	—
8	—	—	—
10	—	—	—
12	—	—	—

SPI = EV/PV
CPI = EV/AC
PCIB = EV/BAC

Summary Graph

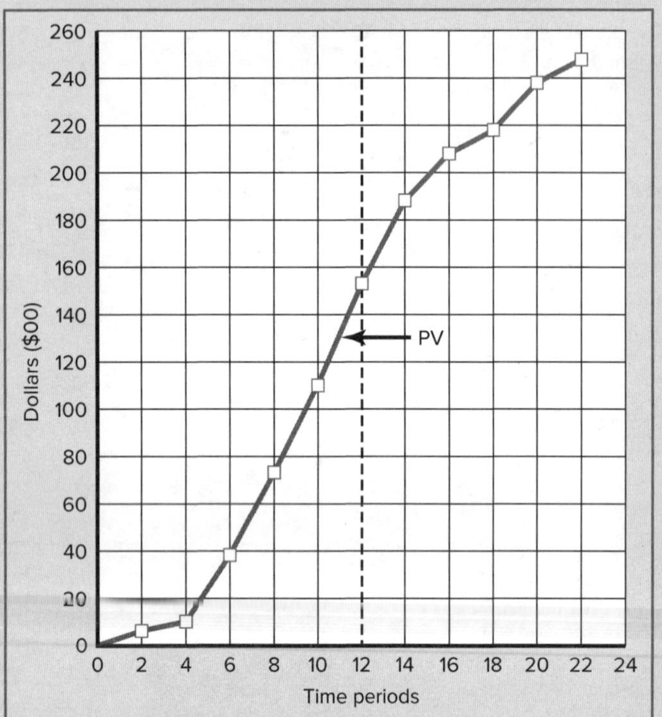

Indexes Periods 2–12

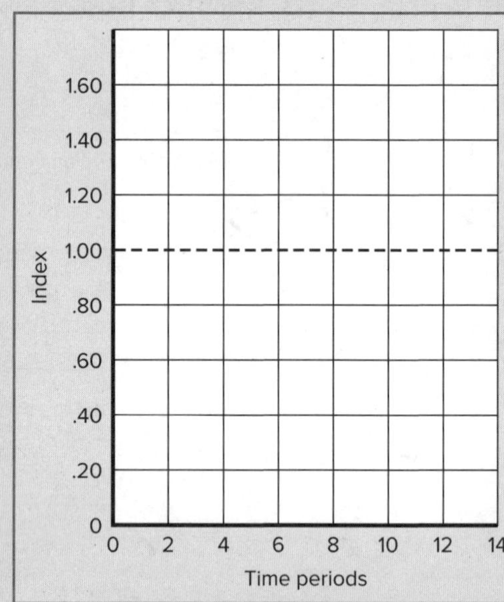

8. Part A.* You are in charge of the Aurora project. Given the following project network, baseline, and status information, develop status reports for periods 1–8 and complete the performance indexes table. Calculate the EAC_f and VAC_f. Based on your data, what is the current status of the project? At completion?

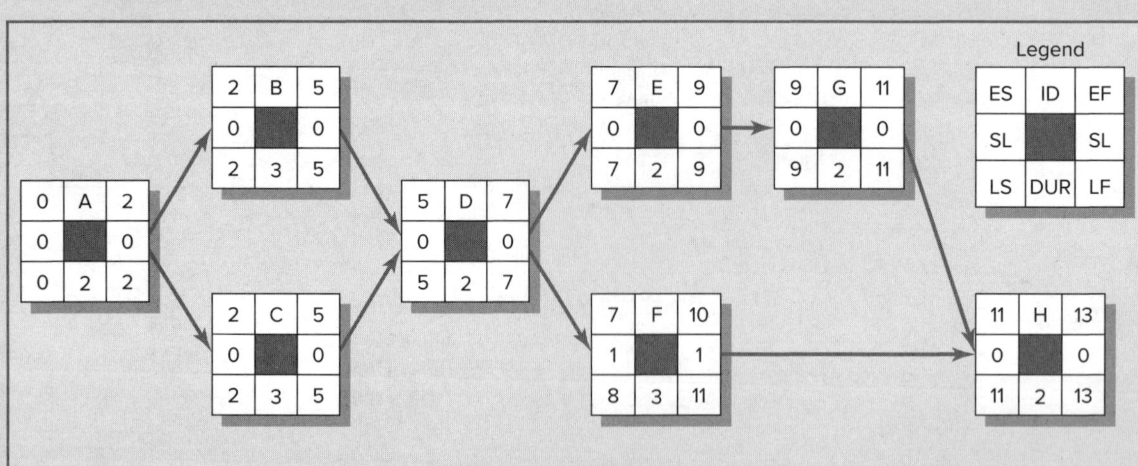

*The solution to this exercise can be found in Appendix One.

ID	Budget ($000)	0–1	1–2	2–3	3–4	4–5	5–6	6–7	7–8	8–9	9–10	10–11	11–12	12–13
A	100	50	50											
B	250			100	50	100								
C	450			150	150	150								
D	200						100	100						
E	300								200	100				
F	300								100	50	150			
G	200										150	50		
H	200												100	100
Total	2000	50	50	250	200	250	100	100	300	150	300	50	100	100
Cumulative		50	100	350	550	800	900	1000	1300	1450	1750	1800	1900	2000

Status Report: Ending Period 1 **($000)**

Task	% Complete	EV	AC	PV	CV	SV
A	25%	—	50	—	—	—
Cumulative Totals		—	**50**	—	—	—

Status Report: Ending Period 2 **($000)**

Task	% Complete	EV	AC	PV	CV	SV
A	50%		100	—	—	—
Cumulative Totals		—	—	—	—	—

Status Report: Ending Period 3 **($000)**

Task	% Complete	EV	AC	PV	CV	SV
A	100%	—	200	—	—	—
B	0%	—	0	—	—	—
C	0%	—	0	—	—	—
Cumulative Totals		—	—	—	—	—

Status Report: Ending Period 4 **($000)**

Task	% Complete	EV	AC	PV	CV	SV
A	100%	—	200	—	—	—
B	60%	—	100	—	—	—
C	50%	—	200	—	—	—
Cumulative Totals		—	**500**	—	—	—

Status Report: Ending Period 5 ($000)

Task	% Complete	EV	AC	PV	CV	SV
A	100%	—	200	—	—	—
B	100%	—	200	—	—	—
C	100%	—	400	—	—	—
Cumulative Totals		—	**800**	—	—	—

Status Report: Ending Period 6 ($000)

Task	% Complete	EV	AC	PV	CV	SV
A	100%	—	200	—	—	—
B	100%	—	200	—	—	—
C	100%	—	400	—	—	—
D	75%	—	100	—	—	—
Cumulative Totals		—	**900**	—	—	—

Status Report: Ending Period 7 ($000)

Task	% Complete	EV	AC	PV	CV	SV
A	100%	—	200	—	—	—
B	100%	—	200	—	—	—
C	100%	—	400	—	—	—
D	100%	—	150	—	—	—
E	20%	—	100	—	—	—
F	5%	—	50	—	—	—
Cumulative Totals		—	**1100**	—	—	—

Status Report: Ending Period 8 ($000)

Task	% Complete	EV	AC	PV	CV	SV
A	100%	—	200	—	—	—
B	100%	—	200	—	—	—
C	100%	—	400	—	—	—
D	100%	—	150	—	—	—
E	100%	—	350	—	—	—
F	10%	—	100	—	—	—
Cumulative Totals		—	**1400**	—	—	—

Performance Indexes Summary

Period	EV	AC	PV	SPI	CPI	PCIB
1	—	—	—	—	—	—
2	—	—	—	—	—	—
3	—	—	—	—	—	—
4	—	—	—	—	—	—
5	—	—	—	—	—	—
6	—	—	—	—	—	—
7	—	—	—	—	—	—
8	—	—	—	—	—	—

EAC_f = ________ VAC_f = ___________

Part B. You have met with your Aurora project team and they have provided you with the following revised estimates for the remainder of the project:

- Activity F will be completed at the end of period 12 at a total cost of $500.
- Activity G will be completed at the end of period 10 at a total cost of $150.
- Activity H will be completed at the end of period 14 at a total cost of $200.

Calculate the EAC_{re} and VAC_{re}. Based on the revised estimates, what is the expected status of the project in terms of cost and schedule? Between the VAC_f and the VAC_{re}, which one would you have the greatest confidence in?

EAC_{re} = ______________ VAC_{re} = ______________

References

Abramovici, A., "Controlling Scope Creep," *PM Network,* January 2000, pp. 44–48.

Anbari, F. T., "Earned Value Project Management Method and Extensions," *Project Management Journal,* vol. 34, no. 4 (December 2003), pp. 12–22.

Bowles, M. "Keeping Score," *PM Network,* May 2011, pp. 50–59.

Brandon, D. M., Jr., "Implementing Earned Value Easily and Effectively," *Project Management Journal,* vol. 29, no. 3 (June 1998), pp. 11–17.

Christensen, D. S., "The Cost and Benefits of the Earned Value Management Process," *Acquisition Review Quarterly,* vol. 5 (1998), pp. 373–86.

Christensen, D. S., and S. Heise, "Cost Performance Index Stability," *National Contract Management Association Journal,* vol. 25 (1993), pp. 7–15.

Fleming, Q., and J. M. Koppelman, *Earned Value Project Management,* 4th ed. (Newton Square, PA: Project Management Institute, 2010).

Kerzner, H., "Strategic Planning for a Project Office," *Project Management Journal,* vol. 34, no. 2 (June 2003), pp. 13–25.

Kim, E. H., W. G. Wells, and M. R. Duffey, "A Model for Effective Implementation of Earned Value Methodology," *International Journal of Project Management,* vol. 21, no. 5 (2003), pp. 375–82.

Naeni, L., S. Shadrokh, and A. Salehipour, "A Fuzzy Approach to the Earned Value Management," *International Journal of Project Management,* vol. 9, no. 6 (2011), pp. 764–72.

Webb, A., *Using Earned Value: A Project Manager's Guide* (Aldershot, UK: Gower, 2003).

Case 13.1

Tree Trimming Project

Layla Fence is a large timber and Christmas tree farmer who is attending a project management class in the spring, her offseason. When the class topic came to earned value, she was perplexed. Isn't she using EV?

Each summer Layla hires crews to shear fields of Christmas trees for the coming holiday season. Shearing entails having a worker use a large machete to shear the branches of the tree into a nice, cone-shaped tree.

Layla describes her business as follows:

A. I count the number of Douglas Fir Christmas trees in the field (24,000).

B. Next, I agree on a contract lump sum for shearing with a crew boss for the whole field ($30,000).

C. When partial payment for work completed arrives (5 days later), I count or estimate the actual number sheared (6,000 trees). I take the actual as a percent of the total to be sheared and multiply the percent complete by total contract amount for the partial payment [(6,000/$24,000 = 25%), (.25 × $30,000 = $7,500)].

1. Is Layla over, on, or below cost and schedule? Is Layla using earned value?
2. How can Layla set up a scheduling variance?

Case 13.2

Ventura Stadium Status Report Case

You are an assistant to Percival Young, president of G&E Company. He has asked you to prepare a brief report on the status of the Ventura Stadium project.

Ventura Stadium is a 47,000-seat professional baseball stadium. Construction started on July 8, 2019, and the stadium is to be completed on February 21, 2022. The project is estimated to cost $320,000,000. There are $35 million management reserves to deal with unexpected problems and delays.

The stadium must be ready for the 2022 major league season. G&E would accrue a $500,000 per day penalty for not meeting the April 3, 2022, deadline.

It is February 25, 2021, the day crews start installing seats.

Tables C13.1 and C13.2 contain information submitted by your counterpart at the Ventura site from which you are to prepare your report. Use the appropriate indexes/information to prepare a report informing Mr. Young on the overall status of the Ventura project in terms of costs and schedule. Note: Mr. Young is not interested in specifics, just how well the overall project is doing and if there is a need to take corrective action.

TABLE C13.1 Ventura Project Earned Value Table as of 2/25/21

	PV	EV	AC	CV	SV
Ventura Stadium	**233,000,000**	**221,000,000**	**232,500,000**	**−11,500,000**	**−12,000,000**
Clear stadium site	10,000,000	10,000,000	12,000,000	−2,000,000	0
Demolish building	2,000,000	2,000,000	1,800,000	200,000	0
Set up construction site	3,000,000	3,000,000	1,700,000	1,300,000	0
Drive support piling	40,000,000	40,000,000	45,000,000	−5,000,000	0
Pour lower concrete bowl	60,000,000	60,000,000	65,000,000	−5,000,000	0
Pour main concourse	25,000,000	25,000,000	28,000,000	−3,000,000	0
Install playing field	5,000,000	5,000,000	6,000,000	−1,000,000	0
Construct upper steel bowl	60,000,000	60,000,000	55,000,000	5,000,000	0
Install seats	4,000,000				−4,000,000
Build luxury boxes					
Install scoreboard					
Stadium infrastructure					
Construct steel canopy					
Light installation					
Build roof supports	10,000,000	10,000,000	11,000,000	−1,000,000	0
Construct roof	10,000,000	3,000,000	4,000,000	−1,000,000	−7,000,000
Install roof tracks	4,000,000	3,000,000	3,000,000	0	−1,000,000
Install roof					
Inspection					

BAC = $320,000,000

TABLE C13.2 Variance Table for Ventura Project as of 2/25/21

Task Name	Start	Finish	Baseline Start	Baseline Finish	Start Var.	Finish Var.
Ventura Baseball Stadium	**Mon 6/10/19**	**Mon 2/21/22**	**Mon 6/10/19**	**Mon 1/31/22**	**0 days**	**15 days**
Clear site	Mon 6/10/19	Fri 8/23/19	Mon 6/10/19	Fri 8/30/19	0 days	−5 days
Demolish building	Mon 8/26/19	Fri 10/11/19	Mon 9/2/19	Fri 10/11/19	−5 days	0 days
Set up construction site	Mon 8/26/19	Fri 10/11/19	Mon 9/2/19	Fri 10/11/19	−5 days	0 days
Drive support piles	Mon 8/26/19	Fri 2/7/20	Mon 9/2/19	Fri 2/14/20	−5 days	−5 days
Pour lower concrete bowl	Mon 2/10/20	Fri 8/28/20	Mon 2/17/20	Fri 7/31/20	−5 days	20 days
Pour main concourse	Mon 8/31/20	Wed 2/24/21	Mon 8/3/20	Wed 1/20/21	20 days	25 days
Installation of playing field	Mon 8/31/20	Wed 1/13/21	Mon 8/3/20	Tue 12/8/20	20 days	25 days
Construction upper steel bowl	Mon 8/31/20	Wed 2/10/21	Mon 8/3/20	Wed 1/20/21	20 days	15 days
Install seats	Thu 2/25/21	Thu 8/12/21	Thu 1/21/21	Thu 8/5/21	25 days	5 days
Build luxury boxes	Thu 2/25/21	Thu 7/1/21	Thu 1/21/21	Wed 5/26/21	25 days	25 days
Install jumbotron	Thu 2/25/21	Wed 4/7/21	Thu 1/21/21	Wed 3/3/21	25 days	25 days
Stadium infrastructure	Thu 2/25/21	Thu 8/12/21	Thu 1/21/21	Thu 7/8/21	25 days	25 days
Construct steel canopy	Fri 8/13/21	Mon 11/29/21	Fri 8/6/21	Fri 11/19/21	5 days	5 days
Light installation	Tue 11/30/21	Mon 1/10/22	Tue 11/23/21	Mon 1/3/22	5 days	5 days
Build roof supports	Mon 8/31/20	Wed 1/6/21	Mon 8/3/20	Tue 12/8/20	20 days	20 days
Construct roof	Wed 12/16/20	Fri 9/17/21	Wed 12/9/20	Thu 8/19/21	5 days	20 days
Install roof tracks	Thu 1/7/21	Wed 5/12/21	Wed 12/9/20	Wed 4/14/21	20 days	20 days
Install roof	Mon 9/20/21	Mon 1/24/22	Fri 8/20/21	Mon 12/27/21	20 days	20 days
Final inspection	Tue 1/25/22	Mon 2/21/22	Tue 1/4/22	Mon 1/31/22	15 days	15 days

Case 13.3

Scanner Project

You have been serving as Electroscan's project manager and are now well along in the project. Develop a narrative status report for the board of directors of the chain store that discusses the status of the project to date (see Table C13.3) and at completion. Be as specific as you can, using the numbers given and those you might develop. Remember, your audience is not familiar with the jargon used by project managers and computer software personnel; therefore, some explanation may be necessary. Your report will be evaluated on your detailed use of the data, your total perspective of the current status and future status of the project, and your recommended changes (if any).

TABLE C13.3

Electroscan, Inc. 555 Acorn Street, Suite 5 Boston, Massachusetts			29 In-store Scanner Project (thousands of dollars) Actual Progress as of January 1				
Name	**PV**	**EV**	**AC**	**SV**	**CV**	**BAC**	**EAC_f**
Scanner project	420	395	476	−25	−81	915	1103
H 1.0 Hardware	92	88	72	−4	16	260	213
H 1.1 Hardware specifications (DS)	20	20	15	0	5	20	15
H 1.2 Hardware design (DS)	30	30	25	0	5	30	25
H 1.3 Hardware documentation (DOC)	10	6	5	−4	1	10	8
H 1.4 Prototypes (PD)	2	2	2	0	0	40	40
H 1.5 Test prototypes (T)	0	0	0	0	0	30	30
H 1.6 Order circuit boards (PD)	30	30	25	0	5	30	25
H 1.7 Preproduction models (PD)	0	0	0	0	0	100	100
OP 1.0 Operating system	195	150	196	−45	−46	330	431
OP 1.1 Kernel specifications (DS)	20	20	15	0	5	20	15
OP 1.2 Drivers	45	55	76	10	−21	70	97
OP 1.2.1 Disk drivers (DEV)	25	30	45	5	−15	40	60
OP 1.2.2 I/O drivers (DEV)	20	25	31	5	−6	30	37
OP 1.3 Code software	130	75	105	−55	−30	240	336
OP 1.3.1 Code software (C)	30	20	40	−10	−20	100	200
OP 1.3.2 Document software (DOC)	45	30	25	−15	5	50	42
OP 1.3.3 Code interfaces (C)	55	25	40	−30	−15	60	96
OP 1.3.4 Beta test software (T)	0	0	0	0	0	30	30
U 1.0 Utilities	87	108	148	21	−40	200	274
U 1.1 Utilities specifications (DS)	20	20	15	0	5	20	15
U 1.2 Routine utilities (DEV)	20	20	35	0	−15	20	35
U 1.3 Complex utilities (DEV)	30	60	90	30	−30	100	150
U 1.4 Utilities documentation (DOC)	17	8	8	−9	0	20	20
U 1.5 Beta test utilities (T)	0	0	0	0	0	40	40
S 1.0 System integration	46	49	60	3	−11	125	153
S 1.1 Architecture decisions (DS)	9	9	7	0	2	10	8
S 1.2 Integration hard/soft (DEV)	25	30	45	5	−15	50	75
S 1.3 System hard/software test (T)	0	0	0	0	0	20	20
S 1.4 Project documentation (DOC)	12	10	8	−2	2	15	12
S 1.5 Integration acceptance testing (T)	0	0	0	0	0	30	30

Appendix 13.1

The Application of Additional Earned Value Rules

LEARNING OBJECTIVES

After reading this appendix you should be able to:

A13.1-1 Apply pseudo-earned value rules to measure progress on a project.

LO A1.1-1

Apply pseudo-earned value rules to measure progress on a project.

The following example and exercises are designed to provide practice in applying the following three earned value rules:

1. Percent complete rule
2. 50/50 rule
3. 0/100 rule

See the chapter for an explanation of each of these rules.

Simplifying Assumptions

The same simplifying assumptions used for the chapter example and exercises will also be used here.

1. Assume each cost account has only one work package, and each cost account will be represented as an activity on the network.
2. The project network early start times will serve as the basis for assigning the baseline values.
3. Except when the 0/100 rule or 50/50 rule is used, baseline values will be assigned linearly, unless stated differently. (Note: In practice, estimated costs should be applied "exactly" as they are expected to occur so measures of schedule and cost performance are useful and reliable.)
4. For purposes of demonstrating the examples, from the moment work on an activity begins, some actual costs will be incurred each period until the activity is completed.
5. When the 0/100 rule is used, the total cost for the activity is placed in the baseline on the early finish date.
6. When the 50/50 rule is used, 50 percent of the total cost is placed in the baseline on the early start date and 50 percent on the early finish date.

Appendix Exercises

1. Given the information provided for the development of a product warranty project for periods 1 through 7, compute the SV, CV, SPI, and CPI for each period. Figure A13.1–1A presents the project network. Figure A13.1–1B presents the project baseline, noting those activities using the 0/100 (rule 3) and 50/50 (rule 2) rules. For example, activity 1 uses rule 3, the 0/100 rule. Although the early start time is period 0, the budget is not placed in the time-phased baseline until period 2 when the activity is planned to be finished (EF). This same procedure has been used to assign costs for activities 2 and 7. Activities 2 and 7 use the 50/50 rule. Thus, 50

percent of the budget for each activity is assigned on its respective early start date (time period 2 for activity 2 and period 11 for activity 7) and 50 percent for their respective finish dates. Remember, when assigning earned value as the project is being implemented, if an activity actually starts early or late, the earned values must shift with the actual times. For example, if activity 7 actually starts in period 12 rather than 11, the 50 percent is not earned until period 12.

Plot the EV and the AC on the PV graph provided (Figure A13.1–1C). Use Figure A13.1–1D to plot the CPI, SPI, and PCIB. Explain to the owner your assessment of the project at the end of period 7 and the future expected status of the project at completion.

FIGURE A13.1-1A

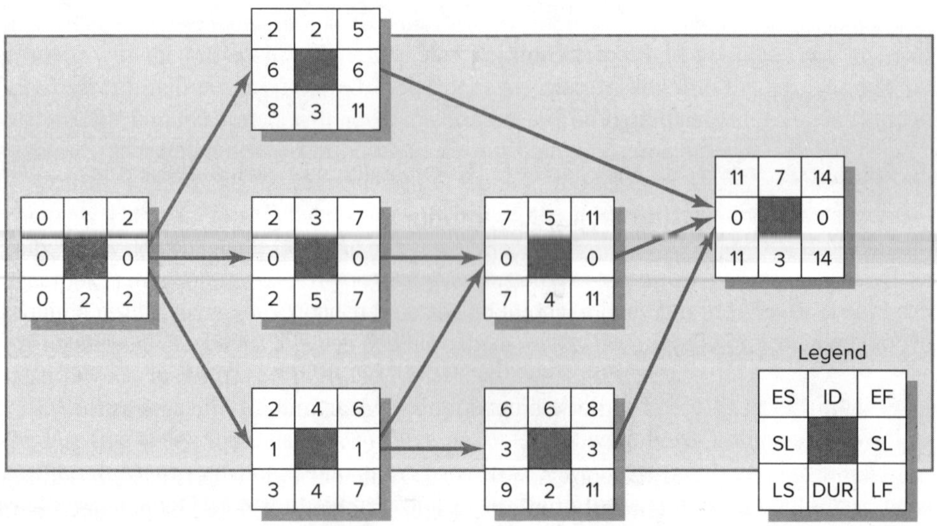

FIGURE A13.1-1B

Schedule information							Baseline budget needs													
							Time period													
EV Rule	ACT/ WP	DUR	ES	LF	SL	Total PV	0–1	1–2	2–3	3–4	4–5	5–6	6–7	7–8	8–9	9–10	10–11	11–12	12–13	13–14
(3)	1	2	0	2	0	6		6												
(2)	2	3	2	11	6	20			10		10									
(1)	3	5	2	7	0	30			9	6	6	6	3							
(1)	4	4	2	7	1	20			8	2	5	5								
(1)	5	4	7	11	0	16								4	4	4	4			
(1)	6	2	6	11	3	18							9	9						
(2)	7	3	11	14	0	8												4		4
Total PV by period							0	6	27	8	21	11	12	13	4	4	4	4	0	4
Cumulative PV by period							0	6	33	41	62	73	85	98	102	106	110	114	114	118

Rule
1 = %complete
2 = 50/50
3 = 0/100

Status Report: Ending Period 1

Task	%Complete	EV	AC	PV	CV	SV
1	0%	—	3	0	—	—
Cumulative Totals		—	**3**	**0**	—	—

Status Report: Ending Period 2

Task	%Complete	EV	AC	PV	CV	SV
1	Finished	6	5	—	—	—
Cumulative Totals		**6**	**5**	—	—	—

Status Report: Ending Period 3

Task	%Complete	EV	AC	PV	CV	SV
1	Finished	6	5	—	—	—
2	0%	—	5	—	—	—
3	30%	—	7	—	—	—
4	25%	—	5	—	—	—
Cumulative Totals		—	**22**	—	—	—

Status Report: Ending Period 4

Task	%Complete	EV	AC	PV	CV	SV
1	Finished	6	5	—	—	—
2	0%	—	7	—	—	—
3	50%	—	10	—	—	—
4	50%	—	8	—	—	—
Cumulative Totals		—	**30**	—	—	—

Status Report: Ending Period 5

Task	%Complete	EV	AC	PV	CV	SV
1	Finished	6	5	—	—	—
2	50%	—	8	—	—	—
3	60%	—	12	—	—	—
4	70%	—	10	—	—	—
Cumulative Totals		—	**35**	—	—	—

Status Report: Ending Period 6

Task	%Complete	EV	AC	PV	CV	SV
1	Finished	6	5	—	—	—
2	50%	—	10	—	—	—
3	80%	—	16	—	—	—
4	Finished	—	15	—	—	—
Cumulative Totals		—	**46**	—	—	—

Status Report: Ending Period 7

Task	%Complete	EV	AC	PV	CV	SV
1	Finished	6	5	—	—	—
2	Finished	—	14	—	—	—
3	Finished	—	20	—	—	—
4	Finished	—	15	—	—	—
5	0%	—	0	—	—	—
6	50%	—	9	—	—	—
Cumulative Totals		—	**63**	—	—	—

Period	SPI	CPI	PCIB
1	—	—	—
2	—	—	—
3	—	—	—
4	—	—	—
5	—	—	—
6	—	—	—
7	—	—	—

SPI = EV/PV
CPI = EV/AC
PCIB = EV/BAC

FIGURE A13.1-1C

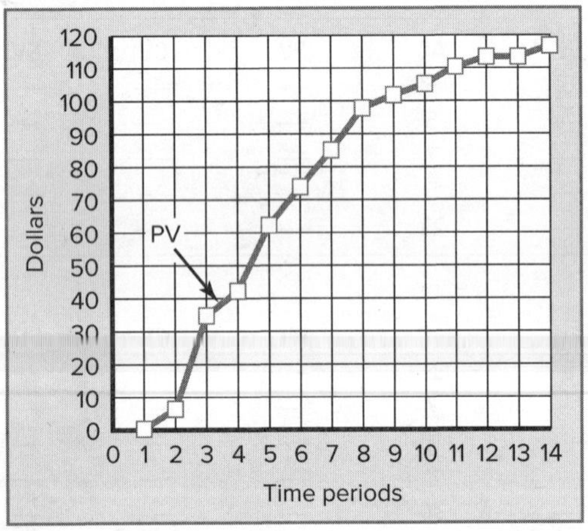

FIGURE A13.1-1D

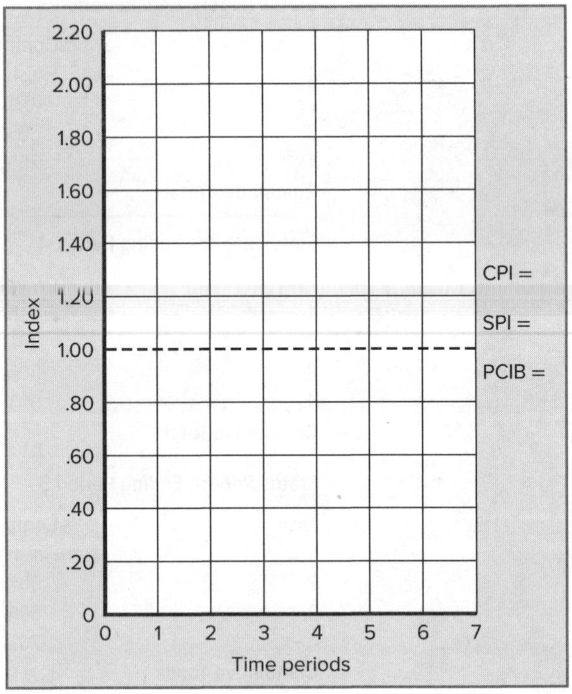

2. Given the information provided for development of a catalog product return process for periods 1 through 5, assign the PV values (using the rules) to develop a baseline for the project. Compute the SV, CV, SPI, and CPI for each period. Assume that PV will be evenly distributed across the activity's duration. Figure A13.1-2A presents the project network, while Figure A13.1-2B displays the project baseline, noting those activities using the percent complete (rule 1), 50/50 (rule 2), and 0/100 (rule 3) rules. Plot the EV and the AC on the PV graph provided (Figure A13.1-2C). Explain to the owner your assessment of the project at the end of period 5 and the future expected status of the project at the completion.

FIGURE A13.1-2A

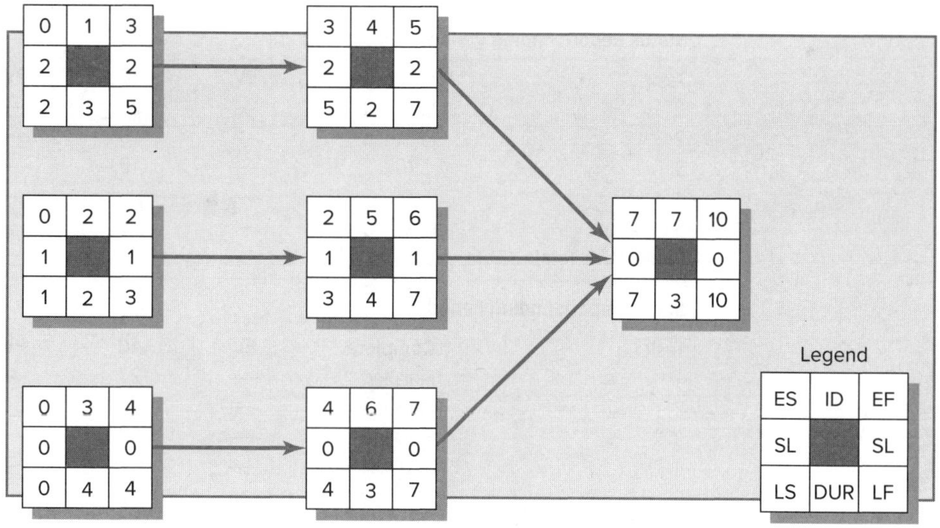

FIGURE A13.1-2B

Schedule information							Baseline budget needs									
							Time period									
EV Rule	ACT/WP	DUR	ES	LF	SL	Total PV	1	2	3	4	5	6	7	8	9	10
2	1	3	0	5	2	30										
3	2	2	0	3	1	20										
2	3	4	0	4	0	30										
3	4	2	3	7	2	10										
2	5	4	2	7	1	40										
1	6	3	4	7	0	30										
1	7	3	7	10	0	60										
Total PV by period																
Cumulative PV by period																

Rule
1 = %complete
2 = 50/50
3 = 0/100

Status Report: Ending Period 1

Task	%Complete	EV	AC	PV	CV	SV
1	40%	—	8	—	—	—
2	0%	—	12	—	—	—
3	30%	—	10	—	—	—
Cumulative Totals		—	**30**	—	—	—

Status Report: Ending Period 2

Task	%Complete	EV	AC	PV	CV	SV
1	80%	—	20	—	—	—
2	Finished	—	18	—	—	—
3	50%	—	12	—	—	—
Cumulative Totals		—	**50**	—	—	—

Status Report: Ending Period 3

Task	%Complete	EV	AC	PV	CV	SV
1	Finished	—	27	—	—	—
2	Finished	—	18	—	—	—
3	70%	—	15	—	—	—
4	0%	—	5	—	—	—
5	30%	—	8	—	—	—
Cumulative Totals		—	**73**	—	—	—

Status Report: Ending Period 4

Task	%Complete	EV	AC	PV	CV	SV
1	Finished	—	27	—	—	—
2	Finished	—	18	—	—	—
3	Finished	—	22	—	—	—
4	0%	—	7	—	—	—
5	60%	—	22	—	—	—
Cumulative Totals		—	**96**	—	—	—

Status Report: Ending Period 5

Task	%Complete	EV	AC	PV	CV	SV
1	Finished	—	27	—	—	—
2	Finished	—	18	—	—	—
3	Finished	—	22	—	—	—
4	Finished	—	8	—	—	—
5	70%	—	24	—	—	—
6	30%	—	10	—	—	—
Cumulative Totals		—	**109**	—	—	—

FIGURE A13.1-2C

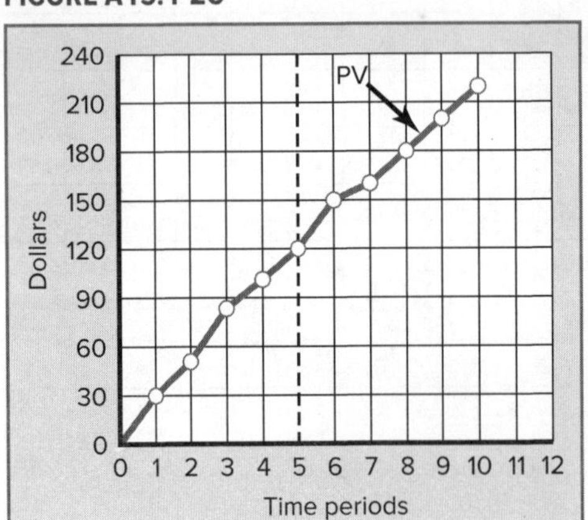

Period	SPI	CPI	PCIB
1	—	—	—
2	—	—	—
3	—	—	—
4	—	—	—
5	—	—	—

SPI = EV/PV
CPI = EV/AC
PCIB = EV/BAC

Design elements: Snapshot from Practice, Highlight box, Case icon: Sky Designs/Shutterstock

CHAPTER FOURTEEN

14 Project Closure

LEARNING OBJECTIVES

After reading this chapter you should be able to:

14-1 Identify different types of project closure.

14-2 Understand the challenges of closing out a project.

14-3 Explain the importance of a project audit.

14-4 Know how to use project retrospectives to obtain lessons learned.

14-5 Assess level of project management maturity.

14-6 Provide useful advice for conducting team performance reviews.

14-7 Provide useful advice for conducting performance reviews of project members.

OUTLINE

14.1 Types of Project Closure

14.2 Wrap-up Closure Activities

14.3 Project Audits

14.4 Project Audits: The Big Picture

14.5 Post-implementation Evaluation

Summary

Appendix 14.1: Project Closeout Checklist

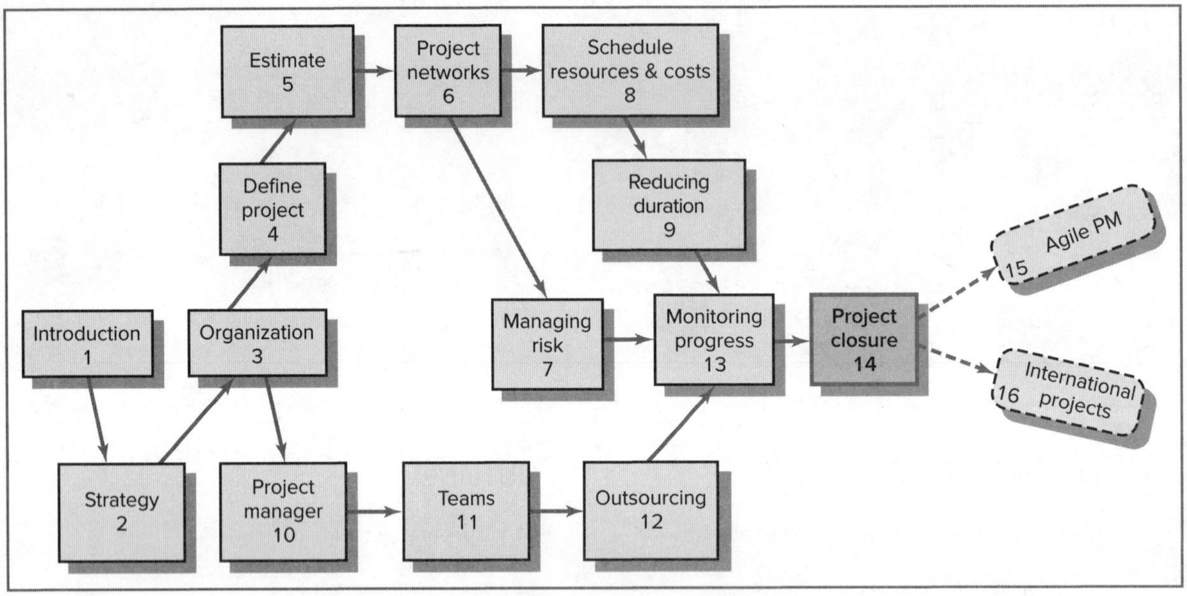

Those who cannot remember the past are condemned to relive it.

—George Santayana, 1863–1952

Every project comes to an end eventually. But how many project participants get excited about closing out a project? The deliverables are complete. Ownership is ready to be transferred. Everyone's focus is on what's next—hopefully a new, exciting project. Carefully managing the closure phase is as important as any other phase of the project. Observation tells us that organizations that manage closure will prosper. Those who don't tend to have projects that drag on forever and repeat the same mistakes over and over.

Closing out a project includes a daunting number of tasks. In the past and on small projects the project manager was responsible for seeing all tasks and loose ends were completed and signed off. This is no longer true. In today's project-driven organizations that have many projects occurring simultaneously, the responsibility for completing closure tasks has been parsed among the project manager, project teams, project office, contracts office, Human Resources, and others. Many tasks overlap, occur simultaneously, and require coordination and cooperation among these stakeholders.

The three major deliverables for **project closure** are as follows (see Figure 14.1):

1. **Wrapping up the project.** The major wrap-up task is to ensure the project is approved and accepted by the customer. Other wrap-up activities include closing accounts, paying bills, reassigning equipment and personnel, finding new opportunities for project staff, closing facilities, and issuing the final report. Checklists are used extensively to ensure tasks are not overlooked. In many organizations, the lion's share of closure tasks is largely done by the project office in coordination with the project manager. The final report writing is usually assigned to one project office staff member, who assembles input from all stakeholders. In smaller organizations and projects, these closure activities are left to the project manager and team.
2. **Project audit.** Audits are post-project reviews of how successful the project was. They include causal analysis and thorough retrospectives that identify lessons learned. These post-project reviews should be held with the team and key stakeholders to catch any missing issues or gaps.

FIGURE 14.1
Project Closure and Review Deliverables

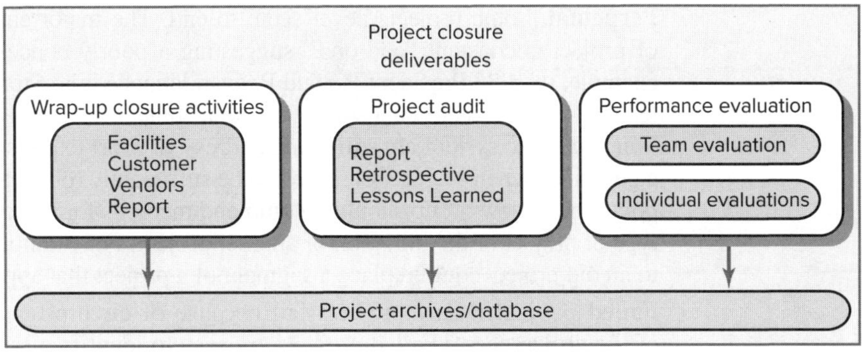

3. **Evaluation of performance and management of the project.** Evaluation includes the team, individual team members, and project manager performance. Vendors and the customer may provide external input. Evaluation of the major players provides important information for the future.

This chapter begins with the recognition that projects are shut down for many reasons. Not all projects end with a clear "Finished" and are turned over to a customer. Regardless of the conditions for ending a project, the general process of closure is similar for all projects, though the endings may differ significantly. Wrap-up closure tasks are noted first. These tasks represent all the tasks that must be "cleaned up" before the project is terminated. Project audits and lessons learned are examined next. Finally, evaluation of individual and team performance is discussed.

14.1 Types of Project Closure

LO 14-1

Identify different types of project closure.

On some projects, the end may not be as clear as would be hoped. Although the scope statement may define a clear ending for a project, the actual ending may or may not correspond. Fortunately, a majority of projects are blessed with a well-defined ending. Regular project reviews will identify projects having endings different from plans. Following are the types of closure.

- **Normal.** The most common circumstance for project closure is simply a completed project. For many development projects, the end involves handing off the final design to Production and creating a new product or service line. For other internal IT projects, such as system upgrades or the creation of new inventory control systems, the end occurs when the output is incorporated into ongoing operations. Some modifications in scope, cost, and schedule probably occurred during implementation.
- **Premature.** For a few projects, the project may be completed early with some parts of the project eliminated. For example, in a new product development project, a marketing manager may insist on production models before testing:

  "Give the new product to me now, the way it is. Early entry into the market will mean big profits! I know we can sell a bazillion of these. If we don't do it now, the opportunity is lost!"

  The pressure is on to finish the project and send it to Production. Before succumbing to this form of pressure, the implications and risks associated with this decision should be carefully reviewed and assessed by senior management and all stakeholders. Too frequently, the benefits are illusory and dangerous, and carry large risks.

- **Perpetual.** Some projects never seem to end. The major characteristic of this kind of project is constant "add-ons," suggesting a poorly conceived project scope. For example, in 1984 President Ronald Reagan launched the Strategic Defense Initiative (SDI). Over 30 years later, many of the technical difficulties with creating a "Star Wars" defense system are still being addressed. Most experts admit they do not have a good idea when such a system would be sufficiently robust to be deployed. At some point, the review group should recommend methods for bringing final closure to this type of project or the initiation of another project. For example, adding a new feature to an old project could replace a segment of a project that appears to be perpetual.
- **Failed project.** Many projects fail because of circumstances beyond the control of the project team. Failed projects are easy to identify after the fact. The machine does not work, the customer rejects our work, or the costs greatly exceed the benefits. Recognizing danger signals and shutting down doom projects in advance can be much more problematic. See the Research Highlight 14.1: Why is it difficult to pull the plug on projects?
- **Changed priority.** Organizations' priorities often change and strategies shift directions. For example, the COVID-19 pandemic shook operations around the world and companies were forced to cancel projects and redirect efforts to face new challenges. Thus, a project may start with a high priority but see its rank erode or crash during its project life cycle as conditions change. When priorities change, projects in the process may need to be altered or canceled. See Snapshot from Practice 14.1: The Wake for a novel response to a canceled project.

Different types of project termination present unique issues. Some adjustments to generic closure processes may be necessary to accommodate the type of project termination you face.

SNAPSHOT FROM PRACTICE 14.1 The Wake[1]

Sally worked as a project manager for a high-tech electronics firm in the late 1980s. The company was using "bubble ink" technology to develop affordable color printers.

Sally was in charge of a team tasked with cutting the prohibitive cost of printers in half. If successful, significant bonuses would be earned and several team members would be given key positions when the product went into production. The team had overcome several difficult technical challenges and was well on its way to accomplishing its objective when the project was canceled. Top management discovered at a trade show that several competitors were about to introduce ink jet printers at a cost one-third the price of printers Sally's team was developing.

What could Sally say to her team? They had worked so hard, and expected so much out of this project. She knew they would be devastated.

Sally knew she had to do something to help her team deal with this bitter disappointment. So she decided to hold a traditional Irish "wake" for the project. She persuaded management to hire a backhoe to dig a grave in the backyard of their office and purchase an actual coffin. After she and the other members gave a brief eulogy about the project, each member dropped something from the project into the coffin. For some members, it was a piece of a printer prototype; for others, it was a memo or a plan. One by one, each member put something personal in the coffin. After the coffin was buried, the team retreated to a local brew pub to imbibe, cry, and share fond memories of the work they had accomplished.

The "wake" became part of the company's folklore and team members still laugh about the experience.

[1] A wake is a party in honor of the deceased that usually involves the consumption of alcohol.

Research Highlight 14.1

Why it is difficult to pull the plug on projects?*

Barry Staw and his colleagues have conducted research directed at answering the question why people continue to pursue a failed coursed of action. Why do people continue to work at jobs that make them unhappy? Or, why do organizations continue to fund bad projects? Their research centers around the concept escalation of commitment.

Escalation of commitment is a human behavior pattern in which an individual or group facing increasingly negative outcomes from a decision, action, or investment, nevertheless, continues the behavior instead of altering course (Staw, 1997).

Through a series of laboratory and field studies, researchers have confirmed that the more people become invested in a project, the less willing they are to abandon it despite increasingly negative results. This investment may be tangible and psychological. Tangible costs include time and resources already spent on the project. "Sunk costs" refers to investment in a project that is not recoverable. Sunk costs are reflected in a project's salvage value and closing costs. An executive could simply terminate an ineffective advertising campaign in midstream, but stopping work on a half-built apartment complex is another story. A project that has very little salvage value and high closing costs—payments to terminated employees, penalties for breached contracts, and losses from the closing of facilities—will be much more difficult to abandon than a project in which expenditures are recoverable and exit is easy.

The problem is many projects are often structured in ways to ensure commitment. First, project managers tend to view each setback as temporary that can be correctable over time with more money and effort. Second, they consider all money spent as investments toward a large payoff they can reap once the project is completed. Third, expenditures as noted earlier are sunk costs and non recoverable if the project is shut down. Sometimes project managers and supporters will feel backed into a corner and perceive they have no alternative but to see the project through.

Staw and colleagues research delved deeper into the question and discovered more subtle, psychological forces at play. One is the need for self-justification, that managers sometimes are unwilling to pull the plug on a project because they consider it a personal failure. People naturally wish to preserve their sense of self-esteem, and when threatened they will continue a project to prove they were right.

Social pressures also come into play. Few like to expose their mistakes to others. No one wants to appear incompetent. When a person's status is tied to a project's success and accepting failure means loss of reputation and even job insecurity, hanging on despite losses makes some sense.

Finally, Staw pointed out that cultural norms often come into play. "Stay the course," "Failure is opportunity," "Stick to your guns" are leadership axioms often embedded in an organization's culture. While often leading to dramatic results, they can also encourage foolish persistence. Staw warned that organizations can become "programmed" to escalate commitment.

Escalating commitment has been attributed to many failures including the 1996 Mount Everest disaster (Alvarez et al., 2011), the Big Dig, aka the exorbitantly over-budgeted Boston Transit project (Sleesman et al., 2012), the continuation of the Vietnam War/Kháng chiến chống M□ (Staw, 1981), and Sony's continued investment in electronics business after $8.5 billion in losses (Woods et al., 2012). It would not be surprising to find many failed project postmortems identifying escalation of commitment as a significant factor behind obvious warning signals being ignored.

So, what can one do?

The most important thing for project managers to realize is that they may be biased toward escalation. For all the reasons mentioned, project managers often delude themselves into thinking that the project will pull through. A second important action is that organizations should separate the decision makers who approve projects from those professionals who assess progress of the projects (remember Gate 5 in Figure 2.3). Independence is key to providing a less bias more objective assessment. Finally, leaders need to assess the role their organization's culture plays. Do the heroes always encourage a "go for broke attitude," or do they recognize that it may take even more courage and loyalty to admit failure and cut losses?

*B. M. Staw, and J. Ross, "Knowing when to Pull the Plug," *Harvard Business Review*, March 1987.

14.2 Wrap-up Closure Activities

LO 14-2

Understand the challenges of closing out a project.

The major challenges for the project manager and team members are over. Getting the project manager and project participants to wrap up the odds and ends necessary to fully complete a project is often difficult. It's like the party is over—now who wants to help clean up? Much of the work is mundane and tedious. Motivation can be the chief challenge. For example, accounting for equipment and completing final reports are perceived as dull administrative tasks by project professionals who are action-oriented individuals.

The project manager's challenge is to keep the project team focused on the remaining project activities and delivery to the customer until the project is complete. Communicating a closure and review plan and schedule early allows the project team to (1) accept the psychological fact the project will end and (2) prepare to move on. The ideal scenario is to have each team member's next assignment ready when project completion is announced. Project managers need to be careful to maintain their enthusiasm for completing the project and hold people accountable to deadlines, which are prone to slip during the waning stages of the project.

Project closure usually includes the following six major activities.

1. Getting delivery acceptance from the customer.
2. Shutting down resources and releasing to new uses.
3. Reassigning project team members.
4. Closing accounts and seeing that all bills are paid.
5. Delivering the project to the customer.
6. Creating a final report.

Administering the details of closing out a project can be intimidating. Some organizations have checklists of over 100 wrap-up tasks! These checklists deal with closure details such as facilities, teams, staff, customer, vendors, and the project itself. A partial administrative closure checklist is shown in Table 14.1.

Getting delivery acceptance by the customer is a major and critical closure activity. Delivery of some projects to the customer is straightforward. Others are more complex and difficult. Ideally, there should be no surprises. This requires a well-defined scope and an effective change management system with active customer involvement. User involvement is critical to acceptance (see Snapshot from Practice 14.2: New Ball Goes Flat in the NBA).

Project managers are not always responsible for all facets of the closeout process. In many organizations, accounts and bills are dealt with by contract offices. Reassignments are managed by the firm's project management office. Disputes are dealt with by lawyers. Sometimes new managers are brought in to close out the project. They specialize in customer relations and/or attention to detail and are often called "terminators" within their organization.

The conditions for completing and transferring the project should be set before the project begins. A completed software project is a good example of the need to work out the details in advance. If the user has problems using the software, will the customer withhold final payments? Who is responsible for supporting and training the user? If these conditions are not clearly defined up front, getting delivery acceptance can be troublesome.

Another delivery tactic (briefly mentioned in Chapter 7) for a project that has been outsourced is known as build, own, operate, and transfer (BOOT). In this type of project, the contractor builds, owns, and operates the project deliverable for a set period of time. For example, Haliburton will operate a hydroelectric plant for six months before

TABLE 14.1
Wrap-up Closure Checklist

	Task	Completed? Yes/No
	Team	
1	Has a schedule for reducing project staff been developed and accepted?	
2	Has staff been released or notified of new assignments?	
3	Have performance reviews for team members been conducted?	
4	Has staff been offered outplacement services and career counseling activities?	
	Vendors/Contractors	
5	Have performance reviews for all vendors been conducted?	
6	Have project accounts been finalized and all billing closed?	
	Customer/Users	
7	Has the customer signed off on the delivered product?	
8	Have an in-depth project review and evaluation interview with the customer been conducted?	
9	Have the users been interviewed to assess their satisfaction with the deliverables? With the project team? With vendors? With training? With support? With maintenance?	
	Equipment and Facilities	
10	Have project resources been transferred to other projects?	
11	Have rental or lease equipment agreements been closed out?	
12	Has the date for the closure review been set and stakeholders notified?	
	Attach comments or links on any tasks you feel need explanation.	

turning over operations to their Indian counterparts. During this time all the bugs are worked out and conditions for delivery are satisfied. Again, the delivery conditions need to be carefully set up before the project begins; if not, wrap-up activities can develop a life of their own.

Releasing the project team typically occurs gradually during the closure phase. For some people, the termination of their responsible activities ends before the project is delivered to the customer or user. Reassignment for these participants needs to take place well before the final finish date. For the remaining team members (full or part-time), termination may result in a new project or a return to their functional job. Sometimes, in product development efforts, team members are assigned to operations positions and play an active role in the production of the new product. For contract people it may mean the end of their assignment to that project; in some cases, there may be follow-up work or user support possibilities. A small number of part-time participants may be recommended to the user organization to train users or operate new equipment or systems.

Since many work invoices are not submitted until after the project is officially over, closing out contracts is often messy and filled with untied ends. For example, it is improbable that all invoices have been finalized, billed, and paid. Further, when contractors are used, there is a need to verify that all the contracted work has been done. Keeping contract records, such as progress reports, invoices, change records, and payment records, is important, should a compliance or lawsuit occur. Too often in the haste to meet deadlines, paperwork and recordkeeping get short-changed, only to create major headaches when it comes time for final documentation.

There are many more wrap-up activities; it is important to complete all of them. Experience has proved time and again that not doing all the little cleanup tasks well

SNAPSHOT FROM PRACTICE 14.2 New Ball Goes Flat in the NBA*

On October 31, 2006, the National Basketball Association (NBA) opened its 57th season with new official game balls. The new ball, manufactured by Spalding, featured a new design and a new material that together were believed to offer better grip, feel, and consistency than the previous leather ball. The material was a microfiber composite with moisture management that provided superior grip and feel throughout the course of a game. Additionally, the new composite material eliminated the need for a break-in period, which is necessary for a leather ball, and achieved consistency from ball to ball.

The NBA and Spalding subjected the ball to a rigorous evaluation process that included a laboratory and on-court testing process. Every NBA team received the new ball and had the opportunity to use it in practice. The ball was also tested in the NBA summer development league.

Ingram Publishing/Alamy Stock Photo

At the press conference announcing the shift from leather to microfiber balls, NBA commissioner David Stern pronounced, "The advancement that Spalding has made to the new game ball ensures that the best basketball players in the world will be playing with the best basketball in the world."

Animal rights advocates applauded the shift from leather to microfiber. Such was not the case for the players who would actually use the new ball. Grumblings emerged immediately when training camps opened in October. Washington Wizards guard Gilbert Arenas said the new basketball "got slippery" when it came in contact with even small amounts of sweat. Then Miami Heat center Shaquille O'Neil said, "It feels like one of those cheap balls that you buy at a toy store."

Some players, including league MVP Steve Nash, began complaining that the new ball was producing small cuts on their hands. "It's awful [the friction burns], it's like an irritant . . . sometimes I even have to tape my fingers in practice." Perhaps LeBron James from the Cleveland Cavaliers best summed up the players' attitudes toward the NBA's introduction of the new ball when he said, "You can change the dress code, you can make our shorts shorter, but when you take our basketball away from us, that's not a transition we can handle."

On December 1, 2006, four weeks into the season, the NBA players union filed an unfair labor practice suit because the league management switched to the new ball without consulting the players. Ten days later, the NBA announced that they would revert to the old leather ball beginning January 1, 2007. In a terse statement, Commissioner David Stern said, "Our players' response to this particular composite ball has been overwhelmingly negative and we are acting accordingly."

The failure to check with the players (the end users) and get buy-in for the new basketball was loudly criticized by the press. "How they could actually even get it that far and not have run it by the players is just an amazing, amazing exercise in ineptitude," Rob Frankel, a Los Angeles–based branding expert, told *Bloomberg News.*

*"NBA Introduces New Game Ball," www.nba.com/news, June 28, 2006; H. Bloom, "The NBA—Uneventful 2006 II," *Sports Business News*, www.sportsbixnews.blogspot.com, December 30, 2006.

will create problems later. Appendix 14.1 presents an example of a closeout checklist used by the state of Virginia.

A final wrap-up activity is some form of celebration. For successful projects, an upbeat, festive celebration brings closure to the enjoyable experiences everyone has had and the need to say goodbye. Celebration is an opportunity to recognize the effort project stakeholders contributed. Even if the project did not reach its objectives, recognize the effort involved and goals that were achieved. If the project was a success, invite everyone who in some way contributed to the project success. Thank the team and each one individually. The spirit of the celebration should be one in which stakeholders are thanked for a job well done and leave with a good feeling of accomplishment.

14.3 Project Audits

LO 14-3

Explain the importance of a project audit.

Project audits are more than the status reports suggested in Chapter 13, which report on project performance. While project audits do use performance measures, they are more inclusive. Project audits not only examine project success but also review why the project was selected. Project audits include a reassessment of the project's role in the organization's priorities and a check on the organizational culture to ensure it facilitates the type of project being implemented. They assess if the project team is functioning well and is appropriately staffed. Audits make recommendations and articulate lessons learned.

Project audits can be performed while a project is in process and after a project is completed. There are only two minor differences between these audits:

- **In-process project audits.** Project audits early in projects allow for corrective changes, if they are needed, on the audited project or others in progress. In-process project audits concentrate on project progress and performance and check if conditions have changed. For example, have priorities changed? Is the project mission still relevant? In some cases, the audit report may recommend shutting down the project or significantly changing the scope of the project.
- **Post-project audits.** These audits tend to include more detail and depth than in-process project audits. Project audits of completed projects emphasize improving the management of future projects. These audits are more long-term oriented than in-process audits. Post-project audits do check on project performance, but the audit represents a broader view of the project's role in the organization; for example, were the strategic benefits claimed actually delivered?

The depth and detail of the project audit depend on many factors. Some are listed in Table 14.1. Because audits cost time and money, they should include no more time or resources than are necessary and sufficient. Early in-process project audits tend to be perfunctory unless serious problems or concerns are identified. Then, of course, the audit would be carried out in more detail. Because in-process project audits can be worrisome and destructive to the project team, care must be taken to protect project team morale. The audit should be carried out quickly, and the report should be as positive and constructive as possible. Post-project audits are more detailed and inclusive and contain more project team input.

In summary, plan the audit and limit the time for the audit. For example, in post-project audits, for all but very large projects, a one-week limit is a good benchmark. Beyond this time, the marginal return of additional information diminishes quickly. Small projects may require only one or two days and one or two people to conduct an audit.

The priority team functions well in selecting projects and monitoring performance—cost and time. However, reviewing and evaluating projects and the process of managing projects are usually delegated to independent audit groups. Each audit group is charged with evaluating and reviewing *all* factors relevant to the project and to managing future projects. The outcome of the project audit is a report.

The Project Audit Process

The following guidelines, which should be noted before conducting a major project audit, will improve your chances for a successful audit.

1. Comments about individuals or groups participating in the project should be minimized. Keep to project issues, not what happened or who did what.
2. Audit activities should be intensely sensitive to human emotions and reactions. The inherent threat to those being evaluated should be reduced as much as possible.
3. The accuracy of data should be verifiable or noted as subjective, judgmental, or hearsay.
4. Senior management should announce support for the project audit and see that the audit group has access to all information, project participants, and (in most cases) project customers.
5. The attitude toward a project audit and its aftermath depends on the modus operandi of the audit leadership and group. The objective is not to prosecute. The objective is to learn and conserve valuable organizational resources where mistakes have been made, learn and elevate future performance when people have succeeded. Friendliness, empathy, and objectivity encourage cooperation and reduce anxiety.
6. The audit should be completed as quickly as is reasonable.

With these guidelines in mind, the project audit process is conveniently divided into three steps: initiation and staffing, data collection and analysis, and reporting. Each step is briefly discussed next.

Step 1: Initiation and Staffing

Initiation of the audit process depends primarily on organization size and project size, along with other factors. In small organizations and projects where face-to-face contact at all levels is prevalent, an audit may be informal and represent only another staff meeting. But even in these environments the content of a formal project audit should be examined and covered, with notes made of the lessons learned. In medium-sized organizations with few projects, the audit is likely to be conducted by someone from management with project management experience. In large companies or organizations with many projects, the audit is under the purview of the project office.

A major tenet of the project audit is that the outcome must represent an independent view of the project. Maintaining independence and an objective view is difficult, given that project stakeholders frequently view audits as negative. Careers and reputations can be tarnished, even in organizations that tolerate mistakes. In less forgiving organizations, mistakes can lead to termination or exile to less significant regions of an organization. Of course, if the result of an audit is favorable, careers and reputations can be enhanced. Given that project audits are susceptible to internal politics, some organizations rely on outside consulting firms to conduct the audits.

Step 2: Data Collection and Analysis

Each organization and project is unique. Therefore, the specific kinds of information that will be collected depending upon the industry, project size, newness of technology, and project experience. These factors can influence the nature of the audit. However, information and data are gathered to answer questions similar to the following.

Organization View

1. Was the organizational culture supportive and correct for this type of project? Why? Why not?
2. Was senior management's support adequate?

3. Did the project accomplish its intended purpose?
4. Were the risks for the project appropriately identified and assessed? Were contingency plans used? Were they realistic? Have risk events occurred that have an impact greater than anticipated?
5. Were the right people and talents assigned to this project?
6. What does evaluation from outside contractors suggest?
7. Were the project start-up and hand-off successful? Why? Is the customer satisfied?

Project Team View

1. Were the project planning and control systems appropriate for this type of project? Should all projects of a similar size and type use these systems? Why or why not?
2. Did the project conform to plan? Is the project over or under budget and schedule? Why?
3. Were interfaces and communications with project stakeholders adequate and effective?
4. Did the team have adequate access to organizational resources—people, budget, support groups, equipment? Were there resource conflicts with other ongoing projects?
5. Was the team managed well? Were problems confronted, not avoided?

The audit group should not be limited to these questions but rather should include other questions related to their organization and project type—for example, research and development, marketing, information systems, construction, or facilities. The preceding generic questions, although overlapping, represent a good starting point and will go a long way toward identifying project problem and success patterns.

Step 3: Reporting

The major goal of the audit report is to improve the way future projects are managed. Succinctly, the report attempts to capture needed changes and lessons learned from a current or finished project. The report serves as a training instrument for project managers of future projects.

Audit reports need to be tailored to the specific project and organizational environment. Nevertheless, a generic format for all audits facilitates the development of an audit database and a common outline for those who prepare audit reports and the managers who read and act on their content. A very general outline common to those found in practice is as follows:

1. *Classification.* The classification of projects by characteristics allows prospective readers and project managers to be selective in the use of the report content. Typical classification categories include the following:

- Project type—for example, development, marketing, systems, construction.
- Size—monetary.
- Number of staff.
- Technology level—low, medium, high, new.
- Strategic or support.

Other classifications relevant to the organization should be included.

2. *Analysis.* The analysis section includes succinct, factual review statements of the project (PMBOK, 2017)—for example,

- Scope objectives, the criteria used to evaluate scope and evidence that the completion criteria were met.
- Quality objectives, the criteria used to assess the project and product/service quality, and reasons for variances.
- Cost objectives, including acceptable cost range, actual costs, and reasons for any variances.
- Schedule objectives, including verification of milestone completion dates, and reasons for variances.
- Summary of risks and issues encountered on the project and how they were addressed.
- Outcomes achieved, including an assessment of how the final product, service, or result addressed the business need identified in the selection process.

3. *Recommendations.* Usually, audit recommendations represent major corrective actions that should take place. Audit recommendations are often technical and focus on solutions to problems that surfaced. For example, to avoid rework, the report of a construction project recommended shifting to a more resilient building material. In other cases, recommendations may include terminating or sustaining vendor or contractor relationships.

4. *Lessons learned.* These do not have to be in the form of recommendations. **Lessons learned** serve as reminders of mistakes easily avoided and actions easily taken to ensure success. In practice, new project teams reviewing audits of past projects similar to the one they are about to start have found audit reports very useful. Team members will frequently remark later, "The recommendations were good, but the 'lessons learned' section really helped us avoid many pitfalls and made our project implementation smoother." It is precisely for this reason that lessons learned in the form of project retrospectives have taken on greater prominence and warrant further discussion. See Snapshot from Practice 14.3: Operation Eagle Claw.

5. *Appendix.* The appendix may include backup data or details of analysis that allow others to follow up if they wish. It should not be a dumping ground used for filler; only critical, pertinent information should be attached.

Project Retrospectives

LO 14-4

Know how to use project retrospectives to obtain lessons learned.

The term **retrospective** has emerged to denote specific efforts at identifying lessons learned on projects. Proponents believe that the traditional audit process focuses too much on project success and evaluation, which interferes with the surfacing and transferal of important lessons learned. They advocate a separate effort toward capturing lessons learned. In many ways, this effort mirrors the auditing process.

Retrospectives vary depending upon the nature of the project, the number of people involved, and the difficulties experienced on a project. On large projects, this would be broken down into relevant teams and management groups. They should include relevant contractors, owners, and other external stakeholders. If these people are not available, then their input should be sought via email or a virtual meeting.

All retrospectives boil down to a small group of people getting together to discuss and identify lessons learned from working on the project together. Focus should not only be

SNAPSHOT FROM PRACTICE 14.3 Operation Eagle Claw*

On November 4, 1979, a mob in Iran stormed the U.S. Embassy and took 52 Americans hostage. After six months of failed negotiation, the green light was given to execute Operation Eagle Claw, a joint military effort to free the hostages.

The plan called for eight Navy RH-53D helicopters to fly 600 miles to a remote site in Iran, code-named Desert One. Under the cover of darkness, the helicopters would be refueled by KC-130 tankers. The helicopters would then fly the assault force to a spot near the outskirts of Tehran, where they would meet up with special agents already in the country. The agents would lead them to a safe house to await the assault on the embassy the next night. Upon rescuing the hostages, the assault team would escort them to a nearby airfield that had already been secured by a second assault team, where they would be flown to safety.

What actually happened was far different from what was planned.

The helicopter pilots were ordered to fly at or below 200 feet to avoid radar. This caused them to run into "haboobs," or dust storms. Two helicopters malfunctioned and turned back. The remainder battled the dust storms and arrived at Desert One one hour late. The rescue attempt was dealt its final blow when it was discovered that a third helicopter had a hydraulic leak and was inoperable. Only five aircraft were serviceable and six were needed, so the mission had to be aborted. Things got worse when one of the helicopters moved into position to refuel and collided with a KC-130 plane. Both aircraft burst into flames. All told, eight soldiers died and dozens were injured. The Iranians scattered the hostages around the country afterward, making any further rescue attempts impossible.

Given the gravity of the situation, a special six-member commission was appointed by the Joint Chiefs of Staff to conduct an audit of the project. They identified a number of issues that contributed to the failure. One issue was the selection of the aircrews. Given the significance of the mission, each military service wanted to be involved. Navy and Marine pilots with little experience in long-range overland navigation or refueling were chosen, even though more than 100 experienced Air Force pilots were available. Another issue was the lack of a comprehensive mission rehearsal program. From the beginning, training was not conducted in a truly joint manner; it was compartmentalized by service and held in different locations across the United States. The limited rehearsals that were conducted assessed only segments of the total mission.

Purestock/SuperStock

The commission concluded that 10 and perhaps 12 helicopters should have been launched to guarantee the minimum of 6 required for mission completion. Finally, the hopscotch method for ground refueling was criticized. If planners had chosen en-route fueling, the entire Desert One scenario could have been avoided. The final report contained several important lessons learned that have contributed to subsequent successful missions, including the one against Osama bin Laden in 2011.

*D. M. Giangreco, and T. A. Griswold, *Delta: America's Elite Counter-terrorist Force* (New York: Motorbooks International, 1992).

on technical lessons (i.e., next time we can skip steps 2–3 and go immediately to step 4) but also on working together issues, such as tech leads need to talk daily to make sure that they are on the same page during the development phase, should be discussed.

In many cases, professionals from the project office are assigned to facilitate the retrospective. This is especially true on controversial projects where there is likely to be a hesitancy in sharing information. Here, trained **facilitators** collect information from interviews and survey data to identify relevant learning opportunities. They then lead the group involved in a discussion of the results and identification of key lessons to be learned. For example, one of the issues identified was a lack of timely decision making and poor coordination between the project team and external groups (i.e., Human Resources (HR), Production, etc.). Through frank discussion, members felt they were getting bombarded with useless information all of the time and they had a hard time sorting through what was important and what could be ignored. A couple of the team members admitted to doing a core dump of all HR e-mails out of frustration. HR and Production admitted that they sometimes felt safer "cc-ing" everyone. Two lessons identified from the discussion included (1) more attention should be devoted when developing the communication plan to carefully delineate who should get what information and (2) two months into a project, whether through an email survey or discussion, the quality and frequency of information exchange should be assessed, and changes made, when necessary.

Even if a project doesn't warrant an outside facilitator, every project manager should take responsibility to see that their project team conducts a retrospective. In fact, no project is complete no matter how small or large without project retrospective taking place. One can simply request that team members submit anonymously responses to three simple questions:

1. What did we do well as a team?
2. What didn't we do well as a team?
3. If you had to do it all over again, what should you/we have done differently?

The project manager reports back their responses and leads the group in a discussion of problems, opportunities, and underlying causes. One would be amazed by the richness of the learning that comes from a discussion.

Such discussions depend upon the level of trust members have in their project manager. Where the threat of mistrust is high, then we would strongly recommend that an outside facilitator be used to conduct the retrospective. Even when trust is high, it is wise to work with a trained facilitator the first time you conduct a retrospective.

Each lesson is assigned an owner, typically a team member who is very interested in and familiar with the lesson. This team member/owner will serve as a contact point for anyone needing information (expertise, contacts, templates, etc.) relating to the lesson. This person often reports lessons learned to larger audiences within their organization that would benefit from the collective wisdom.

Not only is there a contact person but also lessons learned need to be documented and archived in a manner that makes them accessible to and usable by others. Many organizations have created **lessons learned repositories** that store historical information. These repositories use sophisticated search engines that permit others to quickly sort through and access lessons specific to their needs. Failure to do so will produce a system that is undervalued and underutilized.

14.4 Project Audits: The Big Picture

LO 14-5

Assess level of project management maturity.

Project audits and/or retrospectives can yield valuable lessons and recommendations that team members can apply to future project work. When done on a consistent basis, they can lead to significant improvements in the processes and techniques that organizations use to complete projects. A more encompassing look from an

FIGURE 14.2
Project Management Maturity Model

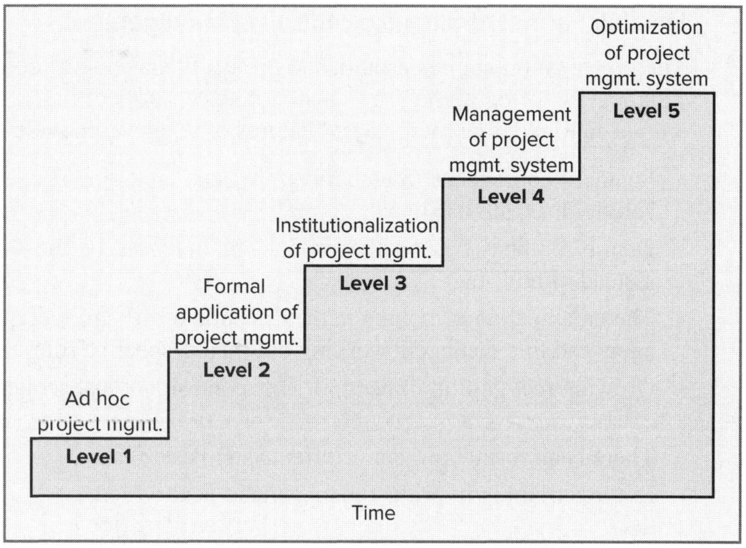

organization-wide point of view is to use a **project maturity model.** The purposes of all maturity models (and there are many available) are to enable organizations to assess their progress in implementing the best practices in their industry and move to improvement. It is important to understand that the model does not ensure success; it only serves as a measuring stick and an indicator of progress.

The term *maturity model* was coined in the late 1980s from a research study by the U.S. government and the Software Engineering Institute (SEI) at Carnegie Mellon University. The government wanted a tool to predict successful software development by contractors. The eventual outcome of this research was the Capability Maturity Model Integration (CMMI). The model focuses on guiding and assessing organizations in implementing concrete best practices in managing software development projects. Since its development, different project maturity models have emerged across industries.

In January 2004, after eight years of development, the Project Management Institute rolled out its second version of the Organizational Project Maturity Model. The latest version is called *OPM3*™. Typically these models are divided into a continuum of growth levels: Initial, Repeatable, Defined, Managed, and Optimized. Figure 14.2 presents one version that borrows liberally from other models, focusing less on a process and more on the state an organization has evolved to in managing projects.

Level 1: Ad Hoc Project Management

No consistent project management process is in place. How a project is managed depends upon the individuals involved. Characteristics of this level include

- No formal project selection system exists—projects are done because people decide to do them or because a high-ranking manager orders them done.
- How any one project is managed varies by individual—unpredictability.
- No investment in project management training is made.
- Working on projects is a struggle because it goes against the grain of established policies and procedures.

Level 2: Formal Application of Project Management

The organization applies established project management procedures and techniques. This level is often marked by tension between project managers and line managers, who need to redefine their roles. Features of this level include

- Standard approaches to managing projects, including scope statements, WBS, and activity lists, are used.
- Quality emphasis is on the product or outcome of the project and is inspected instead of built-in.
- The organization is moving in the direction of the stronger matrix with project managers and line managers working out their respective roles.
- Growing recognition of need for cost control, not just scope and time management, exists.
- There is no formal project priority system established.
- Limited training in project management is provided.

Level 3: Institutionalization of Project Management

An organization-wide project management system, tailored to specific needs of the organization with the flexibility to adapt the process to unique characteristics of the project, is established. Characteristics of this level include

- An established process for managing projects is evident by planning templates, status report systems, and checklists for each stage of the project life cycle.
- Formal criteria are used to select projects.
- Project management is integrated with quality management and concurrent engineering.
- Project teams try to build in quality, not simply inspect it.
- The organization is moving toward a team-based reward system to recognize project execution.
- Risk assessment derived from WBS and technical analyses and customer input is in place.
- The organization offers expanded training in project management.
- Time-phased budgets are used to measure and monitor performance based on earned value analysis.
- A specific change control system for requirements, cost, and schedule is developed for each project, and a work authorization system is in place.
- Project audits tend to be performed only when a project fails.

Level 4: Management of Project Management System

The organization develops a system for managing multiple projects that are aligned with the strategic goals of the organization. Characteristics of this level include

- Portfolio project management is practiced; projects are selected based on resource capacity and contribution to strategic goals.
- A project priority system is established.
- Project work is integrated with ongoing operations.
- Quality improvement initiatives are designed to improve both the quality of the project management process and the quality of specific products and services.

- Benchmarking is used to identify opportunities for improvement.
- The organization has established a project management office or center for excellence.
- Project audits are performed on all significant projects; lessons learned are recorded and used on subsequent projects.
- An integrative information system is established for tracking resource usage and performance of all significant projects.

Level 5: Optimization of Project Management System

The focus is on continuous improvement through incremental advancements of existing practices and by innovations using new technologies and methods. Features include

- A project management information system is fine-tuned; specific and aggregate information is provided to different stakeholders.
- An informal culture that values improvement drives the organization, not policies and procedures.
- There is greater flexibility in tailoring the project management process to the demands of a specific project.

A major theme of this book is that the culture of the organization has a profound impact on how project management methodology operates. Audits and performance evaluations require informed judgment. Good decision making depends not only on the accuracy of the information but also on the right information. For example, imagine how much different your response could be if you made an honest mistake but did not trust management and felt insecure versus if you had confidence and trust in management. Or think how different the quality of the information that would surface from a team would be where trust was divided versus a team that works in a Level 5 environment.

Progress from one level to the next will not occur overnight. The Software Engineering Institute estimates the following median times for movement:

Maturity level 1 to 2 is 22 months.

Maturity level 2 to 3 is 19 months.

Maturity level 3 to 4 is 25 months.

Maturity level 4 to 5 is 13 months.

Why does it take so long? One reason is simply organizational inertia. It is difficult for social organizations to institute significant changes while maintaining business efficacy: "How do we find time to change when we are so busy just keeping our heads above water?"

A second significant reason is that one cannot leapfrog past any one level. Just as children cannot avoid the trials and tribulations of being teenagers by adopting all the lessons learned by their parents, people within the organization have to work through the unique challenges and problems of each level to get to the next level. Learning of this magnitude naturally takes time and cannot be avoided by using quick fixes or simple remedies. See Snapshot from Practice 14.4: 2015 PMO of the Year for how a PMO improved the maturity of project management operations at a large credit union.

SNAPSHOT FROM PRACTICE 14.4 2015 PMO of the Year: Navy Federal Credit Union*

Like many financial institutions, the Navy Federal Credit Union struggled with adapting IT technologies to better serve their over 5 million members. Navy Federal had no clear method of prioritizing projects. Project execution processes were ad hoc. Delivery metrics weren't being tracked. Doomed projects lingered, with no one willing to hit the kill button.

In 2010 things began to change. Navy Federal began developing a team of project professionals who could advocate a standardized project delivery system as well as strategic alignment practices. In 2014 the IT Department opened its project management office (PMO). The office was not greeted with open arms. The team had to work hard to avoid the perception that it was a document engine or needless bureaucracy.

"Throughout our journey, we've certainly faced challenges in terms of buy-in and acceptance of project management," says Kristin Earley, PMP, assistant vice president of the PMO. "We started with small wins. We had to highlight the demonstrated value that we brought in terms of consistent, repeatable delivery of projects."

The impact has been significant. The percentage of projects that closed according to plan jumped from 55 percent in 2014 to 88 percent in 2015. The PMO is now considered an integral part of how Navy Federal does business and was recognized by the Project Management Institute as 2015 PMO of the year.

While the initial push was to standardize project management processes, the PMO realized that not all projects are alike and some may benefit from less traditional methods.

"The PMO started with a one-size-fits-all approach to project delivery. We realized this really wasn't the most effective way to work with our business partners to deliver value frequently throughout the project life cycle," Earley says. "We've tailored our delivery practices to introduce both agile and incremental delivery practices, and that's helped us improve our delivery within the portfolio."

*J. Gantz, "Mission Accomplished," *PM Network*, December 2015, pp. 30–37.

14.5 Post-implementation Evaluation

LO 14-6

Provide useful advice for conducting team performance reviews.

The purpose of **project evaluation** is to assess how well the project team, team members, and project manager performed.

Team Evaluation

Evaluation of performance is essential to encourage changes in behavior and to support individual career development. *Evaluation* implies measurement against specific criteria. Experience corroborates that before the commencement of a project, the stage must be set so expectations, standards, supportive organizational culture, and constraints are in place; if not, the effectiveness of the evaluation process will suffer.

Evaluation of project team performance tends to be based on achieving project objectives according to time, cost, and specifications (scope). It has become more common to add customer/end user satisfaction to the assessment. After all, many argue that the most important indicator of project success is customer satisfaction.

Less common is assessing how well the team worked together and with others. Remember, projects are socio-technical endeavors, and the human dimension should be evaluated along with the technical dimension. Take, for example, a project that was a technical success but emotions and tempers flared toward the end, leaving people swearing they would never work with each other again. Or consider a successful project in which over half of the team was so burned out by the long hours and stress they eventually left the company. Another alternative is an unsuccessful project on which,

TABLE 14.2
Sample Team Evaluation and Feedback Survey

Using the scale below, assess each statement.	Disagree				Agree
1. The team shared a sense of common purpose, and each member was willing to work toward achieving project objectives.	1	2	3	4	5
2. Respect was shown for other points of view. Differences of opinion were encouraged and freely expressed.	1	2	3	4	5
3. All interactions among team members occurred in a comfortable, supportive atmosphere.	1	2	3	4	5

on closer examination, the team should be applauded for achieving what they did, given the hurdles they faced. Important knowledge can be obtained by looking at the underlying behavioral dynamics of a project.

In practice, the **team evaluation** process takes many forms—especially when evaluation goes beyond time, budget, and specifications. The typical mechanism for evaluating teams is a survey administered by a consultant, a staff member from the Human Resources Department, or email. The survey is normally restricted to team members, but in some cases, other project stakeholders interacting with the team are included in the survey. An example of a partial survey is found in Table 14.2. After the results are tabulated, the team meets with the facilitator and/or senior management, and the results are reviewed.

This session is comparable to the team-building sessions described in Chapter 11, except that the focus is on using the survey results to assess the development of the team, its strengths and weaknesses, and the lessons that can be applied to future project work. The results of team evaluation surveys are helpful in changing behavior to better support team communication, the team approach, and the continuous improvement of team performance.

LO 14-7

Provide useful advice for conducting performance reviews of project members.

Individual, Team Member, and Project Manager Performance Reviews

Organizations vary in the extent to which their project managers are actively involved in the appraisal process of team members. In organizations where projects are managed within a functional organization, the team member's area manager, not the project manager, is responsible for assessing performance. The area manager may solicit the project manager's opinion of the individual's performance on a specific project; this will be factored into the individual's overall performance. In a balanced matrix, the project manager and the area manager jointly evaluate an individual's performance. In project matrix and project organizations in which the lion's share of the individual's work is project related, the project manager is responsible for appraising individual performance. One process that appears to be gaining wider acceptance is the multi-rater appraisal, or "360-degree feedback," which involves soliciting feedback concerning team members' performance from all the people their work affects. This would include not only project and area managers but also peers, subordinates, and even customers. See Snapshot from Practice 14.5: The 360-Degree Feedback.

Performance appraisals generally fulfill two important functions. The first is developmental: the focus is on identifying individual strengths and weaknesses and developing action plans for improving performance. The second is evaluative and involves assessing how well a person has performed in order to determine salary or merit adjustments. These two functions are not compatible. Employees, in their eagerness to find out how much pay they will receive, tend to tune out constructive feedback

SNAPSHOT FROM PRACTICE 14.5 The 360-Degree Feedback*

More and more companies are discarding the traditional superior-subordinate performance feedback process and replacing it with 360-degree feedback systems. The 360-degree feedback approach gathers behavioral observations from many sources within the organization and includes employee self-assessment. The individual completes the same structured evaluation process that superiors, project team members, peers, and in many cases external customers use to evaluate a performance. Survey questionnaires, augmented by a few open-ended questions, are typically used to gather information.

Summary results are compared against organizational strategies, values, and business objectives. The feedback is communicated to the individual with the assistance of the company's Human Resources Department or an outside consultant. The technique is used by a growing number of firms, including General Electric, AT&T, Mobil Oil, Nabisco, Hewlett Packard, and Warner-Lambert.

The objective of the 360-degree process is to identify areas for individual improvement. When anonymous feedback solicited from others is compared with the individual's self-evaluations, the individual may form a more realistic picture of his/her strengths and weaknesses. This may prompt behavioral change if the weaknesses identified were previously unknown to the individual. So, for example, a project manager who thinks s/he delegates work effectively finds out that subordinates disagree. This causes him/her to rethink how s/he delegates and to decide to delegate more and sooner.

Many firms obtain feedback from internal and external project customers. For example, a client may evaluate a project manager or member of the project team according to how effectively the individual gets things done without creating unnecessary adversarial relationships. Incorporating customer feedback in the evaluation process underscores collaboration and the importance of client expectations in determining project success.

*B. O'Reilly, "360 Feedback Can Change Your Life," *Fortune*, October 17, 1994, pp. 93–100; R. Hoffman, "Ten Reasons You Should Be Using 360 Degree Feedback," *HR Magazine*, April 1995, pp. 82–85; D. Cochran, "Finally, a Way to Completely Measure Project Manager Performance," *PM Network*, September 2000, pp. 75–80.

on how they can improve their performance. Likewise, managers tend to be more concerned with justifying their decision than engaging in a meaningful discussion on how employees can improve their performance. It is difficult to be both a coach and a judge. As a result, several experts on performance appraisal systems recommend that organizations separate **performance reviews,** which focus on individual improvement, from pay reviews, which allocate the distribution of rewards (cf., Latham & Wexley, 1993; Romanoff, 1989).

In some matrix organizations, project managers conduct the performance reviews, while area managers are responsible for pay reviews. In other cases, performance reviews are part of the project closure process, and pay reviews are the primary objective of the annual performance appraisal. Other organizations avoid this dilemma by allocating only group rewards for project work and providing annual awards for individual performance. The remaining discussion is directed at reviews designed to improve performance because pay reviews are often outside the jurisdiction of the project manager.

Individual Reviews

Organizations employ a wide range of methods to review individual performance on a project. In general, review methods of individual performance center on the technical and social skills brought to the project and team. Some organizations rely simply on an informal discussion between the project manager and the project member. Other organizations require project managers to submit written evaluations that describe and assess an individual's performance on a project. Many organizations use rating scales similar to the team evaluation survey in which the project manager rates the individual according to a certain scale (e.g., from 1 to 5) on a number of relevant performance dimensions (e.g., teamwork, customer relations). Some organizations augment these rating schemes with behaviorally anchored descriptions of what constitutes a 1 rating, a 2 rating, and so forth. Each method has its strengths and weaknesses, and, unfortunately, in many organizations, the appraisal systems were designed to support mainstream operations and not unique project work. The bottom line is that project managers have to use as best they can the performance review system mandated by their organization.

Regardless of the method, the project manager needs to meet with each team member and discuss his/her performance. Following are some general tips for conducting performance reviews.

- Always begin the process by asking the individual to evaluate his/her contributions to the project. First, this approach may yield valuable information that you were not aware of. Second, the approach may provide an early warning for situations in which there is disparity in assessments. Finally, this method reduces the judgmental nature of the discussion.
- Avoid, when possible, drawing comparisons with other team members; rather, assess the individual in terms of established standards and expectations. Comparisons tend to undermine cohesion and divert attention away from what the individual needs to do to improve performance.
- When you have to be critical, focus the criticism on specific examples of behavior rather than on the individual personally. Describe in specific terms how the behavior affected the project.
- Be consistent and fair in your treatment of all team members. Nothing breeds resentment more than if, through the grapevine, individuals feel they are being held to a different standard than are other project members.
- Treat the review as only one point in an ongoing process. Use it to reach an agreement on how the individual can improve his/her performance.

Both managers and subordinates may dread a formal performance review. Neither side feels comfortable with the evaluative nature of the discussion and the potential for misunderstanding and hurt feelings. Much of this anxiety can be alleviated if the project manager is doing his/her job well. Project managers should constantly give team members feedback throughout the project so that individuals can have a pretty good idea of how well they have performed and how the manager feels before the formal meeting. Post-project angst can be avoided if pre-project expectations are discussed before the project and regularly reinforced during project performance.

While in many cases, the same process that is applied to reviewing the performance of team members is applied to evaluating the project manager, many organizations augment this process, given the importance of the position to their organization. This is where conducting the **360-degree review** is becoming more popular. In project-driven organizations, the project office typically is responsible for collecting information on a specific project manager from customers, vendors, team members, peers, and other managers. This approach has tremendous promise for developing more effective project managers.

In addition to performance reviews, data are collected for project retrospectives, which can present situations that may influence performance. In these situations, performance evaluations should recognize and note the unusual situation.

Summary

The goals of project closure are to complete the project and to improve performance in future projects. Implementing closure and review has three major deliverables: wrap-up, audit, and performance evaluation. Wrap-up activities put the project "to bed" and include completing the final project deliverable, closing accounts, finding new opportunities for project staff, closing facilities, and creating the final report. Project audits assess the overall success of the project. Retrospectives are used to identify lessons learned and improve future performance. Individual and team evaluations assess performance and opportunities for improvement. A project should not be considered done until all three activities have been completed. The culture of the organization and the project team will play a major factor in the efficacy of these activities.

Key Terms

Facilitators, *613*
Lessons learned, *612*
Lessons learned repository, *614*
Performance review, *620*
Project closure, *602*
Project evaluation, *618*
Project maturity model, *615*
Retrospective, *612*
360-degree review, *621*
Team evaluation, *619*

Review Questions

1. How does the project closure review differ from the performance measurement control system discussed in Chapter 13?
2. What major information would you expect to find in a project audit?
3. Why is it difficult to perform a truly independent, objective review?
4. Comment on the following statement: "We cannot afford to terminate the project now. We have already spent more than 50 percent of the project budget."
5. Why should an organization be interested in knowing what level they are at in the project maturity model?
6. Why should you separate performance reviews from pay reviews? How do you do this?
7. Advocates of retrospective methodology claim there are distinguishing characteristics that increase its value over past lessons learned methods. What are they? How does each characteristic enhance project closure and review?

SNAPSHOT FROM PRACTICE

Discussion Questions

14.1 *The Wake*

1. What was Sally able to achieve by holding a wake for the canceled project?

14.2 *New Ball Goes Flat in the NBA*

1. How did the culture of the NBA affect this project?
2. What could the NBA have done differently to increase the likelihood of success?

14.3 *Operation Eagle Claw*

1. Assume you are to command a similar mission. What are two things you would insist on, based on what you learned about Eagle Claw?

14.4 *2015 PMO of the Year: Navy Federal Credit Union*

1. How did the project management system evolve at Navy Federal Credit Union?

14.5 *The 360-Degree Feedback*

1. Have you been the subject of a 360-degree review or participated in one? What was it like? How useful was it?
2. What effect do you think 360-degree reviews have on the culture of an organization?

Exercises

1. Consider a course that you recently completed. Perform a review of the course (the course represents a project and the course syllabus represents the project plan).
2. Imagine you are conducting a review of the International Space Station project. Research press coverage and the Internet to collect information on the current status of the project. What are the successes and failures to date? What forecasts would you make about the completion of the project and why? What recommendations would you make to top management of the program and why?
3. Interview a project manager who works for an organization that implements multiple projects. Ask the manager what kind of closure procedures are used to complete a project and whether lessons learned are used.
4. What are some of the lessons learned from a recent project in your organization? Was a retrospective done? What action plans were generated to improve processes as a result of the project?

References

"Annual Survey of Business Improvement Architects," *PM Network,* April 2007, p. 18.

Alvarez, J. F. A., A. Pustina, and M. Hallgren, "Escalating Commitment in the Death Zone: New Insights from the 1996 Mount Everest Disaster," *International Journal of Project Management,* vol. 29, no. 8 (December 2011), pp. 971–85.

Cooke-Davies, T., "Project Management Closeout Management: More Than Simply Saying Good Bye and Moving On," in J. Knutson (ed.), *Project Management for Business Professionals* (Indianapolis, IN: John Wiley and Sons, 2001), pp. 200–14.

Fretty, P., "Why Do Projects Really Fail?" *PM Network,* March 2006, pp. 45–48.

Gobeli, D., and E. W. Larson, "Barriers Affecting Project Success," in *1986 Proceedings Project Management Institute: Measuring Success* (Upper Darby, PA: Project Management Institute, 1986), pp. 22–29.

Kerth, N. L., *Project Retrospectives: A Handbook for Team Reviews* (New York: Dorset House, 2001).

Kwak, Y. H., and C. W. Ibbs, "Calculating Project Management's Return on Investment," *Project Management Journal,* vol. 31, no. 2 (March 2000), pp. 38–47.

Ladika, S., "By Focusing on Lessons Learned, Project Managers Can Avoid Repeating the Same Old Mistakes," *PM Network,* February 2008, pp. 75–77.

Latham, G. P., and K. N. Wexley, *Increasing Productivity through Performance Appraisal,* 2nd ed. (Reading, MA: Addison-Wesley, 1993).

Lavell, D., and R. Martinelli, "Program and Project Retrospectives: An Introduction," *PM World Today,* January 2008, p. 1.

Marlin, M., "Implementing an Effective Lessons Learned Process in a Global Project Environment," *PM World Today,* November 2008, pp. 1–6.

Nelson, R. R., "Project Retrospectives: Evaluating Project Success, Failure, and Everything in Between," *MIS Quarterly Executive,* vol. 4, no. 3 (September 2005), p. 372.

Pippett, D. D., and J. F. Peters, "Team Building and Project Management: How Are We Doing?" *Project Management Journal,* vol. 26, no. 4 (December 1995), pp. 29–37.

Project Management Institute, *Organizational Project Management Maturity Model (OPM3),* 3rd ed. (Newtown Square, PA: Project Management Institute, 2013).

Project Management Institute, *Project Management Body of Knowledge (PMBOK),* 6th ed. (Newtown Square, PA: Project Management Institute, 2017).

Romanoff, T. K., "The Ten Commandments of Performance Management," *Personnel,* vol. 66, no. 1 (1989), pp. 24–26.

Royer, I., "Why Bad Projects Are So Hard to Kill," *Harvard Business Review,*

February 2003, pp. 49–56.

Senge, P., *The Fifth Discipline: The Art and Practice of the Learning Organization* (New York: Doubleday, 1990).

Sheperd, D. A., H. Patzelt, and M. Wolfe, "Moving Forward from Project Failure: Negative Emotions, Affective Commitment, and Learning from the Experience," *Academy of Management Journal,* vol. 54, no. 6 (December 2011), pp. 1229–59.

Sleesman, D. J., D. E. Conlon, G. McNamara, and J. E. Miles, "Cleaning Up the Big Muddy: A Meta-Analytic Review of the Determinants of Escalation of Commitment," *Academy of Management Journal,* vol. 55, no. 6 (2012), pp. 541–62.

Staw, B. M., "Knee-deep in the Big Muddy: A Study of Escalating Commitment to a Chosen Course of Action," *Organizational Behavior and Human Performance,* vol. 16, no. 1 (1976), pp. 27–44.

Staw, B. M., "The Escalation of Commitment to a Course of Action," *The Academy of Management Review,* vol. 6, no. 4 (October 1981), pp. 577–87.

Staw, B. M., "The Escalation of Commitment: An Update and Appraisal," in Z. Shapira (ed.), *Organizational Decision Making* (MA: Cambridge University Press, 1997), pp. 191–215.

Staw, B. M., and J. Ross, "Knowing When to Pull the Plug," *Harvard Business Review,* March 1987, pp. 68–74.

Wheatly, M., "Over the Bar," *PM Network,* January 2003, pp. 40–45.

Woods, J. A., T. Dalziel, and S. L. Barton, "Escalation of Commitment in Private Business: The Influence of Outside Board Members," *Journal of Family Business Strategy,* vol. 3, no. 1 (2012), pp. 18–27.

Yates, J. K., and S. Aniftos, "ISO 9000 Series of Quality Standards and the E/C Industry," *Project Management Journal,*
vol. 28, no. 2 (June 1997), pp. 21–31.

Zaitz, L., "Rail Car Deal Snags Tri Met for Millions," *Oregonian,* December 14, 2008, p. 1, and January 7, 2009, p. D4.

Case 14.1

Halo for Heroes II

You are a member of a project management practicum class. The major assignment for this class is to plan and implement a fund-raising project that will raise at least $1,500 and provide an opportunity to practice project management. You have joined a group of six students who have decided to organize an event based on the popular *Halo* video game. Your professor tells your group that they are in luck because another group did a similar project last year. He hands you a copy of their post-project audit.

Review the document and answer the following questions:

1. What are the two or three most valuable lessons you learned from this report and why?
2. What are one or two important questions/issues that are missing from their report that you wish were addressed? Explain why this information would be useful.
3. Briefly discuss the value of project audits based on this example. Imagine what it would be like if you did not have the audit.

Project Halo Audit

Objective: To raise at least $1,000 for the National Military Families Association by conducting a Halo video game tournament in Kleinsorge Hall on November 16 and 17.

Operation

See tournament information (below) for a detailed description on how the tournament was managed.

Risk Management

Through risk assessment, we were able to identify and mitigate potential risks to the project. We were concerned with technical difficulties in setting up the gaming operations in the different classrooms. We did a trial run three days before the tournament in one of the classrooms to work out the mechanics of connecting consoles to the audio/video equipment in the room. This made setting up things on the first day of the tournament much easier. One surprise was that a few players failed to show up at designated times and we wished we had their cell phone numbers to contact them.

Outcomes

Our final contestant count was marked at 100 contestants, for a total of $1,000 in ticket sales. In addition, we received some cash donations from private sponsors, donated color fliers and equipment rental, 12 cases of Mountain Dew from Pepsi, and several smaller incentives from local businesses. The total valuation of all ticket sales and donated items was $3,113.43. We were unable to locate a business willing to sponsor any large prizes; therefore, we had to purchase these out of our cash proceeds. After the purchase of all prizes and repayment of $500.00 to Prof. X for our seed money, our final net proceeds were $720.00. Despite not reaching our financial goal, the participants enjoyed the experience and we learned a lot about managing a project.

Lessons Learned

Don't advertise specific prizes until you have obtained them. We assumed we could get a local retailer to donate the grand prize (Xbox 360) but ultimately we had to pay for it ourselves.

A multimedia marketing campaign is needed to reach the target audience. We utilized several different strategies to reach our target market, including a dedicated website and PayPal signup, a donation drive web page extended on this site, physical kiosk signups, the development and distribution of 2,500 color fliers, a

MySpace page, a Facebook page, and an announcement on the College of Business website. We actually had contestants from as far away as Portland and Eugene.

Do a walk-through at least one day before the tournament.

Take time out to focus on the team. Team-building exercises we did in class, like "My group as a car," helped us resolve interpersonal issues before they became serious.

Many of us felt the grand prize was a deterrent, with many prospective players opting out because they did not feel they were good enough at playing Halo to compete for such a lofty prize. In retrospect, we felt we could have done just as well by using donated prizes, like tickets for the local movie theaters and gift cards.

Next time we would set up a loser's bracket so that players would have a chance to play against others with comparable ability and win prizes.

You need luck or personal contacts to secure big sponsorships. We had neither. However, we were surprised at how willing local businesses were to donate small prizes to the project.

Take advantage of the contacts you have on your team. Despite our extensive marketing campaign, roughly half of the participants were friends of ours. Your team's social network provides both opportunities and limitations. For example, we had no active members in the Greek community on campus to organize a competition across houses.

Tournament Information

Welcome to the Halo for Heroes Tournament!

By entering this tournament, you agree to the following rules and guidelines.

Important!

This tournament is open to the public and we encourage open competition between all skill levels.

The entire tournament will be played on projected screens in dark rooms. You are more than welcome to bring your own controller to use during the tournament.

You will be able to make your custom profile on our system prior to playing, but we are unable to allow any outside memory to be loaded onto the systems due to time constraints and the "allow one to do it, allow all to do it" problem.

We hope you will have fun, and thanks for supporting Halo for Heroes and the National Military Families Association, Inc.

Reservations

This tournament is by online reservation only on our website, halo4heroes.110mb.com.

Space is limited. If you are unable to register and purchase a ticket online, please contact us. Once you have registered, an event manager will contact you by the e-mail address you provide upon registration within 24 hours. You will be e-mailed a ticket confirmation with an assigned play time, which you will need to enter the tournament. Please keep this, as it has important tournament information. If you are unable to play during the assigned time, please contact us immediately.

Arrival

Show up early! All players who enter the tournament must be ready to play by their respective times as noted on their ticket confirmation. Please arrive at least 15 minutes prior to the scheduled match time to check-in. All players will need to check in at the front lobby of Kleinsorge Hall. All players who are late will forfeit their chance of participating in the tournament. We cannot guarantee parking around campus, so please take ample time to arrive at the event on time. (See the vicinity map.)

Tournament Sequence

All tournament rounds will consist of three matches played on Halo 3® among four individual players. Game style will be "Free for All Slayer" with 25 kills to win the match with a 10-minute time limit per match. All other game rules and options will be Halo 3® default settings. The player with the highest cumulative kill count of all the matches will advance to the next round. All the others will be eliminated from the tournament play.

Round 1 will be conducted on Friday, November 16, and Rounds 2 and 3 will be conducted on Saturday, November 17. All play will be on projection screens. In order to judge the tournament, after a match is over the event managers will need to record the scores. For this reason, please be patient and wait until the event manager gives the okay to proceed with the next game. Below is a map schedule so you can begin practicing.

Halo 3® Map Schedule

Round 1	Round 2	Round 3
Last Resort	Guardian	The Pit
High Ground	Epitaph	Narrows
Snowbound	Isolation	Last Resort

In the event that there is a tie, players will immediately play a single tie-breaking match. "Free for All Slayer" with five kills to win the tie-breaker with a five-minute time limit. The map for the tie-breaker will be "Construct."

Non-Tournament Play

All players who did not receive a position in the tournament can still play! There will be an area set up for non-tournament play. There is a $3.00 charge for all entrants into non-tournament play.

Under-Age Players

Players under the age of 17 must be accompanied by a parent or guardian. The parent or guardian must also sign a Parental Release Authorization and bring it with the child to the event. Any unaccompanied persons who are underage will not be allowed to participate in the tournament.

General Rules

1. Do not damage any hardware and equipment. If you break it, you just bought it.
2. Conduct yourself in a respectful and supportive manner.
3. Unacceptable behavior will result in disqualification.
4. All disputes will be settled by the operators of the event.

Audience

If you have been eliminated and would like to stay and watch the tournament, you are welcome to do so. Family members and friends of contestants are also welcome to attend as an audience. We ask that all audience members be supportive and respectful of all contestants. We reserve the right to dismiss disruptive audience members from the premises.

Prizes and Raffles

The winner of the tournament will receive an Xbox 360. Other finalists will receive various prizes, including games, controllers, and gift certificates. All participants can participate in the event raffles that will be held at the event. Contributions to enter the raffles and the potential prizes will be disclosed at the event.

Refunds

This tournament is to benefit the American Military Families Association, Inc. There will be no refunds under any circumstances. Any dispute must be brought to the attention of the event managers for a decision.

Contact Us

If you have any questions or concerns, contact one of the operators of the event or e-mail us at halo4heroes@hotmail.com. If you need to speak to someone immediately, please call 503-xxx-xxxx.

Thank you for your cooperation, have fun, and good luck!—Halo for Heroes

Case 14.2

Maximum Megahertz Project

Olaf Gundersen, the CEO of Wireless Telecom Company, is in a quandary. Last year he accepted the Maximum Megahertz project suggested by six up-and-coming young R&D corporate stars. Although Olaf did not truly understand the technical importance of the project, the creators of the project needed only $600,000, so it seemed like a good risk. Now the group is asking for $800,000 and a six-month extension on a project that is already four months behind. However, the team feels confident they can turn things around. The project manager and project team feel that if they hang in there a little longer they will be able to overcome the roadblocks they are encountering—especially those that reduce power, increase speed, and use a new technology battery. Other managers familiar with the project hint that the power pack problem might be solved but "the battery problem will never be solved." Olaf believes he is locked into this project; his gut feeling tells him the project will never materialize and he should get out. John, his human resource manager, suggested bringing in a consultant to axe the project.

Olaf decided to call his friend Dawn O'Connor, the CEO of an accounting software company. He asked her, "What do you do when project costs and deadlines escalate drastically? How do you handle doubtful projects?" Her response was "Let another project manager look at the project. Ask, 'If you took over this project tomorrow, could you achieve the required results, given the extended time and additional money?' If the answer is no, I call my top management team together and have them review the doubtful project in relation to other projects in our project portfolio." Olaf feels this is good advice.

Unfortunately, the Maximum Megahertz project is not an isolated example. Over the last five years, there have been three projects that were never completed. "We just seemed to pour more money into them, even though we had a pretty good idea the projects were dying. The cost of those projects was high; those resources could have been better used on other projects." Olaf wonders, "Do we ever learn from our mistakes? How can we develop a process that catches errant projects early? More importantly, how do we ease a project manager and team off an errant project without embarrassment?" Olaf certainly does not want to lose the six bright stars on the Maximum Megahertz project.

Olaf is contemplating how his growing telecommunications company should deal with the problem of identifying projects that should be terminated early, how to allow good managers to make mistakes without public embarrassment, and how they all can learn from their mistakes.

Give Olaf a plan of action for the future that attacks the problem. Be specific and provide examples that relate to Wireless Telecom Company.

Case 14.3

Project Closure of L&T-IBM Semiconductor

The collaboration between L&T Semiconductor Technologies Ltd. (LTSCT) and IBM marks a significant milestone in India's journey toward self-reliance in advanced semiconductor technologies. With global industries becoming increasingly dependent on connected devices, IoT, and electric vehicles, the demand for high-performance, energy-efficient processors has surged. In response, LTSCT and IBM embarked on an ambitious partnership to develop processors tailored for critical sectors such as automotive, renewable energy, and industrial automation. This initiative not only aimed to reduce India's dependence on imported semiconductors but also to strengthen its presence in the global semiconductor landscape.

Upon project completion, LTSCT and IBM successfully delivered the initiative within the planned three-year timeline. Despite facing technical and operational hurdles, the project achieved its key objectives, paving the way for future advancements in India's semiconductor industry.

TABLE 14.3
Final Outcomes vs. Initial Objectives

Objective	Outcome	Achievement Status
Develop processors with 20% improved energy efficiency and 30% higher performance.	Delivered processors with 22% energy efficiency improvement and 31% enhanced performance.	Exceeded expectations
Integrate AI for real-time decision-making and predictive analysis.	Successfully embedded AI capabilities, enabling real-time monitoring and decision-making in processors.	Achieved
Achieve a 15–20% reduction in manufacturing costs.	Achieved a 15% reduction by optimizing fabrication techniques and leveraging local supply chains.	Met expectations
Scale for multiple applications across automotive, energy, and industrial sectors.	Prototypes tested and deployed successfully across the targeted sectors with high adaptability.	Fully achieved
Incorporate eco-friendly manufacturing practices.	Implemented water recycling systems, renewable energy usage, and sustainable waste management.	Fully achieved

HANDOVER AND OPERATIONALIZATION

Handover Process: Final prototypes and technical documentation were delivered to stakeholders, including automotive and industrial OEMs. A comprehensive training program was conducted for client teams, focusing on the operation, integration, and maintenance of the new processors. A technical support team was established to assist with post-deployment troubleshooting and future scalability.

Operationalization: The processors were deployed across pilot projects in the automotive, energy, and industrial sectors. For example, Advanced Driver Assistance Systems (ADAS) in EVs demonstrated improved safety features, while renewable energy grids saw enhanced efficiency using AI-driven optimization. The project entered its mass production phase, with the new processors integrated into the supply chains of key industries.

REFERENCES

1. Ministry of Electronics and Information Technology (MeitY): Semiconductor Manufacturing Incentive Scheme Guidelines. Available at: https://www.meity.gov.in/
2. National Policy on Electronics, 2019. Available at: https://www.meity.gov.in/npe-2019
3. McKinsey & Company: The Semiconductor Industry's Impact on the Global Economy.
4. Available at: https://www.mckinsey.com/
5. Deloitte Insights: 2023 Semiconductor Industry Outlook. Available at: https://www2.deloitte.com/
6. Inc42: L&T Semiconductor Partners with IBM to Design Processors. Available at: https://inc42.com/
7. IBM Research: Semiconductor Innovations and AI Integration. Available at: http://www.ibm.com/research/"www.ibm.com/research/

Appendix 14.1

Project Closeout Checklist

Below is an example of a closeout checklist used by the state of Virginia.

Project Closeout Transition Checklist

Provide basic information about the project, including the following: Project Title—the proper name used to identify this project; Project Working Title—the working name or acronym that will be used for the project; Proponent Secretary—the secretary to whom the proponent agency is assigned or the secretary that is sponsoring an enterprise project; Proponent Agency—the agency that will be responsible for the management of the project; Prepared by—the person(s) preparing this document; Date/Control Number—the date the checklist is finalized and the change or configuration item control number assigned.

Project Title:	________________	*Project Working Title:*	________________
Proponent Secretary:	________________	*Proponent Agency:*	________________
Prepared by:	________________	*Date/Control Number:*	________________

Complete the Status and Comments columns. In the Status column indicate the following: Yes, if the item has been addressed and completed; No, if the item has not been addressed or is incomplete; N/A, if the item is not applicable to this project. Provide comments or describe the plan to resolve the item in the last column.

	Item	**Status**	**Comments/Plan to Resolve**
1	Have all the product or service deliverables been accepted by the customer?		
1.1	Are there contingencies or conditions related to the acceptance? If so, describe it in the Comments column.		
2	Has the project been evaluated against each performance goal established in the project performance plan?		
3	Has the actual cost of the project been tallied and compared to the approved cost baseline?		
3.1	Have all approved changes to the cost baseline been identified and their impact on the project documented?		
4	Have the actual milestone completion dates been compared to the approved schedule?		
4.1	Have all approved changes to the schedule baseline been identified and their impact on the project documented?		
5	Have all approved changes to the project scope been identified and their impact on the performance, cost, and schedule baselines documented?		

(continued)

	Item	Status	Comments/Plan to Resolve
6	Has operations management formally accepted responsibility for operating and maintaining the product(s) or service(s) delivered by the project?		
6.1	Has the documentation relating to operation and maintenance of the product(s) or service(s) been delivered to, and accepted by, operations management?		
6.2	Has training and knowledge transfer of the operations organization been completed?		
6.3	Does the projected annual cost to operate and maintain the product(s) or service(s) differ from the estimate provided in the project proposal? If so, note and explain the difference in the Comments column.		
7	Have the resources used by the project been transferred to other units within the organization?		
8	Has the project documentation been archived or otherwise disposed of as described in the project plan?		
9	Have the lessons learned been documented in accordance with the Commonwealth Project Management guideline?		
10	Has the date for the post-implementation review been set?		
10.1	Has the person or unit responsible for conducting the post-implementation review been identified?		

Signatures

The signatures of the people below relay an understanding that the key elements within the Closeout Phase section are complete and the project has been formally closed.

Position/Title	Name	Date	Phone Number

Source: www.vita.virginia.gov/projects/cpm/cpmDocs/CPMG-SEC5-Final.pdf.

CHAPTER FIFTEEN

15 Agile Project Management

LEARNING OBJECTIVES

After reading this chapter you should be able to:

15-1 Recognize the conditions in which traditional project management versus Agile Project Management should be used.

15-2 Understand the value of iterative, incremental development for creating new products.

15-3 Identify core Agile principles.

15-4 Understand the basic methodology used in Scrum.

15-5 Understand the basic methodology used by Extreme programming.

15-6 Know how to create and use a Kanban board.

15-7 Recognize the limitations of Agile Project Management.

OUTLINE

15.1 Traditional versus Agile Methods

15.2 Agile PM

15.3 Agile PM in Action: Scrum

15.4 Extreme Programming and Kanban

15.5 Applying Agile PM to Large Projects

15.6 Limitations and Concerns

15.7 Hybrid Project Management

Summary

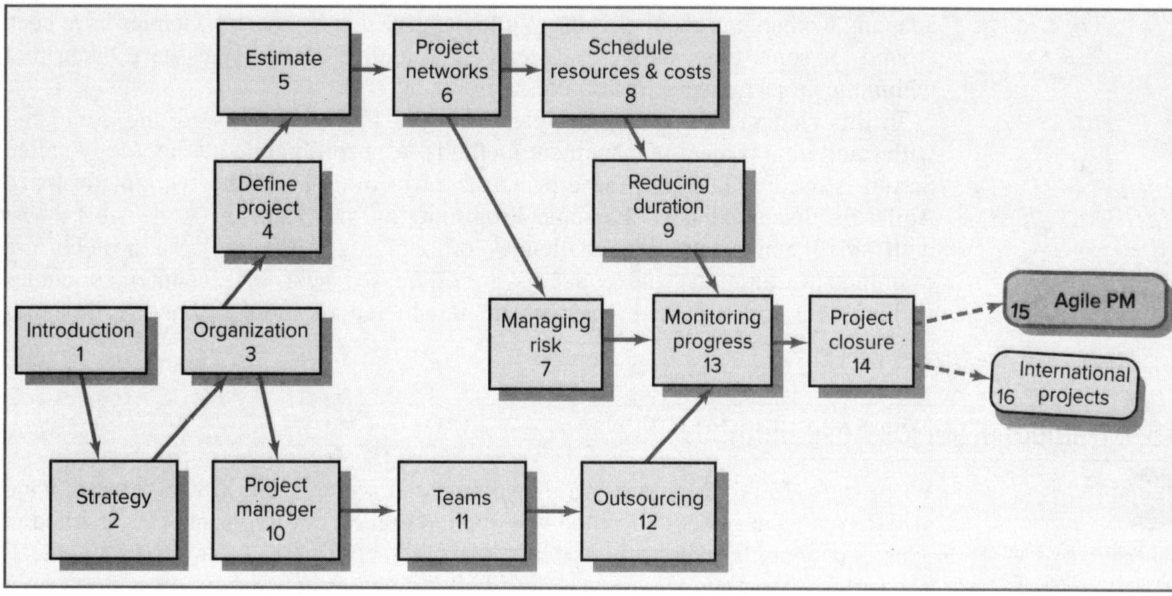

Agile is an attitude, not a technique with boundaries. An attitude has no boundaries, so we wouldn't ask "can I use agile here" but rather "how agile can we be here?"

—Alistair Cockburn, signatory of the Manifesto for Agile Software Development.

As project management entered the new millennium, many professionals recognized that "one size fits all" project management methods did not meet their needs. This was especially true for those working on software and product development projects in which the end product is not well defined and evolves over time. This project environment requires flexibility and the ability to manage changes as more information and learning take place. Enter **Agile Project Management** (Agile PM). Instead of attempting to plan the entire project up front, Agile PM relies on iterative, incremental development cycles to complete projects.

Ken Schwaber uses the analogy of building a house to explain the difference between **iterative, incremental development (IID)** and traditional project management.[1] In the traditional approach, the buyers cannot move into the house until the entire house is completed. The iterative approach would build the house room by room. The plumbing, electrical, and infrastructure would be built for the most important room (e.g., kitchen) first and then extended to each room as it was constructed. Each time a room was completed, the builders and the buyers would assess progress and make adjustments. In some cases, the buyers would realize that they didn't need that extra room they felt they had to have. In other cases, they would add features they didn't realize they needed to have. Ultimately the house would be built to fit the customer's wishes.

Agile PM is ideal for exploratory projects in which requirements need to be discovered and new technology tested. It focuses on active collaboration between the project team and customer representatives, breaking projects into small, functional pieces and

[1] Schwaber, K., *Agile Project Management with Scrum* (Seattle: Microsoft, 2004), p. xviii.

adapting to changing requirements. While iterative development principles have been around for some time, it is only recently that agile methodologies have taken root within the project management profession.

In this chapter, the core principles of Agile PM are discussed and compared with traditional project management methods. A specific agile methodology called Scrum is used to describe these principles in action. Two other variant forms of Agile are discussed next: Extreme Programming and Kanban. Agile works best with small teams, and the challenges of applying Agile to large projects are examined. Limitations and concerns are addressed next. The chapter concludes with a discussion of hybrid arrangements in which both traditional and Agile methods are used.

15.1 Traditional versus Agile Methods

LO 15-1

Recognize the conditions in which traditional project management versus Agile Project Management should be used.

When software products burst on the commercial scene in the 1980s, the traditional plan-driven management approach was applied to their development. This resulted in what is commonly referred to as the "waterfall" approach to software development. The **waterfall method** features a series of logical phases in which progress flows from one phase to the next until completion (see Figure 15.1). The key assumption is that essential requirements can be defined up front so the software can be designed, built, tested, and released. Software projects are completed in a linear, plan-driven fashion, like any other project.

People soon found that software projects were not like other projects and the results proved it. For example, the Standish group reported in 1995 that 31 percent of software projects are canceled each year and only 16 percent are completed on time and budget (The Standish Group International, 1995).

FIGURE 15.1
The Waterfall Approach to Software Development

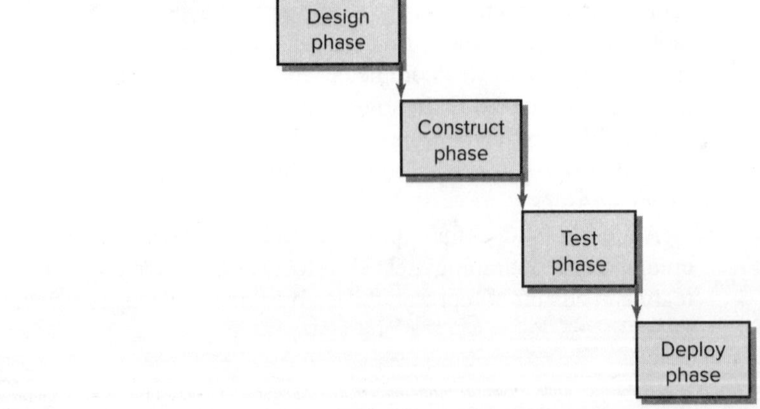

Frustrated by poor results, software engineers began to experiment with more flexible, "agile" approaches to managing software projects. Tensions arose between management who mandated the use of standard templates, and the waterfall method, and the project managers who saw it as a hindrance to their work. A grass roots revolution broke out within the software industry. Several key advocates for change formed the Agile Alliance and published the Agile Manifesto in 2001. The manifesto affirmed a radically different set of values than those being applied by management to projects they were working on:

- Individuals and interactions over processes and tools.
- Working software over comprehensive documentation.
- Customer collaboration over contract negotiation.
- Responding to change over following a plan.

These four values were expanded upon by a set of 12 guiding principles:

1. Our highest priority is to satisfy the customer through early and continuous delivery of valuable software.
2. Welcome changing requirements, even late in development.
3. Deliver working software frequently, from a couple of weeks to a couple of months, with a preference to the shorter timescale.
4. Businesspeople and developers must work together daily throughout the project.
5. Build projects around motivated individuals. Give them the environment and support they need, and trust them to get the job done.
6. The most efficient and effective method of conveying information to and within a development team is face-to-face conversation.
7. Working software is the primary measure of progress.
8. Agile processes promote sustainable development.
9. Continuous attention to technical excellence and good design enhances agility.
10. Simplicity—the art of maximizing the amount of work not done—is essential.
11. The best architectures, requirements, and designs emerge from self-organizing teams.
12. At regular intervals, the team reflects on how to become more effective, then turns and adjusts its behavior accordingly.

The manifesto is a testament for the socio-technical approach to project management. Notice how many of the values and principles relate to the people doing the work. They are a response to an overly controlling, technical approach to software development mandated by the waterfall approach that neither matches the needs of the programmers nor the reality of the work. Furthermore, the manifesto reflects a "mindset," not an elaborate set of tools or procedures. This mindset reflects a culture that values collaboration, trust, embracing change, and customer satisfaction.

To put Agile PM in the proper context, let's revisit the project uncertainty diagram (see Figure 15.2) introduced in Chapter 1. The key point is that traditional project management methods were developed to operate in the predictable zone where the scope is fairly well established and the technology is known. Agile lives in the unpredictable zone. It represents a fundamental shift away from the traditional, plan-driven approach by adopting a more experimental and adaptive approach to managing projects. Projects evolve, rather than are executed. Solutions are discovered, not implemented. Some of the differences between Agile PM and traditional project management are displayed in Table 15.1.

FIGURE 15.2
Project Uncertainty

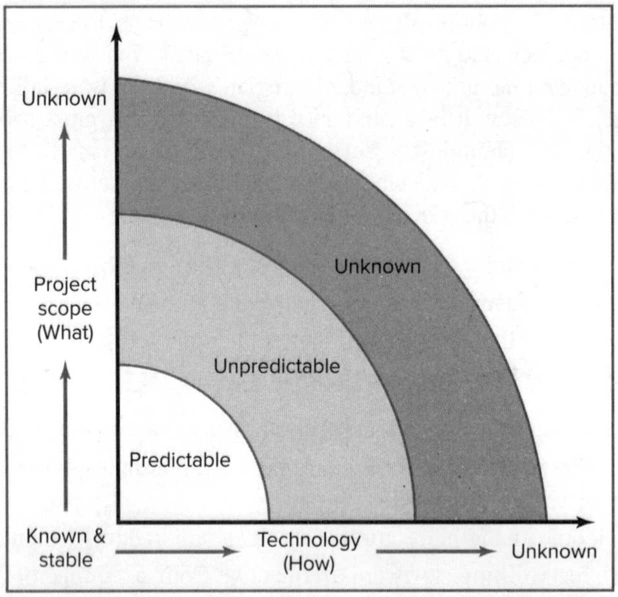

TABLE 15.1
Traditional Project Management versus Agile Project Management

Traditional	Agile
Design up front	Continuous design
Fixed scope	Flexible scope
Deliverables	Features/requirements
Freeze design as early as possible	Freeze design as late as possible
Low uncertainty	High uncertainty
Avoid change	Embrace change
Low customer interaction	High customer interaction
Conventional project teams	Self-organized project teams

15.2 Agile PM

LO 15-2

Understand the value of iterative, incremental development for creating new products.

Fundamentally Agile PM utilizes a rolling wave planning and scheduling project methodology. That is, the final project design is not known in great detail and is continuously developed through a series of incremental iterations over time. Iterations are short time frames ("time boxes") that typically last from one to four weeks. The goal of each iteration is to develop a workable product that satisfies one or more desired product features to demonstrate to the customer and other key stakeholders. At the end of each iteration, stakeholders and customers review progress and re-evaluate priorities to ensure alignment with customer needs and company goals. Adjustments are made and a different iterative cycle begins. Each new iteration subsumes the work of the previous iterations and adds new capabilities to the evolving product (see Figure 15.3) to produce a next, expanded version of the product. See Snapshot from Practice 15.1: IDEO: Masters of Design for an example of iterative development in action.

Iterative development processes provide the following important advantages:

- Continuous integration, verification, and validation of the evolving product.
- Frequent demonstration of progress to increase the likelihood that the end product will satisfy customer needs.
- Early detection of defects and problems.

FIGURE 15.3
Iterative, Incremental Product Development

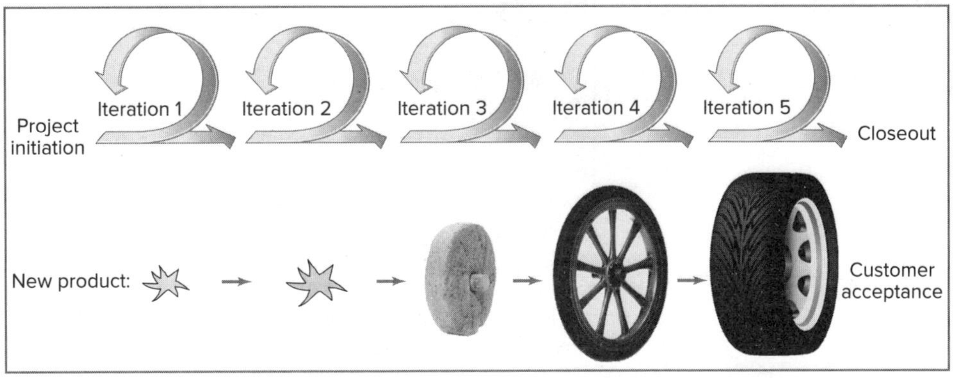

SNAPSHOT FROM PRACTICE 15.1 IDEO: Masters of Design*

IDEO, headquartered in Palo Alto, California, is one of the premier design firms in the world. They are responsible for a wide range of product innovations, including the first Apple mouse, Head's Airflow tennis racket, Zyliss Salad Spinner, and Nokia N-Gage smartphones. IDEO's many clients include Pepsi-Cola, 3M, Logitech, Nike, and HBO. IDEO has won more of the *BusinessWeek/IDSA* Industrial Design Excellence Awards than any other firm.

IDEO's approach to product design relies heavily on an iterative development process in which product prototypes are used to explore and further refine product ideas. CEO Tim Brown states that the goal of prototyping "is to learn about the strengths and weaknesses of the idea and identify new directions that the prototype might take."

For example, IDEO worked with Procter and Gamble to develop a new Crest toothpaste tube. The challenge was to improve the traditional screw-on cap, which always gets gunked up with toothpaste. IDEO's first solution was a pop-on, pop-off cap. However, when designers created rough prototypes and watched people use them, they quickly noticed that users kept trying to unscrew the cap, even though they were told how it worked. The designers concluded that the action was a well-ingrained habit that would probably be impossible to break. So they came up with a hybrid: a twist-off cap that had a short thread but would still be easy to clean.

Focused prototyping resolves critical problems one by one. Brown recommends that prototypes should only take as much time and effort as needed to generate useful feedback and evolve an idea.

Monty Rakusen/Cultura Creative/Alamy Stock Photo

For example, IDEO was working on a chair for Vecta, a high-end office furniture manufacturer. The project had evolved to the point where the height-adjustment lever that tilted with the chair became critical. The team didn't build the whole chair or even the tilt mechanism. They just built the little lever and its interface with the tilt mechanism. It took only a couple of hours. When finished the prototype quickly demonstrated that the principle would work.

"It doesn't matter how clever you are, your first idea about something is never right," Brown says, "so the great value of prototyping—and prototyping quickly and inexpensively—is that you learn about the idea and make it better."

*J. M. Pethokoukis, "The Deans of Design: From the Computer Mouse to the Newest Swiffer, IDEO Is the Firm behind the Scenes," *U.S. News & World Report*, September 24, 2008; T. Brown, "Design Thinking," *Harvard Business Review*, June 2008, pp. 84–95.

Research Highlight 15.1

Product Development Practices That Work*

Alan MacCormack and his colleagues at Harvard Business School conducted a two-year in-depth study of 29 software projects to answer the question "Does evolutionary development, rather than the waterfall model, result in better success?" The waterfall model is the name used in the software industry for the traditional approach to project management in which a process breakdown structure (PBS) is used to first define all the requirements up front and then initiate a design, build, test, and deploy sequence. Conversely, *evolutionary development* is the term used to describe an Agile approach in which customers test early versions of the software, and requirements emerge and are refined after each demonstration.

The results of the study overwhelmingly favored the iterative, Agile approach to software development. Several key practices now associated with Agile Project Management were found to be statistically correlated with the most successful projects:

1. An iterative life cycle with early release of the evolving product to stakeholders for review and feedback.
2. The daily incorporation of new software and rapid feedback on design changes.
3. A flexible product architecture that is both modular and scalable.

MacCormack asserts that uncertainty on software projects dictates short "microprojects"—down to level of features. This is not limited to just software projects but to any new-product endeavor where uncertainty is high and the need for customer feedback and refinement is critical to success.

*A. MacCormack, "Product-Development Practices That Work: How Internet Companies Build Software," *MIT Sloan Management Review*, Vol. 42, no. 2 (2001), pp. 75–84.

There is growing evidence that iterative and evolutionary development is superior to traditional, plan-driven project management when it comes to creating new products. (See Research Highlight 15.1: Product Development Practices That Work.)

It should be noted that Agile PM is not one set method but a family of methods designed to respond to the challenges of unpredictable projects. A few of the more popular ones are listed here:

Scrum	RUP (Rational Unified Process)
Extreme Programming (XP)	Crystal Clear
Agile Modeling	Dynamic Systems Development Method (DSDM)
Lean Development	Rapid Product Development (RPD)

LO 15-3 Identify core Agile principles.

While each of these methods has unique elements and applications, most are based on the following Agile principles:

- **Focus on customer value.** Employ business-driven prioritizations of requirements and features.
- **Iterative and incremental delivery.** Create a flow of value to customers by "chunking" project delivery into small, functioning increments.
- **Experimentation and adaptation.** Test assumptions early and build working prototypes to solicit customer feedback and refine product requirements.
- **Self-organization.** Team members decide among themselves what should be done and who should do it.

- **Servant leadership.** The project manager facilitates rather than directs collaboration.
- **Continuous improvement.** Teams reflect, learn, and adapt to change; work informs the plan.

The Agile methodology known as Scrum will be used to illustrate how these core principles are put into action.

15.3 Agile PM in Action: Scrum

LO 15-4

Understand the basic methodology used in Scrum.

Scrum can be traced back to the work of Hirotaka Takeuchi and Ikujiro Nonaka, who in 1986 described a new holistic approach to developing new products. They were critical of the traditional, relay approach of passing off work from requirements to design to fabricate. Instead, Takeuchi and Nonaka liken new product development to rugby. The scrum metaphor has been expanded and refined into a fairly prescriptive framework that has enjoyed success on high-tech and software development projects (see Snapshot from Practice 15.2: Soul Searching after 9/11).

SNAPSHOT FROM PRACTICE 15.2 Soul Searching after 9/11*

Over 2,792 lives were lost in the collapse of the World Trade Center (WTC) on September 11, 2001. While rescuers labored night and day to recover the bodies, a small team of Michigan software engineers set about salvaging their identities.

New York City hired Gene Codes, an Ann Arbor, Michigan, bioinformatics company, to reinvent the science of DNA mass identification by creating software that would inventory and match the victims' remains and reunite them with their families. They were to do so as soon as possible with no errors. Experts predicted that the violence of the collapse and the intense heat of the fires meant that at best 25 percent of the victims would be identified.

Gene Codes hired William Wake, an independent software coach, to work with their team of eight software engineers on the project. Wake introduced the team to Agile PM. Under Wake's guidance, an environment of intense interaction and communication was created within the programming team by scheduling frequent releases, tempered by constant testing, and feedback from its users. Testing was done before, during, and after the code was written to ensure the same bugs (errors) didn't surface twice.

At the end of each week's iteration, the staff held a retrospective. They listed things that worked well and what needed improvement on fluorescent pink, green, and yellow Post-it® notes, transforming the entire wall into a case of art imitating life. Under "Worked Well," a note said, "Figured out how to use debug form on a wrapped test class." One square under the "Needs Improvement" category merely read, "I'm tired."

Whether out of patriotism or professionalism, the team routinely arrived each day at 7:00 a.m. and worked until midnight. Engineers such as Dave Relyea just wanted to help. "We thought about the victims, the families, and the people at the Office of the Chief Medical Examiner working around the clock. What they were going through made us feel like we could never work hard enough."

The product of their labor was the Mass Fatality Identification System (M-FISys), which contained more than 164,000 lines of code. M-FISys linked all the information in the identification project: 11,641 swab samples from 7,166 family members; 7,681 personal effects (e.g., toothbrushes, hair brushes) and the results of the three types of DNA tests; and nearly 20,000 human remains. The chance of false match was less than 1 in 3.58 million.

In the end, with the help of M-FISys, the New York medical examiner was able to identify 1,521 of the more than 2,792 people who perished in the WTC disaster.

*M. Krause, "Soul Searching," *Bio-IT World.*, www.bio-itworld.com/archive/091103/soul.html. Accessed 3/10/08.

Scrum, like other Agile methods, begins with a high-level scope definition and ballpark time and cost estimates for the project. The scope and cost estimates should be complete enough that management are comfortable with the estimates. The theory is that since requirements evolve over time, detailed up-front planning will be wasted. In place of a product WBS, Scrum uses product *features* as deliverables. A **feature** is defined as a piece of a product that delivers some useful functionality to a customer. In the case of a software project, a feature may be a bank customer being able to change her PIN. In the case of a high-tech product, it may be 5G wireless access. Features are prioritized by their perceived highest value. The project team tackles the highest-priority feasible features first. Priorities are re-evaluated after each iteration. Iterations are called sprints and should last no longer than four weeks. The goal of each sprint is to produce fully functional features. This forces the team to tackle tough decisions early in order to create a workable demonstration.

Specific features are created according to four distinct phases: analysis, design, build, and test (see Figure 15.4). Each feature can be thought of as a mini-project. The first phase is an analysis and review of functional requirements that will be needed to complete the feature. The team commits to meeting these requirements. The second phase is the development of a design that meets the requirements of the feature. The third phase is to build the feature so that it is functional. Finally, the feature is tested and documented. At the end of each sprint, features are demonstrated. Within this sprint framework, Scrum relies on specific roles, meetings, and documents/logs to manage the project.

Roles and Responsibilities

There are three key roles in the scrum process: product owner, development team, and Scrum master.

Product Owner The **product owner** acts on behalf of customers/end users to represent their interests. For commercial development projects, the product owner may be the product manager. For internal projects, the product owner might be the manager of the business group that will benefit from the software. In other cases, the product owner might be a representative of the client organization. They are responsible for

FIGURE 15.4
Scrum Development Process

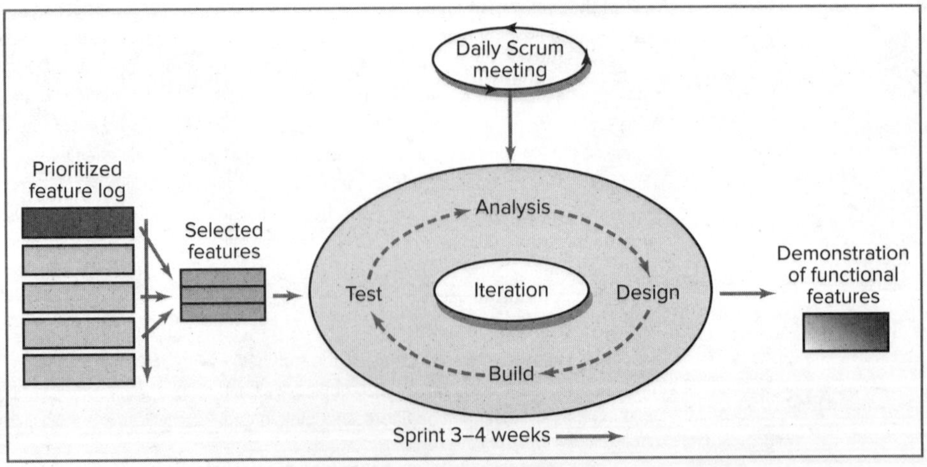

ensuring that the development team focuses their efforts on developing a product that will fulfill the business objective of the project.

The product owner in consultation with others establishes the initial list of product requirements and prioritizes them in the product backlog. Owners often work with the development team to refine features through stories and end user cases (e.g., when the user clicks the F2 key an option drop-down window appears). The product owners negotiate sprint goals and backlog items with the development team. Product owners have the option to change features and priorities at the end of each sprint, if desired. *However, no changes should be made once a sprint has started.* Product owners are the final arbiters on requirements questions and are empowered to accept or reject each product increment. They ultimately decide whether the project is completed. Product owners are the keepers of the product vision and the watchdogs on project cost.

Development Team The team is responsible for delivering the product. A team is typically made up of five to nine people with cross-functional skill sets. There are no designated roles or titles; people take on different responsibilities depending on the nature of the work. The team is a **self-organizing team** in the sense they decide both who does the work and how the work is to be accomplished. Team members should be co-located so that intense face-to-face collaboration occurs. They are responsible for achieving commitments they make at the sprint planning and sprint review meetings.

Scrum Master (Project Manager) The **Scrum master** facilitates the scrum process and resolves impediments at the team and organization levels. The Scrum master is not the leader of the team (the team leads itself!) but acts as a buffer between the team and outside interference. They have no formal authority. Instead, they are responsible for making sure that the scrum process is adhered to. They help the product owner with planning and try to keep the team energized. The Scrum master serves more as a coach than a manager. This servant leadership style empowers the team to complete the project.

Scrum Meetings

Scrum uses a series of coordinated meetings to manage the development process (see Figure 15.5).

Release Planning The purpose of release planning is to establish the goals and general plan for the project. The product owner works with the team, Scrum master, and others to address the question of how the project can meet or exceed the desired customer expectations and return on investment. Outcomes of this meeting include establishing highest-priority product backlog, the major risks, and the overall features and functionality that the released product will contain. The meeting also produces a probable delivery date and initial cost estimates if nothing changes. Management can then monitor progress and make changes to the release plan on a sprint-by-sprint basis.

FIGURE 15.5
Scrum Meetings

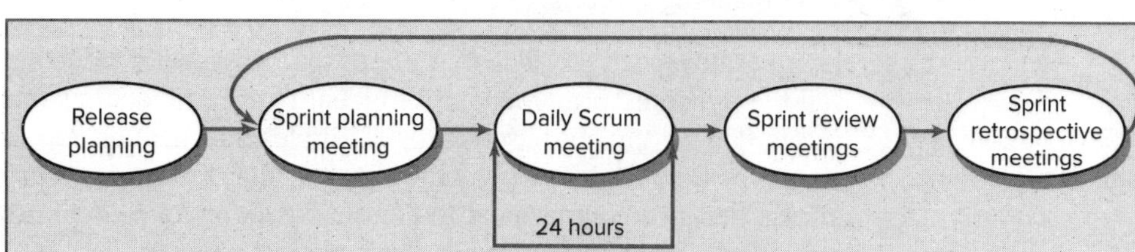

Sprint Planning At the start of each sprint, the product owner and development team negotiate which product backlog items the team will attempt this sprint. The product owner is responsible for identifying which features are most important, and the team is responsible for determining what is possible within the sprint. If it is impossible to complete a certain key item within four weeks, the team works with the product owner to break the feature down into doable pieces. All committed items are recorded in a product backlog. The team uses this backlog to prioritize specific work to be done and assign initial responsibilities. These tasks are recorded in the sprint backlog. Once the meeting has adjourned, the goals for the sprint cannot be changed.

Daily Scrum The heartbeat of an Agile project is the daily meetings, which are commonly referred to as the "Scrum." Each workday at the same time and place, team members stand in a circle and take turns answering the following key questions:

1. What have you done since the last Scrum?
2. What will you do between now and the next Scrum?
3. What is getting in the way of (blocks) your performing your work as effectively as possible?

The daily Scrum, which typically lasts 15 minutes, is held next to a whiteboard, after which time all tasks and blocks are recorded. The Scrum master erases blocks once they have been removed.

The meetings must start on time. A late fine (e.g., $1 to be collected and donated to charity by the Scrum master) is a popular rule. The meeting is limited to just those three core questions. Members stand to create a sense of urgency. Immediately afterward, specific members may meet to resolve issues that surfaced.

The value of the daily Scrum is that it creates a daily mechanism to quickly inform the team about the state of the project. It sustains a sense of team identity that encourages openness and the resolution of problems in real time. Having everyone report what s/he plans to do for that day generates a social promise to the group, thereby building accountability.

Notice again that the team is self-managed. The Scrum master does not assign daily tasks to team members; the team decide among themselves. The Scrum master role is to see that the sprint is running correctly. They are not "master" of the team but, rather, "master" of the process.

Sprint Review At the end of each sprint, the team demonstrate the actual work product increments they have built to the product owner and other relevant stakeholders. Feedback is solicited from the product owner and other relevant stakeholders. The product owner declares which items are "done" and which items need further work and are returned to the product backlog. The team can take this opportunity to suggest improvements and new features for the product owner to accept or reject. The sprint review meeting is an opportunity to examine and adapt the product as it emerges and iteratively refine key requirements. Such refinements will be the subject of the next sprint planning meeting.

Sprint Retrospective The purpose of the retrospective meeting is to reflect on how well the previous sprint went and to identify specific actions that can improve future sprints. The Scrum master typically facilitates this meeting and the team decide which changes will be made in how they work together for the next sprint. The retrospective reflects Scrum's commitment to continuous improvement and the value it places on improving not only products but also team interactions.

See Snapshot from Practice 15.3: *League of Legends* Champions Team to find out how Riot Games adapted Agile methods to video game development.

Product and Sprint Backlogs

Each project has a product backlog and a sprint backlog. The product owner controls the product backlog and the team controls the sprint backlog. The **product backlog** is the customer's prioritized list of key features desired when the project is completed. The product backlog usually defines each feature and estimates time, cost, and work remaining. See Figure 15.6 for a partial product backlog for a software project.

The **sprint backlog** is developed and controlled by the team. It represents the amount of work the team commits to complete during the next sprint. The sprint backlog lists the tasks (activities) that must be completed to deliver a functional feature or segment of a feature. The sprint backlog also serves as a status document by listing the person responsible for each task and the remaining hours of work and by recording the task as *finished, in process,* or *not yet started.* See Figure 15.7 for a partial example of a sprint backlog.

Scrum does not use any of the conventional project management tools, like Gantt charts or network diagrams. Instead, it relies on the daily Scrums and the active involvement of the product owner to manage work flow. Risk is mitigated by short developmental cycles and rigorous testing.

FIGURE 15.6
Partial Product Backlog

Phone-In Prescription Software Project
Product Backlog

ID	Product	Priority	Status	Estimate Hours	Actual Hours
1	Customer Information	2	Complete	100	90
2	Insurance Information	1	Complete	160	180
3	Drug Information	3	Started	80	
4	Doctor Information	5	Not started	40	
5	Inventory status	4	Started	120	

Microsoft Corporation

FIGURE 15.7
Partial Sprint Backlog

Phone-In Prescription Software Project
Sprint Backlog

Sprint Description	Responsible	Actual Hours	Remaining Hours	Defined	In Progress	Tested	Accepted
Drug categories	RT	16	0	X	X	X	✔
Generics	CG	32	0	X	X	X	✔
Branded	AL	24	8	X	X	X	
Design drug inventory system	EL	40	0	X	X	X	✔
Code inventory availability	CE		32				
Code manufacture order	MC		32				
Integrate all inventory systems	LE	4	16	X			

Microsoft Corporation

SNAPSHOT FROM PRACTICE 15.3 *League of Legends* Champions Team*

League of Legends is a very popular multiplayer online battle arena video game developed and published by Riot Games. In *League of Legends*, players assume the role of an unseen "summoner" that controls a "champion" with unique abilities and battle against other controlled champions. When the game was first released in 2009, there were 40 champions. Now there are over 160!

The Champions team at Riot Games creates and updates champions for *League of Legends.* The work is a complex and creative process. Each champ must be emotionally engaging for the players and distinguish itself against the existing roster of champions. Riot Games has adapted Agile methods to create new champions.

CROSS-FUNCTIONAL COLLABORATION

Champions teams comprise 14 types of developers (designers, writers, artists, engineers, QA, producers, etc.). The multidisciplinary team provides a holistic perspective and a tighter, more cohesive product. While differences in perspective can produce creative breakthroughs, they can also lead to conflicts and tension. The Champions team uses the product vision and Scrum rituals to help manage the team.

PRODUCT VISION

One of the early deliverables is a vision statement, or what Riot Games calls "The Dream." The vision statement describes the champions' future state, once the team's work is done. For the champion character "Ivern," the team started off with a basic goal of creating a jungling druid who is a magical friend of the forest. Over time the team began to add different aspects of tree-spirit dryad myth into the character. Ivern's final vision statement became

> *Ivern is a light-hearted and peculiar dryad who is part man, part nature. He roams the world, cultivating his surroundings, and imparting his good nature and unique view of the world to anyone he encounters.*

SCRUM RITUALS

Stand-ups

Daily stand-ups allow the team to communicate updates and identify blockers. Even small tweaks have a cascade effect. For example, if a gameplayer designer changes the length of a spell by a second or even millisecond, the timing can change the mood and clarity of the spell. The sooner the whole team knows a change is coming, the sooner they can react and make sure other assets (animation, spell effect, sounds) support the gameplay needs.

Sprint Review

This is a review where the team members go over planned work and give each other feedback based on the champion's vision statement and other product goals.

Playtest

At least once a sprint, members of the team playtest the champ in a real game situation followed by a team feedback session. These playtests give the whole team a more comprehensive understanding of how it feels to play as, with, or against the champion. For example, midway through Ivern's development, a team member scored a team victory with almost 20 kills from Ivern. While the performance was memorable, it was inconsistent with the product vision of being a benevolent druid, and Ivern was stripped of many of his powers.

Evaluation Review

This is when the team looks at the champion as a whole and evaluates it against the specific fantasy and productwide acceptance criteria using a Likert scale. By quantifying evaluations, the team can see which facets of the champion are in line with Riot Game's standards and which could use more refinement.

Retrospectives

Even though the team created 160 champions over the span of 15 years, retrospectives are conducted every sprint to improve the process. Retrospectives compel the team to keep asking what is and isn't working and make changes to keep creating evocative champions.

*N. L. Torre, and O. Kendall, "Don't Go Chasing Waterfall—Creative Development Using Agile Methods," riotgames.com. Accessed 2/7/19.

Sprint and Release Burndown Charts

Agile favors empirical and value-based measurement instead of predictive measurement. Scrum uses "burndown" charts, which focus on the work remaining and are used to track progress. **Sprint burndown charts** are used to track progress on a daily basis (see Figure 15.8). The vertical axis shows the remaining effort required to complete the sprint backlog, and the horizontal axis contains the number of days until the sprint is completed. The remaining effort is calculated by summing the time estimates for incomplete tasks recorded in the sprint backlog. These estimates are updated on a daily basis.

In Figure 15.8, the circle line shows the ideal scenario if the sprint progresses as predicted by the initial task estimates, and the diamond line shows the actual performance. Ideally, the diamond line should be very close to the solid line. When it is above the circle line the team is behind schedule, and when it is below the circle line the team is ahead of schedule. If the actual remaining line is above the ideal line for an extended period of time, then this signals that adjustments need to be made to the project. This could mean dropping a task, assigning additional resources, or working late. None of these are pleasant, but because of the sprint burndown chart, the team can respond sooner than just before the sprint deadline.

The **release burndown chart** is used to monitor progress toward completion of the project (see Figure 15.9). This chart displays the amount of work remaining across time. Before the start of each sprint, completion estimates are revised in the product backlog and totaled in the release burndown chart. Over time the chart becomes an excellent method for visualizing the relationship between the amount of work remaining and the rate at which the team is reducing this work. Also, the intersection of the trend line for work remaining and the horizontal timeline can be used to estimate the probable completion date. The product owner and team use this information to "what if" the project by removing or adding functionality from the release to achieve a specific completion date or extend the date to include more functionality.

In Figure 15.9, work remaining is recorded for the first six sprints and a trend line is used to revise the expected completion date. Note that in this example the project is expected to be completed later than planned. Does this mean the team is underperforming? No, not necessarily! Remember, the product backlog is dynamic and at the end of each sprint the backlog is revised. Features are added, modified, or deleted. Work estimates are increased or decreased. There is no established baseline in Agile PM.

FIGURE 15.8
Sprint Burndown Chart

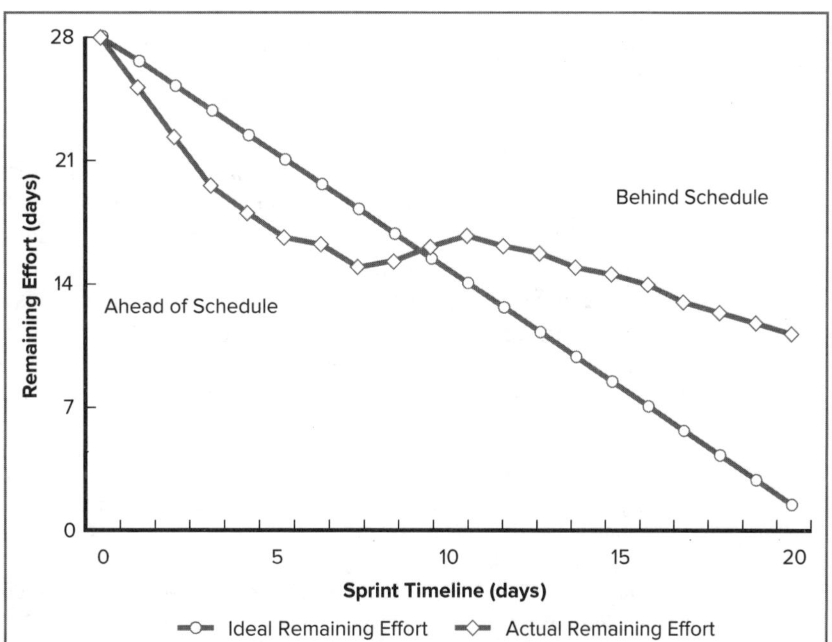

FIGURE 15.9
Release Burndown Chart after Six Sprints

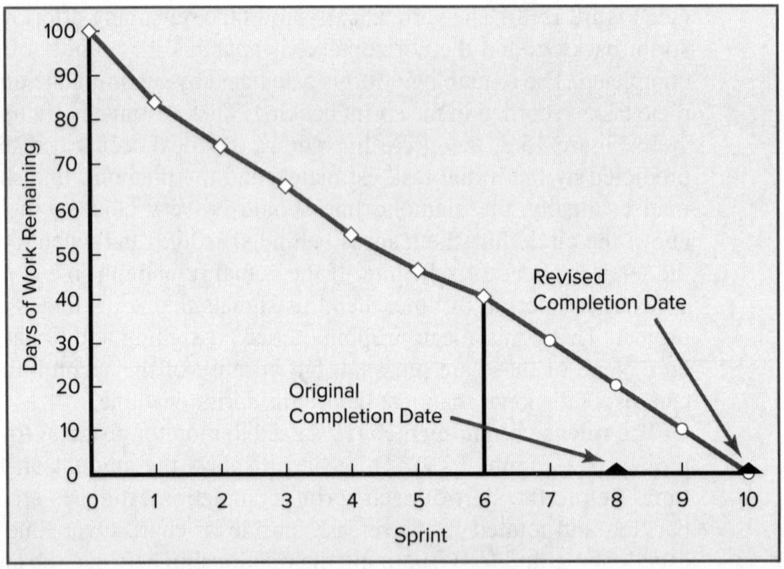

15.4 Extreme Programming and Kanban

LO 15-5

Understand the basic methodology used by Extreme Programming.

Extreme Programming (XP)

Extreme Programming (XP) is a more aggressive form of Scrum that organizes people to produce higher-quality software more efficiently. Originally developed by programmer Kent Beck for the Chrysler Corporation, XP attempts to reduce the cost of changes in requirements by having multiple, short development cycles, rather than a long one (Beck, 1999; Beck & Andres, 2004; Beck & Fowler, 2000). XP considers change a natural, even desirable aspect of software development projects and should be planned for, instead of eliminated. It takes its name from the idea that the software engineering process is taken to "extreme levels" with this approach.

Two of the guiding features of XP are test-driven development and pair programming. The XP approach is that if a little testing can eliminate a few flaws, a lot of testing can eliminate many more flaws. For example, unit tests determine whether a given feature works as intended. Acceptance testing confirms that the requirements as understood by the programmers satisfy the customer's actual requirements, and integration testing detects incompatible basis. Testing occurs on a daily basis. Another unique feature of XP is paired programming. In XP, all code is written in collaboration between pairs of programmers who work side-by-side at the same machine during coding. One, the "driver," writes code while the other, the "navigator," reviews each line of code as it is entered. The two programmers switch roles frequently.

XP is founded on five values:

Communication. The goal is to give all developers a shared view of the system, which matches the view held by the users of the system. To this end, XP favors simple designs, common metaphors, collaboration of users and programmers, frequent verbal communication, and feedback.

Simplicity. XP encourages starting with the simplest solution. Extra functionality can then be added later.

Feedback. Rapid testing reduces errors and ensures work is responsive to customer needs.

Courage. Several practices embody courage. One is the commandment to always design and code for today and not for tomorrow. This is an effort to avoid getting bogged down in design and requiring a lot of effort to implement anything else. Another example of courage is knowing when to throw code away: courage to remove source code that is obsolete, no matter how much effort was used to create that source code.

Respect. This includes respect for others as well as self-respect. Nobody on the team should feel unappreciated or ignored. This ensures a high level of motivation and encourages loyalty toward the team and toward the goal of the project.

XP is not without critics. Some argue that XP requires too much involvement from the user/customer and increases the risk of scope creep, since detailed requirements are not documented (Rosenberg & Stephens, 2003). Proponents argue that customer involvement is the price one pays to avoid unnecessary scope creep.

LO 15-6

Know how to create and use a Kanban board.

Kanban

Kanban is a lean management methodology first developed by Toyota. It has been adapted by Agile practitioners to help manage project work flow.

In its simplest form, Kanban consists of a whiteboard divided into three columns titled Planned, WIP (Work in Progress), and Done. The team identifies the distinct tasks, deliverables, or features associated with their projects. Each is labeled on Post-it® notes or special "Kanban" cards. The cards are prioritized in terms of what needs to be done first and a queue is created in the Next column. The team works on the top-priority items. Once a task or feature has been completed the card is moved to the Done column and the next task is started. Like Scrum, the project team starts each day with a stand-up meeting to update the board, decide what needs to be done, and discuss impediments to progress (Barry & Benson, 2011).

Compared to other project management techniques, Kanban seems a bit too simplistic. Users of this low-tech, high-touch technology attest to its power. Kanban boards provide clear insight into work flow, bottlenecks, blockers, and overall status.

Kanban is based on the idea of *a pull system.* A completed Kanban card signals when the team is ready for more work, which is pulled from the Next list. Work isn't pushed from start to finish. It's only when a task is completed that another task can be started. Limits are set based on the capability of the project team on the number of WIP tasks. For example, no more than three tasks can be in progress at any one time. This reduces the inefficiencies of multitasking and prevents lingering bottlenecks from emerging. Another strength of Kanban is that it helps the team visualize the work flow of the project and focus their attention on the most critical work. Finally, like Scrum, significant time is devoted to solving problems and developing better ways of accomplishing the work (Hammarberg & Sundewn, 2014).

Basic Kanban board
Anathomy/Shutterstock

Depending upon the project, more elaborate mapping schemes can be used. For example, Tarne (2011) described a system for an IT Helpdesk that consisted of six columns: Opened Ticket, In Queue, Root Cause Analysis, Develop Fix, Test, and Deploy. More sophisticated Kanban tools can also be found online.[2]

Kanban is less prescriptive than most Agile approaches, and thus less disruptive. Organizations can begin applying Kanban methods with relative ease and progress toward full implementation if deemed appropriate.

15.5 Applying Agile PM to Large Projects

Scrum and most other Agile methods are ideally suited for distinct projects that can be completed by a small, five-to-nine-person team. Agile methods can be used on larger-scale projects in which several teams are working on different features at the same time. In practice, this condition is called **scaling.** The chief challenge with scaling is integration—making sure that the different features being created work in harmony with each other.

There are no easy solutions to the integration challenge. Significant up-front planning is required to manage the interdependences of different features that will be developed. This is called "staging" and often is the subject of the first development iteration. Here protocols and roles for coordinating efforts and assuring compatibility are established. This is supported by establishing a clear product vision so that trade-off decisions are consistent at the local team level.

Agile advocates recommend creating a hub structure (see Figure 15.10) with overlapping roles and responsibilities to manage large projects. There are several feature

FIGURE 15.10
Hub Project Management Structure

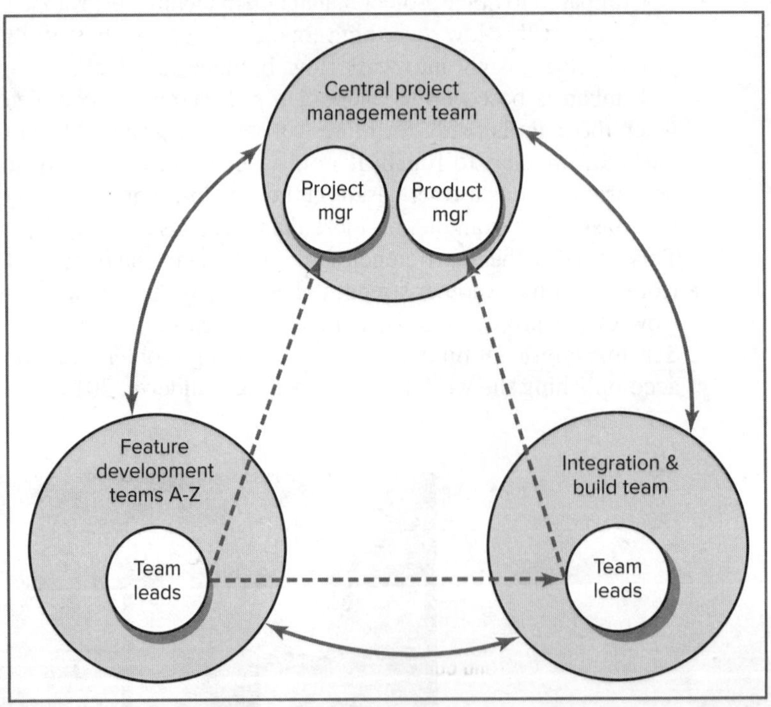

[2] For example, AGILEZEN (agilezen.com) provides a user-friendly, virtual Kanban board, customizable cards/tags and colors, and a performance metrics tracker.

SNAPSHOT FROM PRACTICE 15.4 Adopting Agile Project Management at Infosys and TCS

Agile Project Management has become essential for adaptability in today's dynamic market, enabling companies to pivot quickly while ensuring consistent solution delivery. This study explores how Infosys and Tata Consultancy Services (TCS) transitioned from traditional project management to Agile, analyzing their implementation strategies and challenges. Agile methodologies have revolutionized how Infosys and TCS deliver value, especially in digital transformation. However, scaling Agile across large enterprises presents technical, operational, and cultural challenges.

CHALLENGES IN AGILE IMPLEMENTATION

Scaling Agile Across Large Teams: Infosys struggles with standardizing Agile practices across its globally dispersed teams, leading to inconsistencies. Similarly, TCS faces difficulties in maintaining uniformity as different teams adopt varying Agile approaches.

Client-Centric Challenges: Infosys encounters resistance from clients in traditional sectors preferring waterfall models. TCS faces rigid project scopes due to regulatory constraints, making Agile adoption challenging.

Cultural Resistance: Infosys faces internal resistance, particularly from middle managers accustomed to hierarchical structures. At TCS, employees with longstanding traditional workflows find Agile's collaborative nature uncomfortable.

Talent and Skill Gaps: Infosys requires extensive upskilling in frameworks like Scrum and SAFe, while TCS struggles with retaining Agile practitioners due to industry-wide demand.

Metrics and Performance Measurement: Traditional performance metrics don't always align with Agile. Infosys and TCS face challenges in balancing Agile's dynamic progress tracking with clients' preference for static reports.

Technology and Tool Integration: Infosys experiences difficulties integrating Agile tools with legacy systems, while TCS grapples with maintaining standardization across projects while allowing flexibility.

Quality Assurance and Compliance: Regulatory compliance in sectors like finance and healthcare adds complexity, making it difficult to align Agile's iterative nature with industry standards.

Geographic and Time Zone Differences: Infosys and TCS struggle with real-time Agile ceremonies across distributed teams, causing delays and inefficiencies.

Balancing Customization with Agility: Infosys and TCS face challenges in maintaining Agile principles while accommodating client-specific adaptations, leading to potential inefficiencies.

STRATEGIES USED BY TCS AND INFOSYS FOR OVERCOMING CHALLENGES

1. **Strengthening Agile Training:** Regular organization-wide training, certifications like CSM or SAFe Agilist, and hands-on workshops enhance Agile proficiency.
2. **Fostering an Agile Culture:** Leadership-driven Agile promotion and incentivizing employees help accelerate adoption.
3. **Client Education:** Pilot projects and showcasing Agile benefits improve client collaboration and trust.
4. **Adopting Scaled Agile Frameworks (SAFe):** These frameworks enhance transparency, alignment, and efficiency in large organizations.
5. **Leveraging Collaboration Tools:** Microsoft Teams, Slack, and Confluence facilitate real-time updates and distributed team coordination.
6. **Customizing Agile Metrics:** Hybrid performance indicators combining ROI with Agile-specific metrics align stakeholder expectations.
7. **Integrating Quality and Compliance Checks:** Embedding compliance requirements within Agile workflows ensures adherence without disrupting progress.
8. **Optimizing Communication for Distributed Teams:** Asynchronous tools, scheduled overlapping work hours, and retrospectives improve coordination.
9. **Standardizing While Allowing Customization:** A baseline Agile template provides consistency while enabling slight adjustments for client needs.

Infosys and TCS exemplify Agile's potential to enhance adaptability, innovation, and customer satisfaction. Through structural realignments, training, and Agile integration, both firms improved delivery speed and competitiveness. Despite resistance, they aligned Agile with organizational values, demonstrating that Agile is more than a methodology—it's a transformative framework reshaping project execution and value creation. Their journey offers valuable lessons for businesses embracing Agile in an evolving corporate landscape.

development teams. A separate integration and build team is formed consisting of part-time members of each feature team. This team tackles the sticky integration issue through testing and establishing requirements for the feature teams. To coordinate the multi-team structure a central project team is created consisting of a higher-level project manager, a product manager (who represents the interests of the customer), and the leads ("project managers") from the feature development teams. The project management team provides coordination and facilitates project decision making. Their role is to steer rather than command the other teams. Teams may be real, virtual, or a combination. The entire system requires a spirit of collaboration to work.

The Swedish aeronautics and defense firm Saab AB successfully scaled Agile to their large Gripen jet project. Saab AB deployed over 100 agile teams operating across software, hardware, and fuselage to develop the Gripen fighter jet. Saab coordinates through daily stand-ups. At 7:30 a.m., each frontline agile team meets to flag impediments that can't be resolved by the team and to schedule the work for that day. By 7:45 a.m. these impediments are escalated to the team of teams, where leaders work to settle issues or further escalate the issues. This approach continues, and by 8:45 a.m. the executive action team has a list of critical issues to resolve to keep progress on track. Aeronautics also coordinates things by having a common rhythm of three-week sprints, a project master plan, and co-location of traditionally disparate parts of the organization—for instance, putting test pilots on development teams. The results were dramatic. The Gripen has been recognized as the world's most cost-effective military aircraft (Rigby, Sutherland, & Noble, 2018).

15.6 Limitations and Concerns

LO 15-7

Recognize the limitations of Agile Project Management.

A survey of over 3,900 respondents working in software/IT, financial, and professional services provided a glimpse of the current state of Agile. Ninety-four percent report their firm uses Agile approaches, but only 53 percent report that their agile projects were successful. The biggest reasons for failure were (1) lack of experience with agile methods, (2) company culture at odds with core agile values, (3) lack of management support, and (4) external pressure to follow the traditional waterfall process (Schur, 2015).

One cannot simply install Agile PM into an organization overnight. Agile PM is not a simple methodology. Not only do new techniques need to be learned, but it requires a significant mindset change. Adoption tends to evolve over time. Most companies report gradual introduction of Agile PM. They begin with a couple of pilot projects and with success a few more and so forth. Here the project management office can play a critical role by providing training and coaches to new agile teams.

Many of the Agile principles, including self-organizing teams and intense collaboration, are incompatible with corporate cultures. For example, the principle of self-organizing teams, in which members decide who should do what, regardless of rank or title, contradicts command and control structures. Likewise, intense collaboration is not for everyone. One Agile manager confessed that she had to let several of her top engineers go because their lone-wolf personalities were not compatible with collaboration.

Agile PM does not satisfy top management's need for control. Remember the new house analogy. The buyers got exactly what they wanted but did not know how much it would cost. Nor did they know how long it would take or even what it would look like when it was done. No matter how realistic "it depends" is, management as well as customers are accustomed to working with a greater level of certainty than Agile provides. In response to the financial concerns, many organizations establish "ceilings," which are the maximum budget or time not to be exceeded in the development of a given product or service.

In organizations in which the waterfall process is the dominant methodology there will be a natural tension and pressure to conform. Here Agile skeptics warn that evolving requirements contribute to scope creep. Sprints will produce a never-ending series of requests by product owner/user. They fear that Agile teams will *go native* and identify too much with what the customer wants and not what makes sense from a business point of view.

Another challenge not mentioned in the survey results is that Agile PM requires active customer involvement. Involvement comes in different forms. Designating an internal person to act as a product owner to represent the interests of end users is relatively easy. Soliciting the active participation of external customers can be more problematic. Even though there is consistent evidence that customer participation enhances project success, not all customers want to be that actively involved. Many are simply too busy. Others believe that they hired the project team so they would not have to be involved. Securing the cooperation of customers to devote the requisite time to support Agile PM is often a source of frustration.

Despite the challenges, the repeated success and improvement in software and new-product development projects has led to the acceptance of Agile PM by the traditional project management profession. In 2017 the Project Management Institute (PMI) and the Agile Alliance jointly published the *Agile Practice Guide.*

15.7 Hybrid Project Management

Sometimes organizations use both traditional and Agile methods to complete a project. This is referred to in the world of project management as **hybrid project management.** The most common application is traditional project management being applied to all tasks except for software development which is completed via Scrum teams. However, Agile methods are not exclusive to software development. Businesses are realizing the value of using Agile when the conditions are appropriate (high uncertainty). Here, we are not talking about Scrum per se but applying Agile methods to projects: small, semi-autonomous teams; iterative development; customer engagement; experimentation; and continuous improvement.

Agile PM is often used upfront during the defining phase to resolve scope questions and define key requirements. An Agile team may be used to develop demonstrations of three different interfaces to a client so that this decision can be integrated into the project plan. In essence, IDEO (see Snapshot of Practice 15.1: IDEO: Masters of Design) uses rapid prototyping and iterative development to define key design requirements which are later refined and created by traditional project management methods.

There are also projects where the requirements are known but there is uncertainty regarding how to accomplish (technology) it. In these cases, early in the project execution phase project teams are assigned the task of conducting experiments and building prototypes to test key assumptions and find solutions to technical problems. The results provide the necessary information so that traditional project execution can proceed. For example, in the ever-competitive e-vehicle world, automakers often experiment with 2–3 different battery configurations before deciding which one to use.

Often on projects most of the work is routine and predictable, but there is uncertainty regarding a specific deliverable or task. For example, a construction company secured the contract to build a new facility at a university. The firm had successfully completed similar projects in the past, but there was always a question of which sealing compound to use given weather conditions. While the building was being constructed according to plan, the contractor conducted small-scale installation experiments on the ground to determine the best method and uncover issues early while there was still plenty of time to resolve them. Sometimes traditional PM is used at the tail end of an Agile project. For example, Scrum may be used to develop a company-wide database system, but traditional PM is used to manage the training of 1,000+ users.

Some companies have successfully applied hybrid project management on large projects that combine waterfall and Agile methods. For example, IPC Media, a subsidiary of Time Inc., uses an iterative waterfall approach in which large projects are broken down into sub-projects performed by different teams in parallel. Short sprints and additional checkpoints are used to complete each phase. In essence, each phase is an agile project.

Finally, it is common to find teams using Agile techniques on plan-driven projects. For example, stand-up meetings to coordinate efforts have become commonplace in many organizations. Teams also use shorter iterations and retrospectives to get critical customer feedback. Kanban methods are used by traditional teams to visualize work and identify bottlenecks in the project schedule. This trend is expected to continue. A 2021 survey of project professionals across a wide range of North American industries reported that 23 percent were using a hybrid approach on their projects (PMI, 2021). We expect blended forms of project management to continue to evolve. Hopefully, someone will come up with a better name than simply "hybrid project management."

Summary

Agile Project Management has emerged as a response to the challenges of managing projects with loosely defined scopes and high levels of uncertainty. Agile relies on an iterative, incremental development process in which the scope of the project evolves over time. Development teams create feature-driven working products at the end of each development cycle. Active customer involvement is used to guide this process. Here are some of the key advantages of Agile methods:

- Work is divided into smaller and smaller chunks that are more easily scheduled and controlled.
- Collaboration between the customer and designers is increased, leading to solid change control.
- Methods demand that features be tested and functional when completed.

Agile PM is still evolving. While much of the attention in this chapter has been devoted to software development, Agile PM is being successfully applied to a wide range of unpredictable projects. New methods and approaches will continue to be developed and adapted to meet the specific needs of projects. Stay tuned.

Key Terms

Agile Project Management, *633*
Extreme Programming, *646*
Feature, *640*
Hybrid project management, *651*
Iterative, incremental development (IID), *633*
Kanban, *645*
Product backlog, *643*
Product owner, *640*
Release burndown chart, *645*
Scaling, *648*
Scrum master, *641*
Self-organizing team, *641*
Sprint backlog, *643*
Sprint burndown chart, *644*
Waterfall method, *634*

Review Questions

1. Why is the traditional project management approach less effective when project scope and technology are not well known?
2. What is iterative, incremental development? Why is it useful for developing new products?
3. What are the advantages of Agile PM? What are the disadvantages of Agile PM?
4. What similarities and differences exist between a traditional project manager and a Scrum master?
5. What are the differences between a self-organizing team and a conventional project team?
6. How does a Kanban board work?
7. Why is it difficult to apply Agile PM to large-scale projects?

SNAPSHOT FROM PRACTICE

Discussion Questions

15.1 *IDEO: Masters of Design*

1. What are the advantages of rapid prototyping?
2. Can you think of a personal project that would have benefited from prototyping? How? Why?

15.2 *Soul Searching after 9/11*

1. Why is it useful to hold retrospectives at the end of weekly iterations?

15.3 *League of Legends Champions Team*

1. Why not use the waterfall method to develop new champions?
2. How does having a product vision and using Scrum rituals help teams manage tension and conflict?

Exercises

1. Break into small groups and identify at least two real-life examples of projects in which
   a. The scope and technology are well known.
   b. The scope is well known, but the technology is less well known.
   c. The scope is not well known, but the technology is known.
   d. Neither the scope nor the technology is well known.
2. Break into small groups and discuss the following question:
   What organizational, group, individual, and project factors do you think would promote the successful adoption of Agile PM methodologies like Scrum? Why?
3. Use a project you are currently working on to hold a Scrum meeting according to the steps outlined in Figure 15.5. Designate one member to act as the Scrum master and hold a standing meeting that lasts no longer than 15 minutes. Assess the value of such meetings.
4. Access agilealliance.org and review the subsections Agile 101 and Timeline. What do they have to say about how Agile evolved and gained acceptance in the project management community?
5. Following are four mini-cases from practice. Break into small groups and (1) analyze the case and (2) provide five recommendations for the IT Department.

Project A

You've just taken over a project from another project manager and have come back from a very uncomfortable meeting with your business sponsor. In the meeting, the sponsor told you how dissatisfied she is with the project's performance to date and that she's getting ready to pull the plug on the project entirely. Deadlines keep slipping, the application isn't complete, and the sponsor feels like she can't get in touch with anyone to give her an update on the project's status and progress.

From conversations with your project team, you learn that requirements still haven't been finalized, and the team is waiting for input before being able to proceed on several key parts of the application. Despite that, they've been able to push forward in other areas and are quite proud of the work they've done. However, they haven't had a chance to show it to the sponsor.

To complicate matters further, your boss has made it clear that this project must be completed on schedule, because he needs the resources for another project.

What do you do? What impact do your decisions have on the project's cost, schedule, and performance?

Project B

Your project team has finished gathering the requirements and developing the solution design. Your team is broken into two main groups: the first group consists of the project manager, business analysts, and management and is located in the United States. The second group consists of the development and QA teams and they are located in India.

The WBS was developed based on estimates from the teams in India. The development team agreed to provide daily updates to you about progress against the WBS to make sure that the project's milestones are going to be met.

However, by the time the development team got close to the first milestone, it became obvious that they were behind, even though their daily updates indicated that they were on track. In addition, the team adopted a different design approach than the one agreed upon at the beginning of the project.

The lack of meaningful updates from the development team along with a different design track has jeopardized the whole project by rendering the entire plan obsolete. Your team is now at risk of not delivering the project.

What do you do? What is the impact to cost, schedule, and performance?

Project C

You have just taken over as the program manager of a large program with multiple tracks and a go-live scheduled in three months. At the first meeting with the project sponsors and key stakeholders, you find out that the business requirements are not complete and in some cases not started, the project scope is not realistic to meet the upcoming go-live, and overall the project teams are confused due to lack of communication and understanding of priorities.

What do you do? What impact do your decisions have on the project's cost, schedule, and performance?

Project D

You've just been assigned to take over a new project from an outgoing project manager. The project is a high-visibility project that is using a development methodology that is new to you and to your company. In your transition meetings with the outgoing project manager, he assures you that development is complete and all you have to do is shepherd the project through acceptance testing and release. As a result, several project team members were released as scheduled.

The acceptance testing does not go as smoothly as planned. The application has more defects than anticipated, and some core functionality is not able to be tested. The project team doesn't feel they are getting the direction they need to continue moving forward, and the business sponsor has asked you when she can expect to test application functionality that wasn't a part of the original scope. In addition, your project's deadline is rapidly approaching, and interproject dependencies make it unlikely that you will be able to push your launch date.

What do you do? What impact do your decisions have on cost, schedule, and performance?

References

Barry, T. D., and J. Benson, *Personal Kanban: Mapping Work/Navigating Life* (New York: Modus Cooperandi Press, 2011).

Beck, K., *Extreme Programming Explained: Embrace Change* (Boston: Addison-Wesley, 1999).

Beck, K., and C. Andreas, *Extreme Programming Explained: Embrace Change,* 2nd ed. (Boston: Addison-Wesley, 2004).

Beck, K., and M. Fowler, *Planning Extreme Programming* (Boston: Addison-Wesley, 2000).

Boulter, M., *Smart Client Architecture and Design Guide* (Seattle: Microsoft Press, 2004).

Decarlo, D., *eXtreme Project Management* (Jossey-Bass, 2004).

Gale, S. F., "The Evolution of Agile," *PM Network,* January 2012.

Griffiths, M., *Using Agile Principles Alongside: A Guide to the Project Management Body of Knowledge,* PMI Global Proceedings, Anaheim, California, 2004.

Hammarberg, M., and J. Sundewn, *Kanban in Action* (Shelter Island: Manning Publications, 2014).

Highsmith, J., *Agile Project Management* (Boston: Addison Wesley, 2004).

Hildebrand, C., "Full Speed Ahead," *PM Network,* October 2007, pp. 36–41.

Hobbs, B., and Y. Petit, "Agile Methods on Large Projects in Large Organizations," *Project Management Journal,* vol. 48, no. 3 (2017), pp. 3–19.

Jackson, M. B., "Step by Step," *PM Network,* June 2012, pp. 57–61.

James, M., "Scrum," http://refcardz.dzone.com. Accessed 5/18/09.

Jonasson, H., *Determining Project Requirements* (Boca Raton, FL: Auerbach Publications, 2008).

Kruchten, P., *The Rational Unified Process: An Introduction,* 3rd ed. (Upper Saddle River, NJ: Pearson Education, 2004).

Larman, C., *Agile & Iterative Development: A Manager's Guide* (Boston: Addison-Wesley, 2004).

McConnel, S., *Rapid Development: Taming Wild Software Schedules* (Redmond, WA: Microsoft Press, 1996).

PMI/Agile Alliance, *Agile Practice Guide* (Chicago: Independent Publishers Group, 2017).

Project Management Institute (PMI), "Pulse of the Profession: 10th Global Survey," 2018, pmi.org. Accessed 1/22/19.

Project Management Institute (PMI), "Pulse of the Profession 2021: Beyond Agility," 2021, pmi.org. Accessed 8/5/23.

Reiff, J., and D. Schlegel, "Hybrid Project Management - A Systematic Literature Review," *International Journal of Information Systems and Project Management,* vol. 10, no. 2 (2022), pp. 45-63.

Rigby, D. K., J. Sutherland, and A. Noble, "Agile at Scale," *Harvard Business Review,* May/June 2018, pp. 88–96.

Rigby, D. K., J. Sutherland, and H. Takeuchi, "Embracing Agile: How to Master the Process That's Transforming Management," *Harvard Business Review,* May 2016, pp. 41–50.

Rosenberg, D., and M. Stephens, *Extreme Programming Refactored: The Case against XP* (New York: Apress, 2003).

Schur, M., "The State of Agile," *PM Network,* September 2015, pp. 16–17.

Skarin, M., *Real-World Kanban: Do Less, Accomplish More with Lean Thinking* (Raleigh: Pragmatic Bookshelf, 2015).

Takeuchi, H., and I. Nonaka, "The New Product Development Game," *Harvard Business Review,* January/February 1986.

Tarne, R., "Taking Off the Agile Training Wheels, Advance Agile Project Management Using Kanban," *2011 PMI Global Proceedings,* Dallas, Texas, 2011.

The Standish Group International, *Chaos Report: 1995* (Dennis, MA: Standish Group, 1995).

Vanderjack, B., "21 Methods to Engage and Retain Your Product Owner in an Agile Project," www.pmworldjournal.net, vol. 1, no. 4 (November 2012), pp. 1–6.

Worthen, B., "Try Software on Workers First, Fix It Later," *The Wall Street Journal,* September 25, 2007, pp. B1 and B4.

Case 15.1

Introducing Scrum at P2P

PART A

Kendra Hua worked for six years as a software engineer in the IT Department at Point 2 Point (P2P), a large freight moving company. She liked her job and the people she worked with. While she did some maintenance work, she worked primarily on projects, usually full time. Her work covered a wide range of projects, including system upgrades, inventory control, GPS tracking, billing, and customer databases. These projects were typically able to meet project requirements but were consistently late. Within the IT Department, it was common practice for a betting pool to emerge regarding completion dates. The rule of thumb was to take the original schedule, multiply it by 1.5, and start guessing from then on.

Management decided to try to turn things around by changing the way P2P completed IT projects. Instead of the traditional waterfall approach in which all the requirements were defined up front, the IT Department was to start using Agile Project Management, and more specifically Scrum, to complete their projects.

Kendra had just been assigned to the Big Foot project, which involved developing a system for monitoring P2P's carbon footprint. To prepare for this project, Kendra and her entire team of software engineers would attend a two-day Scrum workshop.

Everyone was given a book on Scrum to prepare for the workshop. At first, Kendra was overwhelmed by terminology—Scrum master, sprints, product manager, sprint logs, and so forth. She questioned the rugby metaphor, since the only thing she knew about the sport was that one of her ex-boyfriends in college would come back to the dorm inebriated and bloodied after a match. And why was the project manager called a master? It seemed demeaning to her. Still, she had heard some good things about Scrum from a friend who was using it in another company. He claimed it gave programmers more freedom to do their work and to work at a faster pace. So she approached the two-day workshop with an open mind.

The workshop was facilitated by a trainer who was well versed in the world of software development. Participants included her other five team members as well as Prem Gupta, a veteran project manager who would now assume the role of Scrum master, and Isaac Smith, who would act as the product manager representing the interests of the customers. At first, everyone gave Prem a hard time by bowing to him, pleading "master, master, master . . ." The facilitator quickly corrected them by saying he was not their master but, rather, master of the Scrum process. The facilitator went on to emphasize that they would work as a self-organizing team. Kendra wasn't exactly sure what that meant, but she felt it had something to do with the team managing itself, not Prem.

The workshop covered all the basic Scrum tools, concepts, and roles. Everyone got to practice the process by completing a simulated project involving the creation of a new board game. Kendra liked the idea of the standing Scrum meeting, since most of her meetings at P2P took way too long. She also liked having the product manager, who was the ultimate decision maker on features and when work was completed. Everyone laughed at the "only one neck to wring" analogy that the facilitator used to describe this role. Overall she thought the process had promise and she was excited about trying it out on the Big Foot project. The Big Foot project was estimated to be completed after five sprints, with each sprint lasting four weeks.

THE FIRST SPRINT

The first sprint planning meeting went pretty much by the book. Isaac, the product owner, had done his homework and came to the meeting with a comprehensive list of features the software needed to provide. There was healthy discussion, and Isaac amended the list to include some features that the team felt was necessary. The afternoon session featured Isaac prioritizing the features in the product backlog with feedback from the team. The final segment was devoted to the team deciding among themselves which high-priority features they would commit to build within the four-week sprint. Prem did a good job of reminding the team that they were expected to build a fully functional feature. This tempered the team's enthusiasm, and in the end, a challenging but doable set of features was assigned to the sprint backlog for the first sprint.

The first couple of daily Scrum meetings were a bit awkward as members were careful not to step on each other's toes. One of the first impediments identified was not having a shared understanding of how a self-organizing team worked. Prem kept emphasizing that it was up to the team to decide who does what and when. Then one morning it just suddenly clicked and members came forward claiming work they felt needed to be done. After that the daily Scrums took on a life of their own, interrupted only when a member had to do five push-ups for every minute late. The pace of work picked up, and there was a shared enthusiasm as tasks and ultimately functional features were completed in rapid fashion. Kendra worked side by side with the other software engineers to solve problems and share what they had learned. Occasionally Isaac was called into the project room to answer questions about specific features and be shown work in progress.

By the time of the first sprint review meeting, the team was able to demonstrate all but one of the designated features to Isaac and even three more that were not on the initial hit list. The team got some useful feedback not only from Isaac but also from a couple of the end users he brought with him. Eighty percent of the features were proclaimed done by Isaac, while the others needed only slight modifications. Everyone agreed that the next Sprint review would be even more successful.

The sprint retrospective meeting was refreshing, as members spoke candidly about both the good and the bad. Everyone agreed that the team needed to do a better job at documentation. Issues regarding fairness and spreading both the fun work and the tough work among the entire team were brought to the surface. Kendra was impressed by how everyone focused on what was best for the project, not just himself or herself.

THE SECOND SPRINT

The second sprint meeting went well. The features that needed rework after the first sprint review meeting were at the top of the backlog. Isaac made appropriate adjustments in priorities, and a couple of new features that were discovered during the sprint review meeting were added. The meeting convened with the team confident that they would be able to complete the work they had committed to.

Project work progressed quickly over the next week. Kendra felt pressure to accomplish what she had said she would at the daily Scrum. At the same time, she felt a tremendous amount of satisfaction reporting work done. The entire team seemed energized. Then one day everything came to a standstill over a sticky integration problem. The team struggled over the next three days, trying to solve the problem, until, at the next Scrum, Prem stepped forward, saying, "I think you should do this. . . ." He then proceeded to outline a specific method for solving the problem, even assigning specific tasks to each team member. During the next two days, Prem went back and forth between team members, coordinating their work and solving problems. While there was some grumbling within the team, his solution worked, and Kendra was grateful to get back on track.

From then on, Prem took a more active role in daily Scrum meetings, often having the final say as to the work agenda for that day. The meetings took on a different tone as members waited for Prem to speak first. Isaac was absent from the project room during this time, as he was visiting sites that would be using the new software. Still, features were being completed and Kendra was happy with the progress. Then one day Isaac showed up at the morning Scrum meeting. He had just gotten back and had fresh information he wanted to introduce into the project. He had rewritten the product log and added several new high-priority features and eliminated a few of the features that the team had been working on. He wanted the team to shift their efforts and complete the new features by the end of the sprint.

The team was shocked because one of the principles they had been taught is that you don't change course midway through a sprint. Prem did his best to explain this to Isaac, but he was insistent. He kept saying that these changes had to be made;

otherwise, much of the sprint output would be a waste of time. He kept repeating that the team needed to be flexible. "After all, isn't that what the Agile approach is all about?" The meeting came to an impasse until Prem came forward with a compromise. The team would agree to do the new work, but the sprint needed to be extended by two weeks. Everyone agreed and Kendra went back to work.

Up until the end of the second sprint, Prem continued to direct project work. When it came for the sprint review meeting, four of the five new features were completed as well as most of the original features. However, the feature demonstrations did not go well. Isaac and several of the end users that were present were critical of the user friendliness of several of the completed features. Kendra and other team members defended their work by saying, "Why didn't you tell us you wanted it to perform that way?" Prem did his best to keep the meeting under control, but the team had little to say when an important feature simply did not work. In the end, only half of the features were accepted as being done.

Kendra walked out of the sprint review discouraged. Tomorrow morning was the sprint retrospective meeting. She had a lot on her mind but wasn't sure what she should say or how to say it at the meeting.

1. How well is Scrum working?
2. What are the issues confronting the Big Foot project?
3. Assume you are Kendra. What would you want to say at the retrospective? How would you say it?
4. What improvements or changes need to be made?

PART B

Prem opened the retrospective by saying he had gotten a call from his boss and she was not happy with the progress. Prem said that he and the team were under the gun to get back on track. The list of things that went well during the second sprint was short, and when it came time to discuss improvements there was an awkward silence. Kendra spoke up and began by saying she had gone back and reviewed the Scrum book. She went on to say that she thought the whole idea behind Scrum was that the team was to work to solve their own problems and it wasn't Prem's role to play task master. A couple of other team members murmured agreement. Prem became defensive and said if he had not intervened it would have taken days for the team to solve the problem.

Another member said he thought it was a mistake allowing Isaac to change the sprint commitments. Prem agreed that in principle that was true but said sometimes you have to bend the rules to do what is right. He admonished the team by saying that they had to practice being more agile. The retrospective ended with few specific recommendations other than that in order to get back on track, Prem felt he would have to get even more involved in the execution of the project.

The subsequent sprint 3 planning meeting was more of a formality. Isaac updated the product backlog with revised priorities, and Prem signed off for the team as to what they would commit to. There was little interaction between the team and Isaac except seeking clarification on performance requirements for specific features.

The team met under Prem's leadership for their daily Scrums. Sometimes the Scrums went beyond the normal 15 minutes as Prem reviewed progress and described in detail what needed to be done that day. Isaac showed up occasionally, changed priorities, reviewed work, and answered questions. Kendra worked hard on her assignments and often received praise from Prem for work well done.

One evening when the team got together for a few beers and sushi, one of the team members pulled out a spreadsheet and asked who wanted to make the first bet on when they thought the project would be done.

After several sprints, Isaac finally signed off on the last feature and declared the project completed. A collective "yahoo" sprang from the team. After the meeting Kendra went around collecting money from each of her teammates—she had predicted that the project would take 12 weeks longer than planned.

1. How would you assess P2P's effort at introducing Scrum?
2. What challenges does an organization face when adopting an Agile approach like Scrum?
3. What could P2P have done to enhance success?

Case 15.2

Graham Nash

Ken Buttrey scratched his head as he looked over an e-mail from John Barbata. Ken was the team lead on the Jasper Jones project. He and 13 other developers were charged with creating Jasper Jones (JJ), a new character to appear in the next edition of the popular video game *Hidden Galaxy. Hidden Galaxy* was the flagship game for NYAS Games. The team was cross-functional and included designers, artists, writers, engineers, QA, and producers. NYAS has applied Agile methods to its projects for the past three years, believing it to be one of the keys to its continued success.

For the most part, Ken was happy with the team and how things were going on the project. There was one big exception: graphic designer Graham Nash. In fact, the e-mail he was reading was another complaint about Graham:

> This is the second time in two weeks that Nash failed to report changes he made in JJ's mobility. This really screws things up. I had to spend most of yesterday adjusting the sound to accommodate the changes.

Unfortunately, this was not the only complaint. Callie Faries, an artist, had just left Ken's cubicle with a similar complaint.

Graham had a reputation at NYAS of being a brilliant designer. He was credited with the creation of the popular Thongor character. In fact, Ken was surprised that his counterpart, Xien Xong, was willing to let him go and work on JJ.

Ken admitted that at times Graham's work could be brilliant and his work ethic was above reproach. But that was part of the problem. He would get so absorbed in his work that he would forget about the rest of the team. This issue kept being raised at the sprint reviews. Graham would agree while making little eye contact with the rest of the team. It didn't help that Graham was an extreme introvert. Rarely did he say anything unless he was asked a question. You have talked to him about being more responsive to the needs of the rest of the team. You also have gotten into the habit of asking him specific questions at the daily stand-up meetings.

1. What options does Ken have in dealing with the Graham Nash situation?
2. What would you recommend Ken do and why?

Case 15.3

Agile Project Management in AEC Industry

AEC (Architecture, Engineering and Construction) industry is one of the most dynamic and fast-developing industries. It encompasses large-scale projects like airports, hotels, towers, entertainment, film cities, hospitals, smart townships, stadiums, etc. While the end goal is somewhat certain in most cases, these projects require Agile Project Management for their successful execution due to the following factors:

- Constant shift in priorities based on the dynamic environment in which they are being constructed.
- Adaptability to change with the situation in such long-term projects is crucial so the governing factor in the initial phase of the project undergoes multiple alterations until it reaches to completion.
- Coordination, communication, and collaboration are required among the various departments as the task cannot be performed by a single team given the deadline constraints, hence, multiple teams simultaneously work on different parts of the project to produce the desire end result.

AEC industry wins project on competitive lowest bidding based on manpower hours and hence, the project is estimated taking into consideration the prevailing market standard rates and prices for various services offered. On successful signing of the Project Charter or contract paper by all the stakeholders and client specifically, a 'Kick-off' meeting is scheduled to discuss the proceedings and finally, the teams start collecting the input files and make plans and roadmaps of project execution, setting pre-declared and client-approved deadlines.

The architecture and structure teams start the project first to provide the basic framework for the MEP-FP (Mechanical, Electrical, Plumbing and Fire Protection) teams. Often, due to time constraints, MEP-FP teams start the work along with ACS (Architecture, Civil and Structure) team. The following factors are of utmost importance to be maintained among the teams as well as in the project execution:

- Sharing progress files, update reports, and latest outputs among teams as there lies a dominant risk of overwork as a particular team may work on a backdated file unaware of the changes made by another team. Hence, time and manpower cost both are wasted in the process.
- Also, certain succeeding activities can only start at the end of a preceding activity, hence, all teams must strictly adhere to the Daily or Weekly Sprints and try to be ahead of their deadlines.
- Assigning specific tasks and goals to different teams to reduce redundancy and overwork.
- Mistakes are identified quickly and easily which allows time and scope for rectification without affecting a major share of the project.
- Proper communication among teams is a must.
- Everyday scrum meeting of 5–15 mins where it is compulsory for the representatives of all the departments to attend.
- Deadlines are sacrosanct and commitments made to the client should be executed to foster professional relationships and converting first-time clients to recurring and loyal clients.

- Proposed frequent changes from clients are a common phenomenon in this business, hence, resources are kept partially dynamic
- Backlogs are maintained for various activities with proper documentation
- COE (Centre of Excellence) and Audit team randomly audit the project to check project health and discrepancies due to manpower negligence or knowledge gaps
- A negative effect of change of skilled manpower in between project life cycle is nullified by the short phase-lives of the project without compromising on quality

DRAWBACKS OF USING AGILE PROJECT METHOD FOR INFRASTRUCTURE PROJECTS

Dynamism brings quality and reduces risk for the project. But using Agile also has some demerits:

- Frequent change in project requirement, scope and deliverables from clients results in mismanagement of manpower and resources often incurring some extra cost over unnecessary activities.
- Any mistake or delay in the sprint from a particular team may affect the output of other teams.
- Some project takes years to complete with a pause or no-work intervals in between which hinders the flow of the project and project sprints thus on resuming, sprints need to review and change.
- At times, the site construction works are in phase with the office design and modelling works. So, an error in the design or modelling work would incur huge costs on the site especially in a country like the United Kingdom, where manpower is very expensive.
- For a small project, where budget is a constraint, using Agile is not recommended as the entire bulk of work can be carried out by a single team only. Hence, if an organization follows Agile methodology, then it has to be very specific in project selection.

Case 15.4

Agile Project Management by Zebra Ltd.

Zebra Ltd. secured an international project. The project is being executed by various departments from different companies (located across multiple countries and continents) operating in different time zones (EST, GMT, GST, IST etc.). The project was awarded to Zebra Ltd., on the basis of the lowest bid with a scope of design and modelling a residential complex in Birmingham, UK. Zebra project team was only given the Electrical part as their scope. For the remaining parts—Mechanical was given to a Korean company, Plumbing was given to a company from Thailand, Fire Protection was their in-house service so they only were doing that and for the Architecture and Structure part, they hired a UK architectural consultant firm.

PROJECT EXECUTION

The project team used to coordinate with the global team twice a week—once for the coordination meeting and again for the project progress and review meeting. The agile project method was followed by all the companies and even the construction work commenced in a week from project kick-off, almost running in parallel to the design and modelling work. The key highlights of the work using Agile were as follows:

- The Zebra team lead kept in track with the changing environment of the site and all companies, adapted to the changes quite quick, though was not easy but the team had to.
- The team lead tried to coordinate with all the different departments from various countries for status updates so that the team didn't fall short of the sprint and also to avoid unnecessary rework.
- The team lead further broke down the part into sprints for the teams and ensured proper coordination and communication among them which resulted in 'Electrical' being the trade with the least clash report among all other trades of the project.
- The project finally came to closure in June 2019 and the building became operational in October 2019.

CHALLENGES IN EXECUTION OF AGILE PROJECT MANAGEMENT

- Agile method was ineffective initially because it took quite some days for all the teams to coordinate among themselves given the diverse working style and time zones.
- Scrum meetings were usually held beyond office hours due to time zones at different locations, so it became quite challenging for teams to incorporate changes quick. It would take some time for the changes to reflect on the other side, for which other teams would have to wait.
- Rework by a team had cost all the other teams considerable loss as by their mistake, all the other teams were working on the last previous update and on synchronizing with the central server, 2–3 days of efforts for all the remaining teams went to vain as it was completely replaced.
- Due to the unavailability of instant telephonic or video-conference communication across the location, meetings were only held on prior mail appointments which also delayed their sprint and progress.
- All companies were not able to deliver quality output, hence, the overall output of the project was affected upto the certain extent.

Case 15.5

Agile in Education Industry

An academic university was running an employee portal called 'Office-Module' but due to restrictions in certain employee demand and needs, a shift was executed from 'Office-Module' to 'Office-360' with a change in database and maintenance service provider as well.

REASONS FOR EMPLOYEE PORTAL CHANGE

- Issue over leave application
- No provision for downloading payslip

- Income tax and other forms had to be manually filled and submitted to HR, instead of uploading in the portal
- Employees were unaware of policy changes in the organization
- Company events and working calendar were not accessible by all employees
- No provision for flexible shift change
- Applications like transfer requests, resignation or promotion/appraisal forms were to be filled manually and submitted to HR
- Absence of employee directory for common employees. It was only made visible to departmental heads and HRs
- Auto-punch attendance was not reflected in the portal
- Process of implementation using Agile Project Management

Separate teams were assigned to execute different tasks and work parallelly in coordination with each other. The entire shift from 'Office-Module' to 'Office-360' was not done in a day. It rather took two months for the test, trial-runs, feedbacks from employees, incorporating those feedback and finally coming up with an employee-centric portal from the earlier one which was more of an employer-centric portal.

Small tasks were created like 'Leave', 'Payslip', 'Policy', 'Employee Directory', 'Working shift', etc., and executed on Sprint basis. Priority activities were taken up first and based upon the internal organizational survey, changed and roadmap was framed. Tasks were executed within the deadline with some preceding defaulters sometimes but most of the tasks were completed on time. Part by part, the database of the employees was shifted to the new portal without hampering the daily office activities. Following that, one service after the other was made accessible for the employees and were asked for a 7-day trial run for each activity, post which feedback were again recorded, sprints were reviewed with modified dates and again those activities were executed with the fresh feedback.

Finally, all the initial and further added needs of the employees were addressed by the new 'Office-360' giving the organization a fresh and dynamic look.

PROBLEMS FACED DURING AGILE PROCESS

The problems faced during the Agile process were:

- Some functional properties were down at times due to maintenance by the sprint team as it caused some hindrance to the employees.
- Once the team executed a task based upon the employees' feedback, again they reverted it as it was not that much by the employees. After a couple of days, the employee felt the need for the same activity, which was finally incorporated before completion. So, a lot of rework had to be incurred.

Design elements: Snapshot from Practice, Highlight box, Case icon: Sky Designs/Shutterstock

CHAPTER SIXTEEN

16 International Projects

LEARNING OBJECTIVES

After reading this chapter you should be able to:

16-1 Describe environmental factors that affect project management in different countries.

16-2 Identify factors that typically are considered in selecting a foreign location for a project.

16-3 Understand cross-cultural issues that impact working on international projects.

16-4 Describe culture shock and strategies for coping with it.

16-5 Understand how organizations select and prepare people to work on international projects.

OUTLINE

16.1 Environmental Factors

16.2 Project Site Selection

16.3 Cross-Cultural Considerations: A Closer Look

16.4 Selection and Training for International Projects

Summary

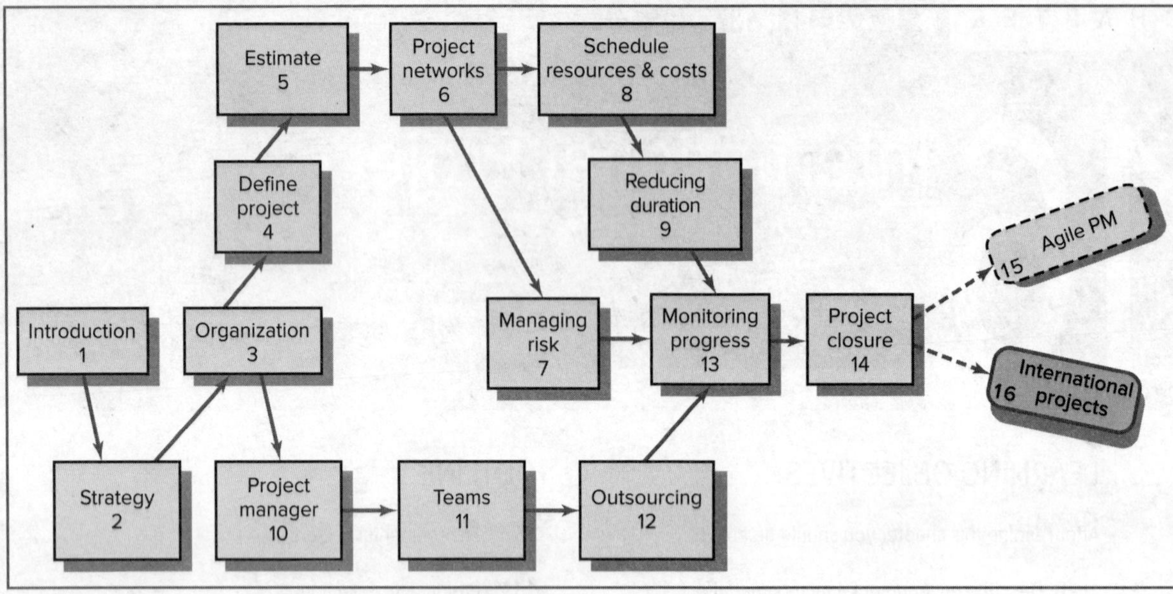

The principal benefit of living abroad is that it enables us to get glimpses of ourselves as others see us and to realize that others' views are more accurate than ours. Progress begins with grasping the truth about ourselves, however unpleasant it may be.

—Russel Ackoff, The Wharton School, University of Pennsylvania

Thanks to technology we live in a "flat world" in which more and more projects have an international element. It might be being sent to Zimbabwe for nine months as a lead contractor on a bridge construction project or flying back and forth across the Atlantic to work on a joint product venture with German engineers. Or it might be relying on a Korean computer supplier on a business expansion project or video conferencing with an Indian counterpart on a software project. This chapter targets the international project manager who must resettle in a foreign land to manage a project. The chapter also provides useful information for professionals whose project work requires interacting either directly or virtually with foreign counterparts from around the world.

There is no generally accepted framework or road map for project managers given overseas assignments. These project managers typically face a difficult set of problems—for example, absence from home, friends, and sometimes family; personal risks; missed career opportunities; foreign language, culture, and laws; and adverse conditions. Of course, there are positives—for example, increased income, increased responsibilities, career opportunities, foreign travel, and new lifetime friends. How the international project manager adapts and approaches challenges encountered in the host country often determines the success or failure of a project.

This chapter focuses on four major issues surrounding the management of international projects. First, major environmental factors that impact project selection and implementation are briefly highlighted. Second, an example of how organizations decide where to expand globally is provided. Third, the challenge of working in a foreign culture is addressed. Finally, how companies select and train professionals for international projects is discussed. Although by no means comprehensive, this chapter provides an understanding of the major issues and challenges confronting managers working abroad on projects. Much of this information is also useful to those working from a distance with foreign counterparts.

16.1 Environmental Factors

LO 16-1

Describe environmental factors that affect project management in different countries.

The major challenge international project managers face is the reality that what works at home may not work in a foreign environment. Too often project managers impose practices, assumed to be superior, from their home country on host-country nationals without questioning their applicability to the new environment. Although there are similarities between domestic and international projects, management practices vary across nations and cultures. It is these differences that can turn an international project into a nightmare. If potential international project managers have a good awareness of differences in the host country's environment from their own domestic environment, the dangers and obstacles of the global project can be reduced or avoided. There are several basic factors in the host country's environment that may alter how projects will be implemented: legal/political factors, security, geography, economic factors, infrastructure, and culture (see Figure 16.1).

Legal/Political Factors

Expatriate project managers should operate within the laws and regulations of the host country. Political stability and local laws strongly influence how projects will be implemented. Typically these laws favor the protection of the local workers, suppliers, and environment. For example, how much control will be imposed from government agencies? What is the attitude of federal and state bureaucracies toward regulations and approval policies that can cause project delays? How much government interference or support can one expect? For example, some governments interpret regulations arbitrarily, depending upon personal interests.

The constraints imposed by national and local laws need to be identified and adhered to. Are local ecological laws restrictive? Will manufacturing a new product in a computer chip plant require exporting toxic waste materials? What are the pollution standards? How will labor laws affect the use of local workers to complete the project?

FIGURE 16.1 Environmental Factors Affecting International Projects

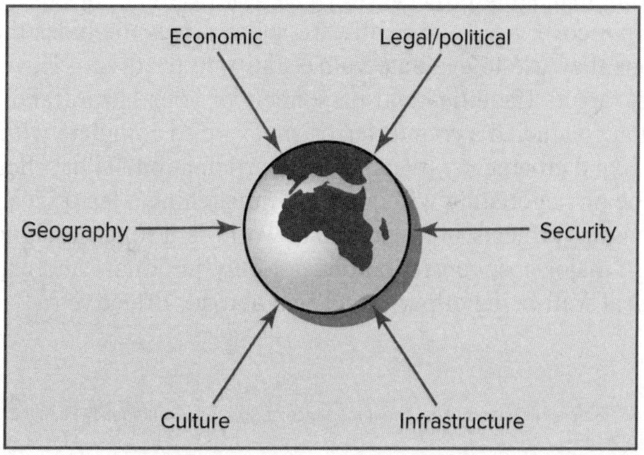

Given that laws that affect business vary widely across countries, qualified legal assistance is essential.

Government corruption is a part of international business. In China, various forms of obligatory "profit sharing" with city officials in the Hainan province have been reported. Employment of relatives, donations, and other "favors" are an expected cost of doing business in that region. A 2022 European Union (EU) study reported that 98 percent of Greek citizens believe corruption is "widespread" in their country. Conversely, just 16 percent of those in Denmark believe that corruption is rampant in their country (Friedman, 2022).

Political stability is another key factor in deciding to implement a project in a foreign country. What are the chances that there will be a change in the party in power during the project? Are the tax provisions and government regulations stable or subject to change with the winds of political change? How are laws made, and what is the past record of fairness? How are labor unions treated in the political realm? Does labor unrest exist? Is there a chance for a coup d'état? Contingency plans need to be established to respond to emergencies.

Security

International terrorism is a fact of life in today's world. Tim Daniel, chief operating officer of International SOS Assistance, Inc., reported that the number of his firm's clients doubled after September 11th. SOS is a security firm that specializes in evacuating expatriates from dangerous situations around the world. The company cites PricewaterhouseCoopers, Nortel Networks Corp., and Citigroup among its clients (Scown, 1993).

Crime is another factor. The growing presence of the Russian Mafia has discouraged many foreign firms from setting up operations in Russia. And piracy is a threat off the coast of Somalia and other parts of the Indian Ocean. Kidnapping of American professionals is also a threat in many parts of the world.

Security nationally involves the capacity of a country's military and police forces to prevent and respond to attacks. In many foreign countries, American firms have to augment the countries' security system. For example, it is common practice to hire tribal bodyguards in such places as Angola and Uzbekistan.

Another cost associated with terrorism is the ease of commerce across borders. Heightened security measures have created border congestions that have expanded the time and cost of moving personnel, materials, and equipment across countries. These constraints need to be factored into the budget and schedule of projects.

Risk management is always a vital part of project management. It plays an even bigger role in managing projects overseas. For example, Strohl Systems Group, a global leader in recovery-planning software and services, includes the following among the questions they use to evaluate vulnerability to terrorism: Have you included possible terrorist targets (facilities and personnel) in your hazard and vulnerability analysis? Have you conducted a counterterrorism exercise complete with law enforcement, fire, medical, and emergency management participation? What should your organization's policy be on negotiating with a person threatening a terrorist act?[1]

Managing projects in a dangerous world is a tough assignment. Security precautions are major cost considerations not only in dollars and cents but also in the psychological well-being of personnel sent abroad. Effective risk management is critical.

[1] Scheier, R., "Before Disaster Strikes: The Importance of Business Contingency Planning," searchcio.techtarget.com. Accessed 2/2/14.

Geography

One factor that is often underestimated until project personnel actually arrive at a foreign destination is the geography of the country. Imagine what it is like to deplane from a modern aircraft and encounter the 105-degree heat and 90 percent humidity of Jakarta, Indonesia, or 3 feet of fresh snow and −22-degree temperatures in Kokkola, Finland. Whether it is the wind, the rain, the heat, the jungle, or the desert, more than one project manager has asserted that the greatest challenge was overcoming the "elements." Mother Nature cannot be ignored.

The planning and implementation of a project must take into account the impact the country's geography will have on the project. For example, a salvage operation off the coast of Greenland can only be scheduled one month out of the year because the waterway is frozen over during the remainder of the year. Construction projects in Southeast Asia have to accommodate the monsoon season, when rainfall can be as high as 50 inches per month.

Geography does not just affect outdoor projects. It can have an indirect effect on "indoor" projects as well. For example, one information systems specialist reported that his performance on a project in northern Sweden declined due to sleep deprivation. He attributed his problems to the 20 hours of daylight this part of the world experiences during summer months.

Finally, extreme weather conditions can make extraordinary demands on equipment. Projects can grind to a halt because of equipment breakdown under the brunt of the wind and sand. Working under extreme conditions typically requires special equipment, which increases the costs and complexity of the project.

Before beginning a project in a foreign land, project planners and managers need to study carefully the unique characteristics of the geography of that country. They need to factor into project plans and schedules such items as climate, seasons, altitude, and natural geographical obstacles. See Snapshot from Practice 16.1: The Filming of *Apocalypse Now* for an example of a poorly planned endeavor in the Philippines.

Economic Factors

Basic economic factors in foreign countries and regions influence choices of site selection and project success. The gross domestic product (GDP) of a country suggests that country's level of economic development. A faltering economy may indicate fewer sources of capital funding. Changes in protectionist strategies of a host country, such as import quotas and tariffs, can quickly alter the viability of projects. Other factors such as balance of payments, taxation, labor laws, safety regulations, and market size can influence project choices and operations.

The skills, access to education, and labor supply prevalent in a host country can determine the choice of a project site. Is project selection driven by low wage levels or the availability of technically skilled talent? For example, one can hire three computer programmers in Ukraine for the price of one programmer in the United States. Conversely, many high-tech companies are willing to endure the additional expense of setting up joint projects in Switzerland and Germany to take advantage of their engineering prowess.

Financial exposure is a significant risk for many international projects. Let's look first at the potential impact of currency fluctuations on project success. For example, a U.S. contractor agrees to build a customized product for a German client. The product will be built in the United States. The contractor estimates that the project will cost \$925,000 and, in order to earn a nice profit, prices the project at \$1 million. To

SNAPSHOT FROM PRACTICE 16.1 The Filming of *Apocalypse Now**

In February 1976, Francis Ford Coppola took his Hollywood film crew to the Philippines to shoot *Apocalypse Now,* a film adaptation of Joseph Conrad's *Heart of Darkness* within the context of the Vietnam conflict. The Philippines was chosen because the terrain was similar to Vietnam's, and the government was willing to rent out its helicopter force for the movie. At the time, the U.S. military was unwilling to cooperate on a film about Vietnam. An additional advantage was cheap labor. Coppola was able to hire more than 300 laborers at $1 to $3 per day to construct elaborate production sets, including an impressive Cambodian temple. *Apocalypse Now* was scheduled for 16 weeks of shooting at a budget of $12 to $14 million.

Months earlier, George Lucas, of *Star Wars* fame, warned Coppola against filming the movie in the Philippines. He said, "It's one thing to go over there for three weeks with five people and scrounge some footage with the Filipino Army, but if you go over there with a big Hollywood production, the longer you stay the more in danger you are of getting sucked into the swamp." His words turned out to be prophetic.

A civil war was going on between government forces and communist rebels. Shooting was repeatedly interrupted because the Philippine military ordered their helicopter pilots to leave the set and fly to the mountains to fight the rebels.

In May 1976, a typhoon struck the Philippine Islands, destroying most of the movie sets. The film team was forced to shut down production and returned to the United States for two months.

The lead character was played by Martin Sheen, who suffered a serious heart attack under the stress and heat of the filming and had to return to the United States. Coppola scrambled to film the scenes that did not require Sheen, but eventually production came to a standstill until Sheen's return nine weeks later.

To make matters worse, actor Marlon Brando showed up greatly overweight, which was totally out of character with the rogue Green Beret he was to portray. Coppola admitted that Brando was too fat to play the scenes as written in the original script. Under immense pressure, Coppola struggled to come up with an ending for his film.

The entire project proved to be a traumatic experience for Coppola, who had enjoyed Academy Award success with his previous *Godfather* movies. "There were times when I thought I was going to die, literally, from the inability to move the problems I had. I would go to bed at four in the morning in a cold sweat."

Film production ended in May 1977 after more than 200 days of shooting. The final cost was about $30 million.

Apocalypse Now opened in August 1979 to mixed reviews, then ultimately critical acclaim. The American Film Institute ranked the movie as the 30th greatest film of all time. The theatrical release grossed over $82 million worldwide.

**Hearts of Darkness: A Filmmaker's Apocalypse* (Paramount Pictures, 1991).

accommodate the German buyer the price is converted to euros. Suppose at the time of the contract the exchange rate is $1.15 per euro, and the price specified in the contract is €869,566.

Ten months later the project is completed as expected, with work costing the estimated $925,000, and the customer pays the agreed-upon price of €869,566. However, the exchange rate has changed; it is now $1.05 per euro. That being the case, the payment equates to €869,566 × 1.05 = $913,044. Instead of reaping a nice profit, the contractor suffers a $(913,044 – 925,000) = $–11,956 loss!

Companies can protect themselves against adverse currency fluctuations in a number of related ways. First, they can *hedge* against this risk by having all parties agree to finalize the deal and make payments at a specified future date. Finance people call this a *forward exchange* or *contract.* Second, they can stipulate in the contract certain conditions based on exchange rates to ensure their profit margin. Finally, many multinational companies who do business in the client country avoid currency exchange and simply use local currency to manage operations in that country. Financiers refer to this as a *natural hedge* (Moffet, Stonehill, & Eiteman, 2012).

Inflation is another significant risk. One of the greatest strengths of the U.S. economy is its relatively low inflation rate (below 3 percent from 1990 to 2012). Other countries do not enjoy such stability. Rapid inflation can strike at any time and have a profound impact on project costs and profits. Suppose that an Italian contractor successfully wins the bid to build a bridge for the Tanzanian government in East Africa. Work starts in 2010 and will be completed by the end of 2011. In 2010 the Tanzanian inflation ratio is less than 6 percent with an average inflation rate of 6.7 over the past decade. The contractor uses what she considers a conservative inflation rate of 9 percent when estimating the costs of the project at 1,800,000 schillings (Tanzanian currency). In order to win the bid and enjoy a solid profit the agreed-upon price is 2 million schillings.

Early in 2011, Tanzania experiences a sporadic rainfall, which, coupled with increased oil prices, causes the inflation rate to jump to over 20 percent! Suddenly costs of certain elements of the project increase dramatically and instead of garnering a nice profit the contractor barely breaks even. Companies can protect against inflation by tying costs to a strong currency such as the U.S. dollar, Kuwait dinar, or euro and/or negotiating cost-plus contracts (see Chapter 12 Appendix) with the client.

Bartering is a form of compensation that is still used by some countries and organizations. For example, one project in Algeria was paid in goat skins. The goat skins were eventually sold to an Italian manufacturer of gloves. A project along the Caspian Sea was paid for in oil. A small group of firms specializes in bartering for project contractors. These intermediaries charge a commission to sell the bartered goods (e.g., oil, diamonds, wheat) for the contractor. However, dealing with commodities can be a risky enterprise.

Infrastructure

Infrastructure refers to a country's or community's ability to provide the services required for a project. Infrastructure needs for a project include communication, transportation, power, technology, and education systems. Power outages are common in many parts of the world. For example, India's burgeoning economy came to a halt during the 2012 summer, when over 670 million people were without power for more than two days. In 2022, about 34 percent of Indian households reported not facing any power outages; however, 28 percent of the households (mostly in rural areas) reported power outages for up to two hours everyday (Statista, 2023). If reliable power is not sufficient, other alternatives need to be considered. For example, construction firms often rely on heavy diesel generators as backups on their projects. Software projects across borders are common today; however, they depend on reliable telecommunication networks. If a project depends on a high ratio of vendor suppliers, good roads, and other transportation modes such as air and seaports, a good infrastructure is imperative.

An example of a project that failed to take into account the needs and infrastructure of the host nation involved a U.S. company that was awarded the contract for building a hospital in Botswana. The local African officials wanted a "low-tech" healthcare facility that would take local traditions and conditions into consideration. Because their relatives generally accompanied patients, space had to be provided for them, too. Electricity was not reliably supplied, and it was doubtful whether well-educated doctors would want to spend careers away from the city. Therefore, the locals wanted a hospital for basic care with minimum technology. The construction company doing the building, on the other hand, had a preconceived notion of what a hospital should be and was not going to be accused of building a second-rate facility. It built a modern hospital that could have stood in any U.S. city. The building was completed; however, even after several years it was not used because the electricity was not sufficient, the air conditioning could not be used, and doctors refused to live in the rural area (Adler & Gunderson, 2007).

Organizations must consider the needs of the families of the personnel they send overseas. Will the facilities and living conditions for the expatriate families place an undue hardship on them? Will schooling for children be available? The welfare and comfort of expatriate families play an important role in retaining good project managers and promoting their peak performance.

Culture

Visiting project managers must respect the customs, values, philosophies, and social standards of their host country. Global managers recognize that if the customs and sociocultural dimensions of the host country are not accommodated, projects will rarely succeed. Too many project audits and final reports of international projects reflect challenges and problems linked to cultural differences.

For most project managers, the biggest difference in managing an international project is operating in a national culture where things are done differently. For example, most economically developed nations use the same project management techniques (CPM, risk analysis, trade-off analysis). However, how activity work is performed can be very different in the host country. For example, a backhoe is used to dig a trench in France, while 20 laborers are used to dig a similar trench in Ethiopia.

Will English be the operating language, or will the project manager need to be fluent in the foreign language? Will translation services be available and sufficient? Communication problems—because of language differences—often become a major problem in carrying out even simple tasks. Although translators can help tremendously, their use does not solve the communication problem completely, because something is lost in translation. For example, consider the disastrous consequences of differences in interpretations and expectations between the Brazilians and Americans highlighted in Snapshot from Practice 16.2: River of Doubt.

Will religious factors influence the project? For example, religious factors touched the spouse of a Scandinavian project manager responsible for building a water desalination plant from seawater in a Middle East country. She was restricted to the living compound for families of foreign guest workers. Going outside the compound to a nearby city meant covering her head, arms, and legs and being accompanied by another woman or, preferably, a man. A physical altercation in the city concerning her clothing was traumatic for her. She left the country and returned home. Her partner requested a transfer back home three months later. The loss of the original project manager set the project back three months.

Not only do project managers have to adapt to the culture of the host country, but often overseas projects require working with people from other different countries. For example, on a light rail project in the Philippines, an American firm was hired to oversee the interests of local real estate companies that were funding the project. The American project manager had to work with Czech representatives who were providing the rail equipment, Japanese engineers responsible for building the rail, Australian bankers who were providing additional financing, and an Indian firm that provided the principal architects, as well as the native Filipinos.

SNAPSHOT FROM PRACTICE 16.2 River of Doubt*

After his crushing election defeat in 1912 as a third-party candidate, former president Theodore ("Teddy") Roosevelt set his sights on a grand adventure, the first descent of an unmapped, rapids-choked tributary of the Amazon aptly titled the "River of Doubt." Together with Brazil's most famous explorer, Candido Mariano da Silva Rondon, Roosevelt accomplished a feat that belongs in the annals of great expeditions.

George Rinhart/Corbis/Getty Images

Along the way, Roosevelt and his men faced an unbelievable series of hardships, losing their canoes and supplies to crushing whitewater rapids and enduring starvation, attacks from indigenous groups, disease, drowning, and even murder within their ranks. Candice Millard brings alive these extraordinary events in her nonfiction thriller *The River of Doubt.* While her account details the ill-fated journey it also reveals insights into international project management as it describes the collaboration between the American and Brazilian cohorts. While each party ultimately earned the respect and admiration of the other, friction between them simmered from the outset.

One source of consternation was the amount of supplies and luggage that the Americans required for the journey. Warned that the luggage requirements of the former president and his party would be extensive, the Brazilian commodore, Rondon, ordered 110 mules and 17 pack oxen to be used for the expedition's overland journey across the Brazilian highland to the great river. Surely, he felt, this would be more than necessary for such a trip.

The Brazilians were astounded by the sheer volume of baggage that was unloaded from Roosevelt's ship, the *Vandycks.* There were mountains of crates: guns and ammunition, chairs and tables, tents and cots, and equipment for collecting and preserving specimens, surveying the river, and cooking meals. An exhausted stevedore elicited a roar of laughter from the onlooking crowd when he announced, "Nothing lacking but the piano!"

Rather than risk embarrassment by telling Roosevelt that they were not prepared to take so much luggage, Rondon scrambled to find additional animals. Extra oxen and mules were located, but they were far from tame. Loaded with supplies, the oxen bucked and threw off the packs. The expedition was delayed as local cowboys endeavored to "break" the animals as quickly as possible.

Within days of finally setting off across the vast highlands, Roosevelt and his men began to experience the harsh realities that were to plague the expedition. After crossing a bone-strewn graveyard of oxen and mules that had starved to death or been eaten during previous expeditions, they were stunned by the sight of unopened supply crates, all clearly marked "Roosevelt South American Expedition." The pack animals, still making their weary away across the plateau ahead of them, had begun bucking off their heavy loads!

As the officers rode slowly past the boxes, they wondered what they were leaving behind and how precious it might become in the months ahead. Little did they know how true those fears would be.

Six weeks into the expedition Roosevelt needed daily attention by the team's physician to deal with a badly infected leg, which at times made him delirious. Ultimately the expedition cut short its mission. Roosevelt staggered out of the jungle having lost over 50 pounds, and he would suffer from recurring bouts of jungle fever for the rest of his life.

*C. Millard, *The River of Doubt* (New York: Doubleday), 2005.

Of all the factors, working within a multicultural environment is most often the greatest challenge for project managers. It will be dealt with in detail later in this chapter.

16.2 Project Site Selection

LO 16-2

Identify factors that typically are considered in selecting a foreign location for a project.

As project managers study the factors contributing to site selection, they will see that inherent in all of them is the risk level that senior management and directors are willing to accept for the potential rewards of a successful international project. One approach for the project manager to digest, clarify, and understand the factors leading to the selection of a specific project is to use a risk matrix similar to those found in Chapter 7.

Figure 16.2 presents a truncated matrix for project site selection of the construction of a laser printer factory in Singapore, India, or Ireland. In this example, political stability, worker skill and supply, culture compatibility, infrastructure, government support, and product-to-market advantage are the major assessment factors. Each project site is compared against each factor. Figure 16.3 depicts a further breakdown of the infrastructure evaluation factor. In this example, transportation, an educated workforce, utilities, telecommunications, and vendor suppliers are considered important to evaluating the infrastructure for each site. The scores given in Figure 16.3 are used to

FIGURE 16.2
Assessment Matrix Project Site Selection

Score legend
5 = excellent
3 = acceptable
1 = poor

	Political stability	Worker skill, supply	Culture compatibility	Infrastructure	Government support	Product-to-market advantage
Singapore	5	4	4	4	4	3
India	3	4	3	3	3	3
Ireland	5	4	5	5	5	5

FIGURE 16.3
Evaluation Matrix Breakdown for Infrastructure

Score legend
5 = excellent
3 = acceptable
1 = poor

	Transportation	Educated workforce	Utilities	Telecommunications	Vendor suppliers
Singapore	5	4	5	5	4
India	3	4	4	4	2
Ireland	5	4	5	5	5

assign values to the infrastructure factor of the assessment matrix, Figure 16.2. In this project, Ireland is the choice. Clearly, Singapore and Ireland are very close in terms of infrastructure and several other factors. However, the major assessment factor of using Ireland to access the European economic community (product-to-market advantage) turned the decision.

Given the macroeconomic factors, the firm's strategic posture toward global projects, and the major considerations for selecting this project, it is imperative the project manager quickly become sensitized to the foreign cultural factors that can spell project success or failure.

16.3 Cross-Cultural Considerations: A Closer Look

LO 16-3

Understand cross-cultural issues that impact working on international projects.

The concept of culture was introduced in Chapter 3 as referring to the unique personality of a particular firm. More specifically, culture was defined as a system of shared norms, beliefs, values, and customs that bind people together, creating shared meaning and a unique identity. **Culture** is a concept created for descriptive purposes and depends on the group that is the focus of attention. For example, within a global context, *culture* can refer to certain regions (e.g., Europeans, Arabs), to specific nations (e.g., French, Thai), or to certain ethnic or religious groups (e.g., Kurds, African Americans). This chapter looks at national cultures; many cultural characteristics are borderless and there is considerable variation within any one country. Still, national cultures provide a useful anchor for understanding different habits, customs, and values around the world.

Right or wrong, Americans have a reputation for not being able to work effectively in foreign cultures. (When we use the term *American,* we are referring to people from the United States.) In the 1960s, the term *ugly American* encapsulated the apparent indifference of Americans to native cultures when working or traveling abroad. Americans are often criticized for being parochial; that is, they view the world solely through their own perspectives. People with a parochial perspective do not recognize that other people have different ways of living and working effectively. American parochial attitudes probably reflect the huge domestic market of the United States, the geographic isolation of the United States, and the reality that English is becoming the international business language in many parts of the world.

It is important that Americans working on international projects anticipate cultural differences. Take, for example, a project manager from a large North American construction company who was given the responsibility for selecting a site for the design and construction of a large fish-processing plant in a West African country. The manager assessed potential sites according to the availability of reliable power, closeness to transportation, nearness to the river for access of fishing boats from the Atlantic Ocean, proximity to main markets, and availability of housing and people for employment. After evaluating alternative sites, the project manager chose the optimum location. Just prior to requesting bids from local contractors for some of the site preparation, the manager discovered, in talking to the contractors, that the site was located on ground considered sacred by the local people, who believed this site was the place where their gods resided. None of the local people upon whom the project manager was depending for staff would ever consider working there! The project manager quickly revised his choice and relocated the site. In this case, he was lucky that the cultural gaffe was discovered prior to construction. Too often these errors are realized only after a project is completed.[2]

Some argue that Americans have become less parochial. International travel, immigration, movies, and the popularity of such international events as the Olympics have made more Americans sensitive to cultural differences. While Americans may be more worldly, there is still a tendency for them to believe that American cultural values and ways of doing things are superior to all others. This ethnocentric perspective is reflected in wanting to conduct business only on their terms and stereotyping other countries as lazy, corrupt, or inefficient. Americans need to make a serious effort to appreciate other ways of approaching work and problems in other countries.

Finally, American project managers have earned a reputation abroad for being very good at understanding technology but not good at understanding people. As one Indonesian engineer put it, "Americans are great at solving technical problems, but they tend to ignore the people factor." For example, Americans tend to underestimate the importance that relationship building plays in conducting business in other countries. Americans have a tendency to want to get down to work and let friendships evolve in the course of their work. In most other cultures just the opposite is true. Before foreigners work with you, they want to get to know you as a person. Trust is not established by credentials but, rather, evolves from personal interaction. Business deals often require a lengthy and elaborate courtship (Arms & Lucas, 1978; Chen & Miller, 2010). For example, it may take five to eight meetings before Arab managers are even willing to discuss business details.

Adjustments

Two of the biggest adjustments Americans typically have to make in working abroad are adapting to the general pace of life and the punctuality of people. In America "time is money," and a premium is placed on working quickly. Other cultures do not share Americans' sense of urgency and are accustomed to a much slower pace of life. They can't understand why Americans are always in such a hurry. Punctuality varies across cultures. For example, Americans will generally tolerate someone being 5 to 10 minutes late. In contrast, among Peruvians, the period before an apology or explanation for being late is expected might be 45 minutes to an hour!

While working on multicultural projects, managers sometimes encounter ethical dilemmas that are culturally bound. For example, the 1999 Olympic site selection scandal featured the sordid details of committee members peddling their votes for a wide range of gifts (e.g., university scholarships for their children, extravagant trips). In many societies such "bribes" or "tributes" are expected and the only way to conduct meaningful business. Moreover, many cultures will not grant a female project manager the same respect they will a male project manager. Should U.S. management increase project risk or violate its own sex-discrimination policy?

These cultural differences are just the tip of the iceberg. There are numerous *How to Do Business in . . .* books written by people who have traveled and worked abroad. Although these books may lack rigor, they typically do a good job of identifying local customs and common mistakes made by outsiders. On the other hand, anthropologists have made significant contributions to our understanding of why and how the cultures of societies are different (see Research Highlights 16.1: Cross-Cultural Orientations and 16.2: Hofstede Framework). Students of international project management are

[2] This incident was cited in Lane, H. W., and J. J. DiStefano, *International Project Management,* 2nd ed. (Boston: PWS-Kent, 1992), p. 27.

Research Highlight 16.1

Cross-Cultural Orientations*

Anthropologists Kluckhohn and Strodtbeck assert that cultural variations reflect how different societies have responded to common issues or problems throughout time (see Figure 16.4). Five of the issues featured in their comparative framework are discussed here.

- *Relationship to nature.* This issue reflects how people relate to the natural world around them and to the supernatural. Should people dominate their environment, live in harmony with it, or be subjugated to it? People from the United States generally strive to harness nature's forces and change them as they need. Other societies, as in India, strive to live in harmony with nature. Still other societies see themselves at the mercy of physical forces and/or subject to the will of a supreme being. Life in this context is viewed as predetermined, preordained, or an exercise in chance.
- *Time orientation.* Does the culture focus on the past, present, or future? For example, many European countries focus on the past and emphasize maintaining tradition. People from the United States, on the other hand, are less concerned with tradition and tend to focus on the present and near future. Paradoxically, Japanese society, while rich with tradition, has a much longer time horizon.
- *Activity orientation.* This issue refers to a desirable focus of behavior. Some cultures emphasize "being" or living in the moment. This orientation stresses experiencing life and seeking immediate gratification. Other cultures emphasize "doing" and emphasize postponing immediate gratification for greater accomplishment. A third alternative is the "control" orientation, where people restrain their desires by detaching themselves from objects. The activity dimension affects how people approach work and leisure and the extent to which work-related concerns pervade their lives. It is reflected in the age-old question "Do we live to work or work to live?"
- *Basic nature of people.* Does a culture view people as good, evil, or some mix of these two? In many Southeast Asian countries, people see themselves as basically honest and trustworthy. Conversely, some Mediterranean cultures have been characterized as taking a rather evil view of human nature. North Americans are somewhere in between. They see people as basically good but stay on guard so as not to be taken advantage of.
- *Relationships among people.* This issue concerns the responsibility one has for others. Americans, for instance, tend to be highly individualistic and believe everyone should take care of themselves. In contrast, many Asian societies emphasize concern for the group or community they are members of. A third variation is hierarchical, which is similar to the group except that in these societies groups are hierarchically ranked, and membership is essentially stable over time. This is a characteristic of aristocratic societies and caste systems.

The Kluckhohn and Strodtbeck framework provides a basis for a deeper understanding of cultural differences. At the same time, they warn that not all members of a culture practice the same behavior all the time and, as in the United States, there is likely to be considerable variation within a given culture.

*F. Kluckhohn and F. L. Strodtbeck, *Variations in Value Orientations* (Evanston, IL: Row, Peterson, 1961).

FIGURE 16.4 Kluckhohn–Strodtbeck's Cross-Cultural Framework

Note: The line indicates where the United States tends to fall along these issues.

Cultural issue	Variations		
Relationship to nature	Domination	Harmony	Subjugation
Time orientation	Past	Present	Future
Activity orientation	Being	Doing	Controlling
Nature of people	Good	Evil	Mixed
Relationships among people	Individualist	Group	Hierarchical

Research Highlight 16.2

Hofstede Framework*

The Hofstede framework grew from a study of 88,000 people working in IBM subsidiaries in 50 countries and 3 multicountry regions. Based on responses to a 32-item questionnaire, Dutch social scientist Geert Hofstede developed different dimensions for examining cultures:

1. *Individualism versus collectivism*—identifies whether a culture holds individuals or the group responsible for each member's welfare.
2. *Power distance*—describes the degree to which a culture accepts status and power differences among its members.
3. *Uncertainty avoidance*—identifies a culture's willingness to accept uncertainty and ambiguity about the future.
4. *Masculinity-femininity*—describes the degree to which the culture emphasizes competitive and achievement-oriented behavior or displays concerns for relationships.

Figure 16.5 shows how he ranked selected countries according to collectivism-individualism and power distance. Wealth appears to influence both factors. Power distance is correlated with income inequality in a country, while individualism is correlated with national wealth (per capita gross national product). As a result, high power distance and collectivism are often found together, as are low power distance and individualism. This can affect decision making on project teams. For example, while the high collectivism may lead a project team in Thailand to operate consensually, the high power distance may cause decisions to be heavily influenced by the desires of the project manager. Conversely, a similar team operating in a more individualistic and low power distance context such as Great Britain or United States might make decisions with more open debate, including challenging the preferences of the project manager.

*G. Hofstede, *Culture's Consequences: Comparing Values, Behaviors, Institutions and Organizations across Nations,* 2nd ed. (Thousand Oaks, CA: Sage, 2001), http://www.geerthofstede.nl.

FIGURE 16.5
Sample Country Clusters on Hofstede's Dimensions of Individualism-Collectivism and Power Distance

Collectivism		Colombia, Peru, Thailand, Singapore, Mexico, Turkey, Indonesia
Individualism	Israel, Finland, Germany, Ireland, New Zealand, Canada, Great Britain, United States	Spain, South Africa, France, Italy, Belgium
	Low power distance	High power distance

encouraged to study these works to gain a deeper understanding of the root causes of cultural diversity. To read how these theories guide e-mail etiquette, see the Snapshot from Practice: Avoiding Communication Catastrophes When E-mailing Across Cultures.

So what can be said to prepare people to work on international projects? The world is too diverse to do justice in one chapter to all the cultural variations managers are likely to encounter when working on international projects. Instead, a sample of some of these differences will be highlighted in this chapter by discussing working on projects in four countries: Mexico, France, Saudi Arabia, and China. We apologize to our readers outside the United States because briefings are presented from the viewpoint of a U.S. project manager working in these countries. Still, in an effort not to be too ethnocentric, we present a fifth scenario for foreign project managers assigned to work in the United States. We should also note that these cultural observations are based on

SNAPSHOT FROM PRACTICE

Avoiding Communication Catastrophes When E-mailing Across Cultures*

E-mailing is an important mode of communication, especially across continents and cultures. It is also an essential part of being a project professional. There are, however, risks involved when sending e-mails across cultures because of miscommunication. Global business expert, Darren Menabney proposed several tips to help project professionals write effective cross-cultural e-mails.

PAY ATTENTION TO TITLES, NAMES, AND GENDER ISSUES.

If the receiver of your e-mail has a title and/or uses post name designations like Ph.D. or Professor, be sure to include these. If you have received an e-mail from this person before, use the same title and designations that were included in the received e-mail. In most very hierarchical cultures, titles mean a lot and not using them can offend. If you are sending a first e-mail to someone whose gender preference is unknown, try to avoid gender-specific pronouns. Additionally, make it clear in your correspondence what gender your gender is if you are expecting a reply e-mail from them.

HOW TO CC.

Some cultures are ones in which a lot of individuals participate in decisions. This is especially true of Japan and South Korea. In these cultures, you will want to CC all who are involved. Leaving off someone who is a part of the reporting chain can offend them.

LOW-CONTEXT COMMUNICATION IS USUALLY BEST.

In some countries that are considered high-context cultures (e.g., India, Brazil), a lot is being communicated by what is not being said. In low-context cultures (i.e., United States, Australia), the words and ideas speak for themselves. The classic example is while Americans feel comfortable saying "no," people in high-context cultures avoid saying "no" but assume the recipient will figure it out. The implication is that it is better to assume a low-context culture by including more information and being more explicit in your writing and the requests that you are asking from the recipient.

BE PERCEPTIVE ABOUT FRANKNESS OR BLUNTNESS.

It is important that you be considerate of your recipient in terms of how they might perceive your choice of words. In some cultures, disagreements are less open. In these cultures, your content must be more subtle, and less straightforward. There are significant differences among cultures as to the explicitness of written communication.

The overriding principle of cross-cultural e-mails is to imagine yourself as the recipient of the e-mail. How would your message be received in the context of the receiver's culture? Do not impose your own cultural norms on the receiver because they can be interpreted very differently by those from different cultures. Therefore, drop your assumptions, your idioms, and think from the perspective of the receiver, their culture, and their interpretation of your message. To do this, it becomes imperative that you learn about the receivers' culture, their communication norms, etc. Determine what is the same and what is different about your way of expressing ideas, thoughts, and theirs.

*Adapted from D. Menabney, "How to Avoid Disaster when Sending E-mails across Cultures," forbes.com, July 12, 2020. Accessed 3/3/23.

significant differentiations about different countries, and there are always exceptions to the rule. Finally, although by no means exhaustive, these briefings provide a taste of what it is like to work in and with people from these countries.

Working in Mexico

The United States developed historically in an environment where it was important for strangers to be able to get along, interact, and do business. On the American frontier, almost everyone was a stranger, and people had to both cooperate and keep their distance. The New England Yankee sentiment "Good fences make good neighbors"[3] expresses this American cultural value well. Conversely, Mexico developed

[3] This expression appears in Robert Frost's poem "The Mending Wall" (1914).

historically in an environment where the only people to trust were family and close friends—and by extension, people who were known to those whom you knew well. As a consequence, personal relationships dominate all aspects of Mexican business. While Americans are generally taught not to do business with friends, Mexicans and other Latin Americans are taught to do business with no one but friends.

The significance of personal relationships has created a *compadre* system in which Mexicans are obligated to give preference to relatives and friends when hiring, contracting, procuring, and sharing business opportunities. People from Canada or the United States often complain that such practices contribute to inefficiency in Mexican firms. While this may or may not be the case, efficiency is prized by Americans, while Mexicans place a higher value on friendship.

Mexicans tend to perceive Americans as being "cold." They also believe that most Americans look down on them. Among the most effective things an American can do to prevent being seen as a typical *Gringo* is to take the time and effort in the beginning of a working relationship to really get to know Mexican counterparts. Because family is all-important to Mexicans, a good way for developing a personal relationship is exchanging information about each other's family. Mexicans will often gauge people's trustworthiness by the loyalty and attention they devote to their family.

The *mañana* syndrome reflects another cultural difference between Americans and Mexicans. Mexicans have a different concept of time than Americans do. Mexicans feel confined and pressured when given deadlines; they prefer open-ended schedules. They generally consider individuals to be more important than schedules. If a friend drops in at work, most Mexicans will stop and talk, regardless of how long it takes and even if chatting makes their work late. This sometimes contributes to the erroneous perception that Mexicans lack a work ethic.

Finally, as in many other cultures, Mexicans do not share Americans' confidence that they control their own destiny. While Americans are taught "When the going gets tough, the tough get going," Mexicans are taught "Taking action without knowing what is expected or wanted can have dangerous consequences." Mexicans tend to be more cautious and want to spend more time discussing risks and potential problems that Americans might dismiss as improbable or irrelevant.

Other useful guidelines for working with Mexicans on projects include the following:

1. Americans tend to be impersonal and practical when making arguments; Mexicans can be very passionate and emotional when arguing. They enjoy a lively debate.
2. Where Americans tend to use meetings as the place to work things out publicly, Mexicans tend to see meetings as the place where persons with authority ratify what has been decided during informal private discussions.
3. While Mexicans can be emotional, they tend to shy away from any sort of direct confrontation or criticism. A long silence often indicates displeasure or disagreement.
4. Speech in Mexico is often indirect. People rarely say no directly but are more likely to respond by saying maybe *(quizas),* or by saying "I will think about it" or changing the subject. Yes *(si)* is more likely to mean "I understand you" than "yes."
5. Titles are extremely important in Mexico and are always used when people are introducing themselves or being introduced. Pay as much attention to remembering a person's title as to remembering their name.

Today, with the North American Free Trade Agreement and increased international business activity in Mexico, old traditions are disappearing. American managers report that cultural differences are less evident in northern Mexico, where many multinational firms operate. There, *hora americana* (American time) rather than *hora mexicana* tends to be used when dealing with foreigners. Project managers should devote up-front effort to understanding how much older mores of Mexican culture apply to their project.[4]

Working in France

Some Americans consider the French the most difficult to work with among Europeans. This feeling probably stems from a reflection of the French culture, which is quite different from that in the United States.

In France, one's social class is very important. Social interactions are constrained by class standing, and during their lifetimes most French people do not encounter much change in social status. Unlike an American, who through hard work and success might move from the lowest economic stratum to the highest, a successful French person might, at best, climb one or two rungs up the social ladder. Additionally, the French are very status conscious and like to provide signs of this status, such as knowledge of literature and arts; a well-designed, tastefully decorated house; and a high level of education.

The French tend to admire or be fascinated with people who disagree with them; in contrast, Americans are more attracted to those who agree with them. As a result, the French are accustomed to conflict and, during negotiations, accept the fact that some positions are irreconcilable and must be accepted as such. Americans, on the other hand, tend to believe that conflicts can be resolved if both parties make an extra effort and are willing to compromise. Also, the French often determine a person's trustworthiness based on their first-hand, personal evaluation of the individual's character. Americans, in contrast, tend to evaluate a person's trustworthiness on the basis of past achievements and other people's evaluations.

The French are often accused of lacking an intense work ethic. For example, many French workers frown on overtime and, on average, have one of the longest vacations in the world (four to five weeks annually). On the other hand, the French enjoy a reputation for productive work, a result of the French tradition of craftsmanship. This tradition places a greater premium on quality than on getting things accomplished quickly.

Most French organizations tend to be highly centralized with rigid structures. As a result, it usually takes longer to carry out decisions. Because this arrangement is quite different from the more decentralized organizations in the United States, many U.S. project managers find the bureaucratic red tape a source of considerable frustration.

In countries like the United States, a great deal of motivation is derived from professional accomplishments. The French do not tend to share this same view of work. While they admire American industriousness, they believe that quality of life is what really matters. As a result, they attach much greater importance to leisure time, and many are unwilling to sacrifice the enjoyment of life for a dedication to project work. Public demonstrations against raising the French pension age from 62 to 64 is an example of this. For many French, retirement is a golden time to travel and enjoy the good things in life.

[4] Adapted from Kras, E., *Management in Two Cultures: Bridging the Gap between U.S. and Mexican Managers,* rev. ed. (Yarmouth, ME: Intercultural Press, 1995); Tuller, L. W., *An American's Guide to Doing Business in Latin America* (Avon, MA: Adams Business, 2008).

Cautions to remember with the French include these:

1. The French value punctuality. It is very important to be on time for meetings and social occasions.
2. Great importance is placed on neatness and taste. When interacting with French businesspeople, pay close attention to your own professional appearance and appear cultured and sophisticated.
3. The French can be very difficult to negotiate with. Often, they ignore facts, no matter how convincing they may be. They can be quite secretive about their position. It is difficult to obtain information from them, even in support for their position. Patience is essential for negotiating with them.
4. French managers tend to see their work as an intellectual exercise. They do not share the American view of management as an interpersonally demanding exercise, where plans have to be constantly "sold" upward and downward using personal skills.
5. The French generally consider managers to be experts. They expect managers to give precise answers to work-related questions. To preserve their reputation, some French managers act as if they know the answers to questions even when they don't.[5]

Working in Saudi Arabia

Project management has a long tradition in Saudi Arabia and other Arab countries. Western interest in oil has contributed greatly to an influx of wealth and subsequent modernization of Arab countries. Despite this tradition, foreigners often find it very hard to work on projects in Saudi Arabia. A number of cultural differences can be cited for this difficulty.

One is the Arabian view of time. In the United States, it is common to use the cliché "The early bird gets the worm." In Saudi Arabia, a favorite expression is "Bukra insha Allah," which means "Tomorrow if God wills," an expression that reflects the Saudis' approach to time. Unlike Westerners, who believe they control their own time, Arabs believe that Allah controls time. As a result, when Saudis commit themselves to a date in the future and fail to show up, there is no guilt or concern on their part because they have no control over time in the first place. In planning future events with Arabs, it pays to hold lead time to a week or less, because other factors may intervene or take precedence.

An associated cultural belief is that destiny depends more on the will of a supreme being than on the behavior of individuals. A higher power dictates the outcome of important events, so individual action is of little consequence. As a result, progress or the lack of progress on a project is considered more a question of fate than effort. This leads Saudis to rely less on detailed plans and schedules to complete projects than Americans do.

Another important cultural contrast between Saudi Arabians and Americans is emotion and logic. Saudis often act on the basis of emotion; in contrast, those in an Anglo culture are taught to act on logic. During negotiations, it is important not only to share the facts but also to make emotional appeals that demonstrate that your suggestion is the right thing to do.

[5] Adapted from Hallowell, R., D. Bowen, and C. I. Knoop, "Four Seasons Goes to Paris," *Academy of Management Executive*, vol. 16, no. 4 (November 2002), pp. 7–24; Hooker, J., *Working across Cultures* (Stanford, CA: Stanford Business Books, 2003); Morrison, T., and W. A. Conaway, *Kiss, Bow, or Shake Hands* (*The Bestselling Guide to Doing Business in More Than 60 Countries*), 2nd ed. (New York: Adams Media, 2006).

Saudis also use elaborate and ritualized forms of greeting and leave-taking. A businessperson may wait far past the assigned meeting time before being admitted to a Saudi office. Once there, the individual may find a host of others present; one-on-one meetings are rare. Moreover, during the meeting there may be continuous interruptions. Visitors arrive and begin talking to the host, and messengers may come in and go out on a regular basis. The businessperson is expected to take all this activity as perfectly normal and to remain composed and ready to continue discussions as soon as the host is prepared to do so.

Initial meetings are typically used to get to know the other party. Business-related discussions may not occur until the third or fourth meeting. Business meetings typically conclude with an offer of coffee or tea. This is a sign that the meeting is over and that future meetings, if there are to be any, should now be arranged.

Saudis attach a great deal of importance to status and rank. When meeting with them, defer to the senior person. It is also important never to criticize or berate anyone publicly. This causes the individual to lose face; the same is true for the person who makes these comments. Mutual respect is expected at all times.

Other useful guidelines for working in Saudi Arabia include the following:

1. It is important never to display feelings of superiority because this makes the other party feel inferior. No matter how well someone does something, the individual should let the action speak for itself and not brag or draw attention to themselves.
2. A lot of what gets done is a result of going through administrative channels in the country. It is often difficult to sidestep a lot of this red tape, and efforts to do so can be regarded as disrespect for legal and governmental institutions.
3. Connections are extremely important in conducting business. More important people get fast service from less important people. Close relatives take absolute priority; nonrelatives are kept waiting.
4. Patience is critical to the success of business negotiations. Time for deliberations should be built into all negotiations to prevent a person from giving away too much in an effort to reach a quick settlement.
5. Important decisions are usually made in person, not by correspondence or telephone. While Saudis seek counsel from many people, the ultimate power to make a decision rests with the person at the top, and this individual relies heavily on personal impressions, trust, and rapport.[6]

Working in China

In recent years the People's Republic of China (PRC, or China for short) has moved away from isolation to encourage more business with the rest of the world. While China holds tremendous promise, many Western firms have found working on projects in China to be a long, grueling process that often results in failure. One of the primary reasons for problems is the failure to appreciate Chinese culture.

Chinese society, like those of Japan and Korea, is influenced by the teachings of Confucius (551–478 B.C.). Unlike America, which relies on legal institutions to regulate behavior, in Confucian societies the primary deterrent against improper or illegal behavior is shame or loss of face. Face is more than simply reputation. There is a Chinese saying: "Face is like the bark of a tree; without its bark, the tree dies." Loss

[6] Adapted from Moran, R. T., P. R. Harris, and S. V. Moran, *Managing Cultural Differences*, 5th ed. (Houston, TX: Gulf, 2010); Hooker, J., *Working across Cultures* (Stanford, CA: Stanford Business Books, 2003).

of face brings shame not only to individuals but also to family members. A member's actions can cause shame for the entire family, hampering that family from working effectively in Chinese society.

In China, "whom you know is more important than what you know." The term *guanxi* refers to personal connections with appropriate authorities or individuals. China observers argue that *guanxi* is critical for working with the Chinese. Chinese are raised to distrust strangers, especially foreigners. Trust is transmitted via *guanxi.* That is, a trusted business associate of yours must pass you along to their trusted business associates. Many outsiders criticize *guanxi,* considering it to be like nepotism, where decisions are made regarding contracts or problems based on family ties or connections instead of an objective assessment of ability.

Many believe that the quickest way to build *guanxi* relationships is through tendering favors. Gift-giving, entertainment at lavish banquets, questionable payments, and overseas trips are common. While Westerners see this as nothing short of bribery, the Chinese consider it essential for good business. Another common method for outsiders to acquire *guanxi* is by hiring local intermediaries, who use their connections to create contacts with Chinese officials and businesspeople.

In dealing with the Chinese, you must realize they are a collective society in which people pride themselves on being a member of a group. For this reason, you should never single out a Chinese person for specific praise because this is likely to embarrass the individual in front of their peers. At the same time, you should avoid the use of "I" because it conveys that you are drawing attention to yourself.

Chinese people do not appreciate boisterous behavior, and when speaking to each other they maintain a greater physical distance than is typical in America. Other cautions include the following:

1. Once the Chinese decide who and what is best, they tend to stick to their decisions. So while they may be slow in formulating a plan, once they get started they make good progress.
2. Reciprocity is important in negotiations. If Chinese people give concessions, they expect some in return.
3. The Chinese tend to be less animated than Americans. They avoid open displays of affection and physical contact; they are more reticent and reserved than Americans.
4. The Chinese place less value on the significance of time and often get Americans to concede concessions by stalling.
5. In Confucian societies, those in position of power and authority are obligated to assist the disadvantaged. In return, they gain face and a good reputation.[7]

For more insights into Chinese culture, see Snapshot from Practice 16.3: Project Management X-Files.

Working in the United States

In the world of international projects, professionals from other countries will come to the United States to manage projects. To them, the United States is a foreign assignment. They will have to adapt their management style to the new environment they find in the States.

[7] Adapted from Graham, J. L., and N. M. Lam, "The Chinese Negotiation," *Harvard Business Review,* October 1, 2003, pp. 82–91; Hooker, J., *Working across Cultures* (Stanford, CA: Stanford Business Books, 2003); Yeung, I., and R. L. Tung, "Achieving Business Success in Confucian Societies: The Importance of Guanxi (Connections)," *Organizational Dynamics,* vol. 25, no. 2 (1996), pp. 54–65.

SNAPSHOT FROM PRACTICE 16.3 Project Management X-Files

Bikeriderlondon/Shutterstock

Americans tend to discount the significance of luck and believe that good fortune is generally a result of hard work. In other cultures, luck takes on greater significance and has supernatural ramifications. For example, in many Asian cultures, certain numbers are considered lucky, while others are unlucky. In Hong Kong, the numbers 7, 3, and especially 8 (which sounds like the word for prosperity and looks like an infinity symbol) are considered lucky, while the number 4 is considered unlucky (because it is pronounced like the word *death*).

Hong Kong businesspeople go to great lengths to avoid the number 4. For example, there is no fourth floor in office and hotel buildings. Business executives have been known to reject ideal sites in heavily congested Hong Kong because the address would contain the number 4. They pay premium prices for suitable sites containing addresses with the lucky numbers. Likewise, Hong Kong business managers avoid scheduling important events on the fourth day of each month and prefer to arrange critical meetings on the eighth day.

Hong Kong is also a place where the ancient art of *Feng shui* (literally "wind water") is practiced. This involves making sure a site and buildings are aligned in harmony with the earth's energy forces so that the location will be propitious. Feng shui practitioners are often called in on construction projects to make sure that the building is aligned correctly on the site. In some cases, the technical design of the building is changed to conform to the recommendations of such experts. Similarly, Feng shui experts have been known to be called in when projects are experiencing problems. Their recommendations may include repositioning the project manager's desk or hanging up mirrors to deflect the flow of unharmonious influences away from the building or site of the project.

In cultures where luck is believed to play a role in business, people who discount luck may not only insult the luck seekers but also risk being thought negligent in not paying enough attention to what is viewed as a legitimate business concern.

Immigration has made the United States a melting pot of diverse cultures. While many are quick to point out the differences between North and South, Silicon Valley and Wall Street, social anthropologists have identified certain cultural characteristics that shape how many Americans conduct business and manage projects.

Mainstream Americans are motivated by achievement and accomplishment. Their identity and, to a certain extent, their self-worth are measured by what they have achieved. Foreigners are often astounded by the material wealth accumulated by Americans and the modern conveniences most Americans enjoy. They are also quick to point out that Americans appear too busy to truly enjoy what they have achieved.

Americans tend to idolize the self-made person who rises from poverty and adversity to become rich and successful. Most Americans have a strong belief that they can influence and create their future, that with hard work and initiative, they can achieve whatever they set out to do. Self-determination and pragmatism dominate their approach to business.

Although Americans like to set precise objectives, they view planning as a means and not an end. They value flexibility and are willing to deviate from plans and improvise if they believe change will lead to accomplishment. Obstacles on a project are to be overcome, not worked around. Americans think they can accomplish just about anything, given time, money, and technology.

Americans fought a revolution and subsequent wars to preserve their concept of democracy, so they resent too much control or interference, especially by governments. While more an ideal than practice, there is deep-rooted belief in American management philosophy that those people who will be affected by decisions should be involved in making decisions. Many foreign businesspeople are surprised at the amount of autonomy and decision-making authority granted to subordinates. Foreign personnel have to learn to interact with American professionals below their rank in their own organizations.

Businesspeople from other countries are amazed and often somewhat distressed at the rapid pace of America. "Getting things done" is an American characteristic. Americans are very time-conscious and efficient. They expect meetings to start on time. They tinker with gadgets and technological systems, always searching for easier, better, more efficient ways of accomplishing things. American professionals are often relentless in pursuing project objectives and expect that behavior of others also.

Americans in play or business generally are quite competitive, reflecting their desire to achieve and succeed. Although the American culture contains contradictory messages about the importance of success (e.g., "It's not whether you win or lose but how you play the game" vs. "nice guys finish last"), winning and being number one are clearly valued in American society. Foreigners are often surprised at how aggressively Americans approach business with adversarial attitudes toward competitors and a desire to not just meet but exceed project goals and objectives.

The following are some other guidelines and cautions for working with Americans on projects.

1. More than half of U.S. women work outside the home; women have considerable opportunity for personal and professional growth, guaranteed by law. It is not uncommon to find women in key project positions. Female professionals expect to be treated as equals. Behavior tolerated in other countries would be subject to harassment laws in the States.
2. In the United States, gifts are rarely brought by visitors in a business situation.
3. Americans tend to be quite friendly and open when first meeting someone. Foreigners often mistake this strong "come-on" for the beginning of a strong reciprocal friendship. This is in contrast to many other cultures where there is more initial reserve in interpersonal relations, especially with strangers. For many foreigners, the American comes on too strong too soon, then fails to follow up with the implicitly promised friendship.
4. In comparison to the rest of the world Americans tend to be informal in greeting and dress, they are a noncontact culture (e.g., they avoid embracing in public usually), and they maintain certain physical/psychological distance between themselves and others (e.g., about 2 feet) in conversations.
5. American decision making is results oriented. Decisions tend to be based on facts and expected outcomes, not social impact.[8]

Summary Comments about Working in Different Cultures

These briefings underscore the complexity of working on international projects. It is common practice to rely on intermediaries—often locals who are foreign educated—to bridge the gap between cultures. These intermediaries perform a variety of functions.

[8] Adapted from Milosevic, D. Z., "Echoes of the Silent Language of Project Management," *Project Management Journal*, vol. 30, no 1 (March 1999), pp. 27–39; Moran, T. T., P. R. Harris, and S. V. Moran, *Managing Cultural Differences*, 5th ed. (Houston, TX: Gulf, 2010).

SNAPSHOT FROM PRACTICE 16.4 Dealing with Customs

Will corruption influence the project? Bribes are illegal in the United States, but in some countries, they are the usual way to do business. For example, one American project manager in a foreign country requested that a shipment of critical project equipment be sent "overnight rush." Two days later, inquiries to the sender confirmed the materials had been delivered to the nearby airport. Further inquiries to the port found the shipment "waiting to pass customs."

Locals quickly informed the American project manager that money paid to the chief customs inspector would expedite clearance. The project manager's response was "I will not be held hostage. Bribes are illegal!" Two more days of calling government officials did not move the shipment from customs.

The manager related his problem to a friendly businessman of the host nation at a social affair. The local businessman said he would see if he could help. The shipment arrived the next morning at 10:00 a.m. The American called his local business friend and thanked him profusely. "I owe you one." "No," replied the local. "You owe me a $50 dinner when I visit you in the States." The use of an intermediary in such situations may be the only avenue available to a manager to reduce the stress and personal conflict with the U.S. value system.

They act as translators. They use their social connections to expedite transactions and protect the project against undue interference. They are used to sidestep the touchy bribery/gift dilemma (see Snapshot from Practice 16.4: Dealing with Customs). They serve as cultural guides, helping outsiders understand and interpret the foreign culture. A growing number of consulting firms perform these functions by helping foreign clients work on projects in their country.

The international briefings also highlight the importance of project managers doing their homework and becoming familiar with the customs and habits of the host country they are going to be working in. As far as possible, the project should be managed in such a way that local-country norms and customs are honored. However, there are limits to the extent to which you should accommodate foreign cultures. Becoming a local is generally not an alternative. After all, it took Russians their entire lives to learn how to be Russians. It would be foolish to think an outsider could learn to be one in six months, two years, or perhaps ever.

The remainder of this chapter focuses on the selection and training of project personnel for international projects. But before these issues are discussed, this section concludes with a discussion of a phenomenon that can have a profound effect on a foreigner's performance on a project in a strange land.

Culture Shock

Stages of Culture Shock

LO 16-4

Describe culture shock and strategies for coping with it.

> My first few weeks in Chiang Mai [Thailand] were filled with excitement. I was excited about the challenge of building a waste treatment plant in a foreign country. I was fascinated with Thai customs and traditions, the smells and sights of the night market. Soon I noticed a distinct change in my attitude and behavior. I started having problems sleeping and lacked energy. I became irritable at work, frustrated by how long things took to accomplish, and how I couldn't seem to get anything accomplished. I started staying up late at night drinking Thai whiskey and watching CNN in my hotel room.

This engineer is experiencing what many would call **culture shock,** a natural psychological disorientation that most people suffer when they move into a culture different from their own. The culture shock cycle has four stages (see Figure 16.6):

FIGURE 16.6
Culture Shock Cycle

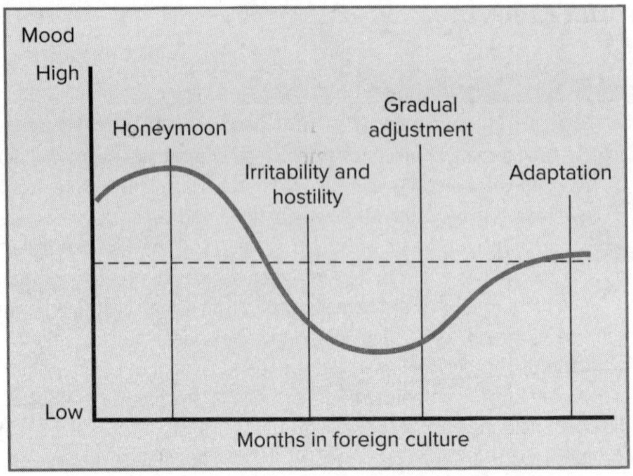

1. **Honeymoon.** You start your overseas assignment with a sense of excitement. The new and the unusual are welcomed. At first, it is amusing not to understand or be understood. Soon a sense of frustration begins to set in.
2. **Irritability and hostility.** Your initial enthusiasm is exhausted, and you begin to notice that differences are greater than you first imagined. You become frustrated by your inability to get things done as you are accustomed to. You begin to lose confidence in your abilities to communicate and work effectively in the different culture.
3. **Gradual adjustment.** You begin to overcome your sense of isolation and figure out how to get things done in the new culture. You acquire a new perspective of what is possible and regain confidence in your ability to work in the culture.
4. **Adaptation.** You recover from your sense of psychological disorientation and begin to function and communicate in the new culture.

Culture shock is not a disease but a natural response to immersing yourself in a new environment. Culture shock results from a breakdown in your selective perception and effective interpretation systems. At a subliminal level, your senses are being bombarded by a wide variety of strange sounds, sights, and smells. At the same time, the normal assumptions you are accustomed to using in your home culture to interpret perceptions and to communicate intentions no longer apply. When this happens, whether in a business context or in normal attempts to socialize, confusion and frustration set in. The local's behavior does not seem to make sense, and even more importantly your behavior does not produce expected results. Frustration occurs because you are used to being competent in such situations and now find you are unable to operate effectively.

Culture shock is generally considered a positive sign that the professional is becoming involved in the new culture instead of remaining isolated in expatriate seclusion. The significant question is how best to manage culture shock, not how to avoid it. The key appears to be managing the stress associated with culture shock.

Stress-related culture shock takes many forms: disappointment, frustration, withdrawal, anxiety, and physiological responses such as fatigue, sleeplessness, and headaches. Stress is induced by the senses being overwhelmed by foreign stimuli and the inability to function effectively in a strange land. Stress is exacerbated when one encounters disturbing situations that, as a foreigner, are neither understood nor condoned. For example, many North Americans are appalled by the poverty and hunger in many underdeveloped countries.

Coping with Culture Shock

There are a wide range of stress management techniques for coping with culture shock. One method does not necessarily work any better than another; success depends on the particular individual and situation involved. Some people engage in regular physical exercise programs, some practice meditation and relaxation exercises, and others find it healthy to keep a journal.

Many effective international managers create "stability zones." They spend most of their time immersed in the foreign culture but then briefly retreat into an environment—a stability zone—that closely re-creates home. For example, when one of the authors was living in Kraków, Poland, with his family, they routinely went to the Polish movie houses to see American movies with Polish subtitles. The two hours spent hearing English and seeing a familiar environment on the screen had a soothing effect on everyone.

On the project, managers can reduce the stress caused by culture shock by recognizing it and modifying their expectations and behavior accordingly. They can redefine priorities and develop more realistic expectations as to what is possible. They can focus their limited energy on only the most important tasks and relish small accomplishments.

After three to six months, depending on the individual and assignment, most people overcome their culture shock "low" and begin living a more normal life in the foreign country. They talk to acquaintances from the host country and experienced outsiders from their own culture to find out how to behave and what to expect. Little by little they learn how to make sense of the new environment. They figure out when "yes" means "yes" and when it means "maybe" and when it means "no." See Snapshot from Practice 16.5: Project X—Namibia, Africa, for further insights into coping with culture shock.

SNAPSHOT FROM PRACTICE 16.5 Project X—Namibia, Africa*

While U.S. reality TV shows focus on finding love, outwitting opponents, and garnering audience support, a Norwegian TV show shone a light on project management under extreme conditions. The plot was deceptively simple: send 10 Scandinavian volunteers 6,000 miles away from home to the dry subtropics of southern Africa and charge them with building a school for orphans and poor children in less than 30 days. Not only would they be forced to adjust to vastly different languages, climates, and cuisines, but only one of the 10 had previous construction experience. The team's trials and tribulations were aired over Norwegian TV in 2009. The marketing blitz for the show, titled *Project X*, played up the drama with the tagline "Can they achieve the mission?"

The team was enthusiastic at the outset, but discontent began as soon as they arrived at the small mining town of Tsumeb in Namibia. The team immediately experienced culture shock—all the while the TV crew followed them, sticking cameras in their faces and asking how they felt.

The sweltering heat, slumlike conditions, and limited cuisine immediately elicited complaints: "I can't sleep." "The food is awful." "Where are the toilets?"

One of the biggest mistakes the volunteers made was applying a Eurocentric sense of time and planning. "I brought my Danish mindset that 'On Friday we will do this and on Saturday we will do that,'" reported Merete Lange, one of the volunteers. "Then I came to understand African time, and that was the biggest surprise."

Hoping to secure local buy-in, Lange arranged for a local carpenter to build desks and tables. A few days before the furniture was needed, she discovered work hadn't even begun.

"I got pretty stressed and tried to be my best at being diplomatic," Lange recalls. "I asked, 'When do you think you will be ready with the furniture?'" The carpenter responded, "Time is unpredictable. I will call you."

Over time, Lange and her teammates were able to adapt to the elements and figure out ways to work with the locals to successfully build the school within 30 days. "The trick is reflecting upon 'where people were coming from, how to meet them there, and how to create a win-win situation that would satisfy both parties.'"

*B. G. Yovovich "Worlds Apart," *PM Network*, October 2010, pp. 24–29.

The vast majority of people eventually make the adjustment, although for some people it can take much longer than three to six months. A smaller number never recover, and their international experience turns into a nightmare. Some exhibit severe stress symptoms (e.g., substance abuse, panic attacks) and must return home before finishing their assignment.

Professionals can use project work as a bridge until they adjust to their new environment. Unfortunately, partners who do not work do not have this advantage. When partners are left to cope with the strange environment on their own, they often have a much more difficult time overcoming culture shock. The effect on partners cannot be underestimated. The number one reason expatriate managers return home is that their partners fail to adjust to the new environment (Tung, 1987).

Project professionals working overseas accept that they are in a difficult situation and that they will not act as effectively as they did at home, especially in the initial stages. They recognize the need for good stress management techniques, including stability zones. They also recognize that it is not an individual problem and invest extra time and energy to help their spouses and families manage the transition. At the same time, they appreciate that their colleagues are experiencing similar problems and are sensitive to their needs. They work together to manage the stress and pull out of a culture shock low as quickly as possible.

It is somewhat ironic, but people who work on projects overseas experience culture shock twice. Many professionals experience the same kind of disorientation and stress when they return home, although it is usually less severe. For some, their current job has less responsibility and is boring compared with the challenge of their overseas assignment. Others have problems adjusting to changes made in the home organization while they were gone. This can be compounded by financial shock when the salary and fringe benefits they became accustomed to in the foreign assignment are now lost, and adjusting to a lower standard of living is difficult. It typically takes six months to a year before managers operate again at full effectiveness after a lengthy foreign assignment (Adler & Gunderson, 2007).

16.4 Selection and Training for International Projects

LO 16-5

Understand how organizations select and prepare people to work on international projects.

When professionals are selected for overseas projects and they do not work out, the overall costs can be staggering. Not only does the project experience a serious setback, but the reputation of the firm is damaged in the region. This is why many firms have developed formal screening procedures to help ensure the careful selection of personnel for international projects. Organizations examine a number of characteristics to determine whether an individual is suitable for overseas work. They may look for work experience with cultures other than one's own, previous overseas travel, good physical and emotional health, a knowledge of a host nation's language, and even recent immigration background or heritage. Prospective candidates and their family members are often interviewed by trained psychologists, who assess their ability to adapt and function in the new culture.

While there is growing appreciation for screening people for foreign assignments, the number one reason for selection is that the personnel assigned are the best people available for the technical challenges of the project (Mendenhall, Dunbar, & Oddou, 1987). Technical know-how takes precedence over cross-cultural sensitivity or experience. As a consequence, training is critical to fill in the cultural gaps and prepare individuals to work in a foreign land.

Training varies widely, depending on the individual, company, nature of the project, and cultures to work with. Project professionals assigned to foreign countries should have a minimal understanding of the following areas:

- Religion.
- Dress codes.
- Education system.
- Holidays—national and religious.
- Daily eating patterns.
- Family life.
- Business protocols.
- Social etiquette.
- Equal opportunity.

An example of a short-term training program is the one developed by Underwriter Laboratories, Inc., to train staff who travel to Japan to work with clients on projects. The program is designed around a series of mini-lectures that cover topics ranging from how to handle introductions to the correct way of interpreting Japanese social and business behavior. The two-day program consists of lectures, case studies, role-plays, language practice, and a short test on cultural terminology; it concludes with a 90-minute question-and-answer period. At the end of the program, participants have a fundamental understanding of how to communicate with people from Japan. More importantly, they know the types of information they lack and how to go about learning more to become effective intercultural communicators.

Other training programs are more extensive. For example, Peace Corps volunteers undergo an intense two- to four-month training program in their country of service. The training includes classes on the history and traditions of the country, intensive language instruction, and cross-cultural training as well as homestays with local families. Many companies outsource training to one of the many firms specializing in overseas and intercultural training.

Figure 16.7 attempts to link the length and type of training with the cultural fluency required to successfully complete the project. Three different learning approaches are highlighted (Mendenhall et al., 1987):

1. The "information-giving" approach—the learning of information or skills from a lecture-type orientation.
2. The "affective" approach—the learning of information/skills that raise the affective responses on the part of the trainee and result in cultural insights.
3. The "experiential" approach—a variant of the affective approach technique that provides the trainee with realistic simulations or scenarios.

According to this framework, the length and level of training depend on the degree of cultural fluency required to be successful. In general, the longer the person is expected to work in a foreign country, the more intensive the training should be. Length of stay should not be the only consideration; high levels of cultural fluency, and therefore more extensive training, may be required to perform short-term, intense projects. In addition, location is important. Americans working in Australia will likely require less cultural fluency than those working on a project in Pakistan.

While English is rapidly becoming the international language for business in many parts of the world, you should not underestimate the value of being able to speak the

FIGURE 16.7 Relationship between Length and Rigor of Training and Cultural Fluency Required

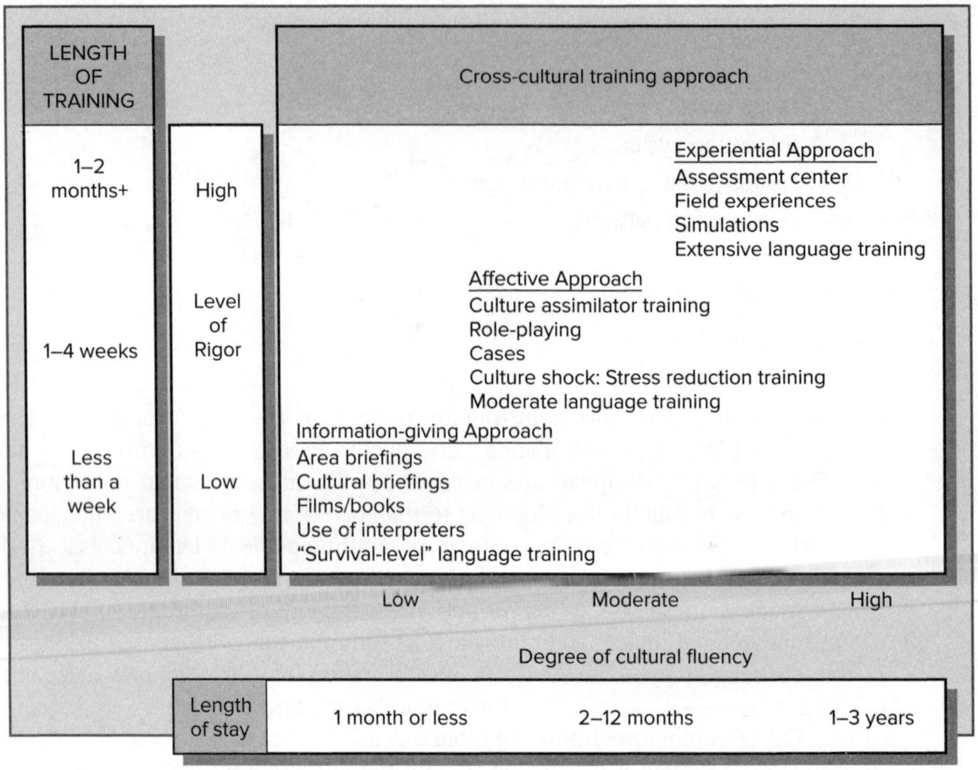

language of the host country. At a minimum, you should be able to exchange basic pleasantries in the native tongue. Most foreigners consider this a sign of respect, and even if you stumble they appreciate the effort.

In many situations, translators are used to facilitate communication. While time-consuming, this is the only way to communicate with non-English-speaking personnel. Be careful in the selection of translators, and do not just assume they are competent. For example, one of the authors enlisted the help of a Polish translator to conduct a meeting with some Polish managers. After the meeting the translator, who taught English at a local university, asked if the author "had good time." I responded that I felt things went well. The translator repeated her question. Puzzled, I reaffirmed that I felt things went well. After the interchange was repeated several times, the translator finally grabbed my wrist, pointed at my watch, and asked again if I "had good time." Doubts arose concerning the accuracy of the meeting translation!**Design elements:** Snapshot from Practice, Highlight box, Case icon: Sky Designs/Shutterstock

Summary

The number of international projects continues to increase. More and more project managers will be needed to implement international projects. Preparing for international projects can be enhanced through training. As a general background, potential international project managers can benefit from a basic international business course that sensitizes them to the forces of change in the global economy and to cultural differences. Learning a foreign language is also strongly recommended.

Further training specific to the host country is a very useful pre-project endeavor. The length and type of training usually depend on the duration of the project manager's assignment. Still, self-learning, on-the-job training, and experience are the best teachers for international project managers.

Preparing for a specific international project requires serious pre-project homework. Understanding the firm's motivation in selecting the project and its site provides important insights. What basic political, geographic, economic, and infrastructure factors were key considerations? How will they impact the implementation of the project?

Finally, preparation and understanding the cultural differences of the host country go a long way toward making positive first impressions with the nationals and managing the project. International projects have distinct personalities. All people are not the same. Differences within and among countries and cultures are numerous and complex. Project managers need to accept these differences and treat them as real—or live with the consequences. What works at home may not work in the foreign country. Americans are regarded as friendly in the global village, but Americans are also noted to be insensitive to differences in local cultures and customs and awkward in our use of languages other than English. Although most attention in foreign projects is focused on technical efforts and their cost, the project must be carried out within the environment of the country's social customs, work practices, government controls, and religious beliefs. In most cultures, sincerity and flexibility will pay off.

Key Terms

Cross-cultural orientations, *677*
Culture, *675*
Culture shock, *687*
Infrastructure, *671*

Review Questions

1. How do environmental factors affect project implementation?
2. What role do local intermediaries play in helping an outsider complete a project?
3. Why is it important to honor the customs and traditions of a country when working on an international project?
4. What is culture shock? What can you do to reduce the negative effects of culture shock?
5. How should you prepare yourself for an international project?

SNAPSHOT FROM PRACTICE

Discussion Questions

16.1 *The Filming of* Apocalypse Now

1. Would more effective risk management have prevented the problems the project encountered?
2. Would you consider the filming of *Apocalypse Now* a success or not?

16.2 *River of Doubt*

1. Why didn't Rondon tell Roosevelt and the Americans that they couldn't take so much luggage on the exploration?

16.3 *Project Management X-Files*

1. Do you have any superstitions that influence how you work? If so, can you explain them?

16.4 *Dealing with Customs*

1. Did the project manager have any other alternatives?

16.5 *Project X—Namibia, Africa*

1. What do you think are the major differences between "Danish time" and "African time"?

Avoiding Communication Catastrophes when E-mailing Across Cultures

1. Have you ever made a mistake sending an e-mail for the first time? If so, how did you resolve the issue?

Exercises

1. Interview someone who has worked or lived in a foreign country for more than six months.
   a. What was the person's experience with culture shock?
   b. What did the person learn about the culture of the country they lived in?
   c. What advice would the person give to someone who would be working on a project in that country?
2. Try as best you can to apply the Kluckhohn–Strodtbeck cross-cultural framework to the five countries discussed in this chapter: Mexico, France, Saudi Arabia, China, and United States. Where do you think these countries lie on each of the cultural issues?
3. Place in order the following countries in terms of what you think would be the least to most corrupt:

   United States, Denmark, Saudi Arabia, Canada, Australia, France, China, Thailand, Botswana, Chile

   Search online for the most recent International Corruptions Perceptions Index (CPI) released by the Berlin-based organization Transparency International.
   a. Check your predictions with the index.
   b. How well did you do? What countries surprised you? Why?
4. Safety is a major concern when working on projects abroad. Select a country that you would consider dangerous to work in and look up the travel advisory provided for that country by the U.S. State Department (http://travel.state.gov/). How safe is it to work in that country?

References

Ackoff, R. L., *Ackoff's Fables: Irreverent Reflections on Business and Bureaucracy* (New York: Wiley, 1991), p. 221.

Adler, N., and A. Gunderson, *International Dimensions of Organizational Behavior,* 5th ed. (Mason, OH: Thomson, 2007).

Arms, P. B., and E. Lucas, "How Do Foreign Clients Really See American Project Managers?" *Proceedings of the 1978 Annual Seminar/Symposium on Project Management* (Newtown, PA: Project Management Institute, 1978), pp. 11K 1–7.

Brett, J., K. Behfar, and M. Kern, "Managing Multicultural Teams," *Harvard Business Review,* November 2006, pp. 85–91.

Cahill, T., "Deadly Business in Moscow," *Bloomberg Businessweek,* March 1, 2010, pp. 22–23.

Chen, M., and D. Miller, "West Meets East: Toward an Ambicultural Approach to Management," *The Academy of Management Perspectives,* vol. 24, no. 4 (November 2010), pp. 17–24.

Deneire, M., and M. Segalla, "Mr. Christian Pierret, Secretary of State for Industry (1997–2002), on French Perspectives on Organizational Leadership and Management," *Academy of Management Executive,* vol. 16, no. 4 (November 2002), pp. 25–30.

Doh, J. P., P. Rodriguez, K. Uhlenbruck, J. Collins, and L. Eden, "Coping with Corruption in Foreign Markets," *Academy of Management Executive,* vol. 17, no. 3 (August 2003), pp. 114–27.

Friedman, A., "98% of Greeks Believe Corruption Is 'Widespread' in Greece: EU Report," greekreporter.com, July 20, 2022. Accessed 4/2/23.

Hodgetts, R. M., and F. Luthans, *International Management: Culture, Strategy, and Behavior,* 5th ed. (Boston: McGraw-Hill/Irwin, 2003).

Hofstede, G., *Cultures Consequences: International Difference in Work-Related Values* (Beverly Hills, CA: Sage, 1980).

Javidan, M., P. W. Dorfman, M. S. de Luque, and R. J. House, "In the Eye of the Beholder: Cross Cultural Lessons in Leadership from Project GLOBE," *Academy of Management Perspective,* vol. 20, no. 1 (2006), pp. 67–90.

Lane, H. W., and J. J. DiStefano, *International Project Management,* 2nd ed. (Boston: PWS-Kent, 1992).

Lewis, R. D., *When Cultures Collide: Leading across Cultures,* 3rd ed. (Boston: Nicholas Brealey International, 2007).

Lieberthal, K., and G. Lieberthal, "The Great Transition," *Harvard Business Review,* October 1, 2003, pp. 71–81.

Mendenhall, M. E., E. Dunbar, and G. R. Oddou, "Expatriate Selection, Training, and Career-Pathing: A Review and Critique," *Human Resource Management,* vol. 26, no. 3 (Fall 1987), pp. 331–45.

Meyer, E., "Being the Boss in Brussels, Boston, and Beijing," *Harvard Business Review,* July/August 2017, pp. 70–77.

Meyer, E., *The Culture Map: Breaking through the Invisible Boundaries of Global Business* (New York: Public Affair, 2014).

Moffett, M. H., I. Stonehill, and D. K. Eiteman, *Fundamentals of Multinational Finance* (Boston: Pearson, 2012).

Neeley, T. "Global Teams That Work," *Harvard Business Review,* October 2015, pp. 74–81.

Rice, C., and A. Zegart, "Managing 21st-Century Political Risk," *Harvard Business Review,* May/June 2018, pp. 130–38.

Ricks, D. A., *Blunders in International Business* (London: Blackwell, 2000).

Saunders, C., C. Van Slyke, and D. R. Vogel, "My Time or Yours? Managing Time Visions in Global Virtual Teams," *Academy of Management Executive,* vol. 18, no. 1 (2004), pp. 19–31.

Scown, M. J., "Managers Journal: Barstool Advice for the Vietnam Investor," *Asian Wall Street Journal,* July 15, 1993.

Statista Research Department, "India: Power Outage Amidst Heatwave and High Temperature 2022," statista.com, February 16, 2023. Accessed 4/2/23.

Tung, R. L., "Expatriate Assignments: Enhancing Success and Minimizing Failure," *Academy of Management Executive,* vol. 1, no. 2 (1987), pp. 117–26.

Case 16.1

AMEX, Hungary

Michael Thomas shouted, "Sasha, Tor-Tor, we've got to go! Our driver is waiting for us." Thomas's two daughters were fighting over who would get the last orange for lunch that day. Victoria ("Tor-Tor") prevailed as she grabbed the orange and ran out the door to the Mercedes Benz waiting for them. The fighting continued in the back seat as they drove toward the city of Budapest, Hungary. Thomas finally turned around, grabbed the orange, and proclaimed that he would have it for lunch. The back seat became deadly silent as they made their way to the American International School of Budapest.

After dropping the girls off at the school, Thomas was driven to his office in the Belvéros area of Budapest. Thomas worked for AMEX Petroleum and had been sent to Budapest four months earlier to set up business operations in central Hungary. His job was to establish 10 to 14 gas stations in the region by purchasing existing stations, building new ones, or negotiating franchise arrangements with existing owners of stations. Thomas jumped at this project. He realized that his career at AMEX was going nowhere in the United States, and if he were going to realize his ambitions, it would be in the "wild, wild east" of the former Soviet empire. Besides, Thomas's mother was Hungarian, and he could speak the language. At least he thought he could until he arrived in Budapest and realized that he had greatly exaggerated his competence.

As he entered the partially refurbished offices of AMEX, he noticed that only three of his staff were present. No one knew where Miklos was, while Margit reported that she would not be at work today because she had to stay at home to take care of her sick mother. Thomas asked Béla why the workmen weren't present to work on finishing the office. Béla informed him that the work had to be halted until they received approval from the city historian. Budapest, anxious to preserve its historical heritage, required that all building renovations be approved by the city historian. When Thomas asked Béla how long it would take, Béla responded, "Who knows—days, weeks, maybe even months." Thomas muttered "great" to himself and turned his attention to the morning business. He was scheduled to interview prospective employees who would act as station managers and staff personnel.

The interview with Ferenc Erkel was typical of the many interviews he held that morning. Erkel was a neatly dressed, 42-year-old, unemployed professional who could speak limited English. He had a master's degree in international economics and had worked for 12 years in the state-owned Institute for Foreign Trade. Since being laid off two years ago, he had been working as a taxicab driver. When asked about his work at the institute, Erkel smiled sheepishly and said that he pushed paper and spent most of the time playing cards with his colleagues.

To date, Thomas had hired 16 employees. Four quit within three days on the job, and six were let go after a trial period for being absent from work, failing to perform duties, or showing a lack of initiative. Thomas thought that at this rate it would take him over a year just to hire his staff.

Thomas took a break from the interview schedule to scan the *Budapest Business Journal,* an English newspaper that covered business news in Hungary. Two items caught his eye. One article was on the growing threat of the Ukrainian Mafia in Hungary, which detailed extortion attempts in Budapest. The second story was that inflation had risen to 32 percent. This last item disturbed Thomas because at the time only one out of every five Hungarian families owned a car. AMEX's strategy in Hungary depended on a boom in first-time car owners.

Thomas collected his things and popped a few aspirin for the headache he was developing. He walked several blocks to the Kispipa restaurant, where he had a supper meeting with Hungarian businessman Zoltán Kodaly. He had met Kodaly briefly at a reception sponsored by the U.S. consulate for American and Hungarian businesspeople. Kodaly reportedly owned three gas stations that Thomas was interested in.

Thomas waited, sipping bottled water, for 25 minutes. Kodaly appeared with a young lady who could not have been older than 19. As it turned out Kodaly had brought his daughter Annia, who was a university student, to act as translator. While Thomas made an attempt to speak in Hungarian at first, Kodaly insisted that they use Annia to translate.

After ordering the house specialty, *szekelygulas,* Thomas immediately got down to business. He told Kodaly that AMEX was willing to make two offers to him. They would like to purchase two of his stations at a price of $150,000 each, or they could work out a franchise agreement. Thomas said AMEX was not interested in the third station located near Klinikak because it would be too expensive to modernize the equipment. Annia translated, and as far as Thomas could tell she was doing a pretty good job. At first, Kodaly did not respond and simply engaged in side conversations with Annia and exchanged pleasantries with people who went by. Thomas became frustrated and reiterated his offer. Eventually, Kodaly asked what he meant by franchising, and Thomas tried to use the local McDonald's as an example of how it worked. He mentioned that Kodaly would still own the stations, but he would have to pay a franchisee fee, share profits with AMEX, and adhere to AMEX procedures and practices. In exchange, AMEX would provide petroleum and funds to renovate the stations to meet AMEX standards.

Toward the end of the meal, Kodaly asked what would happen to the people who worked at the stations. Thomas asserted that according to his calculation, the stations were overstaffed by 70 percent and that to make a profit at least 15 workers would have to be let go. This statement was greeted with silence. Kodaly then turned the conversation to soccer and asked Thomas if it was true that in America girls play "football." Thomas said that both of his daughters played AYSO soccer in America and hoped to play in Hungary. Kodaly said girls don't play football in Hungary and that Annia was an accomplished volleyball player. Thomas pressed Kodaly for a response to his offer, but Kodaly rose and thanked Thomas for the meal. He said he would think about his offer and get back in touch with him.

Thomas left the Kispipa restaurant wondering if he would ever see Kodaly again. He returned to his office, where an urgent message was waiting from Tibor. Tibor was responsible for retrofitting the first station Thomas had purchased for AMEX.

The new tanks had not arrived from Vienna, and the construction crew had spent the day doing nothing. After several phone calls, he found out that the tanks were being held at the border by customs. This irritated him because he had been assured by local officials that everything had been taken care of. He asked his secretary to schedule an appointment with the Hungarian trade office as soon as possible.

At the end of the day, he checked his e-mail from the States. There was a message from headquarters asking about the status of the project. By this time he had hoped to have his office staffed and up and running and at least three stations secured. So far he had only one-third of his staff, his office was in shambles, and only one station was being retrofitted. Thomas decided to wait until tomorrow to respond to the e-mail.

Before returning home Thomas stopped off at the English Pub, a favorite hangout for expats in Budapest. There he met Jan Krovert, who worked for a Dutch company that was building a large discount retail store on the outskirts of Budapest. Thomas and Krovert often talked about being "strangers in a strange land" at the pub. Thomas talked about the interviews and how he could just see in their eyes that they didn't have the drive or initiative to be successful. Krovert responded that Hungary has high unemployment but a shortage of motivated workers. Krovert confided that he no longer interviewed anyone over the age of 30, claiming that what fire they had in their bellies was burned out after years of working in state-run companies.

1. What are the issues confronting Thomas in this case?
2. How well is Thomas dealing with these issues?
3. What suggestions would you have for Thomas in managing this project?

Case 16.2

Phuket A

On December 26, 2004, an earthquake reaching 9.1 on the Richter scale triggered a series of devastating tsunamis off the coast of Indonesia. They spread throughout the Indian Ocean, killing large numbers of people and inundating coastal communities across South and Southeast Asia, including parts of Indonesia, Sri Lanka, India, and Thailand. The 2004 tsunami was one of the deadliest catastrophes in modern history, with more than 220,000 lives lost.

Nils Lofgrin, who had managed several construction projects in Australia and New Guinea, was sent by his construction firm to restore a five-star resort along the Andaman coast in southern Thailand that had been ravaged by this tsunami. Casualties at the resort included 12 staff and 37 guests. This was Nils's first assignment in Thailand.

Nils flew down and toured the site. His assessment of the damage was that it was not as severe as feared. The basic infrastructure was intact but debris needed to be cleared and the resort refurbished. He reported back to headquarters that with a bit of luck he should have the resort up and running in a matter of months. Little did he realize how soon he would regret making such a promise.

The problems began immediately when he was unable to recruit workers to clean up the mess at the resort. Burmese migrant workers made up a significant portion of the workforce in the region. The heavy government presence after the tsunami caused them to flee into the hills out of growing fears of being arrested and deported. Still, there was an ample number of locals available to do the work. Repeated efforts to recruit laborers failed. Even when he offered double wages he was only able to recruit a few Thai people.

1. Why do you think Nils is unable to recruit Thai workers for his project?

Case 16.3

Mr. Wui Goes to America

Wui arrived in Mobile, Alabama, in the middle of summer, unprepared for humidity and heat. The first day he bought a lightweight, breathable business suit. He was helped by salespeople who smiled as they packed the coat and slacks into a box. Americans are nice, Wui decided. He was not worried about his assignment in America. The contract had been negotiated. Wui's job was to work out the details and establish communication protocols.

Wui's firm, DSD, was one of the biggest construction firms in China. Wui was assigned to the Shenzhen Green project, a state-of-the-art, 30-story office building. Wui was sent to Mobile because that is where Katsam Industries had its new electrochromic glass fabrication factory. The factory was producing next-generation glass products, which dramatically improved energy efficiency and occupant comfort. Katsam's global experience was limited, but it had a reputation for being innovative.

When Wui woke up he called Jon Bigelow at Katsam to confirm his 10:00 a.m. meeting. Bigelow's assistant verified the meeting.

Wui arrived at the Katsam office at 10 a.m. sharp. He had brought a pair of sitting foo dogs for Bigelow. The statues were carved from special stone found only near his parent's village. They are cherished by the Chinese for their ability to ward off evil spirits. He would explain the significance to Bigelow later when they knew each other.

When Bigelow's assistant ushered him in, Bigelow stood up immediately and rounded his desk with an outstretched hand. Squeezing Wui's hand, he roared, "How are you? Long trip from Hong Kong? Please sit down, please sit down."

Wui smiled and reached into his jacket for his card. By the time he had presented it, Bigelow was on the other side of his desk. "My card," Wui said with a slight bow.

"Yes, yes," Bigelow answered. He put Wui's card in his pocket without a glance.

Wui stared at the floor.

"Here," Bigelow handed his card.

"Oh, Jon Bigelow, Director of Operations, Katsam Industries, Mobile, Alabama," Wui read out loud while holding the card with both hands. "Katsam has an excellent reputation in China."

"That's me," Bigelow replied. "Pleased to meet you, Wui; I think we will work very well together; won't you sit down?"

Wui smiled and laid Bigelow's card on the table in front of him.

"DSD is pleased to do business with Katsam," Wui spoke slowly. Wui was proud of his English. Not only had he been the top student in his high school and university, but he had also studied business English in evening courses for four years.

Bigelow looked impatient. Wui continued to talk about DSD and Katsam history. "We are the best in the business," Bigelow interrupted. "Ask anyone in the industry, our glass is the best in the world!"

Wui didn't know what to say. He knew Katsam's record—that was why he was in the room. Surely Bigelow knew that. His foot touched the box containing the foo dog statues. Maybe he should give the gift now. No, he thought. Bigelow was still talking about Katsam's achievements. Now Bigelow had switched to his own achievements. "You have to come over to my house. It's a totally renovated 200-year-old colonial mansion with a fantastic view of the bay. You know, I have the greatest wife. She is a superb cook. You come to our house and she'll give you a real taste of Southern cooking: grits, gumbo, sweet tea, you name it."

Wui shifted his weight and said, "Thank you, I would enjoy that very much." He then reached down and picked up the box. "I brought you a present," Wui said, handing him the box containing the foo dogs.

"Thanks," Bigelow answered. He looked genuinely pleased as he tore open the paper and opened the box. Wui looked away while Bigelow picked up a foo dog in each hand and said, "Hey, thanks a lot, I will give one to each of my kids."

Bigelow pushed the statues aside and said, "Give me a second, Wui; I need to send a message to my assistant."

They spent the next hour going over Wui's visit and answering questions about the work Katsam was going to do for DSD. The discussion was interrupted by a tap on the door. Bigelow jumped up and said, "It must be lunchtime!" Bigelow's assistant entered the office caring a brightly colored package. When she handed the package to Wui, Bigelow announced, "Katsam has a present for you." Wui nodded thanks and waited. Bigelow cried, "Aren't you going to open it? I think you are really going to like it. Go ahead, open it."

Wui reluctantly opened the package. He pulled out of the box a light grey shirt with "Atlanta Braves" spelled out on the front and a picture of what appeared to be a tomahawk. On the back was printed the name Aaron and, in big numerals, 44. Bigelow proudly proclaimed, "We heard you guys like baseball, so we thought it would be only fitting to give you a replica of the greatest baseball player to ever come out of Mobile, Alabama, good ole #44, Hammering Hank Aaron." He patted Wui on the back and said, "Now let's go get some food!"

1. How do you think Wui feels about working with Bigelow so far?
2. What mistakes did Wui make?
3. What mistakes did Bigelow make?
4. How could these mistakes have been prevented?

Case 16.4

Bharti Airtel's Expansion into Africa

Bharti Airtel's buyout of Zain's African telecom operations for $8.97 billion was in 2010, that was sought to establish Bharti Airtel as the market leader in telecommunication and expanding its global reach. The deal comprised operations from 15 countries across Africa: Nigeria, Ghana, Kenya, and Uganda, hence providing Airtel with a way to tap over 42 million subscribers. This acquisition was a strategic response to the difficulties Airtel faced in its domestic market, India, amid severe competition, price wars, and market saturation. Africa held significant promise, particularly for the following reasons:

- Low penetration in mobiles, well below the world average as compared in 2010.
- Youthful demographics, with more than 60% of the population under 25 years of age. Africa represented a long-run growth market for telecom services.
- Fast-growing economies in many African nations which boosted demand for mobile connectivity.

KEY STAKEHOLDERS

- **Government Bodies:** The 15 African countries' regulatory authorities played a very crucial role in offering operating licenses and approvals.
- **Private Sector:** Airtel collaborated with the technology providers such as Ericsson and Huawei in the upgrading of infrastructure.
- **End Users:** African customers directly benefited from enhanced connectivity as well as mobile financial services.
- **Workers in the Project:** Local employees contributed to infrastructure setup and customer service.

PROJECT SCOPE AND OBJECTIVES

The project entailed integrating the operations of Zain into the Airtel structure, upgrading telecom infrastructure, and coming up with innovative services such as the Airtel Money. The key objectives were:

- Growing the subscribers of Airtel to 100 million subscribers in three years.
- Creating Airtel as the African telecom market leader.
- Upgrading network infrastructure for 3G and 4G.
- Launching Airtel Money to promote financial inclusion.
- Introducing energy-efficient telecom towers to minimize environmental impact.

PROJECT MANAGEMENT FRAMEWORK

Project Initiation

- **Feasibility Studies:** Airtel conducted a detailed market analysis to understand the telecom landscape in 15 African countries, identifying opportunities for subscriber growth in regions with low mobile penetration.
- **Approvals and Clearances:** Secured operating licenses and approvals from regulatory authorities in all 15 countries, which required alignment with local government policies. Engaged with local leaders and stakeholders to build community trust and ensure smoother entry.

Project Planning

The acquisition and expansion were structured into three key phases:

- **Phase 1:** Infrastructure Development (0–12 months) focused on upgrading network infrastructure, acquiring sites for telecom towers, and deploying modern equipment.
- **Phase 2:** Service Rollout (0–18 months) involved launching Airtel services in all 15 countries and integrating Airtel Money to drive financial inclusion.

- **Phase 3:** Optimization and Expansion (12–36 months) focused on expanding coverage in rural areas, improving service offerings, and optimizing cost structures.

To allocate resources effectively, Airtel invested heavily in modernizing Zain's outdated infrastructure. The company also retained Zain's workforce and provided extensive training to align employees with Airtel's operational standards. Risk management was a crucial aspect of project planning. The primary risks identified included regulatory delays, currency volatility, and operational inefficiencies due to legacy systems. Airtel mitigated these risks by adopting strategies such as currency hedging, phased rollouts, and proactive regulatory engagement.

PROJECT EXECUTION AND RESOURCE MANAGEMENT

Resource Management

- **Procurement:** Airtel partnered with telecom equipment vendors such as Ericsson and Huawei to upgrade legacy infrastructure. The procurement strategy focused on acquiring advanced technologies that could support high-speed data services and improve connectivity in urban and rural areas.
- **Human Resource Planning:** Airtel retained over 6,500 Zain employees to ensure business continuity. The company also introduced leadership training programmes to enhance employee skills and align them with Airtel's operational goals.
- **Technology Management:** Airtel deployed advanced telecom solutions, including modern base stations to improve coverage and unified IT platforms for streamlined operations in billing, customer management, and data analytics.

Communication and Stakeholder Management

- **Internal Communication:** Airtel maintained clear communication channels between project teams in Africa and headquarters in India. Weekly virtual meetings and real-time dashboards facilitated alignment on project goals and issue resolution.
- **External Communication:** Airtel actively engaged with African governments to address regulatory challenges. Public outreach campaigns focused on highlighting Airtel's affordability and service reliability, helping build consumer trust.

PROJECT MONITORING AND CONTROL

Airtel implemented a robust performance tracking system to measure progress based on key performance indicators (KPIs) such as:

- Subscriber growth rate
- Average revenue per user (ARPU)
- Network uptime and service quality

To manage project variances, Airtel took corrective actions such as reallocating resources and renegotiating vendor contracts. Performance indices showed that the Cost Performance Index (CPI) was 0.73, and the Schedule Performance Index (SPI) was 0.7, indicating delays and budget overruns that required adjustments.

PROJECT CHALLENGES AND MITIGATION STRATEGIES

Technical Challenges

- **Legacy Infrastructure:** Zain's obsolete technology limited service quality. Mitigation: Phased upgrades ensured operational continuity.

- **Tech Integration:** Different technological standards across 15 countries required system integration.

  Mitigation: Scalable IT solutions were adopted.

Regulatory Challenges

- **Approval Delays:** Lengthy licensing processes affected timelines.
  Mitigation: Proactive engagement with regulatory authorities accelerated approvals.
- **Impact of Exchange Rate:** Fluctuating exchange rates impacted revenue projections.

  Mitigation: Hedging strategies minimized financial risks.

Environmental and Social Issues

- **Community Resistance:** Concerns over ecological impact delayed infrastructure development. Mitigation: Airtel engaged with local leaders and adopted eco-friendly technologies.

Financial Challenges

- **High Debt Burden:** The acquisition added $10 billion in consolidated debt.
  Mitigation: Airtel negotiated extended repayment terms and optimized cost structures.
- **Low ARPU:** African markets had lower spending power than India.

  Mitigation: Airtel introduced bundled services and focused on high-value customer segments.

PROJECT OUTCOMES AND LESSONS LEARNED

Airtel successfully launched services in all 15 countries within 12 months. The subscriber base grew from 42 million to over 110 million in three years. Airtel Money gained widespread adoption, contributing to financial inclusion. The company also implemented energy-efficient telecom towers, reducing operational costs.

Key Lessons learnt

Localized Approaches: Adapting to cultural and market differences was crucial.
Risk Mitigation: Currency hedging and phased investments helped stabilize operations.
Employee Training: Workforce upskilling improved operational efficiency.

Case 16.5

Tata Motors' Acquisition of Jaguar Land Rover: A Strategic Perspective

In 2008, Tata Motors acquired Jaguar Land Rover (JLR) from Ford for $2.3 billion. This acquisition marked Tata's expansion into the global luxury automotive market, leveraging JLR's technological expertise, strong consumer base, and premium brand recognition. The move diversified Tata Motors' portfolio, reducing its reliance on commercial vehicles and aligning with its aspiration to become a global player. The deal came at a time when JLR was struggling with declining sales, allowing Tata Motors to acquire it at a relatively lower valuation.

PROJECT SCOPE AND OBJECTIVES

The acquisition encompassed JLR's material assets (manufacturing plants, R&D facilities, and distribution network), intellectual property (Jaguar and Land Rover brands, patents), and labour resources (16,000 employees, including engineers, designers, and management teams).

OBJECTIVES

The main objectives of this project were:

- **Brand Reinvention:** Introduce new models and upgrade existing product lines to align with evolving consumer preferences.
- **Market Expansion:** Strengthen JLR's presence in emerging markets like China and India while solidifying its position in North America and Europe.
- **Sustainable Mobility Solutions:** Invest in R&D for electric vehicles (EVs) and hybrid technologies to meet global sustainability standards.
- **Profitability:** Achieve financial turnaround within five years through cost optimization and strategic market penetration.

PROJECT MANAGEMENT FRAMEWORK

Initiation

Tata Motors conducted feasibility studies to assess JLR's market potential, financial health, and operational challenges. Regulatory approvals were obtained from authorities in the UK, EU, and other key markets, while negotiations with trade unions ensured workforce retention.

Planning: Work Breakdown Structure (WBS)

- Phase 1 (0–12 months): Operational integration and financial stabilization.
- Phase 2 (6–24 months): Product development and rebranding.
- Phase 3 (12–36 months): Market expansion and technology investments.

Resource Allocation

- **Financial:** A $3 billion bridge loan funded the acquisition and restructuring.
- **Human:** Retained JLR's experienced workforce and integrated global leadership talent.

Risk Management

Identified risks included luxury car demand fluctuations, high R&D costs, and integration complexities. Strategies such as cost optimization, diversified market focus, and modular product platforms were implemented.

EXECUTION: RESOURCE MANAGEMENT

- **Procurement:** JLR's existing supplier base was maintained while new vendors in China reduced costs.
- **Workforce:** Over 90% of JLR's talent was retained, and leadership appointments ensured strategic alignment.
- **Technology:** Increased R&D investment in EVs and autonomous driving technologies.

COMMUNICATION AND STAKEHOLDER MANAGEMENT

- **Internal:** Regular coordination between JLR and Tata Motors leadership.

- **External:** Collaboration with the British government to secure job retention and R&D incentives.

MONITORING AND CONTROL

- **Performance Tracking:** Financial indicators (EBIT, ROI) and operational KPIs (production timelines, quality standards, market penetration) were monitored.
- **Variance Management:** Budget overruns in R&D were addressed through investment reprioritization, while delayed model launches were streamlined.

SERVICE EXPANSION AND PRODUCT LAUNCHES

New Models

- Range Rover Evoque became a top-seller in the luxury SUV segment.
- Jaguar XF and XJ sedans revitalized the brand's appeal.

Market Diversification

- Expansion into China significantly boosted JLR's global market share.
- Region-specific product offerings catered to local consumer preferences.

PROJECT CHALLENGES

Technical Challenges

- **High R&D Costs:** Required significant investment in EVs and hybrids, mitigated by leveraging government grants.
- **Product Development Complexity:** Ensured alignment between JLR's legacy technologies and Tata Motors' strategic vision through modular platforms.

Operational Challenges

- **Workforce Integration:** Addressed cultural differences through cross-functional leadership teams.
- **Production Constraints:** Established local assembly units in China to meet demand.

Market Challenges

Global Financial Crisis (2008–2009): Declining luxury car sales mitigated by targeting emerging markets.

PROJECT CLOSURE AND EVALUATION

Key Achievements

- **Profitability:** By 2013, JLR reported annual revenue exceeding $20 billion, driven by global market expansion and strong product performance.
- **Successful Product Launches:** Range Rover Evoque pioneered the compact luxury SUV segment, while Jaguar's redesigned XF and XJ models strengthened brand positioning.
- **Market Penetration:** China became JLR's largest market, with significant growth in North America and Europe.
- **Sustainability Milestones:** JLR launched its first fully electric vehicle, the Jaguar I-PACE, ahead of schedule.
- **Brand Revitalization:** Effective marketing strategies enhanced JLR's global reputation, appealing to both legacy customers and new audiences.

LESSONS LEARNED

One of the key factors in the success of Tata Motors' acquisition of JLR was talent retention. Retaining JLR's skilled workforce ensured operational continuity, preserved institutional knowledge, and maintained the high product quality that the brand was known for. This approach helped smoothen the transition and allowed JLR to sustain its legacy of innovation while integrating into Tata Motors' strategic vision. Market diversification played a crucial role in mitigating financial risks. By expanding JLR's presence in emerging economies such as China and India, Tata Motors reduced its dependence on traditional markets like Europe and North America. This strategy provided a buffer against economic downturns in developed markets while tapping into the growing demand for luxury vehicles in high-growth regions.

Another significant aspect was JLR's sustainability focus. Investments in electric vehicles (EVs) and hybrid technologies positioned the company as an industry leader in sustainable mobility. These initiatives aligned with global environmental regulations and shifting consumer preferences, ensuring JLR remained competitive in an evolving automotive landscape. Additionally, cost efficiency became a priority post-acquisition. Tata Motors implemented lean manufacturing and automation to optimize production processes, reduce waste, and improve financial stability. These measures contributed to profitability by enhancing productivity and lowering operational expenses.

Tata Motors' acquisition of Jaguar Land Rover was a transformative move that reshaped both companies. Through effective project management, financial restructuring, and strategic market expansion, JLR evolved into a profitable and globally competitive luxury automotive brand. The key lessons from this acquisition underscore the importance of strategic investment, adaptability, and continuous innovation in achieving long-term success.

Comparison of Bharti Airtel (Africa Expansion) and Tata Motors (JLR Acquisition)

Aspect	Bharti Airtel (Africa Expansion)	Tata Motors (JLR Acquisition)
Objective	Expand telecom footprint in underpenetrated African markets.	Diversify into the global luxury automobile segment.
Acquisition Cost	$8.97 billion for Zain Telecom's African operations.	$2.3 billion for JLR brands, assets, and IP.
Scope	Integration of operations in 15 countries and telecom upgrades.	Workforce retention, product development, and market entry.
Geographic Focus	15 African nations (e.g., Nigeria, Kenya, Uganda).	Global, with a focus on China, Europe, and North America.
Challenges	Regulatory delays, legacy infrastructure, cultural integration.	High R&D costs, financial crisis, cultural differences.
Key Initiatives	Launch of Airtel Money, shared infrastructure models.	Lightweight platform development, EV and hybrid investments.
Revenue Impact	Increased subscriber base to 110 million within three years.	Achieved >$20 billion revenue in five years.
Market Penetration	Covered 75% of rural areas, boosting financial inclusion.	China became JLR's largest market by 2013.
Sustainability Initiatives	Energy-efficient telecom towers for cost optimization.	Early launch of Jaguar I-PACE, an all-electric vehicle.
Profitability Timeline	Achieved breakeven within three years.	Achieved profitability within five years.
Lessons Learned	Importance of localized strategies, cost optimization.	Talent retention, diversification, and lean manufacturing.

APPENDIX ONE

Solutions to Selected Exercises

Chapter 2

2. $$Payback = \frac{Investment}{Annual\ savings}$$

$$Payback_{Project Alpha} = \frac{\$150{,}000}{\$40{,}000} = 3.75\ years$$

$$Payback_{Project Beta} = \frac{\$200{,}000}{\$50{,}000} = 4.00\ years$$

A lower payback is better. Project Alpha has the lower payback and so has the better payback.

5. $$Project\ NPV = I_0 + \sum_{t=1}^{n} \frac{F_t}{(1+k)^t}$$

For Dust Devils Project using the NPV equation:

$$NPV = -\$500{,}000 + \frac{\$50{,}000}{(1+.20)^1} + \frac{\$250{,}000}{(1+.20)^2} + \frac{\$350{,}000}{(1+.20)^3}$$

$$= -\$500{,}000 + \$41{,}667 + \$173{,}611 + \$202{,}546 = -\$82{,}176$$

For Dust Devils Project using Excel:

	A	B	C	D	E	F
1	**Expected ROI**		20%			
2						
3	**Dust Devils**					
4						
5	**Year**	**Inflows**	**Outflows**	**Net flows**	**NPV**	
6	0		$500,000	–$500,000	–$500,000	
7	1	$50,000		$50,000	$41,667	=D7/((1+$C$1)^A7
8	2	$250,000		$250,000	$173,611	
9	3	$350,000		$350,000	$202,546	
10					–$82,176	
11						
12					–$82,176	=D6+NPV($C$1,D7:D9)

Microsoft Corporation

The expected ROI is entered in cell C1 and that will be referenced in the worksheets for the next two projects. Cells E6 to E10 repeat the calculations shown in the previous equations, only using Excel. Cells E7 to E9 perform the three discounting calculations. The equation used is shown in cell F7. The dollar signs in "$C$1" keep that cell from changing when this formula is copied up or down. In Excel, this is called an absolute reference.

Cell E12 performs the NPV calculations as shown in the textbook. Excel gives the same answer either way. Cell F12 shows the formula for the direct NPV calculations.

For Osprey Project using the NPV equation:

$$NPV = -\$250{,}000 + \frac{\$75{,}000}{(1+.20)^1} + \frac{\$75{,}000}{(1+.20)^2} + \frac{\$75{,}000}{(1+.20)^3} + \frac{\$50{,}000}{(1+.20)^4}$$
$$= -\$250{,}000 + \$62{,}500 + \$52{,}083 + \$43{,}403 + \$24{,}113 = -\$67{,}901$$

For Osprey Project using Excel:

	A	B	C	D	E	F
15	**Osprey**					
16						
17	**Year**	**Inflows**	**Outflows**	**Net flows**	**NPV**	
18	0		$250,000	–$250,000	–$250,000	
19	1	$75,000		$75,000	$62,500	=D19/((1+$C$1)^A19)
20	2	$75,000		$75,000	$52,083	
21	3	$75,000		$75,000	$43,403	
22	4	$50,000		$50,000	$24,113	
23					–$67,901	
24						
25					–$67,901	=D18+NPV($C$1,D19:D22)

Microsoft Corporation

For Voyagers Project using the NPV equation:

$$NPV = -\$75{,}000 + \frac{\$15{,}000}{(1+.20)^1} + \frac{\$25{,}000}{(1+.20)^2} + \frac{\$50{,}000}{(1+.20)^3} + \frac{\$50{,}000}{(1+.20)^4}$$
$$+ \frac{\$150{,}000}{(1+.20)^5}$$
$$= -\$75{,}000 + \$12{,}500 + \$17{,}361 + \$28{,}935 + \$24{,}113 + \$60{,}282$$
$$= \$68{,}191$$

For Voyagers Project using Excel:

	A	B	C	D	E	F
28	**Voyagers**					
29						
30	**Year**	**Inflows**	**Outflows**	**Net flows**	**NPV**	
31	0		$75,000	–$75,000	–$75,000	
32	1	$15,000		$15,000	$12,500	=D32/((1+$C$1)^A32)
33	2	$25,000		$25,000	$17,361	
34	3	$50,000		$50,000	$28,935	
35	4	$50,000		$50,000	$24,113	
36	5	$150,000		$150,000	$60,282	
37					$68,191	
38						
39					$68,191	=D31+NPV($C$1,D32:D36)

Microsoft Corporation

The only project SIMSOX should consider is Voyagers. Each of the other two projects would not satisfy the high rate of return SIMSOX expects from its projects.

Chapter 6

3.

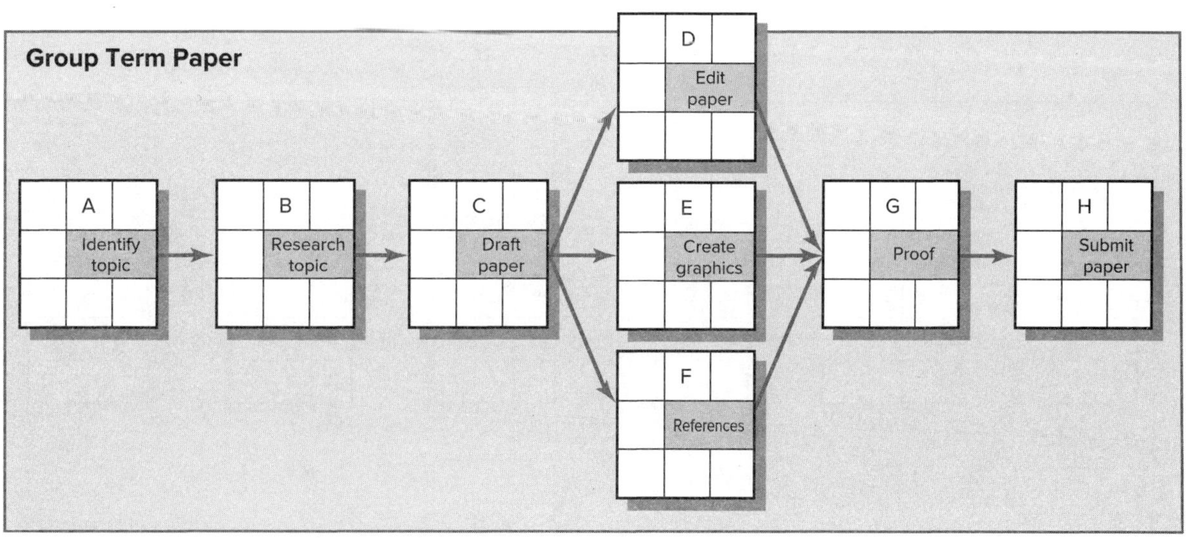

Activity C is a burst activity. Activity G is a merge activity.

11.

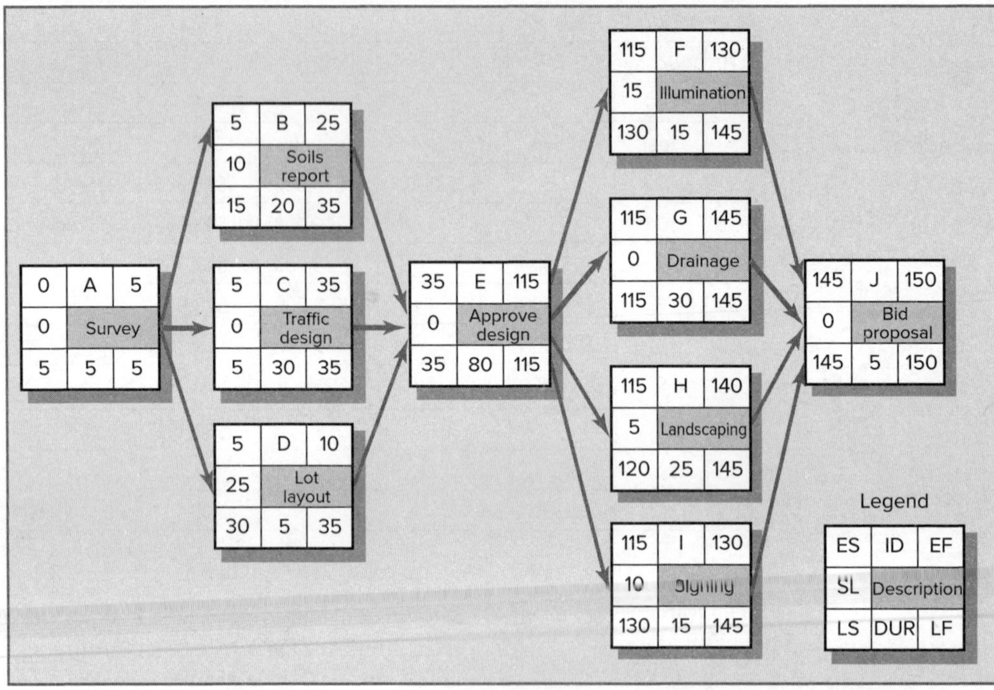

Early start, late start, early finish, late finish, and slack are shown in the diagram above. The completion time is 150 time units. The critical path is A-C-E-G-J.

14.

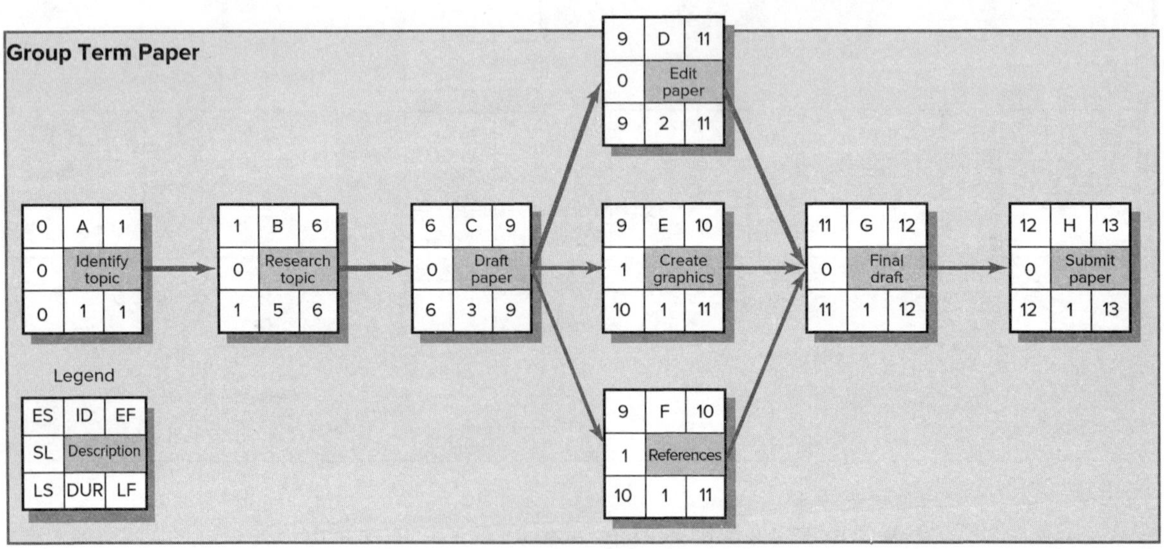

Early start, late start, early finish, late finish, and slack are shown in the diagram above. The Gantt chart is shown below.

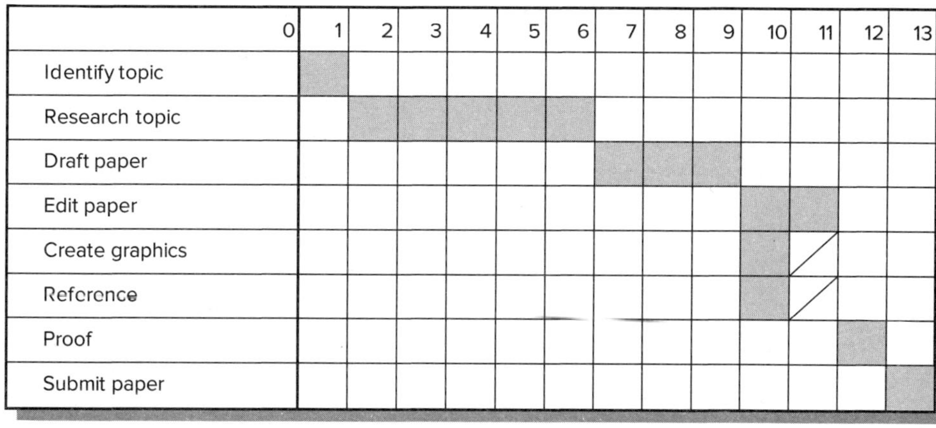

The completion time is 13 time units. The critical path is A→B→C→D→G→H.

22.

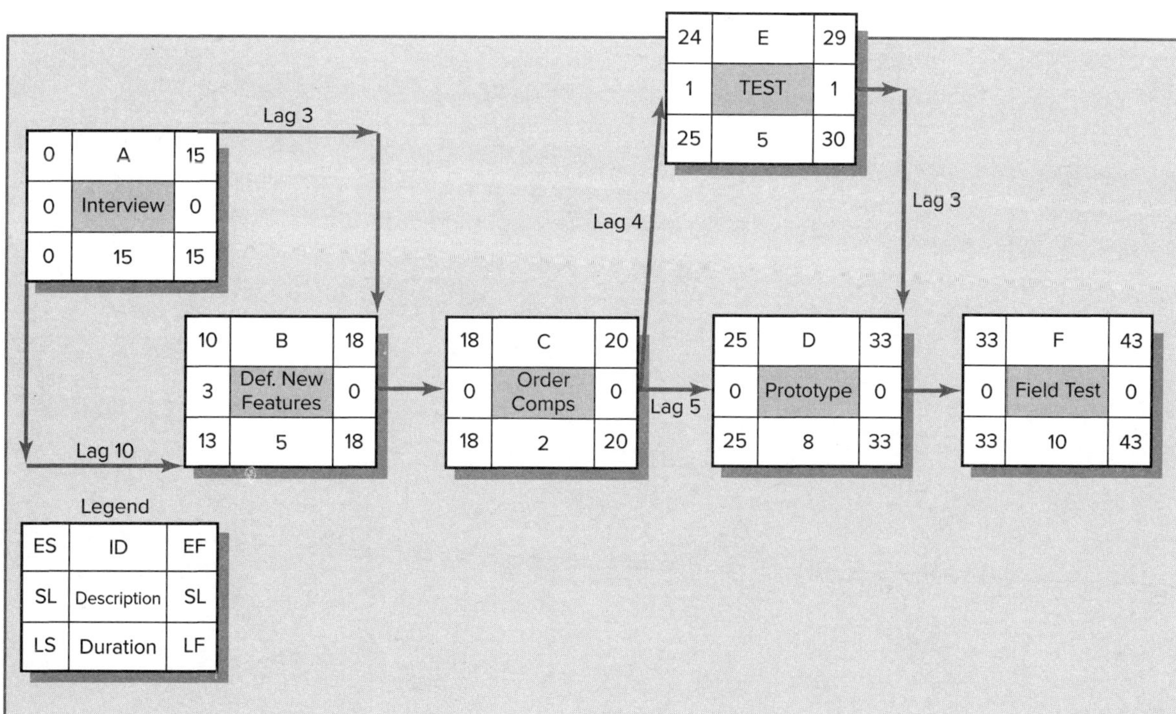

The critical path is A-B (finish only) -C-D-F.

Chapter 8

7. Log of Parallel Method of Scheduling: Exercise 8-7

Period	Activity	Changes
0–1	B	Schedule Activity B (first by minimum slack rule)
	A	Schedule Activity A
1–2	–	No changes
2–3	–	No changes
3–4	–	No changes
4–5	C	Delay ES of Activity C to 5. Reduce slack to 1
5–6	D	Schedule Activity D (minimum slack rule)
	C	Schedule Activity C
	E	Delay ES of Activity E to 6. Reduce slack to 1
6–7	E	Delay ES of Activity E to 7. Reduce slack to 0
7–8	E	Delay ES of Activity E to 8. Reduce slack to –1
	F	Delay ES of Activity F to 11. Reduce slack to –1
8–9	E	Delay ES of Activity E to 9. Reduce slack to –2
	F	Delay ES of Activity F to 12. Reduce slack to –2
9–10	E	Schedule Activity E
10–11	–	No changes
11–12	–	No changes
12–13	F	Schedule Activity F

10. The order in which your activities were scheduled: A, C, B, D, E, F, G, H. You should not spend time planning how you are going to spend your bonus. The schedule will take 16 days.

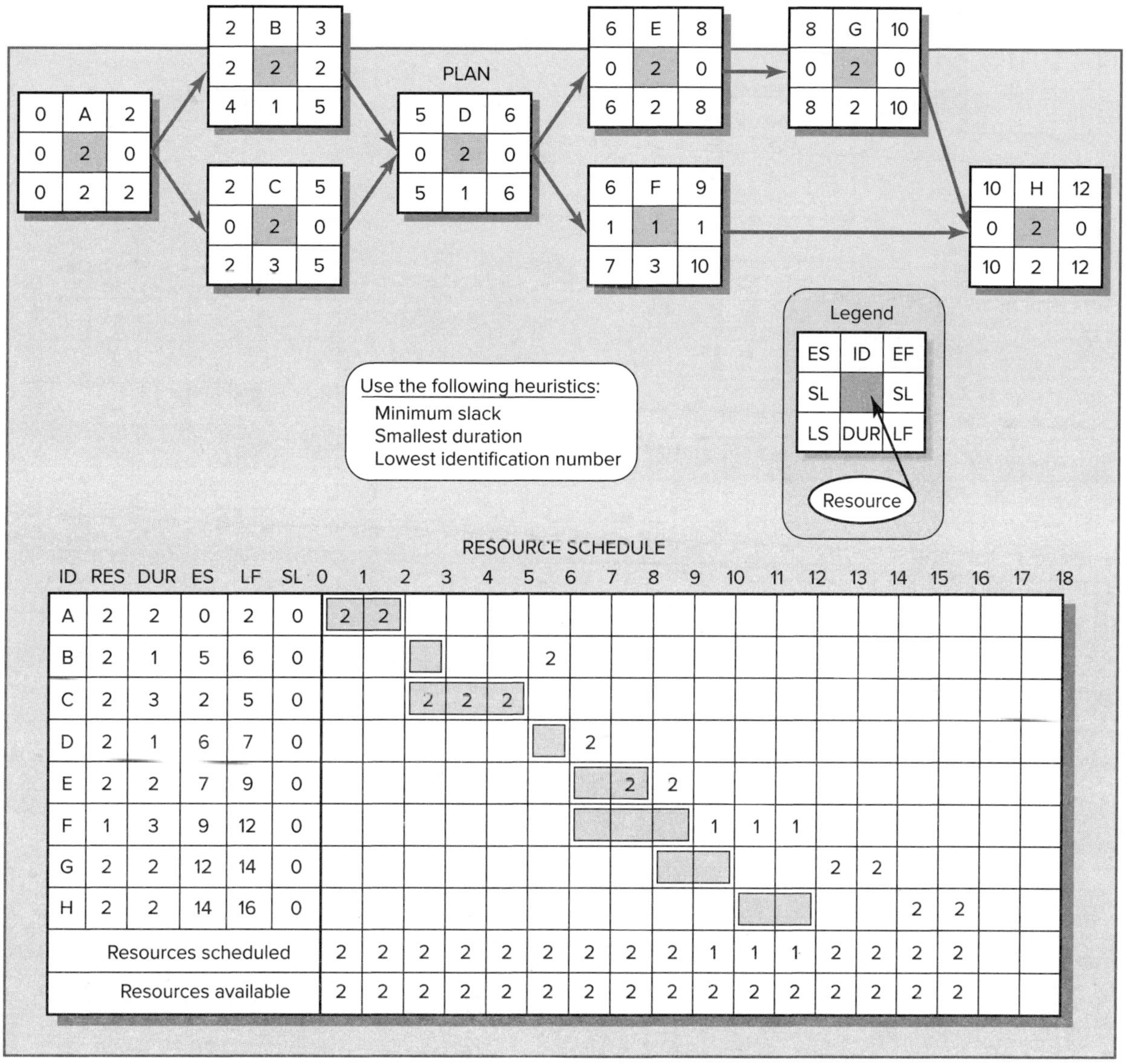

RESOURCE SCHEDULE

ID	RES	DUR	ES	LF	SL	0–1	1–2	2–3	3–4	4–5	5–6	6–7	7–8	8–9	9–10	10–11	11–12	12–13	13–14	14–15	15–16	16–17	17–18
A	2	2	0	2	0	2	2																
B	2	1	5	6	0						2												
C	2	3	2	5	0			2	2	2													
D	2	1	6	7	0							2											
E	2	2	7	9	0								2	2									
F	1	3	9	12	0										1	1	1						
G	2	2	12	14	0													2	2				
H	2	2	14	16	0															2	2		
Resources scheduled						2	2	2	2	2	2	2	2	2	1	1	1	2	2	2	2		
Resources available						2	2	2	2	2	2	2	2	2	2	2	2	2	2	2	2		

13.

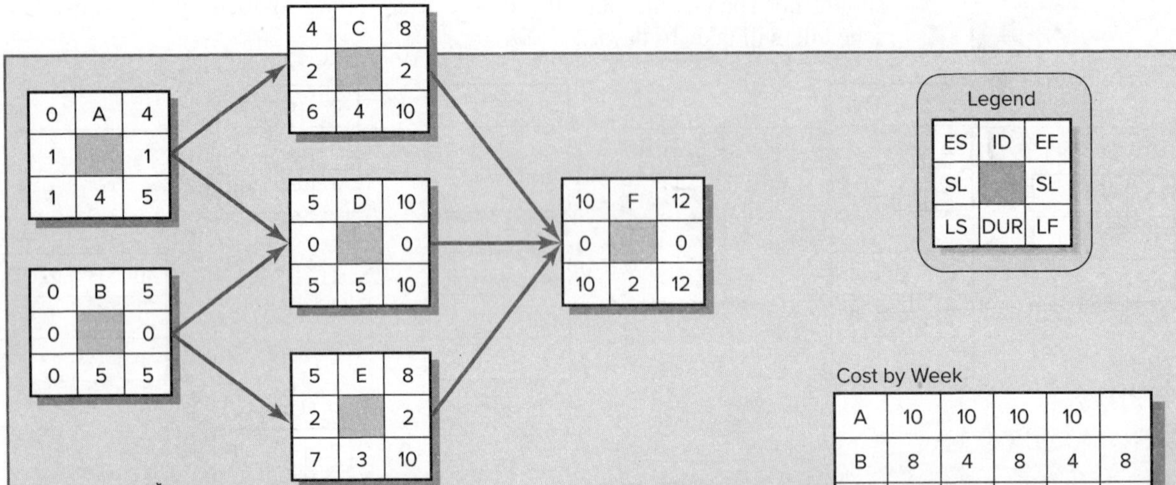

Cost by Week

A	10	10	10	10	
B	8	4	8	4	8
C	12	12	12	12	
D	6	2	2	2	6
E	8	8	12		
F	20	20			

ID	Budget	0–1	1–2	2–3	3–4	4–5	5–6	6–7	7–8	8–9	9–10	10–11	11–12
A	40	10	10	10	10								
B	32	8	4	8	4	8							
C	48					12	12	12	12				
D	18						6	2	2	2	6		
E	28						8	8	12				
F	40											20	20
Total	206	18	14	18	14	20	26	22	26	2	6	20	20
Cumulative		18	32	50	64	84	110	132	158	160	166	186	206

Chapter 9

2.

Act.	Crash Cost (Slope)	Maximum Crash Time	Normal Time	Normal Cost
A	0	0	2	150
B	100	1	3	100
C	50	2	4	200
D	40	1	4	200
E	50	1	3	200
F	0	0	1	150

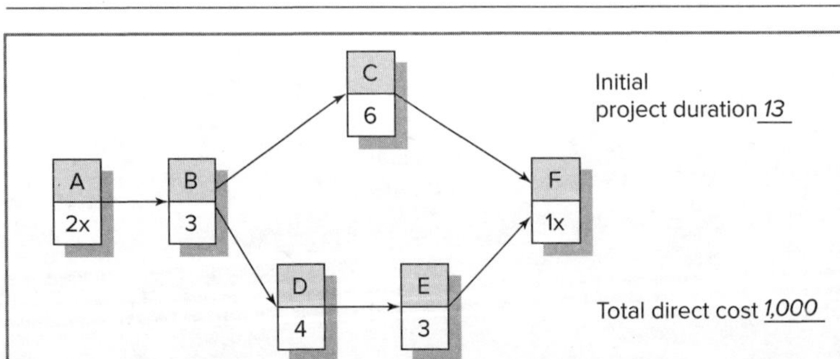

Project duration is reduced from 13 time periods to 10 time periods. Total direct cost goes up from $1,000 to $1,240. The steps are shown below:

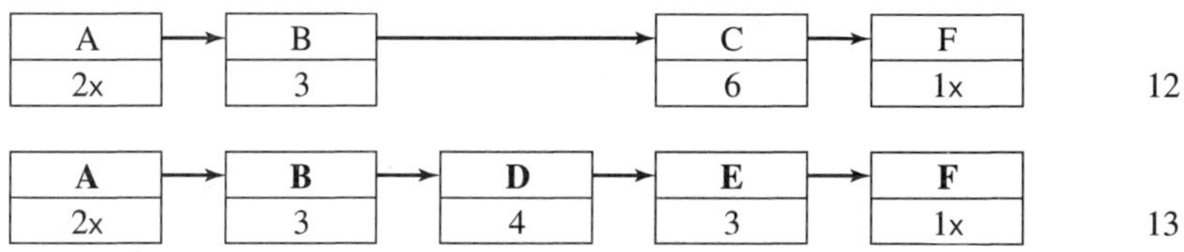

Duration: 13

Direct Cost: $1,000

The project has two paths, A-B-C-F, which takes 12 time periods, and A-B-D-E-F, which takes 13 time periods. This gives the project a duration of 13 time periods. The total direct cost is $1,000.

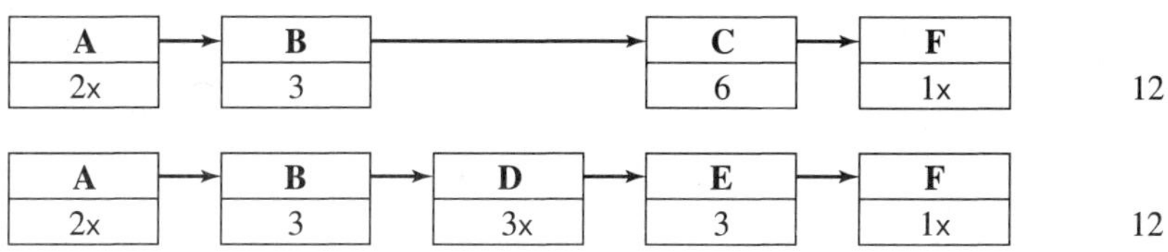

Duration: 12

Direct Cost: $1,040

Activity Changed: D

The cheapest activity to reduce is D at a cost of $40 for one time period. That makes both paths critical. This means that further reductions will require either reducing the same time from an activity on both paths or finding an activity shared by both paths and reducing that activity. Total direct cost goes up from $1,000 to $1,040.

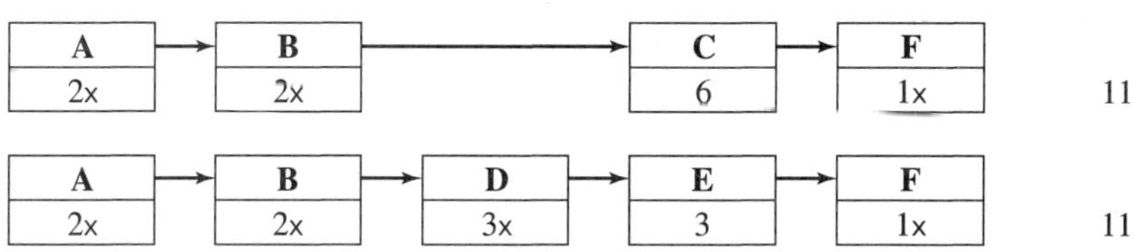

Duration: 11

Direct Cost: $1,140

Activity Changed: B

Activity B is on both paths and can be reduced by one time period at a cost of $100.[1] That lowers the completion time to 11 time periods and raises total direct cost to $1,140.

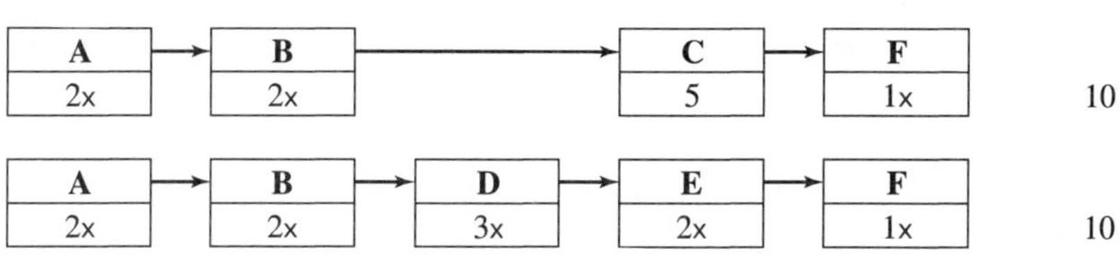

Duration: 10

Direct Cost: $1,240

Activities Changed: C and E

Finally, we can reduce C on the first path at a cost of $50 and E on the second path at a cost of $50. That reduces the completion time to 10 time units and raises total direct

[1] Activities C on the first path and E on the second path also have a combined cost of $100. We select B first since it is usually smarter to crash earlier activities first *and* it is usually smarter to crash one activity rather than two activities.

cost to $1,240. We have reached the crash point for the project. No further reductions are possible.

8.

Activity	Normal Time (weeks)	Normal Cost	Maximum Crash Time (weeks)	Crash Cost (slope)
A	3	150	0	0
B	4	200	1	100
C	3	250	1	60
D	4	200	1	40
E	2	250	0	0
F	3	200	2	30
G	2	250	1	20
H	4	300	2	60
I	2	200	1	200

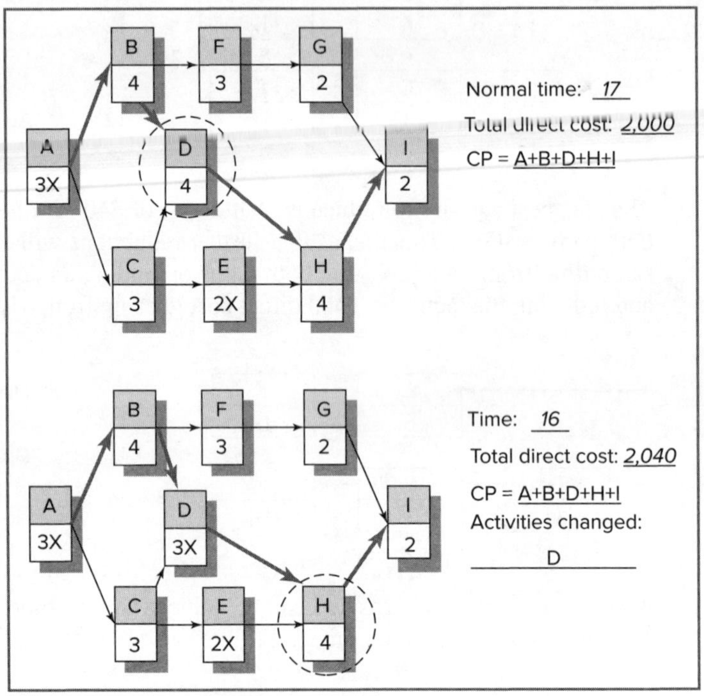

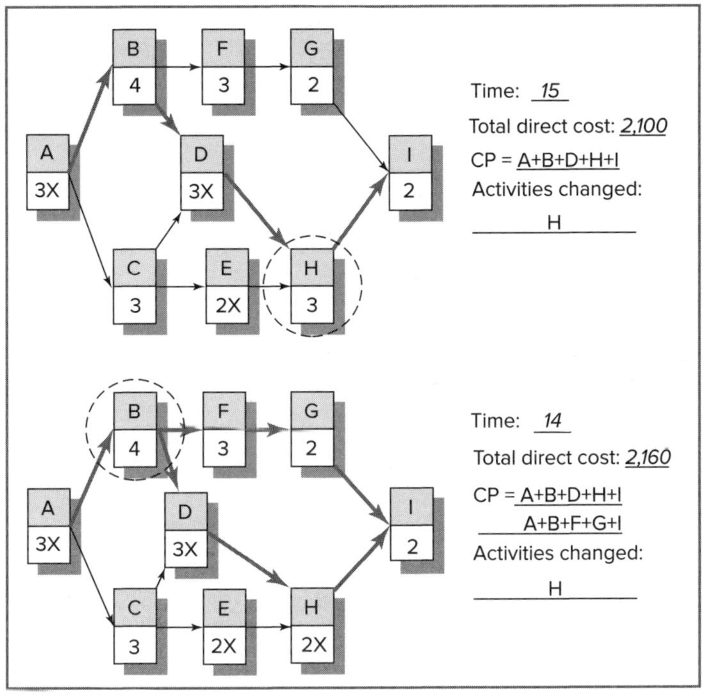

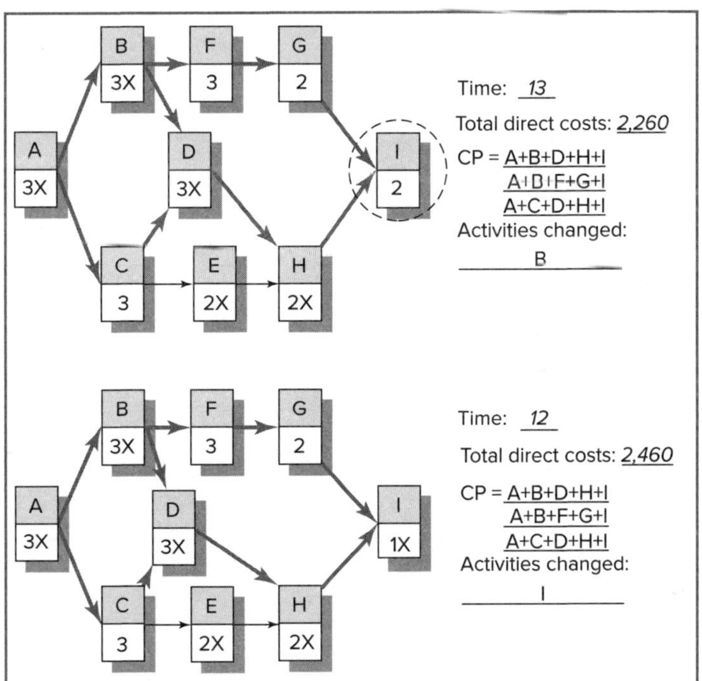

Duration	Direct Cost	Indirect Cost	Total Cost
17	2,000	1,500	3,500
16	2,040	1,450	3,490
15	2,100	1,400	3,500
14	2,160	1,350	3,510
13	2,260	1,300	3,560
12	2,460	1,250	3,710

The optimum time-cost schedule would be 16 weeks at a cost of $3,490.

Chapter 13

8.

Status Report: Ending Period 1 ($000)

Task	% Complete	EV	AC	PV	CV	SV
A	25%	25	50	50	−25	−25
Cumulative Totals		**25**	**50**	**50**	**−25**	**−25**

Status Report: Ending Period 2 ($000)

Task	% Complete	EV	AC	PV	CV	SV
A	50%	50	100	100	−50	−50
Cumulative Totals		**50**	**100**	**100**	**−50**	**−50**

Status Report: Ending Period 3 ($000)

Task	% Complete	EV	AC	PV	CV	SV
A	100%	100	200	100	−100	0
B	0%	0	0	100	0	−100
C	0%	0	0	150	0	−150
Cumulative Totals		**100**	**200**	**350**	**−100**	**−250**

Status Report: Ending Period 4 ($000)

Task	% Complete	EV	AC	PV	CV	SV
A	100%	100	200	100	−100	0
B	60%	150	100	150	50	0
C	50%	225	200	300	25	−75
Cumulative Totals		**475**	**500**	**550**	**−25**	**−75**

Status Report: Ending Period 5 ($000)

Task	% Complete	EV	AC	PV	CV	SV
A	100%	100	200	100	−100	0
B	100%	250	200	250	50	0
C	100%	450	400	450	50	0
Cumulative Totals		**800**	**800**	**800**	**0**	**0**

Status Report: Ending Period 6 ($000)

Task	% Complete	EV	AC	PV	CV	SV
A	100%	100	200	100	−100	0
B	100%	250	200	250	50	0
C	100%	450	400	450	50	0
D	75%	150	100	100	50	50
Cumulative Totals		**950**	**900**	**900**	**50**	**50**

Status Report: Ending Period 7 ($000)

Task	% Complete	EV	AC	PV	CV	SV
A	100%	100	200	100	−100	0
B	100%	250	200	250	50	0
C	100%	450	400	450	50	0
D	100%	200	150	200	50	0
E	20%	60	100	0	−40	60
F	5%	15	50	0	−35	15
Cumulative Totals		**1,075**	**1,100**	**1,000**	**−25**	**75**

Status Report: Ending Period 8 ($000)

Task	% Complete	EV	AC	PV	CV	SV
A	100%	100	200	100	−100	0
B	100%	250	200	250	50	0
C	100%	450	400	450	50	0
D	100%	200	150	200	50	0
E	100%	300	350	200	−50	100
F	10%	30	100	100	−70	−70
Cumulative Totals		**1,330**	**1,400**	**1,300**	**−70**	**30**

Performance Indexes Summary

Period	EV	AC	PV	SPI	CPI	PCIB
1	25	50	50	.50	.50	2%
2	50	100	100	.50	.50	3%
3	100	200	350	.29	.50	5%
4	475	500	550	.86	.95	24%
5	800	800	800	1.00	1.00	40%
6	950	900	900	1.06	1.06	48%
7	1,075	1,100	1,000	1.08	.98	54%
8	1,330	1,400	1,300	1.02	.95	67%

$$EAC_f = \frac{(BAC - EV)}{(EV/AC)} + AC = \frac{(2{,}000 - 1{,}330)}{1{,}330/1{,}400} + 1{,}400 = 2{,}105$$

$$VAC_f = BAC - EAC_f = 2{,}000 - 2{,}105 = -105$$

With two-thirds of the project completed the forecast is that the project will be \$105,000 over budget at completion.

APPENDIX TWO

Computer Project Exercises

In developing the exercises, trade-offs had to be made to enrich the learning experience. One of the major problems students initially encounter is data and detail overload. This reduces their ability to identify project and data problems and to compare alternatives. Although the project found in the exercises is real, it has been reduced and detail has been eliminated many times to concentrate on applying project management principles and understanding linkages. In addition, other simplifying assumptions have been made so that students and instructors can trace problems and discuss outcomes. These assumptions detract from reality, but they keep the focus on the objectives of the exercises and reduce student frustration with software intricacies. Moving from these exercises to real projects is primarily one of increasing detail.

The POM+ Project

Big Kola Company has been concerned that specialized fruit drinks have been eroding their cola market. The CEO mandates that "If you can't beat them, join them." Grape juice was the first product that was successful after an advertising blitz claiming the antitoxin benefits. Lately, competition is compressing grape juice margins and profits. Months of additional market surveys and focus groups have resulted in three potential high-margin drinks: cranberry, blueberry, and pomegranate. All these choices represent antitoxins. The decision is to produce the pomegranate drink that has many health claims. For example, the relative ability of these juices to eliminate harmful free radicals (antitoxins) is 71 percent for pomegranate, 33 percent for blueberry, and 20 percent for cranberry (Technion Institute of Technology). The market potential appears very attractive and should have a higher profit margin than the other potential juice products. Another appeal for pomegranate juice is its familiarity in the Middle East and Asia.

The Priority Matrix for the POM+ Project is:

	Time	Scope	Cost
Constrain			X
Enhance		X	
Accept	X		

Connor Gage, the project manager, has formed his project team and the members have come up with the following work breakdown structure.

1.0 POM+ Project
1.1 R&D product development
  1.1.1 Need survey
  1.1.2 Set product specs

- 1.1.3 Shelf life report
- 1.1.4 Nutrition report
- 1.2 Secure fruit suppliers
- 1.3 Initial production
  - 1.3.1 Equipment rehab
  - 1.3.2 Production trials
  - 1.3.3 Quality trials
  - 1.3.4 Quality metrics
  - 1.3.5 Quality training
- 1.4 Distribution
  - 1.4.1 Market testing
  - 1.4.2 Package design
  - 1.4.3 Select distributors
- 1.5 Legal
  - 1.5.1 Complete FDA certification
  - 1.5.2 Register trademark
- 1.6 Prepare product launch

Part 1

1. Develop the WBS outline using the software available (save your file).
2. Use this file and the information provided below to create a project schedule.
3. The following holidays are observed: January 1, Martin Luther King Day (third Monday in January), Memorial Day (last Monday in May), July 4th, Labor Day (first Monday in September), Thanksgiving Day (fourth Thursday in November), December 25 and 26.
4. If a holiday falls on a Saturday then Friday will be given as an extra day off, and if it falls on a Sunday then Monday will be given off.
5. The project team works eight-hour days, Monday through Friday.
6. The project will begin on January 2, 2025.
7. Based on this schedule, submit a memo that answers the following questions:
   a. When is the project estimated to be completed? How many working days will it take?
   b. What is the critical path?
   c. Which activity has the most total slack?
   d. How sensitive is this network?
   e. Identify two sensible milestones and explain your choice.

   Include the following (one page) printouts:

- A Gantt chart.
- A network diagram highlighting the critical path.
- A schedule table reporting ES, LS, EF, LF, and slack for each activity.

Hint: Change the timescale to months and weeks. The estimated duration of the project is 135 days.

Remember: Save your files for future exercises!

The following information has been derived from the WBS. *Note* that the activity number is what appears in the software with the complete WBS entered.

#	Activity	Duration (days)	Predecessor(s)
3	Need survey	20	None
4	Set product specs	15	3
5	Shelf life report	10	4
6	Nutrition report	5	4
7	Select fruit suppliers	20	5, 6
9	Equipment rehab	30	4
10	Production trials	15	7, 9
11	Quality trials	20	10
12	Quality metrics	5	11
13	Quality training	15	12
15	Market testing	30	5, 6
16	Package design	15	15
17	Select distributors	25	5, 6
19	Complete FDA certification	15	7, 15
20	Register trademark	5	7, 15
21	Prepare product launch	15	13, 16, 17, 19FS + 25 days, 20FS + 15 days

FS = Finish to Start lag.

Part 2

Remember the old saying, "A project plan is not a schedule until resources are committed." This exercise illustrates this sometime subtle, but important point.

Using your files from Part 1, input resources and their costs if you have not already done so. All information is found in Tables A2.1 and A2.2.

Prepare a memo that addresses the following questions:

1. Which if any of the resources are overallocated?
2. Assume that the project is time constrained and try to resolve any overallocation problems by leveling within slack. What happens?

TABLE A2.1 Resource Assignments

Activity	Resources
Need survey	MRKT (500%)
Set product specs	R&D (400%), MRKT (200%)
Shelf life report	R&D (300%)
Nutrition report	R&D (300%)
Select fruit suppliers	PURCH (100%)
Equipment rehab	ENG (1,000%), PROD (2,000%)
Production trials	PROD (1,500%), PURCH (100%), ENG (1,000%)
Quality trials	QUAL (300%), PROD (500%)
Quality metrics	QUAL (300%), PROD (100%)
Quality training	QUAL (300%), PROD (1,500%)
Market testing	MRKT (500%)
Package design	DESIGN (300%), MRKT (100%)
Select distributors	MRKT (500%)
Complete FDA certification	LEGAL (300%)
Register trademark	LEGAL (300%)
Prepare product launch	QUAL (300%), PURCH (200%), PROD (1,500%), MRKT (500%), ENG (500%), R&D (100%)

TABLE A2.2
Resources Availability and Pay Rates

Resource	Abbrev	Available	Hourly rate
Marketing staff	MRKT	5	$80/hr
R&D	R&D	5	$80/hr
Engineering	ENG	10	$100/hr
Purchasing	PURCH	2	$60/hr
Quality engineers	QUAL	3	$80/hr
Designers	DESIGN	3	$60/hr
Legal staff	LEGAL	3	$120/hr
Production	PROD	20	$60/hr

3. What is the impact of leveling within slack on the sensitivity of the network?

   Include a Gantt chart with the schedule table after leveling within slack.

4. Assume the project is resource constrained and resolve any overallocation problems by leveling outside of slack. What happens?

   Include a Gantt chart with the schedule table after leveling outside of slack.
   Note: No splitting of activities is allowed.
   Note: No partial assignments (e.g., 50 percent). All resources must be assigned 100 percent.

Part 3

Top management has accepted the July 21st completion schedule created at the end of Part 2. Prepare a brief memo that addresses the following questions:

1. How much will the project cost? What is the most expensive activity?
2. What does the cash flow statement tell you about how costs are distributed over the life span of the project?

   Include a monthly estimated cash flow for the project.
   Once you are confident that you have the final schedule, save the file as a baseline.

Hint: Save a backup file just in case without baseline!

Part 4 A

Assume that today is March 31, 2025, and Table A2.3 contains the tracking information for the project up till now. Enter this information into your saved baseline file and prepare a status report for the first three months of the POM+ project.

TABLE A2.3
Status Report March 31, 2025

Activity	Actual Start	Actual Finish	Actual Duration	Remaining Duration
Need survey	1/2/25	2/3/25	22	0
Set product specs	2/4/25	2/28/25	19	0
Shelf life report	3/3/25	3/14/25	10	0
Nutrition report	3/17/25	3/20/25	4	0
Equipment rehab	3/3/25		23	12

Your status report should also address the following questions:

1. How is the project progressing in terms of cost and schedule?
2. What activities have gone well? What activities have not gone well?
3. What do the PCIB and PCIC indicate in terms of how much of the project has been accomplished to date?
4. What is the forecasted cost at completion (EAC_f)? What is the predicted VAC_f?
5. Report and interpret the TCPI for the project at this point in time.
6. What is the estimated date of completion?
7. How well is the project doing in terms of its priorities?

Try to present the above information in a form worthy of consideration by top management.

Include an Earned Value table and a Tracking Gantt Chart.

Note: Insert March 31, 2025, as the status date in the Project Information box.

Part 4 B

Assume that today is May 30, 2025, and Table A2.4 contains the tracking information for the project up till now. Enter this information into your saved baseline file and prepare a status report for the POM+ project.

Your status report should address the following questions:

1. How is the project progressing in terms of cost and schedule?
2. What activities have gone well? What activities have not gone well?
3. What do the PCIB and PCIC indicate in terms of how much of the project has been accomplished to date?
4. What is the forecasted cost at completion (EAC_f)? What is the predicted VAC_f?
5. Report and interpret the TCPI for the project at this point in time.
6. What is the estimated date of completion?
7. How well is the project doing in terms of its priorities?

Try to present the above information in a form worthy of consideration by top management.

Include an Earned Value table and a Tracking Gantt Chart.

Note: Insert May 30, 2025, as the status date in the Project Information box.

TABLE A2.4
Status Report May 30, 2025

Activity	Actual Start	Actual Finish	Actual Duration	Remaining Duration
Need survey	1/2/25	2/3/25	22	0
Set product specs	2/4/25	2/28/25	19	0
Shelf life report	3/3/25	3/14/25	10	0
Nutrition report	3/17/25	3/20/25	4	0
Select fruit suppliers	4/4/25	5/1/25	20	0
Equipment rehab	3/3/25	4/14/25	31	0
Production trials	4/17/25	5/8/25	14	0
Quality trials	5/12/25	6/5/25	18	0
Market testing	4/7/25	5/9/25	25	0
Package design	5/12/25	5/28/25	12	0
Select distributors	5/28/25		3	20
Complete FDA certification	5/12/25	5/30/25	14	0

Red Zuma Project

The ARC Company specializes in developing and selling a wide range of high-quality scooters. Sales representatives report that there is a growing demand for racing scooters. ARC's president, Robin Lane, is excited about the possibilities and predicts that one day these kinds of razor scooters will be featured in X-Game events. ARC is a small company and uses a strong matrix to optimally utilize limited manpower.

The Project Priority Matrix for the Red Zuma Project is:

	Time	Scope	Cost
Constrain		X	
Enhance	X		
Accept			X

Part 1

You are a member of a project team assigned to develop the new razor scooter code named "Red Zuma." Table A2.5 contains the information necessary to create a project schedule. For the purpose of this case assume the following:

1. The project begins January 2, 2015.
2. The following holidays are observed: January 1, Martin Luther King Day (third Monday in January), Memorial Day (last Monday in May), July 4th, Labor Day (first Monday in September), Thanksgiving Day (fourth Thursday in November), December 25.
3. If a holiday falls on a Saturday, then Friday will be given as an extra day off, and if it falls on a Sunday, then Monday will be given as a day off. If December 25th falls on a Friday then Monday will not be given a day off.
4. The project team works eight-hour days, Monday through Friday.

TABLE A2.5
Red Zuma: Project Schedule

ID	Task Name	Duration	Predecessors
1	1 Red Zuma Project	260 days	
2	1.1 Market Analysis	25 days	
3	1.2 Product Design	30 days	2
4	1.3 Manufacturing Study	20 days	2
5	1.4 Product Design Selection	10 days	3, 4
6	1.5 Detailed Marketing Plan	15 days	5
7	1.6 Manufacturing Process	30 days	5
8	1.7 Detailed Product Design	45 days	5
9	1.8 Build Prototypes	25 days	8
10	1.9 Lab Test Prototypes	10 days	9
11	1.10 Field Test Prototypes	15 days	9
12	1.11 Finalized Product Design	20 days	7,10,11
13	1.12 Final Manufacturing Process	10 days	12
14	1.13 Order Components	7 days	12
15	1.14 Order Production Equipment	14 days	13
16	1.15 Install Production Equipment	35 days	14FS+20 days,15FS+30 days
17	1.16 Celebrate	1 day	6, 16

Note: FS refers to a Finish-to-Start lag.

Construct a network schedule for this project and prepare a memo that answers the following questions:

1. When is the project estimated to be completed? How long will the project take?
2. What is the critical path for the project?
3. Which activity has the greatest amount of slack?
4. How sensitive is this network?
5. Identify two sensible milestones and explain your choices.

Include the following printouts:

- A Gantt chart.
- A network diagram highlighting the critical path.
- A schedule table reporting ES, LS, EF, LF, and slack for each activity.

Part 2

The following personnel have been assigned full-time to the Red Zuma project team:

4 marketing specialists
4 design engineers
4 development engineers
4 industrial engineers
4 test riders
2 purchasing agents

Use the file from Part 1 and the information contained in Tables A2.6 and A2.7 to assign resources to the project schedule.

Part A

Prepare a memo that addresses the following questions:

1. Which if any of the resources are overallocated?
2. Assume that the project is time constrained and try to resolve any overallocation problems by leveling within slack. What happens?
3. What is the impact of leveling within slack on the sensitivity of the network?

   Include a Gantt chart with the schedule table after leveling within slack.

4. Assume that the project is resource constrained and no additional personnel are available. How long will the project take given the resources assigned? (Hint: Undo leveling performed in Part A before answering this question.)

Note: No splitting of activities is allowed.

TABLE A2.6
Red Zuma Project Resources

	$	Number available
Marketing specialist	$80,000/yr	4
Design engineer	$125,000/yr	4
Development engineer	$110,000/yr	4
Industrial engineer	$100,000/yr	4
Purchasing agent	$75,000/yr	2
Test rider	$70/hr	4

Note: MS Project considers resources in terms of percentages with one full-time worker being 100%.

TABLE A2.7 Red Zuma Resource Assignments

Task Name	Resource Names
Red Zuma Project	
Market Analysis	Marketing Specialist [400%]
Product Design	Marketing Specialist, Design Engineer [400%], Development Engineer [200%], Industrial Engineer, Purchasing Agent
Manufacturing Study	Industrial Engineer [400%], Development Engineer [200%]
Product Design Selection	Marketing Specialist [200%], Design Engineer [300%], Development Engineer [200%], Industrial Engineer [200%], Purchasing Agent [25%]
Detailed Marketing Plan	Marketing Specialist [400%]
Manufacturing Process	Design Engineer, Development Engineer [200%], Industrial Engineer [300%]
Detailed Product Design	Marketing Specialist [200%], Design Engineer [400%], Development Engineer [200%], Industrial Engineer [200%], Purchasing Agent [25%]
Build Prototypes	Design Engineer [200%], Development Engineer [200%], Industrial Engineer [400%]
Lab Test Prototypes	Design Engineer [200%], Development Engineer [200%], Test Rider
Field Tests	Marketing Specialist, Design Engineer [200%], Development Engineer, Industrial Engineer, Test Rider [300%]
Finalized Product Design	Marketing Specialist [200%], Design Engineer [300%], Development Engineer [300%], Industrial Engineer [200%], Purchasing Agent [25%]
Final Manufacturing Process	Industrial Engineer [300%], Design Engineer, Purchasing Agent [25%]
Order Components	Purchasing Agent
Order Production Equipment	Purchasing Agent
Install Production Equipment	Design Engineer, Development Engineer [300%], Industrial Engineer [400%]
Celebration	Design Engineer [400%], Development Engineer [400%], Industrial Engineer [400%], Marketing Specialist [400%], Purchasing Agent [200%]

Note: Resource assignments without brackets are 100%.

5. How does the new duration compare with the estimated completion date generated from Part 1? What does this tell you about the impact resources can have on a schedule?

Include a Gantt chart with a schedule table displaying free and total slack depicting the resource-constrained schedule.

Part B

Top management is not happy with the resource-constrained schedule. Robin Lane, the president, has promised retailers that ARC will begin production in time for the major trade show in Las Vegas on January 22, 2016, which means the project needs to be completed by January 17, 2016. She has authorized working the first available Saturday of each month to help the project get completed sooner. She realizes that this will only reduce the project duration by 12–13 days.

After talking to the engineers, everyone agrees that they do not have to wait for the Detailed Product Design to be 100% completed before starting to build the prototype. The consensus is that Building the Prototype can start 30 days after the start of the Detailed Product Design. Likewise, the Final Manufacturing Process can start 15 days after the start of Finalized Product Design.

Dewey Martin, director of product development, is also willing to add personnel to the project. He is willing to make available at least one more Development, Design, and/or Industrial Engineer to the project as well as Marketing Specialist. Since there is an acute shortage of personnel at ARC he requests that you only use additional manpower that will help meet the deadline. Your objective is to develop a schedule that will satisfy the deadline with minimum additional resource usage.

Prepare a memo that addresses the following questions:

1. What was the impact of introducing Start-to-Start lags to the schedule and budget?
2. Which, if any additional personnel assignments, would you choose to complete the project before the January 17th deadline? Explain your choices as well as the reasons for not choosing other options.
3. How have these changes affected the sensitivity of the network and the critical path?

Include a Gantt chart with a schedule table displaying free and total slack for the new schedule.

Note: Do not assign new personnel to specific tasks, simply add them to the Resource Sheet. All new personnel are available full time (100%).

> At first glance—this appears to be a very complicated, difficult assignment, but if you enter the information correctly, the computer is able to generate the answers with a few simple clicks.

Part 3

Top management has accepted the schedule created at the end of Part 2. Prepare a brief memo that addresses the following questions:

1. How much will the project cost? What is the most expensive activity?
2. What does the cash flow statement tell you about how costs are distributed over the life span of the project?

Include a monthly cash flow for the project.

Once you are confident that you have the final schedule, save the file as a baseline.

Hint: Save a backup file just in case without baseline!

Part 4

Part A

Today's date is July 8, 2015, the milestone date for the completion of the Prototype. You are charged with preparing a status report for top management. Table A2.8 summarizes progress on the Red Zuma project.

Submit a professional status report to Robin Lane that addresses the following questions:

1. How is the project progressing in terms of cost and schedule?
2. What activities have gone well? What activities have not gone well?
3. How much of the project has been accomplished (PCIB)?
4. What is the forecasted cost at completion (EAC_f)?
5. What is the estimated completion date?
6. How is the project doing in terms of priorities (see Part 1)?

Report and interpret relevant Earned Value metrics in your report.

Include a Tracking Gantt chart as well as an Earned Value Table with your memo.

TABLE A2.8 Red Zuma Project Update

	Task Name	Act. Start	Act. Finish	% Comp.	Phys. % Comp.	Act. Dur.	Rem. Dur.
1	**1 Red Zuma**	**Fri 1/9/15**	**NA**	**46%**	**0%**	**125.85 days**	**146.4 days**
2	1.1 Market Analysis	Fri 1/9/15	Thu 2/12/15	100%	0%	25 days	0 days
3	1.2 Product Design	Fri 2/13/15	Wed 4/1/15	100%	0%	35 days	0 days
4	1.3 Manufacturing Study	Fri 2/13/15	Fri 3/6/15	100%	0%	16 days	0 days
5	1.4 Product Design Selection	Thu 4/2/15	Fri 4/17/15	100%	0%	13 days	0 days
6	1.5 Detailed Marketing Plan	NA	NA	0%	0%	0 days	15 days
7	1.6 Manufacturing Process	NA	NA	0%	0%	0 days	30 days
8	1.7 Detailed Product Design	Mon 4/20/15	Wed 6/24/15	100%	0%	49 days	0 days
9	1.8 Build Prototypes	Wed 6/10/15	NA	39%	0%	9 days	14 days
10	1.9 Lab Test Prototypes	NA	NA	0%	0%	0 days	10 days
11	1.10 Field Test Prototypes	NA	NA	0%	0%	0 days	15 days
12	1.11 Finalized Product Design	NA	NA	0%	0%	0 days	20 days
13	1.12 Final Manufacturing Process	NA	NA	0%	0%	0 days	10 days
14	1.13 Order Components	NA	NA	0%	0%	0 days	7 days
15	1.14 Order Production Equipment	NA	NA	0%	0%	0 days	14 days
16	1.15 Install Production Equipment	NA	NA	0%	0%	0 days	35 days
17	1.16 Celebrate	NA	NA	0%	0%	0 days	1 days

Part B

You have told Robin Lane that based on what you know now you need to revise the estimates for some of the remaining activities. Finalized Product Design is expected to take 3 days longer than planned. Final Manufacturing Process is expected to take 2 days less than planned, while Install Production Equipment is now expected to take only 30 days. You also report that Detailed Marketing plan will be completed before the end of the New Year. She is insisting that the project be completed by January 17th in order to be ready for the Las Vegas show. She is willing to spend $50,000 from Management Reserves to expedite shipping if necessary. $25,000 would reduce the shipping of components by 5 days and/or $25,000 would reduce the shipping of manufacturing parts by 5 days. (Hint: Adjust lag.) Prepare a memo to Robin that addresses the following questions:

1. What is the impact of the revised estimates for Finalized Product Design and Install Production Equipment on the project schedule and cost?
2. Would you recommend authorizing the expenditure of $50,000? Explain.
3. What, if any other recommendations, would you make so that the project can achieve Robin's deadline? Justify your recommendations.

Include a Tracking Gantt chart with variance schedule that depicts your final recommendations and revised schedule.

Hint: After adjusting the Installation of Production Equipment and Finalized Product Design, level outside of slack to eliminate any resource over allocation problems.

Conveyor Belt Project

Part 1

Project Description

The new computer-controlled conveyor belt is an exciting project that moves and positions items on the conveyor belt within <1 millimeter. The project will produce a new system for future installations, and for replacement of those in the field, at a low cost. The computer-controlled conveyor belt has the potential to be a critical unit in 30 percent of the systems installed in factories. The new system is also easier to update with future technologies.

The Project Priority Matrix for the Conveyor Belt Project (CBP) is:

	Time	Scope	Cost
Constrain	X		
Enhance		X	
Accept			X

Table A2.9 has been developed for you to use in completing the project exercises.

Assignment

Develop the WBS outline using the software available to you.

Question

Does this information (WBS) allow you to define any milestones of the project? Why or why not? What are they?

Remember: Save your file for future exercises!

TABLE A2.9 Conveyor Belt Project; WBS

Conveyor Belt Project	
Hardware	Hardware specifications
	Hardware design
	Hardware documentation
	Prototypes
	Order circuit boards
	Assemble preproduction models
Operating system	Kernel specifications
	Drivers
	Disk drivers
	Serial I/O drivers
	Memory management
	Operating system documentation
	Network interface
Utilities	Utilities specifications
	Routine utilities
	Complex utilities
	Utilities documentation
	Shell
System integration	Architectural decisions
	Integration first phase
	System hard/software test
	Project documentation
	Integration acceptance testing

Part 2

Use your file from Part 1 and the information provided below to complete this exercise. (See Table A2.10.)

1. Each work package will represent an activity.
2. The project begins January 5, 2026.
3. The following holidays are observed: January 1, Memorial Day (last Monday in May), July 4th, Labor Day (first Monday in September), Thanksgiving Day (fourth Thursday in November), December 25.
4. If a holiday falls on a Saturday then Friday will be given as an extra day off, and if it falls on a Sunday, then Monday will be given as a day off.
5. The project teams work eight-hour days, Monday through Friday.

Warning: Experience has taught students to frequently make separate backup files for each exercise. The software is never as friendly as users expect!

Construct a network schedule for the conveyor belt project and prepare a memo that addresses the following questions:

1. When is the project estimated to be completed? How long will the project take?
2. What is the critical path(s) for the project?
3. Which activity has the greatest amount of slack?
4. How sensitive is this network?
5. Identify two sensible milestones and explain your choices.
6. Compare the advantages/disadvantages of displaying the schedule as a network versus a Gantt chart.

TABLE A2.10 Conveyor Belt Project; Schedule

Activity	Description	Resource	Duration (days)	Preceding Activity
1	Architectural decisions	Design	25	—
2	Hardware specifications	Design, Development	50	1
3	Kernel specifications	Design	20	1
4	Utilities specifications	Design, Development	15	1
5	Hardware design	Design, Development	70	2
6	Disk drivers	Assembly/test, Development	100	3
7	Memory management	Development	0	3
8	Operating system documentation	Design, Documentation	25	3
9	Routine utilities	Development	60	4
10	Complex utilities	Development	80	4
11	Utilities documentation	Design, Development	20	4
12	Hardware documentation	Design, Development	30	5
13	Integration first phase	Assembly/test, Development	50	6, 7, 8, 9, 10, 11, 12
14	Prototypes	Assembly/test, Development	80	13
15	Serial I/O drivers	Development	130	13
16	System hard/software test	Assembly/test	25	14, 15
17	Order circuit boards	Purchasing	5	16
18	Network interface	Development	90	16
19	Shell	Development	60	16
20	Project documentation	Development, Documentation	50	16
21	Assemble preproduction models	Assembly/test, Development	30	17F-S, lag 50 days
22	Integrated acceptance testing	Assembly/test, Development	60	18, 19, 20, 21

Note: F-S refers to a Finish-to-Start lag.

Include the following printouts:

- A Gantt chart.
- A network diagram highlighting the critical path.
- A schedule table reporting ES, LS, EF, LF, and slack for each activity.

Hint: The project should be completed in 530 days.

Remember: Save your file for future exercises!

Part 3

Remember the old saying, "A project plan is not a schedule until resources are committed." This exercise illustrates this subtle, but very important, difference.

Part A

Using your files from Part 2 input resources and their costs if you have not already done so. All information is found in Tables A2.10 and A2.11.

Prepare a memo that addresses the following questions:

1. Which if any of the resources are overallocated?
2. Assume that the project is time constrained and try to resolve any overallocation problems by leveling within slack. What happens?
3. What is the impact of leveling within slack on the sensitivity of the network?

   Include a Gantt chart with the schedule table after leveling within slack.

4. Assume the project is resource constrained and resolve any overallocation problems by leveling outside of slack. What happens? What are the managerial implications?
5. What options are available at this point in time?

   Include a Gantt chart with the schedule table after leveling outside of slack.

Note: No splitting of activities is allowed.

Note: No partial assignments (e.g., 50 percent). All resources must be assigned 100 percent.

Part B

When you show the resource-constrained network to top management, they are visibly shaken. After some explanation and negotiation they make the following compromise with you:

- The project must be completed no later than February 1, 2028 (530 days).
- You may assign two additional development teams.
- If this does not suffice, you may hire other development teams from the outside. Hire as few external teams as possible because they cost $50 more per hour than your inside development people.

TABLE A2.11 Organization Resources

Name	Group	Cost ($/hr)
Design	R&D (2 teams)	$100
Development	R&D (2 teams)	70
Documentation	R&D (1 team)	60
Assembly/test	R&D (1 team)	70
Purchasing	Procurement (1 team)	40

Internal Development

Add as many development units (teams) as needed to stay within the 530 days. If you need more than two internal development units, then hire as few external teams as necessary. Select the cheapest possibility! Change as few activities as possible. It is recommended you keep work packages that require cooperation of several organizational units inside your company. You decide how best to do this.

Hint: Undo leveling prior to adding new resources.

Once you have obtained a schedule that meets the time and resource constraints, prepare a memo that addresses the following questions:

1. What changes did you make and why?
2. How long will the project take?
3. How did these changes affect the sensitivity of the network?

Include a Gantt chart with a schedule table presenting the new schedule.

Part 4

Based on the file created at the end of Part 3, prepare a memo that addresses the following questions:

1. How much will the project cost?
2. What does the cash flow statement tell you about how costs are distributed over the life span of the project?

Include a monthly cash flow and a cost table for the project.

Once you are confident that you have the final schedule, save the file as a baseline.

Hint: Save a backup file just in case without baseline!

Part 5

Prepare status reports for each of the first four quarters of the project, given the information provided here. This requires saving your resource schedule as a baseline and inserting the appropriate status report date in the program. Assume that no work has been completed on the day of the status report.

Your status report should include a table containing the PV, EV, AC, BAC, EAC, SV, CV, and CPI for each activity and the whole project. The report should also address the following questions:

1. How is the project progressing in terms of cost and schedule?
2. What activities have gone well? What activities have not gone well?
3. What do the PCIB and PCIC indicate in terms of how much of the project has been accomplished to date?
4. What is the forecasted cost at completion (EAC_f)? What is the predicted VAC_f?
5. Report and interpret the TCPI for the project at this point in time.
6. What is the estimated date of completion?
7. How well is the project doing in terms of its priorities?

Try to present the above information in a form worthy of consideration by top management.

Include a Tracking Gantt chart with each report.

First Quarter, March 31, 2026

Table A2.12 summarizes the information regarding activities accomplished to date.

Be sure to save your file after each quarterly report and use it to build the next report!

Second Quarter, June 30, 2026

Table A2.13 summarizes the information regarding activities accomplished since the last report.

Third Quarter, September 30, 2026

Table A2.14 summarizes the information regarding activities accomplished since the last report.

TABLE A2.12
March 31, 2026

Activity	Start Date	Finish Date	Actual Duration	Remaining Duration
Hardware specifications	2/10/26		36	9
Kernel specifications	3/23/26		7	13
Utilities specifications	2/9/26	2/27/26	15	0
Routine utilities*	3/23/26		7	53
Complex utilities	3/23/26		7	73
Architectural decisions	1/5/26	2/26/26	25	0

* The project manager for the external development team was hired to perform routine utilities reported that due to commitments to other clients they would be able to start on that activity 3/23/26.

TABLE A2.13
June 30, 2026

Activity	Start Date	Finish Date	Actual Duration	Remaining Duration
Hardware specifications	2/10/26	4/13/26	45	0
Hardware design	4/14/26		55	12
Kernel specifications	3/23/26	4/24/26	25	0
Disk drivers	4/27/26		46	64
Memory management	4/27/26		46	50
Op. systems documentation	5/18/26	6/22/26	25	0
Utilities specifications	2/9/26	2/27/26	15	0
Routine utilities	3/23/26	6/22/26	65	0
Complex utilities	3/23/26		71	20
Utilities documentation	4/27/26	5/27/26	22	0
Architectural decisions	1/5/26	2/26/26	25	0

TABLE A2.14
September 30, 2026

Activity	Start Date	Finish Date	Actual Duration	Remaining Duration
Hardware specifications	2/10/26	4/13/26	45	0
Hardware design	4/14/26	7/17/26	67	0
Hardware documentation	7/20/26	8/21/26	25	0
Kernel specifications	3/23/26	4/24/26	25	0
Disk drivers	4/27/26	9/15/26	99	0
Memory management	4/27/26	9/7/26	93	0
Op. systems documentation	5/18/26	6/22/26	25	0
Utilities specifications	2/9/26	2/27/26	15	0
Routine utilities	3/23/26	6/22/26	65	0
Complex utilities	3/23/26	7/28/26	90	0
Utilities documentation	4/27/26	5/27/26	22	0
Architectural decisions	1/5/26	2/26/26	25	0
Integration first phase	8/24/26		27	23

Fourth Quarter, December 31, 2026

Table A2.15 summarizes the information regarding activities accomplished since the last report.

Part 6

You have received revised estimates for the remaining activities at the end of the fourth quarter:

- Prototypes will be completed on 3/8/27, which is 5 days early.
- Serial I/O drivers will be completed on 6/22/27, which will take 20 days longer than planned.
- System hardware/software test will start on 7/1/27 and take 25 days.
- Order circuit boards will start on 8/6/27 and take 5 days.
- Assemble preproduction model will begin on 9/16/27 and take 18 days.
- Project documentation is expected to start on 8/6/27 and will take 55 days.
- Network interface is expected to start on 8/6/27 and will take 99 days.
- Shell is expected to start on 8/6/27 and will take 55 days.
- Integrated acceptance testing is expected to start on 12/29/27 and will take 54 days. Prepare a memo that addresses the following questions:

1. What is the new EAC for the project? How long should the project take given these revised estimates?
2. How happy will top management be with these forecasts given the priorities of the project?
3. What recommendations would you make?

Include a revised schedule, a Tracking Gantt chart, and cost table with your memo.

TABLE A2.15
December 31, 2026

Activity	Start Date	Finish Date	Actual Duration	Remaining Duration
Hardware specifications	2/10/26	4/13/26	45	0
Hardware design	4/14/26	7/17/26	67	0
Hardware documentation	7/20/26	8/21/26	25	0
Prototypes	11/19/26		29	51
Kernel specifications	3/23/26	4/24/26	25	0
Disk drivers	4/27/26	9/15/26	99	0
Serial I/O drivers	11/19/26		29	111
Memory management	4/27/26	9/7/26	93	0
Op. systems documentation	5/18/26	6/22/26	25	0
Utilities specifications	2/9/26	2/27/26	15	0
Routine utilities	3/23/26	6/22/26	65	0
Complex utilities	3/23/26	7/28/26	90	0
Utilities documentation	4/27/26	5/27/26	22	0
Architectural decisions	1/5/26	2/26/26	25	0
Integration first phase	8/24/26	11/18/26	46	0

GLOSSARY

A

acceptance criteria A list of conditions that must be met before deliverables are accepted.

accuracy of estimate Refers to how correct the estimate is.

activity Task of the project that consumes time while people/equipment either work or wait.

activity-on-arrow AOA A method for drawing project networks. The activity is shown as an arrow.

activity-on-node AON A method for drawing project networks. The activity is on the node (rectangle).

Agile Project Management (Agile PM) A family of interative, incremental development methods for completing projects.

apportionment The Costs allocated to a specific segment of a project by using a percentage of planned total cost—for example, framing a house might use 25 percent of the total cost, or coding a teaching module 40 percent of total cost.

avoiding risk Eliminating the risk caused before the project begins.

B

balanced matrix A matrix structure in which the project manager and functional managers share roughly equal authority over the project. The project manager decides what needs to be done; functional managers are concerned with how it will be accomplished.

baseline A concrete document and commitment; it represents the first real plan with cost, schedule, and resource allocation. The planned cost and schedule performance are used to measure actual cost and schedule performance. Serves as an anchor point for measuring performance.

best alternative to a negotiated agreement (BATNA) Strong or weak BATNA indicates your power to negotiate with the other party.

bottom-up estimates Detailed estimates of work packages, usually made by those who are most familiar with the task (also called micro estimates).

brainstorming Generating as many ideas/solutions as possible without critical judgment.

budget at completion (BAC) Budgeted cost at completion. The total budgeted cost of the baseline or project cost accounts.

burst activity An activity that has more than one activity immediately following it.

C

Certified Associate in Project Management (CAPM) A credential offered by the Project Management Institute to an entry level person starting a career as a project manager. An individual who met specific education requirements without project management experience can sit for an examination administered by the Project Management Institute. *See also* Project Management Professional (PMP).

change management system A defined process for authorizing and documenting changes in the scope of a project.

co-location A situation in which project members including those from different organizations work together in the same location.

concurrent engineering Cross-functional teamwork in new-product development projects that provides product design, quality engineering, and manufacturing process engineering all at the same time.

confidence in estimate Refers to the degree one trusts the estimate.

contingency plan A plan that covers possible identified project risks that may materialize over the life of the project.

contingency reserves Financial reserve setup to cover identified risks that may occur and influence baseline time and costs. These reserves are typically controlled by the project manager and project team. *See also* management reserves.

control chart A chart used to monitor past project schedule performance and current performance as well as estimate future schedule trends.

cost account A control point of one or more work packages used to plan, schedule, and control the project. The sum of all the project cost accounts represents the total cost of the project.

cost performance index (CPI) The ratio of work performed to actual costs (EV/AC).

cost variance (CV) The difference between EV and AC (CV = EV − AC). Tells if the work accomplished cost more or less than was planned at any point over the life of the project.

crash To shorten an activity or a project.

crash point The most a project activity time can realistically be compressed with the resources available to the organization.

crash time The shortest time an activity can be completed (assuming a reasonable level of resources).

critical path The longest activity path(s) through the network. The critical path can be distinguished by identifying the collection of activities that all have the same minimum slack.

cross-cultural orientations A framework that describes and/or explains cultural differences.

culture The totality of socially transmitted behavior patterns, beliefs, institutions, and all other products of human work and thought characteristic of a community or country.

culture shock A natural psychological disorientation that most people suffer when they move to a culture different from their own.

D

dedicated project team An organizational structure in which all of the resources needed to accomplish a project are assigned full time to the project.

Delphi method A group method to predict future events—for example, time, cost.

direct costs Costs that are clearly charged to a specific work package—usually labor, materials, or equipment.

dysfunctional conflict Disagreement that does not improve project performance.

E

early time The earliest an activity can start or finish based on network logic, the data date, and any schedule constraints.

earned value (EV) The physical work accomplished plus the authorized budget for this work. Previously this was called the budgeted cost of work performed (BCWP).

Earned Value Management (EVM) A methodology that combines scope, schedule, and resource measurements to assess project performance and progress.

emotional intelligence (EQ) The ability or skill to perceive, assess, and manage the emotions of oneself and others.

escalate opportunity Notify the appropriate people of an opportunity that is outside the scope of the project or exceeds the authority of the project manager.

escalate risk Notify the appropriate people of a risk that is outside the scope of the project or exceeds the authority of the project manager.

escalation A control mechanism for resolving problems in which people at the lowest appropriate level attempt to resolve a problem within a set time limit or the problem is "escalated" to the next level of management.

Estimate To forecast or approximate the time and cost of completing project deliverables.

estimated cost at completion (EAC) The sum of actual costs to date plus revised estimated costs for the work remaining in the WBS. The text uses EACre to represent revisions made by experts and practitioners associated with the project. A second method is used in large projects where the original budget is less reliable. This method uses the actual costs to date plus an efficiency index (CPI = EV/AC) applied to the remaining project work. When the estimate for completion uses the CPI as the basis for forecasting cost at completion, we use the acronym EAC_f, where $\mathbf{EAC_f}$ = estimated costs at completion. Includes costs to date plus revised estimated costs for the work remaining. (Uses formula to compute EAC.)

Extreme Programming (XP) An aggressive form of agile that features test-driven development and pair programming.

Extrovert A person who tends to be talkative, outgoing, and enjoys social interaction.

F

facilitator A guide who leads the project team through an analysis of project activities that went well, what needs improvement, and development of a follow-up action plan with goals and accountability.

fast tracking Accelerating project completion, typically by rearranging the network schedule and using start-to-start lags.

feature A piece of a product that delivers some useful functionality to a customer.

force majeure Acts of nature (i.e., earthquakes, hurricanes, etc.).

forecasted total cost at completion (EAC_f) The expected total cost of the project expressed as the sum of actual costs to date and forecasted estimate of the cost of remaining work based on the current CPI.

free slack The maximum amount of time an activity can be delayed from its early start (ES) without affecting the early start of any activity immediately following it.

function points Points derived from past software projects to estimate project time and cost, given specific features of the project.

functional conflict Disagreement that contributes to the objectives of the project.

G

Gantt chart A bar chart of schedule information where activities are listed on the vertical axis, dates are shown on the horizontal axis, and activity durations are shown in horizontal bars placed according to start and finish.

gold plating The addition of any feature or enhancement not considered in the original scope plan or product description at any point in a project.

groupthink A tendency of members in highly cohesive groups to lose their critical evaluative capabilities.

H

hammock activity A special-purpose, aggregate activity that identifies the use of fixed resources or costs over a segment of a project—for example, a consultant. It derives its duration from the time span between other activities.

heuristics A rule of thumb used to make decisions. Frequently found in scheduling projects. For example, schedule critical activities first; then schedule activities with the shortest duration.

hybrid project management A management approach that blends agile and traditional project management practices to complete a project.

I

implementation gap The lack of consensus between the goals set by top management and those independently set by lower levels of management. This lack of consensus leads to confusion and poor allocation of organizational resources.

indirect costs Costs that cannot be traced to a particular project or work package.

infrastructure Basic services (e.g., communication, transportation, power) needed to support project completion.

inspiration-related currencies Influence based on inspiration (opportunity to do good, be the best, etc.).

Introvert A person who is more reserved and likes alone time to engage in more reflective thinking.

iterative, incremental, development (IID) A cyclical development process in which a project gradually evolves over time.

K

Kanban A Japanese lean management approach that helps a team prioritize and manage work flow.

L

lag relationship The relationship between the start and/or finish of a project activity and the start and/or finish of another activity. The most common lag relationships are (1) finish-to-start, (2) finish-to-finish, (3) start-to-start, and (4) start-to-finish.

late time The latest an activity can start or finish without delaying the completion of the project.

law of reciprocity People are obligated to grant a favor comparable to the one they received.

learning curve A mathematical curve used to predict a pattern of time reduction as a task is performed over and over.

lessons learned An analysis carried out during and shortly after the project life cycle attempting to capture positive and negative project learning.

lessons learned register A document used to record knowledge gained during a project so that it can be used in the current project and entered into the lessons learned repository.

lessons learned repository A database containing historical information about lessons learned.

leveling Techniques used to examine a project for an unbalanced use of resources and for resolving resource overallocations.

M

management by wandering around (MBWA) A management style in which managers spend the majority of their time outside their offices, interacting with key people.

management reserve index (MRI) The percentage of the management reserves that have been used to date.

management reserves A percentage of the total project budget reserved for contingencies. The fund exists to cover unforeseen, new problems—not unnecessary overruns. The reserves are designed to reduce the risk of project delays. Management reserves are typically controlled by the project owner or project manager. *See also* contingency reserves.

matrix Any organizational structure in which the project manager shares responsibility with the functional managers for assigning priorities and for directing the work of individuals assigned to the project.

mentor Typically a more experienced manager who acts as a personal coach and champions a person's ambitions.

merge activity An activity that has more than one activity immediately preceding it.

met expectations Customer satisfaction is a function of the extent to which perceived performance exceeds expectations.

milestone An event that represents significant, identifiable accomplishment toward the project's completion.

mitigating risk Action taken to either reduce the likelihood that a risk will occur and/or the impact the risk will have on the project.

N

net present value (NPV) A minimum desired rate of return discount (e.g., 15 percent) is used to compute present value of all future cash inflows and outflows.

nominal group technique (NGT) A structured problem-solving process in which members privately rank-order preferred solutions.

O

opportunity An event that can have a positive impact on project objectives.

optimism bias The belief that your chances of experiencing negative events are lower and your chances of experiencing positive events are higher than those of your peers.

organization breakdown structure (OBS) A structure used to assign responsibility for work packages.

organizational culture A system of shared norms, beliefs, values, and assumptions held by an organization's members.

organizational politics Actions by individuals or groups of individuals to acquire, develop, and use power and other resources to obtain preferred outcomes when there is uncertainty or disagreement over choices.

outsourcing Contracting for the use of external sources (skills) to assist in implementing a project.

overhead costs Typically, organization costs that are not directly linked to a specific project. These costs cover general expenses such as upper management, legal, market promotion, and accounting. Overhead costs are usually charged per unit of time or as a percentage of labor or material costs.

oversight A set of principles and processes to guide and improve the management of projects. The intent is to ensure projects meet the needs of the organization through standards, procedures, accountability, efficient allocation of resources, and continuous improvement in the management of projects.

P

parallel activities Activities that can be carried on concurrently or simultaneously.

partnering charter A formal document that states common goals as well as cooperative procedures used to achieve these goals that are signed by all parties working on a project.

path A sequence of connected activities.

payback The time it takes to pay back the project investment (investment/net annual savings). The method does not consider the time value of money or the life of the investment.

percent complete index actual costs (PCIC) The amount of work accomplished based on actual costs and revised estimates (AC/EAC).

percent complete index budgeted costs (PCIB) The amount of work accomplished based on project budget (EV/BAC).

performance review In general, all review methods of individual performance center on the technical and social skills brought to the project and team. These reviews stress personal improvement and are frequently used for salary and promotion decisions.

personal integrity Adherence to moral and ethical principles.

personal-related currencies Influence based on enhancing another person's self-esteem.

phase estimating An estimating method that begins with a macro estimate for the project and then refines estimates for phases of the project as it is implemented.

phase gate model A structured process to review and evaluate each project phase to determine whether to continue, revise, or cancel the project.

planned value (PV) The planned time-phased baseline of the value of the work scheduled. Previously, this was called the budgeted cost of work scheduled (BCWS).

portfolio management Centralized selection and management of a portfolio of projects to ensure that allocation of resources is directed and balanced toward the strategic focus of the organization.

position-related currencies Influence based on the ability to enhance someone else's position within an organization.

positive synergy A characteristic of high-performance teams in which group performance is greater than the sum of individual contributions.

precision of estimate Refers to the degree of exactness of the estimate.

principled negotiation A process of negotiation that aims to achieve win/win results.

priority matrix A matrix that is set up before the project begins, establishes which criterion among cost, time, and scope will be enhanced, constrained, or accepted.

priority system The process used to select projects. The system uses selected criteria for evaluating and selecting projects that are strongly linked to higher-level strategies and objectives.

priority team The group (sometimes the project office) responsible for selecting, overseeing, and updating project priority selection criteria.

process breakdown structure (PBS) A phase-oriented grouping of project activities that defines the total scope of the project. Each descending level represents an increasingly detailed description of project work.

product backlog A prioritized list of project requirements with estimated time to turn them into complete product functionality.

product owner The person responsible for managing the product backlog in Scrum so as to maximize the value of the project. The product owner represents all stakeholders.

product scope description A detailed description of the product, service, or outcome of the project.

program A group of related projects designed to accomplish a common goal over an extended period of time.

project A temporary endeavor undertaken to create a unique product, service, or result.

project charter A document that authorizes the project manager to initiate and lead a project.

project closure All of the activities of shutting down a project. The major activities are evaluating project goals and performance, developing lessons learned, releasing resources, and preparing a final report.

project cost-duration graph A graph that plots project cost against time; it includes direct, indirect, and total costs for a project over a relevant range of time.

project evaluation The process of assessing, verifying, and documenting project results.

project kick-off meeting Typically the first meeting of the project team.

project life cycle The stages found in all projects—definition, planning, execution, and closing.

project management office (PMO) A centralized unit within an organization or a department that oversees and improves the management of projects.

Project Management Professional (PMP) An individual who has met specific education and experience requirements set forth by the Project Management Institute, has agreed to adhere to a code of professional conduct, and has passed an examination designed to objectively assess and measure project management knowledge. In addition, a PMP must satisfy continuing certification requirements or lose the certification. *See also* Certified Associate in Project Management (CAPM).

project maturity model A framework that details different levels of development in an organization's project management practices and methods.

project portfolio A group of projects that have been selected for implementation, balanced by project type, risk, and ranking by selected criteria.

project sponsor Typically a high-ranking manager who champions and supports a project.

project vision An image of what the project will accomplish.

projectitis A condition in which team members become strongly attached to their project and disconnected from the larger organization.

projectized organization A multiproject organization in which project managers have full authority to assign priorities and direct the work of persons assigned to their project.

R

range estimating An estimating technique in which multiple estimating points are given based on some logic (e.g., high vs. low or best case, worst case, and most likely case).

ratio method A method that uses the ratio of past actual costs for similar work to estimate the cost for a potential project. This macro method of forecasting cost does not provide a sound basis for project cost control, since it does not recognize differences among projects.

reference class forecasting (RCF) A sophisticated forecasting method in which you take an external view and forecast project costs based on actual outcomes of similar projects.

relationship-related currencies Influence based on friendship.

release burndown chart The trend of work remaining across time. In a release or product, the source of data is the product backlog with work remaining tracked on the vertical axis and number of sprints on the horizontal axis.

Request for Proposal (RFP) A type of procurement document used to request proposals from prospective sellers of products or services.

resource smoothing A technique that uses slack to reduce peak resource demand to increase resource utilization.

resource-constrained project A project that assumes resources are limited (fixed) and therefore time is variable.

resource-constrained scheduling Scheduling a project in which resources are inadequate.

responsibility matrix A matrix whose intersection point shows the relationship between an activity (work package) and the person/group responsible for its completion.

retaining When a conscious decision is made to accept the risk of an event occurring (i.e., if risk is too large, if the chance of occurring is slim, or if the contingency reserves can simply absorb the risk if it materializes).

retrospective A methodology that analyzes a past project event to determine what worked and what didn't, develops lessons learned, and creates an action plan that ensures lessons learned are used to improve management of future projects.

revised estimated cost at completion (EAC_{re}) The expected total cost of the project expressed as the sum of actual costs to date and revised estimates of the cost of remaining work based on the judgment of those doing the work.

risk The chance that an undesirable project event will occur and the consequences of all its possible outcomes.

risk breakdown structure (RBS) A hierarchical depiction of the identified project risks, arranged by risk category and subcategory, which identifies the various areas and causes of potential risks.

risk profile A list of questions that address traditional areas of uncertainty on a project.

risk register A register detailing all identified risks, including descriptions, category, probability of occurring, impact, responses, contingency plans, owners, and current status.

risk severity matrix A tool used to assess the impact of risks on a project.

S

sacred cow A project that is a favorite of a powerful management figure, who is usually the champion for the project.

scaling Adapting Agile PM to large, multi-team projects.

scenario analysis Technique for analyzing risks where team members assess the significance of each risk event in terms of probability and impact of the event.

schedule variance (SV) The difference between the planned dollar value of the work actually completed and the value of the work scheduled to be completed at a given point in time (SV = EV − PV). Schedule variance contains no critical path information.

scheduling performance index (SPI) The ratio of work performed to work scheduled (EV/PV).

scope creep The tendency for the scope of a project to expand once it has started.

scope statement A definition of the end result or mission of a project. Scope statements typically include project objectives, deliverables, milestones, specifications, and limits and exclusions.

Scrum master The person responsible for the Scrum process and its correct application.

self-organizing team A semi-autonomous team that manages itself.

sensitivity A function of the number of critical or near-critical paths.

social network building The process of identifying and building cooperative relationships with key people.

splitting A scheduling technique in which work is interrupted on one activity and the resource is assigned to another activity for a period of time, then reassigned to work on the original activity.

sprint backlog A list of tasks that define a Scrum team's work for a sprint. Each task identifies those responsible for doing the work and the estimated amount of work remaining on the task on any given day during the sprint.

sprint burndown chart The trend of work remaining across time in a sprint. The source of data is the sprint backlog with work remaining tracked on the vertical axis and days of a sprint on the horizontal axis.

stakeholders Individuals and organizations that are actively involved in a project, or whose interests may be positively or negatively affected as a result of project execution or completion. They may also exert influence over the project and its results.

strategic management The process of assessing "what we are" and deciding and implementing "what we intend to be and how we are going to get there." Strategy describes how an organization intends to compete with the resources available in the existing and perceived future environment.

strong matrix A matrix structure in which the project manager has primary control over project activities and functional managers support project work.

systems thinking A holistic approach to viewing problems that emphasizes understanding the interactions among different problem factors.

T

task-related currencies Influence based, helping others do their work.

team building A process designed to improve the performance of a team.

team evaluation Evaluating the performance of the project team using a minimum core of conditions in place before the project began. Evaluation practices should emphasize the team as a whole, while minimizing individual performance.

team rituals Ceremonial actions that reinforce team identity and values.

template method A method that uses a prepared form to develop project networks, costs, and time estimates.

360-degree review A multirater appraisal system based on performance information that is gathered from multiple sources (superiors, peers, subordinates, customers).

time and cost databases Collections of actual versus estimated times and costs of work packages over many projects, used for estimating new project tasks and their expected possible error.

time buffer A contingency amount of time for an activity to cover uncertainty—for example, availability of a key resource or merge event.

time-constrained project A project that assumes time is fixed and if resources are needed, they will be added.

time-phased budget baseline A cost baseline that is derived from the WBS and project schedule. The budgeted costs are distributed to mirror the project schedule.

to complete performance index (TCPI) The calculated cost performance index that must be achieved on the remaining work in order to meet the project budget (BAC – EV)/(BAC – AC).

top-down estimates Rough estimates that use surrogates to estimate project time and cost (also called macro estimates).

total slack The amount of time an activity can be delayed and not affect the project duration (TS = LS – ES or LF – EF).

tracking Gantt A Gantt chart that compares planned versus actual schedule information.

transferring risk Shifting responsibility for a risk to another party.

U

uniqueness bias The tendency to see yourself as more singular than they actually are.

V

variance at completion (VAC) An indication of expected actual cost over- or underrun at completion (VAC = BAC – EAC).

virtual project team A spatially separated project team whose members are unable to communicate face-to-face. Communication is usually by electronic means.

W

waterfall method A linear, sequential approach to software development.

WBS dictionary A dictionary that provides detailed information about each element in the WBS. The dictionary typically includes the work package level (code), name, and functional description.

weak matrix A matrix structure in which functional managers have primary control over project activities and the project manager coordinates project work.

white elephant A burdensome possession that is not easily disposed of and whose cost (particularly upkeep) is out of proportion with its usefulness.

work breakdown structure (WBS) A hierarchical method that successively subdivides the work of the project into smaller details.

work package A task at the lowest level of the WBS. Responsibility for the package should be assigned to one person and, if possible, limited to 80 hours of work.

ACRONYMS

AC	Actual cost of work completed
ACWP	Actual cost of work performed
AOA	Activity-on-arrow
AON	Activity-on-node
BAC	Budget at completion
BATNA	Best alternative to a negotiated agreement
BCWP	Budgeted cost of work performed
BCWS	Budgeted cost of work scheduled
BOOT	Build-own-operate-transfer
CAPM	Certified Associate in Project Management
CCPM	Critical-chain approach to project planning and management
CMMI	Capability Maturity Model Integration
CPI	Cost performance index
CPM	Critical path method
CV	Cost variance
DUR	Duration
EAC	Estimate at completion (with revised cost estimates)
EF	Early finish
EQ	Emotional intelligence
ES	Early start
ETC	Estimate to complete
EV	Earned value
FAC	Forecast at completion
FS	Free slack
IFB	Invitation for bid
KISS	Keep it simple, stupid
LF	Late finish
LS	Late start
MRI	Management reserve index
MBWA	Management by wandering around
NIH	Not invented here
NPV	Net present value
OBS	Organization breakdown structure
PCI	Percent complete index
PCIB	Percent complete index—budget costs
PCIC	Percent complete index—actual costs
PDM	Precedence diagramming method
PERT	Project evaluation review technique
PMP	Project Management Professional
PMO	Project management office
PV	Planned value of work scheduled
RBS	Risk breakdown structure
RM	Responsibility matrix
SL	Slack
SPI	Schedule performance index
SV	Schedule variance
TCPI	To complete performance index
VAC	Variance at completion
WBS	Work breakdown structure
XP	Extreme programming

PROJECT MANAGEMENT EQUATIONS

$$PCIB = \frac{EV}{BAC}$$

$$CV = EV - AC$$

$$CPI = \frac{EV}{AC}$$

$$EAC_f = \frac{(BAC - EV)}{\left(\frac{EV}{AC}\right)} + AC$$

$$EAC_{re} = AC + ETC_{re}$$

$$MRI = \frac{CV}{MR}$$

$$t_e = \frac{a + 4m + b}{6}$$

$$\sigma_{t_e} = \left(\frac{b - a}{6}\right)$$

$$TCPI = \frac{(BAC - EV)}{(BAC - AC)}$$

$$PCIC = \frac{AC}{EAC}$$

$$SV = EV - PV$$

$$SPI = \frac{EV}{PV}$$

$$VAC_f = BAC - EAC_f$$

$$VAC_{re} = BAC - EAC_{re}$$

$$\sigma_{T_E} = \sqrt{\sum \sigma_{t_e}^2}$$

$$Z = \frac{T_S - T_E}{\sqrt{\sum \sigma_{t_e}^2}}$$

A Socio-Technical Approach to Project Management

The Technical and Sociocultural Dimensions of the Project Management Process

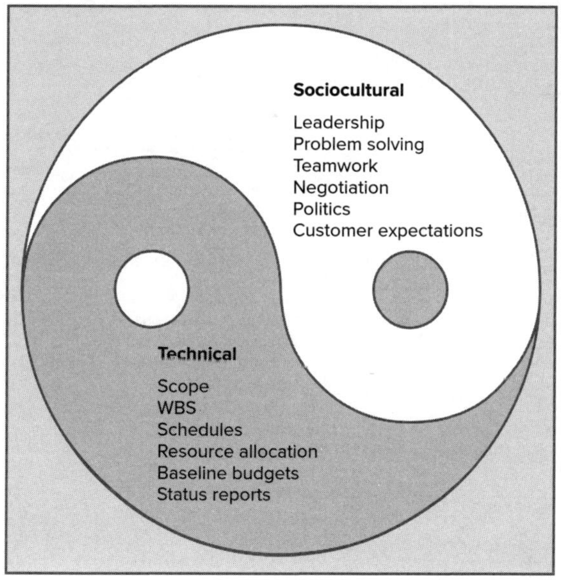

Project Life Cycle

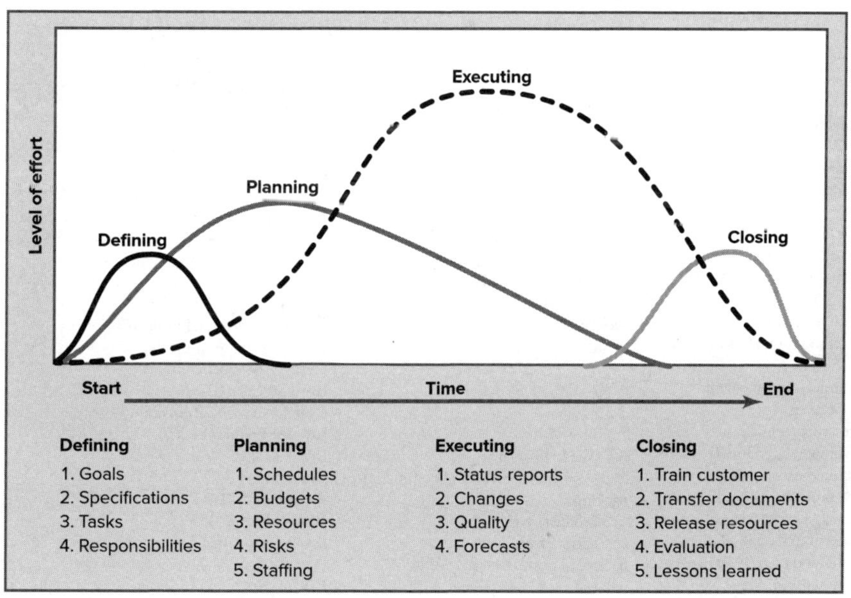

Index

Bold page numbers indicate definitions of terms.

A

AC. *See* actual cost
acceleration. *See* duration of projects, reducing
acceptance criteria, **130.** *See also* delivery acceptance
Ackoff, Russel, 666
acronyms, in earned value management, 551, 552
activities, **199, 201.** *See also specific types*
  level of detail for, 213
  numbering of, 213-214
  in project networks, 198-201
  splitting, 306, 320, 359
  types of, 201
activity-on-arrow (AOA) networks, **202**
activity-on-node (AON) networks, 202-205
  computation process for, 205-209
  fundamentals of, 202-205
  start-to-start lags in, 218-219
activity orientation, cultural differences in, 677
actual cost (AC), **552**
Adams, J. R., 471
adjourning stage of team development, 455
Adler, N., 672, 690
administrative support groups, as stakeholders, 414
Agile Alliance, 635,651
Agile Manifesto, 635
Agile Practice Guide, 651
Agile Project Management (Agile PM), 632-652
  definition of, **12, 633**
  Extreme Programming method of, 646-647
  hybrid project management, 651-652
  iterative, incremental development, 636-637
  Kanban method of, 646-647
  for large projects, 648-649
  limitations of, 650-651
  principles of, 635, 638–639, 649
  Scrum method of, 639- 646
  vs. traditional PM, 12–13, 637–640
AGILEZEN, 648n2
AI. *See* artificial intelligence
Airbnb, 46
Air France, 180
airplane production, 356, 407-408
Albaugh, Jim, 508
Alexander, R. C., 48n4
Alicke, M. D., 45
Allen, Roger E., 126
Allen, Stephen D., 126
allocation. *See* resource allocation
alternatives, in team decision making, 470
ambition, as criteria for team membership, 459
Americans
  cross-cultural factors in working with, 684-685
  international reputation of, 675-676
Andersen, Arthur E., 431,432
Andres, C., 646anger, in negotiations, 521
AOA. *See* activity-on-arrow
AON. *See* activity-on-node
Apocalypse Now (film), 670
Apollo 18
appendices, of audit reports, 612
Apple, 48, 65, 95, 505Applebaum, Jeffrey, 516
apportionment, 167
arbitration, 474
Arenas, Gilbert, 608
Arms, P. B., 676
Arrow, K. J., 308
Arthur Andersen, 431, 432
artificial intelligence (AI), 16, 41
assignments
  in resource scheduling, 322
  as reward for individual performance, 469
AT&T, 39, 88
Audi, 15
audits, project, **602,** 609-618
  in-process, 609
  and maturity models, 614-616
  post-project, 609
  process of, 610-612
availability, as criteria for team membership, 459
Avatar (film), 482n11
avoidance, risk, **263**
awards, 567, 620

B

BA. *See* British Airways
BAC. *See* budgeted cost at completion
backlogs
  product, **643**
  sprint, **643**
backward pass, 208, 212, 221
balance
  of portfolios, 64-66
  in project managers, 435
balanced matrix organization structure, 98
Barnes, R., 360
Barry, T. D., 647
bartering, 671
baseline changes, 570-574
baseline plans, 546
baselines, budget. *See* budget baselines
basketball, 453, 608
BATNA. *See* best alternative to a negotiated agreement
Beck, Kent, 646
behavioral biases, 45-47
Bell Aircraft, 269
Bennis, W., 436
Benson, J., 647
Berkun, S., 465n6
best alternative to a negotiated agreement (BATNA), 523-524
bets, motivation through, 385
Beyer, J. M., 105n5
bias, optimism, 180
big picture, 435
bio-tech industry, 373
Black, J. H., 196
bodyguards, 668
Boeing, 15, 178, 507-508
Bogart, Humphrey, 505
Bolman, Lee, 39
Bolman, L. G., 465n3
bonuses, in reward systems, 468
BOOT. *See* build, own, operate, and transfer
bottlenecks, resource, 355
bottom line, triple, 16
bottom-up estimates, **164, 173**
  methods for, 170-171
  vs. top-down estimates, 164, 169-171, 178
Bourne, Lynda, 146n2, 416n1
Bowen, D., 682n5
Bowen, H. K., 98,111, 465
Bradford, D. L., 417
Bradley Fighting Vehicle (BFV), 132
brainstorming, **470**
  of cost savings options, 400
  in team decision making, 470
Brando, Marlon, 670
Brandt, S. E., 471
Brazil, international projects in, 673
bread-and-butter projects, 65
bribery, 684, 687
Brin, Sergey, 107
British Airways (BA), 257
Brooks, Frederick, 372, 372n1, 544
Brooks's law, 372
Browning, T., 273
Brown, K., 40
Brown, Larry, 453
Brown, Tim, 637
Bruzelius, N., 179
Bryant, Kobe, 453
budget baselines
  costs included in, 553
  development of, 324-329
  time-phased, 302, 324-329
budgeted cost at completion (BAC), **552**
budget estimates. *See also* cost estimates
  contingency reserves in, 271, 272
Buehler, R., 177
buffers
  vs. slack, 359
  time, **272,** 355
build, own, operate, and transfer (BOOT), 606
bulletin boards, electronic, 479
bureaucratic bypass syndrome, 481-482
burndown charts
  release, 645-646
  sprint, 644-655
burst activities, **201,** 204
business case, 128
Button, S., 360

C

Cabanis, J., 431n5
Caldwell, D. F., 105n5
calendar dates, 211
Calhoun, Chad, 375
California Department of Transportation (CalTrans), 372
Callaway Golf Equipment, 129
Canan, Crystal, 516
cancellation, project, contingency plans for, 269
Cao, Q., 104n4
Capability Maturity Model Integration (CMMI), 615
CAPMs. *See* Certified Associates in Project Management
Captain Marvel (film), 15
Carnegie Mellon University, 615
Carrier Transicold, 267-268
Carroll, Pete, 7
case studies
  The Accounting Software Installation Project, 531-532
  Advantage Energy Technology Data Center Migration, 237-238, 298-300
  Ajax Project, 490-491
  Alaska Fly-Fishing Expedition, 280-281
  AMEX, Hungary, 696-698
  Blue Mountain Cabin, 345
  The Blue Sky Project, 443-446
  Buxton Hall, 533-535
  The CCPM Dilemma, 362
  Celebration of Colors 5K, 155-156
  Cerberus Corporation, 447-449
  A Day in the Life, 22-24
  Film Prioritization, 74, 77
  Franklin Equipment, Ltd., 492-494
  Fund Raising Project Selection, 77- 80
  Goldrush Electronics Negotiation Exercise, 535-536
  Graham Nash, 660
  Halo for Heroes II, 625-627
  Hector Gaming Company, 73-74
  The Hokies Lunch Group, 24-27

The Home Improvement Project, 156-157
Horizon Consulting, 121-124
International Capital, Inc., 297-298, 395
Introducing Scrum at P2P, 656-660
Kerzner Office Equipment, 448-490
Maximum Megahertz Project, 628
Midnight Sun II Project, 352-353
Moss and McAdams Accounting Firm, 119-121
Mr. Wui Goes to America, 699-700Nightingale Project, 398-400
The "Now" Wedding, 402-403
Phuket A, 698-699
Post-Graduation Adventure, 188
Power Train, Ltd., 345-347
Scanner Project, 594
Sharp Printing, AG, 187-188
Shell Case Fabricators, 530-531
Silver Fiddle Construction, 281-282
Sustaining Project Risk Management during Implementation, 285-287
Tham Luang Cave Rescue, 347-351
Tom Bray, 446-447
Trans LAN Project, 282-283
Tree Trimming Project, 592
Umdanso Project, 537
Ventura Baseball Stadium, 240, 395-396,593
Whitbread World Sailboat Race, 396-398
X3U Spring Concert, 284-285
Casey, W., 101
cash bonuses, 468
C. C. Myers, Inc., 372
CCPM. *See* critical-chain project management
celebrations, of project closure, 608-609
centralized scheduling, 323
certainty. *See* uncertainty
certification, project management, 3
Certified Associate in Project Management (CAPM), 3
Chafkin, M., 15
chains of command, 428
change control management, 273-276
for contracts, 538-540
and scope creep, 130
change management systems, 274
change request forms, 274change request logs, 274, 276
change, types of, 273
Chaparral Steel, 104, 111
character ethic, 433
character, trust as function of, 433-434
charters
partnering, 514, 515
project, **130**
team, 462
charts
control, 547- 548
Gantt, 214, 214n3, 216
tracking Gantt, 547
Chatman, J., 105n5
checklist models of project selection, 54-55
checklists
process breakdown structure, 142
project closure, 602, 606, 607, 630-631
project scope, 127-130
Chen, M., 676
Chetty, T., 180
Chevy Volt, 220
China, cross-cultural factors in, 668, 683-684
Christensen, D. S., 566
Chrysler, 686
Chunnel, 179, 504
Churchill, Winston, 159
Clark, J., 465
classes, project management, 4–5
closure, project, 601–631, **602**
audits in, 602, 609-618
checklists for, 602, 606, 607, 630-631
performance evaluation in, 603, 618-621
in project life cycle, 9
responsibility for tasks of, 602
types of, 603-604
wrap-up tasks in, 602, 606-609
CMM. *See* Capability Maturity Model
Coady, Gerry, 56
Cochran, Dick, 620
Cockburn, Alstair, 633
code names, project, 65
codes of conduct, 431
for virtual teams, 479
coding systems, for work breakdown structure, 141-142
Coggan, D., 15
Cohen, A. R., 417
Colangelo, Jerry, 453
collectivism, 678
College of Oceanography (CoO), 551
Collins, J. C., 111
co-location
in outsourcing, 517-518
of team members, 464
command and control center PMOs, 102
commendation, letters of, 469
communication
in customer satisfaction, 524-526
by effective project managers, 435
with outsourcers, 513
within virtual teams, 476-481
communication plans, 146-148
compadre system, 680
competence
emotional, 436
trust as function of, 433, 434
complexity, in project estimation, 161
compliance projects, **49**
computer-aided design (CAD) software, 268
computers. *See also* software
in network development, 214-216
in resource-constrained scheduling, 313-320
Conaway, W. A., 682n5
Concorde, 180
concurrent activities. *See* parallel activities
concurrent engineering, 219, 220
conduct, codes of, 431
for virtual teams, 479
conductors, project managers as, 416
conference calls, virtual teams' use of, 479
confidence, 436
confidence in estimate, 160
conflict, in outsourcing, 507, 514, 516
conflict, within teams, 471-474
dysfunctional, 473- 474
functional, 473-474
management of, 471-474
sources of, 471-473
in storming stage of team development, 454-455
conformity, in groupthink, 481
Confucius, 683
Conrad, Joseph, *Heart of Darkness,* 670
consensus
in team decision making, 470
in time and cost estimates, 166
consensus method, **166**
consistency, of character, 433
constraints. *See* resource-constrained projects; time-constrained projects
contingencies, in project estimation, 163
contingency funding, 270-272
contingency plans, 265-269
contingency reserves, **271**
contract(s), 538-542
closing out, 607
cost-plus, 510, 538, 540-541
fixed-price, 510, 538-540
forward, 670
incentive, 371, 372, 518, 540-541
performance-based, 518
redetermination, 539-540
risk in, 263, 541
contract change control systems, 541-542
contract management, 537-542
contractors. *See also* outsourcing
as stakeholders, 415
control charts, 547-548
control, loss of, in outsourcing, 506
control management. *See* change control management
control systems, project, 544, 546-547
control tower PMOs, 100
Conveyor Belt Project (CBP), 730-735
CoO. *See* College of Oceanography
cooperation
exchange view of influence and, 417-420
leading by example with, 430
coordination, in outsourcing, 506
coping, with culture shock, 689-690
Coppola, Francis Ford, 670
core project teams. *See* dedicated project teams
Corning, 518
corporate culture. *See* organizational culture
corruption, 668, 687
cost(s). *See also specific types*
methods for reducing, 386-387, 506
nature of, 376
with outsourcing, 387, 506
of risk events, 253
types of, 175-176
cost accounts, 135, **139**
cost baselines. *See* budget baselines
cost-duration graphs, project, 376-384
constructing, 379-383
example of, 380-383
types of costs in, 376-378
using, 383-384
cost estimates, 158-183
accuracy by type of project, 172
bottom-up, 164-166
databases for, 178-179
definition of, **159**
factors influencing quality of, 160-162
guidelines for, 162-163
importance of, 159-160
learning curves for, 169-170, 179-182level of detail in, 173-174
with mega projects, 179-182
methods for revising, 565-567
refining, 175-177
top-down, 164
types of costs in, 175-176
in work breakdown structure, 136
cost performance index (CPI), **562,** 571, 573
cost performance, monitoring, 546
cost-plus contracts, 510, 538, 540-541
cost risks, contingency plans for, 268
cost scheduling, 302-303. *See also* resource scheduling
in Request for Proposals, 510
cost-sharing ratio (CSR), 540
cost variance (CV), **552,** 554-555
countercultures, 106
Coutu, D. L., 479
Covance, 373
Covey, Stephen, *Seven Habits of Highly Effective People,* 433, 436n9, 522, 522n4
COVID-19 pandemic, 45, 46, 252, 270, 370, 412,426,506,537,570,604
vaccines, 49, 219, 376, 377
virtual project teams, 476
Zoom fatigue, 426
Cowan, C., 511n1
CP. *See* critical path
CPI. *See* cost performance index
CPM. *See* critical path method
crash, 268, **379,** 384–385. *See also* duration of projects, reducing
crash costs, **379**
crash points, **380**
crash times, **379**–381, 384
Crawford, L., 49n5
creatively-led projects, 46
credibility, as criteria for team membership, 459
creep, scope, 130-131, **569**
crime, and international projects, 668
critical chain, **353**
critical-chain project management (CCPM), 353-361
reducing project duration with, 375
and splitting tasks, 359
vs. traditional scheduling, 359-359
criticality index, 262
critical path (CP), **201, 206**

- identifying, 206, 210-211
- critical path method (CPM), 211
- cross-cultural factors. *See* cultural differences
- cross-cultural framework, Kluckhohn-Strodtbeck, 677
- crowdsourcing, 162
- CSR. *See* cost-sharing ratio
- Cuddy, J. A., 434
- cultural differences, 675-690
  - adjustments needed for, 676, 678-679
  - in China, 604, 683-684
- culture shock and, 687-690
  - in France, 681-682
  - intermediaries for, 686-687
  - in Mexico, 679-681
  - in outsourcing, 513
  - overview of, 672-673
  - in Saudi Arabia, 682-683
  - in United States, 684-686
- cultural fluency, 691, 692
- culture, 672-673, **675.** *See also* organizational culture
- culture shock, 687-690
- coping with, 689-690
  - definition of, **687**
  - stages of, 687-688
- Culver, Irvin, 93
- C.U.R.E., Project, 15
- currencies, 418-421
  - inspiration-related, **418, 421**
  - personal-related, **418, 421**
  - position-related, **418, 420**
  - relationship-related, 418, 421
  - task-related, **418-419**
- currency exchange rates, 670-671
- customers
  - in Agile Project Management, 650-651
  - delivery acceptance by, 130, 606, 607
  - as stakeholders, 413, 415
- customer satisfaction
  - increased focus on, 16
  - met-expectations model of, 524-525
  - in outsourcing, 524-526
- CV. *See* cost variance

D

- daily Scrums, 643
- DaimlerChrysler, 505
- Dalangin, Marc, 519
- dangler paths, 214
- Daniel, Tim, 668
- dashboards, **567**
- databases, time and cost, 178
- data collection
  - for progress and performance measurement, 544
  - for project audits, 610
- Data General Corporation, 466
- Davis, E. W., 309
- deadlines
  - imposed, 371
  - in outsourcing, 513
- Deal, T. E., 105, 462n3
- de Castro, Edson, 466
- deception, in estimates, 180
- decision making, team, 469-471
  - ground rules for, 460-461
  - nominal group technique for, 482
  - steps in process of, 470-471
- decision trees, 261
- dedicated project teams, 88, 91-96
  - considerations in choice of, 102-104
  - definition of, **91**
  - nature of, 91-93
  - pros and cons of, 91-94
  - reducing project duration with, 374
- Defense, U.S. Department of (DoD), 490, 519
- Defiant project, 15
- defining stage of projects, 125-157. *See also* work breakdown structure
  - communication plans in, 146-148
  - priorities in, 132-134
  - process breakdown structure, 142-143
  - in project life cycle, 8
  - responsibility matrices, 143-145
  - scope in, 127-132
  - work breakdown structure, 134-142
- deliverables, **128**
  - features as, 640
  - for project closure, 602-603
  - in project scope definition, 127, 128
  - in Request for Proposals, 509-510
  - in work breakdown structure, 134
- delivery acceptance
  - criteria for, in project scope definition, 130
  - in project closure, 606–607
- Deloitte Consulting, 47
- Delphi Method, 167, 258n2
- demand, smoothing resource, 306-308
- DeMarco, T., 373
- Denver International Airport, 179
- dependencies, among stakeholders, 413-415, 422-424
- DeRosa, D., 476
- detail, level of
  - for activities, 213
  - in project estimation, 173-174
  - in Request for Proposals, 509
- detection difficulty, 260
- *Developing Products in Half the Time* (Smith and Reinertsen), 268
- development teams, in Scrum, 641
- Dexter, Susan, 373
- dictionaries, WBS, **142**
- Digital Equipment Corporation, 466
- direct costs, **175, 378**
  - in cost estimates, 175
  - in project cost-duration graphs, 376-383
- dissemination modes, in communication plans, 147
- dissent, healthy, 473
- DiStefano, J. J., 676n2
- DNA identification, 639
- documentation. *See also* reports
  - of lessons learned, 612
  - of requirements in outsourcing, 513
  - scope, 127, 130
- DoD. *See* U.S. Department of Defense
- Dooley, K. J., 459
- Doran, G. T., 44
- dovetailing, 522
- Drexler, John A., 492n
- dropped batons, 354
- Dunbar, E., 690
- Duncan, David, 432
- duration of projects, reducing, 368-404
  - cost-duration graphs in, 376-384
  - methods for, 371-376
  - with outsourcing, 373, 506
  - practical considerations in, 383-386
  - rationale for, 372-373
  - *vs.* reducing cost of projects, 388-389
- duration of tasks, 174
- Dvie, D., 40n1
- Dvir, D., 103, 104n3, 360
- dysfunctional conflict, 473, 474

E

- EAC. *See* estimated cost at completion
- EAC_f. *See* forecasted total cost at completion
- EAC_{re}. *See* revised estimated cost at completion
- Earley, Kristin, 618
- early finish (EF), 206-208, 212
- early start (ES), 206-208, 212
- early times, **200**
- earned value (EV), **546, 552**
  - additional rules for, 564-565, 595-600
  - origins of concept, 451
  - percent complete rule for, 453, 575, 595-600
  - in performance measurement, 546, 549-555
  - in resource scheduling, 317
- earned value management (EVM), 549-555, 570-571
- earthquakes, 372
- economic factors, in international projects, 669-671
- education, project management, 4-5. *See also* training
- EF. *See* early finish
- efficiency of teams, increasing, 374
- electronic bulletin boards, 479
- Eliyahu Goldratt Institute, 360n3
- e-mailing, 679
- e-mail, virtual teams' use of, 479
- emergency projects, 49
- emotional intelligence (EQ), **436**
- *Emotional Intelligence* (Goleman), 436
- empathetic listening, 522
- empathy, 436
- energy, as criteria for team membership, 459
- English language, 513, 672, 691-692
- Enron, 431, 432
- environmental factors, in international projects, 667-673
- EQ. *See* emotional intelligence
- equations, 674
- equipment, as resource constraint, 305-306
- ES. *See* early start
- escalation, **514**
  - risk, **265**
- estimated cost at completion (EAC), **552**
  - revised (EAC_{re}), **565**
- estimated cost to complete remaining work (ETC), **552**
- estimation, project, 158-192. *See also* cost estimates; time estimates
  - databases for, 168-169
  - definition of, **159**
  - factors influencing quality of, 160-162
  - guidelines for, 162-163
  - importance of, 159-160
  - learning curves for, 169-170, 189-192
  - level of detail in, 173-174
  - with mega projects, 179-182
  - methods for, 166-173
  - refining of, 176-178
- ETC. *See* estimated cost to complete remaining work
- ethics, 432-434
  - in international projects, 676
  - leading by example with, 432-433
  - personality *vs.* character, 435
  - of project managers, 433-434
- Ettenson, R., 40
- Euro, 18
- European Union (EU) (2022) study, 668
- EV. *See* earned value
- evaluation criteria, in Request for Proposals, 510
- evaluation, project, 618-621. *See also* performance measurement; progress measurement
- Evans, J., 320
- *Everest* (film), 267
- EVM. *See* earned value management
- evolutionary development, 638
- example, leading by, 430-433
- exchange, influence as, 417-420
- exchange rates, 670-671
- exclusions, in project scope definition, 129-130
- executing stage of projects, 8-9
- expectancy theory of motivation, 385, 385n
- expectations, management of
  - of customers, 524-525
  - of stakeholders, 423
- expectations, met, 524-525
- expected time (TE), 206-208
- experience
  - in cost and time estimates, 160
  - in Request for Proposals, 510
- experience curves, 169, 193. *See also* learning curves
- expertise
  - as criteria for team membership, 459
  - outsourcing for, 506
- external risks, 254
- Extreme Programming (XP), 646-647
- extroverts, 480-481

F

- face, saving, 683
- failed projects, closure of, 604, 605
- failure mode and effects analysis (FMEA), 261
- fairness, in outsourcing contracts, 518

familiarity, as criteria for team membership, 459
fast tracking, 220, **374**
features, **640**
feeder buffers, 355
feminine orientation, 678
Fendly, L. G., 309
Feng shui, 685
FIFA, 180
50/50 estimates, 354-361
50/50 rule, 564, 595-600
film industry, 505
final cost, forecasting, 565-567
financial selection criteria, 52-54, 58
Financial Solutions Group of Mynd, 425
finesse, 425
finish-to-finish relationship, 221
finish-to-start relationship, 217, 218
Fisher, R., , 520, 520n2, 521, 523, 524
five-stage team development model, 454-456
fixed-price (FP) contracts, 263, 510, 538-540
flat world, 666
Fleming, Q., 562n1, 566
flexibility
    outsourcing for, 506
    of project managers, 435
    as reward for individual performance, 469
float. *See* slack
Flyvbjerg, B., 45, 47, 179-180
FMEA. *See* failure mode and effects analysis
football, 7
Force majeure, **570**
Ford, 462
Ford, Henry, 452
forecasted total cost at completion (EAC_f), 565-566
Forest Service, U.S. (USFS), 321, 575
forming stage of team development, 454
forms, change request, 274, 275
forward exchanges, 670
forward pass, 206-208, 212, 221-222
Foti, R., 54
Fowler, M., 646
FP. *See* fixed-price
Frame, J. D., 464
France, cross-cultural factors in, 681-682
Frankel, Rob, 608
free slack (FS), 211-212
Friedman, A., 668
Fritz, Robert, 465
Frontier Airlines, 56
FS. *See* free slack
functional conflict, 473-474
functional managers
    in matrix organization structure, 96, 98
    vs. project managers, 9–10
    as stakeholders, 414-415
functional organization structure, 88-91
    considerations in choice of, 103-104
    nature of, 89
    pros and cons of, 89, 91
function point methods, 168-169
funding, contingency, 270-272
funding risks, contingency plans for, 268-269

G

Gantt charts, 214, 214n3, 216
tracking, 547
Gantt, Henry, 214n3
Gardner, H. K., 49
GDP. *See* gross domestic product
Gene Codes, 639
general and administrative (G&A) overhead costs, 175-176
General Electric, 39
General Motors, 220
geography, in international projects, 669
Gersick, Connie, 457
gift-giving, 684
Girouard, Dave, 369
givers, 420
Global Polio Eradication Program, 18
global projects. *See* international projects
global teams, virtual, 476
global warming, 16
goals, in strategic management, 40, 42
Goal, The (Goldratt), 353
Gobeli, D. H., 98, 103, 127
going local, 482-483
going native, 651
Goldberg, Aaron, 95
Gold, Dan, 373
Golden Gate Bridge, 305
gold plating, **130**
Goldratt, Eliyahu, 320, 353-354, 360
Goleman, Daniel, *Emotional Intelligence,* 436
Google, 107, 322
Gordon, R. L., 372n2
governance team, in portfolio system management, 64
government agencies, as stakeholders, 415
government corruption, 668
Govorun, O., 45
Graham, J. L., 684n7
Grant, Adam, 417, 420
graphs, project cost-duration, 383-386
Gray, C., 103
Gray, C. F., 511n1
Gray, Clifford, 8, 302
Griffin, D., 177
gross domestic product (GDP), 669
ground rules, team, 460
group range estimating, 171
groups. *See* team(s)
groupthink, **481**
Gryglak, Adam, 463Gu, V. C., 104n4
guanxi, 684
A Guide to the Project Management Body of Knowledge (PMBOK Guide), 34-37
Gunderson, A., 672, 690

H

Habitat Affiliate Mannakau, 375
Haliburton, 606-607
Hallowell, R., 682n5
Hammarberg, M., 647
hammock activities, 222-223, 223n4
hands-off *vs.* hands-on approach, 435
Harris, P. R., 683n6, 686n8
Harrison, M. T., 105n5
Hartman, Frances, 464n4
Harvard Business School, 638
Harvard Negotiation Project, 520
Heart of Darkness (Conrad), 670
Heathrow Airport, 256
hedges, 670
Helmstetter, Richard C., 129
Henricks, Paul, 373
Henry, R. A., 255
heuristics, **309**
Hewlett Packard, 88, 424,482
Hirschman, A. O., 180
Hobbs, B., 49n5, 103
Hoffman, J. J., 104n4
Hofstede framework, 676
Hofstede, Geert, 678
Homans, G. C., 456n2
Hong Kong, cross-cultural factors in, 685
Hooker, J., 682n5, 684n7
horizons, planning, 160-161
Howard, Dwight, 453
hub structure, 648
Human Genome Project, 18
human resources. *See also* people
    as resource constraint, 304-305
Hurowicz, L., 308
hybrid project management, 651-652
hybrid project teams, 480-481
Hyer, N., 40

I

IBM, 41, 111,178,372,678
IBM Global Services, 477
identification codes, activity, 213
identity, team, establishment of, 464
IDEO, 637
IFBs. *See* invitation for bids
IID. *See* iterative, incremental development
impact scales, 259
implementation. *See also* project management structures
    of negotiated agreements, 520
    of organization strategies, 45
implementation gap, **47**
imposed deadlines, 371
improvement curves, 169,193. *See also* learning curves
incentive contracts, 371,388,540
incentives, in reward systems, 467
independent tasks, 163
indexes, for monitoring progress, 561-565
India
    infrastructure of, 671
    outsourcing in, 503
indirect costs, **377**
    in project cost-duration graphs, 376-379
individualism, 678
individual performance
reviews of, 619-621
rewards for, 468-469
industrial progress curves, 169, 193. *See also* learning curves
infatuation, team, 482
inflation, 671
influence
    exchange view of, 417- 420
    trust building and, 432
information needs, in communication plans, 147
information sources, in communication plans, 147
infrastructure, **671**
    estimates for building, 179
    in international projects, 671-672
initiative taking, as criteria for team membership, 459
innovation, by project managers, 434
in-process project audits, 609
insensitive networks, 386
Inside Arthur Andersen (Squires et al.), 432
inspiration-related currencies, **417, 421**
insurance, risk transfer through, 363-264
integrity, of effective project managers, 436
Intel, 39, 504
Intel 4004, 18
intelligence, emotional, **436**
interaction costs, 177
intermediaries, 684-685
international projects, 665-693
    See also cultural differences
    environmental factors in, 667-673
    personnel selection for, 690-692
    site selection for, 674-675
    training for, 690-692
International SOS Assistance, Inc., 668
interpersonal competence, 434
interpersonal relationships
    cultural differences in, 677
    in negotiation, 520-521
    between top management and project managers, 415, 427-428
introverts, 480
Intuitive Surgical, Inc., 15
invitation for bids (IFBs), 539
invoices, 607
iPod, 18
Iranian hostage crisis, 613
Irix Pharmaceuticals, 373
iterative, incremental development (IID), **633.** *See also* Agile Project Management

J

Jago, A. G., 469
James, LeBron, 453,608
Janis, I. L., 481
Jelen, F. C., 196
Jensen, M. C., 454
Jeopardy (tv series), 41
Jobs, Steve, 95
Johansen, R., 482
Johnson, Clarence L. "Kelly," 93
Johnson, Magic, 453
Jordan, Michael, 453
jujitsu negotiation, 523
justification, in project scope definition, 128

K

Kahneman, D., 45, 177
Kalaritis, Panos, 373Kanban, 647-648
Kanter, R. M., 434, 504
Kaplan, R. E., 417
Katzenbach, J. R., 462n3
Katz, R., 462n3, 464
Keifer, S., 569n2
Kennedy, A. A., 105
Kerzner, H., 104n4
kick-off meetings, project, **460**
Kidder, Tracy, *The Soul of a New Machine,* 466, 468n7
Kidd, Jason, 453
kidnapping, 668
"kill the messenger" syndrome, 430n4
King, Jon, 430n4
Kipling, Rudyard, 198
Kirk, Dorothy, 425
Kluckhohn, F., 677
Kluckhohn-Strodtbeck cross-cultural framework, 677
Knoop, C. I., 682n5
knowledge explosion, 16
Kohu, M., 434
Kolawa, Adam, 513
Koppelman, J. M., 562n1, 566
Kotter, J. P., 412
Kouzes, J. M., 428
Kras, E., 681n4
Krupp, Goran, 267
Krzyzewski, Mike, 453

L

laddering, **217**
lag relationship, 218-222
lags, 217-220
Lamb, J. C., 372n2
Lam, N. M., 684n7
Landau, E., 254n1
Lane, H. W., 676n2
Lansing, Alfred, 429
large-scale projects
  Agile Project Management with, 648-649
  estimation with, 179
  vs. small projects, 16-17
Larson, Brie, 15
Larson, E. W., 89,93,98,103,127, 430n4, 511n1
late finish (LF), 208, 209
late start (LS), 206, 208-209, 212
late times, **200**
Latham, G. P., 620
law of reciprocity, **417**
Lawrence of Arabia (film), 482n11
laws, in international projects, 667
Leach, L. P., 355n2
leadership
  by example, 428
  vs. management, 424
  need for, 412-413
Leadership in Energy and Environmental Design (LEED), 16, 16n2
Leading at the Edge (Perkins), 429
League of Legends (video game), 643
learning curves, 169, 193
Leavitt, H. J., 482
LEED. *See* Leadership in Energy and Environmental Design
legal factors, in international projects, 667-668
Leonard, Randy, 165
lessons learned, **612**
lessons learned repositories, **614**
letters of commendation, 469
leveling, resource, 306, 308
Levy, S. L., 468, 468n8
LF. *See* late finish
Libanovnos, Christos, 181
life, cultural differences in pace of, 676
life cycles
  product, 15
  project, **8**–9
Likert, R., 454n1
Lilly, Bonnie, 375
limits, in project scope definition, 129-130
Lincoln, Abraham, 420
linearity assumption, 384, 384n3
linear responsibility charts, 143-144
Lipman-Blumen, J., 482
Lipsinger, R., 476
listening, empathetic, 522
Loader, Rob, 101
Lockheed Martin, 92, 253
logic errors, network, 213
logs, change request, 274, 276
Loizeauz, Mark, 264
London Heathrow Airport, 257
long-term outsourcing relationships, 518
Lonza Biologics, 373
looping, 213
Lovallo, D., 177
low-priority projects, team management in, 472
loyalties, team *vs.* organizational, 435
LS. *See* late start
Lucas, E., 676
Lucas, George, 670
luck, 685
lump-sum contracts. *See* fixed-price contracts

M

MacCormack, Alan, 638
MacIntyre, J., 47, 47n2
Magnetic Resonance Imaging (MRI), 18
Maier, N. R. F., 470n9
management by wandering around (MBWA), 424-425, 469
management reserve index (MRI), **563**
management reserves, **271**
management structures. *See* project management structures
managers. *See* project managers
mañana syndrome, 680
Mantel, S. K., 427n3
maps, of stakeholder dependencies, 422-424
Marvel Studios, 15
masculine orientation, 678
Mass Fatality Identification System (M-FISys), 639
matchers, 420
materials, as resource constraints, 305
Matheson, D., 65, 65n8
Matheson, J., 65, 65n8
matrices
  priority, 133-134
  responsibility, 126, 143-145
  risk response, 266
  risk severity, **260-261**
  site selection, 674-675
matrix organization structure, 88, 96-100
  considerations in choice of, 103-105
  nature of, 96-98
  pros and cons of, 98-100
  types of, 98-100
maturity models, project, 614-617, **615**
MBWA. *See* management by wandering around
McNerney, Jim, 508
mediation, 474
meetings, project, 459-461
  guidelines for effective, 462-463
  kick-off, **459**
  Scrum, 641-644
  and team identity, 464
  types of, 462-463
  vision-building, 467
  mega projects, **179**
  estimation with, 179-182
Ménard, P., 103
Mendenhall, M. E., 690
merge activities, **201,** 204
met expectations, 524-525
metrics, performance, 544-545
Mexico, cross-cultural factors in, 679-681
Meyer, D., 320
micromanagers, 413
Microsoft, 504
milestones, **128**
  guidelines for setting, 550
  merge activities as, 204
  in project scope definition, 128
  schedules of, 548-550
Millard, Candice, *The River of Doubt,* 679
Miller, D., 676
Milosevic, D. Z., 686n8
misrepresentation, strategic, 177
mission, organizational, 40,42,43
mitigation, risk, 262-263, 266
mixed project teams, 476
Moffitt Cancer Center, 101
Molloy, E., 180
Monarch platform, 15
monitoring information systems, project, 544-546
Monroe, Marilyn, 505
Moran, James, 237n
Moran, R. T., 683n6, 686n8
Moran, S. V., 683n6, 686n8
Morgan, Pat, 463
Morigeau, Stuart, 280n
Morrison, T., 682n5
Mortensen, M., 119
motivation
  expectancy theory of, 385, 385n
  project managers' role in, 385, 435
  self-, 436
Motorola, 505
Mount Everest, 267
MRI. *See* management reserve index
MS Project. *See* software
Müller, R., 431, 435
multiproject resource schedules, 323-324
multi-rater appraisals, 619
multitasking
  excessive, 354
  and project selection, 48-49
multi-weighted scoring models, 55-58
Murphy, C., 465
mutual gain, options for, 522-523

N

names
  project code, 65
  team, 464
NASA Mars Climate Orbiter, 253
Nash, Steve, 608
National Basketball Association (NBA), 608
national cultures, 675
National Football League (NFL), 7
National Science Foundation (NSF), 551
native, going, 651
natural hedges, 671
nature, cultural differences in relationship to, 677
Navistar, 463
Navy Federal Credit Union, 618
Navy, U.S., 509
NBA. *See* National Basketball Association
NEC, 39
Neffinger, J., 434
negative synergy, 452, 453
negotiations, 519-524
noncompetitive view of, 520
  principled, 516, 520-524
Nelson, K., 432n6
net present value (NPV) model, 52-54,261
network development, 197-250
  activity-on-arrow, 202
  activity-on-node. *See* activity-on-node networks
  computation process for, 205-212
  computers in, 214-216
  extended techniques for, 217-223
  importance of, 198-199
  level of detail in, 213
  practical considerations in, 213-217
  rules for, 201,213
  terminology of, 201
  from work breakdown structure, 198-200
network, project, **198**
  sensitivity of, 211, 386
network, social, of project managers, 422-431
NFL. *See* National Football League
NGT. *See* nominal group technique
  NIH. *See* not invented here
1985 Live Aid Concert project, 18
9/11 terrorist attacks, 639
Nintendo, 65
Noble, A., 650
Nofziner, B., 435
nominal group technique (NGT), **482**
Nonaka, Ikujiro, 639

nonfinancial selection criteria, 52,54
nonproject factors, in project estimation, 162
Noriega, Manual, 65
normal conditions, in project estimation, 163-163, 177
normal project closure, 603
normal times, in project cost-duration graphs, 379-380, 384
norming stage of team development, 455
norms, team, establishment of, 461-463
Northridge Earthquake, 372,541
not invented here (NIH) culture, 456
NPV. *See* net present value
NSF. *See* National Science Foundation
numbers
  assigned to activities, 213-214
  lucky, 685

O

objective criteria, in negotiations, 523
objectives
  as defining characteristic of projects, 8
  in project scope definition, 127, 128
  in strategic management process, 44
OBS. *See* organization breakdown structure
Oddou, G. R., 690
offices, project management (PMOs), 100-102, 100n2
Ohio School Facilities Commission, 516
OHSU. *See* Oregon Health & Science University
Olympics, 181,453, 676
O'Neil, Shaquille, 608
openness, 433
operational projects, 49, 50
Operation Eagle Claw, 612
opportunities, **269**
  management of, 269-270
  in strategic management process, 44
optimism bias, 45, 180
optimism, of project managers, 437
Oregon Health & Science University (OHSU), 165
Oregon State University (OSU), 551, 570
O'Reilly, C. A., 105n5
organizational competence, 434
organizational culture, 105-112
  and Agile Project Management, 650
  characteristics of, 105
  and critical-chain approach, 360
  definition of, **88, 105**
  diagnosis worksheet, 108
  and ethical behavior, 431-432
  functions of, 106
  identifying, 107-109
  implications for project organization, 109-111
  in project estimation, 161-162
  and project management structures, 103, 108-111
  and risk management, 273
  subcultures and countercultures within, 106
organizational mission, 43
Organizational Project Maturity Model, 615
organization breakdown structure (OBS), **139**
organization politics, 47-48
organization strategy, 38-67
  importance of understanding, 40, 41
  strategic management process in, 40-45
organization structure. *See* project management structures
outsourcing, 503-542
  best practices in, 511-519
  conflict management in, 507, 514, 516
  contract management in, 537-542
  customer satisfaction, 524-526
  definition of, **504, 505**
  negotiation in, 516, 519-524
  partnering approach to, 511-519
  pros and cons of, 506-507
  reducing project cost with, 376, 506
  reducing project duration with, 375, 506
  Request for Proposals in, 509-511
  for resource allocation problems, 324
overhead costs, 175-176
  direct, **175**
  general and administrative, 175
overtime, reducing project duration with, 373
oyster projects, 66

P

padding estimates, 161
pair programming, 646
parallel activities, 201, 203
parallel scheduling method, 310
parametric methods, 166, 170
Parker, Ron, 10–11
Parkinson's law, 354
parochialism, 675
partnering approach to outsourcing, 511-516
partnering charters, 514
past experience. *See* experience
Patel, B., 102
Patheon, Inc., 373
paths, **214**
Patterson, J., 309
Patterson, J. H., 308
Paulus, P. B., 456n2
payback model, 52
payment schedules, in Request for Proposals, 510
PBS. *See* process breakdown structure
PCIB. *See* percent complete index budgeted costs
PCIC. *See* percent complete index actual costs
Peace Corps, 691
pearl projects, 65
Peck, W., 101
peer pressure, 354
people
  cultural differences in basic nature of, 677
  as factor in project estimation, 161
  as resource constraints, 304-305
  unreasonable, 523-524
People's Republic of China (PRC). *See* China
percent complete index actual costs (PCIC), **563**
percent complete index budgeted costs (PCIB), **563**
percent complete rule, 553, 564
percent complete with weighted monitoring gates, 564
performance-based contracts, 518
performance measurement, 544-576
  cost performance in, 546
  critical-chain approach to, 359-360
  data collection for, 544-545, 574-575
  earned value management in, 547-553
  forecasting final project cost in, 565-567
  indexes for, 562
  in project closure, 603, 618-621
project control system in, 544, 546-547
project monitoring information system in, 544-546
  reporting on, 544-546, 556-561
  scope changes in, 570-574
  technical performance in, 567, 569
  time performance in, 546-549
performance reviews, **619-620**
performance standards, leading by example with, 453
performing stage of team development, 455
Perkins, Dennis, *Leading at the Edge*, 429
perpetual project closure, 604
personal integrity, of effective project managers, 436
personality ethic, 433
personal-related currencies, **421**
personnel selection, for international projects, 687-689
PERT, 292
Peters, Lawrence, 466
Peters, T., 428
phase estimating, 171-172
phase gate model of project management, 50-52
Philippines, international projects in, 669, 670
Pinto, J., 360
Pinto, J. L., 427n3
piracy, 668
planned value (PV), **317**, 551, **552**
planning horizons, 160-161
planning stage of projects, 8
  in Agile *vs.* traditional project management, 12–13
PMBOK. *See* Project Management Body of Knowledge
PMI. *See* Project Management Institute
PMOs. *See* Project Management offices
PMPs. *See* Project Management Professionals
politics
  in criteria for team membership, 459
  in international projects, 667-668
  organization, 47-48
  of outsourcing, 507
POM+ Project, 720-724
Porras, J. I., 111
portfolio management, 64-66
  balancing projects in, 64-66
  benefits of, 49
  need for, 45
  roles and responsibilities in, 64
  senior management input,64
portfolio, project, **45**
Portland Aerial Tram, 164
Portland General Electric Company, 567
position-related currencies, **420**
positions, *vs.* interests, in negotiations, 521-522
positive risks, 269
positive synergy, **452, 454**
Posner, B. Z., 428, 435, 471
Post-it stickers, 202
post-project project audits, 609
power distance, 678
PRC. *See* China
precision of estimate, 160
predecessor activities, **203**
predictability, 12
premature project closure, 603
price. *See* cost
price risks, contingency plans for, 268
principled negotiation, 516, 519-522
priorities
  changed, project closure due to, 604, 605
  in leading by example, 429-430
  in low-priority projects, 472
  in multi-weighted scoring models, 55-56
  within projects, 132-134
  in project selection, 63
priority matrices, 133
priority system, project, 45-49
priority teams, 55
Prius Automobile, 18
proactivity, of effective project managers, 436
probabilities, risk, 257-261
probability analysis, 261-262
problem identification, in team decision making, 470
problem solving
  as criteria for team membership, 459
  leading by example with, 430
process breakdown structure (PBS), 126, 142-143, 638
Process Groups: A Practice Guide, 269n4
process projects, 142
procrastination, 355
Procter and Gamble, 39,637
procurement management, 538
product backlogs, **643**
product life cycle, 15
product owners, 641
product scope, in project scope definition, **128**

Professionals, Project Management (PMPs), **3**
profiles, risk, 256-257
program(s), **8**
vs. projects, 8
program evaluation and review technique. *See* PERT
program management, 8
progress measurement, 543-
cost performance in, 546
data collection for, 544-545, 574-575
earned value management in, 549-555
forecasting final project cost in, 565-567
indexes for, 561-565
project control system in, 544, 546-547
project monitoring information system in, 544-546
reporting on, 544-546, 554-559
technical performance in, 567, 569
time performance in, 546-549
project(s), **5**–12
characteristics of, 6
classification of, 49-50, 57-58
vs. everyday work, 6, 8
examples of diversity of, 4
vs. programs, 8
small *vs.* large, 16-17
project buffers, 355
project charter, **130**
project cost-duration graphs. *See* cost-duration graphs; cost-duration graphs, project
Project C.U.R.E., 15
project duration. *See* duration
project estimation. *See* estimation
projectitis, **95**
projectized organization, 93-94
project kick-off meetings, **459**
project life cycle, **8**–9. *See* also *specific stages*
project management
Agile. *See* Agile Project Management
certification in, 3
classes on, 4–5
current drivers of, 15-16
importance of, 2–5
phase gate model of, 50-52
principles of, 34
vs. project leadership, 412-413
socio-technical approach to, 17-18, 635
Project Management Body of Knowledge (PMBOK), 3, 34-37, 612
Project Management Consultants, 516
Project Management Institute (PMI), 3
on Agile Project Management, 650, 651
awards given by, 567,618
on definition of project, 5
growth of, 3
50 most influential projects, 17, 18
Organizational Project Maturity Model of, 615
PMBOK Guide, 34-37
on PMOs, 100
on project managers, 416
on project sponsors, 48, 48n3
on stakeholders, 414
website of, 20
project management offices (PMOs), 100-102, 102n2, 618
Project Management Professionals (PMPs), **3**
project management software. *See* software
project management structures, 89-100
considerations in choice of, 102-104
dedicated team, 89, 91-96
functional, 89-92
matrix, 89, 98-100
and organizational culture, 104-106
and project estimation, 161
and project management offices, 100-102
project managers, 410-447
charters authorizing, 129
as conductors, 416
ethical behavior of, 431-432
influence as exchange for, 417-420
in matrix organization structure, 96,98
in performance reviews, 619-621
PMI certification of, 3
vs. project leaders, 412-413
qualities of effective, 434-437
roles of, 9–10, 526
as Scrum masters, 641
social network building by, 417-426
stakeholder engagement by, 413 -416
as stakeholders, 414
trust building by, 432
understanding of organization strategy, 40
without title of project manager, 4
project maturity models, **614-617, 615**
project monitoring information systems, 544-546
project network. *See* network
Project of the Year, 567
project percent complete indexes, 563
project portfolio, **45.** *See also* portfolio management
project proposals. *See* proposals
project scope. *See* scope
project selection. *See* selection; selection of projects
project sponsors. *See* sponsors, project
project teams. *See* team(s)
proposals, 58-63
in phase gate model, 50-51
screening and ranking of, 60-63
sources and solicitation of, 59-60
prototyping
in iterative development, 637
in outsourcing, 513
in risk management, 262, 266
pseudo-earned value percent complete approach, 574
public recognition, for individual performance, 469
pull, 646
punctuality, 675
punctuated equilibrium model of group development, 457
purpose, sense of, 433
PV. *See* planned value

Q

quality, reducing project duration by compromising, 376
quid pro quo, 417

R

Ramasesh, R. V., 273
Ramsden, Sam, 7
RAND Corporation, 167
range estimating, 170-171
ratio methods, **166**
Raz, T., 360
RBSs. *See* risk breakdown structures
RCF. *See* reference class forecasting
Reagan, Ronald, 604
reciprocity, law of, **417**
recognition, public, for individual performance, 469
recommendations, audit, 612
Reconciliation Commission, 18
recruitment, of team members, 458-459
redetermination contracts, 539-540
Red Zuma Project, 725-729
reference class forecasting (RCF), **182**
regional coastal research vessels (RCRV) project, 570-573
cost/schedule graph, 571, 572
earned value management, 570-571
SPI and CPI, 571, 573
register, risk, **272**
Reinertsen, D. G., 116, 268, 468
rejuvenation, of teams, 474-476
relationship-related currencies, 417, 419-420
relationships
interpersonal. *See* interpersonal relationships
lag, 218-223
long-term outsourcing, 518-519
release burndown charts, 644-645
release planning, in Scrum, 641
religious factors, in international projects, 672, 682-683
Relyea, Dave, 639
reports
audit, 611-613
progress, 544-546, 556-561
repositories, lessons learned, **614**
Request for Proposals (RFPs), 509-511
contents of, 509-510
in outsourcing, 509-511
in project selection process, 59
selection of contractors from, 510-511
requirements, in outsourcing, 509-512
reserves
contingency, **271**
management, **271**
resource(s), **304**
reducing project duration by adding, 371-373
resource allocation, 306-313
assumptions in, 306
multiproject, 322-323
outsourcing in, 323
in resource-constrained projects, 308-313
in time-constrained projects, 306-308
resource buffers, 355
resource-constrained projects, **306**
options for reducing duration of, 374-376
resource allocation methods for, 308-313
vs. time-constrained projects, 306
resource-constrained scheduling, 303-305
benefits of, 321
computer demonstration of, 313-320
impacts of, 317,320
overview of, 303-305
resource constraints, types of, 304-306
resource demand, smoothing, 306-308
resource estimates, guidelines for, 162-163
resource pool PMOs, 102
resource scheduling, 301-362.
See also resource-constrained scheduling
assigning project work in, 322
benefits of, 321
centralization of, 323-324
classification of projects in, 306
critical-chain approach to, 353-361
in development of budget baselines, 324-329
multiproject, 323-324
need for, 303
overview of, 303-305
in planning process, 302-303
resource allocation methods in, 306-313
splitting activities in, 306,320
resource sharing, and project selection, 49
resource smoothing, **303,** 306-308
responsibility matrices (RMs), 126, 143-144
retention, risk, **365**
retrospective meetings, sprint, 643-645
retrospectives, project, 612-614
reviews, performance, 619-621, **620**
revised estimated cost at completion (EAC_{re}), **565**
reward systems, 467- 469
RFP. *See* Request for Proposals
Rigby, D. K., 650
Riot Games, 644
risk(s), **252**
balancing portfolios by, 64-66
causes and consequences of, 252
in contracts, 263, 541
external sources of, 254
risk appetite, 265
risk assessment/analysis, 258-260
methods of, 258-260
in project estimation, 163
of proposals, 59, 61
risk avoidance, **263**

risk breakdown structures (RBSs), 255-256
risk escalation, **265**
risk identification, 254-258
risk management, 251-296
contingency funding in, 270-272
contingency planning in, 265-269
cost of errors in, 253-254
definition of, **252**
in international projects, 669
model of, 253
opportunity management in, 269-270
overview of process of, 253-254
proactive approach in, 254
risk assessment in, 258-230
risk identification in, 254-258
risk response control in, 272-276
risk response development in, 262-269
time buffers in, 272
risk mitigation, 262-263, 266
risk profiles, 256-258
risk register, **272**
risk response control, 272-276
risk response development, 262-269
contingency planning in, 265-269
types of responses in, 262-263
risk response matrices, 266
risk retention, **265**
risk severity matrices, **260-261**
risk tolerance, 265
risk transfer, 262-264
Ritti, R. R., 468, 468n8
rituals
in project closure, 604
team, 464, 472, 475
River of Doubt, The (Millard), 673
Rizova, Polly S., 112
RMs. *See* responsibility matrices
Rockwood, K., 15
rolling wave approach, 13 , 636
Romanoff, T. K., 620
Rondon, Candido Mariano da Silva, 673
Roosevelt, Theodore, 673
Rosenberg, Doug, 647
Ross, M., 177
Rothengatter, W., 179
Rubinstein, J., 320
Russia, international projects in, 668
Rwanda National Unity, 18

S

Saab AB, 650
sacred cow projects, 56
Sanborn, J., 181n1
Santayana, George, 602
Saudi Arabia, cross-cultural factors in, 682
Sayles, Leonard R., 425n2, 427, 435
scaling, **648**
scenario analysis, 258-260
schedule, project, 197-240
checklist for, 127-129
milestones in, 128, 548-550
in Request for Proposals, 510
schedule risks, contingency plans for, 268
schedule variance (SV), **552,** 554-555
scheduling performance index (SPI), **562,** 571, 573
Scheier, R., 668n1
Schein, E., 105n5
Schein, E. H., 454n1
Schkade, J., 456n2
Schmidt, Eric, 322
Schniederjans, M. J., 104n4
Schur, M., 650
Schwaber, Ken, 633, 633n1
scope, project, 127-132
changes to, 159, 570-574
creep in, 130-131, **569**
defining, 127-132
documentation of, 127, 130
vs. project vision, 465
reducing project cost by reducing, 387
reducing project duration by reducing, 376
in Request for Proposals, 508
scope statements, **130**
Scown, M. J., 668
screening, of proposals, 60-63
Scrum, 639-646
Extreme Programming form of, 646-647
meetings in, 641-644
product and sprint backlogs in, 643
roles and responsibilities in, 640-641
sprint and release burndown charts in, 644–646
Scrum masters, **541**
Sculley, John, 95
SDI. *See* Strategic Defense Initiative
Seattle Kingdome, 263
SEC. *See* Securities and Exchange Commission
Secret of Success, The (Rizova), 112
Securities and Exchange Commission (SEC), 432
security
in international projects, 668
in outsourcing, 507, 512
SEI. *See* Software Engineering Institute
selection
of contractors, 410-411
of international sites, 674-675
of personnel for international projects, 690-692
selection of projects, 50-91
classification of projects in, 49-50, 57-58
financial criteria for, 52-56, 58
multi-criteria models for, 55-58
nonfinancial criteria for, 52, 54
portfolio management in, 63-65
priority system in, need for, 45-49
proposals in, 57-62
self-awareness, 436
self-esteem, 421
self-motivation, 436
self-organizing teams, **641**
self-protection, 354
self-regulation, 436
Senge, Peter M., 436n8, 464n5
senior management. *See* top management
sensitivity, network, **211,** 386
Seta, J. J., 456n2
Seven Habits of Highly Effective People (Covey), 433, 436n9, 522n4
sex discrimination, 676
Shackleton, Ernest, 429
Shanahan, S., 309
sharing, resource, 49
Sheen, Martin, 670
Shelby County Habitat for Humanity, 375
Shenhar, A., 40, 40n1
Shenhar, A. J., 104n3, 435
Sherif, M., 456n2
Sikorsky, 15
Singer, Carl A., 477
Singles Day, 18
site selection, in international projects, 674-675
skills. *See also specific types*
of project managers, 435-437
of team members, 459
Skilton, P. F., 459
skunk works, 93
slack (or float) (SL), 204, 207-210
vs. buffers, 359
in critical-chain approach, 353-361
free, 209-210
in reducing project duration, 386
total, 207-210
Sleeping Dictionary, The (film), 482n11
Sloan, John, 447n
small projects, 16-17
SMART objectives, 44
smartphone industry, 372
Smith, B. J., 467
Smith, D. K., 48n4, 462n3
Smith, P. G., 122, 268, 468
smoothing, resource, **303,** 306-308
Snapple Company, 253
Snizek, J. A., 255
social class, in France, 681-682
social network building, by project managers, 421-431
social skills, 436
socio-technical approach, 17-19, 635
Software Engineering Institute (SEI), 615, 617
software, project management
for cost/schedule systems, 563-564
in network development, 212-214
in project communication plans, 147
in resource allocation, 313
in resource-constrained scheduling, 313-320
Soul of a New Machine, The (Kidder), 466, 468n7
SOWs. *See* statements of work
Spalding, 608
SPI. *See* scheduling performance index
Spirit Aero Systems, 356
splitting activities, **306,** 320, 359
sponsors, project, **48**
project managers' relationship with, 415, 427
in project selection, 48
as stakeholders, 415
sprint backlogs, **643**
sprint burndown charts, 644-645
sprints, 640
planning of, 642
review of, 642
Squires, Susan, *Inside Arthur Andersen,* 432
stability, maintenance of, 434
stability zones, 689
staging, 648
stakeholder(s), **414**
analysis of, in communication plans, 146-147
dependencies among, 413-415, 421-423
managing expectations of, 424
project managers' engagement of, 413-416
in project managers' social network, 421-423
in risk identification, 257
Standard for Project Management (SPM), 34-35
Standish Group, The, 12, 634
start-to-finish relationship, 221
start-to-start relationship, 218-219
statements of work (SOWs), 130, 509
status updates, in outsourcing, 516-517
Staw, Barry, 605
Stephens, Matt, 647
stereotypes, in groupthink 482
Stern, David, 453, 608
storming stage of team development, 454-455
Strategic Defense Initiative (SDI), 604
strategic management, 40-45
strategic misrepresentation, 177
strategic projects, **49**
strategy, organization. *See* organization strategy
stress, and culture shock, 688, 689
Strodtbeck, F. L., 677
Strohl Systems Group, 668
strong matrix organization structure, 98, 99
Stubbs, David, 181
student syndrome, 355
subcontracting. *See* outsourcing
subcultures, 96
subdeliverables, 135,136,138
successor activities, **203**
Suis, J., 45
Sullivan, Stacy Savides, 107
Sundewn, J., 647
sunk costs, 605
suppliers, as stakeholders, 415
surveys, online, in outsourcing, 517
sustainable business practices, 16
Sutherland, J., 650
SV. *See* schedule variance
Sweden, international projects in, 669
SWOT analysis, 44
synergy
negative, 452, 453
positive, **452, 454**
systems thinking, in effective project managers, 436-437

T

takers, 420
Takeuchi, Hirotaka, 639
Talbot, B. F., 308
tangible costs, 605
Tarne, R., 648
task duration, 174

- task-related competence, 434
- task-related currencies, **417, 419**
- TCPI. *See* to complete performance index
- TE. *See* expected time
- team(s), 451-502
  - common problems facing, 481-483
  - conflict in, 454-455, 471-474
  - decision making in, 460-461, 469-471
  - dedicated. *See* dedicated project teams
  - evaluation of, at project closure, 618-621
  - five-stage development model for, 454-456
  - governance, in portfolio system management, 64
  - hybrid project, 480-481
  - identity of, 464
  - increasing efficiency of, 374
  - meetings of, 459-461
  - mixed project, 480
  - norms for interaction in, 461-463
  - at project closure, 606, 607,618-621
  - punctuated equilibrium development model for, 457
  - recruiting members for, 458-459
  - rejuvenating, 474-476
  - reward systems for, 467-469
  - risk management, 254-255
  - role of, 11–12
  - in Scrum, 640, 641
  - self-organizing, 641
  - shared vision of, 465-467
  - situational factors in development of, 456
  - as stakeholders, 414
  - synergy in, 452-454
  - virtual, 476-481
- team-building, **475**
  - in outsourcing, 513-515
  - rejuvenation of teams with, 475-476
- team performance
  - evaluation of, at project closure, 618-621
  - rewards for, 467-469
- technical constraints, 304
- technical dimension of project management, 17-19
- technical performance measurement, 567, 569
- technical requirements, in project scope definition, 128
- technical risks, contingency plans for, 267-268
- technological expertise, as criteria for team membership, 459
- Telstra, 101
- template methods, **170**
- termination, project. *See* closure
- terminators, 606
- terrorism, international, 668
- testing
  - development driven by, 646
  - in risk management, 262
- Thamhain, H., 268, 272
- Thamhain, H. J., 471
- threats. *See also* risk(s)
  - in strategic management process, 43-44
  - use of term, 254
- 360-degree feedback, 619
- 360-degree reviews, **6213**M, 55, 11, 479
- time and cost databases, **178**
- time buffers, 272, 355
- time-constrained projects, **300**
  - resource allocation methods for, 306-308
- time, cultural differences in concepts of, 676, 680-686
- time estimates, 158-196. *See also* duration
  - accuracy by type of project, 172
  - bottom-up, 164-166
  - in critical-chain approach, 353-361
  - databases for, 178-179
  - definition of, **159**
  - factors influencing quality of, 160-162
  - guidelines for, 162-163
  - importance of, 159-160
  - learning curves for, 169-170, 193-196
  - level of detail in, 173-174
  - with mega projects, 179-182
  - milestones in, 128
  - refining, 176-178
  - top-down, 164-170
  - in work breakdown structure, 136
- time management, by project managers, 437
- time performance, monitoring, 546-549
- time-phased budget baselines, 302,324-329
- time-to-market, 15, 370
- time units, 163
- time zones, and virtual global teams, 477-478
- to complete performance index (TCPI), **566**
- tolerance, risk, 265
- top-down estimates, **159, 164**
  - *vs.* bottom-up estimates, 159, 164-166, 173
  - methods for, 166-170
- top management
  - in portfolio system management, 64
  - project managers' relationship with, 415, 427-428
  - projects prioritized by, 63
  - as stakeholders, 415
- Torti, M. T., 526
- total costs, 376
- total quality management (TQM), 49
- total slack, 209-212
- Toyota, 39, 505, 518, 647
- TQM. *See* total quality management
- tracking Gantt charts, **547,** 548
- traditional project management
  - *vs.* Agile Project Management, 12–13, 633-636
  - in hybrid project management, 651-652
- training
  - for international projects, 690-692
  - in outsourcing, 513-514
- traits, of effective project managers, 435-437
- transfer, risk, 263-264
- translators, 692
- transparency, ethical issues with, 431
- travel, by virtual team members, 479
- Trevino, L., 452n6
- triple bottom line, 16
- Trojan Nuclear Plant, 567, 568
- tropical forest restoration, 15
- trust building
  - by project managers, 432-434
  - within virtual teams, 476, 478
- trust, meaning of, 433
- Tuckman, B. W., 454
- Tuller, L. W., 681n4
- Tung, R. L., 684n7,690
- Turner, J. R., 49n5,435
- Turtle, Q. C., 219

U

- ugly Americans, 675
- uncertainty
  - and Agile Project Management, 12-13, 635, 637
  - in cost and time estimates, 159
  - need for leadership with, 412
- uncertainty avoidance, 678
- Underwriter Laboratories, Inc., 691
- uniqueness bias, **45**
- United States, cross-cultural factors in, 684-686
- United States Golf Association (USGA), 129
- unreasonable people, 523-524
- urgency, sense of, 430
- Ury, W., 520, 520n2
- U.S. Department of Defense (DoD), 52, 519, 551
- U.S. firms, 507
- U.S. Forest Service (USFS), 321, 575
- USGA. *See* United States Golf Association
- U.S. Navy, 509

V

- VAC. *See* variance at completion
- value engineering, 578
- variance
- cost, **552,** 554-555
- schedule, **552,** 554-555
- variance analysis, methods of, 454-455
- variance at completion (VAC), **552, 554**
- Vecta, 637
- vendors, as stakeholders, 415
- Versatec, 109
- videoconferencing, 479
- virtual project teams, 476-481
- visions, project, **465**
  - in conflict management, 473
  - creation of shared, 465-467
- vision statements, 467
- volunteers, for team membership, 458
- Vroom, V. H., 385,469

W

- Wake, William, 639
- Walt Disney, 15, 18
- Wan, C. K., 45
- warmth, 434, 434n7
- waterfall method, 142,634-635,652
- Watson's *Jeopardy* Project, 41
- WBS. *See* work breakdown structure
- WBS dictionaries, **142**
- weak matrix organization structure, 98, 99
- weather, and international projects, 669
- weather station PMOs, 101
- Webber, S. S., 526
- weighted scoring models, 55-58
- Weiler, Ed, 253
- Wells Fargo, 431
- West, Tom, 466
- Wexley, K. N., 620
- whiteboards, Kanban, 647
- white elephant projects, 66, 180-181
- Whitten, Danny, 385
- Wikipedia, 18
- Wilemon, D. L., 471
- Wilson, Pete, 372
- women, in international projects, 676
- Woodworth, B. M., 309
- work breakdown structure (WBS), 126-127, 134-142
  - coding system for, 141-142
  - development of, 126, 134-139
  - integration of OBS with, 139-141
  - level of detail in, 164
  - networks developed from, 198-200
  - *vs.* process breakdown structure, 142-143
  - *vs.* responsibility matrices, 143-145
  - in risk identification, 255
- work packages, **136,** 138, 199-200
- Worldcom, 431
- World Cup, 180
- World Trade Center (WTC), 639
- World Wide Web, 18
- wrap-up closure tasks, 602, 604-607

X

- Xerox, 48, 109
- XP. *See* Extreme Programming

Y

- Yazici, H., 104n4
- Yeung, I., 648n7
- Young, Bruce, 385

Z

- Zalmanson, E., 360
- Zander, A., 456n2
- Zaphiropoulos, Renn, 109
- Zenisek, Joseph, 356
- 0/100 rule, 564, 595-600
- Zoom fatigue, 426
- Zuckerberg, Mark, 252